1975-1998   Volume 1   **STEVEN HOLL**

Copyright © 2012 A.D.A. EDITA Tokyo Co., Ltd.
3-12-14 Sendagaya, Shibuya-ku, Tokyo 151-0051, Japan
All rights reserved. No part of this publication may be reproduced,
stored in a retrieval system, or transmitted, in any form or by any means,
electronic, mechanical, photocopying, recording, or otherwise,
without permission in writing from the publisher.

Copyright of photographs except as noted
©2012 GA photographers
Copyright of drawings and renderings
©2012 Steven Holl Architects

Logotype design: Gan Hosoya

Printed and bound in Japan

ISBN978-4-87140-432-7 C1352

STEVEN HOLL

1975-1998 Volume 1

Edited by Yukio FUTAGAWA
Introduction by Toyo ITO

企画・編集:二川幸夫　序文:伊東豊雄

A.D.A. EDITA Tokyo

STEVEN HOLL

1947	Born in Bremerton, Washington
1970	Graduated from University of Washington; B. Arch
1970	Studied architecture in Rome
1976	Postgraduate studies at Architectural Association School, London
1976	Established Steven Holl Architects in New York
1981	Became Adjunct Professor at Columbia University
1985	AIA New York Chapter Award for Cohen Apartment, New York
1986	AIA New York Chapter Award for Pace Collection Showroom, New York
1988	AIA New York Chapter Awards for Urban Proposal for Porta Vittoria District, Milan and Giada Showroom, New York
1989	Became Tenured Professor at Columbia University
	Published *Anchoring*
	Participated in a Two-Man Show at Museum of Modern Art
	AIA National Honor Award for Berkowitz-Odgis House, Martha's Vineyard
1990	Arnold W. Brunner Prize for Achievement in Architecture for American Academy and Institute of Arts and Letters
1991	AIA National Honor Award for Hybrid Building, Seaside
	"Architecture Tomorrow" exhibit at Walker Art Center
1992	AIA New York Chapter Honor Award for "Void Space/Hinged Space" Housing, Fukuoka, Japan
	AIA National Honor Award for D.E. Shaw & Co., New York
1993	AIA National Honor Award for Stretto House, Dallas
1995	New York AIA Design Awards for Cranbrook Institute of Science, Bloomfield Hills
	Chapel of St. Ignatius, Seattle University, Seattle
1996	Published *Intertwining*
1997	New York AIA Medal of Honor Award
1998	National AIA Design Award for Chapel of St. Ignatius, Seattle University, Seattle
	Alvar Aalto Medal
	Chrysler Award for Innovation in Design

1975-1998 Contents
Volume 1

8	An Architecture Adrift in Time: A Message to Steven Holl
	Toyo Ito
12	Phenomena and Idea
	Steven Holl
18	**1. Light, Material and Detail**
20	Cohen Apartment, New York, New York, U.S.A., 1982-83
28	Pace Collection Showroom, New York, New York, U.S.A., 1985-86
32	MoMA Tower Apartment, New York, New York, U.S.A., 1986-87
36	Objects, Swid Powell / Carpets, V'Soske, New York, New York, U.S.A., 1986
38	Giada Showroom, New York, New York, U.S.A., 1987
42	Metropolitan Tower Apartment, New York, New York, U.S.A., 1987-88
48	D.E. Shaw & Co. Offices, New York, New York, U.S.A., 1991
52	Storefront for Art and Architecture, New York, New York, U.S.A., 1992-93
56	Sarphatistraat Offices, Amsterdam, The Netherlands, 1996-2000
62	**2. Houses**
64	Sokolov Retreat, St. Tropez, France, 1976
66	Telescope House, Still Pond, Maryland, U.S.A., 1978-79
68	Metz House, Staten Island, New York, U.S.A., 1980-81
70	Pool House and Sculpture Studio, Scarsdale, New York, U.S.A., 1980-81
74	Berkowitz-Odgis House, Martha's Vineyard, Massachusetts, U.S.A., 1984-88
80	Residence, Cleveland, Ohio, U.S.A., 1988-90
84	Stretto House, Dallas, Texas, U.S.A., 1989-92
96	"Y" House, Catskill Mountains, New York, U.S.A., 1997-99
102	**3. Housing and Hybrid Buildings**
104	Gymnasium Bridge, South Bronx, New York, U.S.A., 1977-78
108	Bridge of Houses, New York, New York, U.S.A., 1979-82
110	Autonomous Artisans' Housing, Staten Island, New York, U.S.A., 1980-84
112	Hybrid Building, Seaside, Florida, U.S.A., 1984-88
120	Void Space/Hinged Space Housing, Fukuoka, Japan, 1989-91
128	Town Square, Four Houses and Chapel, Port Ludlow, Washington, U.S.A., 1991-92
130	Makuhari Bay New Town, Chiba, Japan, 1992-96
140	Hypo-Bank Offices and Art Hall, Munich, Germany, 1994
144	Manifold Hybrid, Amsterdam, The Netherlands, 1994
146	**4. Ontology of Institutions**
148	Berlin AGB Library, Berlin, Germany, 1988
156	College of Architecture and Landscape Architecture, University of Minnesota (early scheme), Minneapolis, Minnesota, U.S.A., 1988-91
158	Palazzo del Cinema, Venice, Italy, 1990-91
162	Cranbrook Institute of Science, Bloomfield Hills, Michigan, U.S.A., 1992-99
172	Chapel of St. Ignatius, Seattle University, Seattle, Washington, U.S.A., 1994-97
180	Knut Hamsun Center, Hamarøy, Norway, 1994-2009
186	Museum of the City of Cassino, Cassino, Italy, 1996
188	Museum of Modern Art Expansion, New York, New York, U.S.A., 1997
196	Bellevue Art Museum, Bellevue, Washington, U.S.A., 1997-2000
204	College of Architecture and Landscape Architecture, University of Minnesota, Minneapolis, Minnesota, U.S.A., 1997-2002
210	Higgins Hall Center Section, Pratt Institute School of Architecture, Brooklyn, New York, U.S.A., 1997-2005
216	**5. Edge of a City**
218	Urban Proposal for Porta Vittoria District, Milan, Italy, 1986
224	Erie Canal Edge, Rochester, New York, U.S.A., 1988
226	Spatial Retaining Bars, Phoenix, Arizona, U.S.A., 1989
228	Parallax Towers, New York, New York, U.S.A., 1990
230	Stitch Plan, Cleveland, Ohio, U.S.A., 1989
232	Spiroid Sectors, Dallas/Fort Worth, Texas, U.S.A., 1990
234	**6. Fusion: Landscape, Urbanism and Architecture**
236	Riverfront Flint Fountain, Flint, Michigan, U.S.A., 1975-77
238	Kiasma, Museum of Contemporary Art, Helsinki, Finland, 1992-98
250	Whitney Water Purification Facility and Park, Connecticut, U.S.A., 1998-2005
254	**List of Works 1974-98**

8	時を漂う建築——スティーヴン・ホールへのメッセージ	146	4章　公共建築の存在論
	伊東豊雄	148	ベルリン・アメリカ記念図書館　ドイツ, ベルリン, 1988年
		156	ミネソタ大学 建築＋ランドスケープ学部棟(初期案)　ミネソタ州ミネアポリス, 1988〜91年
12	現象と理念	158	パラッツォ・デル・チネマ　イタリア, ヴェネツィア, 1990〜91年
	スティーヴン・ホール	162	クランブルック科学研究所　ミシガン州ブルームフィールド・ヒルズ, 1992〜99年
		172	シアトル大学聖イグナティウス礼拝堂　ワシントン州シアトル, 1994〜97年
18	1章　光, 材料, ディテール	180	クヌート・ハムスン・センター　ノルウェー, ハマロイ, 1994〜2009年
20	コーエン・アパートメント　ニューヨーク州ニューヨーク, 1982〜83年	186	カッシーノ市立美術館　イタリア, カッシーノ, 1996年
28	ペース・コレクション・ショールーム　ニューヨーク州ニューヨーク, 1985〜86年	188	MoMA／ニューヨーク近代美術館増改築案　ニューヨーク州ニューヨーク, 1997年
32	MoMAタワー・アパートメント　ニューヨーク州ニューヨーク, 1986〜87年	196	ベルヴュー・アート・ミュージアム　ワシントン州ベルヴュー, 1997〜2000年
36	オブジェ, カーペットのデザイン　ニューヨーク州ニューヨーク, 1986年	204	ミネソタ大学 建築＋ランドスケープ学部棟　ミネソタ州ミネアポリス, 1997〜2002年
38	ギアダ・ショールーム　ニューヨーク州ニューヨーク, 1987年	210	プラット・インスティテュート建築学科 ヒギンズ・ホール中央セクション
42	メトロポリタン・タワー・アパートメント　ニューヨーク州ニューヨーク, 1987〜88年		ニューヨーク州ニューヨーク, 1997〜2005年
48	D・E・ショウ社オフィス　ニューヨーク州ニューヨーク, 1991年		
52	ストアフロント美術建築ギャラリー　ニューヨーク州ニューヨーク, 1992〜93年	216	5章　都市の周縁
56	サルファティストラートのオフィス　オランダ, アムステルダム, 1996〜2000年	218	ポルタ・ヴィットリア計画　イタリア, ミラノ, 1986年
		224	エリー運河畔計画　ニューヨーク州ロチェスター, 1988年
62	2章　住宅	226	スペイシャル・リテイニング・バー　アリゾナ州フェニックス, 1989年
64	ソコロフ邸の隠れ家　フランス, サントロペ, 1976年	228	パララックス・タワー　ニューヨーク州ニューヨーク, 1990年
66	テレスコープ・ハウス　メリーランド州スティル・ポンド, 1978〜79年	230	スティッチ・プラン　オハイオ州クリーヴランド, 1989年
68	メッツ邸　ニューヨーク州スタテン・アイランド, 1980〜81年	232	スピロイド・セクター　テキサス州ダラス／フォートワース, 1990年
70	プール・ハウス／彫刻スタジオ　ニューヨーク州スカースデール, 1980〜81年		
74	バーコヴィッツ＝オッジス邸	234	6章　融合：ランドスケープ, 都市, 建築
	マサチューセッツ州マーサズ・ヴィニヤード, 1984〜88年	236	フリント河岸の噴水公園　ミシガン州フリント, 1975〜77年
80	クリーヴランドの住宅　オハイオ州クリーヴランド, 1988〜90年	238	Kiasmaヘルシンキ現代美術館　フィンランド, ヘルシンキ, 1992〜98年
84	ストレット・ハウス　テキサス州ダラス, 1989〜92年	250	ホイットニー浄水施設＋公園　コネチカット州, 1998〜2005年
96	"Y"ハウス　ニューヨーク州キャッツキル・マウンテン, 1997〜99年		
		254	作品リスト　1974〜98年
102	3章　ハウジングとハイブリッド・ビルディング		
104	ジムナジウム・ブリッジ　ニューヨーク州サウス・ブロンクス, 1977〜78年		
108	ブリッジ・ハウス　ニューヨーク州ニューヨーク, 1979〜82年		
110	様々な職人のハウジング　ニューヨーク州スタテン・アイランド, 1980〜84年		
112	ハイブリッド・ビルディング　フロリダ州シーサイド, 1984〜88年		
120	ヴォイド・スペース／ヒンジド・スペース・ハウジング　福岡県福岡市, 1989〜91年		
128	タウン・スクエア——四つの住宅＋礼拝堂　ワシントン州ポート・ラドロー, 1991〜92年		
130	幕張ベイタウン・パティオス11番街　千葉県千葉市, 1992〜96年		
140	ヒポ・バンク——オフィス＋アート・ホール　ドイツ, ミュンヘン, 1994年		
144	マニフォールド・ハイブリッド　オランダ, アムステルダム, 1994年		

TOYO ITO
An Architecture Adrift in Time: A Message to Steven Holl

時を漂う建築：スティーヴン・ホールへのメッセージ｜伊東豊雄

Dear Steven:

It has been a year since I visited the apartments (with their Void Space/Hinged Space Housing, Fukuoka, 1989-91) that you designed for Nexus World. I was impressed then mostly by their extraordinarily delicate beauty, but having had a chance to go through *Anchoring*, the volume of your works that you sent me recently, I now understand that the basic concept of the project in Fukuoka is the product of many years of thought. The qualities that have characterized your projects from the start are, I believe, most fully developed in that building.

The most impressive feature of the Fukuoka project is the open passageway penetrating the five wings of the building. Similar spatial experiences—that is, movements perpendicular to, and through, volumes of the same size located at equal intervals—are offered by the Bridge of Houses (1979-82) built over the regularly spaced blocks of New York, the Autonomous Artisans' Housing (1980-84) for New York's Staten Island, and a portion of the Urban Proposal for Porta Vittoria District (1986) for Milan.

Is the orderly repetition of mass and void—the preoccupation with formality—an *hommage* to the various urban projects of Le Corbusier? Or is it to be traced back to the agreeable repetition of blocks in Manhattan? I remember sitting through lectures on the planning of public housing as a university student and thinking how tedious the inevitably orderly and formal site plans were, but you have made those qualities a virtue. I feel that is a significant point in considering your architecture.

スティーヴン・ホール様

Nexus Worldであなたの設計されたアパートメント（ヴォイド・スペース／ヒンジド・スペース・ハウジング，福岡，1989-91）を見せてもらってから，もう1年経ちました。あの時には異常な程に繊細な美しさだけが印象に残りましたが，最近あなたが送ってくれた作品集『Anchoring』を見て，福岡のプロジェクトの基本的なコンセプトはあなたが長年考え続けてきたことの結実であることがよくわかりました。本当に，あの建築には，あなたがつくり始めてからの数々のプロジェクトに繰り返しあらわれる特質が集大成されているように思われます。

例えば福岡のプロジェクトで最も印象的なのは五つの住居棟を貫く屋外通路です。全く等間隔に置かれた同一サイズのヴォリュームを横断してゆく空間体験，それはニューヨークの規則的な街区を縦断して架けられたブリッジ・ハウス（1979-82）や同じくニューヨークのスタテン・アイランドのプロジェクト，様々な職人のハウジング（1980-84），或いはミラノのためにつくられたプロジェクト，ポルタ・ヴィットリア計画（1986）の一部などに典型的に見ることができます。

マスとヴォイドの規則的な繰り返し，その形式性への執着はル・コルビュジエのさまざまなアーバン・プロジェクトへのオマージュに由来するのでしょうか，それともマンハッタンの規則的な街区の繰り返しの心地良さから来るのでしょうか。かつて僕らは大学の住宅地計画のレクチュアで，パブリック・ハウジングに於ける住棟配置のあまりの規則性，形式性にうんざりした記憶がありますが，その退屈さをあなたは徹底的にポジティブな空間へと置き換えておられますね。このことはあなたの建築について考える時にとても重要な意味を持っているように思われます。

つまり，今世紀初めの近代の建築計画や都市計画にしばしば見られる均

In other words, up to now our sole concern has been to introduce variety into the homogeneous environments created by modern architectural design and city planning in the early part of this century. You, however, seem to have been attracted precisely to the homogeneity and formality that were beginning then to characterize society.

What is new about the homogeneity and formality of your projects, that is, what distinguishes your site plans for housing from those of Le Corbusier, is their level of abstraction. Le Corbusier's plans are quite abstract and rarefied in drawings, but the realized buildings from not only his later years but even the 1920s and 1930s impress one by their substance and depth. They are characterized by sharp contrasts between massive volumes and voids or between light and shadow. Despite the abstract quality of his work on a conceptual level, Le Corbusier seems to have been drawn to the material and massive qualities of actual buildings, the thickness of walls, the stoutness of columns, and the power or dynamism of spaces scooped out of mass.

To experience a work by Le Corbusier is to wander through spaces defined by weightless lines and planes but to remain conscious at the same time that the structure is firmly rooted in the land. Just as an astronaut in space is sustained by the conviction that he will eventually return to earth and its gravity, we are sustained by the knowledge that ultimately the conceptual weightlessness of architecture will be reconciled with nature. Ultimately, the voyage comes to an end.

However, the spatial experience in your architecture, Steven, is quite unique. It's as if one were dreaming about modern architecture, particularly the architecture of Le Corbusier. In the case of your buildings, the actual work seems to be even more rarefied than the drawings and models. You must study each choice or detailing of material very carefully, but any hint of effort vanishes in the realized building. One is left in an abstract space. There may be a sequence of masses and voids, but it does not offer the sharp contrast of light versus darkness, or of the substantial versus the insubstantial, to be found in Le Corbusier's works. One is always drifting in a weightless world created out of planes without thickness.

The verb "to drift" suits your architecture perfectly. In dreams, space is often weightless, and one travels on a voyage without conclusion. For example, when one steps into the entrance hall of the Fukuoka project one has already embarked on an endless journey. The irregularly articulated and subtly bending sashwork, the crisscrossing brass bars embedded in the terracotta walls, the floor with its slight changes in level and material, and the stairs—all these lead eventually to an open, linear passageway. This passageway, which parallels the street in front and curves gently, is striped by a regular succession of light and shadow. However, this rhythm of light and darkness is a sophisticated surface effect, suggesting a sheet of paper that has been divided into white and gray areas by computer graphics. The facades of the wings that are at right angles to the passageway are, on one side, sheets of corrugated aluminum in a concrete frame, and on the other, finished in exposed concrete. On both sides, windows of diverse sizes establish a light rhythm and create planes without depth. Moreover, these repeated, abstract planes are re-

質さ、我々は久しくその均質さにどのようなバリエーションを与えるかということばかりを考えてきたのですが、あなたは、その頃既に今日の社会に浸透しつつある新しい均質さや形式性にこそ魅力を感じておられたのではないでしょうか。

あなたのプロジェクトに見られる均質性や形式性の新しさ、即ちル・コルビュジエの住棟配置との違いは抽象性の差にあります。図面で見る限りはコルのプランもきわめて抽象度の高いドライなものですが、実際につくられた建築は、晩年は言うに及ばず、20〜30年代の作品でも、もの自体の持つ実体感や奥行きを感じさせます。それはマッシヴなヴォリュームとヴォイドな部分との強いコントラストや、光と陰の強いコントラストに典型的に示されています。恐らくコルはコンセプチュアルなレベルでの抽象性にも拘らず、実体としての建築の持つ素材感や重量感、壁の厚さや柱の太さ、マッスのなかを繰り抜いたヴォイドなスペースなどの強さやダイナミズムに惹かれていたに違いありません。

したがってコルの建築を体験する時我々は、一方で重さを持たない線や面の空間をさまよいつつ、他方では大地にしっかりと根をはやした構造物への信頼に引き戻されるという両義性を味わうことになる訳です。つまり宇宙に投げ出された宇宙飛行士も必ず重力を持つ地球に帰ってくるという確信に支えられているように、建築という観念内部の無重力状態も常に自然との調和した関係に最終的には到る。結局、いつでも旅が終わるのです。

しかしスティーヴン、あなたのつくった建築のなかに浸っていると、その空間体験は実に不思議なものです。私はまるで近代建築、特にル・コルビュジエの建築の夢をみているようです。あなたの建築の場合、実作に感じられる存在感の希薄さはむしろ図面や模型以上です。素材の選択やディテールには吟味に吟味を重ねているのでしょうが、それらは消え去って、あなたの建築のなかで私は抽象的な「空間」のなかにいます。マッスとヴォイドの繰り返しを経ても、その体験は決してコルの場合のようなはっきりとした明暗のコントラストではないし、密実なものと空疎なものとのコントラストでもない。いつでも私は厚さのない面だけが織りなす無重力の世界に漂っています。

正しく、漂うという言葉があなたの建築にはぴったりです。夢の空間はしばしば無重力だし、帰結のない旅をしているからです。例えば福岡プロジェクトのエントランスホールに入ると、既にそこはあてのない旅の始まりです。不規則に分節された微妙に折れ曲がるサッシュワーク、テラコッタの壁面を飛び交う象嵌された真鍮のバー、わずかにレベルや素材を変える床、階段を上がると自然に我々はリニアな屋外通路へと導かれます。前面道路と平行に緩やかにカーブしたこの通路では光と陰の規則的なストライプが繰り返されます。しかしこの明暗のリズムは、白とグレーにコンピュータ・グラフィックで塗り分けられた紙のように表層的でソフィスティケートされたものです。そして通路と直交して姿をあらわす住棟のファサード、一方はコンクリートのフレームの間にアルミの波板が貼られ、他方はコンクリートの打ち放しで仕上げられていますが、いずれの面もさまざまなサイズの開口が軽やかなリズムをつくりながら奥行きのない面を構成しています。しかも繰り返されるそれらの抽象的な面は池の水に映り込み、或いは水面からの反射光を浴びて繊細きわまりない輝きを放っています。水もまた、ここではアルミパネルと同じように奥行きのない平滑なひとつの面でしかありません。

明るい通路から住戸に歩を進めると、さまざまな要素の絡み合いは一層複雑かつ微妙になります。色を変え、レベルを変え、小さく折れ曲がりながら、空間の流れはとどまることがありません。外部空間で重要な要素であっ

flected on the pond and are bathed by reflected light, so that they radiate an extremely delicate light. The water here is also simply a smooth plane without depth like the panels of aluminum.

As one walks down the passageway, the interplay of diverse elements becomes even more complex and subtle. Colors may change, the level may change, and the passageway may bend slightly, but the flow of space never ceases. The windows, which play an important role in giving the exterior space a rhythm, introduce light into each unit from many directions and give even greater variety to the diverse interior compositions of planes.

Your architecture is more aural than visual, more temporal than spatial. An analogy is often drawn between the rhythm of your architecture and the rhythm of sounds. However, when I say that your architecture is aural, I mean that I always sense in your spaces a transparent quality. I sense this transparency not so much in the way void spaces are composed but in the planes. For example, when multiple windows are introduced rhythmically into a single facade, I sense a transparency in the concrete or aluminum wall planes that form the ground for those figures. Like the intervals between sounds in music, the wall planes, be they concrete or aluminum, are fated to vanish in the distance leaving only figural elements.

Your architecture is characterized by such a transparency. Transparency of space makes one unaware of the material quality of volumes, no matter how many of them are layered. Only those elements that are figures emerge in the transparent space. In that transparent space, the elements respond and resonate to each other, and create a world of sounds. However, the spaces you create never feature discordant sounds. The elements never repulse, clash against, or pierce each other. Each element seeks the most agreeable place for it and floats in space, composing a space of tranquil relationships.

A temporal architecture is an architecture of sequences. In moving from one place to the next, and then to the next again, space appears and disappears as if marking the passing of time. The architecture does not appear all at once but becomes manifest phenomenally to the people who experience it.

Toru Takemitsu, Japan's best-known composer of contemporary music, once stated his intentions as follows: "Words like harmony and balance do not mean conformity to existing standards. Simple functionalism must be transcended. The objective is to make new discoveries in the world using your own criterion." He has also said, "I want to free 'sound' from the petty, schematic rules that have bound it and to endow it with a movement that is as true as breathing in and breathing out. I believe the conceptual, inner form of expression that prevails today is not real music. Music ought to be profoundly related to nature; it is at times elegant and at other times brutal."

The architecture you are seeking seems to me to be quite close to what he describes. Many people can sense in your architecture an attempt, not to introduce preconceived schemas into the spatial composition, but to inscribe in that composition a fresh rhythm expressive of the age.

A nostalgia for the vernacular townscape of Italy reappears in the dreamlike, early projects of Aldo Rossi, but with your architecture, Steven, it is as if the modernist spaces depicted by Le Corbusier

---

たリズムを織りなす開口は,住居の内部にあってもさまざまな方向からの光を導き多様な面の構成に一層の変化をもたらしています。

あなたの建築は視覚的と言うより聴覚的であり,空間的と言うよりは時間的な建築です。あなたの建築に感じられるリズムはしばしば音のリズムとの類似性を指摘されていますから,聴覚的であるのは当然かもしれません。しかし私は聴覚的建築と言う時には,必ずその空間に透明性を感じるのです。それはヴォイドなスペースのつくり方,というよりもむしろ面に感じられる透明性です。つまり例えばひとつのファサードのなかに複数の開口がリズムをつくりながら採られているとすると,地を構成しているコンクリートやアルミの壁面に感じられる透明性なのです。音楽に於ける音と音との間の余白のように,いかにコンクリートであろうとアルミが貼られていようと,その壁面は図を構成する要素の彼方に消え去っていかねばならないのです。

あなたの建築はそうした透明さを備えています。したがっていくらヴォリュームが重なっていようと,それらの質感は消え去って透明な空間のなかに図としての要素だけが浮かび上がってくるのです。そして透明な空間のなかで要素は互いに呼応し合い,響き合って聴覚的な世界を奏で始めるのです。しかしあなたのつくり出す空間は決して不協和音の空間ではありません。要素が反発し合ったり,衝突し合ったり,鋭角的に要素が交差することはありません。各要素はそれぞれに自らの最も心地良い場所を求めて空間を漂い,穏やかな関係の空間を構成しています。

時間的な建築,それはシークエンスの建築です。或る場所から別の場所へ,さらに次の場所へと空間は時間的な経緯を伴ってあらわれ,消えてゆきます。建築は一気に全体像としてあらわれるのではなく,体験する人々とともに現象するのです。

日本を代表する現代作曲家,武満徹はかつて自らの作曲への意志を次のように語っています。「調和とか均衡とかいう言葉は,既成の尺に律せられるという意味ではない。それは,たんなる機能主義を超えたものである。自らのモデュールによって世界に新しい発見をすることだ」。或いはまた次のようにも述べました。「図式的なおきてにくみしかれてしまった音楽のちゃちな法則から〈音〉をときはなって,呼吸のかようほんとうの運動を〈音〉にもたせたい。音楽の本来あるべき姿は現在のように観念的な内部表白だけにとどまるものではなく,自然との深いかかわりによって優美に,時には残酷になされるのだと思う」。

恐らくあなたの建築に求めているものはこの言葉にきわめて近いのではないでしょうか。あなたが既成の図式を空間構成に持ち込むのではなく,そこに新鮮な時代の息づかいをリズムとして刻もうとしているのを多くの人々があなたの建築から感じとることができるからです。

アルド・ロッシの初期のプロジェクトには,イターリーのヴァナキュラーな街へのノスタルジーが夢にあらわれる建築のように再現されていますが,スティーヴン,あなたの建築はル・コルビュジエやマレヴィッチなどが描いたモダニズムの空間を夢のなかで再現したかのように感じられるのです。つまり夢が現実と非現実の世界の境界を彷徨するように,あなたの建築も抽象的な空間と現実の生なもので構成される空間の狭間で帰結のない旅を続けているように見えるのです。あなたはコルのように大地に帰還することは出来ない,しかしあなたは虚空に投げ出されたままに,完璧な抽象の世界にとどまることもできない。あなたのプロジェクトを見ていると,宇宙船が地球に近づきながら大気圏に突入し得ないでその周囲を漂っているような印象を受けます。

恐らくそれはあなたの建築への,そして人間への決して裏切ることのでき

or Malevich had reappeared in a dream. Just as a dream wanders on the border between reality and unreality, your architecture travels on an endless journey between abstract spaces and palpable spaces. Unlike Le Corbusier, you cannot return to the earth, yet you cannot remain completely in a world of abstraction either. Looking at your projects, I think of a ship that approaches the earth after traveling in space but, unable to penetrate the atmosphere, is adrift on its fringes.

Perhaps that is because you cannot stop trusting architecture or humanity. The reason I believe in you as an architect is that you are sincere. However, our architectural or artistic images are transcending real life and advancing inexorably into an inanimate, unfeeling world. In contrast, our bodies cannot change, and our actions cannot be free of gravity. Our society, in the meantime, continues to abide by conventions so as to maintain order. Our images are alert to the spirit of the era and capture its essence. They rush headlong into a weightless world or a space that is insatiably homogeneous and abstract. As a result, architects like you with a well-honed sensibility are torn between a cutting-edge world of images and the conservative world of the body, which cannot change as easily. You put too much trust in human beings to try to realize the conceptual avant-garde world. To put it bluntly, you are too gentle. That is why your architecture neither vanishes into the distance beyond the sky nor lands on the earth but instead floats somewhere at the limits of the atmosphere.

I find the new homogeneous spaces attractive. I feel something of their quality in the convenience stores that are scattered everywhere in both the United States and Japan. Generally speaking, the spaces in convenience stores are quite meager. The food products displayed on neutral racks that suggest the inside of a huge refrigerator, the everyday goods that are arranged matter-of-factly as in a warehouse—practically everything that is needed for everyday life is stocked. Everything in that space seems to be of similar quality. The situation is the very opposite of what one finds in department stores or specialty stores that sell brand products. In department stores and specialty stores, each product is displayed to show how it is different and unique. A convenience store, on the other hand, seems to be saying it is really all the same, no matter what you eat, what you wear, and what you use to clean or wash. The message it seems to be transmitting is that everything is the same quality and neutral, and that the individuality or the difference in quality we set so much store by amounts actually to very little. It is a space that anticipates an ultimate condition of entropy.

This space goes beyond mere rationalization or functionality and gives us a glimpse of the arrangement by which our lives today are controlled. We are drawn, after all, not just to utopian spaces but to their opposite. An image of cool homogeneity in its extreme form always gives us as much a frisson as the universal space depicted by Mies. Only a thin line separates the extreme of poverty from abundance.

Your architecture is adrift in a condition of gentleness, but that cannot continue indefinitely. It must either land on earth or depart, vanishing into emptiness. Awaiting that moment, I give myself up in the meantime to your agreeable spaces.

1992

ない信頼に因るのではないでしょうか。私がスティーヴンを一人の建築家として信用できるのはあなたのその誠実さです。しかし我々の建築的，或いは芸術的イメージは現実の生活を超えて，非情な世界へとどんどん踏み込んでいってしまいます。我々の生な身体が変わることはないし，我々の行動は重力に逆らうことはできない。また我々の社会は秩序を維持するためには慣習的であり続けようとします。それに対し，我々のイメージは時代の空気を敏感に感じとってひたすらそれを尖鋭化させます。無重力の世界やあくなき均質で抽象的な空間のイメージへと突き進んでいってしまうのです。その結果，あなたのように研ぎすまされた感性を備えた建築家は，イメージの世界での先端性と容易には変わり得ない身体自体の保守性との間の拡大されたギャップに引き裂かれることになるのです。観念内部のアヴァンギャルドの世界を実体化しようと突き進んでしまうには人間を信頼し過ぎている，端的に言えば，やさし過ぎるのです。だからこそあなたの建築は虚空の彼方に消え去ってしまうこともなく，かと言って大地に着地することもなく，大気圏の周辺を漂うことになるのではないでしょうか。

今日，新しい均質な空間は魅力的だと言いましたが，私はあなたの国や日本ならば到るところに散在するコンビニエンス・ストアにそのような性格を感じます。一般的に言えばコンビニエンス・ストアの空間はきわめて貧しい空間です。大きな冷蔵庫の内部のようにニュートラルなラックに並列された食料品の数々，或いは倉庫の内部のように素っ気なく並べられた日用品の数々，そこには住生活に必要なほとんどすべてのものが取り揃えられていますが，この空間の内部であらゆるものは均質に見えます。それはデパートやブランド品を売る専門店とは全く逆の空間です。デパートや専門店では，各品物は隣の品といかに違うか，それ自体が個性の輝きを放っているかをディスプレイしようとしますが，コンビニエンス・ストアでは何を食べようが，何を着ようが，掃除や洗濯をするのに何を使おうが，結局すべて同じなんだと言っているように見えるのです。あらゆるものは均質でニュートラルで，我々が固執してきたさまざまなものの個性とか質の違いはほんの微差に過ぎないんだ，というメッセージを発しているように思われてしまうのです。すべての運動はエントロピーの究極状態へ向かっているんだという予言の空間のように感じられるのです。

恐らくこの空間は，単に販売の合理性とか機能性といった次元を超えて，我々の今日の生活がどれ程コントロールされたものであるのか，その仕組みを垣間見せているのではないでしょうか。我々はユートピアの空間にのみ惹かれる訳ではなく，その逆にも取り憑かれてしまうのです。かつてミースが描いたユニヴァーサル・スペースのように，冷徹な均質さの極限のイメージは常に我々をぞくぞくさせる程の魅力に満ちているのです。貧しさの極致は豊かさといつも紙一重です。

あなたの建築が漂っている状態はやさしさに溢れていますが，このまま永久に漂い続けるわけにはいかないでしょう。それはいつか大地に着地するのか，それとも虚空の彼方に飛び去ってしまうのか，その瞬間を見ることを心待ちしながら，私はあなたの心地良い空間に身を任せています。

1992年

STEVEN HOLL
Phenomena and Idea

現象と理念｜スティーヴン・ホール

Experience of phenomena—sensations in space and time as distinguished from the perception of objects—provides a "pre-theoretical" ground for architecture. Such perception is pre-logical i.e., it requires a suspension of a priori thought. Phenomenology, in dealing with questions of perception, encourages us to experience architecture by walking through it, touching it, listening to it. "Seeing things" requires slipping into a world below the everyday neurosis of the functioning world. An underground city for which we have keys without locks, it is full of mysteries.

Phenomenology as a way of thinking and seeing becomes an agent for architectural conception. While phenomenology restores us to the importance of lived experience in authentic philosophy, it relies on perception of pre-existing conditions. It has no way of forming a priori beginnings. Making a non-empirical architecture requires a conception or a formative idea. In each project we begin with information and disorder, confusion of purpose, program ambiguity, an infinity of materials and forms. All of these elements, like obfuscating smoke, swirl in a nervous atmosphere. Architecture is a result of acting on this indeterminacy.

To open architecture to questions of perception, we must suspend disbelief, disengage the rational half of the mind, and simply play and explore. Reason and skepticism must yield to a horizon of discovery. Doctrines cannot be trusted in this laboratory. Intuition is our muse. The creative spirit must be followed with happy abandon. A time of research precedes synthesis.

In music one says that something is "meant" by a particular movement. Do architectural thoughts have equivalent "meanings?" Is there a way of thinking in the material of construction? A way of thinking in materials which may yield a coupling of thinking-making specific to architecture? Making architecture involves a thought that forms itself through the material in which it is made. The thinking-making couple of architecture occurs in silence. Afterward, these "thoughts" are communicated in the silence of phenomenal experiences. We hear the "music" of architecture as we move through spaces while arcs of sunlight beam white light and shadow.

現象を体験すること——自分の外にある対象として知覚するのではなく，空間と時間の中に身を置くことで得られる感覚——は，建築の「理論以前」の領域に踏み込むことである。このような知覚は論理にかなうか否かを問う以前のものであるから，このときには，演繹的な思考を停止しなければならない。現象学，つまり知覚したことについての問いを抱くという方法は，建築の中を自らの足で歩き，手で触れ，耳で聴くことによって建築を実感しようとする時に，私たちの役に立つはずである。「物を観る」には，機能世界の日常的な神経症的状況の下に隠された世界に入り込むことが欠かせない。私たちが入り口の鍵を与えられている地下の都市は，神秘に満ちているのだから。

思考と観察の一方法としての現象学は，建築を理解するための仲介者となってくれる。哲学の分野でいえば，現象学とは，生きる中で得られる経験の重要性を私たちに再認識させるものであるとともに，まだ実在しない状況を感知しようとするものでもある。したがって演繹的な意味での出発点となるものは持たない。経験主義に基づかずに建築をつくろうとすれば，コンセプト，つまり造形上の理念が必要である。プロジェクトにとりかかる時には私たちはいつも予備知識を集めるけれど，はじめのうちそれらは未整理であるから目的は混乱し計画はあいまいだが，それだけに，材料にせよ形態にせよこの時点では限りない可能性が残されている。これらの要素のことごとくは煙幕のように，神経質な雰囲気を漂わせながら渦巻いている状態にある。建築とは，このような不確実な状態にはたらきかけた末にやっとつくり出される結果なのである。

知覚によって生じた疑問に対して，開かれた状態に建築を置こうとするなら，猜疑心をひとまずおいて，心の半分を占める合理性から離れて虚心に遊びながら探索することだ。理性と懐疑論は，果てしない地平の中で何も発見することなく屈するにちがいない。この実験では，何であれ教条主義に陥ることなく，直観を創造の神にする。独創的な精神には，幸福な放縦がともなう。統合に至る前にまず調査の時が必要なのだ。

音楽では，どの楽章をとっても何かの「意味がある」と言われている。建築でもそれに相当するような「意味」があるだろうか。構造材料についての考え方は確立しているだろうか。考えることとつくることを結びつけるものである素材について考える方法は，建築に特有のものがあるのだろうか。建築をつくるにあたっては，それをつくる素材を通じて自ずと形成される思想を必要とする。建築について考えることは，つくることと平行して，自然のうちに進んでゆく。のちになって，こうして

In a "zero ground" without site, program, or time, certain types of perception emerge as "phenomenal zones." Experimental territories, these zones of intensely charged silence lie beyond words. In opposition to those who insist on speech, on language, on signs and referents, we strive to escape language-time bondage. To evolve theoretically in active silence encourages experimentation. Silent phenomenal probes haunt the polluted sea of language like submarines gliding along the sandy bottom, below the oil-slick of rhetoric.

Certain physical interactions offer zones of investigation:

Color projection is experienced when light, reflected off a brightly colored surface, then bounced onto a neutral white surface, becomes a glowing phenomena that provokes a spatial sense. Reflected color is seen indirectly; it remains, with a ghostlike blush, the absent referent to an experience. In experiments with these phenomena we have discovered an emotional dimension that suggests a "psychological space."

A sponge can absorb several times its weight in liquid without changing its appearance. Cast glass seems to trap light within its material. Its translucency or transparency maintains a glow of reflected light, refracted light or the light dispersed on adjacent surfaces. This intermeshing of material properties and optic phenomena opens a field for exploration. Phenomenal zones likewise open to sound, smell, taste, and temperature as well as to material transformation.

Overlapping perspectives, due to movement of the position of the body through space create multiple vanishing points, opening a condition of spatial parallax. Perspectival space considered through the parallax of spatial movement differs radically from the static perspectival point of Renaissance space and the rational positivist space of modern axonometric projection. A dynamic succession of perspectives generates the fluid space experienced from the point of view of a body moving along an axis of gliding change. This axis is not confined to the x-y plane but includes the x-y-z dimensions manifesting themselves in the other dimensions, gravitational forces, electromagnetic fields, time, etc. Perspectives of phenomenal flux, overlapping perspective space is the "pure space" of experiential ground.

Architecture is born when actual phenomena and the idea that drives it intersect. Whether a rationally explicit statement or a subjective demonstration, a concept establishes an order, a field of inquiry, a limiting principle. The concept acts as a hidden thread connecting disparate parts with exact intention. Meanings show through at this intersection of concept and experience.

A structuring thought requires continuous adjustment in the design process to set manifold relations among parts within the larger whole. As dimensions of perception and experience unfold in the design process, constant adjustments aim at a balance of idea and phenomena.

"Kajitsu"
Japanese Zen poets developed a vocabulary to discuss *Kajitsu* or a poem's aspect and form. *Ka* is the beautiful surface of a poem while *jitsu* is its substantial core. An organic fusion of spirit and intellect opens a path toward inspiration, awareness, and *yugen*, the Buddhist term for

浮かんだ「思想」は現象的な経験のうちに、いつしか伝えられる。太陽の弧を描く白い光とそれぞれがつくる影の中、空間を動いてゆくと、建築の奏でる「音楽」が聞こえてくるようになるのだ。

敷地もプログラムも時間もない「ゼログラウンド」では、ある種の知覚が「現象ゾーン」として現れる。実験的な領域は、言葉を超越して、沈黙が支配するゾーンである。弁舌や言語や記号や引用などに力をいれる連中とは反対に、私たちは言語と時間の結びつきを避けようとする。あえて沈黙のうちに理論を進化させることによって実験は黙々と進められるからである。現象についての調査は潜水艦よろしく、レトリックが油膜のように水面に浮かぶ下を、汚染された言語の海の底を静かに航行する。

ある種の物理的な相互作用が研究の領域を提供することもある。

色彩の投影を経験するには、鮮やかな色の面で光を反射させて、それを色のない白い面にあてると、白熱する光がにじみだし、それによって空間が実感される。このとき、反射光は間接的にしか見えない。そのぼうっとした明かりは、経験に照らしても思い当たるものがない新たな体験である。このような現象を扱う実験によって、私たちは「心理的空間」を示唆する情緒の次元を発見したのである。

海綿は、その重量の数倍もの液体を吸い込みながら外には変化を見せない。キャストグラスは、その中に光を閉じ込める。あるいは半透明な、あるいは透明なこのガラスは、反射した光や閉じ込めた光の輝きや、となりあわせた表面で拡散された光の輝きをたくわえる。物質の領域と光学的な領域がこのように重なり合うと、また探求すべき分野が開かれる。現象ゾーンは、物質の変化に対するのと同じように音、香り、味、温度などにも開かれている。

空間の中、身体の位置を動かすにしたがってパースペクティブが重なり、多くの消失点が生じ、空間の中の視差の状態が開かれる。空間を動く視点から検証するパースペクティブな空間は、ルネッサンスの空間の固定した視点とも、現代のアクソノメトリックの合理的実証主義の空間とも根底的な差異がある。パースペクティブを連続的に移動させることによって、そこには流動的な空間が生じ、すべるように変化する軸に沿って動く身体の視点からそれを経験することができる。この軸はＸＹ平面だけでなく、Ｘ, Ｙ, Ｚの次元を含む諸々の次元、たとえば重力、電磁場、時間などで表される。パースペクティブな空間に重なるようにして、現象がパースペクティブに変化すると、そこには実験の場としての「純粋空間」が生じるのである。

現象と、それを動かす理念が交わる時に建築が生まれる。合理的で明白な形で表明されるものであれ主観的な主張であれ、コンセプトによって秩序や研究の分野や原則を確かなものにする。コンセプトは表立たずに裏糸のようにして、別個のものであるそれぞれの部分を明白な意図によって結ぶ。このようにして、コンセプトと経験が交わるときに意味が表れるのである。

思考を体系づけるには、デザインの過程で絶えず調整を続けながら、全体をなす大きなものの中にあるそれぞれの部分のうちに、多面的な関係をつくりあげてゆくことが必要である。デザインの過程では、知覚と経験の次元が展開してゆくに伴って、理念と現象の間のバランスをとるために常に調整がつづけられる。

［花実］
日本の禅の詩人たちのつくったあるヴォキャブラリーが議論を生んだ。花実、すなわち、詩の伝えるものと形式である。「花」は詩の美しい表面であるのに対して、「実」は本質をなす中心を意味する。精神と知の有機的な融合がインスピレーションや悟りあるいは幽玄（「意味の奥深さ」とでもいった仏教用語）へ至る道を開く。

建築のとらえどころのない本質、深いところにある意味や、本質的な中心を見つけるには情熱と熱中が必要

"depth of meaning."

Uncovering the elusive essence of architecture, its depth of meaning or substantial core, requires passion and enthusiasm. The search for meaning demands a resistance to empty formalism, textual obfuscation and commercialism. Focusing on ideas early in the design process sets the substantial core ahead of the surface.

If there is life in ideas, a passion for architecture is renewed in the clarification of these ideas. For what is an architectural concept if not the material and spatial expression of spiritual intentions?

Intertwining of intellect and feeling is inherent in thought intuitively developed, thought that seeks clarity rather than possesses truth, thought that searches and is open to the changing field of culture and nature that it expresses. Although intuition cannot be explicitly expressed, we cannot condemn intuitive work to ambiguity. Architecture, perhaps more than any other form of communication, possesses the power of uniting intellectual and intuitive expression. Fusing the objective with the subjective, architecture can stitch our daily lives together by a single thread of intensity. It can possess both the core depth and the radiant surface by which to concretize the spirit. We must look beyond the *ka* of a beautiful surface to contemplate the *jitsu* of the core substance.

Soul

Soul is essential to architecture. A building stands in mute solitude, yet receptive individuals silently perceive the soul instilled in the work. Soul lies in attention to detail distilled in space and concretized in the love of construction. This love can take the form of shimmering icicle prisms or perspectives of steel.

In the thirteenth century, Saint Thomas Aquinas developed teachings linking theology and philosophy which held that all knowledge begins with sense perception. The direct connection of soul and perception was taught in "clear sighted penetration of the soul into objects of perception...."

Nourishment of soul begins by allowing greater expression of the language of the imagination, by suspending disbelief in favor of experiment, and by seeing things. Cultivating of a metaphorical sense of reality ... a mythopoetic understanding of indefinable experiences and mysteries enriches the soul. Just as the unconscious and the intuitive can be intentionally brought to bear on thoughts and decisions, the intense exploration of a particular locus, together with material, can endow form with greater psychological significance. Like an electrical charge, soul passes from the artist into objects, and through eyes from the object to the viewer.

Reflection on perception in the design process considers all scales, including the micro scale of material properties. Even the most common seemingly inert material must be allowed to "speak" its essence. Kandinsky addresses this approach: "Everything that is dead quivers. Not only the things of poetry, stars, moon, wood, flowers, but even a white trouser button glittering out of a puddle in the street. Everything has a secret soul, which is silent more than it speaks."

Triumphant expressions of life often emerge despite the cycles of death by which

である。意味を探るには，内容のない形式主義に陥ったり，原点に固執するあまりに目を曇らせたり，商業主義に堕することは慎まねばならない。デザインの初期のプロセスの中で理念を中心にすえることは，表面よりも，本質的な中心を前にすえるということを意味するのである。

理念が真に生命を持つものであるなら，建築に対する情熱は，これらの理念を明らかにすることでまた新たに再生するはずだ。精神の目指すものが，物質と空間によって表現したものと一致しないとしたら，建築のコンセプトなど何の役にも立たなかったことになる。

知と情が織りなされている状態は，直観に基づいて展開された思想，たとえば真実を固定したものとして所有しようとするのではなく明晰さをあくまでも追求しようとする思想，あるいは文化と自然の領域の変化するありかたを探り，それを受け入れようとする思想などに固有のものである。直観力というものが明確な形で表すことができないとしても，直観に基づく仕事はあいまいなものだといってとがめるわけにはゆかない。建築は，おそらく他のどんなコミュニケーションの形式にもまして，知的な表現と直観的な表現を結ぶ力を持っているのだ。建築が客観的な立場と主観的な立場を融合させることができれば，私たちの日々の生活を，丈夫なことこのうえない一本の糸を使って縫い合わせることができるのである。そのとき，建築は，深いところにある中心と，精神をにじませて光芒を放つ表面を二つながらに持つことになる。美しい表面である「花」を貫いて観る目をもって，本質をなす「実」にまで思考を深めねばならない。

［魂：ソウル］

魂は建築になくてはならないものだ。建築は一言も発するわけでもなく孤独に立っているだけであるけれど，感受性をそなえた人は，そこに潜む魂の存在を無言のうちに感じとることができる。魂は，あるときは空間の中で熟成されたディテールに注がれた思い入れの中に潜み，あるいは建築をつくりあげてゆくことへの愛情の中で具体化される。このような愛情は，ほのかに光るつららのプリズムのような形をとることもあれば，時にはスティールが見せるパースペクティブとなることもある。

13世紀，聖トマス・アクィナスは神学と哲学を結びつけ，あらゆる知識は感性による知覚から始まるのだという教えを展開した。魂と知覚を直接に結びつけることをこう教えたのである。「魂が知覚の対象のなかへ，目を見開きながら入り込んでゆくことだ」と。

魂を育てるには，想像をこめた言葉で表現するのを認めること，なにごとも体験で確かめようとする姿勢をひとまず採ること，物事を自分の目で見ることなどから始める。現実の中にメタファーを読みとる感覚を培う——説明のつかない経験や神秘的な事象を神話詩的に理解することが魂を豊かなものにするからだ。無意識や直感力を意図的に思想や判断に持ちこむのと同じように，物質を含む特定のものに焦点を合わせて真剣な探求をすすめれば，心理的な意味を大きくした形態を生み出すことが出来る。充電をするときのように，魂は芸術家から作品へと移り，作品から鑑賞者へと目を経て伝えられるのである。

デザインの過程での知覚について考えると，物質の領域での微妙な世界まで含んだあらゆるスケールに及ぶ。たとえ，このうえなくありふれた，浅薄でつまらない物質であれ，その本質を「物語る」ことが許されねばならない。カンディンスキーは，このようなアプローチについてこう書いている。「生命なきものさえ，あらゆるものが身を震わせる。星や月や森や花のような詩的なものたちは言うにおよばず，道端の水たまりでキラキラしているズボンの白いボタンのようなものでもその例外ではない。あらゆるものが秘めた魂を持ちながら語ろうとせずに沈黙を守るのである」。

生命あるものは，やがて巡ってくる死に囲まれながら

they are surrounded. The question of soul is a question of will. The spirit of a community or society as well as that of an individual is often a pathologized territory. New investigations and new projects must be undertaken. Today the urgency of the soul is provoked by unprecedented human coldness.

An inexplicable modern soul unfolds from tragedy and absurdity. Hope rises on the ground of desperate conditions indifectly proportional to the emotional intensity of the situation: in the writings of Franz Kafka, and André Breton, the tragic and seemingly absurd are taken to extremes, yielding a strange existential hope. Humiliating circumstances and absurd predicaments are a part of everyday life in the modern metropolis, yet these conditions fuel the modern soul.

To embrace the unique anxieties of our time, one must avoid false optimism and the phantoms of nostalgia. Our challenge is to make spaces of a serenity and exhilaration that allow the modern soul to emerge. Our everyday lives include the upside-down view of the earth, in a live television broadcast in which figures walk without gravity, or stroll along a sidewalk past barrels of live crabs fighting each other. The modern soul, its unprecedented spirit, must have an architecture.

Meshing Sensation and Thought

If I walk along a shore towards a ship which has run aground, and the funnel or masts merge into the forest bordering on the sand dune, there will be a moment when these details suddenly become part of the ship; and indissolubly fused with it. As I approached, I did not perceive resemblances or proximities which finally came together to form a continuous picture of the upper part of the ship. I merely felt that the look of the object was on the point of altering, that something was imminent in this tension, as a storm is imminent in storm clouds.
—M. Merleau-Ponty

Perception of architecture entails manifold relations of three fields; the foreground, middle ground and distant view are united in one experience as we observe and reflect while occupying a space. Mergings of these fields of space bracket very different perceptions. In the intertwining of the larger space with its forms and proportions and the smaller scale of materials and details lies architecture's power to exhilarate. Such phenomenal territory cannot be indicated in plan/section methods. Photography can only present one field clearly, excluding changes in space and time.

The weak link from perception back to inception must be scrutinized and strengthened. The traditional drawing of a plan is a blind notation, nonspatial and nontemporal. Perspectives of overlapping fields of space break this short circuit in the design process. Perspective precedes plan and section to give a priority to bodily experience and binds creator and perceiver. The spatial poetry of movement through overlapping fields is animated parallax.

To work simultaneously in foreground, middle ground, and distant view, an architect must constantly think of the next smaller and the next larger scales. The master plan of a campus space, for example, must consider the space between and within buildings as well as details of materials, glossy or dull or luminescent. Models constructed in plaster, wire, acid-transformed brass, and other

---

も、生命のよろこびを示すのである。魂の発する問いは意思の抱く問いでもある。コミュニティや社会の精神は、人間ひとりひとりのそれと同じように、時には病に至ることが少なくない。それを守るための、新しい研究と新しいプロジェクトが進められるべきだ。今日、魂が追い詰められているのも、かつてない人間の冷たさのせいなのだから。

悲劇や不条理の中で見ると、名状しがたい現代の魂さえも明らかになってくる。希望は、絶望的な状況という大地から芽を伸ばすものだが、それは、状況が感情に訴える強さに間接的に比例したものである。フランツ・カフカやアンドレ・ブルトンの著作では、悲劇やあからさまな不条理がある限界に達すると、不思議な実存的な希望が湧いて来る。屈辱的な環境や不条理に満ちた境遇は、現代の大都市では日々の生活の一部を占めているのだが、それが、現代人の魂に火を点すのである。

私たちの時代に特有の苦悩と正面から取り組もうとすれば、偽りのオプティミズムやノスタルジアの亡霊に囚われることは避けねばならない。私たちが目指しているのは、静寂に満ちていながら活気を溢れさせて、現代の魂の生まれるのを促すような空間をつくることである。日常的な生活の中でも、テレビジョンの生放送では地球の裏側の光景が映し出され、無重力状態で人間が歩いたり、夥しい数の生きたカニが戦いをくりひろげるかたわらの歩道を人がぶらついたりするのだ。このような現代の魂という、かつてなかった精神は、それ自身にふさわしい建築を持たねばならない。

［感覚と思考を織り合わせる］
「私が渚づたいに或る難破船の方へ歩いて行って、その船の煙突なり帆柱なりが砂丘を縁どる森と溶け合って見えるという場合、やがてこれらの細部が生き生きとその船と合体し、その船に接合される或る瞬間が来るだろう。だが、もっと近づくにつれて私の知覚したものは、この船の上部構造を最後には一つの連続した図面の中に再結合してしまうであろうような、相似または近接の関係ではない。私が感得したところは、ただ、対象の様相が変化して行ったこと、あたかも雲が嵐の逼迫を告げているようにこの緊張が何ものかの到来を告げていたということ、これである。」
——M・メルロー＝ポンティ著、『知覚の現象学1』、竹内芳郎、小木貞孝 共訳

建築の知覚には、三つの領域相互の多面的な関係を伴う。ある空間の中に立って観賞していると、近景と中景と遠景が結ばれて一つの経験として残される。三つの空間領域が合体することは、全く異なった知覚を一つに括りこむことである。人を活気づける建築の力は、形態やプロポーションが大きなスペースに、材質やディテールが小さなスケールに織りこまれたところに生まれるのだ。このような現象になると、平面や断面図による方法では伝えることができない。写真にしても、せいぜいひとつの場をはっきりと表現することができるだけで、空間と時間の変容となると手に負えるものではない。

知覚することと、知覚に至るその発端は弱く結ばれているにすぎないことを綿密に調べ、それを強めなければならない。平面図という伝統的な図面は、不十分な表現法であるから空間と時間を伝えることができないが、空間の重なりを表現するパースであれば、デザインのプロセスの中でこのような短絡を断ち切ることができる。平面や断面図の前にパースを描けば身体的な経験を優先させることによって、建築家はつくる人間であると同時にそれを感知する立場に立つことができる。重なる領域の中で、動きによって、空間の詩は生き生きとした視差をつくる。

近景、中景、遠景を同時に考えながらつくれば、建築家は、常にひとつ小さいスケールから一段大きいスケールまで考え続けることになる。たとえばキャンパスのマスタープランをつくるにあたっても、建物の間や中のス

construction materials balanced against a range of perspective views set an intermeshing design process in motion.

The phenomenal merge of object and field is accomplished via attention to individual site and situation. The hackneyed terms *contextualism* or *context* have encouraged an operation whereby a new building, chameleonlike, takes characteristics from each of its neighbors without maintaining internal integrity.

Rather, actual experience envisioned in light, perspective and material must be cross-referenced in an analytic process open to a new architecture that may not yet be understood. Architecture inserted into an existing situation may not strive to replicate or to achieve autonomy via contrast. Meshing of site and situation with an integrally conceived new architecture yields a third condition; a new interrelation—a new "place" is formed.

Time's Multiplicity

As the imperceptible downward flow of glass in the lower portion of window panes measures the passage of time, architecture also serves as an index of time. Second, minute, hour, month, year, decade, epoch, millennium all are focused by the lens of architecture. Architecture is among the least ephemeral, most permanent expressions of culture.

Nostalgia, an irrational yearning for the return to another time, dominates American architecture today. Preservation of the past continues in the mind in books, in photographs and films, and in the conservation of past construction but simulating the past is a travesty of the present. This return to a romanticized time avoids the existential burden of time—its angst and its joy.

A certain resistance, a "negative capability," is necessary to exist and act in the present. It is important to think and to act on our thinking in the present. We are not merely of our time, we *are* our time. In our time the nature of speed itself has transformed the definition of space. The acceleration of fluctuating trends renders it impossible to meet ever-changing appetites. To last, to endure, is a primary challenge to architecture conceived today.

Strategies transcending the novel and image-driven in architecture counter the ongoing historical time of Western culture with a cyclical time of particular place and individual circumstance. For each distinct situation there is a time, yielding a "multiplicity of times." For example, for Islamic theologians time is not a continuous flow but a galaxy of instants. Space is nonexistent except in points. Alternately, from Bergson's point of view, space is the "impure combination of homogeneous time." Bergson's idea of "duration" includes a "multiplicity of secession, fusion and organization." These two ideas of time—as space or as continuous multiplicity and flow—correspond roughly to the strange cultural conditions of the world today.

While a global movement electronically connects all places and cultures in a continuous time-place fusion, the opposite tendency coexists in the uprising of local cultures and expression of place. In these two forces—one a kind of expansion, the other a kind of contraction—time-space is being formed. A new architecture must be formed that is simultaneously aligned with tran-

---

ペースを考えつつ, 細部の材料を艶ありにするか艶消しにするか, それとも発光性のものにするかなどを考えねばならない。プラスターであれワイヤーや酸化処理をした真鍮であれ, 諸々の建築材料を使った模型とある範囲のパースペクティブとをバランスをとりながら, 進行中のデザインプロセスに織り込んでゆく。

物と背景を現象として融け合わせるには, 個々の敷地と状況に対する関心を持つことが必要である。紋切り型のコンテクスチュアリズムとかコンテクストといった言葉を使うことですすめられてきた方法といえば, 新しい建物をカメレオンさながらに, 隣の建物の性格をもらいうけて建てるばかりで, 内部から滲み出すそれ自身の性格を守ろうとはしない。

それよりも, 光, パースペクティブ, 材料によって思い描いたものの現実の経験を, 未知の新しい建築への道を開く分析のプロセスの中で, 相互参照してゆかねばならない。そこにあるがままの状況の中に挿しこまれた建築は, 周囲を複製しようともせず, さりとて対比をきわだたせて自己主張をしようともしないだろう。敷地と周囲の環境の網目に織り込むように有機的に考えてつくられた新しい建築は, 第三の状況を産む。新たな相互関係――新たな「場所」が形成されるのである。

[時間の多様性]

窓のガラスの下の部分では, 下に向かうガラスの微細な流れが時間の経過を計るので, 建築は時間の指標でもある。秒, 分, 時間, 月, 年, 10年, 一時代, 千年という時を建築というレンズによってのぞくことができるのだ。建築は, はかない命とはいい難いものの中でも, 最も永遠に近い時間にわたって, 文化を表現しつづける。

ノスタルジア, すなわち, 過去のある時代に回帰したいという不合理なあこがれが, 今日のアメリカの建築を支配している。人間の心の中に, 書物や写真やフィルムの上に, あるいは古い建物の保存という形で過去を残そうとする動きは続けられているけれど, 過去を模倣しようという試みは, 所詮現在のパロディ化にほかならない。美化された時代に回帰しようという企ては, 実存する時間の重荷――その苦悩や歓びを回避しようとするものである。

現代に存在し, 行動するには, ある種の抵抗,「負の能力」が必要である。現在という時に思考し行動することこそ重要なのである。私たちは, この時代に属するだけではない, 私たち自身が私たちの時代そのものなのだ。この時代は, スピードという性質が空間の定義を変形させてしまった。ますます速度を増して変化をつづける傾向の中では, 変化してやまない欲望にすべて応えることは不可能になっている。だとすれば, 持続することこそ, 今日の建築にとっては主要な挑戦となるのだ。

新しさばかりを追い求めたり, イメージを拡大したりすることでつくられる建築を超越しようとするには, 西欧文明の歴史を流れている時間に対して, 特定の場所と特定の人に固有の, 回帰する時間を対置しなければならない。どのような状況の中にも,「時間の多様性」を持つ時間というものがある。たとえば, イスラム教の神学者にとっては, 時間とは連続的な流れではなく, 無数の瞬間が銀河のように集合したものである。空間は, 個々の点にしか存在しないのである。ベルクソンによれば, 空間は「均質な時間の, 雑多な組み合わせ」である。ベルクソンの「時間の持続」という観念は,「離脱と混在と組織化の多様性」を含むものである。時間についてのこれら二つの考え方――空間あるいは連続的な多様性と流れであるという捉え方――は, 今日の世界の不思議な文化状況にほぼ合致する。

電子技術を駆使して, あらゆる場所と文化を結び, 時間と場所が連続的に混在する世界にしようとする世をあげての動きがある一方で, 地方の文化やその場所に固有の表現の反乱という, それとは逆の傾向も共存している。この二つの力――一方は広がってゆこうとし, 他方は凝縮しようとする――が拮抗する中で, 時空間は形

scultural continuity and with a poetic expression of individual situation and community.

Expanding toward an ultra-modern world of flow while condensing sunlight or the texture of stone, on a single plot of land, this architecture aspires to Blake's admonition "to see the universe in a grain of sand." Poetic illumination of unique qualities of places, individual culture and individual spirit reciprocally connects to the transcultural, trans-historical present.

Architecture is a transforming link. An art of duration, crossing the abyss between ideas and orders of perception, between flow and place, it is a binding force. It bridges the yawning gap between the intellect and senses of sight, sound, and touch, between the highest aspirations of thought and the body's visceral and emotional desires. A multiplicity of times are fastened, a multitude of phenomena are fused, and a manifold intention is realized.

Idea

It is precisely the realm of ideas—not of forms or styles—that presents the most promising legacy of twentieth-century architecture. The twenty-first century propels architecture into a world where meanings cannot be completely supplied by historical languages. Modern life brings with it the problem of the meaning of the larger whole. The increased size and programmatic complexity of buildings amplify the innate tendency of architecture toward abstraction. The tall office building, the urban apartment house, and the hybrid of commercial complex call for more open ideas more imaginative organization of a work of architecture. Organization of overall form depends on a central concept to which other elements remain subordinate.

In the experimental work of tentative investigations we remain explorers. This new freedom produces an anxiety that must be embraced with enthusiasm. The practice of a refined methodology, a technical skill, has now seeped through the osmotic membrane of a narrow profession into the open sea and must be nourished with a passion for discovery. New architectures can only be born if we leave habitual ways of working and reject unthinking methods.

Easily grasped images are the signature of today's culture of consumer architecture. Subtle experiences of perception as well as intellectual intensity are overshadowed by familiarity. A resistance to commercialism and repetition is not only necessary, it is essential to a culture of architecture.

The experience of space, light, and material as well as the socially condensing forces of architecture are the fruit of a developed idea. When the intellectual realm, the realm of ideas, is in balance with the experiential realm, the realm of phenomena, form is animated with meaning. In this balance, architecture has both intellectual and physical intensity, with the potential to touch mind, eye, and soul.

1992

成されることになる。したがって, 新しい建築は, 多くの文化の共通項を持ちつつ, 同時に, そこだけにしかない状況やコミュニティを詩的に表現するものでなければならない。

超現代の, 流動する世界に向かって拡がる一方で, 太陽の光や石の肌合いなどを大切にする小さな世界を, ひと切れの土地につくろうとするこの建築は, ブレイクの「砂のひとつぶの中に宇宙を見る」という言葉を意図している。場所の持つユニークな性格や個人ひとりひとりの持つ文化, ひとりの人間の精神性などの持つ詩的な輝きが, 文化の違いを超え歴史を超えた現在といろいろな形で結ばれる。

建築とは, 変形させながら結びつける絆である。頭に抱いた考えと感じとったものの間に横たわる深淵を越え, あるいは流れと場所の間を結ぶ力, 持続する芸術である。知性と視覚, 聴覚, 触覚の間, 思想の目ざす高みと肉体の本能的, 情緒的な欲望の間の, 退屈なまでのギャップに建築は橋渡しをする。多様な時間をまとめ, 雑多な現象を融合し, 多種多様な意図を実現する。

[理念]

20世紀の建築では, 最も期待できる神話を生むのは, 形態でも様式でもない, それはきっと理念の分野だろう。21世紀が建築を送り出す世界は, 歴史的な言語では意味をまかなえなくなっているだろう。現代生活は, さらに広範な全体像を必要としている。建築がますます大きくなり, 計画の複雑さを増すとともに, 建築は抽象化する傾向を強める。高いオフィスビル, 都市のアパートメント, 複合的な機能を持つ商業施設などは, より開放的な考え方, より豊かな想像力を秘めた建築の構成を求めている。全体の形式の構成は, それぞれの中心に据えられるコンセプトの如何にかかっている。

一時的な研究にすぎないような実験的な仕事では, 私たちは探検家であることに安住してしまう。ここで手にいれる新しい自由は, 熱情のとりこになるという新たな悩みを生むことになる。洗練された方法論, 磨かれた技術の実践は, せまい職能に納まらずに, 外海に浸み出すので, 発見する情熱という養分を与えられなければならない。我々が, 旧態依然たる仕事のしかたを脱し, 思考を伴わないやり方を退けようとしないかぎり, 新しい建築は生まれない。

容易に手にすることのできるイメージなど, 消費におもねた建築のつくる今日の文化のしるしにすぎない。そこで感知した微妙な経験は, 知的な力と同じように, やがては馴れによって色褪せたものになる。コマーシャリズムや繰り返しに対して抵抗することは必要であるどころか, 建築の文化の本質をなすものである。

空間と光と材質の経験は, 社会的な問題に対応しうる建築の力と同じように, 理念を発展させたことの成果である。知性の領域, すなわち理念の領域が, 経験の領域, 言いかえれば, 現象の領域との間にほどよいバランスを保つことができれば, 形態は意味によって生命を与えられる。このバランスがあるかぎり, 建築は知的であるとともに物理的な強さを持ち, 心と目と魂に触れる力を秘めたものであり続ける。

1992年

1 Light, Material and Detail
光, 材料, ディテール

Architecture intertwines the perception of time, space, light, and materials, existing on a "pre-theoretical ground." The phenomena which occur within the space of a room, like the sunlight entering through a window, or the color and reflection of materials on a surface, all have integral relations in the realm of perception. The transparency of a membrane, the chalky dullness of plaster, the glossy reflection of opaque glass, and a beam of sunlight intermesh in reciprocal relationships that form the particular experience of a place.

Materials produce a psychological effect such that mental processes, feelings and desires are provoked. They stimulate the senses beyond acute sight towards tactility. In the perception of details, colors and textures, psychological and physiological phenomena intertwine. Phenomena that can be "sensed" in the material and detail of an environment exist beyond that which can be intellectually transmitted.

The materials of architecture communicate in resonance and dissonance, just as musical instruments in composition. Architectural transformations of natural material, such as glass or wood, have dynamic thought and sense provoking qualities. Analogous to woodwinds, brass and percussion instruments, their orchestration in an architectural composition is as crucial to the perception and communication of ideas as the orchestration of musical instruments is for a symphonic work.

Like a musician's breath to a wind instrument or touch to a percussion instrument, light and shadow bring out the rich qualities of materials which remain mute and silent in darkness. Glass becomes radiant when its functional role is altered in transformed states of the material. Bending induces dazzling variations to a simple plane with the geometric curvature of reflected light. Cast glass with its mysterious opacity traps light in its mass and projects it in a diffused glow. Sandblasted glass, likewise, has a luminescence which changes subtly depending on the glass thickness and type, and the grain size of the silica sand used.

Metals can be significantly transformed by sandblasting, bending and acidoxidization, to create rich materiality of surface and color. Integral to materials and their weathering change in time, the beauty of various colors and textures of oxidation also gives details a painterly dimension. Cast metals, aluminum bronze, and brass also add to the palette of alternative materials, expanding the range of details. A variety of metals, such as copper, nickel and zinc, can now be electronically atomized, and sprayed nearly cold in a thin layer over a surface of a different material, opening up new possibilities for finished and plastic details.

The texture of a silk drape, the sharp corners of cut steel, the mottled shade and shadow of rough sprayed plaster or the sound of a spoon striking a concave, wooden bowl, reveal an essence which stimulates the senses.

The experience of material transformations is immersed in the human dimension and the necessity for beauty. Materials form the tools that allow communication of a concept in the experience of an architectural work, regardless of its size. In material and detail, an intensity of quality, rather than quantity, stimulates the perceiver's senses, reaching beyond acute sight to tactility, reviving the haptic realm. The joy of living, and the enhanced quality of everyday life is argued in a quality architecture. It is whispered in material and detail and chanted in space.

Steven Holl

Stretto House

建築では、「理論以前の領域」で時間と空間と光と材料が人に語りかけて、そこにひとつの世界をつくりだす。部屋という空間で生じる現象、たとえば窓から射しこむ日の光、さまざまな材料の表面の色や反射、そうしたものがひとつになって、知覚領域のなかで互いに切り離せない関係が生じるのだ。透けて見える材料、プラスターの落ち着いた白、つややかに光をうつす乳白ガラス、そして一条の太陽光線などが織りなされ、高めあってそこにしかない経験の場をつくりだす。

このようにして材料は、精神作用、感情、欲望をかきたてるほどの心理的効果をもたらす。それらは感覚を刺激し、視覚を超えて、聴覚へと運んでゆく。ディテール、色彩、質感の語るものには、心理的現象と生理的現象が絡み合っている。ある環境を構成している材料やディテールのうちに〈感知〉する現象は、知的に伝達されるものを超えたところにあるのだ。

建築における材料の役割は、ちょうど作曲における楽器のようなものである。ときに美しく響き合い、ときに不協和音をたてる。ガラスや木材のように、自然の材料が形を変えて建築に使われると、思考や感覚を人に引き起こすような性質を備えはじめる。また、建築にとって種々の材料の組み合わせ方が、設計の意図を感じとらせて、それを伝えることに決定的な意味を持つのは、木管楽器や金管楽器や打楽器などの編成が、交響曲に対して持つ意味と同じようなものである。

演奏家の息が管楽器に吹きこまれ、打楽器に一振りが加えられるときのように、光と影は、さもなくば沈黙の闇に潜まざるをえない素材の持つ豊かな性質を引き出してくる。ガラスが機能的な役割から一歩を踏み出して、素材としての別のありかたをするようになると、自ずから輝きを増してくる。たとえば平面ガラスを曲げるだけで、その表面で反射される光は幾何学的な曲面を浮び上がらせて、眩しいバリエーションが生まれる。キャストグラスは、あたかもその塊の中に光を封じ込めたような、不思議な不透明さのあるひそやかな光を沁み出させる。サンドブラスト加工をほどこせば、ガラスの厚さとタイプや吹きつける珪砂の粒径に応じて微妙に光り方を変える。

金属の場合にもサンドブラストや、曲げ加工あるいは酸化などの加工をほどこすことによって生じる著しい変化が、表面や色に豊かな質感を生む。材料の種類に加えて経時変化などが生じると、酸化のもたらす種々の色とテクスチュアによって、ディテールに絵画的な次元が加わることになる。アルミニウム、ブロンズ、真鍮などの鋳物も、材料のパレットに色を加えるので、ディテールはその表現の範囲をさらに拡げてゆく。銅、ニッケル、亜鉛などの種々の金属は、最近ではエレクトロニクス技術によって霧状にすることが可能になり、さほど熱を加えずに他の材質の表面に薄い膜をつくることができるようになって、自由な造型と仕上げをもったディテールに新たな可能性が開かれた。

絹のドレープの風合い、切断されたスティールの鋭い角、荒く吹き付けたプラスターのまだらな陰影、あるいは彫り出しの木のボウルにあたるスプーンの音、そういったものを思い浮かべれば感覚を刺激するもののエッセンスとは何かが明らかになってくる。

材料を変形するという作業は、人間の尺度に合わせつつ美しさを求めるためには欠かすことができない。材料とは、建築の大小を問わず、そのうちにこめられたコンセプトを伝える道具なのだ。材質やディテールについては、量よりも質が人の知覚を刺激して、目に見えるものを超え、触覚の領域を甦らせるからである。生きるよろこびと、日々の生活の質を高めることこそ、すぐれた建築との語らいがもたらすものだが、素材やディテールの中では、ささやかに交わされていた言葉が空間という場を得ると、高らかな歌声なって響きわたるのである。

（スティーヴン・ホール）

1982-83 Cohen Apartment
New York, New York, U.S.A.

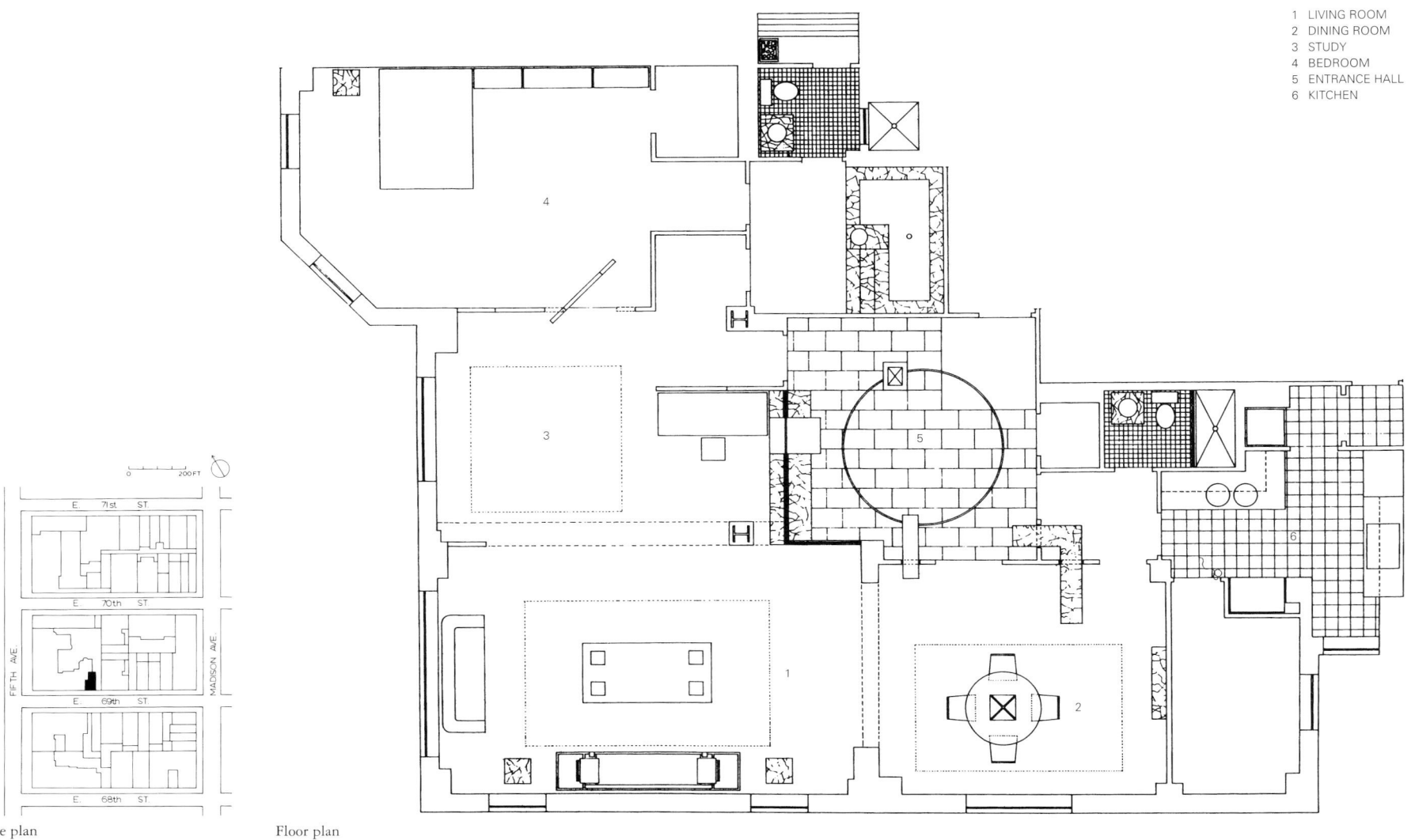

Site plan

Floor plan

1 LIVING ROOM
2 DINING ROOM
3 STUDY
4 BEDROOM
5 ENTRANCE HALL
6 KITCHEN

The existing rooms were removed, exposing an uneven slab and beam system (1939) in the L-shaped apartment. All views from the apartment are characterized by vertical buildings in the near distance.

A brass channel horizon line is set into the wall all around the "L." Above the channel (which is also a plaster screed), integral-color blue plaster is applied to the random beam and plate configuration, resulting in an Euclidian cloud formation. The plaster sky with flying lamps hovers over a floor of waxed cork. Inside the "L" an investigation of elemental architectural composition is explored in three modes: the linear, the planar, and the volumetric.

The dining area is of a linear mode: a linear chandelier is made of three types of lines, a linear table with four linear chairs sits on a carpet patterned with a great variety of lines.

The living area is of a volumetric mode with stuffed cylindrical sofa cushions, a volumetric coffee table and a volumetric carpet.

The studio and bedroom are in a planar mode with a planar drawing board, planes of walls that unfold becoming doors, and a carpet with woven planar elements.

An L-shaped wall dividing the apartment from the entrance foyer records this investigation in a progression of sandblasted glass drawing: planar, volumetric, linear.

Living room and study: view toward bedroom

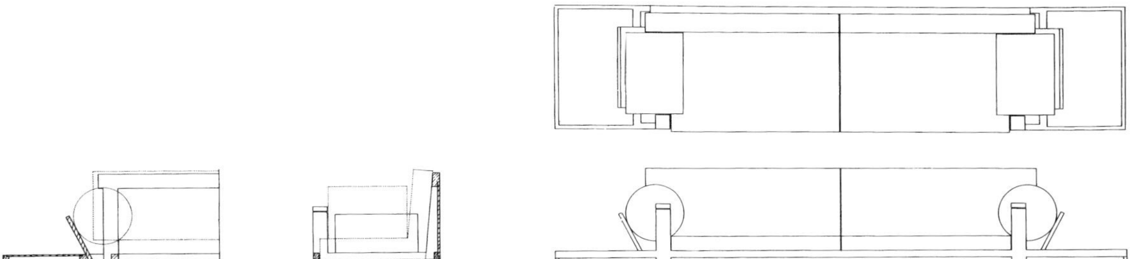

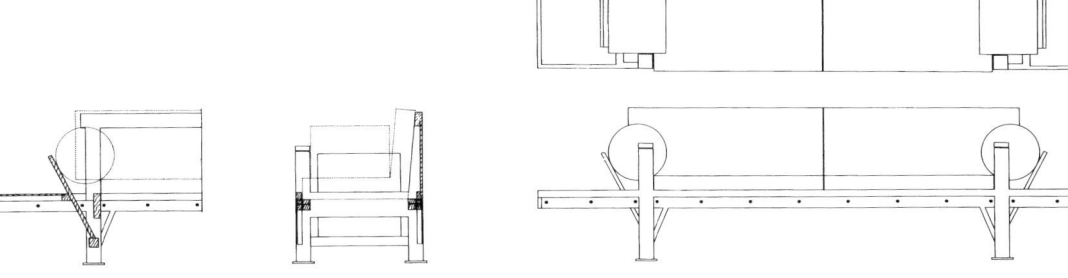

Sofa

I-21

Perspective: view from living room toward study and bedroom

View from living room toward dining room

I-22

Sketch: planar/linear

コーエン・アパートメント

部屋は内装を取り除かれ,床はデコボコのスラブで天井には梁が露出しているという,L型プランのアパートメントだった(つくられたのは,1939年)。外を見ると,垂直にそそり立つビルが間近に並ぶ景観が印象深い。

このL型プランの壁全体に,真鍮のチャンネルを一本,水平に巡らした。このチャンネル(それがプラスター塗の定木の役割も果たした)の上の壁,天井,不揃いの梁の部分にブルーのカラープラスターを塗ると,ユークリッドの雲型模様が浮かんだ。プラスターの空を背景にして,照明はワックスがけのコルクの床の上空を翔ぶ。L型平面を,建築を構成する基本要素によって三つに分類して構成した。線と面と立体である。

食堂は直線のモードである。線形のシャンデリアは三つのタイプの線でつくられ,線形で構成する椅子を四つ並べた線形のテーブルが,ありとあらゆる線のパターンを織込んだカーペットの上に置かれる。

居間は立体のモードだから,詰め物を入れた円筒形のクッションや,立体感を強調したコーヒーテーブルやカーペットが置かれる。

スタジオと寝室は平面のモードである。製図板は平面だし,開けばドアになる壁も平面,カーペットは平面の要素で織ったものだ。

アパートメントを玄関から分かつ「L」型の壁に,こうしたコンセプトをまとめるまでの過程がサンドブラストによってガラスに描かれている。面と立体と線。

Dining room

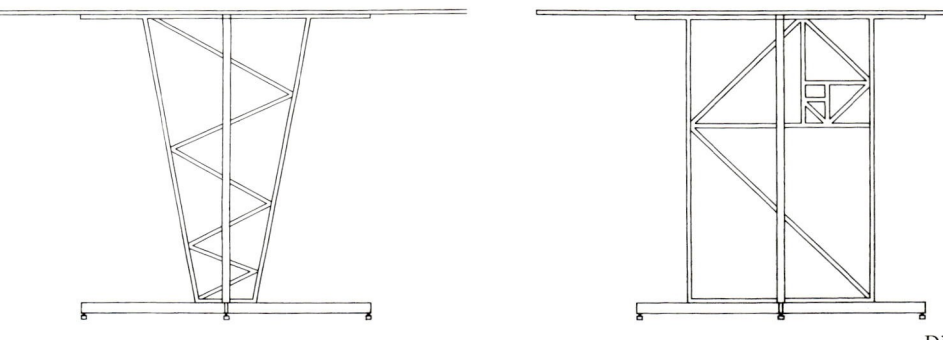

Dining table

I-23

View toward entrance hall

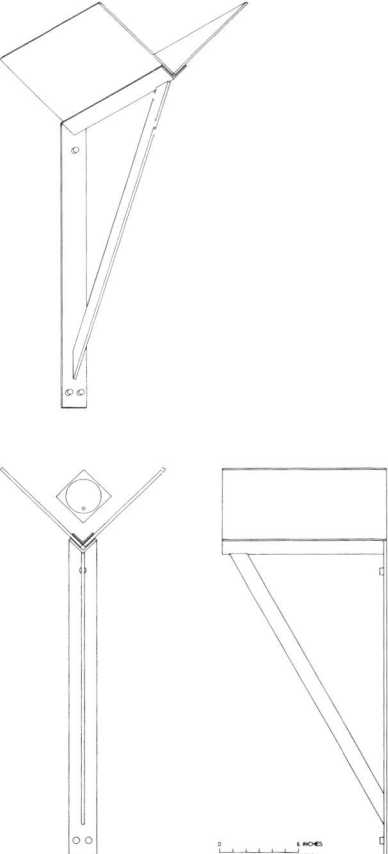

Lighting fixture

Bedroom door: opened (above), closed (below)

View from bedroom toward study and living room

I-25

Ceiling light and sandblasted glazed wall

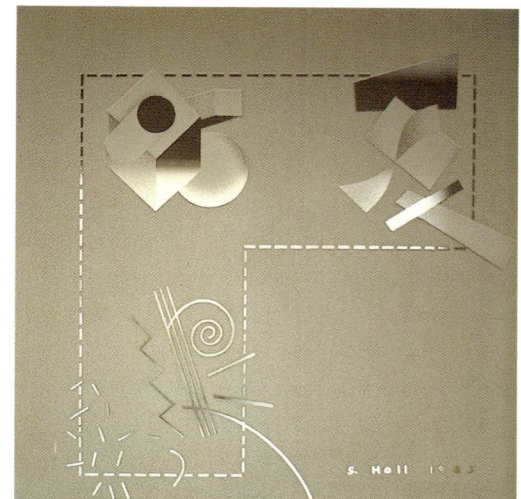

Bedroom on left

Detail of sandblasted glazed wall

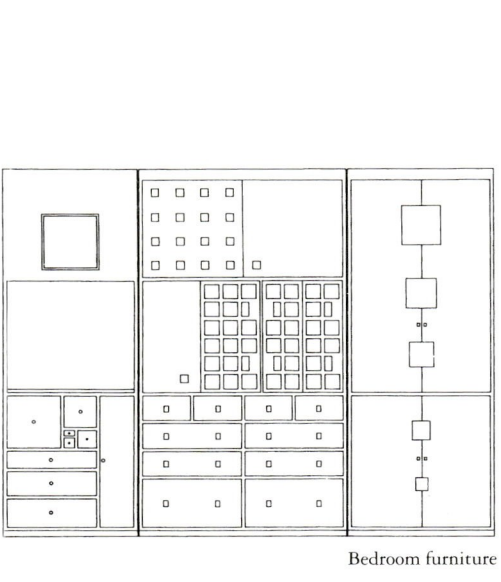

Bedroom furniture

Bedroom

I-27

The site for the Pace Collection showroom is an existing two-story limestone structure with the corner of the building sliced back. A new foundation at the edge of the urban grid was set for the new showroom, completing the corner with a steel-mullioned window affording the maximum showroom glass.

An individual standing on a corner of a Manhattan intersection like Madison Avenue and 72nd Street is exposed to a hyperactive view of alternating forces of movement. The intersection is a counterpoint of one thing against another—fast against slow, stop against go—with the ominous command from the metropolitan authority, "Don't block the box."

An idea of counterpoint (note against note) characterizes the essentially linear architecture. Small sandblasted amber glass panels are set against the horizontal steel bars of the main mullions. Along 72nd Street, the bars are predominantly horizontal, while along Madison they are predominantly vertical. The sandblasted glass drawings carry the contrapuntal idea to the detail scale. Along Madison Avenue, these drawings are in lines, while the 72nd Street facade shows the same drawings extruded

Elevation on 72nd Street

Pace Collection Showroom
1985-86   New York, New York, U.S.A.

I-28

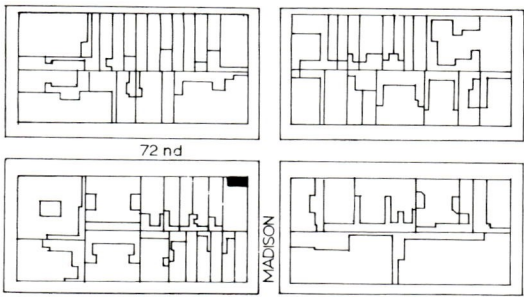

Site plan

into planes. It is as if the shop itself were a block of wood with end grain and edge grain differentiation. Each glass drawing freely interprets counterpoint in a different way, contrasting two kinds of lines, straight against curved, free-form against arc, arc against zigzag, arc against chord, etc. The awning is a curve against the straight lines of the mullions. Inside, the idea is carried further in the guardrail where a curve fuses against simple horizontal bars dislocating them vertically to miss connecting along the curve. The ceiling is a free contrapuntal arrangement of rectangular voids (containing lighting and A.C.) set against the flat horizontal plane.

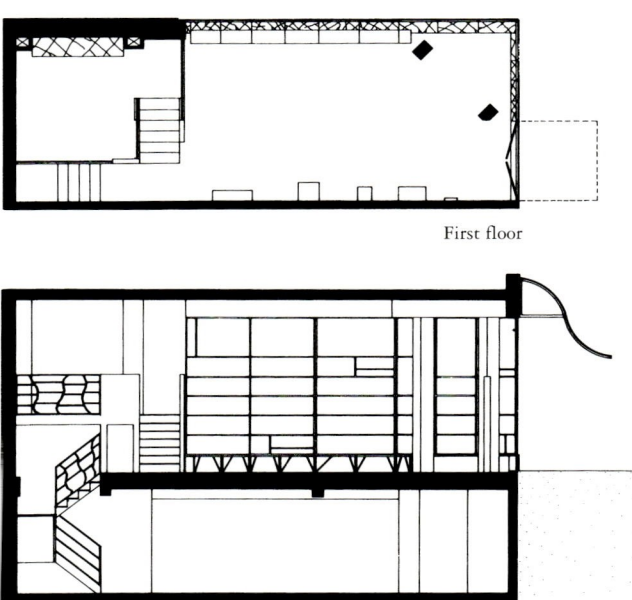

First floor

Longitudinal section

Entrance on Madison Avenue

View from mezzanine

I-29

Night view from 72nd Street

Mezzanine

View toward mezzanine

ペース・コレクション・ショールーム

ペース・コレクションのショールームが入るのは、角のところが切り取られて後退している、石灰岩の2階建の既存の建物である。区画の縁に沿って新たに基礎をつくり、スティールの方立で包んで最大限のガラス面を確保した。

マディソン・アベニューと72丁目の交差点のような、マンハッタンの街角に立つと、ひきもきらず行き交うとてつもない動きと力にさらされる。こうした交差点はものとものを対比的に見せる場なので——速く動くものと緩やかなもの、停止と前進——そこには、「交差点をふさぐべからず」などという市当局のご託宣がある。

そこで、対位法（音と音の対比）に則って、この建築の線形という性格を表現することになった。細かく割り付けたアンバー色のガラスパネルを、メインとなる方立の水平のスティール・バーにはめ込む。72丁目側では、水平方向が強く、マディソン・アベニューに面するところでは垂直方向のラインが強調される。サンドブラストによるガラスのドローイングは、ディテールのスケールに至るまで対位法の考え方が一貫している。マディソン・アベニュー側のドローイングは線で描かれるが、72丁目側のファサードは同じドローイングが面に形を変える。さながら、この店が木のかたまりで、一方には木口の年輪を見せ、他方が柾目を見せているようなものだ。ガラスに描かれた各々のドローイングは、二種の線でそれぞれに異なる形で対位法を表現する。曲線に対して直線、円弧に対比する自由曲線、ジグザグに円弧、直線の弦には円弧といった具合だ。庇は、方立の直線に対置する曲線である。内部に目を向けると、これが手摺りにも表われて、曲線がシンプルな水平線に溶け込み、それが垂直方向に位置を変えて曲線とのつながりを断つ。天井には長方形の掘り込み（照明や空調が納められる）が散在する。これも水平に対する対位法なのである。

1986-87 MoMA Tower Apartment
New York, New York, U.S.A.

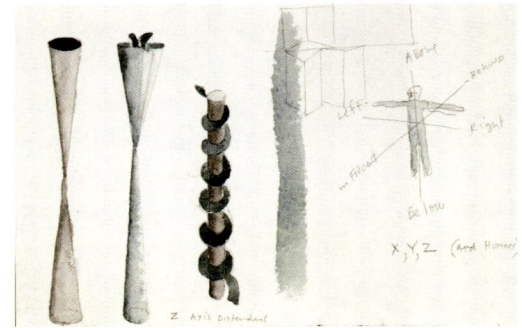
Concept sketch

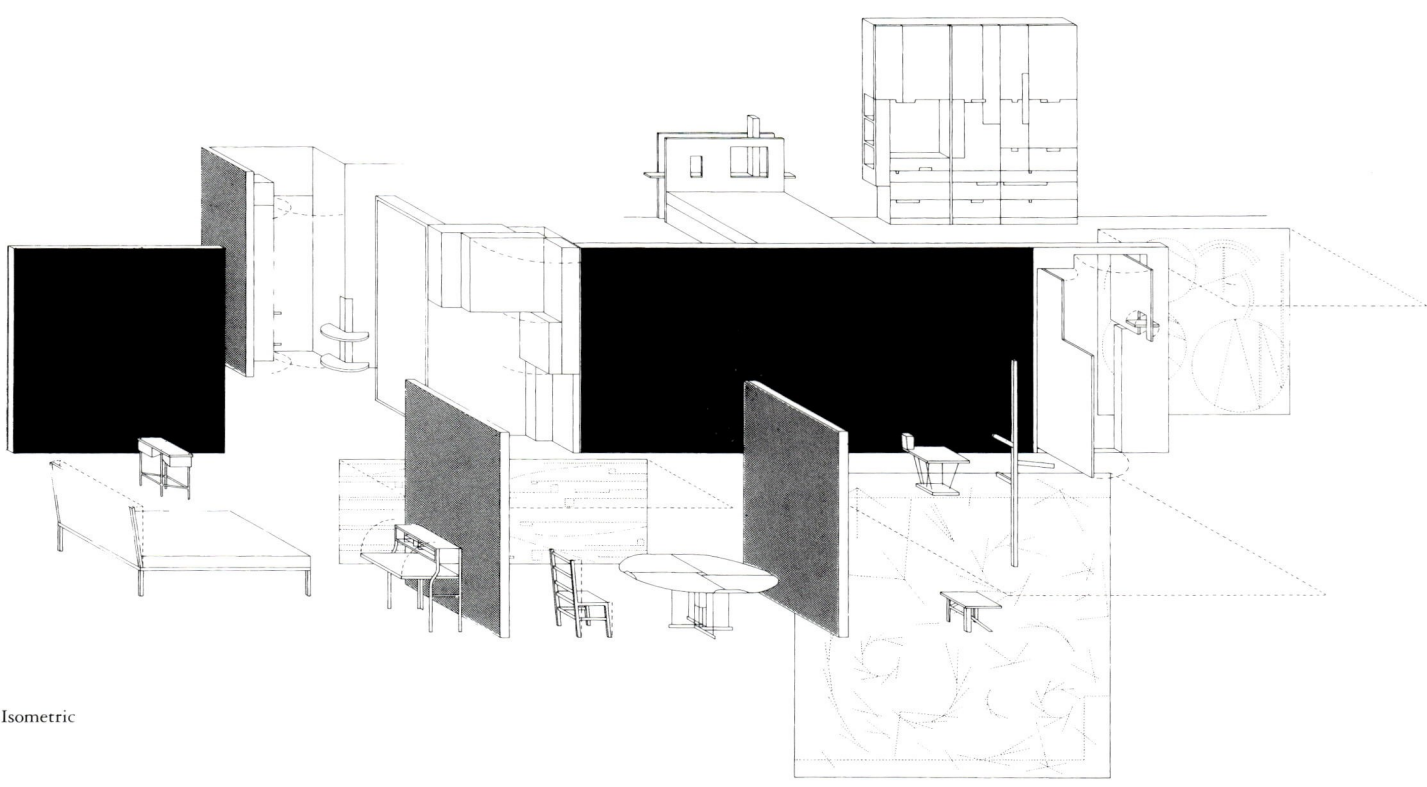
Isometric

The interior renovation and design of fixtures and furniture began with a simple concept arrived at during the first encounter with the Manhattan site. The apartment tower rises directly up from its lot line, intensifying the experience of the Manhattan grid. Standing in the front corner window, the north/south and east/west geometry of the urban perspectives outside are particularly emphasized by the vanishing point in the Z (vertical) dimension. (From here the tower appears to be leaning over 53rd Street.)

This experience inspired the organization of all the elements in the apartment according to a lyrical illumination of the X, Y, and Z directions.

Plaster walls in the X direction are charcoal black integral color, while plaster walls in the Y direction are yellow. The Z dimension is emphasized in a long narrow corner lamp at the entry, in an intersected pole lamp near the main corner window, and in linear verticals in the furniture. Three wool carpets are fabricated for the apartment, one based on the X, one on the Y, and one on the Z dimension. Furniture specially designed for the apartment includes a

Sketch: living and dining room

dining table in which the XYZ dimension is emphasized at its steel center while its edges are vaguely free form.

The elements present the original idea in a variety of ways—literal, poetic, systematic, intuitive. Seen together they do not become a collection of more or less equivalent examples; the differences in means prevent this. Their association is less didactic and more mysterious; the elements serve to form a ground for each other. Only in this indirect way does the original XYZ idea prepare a relation between the parts.

This relation is spatial. That which is the object in one position is the reference in another. Their common result is a kind of suspension—a consequence of the suspended site, the vertiginous view.

Concept sketch

Sketch: living room

Sketch: entrance hall

Sketch: carpet

Bedroom: view toward entrance hall

Bedroom door and closet

I-33

Bookshelf

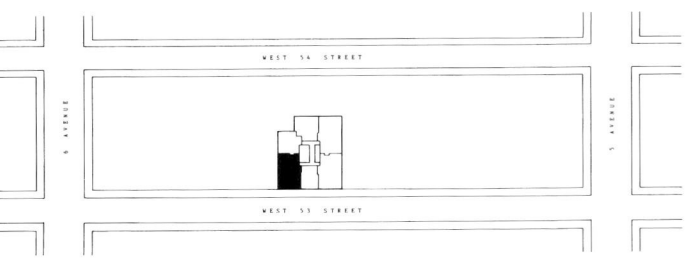

Site plan

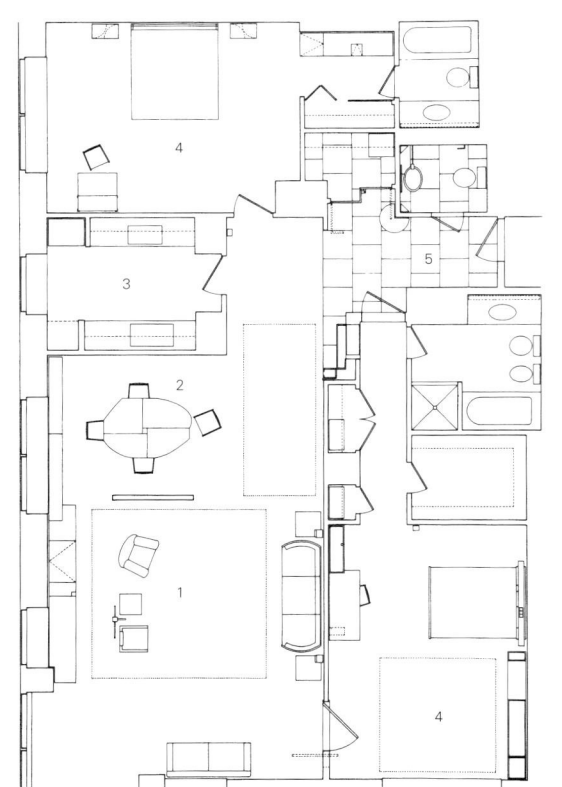

1 LIVING ROOM
2 DINING ROOM
3 KITCHEN
4 BEDROOM
5 ENTRANCE HALL

Floor plan

View from dining room toward entrance hall

Dining room

Writing desk

Door detail

Shelves

Corner detail

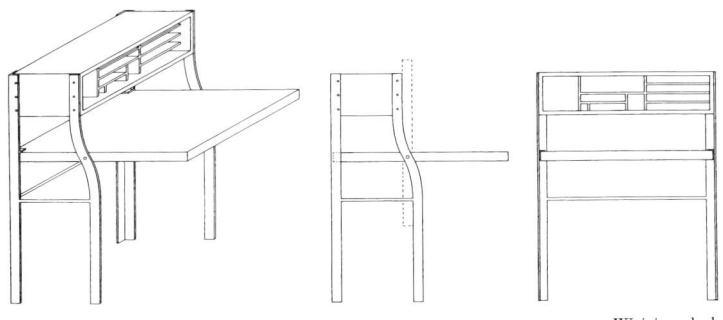

Writing desk

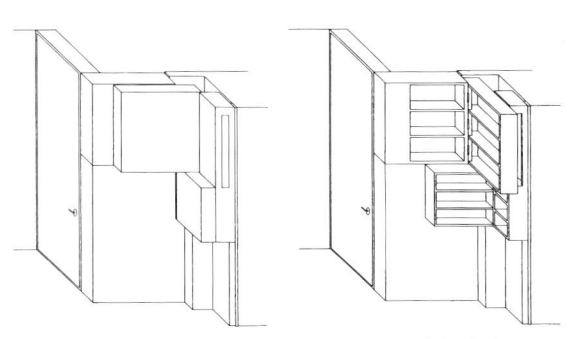

Bookshelf: close/open

MoMAタワー・アパートメント
設備や家具のデザインを含んで，インテリアを改装するためのデザインは，マンハッタンのこの場所にはじめて立った時に胸に浮かんだシンプルなコンセプトが始まりだった。このアパートメント・タワーは敷地の境界線から直かに立ち上がってマンハッタンの街路のグリッドを強調していた。道路側の角の窓際に立って外に目を向けると，この都会のもつ，東西と南北に走る街路の幾何学的パターンのパースペクティブが，とりわけZ（垂直）方向の消失点によってますます強められるのが感じられる（ここから見下ろすと，タワーは53丁目の通り側に傾いているように感じられる）。

このような体験がもとになって，このアパートメントのあらゆる要素にX, Y, Zの三つの方向性を用いた叙情的な光をあてることでデザインを構成しようと考えたのである。

X方向の壁はチャコール・ブラック，Y方向は黄色のプラスターを塗った。Z方向の要素は細長いコーナーランプが玄関に，コーナーウィンドウのそばには照明を直交させてつけたポールランプがあるし，家具では垂直方向のラインが強調される。三ヵ所に敷かれたウールのカーペットは特注で織った物で，それぞれX, Y, Zの三つの次元にもとづいてデザインされている。家具も，この住まいのためにデザインされた。中でも食卓は，天板の周辺部分は自由な形態だがスティール製の中央部分では，X, Y, Zの方向性が強調されている。

様々な要素が，中心となる考え方を様々な形で表現する──あるものは文学的に，詩的に，あるいはシステマティックに，時には直観的に。それらをひとつのまとまりとして見ると，同等のものの単なる集合には感じられない。やり方がそれぞれに違うからだ。それら全体の，ひとつのまとまりとしての印象は，何かを伝えてくるというのではなく，神秘的なものである。各要素が，それぞれ互いに他の背景となるのだ。このような間接的な形で，X, Y, Zという基本概念が，部分部分を関係づけるのである。

この関係は空間的である。ある所では主役を演じるものが，別の場では引立て役をつとめる。その結果，常に浮遊状況が生じる。マンハッタンに浮遊したこの場所と目も眩む景色がそれを生んだのだろう。

1986 Objects, Swid Powell / Carpets, V'Soske
New York, New York, U.S.A.

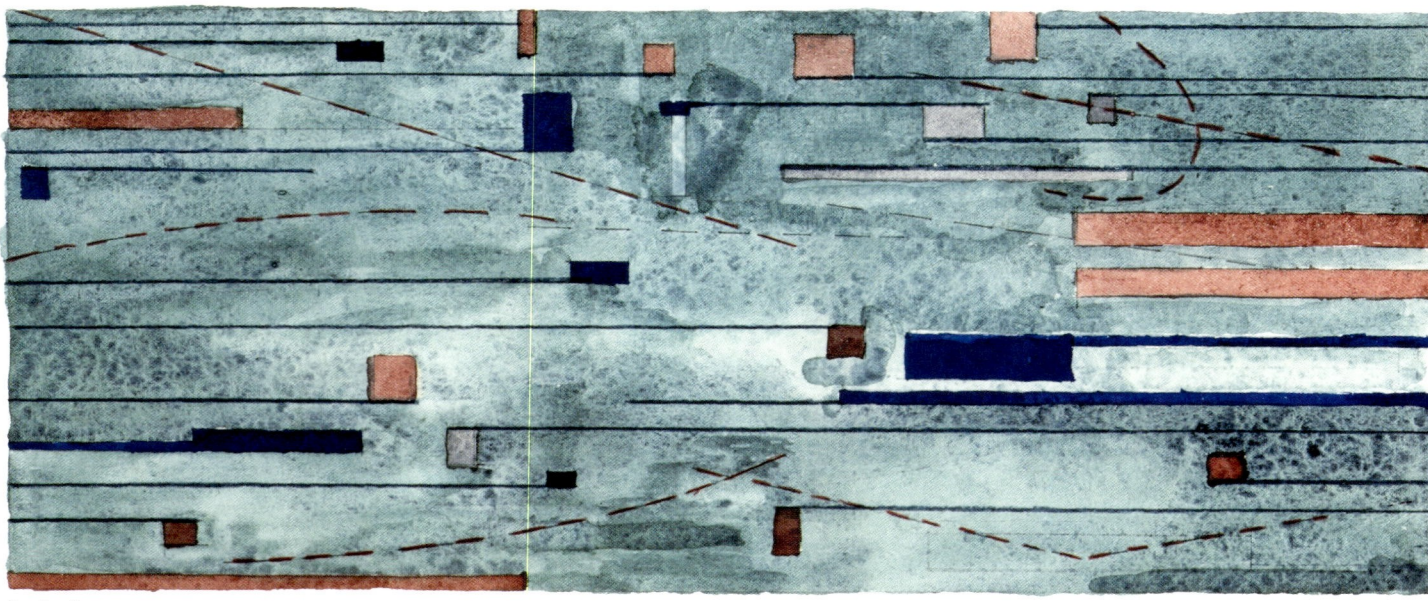

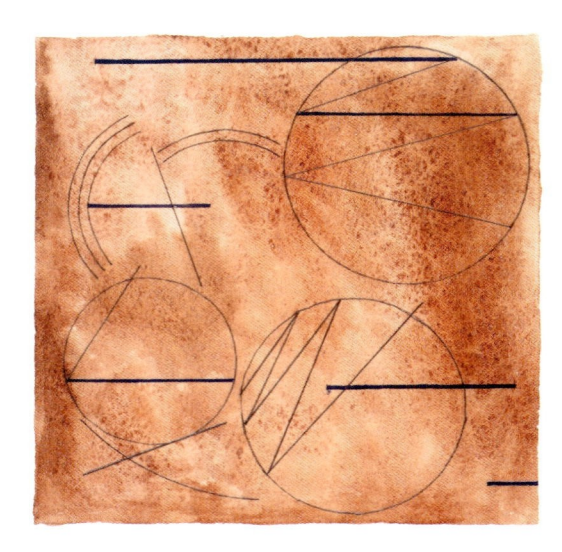

Studies for carpets

As an exercise in elemental composition from line to plane and volume, several household objects were designed, and produced by Swid Powell beginning in 1984. An open language of composition from micro to macro implies a shift in scale. Possible combinations of lines, planes, and volumes in space remain disconnected, trans-historical and trans-cultural. They float about in a zero-ground of form without gravity but are precursors of a concrete architectonic form. They are proto elements:

Lines
Stems of grass, twigs, cracks in mud, fissures in ice, veins in a leaf, woodgrain, nodal lines, spiderwebs, hair, ripples in sand...the astonishing Gothic stone tracery of King's College Chapel, of Westminster Abbey, or of Gloucester Cathedral. The steel linearity of Paxton's Crystal Palace...

Planes
Ribbons of seaweed, palm leaves, cabbage, sediments, stone, elephant ears, sheets of water, wings, feathers, papyrus... the planar wall architecture of ancient Egypt; the temple of Luxor. The wonderful superimposed lyrical planarity of Terragni's Casa Giuliani-Frigerio or of Rietveld's Schröder House.

Volumes
Nautilus shells, pumpkins, watermelon, tree trunks, icebergs, endomorph crystals, cactus, the volumetric intensities of Roman architecture, the stone drums, the pure pyramid of Cestius or the Romanesque interior volumes of St. Front at Périgueux.

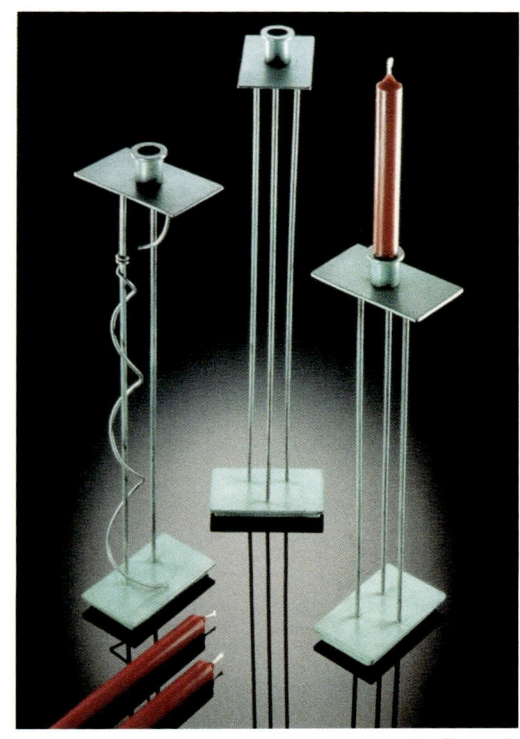

Frame/clip box/vase

Candle stands

Planar plate

Volumetric plate

Linear plate

オブジェ、カーペットのデザイン
線から面，面から立体へと至る基本的な構成の習作として，いくつかの家庭用品をデザインし，その製品化がスウィッド・パウエル社によって，1984年に始められた。ミクロからマクロまでの様々な構成がつくる言語は，そのまま種々のスケールを物語る。空間の中で，線と面と立体のそれぞれが組み合わされたものを，あらゆる歴史と文化にわたって無作為に並べると，これらは重力のない形態のゼロ・グラウンドに漂っている。けれどもそれが，具体的な建築形態を生む萌芽，つまりプロト・エレメントなのである。

［線］
グラスの脚，小枝，乾いた泥地に走るひび，氷の裂け目，葉脈，木目，波紋，クモの巣，髪の毛，砂の風紋……キングスカレッジのチャペル，ウェストミンスター大聖堂，そしてグロスター・カテドラルなどの，石でつくられた驚くべきゴシックのトレイサリー。パクストンのクリスタルパレスを支えるスティールの細長い構造体……。
［面］
リボンのような海草，ヤシの葉，キャベツ，水の底に降り積もった堆積物，象の耳，水の膜，翼，羽根，パピルス……古代エジプトの建築の平らな壁，ルクソール寺院。テラーニのジュリアーニ・フリジェリオ邸やリートフェルトのシュローダー邸の，面が重なり合って詩的に語りかけるすばらしさ。
［立体］
オーム貝，カボチャ，西瓜，木の幹，氷山，内に結晶を秘める水晶，サボテン，宇宙に浮かぶ惑星，古代ローマ建築のヴォリュームのある力強さ，ドームを支える石造のドラム，セシウス神殿のピラミッドの純粋な幾何学的形態，ペリグーにあるサン・フロン聖堂のロマネスク様式による内部空間の造形。

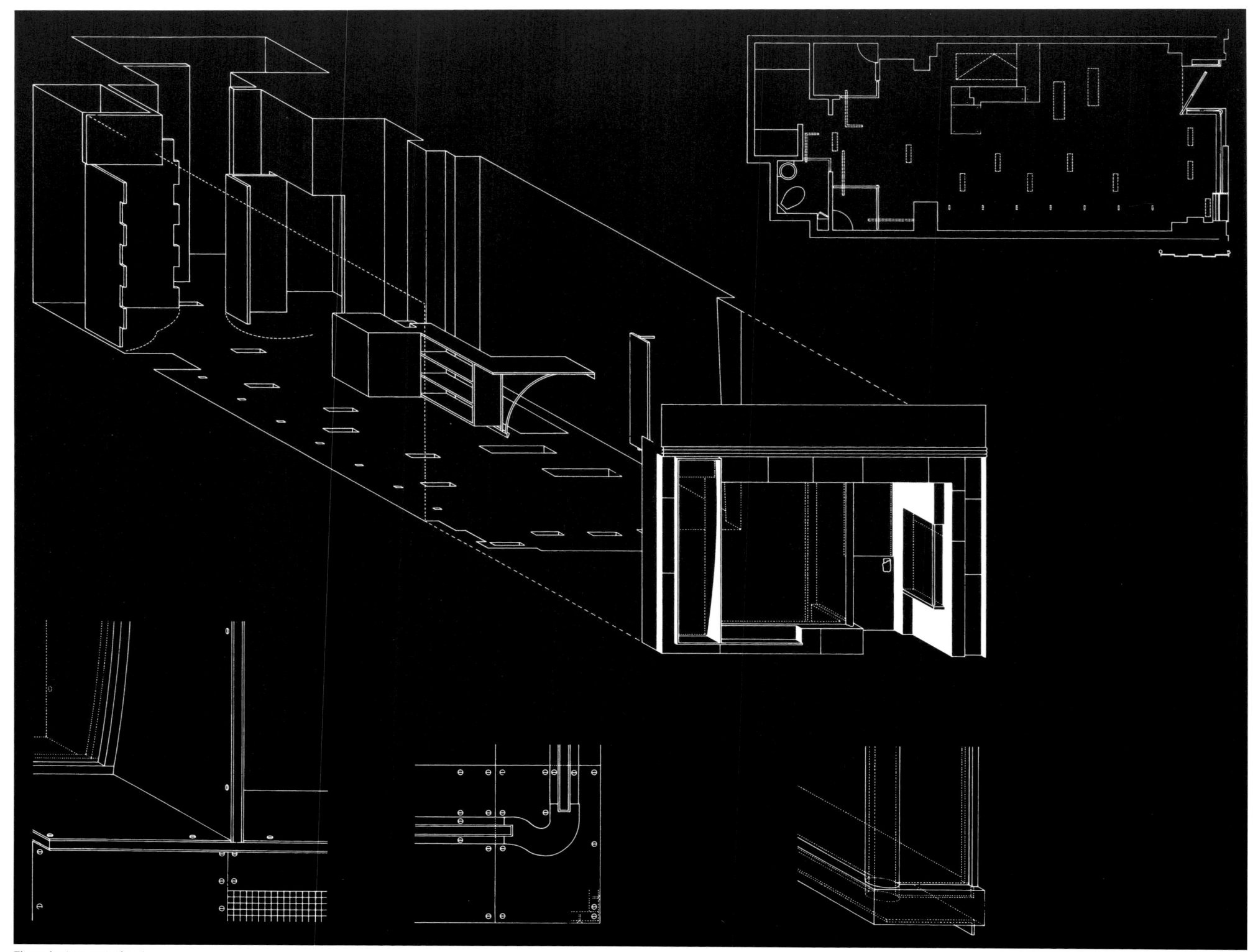

Floor plan/isometric/details

Giada Showroom

1987 New York, New York, U.S.A.

Site plan

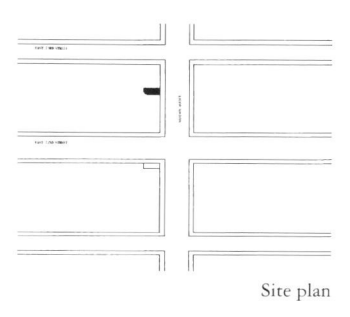

The site is on a busy section of Madison Avenue, midblock between 72nd and 73rd Streets. The absolutely compressed condition of the 14- by 30-foot shop is situated with a large building above bearing down with more than gravitational force; economic pressure and time pressure together act like an invisible vise grip pressing the space in a psychological densification. The idea was to express the compression on the exterior and relieve it on the interior. All proportions are organized according to a logarithmic spiral of relations to the section.

On the exterior, cast glass, three-inch slab glass, and brass plates express densification. The brass plates that contain and define the front are acid-etched to a dull red with flat-head and round-head screws spaced according to conceptual pressure. Bulging and bending shapes are heavy in contrast to interior elements.

Interior materials, bronze wire screen, brass mesh, and spun aluminum, express the light-weight. An eight-inch void below a "floating" terrazzo floor in cloud-like, hand-sprinkled terrazzo has pockets and trap doors opening up for various exhibit devices. When the wire skeleton mannequins with their cast glass shoulders are moved from pocket to pocket, the spaces below are being activated as anti-compression devices. Light ash doors at the changing rooms turn inside-out when not in use, giving their interior volumes back to the overall space.

Storefront on Madison Avenue

Sketch: display stands

Sketch: storefront

Interior

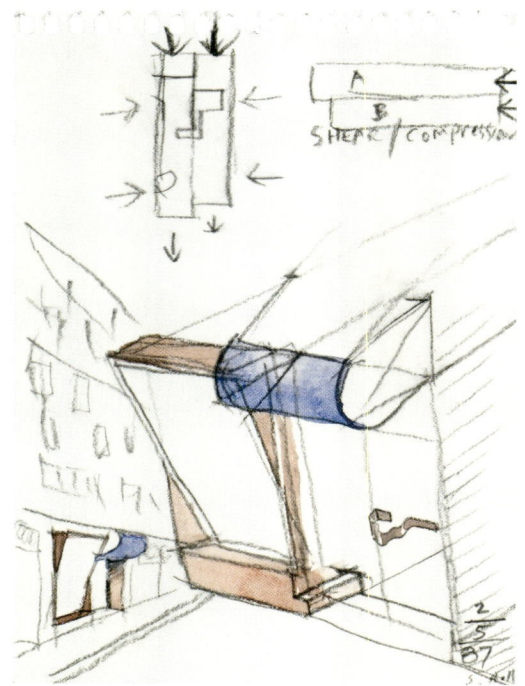

Sketch: storefront

Entrance

ギアダ・ショールーム

敷地はマディソン・アベニューの72丁目と73丁目に挟まれるブロックの中央というにぎやかなところにある。14フィート×30フィートの広さに圧縮されたこの店が支えているその上の巨大なビルの重さは,物理的な重力だけではない。経済的な圧力と時間の圧力がもろともに,さながら目に見えぬ万力のように締めつけては心理的な密度をあげるからだ。そこで,外部に対してはこの圧力を表現しながら,インテリアではそれを解き放つという意図でデザインを進めることにした。プロポーションはすべて,対数曲線に基づいて断面を決定し,構成した。

エクステリアでは,3インチ厚のガラスと真鍮板が密度を表現する。正面の一部を構成する真鍮板は酸で表面を腐蝕させて,沈んだ赤味を帯びさせ,そこに皿ビス

Interior

Shelf

Shelf detail (above), door pull (below)

や丸頭ビスを取付け, その間隔を想定上の圧力に対応させた。外部に膨らみながら傾いた形は, インテリアの要素と強いコントラストを示す。

　インテリアは, ブロンズ・ワイヤー製のスクリーン, 真鍮の網, 削り出しのアルミなどの材料を使い, 軽やかさを表現する。下に8インチの隙間をとって浮かぶ, 雲状の模様をちりばめたテラゾーの床には, そこここにポケットやはね上げ戸を配した。様々な催しが行われる時にはそこを開けて利用する。たとえば, 針金の胴体にガラスの肩を持つマネキンが, ポケットからポケットに移動されるとき, 床下のスペースは圧力に対抗するしかけとして働く。試着室の軽いトネリコのドアは, 使われない時には裏を出して開けておけば, そのスペースも全体の一部となる。

1987-88 Metropolitan Tower Apartment
New York, New York, U.S.A.

Site plan/floor plan

In the gridded city of Manhattan, ruthless economic forces have inserted a tall, sharp-pointed wedge of glass midblock between 56th and 57th Streets. The point that rises up from the street edge becomes the crucial character of the interior, its shrill angle of 40 degrees analogous to a shrill sound high in pitch (high in elevation).

The interior design is an intensification of this event or condition rather than a criticism or negation. No apparent traditional domesticity, no static rectilinearity or symmetry should attempt to reverse the direction already taken. Rather, what has started can take a more lyrical tone, increasing its non-rectilinearity and indeterminacy. A free floating spatial tilting is characterized by the four-degree tilt of walls that accompany the acute angle of the existing plan. A floating cloud-like black and white terrazzo floor underlies the new free-form walls. The slight folds in the curved walls are like folds in a paper airplane. In a range of sandblasted glass fixtures, interior night-lighting is diffused and indeterminant. An ultra-light curved wall fragment constructed in basswood and airplane silk is a kind of "Icaran wing" dividing the sleeping (dreams) area from the conscious area. Carpets are drawn from an intuited version of a piece of music, "Landscapes of the Mind," based on a painting by Georgia O'Keefe, "Sky Above Clouds." A floating cloud-like habitat striving for immateriality, this dwelling is in the evaporative dream state above the metropolis.

Sketch: entrance hall

メトロポリタン・タワー・アパートメント

マンハッタンの格子の都市の只中,仮借ない経済の力学ゆえに,高くそびえる鋭角をもったガラスのくさびが56丁目と57丁目の間のブロックの中に差し込まれている。道路の間際から立ち上がるくさびの先端にこの部屋があるということで,内部空間が性格づけられた。その40度という鋭角は,高く鋭い音(エレベーションの高い所に位置する)のアナロジーかもしれない。

このインテリアデザインは,このようなできごと,もしくは条件を,あえて批評もせず否定することもなく強調することであった。

伝統的な家庭らしさや静止的な直交性や対称性といったもので,すでに存在している方向を転換しようなどとするべきではない。むしろ,そこにある条件は,詩的な調子をさらに加え,非直角性と不確定性を増幅するという方向をとることのできるものだ。自由に漂う空間の傾斜は,平面のなす鋭角に加えて4度というわずかな壁の傾きで強められた。空に浮かぶ雲のような黒地に白のパターンを散らしたテラゾーの床が,新たに構成された自由な形態の壁の足元に広がる。曲面をなす壁には,紙飛行機の折り目のようなすじがある。サンドブラストのガラスの照明器具が放つ光で,夜の光は拡散されおぼろに広がる。曲線を描く非常に軽い壁の一部は,しなの木と飛行機用のシルクでつくられているので,「イカルスの翼」を思わせながら,眠り(夢)の空間を覚醒のエリアから分かつのである。カーペットの模様は,ジョージア・オキーフの「雲の上の空」と題する絵をもとに作曲された「心の景色」という音楽の一部を感覚的に表現したものだ。空を漂う雲のような非物質性を,あくまでも追い求めたこの生活空間は,メトロポリスの上空高く浮かぶ,儚い夢の国の住まいなのだ。

Entrance hall

Concept sketch

Living and dining room

Sketch: dining room

I-44

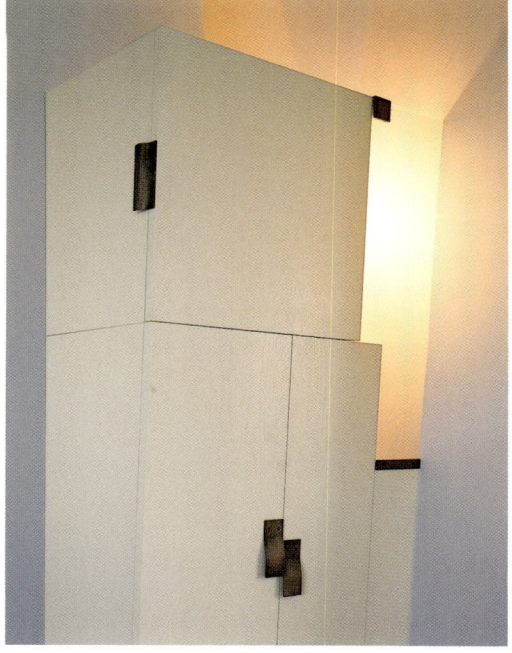

Living room

Furniture

Living room

View toward living room

Partition wall: bathroom behind

Partition wall: view toward dining room

Furniture of living room

Cast-glass lighting fixture

I-46

View from bedroom corner toward Central Park

Sketch: light shafts of reception

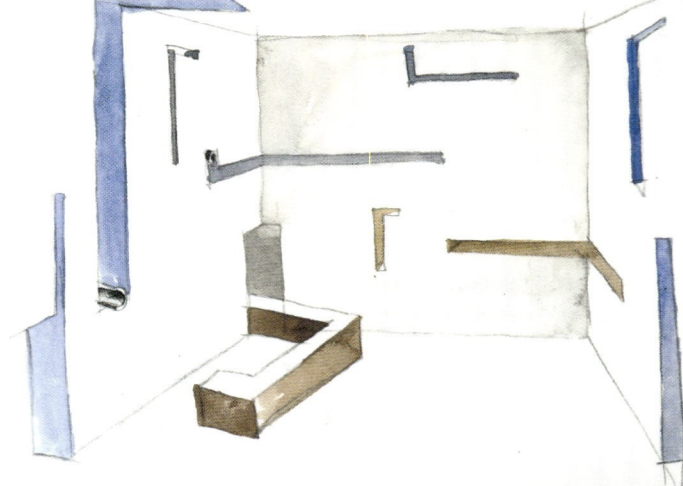

Sketch: reception

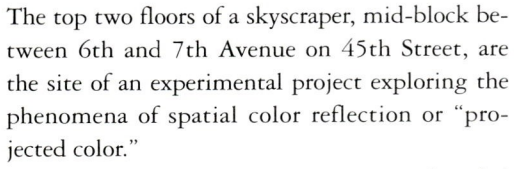

The top two floors of a skyscraper, mid-block between 6th and 7th Avenue on 45th Street, are the site of an experimental project exploring the phenomena of spatial color reflection or "projected color."

D.E.Shaw & Co., a young company founded and invented by a doctor in physics, works with the miniscule drift of numbers and percentages as measured in short intervals of time. Their extensive series of computers are hooked up by telephone lines and working 22.5 hours per day, at rest only between the time the Tokyo exchange has closed and the London exchange has not yet opened. One room in the facility contains more than 200 small computers. This curious and invisible program was given a parallel in the design concept of the interior. The metal framing and sheet-rock with skim-coat plaster was carved and notched at precise points around the central 31-foot cube of space at the entry. Color was applied to the backsides of surfaces, invisible to the viewer within the space. Natural and artificial lights project this color back into the space around walls and fissures. As the phenomena greatly reduces the intensity of the color being reflected, a range of fluorescent colors could be utilized on the unseen surfaces. One consequence of the exploration was the presence of the project seen from the street as a fluorescent green backside on the top floors of the tower.

The interior has a mysterious calm glow with surprising views as one moves around observing one field of reflected color through another and vice versa.

Reception

1991

D.E. Shaw & Co. Offices
New York, New York, U.S.A.

Reception with various coloured light

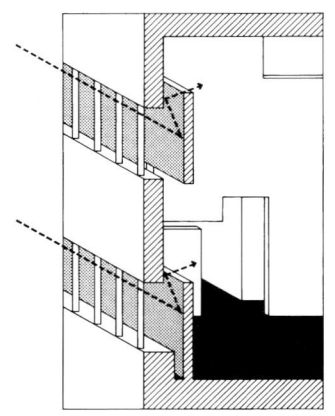

Diagram of daylight color projection

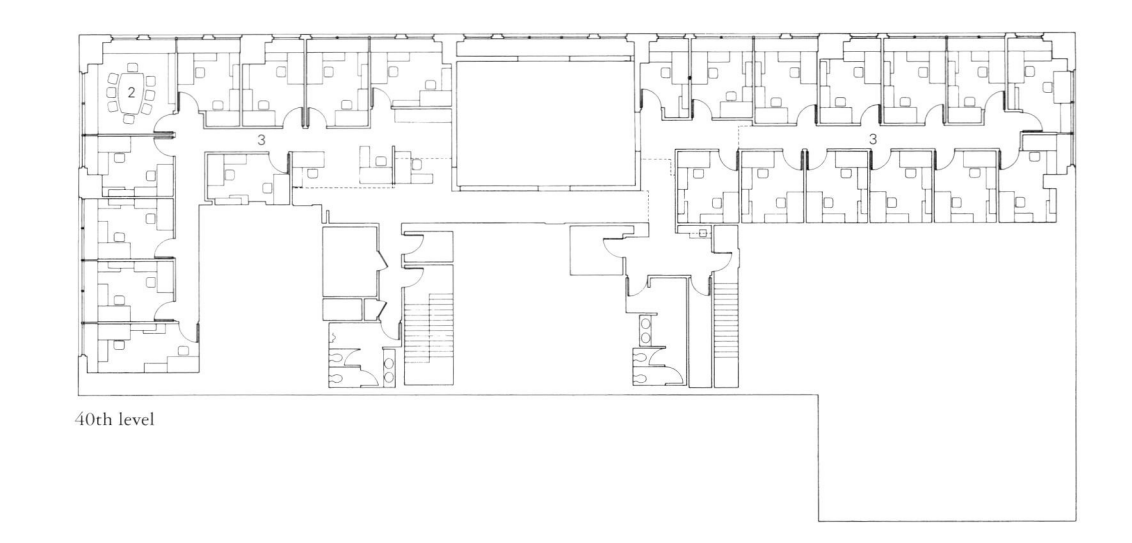

D・E・ショウ社オフィス

6番街と7番街の間の45丁目,超高層ビルの最上階の2層を使って,色彩を空間に投射して,「投影された色彩」という現象を探求する実験的な計画のための場がつくられた。

ある物理学博士が創設した若い会社であるD・E・ショウ社では,ひっきりなしに流れてくる細かい数字やパーセンテージを扱っている。彼等のコンピュータ・ネットワークは電話回線で結ばれて,一日のうち22時間半動き続け,東京の株式市場が閉まりロンドン市場が開くまでの間だけが束の間の休止時間である。この施設のある部屋には200を越える小型コンピュータがある。コンピュータの目に見えぬプログラムが,このインテリアデザインのコンセプトのもとになった。金属の下地にプラスターボードを張り,プラスターの薄塗を施してエントランスの中心に置いた31フィートの立方体の周りには,厳密に決めた位置に模様をつけV形の溝を刻んだ。立方体の外側の面に色を塗るので,スペースの中にいる人には直接目に触れない。自然光や人工照明の光がこの色を塗った裏側にあてられると,光はまわりの壁や割れ目から入りこんでくる。色は反射されて漏れて来るにすぎないからすっかり弱められてしまうので,見えないスクリーンには蛍光色が使われる。この実験の結果,街路から見ると蛍光色のグリーンに塗られた壁の背面がタワーの最上階にあらわれた。

中に入って反射光を受ける場所を観察しながらひと巡りすると,神秘的で静けさをたたえた光芒の醸し出す光景に驚かされる。

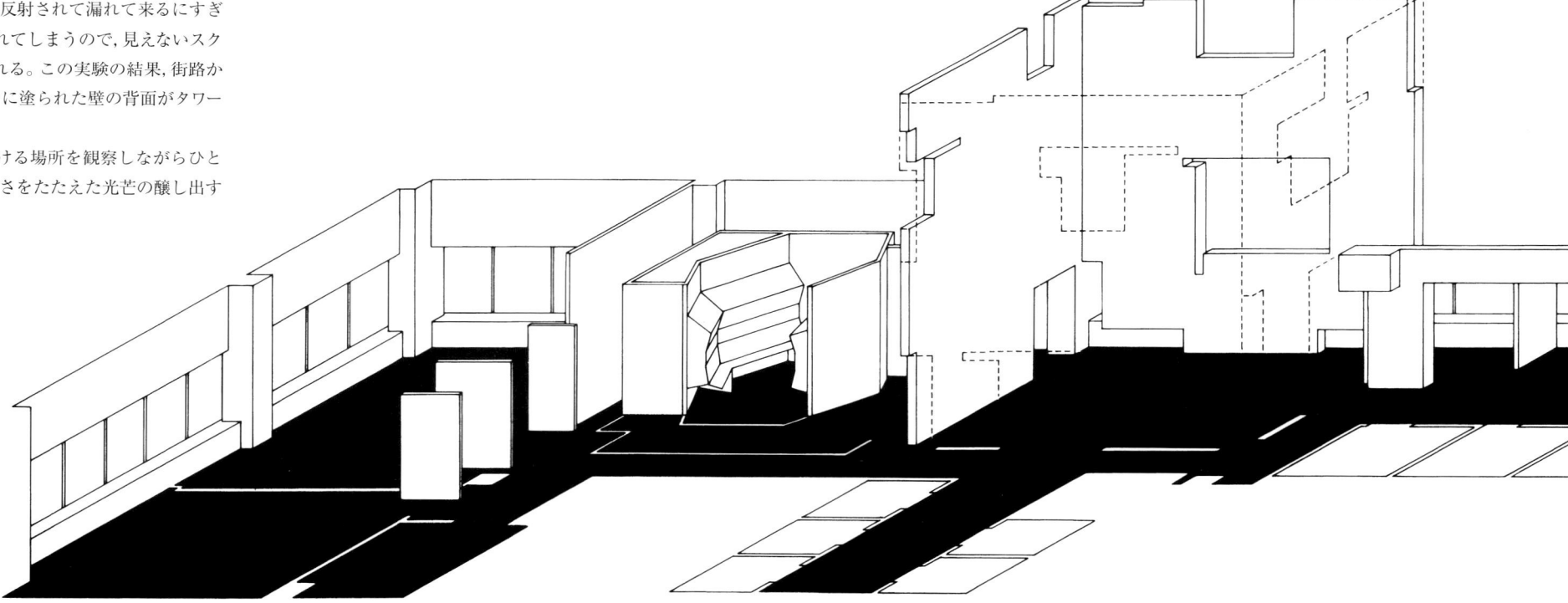

40th level

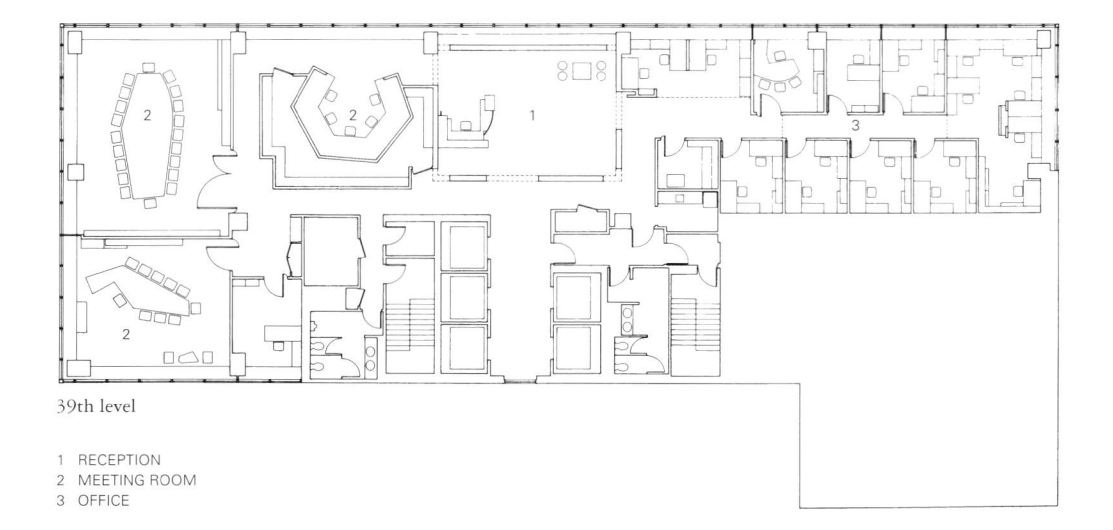

39th level

1 RECEPTION
2 MEETING ROOM
3 OFFICE

Isometric

Meeting room. Table designed by Steven Holl

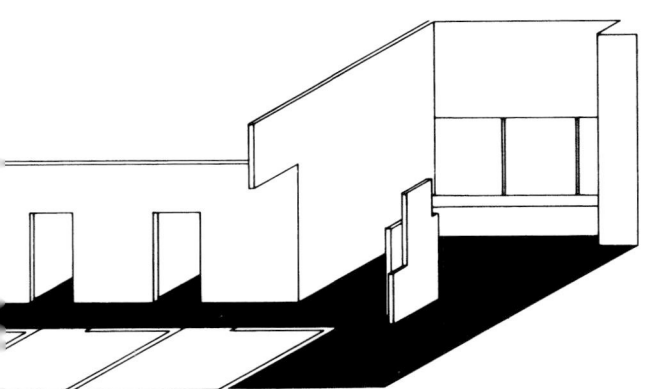

Reception

Site plan

Storefront on Kenmare Street

Storefront for Art and Architecture
1992-93   New York, New York, U.S.A.

I-52

Storefront: door opened

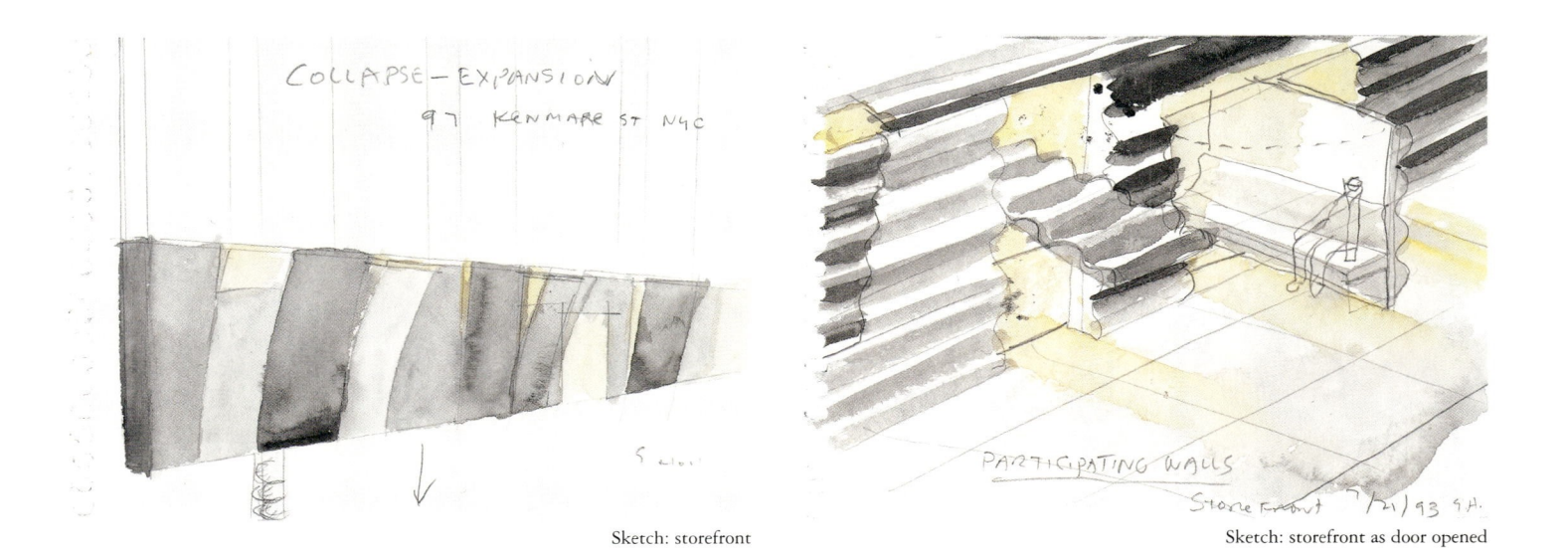

Sketch: storefront

Sketch: storefront as door opened

I-53

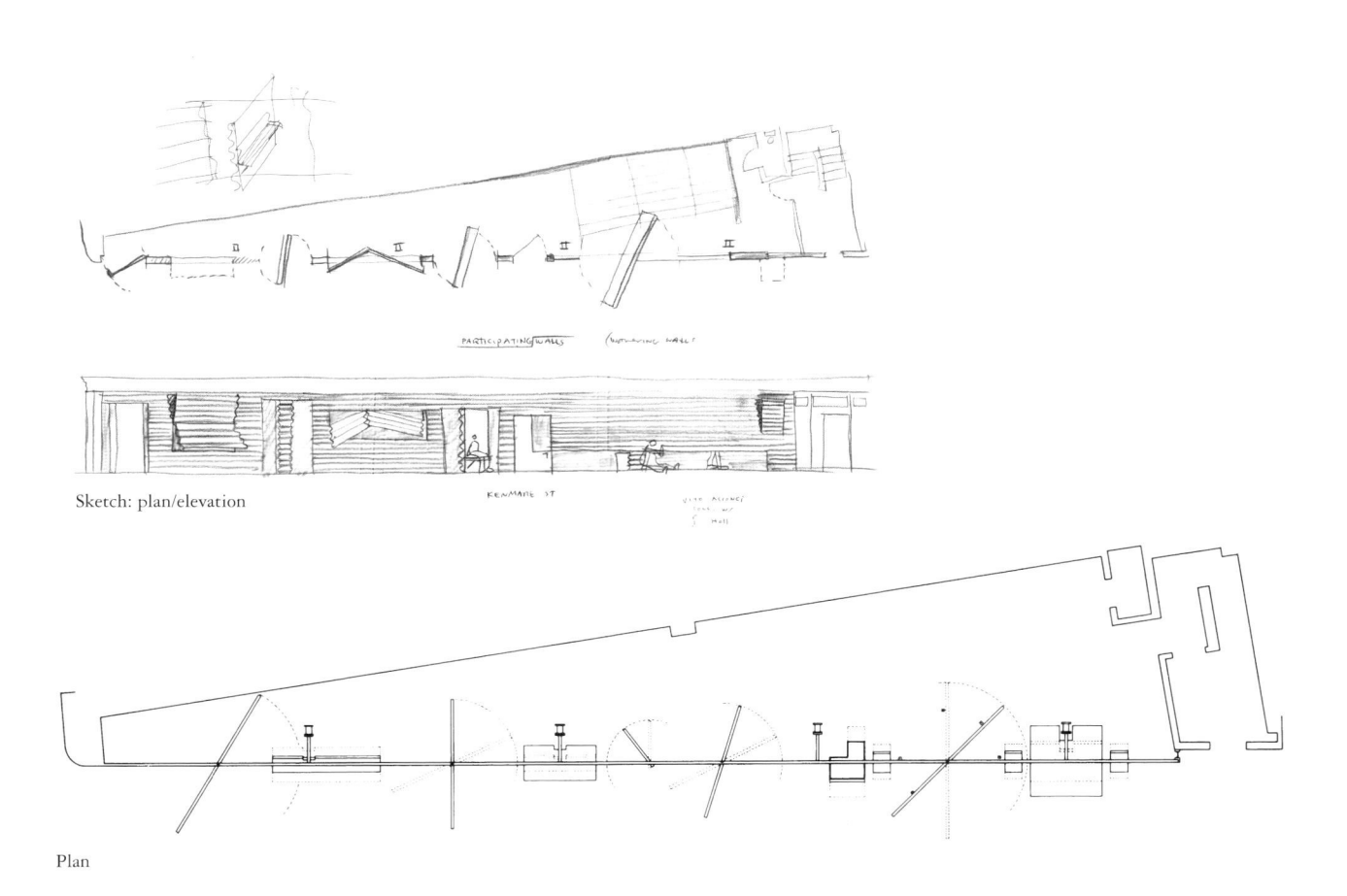

Sketch: plan/elevation

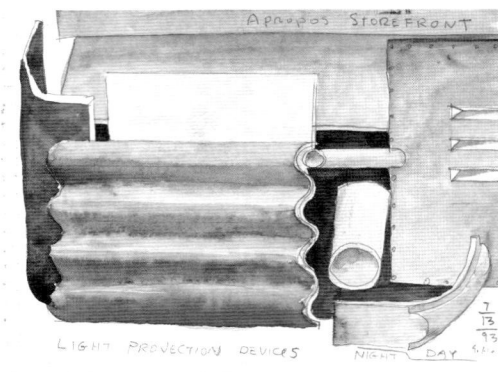

Sketch: light projection devices

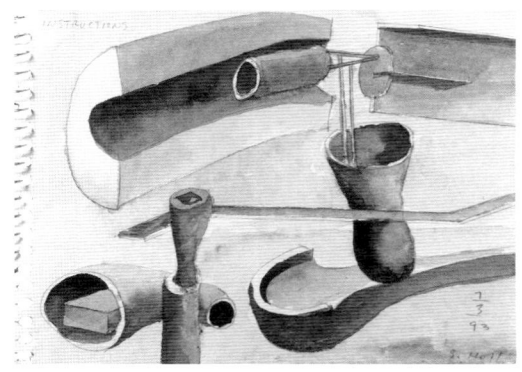

Plan

Sketch: detail

In 1992, Steven Holl and artist Vito Acconci were commissioned as a collaborative team to renovate the aging facade of the Storefront for Art and Architecture, one of few galleries dedicated to the exhibition of young architects in New York City. The Storefront project is the second collaborative effort by Holl and Acconci; their first work together was a 1988 urban plan for a growing arts community in downtown Washington D.C. sponsored by the Pennsylvania Avenue Development Corporation.

The Storefront for Art and Architecture is situated on the corner of a block that marks the intersection of three distinct neighborhoods: Chinatown, Little Italy and SOHO. The gallery itself is a limited, narrow wedge with a triangulated exhibition interior, such that the most dominant structure for the Storefront for Art and Architecture is the building's long facade. In fact, the history of exhibitions at the gallery was marked in the various cuts and layers of paint which exhibiting architects had imposed on and through this once-uniform surface.

Drawing from this history, neither Acconci nor Holl were interested in the permanence of the facade or the idea of a static gallery space. Seeking to introduce improbability and to puncture the facade, Acconci and Holl challenged this symbolic border which underlines the exclusivity of the art world, where only those on the inside belong. Using a hybrid material comprised of concrete mixed with recycled fibers, Holl and Acconci inserted a series of hinged panels arranged in a puzzle-like configuration. When the panels are locked in their open position, the facade dissolves and the interior space of the gallery expands out on to the sidewalk. If the function of a facade is to create a division separating the inside from the outside space, this new facade, in the words of director Kyong Park, is "No Wall, No Barrier, No Inside, No Outside, No Space, No Building, No Place, No Institution, No Art, No Architecture, No Acconci, No Holl, No Storefront."

Storefront

Sketch: interior walls

ストアフロント美術建築ギャラリー
スティーヴン・ホールと芸術家ヴィト・アコンチが老朽化したストアフロント美術建築ギャラリーのファサード改修の共同設計者に指名されたのは,1992年のことである。ここはニューヨーク市内でも,若手建築家が展覧会を開くことのできる数少ないギャラリーのうちのひとつである。ストアフロント・ギャラリーはホールとアコンチによる2度目の共同作業である。ふたりの初めての取り組みは,ワシントンDC中心部の芸術家のコミュニティのために行ったペンシルヴァニア・アベニュー開発公社の1988年の都市計画である。

ストアフロント美術建築ギャラリーは,チャイナタウン,リトルイタリーおよびソーホーの3つに隣接した地区の目印となる交差点に位置している。ギャラリー自体は狭くて幅もなく,内部も展示空間が三角形に分割されたくさび型の空間である。そのため最も重要な構造は,この建物の細長いファサードということになる。一方で,元々平滑であった壁面に対してこれまでに出展してきた建築家が幾重にも塗り重ねてきたペイントの跡が,このギャラリーの歴史を物語っている。

そのような歴史的経緯からアコンチとホールは,ファサードの機能性や,変化に乏しいギャラリー空間に対して関心を示すことはなかった。意外性を求めてファサードを穿孔することによって,アコンチとホールは内輪で占められる美術界に対し,その排他性を強く暗示する象徴的境界線に挑んだのだ。ファイバーコンクリートを使った再資源複合素材で,ホールとアコンチは幾つもの回転パネルをパズル状の構成に並べて挿入した。開放された状態でパネルがロックされるとファサードは消失し,ギャラリーの内部空間は歩道に対し拡張される。ファサードの機能が内部空間を外部空間から分け隔てるものだとすれば,この新しいファサードはディレクターのパク・キョンが言うように「ノー・ウォール,ノー・バリア,ノー・インサイド,ノー・アウトサイド。空間も,建物もない。その場所も,ギャラリーも,アートも,建築もない。アコンチも,ホールも,ストアフロントもない」のだ。

Interior

Sarphatistraat Offices
1996-2000   Amsterdam, The Netherlands

View across canal

Sketch: view across canal

Sketch

Entrance

Exterior view of southwest corner

Interior view of southwest corner

In Amsterdam, on the Singel Gracht, the renovated building is the former Federal Warehouse of Medical Supplies. The main structure is a four-story brick "U" merging it internally with a new "sponge" pavilion on the canal. While the exterior expression is one of complimentary contrast (existing brick adjacent to new perforated copper) the interior strategy is one of fusion. The complex at 410 Sarphatistraat is entered through the original 19th century brick courtyard. Passing through the interior reveals gradually more porous spaces until reaching the "Menger Sponge" pavilion overlooking the canal. While the major portion of the 50,000 sq.ft. project is workspace for the Social Housing Company's 268 employees, the large sponge space is open to receive all uses from public gatherings to performance events. Given back to the community, the immediate canal edge has a new boardwalk.

The porous architecture of the rectangular pavilion is inscribed with a concept from the music of Morton Feldman "Patterns in a Chromatic Field." The ambition to achieve a space of gossamer optic phenomena with chance-located reflected color is especially effective at night when the color patches paint the Singel Canal in reflections.

The layers of perforated materials, from copper on the exterior to plywood on the interior, contain all services such as lighting, supply and return air grilles. The perforated screens developed in three dimensions are analogous to the "Menger Sponge" principle of openings continuously cut in planes approaching zero volume.

"Chromatic Space" is formed by light bounced between the building's layers. At night light trapped between screens sometimes appears as thick floating blocks of color. At other times the passing sun creates a throbbing color wash, or moiré patterns are created in the moving view.

Below the pavilion an automatic car parking machine which takes the cars one at a time and returns them turned around is made possible on a steel framework with self lubricating nylon wheels.

I-57

Sections

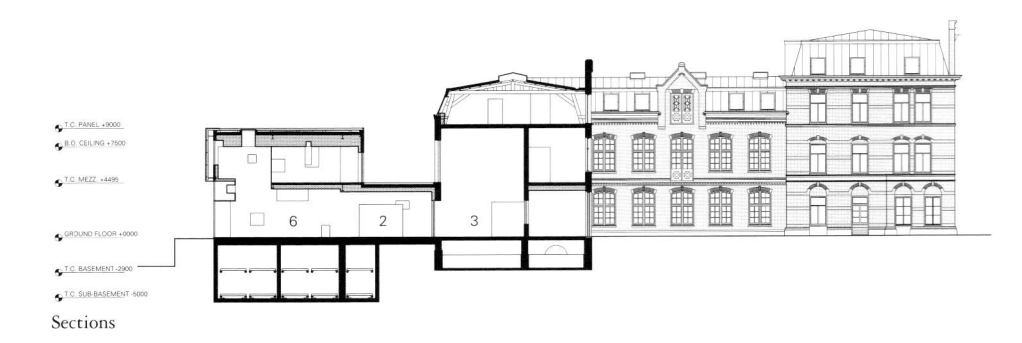

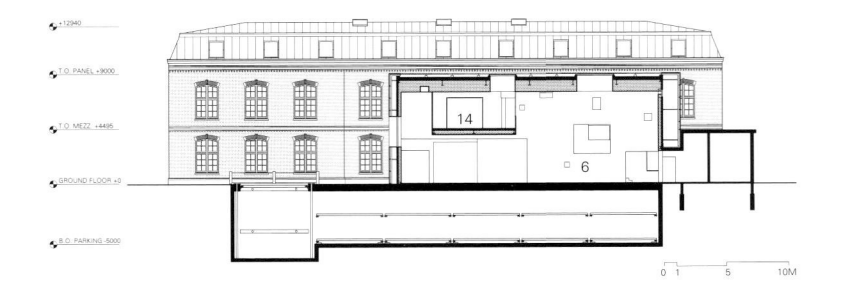

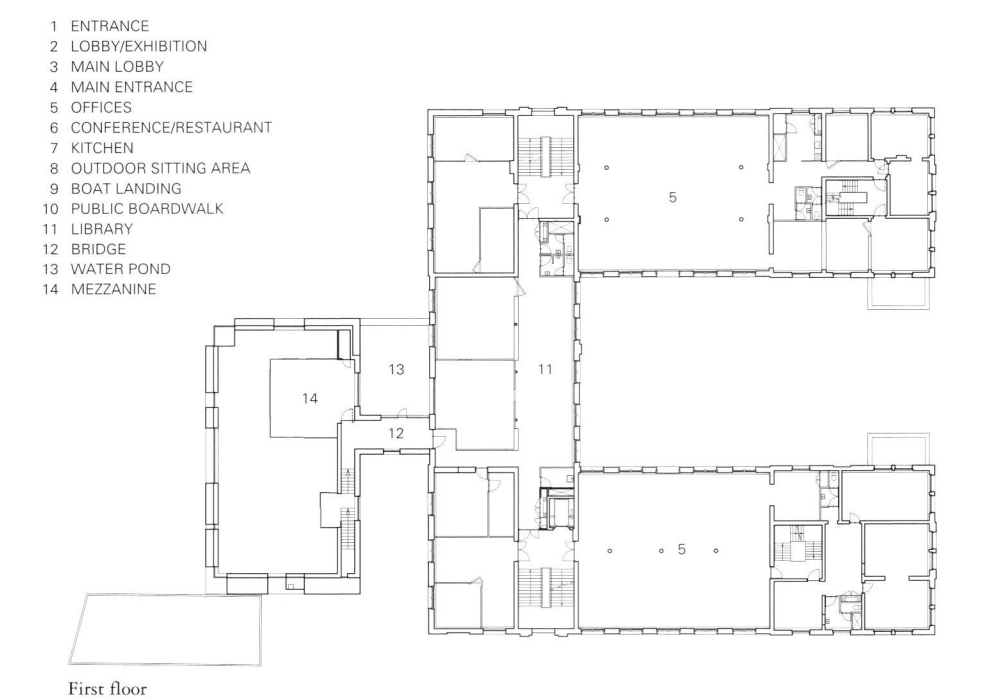

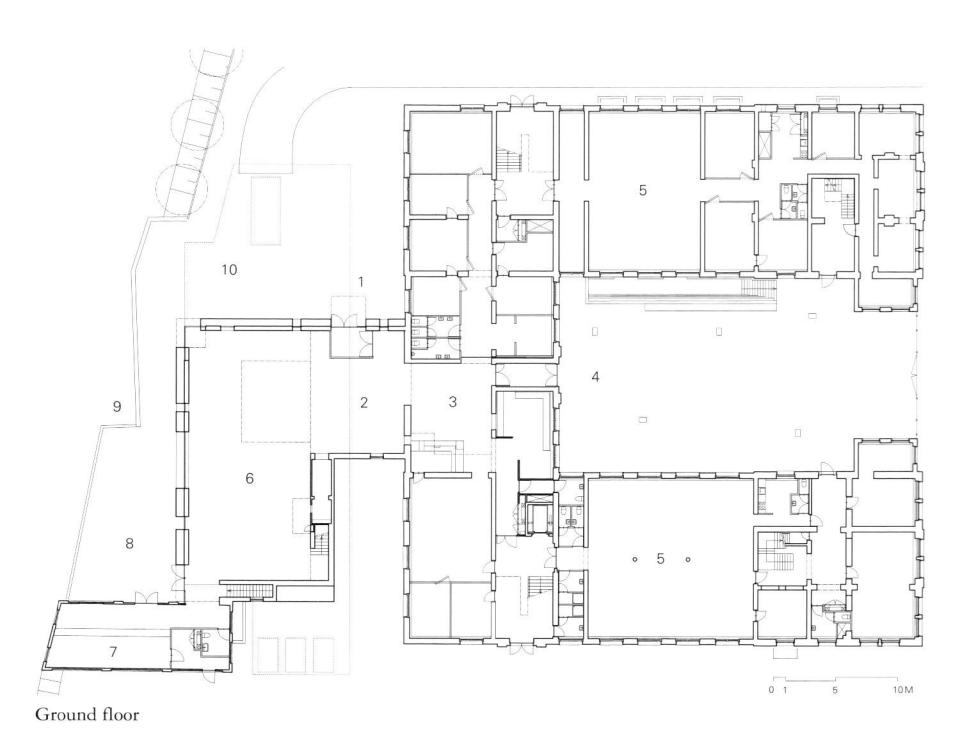

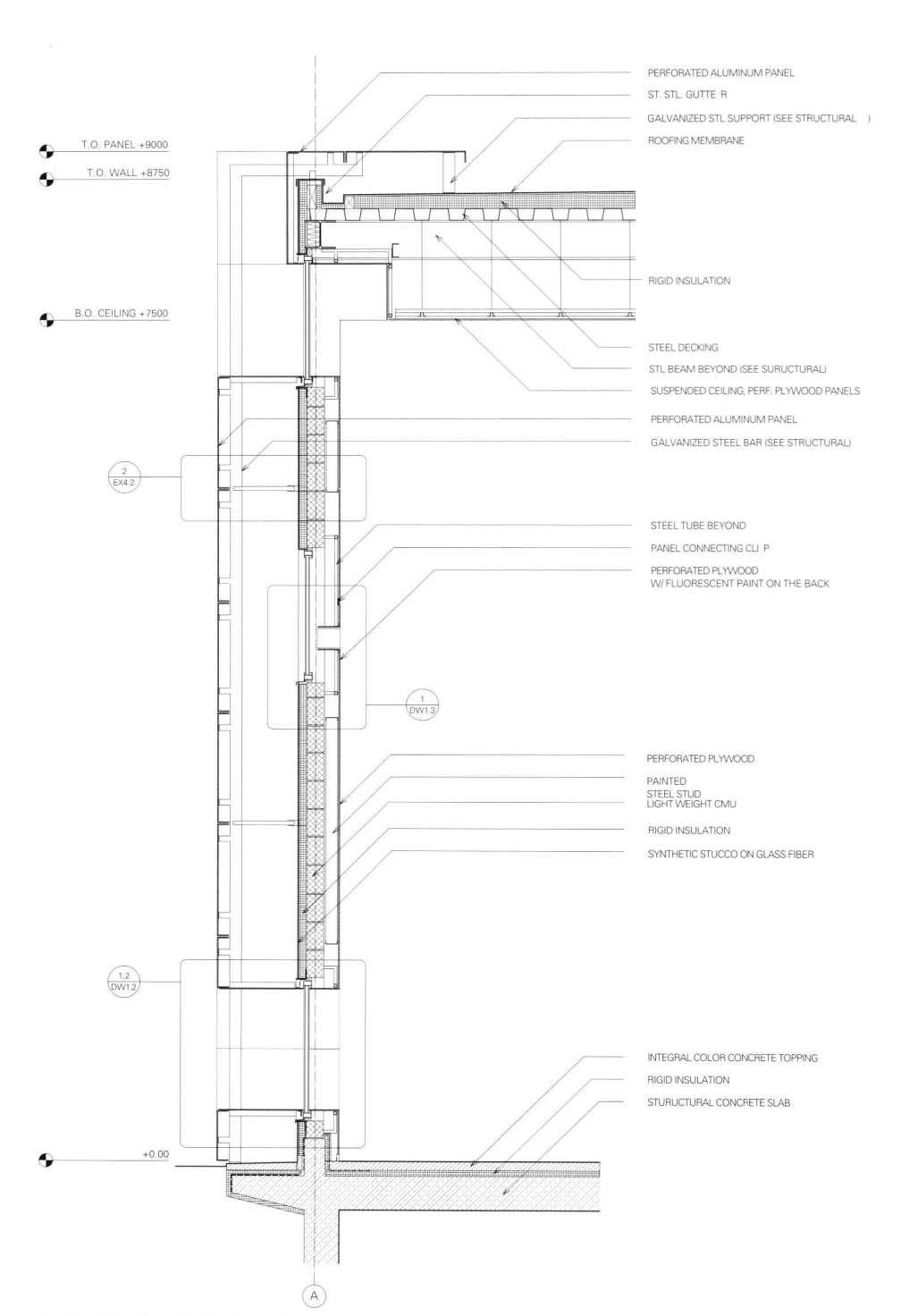

1 ENTRANCE
2 LOBBY/EXHIBITION
3 MAIN LOBBY
4 MAIN ENTRANCE
5 OFFICES
6 CONFERENCE/RESTAURANT
7 KITCHEN
8 OUTDOOR SITTING AREA
9 BOAT LANDING
10 PUBLIC BOARDWALK
11 LIBRARY
12 BRIDGE
13 WATER POND
14 MEZZANINE

First floor

Ground floor

Sectional detail: wall of conference/restaurant

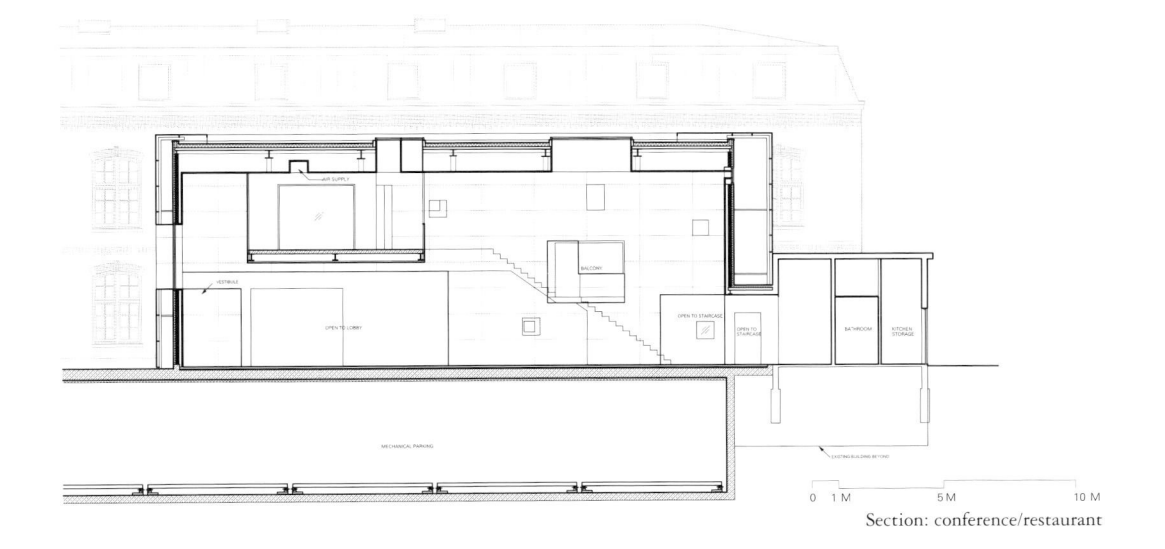

Conference/restaurant

Section: conference/restaurant

I-59

Main Lobby

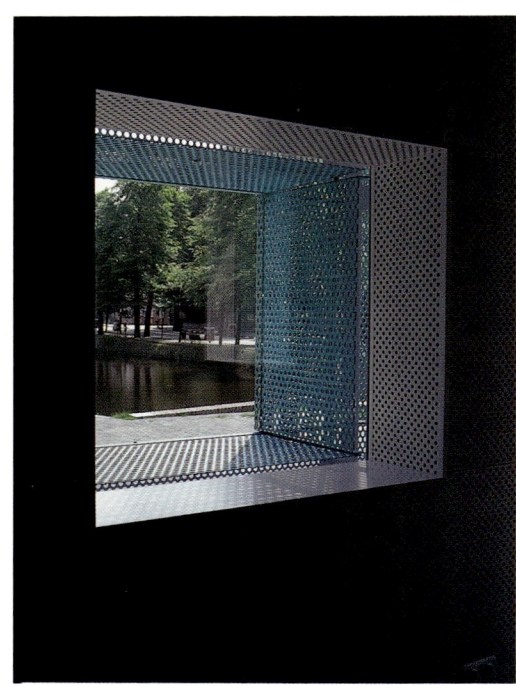

Window detail

サルファティストラートのオフィス

アムステルダムのシンヘル運河に面して建つ,連邦政府の医療品保管倉庫であった建物の改造である。主屋は煉瓦造の4階建ての建物で,運河に面して新設された"スポンジ"パヴィリオンと内部で一体化されている。外観の表現が補完的な対比(新しい棟の銅の有孔パネルと並置する既存棟の煉瓦)である一方,内部のストラテジーは融合である。

サルファティストラート410番地の複合建築へは19世紀に遡る煉瓦敷きのコートヤードから入る。内部を進むと,運河を見晴らす"メンガー・スポンジ"パヴィリオンに至るまで,徐々に多孔性の空間が展開していく。5万平方フィートの建物の主要部分はソーシャル・ハウジング・カンパニーの職員268人の仕事場であるが,広いスポンジ・スペースは公共的な集会からパフォーマンスなどの催しまであらゆる用途に使える。近隣地区への返礼として,傍らの運河沿いにはボードウォークが新設された。

正方形パヴィリオンを構成する多孔性建築には,モートン・フェルドマンの作曲した"Patterns in a Chromatic Field"からとったコンセプトが刻み込まれている。偶発的に配された反射する色彩によって,薄く軽い布地のような光学現象が生まれる空間をつくるという野心的試みは,色彩のまだら模様が運河の水を反射光で染める夜は特に効果的である。

外部に使われている銅から内部の合板まで,多孔性物質の重なりのあいだには,照明や給排気グリルなど,すべてのサービス設備が内包される。三次元に展開されたこれらの有孔スクリーンは,ゼロ・ヴォリュームへ近づきながら,面に連続的に開口をうがつ,"メンガー・スポンジ"法則に相似するものである。

"色彩空間"は,建物の層構成のあいだに反射する光がつくりだす。夜になると,光はこれらのスクリーンのあいだに捕えられ,時々,色彩の厚い塊となって漂う。またある時は,移動する日射しが,どきどきするような色彩の奔流を生み出したり,動いて行く光景のなかにモワレ模様をつくりだす。

パヴィリオンの下には,ナイロン・ホイールと油圧式エレベータを組み合せた,鉄骨造の駐車施設が設置される。

Staircase

Mezzanine

Balcony of conference/restaurant

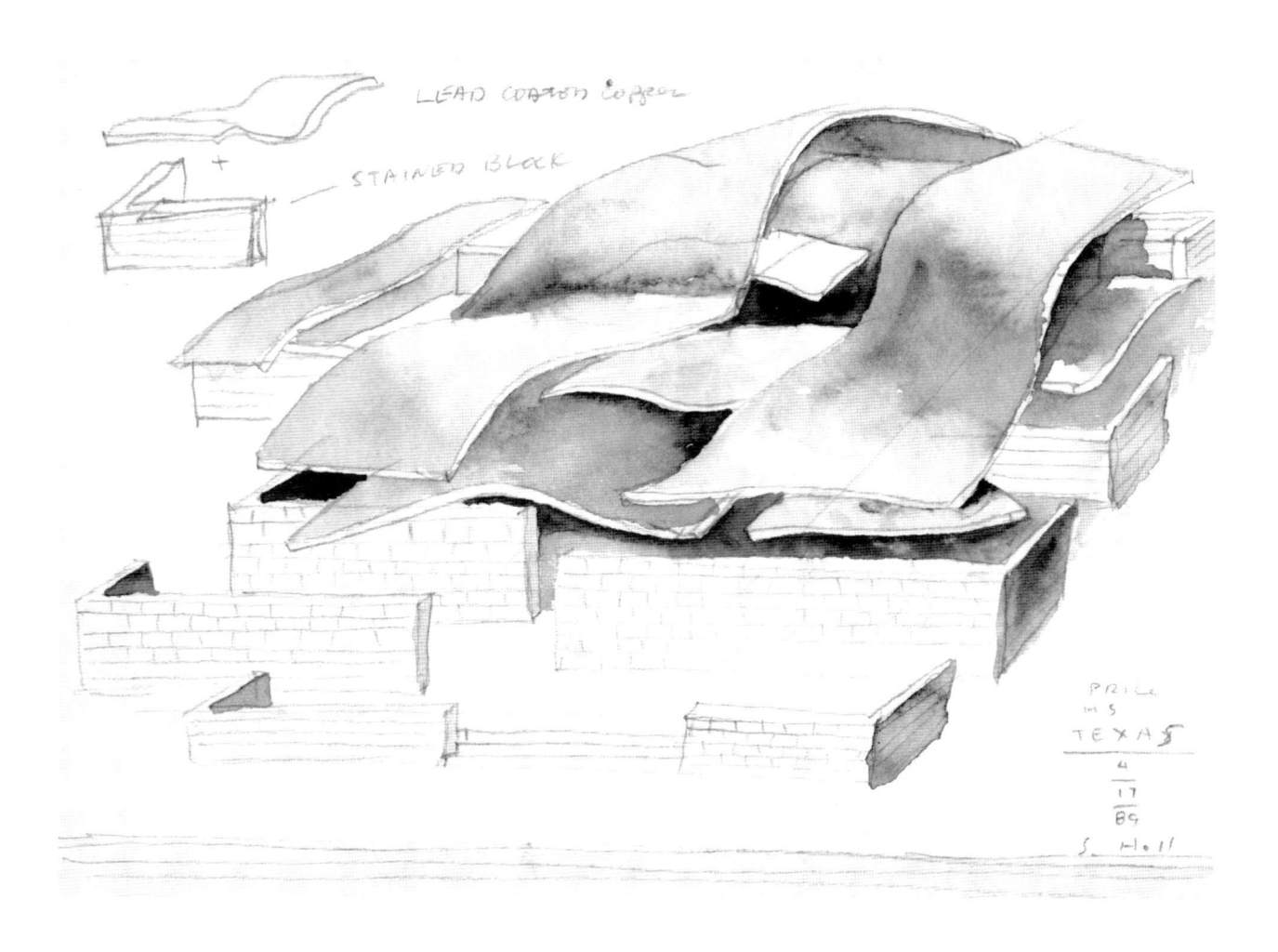

2 Houses
住宅

The challenge of designing houses depends on the particular intensity with which characteristics of place, spatial and material ideas are developed. Experiencing the poetry of light and space is a confirmation of the exhilarating potential of architecture as a vessel for everyday life. From meditative spaces to inspiring details, architecture holds the potential to change the way we live.

Space is a plastic medium. From the absolute stillness of the underwater chambers of the 1976 Sokolov Retreat, which drift in a wash of gently moving sunlight to the cubic shift of space in the Metz House of 1980, and the sheared space of the Residence in Cleveland, 1988, architectural space and its unique relation to site is explored.

With a pairing of Solid and Void, or Cavity and Mass, the Metz House is an exploration of a program where concavities become convexities. Here, space is conceived as blocks of ice shearing past one another, yet overlapping—a study in principles which Adolf Loos developed in the "Raum Plan."

Space becomes fluid in the 1989 Stretto House in Dallas, Texas. The reading of the existing stream and pools of water created by dams on the site is transformed into "aqueous space." A light steel and glass structure "flows" through four concrete-block "spatial dams." An obsession with the relation of music and architecture has shown promising ground for research since the "Music and Architecture" design experiments were begun in the fall of 1984 at Columbia University. The Stretto House, constructed as an analogue of Bela Bartok's *Music for Strings, Percussion, and Celeste*, concretizes liquid spatial concepts and explores new possibilities for domestic space.

"Hinged Space," or the space of "participating walls," was developed as a means of opening cramped interiors in Manhattan Apartments in the 1982 Cohen Apartment renovation. Lightweight hollow core doors and pivot hinges allowed the transformation of interior spaces by the inhabitants. This dynamic spatial shifting was taken to a large scale in "Void Space/Hinged Space" housing in Fukuoka, Japan in 1989.

The space of the oceanic horizon embraced in the body of the house became a point of departure for two ocean-front houses designed in 1984. In the Leucadia Oceanfront House, the central portion of the house is removed to form a void which brackets the Pacific Ocean horizon. The Martha's Vineyard House (Berkowitz-Odgis House, 1984-88) is the metaphor of a skeleton. The horizon is always seen through the delicate ribs of its linear structure. In each of these projects, an economy of means fuses with the desire for a spiritual connection to the site.

The house is a home for the soul, the heart and the spirit. It is a container for the day's light, from the pale yellow of dawn to the deep blue of twilight. It is a box for the existential objects of life. It is a vessel for imagination, laughter, ant motion... and a silent space for the poetic sense of life.

Steven Holl

Stretto House

住宅の設計に挑戦するには，場所の持つ特性や，空間と材料についての思考を展開することに，並々ならぬ熱意を注がなければならない。光と空間の詩を体験するということは，日常生活の器としての建築の，人を鼓舞する能力を知ることである。瞑想的な空間から，生気に満ちた空間にいたるまで，建築には私たちの生き方を変える力が秘められている。

空間とは，造型的なメディアである。1976年のソコロフ邸の隠れ家の水面下の部屋のように，おだやかにたゆたう日の光に洗われて漂う孤絶の中の静寂から，1980年のメッツ邸でのキュービックな空間への転換，1988年の，切り分けるような形でつくったクリーヴランドの住宅に至るまで，建築空間と敷地との間のユニークな関係のあり方を探求してきた。

虚と実，あるいは，空洞とマッスを組み合わせるプランニングによって，凹面が凸面に姿を変えてゆく構成を求めたのがメッツ邸であった。ここでは，空間を，互いに切り込まれ重なり合う水の固まりと考え，アドルフ・ロースが「ラウム・プラン」で展開した原理の演習を試みた。

1989年のテキサス州ダラスのストレット・ハウスでは，空間が流体になる。敷地を流れる小川と，それをせきとめてつくられていた池を読みとって，それを「水の空間」という形にした。軽量鉄骨とガラスの構造がコンクリート・ブロックでつくられた四つの「空間ダム」を「流れる」のである。1984年の秋，コロンビア大学で始めたデザイン実験以来とりつかれてきた，音楽と建築の関係の探求に明るい地平を開くことができたのがこの住宅である。ベラ・バルトークの「弦楽器と打楽器とチェレスタのための音楽」になぞらえてつくられたストレット・ハウスは，流体空間というコンセプトを実現して住空間の新たな可能性を探るものである。

「ヒンジド・スペース」あるいは「参加する壁」のある空間は，1982年のコーエン・アパートメントの改装で，マンハッタンのアパートメントの狭く閉ざされた内部空間を開放する手段として考え出されたものだった。軽いフラッシュ・ドアとピボット・ヒンジを使うことで，住人が自分の手で内部空間を変えることを可能にした。この動的な空間転換の仕掛けを大規模に試みたのが1989年の福岡のハウジング「ヴォイド・スペース／ヒンジド・スペース」である。

外洋の水平線を住宅の中に抱き込む空間をつくろうという意図が出発点になって，外洋に面する二つの住宅が，1984年に設計された。リューカディア・オーシャンフロント・ハウスでは，住宅の中央部を取り去って，その中から見ると太平洋の水平線を開口の端から端にかけ渡したように見える空間をつくった。マーサズ・ヴィンヤードの家（バーコヴィッツ＝オッジス邸，1984-88）は，骨格のメタファーとしてつくられた。直線で表現したこの家の，肋骨のように並ぶ細い列住を通して，常に水平線が望める。この二つの住宅はいずれも，費用を切りつめることが敷地との精神的な結びつきを求めることと，うまく融合したものだった。

住宅とは，魂と心と精神の拠り所となるものだ。夜明けの青みを帯びた淡黄色からはじまって，たそがれ時の深い青に至る，日の光の容れ物でもある。生活のための物たちを仕舞う箱。想像力と笑いと感動のための器……そして生活の中の詩的な感覚に捧げられた静謐な空間。

（スティーヴン・ホール）

1976 Sokolov Retreat
St. Tropez, France

The noise and confusion of vacation crowds in the harbor of St. Tropez suggested the need for a retreat from a vacation house. The retreat is easily accessible from the client's waterfront house. Silence and solitude are primary concerns.

The retreat is underwater, anchored in front of the existing house at the edge of the harbor. Floating four centimeters below the surface of the water, the chamber is invisible except for the hollow glass block towers for light and air. The towers extend upwards to guard against waves and to increase air circulation via the principle of the chimney draft.

The effort required for entry contributes to the sensation of a retreat; one must row from the mainland, secure the rowboat, and, with shoes off and trousers rolled, cross the submerged deck to the tower containing the entry stair.

The area of the plan stretches into a cruciform, like a catamaran leaning in two directions, to minimize rocking. Within the plan, one can retreat toward the ends to the hammocks or sit in the central meeting area, which has a glass bottom. The hollow glass block towers are at the endpoints of the plan for the best distribution of light and air. One tower is equipped with a ladder allowing eccentric guests the opportunity to dive off into the bay.

The structure is resin-coated ferroconcrete, a thin shell construction with layered wire mesh. Automatic sump pump and adjustable ballast in the double bottom maintain flotation and protect against overloading and listing. The towers are steel-secured glass block with silicone joints and acrylic rain flaps. Floors and walls are polished pigmented concrete. The hammocks are uncolored canvas.

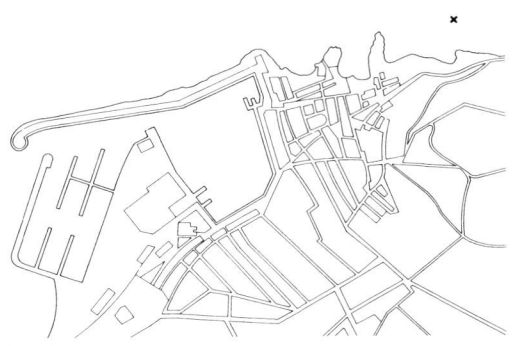

Site plan

ソコロフ邸の隠れ家

サントロペの港の喧騒と混乱のほどは,別荘からさらに引きこもることのできる隠れ家が欲しいという要望にうなずかせるに充分なものがあった。隠れ家へは,海辺に建つクライアントの別荘から,たやすくアクセスができる。そこでは,静けさの中で孤独にひたれることが,すべてに優先した。

隠れ家は水面下にあって,港のはずれにある別荘の目の前に繋留される。水面下4cmに浮かぶ部屋は外からは見えない。水面の上には光と空気を採り入れるガラスブロックの塔が立つのが見えるだけだ。上にのびる塔は,打ち寄せる波をかわし,煙突効果で空気の循環を促すのである。

ここに辿り着くには,多少の手間をかけねばならないために,いっそう隠れ家らしさが増すことになった。岸から漕いでやって来たボートを繋ぎ止めると,まず靴を脱ぎ,ズボンの裾を折り上げてから水面下にかくれたデッキを渡って,階段のある塔に行く,という具合なのだ。

平面形は十字をなし,さながら双胴船のように二方向に伸ばすことで揺れを軽減させるのである。中に入ると,ハンモックを吊った奥の方に潜むか,中央の,ガラス張りの床の居間に腰を下ろす。十字型プランの各先端に立つガラスブロックの中空の塔は,光と空気をできる限り行きわたらせようとしている。そのひとつには梯子があって,変わり者の客が湾に飛び込みたいなどと言い出しても,要望に応えることができるというわけだ。

構造は,レジンを塗ったフェロコンクリートの薄いシェル構造体で,ワイヤーメッシュを重ねて入れる。二重底の中にある自動揚水ポンプの働きとバラストの増減によって浮力を安定させ,荷重の超過や減少による転倒を防ぐことができる。塔は,鉄筋で補強したガラスブロック。目地にはシリコンのコーキング,アクリルの雨よけも備える。床と壁は,コンクリートに光沢のある塗料を塗る。ハンモックは,生成りのキャンヴァスである。

Section

Roof

Plan

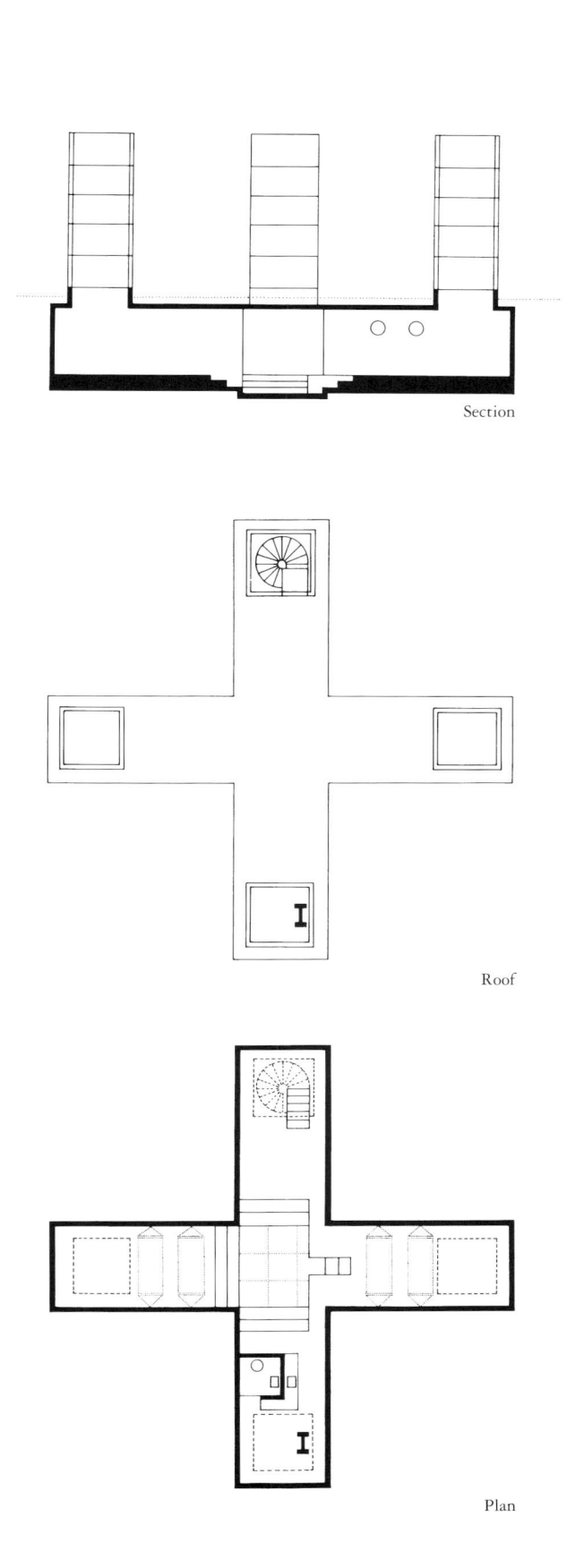

Perspectives

Night view

I-65

1978-79 Telescope House
Still Pond, Maryland, U.S.A.

With this project we launched our debate against eclecticism and against the importation of history. Eclecticism provokes the fragmentation of the past and the obfuscation of the present. This project is for us its opposite; it is a kind of distilled modern interpretation of certain cultural developments.
—Excerpt from exhibition, Yale University 1979

A retired couple with a very narrow site on Chesapeake Bay required a house in portions that could be closed off when not in use. This coincided with certain configurations observed in the history of Eastern Shore architecture. We fused a model of a particular type, the telescope house, with the program. Telescope houses, evolving since the early 1700s, received their name from their external appearance resembling a spyglass or telescope. Some were built large section first, descending, some small section first, ascending, and some, all sections at once.

The proposed house is in three portions corresponding to frequency of use: a) the basic house for two persons, used year round; b) the formal entertainment rooms for visiting family; and c) the guest rooms, closed off when not in use.

The plan responds to a thin lot (160 by 493 feet) which is narrowed further by a 60-foot setback from the water edge and from the street. The house is approached from a long driveway framed with trees, which offers a glimpse of the bay before passing parallel to the house and court. Walking through the court onto the screened front porch, a grid of steel windows with double doors leads to the entrance hall and sitting room beyond. Moving through the house gives a feeling of crossing strips of sunlight aligned with views of the water, as each major room has both north and south windows of identical exposure. The second level observatory can be reached by an interior stair or by way of the roof that ascends parallel to the water's edge. Magnificent vantage points facing the bay and the wildlife preserve on the adjacent site can be found along the roof, in the observatory, and along the deck overlooking the courtyard. The house does not so much fill the site as create a new, synthetic one, looking over the trees to the Chesapeake.

The structure is of stained concrete block with wooden roof and floor joists. The rubber-membrane roof is of the type developed for commercial construction, eliminating the need for any roof flashing. Windows are painted steel with insulated glass. The cerulean blue concrete pavers of the entrance court lead to an entrance hall of honed marble slabs, which gives way to an assymetrical black slate stair leading to the observatory.

テレスコープ・ハウス
「このプロジェクトで,私たちは折衷主義と歴史の転用に対して議論を挑むつもりだ。折衷主義は過去を切り刻み,現在を曖昧なものにする。それに対してこのプロジェクトは,私たちに言わせればそれとは対極にあるものだ。つまり,発展の過程にある文化に対して,現代という時点に立って解釈を加え,それを精製したものなのである。」
(1979年イエール大学に於ける展覧会より)

チェザピーク・ベイに細長い土地を持つ,引退した夫妻は,家の一部を使用しない時には閉め切ることができるよう希望した。東海岸の建築の歴史には,このような形式にぴったりのものがあるので,私たちはテレスコープ・ハウスと呼ばれる形式をこの住宅にあてはめることにした。これは,1700年代初頭から始まったものだが,その名はスパイ・グラスや望遠鏡に似た外見から採ったものだ。あるものは大きい部分をはじめにつくって,徐々に小さい部分に移り,またあるものは逆に小さい部分をはじめに手がけてから大きい方へ取りかかったし,中には全ての部分を同時につくりあげるものもあった。

この住宅の計画案では,使用頻度に応じて全体を三つの部分に分けた。a) 一年を通じて使われる,二人の住み手のための,住宅の中心をなす部分,b) 家族づれの来客を迎えるための,正式なもてなしの部屋,c) 使用されない時は締め切っておくゲストルームである。

もともと細長い敷地の形(160フィート×493フィート)から,

水際と道路の両方から60フィート、セットバックすると、平面はなお狭められた。樹木に囲まれた車寄せを抜けて走るアプローチの途中、家と中庭に平行な方向に向きを変えようとする時に、湾を垣間見ることができる。中庭を経て、スクリーンで囲われた玄関ポーチに至ると、格子状のスティールの窓の中に設けられた両開きのドアから、玄関ホール、その奥の居間へと続く。家を通り抜ける途中、片側に太陽の光、片側に水面の景色があるので、連続する光の帯を次々に通りすぎるような思いを抱かされる。主な部屋は、そのどれもが南北両面に同じ大きさの窓があるからなのだ。2階の展望台へは室内の階段、もしくは湖面に平行に高さを変える屋根づたいにアクセスできる。湾や、隣接する野生生物保護区を一望にする絶好の見晴しは、屋根の上にも展望台にも、中庭を見下ろすデッキにも、こと欠きはしない。この住宅では、敷地いっぱいに建てるというよりも、木々の梢越しにチェザピークを望めるような、敷地との新しい関係をつくりだそうとした。

構造はステイン塗りのコンクリートブロックに木造の屋根と床梁を架けたものだ。ゴム系の屋根材は商業建築のために開発されたもので、水切などを必要としない。窓はスティールに塗装、ペアグラスを入れる。セルリアン・ブルーのコンクリート舗装を施されたエントランス・コートから水磨きの大理石の玄関ホールにつづき、それが、展望台への非対称のスレート貼りの階段へ至る。

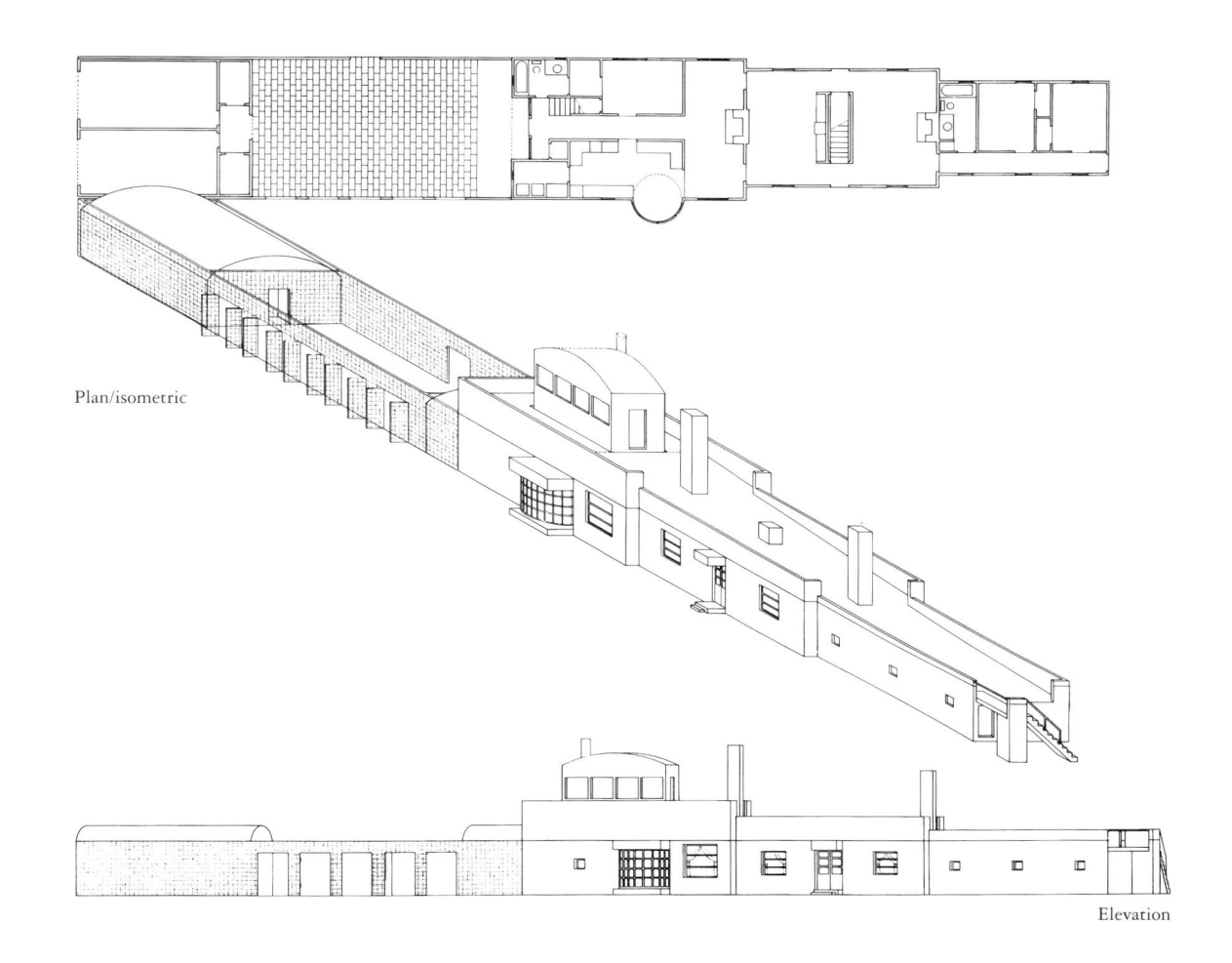

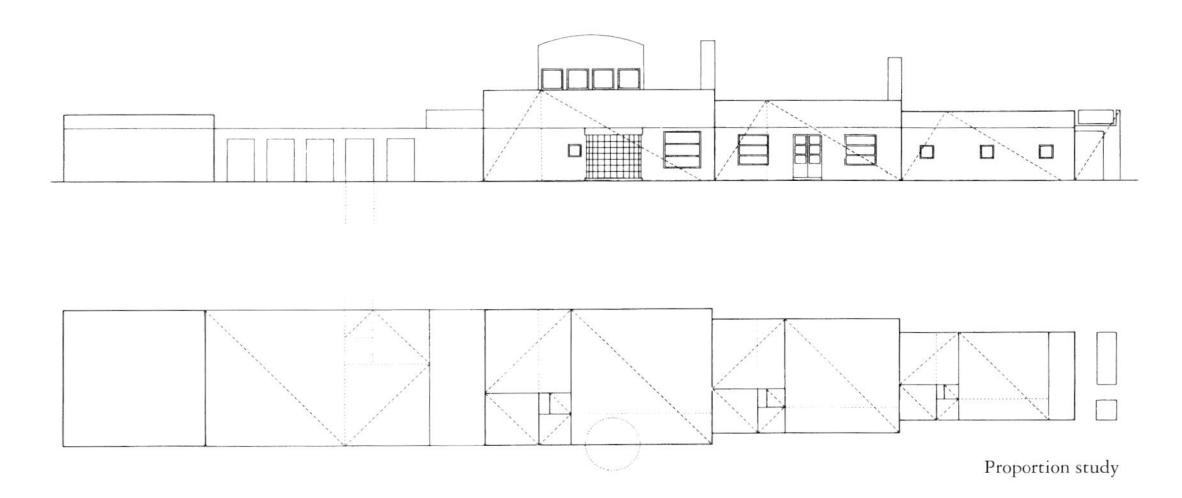

Plan/isometric

Elevation

Proportion study

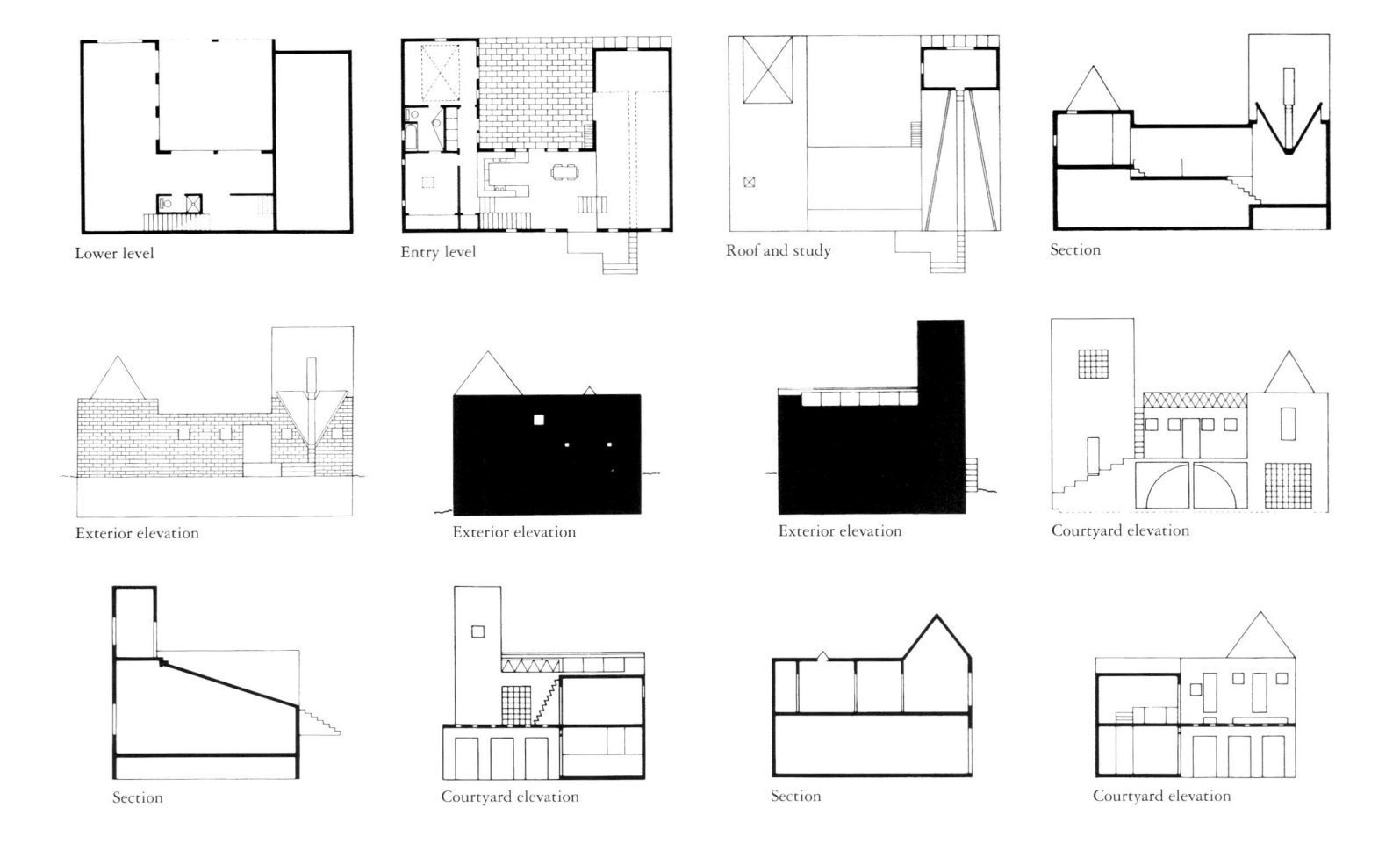

Lower level · Entry level · Roof and study · Section

Exterior elevation · Exterior elevation · Exterior elevation · Courtyard elevation

Section · Courtyard elevation · Section · Courtyard elevation

The site for this project is a thickly wooded lot on Staten Island overlooking a forested ravine. It is an inexpensive house for a young couple, both artists. Conventional living and dining rooms are excluded in favor of two larger studios and a large kitchen. The studio's requirements reflect the nearly opposite sensibilities of the two artists: husband (sculptor) and wife (painter). She makes floral paintings, loves sunlight and plants, and has several cats. He makes black concrete sculpture, hates cats and house plants, and doesn't care to have natural light in his studio as he works mostly at night. One bedroom is for a teenage daughter who desires privacy. The client expressed dislike of the suburban image of local developments, favoring an approach that leaves all natural vegetation on the site untouched.

The house is a dialectic of two parts based on a traditional U-type courtyard plan. An introspective outdoor court opens to the sun and a view of the ravine. The analogy of an urban building type, like an island in the forest, is carried out in all the elevations: the front facade is articulated in integral color concrete blocks, the side walls are painted black like the party walls in a city, and the courtyard is painted white for maximum light.

Each wing of the "U" contains one of the studios, whose character is expressed by the contrast between the two wings. In the right wing is the painting studio with skylight providing indirect light. Above the monitors is a ramp to the solitude of the study. In the lower part of the left wing is the sculpture studio, opening to the grotto and outdoor work area. The grotto receives light from cylindrical glass block elements cast in the slab of the courtyard. In the center of the main level are the common areas of the kitchen/dining and entrance foyer. The teen-ager's bedroom has a special roof, giving her the feeling of being in a separate little house.

Construction is insulation-filled concrete block with plaster interiors applied directly to the block. Floors are industrial grade pine with an oiled finish. The roof is insulated wood framing with composite roll-roofing. Interior stairs in the entrance foyer are black slate alternating with white marble, creating an effect like the black and white keys of a piano.

Metz House
1980-81   Staten Island, New York, U.S.A.

Isometric

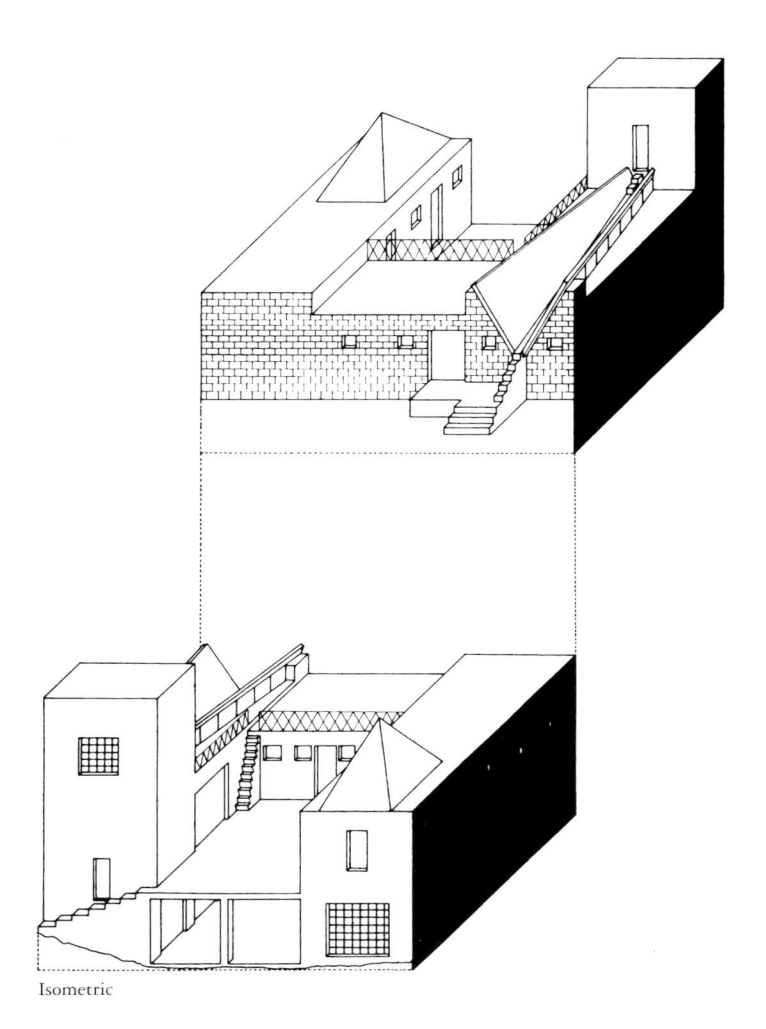

メッツ邸

この計画の敷地は, スタテン・アイランドの樹影の濃い峡谷を見下ろす土地である。いずれも芸術家である若いカップルのための, 工費を抑えた住宅である。居間や食堂といった伝統的なものはつくらず, 大きめのスタジオを二つと広いキッチンが求められた。スタジオについての要求には, 二人の芸術家は正反対というくらい感性の違いを示した。夫は彫刻家, 妻は画家である。彼女は花を描くので, 日の光と植物を愛し, 猫を何匹も飼っている。夫は黒いコンクリートの彫刻をつくる。こちらは猫も, 園芸植物も大嫌いで, スタジオに自然光はいらないという。ほとんど夜に制作するからだ。ひとつしかない寝室は, プライバシーを欲しがるティーンエイジャーの娘の部屋だ。クライアントは, 地元のディベロッパーのつくるような郊外風を嫌って, 敷地にあった植物を全て残すよう望んだ。

この住宅は, 伝統的なU字の中庭型プランをもとにして, その両翼を発展させたものである。内向的な中庭は太陽を抱き入れ, 渓谷の景色に向かって開いている。森の中に浮かぶ島のような家をつくるつもりで, 都市の建物のようにエレベーションを描いていった。正面のファサードはカラー・コンクリート・ブロック, 側面の壁は都市の建物の隣地との共同壁であるかのように黒く塗り, 中庭はできるだけ光を採り入れるために白い塗装とした。

U型をなす二つのウイングは, それぞれにひとつずつスタジオがあって, その性格がそのまま二つのウイングの対照的な形にあらわれている。右のウイングには, 間接光を取入れるスカイライトのついた, 絵画用のアトリエがある。屋根の上のスロープは独立した書斎に続く。左のウイングの下の階は彫刻のスタジオである。ここは, グロットと屋外作業場に続く。グロットには, その上の中庭の床スラブに埋め込まれた円形のガラスブロックを通して光が落ちてくる。メインレベルの中央には, キッチンとダイニングそして玄関がある。ティーンエイジャーの寝室には特別の屋根が載せられているので, 独立した小さな家にいるようだ。

構造は断熱材を充填したコンクリート・ブロックに, 内部は直かにプラスターを塗る。床は量産の松の板にオイルフィニッシュ。屋根は木造で, 断熱を施したうえ長尺の合成屋板材で仕上げる。玄関ホールの階段は玄昌石の黒と大理石の白が交互に混ざり, ピアノの黒鍵と白鍵を思わせる。

Isometric

Sectional perspective

Overall view from southeast. Main house on right

Pool House and Sculpture Studio
1980-81   Scarsdale, New York, U.S.A.

Poolside elevation on south

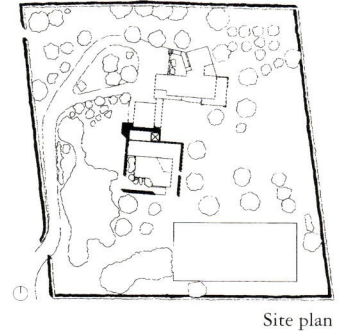

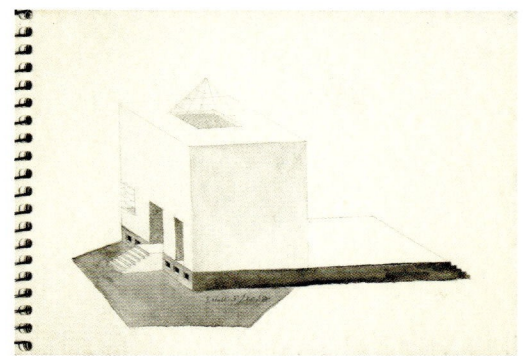

Site plan

Sketch

Entrance door with sandblasted glasses

I-71

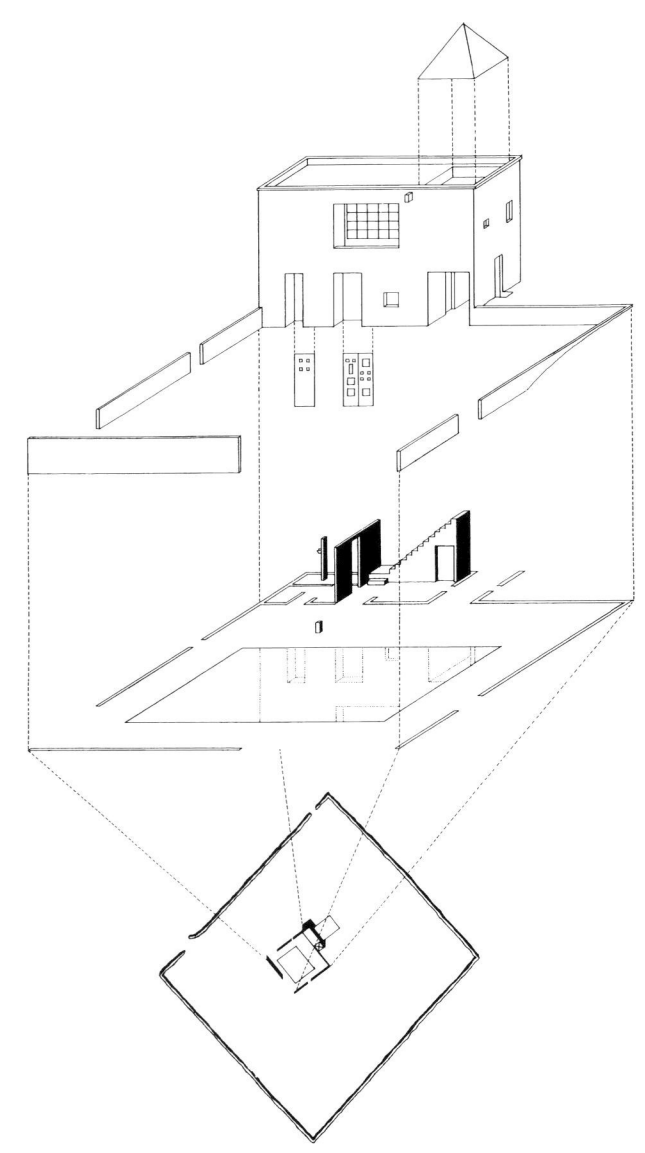

Exploded isometric

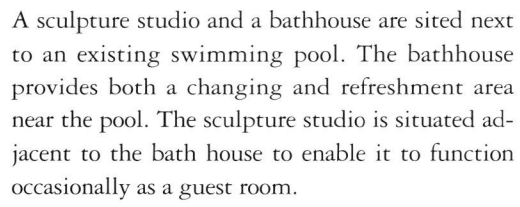

Sculpture studio on second floor

A sculpture studio and a bathhouse are sited next to an existing swimming pool. The bathhouse provides both a changing and refreshment area near the pool. The sculpture studio is situated adjacent to the bath house to enable it to function occasionally as a guest room.

The site in Scarsdale, New York has a history that dates from the transference of property rights by King George in the early eighteenth century. The land is marked by stone walls that were used to define its boundaries.

The project is organized with the idea of "walls within walls". New walls enclosing the existing pool form a courtyard recalling the ancient stone boundary wall around the site. On the north wall of the new court, the pool house and sculpture studio form a two-story pavilion. The sculpture studio on the upper level receives light from two major windows and a pyramid skylight, which also marks the major axes on the site.

Construction is of insulation-filled concrete block with smooth plaster interiors and luminous gray stucco exteriors. Red integral-color concrete pavers in the courtyard provide contrast with the dark green marble of the details and countertops. The floor of the bathhouse is flesh-colored marble. The white ceramic tile of the shower room is broken by a green marble water column with brass shower fixtures. Glass openings in the lower doors have sandblasted drawings carved in them that relate to the history of the site and the architectonic ideas.

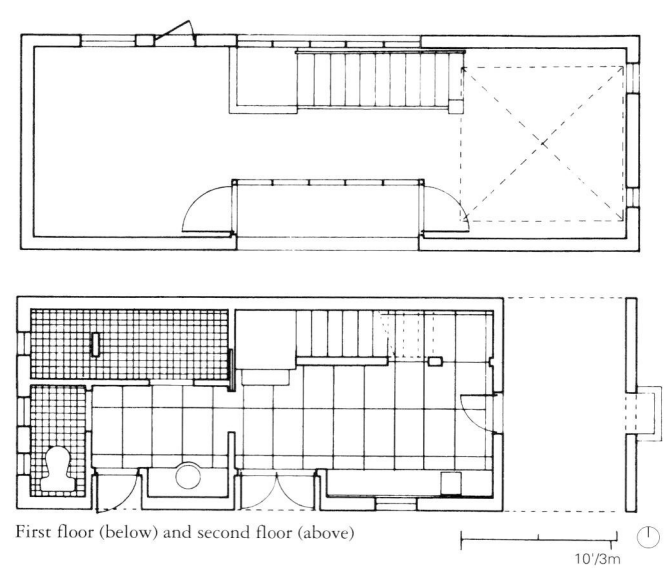

First floor (below) and second floor (above)

I-72

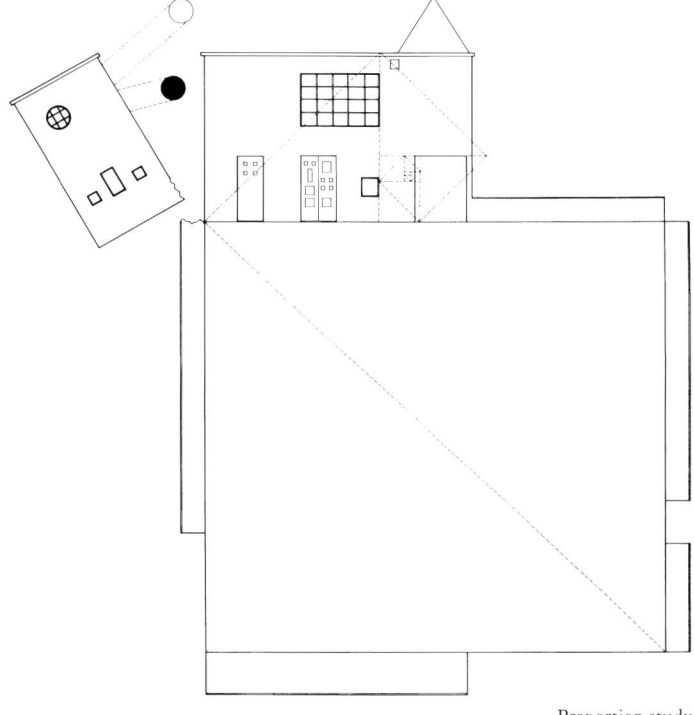

Second floor

Proportion study

プールハウス／彫刻スタジオ
彫刻のスタジオ／バスハウスがプールの脇につくられた。バスハウスはプールの近くにあるので着替えにも，休息にも使うことができる。彫刻スタジオはバスハウスの上にあるので，必要とあらば時にはゲストルームとして使われる。

ニューヨークのスカースデールにある敷地は，18世紀のジョージ王朝による土地所有権の移譲まで遡る歴史をもっている。この土地は，かつて境界を表示するために使われた石積の壁で囲われている。

計画は「壁の中の壁」という考え方によってつくられた。既存のプールを囲む新しい壁は中庭を形成し，敷地の周囲の旧い壁を思わせる。この新しい中庭の壁の北側の一部を構成してプールハウスと彫刻スタジオの2階建のパヴィリオンがある。2階の彫刻スタジオは二つの大きな窓とピラミッド型のスカイライトから採光する。このピラミッドは，敷地の主要な軸をなす。

断熱材充填のコンクリート・ブロックに，内部はプラスター塗り，外部は光沢のあるグレイのスタッコ仕上げである。中庭の床に使われたカラーコンクリートの赤は，ディテール各部とカウンターの天板に使われるダークグリーンの大理石とコントラストをなす。バスハウスの床は肌色の大理石。シャワールームの白いタイルは，真鍮のシャワーをとりつけた柱のグリーンの大理石がひきたてる。1階の開口部のガラスにはサンドブラストのレリーフで，この地の歴史と，この建築の理念が描かれている。

1984-88 **Berkowitz-Odgis House**
Martha's Vineyard, Massachusetts, U.S.A.

Overall view from northwest

Site plan

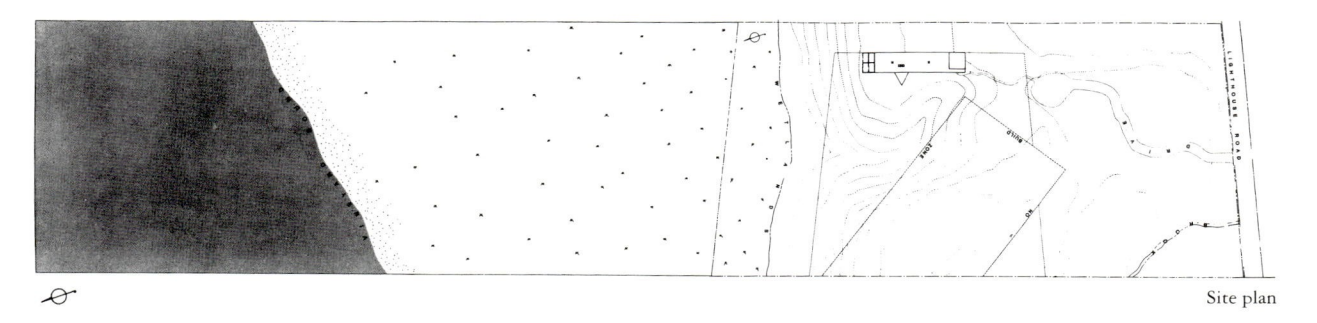

Concept sketch

View from west

View from northeast

Perspective: the Atlantic Ocean and house

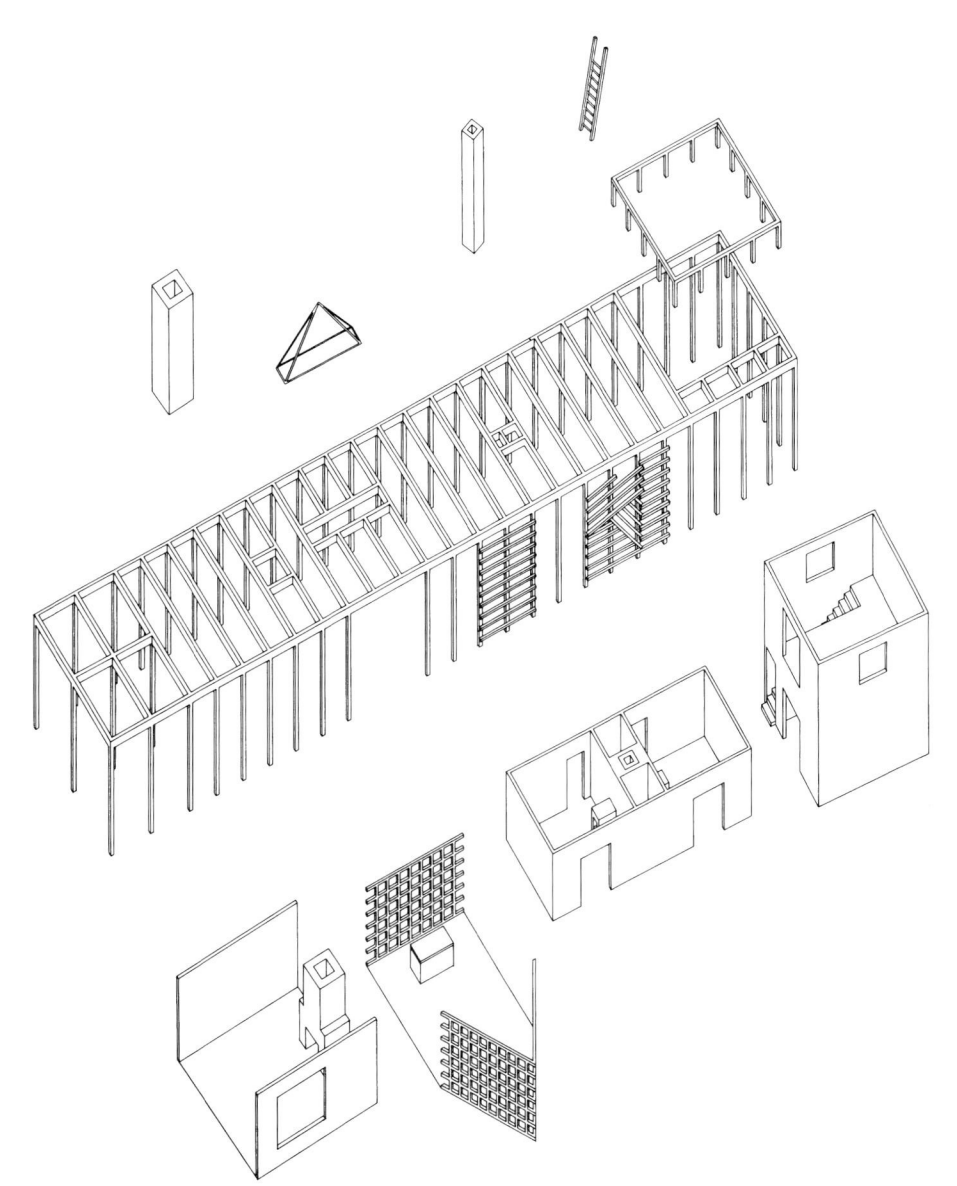

Second floor

1 LIVING ROOM
2 KITCHEN
3 DINING ROOM
4 BEDROOM
5 PORCH

First floor

Section

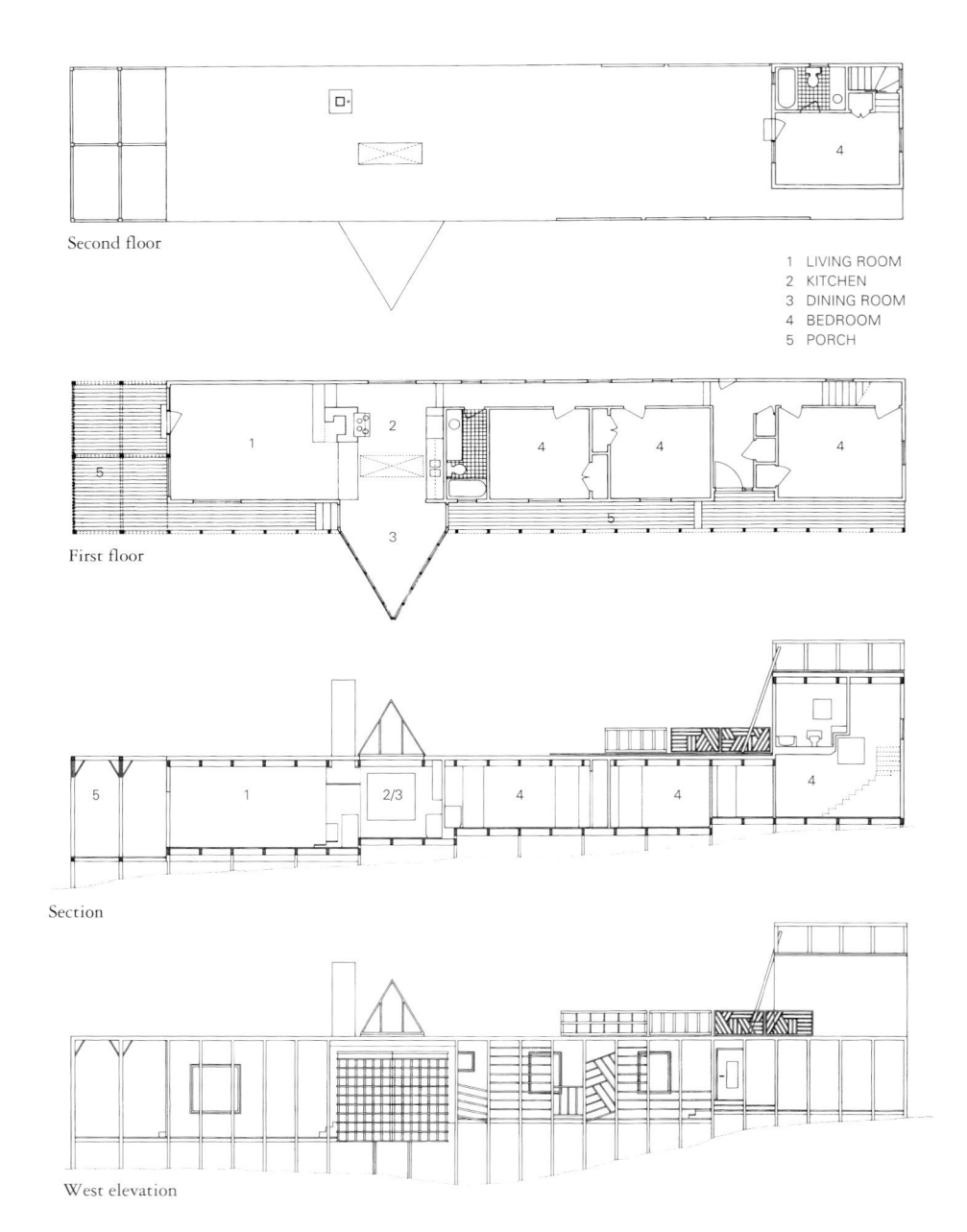

West elevation

Exploded axonometric

I-76

Porch on west

Living room

Porch

Door detail

Porch: view toward the Atlantic Ocean

Living room. Kitchen behind

In looking at things spiritual, we are too much like oysters observing the sun, through the water, and thinking that thick water the thinnest of air.
—H. Melville, *Moby Dick*

The site is a hill overlooking the Atlantic Ocean. The ground, densely overgrown with brush, is cut by a gully that descends to an unobstructed bog. The steep terrain and other building restrictions strictly limit the siting and construction material as well as the building height for the vacation home.

According to Melville's *Moby Dick*, the Indian tribe that originally inhabited Martha's Vineyard created a unique dwelling type. Finding a whale skeleton on the beach, they would pull it up to dry land and stretch skins or bark over it, transforming it into a house.

The house is an inside-out balloon frame of wooden construction: a skeleton house whose modern bones define a veranda. Along this continuous porch, wooden members receive the natural vines of the island, which transform the straight linear mode of the architecture.

The structural frame exposed inside and out meets the undisturbed sand dune on point foundations rather than on a common perimeter footing. Roofing is a rubber membrane unrolled over the frame, analogous to the skins over the whale skeleton.

Dining room

East elevation: view toward dining room

バーコヴィッツ＝オッジス邸
「おれ達が霊的な物事をながめる時において，まるで牡蛎が水の底から太陽を覗きながら，どろどろした水を澄明な空気だとおもっているようなものかもしれないぞ。」
——H・メルヴィル著『白鯨』，阿部知二訳

敷地は，大西洋を見下ろす丘にある。地表はびっしりと潅木が生い茂り，一方は削りとられたような斜面が沼地に向かい，景観を遮るものはない。土地の傾斜が急なうえ，建築規制があるために，この別荘は高さはもとより，配置や構造も非常に限定されることになった。

メルヴィルの『白鯨』によれば，マーサズ・ヴィンヤードの先住民だったインディアンの部族が考え出した大変ユニークな住まいがあるそうだ。海岸に打ち上げられた鯨の骨格を見つけると，彼等はそれを乾燥した土地まで引き上げて毛皮や樹皮を張って家に変身させたのだという。

この住宅は，バルーン・フレームを裏返しにしたような木造建築である。現代製の骨がベランダの周囲を包む，骨組みの家だ。周囲を巡るこのポーチの柱や梁にこの島に自生するツタがからみ，建築の直線的な性格を変身させてしまうのである。

内側，あるいは外に露出する構造体は，布基礎に代えて使われた円柱形の独立基礎だけで整地しないままの砂丘と接する。屋根には長尺のゴム系の屋根材を，さながら鯨の骨の上に巡らした皮のように張った。

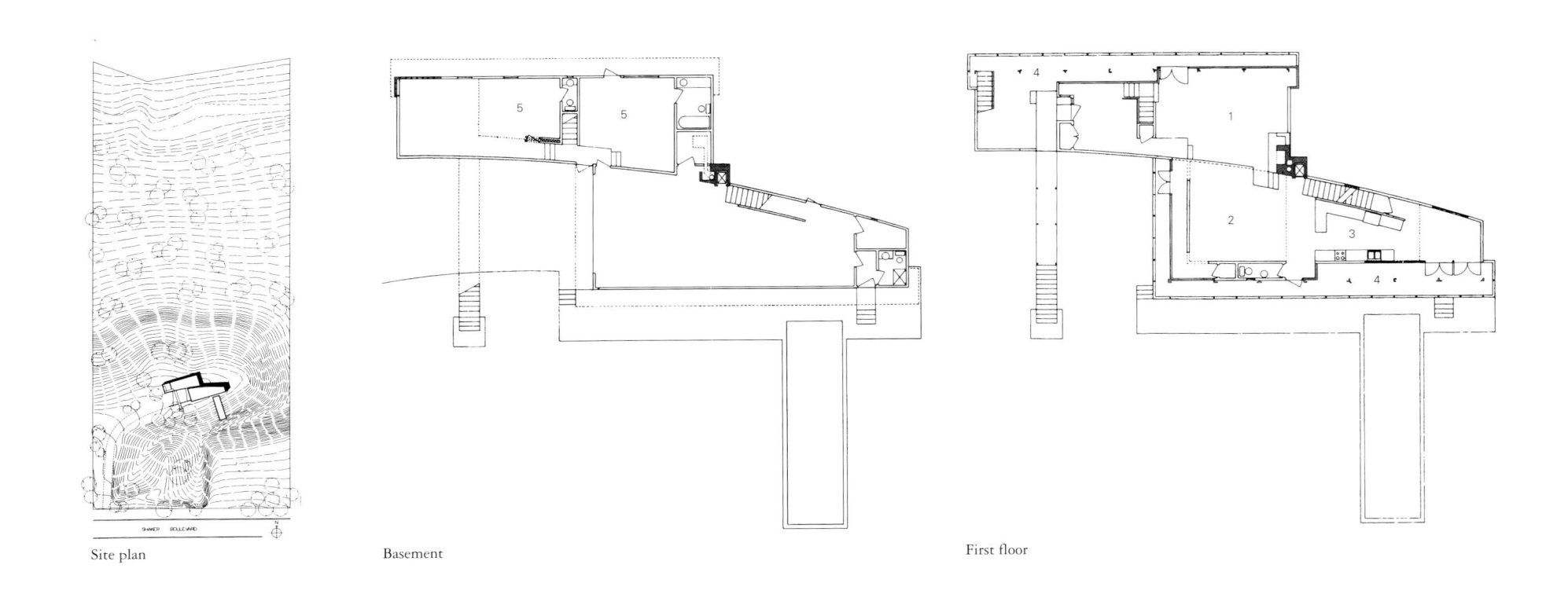

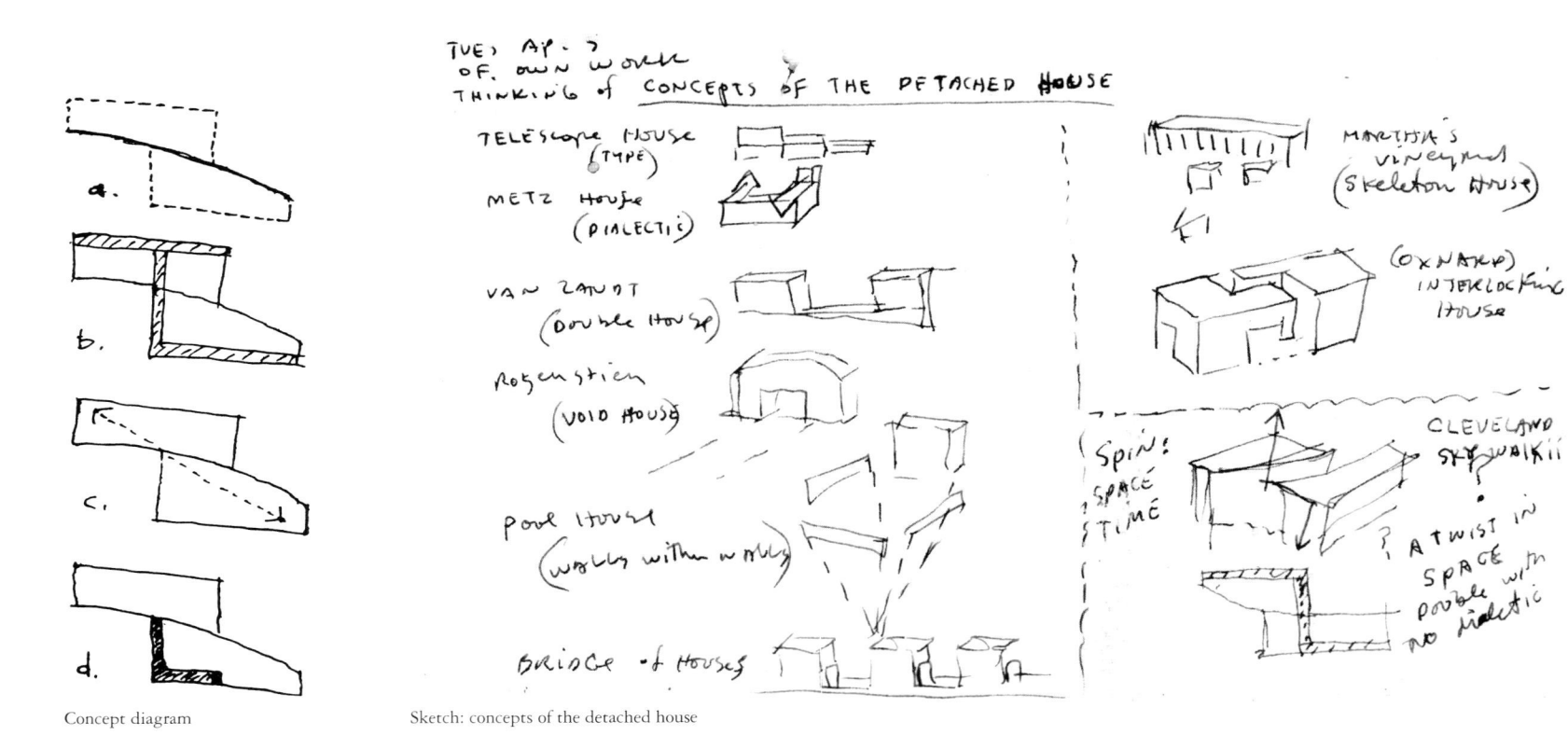

Site plan · Basement · First floor

Concept diagram · Sketch: concepts of the detached house

Residence

1988-90 Cleveland, Ohio, U.S.A.

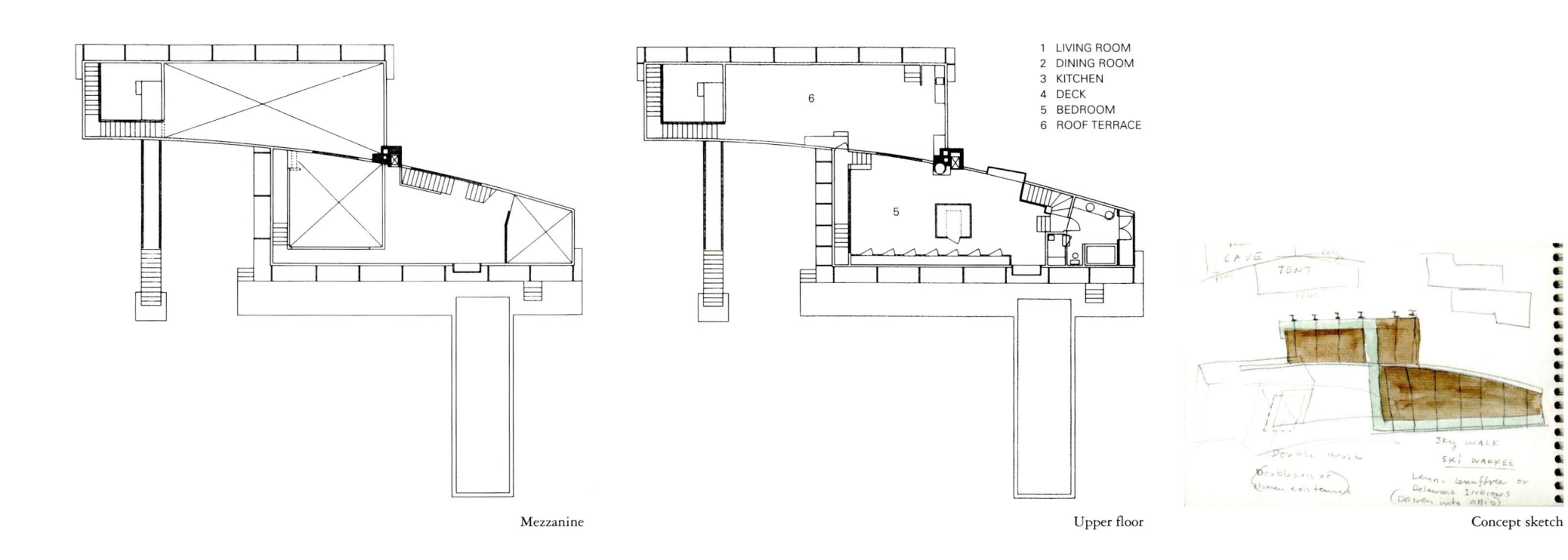

Mezzanine	Upper floor	Concept sketch

1 LIVING ROOM
2 DINING ROOM
3 KITCHEN
4 DECK
5 BEDROOM
6 ROOF TERRACE

Perspective: living room and dining room

Perspective: living room

Perspective: deck and staircase

Perspective: deck and roof terrace

I-81

Model: north elevation

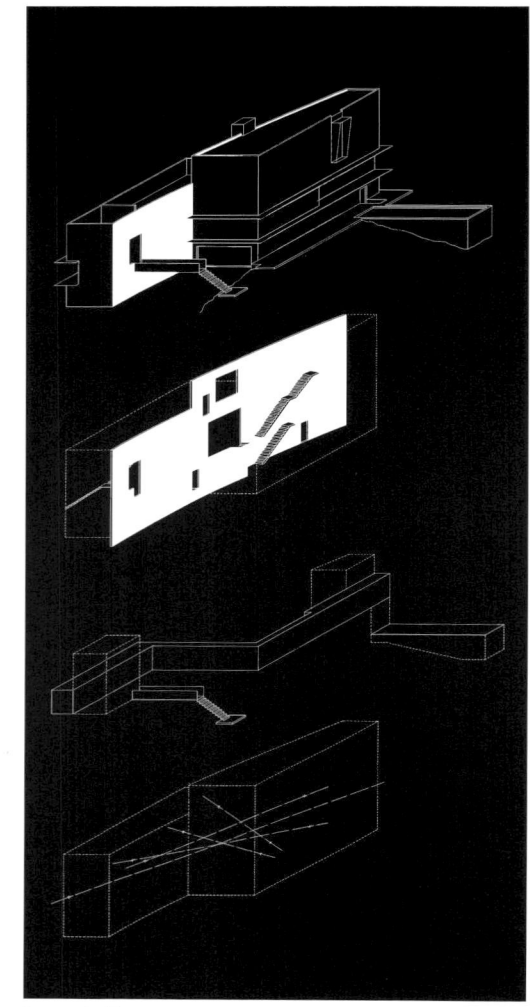

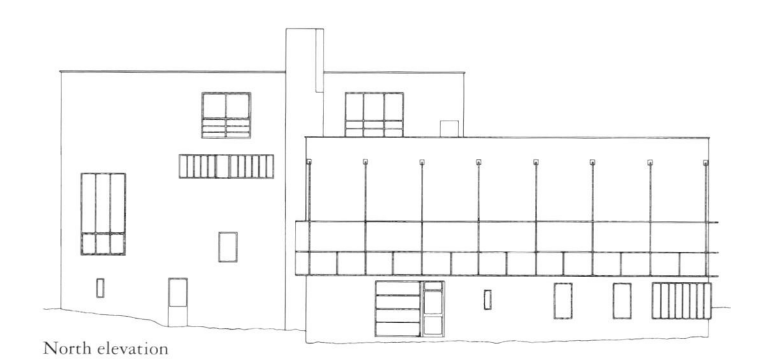

North elevation

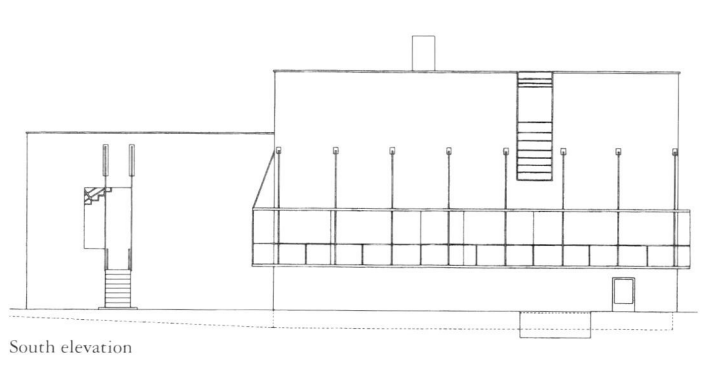

South elevation

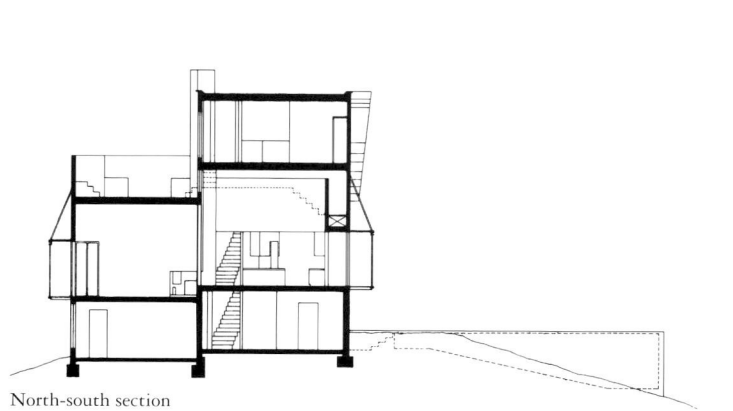

North-south section

East-west section

Isometric diagrams

I-82

A thickly wooded site east of Cleveland characterized by ravines and steep grades is the site for a house for a lawyer and his wife, a painter. Large open spaces and a vertical emphasis were requested, along with a three-car garage. The house has a multilevel section shifted along a curve, which coincides with the central ravine on the site. A series of conditions erase the dialectic nature of the house's double-form:

a) The double form is displaced along the entrance plane of the house. Distinct from the other elevations, this blackened plane makes a "front" on the inside and the outside, north and south.

b) A "skywalk" suspended from the facade traverses both halves of the house, joining them in a continuous steel deck view of the trees.

c) Diagonal views of interior space, 100 feet in length, join both halves of the house.

d) Sleepwalk passage: above the "skywalk," a blind passage leads from the mezzanine to a roof terrace. This passage was inspired by C. Brockden Brown's novel, *Memoirs of a Sleep Walker*, published in 1779. The novel is based on his unpublished work *Sky Walk* (a corruption of "skiwakkee," the name given to the Delaware Indians, who were later driven into Ohio). Sleepwalking and a cave are metaphors Brown uses for subconsciousness. The novel revolves on dualities, coupling, intertwining, etc. Here the psycho-symbolic program of sleep-walking finds an architectural equivalent.

Cleveland's steel industries are employed in the steel construction. Varying automotive channel sections are rolled straight and spaced at eight feet on center along the "skywalk." The remaining structure is plywood reinforced metal studs, steel-suspended walks, and steel windows.

Model: southeast view

Model: west elevation

クリーヴランドの住宅

幾筋もの沢と急傾斜が特徴的な,クリーヴランドの東部に位置する樹影の濃い敷地には,弁護士である夫と画家の夫人というカップルのための住宅が建てられる。広々としたオープンスペースを持ち垂直性を強調した空間であること,3台の車のガレージを備えることが要望された。この住宅は,曲線に沿ってレベルを変化させ,その曲線は敷地の中心にある沢に合わせたものである。一連の状況を設定することによって,この住宅のもつダブル・フォームという論証的側面を消去する。

a) ダブル・フォームは,この住宅の玄関の壁面に沿って反転される。他の立面とははっきり区別されたこの黒い壁面は,内に外に,北に南に一枚の正面ファサードを構成する。

b) ファサードに吊る「スカイウォーク」は,二つに分けられた住宅の両方を横断して,どちらからも,森の景色をスティールのデッキから森の景色を楽しめるようにしている。

c) 内部空間を対角方向に見ると100フィートに及ぶ奥行きを持ち,二分割されたこの住宅の双方にまたがっている。

d) 夢中歩行者の通路――「スカイウォーク」の上の窓のない通路は,中2階からルーフテラスへ続く。この通路はC・ブロックデン・ブラウンの『夢遊病者の記憶』(1779年出版)という小説をもとにした。この小説は,未刊行の作品『スカイウォーク』を発展させたものである(後にオハイオに移住させられたデラウェア・インディアンに与えられた名である「スキワキー」の堕落が描かれている)。夢中歩行と洞窟を,無意識に対するメタファーとして用いた。この小説は二重性を中心にして循環する。ときには二つが結び合い,ときにはそれらがもつれ合う。これは,夢中歩行の精神状態を建築によって象徴的に表現したものである。

鉄骨工事には,クリーヴランドの鉄鋼業者が使われた。種々の量産のチャンネル鋼を「スカイウォーク」の中央に8フィートおきに巻付けた。その他の構造は合板で補強したメタルスタッドと,スティールで吊った通路,それにスティールの窓である。

1989-92   **Stretto House**
            Dallas, Texas, U.S.A.

View from south approach

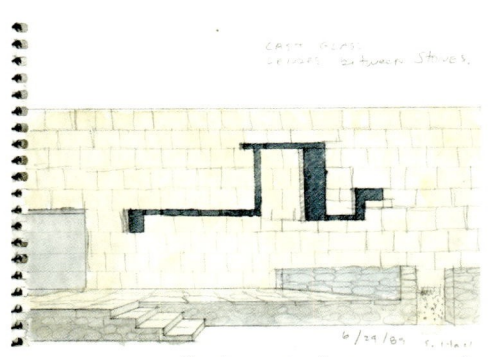

Sketch: cast glass between stone walls

Entrance terrace

Entrance

I-85

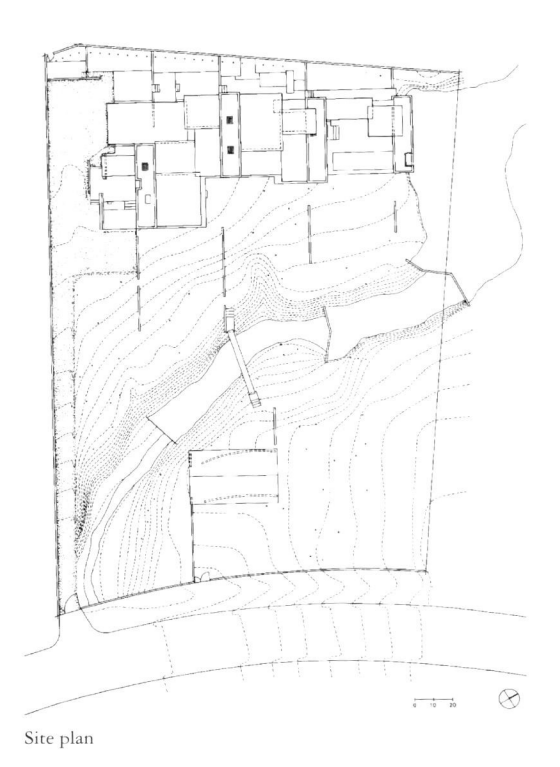

Site plan

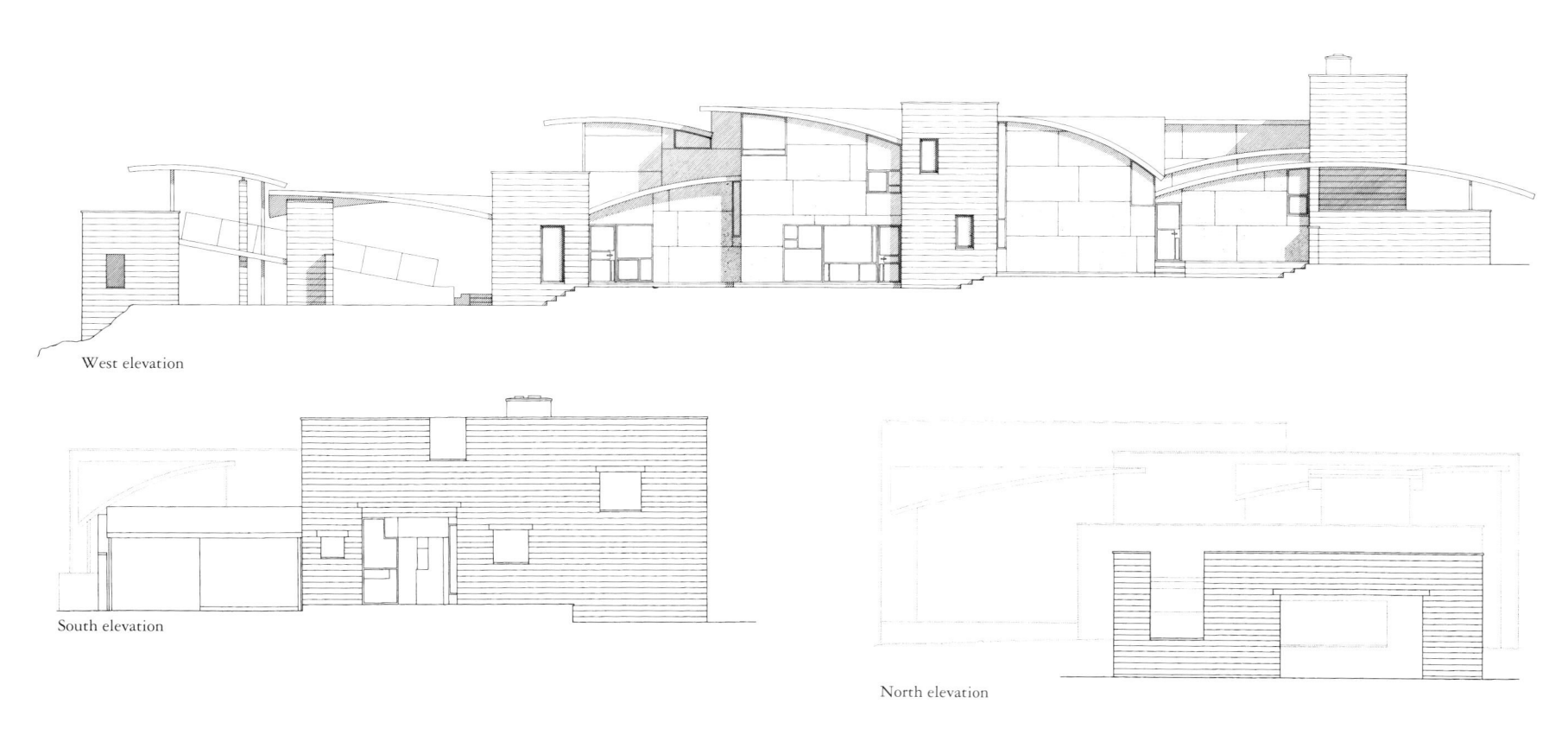

West elevation

South elevation

North elevation

I-86

View from east

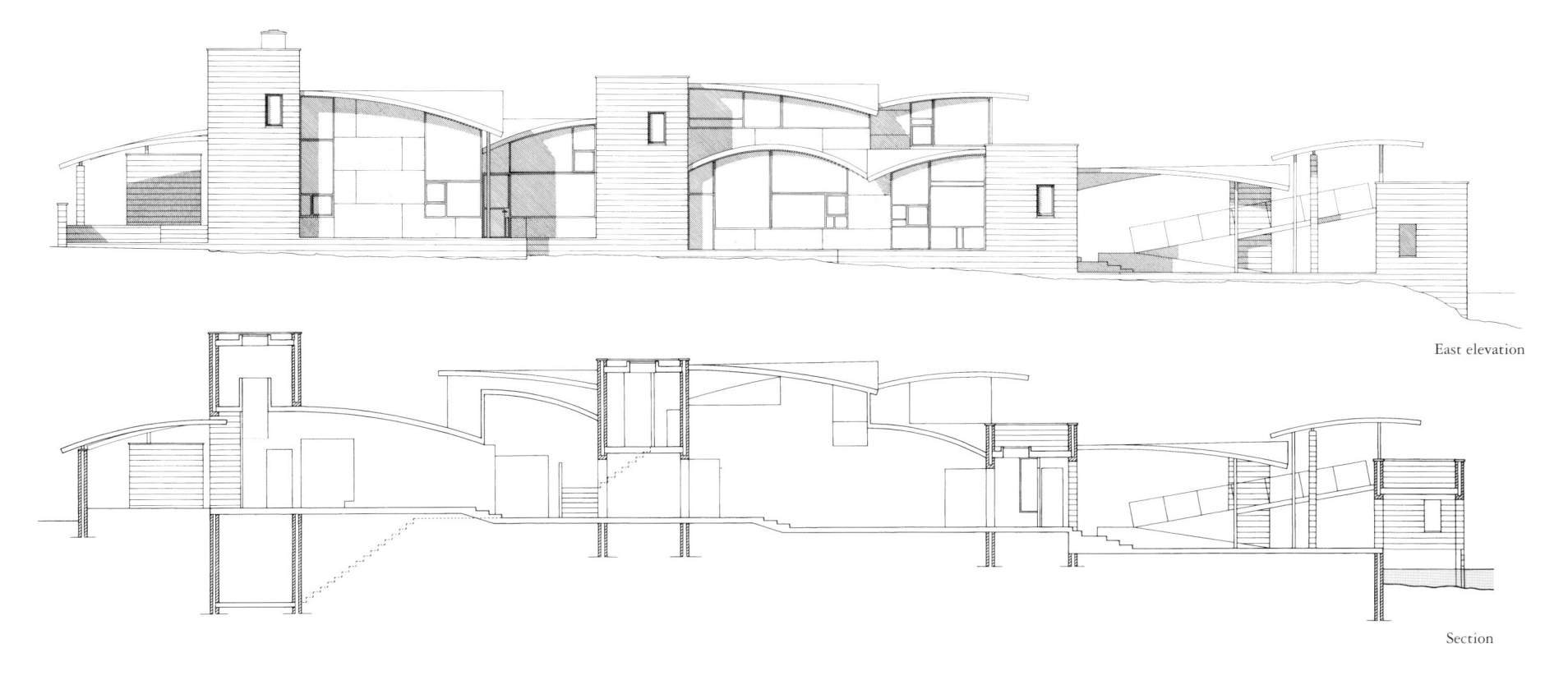

East elevation

Section

View toward living room

Sketch: roof on concrete block

Sited adjacent to three spring-fed ponds with existing concrete dams, the house projects the character of the site in a series of concrete block "spatial dams" with metal-framed "aqueous space" flowing through them. Coursing over the dams, like the overlapping stretto in music, water is an overlapping reflection of the space of the landscape outside as well as the virtual overlapping of the space inside.

A particular music with this "stretto," Bartok's *Music for Strings, Percussion and Celeste*, was a parallel on which the house form was made. In four movements, the piece has a distinct division between heavy (percussion) and light (strings). Where music has a materiality in instrumentation and sound, this architecture attempts an analogue in light and space, that is

$$\frac{material \times sound}{time} = \frac{material \times light}{space}$$

The building is formed in four sections, each consisting of two modes: heavy orthogonal masonry and light, curvilinear metal (the concrete block and metal of Texas vernacular). The plan is purely orthogonal; the section, culvilinear. The guest house is an inversion with the plan culvilinear and section orthogonal, similar to the inversions of the subject in the first movement of the Bartok score. In the main house aqueous space is developed by several means: floor plans pull the level of one space through to the next, roof planes pull space over walls, and an arched wall pulls light down from a skylight. Materials and details continue the spatial concepts in poured concrete, glass cast in fluid shapes, slumped glass, and liquid terrazzo.

Arriving at the space via a driveway bridging over the stream, a visitor passes through overlapping spaces of the house, glimpsing the flanking gardens, arriving at an empty room flooded by the existing pond. The room, doubling its space in reflection, opening both to the site and the house, becomes the asymmetrical center of two sequences of aqueous space.

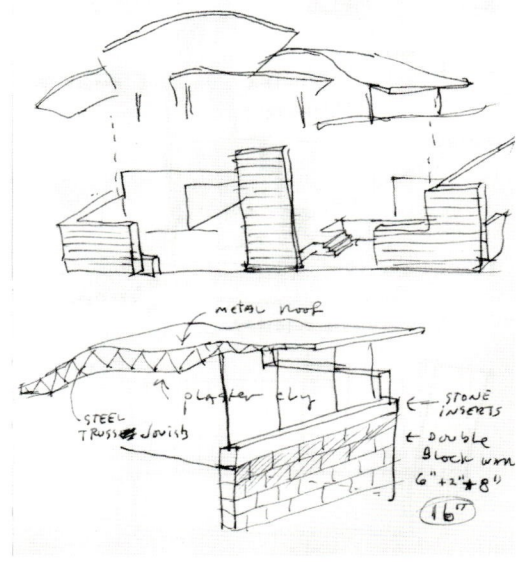

Sketch: metal roof and concrete block

View toward flooded room

ストレット・ハウス

湧水の流れ込む三つの池にはコンクリートの堰がある。その池のほとりの家は、そうした敷地の性格を反映して、コンクリート・ブロックの「空間を貯えるダム」が並び、金属フレームの「水のような空間」が、その上を乗り越えて流れるという構成である。音楽のストレットが重なるように、ダムを乗り越える水は、外の景観の様子と重なり、内部空間では同じようにして文字通り、空間が重なり合う。

バルトークの「弦楽器と打楽器とチェレスタのための音楽」という、この「ストレット」の手法を使った曲を下敷に、この住宅の形態はつくられた。四つの楽章から成るこの曲は、重さ(打楽器)と軽さ(弦楽器)にはっきりと分けられている。音楽の場合の楽器編成と音における物質の位置をこの建築では光と空間におきかえてアナロジーを試みた。つまり次のような関係である。

$$\frac{物質 \times 音}{時間} = \frac{物質 \times 光}{空間}$$

この建築は四つの部分から構成されるが、それらがまた各々二つに分節される。直角で形成される重い組積造と、曲線を描く軽い金属(テキサスでよく見かけるコンクリート・ブロックと金属の組み合わせ)である。平面形は純粋な曲線で構成されるが、断面は直角をなす。逆にゲストハウスでは、平面に曲線をとりいれ断面を直角にするという転倒を行った。これはバルトークの楽譜の第一楽章での主題の転回のようだ。母屋では、水のような空間が種々の方法で展開される。プランは隣より空間のレベルを持ち上げ、屋根の面は空間を壁の上まで引き上げるし、アーチを描く壁はスカイライトから落ちる光を下に呼びこむ。材質とディテールは空間コンセプトを連続させながら、現場打ちコンクリート、液体のような形にしたガラス、前傾したガラス、流し込みのテラゾーと続く。

小川をまたぐ車道を経て建物に着き、この家の重なり合う空間を通りながら横の庭を視界にとらえつつ進むと、池から水を引いたプールのある、吹きさらしの部屋に至る。水面に姿を映して、二倍の大きさを感じさせるこの空間は庭と家の両方をむすび、二つの水の空間の、非対称な中心という位置を占めることになる。

Flooded room

Flooded room

View through library toward entrance hall

View toward entrance hall

1	TERRACE	9	BREAKFAST AREA
2	GARAGE	10	KITCHEN
3	ENTRANCE	11	WALLED GARDEN
4	LIVING ROOM	12	POOL
5	ART STORAGE ROOM	13	FLOODED ROOM
6	LIBRARY	14	BEDROOM
7	STUDY	15	SITTING ROOM
8	DINING ROOM	16	ROOF TERRACE

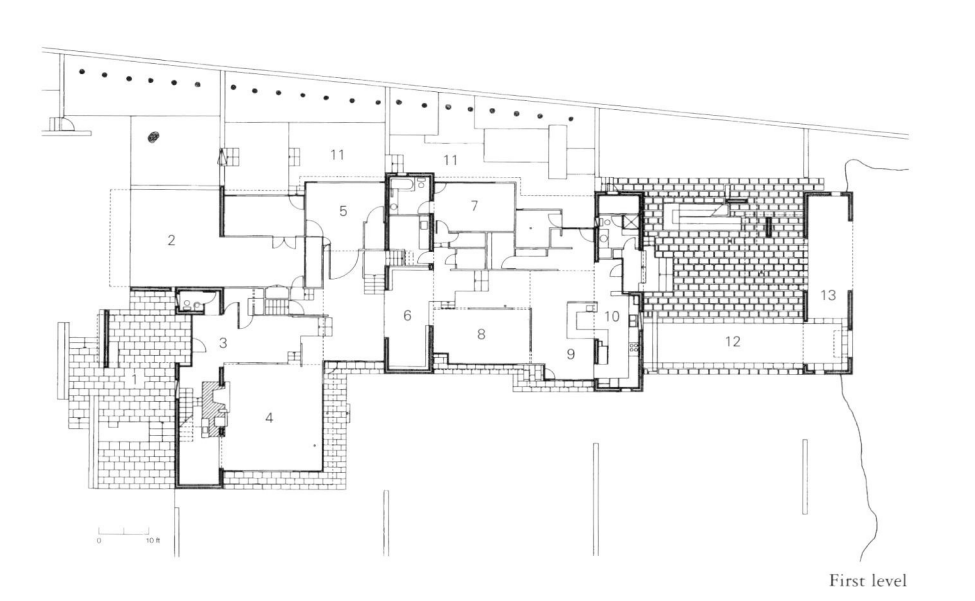

First level

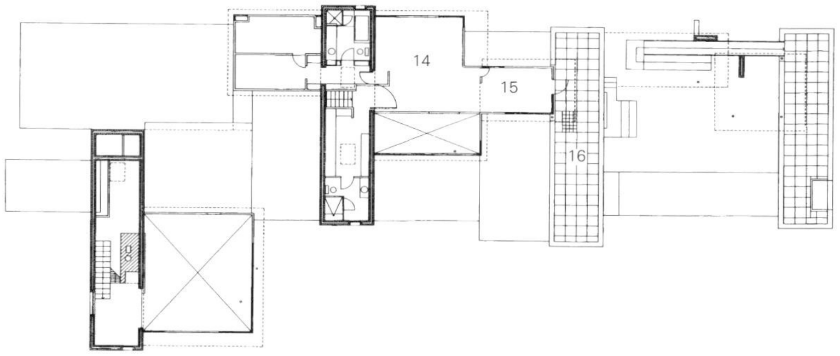

Second level

I-91

Living room

Living room

View toward art storage room

Dining room on right

View from living room

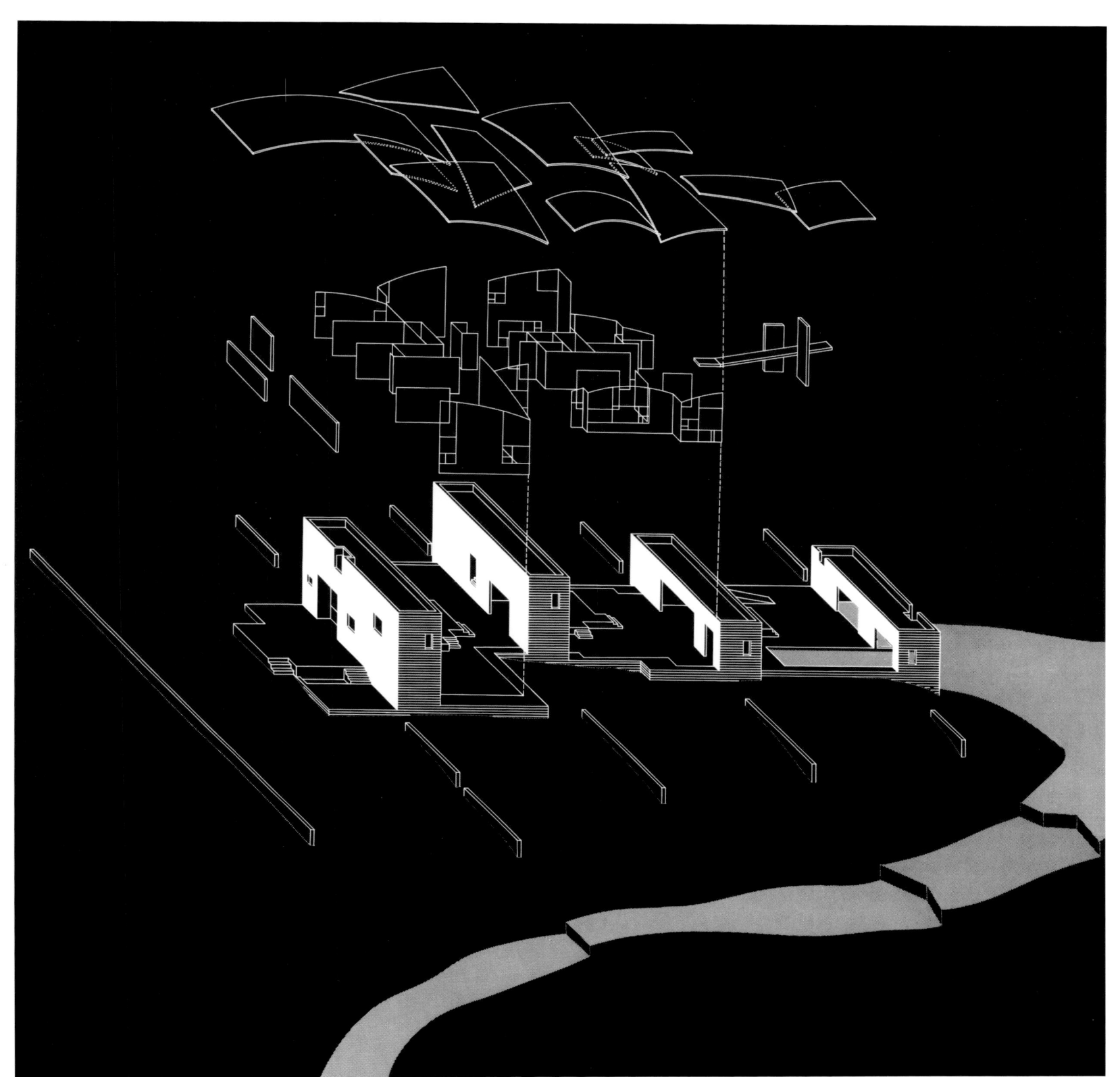

Exploded isometric

I-95

Overall view from southwest

"Y" House
1997-99   Catskill Mountains, New York, U.S.A.

Site plan

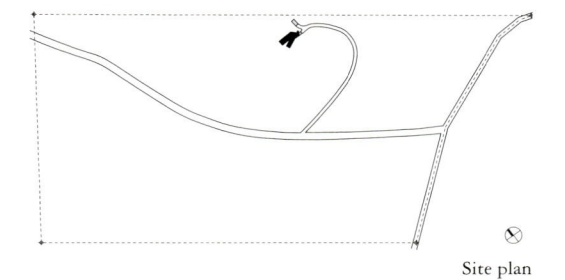

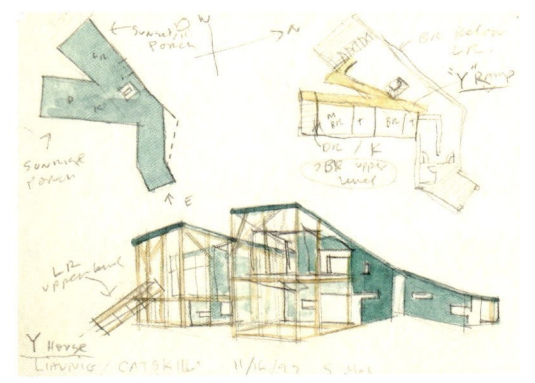

Concept sketch

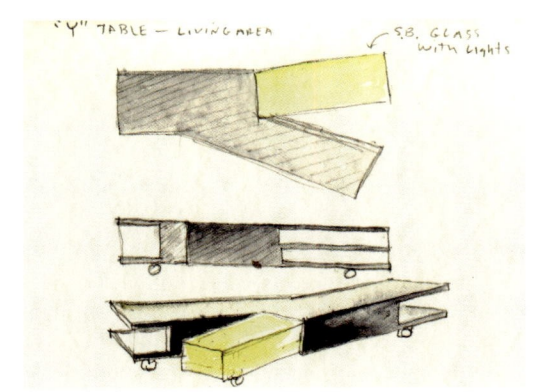

Furniture sketch

Program: A weekend retreat for a European family with three bedrooms, a kitchen and living space. The house is designed to integrate a large collection of modern art.

On a hilltop site of 11 acres in a remote section of the Catskill Mountains, the "Y" House continues the ascent of the hill, its thrusting form splitting to form two arms which end in balconies. The "Y" cuts a slice of sky and draws the sun into the heart of the house. The slow passing of time from early morning to sunset is to be a primary experience as different areas of the house become activated by the path of the sun, the geometry allowing light and shadows to "chase still time" with the diurnal movement of the sun across the walls of the "Y."

The "Y," like a found forked stick, makes a primitive mark on the vast site, its reaching view extending in several directions. As an alternative to an upside-down section with bedrooms (night) below and living (day) above, the geometry of the "Y" contains a sectional flip of public/private or day/night zones. In the North arm, the day zone is above and night zone below while the South arm is reversed with night above and day below. In section these zones are joined by a central "Y" ramp. Maximum wall hanging space to accommodate a large modern art collection is balanced with windows sliced to frame special distant views.

The house occupies the hill and site through three primary relationships: "in the ground," "on the ground," and "over the ground." The portion "over the ground" suspends cantilevered above the portion "in the ground" which opens to a stone court.

The deep balconies facing nearly due south act as passive solar devices allowing the warming winter sun to penetrate the interiors while excluding the hot summer sun. Various slopes of the metal roof channel rainwater to a single water cistern to the north of the house.

Steel framing and steel roof are iron-oxide red, siding is red-stained cedar while interiors are white with black ash floors.

View from south

View from north

View toward entrance

"Y" staircase to living room and master bedroom

Kitchen/dining room

Hall: view toward entrance

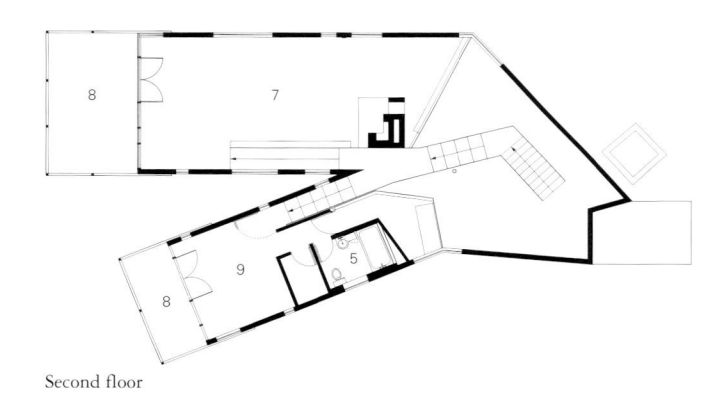

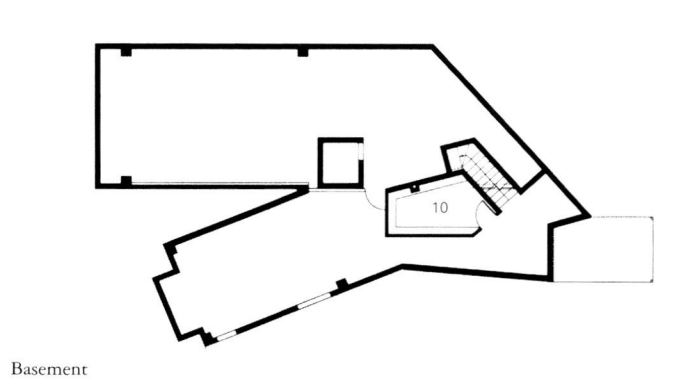

Second floor

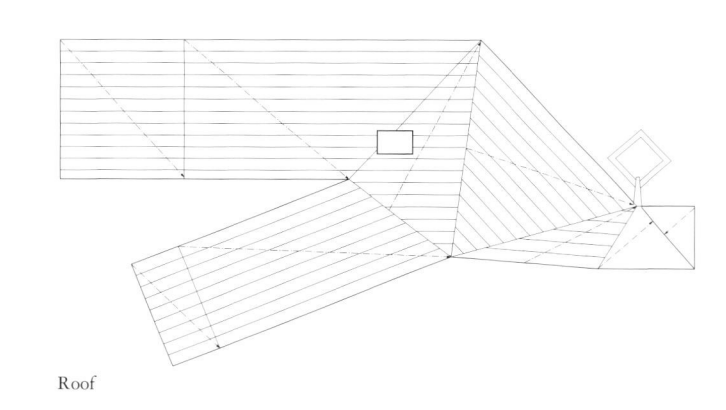

Roof

Basement

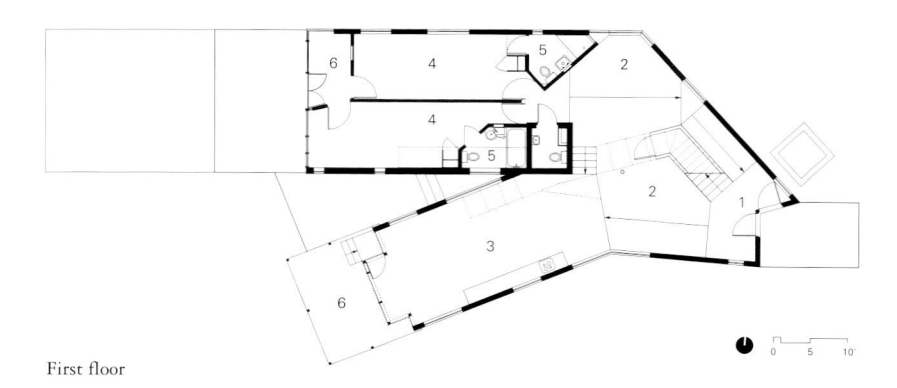

First floor

1 ENTRANCE
2 HALL
3 DINING ROOM
4 BEDROOM
5 BATHROOM
6 VERANDA
7 LIVING ROOM
8 BALCONY
9 MASTER BEDROOM
10 WINE CELLAR

Central "Y" staircase and ramp

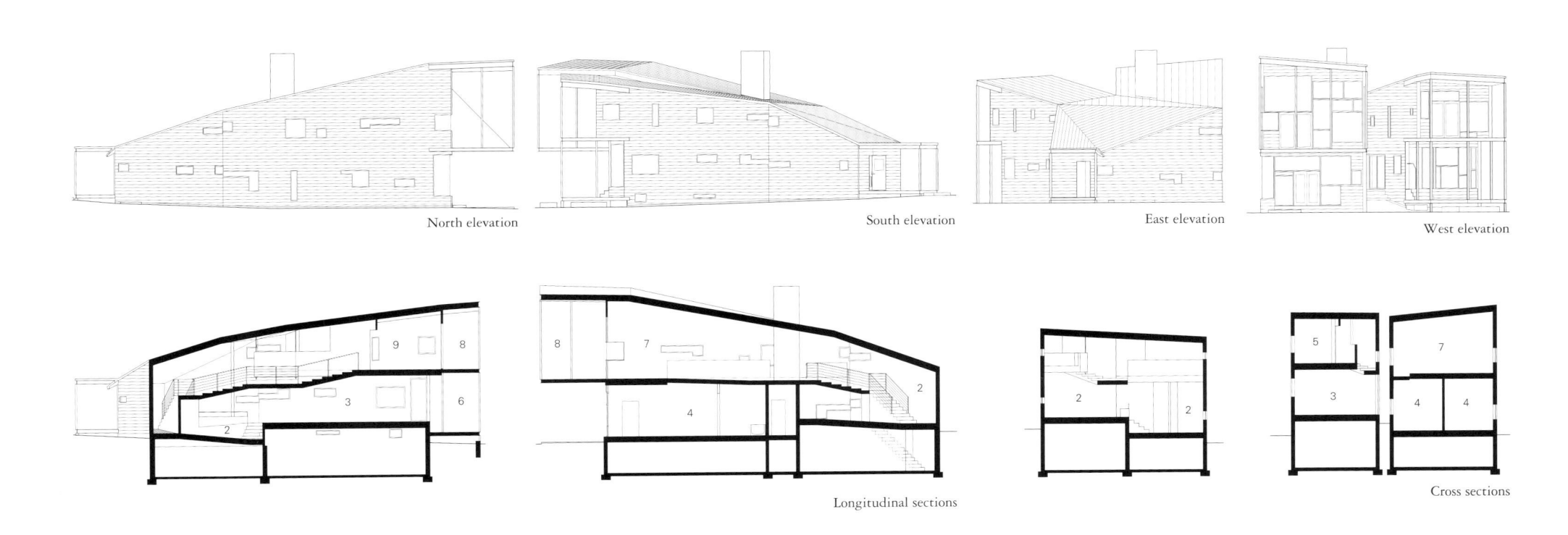

North elevation

South elevation

East elevation

West elevation

Longitudinal sections

Cross sections

I-99

Living room: view toward balcony

Bedroom on first floor

Living room

Master bedroom on second floor

"Y"ハウス
プログラム：3寝室，キッチン，リビング・スペースから成る，ヨーロッパ人一家のための週末住宅。現代美術の大規模なコレクションと融合するデザインが求められる。

キャッツキル山脈の人里離れた丘の頂きに広がる，11エーカーの敷地に建つ"Y"ハウスは，丘の登り勾配に沿って延びている。斜面から突き出した部分は，分岐して2本のアームを構成し，その先端はバルコニーである。"Y"形は空の一片を切り取り，家の中心に日差しを引き入れる。住宅内の様々なエリアが太陽軌道の動きによって生き生きと目覚めるにつれて，早朝から夕暮れへとゆっくりと進む時間がこの住宅での主要な体験となる。その幾何学形態によって，"Y"の壁面を横断していく陽光の一日の動きと共に，光と影は「静止した時間を追いかける」。

二股に分かれた木の枝を拾ってきたような"Y"は，広大な敷地にプリミティブな標識をつくり，いくつもの方向に広がる眺めへと手を差し伸べる。寝室（夜）が下に，リビング（昼）が上にという上下逆転した構成に代わって，"Y"の幾何学形態にはパブリック／プライベート，つまり昼／夜の領域が2本のアームの間で逆転している。北側のアームには昼のゾーンが上に，夜のゾーンが下にあり，南側のアームでは反対に夜のゾーンが上に，昼のゾーンが下にある。断面上ではこれらのゾーンは"Y"ランプによって連結されている。現代美術の大きな作品を飾るため壁を最大限広くとったスペースは，遠くの美しい風景を枠取るように細く切り取られた窓によって均衡がとられる。

家は，この丘と敷地を，「地の中」，「地上」，「地の上方」，という主要な三つの関係性によって占拠する。「地の上方」の部分は，石の中庭に面した「地の中」の部分の上に片持ちで張り出している。ほぼ真南を向いた深いバルコニーは，暖かい冬の日差しを室内に浸透させ，夏の暑い日差しを跳ね返して，パッシブ・ソーラーとして働く。様々な勾配をもつメタルルーフが雨水を家の北側にある水槽に流す。

鉄骨枠組と鋼板の屋根は酸化鉄の赤，外壁はシーダーに赤いステインを塗り，内壁は白で，床はクロトネリコ材である。

Balcony of living room: looking south

3 Housing and Hybrid Buildings
ハウジングとハイブリッド・ビルディング

The concentration of many social activities within an architectural form distends and warps a pure building type. Previously neglected forms of association are wrenched together in the modern city generating buildings which might stand as an "anti-typology." Building functions are mixed, and disparate uses are combined, forming "Hybrid Buildings."

There are examples of combined-function buildings throughout history, for example, the house over the shop is prevalent in many ages and cultures. However, hybrid buildings have appeared predominantly within the 19th century. The modern city has acted as a fertilizer for the growth of architecture, from the homogeneous to the heterogeneous in regard to use. Urban densities and evolving building techniques have effected the mixing of functions, piling one atop another, defying those who contend that a building should "look like what it is."

The 1977 project for a Gymnasium Bridge in the Bronx (1977-78), New York, fused diverse programs and typological characteristics forming a hybrid building. In 1985 we began construction of the Hybrid Building in Seaside, Florida (1984-88), which formed the edge of a new town square in a condensation of five diverse shops, offices and eight residences based on a mythopoetic division between boisterous types and melancholic types. Exploration of the formation of urban space and the edges of the public space of the street, with a hybrid building of several functions, is continued with the Void Space/Hinged Space Housing of Fukuoka (1989-91), Japan, completed in 1991.

A hybrid combination of functions in buildings can be more than a mute mixture of uses. These juxtapositions may be "social condensers" creating primary interactions of vitality within the city, increasing the role of architecture as a catalyst for change.

Steven Holl

Makuhari Bay New Town

数多くの社会活動をまとめて、一つの建築形態の中におさめると、建築のタイプは純粋なものではなく、膨張したりねじれたりしたものになってくる。それまでは省みられることのなかった集合形態が現代都市の中にねじり合わされ、「反類型的」な建築が生まれてくる。建築の機能が混在し、共通するもののない用途が組み合わされると「ハイブリッド・ビルディング」が形成される。

さまざまな機能を組み合わせた建築の例は、歴史を通じていつの時代にも存在してきた。たとえば、商店の上に住宅を重ねる形式は、多くの時代、多くの文化を通じてよく見られる。複合ビルは、19世紀になって目につくようになってきたタイプである。単一の機能から複合機能へと建築が成長するにあたっては、現代都市が肥料の役割を果たしたのである。都市の密度が上昇し建築技術が進化したことが影響を及ぼして、機能が混ざり合い、次々と重ねられてゆくようになり、その結果、建築は「それらしく見える」ものでなければならないと考える人達を無視するようになった。

1977年のニューヨーク、ブロンクスのジムナジウム・ブリッジのプロジェクト(1977-78)では種々のプログラムと類型を融合させて複合ビルをつくった。1985年には、フロリダ州シーサイドのハイブリッド・ビルディング(1984-88)の建設に取りかかった。新しくつくられた広場の一辺を形成して五つの業種からなる独立した店舗とオフィス、8戸の住宅を集合させた。住宅は想定した住人に神話詩的な分類をほどこし、躁タイプとメランコリータイプに分けて考えた。都市空間の組み立て方と街路に面するパブリック・スペースの境界のありかたを探り、複数の機能をもつ複合ビルを配するという方法は、1991年に完成した福岡のハウジング、ヴォイド・スペース／ヒンジド・スペース・ハウジング(1989-91)に引きつがれる。

建築に異質の機能を盛り込むことは、ただ用途を混合させるというだけのものではない。これはいわば「ソーシャル・コンデンサー」の働きをして、都市に生き生きとした活力を引きおこし、建築が変化のための触媒としての役割を増すことになるだろう。

(スティーヴン・ホール)

Perspective

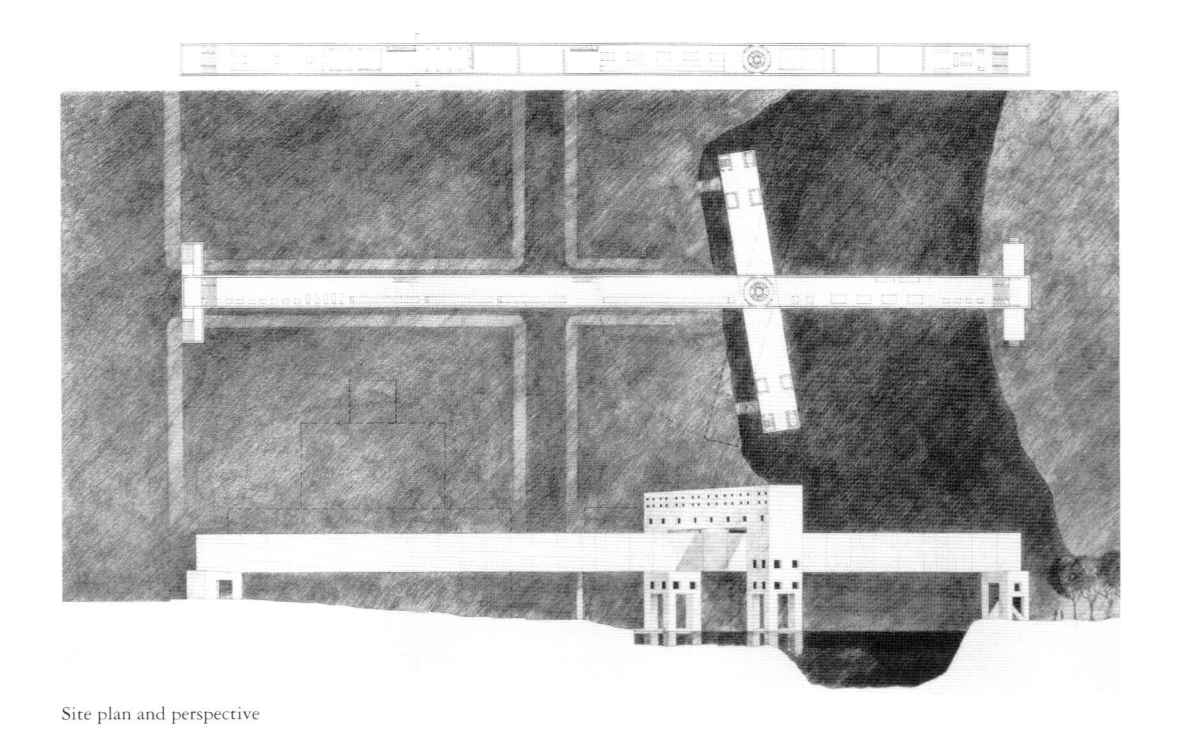

Site plan and perspective

Gymnasium Bridge

1977-78   South Bronx, New York, U.S.A.

Night view

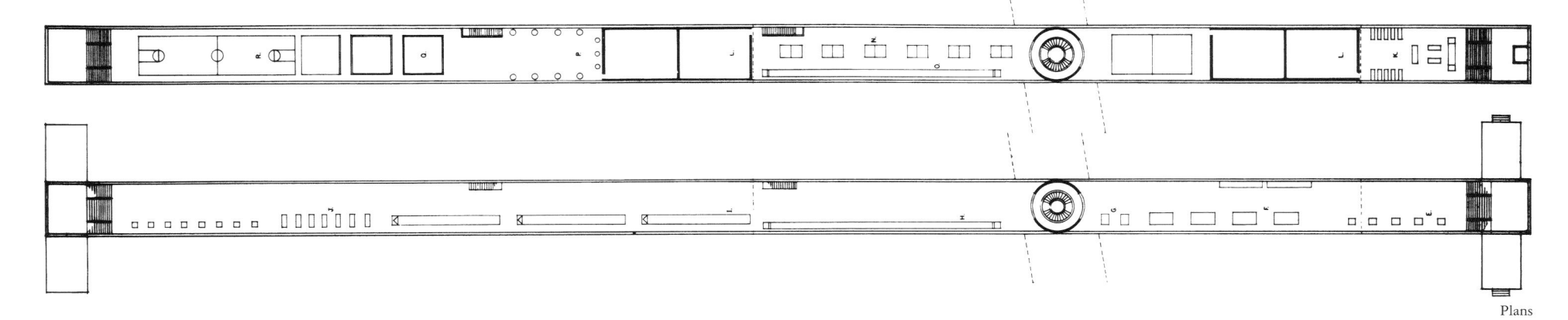

Plans

I-105

Penn Central's South Bronx railroad yards have fallen into disuse. The site is boxed in by bridges and elevated highways with a ceiling formed by the flight patterns of planes landing and taking off from La Guardia Airport.

The program called for "ideas or strategies that would yield incremental benefits for the immediate neighborhood." The only explicit requirement is a pedestrian bridge from the South Bronx to the park on Randall's Island. The bridge "must not assume a form that would jeopardize the future development of the site for commercial or industrial purposes, including deep water ship movement in the canal." The immediate neighborhood of the South Bronx with a population of approximately 400,000 has unemployment of 45 to 50 percent.

The Gymnasium-Bridge is a hybrid building synthesized as a special strategy for generating positive economic and physical effects. The Gymnasium-Bridge condenses the activities of meeting, physical recreation, and work into one structure that simultaneously forms a bridge from the community to the park on Randall's Island.

Along the bridge, community members participate in competitive sports and physical activities organized according to a normal work day with wages provided by a branch of the Urban Jobs Corp or a reconstituted WPA. While earning enough money to become economically stable, community members gain physical and moral strength and develop a sense of community spirit. The bridge becomes a vehicle from which destitute persons can reenter society, become accustomed to a normal work day, and help gain the strength to develop their full individual potential.

The form of the architecture is a series of bridges over bridges. The small entrance bridges at each end of the main span preserve the view down Brook Street to the canal, and from Randall's Island up Brook Street. The main span is aligned with this axis and is crossed by a fourth and highest bridge. In water rather than over water, this bridge acts as a structural pivot from which the turn-bridge portion of the main span rotates to allow future ship passage in the waterway. At its base are floats for competition rowboats, which are an extension of the activities and payroll of the Gymnasium.

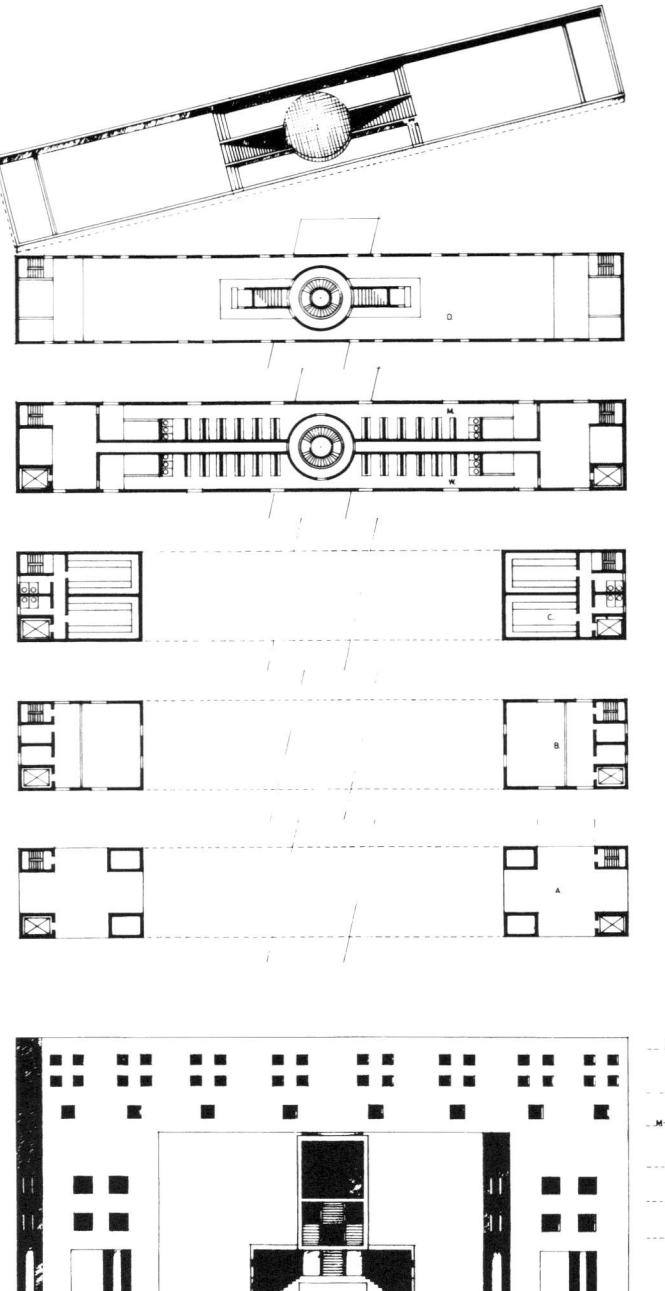

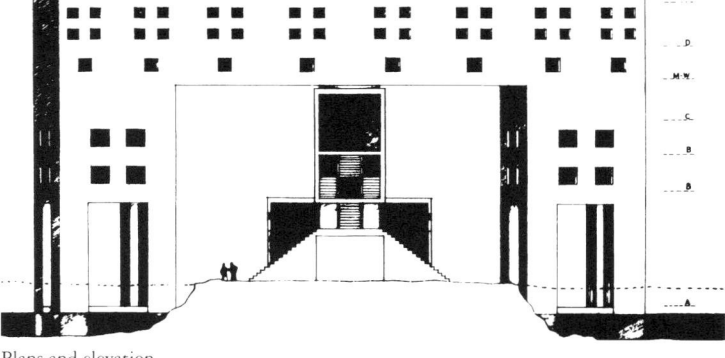

The structure is a two-story steel truss covered in translucent white insulated panels. The panels at eye-level may be opened outward forming awnings over their sills. At night the interior lighting produces a glowing effect, lighting the axis and pathway below the bridge.

Plans and elevation

Perspective

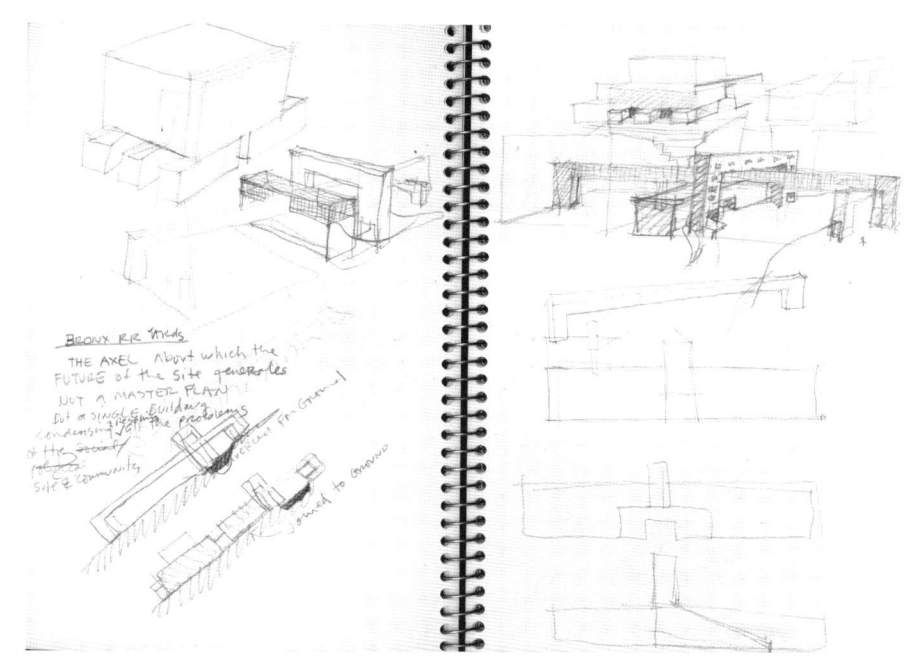

Concept sketch

ジムナジウム・ブリッジ

ペン・セントラルの,サウス・ブロンクス鉄道の用地はすっかりさびれてしまい,使用されることもなくなった。この敷地は橋と高速道路に四方を囲まれ,ラガーディア空港に離着陸する飛行機の航路が,さながらそこに架けられた天井のようである。

これは「隣接地域の利益を増進する戦略」と呼ばれる計画である。ただひとつの明快な要望は,サウス・ブロンクスからランドールズ島の公園に向かう歩行者用の橋をつくることであった。この橋は「この地域の将来の商工業の発展や,河を航行する船の活動を阻害するようなものであってはならない」という。サウス・ブロンクスの隣接地域は,およそ40万の人口をかかえ,失業者がその45%から50%を占めていた。

ジムナジウム・ブリッジは,経済的にも心身の上でも積極的な効果の期待される,それらを融合させた複合的な建物なのだ。集会,スポーツやトレーニングなどの活動を凝縮して,それを建築物という形にしたもので,同時に,この地域からランドールズ島の公園へ渡る橋でもある。

この橋を渡って,地域の住民たちは競技スポーツや体育活動に参加する。これらはウィークデーに行われ,都市職業協会の出張所や再建されたWPA(事業企画庁)によって賃金が支払われる。経済的安定を得るだけの金を手に入れるかたわら,地域住民は肉体的にもモラルの上でも強化されて,コミュニティ意識を育てられてゆくことになる。この橋は人を乗せる乗物のようなものかもしれない。これを降りる時には,貧しい人々が社会に戻って,日々労働し,ひとりの能力を充分に発揮できるような力を得る手助けをするのだ。

建築の形態は,橋の上に橋を載せるという形の連続である。主要部の両端にある,エントランスとなる小さなブリッジからは,ブルック通りの側から運河を望み,ランドールズ島側からはブルック通りを見通すことができる。主要部はこれを結ぶ軸に沿って渡り,それと交差する形で四つ目の,一番高いブリッジがある。水の上というより,水の中に建つこのブリッジを中心にして,主要部分の一部が回転し,将来,運河で船が航行すれば回転橋になる。橋の足許には競技用のボートの浮桟橋がある。このボートはジムナジウムの活動と報酬支払事業の一部として運営される。

構造は,2層のトラスを透光性の白いパネルで包んだものだ。その一部,目線の高さにあるパネルは,突出し窓として開けることができる。夜になると,内部の明りがにじみだし,ブリッジそのものが発光体となってその下の通路も照らし出される。

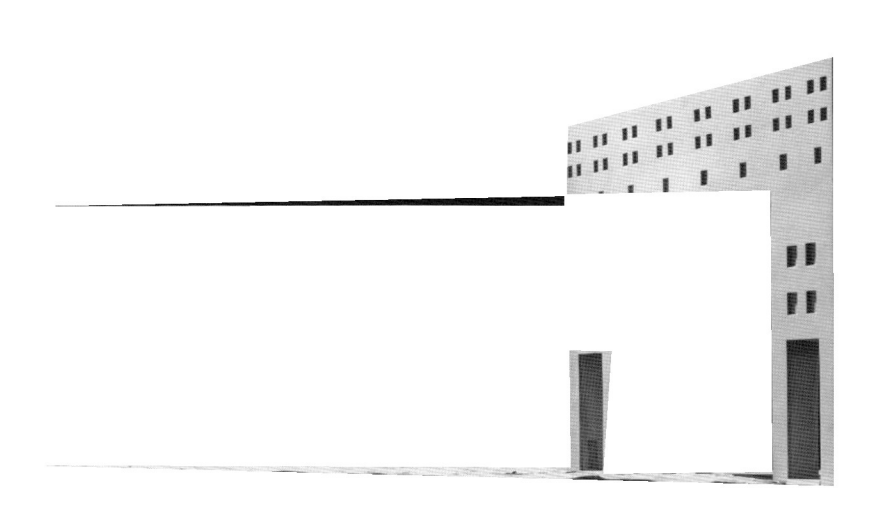

Model

1979-82 Bridge of Houses
New York, New York, U.S.A.

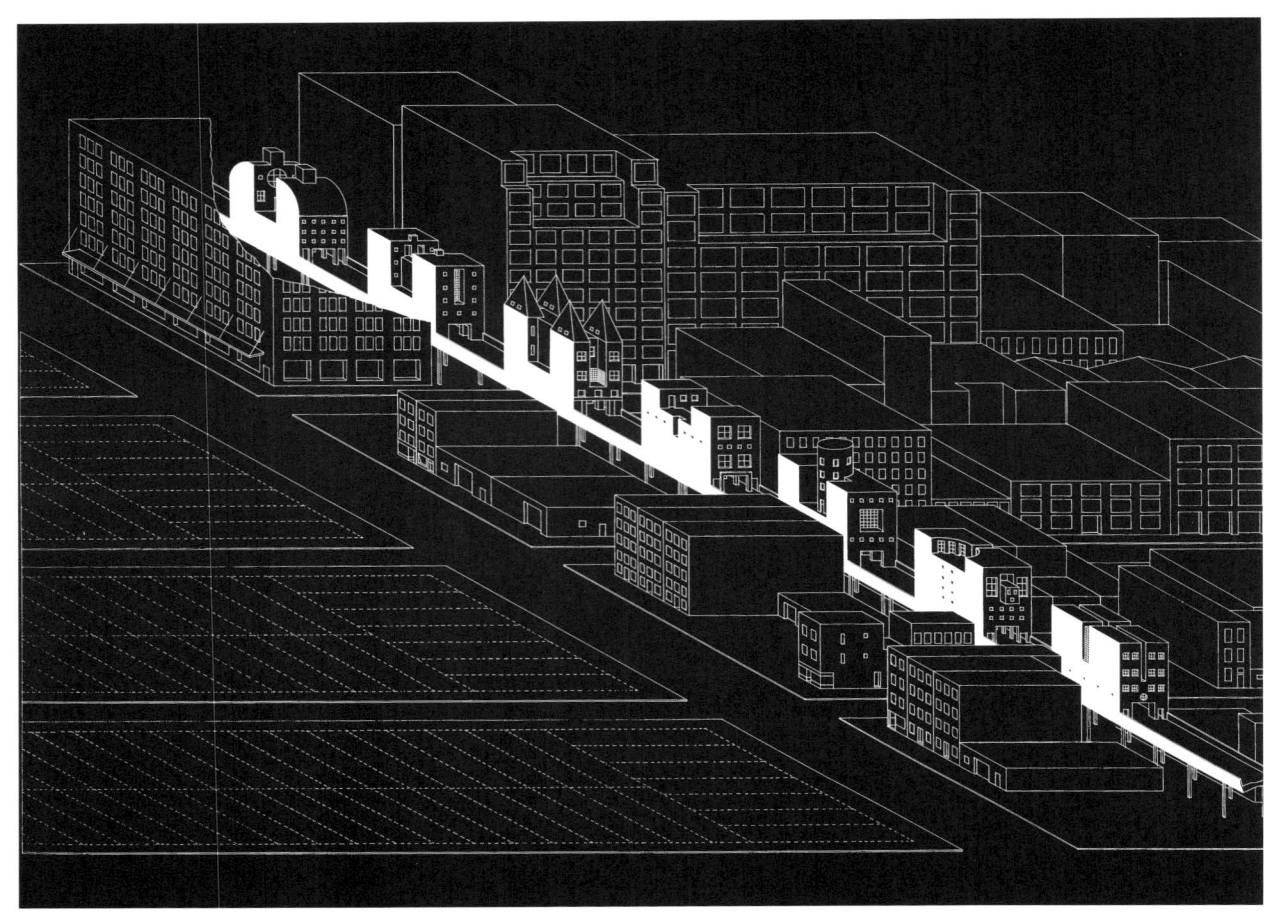

Isometric: site

Perspective: street

The site and structural foundation of the Bridge of Houses is the existing superstructure of an abandoned elevated rail link in the Chelsea area of New York City. This steel structure is utilized in its straight leg from West 19th Street to West 29th Street parallel to the Hudson River.

West Chelsea is changing from a warehouse district to a residential area. With the decline of shipping activity on the pierfront, many vacant warehouses are being converted to residential lofts. The Bridge of Houses reflects the new character of the area as a place of habitation. Re-use rather than demolition of the existing bridge would be a permanent contribution to the character of the city.

This project offers a variety of housing types for the Chelsea area, as well as an elevated public promenade connecting with the new Convention Center on its north end. The structural capacity and width of the existing bridge determine the height and width of the houses. Four houses have been developed in detail, emphasizing the intention to provide a collection of housing blocks offering the widest possible range of social-economic coexistence. At one extreme are houses of single-room-occupancy type, offered for the city's homeless; each of these blocks contains twenty studio rooms. At the other extreme are houses of luxury apartments; each of these blocks contains three or four flats. Shops line the public promenade level below the houses.

The new houses are built in an alternating pattern with a series of 2,000-square-foot courtyards (50% open space). All new houses align with the existing block front at the street walls, reinforcing the street pattern. The ornamental portions of the rail bridge that pass over the streets remain open.

Construction consists of a lightweight metal frame with a reinforced exterior rendering on wire lath and a painted finish. Windows have a baked enamel finish, while doors are made of solid core wood with sandblasted glass drawings on the entrances and brass lever handles.

Site plan

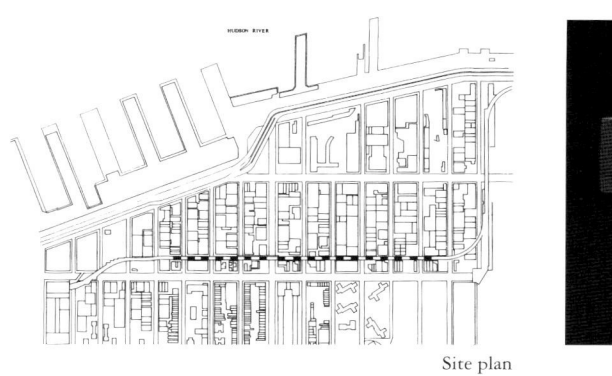

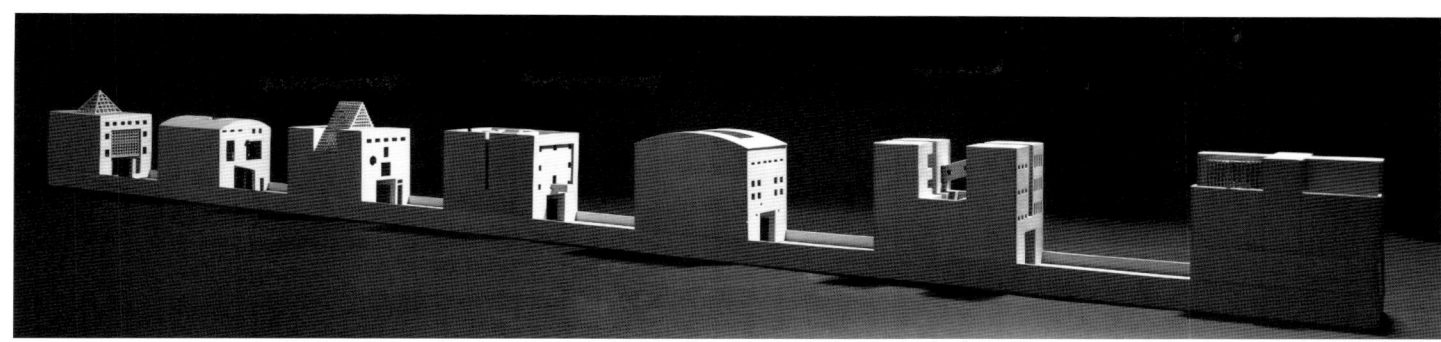

Cutaway isometrics/sections/elevations/plans

ブリッジ・ハウス

ブリッジ・ハウスの場合,敷地というか,基礎というか,それは,ニューヨーク市のチェルシー地区にある高架鉄道の,今では使われなくなった既存の構造物なのだ。スティール製の構造物は,西19丁目から西29丁目まで,ハドソン河に平行な直線をなしている。

ウエスト・チェルシー地区は,倉庫街から居住地域へと変貌しつつある。埠頭がかつてのにぎわいを失うにつれて,使われなくなった倉庫の多くが住宅用のロフトに変わっているのだ。ブリッジ・ハウスは,この一帯の住居地域化という新たな性格の変化に応じたものである。もともとある高架線を取り壊すよりは,再利用を図るほうが,この都市の本来の性格を守るのに役立つはずである。

この計画は,高架線上にチェルシー地区のために種々のタイプの住宅をつくり,その建物の足元には空中プロムナードを通し,北端にはコンベンション・センターをつくるというものである。既存ブリッジの構造上の余力と寸法によって住宅の高さと幅は決定される。四つの住宅棟が詳細にわたりつくられた。居住対象となる住民を,社会的にも経済的にも幅の広いものにしたいと私たちは考えた。一方の極には,ワンルームで,ホームレスのためのタイプがある。これには1棟に20戸のワンルーム・タイプが収まる。もう一方の極には,豪華なアパートメントがある。こちらは1棟が3戸から4戸のフラットで構成される。住居の下のプロムナードのレベルには店舗が軒を連ねる。

新しい住宅は,2,000平方フィートの中庭(50%のオープンスペース)と交互に建てられる。これらは全て,街のグリッドに合わせて,通り沿いの壁と整列させ,街路のパターンを強めることになる。街路をまたぐ高架橋の装飾もそのまま残される。

構造は軽量鉄骨にワイヤラス下地で外部仕上げのうえ塗装する。窓はエナメル焼付塗装,無垢の木製の玄関ドアは,ガラスにサンドブラスト仕上げでドローイングを描き真鍮のレバーハンドルを取り付ける。

Perspective: promenade

1980-84 Autonomous Artisans' Housing
Staten Island, New York, U.S.A.

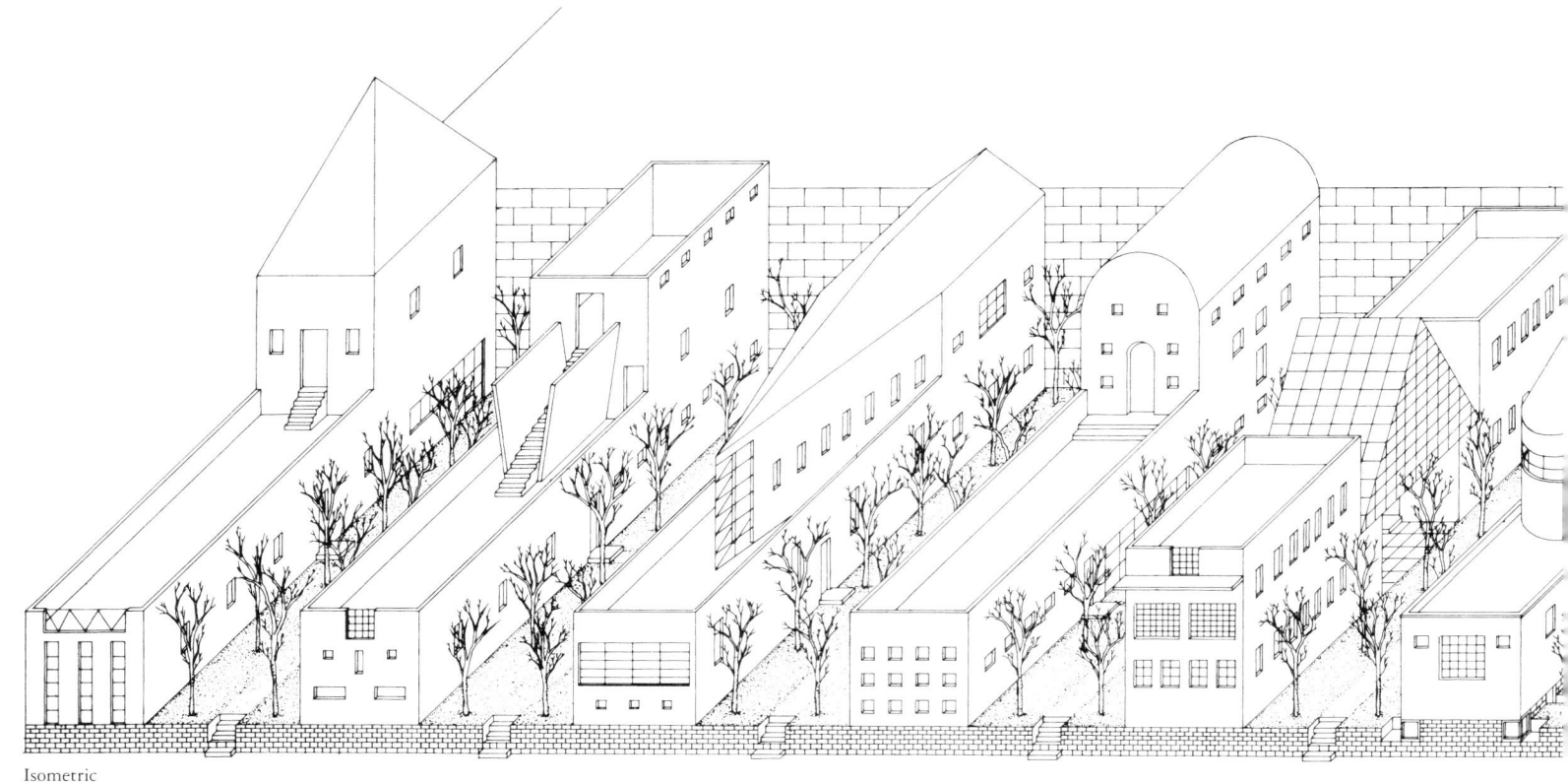

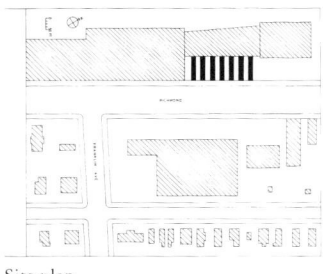

Site plan

Isometric

1 ENTRANCE
2 PRIVATE GARDEN
3 ROOF TERRACE

Second floor

First floor

An existing warehouse is converted to work space held in common by artisans working in several disciplines. Against the warehouse wall, houses are built in a pattern allowing for private gardens between each house. The plan/section is based on the "shotgun" type.

The individual autonomous artisan's craft is expressed in the second level of each house: the paper maker's house has a roof terrace shaped specifically for drying paper; the wood worker's house displays the skills of a boat builder; the mason has a brick barrel vault roof. A roof of etched glass covers the glass etcher's entry way. Similarly, expressions of craft exist in the plasterer's and metal worker's houses.

Outdoor areas include private gardens between each of the houses, as well as roof terraces. The urban street edge is maintained with the alignment of the front walls. Construction of the foundation level of each house is insulation-filled concrete block and wood floor joists. Roofs and second level elements are in different materials according to each artisan/occupant.

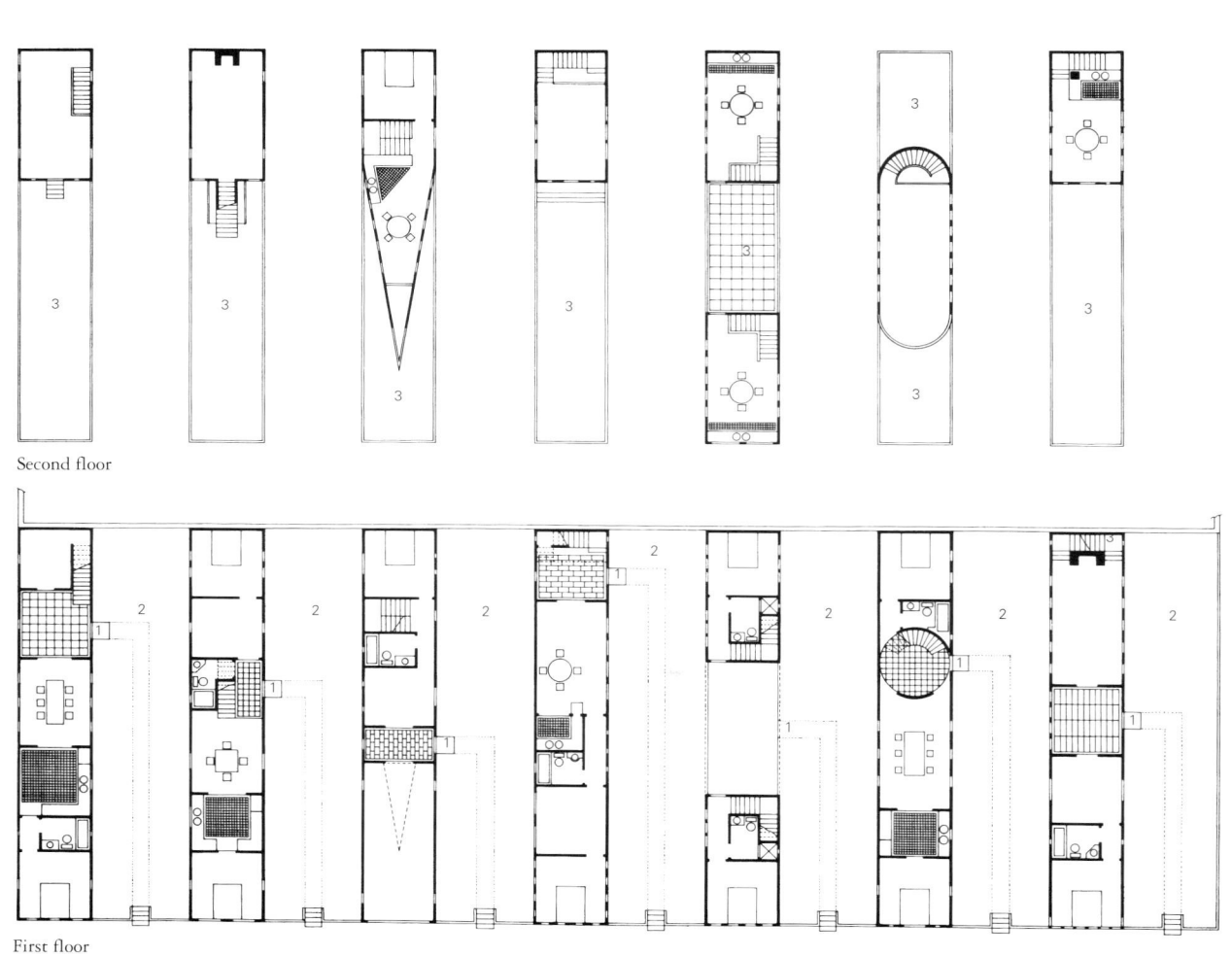

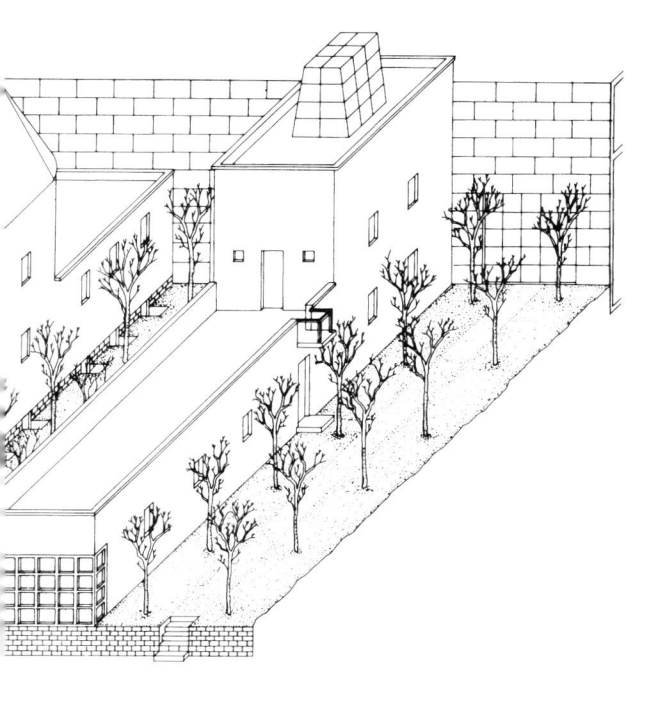

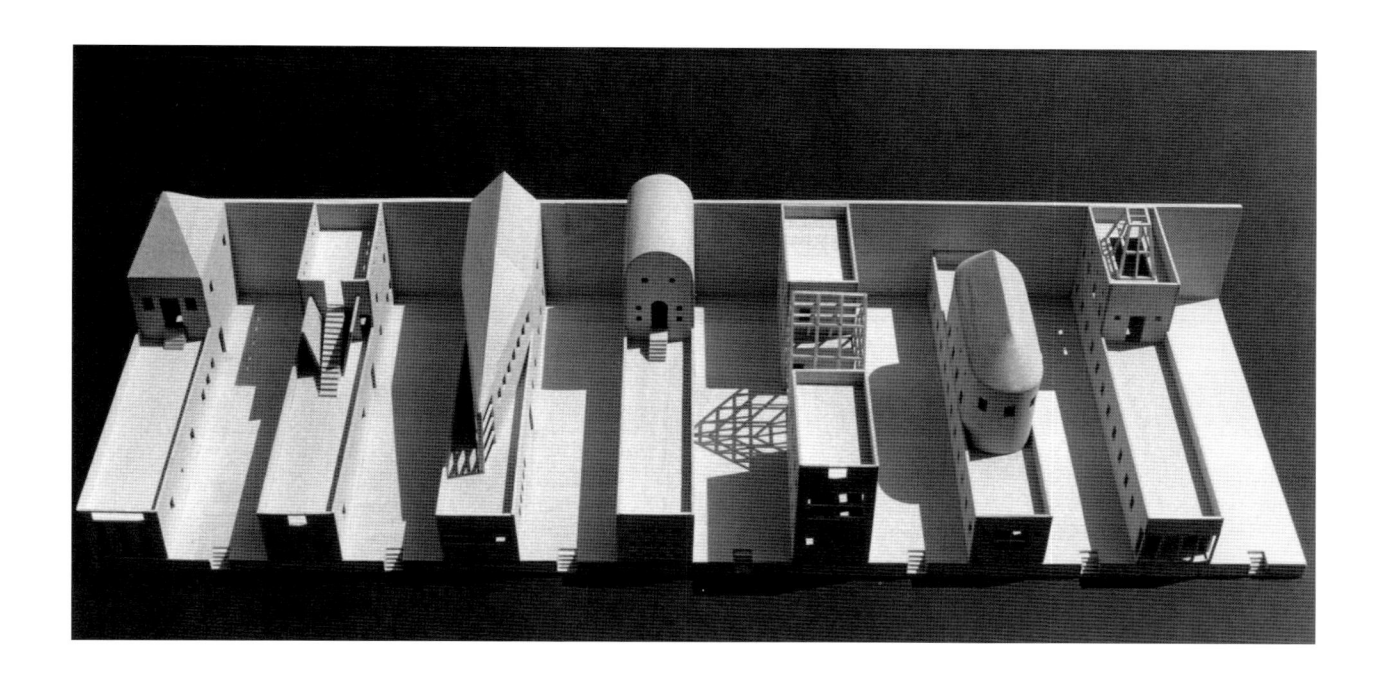

Perspective

Sketch

様々な職人のハウジング
既存の倉庫を,それぞれ分野を異にする職人が共有する仕事場に改造し,その倉庫の壁を背にして住宅が建てられる。住棟の配置は,各戸の間に専用の庭をはさみこんでゆくというものだ。平面と断面はショットガン・タイプを基にしてつくられた。

様々な職人のひとりひとりの仕事が,各々の家の2階に表現される。たとえば紙漉き職人の家には,紙の乾燥台の形をしたルーフテラスがあるし,木工職人の住まいでは船大工の腕前を見せる。石工の家の屋根にはレンガ造のヴォールトがかけられるかと思えば,エッチングを施したガラス屋根が,エッチング職人の家の入口を覆う。そんな具合に,左官や金工職人の住まいにも彼らの腕を示すものがつくられる。

屋外スペースは,各戸の間を分ける専用庭の他にルーフ・テラスがある。道路側の面は壁の位置を揃えて並ぶ。1階レベルの構造は断熱材入りのコンクリート・ブロックに木造の梁だが,屋根と2階の各部は,職種に応じてそれぞれに異なった材料が使われる。

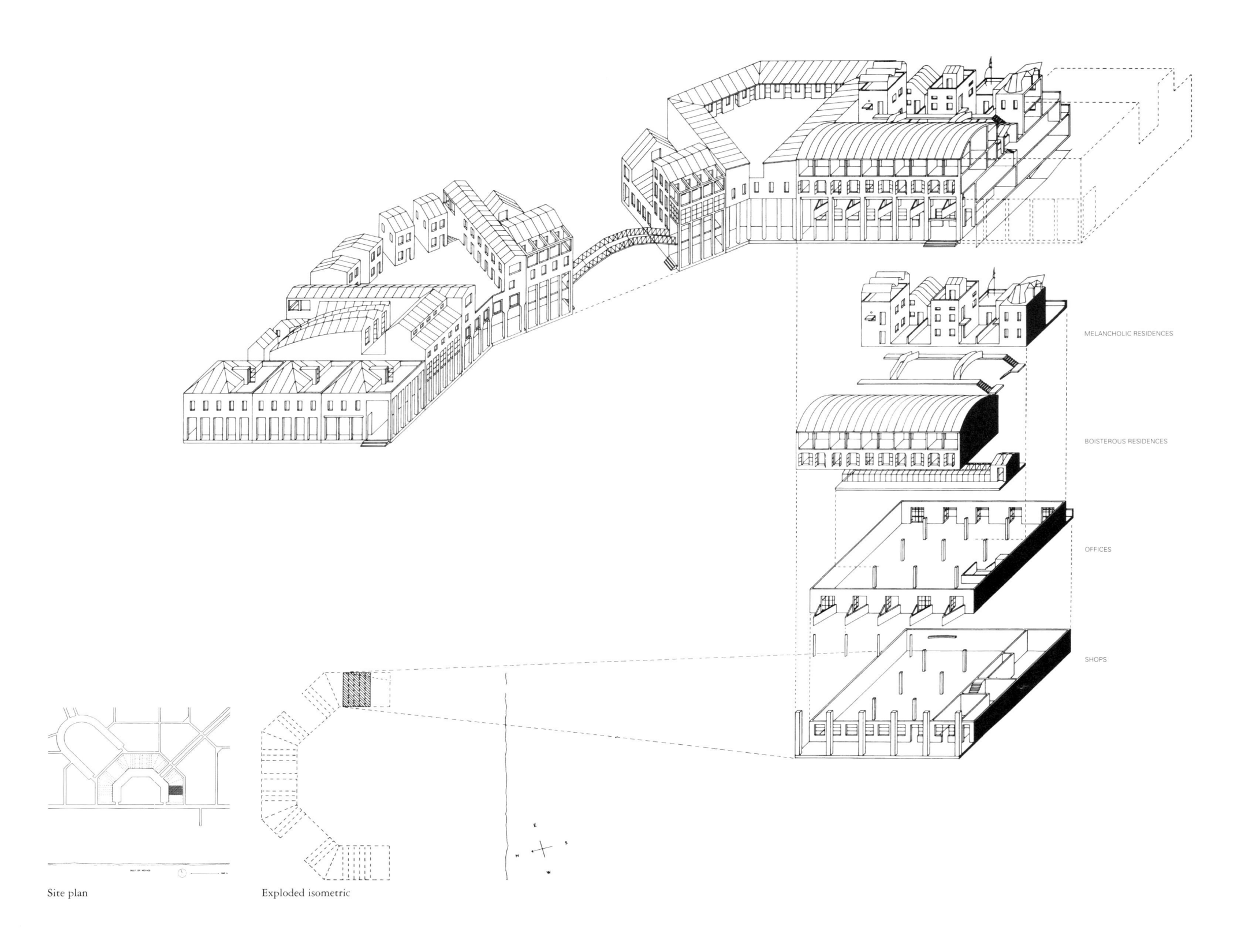

MELANCHOLIC RESIDENCES

BOISTEROUS RESIDENCES

OFFICES

SHOPS

Site plan

Exploded isometric

Hybrid Building

1984-88   Seaside, Florida, U.S.A.

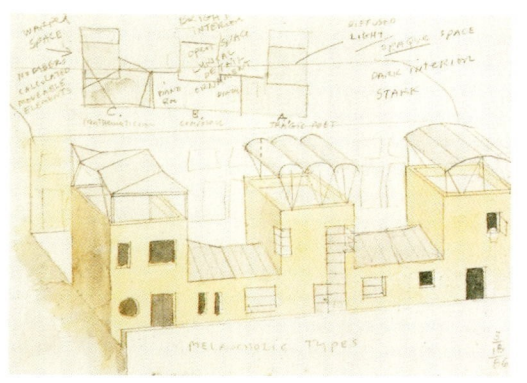

Study

Concept sketch

View from southeast

Courtyard on residential level

Perspective: courtyard

Seaside is a new town on the Gulf of Mexico. The planners have established height restrictions, design guidelines, and easements. By their code, this project and adjoining buildings are required to form a continuous public arcade around the square.

The Hybrid Building combines retail, office, and residential uses. The concentration of disjointed programs forms an incidental urbanism. Along with intensification of an urban condition, the building expresses the idea of a "society of strangers." The building forms split at the upper levels into east and west types. Rooms facing the setting sun and central square are for boisterous types, late risers who enjoy watching the action, toasting the sunset, etc. All of their two-level flats are identical. They contain luxury bathrooms, microwave ovens, and space for parties.

Facing east to the rising sun are rooms for melancholic types. These individuals are early risers, inclined to silence and solitude. Melancholic types are imagined as: a tragic poet, a musician, and a mathematician. The plans and sections of the three rear flats are characterized accordingly. The house of the tragic poet has dim light; every window is of the same narrow and tall dimension. The awning at the roof is like a rag on a peasant's table. In the house of the musician, light is cast down from the corner windows on the upper level. A black plaster wall slips from the lower to the upper floor, enhancing the flowing nature of the space. In the house of the mathematician everything is slightly warped. The stair to the second level warps over the bathroom. The warp over the ceiling joists forms a slight doubly-curved surface. At the second level is a calculating table with a skull shelf, in homage to Johannes Kepler.

Construction is of precast concrete columns and beams, and hollow-core planks. Walls are integral-color stucco on concrete block; roofs are galvanized metal.

View from northwest

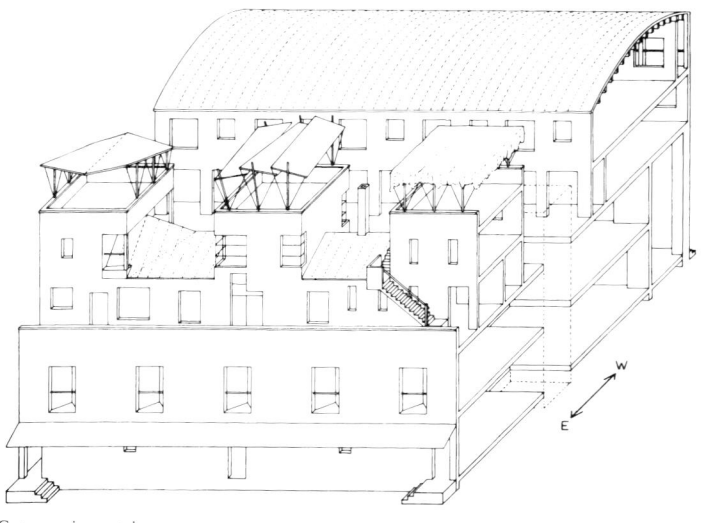

Cutaway isometric

Boisterous residence: view of courtyard on third floor

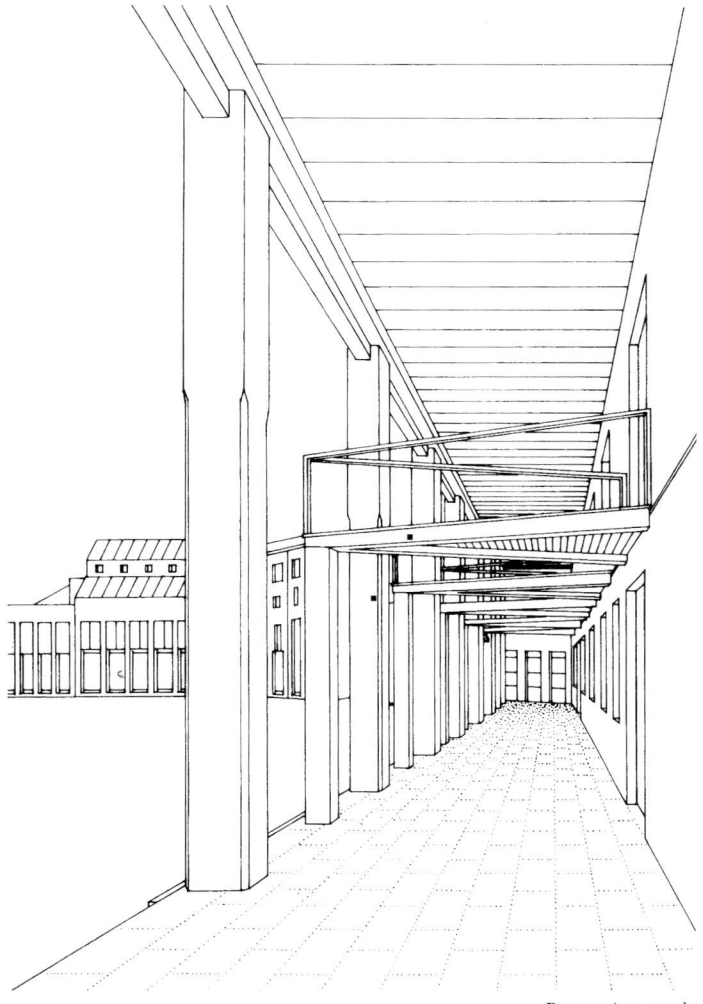

Perspective: arcade

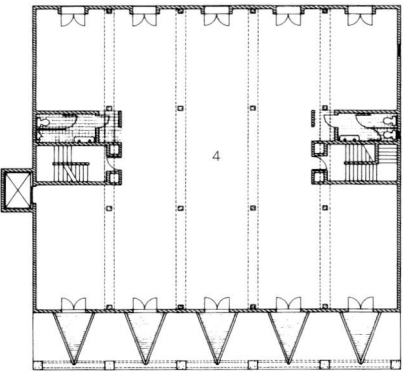

1 ARCADE
2 LOBBY
3 SHOP
4 OFFICES
5 COURTYARD

A HOUSE OF MATHEMATICIAN
B HOUSE OF MUSICIAN
C HOUSE OF TRAGIC POET
D BOISTEROUS UNIT

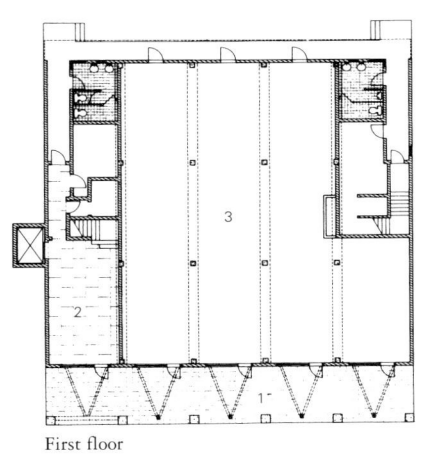

Second floor

Fourth floor

First floor

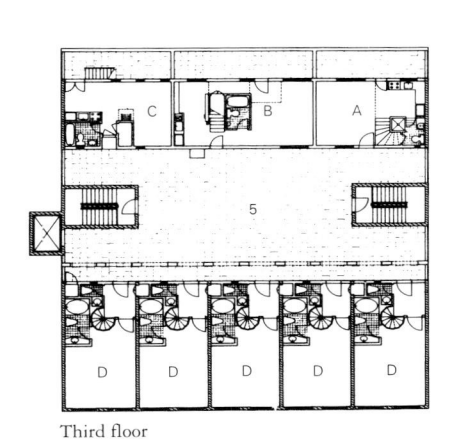

Third floor

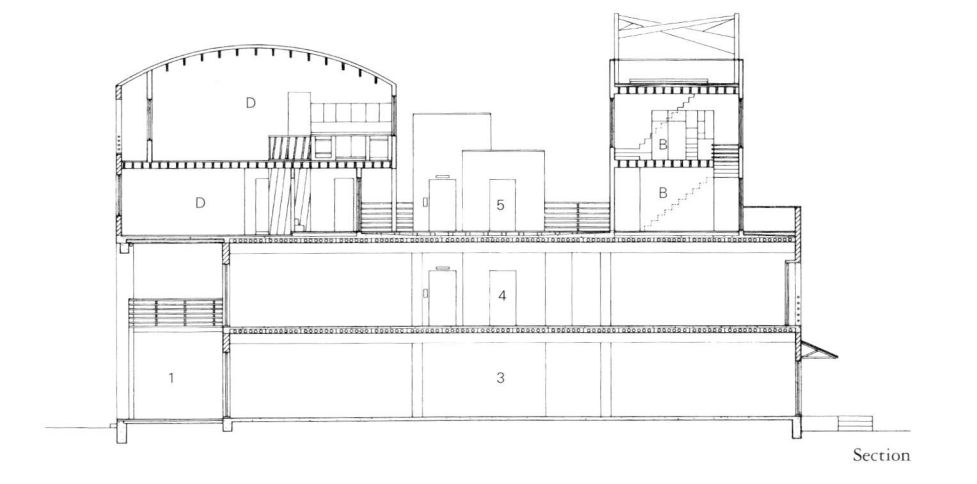

Section

I-115

Lobby on first floor

Detail: staircase to second floor

Boisterous Unit

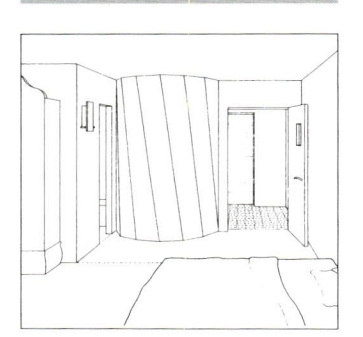

Perspective: lower floor

Upper floor: spiral staircase on center

Lower floor: spiral staircase inside

I-116

House of Musician

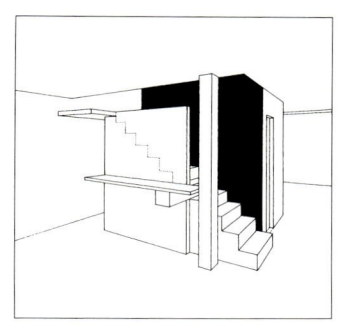

Perspective: staircase on lower floor

Detail: handrail of staircase

Lighting fixture

Kitchen

House of Mathematician

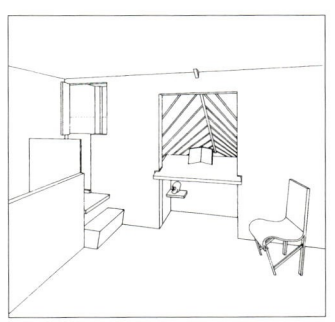

Perspective: lower floor

Lower level: kitchen on left

Staircase

I-117

House
of
Tragic Poet

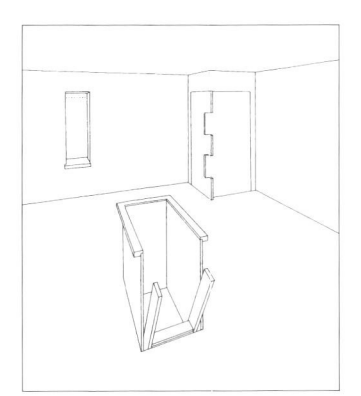

Perspective: upper floor

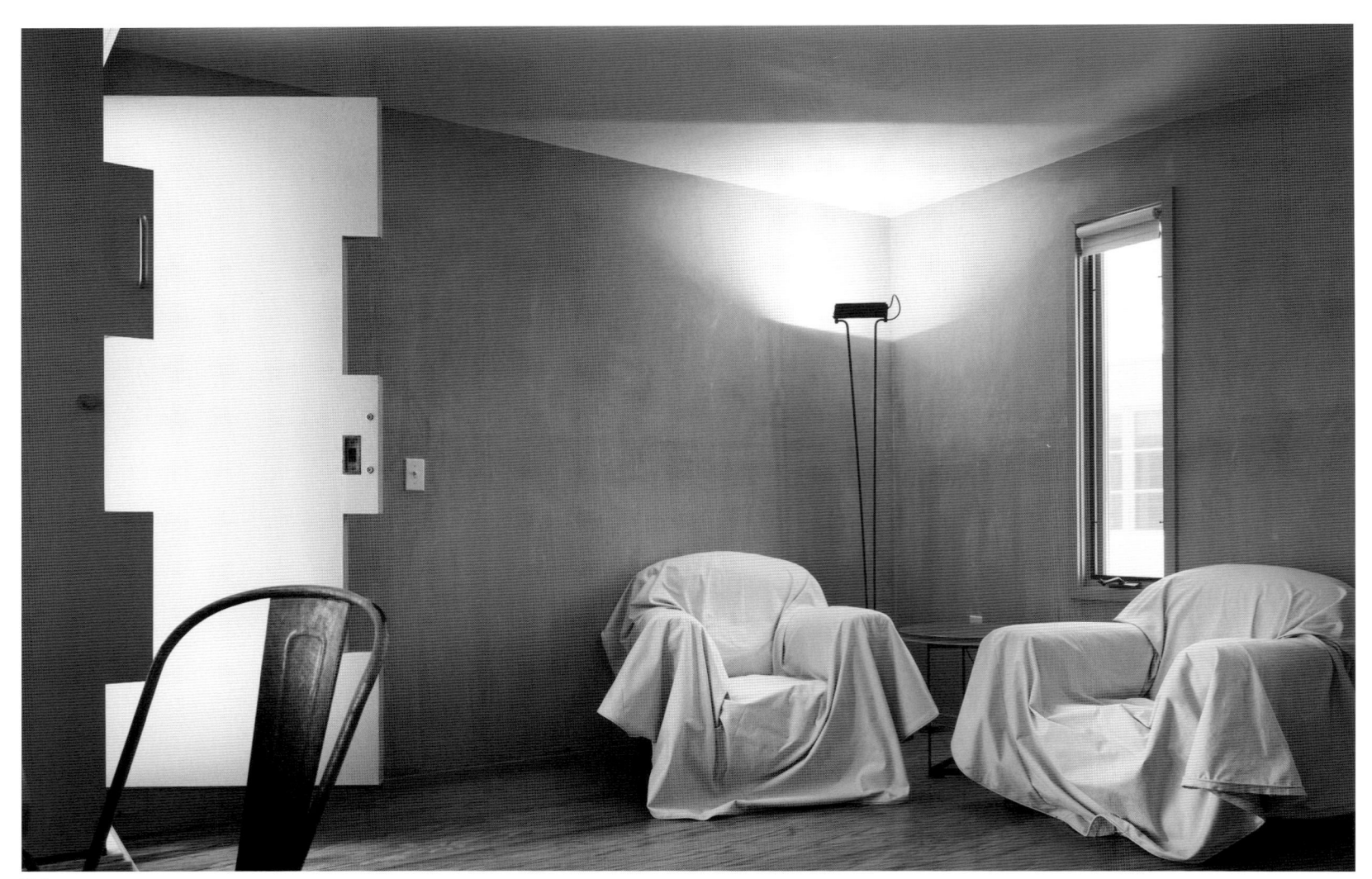

Living room

Lower floor: ladder to upper floor behind

Upper floor

Upper part of building: view from stairs of House of Tragic Poet

Roof terrace: view toward the ocean

ハイブリッド・ビルディング

シーサイドは,メキシコ湾に臨むニュータウンである。これをつくるにあたって,高さ制限,デザイン・ガイドライン,地役権などの規定をプランナーは用意した。この協定によって,この建物と隣につづく建物は,広場を囲むアーケードを連続させてることを求められた。

ハイブリッド・ビルは,小売り店舗,オフィス,住宅などで構成される。個々の独立性を重んじる設計に専心した結果,都市的な雰囲気が生じることになった。都市的な状況を強調すると同時に,「見知らぬ者たちの社会」というテーマを表現する。上層の階は,東向きと西向きのタイプに分かれる。夕陽を望み広場に面した部屋は,にぎやかなのが好きなタイプ,朝は遅く起きて街のにぎわいや燃える夕陽を眺めるのを楽しむ人たち向きだ。2層からなるフラットは,すべて同じ形式である。豪華なバスルームと電子レンジを備え,パーティーのためのスペースも用意される。

朝日を望む東向きの部屋は,メランコリー気質の人の部屋だ。この人たちは早起きで静けさを好み孤独にひたる。たとえば悲劇詩人,音楽家,数学者などである。裏側の3戸のフラットは,このようにして性格付けされた。悲劇詩人の住まいはうす暗い。窓は,どれも細長い。屋上の日除けは農夫のテーブルにかける布のようだ。音楽家の住まいには,上の階の角の窓から光が落ちる。黒いプラスターの壁が下の階から上まで続いて空間の連続を強調する。数学者の住まいでは,すべてがわずかにねじれている。階段はバスルームの上をねじれながら昇ってゆく。その天井は垂木をねじらせることで,二重曲面とした。上階には,ヨハネス・ケプラーを讃えて,頭蓋骨をのせるための棚を備えた,計算用のテーブルがある。構造は,プレキャスト・コンクリートの柱梁にヴォイド・スラブ。壁はコンクリート・ブロックにカラースタッコ塗,屋根は亜鉛メッキ板である。

Overall view from south

Void Space/Hinged Space Housing
1989-91 Fukuoka, Japan

Sketch: west view

Sketch: courtyard

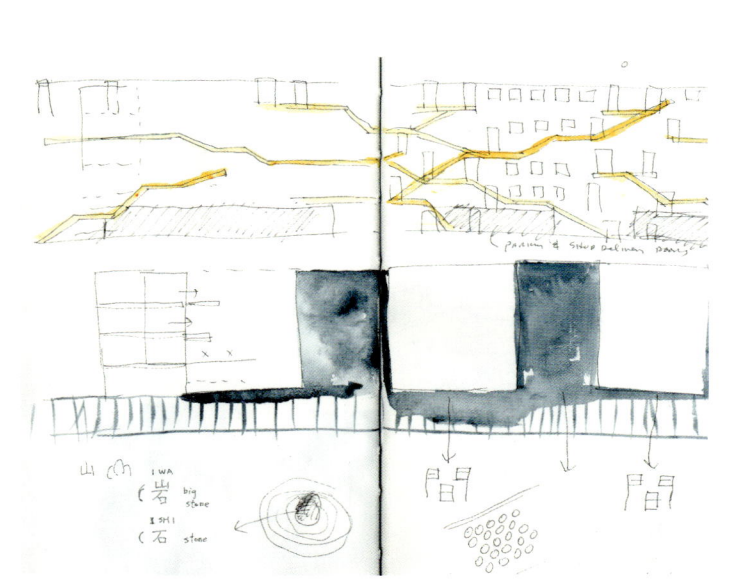

Concept sketch: void

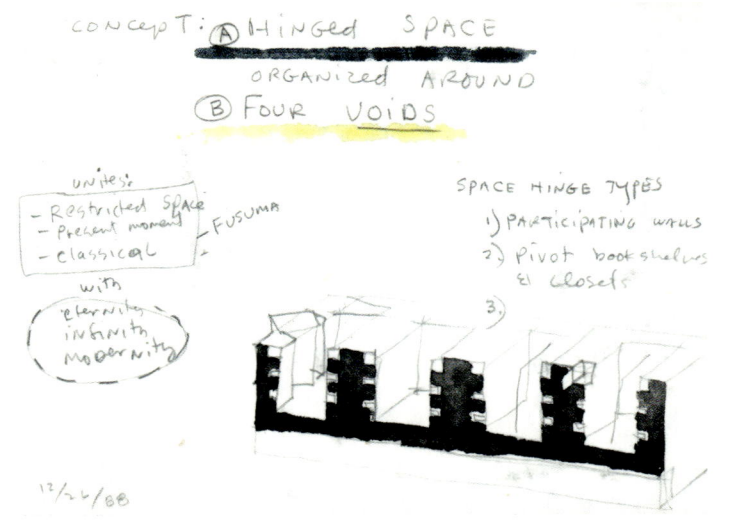

Concept sketch: hinged space and four voids

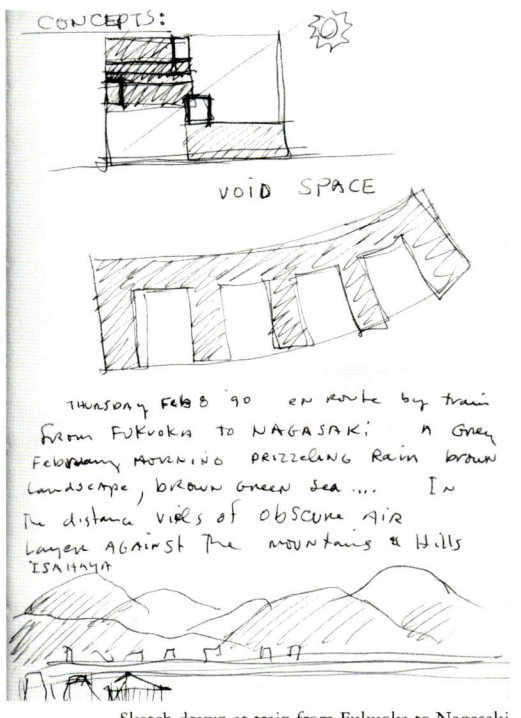

Sketch drawn at train from Fukuoka to Nagasaki

I-121

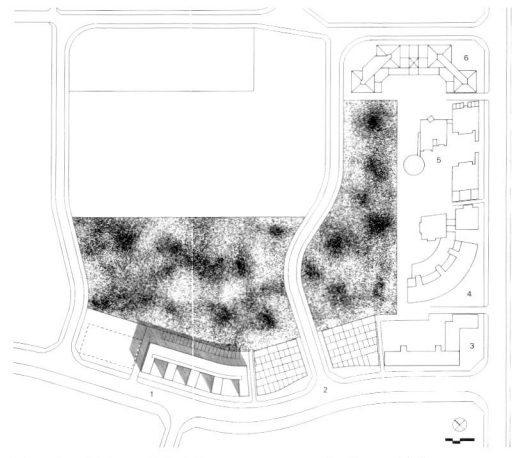

Site plan (Nexus World)
1 Steven Holl
2 Rem Koolhaas
3 Mark Mack
4 Osamu Ishiyama
5 Christian de Portzamparc
6 Oscar Tusquets

Water court on second floor

Concept: From hinged space to the silence of void space

Four active north-facing voids interlock with four quiet south-facing voids to bring a sense of the sacred into direct contact with everyday, domestic life. To ensure emptiness, the south voids are flooded with water; the sun makes flickering reflections across the ceilings of the north courts and apartment interiors.

Interiors of the 28 apartments revolve around the concept of "hinged space," a development of the multi-use concepts of traditional *Fusuma* taken into an entirely modern dimension. One type of hinging—diurnal—allows an expansion of the living area during the day, reclaimed for bedrooms at night. Another type—episodic—reflects the change in a family over time; rooms can be added or subtracted to accommodate grown children leaving the family or elderly parents moving in.

An experiential sense of passage through space is heightened in the three types of access, which allow apartments to have exterior front doors. On the lower passage, views across the water court and through the north voids activate the walk spatially from side to side. Along the north passage one has a sense of suspension with the park in the distance. The top passage has a sky view under direct sunlight.

The apartments interlock in section like a complex Chinese box. Individuation from the standpoint of the individual inhabitant has an aim in making all 28 apartments different. Due to the voids and interlocking section, each apartment has many exposures: north, south, east and west.

The structure of exposed bearing concrete is stained in some places. A lightweight aluminum curtain wall allows a reading of the building section while walking from east to west along the street; an entirely different facade of solids is exposed walking from west to east.

The building, with its street-aligned shops and intentionally simple facades, is seen as part of a city in its effort to form space rather than become an architecture of object. Space is its medium, from urban to private, hinged space.

Fifth floor

Forth floor

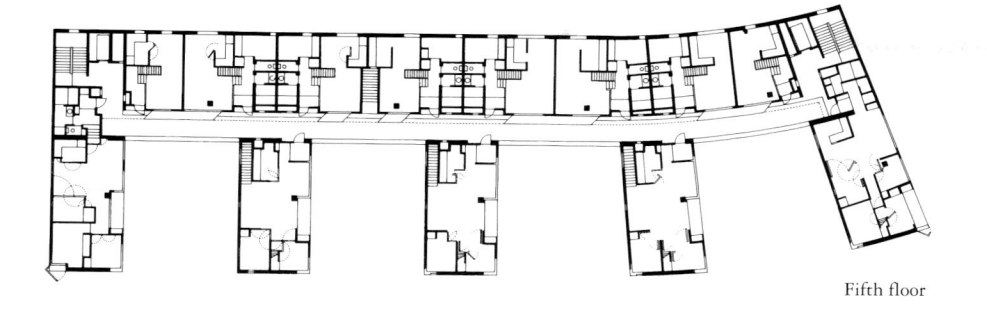

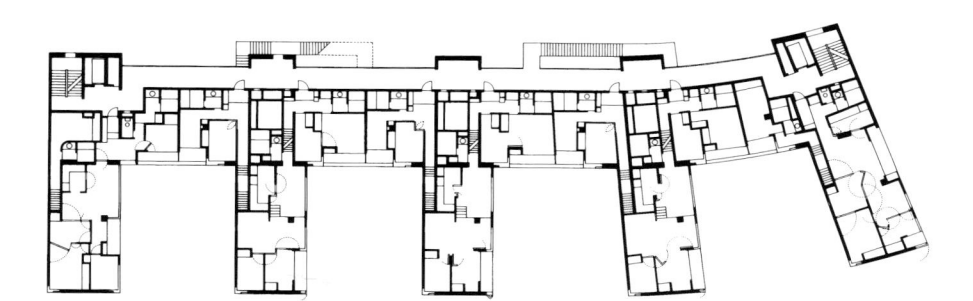

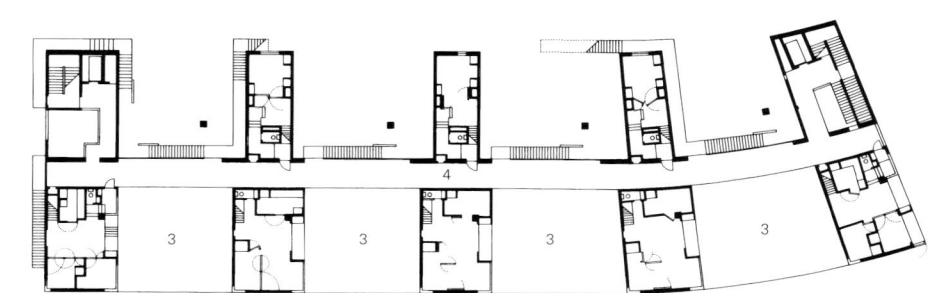

Third floor

1 MAIN ENTRANCE
2 ENTRANCE HALL
3 WATER COURT
4 PASSAGE

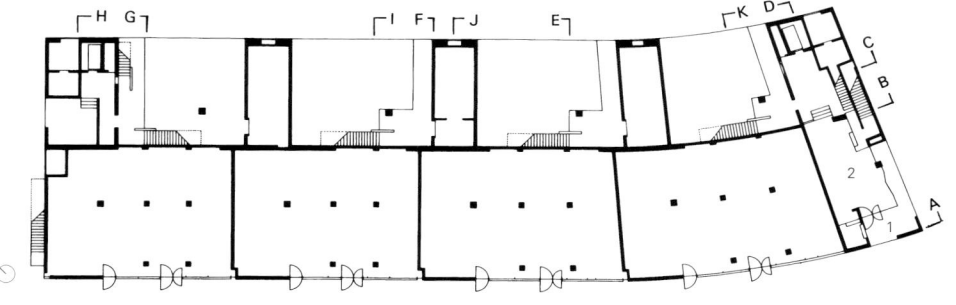

Second floor

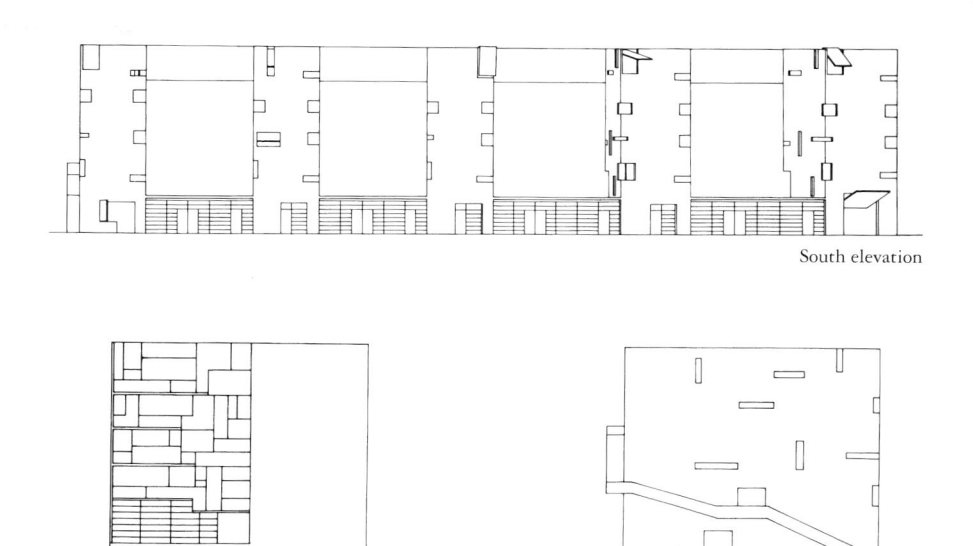

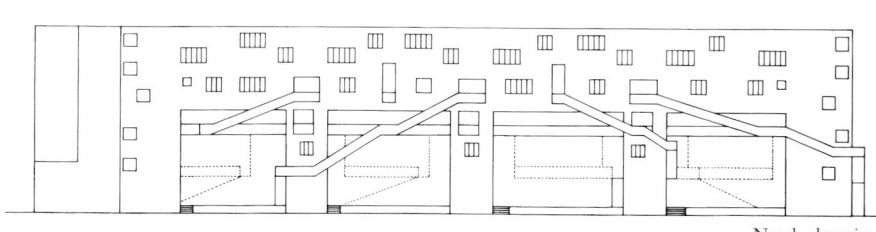

First floor

South elevation

East elevation

West elevation

North elevation

ヴォイド・スペース／ヒンジド・スペース・ハウジング
[コンセプト：ヒンジのつくる空間から吹抜けの静寂まで]
南と北の両側にそれぞれ四つの吹き抜けがある。北側は動的で南側は静的な性格を持ち，それらをかみ合わせることで，日々の家庭生活と神聖な感覚を直接に結びつけようとした。空間が何もないままに守られるよう，南側の吹抜けの下のスラブには水を張る。ここに反射したきらめく光は，北の吹抜けの天井やアパートメントの室内の天井にまで届く。

28戸のアパートメントは，「転換する空間／ヒンジド・スペース」というコンセプトを軸に展開する。これは，日本の伝統的な襖の多用途のコンセプトを現代的な次元に高めたものである。転換の第一の形式——毎日の——は，日中には生活空間を広くして，夜には一部を寝室に改めるというものだ。次の形式——時々起こる——は，家族の変化への対応である。成人した子供たちが家を出たり，逆に年老いた親などがやって来たりするのに応じて，部屋数を増やしたり減らしたりすることができる。

三つのタイプが設けられたアクセスルートを通ってゆくと，空間の中をめぐってきたという実感が高められるし，このルートのおかげで，各戸には直接外に面した玄関がつけられる。下の廊下を歩けば，水の中庭ごしの景観と吹抜けを間にした北の景色が眺められるので，空間は生き生きとしたものになる。北側沿いの廊下を歩くと，遠くの公園と一緒に宙に浮かぶような思いにとわれるし，最上階の廊下に立てば，陽を浴びながら空を眺められるのだ。住戸はさながら複雑なパズルのように断面が噛み合う。それぞれの住人の立場に立って個性を守るために28戸のアパートメント全てを違うものにしようという目的があった。吹抜けと組み合わせる断面のおかげで，どのアパートメントにも数多くの開口が可能になった。北にも南にも，そして東も西も。

打放しコンクリートの構造体は，所々ステインを塗ってある。道を東から西へ歩いて建物を見ると，軽量のアルミのカーテンウォールによって構造体の断面の形を読みとることができる。逆に，西から東に向って歩くと，それぞれに全く違ったファサードが見えてくる。

道路に面して店舗を並べ，ファサードをあえて単純なものにしたことで，建築が都市の一部として感じられる。それは，オブジェとしての建築ではなく，スペースをつくることを意図したからに他ならない。空間とは，都市とひとりの人間の間にあって両者を結ぶヒンジのような媒体(メディア)なのだ。

Main entrance

Entrance hall

Entrance hall

I-124

Entrance hall

View from living room

View from dining room

Living room

Entrance

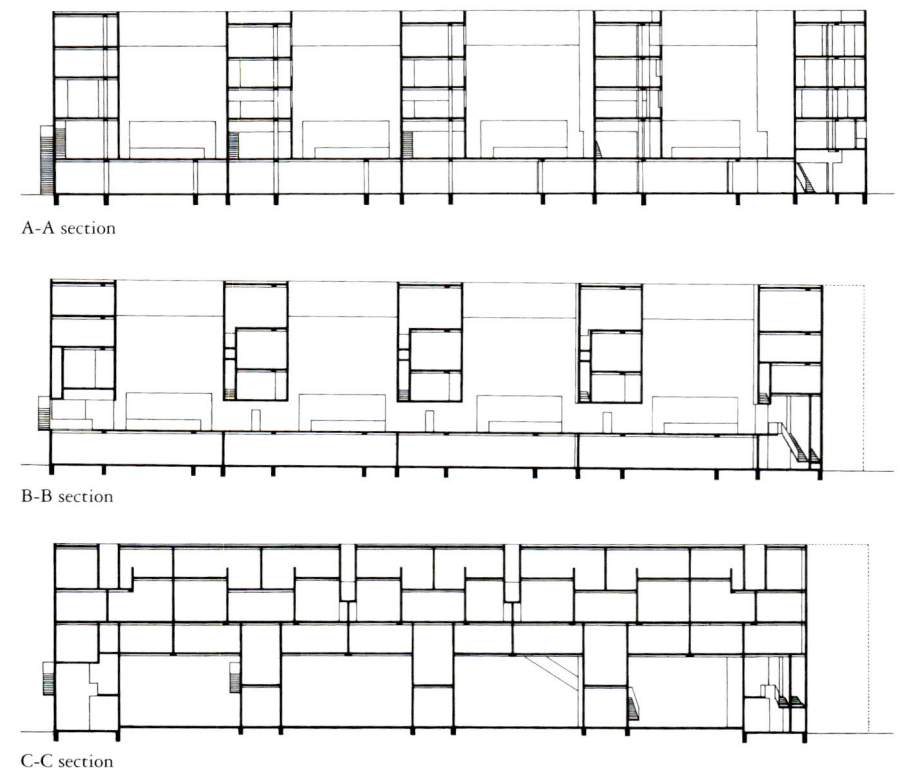

A-A section

B-B section

C-C section

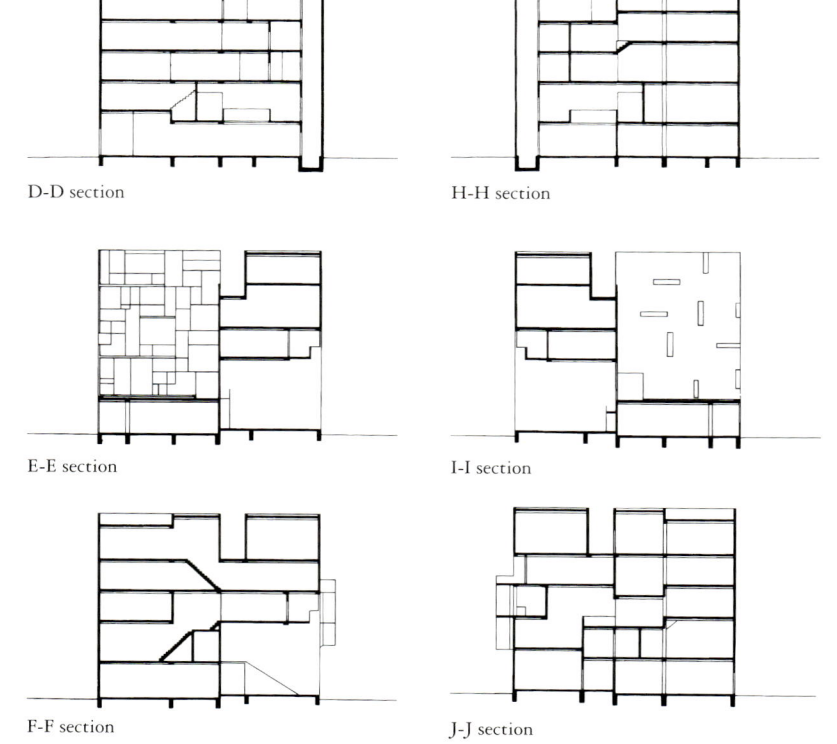

D-D section

E-E section

F-F section

H-H section

I-I section

J-J section

Living room

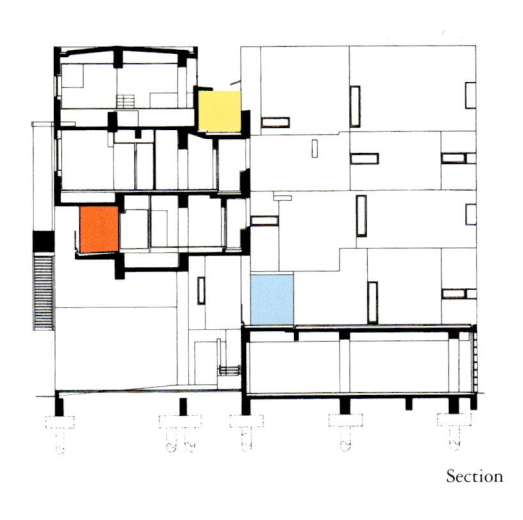

Section

Cabinet

Hall

I-127

1991-92 Town Square
Four Houses and Chapel
Port Ludlow, Washington, U.S.A.

Sketch: chapel

Port Ludlow is a new community being built on the site of a former saw mill, on a small, deep-water bay in Washington State. Different architects are at work on various parts of the town. The town square by Steven Holl and Don Carlson, is a parallelogram with its acute angles oriented to Admiralty Bay to the north and the Cascade Mountains to the south-west.

One side of the town square is formed by four houses which are a four part "Ode to the Pacific Northwest": 1) "A walk through the forest," 2) "Melancholia" 3) "Free spirit," and 4) "A gaze at the mountains."

The exteriors reinforce a collective space while the interiors are individually developed.

The Chapel is programmed as a duality. As a place of silence and reflection, it accommodates sacred events, such as small weddings, vigils or last rights. As a meeting house it accommodates receptions, and concerts, etc.

The dual form of the building, curved and square, recalls the transformation of timber from the cylindrical trunks of the big Douglas firs to their final milled form, rectangular in section. The round tower is also inspired by the old saw mill burners, such as the one that existed in Port Ludlow.

The curved space recalls the mythical time of the ancient trees and the first inhabitants of the site. The square section embodies the profane: on-going historical time. The curved wall of the round tower is washed by sunlight from the tall south-facing window. The square tower is lit by the morning light from the east, which filters through a window of clear and cast colored glass, playing onto interior walls and the stained concrete floor. A light wooden stair, passing inside the curved wall, leads to the upper roof.

From the observation point at the top, one can see the whole bay of Port Ludlow and beyond to the mountains. The steel structure, with scratch-coat stucco interior, will be skinned in lead-coated copper; weathered to a silvery blue gray.

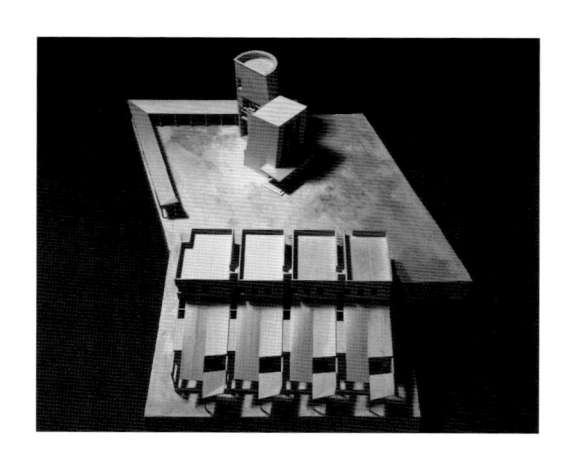

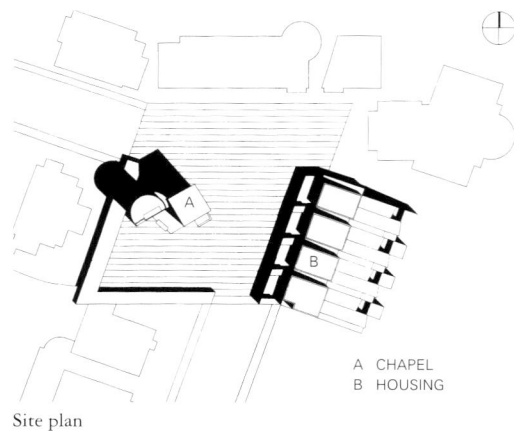

Site plan
A CHAPEL
B HOUSING

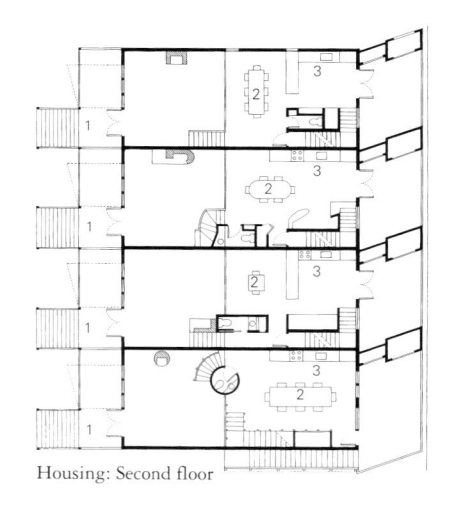

Housing: Second floor

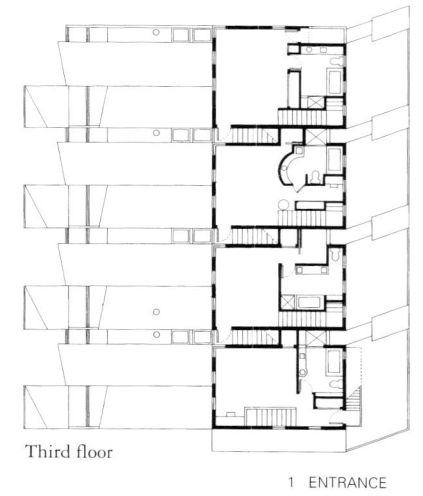

Third floor

1 ENTRANCE
2 DINING ROOM
3 KITCHEN
4 OFFICE

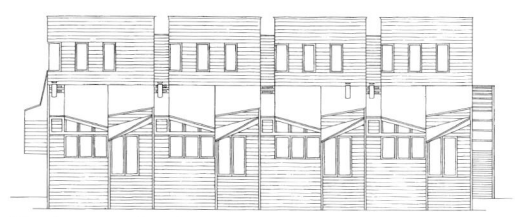

Housing: west elevation

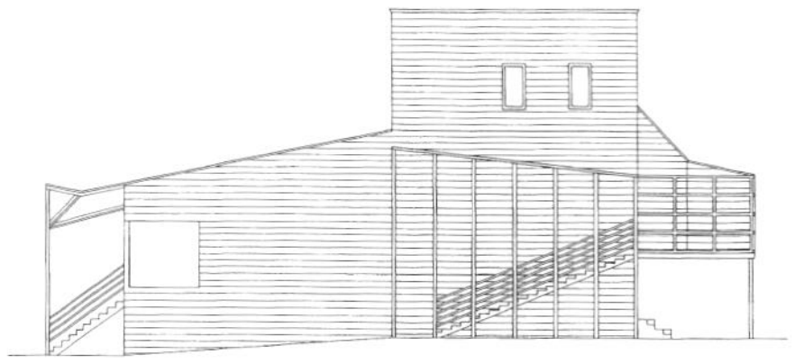

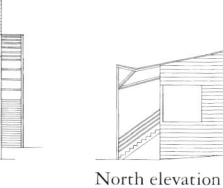

North elevation

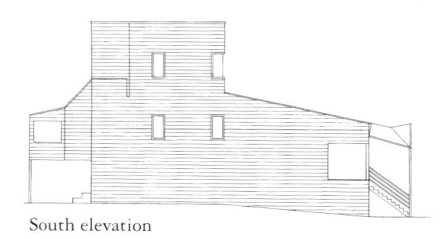

South elevation

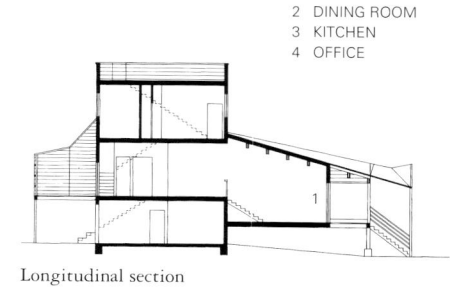

Longitudinal section

タウン・スクエア――四つの住宅＋礼拝堂

ポート・ラドローは，かつて製材加工場のあった土地で，ワシントン州の，小さな奥まった湾に面するこじんまりとしたコミュニティである。町の各所ではいろいろな建築家が仕事をしている。スティーヴン・ホールとドン・カールソンによるタウン・スクエアは平行四辺形をなし，その鋭角のひとつは北のアドミラルティ湾を指し，もう一方は南西のカスケード山を向いている。

広場の一辺は，4部構成の「北西太平洋沿岸州の頌歌」と呼ぶ四つの住宅で構成され，それぞれ，1）森を歩く，2）メランコリア，3）自由な精神，4）山々を見つめる，と名づけられた。

住宅の外形は広場の公共の性格を強めるものでありながら，内部はそれぞれに個性的である。

チャペルは二重の性格を持つよう計画された。静寂と思索の場として使われる時には，小規模な結婚式，徹夜の祈り，葬式などの宗教的な儀式が行われるが，にぎやかな集会場としては，レセプションやコンサートが催される。

曲線と四角で構成されるこの建築のもつ二重の形態は，ダグラスファーの巨木の円筒形が製材されて直角の断面に形を変える様を思わせるところがある。円筒形の塔は，ポート・ラドローにあった製材工場の焼却炉をもとにしたものである。

曲線でつくられた空間は，太古の樹々とともにこの地の先往者が暮した神話時代を思わせる。正方形の断面は世俗の世界，現代を含めて歴史に記された時代をあらわす。円筒形の塔の曲面が南向きの高窓から降り注ぐ陽の先に照らされ，四角い塔は，東からの朝の光に洗われて，透明ガラスと色ガラスの窓に濾された光が内壁とステイン塗のコンクリートの床に戯れる。その中を軽やかな木の階段が内壁の曲面に沿って上の屋根へ昇ってゆく。

屋上の展望台に立てば，ポート・ラドローの湾とその向こうの山並みを一望に納める。鉄骨の構造体にスタッコのかき落しで内壁を仕上げ，銀色を帯びたブルーグレーに腐蝕させた鉛を張った銅板で外壁を包む。

Model: housing (left) and chapel (right)

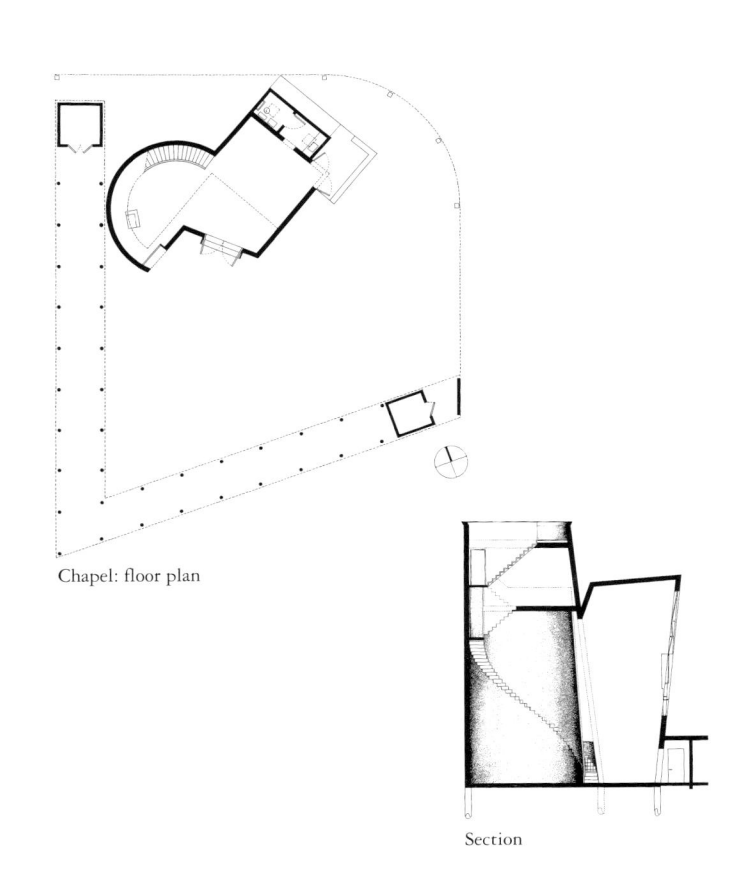

Chapel: floor plan

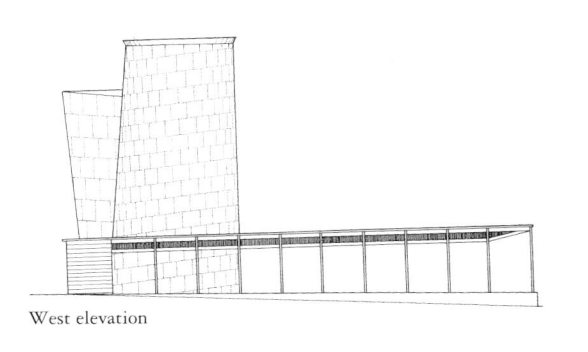

Section

West elevation

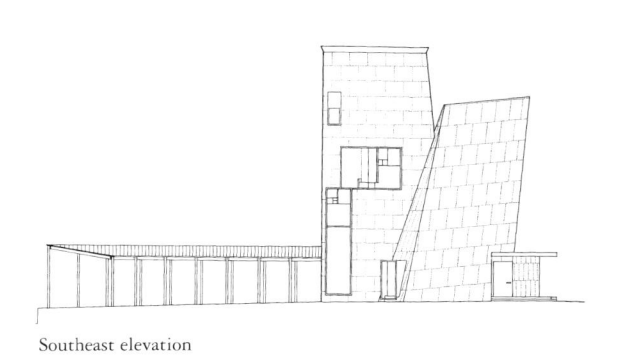

Southeast elevation

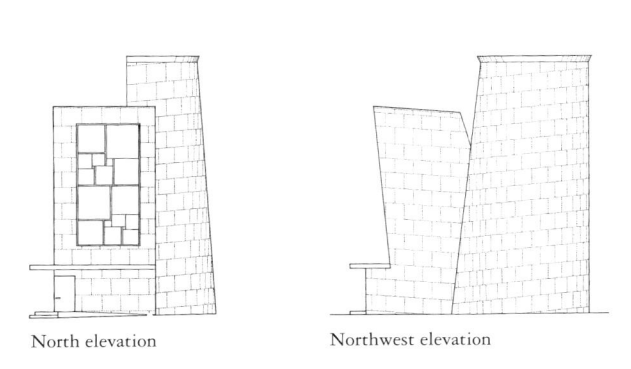

North elevation

Northwest elevation

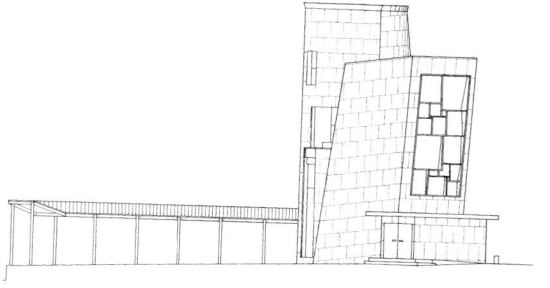

East elevation

South gate

Makuhari Bay New Town
1992-96   Chiba, Japan

Site plan

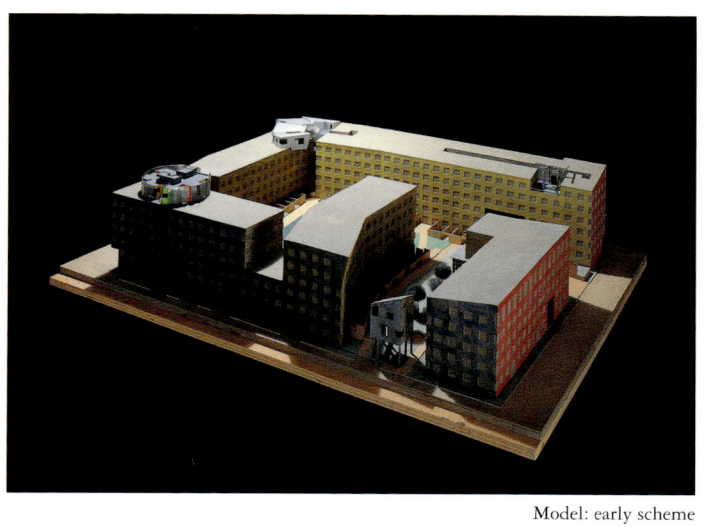

Model: early scheme

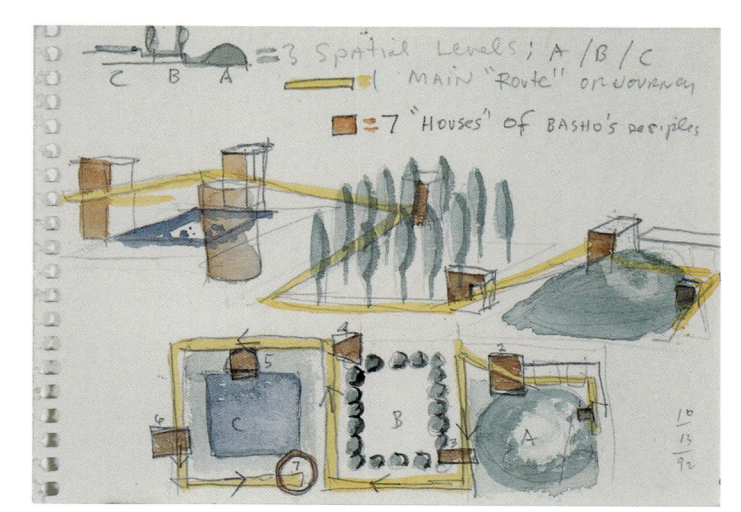

Concept sketch

West gate

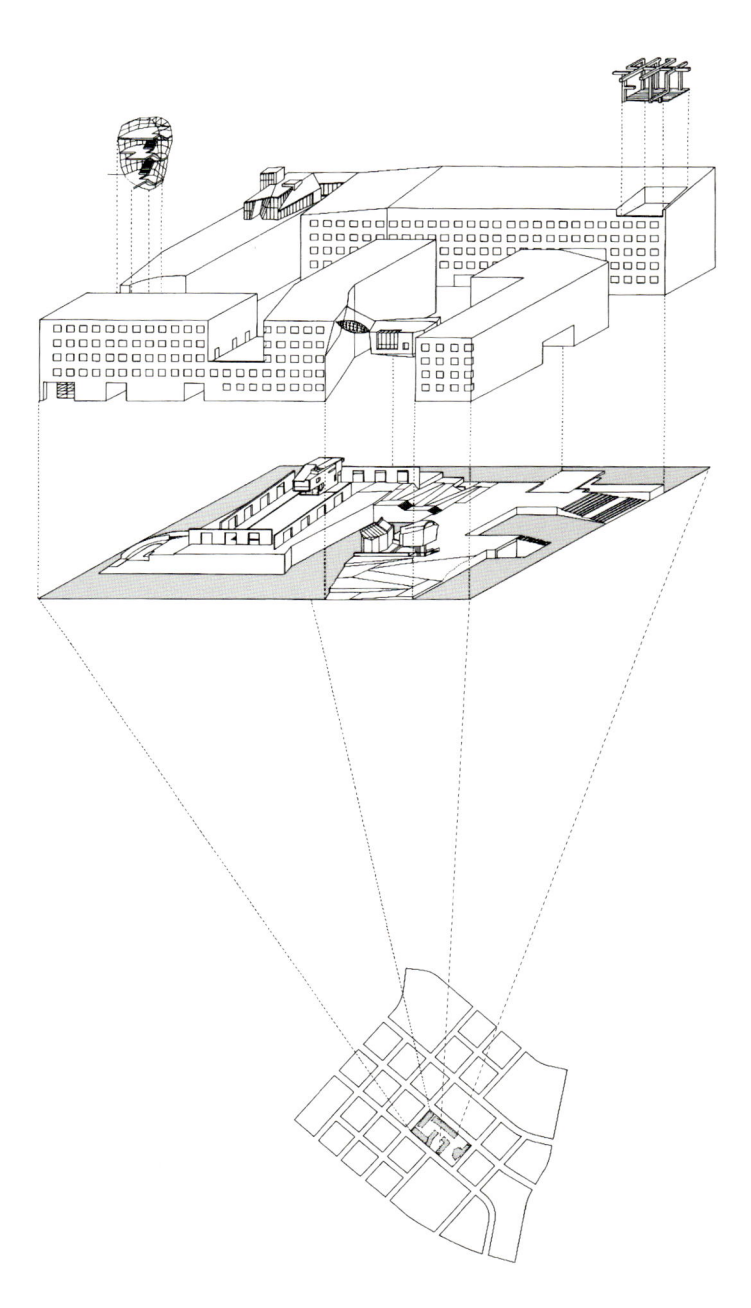

Exploded isometric: early scheme

I-131

A East Gate House
B South Gate House
C West Gate House
D North Gate House
E North Court House
F South Court House
G Reflecting Pool

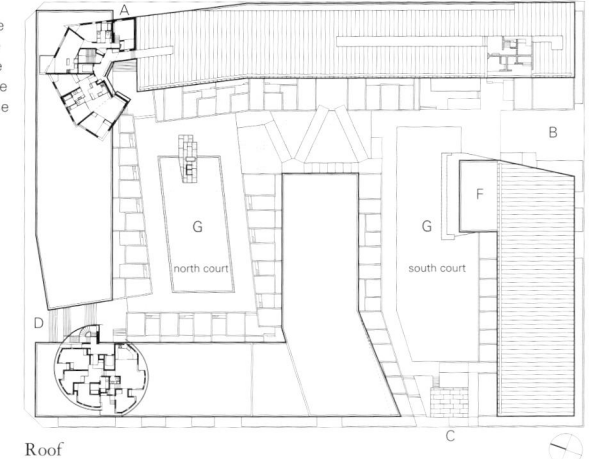

Roof

Longitudinal section

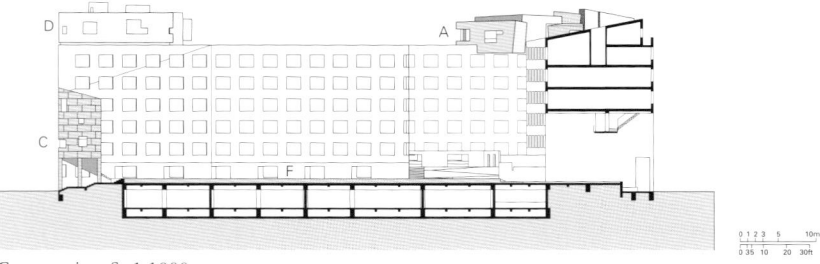

Cross section S=1:1000

Third floor

North Court House

1 ENTRANCE
2 TEA ROOM
3 KITCHEN
4 REFLECTING POOL

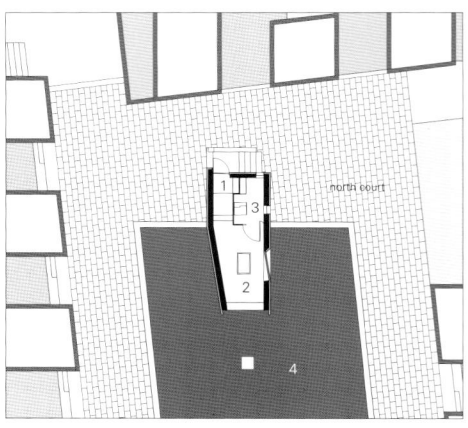

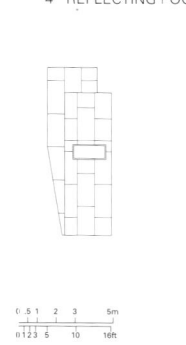

North court house: first floor and roof S=1:400

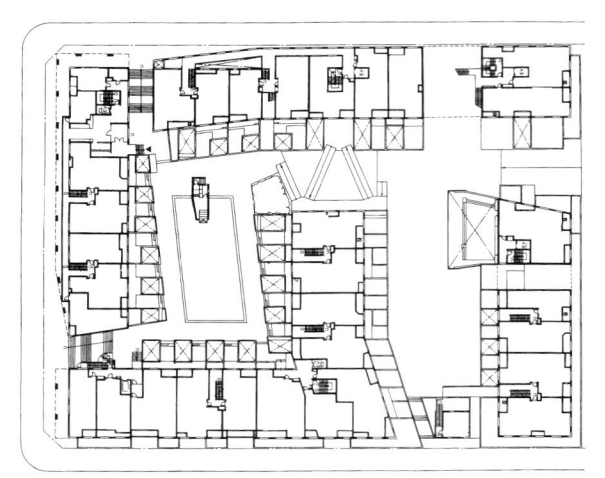

Second floor

1 ENTRANCE/LOBBY
2 SHOP
3 BICYCLE PARKING
4 ENTRY TO CAR PARKING
5 UPPER PART OF CAR PARKING
6 HOUSING
7 POND

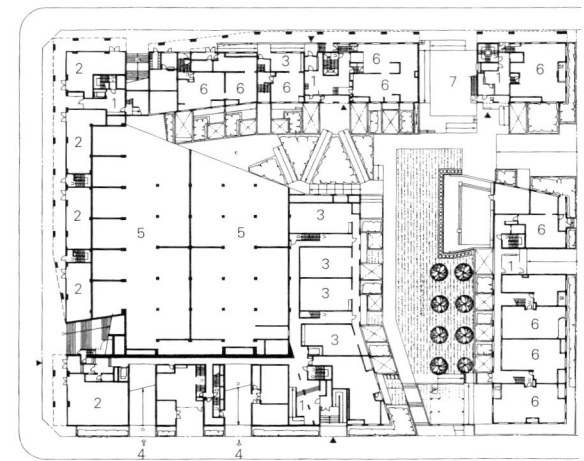

First floor S=1:1400

Downward view of north court: north court house (left) and reflecting pool

I-132

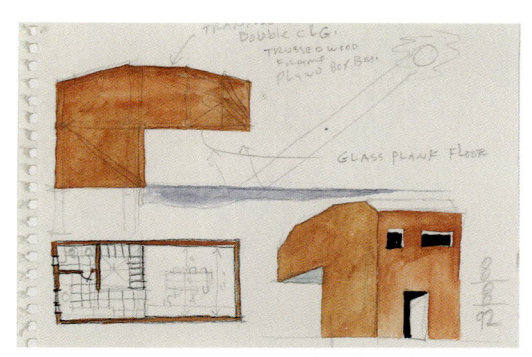

Sketch: north court house

Sketch: court with reflecting pool

North court house and reflecting pool. North gate house on left above

View from north court house toward reflecting pool

North court house and east gate house above

Lightweight = Activists = Sounds
Heavyweight = Bracketing Blocks = Silence

The new town of Makuhari is sited on dredged fill at the rim of Tokyo Bay. The urban planners have set rules for building height limits, tree-lined streets, areas for shops, etc. Each city block is to be designed by 3 or 4 different architects in an effort to achieve variety.

Our concept proposes the interrelation of two distinct types: silent heavyweight buildings and active lightweight structures.

The silent buildings shape the forms of urban space and passage with apartments entered via the inner garden courts. The concrete bearing wall structures have thick facades and a rhythmic repetition of openings (with variation in window or deck.) Slightly inflected, according to sunlight rules they gently bend space and passage, interrelating with movement and the lightweight structures.

Celebration of the miniature and natural phenomena are taken up in the lightweight activist force of individual characters and programs.

These individuated "sounds" invade the heavyweight "silence" of the bracketing buildings.

Inspired by Basho's *The Narrow Road to the Deep North*, the semi-public inner gardens and the perspectival arrangement of activist houses form an inner journey.

While the interiors of apartments in the silent buildings are designed by Koichi Sone and Toshio Enomoto (Kajima Design), the activist structures by Steven Holl include:

1. East Gate House
   Sunlight Reflecting House
2. North Gate House
   Color Reflecting House
3. North Court House
   Water Reflecting House
4. South Court House
   Public meeting room, House of Blue Shadow
5. West Gate House
   House of Fallen Persimmon
6. South Gate House
   Public Observation Deck
   House of Nothing

I-133

Gate between north wing (right) and east wing (left)

South Court House

1 ENTRANCE
2 STORAGE
3 MEETING ROOM

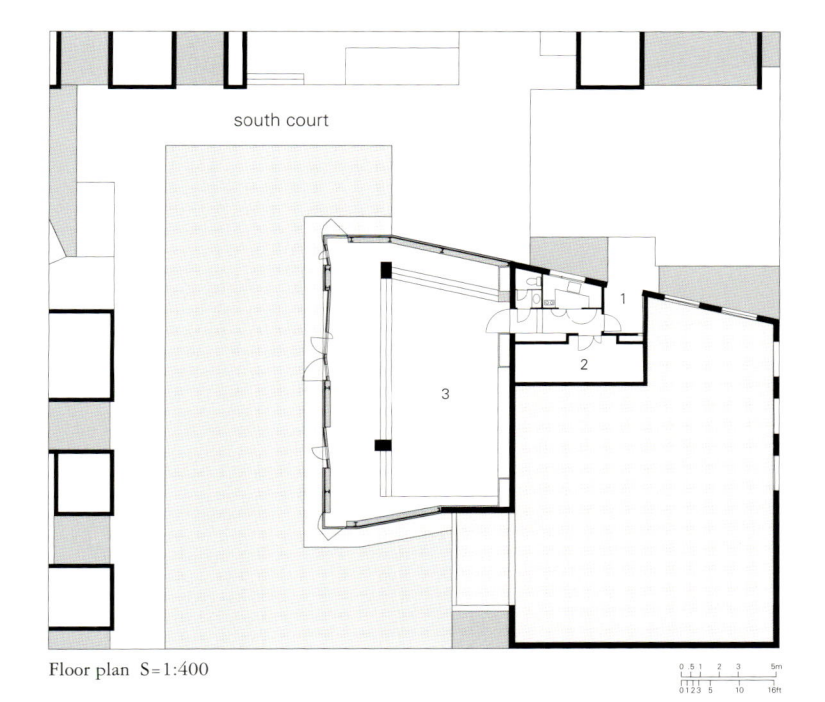

Floor plan S=1:400

South court

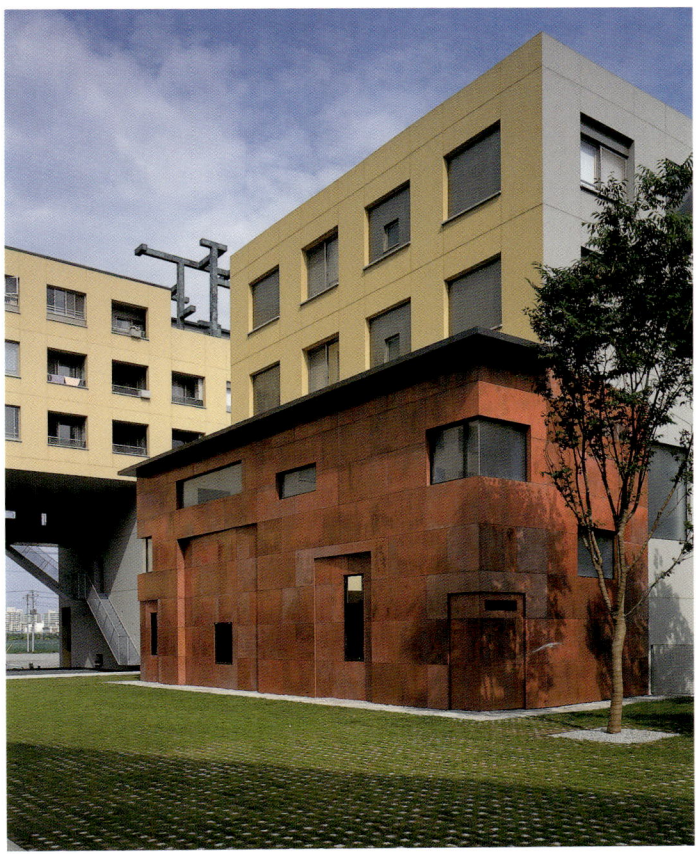

South court house

South court house: meeting room

I-135

West Gate House

West gate house

West gate house: upper floor

1 ENTRANCE
2 LIVING/DINING ROOM
3 KITCHEN

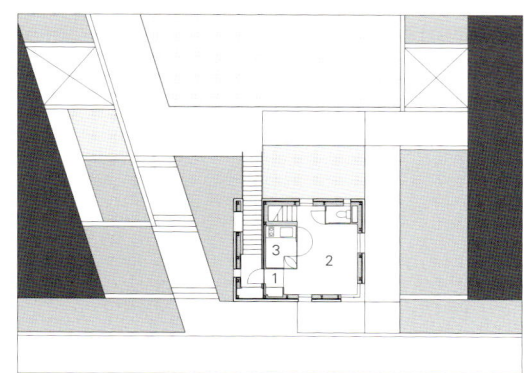

First floor S=1:400

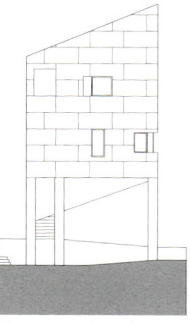

Elevations S=1:400

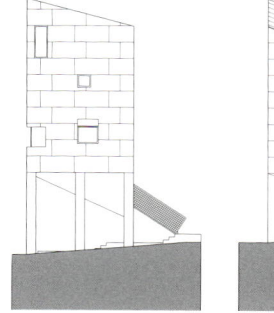

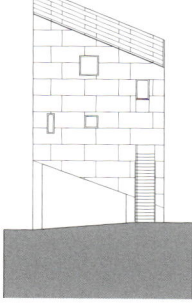

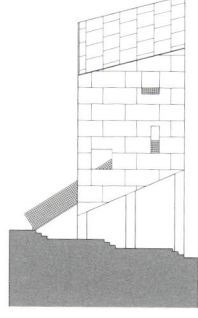

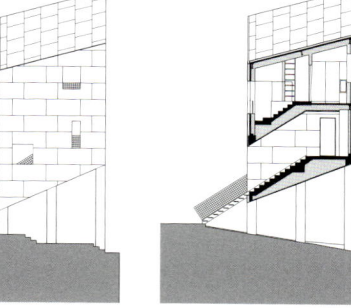

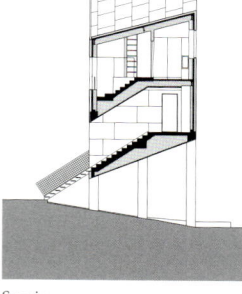

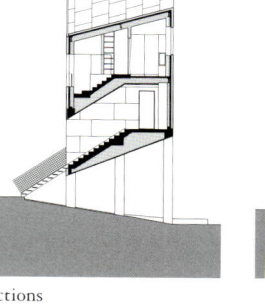

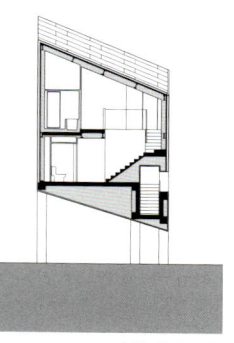

Sections

North Gate House

North gate house

North gate house: north elevation

Living room

1 ENTRANCE
2 AISLE
3 LIVING ROOM
4 DINING ROOM
5 KITCHEN
6 BEDROOM
7 BATHROOM
8 WC
9 BALCONY

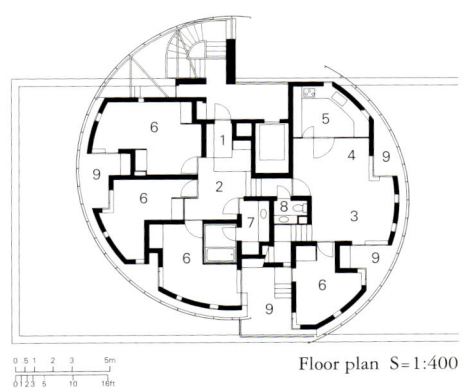

Floor plan S=1:400

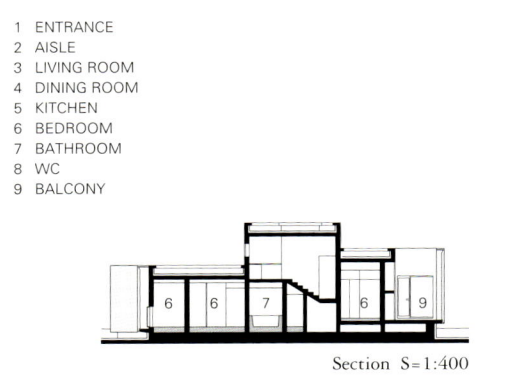

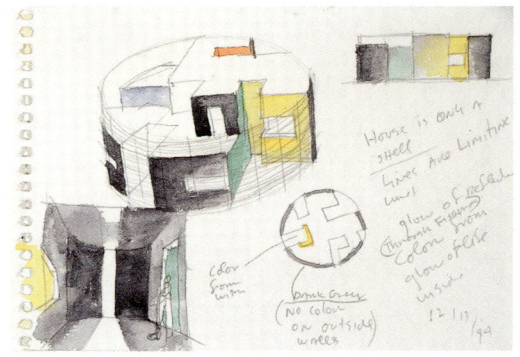

Section S=1:400

Concept sketch

West elevation

Living room (east side)

East Gate House

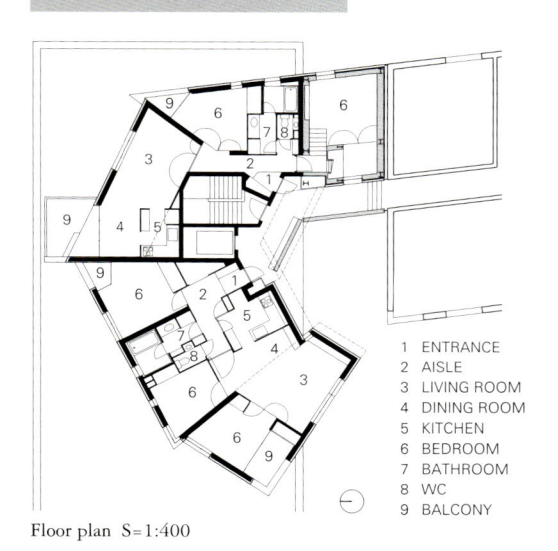

Floor plan S=1:400

1 ENTRANCE
2 AISLE
3 LIVING ROOM
4 DINING ROOM
5 KITCHEN
6 BEDROOM
7 BATHROOM
8 WC
9 BALCONY

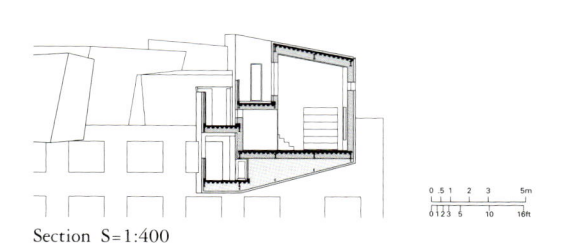

Section S=1:400

Living room (west side): kitchen on left

Living room (west side)

South Gate House

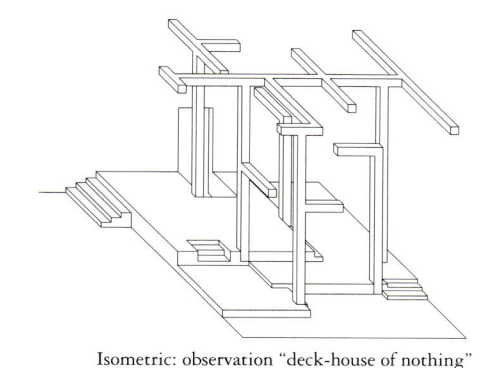

Isometric: observation "deck-house of nothing"

幕張ベイタウン・パティオス11番街
［ライトウェイト＝アクティビスト＝サウンド］
［ヘビーウェイト＝ブラケット・ブロック＝静寂］
幕張ニュータウンがあるのは東京湾岸の埋め立て地である。都市計画では建築の高さ制限，並木道，商業地域を定めることといったルールが定められていた。多様性を獲得することを目的として，3，4人の別々の建築家によって各々の街区は設計された。

この構想は異なる2種類の空間，すなわち静寂のヘビーウェイトの建築と，活気あるライトウェイトの構造の相互関係性に対する提案である。

サイレント・ビルディングを形成するのは都市空間とパッサージュ，内部の庭園からアクセスすることのできる集合住宅である。コンクリートの耐力壁のファサードは厚く，(窓やデッキといった，様々な)開口部がリズミカルに反復している。太陽光の動きに従いわずかに屈折した壁面は，緩やかに空間とパッサージュを折り曲げるようにして，リズミカルなライトウェイト構造へと結びついている。

細緻さと自然現象に対する祝福は，個々の空間の性格やプログラムが持つ軽やかで活動的な力として結実する。個々に峻別された「サウンド」は一括りの建築の持つ重厚な「静寂」の中へと侵入する。

松尾芭蕉の『奥の細道』は着想の源である。セミパブリックである内部の庭園と躍動する住宅の透視図法的空間構成が，内なる旅を生み出している。

サイレント・ビルディングのインテリアは曽根幸一氏と榎本敏男氏(鹿島建設)によるもので，スティーヴン・ホールによるアクティビスト・ストラクチュアは以下の住戸を含む：
1. イースト・ゲート・ハウス──陽光を映す家
2. ノース・ゲート・ハウス──色を映す家
3. ノース・コート・ハウス──水を映す家
4. サウス・コート・ハウス──集会室，青影の家
5. ウエスト・ゲート・ハウス──落柿の家
6. サウス・ゲート・ハウス──展望デッキ，無空の家

View from northwest

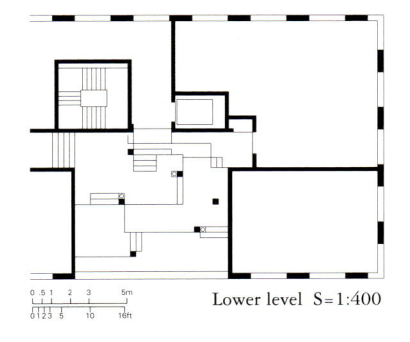

Lower level S=1:400

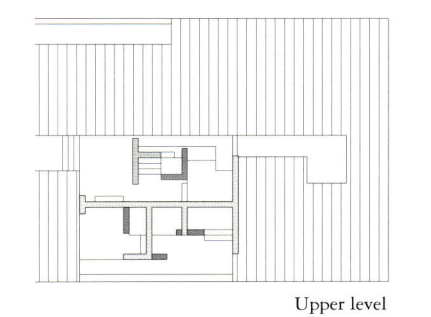

Upper level

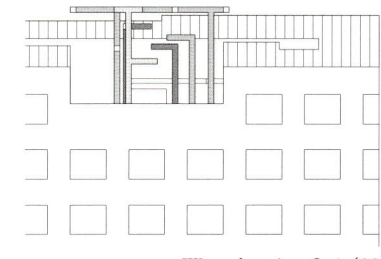

West elevation S=1:400

1994

Hypo-Bank Offices and Art Hall
Munich, Germany

Elevation study

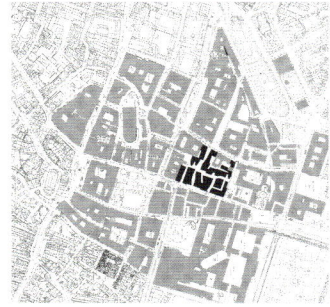

Site plan

The site is the better portion of a city block fronting on Theatinerstrasse in the heart of the old city center of Munich. The project is a hybrid of many functions: offices, a banking hall, shopping facilities, apartments, an art hall, and related facilities such as parking. The plans of the lower voids are extruded upwards, forming a glass-peaks level of glazed apartments.

As a counter-offering against the banal qualities of the tourist-oriented "shopping mall" transformation of old European city centers, this project organizes life in three overlaps of function and time and in the following priority: time one, permanent community of in-city residents; time two, semi-transient office workers and urban commuters; time three, transient tourists and passing shoppers.

To organize the maximum quality and range of living spaces and experiences for the described time layers, a heuristic device was adapted: a musical score by Karl Stockhausen for a piece entitled *Gruppen* (inspired by a view of the Alps). The score shows a mountain range in the first three measures and shaped voids in the remaining four measures.

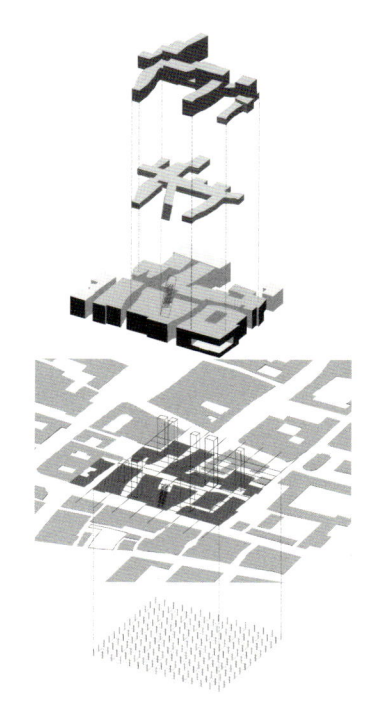

Isometric

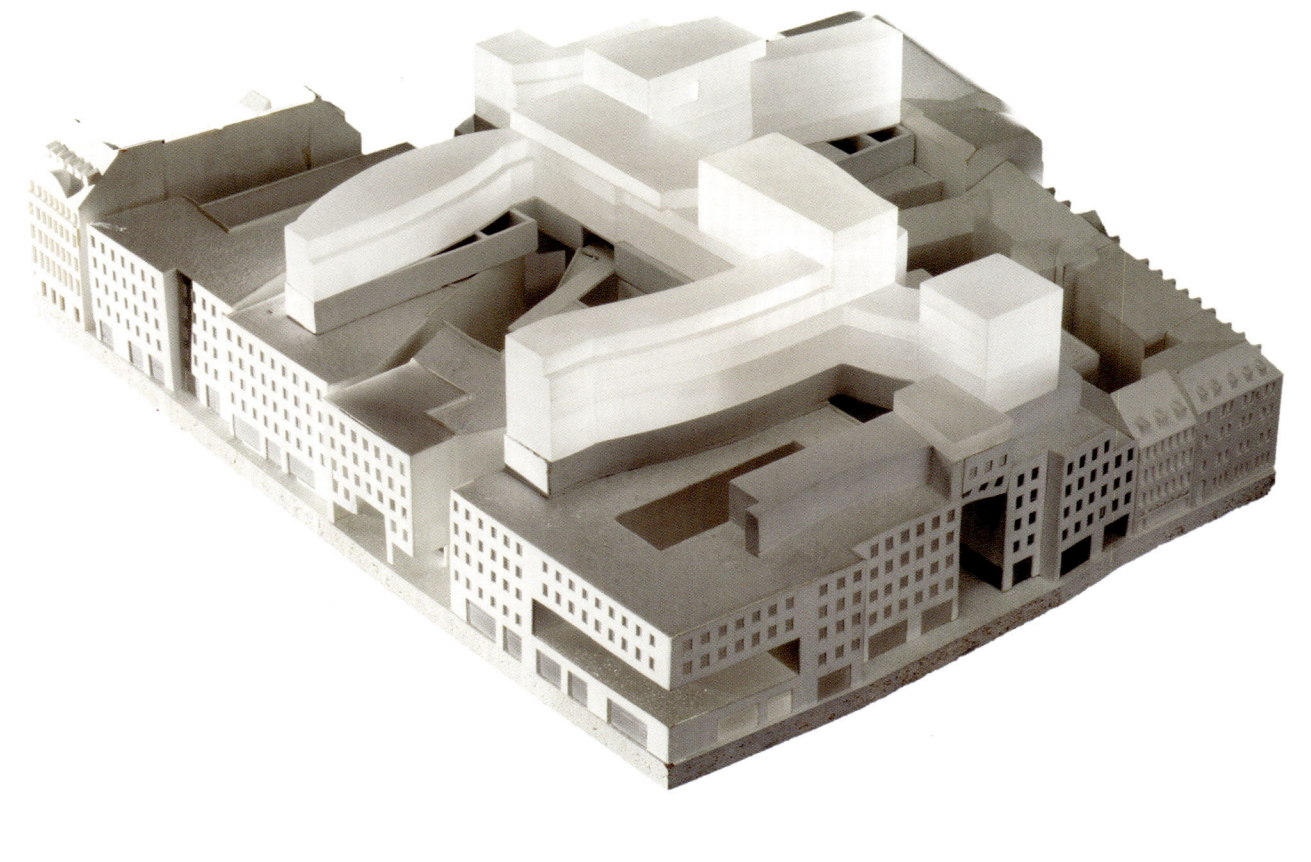

Concept sketch

Concept sketch

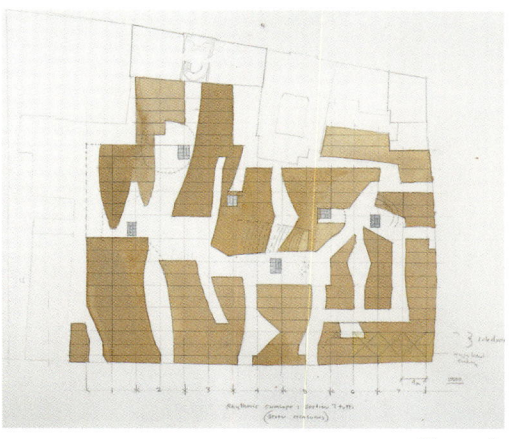

Plan study

ヒポ・バンク―オフィス＋アート・ホール
敷地はミュンヘン旧市街中心部のテアティナー通りに面した品の良い街区の一画にある。オフィス, 銀行のホール, 商業施設, 集合住宅, 美術ホール, 及びこれらのための駐車場という具合に, この計画は複数の機能を持った複合建築である。低層部のヴォイド・プランは上に向かって引き延ばされ, 頂部でガラスの集合住宅を形成している。

歴史あるヨーロッパの中心市街地を, ツーリスト向けの凡庸な「ショッピングモール」へと仕立て上げる代わりに, この計画では次のような優先順位に従って, 三期にわたって重複的に機能が組織される。

第1期：市内居住者の恒久的コミュニティ。第2期：中短期的に滞在するオフィスワーカーや通勤者。第3期：短期滞在するツーリストと通りゆく買い物客。

この時間軸に沿って居住空間と空間体験の質と多様性を最大限まで引き出すために, 自己発展的デバイスが導入された。すなわち, (アルプスの眺望に触発された)「グルッペン」と題する楽曲のためにカール・シュトックハウゼンの描いた楽譜である。初めの三小節では山脈の連なりを, 残りの四小節では形ある空隙を, その譜面は指し示している。

I-141

Concept sketch

Concept sketch

Ground level

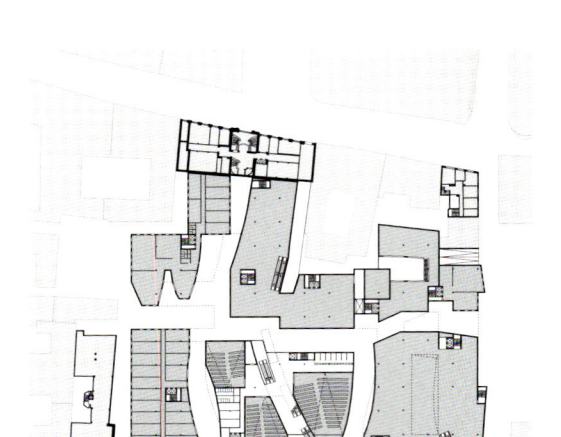

Art hall level

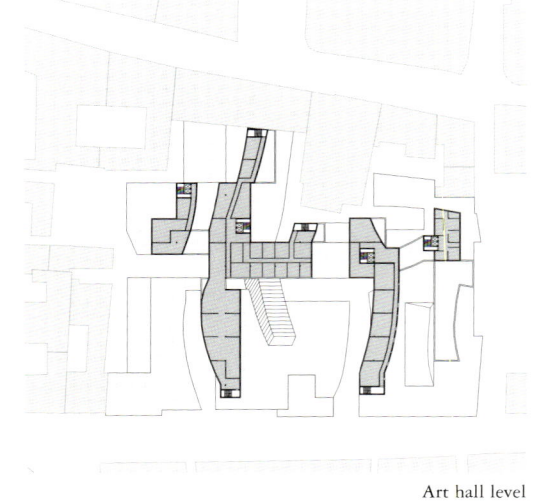

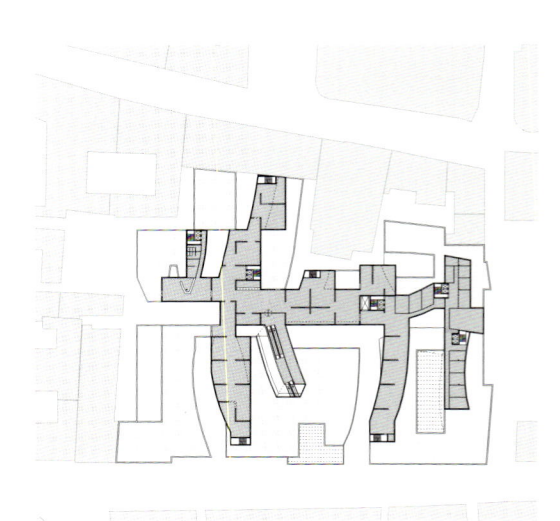

Apartments level

Sketch: roof garden

Sketch: ground level

Sketch: void space

Sketch: banking hall

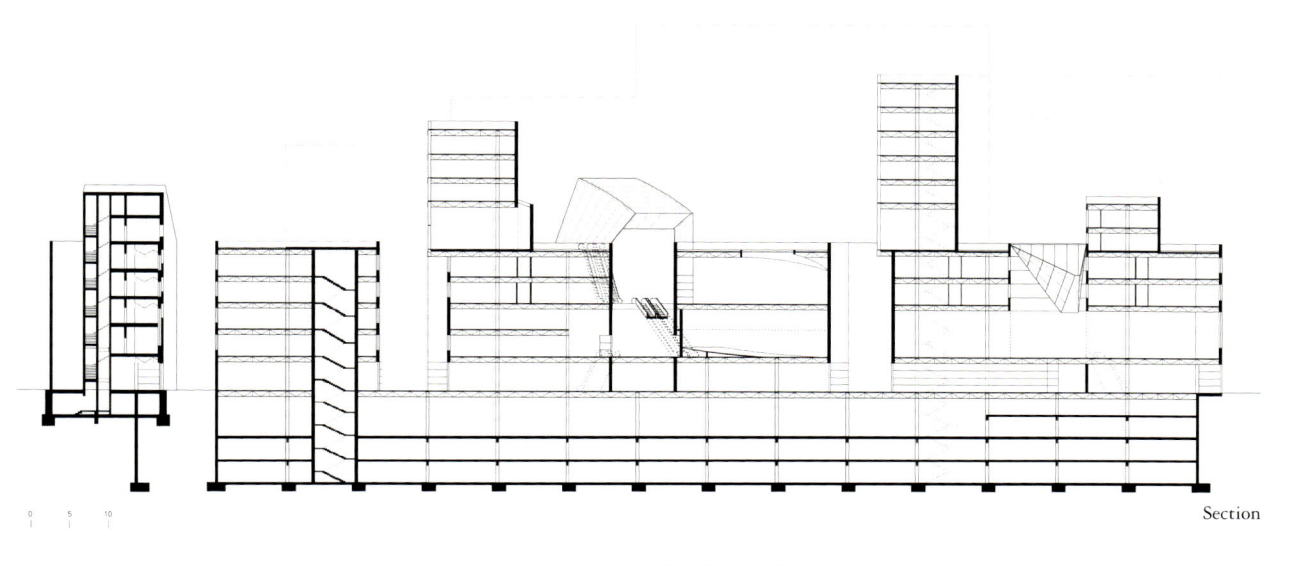

Section

Sketch: art hall

Sketch : passage

Sketch: escalator hall

I-143

Sketch: overall view

Model

Concept

Manifold Hybrid
1994 Amsterdam, The Netherlands

Site model

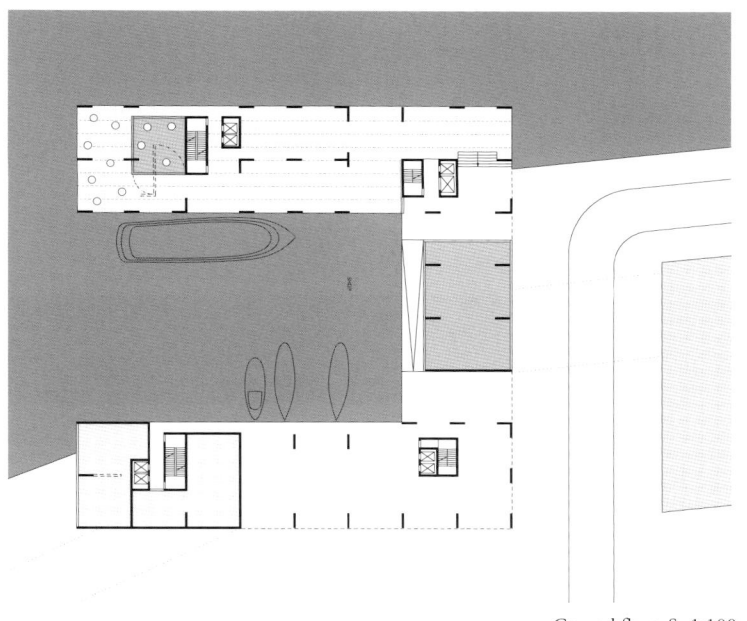

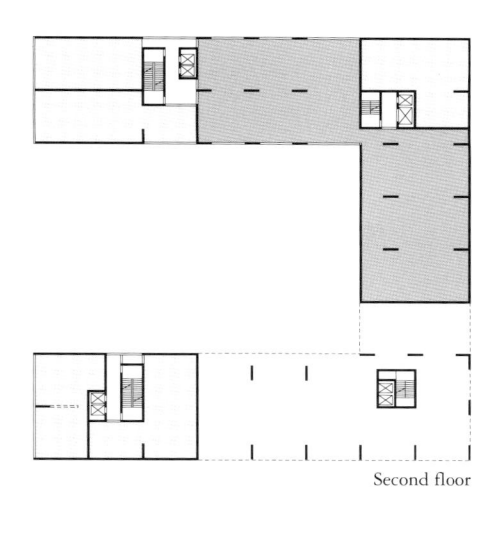

Ground floor S=1:100

Second floor

Seventh floor

Situated on the reused shipping quays overlooking the canal Erts, this large housing block of 182 apartments is part of an urban plan for housing which calls for three large super blocks in a lower urban field of garden row houses. The new 18-story block is envisioned as a section of a new city with several functions: offices a small art gallery, a restaurant, a boat house, a deli, and a health club. Eleven different apartment types are accessed by very different paths.

As a 56 m cube, the rotations and translations of this manifold building are seen from below as colored folds. The heart of the block is a huge water court which can accommodate visiting houseboats in the Amsterdam tradition. The penetrating stain on the concrete is of black, blue, and yellow colors which guide visitors on the multiple routes within.

The horizon view of Amsterdam is an important asset to these apartments, while the interlocking geometry of the sections adds a unique dimension to the interiors. Just as the interior is a harbor of the soul, the "U" shaped building is itself a harbor with a section of a small city surrounding it on three sides.

マニフォールド・ハイブリッド
エルツ運河を見渡す貨物埠頭の再生地区に位置する巨大な182住戸の居住ブロックは、庭付きのタウンハウスが並ぶ低層居住区域に三つの巨大なスーパーブロックをつくる都市居住計画の一部である。新しい18層のブロックは、オフィス、小規模アートギャラリー、レストラン、ボートハウス、デリカテッセン、スポーツクラブなど、多機能的で新しい都市の一部になる。11種類の異なるタイプの住宅は、全く異なる通路からアクセスすることができる。

一辺56mの立方体を回転し並進させた多様体建築は、下から見上げると色鮮やかに折り畳まれた空間に見える。ブロックの中央にある巨大な噴水広場はアムステルダム伝統のハウスボートを迎えることができる。コンクリートには黒、青、黄色の着色染料が使われ、内部へと続く複数の通路に来館者を導いている。

水平に広がるアムステルダムの眺望は、これらの住居の資産である。その一方でそれぞれの用途が絡み合うジオメトリは、内部空間に独特のスケールを付与している。内部空間が心の港であるように、「U」字型のこの建築はそれ自身、三面を取り囲む小都市の機能を担う港のような存在である。

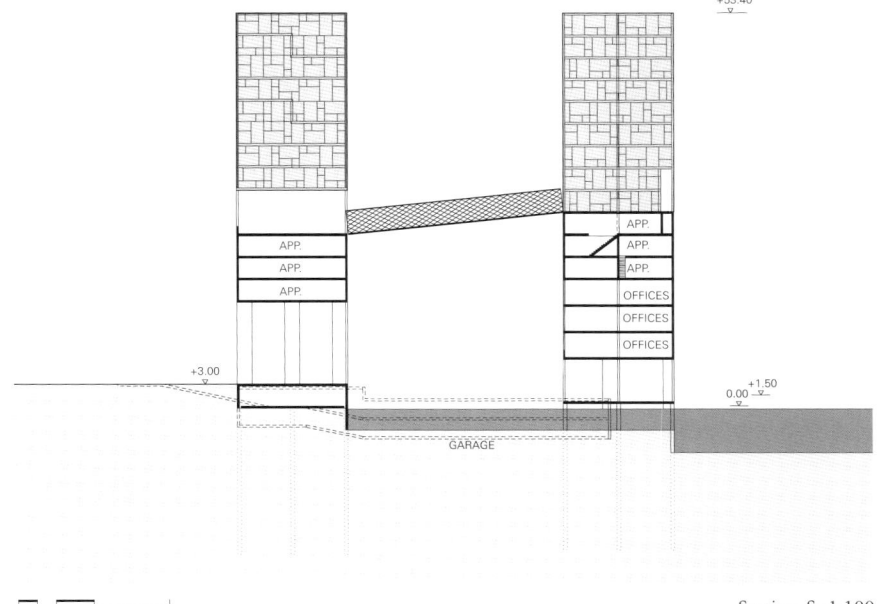

Section S=1:100

4 Ontology of Institutions
公共建築の存在論

In a tentative search for expression, an architecture of public institutions seeks to open barriers between the individual and the institution, between the teacher and the child, between the reader and the book. This openness exists in steps between the micro and macro scales, moving from the intimacy of fingers touching a handrail to the cultural connections of a city, to the green landscape of a campus, to the connection between earth and sky.

Monumental architecture of institutions of the past have expressed the philosophical preoccupations of their time. A belief in reason and the perfectibility of man in relation to an exalted view of past civilizations provoked monumental classical architecture. Bourgeoisie cultural desires for "ennobling edifices" placed institutions on a higher plane, apart from the vulgar day-to-day. Gradually this symmetrical stone monumentality has given way to desires for openness and public accessibility. Compared to the civilizations of the past, (for example, Athens, at its cultural apex, had a population of a mere two hundred and fifty thousand) ours is a society larger in numbers, more open in spirit and fostering freedom of passage and access. Along with this general opening-up, which is political as well as physical, society is questioning the environmental degradation of our times, which has occurred due to our disregard of the interrelation of all things.

Today, questioning past habits and exploring new ways of thinking and making is fundamental. The nature of being, the order of our cultural reality and the nature of our institutions is open to inquiry. This questioning at all scales should involve the individual as well as the institution. An ontology of institutions as a fundamental reconsideration is being written by our society in the dreams and proposals for new public programs and an open architectural expression of those programs. As yet unformulated, new ideas and new technologies may lead to new institutions. The self-assured certainty of monumental classical expression is giving way to tentative expressions of openness, uncertainty and new freedoms.

Steven Holl

Parthenon, Athens

表現を実験的に追求する過程で、公共建築の分野では、個人と組織や施設、教師と子供の間、読者と本の間をさえぎるようなものを取り払おうとしはじめている。このような開放化は小さなスケールから大きなものまで何段階も存在している。手摺と触れあう指の親密なかかわりから都市の文化的なつながり、キャンパスの緑のランドスケープ、大地と空の間のつながりにまでおよぶ。

かつては、公の建築は時流に乗った思想を表現するものだった。ある時は、理性と人間の完全性に対する信仰が、過ぎ去った数々の文明への賛美を伴ってモニュメンタルな古典建築をつくらせた。ブルジョワ文化は「高貴な殿堂」を望むあまり、公を高い位置にすえ、庶民の日常からかけはなれたものにしようとしてしまった。こうした対称性を重んじたかつての石造の記念碑は、開放的で誰もが近づけるものを求める趨勢に道をゆずることになった。過去の文明と比較すると（たとえば、アテネはその文化が頂点を極めた頃で、25万の人口にすぎない）、私たちの社会は、はるかに人口も多く、精神も開放的で、移動の自由をはぐくんできた。分野を問わず、政治的にも物理的にも開放化が進められるにつれて、我々の時代になって環境の悪化が社会的に問われるようになった。世の中のあらゆるものが互いの関わり合いを持ちながら存在するという事実を我々が無視してきたことがその原因となっていたのである。

これまで続けてきたことを問い直しながら、考えること、つくることの新たな方式を探ることは、今日の基本的な課題である。存在の本質、私たちの文化的現実、時代をつらぬくものの本質が問われている。規模を問わず、このような問い直しには、個人から組織に至るまでを巻き込む必要がある。根源的な再検討を必要とする公共建築の存在論は、新たな公共計画の夢や提案、それを実現するための開放的な建築という形で描かれだしている。未だ確立されるには至らないが、新たな思想と技術が新しい公共建築を導きだすことになるのかもしれない。モニュメンタルな古典的表現の自己過信的なまでの普遍性を求める姿勢は、今や、開放的で、不確かさを許容しながら、新たな自由を目指す実験的な表現に道をゆずろうとしている。

（スティーヴン・ホール）

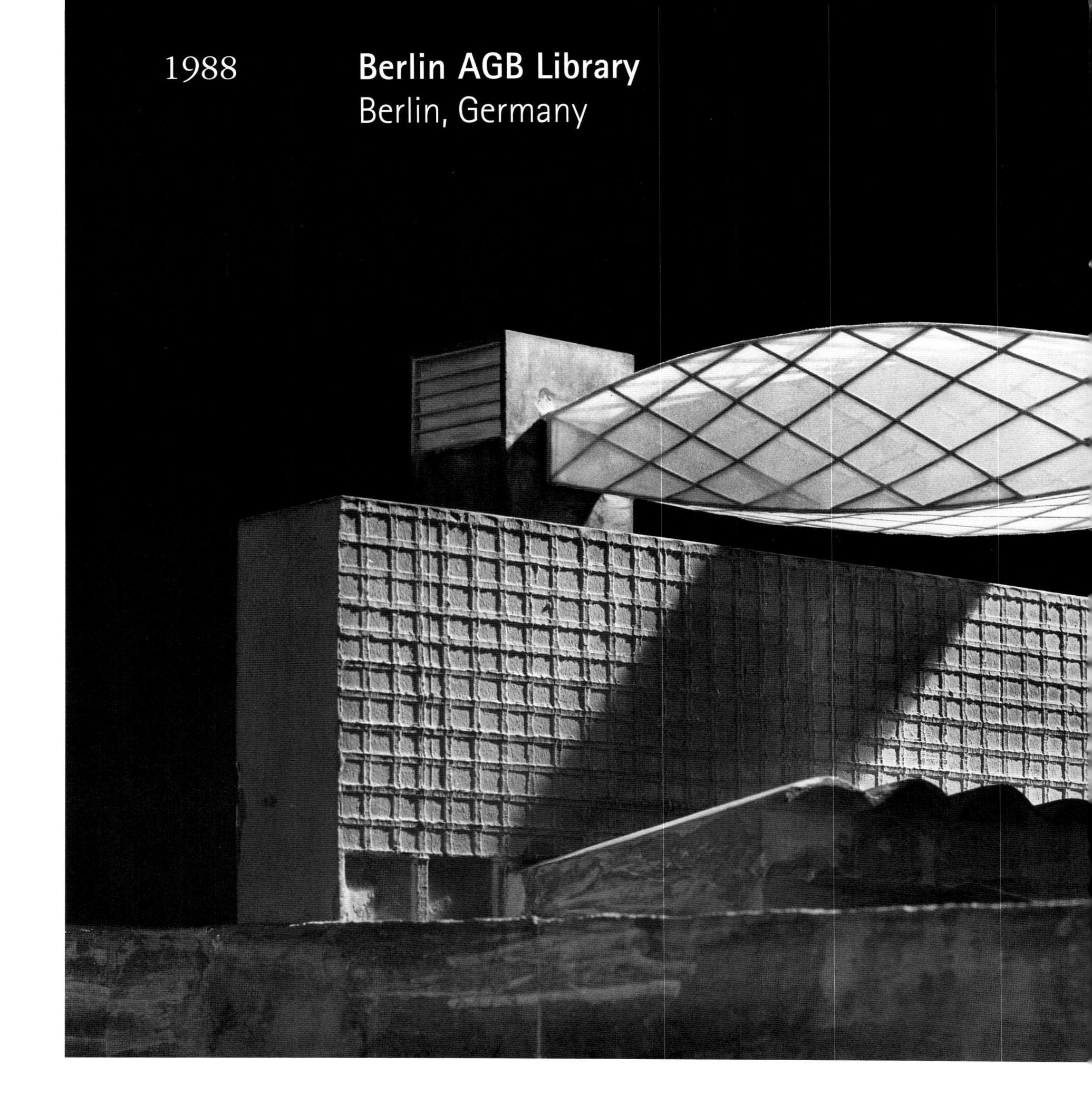

1988 Berlin AGB Library
Berlin, Germany

I-149

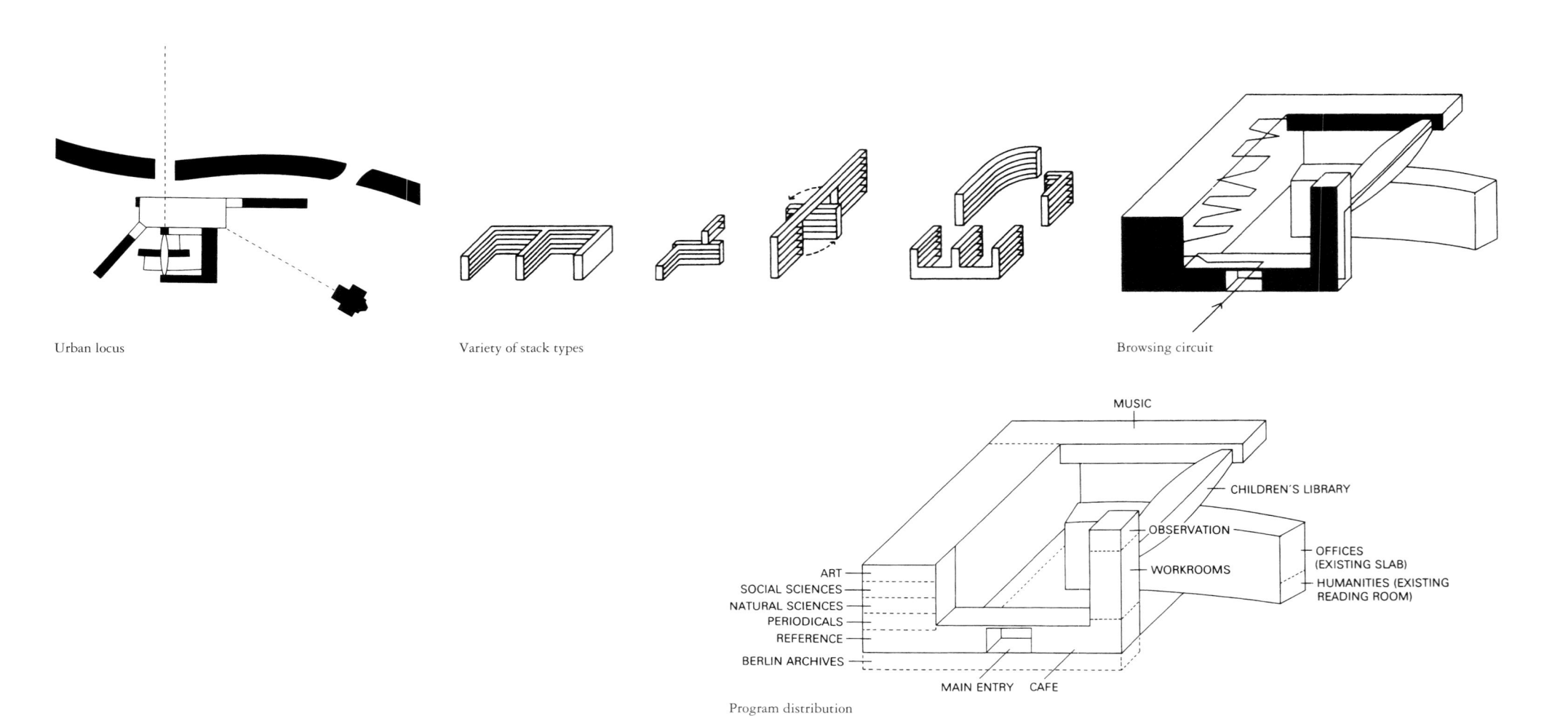

Urban locus

Variety of stack types

Browsing circuit

Program distribution

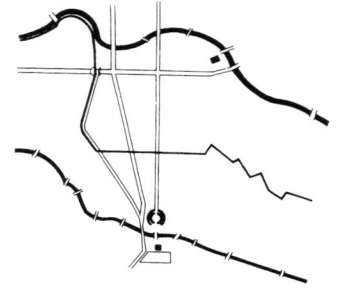

Site: Berlin

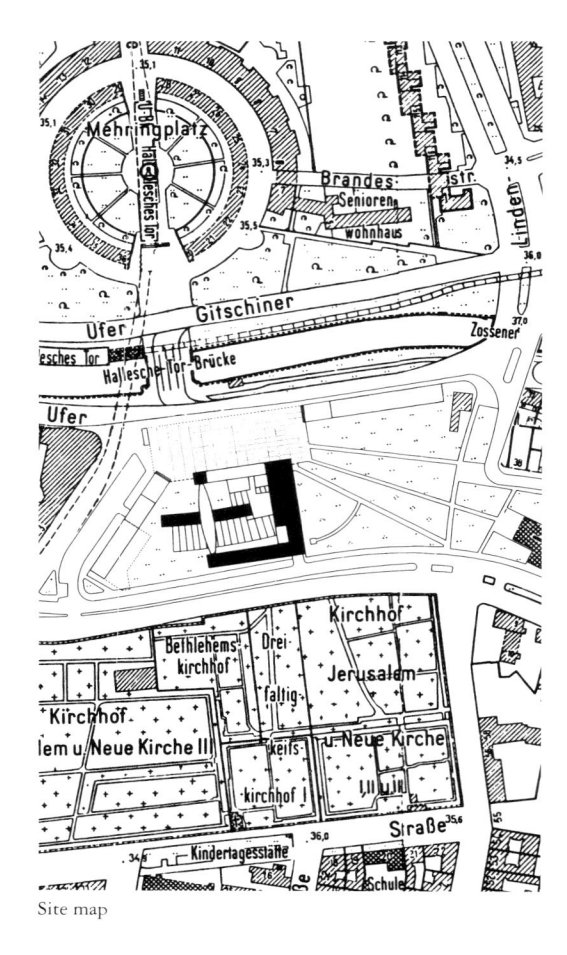

Site map

This project is a competition entry for an addition to the Amerika Gedenk Bibliothek in Berlin and surrounding area.

The design extends the philosophical position of the open stack—the unobstructed meeting of the reader and the book—by organizing the offerings along a browsing circuit. The circuit is a public path looping the building, presenting the collection of the entire library. The library stacks are developed as furniture, giving different characteristics to areas of the open plan. The concept of a browsing circuit is given memorable variety by these different stack arrangements.

The circuit forms a slipped ring bracketing the original building. The extension holds the original building in space without overpowering or deferring to it. Proportions of all major architectural elements, including interior and exterior spaces and structural grid, are determined by a single series (1:1.618) based on the height of the existing building.

The importance of the site within the city plan is expressed by making the library a major urban element, analogous to a city gate. The north face of the library addition defines the south edge of the new Blücherplatz. Additional buildings to the east and west, containing public programs, complete the definition of space. A clearly defined park to the east and west strengthens the connection to the Holy Cross Church. The tower offers a public observation point—a lens focused on the city—and supports the children's library. Suspended over the original building, the library elevates children to caretakers of the city. It has sloped floors for reading while lying down. The structure is a lattice truss sheathed in sandblasted glass with vision panels.

The main structure is an exposed concrete frame with glass curtain walls of sandblasted white, amber, and blue glass set off by areas of lead or stainless-steel covered panels. Under the gray skies of Berlin, the effects of east and west light in the library will be highly varied according to the sandblasted lines and mullion patterns in the curtain walls. For the interior, careful attention has been given to acoustics to assure silence, while natural materials and subdued colors have been selected for their contributions to a serene and reflective mood.

Site plan

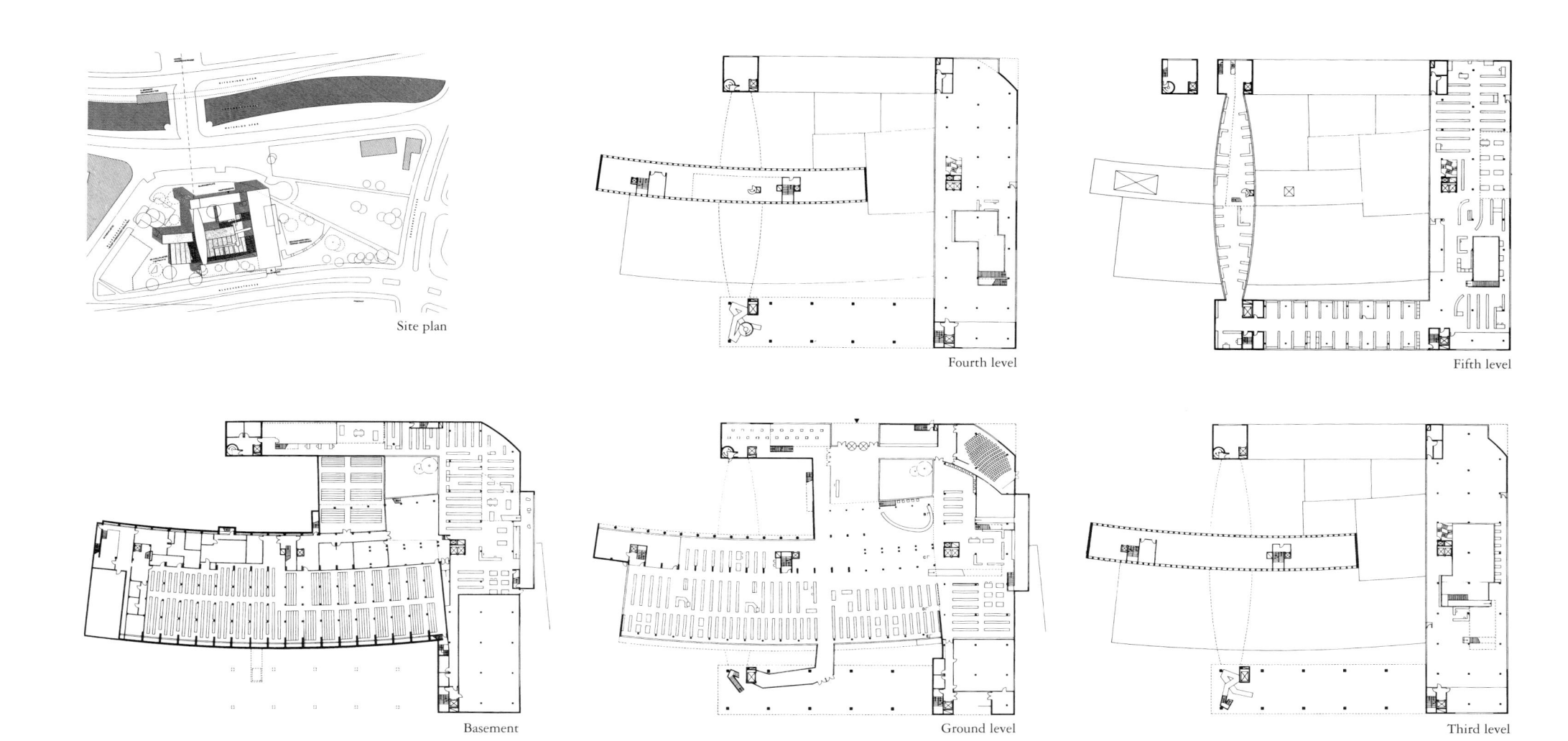

Fourth level

Fifth level

Basement

Ground level

Third level

ベルリン・アメリカ記念図書館

ベルリンのアメリカ記念図書館の増築とその周辺計画のための設計競技案である。

　読者と本が直接出会うことのできる開架式のアイディアを発展させ，本を眺めながら全体を一巡りできるよう書架を配した。このルートは，図書館全体の蔵書を見せるとともに，建物を一周するための出入り自由な通路でもある。書架は家具として扱い，連続する空間の中で各エリアに相応しい性格を与える。このようにして，独自の本棚を各々に設けることによって，ブラウジング・サーキットにはそれぞれの場所が心に留まりやすくなるような多様な性格が与えられる。

　このサーキットは，既存の建物の上をまたいで，ややねじれた環状をなす。増築は旧館の建物を圧倒することもなく，異質に見せることもなく，旧館をとりこんでいる。建築の主な要素は，内部空間，外部空間にかかわりなく，構造体のグリッドに至るまで，そのプロポーションは旧館の建物の高さをもとにした一貫した比率(1:1.618)で構成される。ベルリンの都市計画に占めるこの敷地の重要性を示すために，この図書館を都市の門になぞらえることでその主な要素の地位に引き上げようとした。図書館の新しい北側ファサードは，新しくつくられるブリューヒャー広場の南端を形成する。公開の催し物も行われる東西の増築部でこの空間が完結する。東西に広がる公園によって聖十字教会との結びつきは強められる。塔状の部分は，展望台——レンズはベルリンに焦点を合わせる——であると同時に，子供図書館の部分を支持する構造体でもある。旧館をまたぐ子供図書館は，子供たちをこの都市の守護神に押し上げる。横になって本を読めるよう，床は傾斜している。ラチストラスの構造体をサンドブラストのガラスで包み，所々に外を見るためのガラスがはめこまれる。

　打放しコンクリートを主な構造体として，そこに白やアンバーあるいはサンドブラスト処理されたブルーのガラス・カーテンウォールが，鉛やステンレスのパネルより表面を下げて取り付けられる。ベルリンの灰色の空の下で，図書館の照明を滲み出させる東西面は，サンドブラストで刻まれる線やカーテンウォールの方立のパターンによって変化に富んだものになる。内部については，静けさを保つための音響上の配慮が注意深くなされ，同時に自然の素材やくすんだ色彩を選んで静寂と内省的な雰囲気づくりに役立てられる。

I-151

West elevation

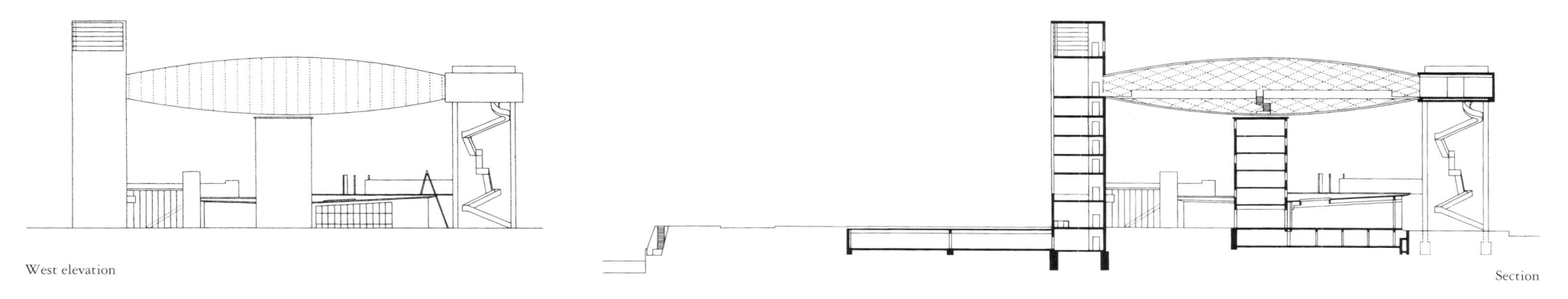

Section

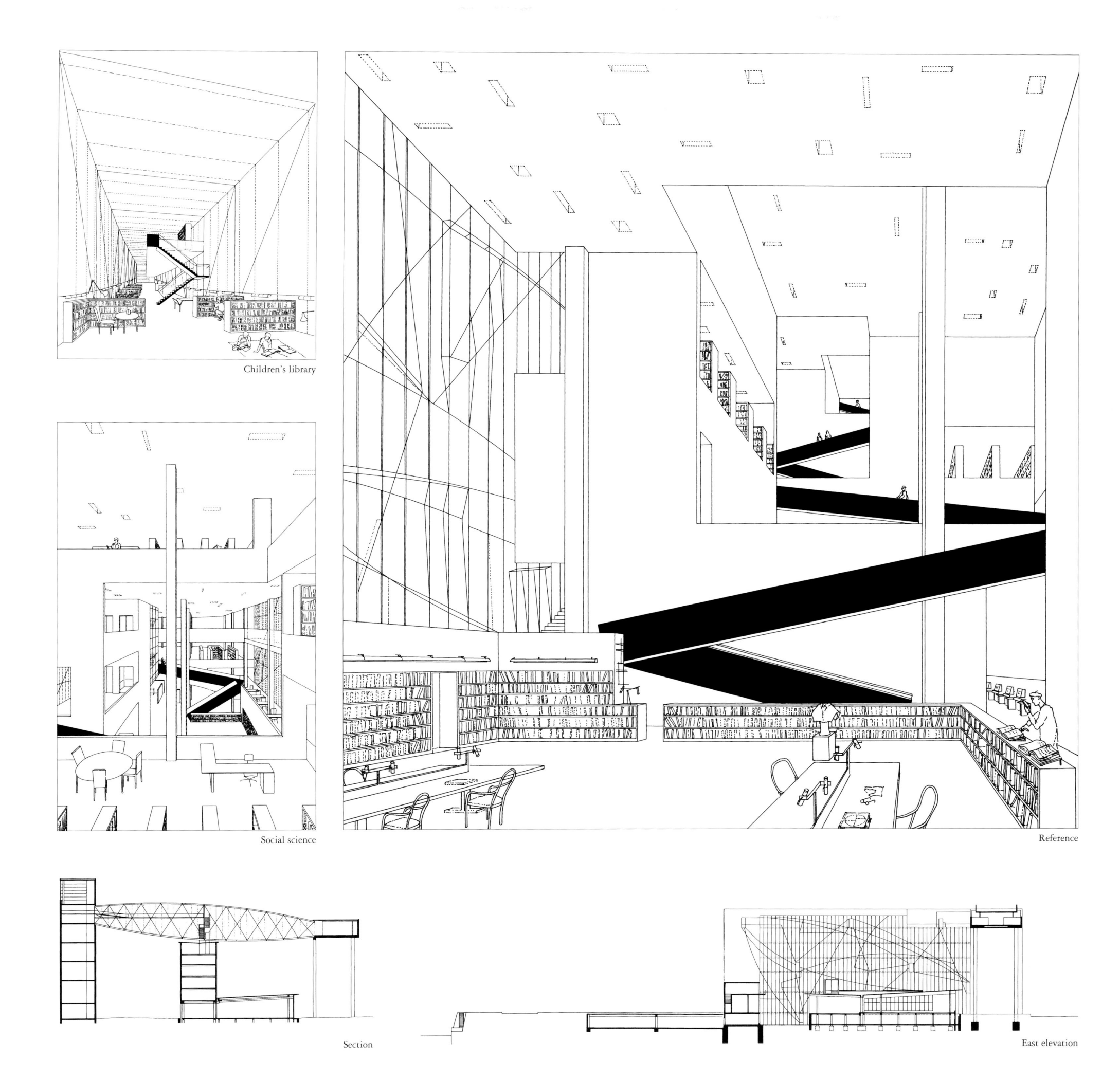

Children's library

Social science

Reference

Section

East elevation

I-153

I-154

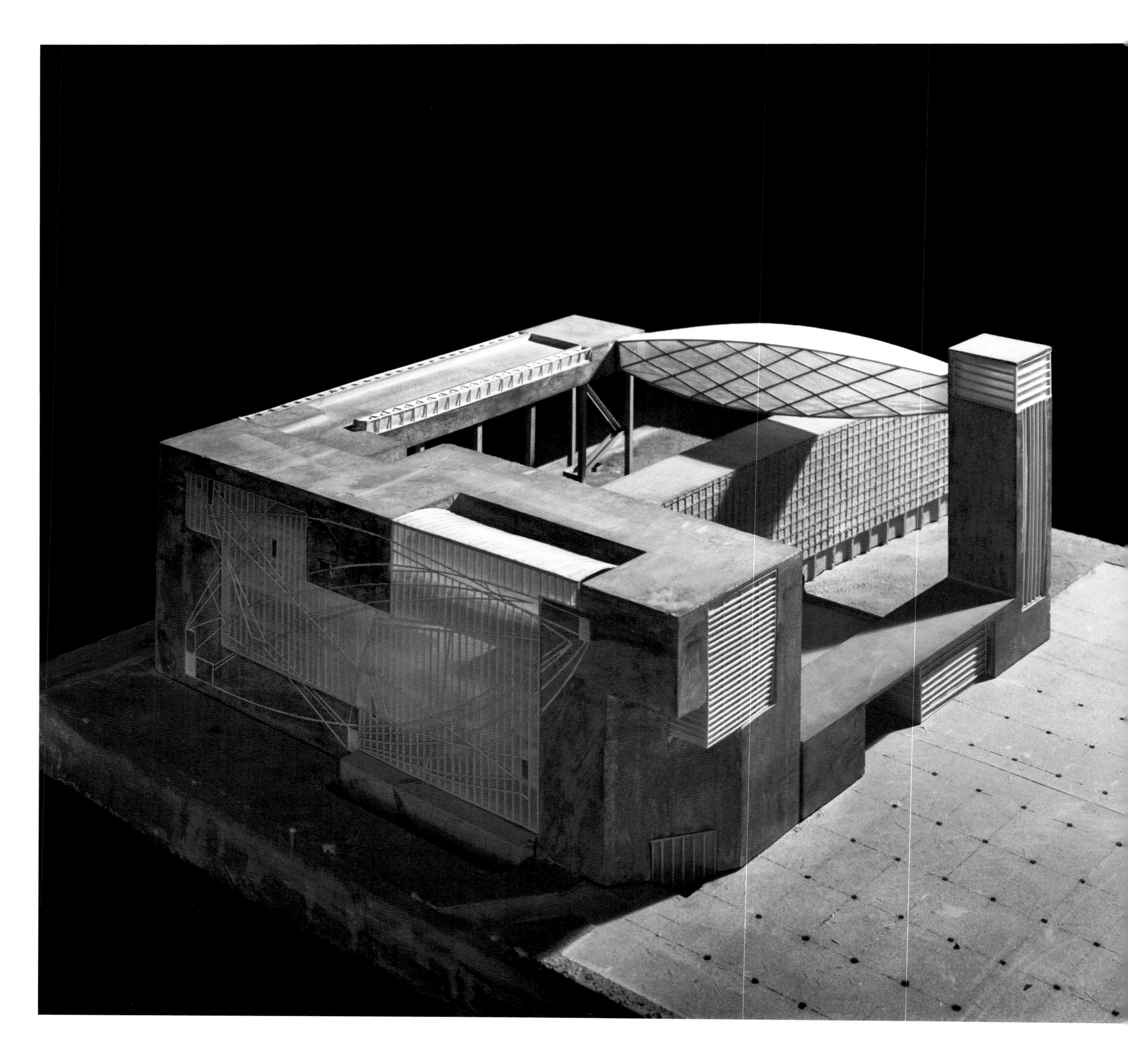

Sketch: section study

Night view

Concept sketch

Sketch: view toward suspended zones

I-155

1988-91 College of Architecture and Landscape Architecture University of Minnesota (early scheme)
Minneapolis, Minnesota, U.S.A.

The site on the University of Minnesota campus is to the north and west of the existing School of Architecture. The existing building (1958, Thorshov and Cemy) is 200 feet square and 29 feet high, with a 100-foot-square central atrium.

The program calls for a 90,000-foot-square addition of studio space, offices, a library, and an auditorium, allowing the Schools of Landscape Architecture and Architecture to be housed in one building.

Two Centers
Analogous to the joining of the architecture and the landscape architecture programs, the new building is formed around two centers: the existing center is a static interior space of hard surfaces; the new center is an elastic exterior space of complex surfaces.

Towers of Light
Shafts of campus space are marked by four masonry towers. Placed at the conjunction of campus routes, these towers mark new entrances to the building. The towers are laboratories of daylight; each captures a different light condition. North, east, west, and south light are variously screened and projected into the upper studios in the towers.

"Figure 8" Promenade
A ramp rising from the north entry through the east wing to the second level of the existing building begins a "figure 8" promenade through the building. This promenade links all major spaces of school, joining the studios on the top with offices, jury rooms, and the library below. The last passages of the promenade take the form of catwalks over the roof of the existing building.

The construction of the addition has a didactic intention, expressing the heavy construction of the towers and lightweight construction of the curving wings. The towers are concrete frame with a concrete-block cavity wall. The curving wings are exposed light-weight steel frame, with steel windows and an aluminum skin.

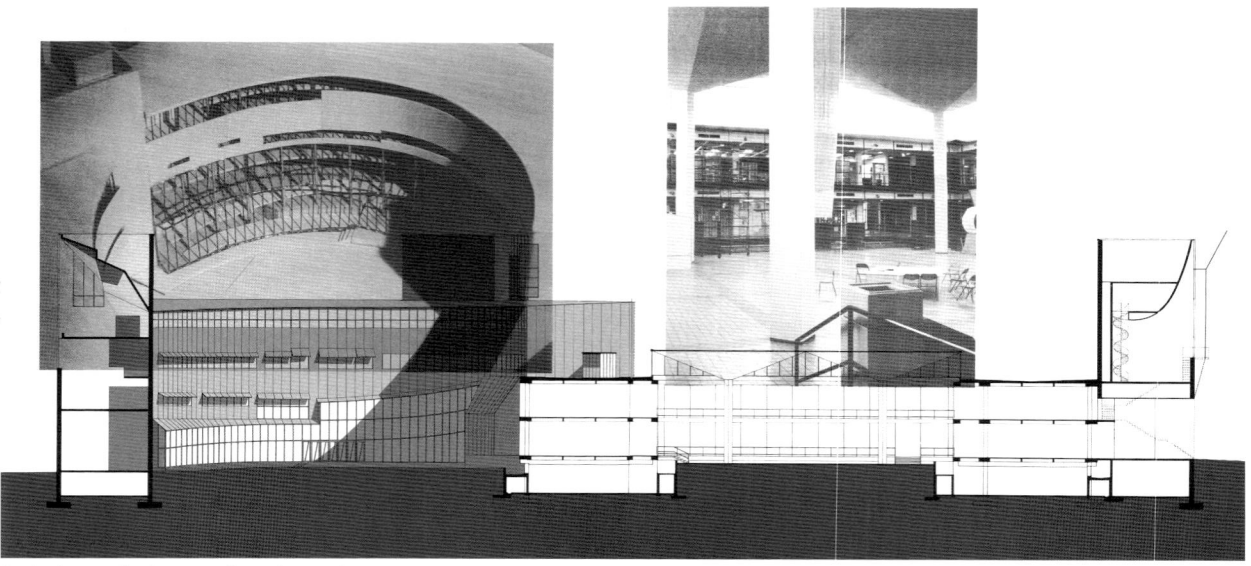

Study: longitudinal section through central axis

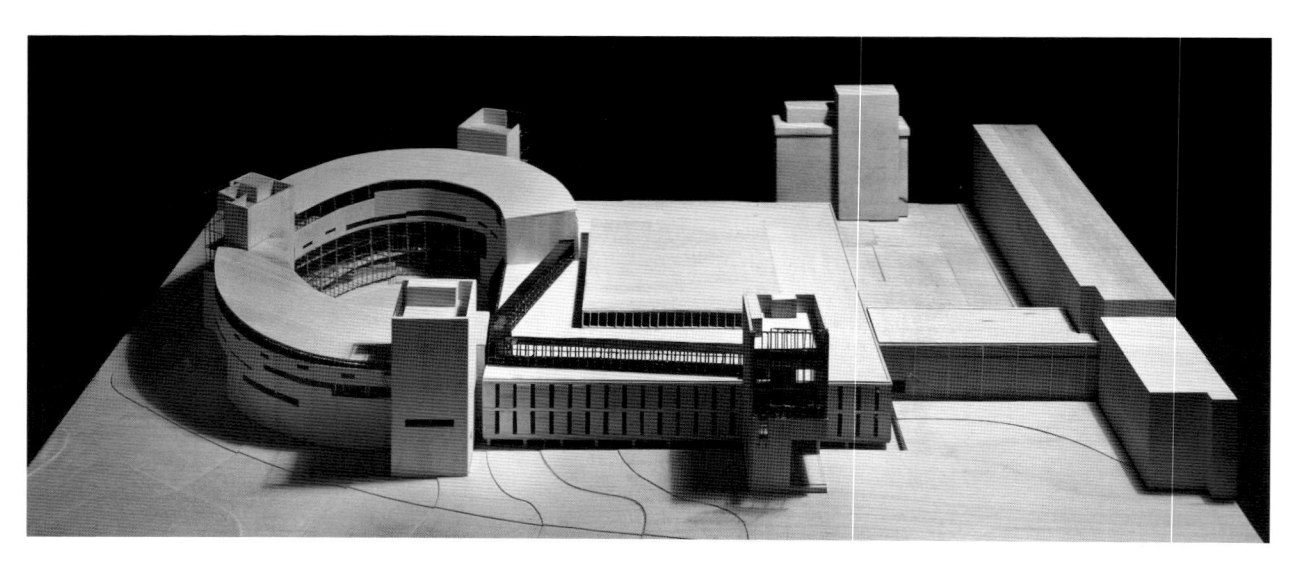

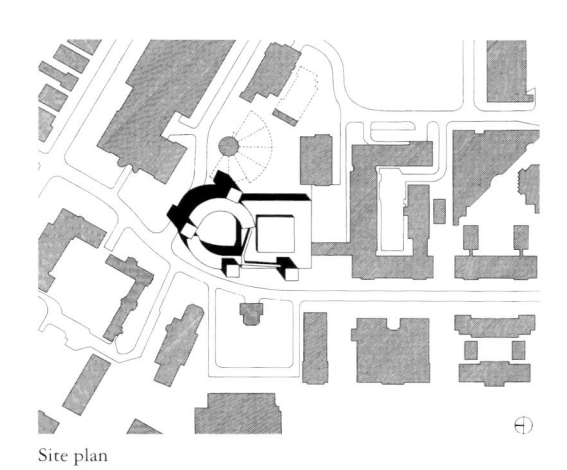

Site plan

1 EXTERIOR GARDEN
2 INTERIOR COURTYARD
3 AUDITORIUM
4 ENTRANCE LOBBY
5 LIBRARY
6 COMMON AREA
7 RESEARCH CENTER
8 STUDIO
9 JURY ROOM
10 FACULTY OFFICES
11 ADMINISTRATION
12 PROMENADE RAMP FROM NORTH ENTRY

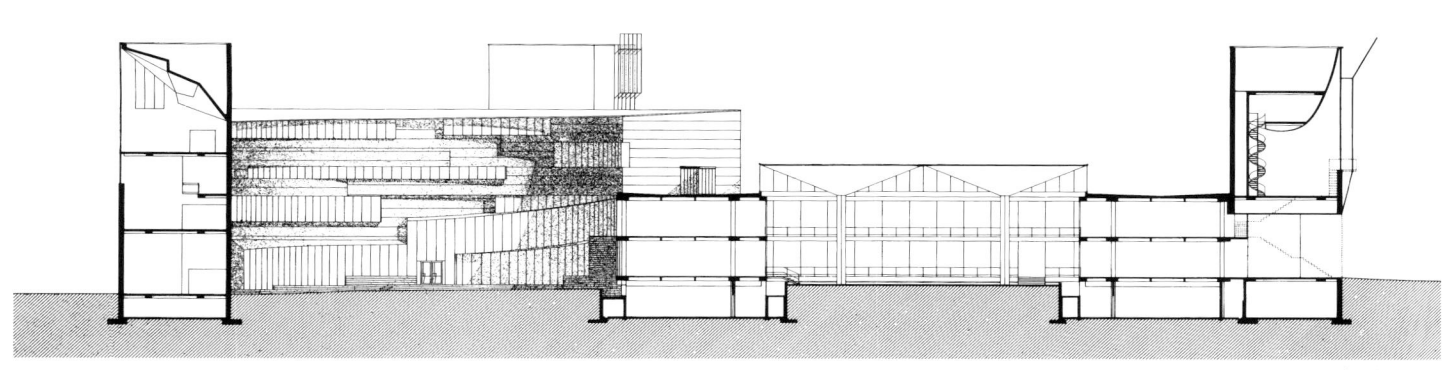

First floor

Second floor

Third floor

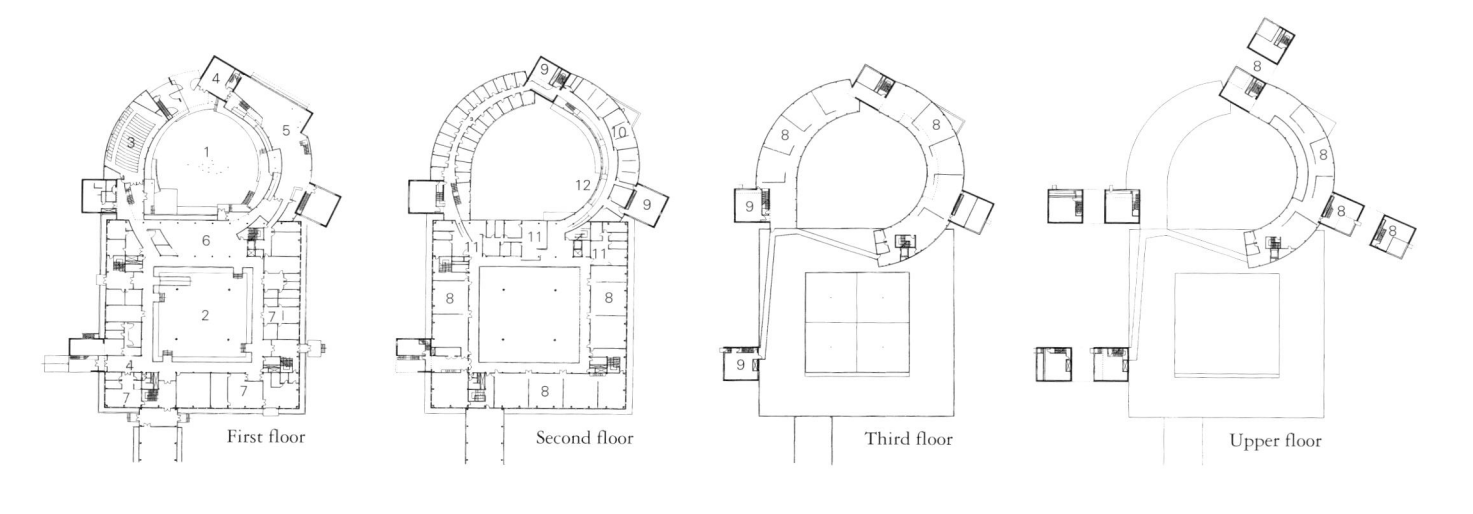

Upper floor

Longitudinal section

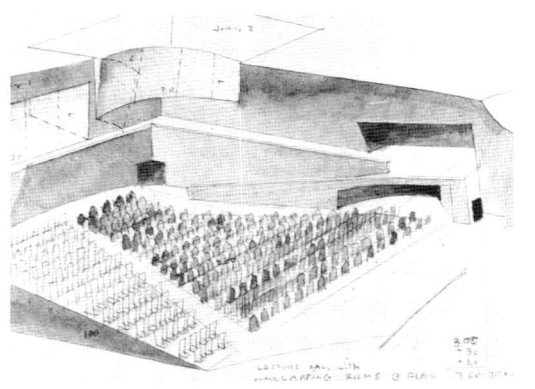

Study sketch: auditorium

Ramp

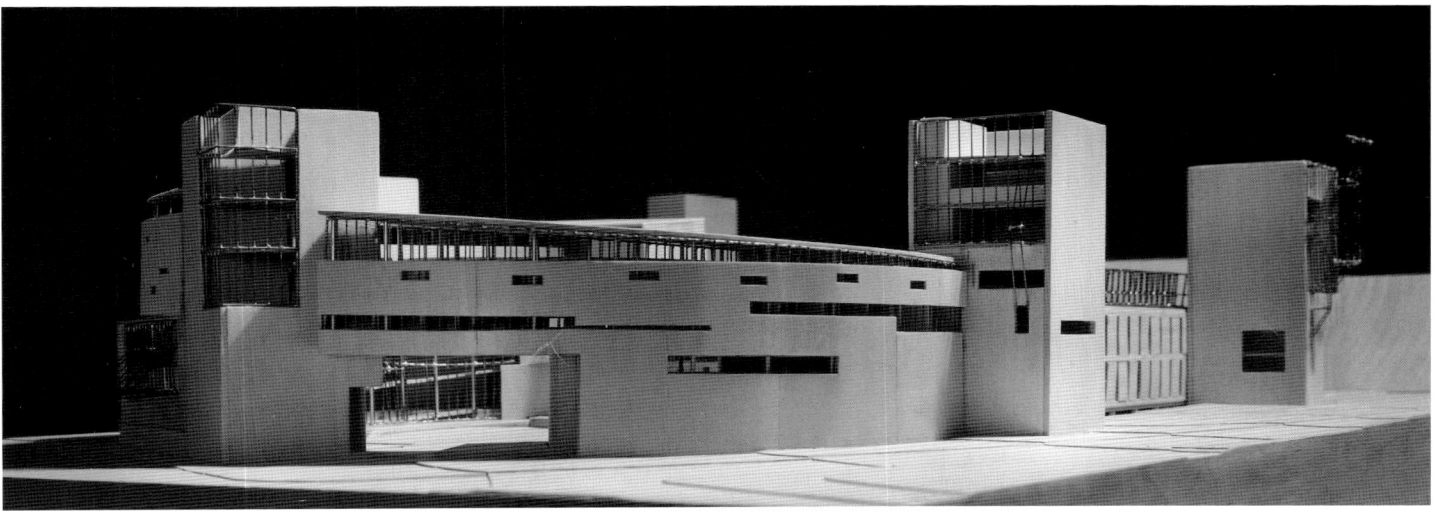

View from northwest

ミネソタ大学建築＋ランドスケープ学部棟（初期案）

ミネソタ大学のキャンパス内にある敷地は，現在の建築学部の北と西にあたる。既存の建物（1958年，ソーショフとシーミーの設計）は200フィート角で高さ29フィート，中央に100フィート角のアトリウムがある。

計画では，90,000平方フィートの増築によって，スタジオ，オフィス，図書館，オーディトリアムを含み，ランドスケープ学部と建築学部を一つの建物に納めるというものである。

［二つの中心］
ちょうど，建築とランドスケープの学部が一緒になるのと同じように，新しい建物は二つの中心の周りにつくられる。既存部の中心は固い表面をもつ静的な内部空間，新しい中心はいろいろな表面を持つ自在な外部空間である。

［光の塔］
キャンパスの空間全体を支える柱のような，組積造の四つの塔がある。キャンパス内の動線の節目に位置するこれらの塔は，建物への新しい入口の印でもある。塔は太陽光の実験室で，それぞれが異なった日射条件にある。北，東，西，南の光をいろいろな形で遮ったり，塔の上部のスタジオに光を当てたりする。

［「8の字型」のプロムナード］
北の入口から入り，東棟を抜けて既存部の2階に達するルートは，建物を巡る8の字型のスロープとなる。このプロムナードは，主要なスペースを結び，最上階のスタジオやオフィス，審査員室，下にある図書館までをつなぎ，最後には，既存建物の上にかかるキャットウォークになる。

増築部の構造は，あえて教育的な意図を表に出した。塔の重い構造と曲線部分の軽い構造を対比的に表現したのである。塔はコンクリートの柱梁にコンクリート・ブロックの壁。円形の棟は鉄骨を露出して，スティールのサッシにアルミの壁である。

1990-91 **Palazzo del Cinema**
Venice, Italy

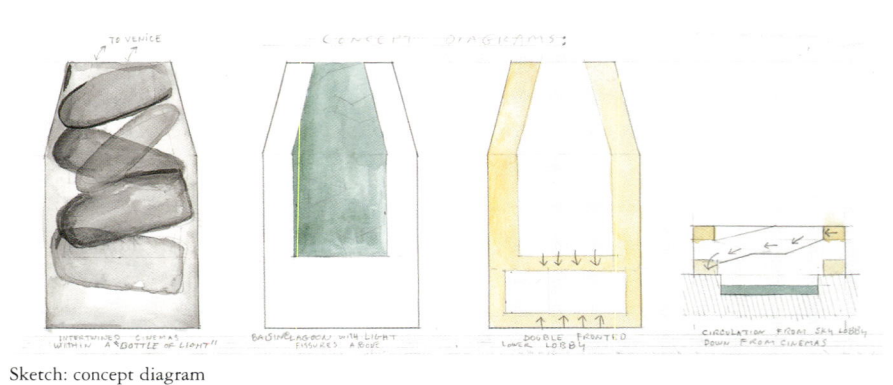

Sketch: concept diagram

Sketch: study of east elevation

Concept sketch

Sketch: lagoon basin

West elevation

Sketch: lagoon basin

Sketch: section through cinema hall

I-159

1	LAGOON BASIN
2	BOAT LANDING
3	MAIN LOBBY
4	UPPER LOBBY
5	PRESS OFFICE
6	CINEMA HALL 1
7	CINEMA HALL 2
8	CINEMA HALL 3
9	CINEMA HALL 4

A-A Section

B-B Section

C-C Section

Level +16.00 m

Level +11.00 m

Level +0.00 m

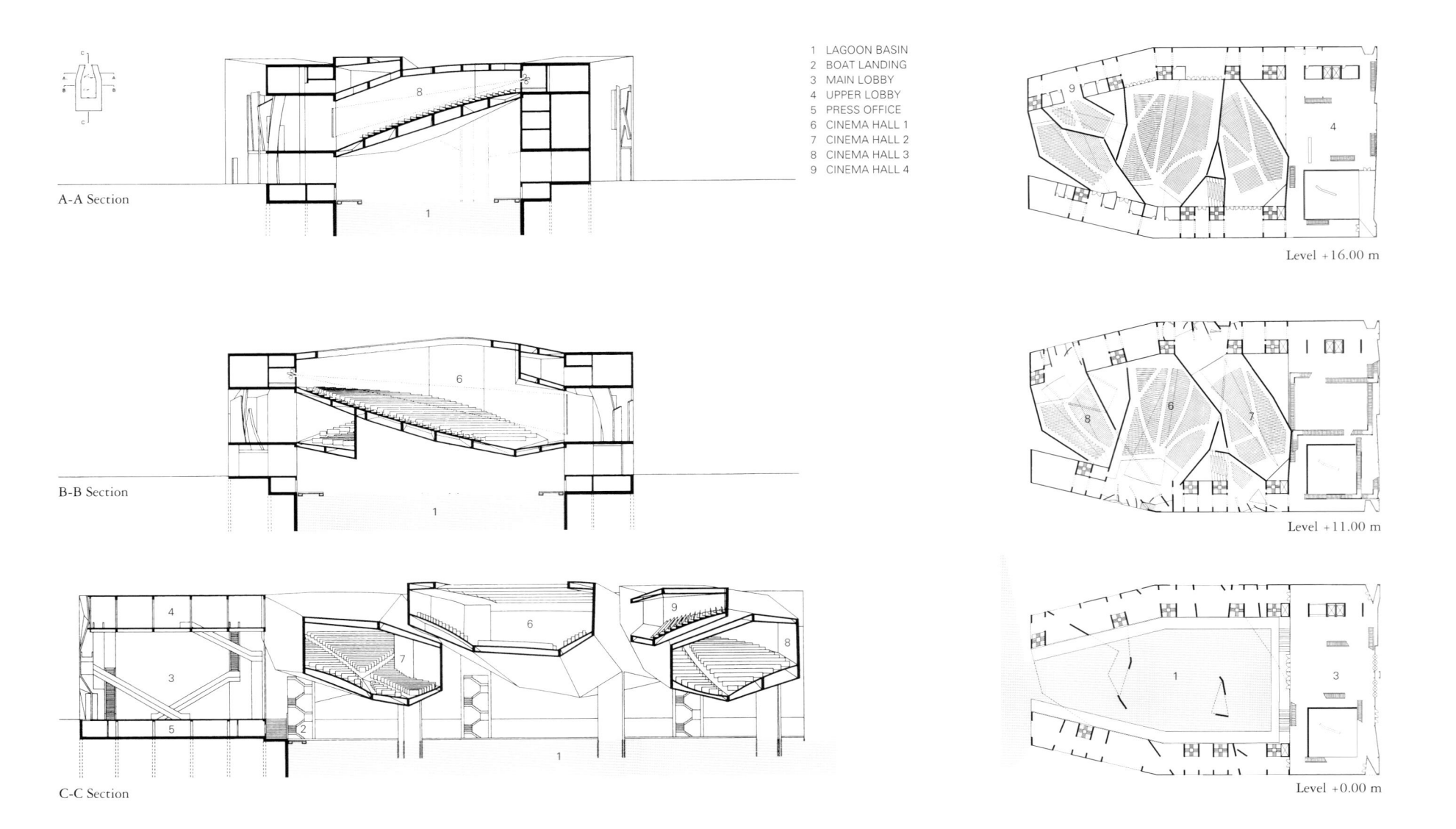

An invited competition for the rebuilding of the Venice Film Festival building on the Lido in Venice. Among the ten invited architects were: Aldo Rossi, Italy; Rafael Moneo, Spain; Sverre Fehn, Norway; James Stirling, U.K., and Jean Nouvel, France. Steven Holl represented the United States.

The connection of the Lido site to Venice by water is emphasized by a grand arrival of space on the lagoon. Filled with diaphanous light from gaps between the cinemas above, this space—a homage to Venice—would also be a place for the Lido community. During the months when there is no cinema festival, this public grotto might have shops along the arcade or marina functions coexisting with the Palazzo del Cinema.

Time in its various abstractions links architecture and cinema. The project involves three interpretations of time and light in space:
1) Collapsed and extended time within cinema is expressed in the warp and extended weave of the building, analogous to cinema's ability to compress (20 years into 1 minute) or extend (4 seconds into 20 minutes) time.
2) Diaphanous time is reflected in sunlight dropping through fissure space between the cinemas into the lagoon basin below. Ripples of water and reflected sunlight animate the grand public grotto.
3) Absolute time is measured in a projected beam of sunlight that moves across the "cubic pantheon" in the lobby.

The projection of light in space, light in reflection, and light in shade and shadow are seen as programs to be achieved parallel to solving functional aspects.

A vessel for "filmic time" and "filmic space," the building's perimeter is bottle-shaped with the mouth open to the lagoon towards Venice. The cinemas interlock within this frame, creating essential crevices and fissures that allow sunlight to the water below. In section, like interlocking hands, the cinemas turn slightly, changing their interior and exterior aspects of space.

The lobby at the end of the covered boat basin joins arrival from the east with arrival from the west. Escalators take ticketed people to the upper level lobby, which has a cafe and a horizontal view of the Adriatic. The escalators pass through the lobby space in sections like the weave of theaters over the lagoon. The main facade of cable-reinforced, sandblasted acrylic responds to this warp and weave.

The main structure is of concrete in "planar" form. Metal formwork for the concrete is retained on the exterior facade. Made of a brass alloy, this metal acquires a red patina.

In some areas the cinema screens can be withdrawn, and the cinema images projected onto warped concrete planes of the structure; the images appear as dissected colors and light on the exterior. The monolithic red patina of the exterior is interrupted by these warped projection zones. Here cinema burns holes in architecture.

Sketch: light through gaps

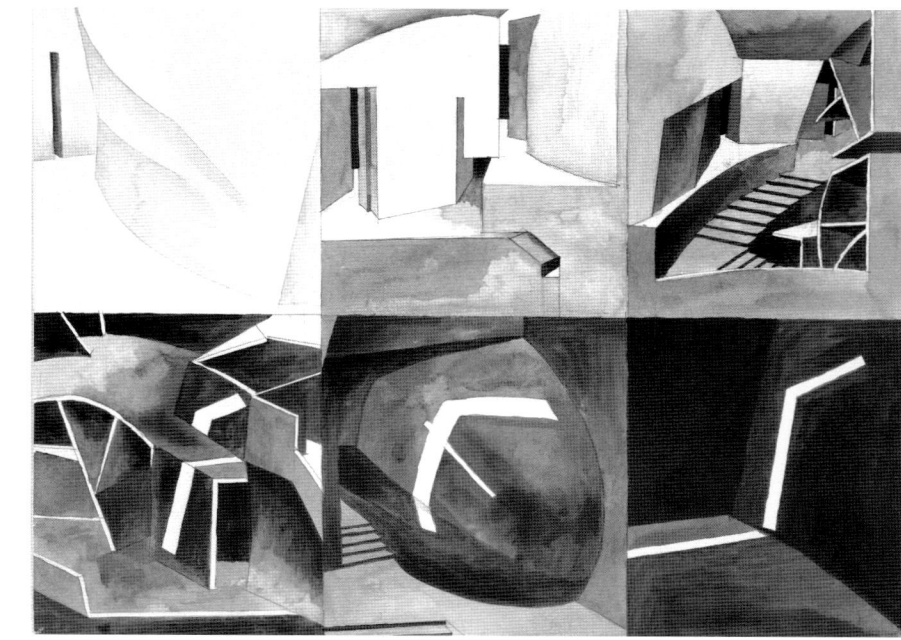

Interior sketches

パラッツォ・デル・チネマ

ヴェネツィアのリド島にあるヴェネツィア映画祭の建物を建て替えるための指名コンペである。指名された10人の中には、イタリアのアルド・ロッシ、スペインのラファエル・モネオ、ノルウェーのスヴェーレ・フェーン、イギリスからジェイムズ・スターリング、フランスのジャン・ヌヴェルなどがいた。スティーヴン・ホールがアメリカを代表することになった。

リド島の大地とヴェネツィアの水による結びつきは、干潟に面する空間に堂々と舟を乗りつけることで強調される。上を覆う映画館の狭間から漏れ落ちる、透けるような光に満たされるこの空間——ヴェネツィアへの賛歌——は、同時にリド島のコミュニティのための場所でもある。映画祭の行われない何ヶ月もの間は、出入り自由な、この岩屋のような空間にはアーケード沿いに店が並んでもいいし、パラッツォ・デル・チネマと併設されるマリーナで利用されるのもいい。

時間をいろいろな形で抽象化するという点で、建築と映画には通じるところがあるのだが、このプロジェクトでは、空間の中の時間と光について三つの解釈がとられている。

1）映画では時間が縮んだり伸びたりするが、それが建築のゆがみや引き伸ばしという形で表現される。それは、時間を圧縮したり(20年を1分に)、伸ばしたり(4秒を20分に)することの可能な映画のアナロジーなのである。

2）稀薄な時間は、映画館の間のすき間から干潟の水面に落ちる日の光に反映される。小波とそれに反映する光が、広い岩屋に生命を吹き込む。

3）絶対的時間は、ロビーの「キュービック・パンテオン」に射しこむ光の移動によって計られる。

空間に鋭く射し込む光、反射光、影の中を舞う微妙な光は、機能的な側面を解決することと平行して考えるべきものとみなした。

「映画のような時間」と「映画のような空間」を満載した船であるこの建築は、外から見ればヴェネツィアの方向に向いて干潟に口を開いた瓶のようでもある。この外殻の中に映画館をいくつも組み合わせて、所々に裂け目や隙間を生じさせ、そこから太陽の光を下の水面に導くのである。断面は、手を組み合わせたような形になっているので、映画館は少しずつ向きを変えながらその内部と外部の空間の様相を変化させる。

建物に覆われた船着場の奥にあるロビーで、東から来る人たちと西から来る人々が一堂に会することになる。入場券を手にした人々はエスカレータで、その上階のロビーへ運ばれる。そこには、水平線に消えるアドリア海を望むカフェがある。このエスカレータは、ロビーの空間を浮かんで上昇し、さながら干潟とその上に浮かぶ映画館とを編みこんでいるようだ。金属線で補強されたアクリルにサンドブラストした正面ファサードは、空間のこのようなねじれを表わしたものだ。

主要な構造体は、「ブラナー」型枠を使ったコンクリートである。金属製の仮枠はそのまま外壁に残される。真鍮の合金でつくられた金属板枠は赤い緑青を生じる。

一部には、映写スクリーンを取り外すと、ねじれたコンクリートの構造壁に映画を映すことができるところがある。色と光が外壁を切り裂いたかのように映像が外壁に映し出されると、大きな塊として見える赤い緑青の外壁には、所々このようなねじれた映写ゾーンが挟みこまれる。ここは、映画が建築にあけた、焦げ穴というわけだ。

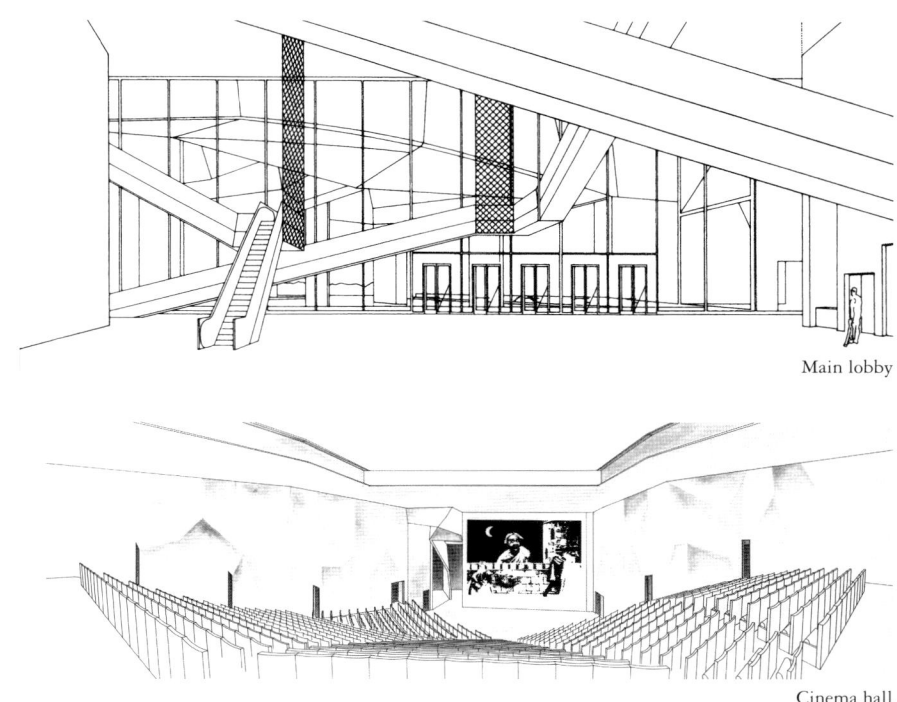

Main lobby

Cinema hall

Main entrance

Cranbrook Institute of Science
1992-99   Bloomfield Hills, Michigan, U.S.A.

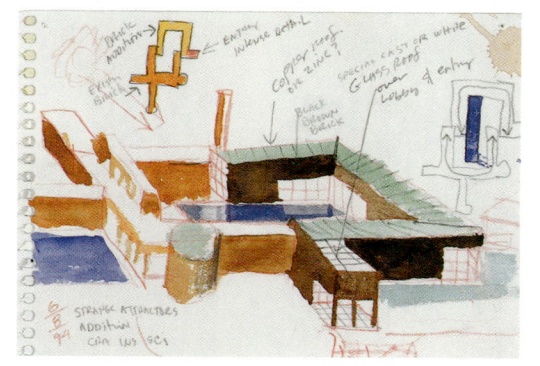

Concept sketch

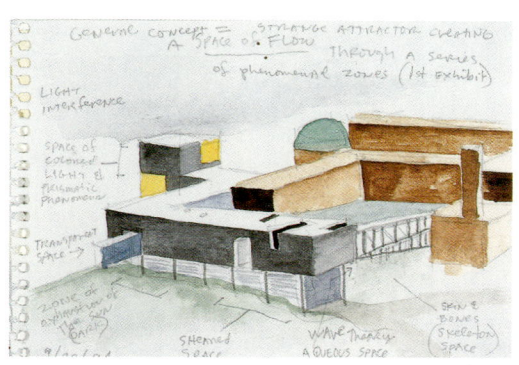

Concept sketch

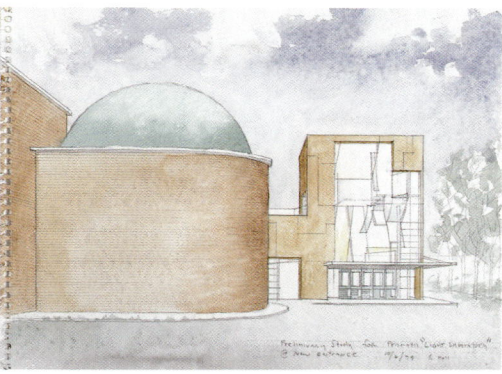

Sketch: entrance

Main entrance

I-163

Science garden

1	SCIENCE GARDEN
2	HOUSE OF ICE
3	EXISTING AUDITORIUM
4	EXISTING MECH/STORAGE
5	AUDITORIUM VESTIBULE
6	LOWER LOBBY
7	MUSEUM SHOP
8	CHANGING EXHIBITION HALL
9	SERVICE VESTIBULE
10	MECHANICAL PLENUM
11	MECHANICAL
12	STORY OF WATER
13	HOUSE OF VAPOR
14	RECEIVING STORAGE
15	EXISTING WORKSHOP
16	EXISTING EXHIBITION HALL
17	LIGHT LABORATORY/ENTRY VESTIBULE
18	LOBBY
19	GARDEN TERRACE
20	LONG TERM EXHIBITION HALL
21	STUDY GALLERY
22	CLOAK ROOM
23	BATHROOM
24	ROOF TERRACE
25	MEZZANINE
26	EXISTING ROOF

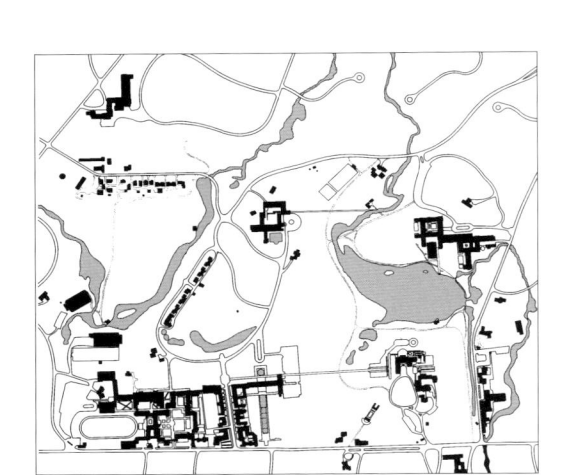

Site plan

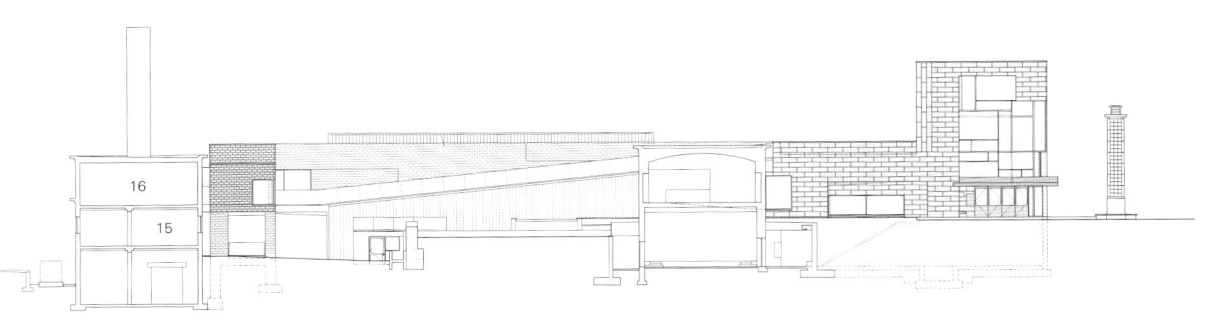

South elevation / Section

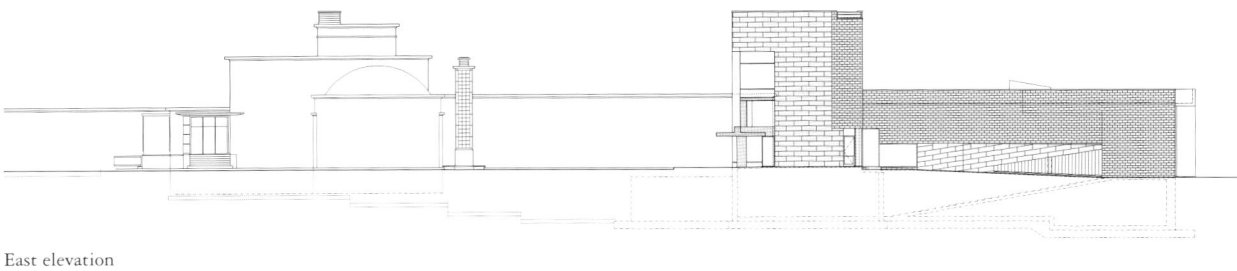

East elevation

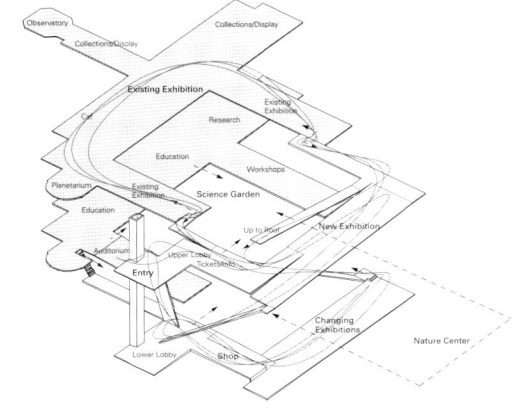

Floor diagram: circulation

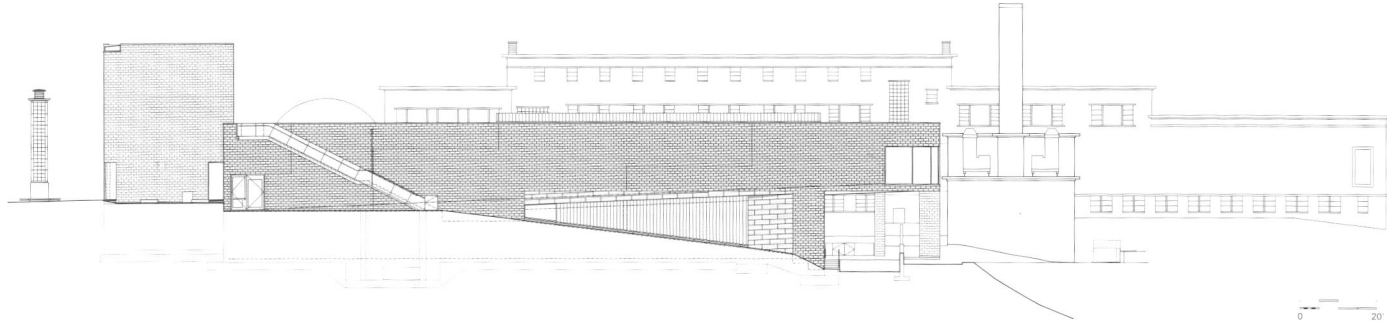

North elevation

Roof

First floor

Ground floor

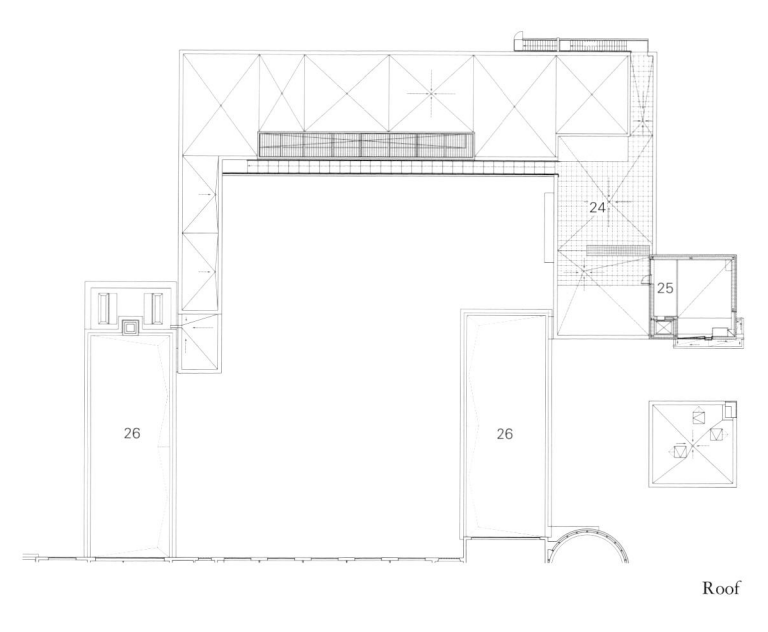

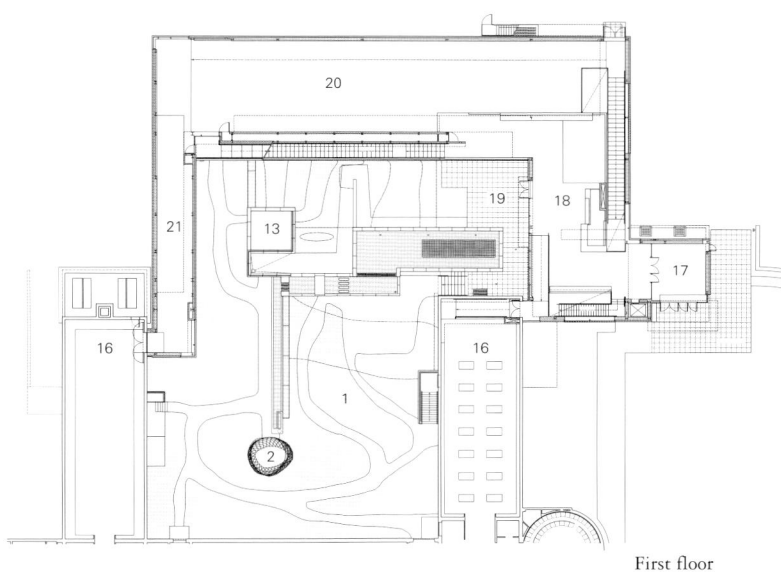

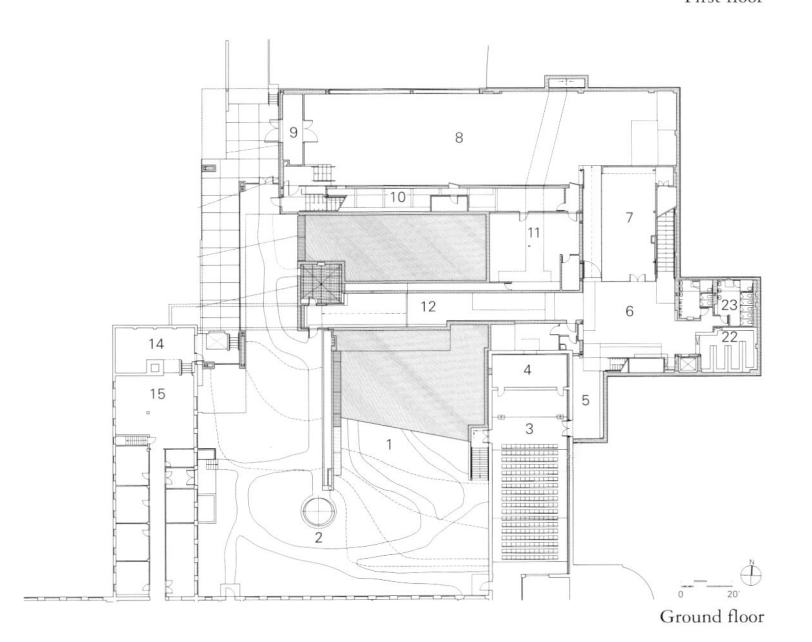

Pool at garden terrace: view toward lobby

Site Strategy
The bracketing and shaping of exterior spaces with buildings which characterizes the Cranbrook campus is continued in our addition to the Cranbrook Institute of Science. Our aim is to make the least intrusion on the architecture of the original Saarinen building while maximizing the potential for circulation and visiting experiences with the addition.

The new inner garden has a gently sloping and folding connection to the exterior campus grade. At the northwest corner the new addition passes above the ground, allowing a "permeable" campus grade connection which provides orientation to garden exhibits, and an open and inviting feeling.

An axis called "Stairway of Inexplicables" is formed from the new entry, roughly parallel to the existing "Ramp of the Chinese Dog." This new line of view and movement connects the Institute to existing nature trails along the sloping ground to the east.

Building Concept
The new addition opens up the dead end circulation of the existing 1937 galleries; the Hall of Minerals and the Hall of Man. A slipped "U" shape, like the scientific diagram for "Strange Attractors," allows for multiple paths within the exhibitions and other programs of the Institute. The term "Strange Attractors" (by the meteorologist Edward Lorenz) has both geometric and experiential potential. With this concept as an analog, we aim for a free and open-ended addition which can easily adapt to change. It has unique qualities in its various circuits and routes which allow for the potential that no visit to the new science museum will be a repeat experience. Each engagement is provocative and unpredictable.

The new Institute is centered around an inner garden where scientific phenomena are exhibited in the open air. Within this "Science Garden" is the Story of Water; water in liquid, solid and vapor is featured in flow pools, a "House of Ice," and a "House of Vapor." Upon entering, and throughout the exhibition loops, views of the science garden orient the museum visitor.

A new entry lobby forms a "Light Laboratory" with a south-facing wall of many types of glass. Different phenomena of light such as refraction and prismatic color are displayed on the lobby walls as the sunlight changes.

The basic structure of the addition is formed of steel truss frame spanned in pre-cast concrete planks which carry services and distribute air in their hollow cores. The exterior is clad in yellow Kasota Stone at the entry elevation, but gradually it changes to integral color concrete block on the North. The relation of stone to block is analogous to "phase space" which is a property of Strange Attractors.

Science garden

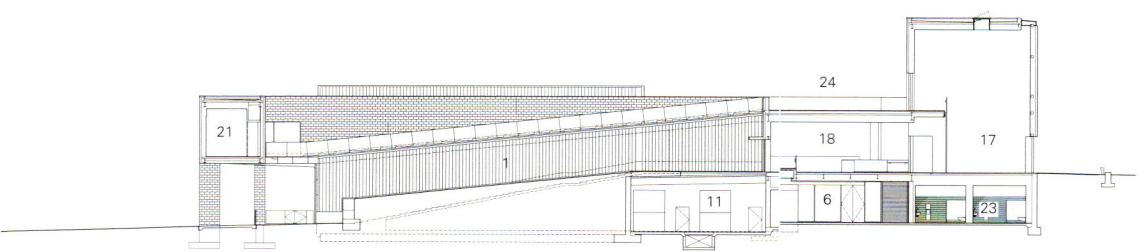

Section through Science garden, looking north

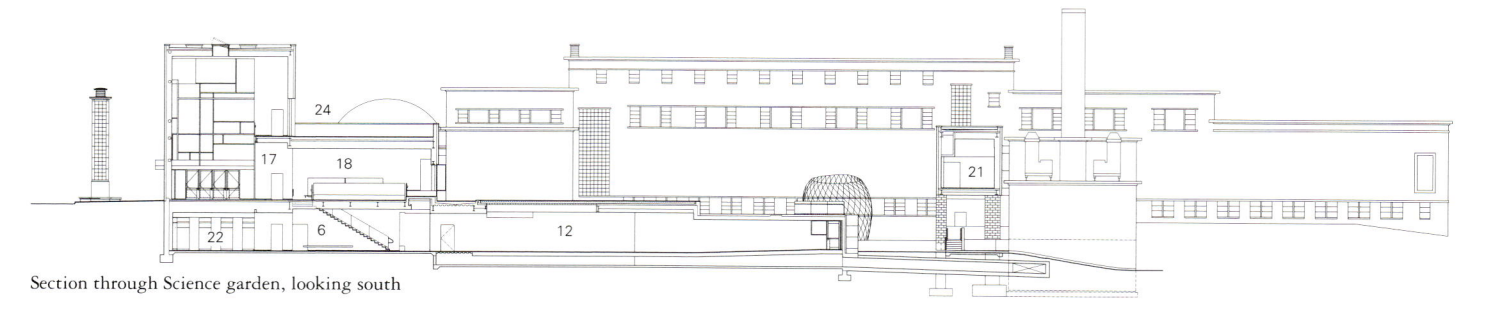

Section through Science garden, looking south

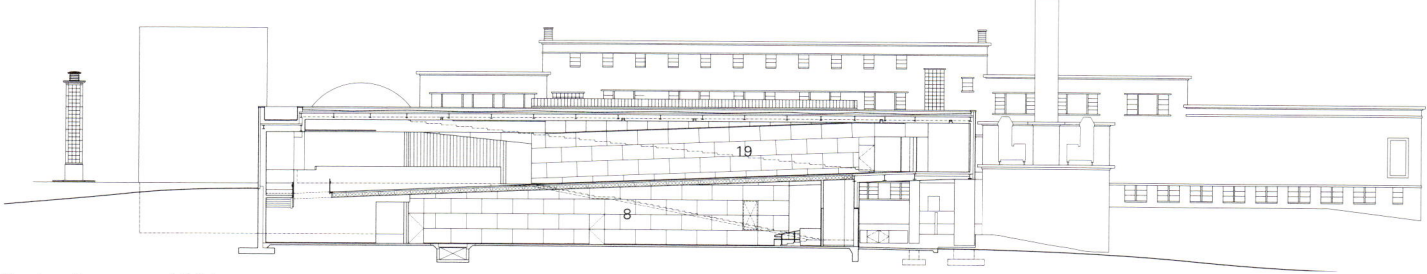

Section along new exhibition spaces

I-166

House of ice

Science garden

House of vapor

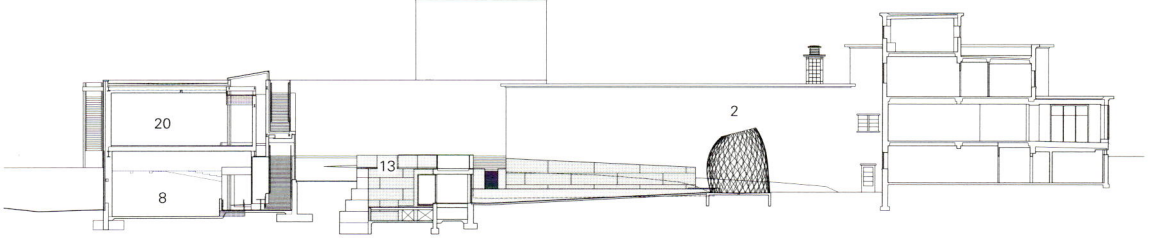

Section through Science garden, looking east

I-167

Entrance hall: "light laboratory"

"Light laboratory"

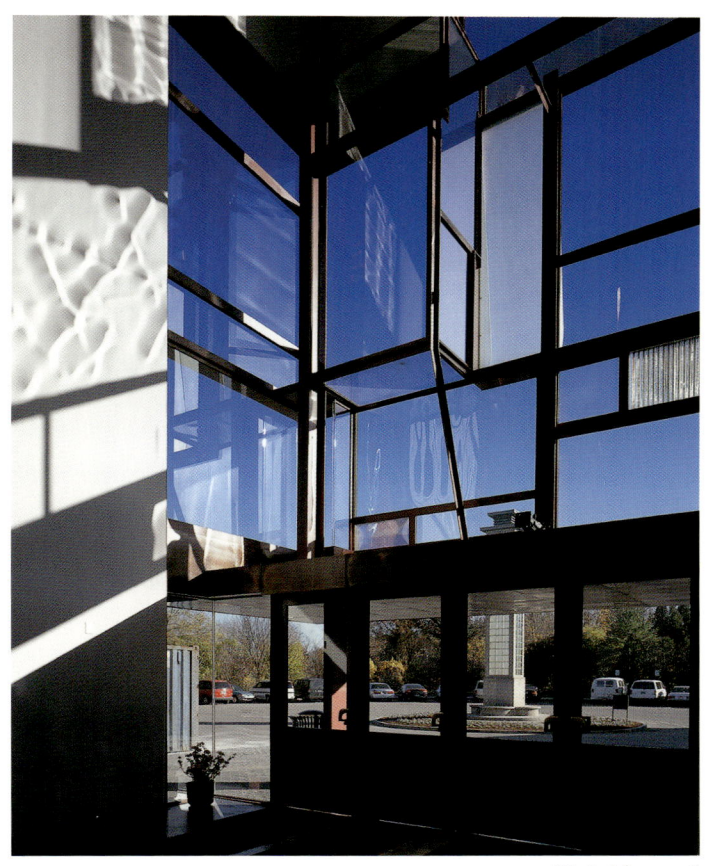

View toward garden terrace from lobby

Lobby

Staircase to lower lobby

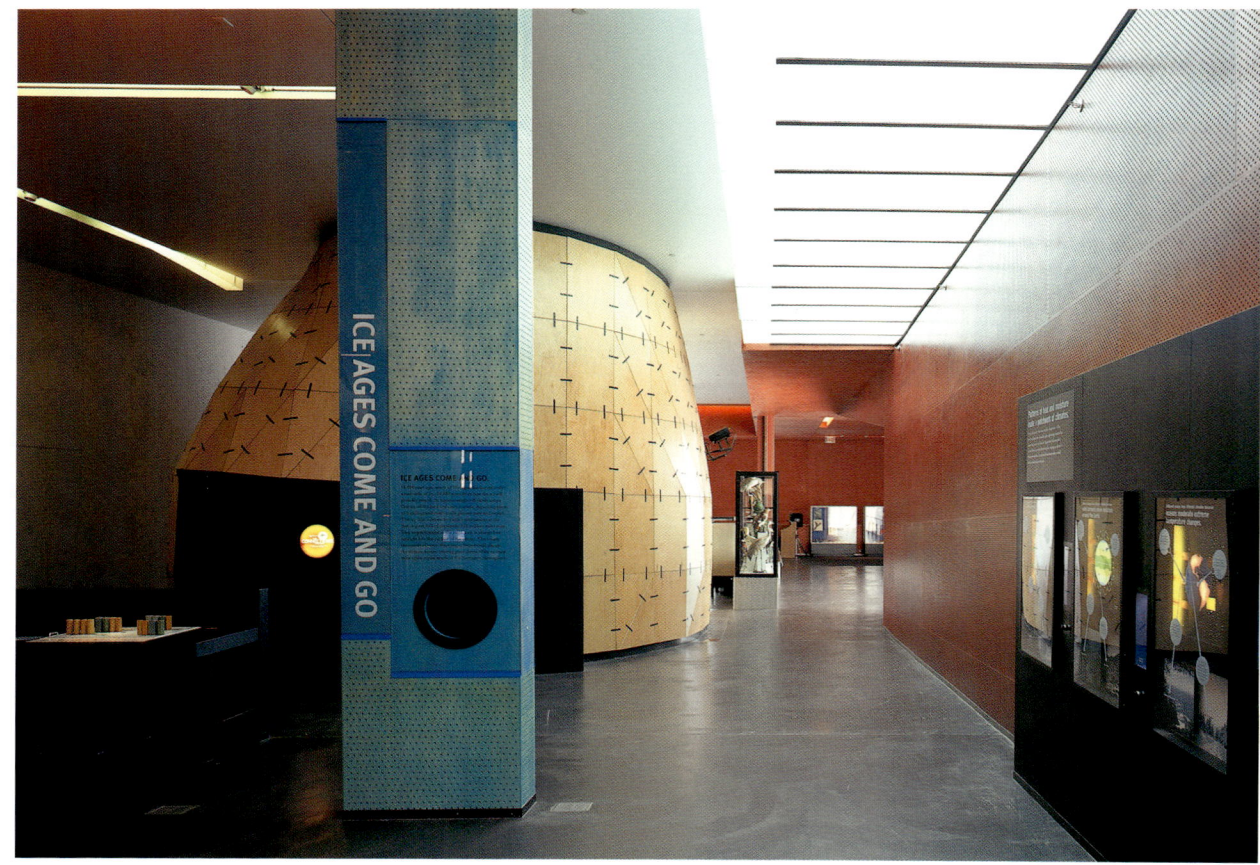

Long term exhibition hall

クランブルック科学研究所
[敷地に対するストラテジー]
クランブルック・キャンパスの特徴である,建物によって外部空間を挟みながら形成していく方法は,クランブルック科学研究所に対する増築においても継続されている。われわれの目的は,オリジナルの建物であるサーリネン設計の棟に対する侵犯を最小限に抑えながら,増築部による動線構成の可能性,つまりそこを訪れることで得られる体験の豊かさを最大限に高めることである。

新しく構成された内庭は,緩やかに傾斜し,その外に広がるキャンパスへつながって行く。北西角部で,新たな増築部は地盤を離れて上方を延びて行くので,そこから,キャンパスとの「透過性をもった」接続部が生まれ,庭園内の展示への方向性が提示され,開かれ,迎え入れる雰囲気がつくりだされる。

「不可解な階段」と呼ばれる軸線が,既存の「中国犬の斜路」とほぼ平行して新しいエントランスを起点に形成される。眺望と動線を提供するこの新しい軸線によって,建物は東に傾斜する地盤に沿って延びる自然の小道と結びつけられる。

[建物をめぐるコンセプト]
この度の増築では,1937年につくられたギャラリー——「鉱物のホール」と「人類のホール」の,行き止まりで閉じられていた動線を開放する。「ストレンジ・アトラクターズ」(気象学者,エドワード・ローレンツの用語)のための科学的ダイアグラムに似た,解き放たれたU形は,展覧会や学校主宰によるその他の企画が行われる際に,多様な道筋をとることを可能とする。ストレンジ・アトラクターズは幾何学的および経験的な可能性を共に備えている。ストレンジ・アトラクターズと相似するコンセプトによって,変化に簡単に対応できる自由でオープンエンドな増築を行うことが設計目標である。多様な回路や順路によって,この新しい科学研究所を訪れることが,反復的な経験にはならないように特別な性格をもたせること。訪れる一回一回が,興味深く,意外性に満ちたものとなるようにすること。

新しい建物は,科学現象が野外に展示されている内庭を中心に構成されている。この「サイエンス・ガーデン」に展示されているのは,いわば水の物語である。液体,個体,気体の状態にある水が,流れるプール,「氷の家」,「蒸気の家」というかたちで提示されている。エントランスから,そして展示回路のどこからでも見えるこのサイエンス・ガーデンが,来館者を導いて行く。

新しいエントランス・ロビーは,さまざまなタイプのガラスをはめた南面する壁をもつ「光の実験室」を形成する。日射しの変化につれて,屈折や虹色など,光のさまざまな現象がロビーの壁に見られる。

増築部の基本構造は,プレキャスト・コンクリートに,スティール・トラス・フレーム架構。コンクリート・コアの中空部にはサービスや給排気管が通っている。外壁は,エントランス廻りは黄色のカソタ・ストーンで被覆されているが,北に向かって徐々に,カラー・コンクリート・ブロックに変化する。こうした,石からブロックへと引き継がれて行く関係は,ストレンジ・アトラクターズの領域である「位相空間」に似たものとなる。

Detail of column and bench

Long term exhibition hall

1994-97 **Chapel of St. Ignatius, Seattle University**
Seattle, Washington, U.S.A.

View from south: entrance on left

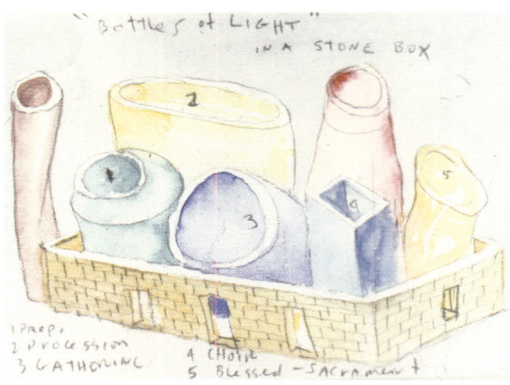

Concept sketch: "Bottles of Light" in a Stone Box

Concept sketch

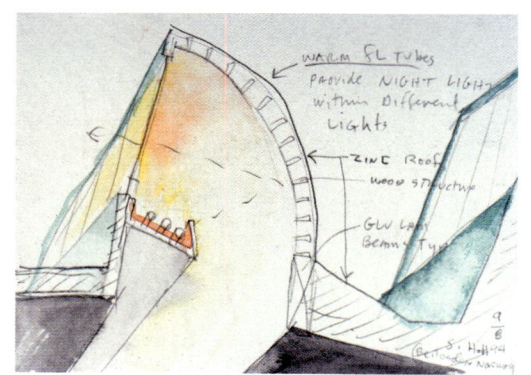

Sketch: roof detail

View from southwest

Site plan

View from southeast

View from lobby toward bell tower

I-173

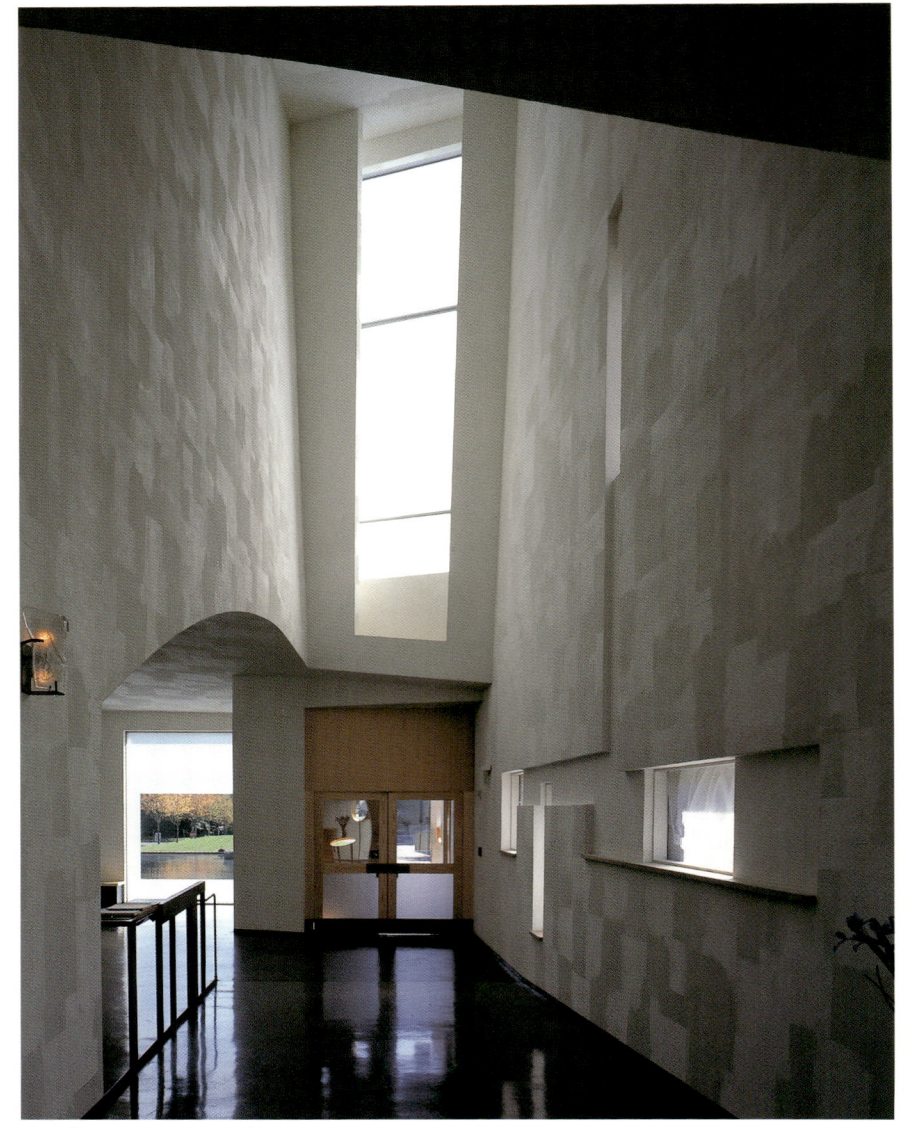

View from procession toward entrance

Narthex

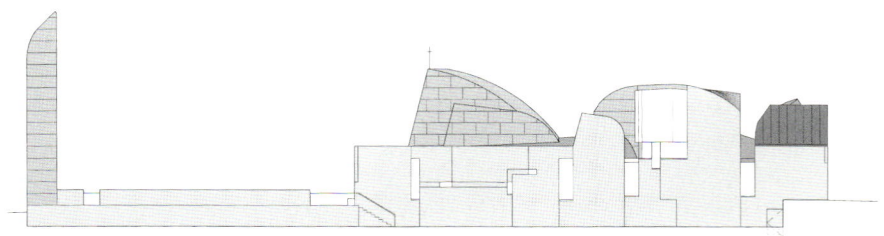

East elevation

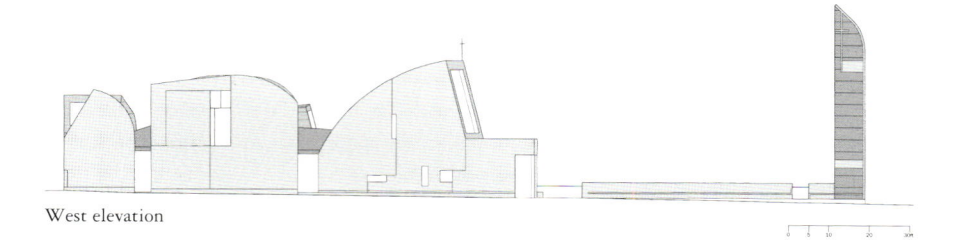

West elevation

1 ENTRANCE
2 PROCESSION (ramp)
3 NARTHEX (lobby)
4 ENTRY TO NAVE
5 PEWS
6 ALTAR
7 VESTING SACRISTY
8 BRIDE'S ROOM
9 RECONCL CHAPEL
10 BAPTISTRY
11 BLESSED SACRAMENT CHAPEL

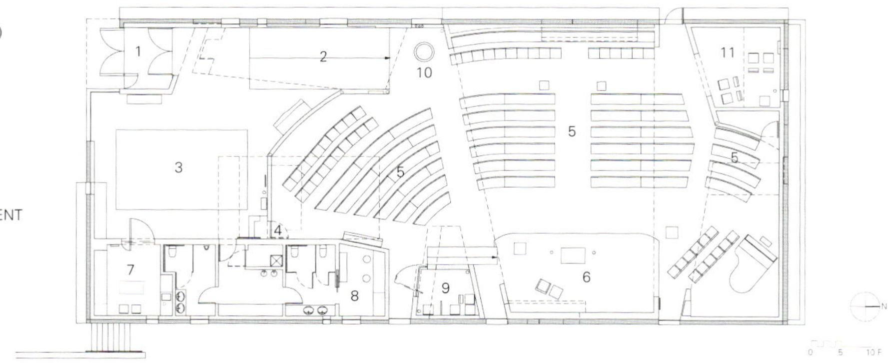

Plan

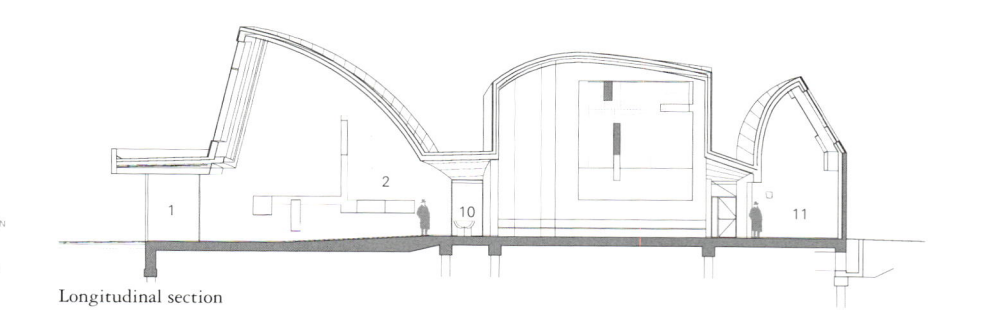

Longitudinal section

Narthex: door to nave

In the Jesuits "spiritual exercises", no single method is prescribed—"different methods helped different people...".

Here a unity of differences is gathered into one. The light is sculpted by a number of different volumes emerging from the roof. Each of these irregularities aims at different qualities of light. East facing, South facing, West and North facing, all gather together for one united ceremony.

Each light volume corresponds to a part of the program of Jesuit Catholic worship. The south-facing light corresponds to the procession, a fundamental part of the mass. The city-facing north light corresponds to the Chapel of the Blessed Sacrament and to the mission of outreach to the community. The main worship space has a volume of east and west light. The concept of Different Lights is further developed in the dialectic combination of a pure colored lens and a field of reflected color within each light volume.

A baffle is constructed opposite the large window of each "bottle of light." Each of the baffles is back painted in a bright color; only the reflected color can be seen from within the chapel. This colored light pulses with life when a cloud passes over the sun. Each bottle combines the reflected color with a colored lens of the complementary color. At night, which is the time of gatherings for mass in this university chapel, the light volumes shine in all directions out across the campus like colored beacons. On occasion, for those in vigilant prayer, light will shine throughout the night. The visual phenomena of complementary colors can be experienced by staring at a blue rectangle and then a white surface. One will see a yellow rectangle; this complimentarily contributes to the two-fold merging of concept and phenomena in the chapel.

The concept of "Seven Bottles of Light in a Stone Box" is expressed through the tilt-up method of construction. The integral color tilt-up concrete slab provides a more direct and economical tectonic than stone veneer. The building's outer envelope is divided into 21 interlocking concrete panels cast flat on the chapel's floor slab and on the reflecting pond slab. Over the course of two days these panels were put in place by a hydraulic crane, which strained at the ponderous weights of up to 80,000 lbs. "Pick pockets," or hooks inset into the panels were capped with bronze covers once the panels were upright. Windows were formed as a result of the interlocking of the tilt-up slabs, allowing the 5/8" open slab joint to be resolved in an interlocking detail.

The chapel is sited to form a new campus quadrangle green space to the north, the west, and in the future, to the east. The elongated rectangular plan is especially suited to defining campus space as well as the processional and gathering space within. Directly to the south of the chapel is a reflecting pond or "thinking field."

Nave: view toward altar through pews

Nave with natural light through slits

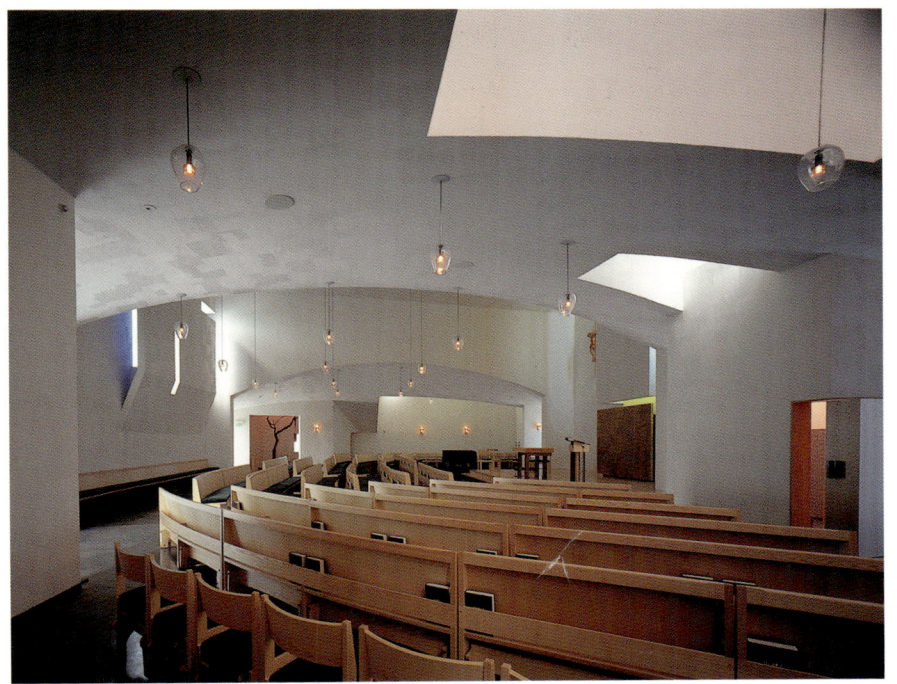

Nave: view toward north

Nave: view toward south. Altar (left) and pews (right)

I-177

Blessed Sacrament Chapel

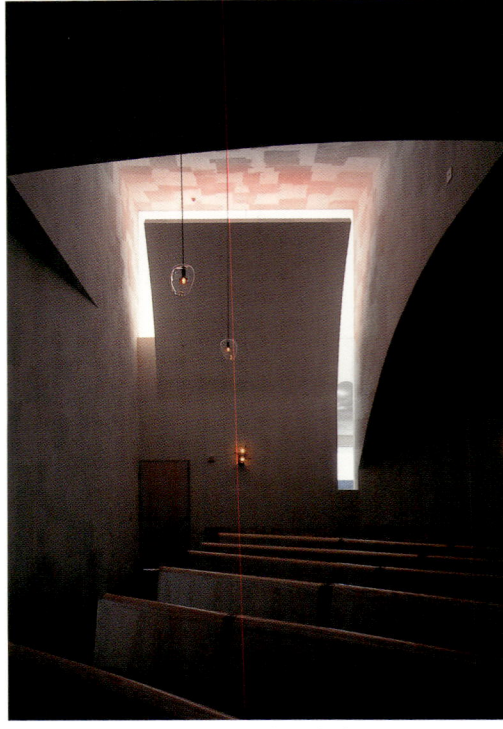

Pendent lamp and natural light through slits

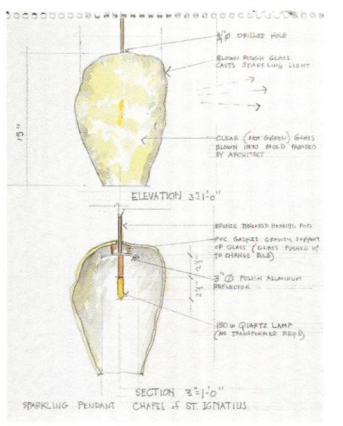

Sketch: lighting fixtures

View toward altar with natural light through windows behind

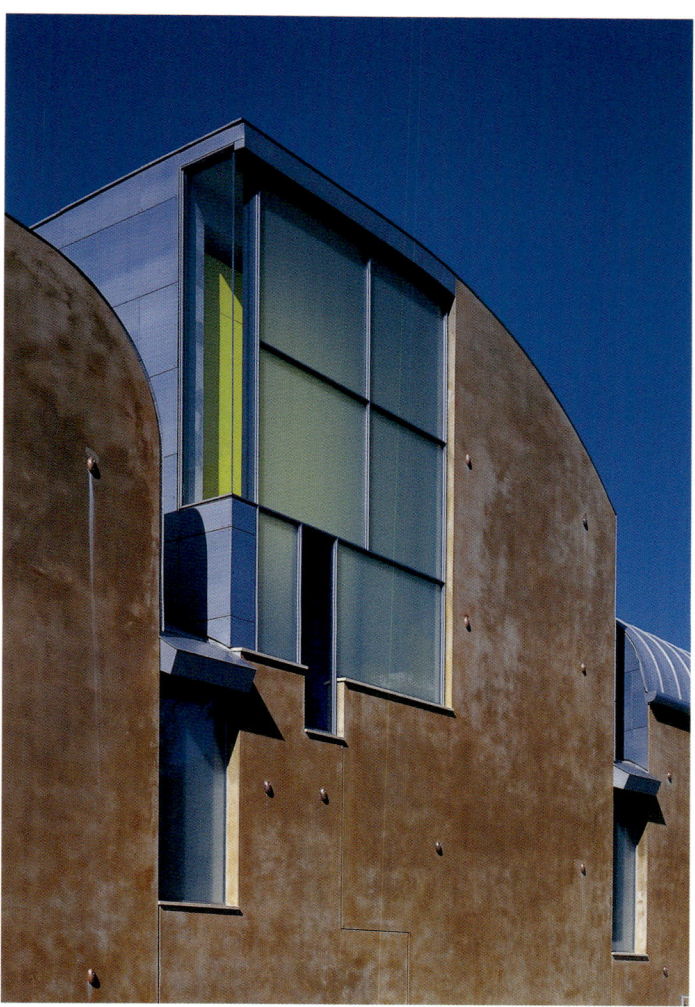

Windows of altar

シアトル大学聖イグナティウス礼拝堂

イエズス会の「霊的修養」には、あらかじめ定められた方法論がない。「救済はそれぞれの人に用意されている…」。

ここには差異の調和がひとつに集められている。光は屋根から生まれた幾つもの異なるヴォリュームによって彫刻される。各々のヴォリュームが不規則なのは、異なる光を引き入れるためである。東西南北のそれぞれの壁面は全て祝福のため、ひとつに集められる。

各々の光のヴォリュームはイエズス会のカトリック礼拝のプログラムに相当している。南ファサードの光はミサの基礎となる聖体行列に相当する。市街に面した北ファサードからの光は、聖体礼拝堂と地域コミュニティへの奉仕活動に相当する。主礼拝室にあるのは東西の光のヴォリュームである。純粋な着色レンズと、各々の光のヴォリュームのなかで反射する光の場との弁証法的結びつきのなかに、差異化する光という構想がより一層深く追求される。

各々の「光のボトル」の大ウィンドウの向かいには隔壁が立てられる。それぞれの隔壁は鮮やかな色で背後が塗装されている。教会の中からはその反射光の色のみが見える。群衆が太陽の前を通り過ぎる度に光の色は生きているように脈動する。各々のボトルは反射光の色と着色レンズの補色を組み合わせたものである。夜、大学教会のミサや集会の時間になると、キャンパス中のあらゆる場所を灯台のように光で照らす。夜を徹した礼拝に来る人々のために、時として一晩中光が灯される。青色の長方形から白色の表面に凝視した視線を移すと、補色の視覚的効果を経験することができる。目にする黄色の長方形もまた、教会の思想と現象の両義的融合を補完している。

「石の箱に収められた七つの光のボトル」という構想は、ティルトアップ工法による建設工程を通して表現される。着色された完全なティルトアップ・コンクリートは化粧貼りの石と比べて直接的、経済的な構造である。建築の外形となるのは教会の床とリフレクティング・プールの両方のスラブの上で平滑に打設された、21枚からなるインターロッキング・コンクリートパネルである。80,000ポンド(約36 t)の荷重を2日間かけて吊り上げ、これらのパネルは油圧クレーンで所定の位置に設置された。パネルが垂直に建てられると、パネルの「ピックポケット」と呼ばれるフックはブロンズ製のカバーで覆われた。スラブのオープンジョイントは5/8インチ(約1.6cm)である。この接合ディテールを解決するために、開口部はティルトアップ・スラブを組み合わせて構成された。

この教会は北と西、そして将来は東へと、新しいキャンパスの中庭に緑の空間を形成するように配置されている。細長い長方形の平面計画は特にキャンパスの空間だけでなく、内部で行われる聖体行列や集会にも適している。教会の南側に直接面しているのは、「黙想の場」と呼ばれるリフレクティング・プールである。

1994-2009 **Knut Hamsun Center**
Hamarøy, Norway

Northwest view

Fourth floor

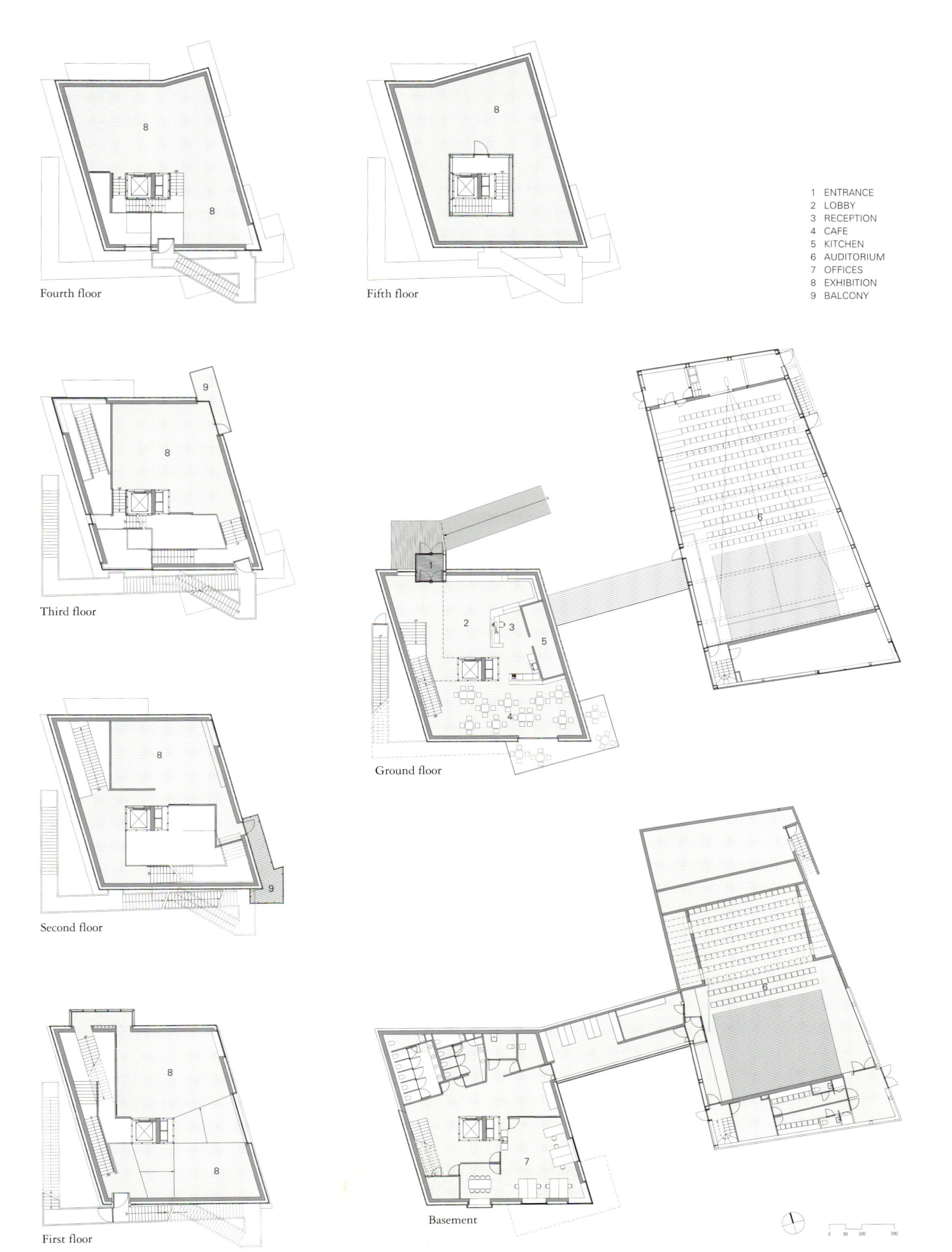

Fifth floor

1	ENTRANCE
2	LOBBY
3	RECEPTION
4	CAFE
5	KITCHEN
6	AUDITORIUM
7	OFFICES
8	EXHIBITION
9	BALCONY

Third floor

Ground floor

Second floor

First floor

Basement

Knut Hamsun, Norway's most inventive twentieth-century writer, fabricated new forms of expression in his first novel Hunger. He went on to found a truly modern school of fiction with his works Pan, Mysteries, and Growth of the Soil. This center dedicated to Hamsun is located above the Arctic Circle near the village of Presteid of Hamarøy near the farm where the writer grew up. The 2,300-square-meter center includes exhibition areas, a library and reading room, a cafe, and an auditorium equipped with the latest film projection equipment. (Hamsun's writings have been particularly inspiring to filmmakers, which is evident in the more than 17 films based on his work.)

The building is conceived as an archetypal and intensified compression of spirit in space and light, concretizing a Hamsun character in architectonic terms. The concept for the museum, "Building as a Body: Battleground of Invisible Forces", is realized from inside and out. Here the wood exterior is punctuated by hidden impulses piercing through the surface: An "empty violin case" balcony has phenomenal sound properties, while a viewing balcony is like the "girl with sleeves rolled up polishing yellow panes".

Many other aspects of the building use the vernacular style as inspiration for reinterpretation. The stained black wood exterior skin is characteristic of the great wooden stave Norse churches. On the roof garden, long grass refers to traditional Norwegian sod roofs in a modern way. The rough white-painted concrete interiors are characterized by diagonal rays of light calculated to ricochet through the section on certain days of the year. These strange, surprising, and phenomenal experiences in space, perspective, and light provide an inspiring frame for exhibitions.

Distant view from northeast

Concept sketches

Concept sketch

I-182

View from northeast toward entrance

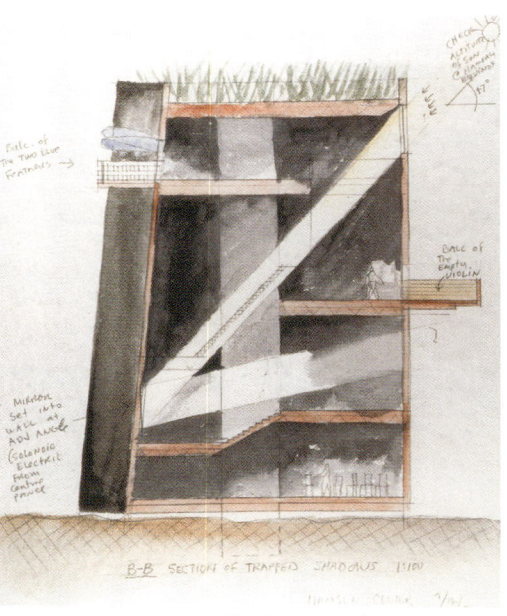

Sketch: section of trapped shadows

Balcony on third floor:
"girl with sleeves rolled up polishing yellow panes"

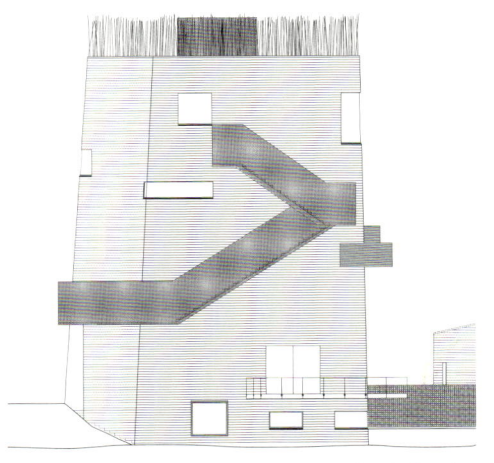

South elevation 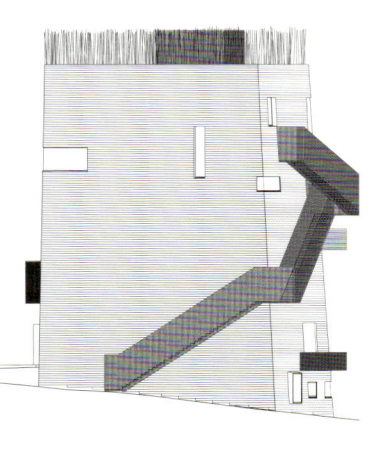   West elevation 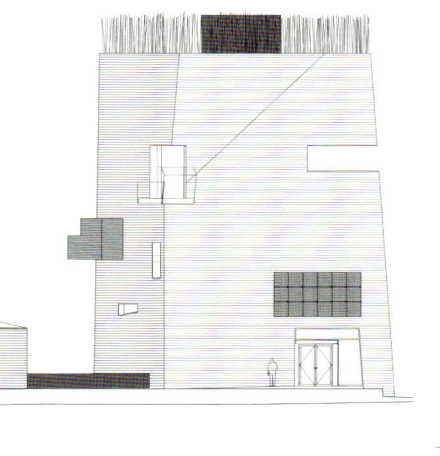   North elevation 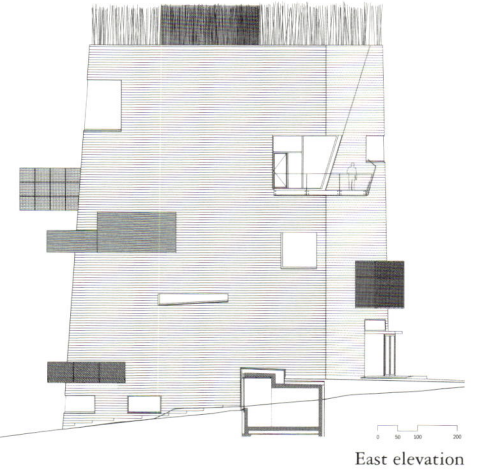   East elevation

I-183

External staircase with brass cage

Interior of staircase

クヌート・ハムスン・センター

ノルウェーの最も独創的な20世紀の作家クヌート・ハムスンは、彼の処女小説『飢え』で新しい表現様式をつくり上げた。彼は、『牧神』、『神秘』、『土の恵み』等の作品を通じて、小説の分野で真の近代学派の礎を築き続けた。ハムスンに捧げられたこのセンターはハーマレイ島のプレスティド村に程近い、この小説家が幼少期を過ごした農場の近くにあり、北極線以北に位置している。2,300平米のセンターには展示エリア、図書館、読書室、カフェ、そして最新のフィルム映写設備を備えた劇場が設けられている。(ハムスンの作品がとりわけ映画制作者達をインスパイアしてきたことは、彼の小説を題材とする映画が17本以上もつくられていることからうかがわれる。)

建物は、空間と光に宿る魂をそのままの形で最大限に濃縮するという着想で、ハムスンのキャラクターの一面を建築学的表現で具象化している。ミュージアムのコンセプト「人体としての建物:見えない力の戦場」は、建物の内側でも外側でも、至る所で実現化されている。秘められた衝動が外表をも突き破り、木製の外観を裁断してしまっているのが分かるだろう。すなわち、「空のバイオリン・ケース」のバルコニーは素晴らしい音響を備え、一方、展望バルコニーは、「腕まくりをして黄色い窓枠を磨く少女」のように見える。

再解釈へのインスピレーションとして、他にも建物のあらゆる面で、土地特有のスタイルが用いられている。黒塗りの木製外板は、古代スカンジナビアの教会に使われていた大きなたる板の特徴を示している。屋上庭園に植えられた長い草は、ノルウェーの伝統的な芝草屋根の現代的解釈である。白く塗られた荒仕上げのコンクリートの内装は、一年のうち数日、差し込む陽光がその断面を対角線上に突き抜けるように設計されている点が個性的だ。空間、景色、光の中でのこのような奇妙な、驚くべき、素晴らしい体験は、見せることに対する発想の枠組みを提供してくれる。

Exhibition room on third floor

First floor: looking east

First floor: looking west

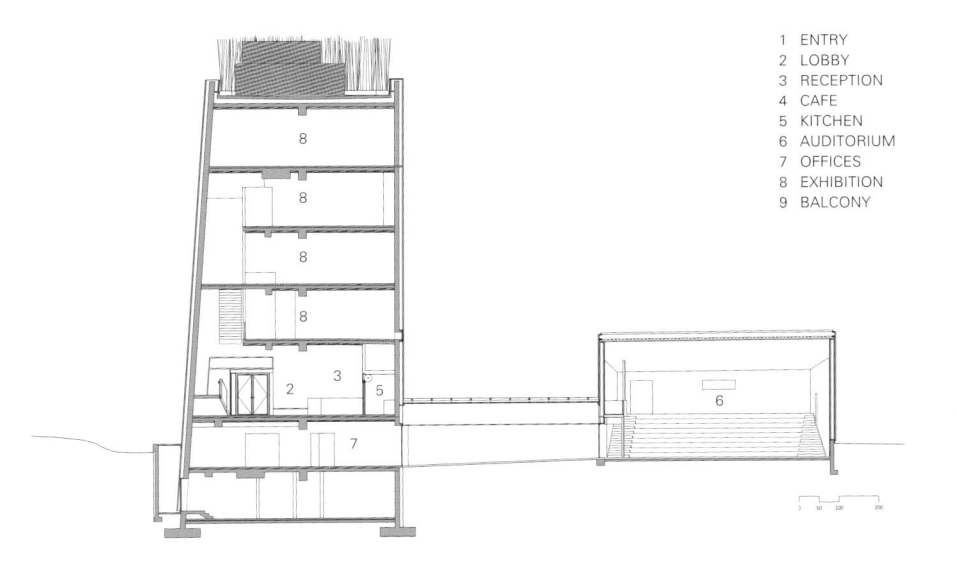

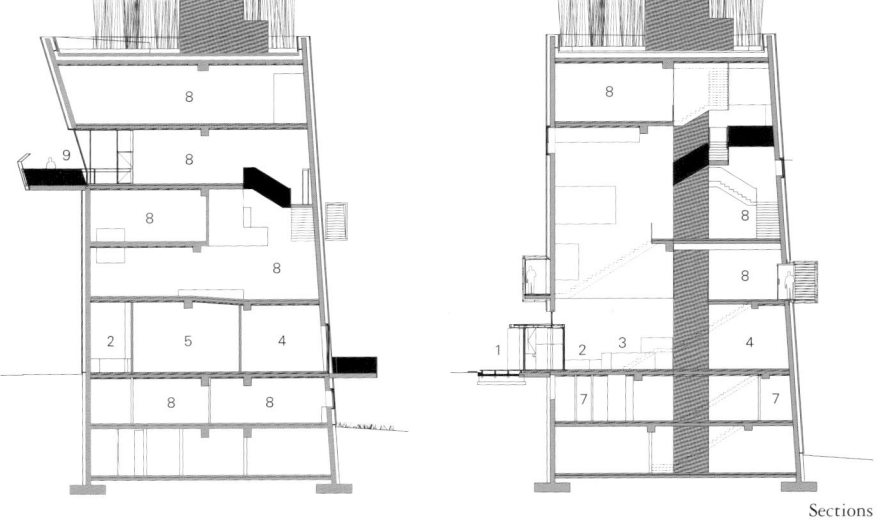

1 ENTRY
2 LOBBY
3 RECEPTION
4 CAFE
5 KITCHEN
6 AUDITORIUM
7 OFFICES
8 EXHIBITION
9 BALCONY

Sections

Level 2

Level 1

Level -1

Study: pattern of natural light through slits and skylights

1 MAIN ENTRY	9 ADMINISTRATION/STORAGE	17 PREPARATOR'S SHOP
2 LOBBY	10 KITCHEN/STORAGE	18 WORK AREA/OFFICES
3 INFORMATION DESK	11 FOUNTAIN COURT	19 LIBRARY
4 CLOAK	12 EV	20 STAGING/STORAGE
5 GALLERY	13 WC	21 SERVICE
6 CAFE	14 OUTDOOR GALLERY/TERRACE	22 LOADING DOCK
7 MUSEUM SHOP	15 SKYLIGHT	23 UNDERGROUND PARKING
8 RAMP	16 LOWER LOBBY	24 MECHANICAL

Site plan

Sketch: interior

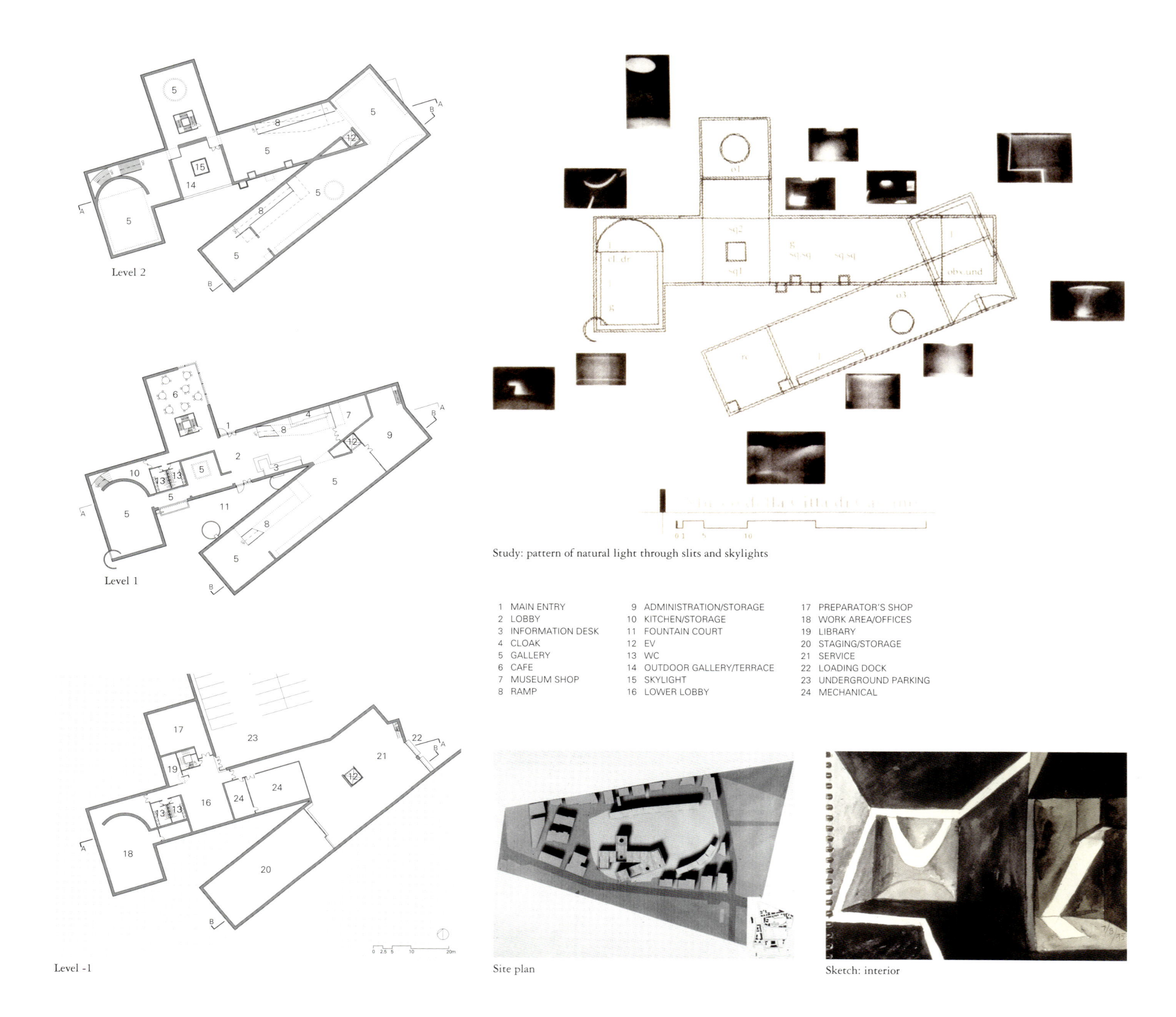

Museum of the City of Cassino
1996   Cassino, Italy

Longitudinal section AA

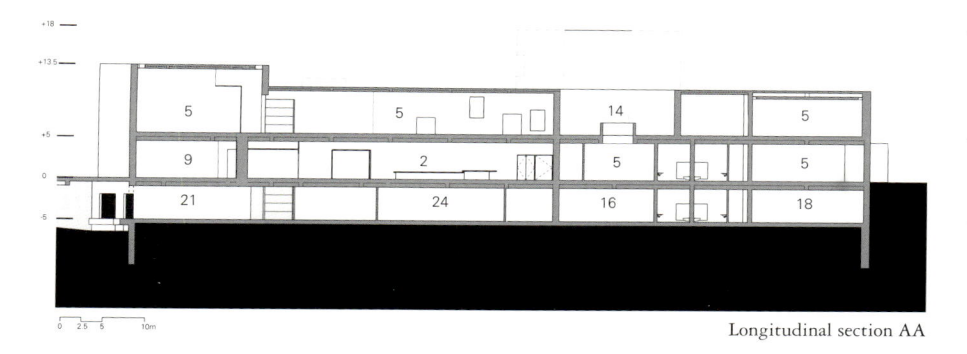

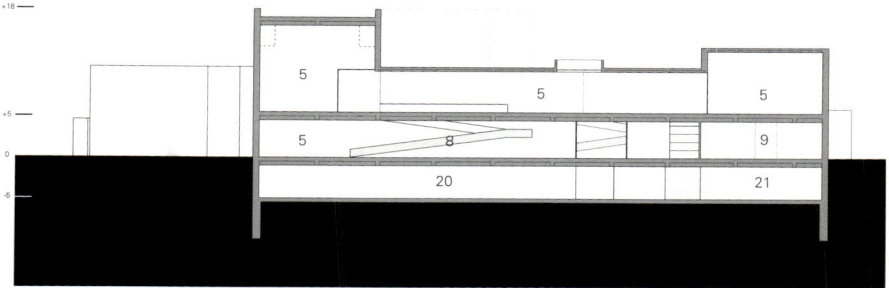

Longitudinal section BB

Following the Allied destruction of the City of Cassino during WWII, reconstruction efforts began. Like the town below, the Abbey located at the top of Mount Cassino was leveled. The City of Cassino is located in the mountainous region of Italy, south of Rome. The site for the Museum lies beneath the mountain and is currently used as a fairground. The plan of the 12,000 square meter building frames a town square with new housing blocks to the north and south east. In the galleries above the entrance, visitors will see exhibits of artifacts from the formerly destroyed Abbey as well as direct views of the reconstructed building on the mountain top.

The Museum is to stand both as a historical museum—documenting the city through artifacts—and as an art museum with permanent and changing exhibitions. The collection will be presented in the following order: according to time period: Gallery 1, Sabini; Gallery 2, Romans; Gallery 3, Medieval; Gallery 4, Monastic; Gallery 5, Destruction; Gallery 6, Contemporary; Gallery 7, Temporary. The Museum will also house a cafe, library and administrative offices.

カッシーノ市立美術館
連合軍によって破壊されたカッシーノの町の再建が進められたのは第二次大戦後のことである。ふもとの町と同様に、モンテ・カッシーノの山頂にある大修道院もまた破壊された。カッシーノの町はローマの南のイタリア山岳地帯に位置している。美術館の敷地は山の麓の、今では遊園地の敷地として利用されている場所である。12,000平米の建築の平面計画は北と南東の新しい居住ブロックで町の広場を縁取るように取り囲んでいる。エントランス上部のギャラリーでは、山頂に再建された建築を直接眺めながら以前破壊された大修道院の工芸品の展示を見ることができる。

この美術館は工芸品を通してカッシーノの町のことを記録する歴史博物館として、また、常設と企画の展示を行う美術館としてつくられる。コレクションは歴史区分に応じ、次の順序で展示される。ギャラリー1はサビーニ文化、ギャラリー2はローマ時代、ギャラリー3は中世、ギャラリー4は修道院、ギャラリー5は破壊の時代、ギャラリー6は現代、ギャラリー7は企画展示である。また、美術館にはカフェ、図書館、管理事務所も含まれる。

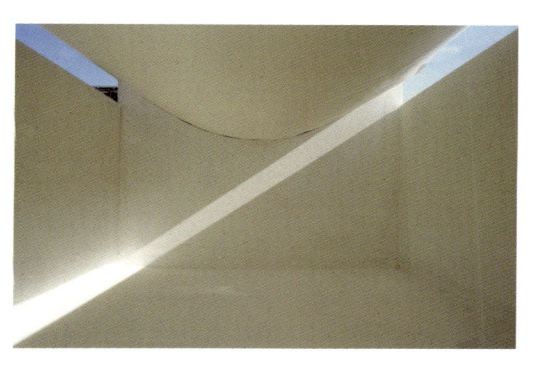

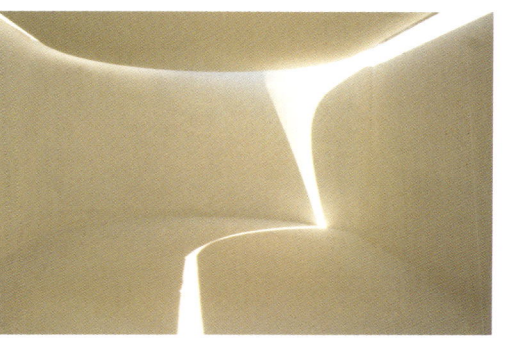

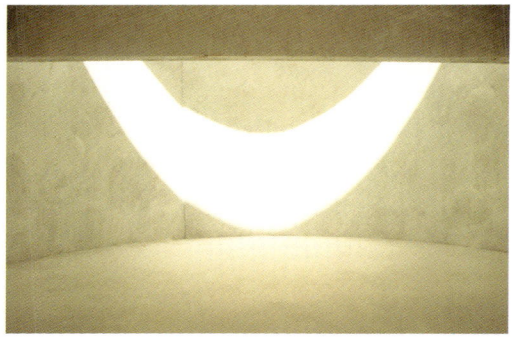

Pattern of light through slit

Sectional model

I-187

1997 Museum of Modern Art Expansion
New York, New York, U.S.A.

Concept sketch

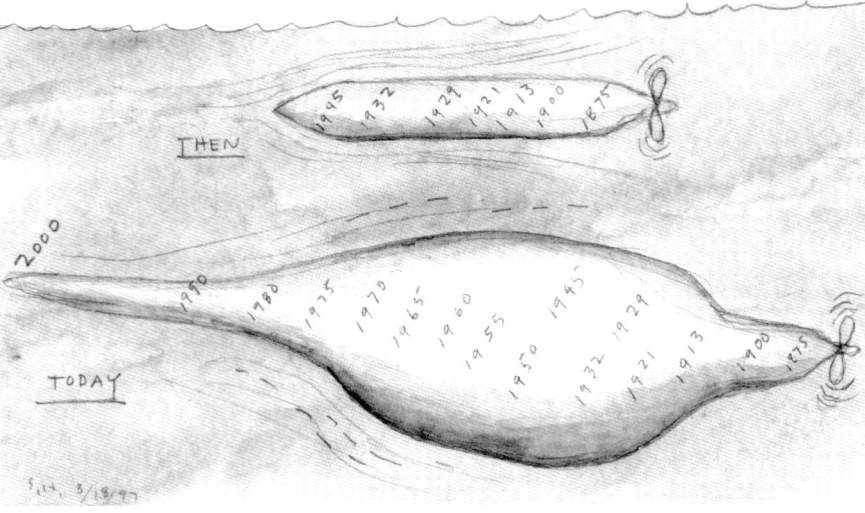

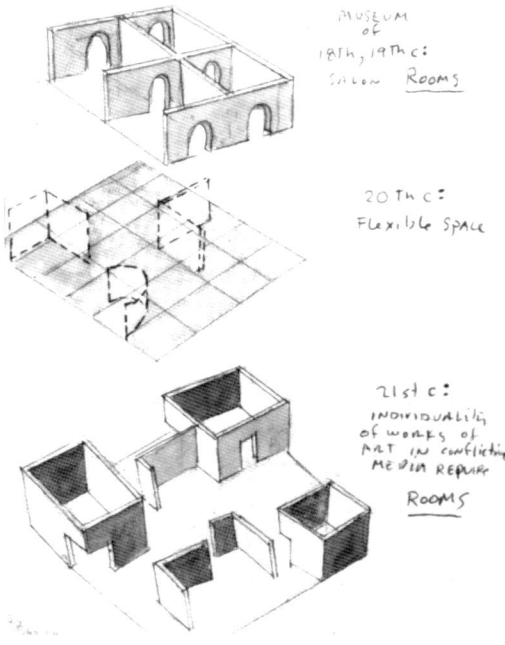

Concept sketch: "the collection: space to place"

The invited competition for the expansion and renovation of the Museum of Modern Art provoked many questions about the future of the institution. The origin of museum as a room of the muse, a place to think and consider deeply and at length, is an idea to contemplate as we are faced with a major transformation of the Museum of Modern Art.

Architectural concepts at this stage of MoMA's redefinition provoke rather than resolve many questions. We adopted a comparative method, devising two concepts as heuristic devices enabling a better understanding of the potential of MoMA's expansion. These two concepts are dialectical: Concept A, 'Cutting', is vertically organized while Concept B, 'Bracketing', is horizontally organized. Concept A adopts an 'evolutional' architectural and urban form while Concept B 'brackets' the entire campus.
—Evolution vs. Involution?
Is the growth of MoMA Evolutional or Involutional? If each successive building addition attempts to swallow the earlier buildings, isn't the expression turning inward? To roll up or wrap in a new envelope is to decline the evolutional expression of a succession. If a strategy for an overall envelop is adopted, what about the potential of further additions?
—Eclipse of the Modern?
Has there been an eclipse of the idea of the institution or does a transformed version continue? Has there been a break between the historical explanation of 'modern' and our narrative understanding? Can we locate the epistemological break in time: 1960? 1964? 1966? 1970? Is this period analogous to a natural eclipse—a partial darkening with transformation and recurrence?
—Art in our time?
The original sign welcoming visitors to the young Museum of Modern Art in 1939 read "Art in Our Time". As the much-expanded institution prepares for the next century of art, it must balance its commitment to its historic collection with its original mission statement.
—Multi-Departmental Structure
Is the present multi-departmental structure actually contradictory to the original mission of 'art in our time', given the present challenges to distinct and traditional art categories? Should the structure be extended to more departments? Could a revolutionary closure of the present categories give birth to a cross-department hybrid?
—Rooms vs. Flexible Space
Rooms, which were the gallery character of museums in the eighteenth and nineteenth centuries were supplanted by flexible space and moveable partitions in the twentieth century. On the cusp of the twenty-first century, the new diversity of contemporary art media requires the acoustic and spatial separation of a gallery of rooms.

Art as Fundamental
—The Collection: Space to Place
The collection is mysterious and full of feeling. New galleries for the collection could be formed especially for individual works. The architectural space could provide for masterworks of art the place in which they belong. To recognize the place of a masterpiece in a museum is to keep the museum with you wherever you go. A special room for *Les Desmoiselles d'Avignon*, a place for Brancusi's *Bird in Space, Fish, Magic Bird*, and

Concept sketch: "new art: toward an unknown"

Socrates. A special room for Giacometti's works in natural light. Great spaces of contemplation to which one can always return would deepen the presence of MoMA. The materiality of the walls and ceiling could be plaster, for example, reinforcing the fundamental solidity and quality of these spaces. Detail where the wall meets the ceiling and where the wall meets the floor are essential in a contemplative gallery. These subtle conditions come to the foreground and intermesh with the experience of the art, establishing an important role for architecture; the subtle realm of touch; the haptic realm.
— New Art: Toward an Unknown
Evolutional or experimental galleries would be offered in which any form of media could be utilized by artists. These spaces would be wired and equipped for projection devices from ceilings, walls and floors. Ceiling structure would have the capacity for suspension of various screens and platforms. Artificial illumination would be adjustable, reaching theatrical nature if necessary. These evolutional spaces (or non-spaces) can be fused into one another or alternately closed off.

Concept A: Cutting

In Concept A, the new site's zoning envelope is taken as a "ready made" form, which is cut for natural light. A major cut is made for the main lobby connecting 53rd Street, 54th Street, and the garden. This is a large public space with a ramp down to the cinemas and up to the galleries. In raising the issue of the evolutional nature of MoMA's campus, Concept A accepts each building phase as evolution expressed. The zoning envelope, itself a consequence of building density and light, is incised creating internal light.

The volume is built out to the color area allowed of 216,000 sq.ft., offering some loft galleries with exceptionally high volumes. This expanded area could concentrate all the galleries; one could move from the new collection galleries below to 'evolutional' or experimental galleries above. Staff offices are relocated in the former gallery floors. All work spaces receive natural light from the original façade and a few selective cuts from above. In the upper levels, truss space on sloped exteriors double as light baffle zones and mechanical duct space. The deep cuts could contain all intake air, exhaust grills, etc.
—Urbanism
The public lobby connecting garden views with 53rd and 54th Streets has true urban proportions. A thru-block connection between 54th and 53rd Streets would be a neighborhood contribution, cutting the pedestrian distance in the 950' long block as well as presenting the passing public with MoMA programs. The vertical character of (A) affords a public roof garden at the top of the building with fine urban views.
—Light
The potential of natural light to affect the experience of the museum is central to the psychological space of Concept A. Natural light provides a sense of the time of day, a sense of orientation in space, and a biological connection which can fuse subjective and objective into pure feeling. In the cutting concept, the potential of natural light is introduced into many of the galleries. This would be a non-glaring diffused natural light, bounced off ceilings through the use of special shaped baffles. All galleries with natural light have blackout screens which are electrically operated and allow the light to be individually adjusted for particular works.
—Circulation
The through-block public lobby opens a free flow of public circulation to all main areas. A direct ramp down to the cinemas prevents back-up in the lobby and facilitates changing programs between day and evening. Elevators carry the public to upper galleries with open stairs and ramps allowing a walk down. The staff entrance is through a reconstruction of the original 1939 MoMA entry. Stairs interconnect staff offices and allow natural light to enter from above. The current escalators are replaced by a new 'hall of reverie' running transversely the length of the garden. Here the view of the garden is enhanced along its full length. Benches for sitting and reflecting afford views to the rain glossy marble paving, or the winter snow. This would be a special hall for receptions, open to the garden in summer.

Concept B: Bracketing

In Concept B, a maximum connectivity of gallery circuits is envisioned within an outer bracket, with the garden as the main focus at its center. The horizontally organized concept proposes lifting the garden 11 feet and shifting it +/- 70 feet west. This affords a more central position for the original 1939 building as well as two new below-garden experimental exhibition areas of 21,000 square feet each. Access is enhanced from all sides. The garden is perfectly rebuilt with the addition of glass bottoms in the pools of water and water year-round (dissolving snow from skylight to below). Staff offices are located in the thin floor plates of the upper levels of the bracketing scheme providing light and art to all offices. The staff café would have a roof garden.
—Urbanism
The reconfigured site provides an overall identity for the Museum within the city. Lobby and thru-block connections are offered as in (A). Public

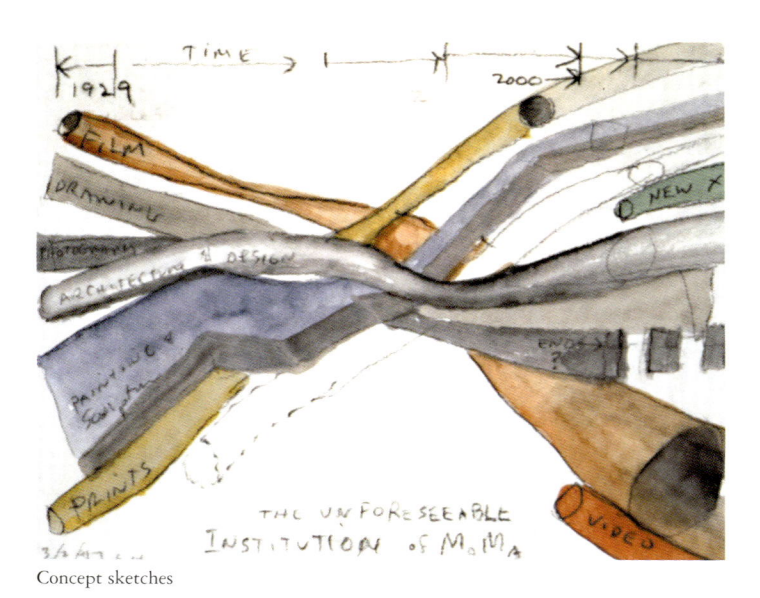

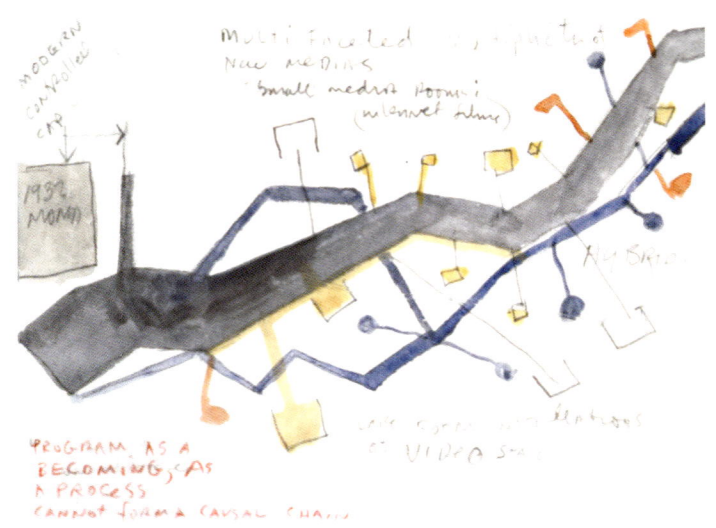

Concept sketches

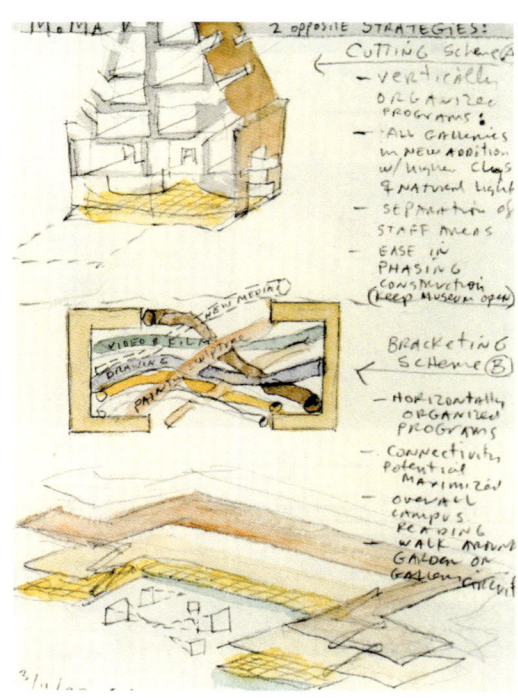

Concept sketch: opposite strategies—concept A as cutting scheme (above) and concept B as bracketing scheme (below)

view windows along 54th to the lobby gallery would enliven the currently blank street wall. The public roof area would be larger however lower in elevation than in (A). The proposed moving rubber ramps would connect to this upper garden directly.

—Art Underground

The underground or 'Orpheum' space gained in Concept B is an experimental space of vast proportions. This 21,000 square foot below ground volume corresponds to an underground focus on art of any and all media. This space, added to the given program, provides the volumetric equivalent of a prediction for a very active "art of our time" in the future.

—Darkness

The mysteries of darkness and unknown are an aspect of Concept B. Natural light plays a much subtler role in the horizontal organization. The horizontal promenade is bracketed by natural light at turning points in the sequence of galleries. The Orpheum underground space is characterized by darkness with glowing bits of light.

—Circulation

A through block lobby contains quiet moving ramps lifting the public to the horizontal gallery floors and finally to the roof garden. The horizontal circulation interlocks with the existing gallery floors and allows the garden to be an orientation point along the gallery circuit. The shifting and raising of the garden unblocks the entire circulation. Two new areas are created complimenting the given program. The staff (and public library) entrance is east of the garden on 53rd Street with separate elevators. The art and the service loading docks are reached at opposite ends on 54th Street.

Conclusion

Phenomenology of Art and Architecture. By unifying foreground, middle ground and distant views, Architecture ties perspective detail and materials to space. Our sensations combine within one complex experience, which becomes articulate and specific, though wordless. Art and architecture speak through perceptual phenomena. Early modern architects rationalized the use of light in their buildings. Today we understand the importance of subtle and psychological differences within the vast spectrum of light. With this new understanding, we give attention to darkness and the secrets of light and dark. Awareness of the role of perception affords a reconsideration of how physicalities become the subject of the senses. The tactile, aural, cognitive, visual and olfactory become essential to the development of new architecture.

In this spirit, the new architecture for the Museum of Modern Art will establish a presence connecting the individual and the art. We envision architecture realized with the capacity of revealing and establishing experience as central to the meaning of the museum.

Concept A
Cutting

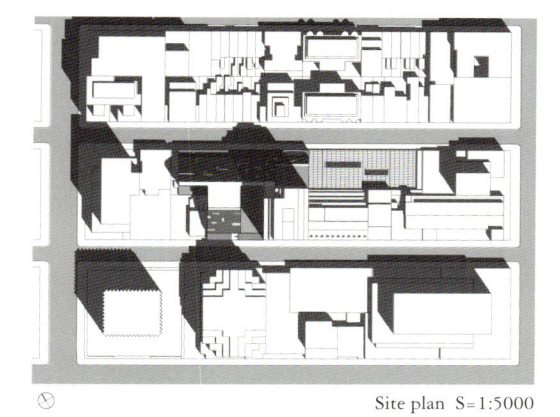

Site plan S=1:5000

A. URBANISM:
1) Public Rooftop Garden
2) Public space scaled street lobby
3) Open pedestrian 53-59 connection

950' long block is split open

Sketch: whole volume

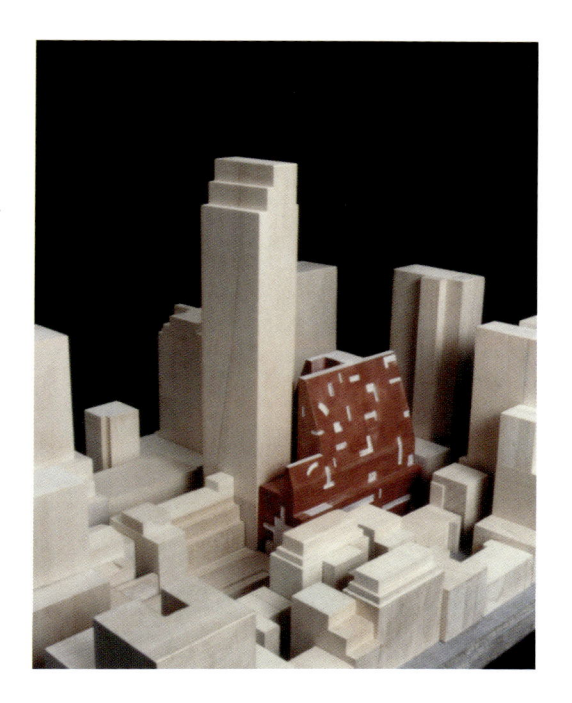

Sketch: section and interior

Sketch: ground floor and interior (lobby)

I-191

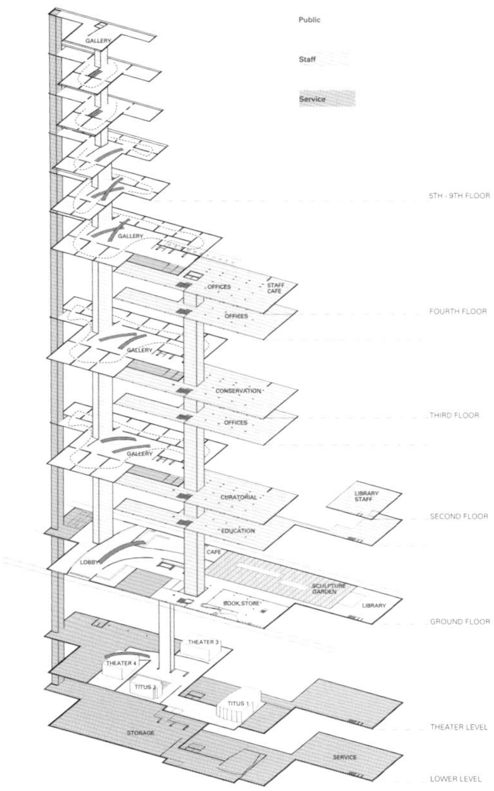

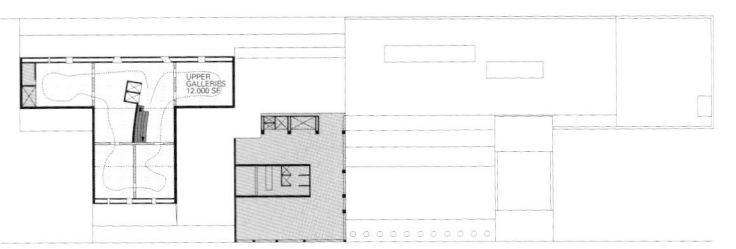

Typical upper gallery level (+209'4")

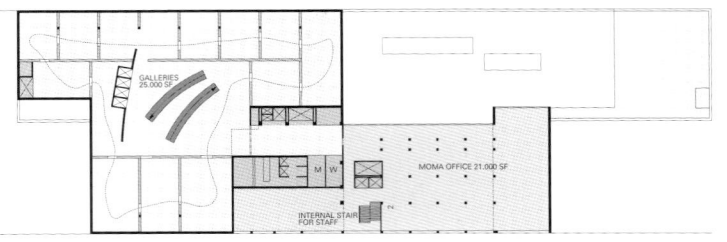

Typical gallery level (+124'8")

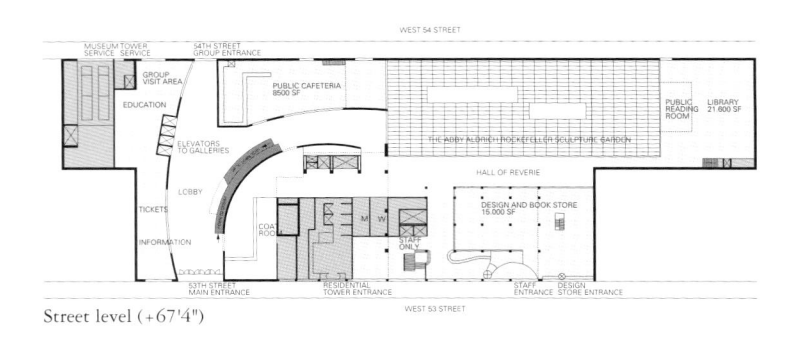

Street level (+67'4")

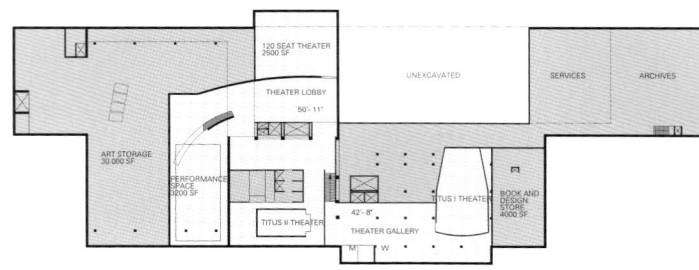

Theater level (+50'11", +42'8") S=1:2000

Exploded isometric: diagram

Interior sketch

Interior sketch: ramp of lobby

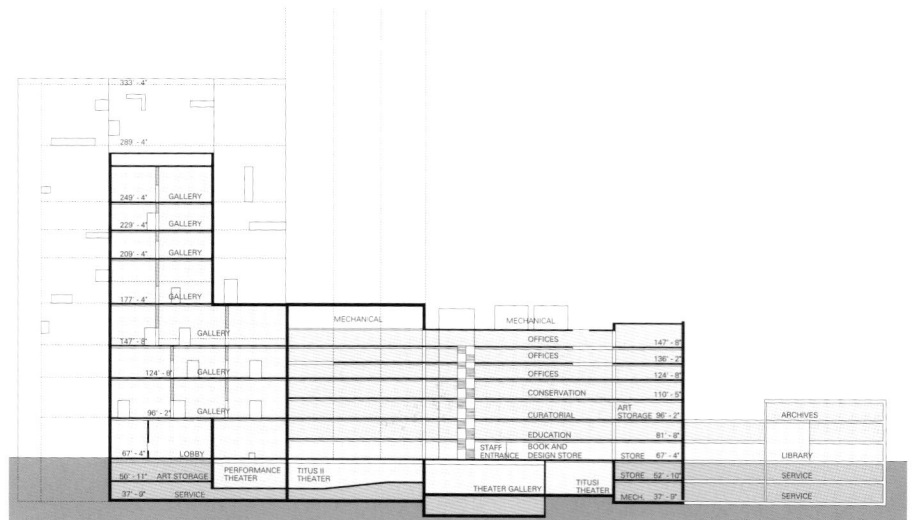

Longitudinal section S=1:1600

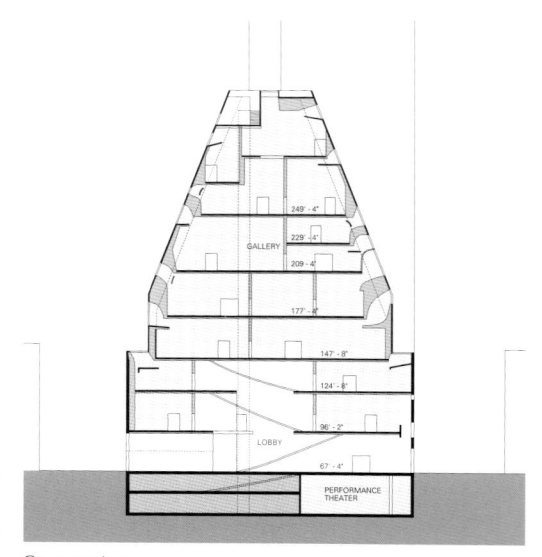

Cross section

I-192

Concept B
Bracketing

Site plan S=1:5000

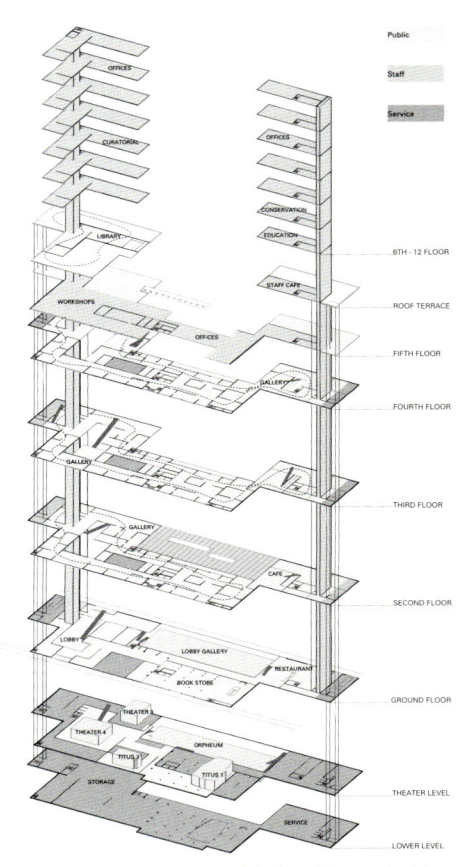

Exploded isometric: diagram

Exterior sketch: garden

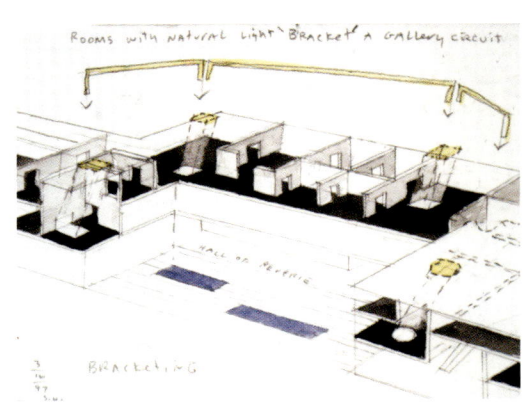

Concept sketch

Sketch: section

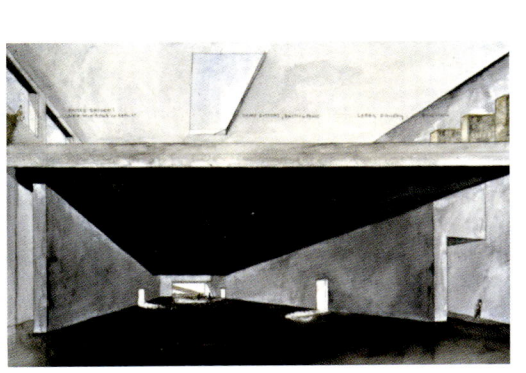

Interior sketch: orpheum under garden

Interior sketch: cinema lobby

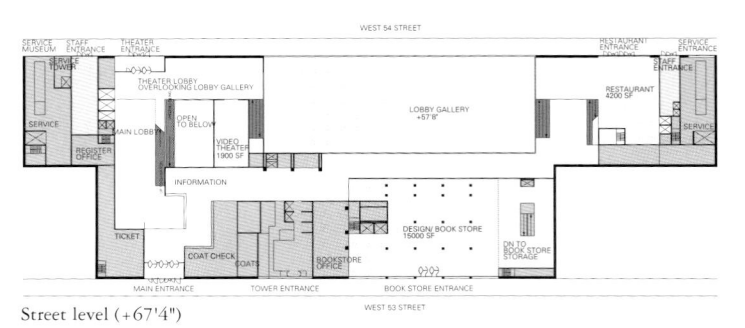

Street level (+67'4")

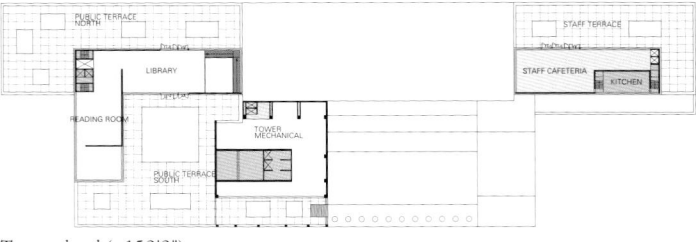

Terrace level (+152'2")

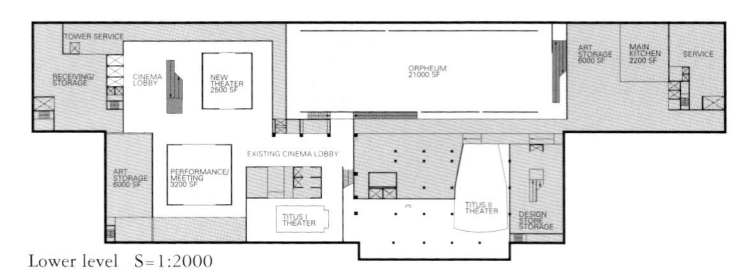

Lower level　S=1:2000

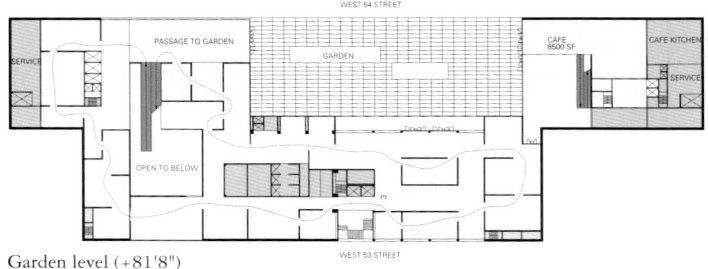

Garden level (+81'8")

MoMA／ニューヨーク近代美術館増改築案

ニューヨーク近代美術館増改築案のための指名コンペは，この美術館の未来について多くの疑問をかき立てるものであった。この美術館の原点を沈思黙考の空間，深く細緻に思索するための場として捉えることは，ニューヨーク近代美術館の重要な変革を前に熟考に値するものである。

MoMAを再定義するこの度の建築の構想は，多くの疑問をひとつに解決するよりも，多くの疑問を引き起こす。私たちが採用したのは相対的方法論，すなわちMoMAの次世代の増築に対する潜在的理解を深めることを可能にする自己学習的デバイスとして，二つのコンセプトを提案することである。これらは弁証法的だ。コンセプトAの「切断／Cutting」が垂直的に構成されるのに対し，コンセプトBの「ブラケット／Bracketing」は水平的に構成される。コンセプトAは建築や都市の「進化する」形態であるのに対して，コンセプトBは敷地全体を「包み込む」ものである。

〈進化なのか，退化なのか？〉
MoMAの発展は進化なのか，退化なのか？　過去を継承して各々増築される建築がそれまでの建築を飲み尽くすようなら，それは内向きの表現とはならないだろうか？　古いものを新しい外皮で覆い隠すということは，表現の継承的進化を弱体化させるものである。もし外皮の戦略が全体に及ぶものであれば，今後の増築の潜在的可能性はどうなるだろうか？

〈近代の衰退か？〉
美術館の思想は退潮を迎えているのだろうか，あるいは姿を変えた存在として存続してゆくのだろうか？「近代」に対する歴史の言及と，私たちのこの物語への理解とのあいだに断絶がないだろうか？　1960年，1964年，1966年，1970年。これらの年を認識論的断絶として位置づけることは可能だろうか？　この時代は変容と循環を伴い，時折翳る日差しのような，自然界の退潮へのアナロジーなのだろうか？

〈現代の芸術か？〉
1939年当時，まだ新しいニューヨーク近代美術館で来場者を迎えるサインには「現代の芸術」と記されていた。大規模に拡張された美術館として新しい時代の芸術に備えるとともに，設立時の基本理念と歴史的コレクションに対する責任をふまえて調和したものとならなければならない。

〈複数の組織部門構造〉
明瞭で伝統的な芸術のカテゴライズに対する現在の様々な試みを考慮すると，現在の複数からなる組織部門構造は，事実上「現代の芸術」という設立時の基本理念とは矛盾したものなのではないか？　この構造はより多くの部門へと拡張されるべきか？　現在のカテゴリーを革命的に閉鎖することで，部門を越えたハイブリッドな組織を生み出すことが可能だろうか？

〈展示室か，フレキシブル・スペースか〉
18世紀から19世紀の美術館展示の特徴である部屋ごとの展示の代わりに，20世紀に入るとフレキシブル・スペースと可動式パーティションがその地位を占めた。21世紀の転換期を迎えて新しい多様な現代芸術メディアは，ギャラリーの展示室を音響的にも空間的にも分離することを求めている。

[芸術の基本]
〈コレクション：空間から場所性へ〉
展示コレクションは神秘的で情感に溢れたものである。展示コレクションのための新しいギャラリーは，個別の作品ごとに特別なものとなる。建築空間は最高の芸術作品のために，その作品が設置される場を提供するようになるだろう。いつ来ても美術館には決まった場所に名作が置いてある。美術館は絶えず来館者の傍にあるのだ。「アヴィニョンの娘たち」の特別展示室，ブランクーシの「空間の鳥」，「魚」，「魔法の鳥」，「ソクラテス」といった作品を展示する場所。自然光の入るジャコメッティの作品の特別展示室。沈思黙考するため，大空間にすぐ戻ることができる。そのことがMoMAの存在感を一層深めている。壁面と天井面の素材はプラスター仕上げである。それは例えば基本となる連帯感や，これらの空間の本質を一層強めるものである。展示ギャラリーの静謐は，壁面と天井面，あるいは壁面と天井面の取り合いのディテールに宿る。これらの繊細さが前面に現れ，芸術体験へと組み込まれる。手で触れられるような繊細な世界，触覚の世界をつくるのは建築の重要な役割である。

〈新しい芸術：未知なるものにむけて〉
進化的，実験的な展示ギャラリーで，芸術家はあらゆる形態のメディアを利用することができる。これらの空間には天井や壁，床から配線が走り，映写機が取り付けられる。天井の構造からは，多種多様なスクリーンや舞台を吊ることができる。人工照明は必要な場合には演劇向けに，調整可能である。これらの進化する空間（あるいは非空間／non-space）は互いに溶融し，また閉じることができる。

[コンセプトA：切断／Cutting]
コンセプトAにとって，新しい敷地の斜線制限は「レディ・メイド」である。これは自然光を引き入れる切断面である。主断面は53丁目，54丁目，及び庭園とを結ぶメイン・ロビーのためのものである。これは巨大なパブリック・スペースで，斜路を下ると映画館に，上がるとギャラリーへと続く。進化する美術館というMoMAの本質に取り組む際に，コンセプトAはそれぞれの棟の建築過程で進化を表現したものである。建築密度と採光がもたらす斜線制限は，同時に内部に光をもたらすための切断面となる。

ヴォリュームは216,000平方フィート（約20,000平米）増築され，非常に背の高いヴォリュームの中はロフト・ギャラリーになっている。この拡張部分にはすべてのギャラリーが集約される。下階の新しいコレクション・ギャラリーから上階の「進化的」，実験的なギャラリーへと人は移動できる。事務局は以前，ギャラリーのあったフロアに再配置される。ワークスペースでは全て，本来のファサードと上部に選択的に設けられた複数の開口から自然光を取り入れている。上層階の傾斜した外部空間にはトラスが組まれ，反射板のゾーンと機械ダクトスペースの二層構

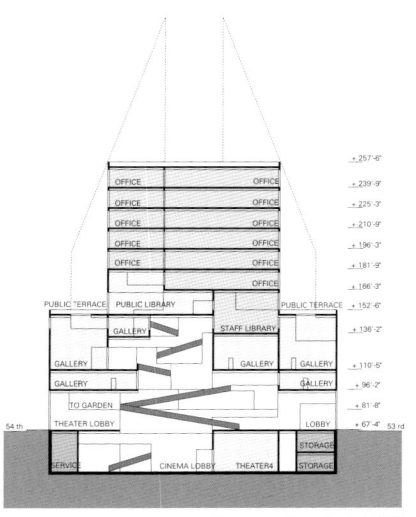

Cross section　S=1:1600

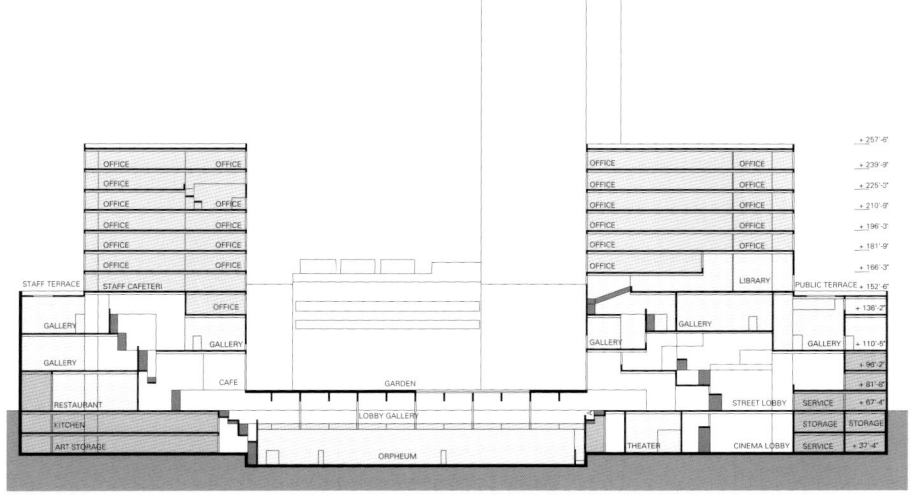

Longitudinal section

造になっている。深い開口部には全ての吸気口,排気用ガラリなどが収容されている。

〈アーバニズム〉
庭園の眺望と,53丁目と54丁目とをつなぐパブリック・ロビーは真に都市的なものである。ブロックを通り越して53丁目と54丁目を繋ぐことは,周辺環境に対する貢献である。これは歩行距離を950フィート(約290m)縮め,通り過ぎる人にMoMAのプログラムを提供することができる。コンセプトAは垂直に聳え,建築頂部のパブリックな屋上庭園からは都市への眺望が広がっている。

〈光〉
美術館体験を深く印象づける自然光の潜在的可能性こそが,心理的空間としてのコンセプトAの中心概念である。自然光が与えるのは,一日の時間の流れ,空間の方位,及び主体と客体を純粋な感性へと融合する生物的結合である。切断という構想によって,自然光の潜在的可能性が多くのギャラリーにもたらされる。自然光はノングレアで拡散し,特殊な形状の反射板で天井面に反射する。自然光の入るギャラリーには全て電動式の暗幕が設けられ,光を個別の作品ごとに調節することができるようになっている。

〈動線〉
街区を貫通するパブリック・ロビーは,全ての主要エリアへの公共動線を自由に開放している。映画館へと直接続く斜路は,昼と夜とでプログラムが変わるたびにロビーなどの施設で起きる行列を防ぐ。エレベータは人々を上階のギャラリーに運び,開放的な階段と斜路は歩いて降りてくるのに利用される。スタッフ用エントランスのためにMoMA本来の1939年のエントランスが改修される。階段は事務局を内部で繋ぎ,自然光を上から採光する。現在のエスカレータは庭園の全長にわたって空間を横断する新しい「想像の間」へと改修される。今や庭園からは,その全長にわたって眺望が広がっている。ベンチに座り,考え事をしていると,雨露に光る大理石舗装や,冬の日の雪が視界に入る。ここは夏の日には庭園へと開放される,レセプションに相応しい特別なホールである。

[コンセプトB:ブラケット／Bracketing]
コンセプトBでは,外部ブラケットでギャラリー動線の連続性を最大化することが構想された。ここでは中央にある庭園が主な関心の対象である。水平に組織化されたこの提案は,庭園を11フィート(約3.3m)持ち上げ,約70フィート(約21m)西側に水平移動するものである。このことによって,庭園の下にある各々21,000平方フィート(約1,950平米)の二つの新しい実験的な展示空間と同じ様に,1939年の建設当時の建築が敷地の中央を占めるようになり,全ての場所からのアクセスが増える。プールの底にガラスを取り付け,庭園は完全に再構築される。年間を通して水の張られたプールの水は,天窓から下に落ちてくる雪を溶かす。事務局は上階の薄いフロアプレートに位置し,ブラケット構成が光と芸術作品を全ての事務室に引き入れている。スタッフ用カフェには屋上庭園が設けられる。

〈アーバニズム〉
新しい敷地は都市のなかの美術館に,全く新しい個性を与えている。コンセプトAではロビーと,ブロックを貫通する都市の連続性が提案された。54丁目に沿ってロビー・ギャラリーを見るパブリック・ウィンドウは,現在何もない通りに彩りを与える。パブリック・ルーフはコンセプトAよりもずっと大きく,かつ,より低いものとなる。ラバー製の動く斜路は上階の庭園に直接,接続している。

〈アート・アンダーグラウンド〉
コンセプトBの地下空間,「オルフェウム」は奥行きのあるプロポーションの実験空間である。この21,000平方フィート(約1,950平米)の地下のヴォリュームは,ありとあらゆるメディア芸術のアンダーグラウンドの関心と呼応するものである。所与のプログラムに加えてこの空間は,未来の躍動的な「現代の芸術」への予言と同義的なヴォリュームでもある。

〈暗闇〉
暗闇と未知への神秘はコンセプトBの側面のひとつである。自然光は水平の構成では,より一層繊細な役割を果たす。水平のプロムナードはギャラリーのシークエンスが切り替わるところで自然光に包まれる。オルフェウムの地下空間は暗闇とささやかな光の輝きがその特徴である。

〈動線〉
エントランス・ロビーの静かに動くスロープから水平のギャラリー階を通り,最後には屋上庭園へと上がることができる。既存のギャラリーフロアは水平動線に組み込まれている。庭園はギャラリー動線に沿って順路を指し示すための基準点となる。庭園を水平方向に移動し,持ち上げることで,動線全体の障害が取り除かれる。所与のプログラムに敬意を払うように,二つの新しい区画が生み出される。スタッフ(及び公共図書館)のエントランスは53丁目に面した庭園の東側にあり,別のエレベータで上がる。作品の搬入とサービス用ドックは反対側の54丁目側からアクセスすることができる。

[結論]
芸術と建築の現象学。前景,中景,遠景とを統合することで,建築は遠近法的ディテール,素材,及び空間とをひとつに結びつけることができる。私たちの感覚はひとつの複合的経験に結合する。そのような経験は沈黙のうちに分節化し,明瞭化するものである。芸術と建築が物語るのは,知覚的現象である。初期の近代の建築家は,自分たちの建築のなかで合理的に光を取り扱った。今日私たちが理解しているのは,非常に幅のある光のスペクトラムのなかの繊細な心理的差異の重要性である。この新しい理解のもとで,私たちは暗闇と,光と闇の秘密について関心を払ってきた。認識の持つ役割への理解によって,身体性こそが感覚的なるものの主題であることについて再考することが可能になる。触覚,聴覚,経験的認識,視覚及び嗅覚が,新しい建築の発展の基礎となるものである。

この精神のもとに,ニューヨーク近代美術館の新しい建築は人間と芸術との結びつきを確立するものである。美術館の意義の中心には経験がある。その経験を示現し,確立することをいかに実現しうるかが私たちの描いた構想である。

Overall view from west

Bellevue Art Museum
1997-2000   Bellevue, Washington, U.S.A.

View from street

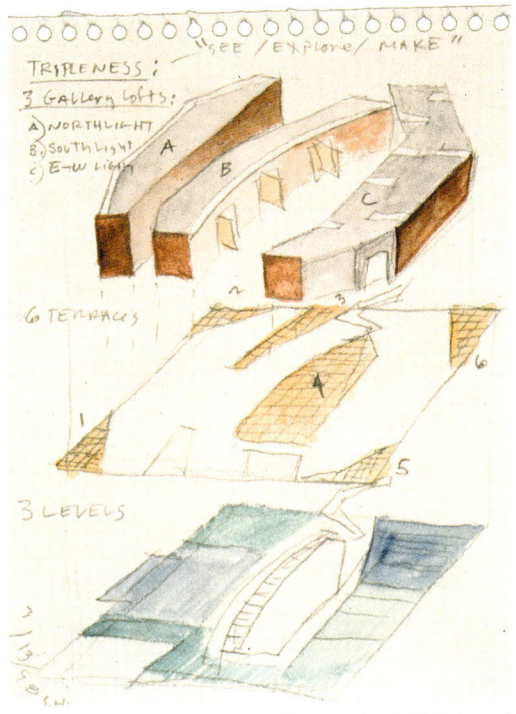

Concept sketch: "Tripleness"

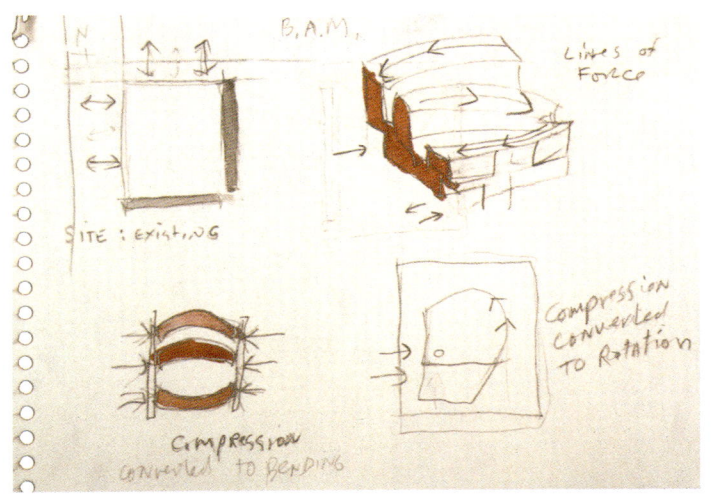

Concept sketch: composition

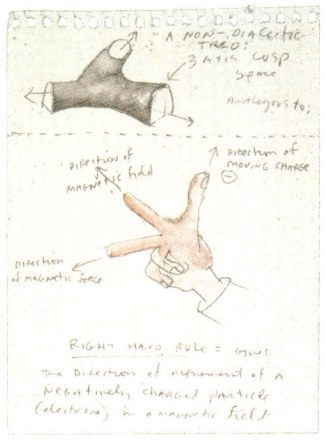

Concept sketch: "Right Hand Rule" on outdoor terrace

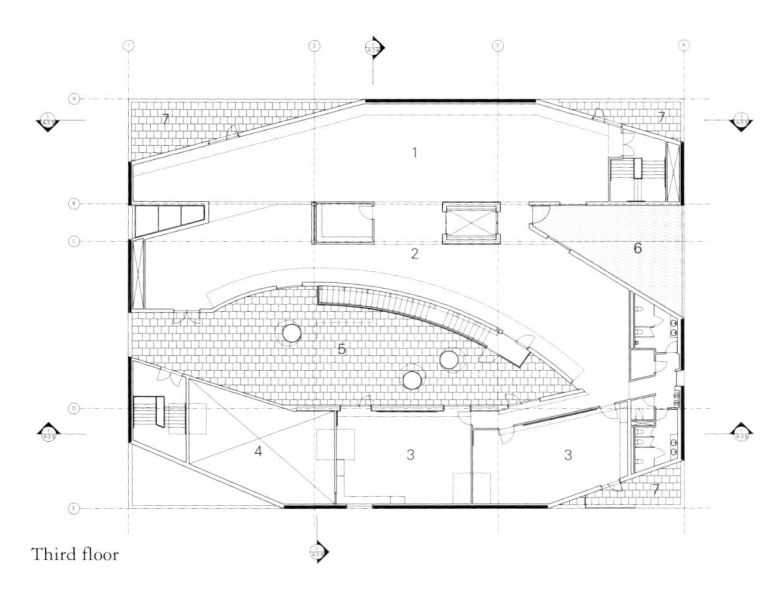

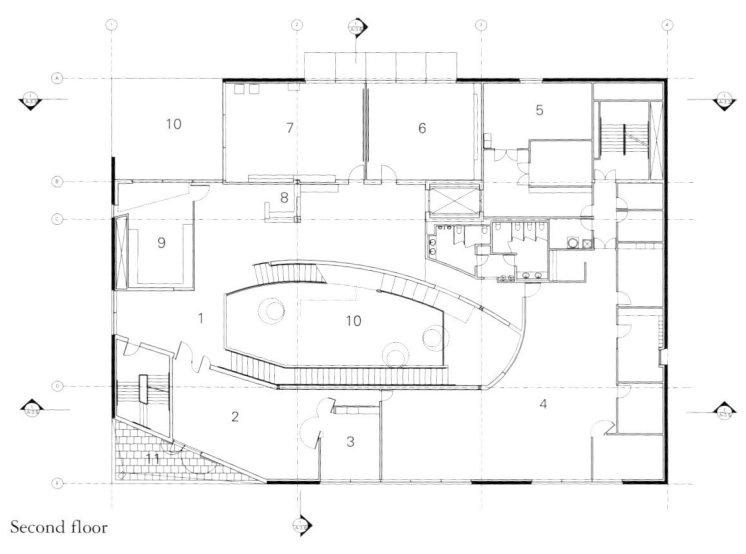

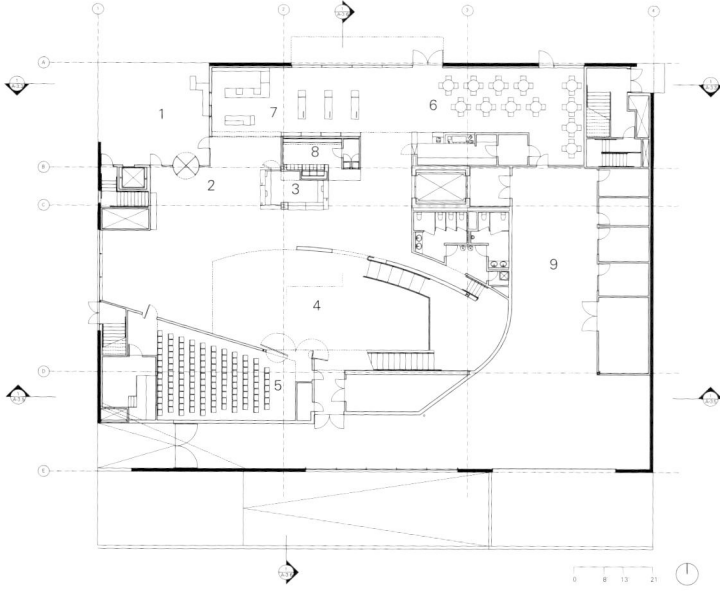

First Floor	Second Floor	Third Floor
1 ENTRY	1 UPPER LOBBY	1 NORTH LIGHT GALLERY
2 LOBBY	2 EAST / WEST / LIGHT GALLERY	2 SOUTH LIGHT GALLERY
3 INFORMATION	3 ARTIST-IN- RESIDENCE	3 STUDIO
4 FORUM	4 ADMINISTRATION	4 OPEN TO BELOW
5 AUDITORIUM	5 EXHIBITION PREPARATION	5 COURT OF LIGHT
6 CAFE	6 STUDIO	6 COURT OF WATER
7 MUSEUM SHOP	7 CERAMICS STUDIO	7 TERRACE
8 CLOAK	8 SCHOOL RECEPTION	
9 LOADING	9 LIBRARY	
	10 OPEN TO BELOW	
	11 TERRACE OF PLANETARY MOTION	

Third floor

Second floor

First floor

The Bellevue Art Museum focuses on education and outreach rather than collecting. In fact the museum maintains no permanent collection but rather collaborates with local arts and educational institutions to provide innovative arts programming and changing temporary exhibitions. As an "art garage" open to the street, the museum provides a new pedestrian city scale at the center of Bellevue as well as an active workshop for new art projects.

Concept

Tripleness is the organizing concept for the building. A non-dialectic openness of experience, thought and contact give character to space on three levels, in three galleries, with three different light conditions and three circulation options.
Tripleness (non-dialectic openness):
- 3 gallery lofts
- 3 light qualities
- 3 actions—see/explore/make (art, science, technology)
- 3 main levels
- 3 circulation directions

The spirit of openness of the Bellevue Art Museum is expressed in the three main lofts which are each slightly warped and gripped by the end wall structures. The outer walls in a special "shot crete" construction support the inner lightweight steel framework. The three distinct lighting conditions of the three gallery lofts are analogous to three different conditions of time and light. *Linear Ongoing* Time is expressed in the evenness of the light in the north loft. *Cyclic Time* has its parallel in the arc of south light gallery. Its plan geometry corresponds roughly to the arc of the sun at 48° north latitude. *Fragmented or Gnostic Time* is reflected in the east-west skylights of the studios loft.

Outdoor Terraces

The Bellevue Art Museum originated as an exterior experience in the street fair. In this spirit, outdoor terraces extend the museum's top level. With sunlight and views, these terraces accommodate outdoor classes as well as exhibitions and events on summer evenings. The twilight sky will be particularly inspiring from these spaces. The open attitude of *tripleness* is realized in a semi-permanent exhibit program for each of the terraces:
l. "Right Hand Rule"
The properties of movement of a negatively-charged particle (electron) in a magnetic field are characterized by the "Right Hand Rule". The symbol in three fingers (digits) connects the hand crafted past of the Bellevue Art Museum to its digital future.
2. Terrace of Planetary Motion
Beginning with Kepler's three laws of planetary motion, this terrace exhibits recent cosmological discoveries via Hubbell Telescope and electronic digital telescopes. The Hubbell images are projected on the inflected street-facing facade.
3. Court of Light
The debate in physics concerning whether light is a wave or a particle is eventually opened: light is both a wave and a particle, depending on, one's perspective. Here sunlight generates various unpredictable light phenomena.
4. Chromatic Terrace: Light projection
From blue, red and green white light is formed.
5. Court of Water
With east exposure the reflected light from a 2" deep water court dapples the gallery ceilings. Rain drops provide reflective patterns on rainy days.
6. Terrace of Wind and Shadow
Light projected from special fixtures captures the drama of the wind in moving shadows cast on the wall.

Forum

A stepped ramp up to the galleries pauses in a landing which double functions as a stage. Ascending to the next level one arrives at the Explore Gallery, a double-height skylit space with an adjacent artist-in-residence studio. Passing by the overlook to the Forum, the stepped ramp leads to the top level main loft galleries and the Court of Light.

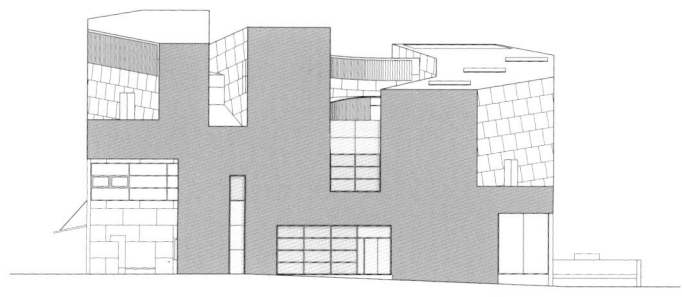

West elevation

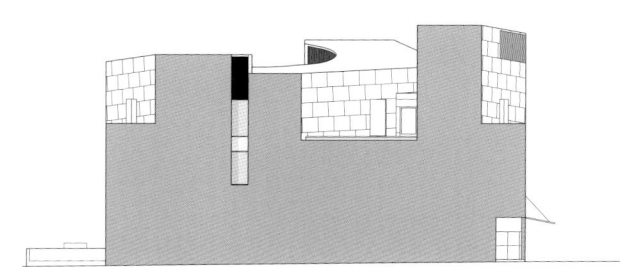

East elevation

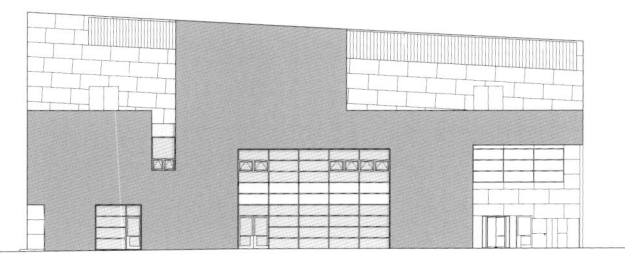

North elevation

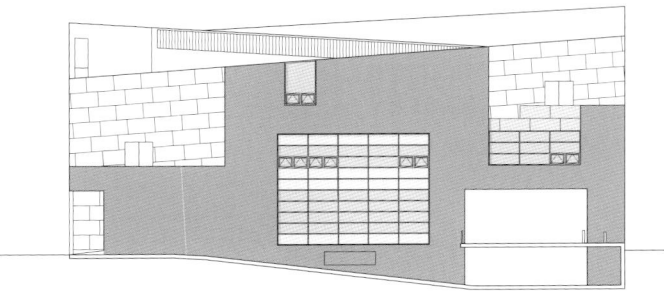

South elevation

ベルヴュー・アート・ミュージアム
ベルヴュー・アート・ミュージアム(BAM)は,作品蒐集よりも,教育と地域社会へ向けた奉仕活動に主軸とする。事実,パーマネント・コレクションは持たず,地域の芸術・教育機関と協力しあい,革新的なアート・プログラムや種々の企画展を行う。街路に開いた「アート・ガレージ」として,ベルヴュー市の中心に,新たな歩行者規模の都市空間,新しいアート・プロジェクトのための活発なワークショップとなる場所を提供する。

[コンセプト]
「三重性」が建物のコンセプトである。体験すること・考えること・触れ合うことから成る非弁証法的な開放性が,3つのレベルに展開する,3つのギャラリー,3つのそれぞれに異なる光の状態,3つの進路選択肢をもつ空間を特徴づける。

三重性(非弁証法的開放性):
・3つのギャラリー・ロフト
・3つの光の質
・3つの行為――見る/探る/つくる(芸術・科学・技術)
・3つの主階
・3つの進行方向

BAMの開かれた在り方は,それぞれが微妙にワープし,妻壁によってしっかり押さえられた3つのギャラリー・ロフトが表現する。特殊な〈ショットクリート〉でつくられた外周壁は,内側の軽量鉄骨枠を支持している。3つのギャラリー・ロフトでそれぞれ違う3種の光の状態は,時間と光における3種類の状態と相似する関係にある。「直進する時間」は北ロフトの均質な光が表現する。「循環する時間」には,南側,光のギャラリーの弧が対応する。その幾何学プランは,北緯48度の太陽軌道にほぼ一致する。断片化された,つまり認識された時間はスタジオ・ロフトの東西に延びるスカイライトに反映される。

[屋外テラス]
BAMのそもそものルーツは,露店市での屋外体験である。この精神において,幾つもの屋外テラスによってミュージアムの最上階を拡げる。陽射しを浴び,見晴らしのきくこれらのテラスは,屋外教室,展示,夏の夕方のイベントなどに使われる。ここから見る薄明の空は,とりわけ印象深いことだろう。「三重性」という開かれた在り方は,それぞれのテラスで開かれる半恒久的な展示計画により実感される。

1.「右手の法則」のテラス
磁場のなかにおける陰電気を帯びた粒子の運動属性は「右手の法則」によって特徴づけられる。3本指のシンボルは,BAMの手工芸的過去とデジタルな未来を結ぶ。

2.惑星運動のテラス
惑星運動に関するケプラーの3法則に始まり,このテラスでは,ハッブル宇宙望遠鏡やデジタル型電子望遠鏡による,宇宙をめぐる最近の発見を展示する。ハッブルの捉えた映像は,道路側の内側に屈曲したファサードに投影される。

3.光のコート
光は波長であるか粒子であるか,という物理学上の論争がようやく始まった。見方によって,光は波長でもあり,粒子でもある。このテラスでは,陽光が,様々な予測不可能な光の現象を発生させる。

4.色彩のテラス:光の投射
青・赤・緑から白い光が形成される。

5.水のコート
東側の開口から入り,深さ2インチの水のコートに反射した光が,ギャラリーの天井に斑模様を描く。

6.風と影のテラス
特殊な装置から投射された光が,ゆらめく影を壁に投影し,風のドラマを捉える。

[フォーラム]
ギャラリーまで上がって行く,ステップを刻んだランプが踊り場で小休止し,そこは舞台としても使え,二重の機能を持つ。さらに次のレベルまで上がると,探査のギャラリーへ出る。そこは2層の高さがある空間で,隣にイン・レジデンスの芸術家専用スタジオがある。フォーラムを見下ろしながら,さらに上がると,そこが,最上階のロフト・ギャラリーと光のコートである。

Information

Forum on first floor

Bench at entrance

Glazed staircase above

Forum: looking west

I-201

Forum: view from upper lobby on second floor

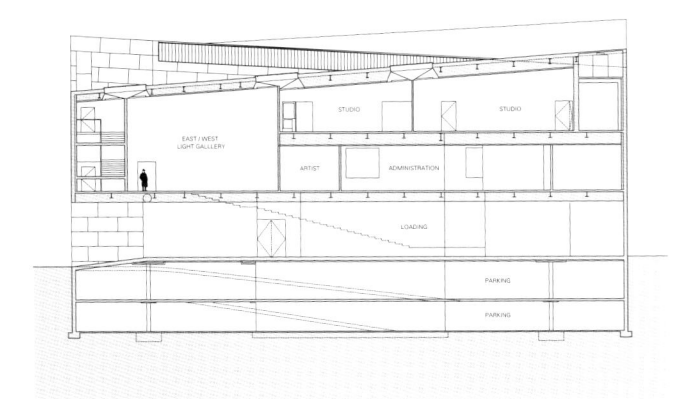

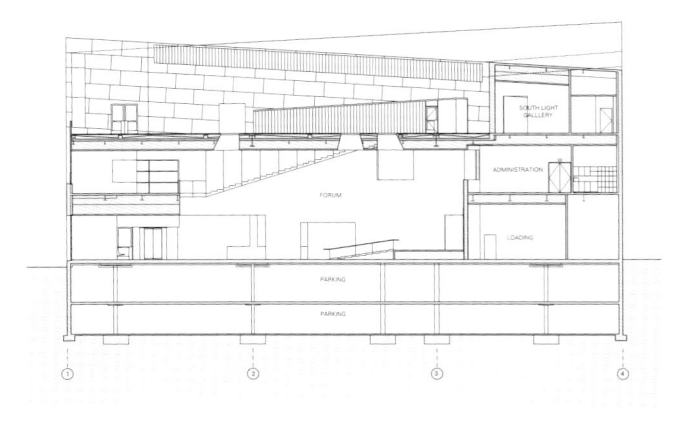

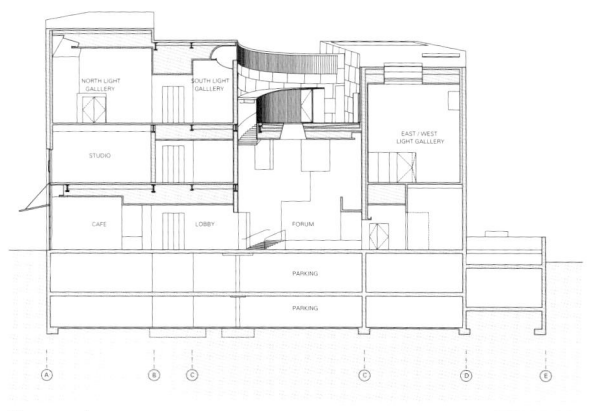

Longitudinal sections

Cross section

I-202

"North Light Gallery"

Upper lobby

"Court of Light"

1997-2002 **College of Architecture and Landscape Architecture University of Minnesota**
Minneapolis, Minnesota, U.S.A.

West view

North view

With both its interior and exterior spaces, the expansion to the College of Architecture and Landscape Architecture promotes campus activity and pedestrian circulation while providing a unified facility for the architecture and landscape architecture schools on campus.

The addition becomes a counterpoint and a complement to the existing 200-foot square building with its centralized 100′ x 100′ atrium built in 1958 by Thorshov and Cerny. While the existing building is centralized and homogeneous, the new addition offers peripheral views and morphological multiplicity. The existing building is centripetal, with four right angles framing four views onto the same court; the addition is centrifugal, with four obtuse angles opening to views on four different exterior landscapes. In compliment to the horizontal facade of the existing building, the new addition has vertical elevations at the ends of each arm which stand as virtual towers, "shafts of space" activating the campus site.

The addition consists of two overlaid "L-shaped" masses including a new library, auditorium, seminar rooms, office and studio space. The basement and first two levels correspond with the existing building levels, and all four levels will be accessible via an elevator in the existing building.

The main entry to the west on Church Street and the entry from the "Boreal Garden" to the north on Pillsbury Drive both lead into a double-height central arrival space with an informal gallery and auditorium access. This dynamic center of the new addition is formed vertically in the overlap of two "L-shaped" voids, with a central stair leading to the library entry above. The top floor of studio space will be a large, open loft area in close proximity to the library below and studios in the adjacent existing building.

The thin plan section of each arm of the new building allows natural cross ventilation and natural light for all spaces. The addition is built with exposed precast concrete structural elements and integral color concrete floors. The horizontal inner facades are developed in naturally weathering copper with 1″ horizontal standing seams. The soft texture of the patina green weathered copper will have the relief of shadows of the horizontal seams. During winter, strips of snow will enliven the facades with sparkling white horizontal lines.

Concept sketch: centripetal existing building and centrifugal addition building

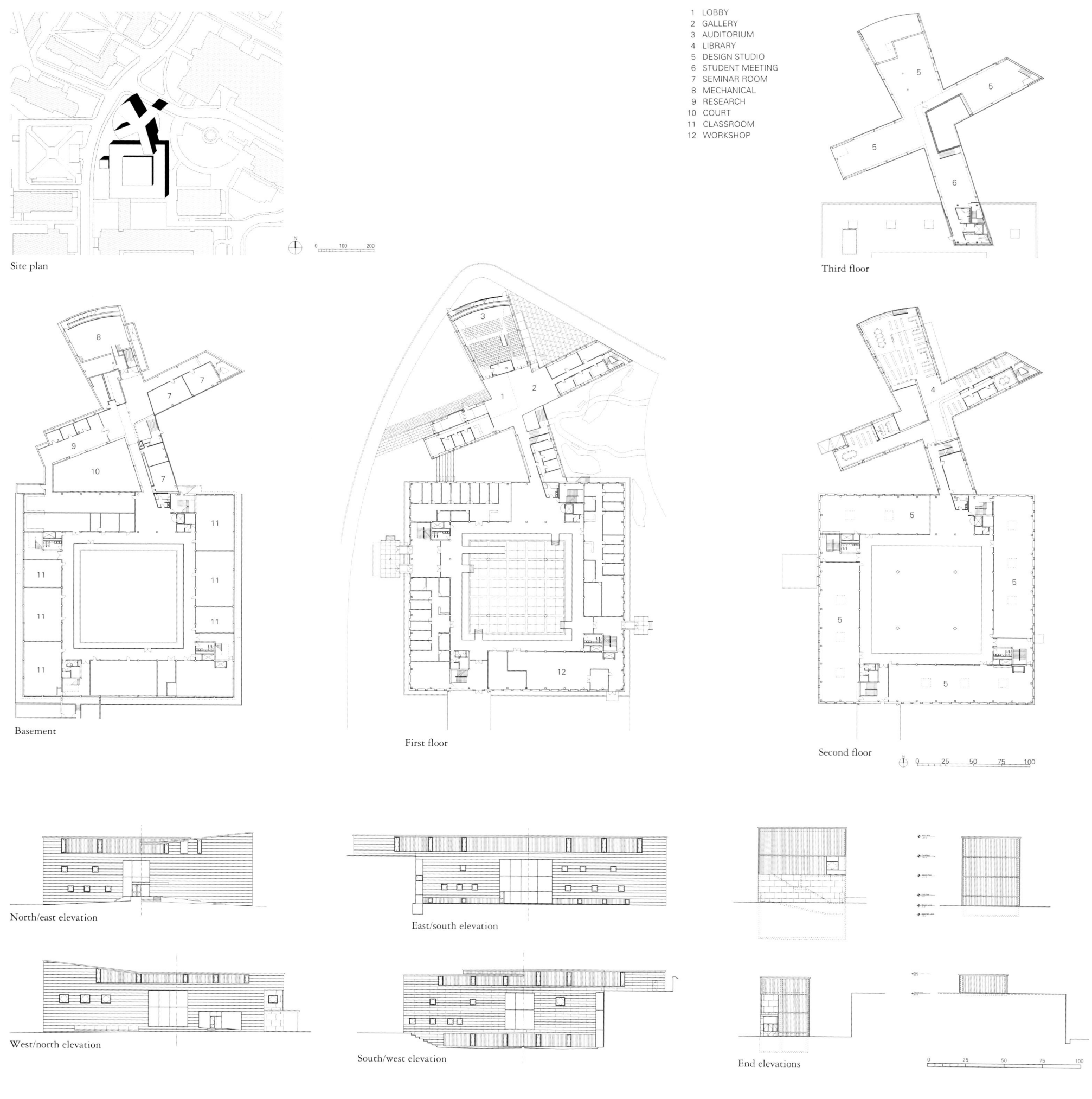

#	
1	LOBBY
2	GALLERY
3	AUDITORIUM
4	LIBRARY
5	DESIGN STUDIO
6	STUDENT MEETING
7	SEMINAR ROOM
8	MECHANICAL
9	RESEARCH
10	COURT
11	CLASSROOM
12	WORKSHOP

Site plan

Third floor

Basement

First floor

Second floor

North/east elevation

East/south elevation

West/north elevation

South/west elevation

End elevations

ミネソタ大学建築＋ランドスケープ学部棟

建築及びランドスケープ学部への増築は，その内部と外部構成の両面で，2つの学部を統合する施設を提供する一方で，キャンパス内の活動や歩行者のサーキュレーションを活性化する。

　増築棟は，1958年にソーショフとシーミーの設計でつくられた，縦横100フィートのアトリウムが中心になった200平方フィートの既存建物とは，対比的であり補足的な存在になる。既存棟は集中的で均質な性格を備える一方で，増築棟は周縁部の眺めを取り込み，多様な形態構成を備えている。既存棟は求心的で，4つの方形の開口が同じコートに向かって4つの眺めを枠取っている。増築棟は遠心的で，鈍角で枠取られた4つの開口が4つの違う屋外風景に向いている。既存棟の水平に広がるファサードを補足して，増築棟は各アームの終端部が垂直的な立面を備え，キャンパス・サイトを活性化するバーチャルなタワー，つまり"空間のシャフト"として立ち上がる。"L形"を2つ組み合わせた新棟には，図書室，オーディトリアム，セミナー室，オフィス，スタジオ・スペースが配置されている。地階とその上2層は既存棟の各階に対応し，4層すべては既存棟のエレベータでアクセスできる。

　西側のチャーチ・ストリートに面したメイン・エントリーも，北側のピルスベリー・ドライヴに面した「ボリアル・ガーデン」からのエントリーも，共にインフォーマルなギャラリーとオーディトリアムへ導く2層の高さを持つ中央空間へ通じている。増築棟のこのダイナミックな中心は，2つの「L形」が重なる部分に垂直のヴォイドを形成し，中央の階段を上がると図書室の入口である。スタジオ・スペースの最上階はその下の図書室と，隣接する既存棟内のスタジオに近接した広いオープンなロフト・エリアとなっている。

　新棟を構成する4本のアームの平面は幅が狭く，すべての部屋で自然換気と自然採光が可能である。構造体は打放しプレキャスト・コンクリートに，着色コンクリートの床。アーム長手側の壁には，銅板が1インチの立ちはぜ継ぎで水平に張られている。風化して緑青色に変色した銅のやわらかなテクスチャーに，水平に延びる立ちはぜ継ぎの落とす影がレリーフをつくり，冬には，継ぎ目に積もる雪の細長い帯が，白く輝く水平の線を描き，ファサードを生き生きさせるだろう。

East view

North-south longitudinal section

East-west longitudinal section

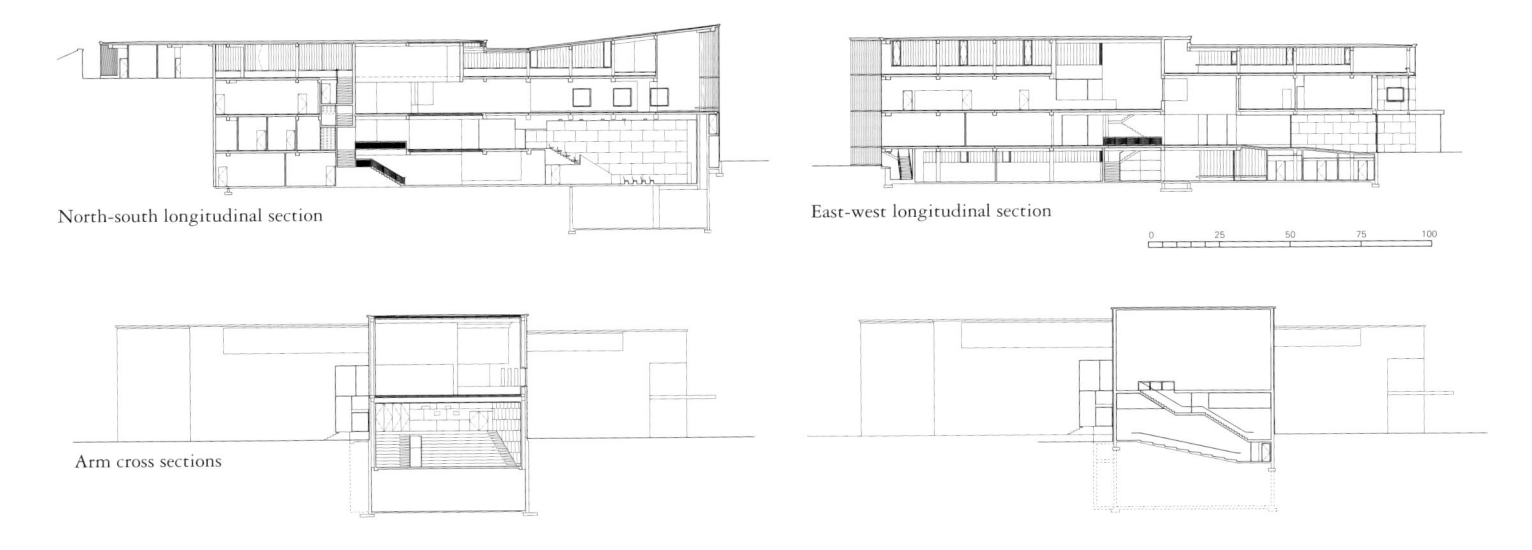

Arm cross sections

Entrance hall on fisrt floor

Main entrance

Basement: research

Corridor beside courtyard on basement

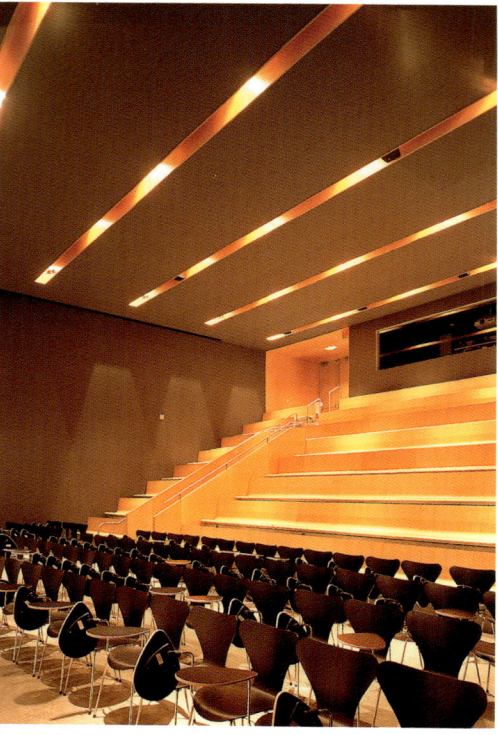

Auditorium

Library on second floor

Studio on third floor

Bench on second floor

Entrance court: new entrance between two existing buildings

Higgins Hall Center Section
Pratt Institute School of Architecture
1997-2005   Brooklyn, New York, U.S.A.

1 LECTURE HALL
2 LOWER LOBBY
3 CLASSROOM
4 ENTRANCE COURT
5 RECEPTION/LOBBY
6 GALLERY
7 SCULPTURE TERRACE
8 STUDIO
9 ROOF TERRACE
10 MECHANICAL

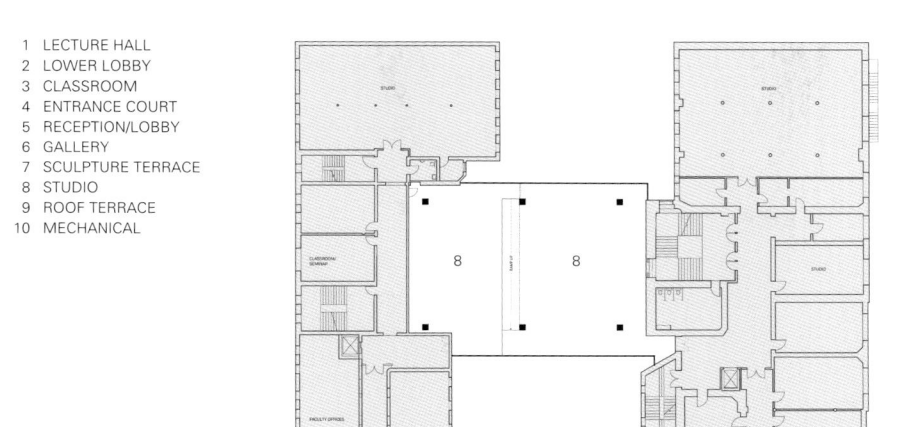

Second floor

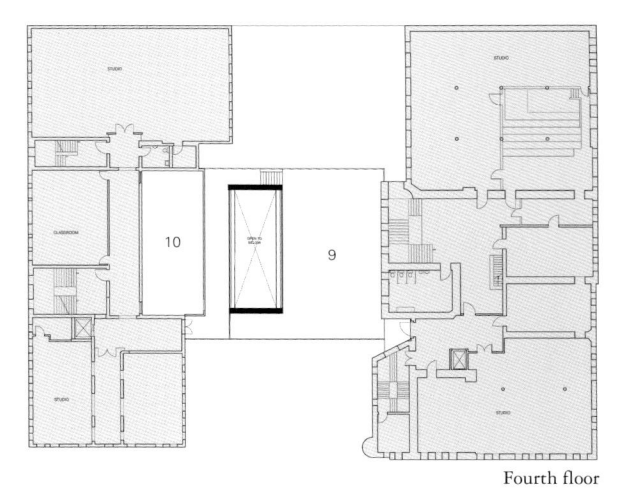

Fourth floor

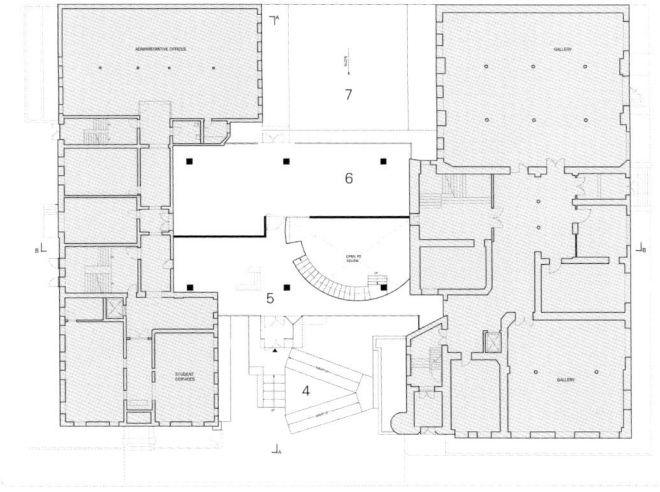

First floor

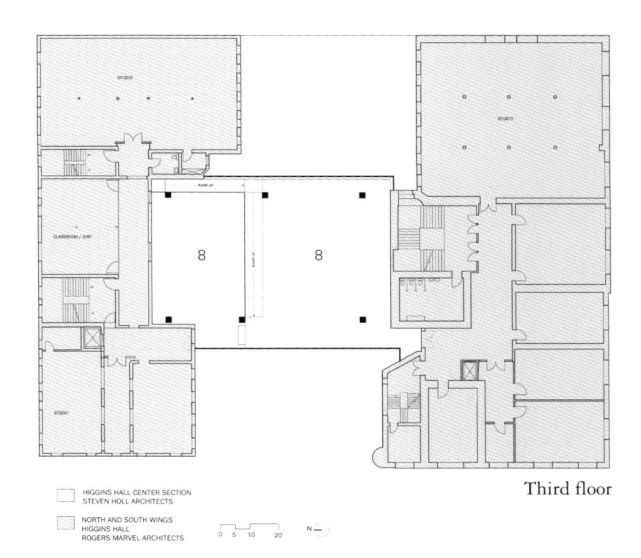

Third floor

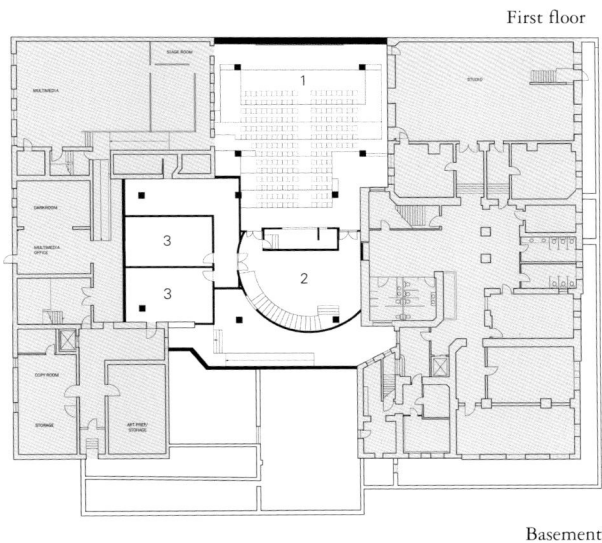

Basement

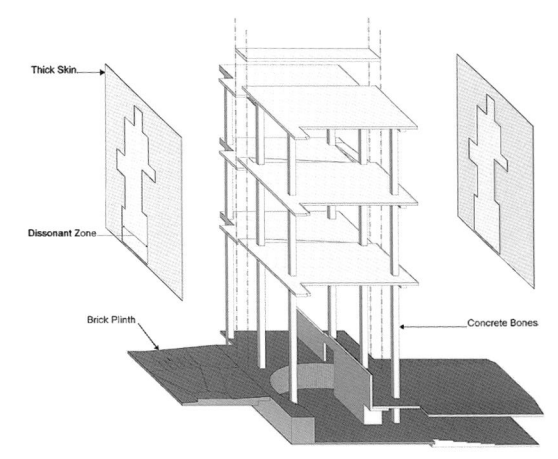

Isometric diagram

The new Higgins Hall Center Section replaces a building that was lost to a fire in 1996.

The new Higgins Hall Center Section is an urban insertion which draws from the sections of the two adjacent historic land-marked buildings. Floor plates of the north and south wings do not align. By drawing this misalignment into the new glass section to meet at the center a "dissonant zone" is created which marks the new entry to the school.

The two masonry buildings together with the new glass insertion form an "H" in plan. New courts facing east and west are paved in the reused red brick which was salvaged following the fire that took place in 1996. The east facing court overlooks the green yards of the inner block, while the west court is shaped as the main front on St. James Place.

Rising from this red brick plinth, the glass center is supported on six pre-cast concrete columns. Fabricated in Canada the thick steel beams and columns form stone-like bones, while the "U" shaped structural glass planks with translucent white insulation form a thick glowing skin. The thick skin is interrupted by clear glass at the dissonant zone, which is aligned with the internal ramps, turning the circulation north and south for views out.

The misalignment in floors can be seen in the dissonant zone which varies increasingly as it moves vertically in section: on the first floors, the misalignment is 1/2 inch; on the second floors it is 1 foot 8 inches, on the third floors it is 4 feet 9 inches, and on the fourth floors it is 6 feet seven inches. Thus, the dissonance moves from the detail thickness of a finger to human scale.

A two-throated skylight marks the top of this center wing, joining two types of light; south light and north light, analogous to harmonious sounds in a dissonant chord.

Rebuilding the center allows a new arrangement of the School of Architecture under the direction of Dean Thomas Hanrahan. For the first time the north and south wings are functionally connected, and the School of Architecture a single, clearly-oriented entrance and central entrance court.

The new functional spaces include: New design studio spaces, classrooms and media office, the Leo Kuhn entrance/reception area, a new auditorium with overflow seating for digital projection, and the new Robert H. Siegel Architecture Gallery.

With President Tom Schutte's leadership, the collaboration of Rogers Marvel Architects, and the skill of Sciame Construction, a great architecture school will glow here at night.

Entrance court: evening view

プラット・インスティテュート建築学科
ヒギンズ・ホール中央セクション
ヒギンズ・ホールの新しいセンター・セクションは，1996年に焼失した建物に代わるものである。

この中央部分は，隣接する2棟の歴史的なランドマーク・ビルの一部から引き出された都市的な挿入部である。北と南の棟の床面の高さは互いにずれがあり，このずれを中央で整合させるために新設されたガラス張りのセンター・セクションの中へ引き込むことによって，学部への新しいエントリーを構成する「不整合ゾーン」がつくりだされる。

2棟の煉瓦造の建物は，新しいガラスの挿入部と共に「H」型平面を形成する。東側と西側に面して新たに生まれたコートには，1996年の火災跡から回収した赤煉瓦が敷き詰められる。東面するコートは奥のブロックの芝生の中庭を見晴らし，西のコートはセント・ジェイムズ・プレイスに面した正面ファサードを形成する。

この赤煉瓦の台座から立ち上がる中央のガラス棟は，6本のプレキャスト・コンクリートの柱で支持されている。カナダで製作されたスティールの厚い梁と柱は，石に似た骨格をかたちづくり，半透明の白い断熱材の入った厚板ガラスの「U」型をした構造材が厚い白熱する皮膜をかたちづくる。厚い皮膜は「不整合ゾーン」のところで透明ガラスによって遮られる。透明ガラスは，外側の眺めに向かって，北と南に動線を転換しながら内部スロープと整列する。

床の高さのずれは「不整合ゾーン」で目視できる。ずれは垂直方向に変化の度合いを増す。1階では1/2インチ。2階では1フィート8インチ，3階では4フィート9インチ。4階では6フィート7インチ。こうして高さのずれは1本の指に等しい厚さから人間の尺度まで進展する。

2本の管の付いたスカイライトがこの中央棟の頂部を飾り，不協和音のなかに響く耳に快い音のように，南と北からの2種類の光を結び合わせる。

トーマス・ハンラハン学部長の監督下，中央部の再建

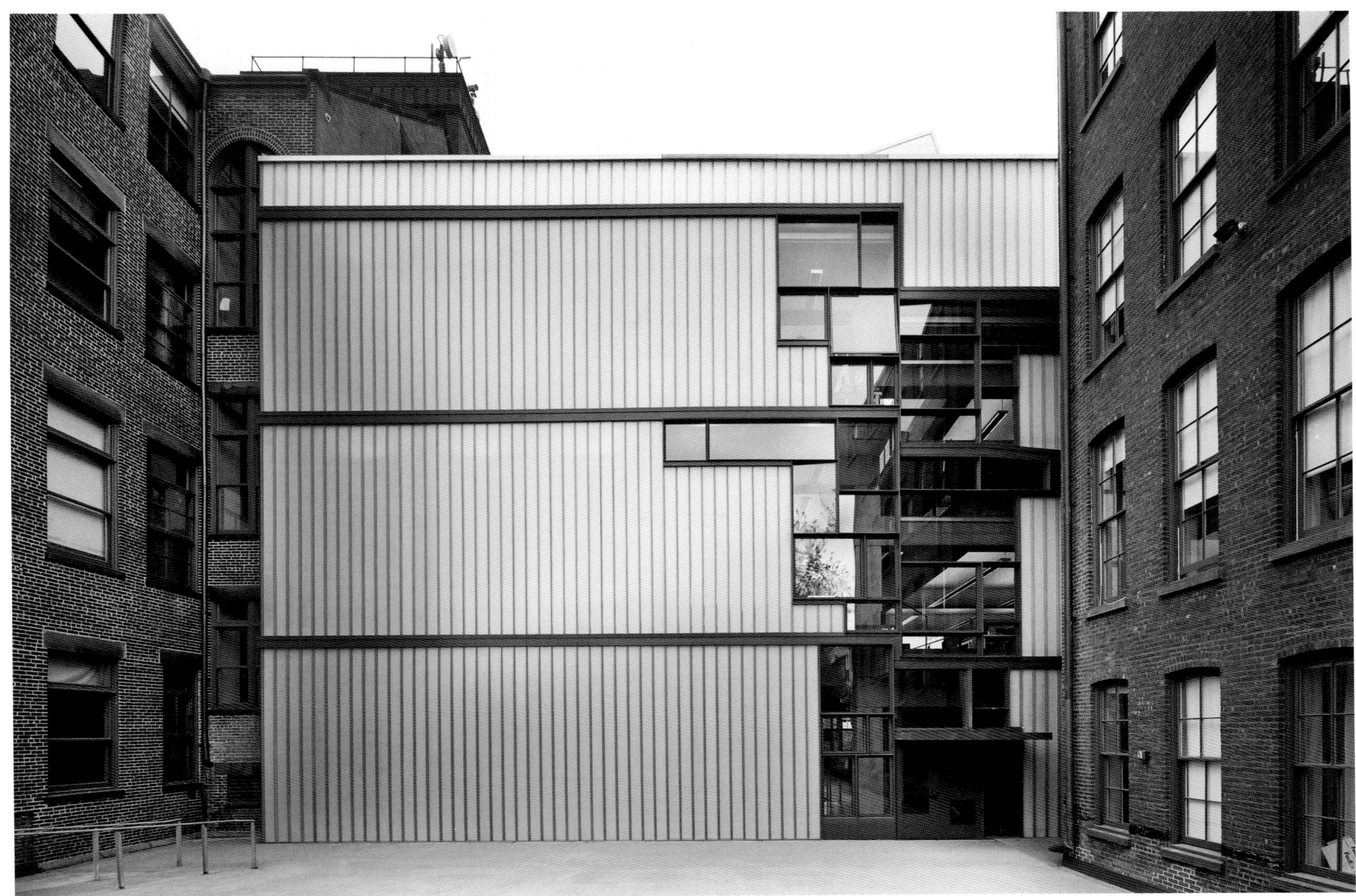

Sculpture terrace

により建築学部の新たな再編が可能となる。初めて北棟と南棟が機能的に結合され，建築学部は，明快に方向づけられた中央エントランス・コートを持つことになる。

新しい機能として次のものが含まれる。デザイン・スタジオ，教室，メディア・オフィス，レオ・クーン・エントランス／レセプション・エリア，デジタル映写の際，かつては入りきれなかった人数分の席を備えたオーディトリアム，新しいロバート・H・シーゲル建築ギャラリー。

学長のトム・シュットの指導の下，ロジャーズ・マーヴェル・アーキテクツの協力と，シアム・コンストラクションの技術によって，この名高い建築学部棟は，夜も輝くことだろう。

Dissonant levels

Entrance

Lower lobby

Entrance: view from lobby

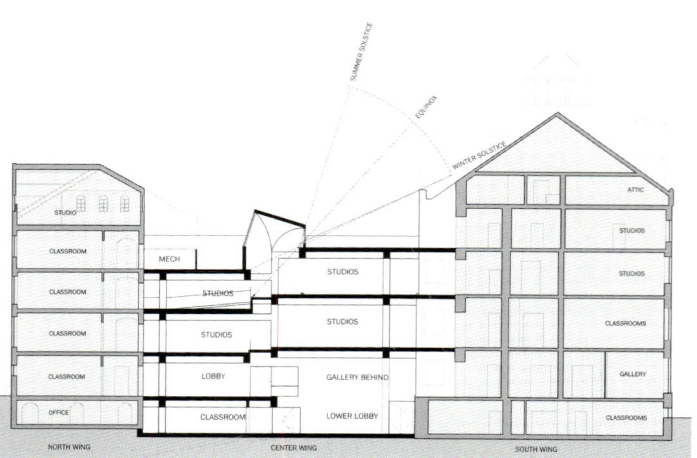

North-south section

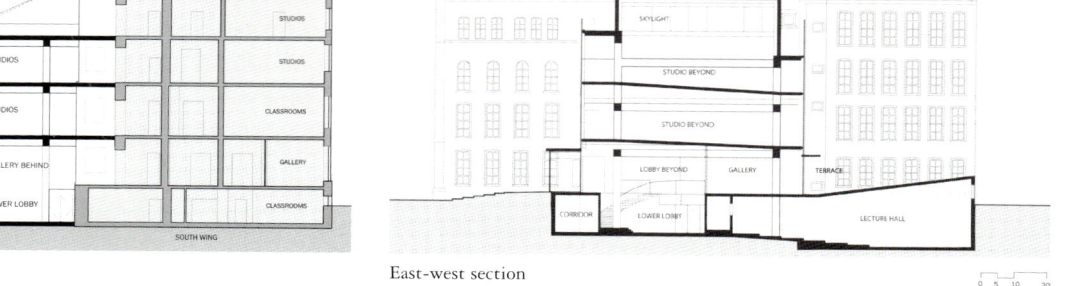

East-west section

Studio

Lecture hall

5 Edge of a City
都市の周縁

The health of the eye seems to demand a horizon. We are never tired so long as we can see far enough.
——Ralph Waldo Emerson

On the fringe of the modern city, displaced fragments sprout without intrinsic relationships to existing organization, other than that of the camber and loops of the curvilinear freeway. Here, the "thrown away" spreads itself outward like the nodal lines of a stone tossed into a pond. The edge of a city is a philosophical region, where city and natural landscape overlap, existing without choice or expectation. This zone calls for visions and projections that delineate the boundary between the urban and the rural. Visions of a city's future can be plotted on this partially spoiled land, liberating the remaining natural landscape, protecting the habitats of hundreds of species of animals and plants that are threatened with extinction. What remains of the wilderness can be preserved; defoliated territory can be restored. In the middle zone between landscape and city, there is hope for a new synthesis of urban life and urban form. Traditional planning methods are no longer adequate. Looking back at the city from the point of view of the landscape, these projects consider untested programs and new kinds of urban spaces.

  The exponential changes brought about by air travel over 20th century exemplify how experiences of space and time change from city to city. Within hours we are transported from one climate and time zone to another. Formerly, entering a city occured along the earth via a bridge or a portal. Today, we circle over then jet down to an airstrip on a city's periphery. Consequently, in making plans and projections for new city edges, it is necessary to discard old methods and working habits and begin with basic research.

  The exploration of strategies to counter sprawl at the periphery cities ——the formation of spaces rather than the formation of objects ——are primary aims of the Edge of a City projects. The expanded boundary of the contemporary city calls for the synthesis of new spatial compositions. An intensified urban realm could be a coherent mediator between the extremes of the metropolis and the agrarian plain.

  In each proposal, living, working, recreational and cultural facilities are juxtaposed in new pedestrian sectors that might act as social condensers for new communities. From Spatial Retaining Bars (1989) that protect the desert at the edge of Phoenix, Arizona, to Spiroid Sectors (1990) that densify suburban settlement, preserving the natural landscape, the proposals presented here entwine a new social program with existing circumstances. Though they differ in form, these proposals share a "pre-theoretical ground" of psychological space, program, movement, light quality and tactility.

Steven Holl

New York City

「目の健康には水平線が必要なようだ。遠くが見えるかぎり私たちは疲れを覚えることはない。」
——R・W・エマーソン

現代都市の周縁では,あちらこちらで,既存の周辺環境との関わりを無視した新しい建物への建て替えが進んでいる。それはまた,高速道路の曲線の描く傾きやループとも別種のものなのだ。そこでは,これらの「投げ捨て」建築が,池に投じられた石のつくりだす波紋のように外へ外へと広がってゆく。こうした都市の周縁は,都市と自然の景観が混在し,選択の自由もなく将来の期待ももてない,根源的な考察を要する地域である。このような一帯には,都市と田園地帯の境界についての輪郭を描けるようなヴィジョンと提案が待望されている。破壊されかけているこの土地に,残された自然景観を保存しながら,絶滅の危機に瀕した何百という種の動植物が生息する環境を護るような形で,都市の未来像を描くこともできるはずだ。残る未開の土地は保護し,枯れた土地は回復させる。自然景観と都市の間に横たわる中間地帯には,都市生活と都市形態のあいだに新たな統合を生みだせる望みがある。そこでは伝統的な計画手法はもはや適合しない。ここにあげるプロジェクトは,ランドスケープという視点から都市を見直して,未だ試みられたことのない計画や新しい種類の都市空間について考察したものである。

20世紀に入って,飛行機旅行によってもたらされた変化の代表的なものは,都市から都市への空間と時間を移動する時の体験である。今では,数時間のうちに,気候も時刻も違う所へ移動するが,かつては,よその都市に入ってゆくといえば地上を移動して橋を渡り,門をくぐってゆくものだった。それが今日では,ジェット機が空を旋回して,都市の郊外にある空港の滑走路めがけて下降するのだ。だとすれば,都市の周辺部に新たな計画をつくり提案するには,古い方法や現行の慣習を捨て去り,根本的な調査からはじめなければならないだろう。

都市の周縁部のスプロールに対処する戦略を練るにあたって,オブジェを配するという形ではなく,空間をどう配置するかが,「エッジ・オブ・シティ」の諸計画の目標である。現代都市の,外へ広がり続ける境界地域では,新たに空間を構成する統合の方法を求めている。都市の膨脹部は,大都市のいちばん外れと農業地帯の間を一体とする仲介者に転ずるに違いない。

ここにあげたどの提案をとっても,生活,労働,余暇や文化のための施設が,新しいコミュニティのための「コンデンサー」となる新たに構成された歩行者の中に置かれている。アリゾナ州フェニックスの外れに広がる砂漠を保護するスペイシャル・リテイニング・バー(1989)から,郊外地の居住密度をあげつつ自然を残そうというスピロイド・セクター(1990)に至るまで,これらの提案は,新しい社会政策と既存の環境との調和を示すものだ。それぞれ形は違っているにしても,心理的な空間,プログラム,動き,光の質,触感という,「理論以前の領域」を共有しているのである。

(スティーヴン・ホール)

1986 Urban Proposal for Porta Vittoria District
Milan, Italy

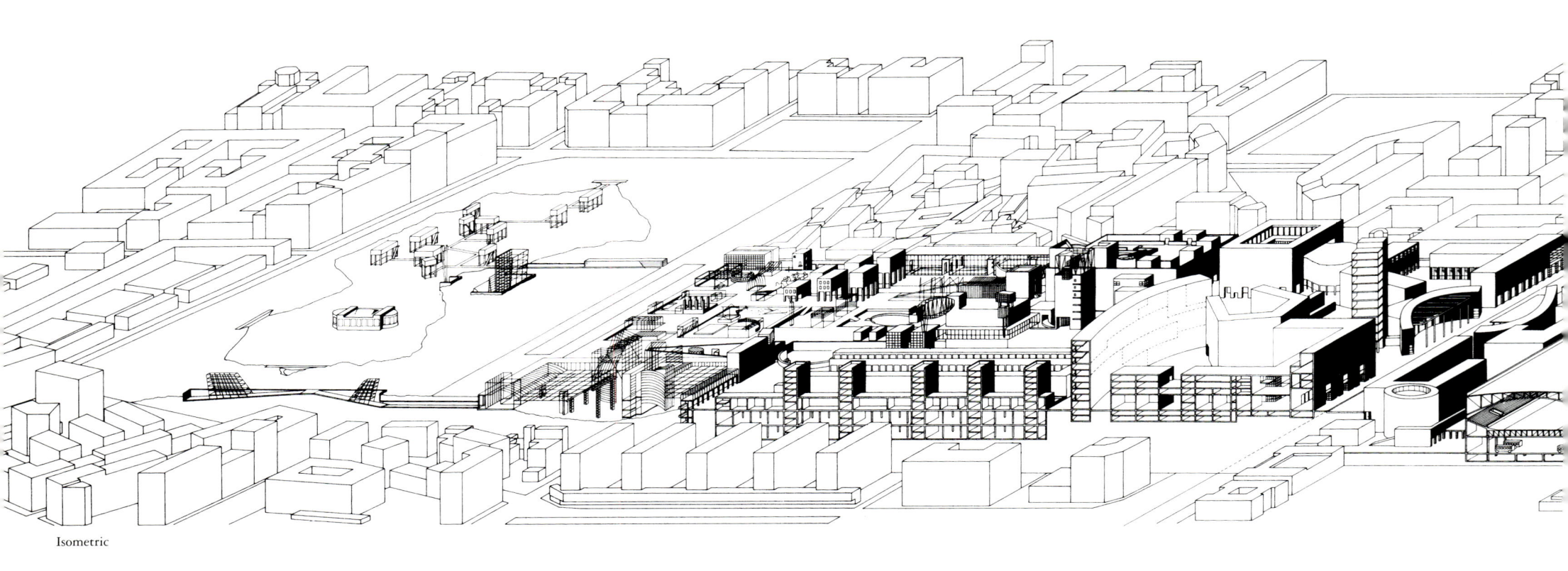

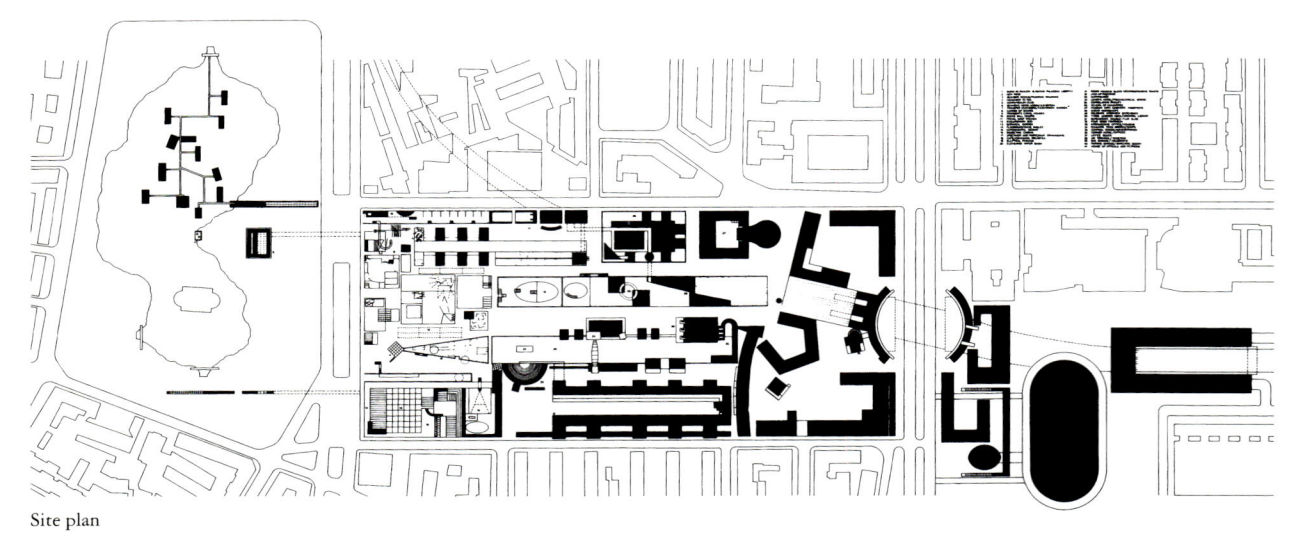

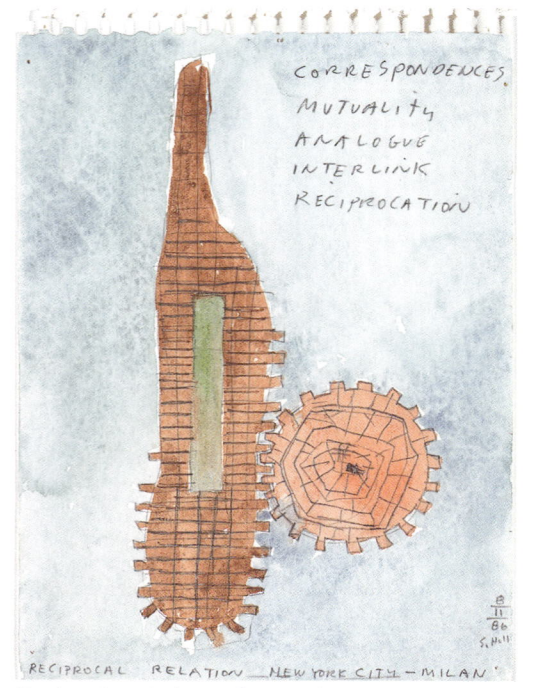

Isometric

Site plan

Sketch: reciprocal relation of New York City and Milan

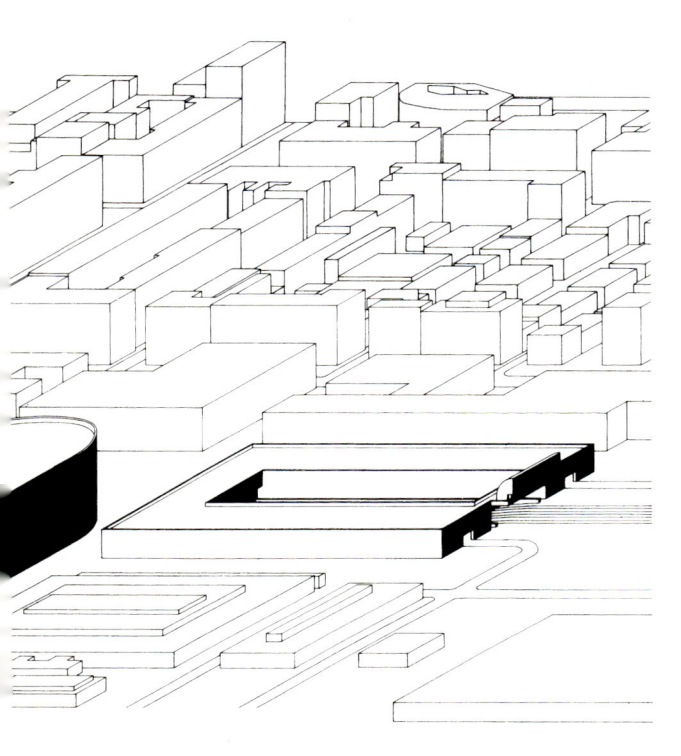

Long basin for aquatic activities below, truss footbridge and suspended chapel above

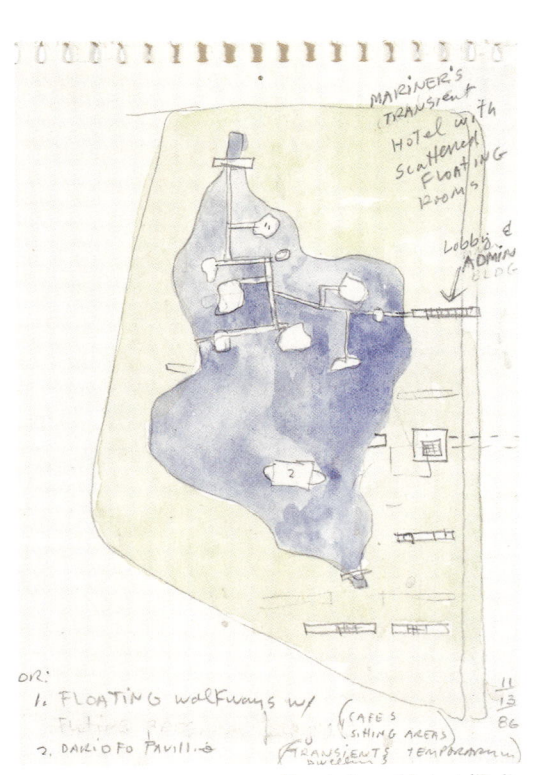

Sketch: Largo Marinai d'Italia

Sketch: monument at Largo Marinai d'Italia

I-219

Sketches: elliptical passsage

New subway station

Passage

The site for this project, commissioned by the 17th Triennale of Milan, is a disused freight rail yard (part of Milan's old railroad belt) bordered by blocks of different housing types. It is in the nineteenth-century gridded portion of Milan, outside the historical center.

The program required keeping only the new "Passante" subway station, provoking the redevelopment of the area. Other functions to be located at the site include a bus station and garage for thirty buses, an air terminal station, hotels, offices, and housing. The proposal is also meant to provoke consideration of other programs for the reclamation of this metropolitan site.

The conviction behind this project is that an open work—an open future—is a source of human freedom. To investigate the uncertain, to bring out unexpected properties, to define psychological space, to allow the modern soul to emerge, to propose built configurations in the face of (and fully accepting) major social and programmatic uncertainty: this is our intention for the continuation of a "theoretical Milan."

From a dense center, Milan unfolds in circles ringed by a patchwork grid that finally sprawls raggedly into the landscape. Against this centrifugal urban sprawl (from dense core to light periphery), a reversal is proposed: light and fine-grained toward the center, heavy and volumetric toward the periphery. This proposal projects a new ring of density and intensity, adjoining the rolling green of a reconstituted landscape.

Three traditional urban strategies were rejected. The flexible planning device of the grid was suspended, because of its tendency to render everything as a measure of block-by-block infill. Secondly, the method that organizes historically modeled building types according to the existing morphology of the city was suspended. Finally, the whole method of drawing a plan layout, followed later by a three-dimensional form, was rejected.

The strategy used reverses the usual method of design in architecture (from plan to section, elevation, perspectival space). Instead, perspective sketches of spatial conditions are cast backward into plan fragments, which are then reconciled in an overall layout.

By its nature the perspective drawing implies associations between elements. These spatial configurations are taken as evidence of particular activity, clues for reconstructing a program. Images of human activity, collected from diverse sources, are held alongside the perspective views to provoke the analysis.

For the existing park, Largo Marinai d'Italia, a giant pond is proposed to reconcile the park with its name. The Palazzina Liberty is restored as the Dario Fo Pavilion and is accessible by rowboat only. A series of floating walkways connects a seaman's exhibition. Residential apartments hover over tiny objects: an oar, a horn, a carving. Old sailors discuss the artifacts with passing visitors; stories are the material of the floating exhibition.

At the edge of the pond is a large metronomelike Monument to Toil, in memory of the loading and unloading of goods that once filled this site. As the slow movement of each pipe beam reaches the end of a beat, a drop of water is emitted from its top. Nearby, an aviary housing two white doves juts out of the park, bringing light to an underground assemblage.

Across Viale Umbria, in a Garden of Sounds, the park infiltrates the urban area.

Largo Marinai d'Italia

Long basin for aquatic activities

Long basin for aquatic activities

Within the garden is a seasonal children's zoo whose animals require a variety of cages and enclosures (the goat, the chicken, the cow, etc.). Other little programs are implied by the titles of the various areas: The See-Saw, Fishing, The Picnic, The Water-Chute, The Sleigh, La Commedia Italiana, The Octopus, Hunting, Fireworks, Bocci Ball.

To the south of the site is a large public Botanical Garden with glass-roofed forms in a sprouting diversity parallel to the vegetation within. Over the sloping earthen floor of the interior are areas for experimental botany, checker and chess tables, and meeting tables. These are scattered throughout the green density of the vegetation. On the ground of the eastern portion is a darkened hall containing a cinema that dissects its interior. The public is exposed to back-projection on constructed objects, multiple separation, and other cinematic experiments.

Bounding the Botanical Garden is a large public fountain that is negotiated via stone steps and passages interwoven with cascades of water. The fountain opens onto a long basin for aquatic activities and barge-borne theatrical events. At the edge of this opening is a hotel for unhappy lovers. The plan has no interior corridors, setting the rooms of the hotel back-to-back. One large glass corridor belts the building. At the top is a crooked cafe-lounge and a wiry truss containing a foot-bridge to a suspended chapel. On the northwest portion of the site, a water channel is flanked by rudimentary housing for the homeless. Nearby, a public gymnasium is organized in a strip interwoven with spectator areas. To the east is a school of the humanities. Its central block of lecture rooms is banded by study room towers; visiting professors live in the upper portions. From the main building, a walkway connects to two wedge-shaped interrelated workshop-studios. To the west, a ramp cycles through a two-part correlating facility, leading upward into spaces more and more remote, arriving at a mechanical rooftop simulating teleological suspension.

Near Via F. Rezzonico is a sanctuary of the muses filled with ancient stone fragments. A modern cinema is inserted from the east. The public can move back and forth from celluloid simulation to stone materiality.

The new subway station opens to the west onto an elongated gap. Here the visitor passes through several activities, rising through an elliptical passage to the Garden of Sounds. Bureaucratic and administrative activities (formless and always in flux) are given specific urban character in a thin tower, a four-sided pentagon, a double-flux slab (whose section can be altered), and large galleries along the water basin. The three lobbies of these work areas are connected by a central neckshaped space.

Across Viale Mugello, to the east, larger programs fit into the existing city fabric. The airport connection station sits here; adjacent is the bus garage, housed below a public arena and velodrome.

Of these specific ideas, several might be realized, and yet the overall strategy and intention depends on none of them. They serve only as examples for the figure in the landscape of this city for which the unknown is a source of optimism. To affirm the joy of the present, to find lines of escape, to subvert an overall urban plan from within—via architecture—is part of projecting an open future as a source of freedom.

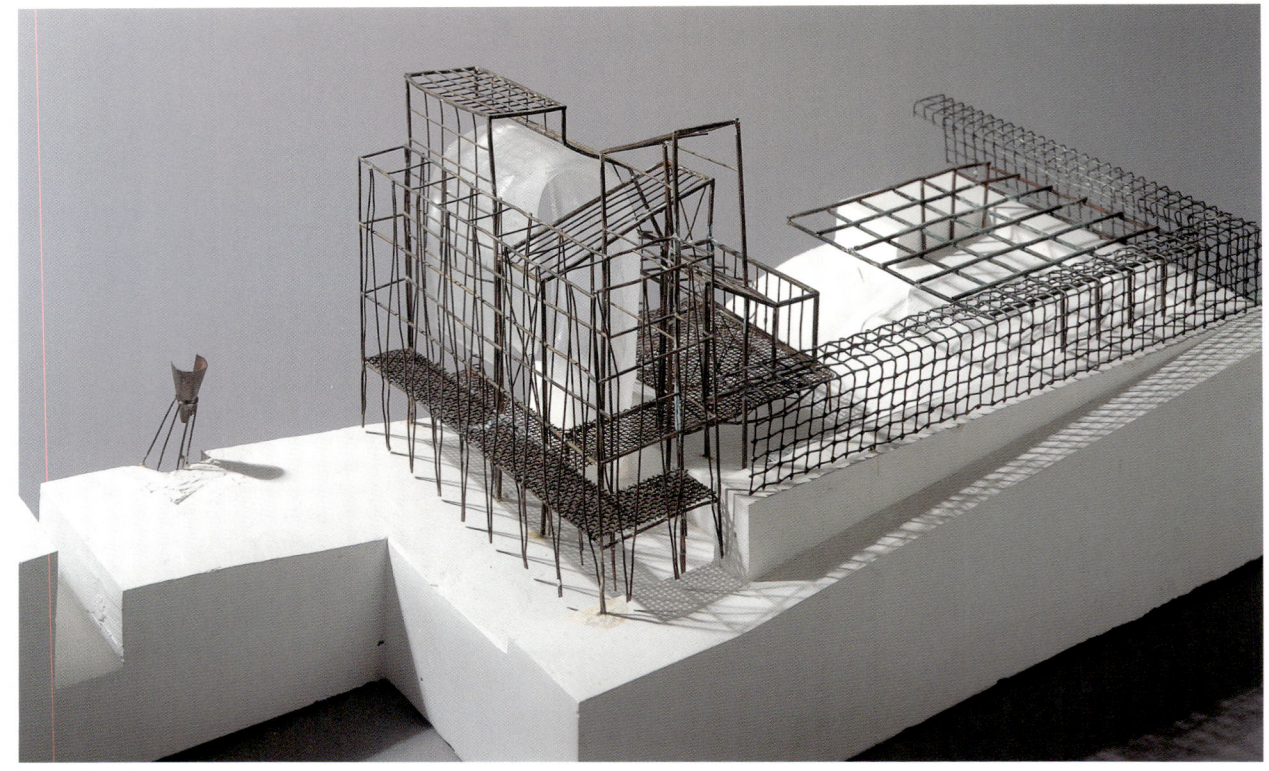

Botanical garden

New subway station (above and bottom)
School of humanities and study room towers (middle)

ポルタ・ヴィットリア計画

ミラノの第17回トリエンナーレに依頼されたこの計画の敷地は,使われなくなった貨物線の鉄道駅の跡地で(ミラノの旧鉄道の一部),それぞれに表情を異にする住宅の建つブロックで周囲を固められている。このあたりは19世紀になって,格子状に区画された地域で,ミラノの歴史的な中心部からははずれた所である。

この計画では,新しい地下鉄「パッサンテ」の駅を,あたりの再開発の起爆剤として取り込むことが望まれた。敷地内につくる施設の概要は,バスの停留所と30台のバスを収容するガレージ,空港の駅,ホテル,オフィス,それに住宅である。提案には,この都市の再開発を計る他の諸々の計画にも目を向けさせようという意図も込められている。

この計画の背後には,ひとつの信念がある。開放的な働き方——開放的な未来——は,人間の自由の根源をなすものであるということだ。不確かなものに投資すること,思いがけない資質に目の光を当てること,精神的な空間とは何であるかを示すこと,時代の魂を目に見えるものにすること,建物を配置することで,重要なものではありながら社会的にはまだ認識されていない計画を目の前に(充分に受け入れ可能な形で)提示することである。これが,「あるべきミラノ」像をどう伝えるべきかということについての私たちの見解である。

高密度の中心部から外にゆくにつれて,現在のミラノは密度がゆるやかになり,やがて周囲の景観の中に不揃いに食い込んで終わる。このような遠心的なスプロール(濃密な中心部から稀薄な周辺部へ)とは反対の形を私たちは提案したのである。中心に向かうにつれ,小さなものを疎らに配し,周辺を大規模な建築が高密度に占めるのだ。ここでは,高密度で強い性格をもつ環状地帯を新たにつくり,景観にも手を加えて,なだらかに起伏する緑を加える。

私たちは都市計画の三つの常套手段を退けた。まず,格子によるプランニングは控える。とかく,何もかもブロック単位で量りながら空間を埋めてゆき,それだけで満足しがちだからである。次に,この都市をなぞるようにして歴史的な形の建築をつくるという手法もとらない。また全体のプランを描いて,その後で三次元の形態をつくるという方法も退けた。

この方法は建築デザインの常道(平面図から断面,立面,パースペクティブな空間へ)の逆をゆくものであった。つまり,空間の状況を示すパースペクティブなスケッチからとりかかって,部分的な平面に進み,その後で全体の配置と調整をはかるのである。

その性質上,パースは様々な要素の相互のかかわり方を伝える。したがって,こうした空間上の配置は,ある特定の行動を示すものとなり,それが,何らかのプログラムを組み立てる糸口になるのだ。広く集められた人間の行動のイメージは,パースに基づいて把握されて分析を促すことになる。

既存の公園,ラルゴ・マリナイ・ディターリア(イタリアの船員達の広場)にはその名に恥じぬように大きな池を提案にとりいれた。パラッツィーナ・リベルティは修復してダーリオ・フォー・パヴィリオンに名を改める。これは池の中にあるので,ボートを漕いで行くほかに近づけない。船員

Sketch: passage

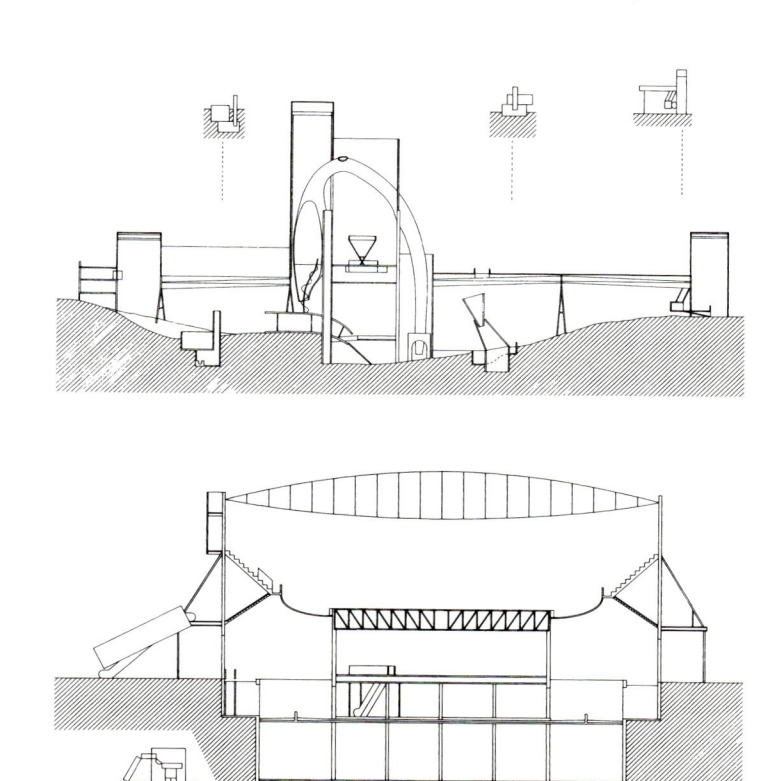

Sections

に関するものを納める展示場は,浮桟橋伝いに結ばれる。こまごまとした物たち,たとえばオール,霧笛,彫刻などを展示するフロアの上の階にはアパートメントが置かれる。年老いた船員たちがここを訪れる人々を相手に,展示された物について言葉を交わす。彼らの語る物語も水上の展示物の一部なのだ。

池の縁に,巨大なメトロノームを思わせる形をした,かつての重労働のモニュメントが建っており,この地を埋めつくした貨物の揚卸の作業を偲ばせるよすがになっている。それぞれのパイプが,ゆるやかな動きで受持ち範囲の端にゆくと,その先端から水が流れ出るという仕掛けだ。その傍らには,2羽の白い鳩を入れる鳥小舎が公園の上に突き出して,そこからは地下の集会場に光を届ける。

ウンブリア通りを横切って,ガーデン・オブ・サウンドに入ると,公園は,都市の様相を帯びる。庭の一部には,季節によって開かれる子供動物園があるので,様々な檻や囲いが必要だ(山羊,にわとり,雌牛などがいるのだ)。その他のこまごまとしたものは,それぞれの呼び名で内容がわかるだろう。たとえばシーソー,魚つり,ピクニック,ウォーターシュート,ソリ,イタリア喜劇,オクトパス,狩り,花火,ボッチボールといった具合だ。

敷地の南には広い植物園があって,中の植物に応じた様々な形のガラス屋根がある。傾斜を残したままの土の床には,植物学上の実験に使われる一帯もあれば,チェッカーやチェスのテーブルや談笑するためのテーブルなどの置かれるところもある。これらが,鬱蒼と生える植物の間に点在しているのだ。東側には,内部が細分された映画館を納めた暗いホールがある。入場者は背面映写のマルチスクリーンなどの実験的映像に目を奪われる。

植物園の縁には,石の階段や歩道が滝とともに織りなされた噴水池があって,それが細長い池に向かって開いている。ここでは水上の催し物や,船上のようにつくられた舞台での催しが繰り広げられる。そのほとりに,幸せになれない恋人たちのためのホテルがある。ホテルの平面は,内部に廊下というものがない。客室は全て,背中合せに並んでガラス張りの長い廊下が周りを囲むからだ。その屋上に,カフェラウンジがあって,さらにそこからはトラスのブリッジが延びてゆき,その先端の吊られたチャペルへ導く。敷地の北西部には,水路の縁にホームレスのための住居がある。その隣に,観客席と組合わされた体育館が帯状に並ぶ。その東には人文科学の学校がある。中央に位置する講義室棟を囲むようにして塔状の研究室棟が建つ。客員教授たちは,その上部を住居にすることになる。中央棟からは,くさび形を組合わせた平面の工作室スタジオへ通路で結ばれる。その西では,螺旋形をなすスロープが二つの建物を行きつ戻りつして,次々と空間を経て昇りつづけると,屋上で行き止まる。本来,原因に達することなどできはしない目的論的思考が,いずれ中断せざるをえないことを表現したものだ。

F・レッツォニコ通り沿いの瞑想のための聖域には古代の石の破片が豊富にある。その東側には,映画館が挿し込まれるようにして続いている。映画という虚像と石の実像との間を行き来できるというわけだ。

新たにつくられる地下鉄駅は西の方にも出入口があって,そこからは細長い広場に続く。ここで様々な仕掛けに出会いながら長円形をなす通路を経てガーデン・オブ・サウンドに至る。役所や管理組織(固定せず常に流動的な形式にする)のためには,それぞれにふさわしい都市的な形態が与えられる。細い塔状や一辺の欠けた五角形もあれば,二層ごとに床を可変にしたり(断面の形が変えられる),あるものは水に沿って長いギャラリーがある。これらオフィス部分の三つのロビーは中央にある首のような形をしたスペースで結ばれる。東側,ムジェッロ通りを挟んだ向い側には,既存の都市の機能につなぐための大規模な計画もある。空港の駅がここに来るし,隣にはバスの車庫があって階下には体育館と自転車の競技場が含まれる。

これら数々のアイディアのうちで,いくつかは実現するかもしれないが,この都市全体の戦略や意図がそのうちのどれかによって左右されることはないかもしれない。ただ,これまで思いもしなかったものが楽天的な気分の源になれるような,ミラノの都市景観の一例として役立てればいいと思う。現在の喜びを確実なものにしたり,あるいは別の世界へ脱出する拠り所を提供したり,都市計画をすっかり転覆させたりすることが内側から──建築を通じて──できるなら,それは,自由の源泉としての解放された未来を,その一部なりとも人々に示せたということだ。

1988 Erie Canal Edge
Rochester, New York, U.S.A.

The Erie Canal, a grand work that secured the growth of New York and of cities along its route, is now an undistinguished trench to the south of Rochester. The project is a cross-sectional study which redefines the canal and reinforces the city edge.

"Canal House" types rest on the top and bottom of the embankment, like dogs at the dinner table. On the north side of the canal, the houses form a continuous wall and an intermittent arcade; on the south, they are dis-aligned and open to the rural.

The northern urban edge is characterized by a workplace building, which anticipates new programs not requiring horizontal floors. Operation occurs via walkway beams analogous to the former work walks along the Erie Canal.

Between the work building and the canal houses are a series of social and cultural facilities: a group of cinemas, a music school, and housing for the elderly with a connecting cultural gallery.

Site plan

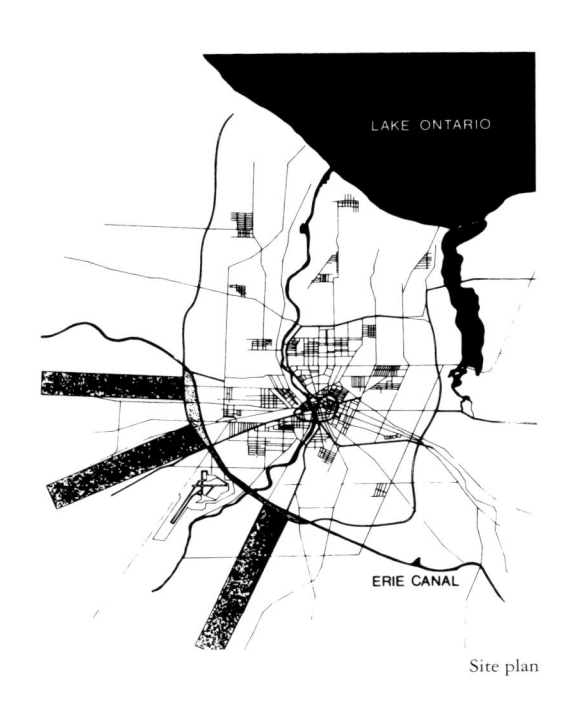

エリー運河畔計画

これまでニューヨークと運河沿いの都市の成長を護って来たエリー運河だが, それが今日ではロチェスターの南を縁取るだけの目立たぬ堀にすぎない有様だ。これは, 運河を見直して都市の周縁部を強化しようという運河の両岸にわたる計画である。

「カナルハウス」タイプの住宅が堤防の上下に, さながらダイニングテーブルに前足をかけている犬のように置かれる。運河の北側には住宅の連続する壁をつくり, その所々にアーケードが設けられる。南岸では住宅は疎らに並ぶので, 背後の田園に対して空間は開かれている。

運河の北の, 都市の縁を形成する側に特徴的なものはワーク・プレイス・ビルディングである。水平の床を必要としない新しい計画が生まれることを予測して, かつてエリー運河沿いにつくられていた作業用の通路になぞらえた歩行用の梁が渡されている。

ワークビルディングとカナルハウスの間には文化施設がある。映画館, 音楽学校, それにカルチャー・ギャラリーを備えた老人用のハウジングなどだ。

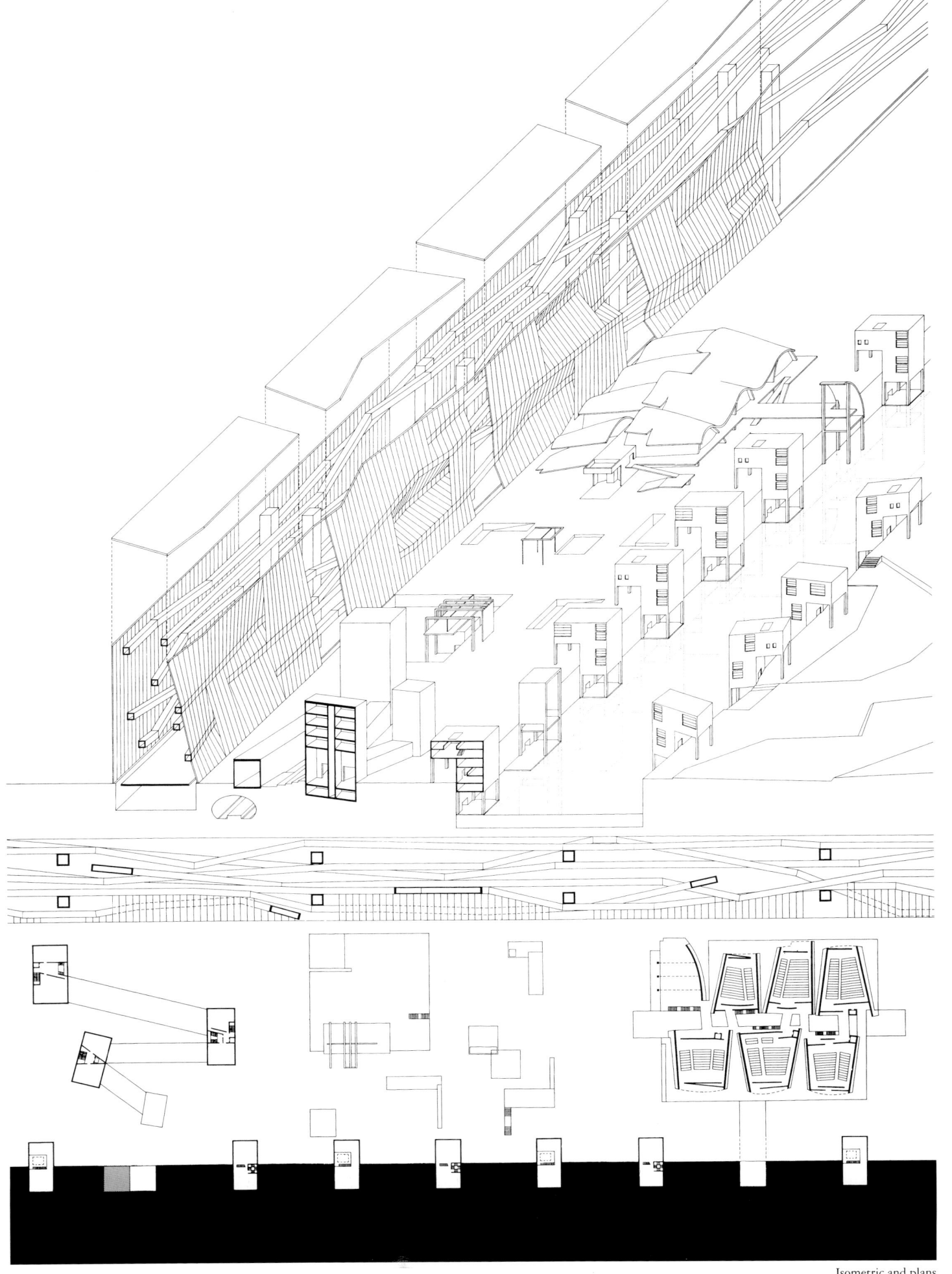

Isometric and plans

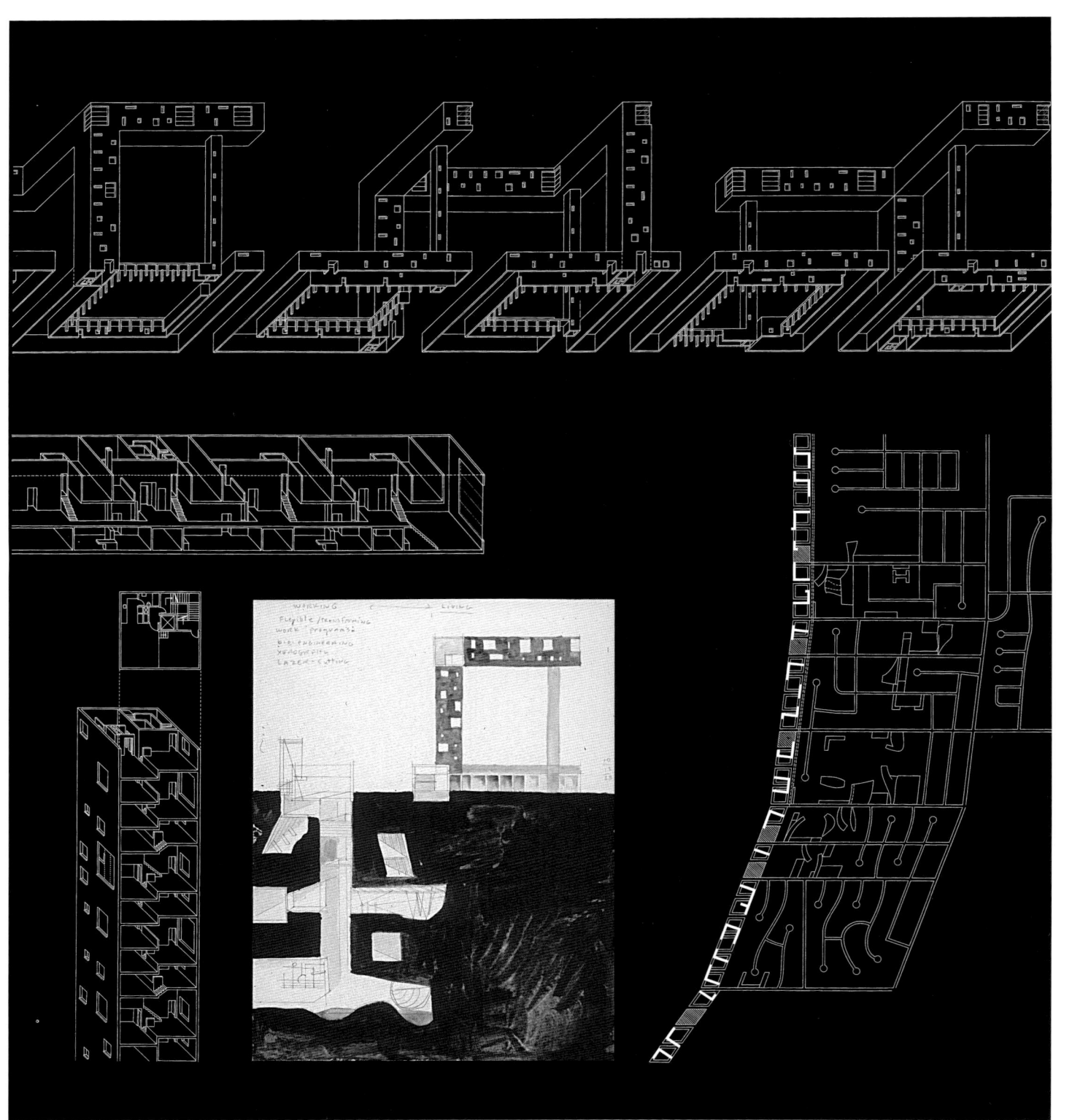

Axonometric, plan and sketch

The most prominent aspect of the history of Phoenix is the mysterious disappearance of the Hohokum Indian civilization after their cultivation of the valley with 250 miles of thirty-foot canals for 1,000 years.

Sited on the periphery of Phoenix, a series of spatial retaining bars infers an edge to the city, a beginning to the desert. Each structure inscribes a 180-foot-square space while it rises to frame views of the distant mountains and desert.

Loft-like living areas hang in silent isolation, forming a new horizon with views of the desert sunrise and sunset. Communal life is encouraged by entrance and exit through public squares at grade. Work is conducted electronically from loft spaces adjoining dwellings. Cultural facilities are suspended in open-frame structures.

The thirty-foot-square building sections act as hollow, reinforced concrete beams. Exteriors are made of pigmented concrete with the undersides of the arms polished to a high gloss. In the morning and evening these undersides are illuminated by the red desert sun—a hanging apparition of light once reflected by the water of the Hohokum canals.

Spatial Retaining Bars

1989   Phoenix, Arizona, U.S.A.

Montage

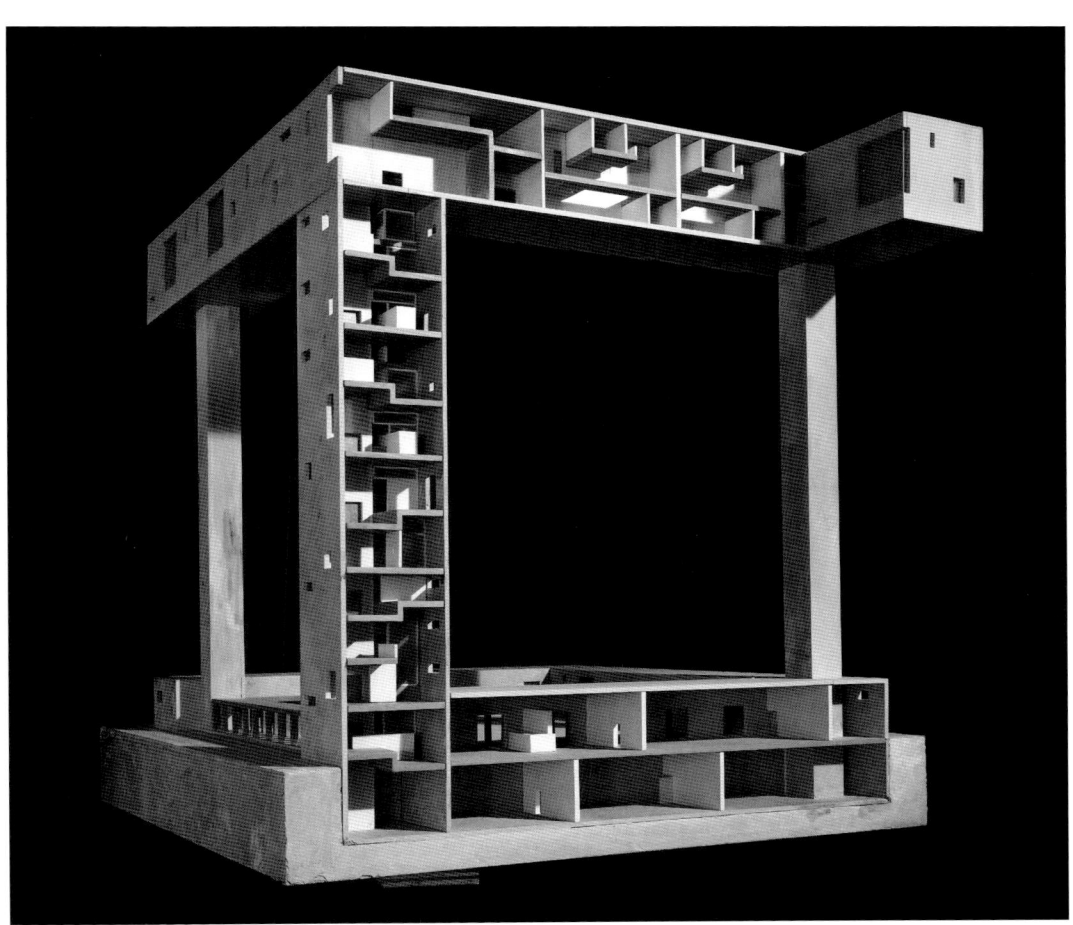

スペイシャル・リテイニング・バー

フェニックスの歴史上で何より際立つのは、幅30フィートの運河を延べ250マイルにわたって巡らせ、山あいの平地を耕作していたホホカム・インディアンの文明が千年の長きにもわたって栄えながら、忽然と消え去ってしまったというミステリーである。

フェニックスの外周部に位置する、中に空間を抱いた、柱と梁だけで構成されたような建築の連なりは、これが都市の端であり、砂漠の始まりであることを伝える。ひとつの単位がそれぞれ180平方フィートの土地を囲み、それが垂直方向にも立ち上がって、彼方の山並みと砂漠のつづく景色を、さながら額縁のように切りとる。

ロフトのような生活空間が、静寂と孤独の中で宙に浮かび、砂漠の日の出と日没を従えた、新たな地平線を形づくる。コミュニティの一員として生活しているという思いは、地表に並ぶ広場を通り抜けて出入りするたびに高められる。設備の操作は、住居に隣接するロフトのスペースから電気的に行われる。文化的な施設は壁のないフレームの中に、吊られるようにして設置される。

30フィート角の断面を持つ建物全体が、中空の鉄筋コンクリートでつくられ、下面はつややかに磨かれているので、明け方や夕暮れ時ともなれば、下側の面は砂漠に赤く輝く太陽に照り映えて、かつてホホカム運河の水面で反射された光が中空に現出したかのように見える。

Retaining bar

A series of spatial retaining bars

1990 **Parallax Towers**
New York, New York, U.S.A.

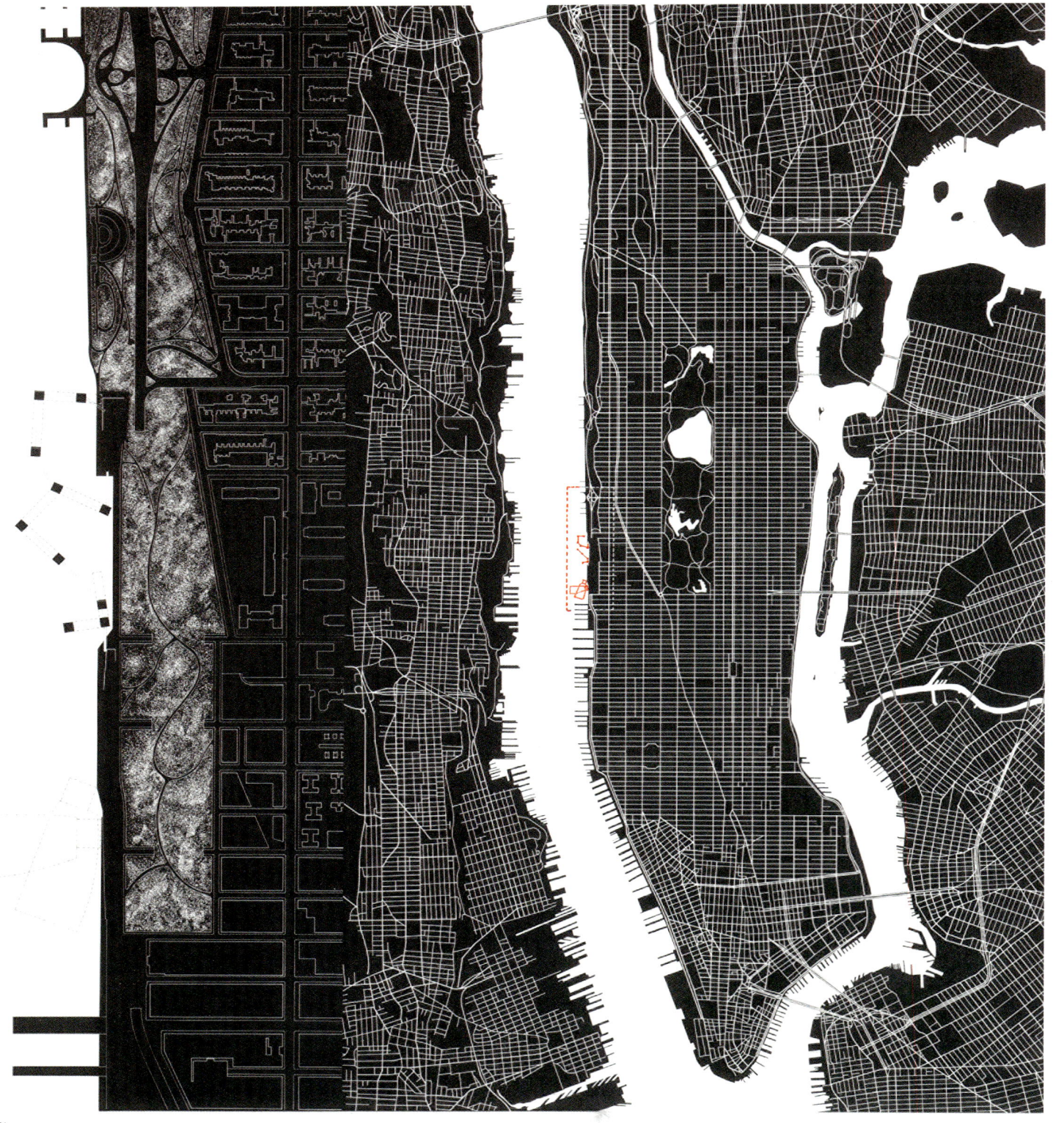

Site map

In this proposal, the existing 72nd Street train yards would be transformed into a new city-edge park in the spirit of Frederick Law Olmsted. The existing dense development to the east looks out over this new open park, which extends to the Hudson River's edge.

On the river, ultrathin skyscrapers bracket the view and create a new kind of framed urban space over water. Hybrid buildings with diverse functions, the towers are linked by horizontal underwater transit systems that connect underwater parkside lobbies to high-speed elevators serving upper transfer lobbies. Occupants are within walking distance of the 72nd Street subway entrance or express ferries to the Jacob K. Javits Convention Center, Wall Street, and La Guardia Airport.

In counterbalance to the ultrathin towers, an ultrathick floating public space is used as a concert stadium, large-screen movie theater complex, or grand festival hall.

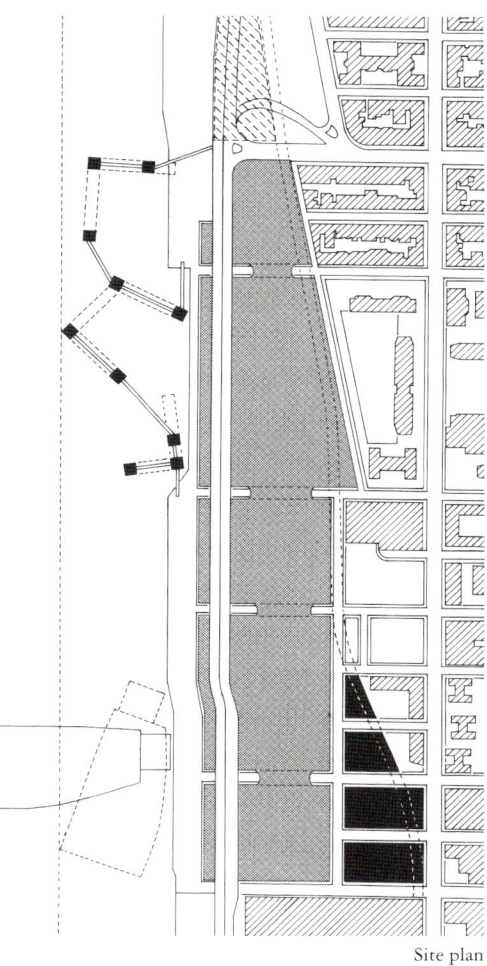

Sketch: west elevation

パララックス・タワー

この計画は72丁目の鉄道操作場の敷地を，フレデリック・ロウ・オルムステッドの精神を受け継ぐ，シティ・エッジ・パークに生まれ変わらせようというものだ。東側の高密度に開発された区域から見ると，ハドソン河岸までひろがるこの新しい公園越しの景色が広がる。

川面に極細型の高層ビル群が景色を包み込むようにして建ち並ぶと，水面に新しい種類の都市空間が浮かぶ。様々な機能を内包した複合ビルである複数のタワーを地下で水平方向に結び，これがやはり水中にある公園側のロビーに続いて，そこから高速エレベータで上階の乗り換えロビーと結ばれる。ビルの利用者は72丁目の地下鉄の入口をはじめ，ジェイコブ・K・ジェイヴィツ・コンベンションセンターやウォールストリート，ラガーディア空港などへ行く高速フェリーの乗り場へも歩いて通える。

極細型の高層ビルと対比させるように，ヴォリュームのあるボ上パブリック・スペースは，コンサート・スタジアムや巨大スクリーンの映画館，グランド・フェスティバル・ホールなどとして使われる。

Site plan

Montage

1989 Stitch Plan
Cleveland, Ohio, U.S.A.

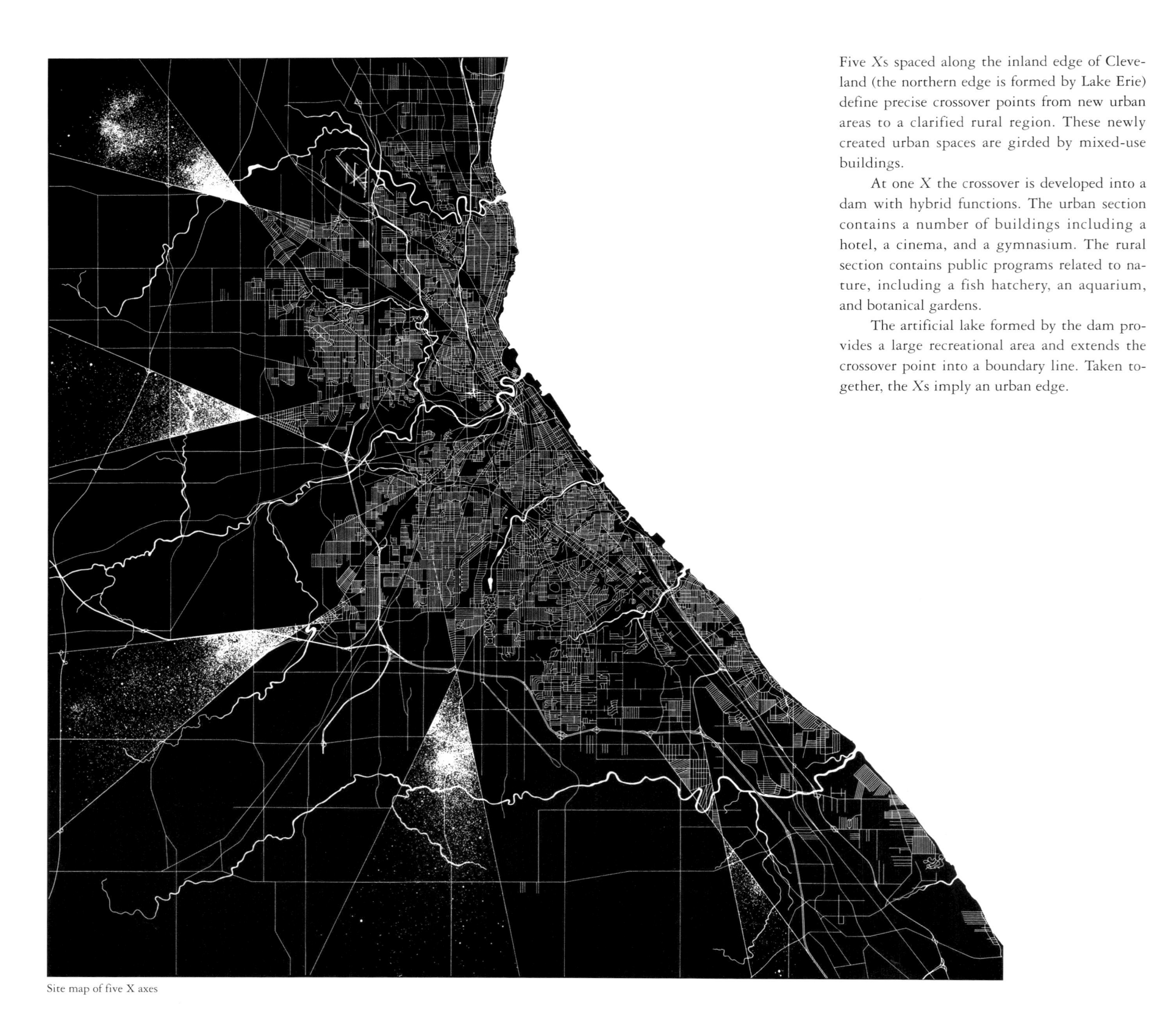

Five Xs spaced along the inland edge of Cleveland (the northern edge is formed by Lake Erie) define precise crossover points from new urban areas to a clarified rural region. These newly created urban spaces are girded by mixed-use buildings.

At one X the crossover is developed into a dam with hybrid functions. The urban section contains a number of buildings including a hotel, a cinema, and a gymnasium. The rural section contains public programs related to nature, including a fish hatchery, an aquarium, and botanical gardens.

The artificial lake formed by the dam provides a large recreational area and extends the crossover point into a boundary line. Taken together, the Xs imply an urban edge.

Site map of five X axes

Section

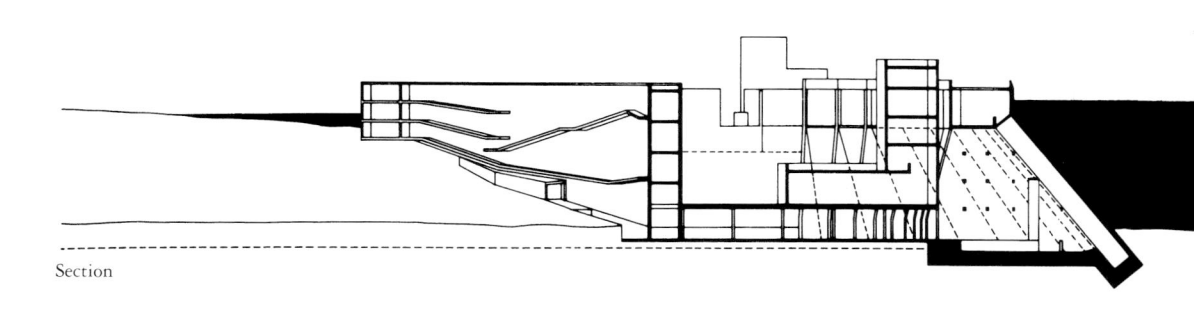

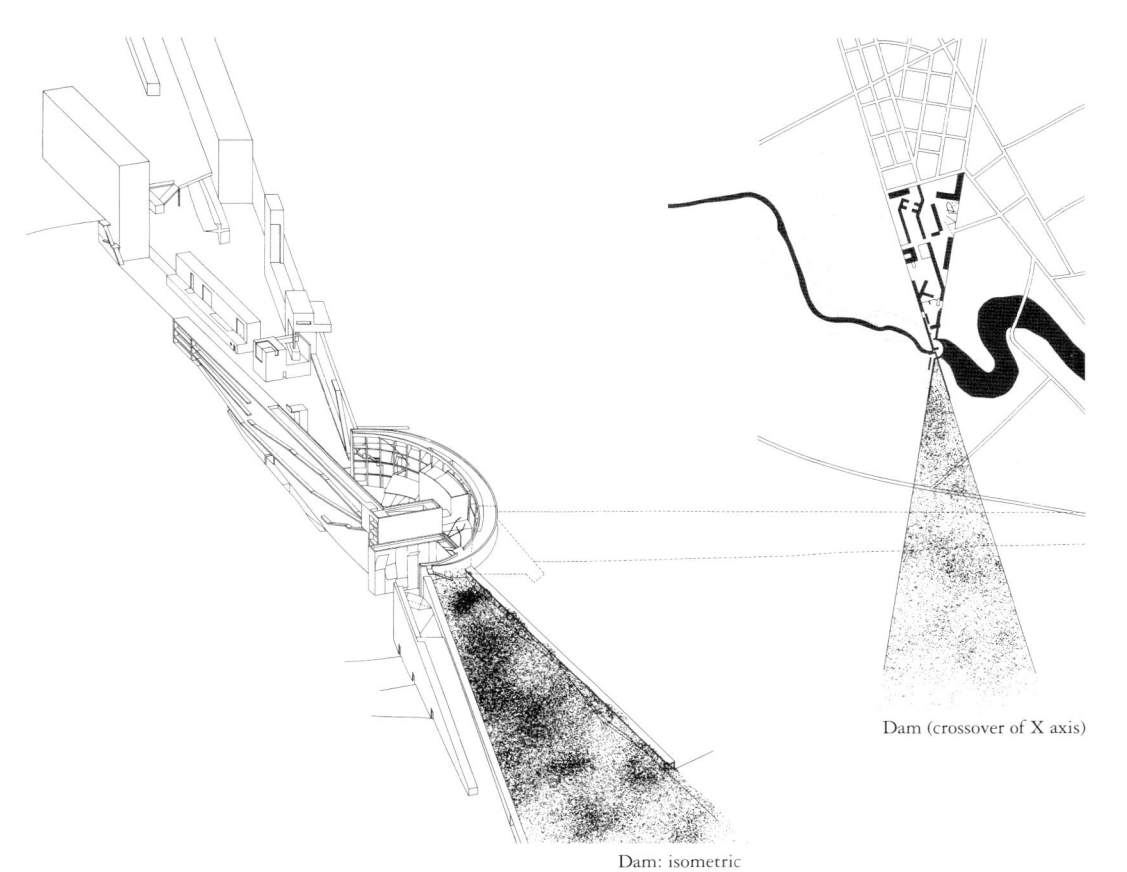

スティッチ・プラン

クリーブランドの内陸側の周縁部(北端はエリー湖に面する)に沿って,間隔をおいて並ぶ5つのX型は,新興の都市域から田園地域へと変わる交差部を明確に定めている。5つのX型の内側につくられる新しい都市域側には,種々の用途をもつ建物が建ち並ぶ。

X型のひとつは,その交差部に様々な機能を複合させたダムになる。その都市側には数多くのビルが建ち並び,ホテル,映画館,体育館などがある。それに対して,田園地帯側は,自然を生かした公共的な計画,たとえば魚の孵化場,水族館,植物園といったものである。ダムが形づくる人造湖は,広いレクリエーション地域となるので,交差部は引き伸ばされて,点ではなく境界線を形成する。また,X型をひとつながりとして見ると,それは都市の縁を暗示するものとなる。

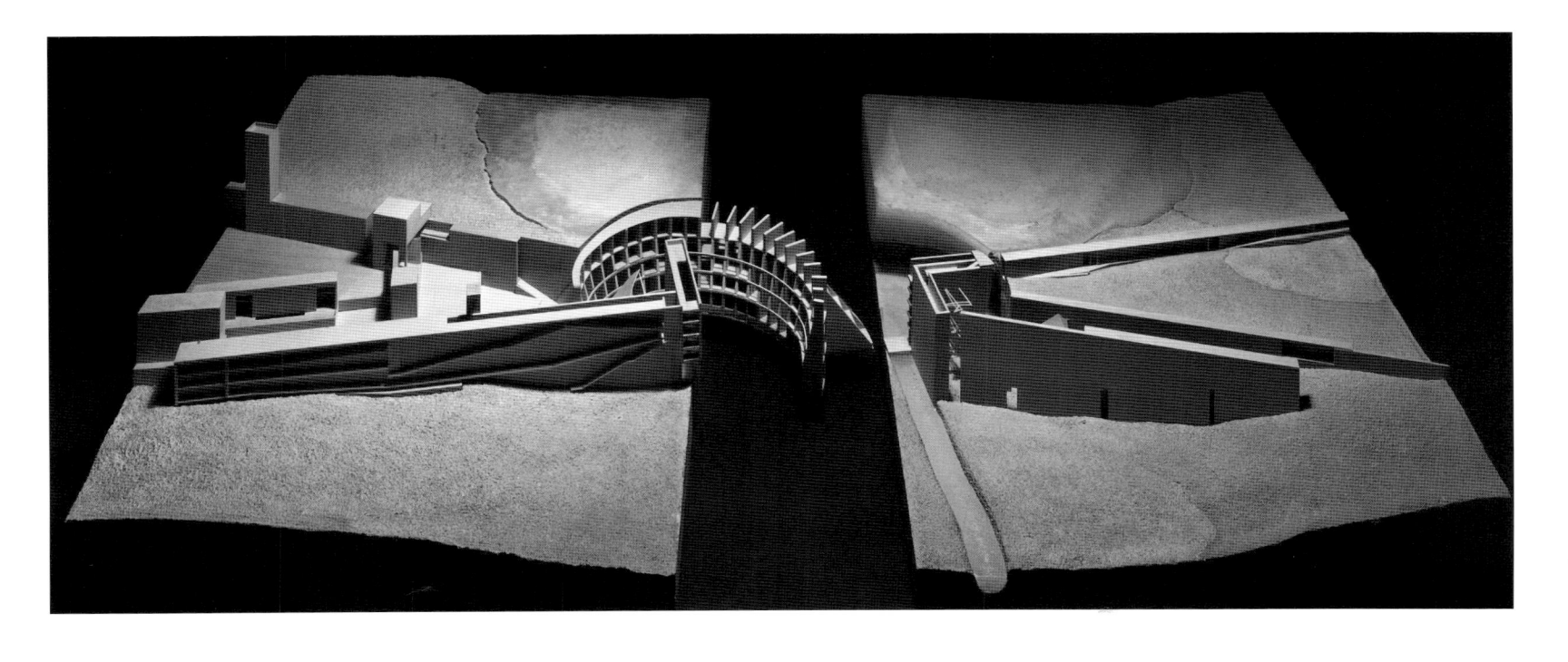

Dam: isometric

Dam (crossover of X axis)

Isometric

Concept sketch

Concept sketch

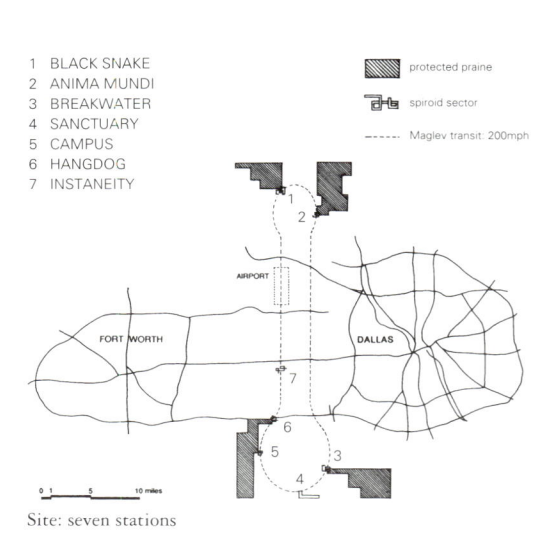

1 BLACK SNAKE
2 ANIMA MUNDI
3 BREAKWATER
4 SANCTUARY
5 CAMPUS
6 HANGDOG
7 INSTANEITY

protected prairie
spiroid sector
Maglev transit: 200mph

Site: seven stations

Spiroid Sectors

1990   Dallas/Fort Worth, Texas, U.S.A.

Sketch: coiling continuous space

Protected Texas prairie is framed by new sectors that condense living, working, and recreational activities. Future residents are transported to new town sectors by a high-speed Maglev transit from the Dallas/Fort Worth Airport.

A new hierarchy of public spaces is surrounded by armatures knotted in a continuous space-forming morphology. Various public passages along the roof afford a shifting ground plane, invigorating the interconnected experience of the sector's spaces.

The coiling armatures contain a hybrid of macroprograms: public transit stations, health clubs, cinemas, and galleries, with horizontal and vertical interconnected transit. Micro-programs of domestic activities are in smaller adjacent structures. The smallest spiroids form low-cost courtyard housing in experimental thin/thick wall construction.

Montage

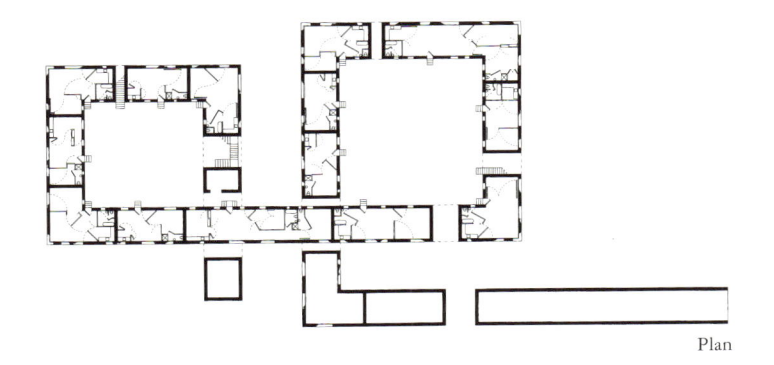

Plan

スピロイド・セクター
テキサスで保護地域に指定されているプレイリーのまわりの一帯は,住居やビジネスやレクリエーションなどの施設で埋められようとしている。将来の住民たちは,ダラス／フォートワース空港からマグレヴ高速鉄道でニュータウン地域に帰る。

ここではパブリック・スペースを構成する新しいヒエラルキーは,連続的な空間をつくる建築を随所に配して周りを囲むという形をとる。種々の交通ルートが高架で設けられるために,地上面の動きが自由になって,各区域を結ぶ活動を促すことになる。

螺旋形をなす建物の中には広い地域を対象にする施設が混在する。たとえば鉄道の駅,ヘルスクラブ,映画館,ギャラリーなどが入り,それらが,文字通り縦横に結ばれる。住宅関連の小規模な活動は隣接する小さな建物が引き受ける。最も小さい螺旋形は,薄壁と厚壁による実験的な壁構造のローコストのコートハウスである。

6 Fusion: Landscape, Urbanism and Architecture
融合：景観, 都市, 建築

The fusion of architecture, urbanism, and landscape can be realized in city fragments when all aspects are conceived integrally. This integration should carry over into texture, material, color, translucency, transparency, and reflection. Landscape design ordered as an afterthought cannot effectively fuse with architecture and urbanism.

The Zen gardens of Japan are an inspiring example of the indefinite boundary of architecture and gardens: bodies of water, illusions of distance, and edifices floating on their own reflections are part of a tradition of slow development. Japanese culture merged the arts of gardening, painting, sculpture, and architecture.

Our aim to fuse landscape with urbanism and architecture began with riverfront fountains in a 1975-1977 projects in Flint, Michigan, in conjunction with Lawrence Halprin landscape architects. Here, a "sunken building" is carved into the Riverfront with grotto rooms characterized by different water phenomena. An "Archimedes Screw" lifts the water naturally into a flume and "U tube" which feed a water-wall defining the public space.

In our 1979 proposal "Bridge of Houses", the High Line in New York is first proposed as a public promenade. Thirty years later this public space has been realized and the strip of public green that is the high line has become an important new public space fusing landscape and architecture.

The competition drawings for Kiasma:, Museum of Contemporary Art in Helsinki, in 1993 propose a water extension from Töölö Lake, which intertwines with and passes through the Museum. The intertwining of the geometry of the city and the landscape are reflected in the building. In the extended landscape plan, the horizontal light of the Northern latitudes is enhanced by a waterscape that would serve as "urban mirror".

Maurice Merleau-Ponty described an "in-between" reality, or ground, on which it is universally possible to bring things together. The aim of fusing landscape, urbanism , and architecture is an "in-between" measured by the overlapping perspectives of the body moving through space. In this phenomena, there is no beginning to architecture, no beginning to urbanism, and no end to landscape architecture.

Steven Holl

Kiasma, Museum of Contemporary Art, Helsinki

建築・都市・景観の融合は,すべての様相が一体化されたものとして着想された場合に限り,都市の断片において実現可能であり,質感,素材,色,透光性,透明度,そして反射に至るまでを含む一体化でなければならない。後から思いついたような景観デザインでは,建築や都市との効果的な融合は望めない。

日本の禅庭は,建築と庭との曖昧な境界という意味で示唆的な一例である。様々な水辺,距離感の錯覚,そして自らの鏡像の上に浮かぶ建造物などは,日本文化が園芸,絵画,彫刻,建築といった芸術を統合させてきた,ゆるやかな展開の伝統の一端を示している。

景観を都市と建築に融合させるという我々の目的は,ランドスケープ・アーキテクトのローレンス・ハルプリンと協同した,ミシガン州のフリント河岸の噴水公園(1975-1977)に端を発した。そこでは,異なる水の現象に特色づけられた洞窟風の部屋を持つ「サンクン・ビルディング」が河岸に掘られ,「アルキメデスの螺旋」による自然な流れが水を人工水路へと持ち上げ「U字管」へと運び,それが滝となり公共スペースを特徴づけている。

1979年のブリッジ・ハウスは,ニューヨークのハイラインを公共の遊歩道として提案した最初の計画である。30年後,この公共スペースは実現化され,かつての高架鉄道の軌道は一筋の緑道となり,景観と建築とを融合する影響力のある新たな公共の場となったのである。

Kiasmaヘルシンキ現代美術館のコンペ案ドローイング(1993)ではトゥーリョ湖からの延長として美術館にまとわり通り抜けて行く水の流れを提案し,景観と街が絡み合う形状を建物に反映させた。拡張された景観プランでは,「都市的な鏡」としての水辺風景が,高緯度地における水平線の光を引き立てている。

モーリス・メルロー=ポンティが唱えた「はざま」の現実,あるいは場では,様々な物を結びつけることが普遍的に可能である。景観,都市,建築を融合させる目的とは,空間内を移動する身体による交差し合う視点が定義する「はざま」であり,この現象においては建築の始点も都市の始点も,また景観設計の帰着点も存在しない。

(スティーヴン・ホール)

1975-77 Riverfront Flint Fountain
Flint, Michigan, U.S.A.

Subterranean Fountain

Subterranean Fountain

The 1975-1977 project for the Flint Michigan Riverfront Fountains began as an alternative to the Army Corps of Engineers flood control walls. In conjunction with Lawrence Halprin Landscape Architects, three different riverfront fountains were realized. An Archimedes Screw connected to a hydraulic pump on the face of an existing dam naturally lifts water into a flume passing it under a street via a "U" tube and then to a waterwall. The largest fountain; a "sunken building" is a public space with water rushing in and falling in several directions. Proportions of all elements of the "sunken building" are according to the Fibonacci sequence: 3, 5, 8, 13, 21, 34 & 55.

Subterranean Fountain

フリント河岸の噴水公園

1975年から1977年のフリント河岸の噴水公園は、陸軍工兵司令部の治水事業に代わる計画として始められたものである。ランドスケープ・アーキテクトのローレンス・ハルプリンとの協同作業で、三つの噴水が完成した。既存の護岸面の水圧ポンプに取り付けられたアルキメディアン・スクリューは自然の力でこの水路へと揚水を行う。水は道路の下で「U」字管を通り、水壁へと注ぎ込まれる。最も大きな噴水は「サンクン・ビルディング」と呼ばれ、このパブリックスペースに注がれた水はあらゆる方向へと水壁から落ちる。3, 5, 8, 13, 21, 34, 55と続くフィボナッチ数列が「サンクン・ビルディング」の建築要素のプロポーションである。

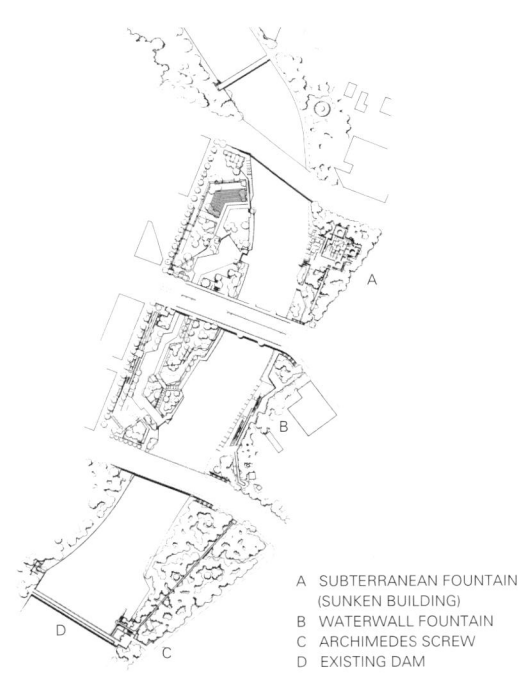

A SUBTERRANEAN FOUNTAIN (SUNKEN BUILDING)
B WATERWALL FOUNTAIN
C ARCHIMEDES SCREW
D EXISTING DAM

Site plan

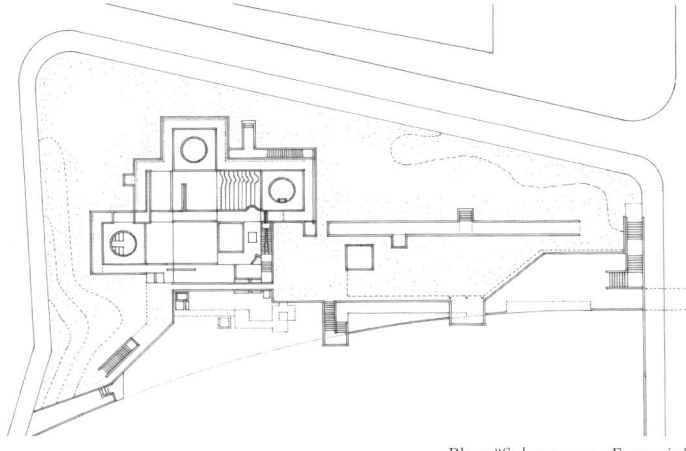

Plan: "Subterranean Fountain"

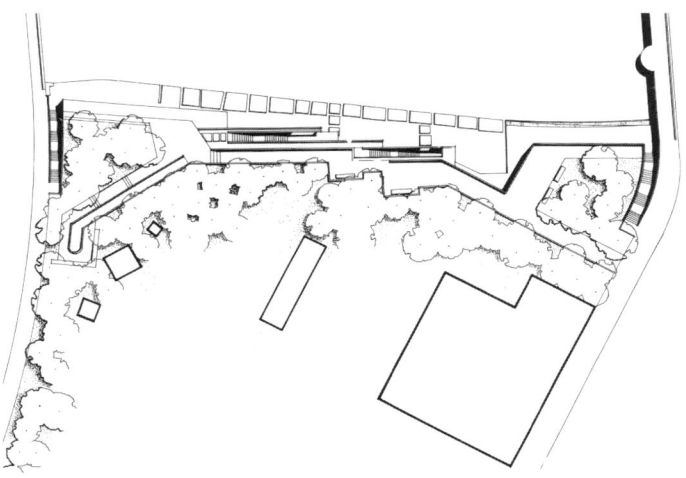

Plan: "Waterwall Fountain"

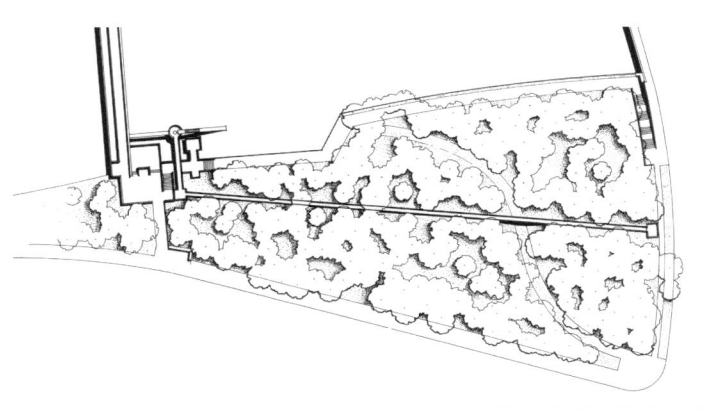

Plan: "Archimedes Screw"

1992-98   Kiasma, Museum of Contemporary Art
Helsinki, Finland

Overall view from southeast

View from northwest

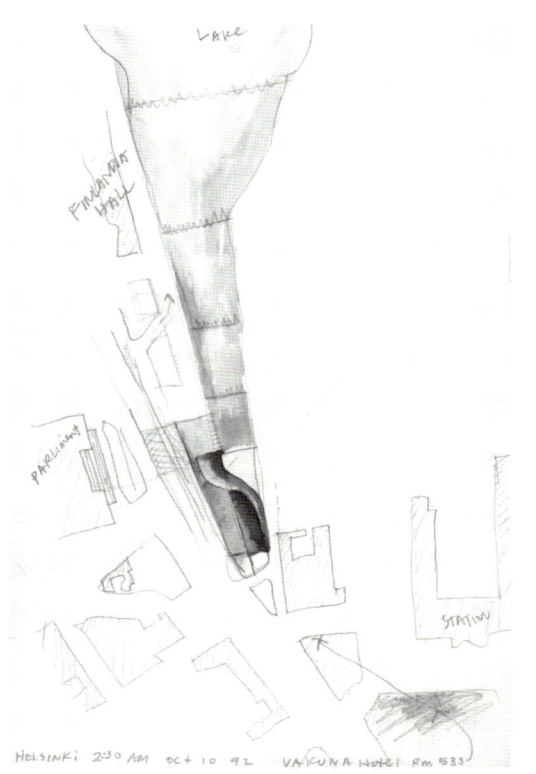

Concept sketch: water extension from Töölö Lake

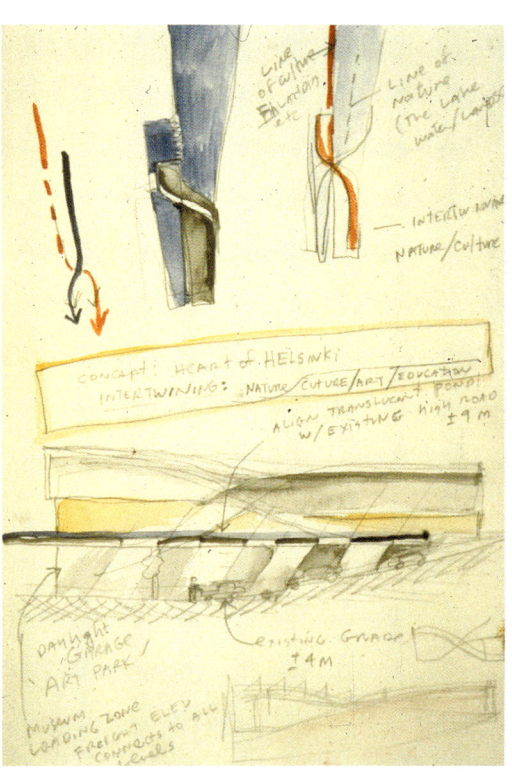

Concept sketch

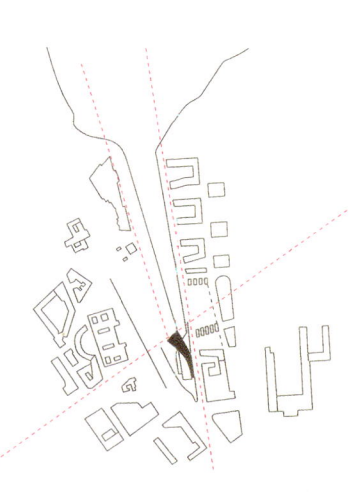

INTERTWINING
engage geometry of the city

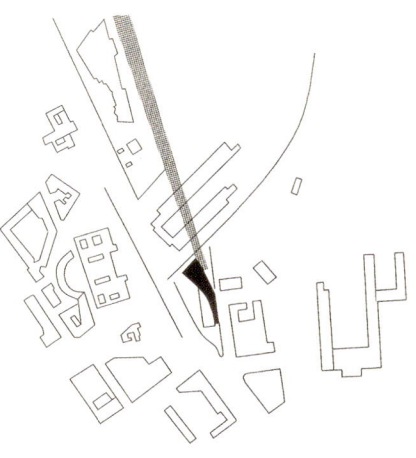

MASTER PLAN
open sight lines

Concept

I-239

1 ENTRANCE
2 ATRIUM
3 INFORMATION
4 CAFETERIA
5 BOOKSHOP
6 CLOAK
7 AUDITORIUM LOBBY
8 AUDITORIUM
9 PERMANENT COLLECTION ROOM
10 OFFICE
11 EXHIBITION ROOM
12 WORKSHOP FOR CHILDREN
13 MECHANICAL

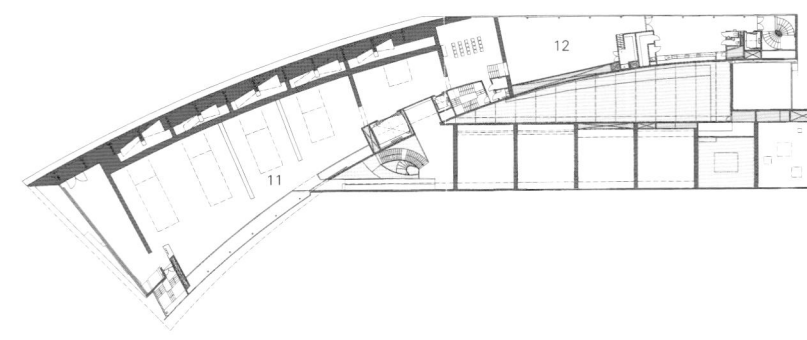

Fourth floor

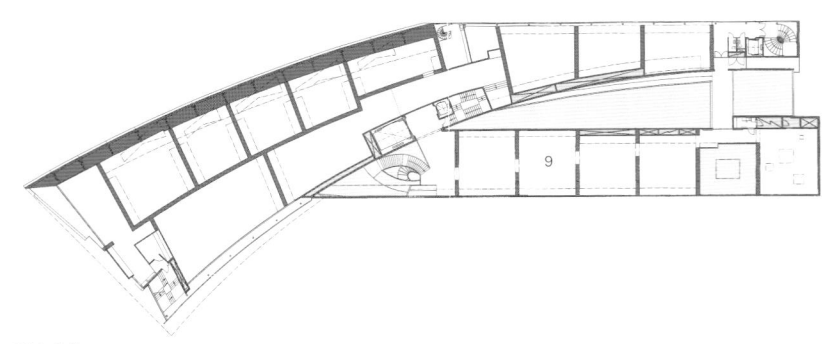

Third floor

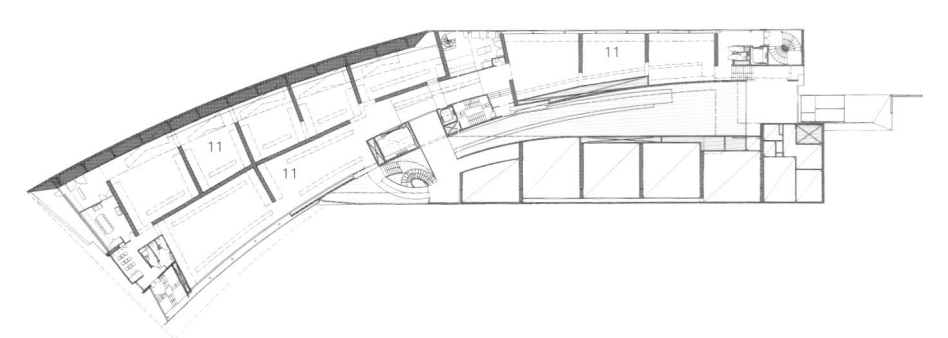

Second floor

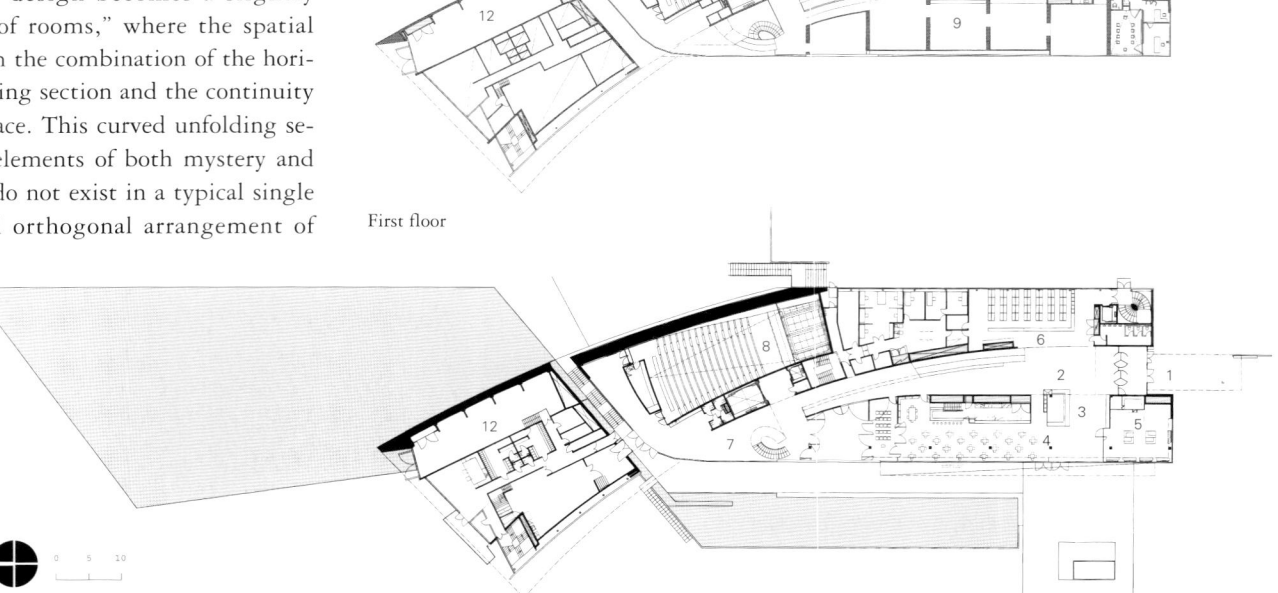

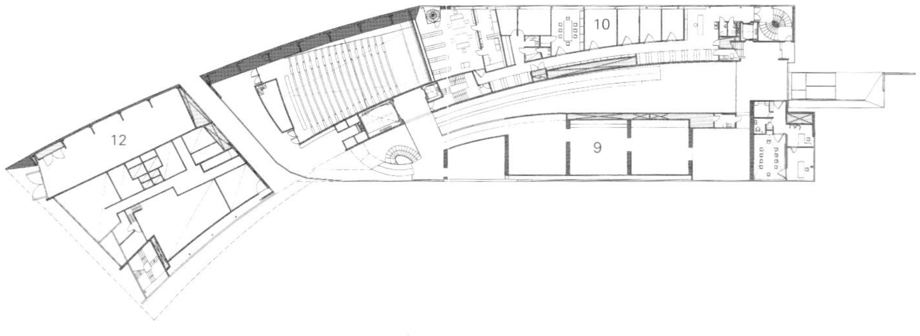

First floor

Ground floor

The site for Kiasma lies in the heart of Helsinki at the foot of the Parliament building to the west, with Eliel Saarinen's Helsinki Station to the east, and Alvar Aalto's Finlandia Hall to the north. The challenging nature of this site stems from the confluence of the various city grids, from the proximity of the monuments, and from the triangular shape that potentially opens to Töölö Lake in the distance.

The concept of Kiasma involves the building's mass intertwining with the geometry of the city and landscape which are reflected in the shape of the building. An implicit cultural line curves to link the building to Finlandia Hall while it also engages a "natural line" connecting to the back landscape and Töölö Lake. In the landscape plan, extending the lake up to the building will provide an area for future civic development along this tapering body of water, which also serves as a reflecting pool for the Finlandia Hall and new development along the south edge of the water. The horizontal light of northern latitudes is enhanced by a waterscape that would serve as an urban mirror, thereby linking the new museum to Helsinki's Töölö heart, which on a clear day, in Aalto's words, "extends to Lapland." The changes in elevation proposed with the water extension and its shallow depth would allow for parking decks and/or highway linkages which are presently part of various planning considerations.

This water extension from Töölö Lake intertwines with and passes through the museum. The rectangular pool along the west elevation is the source of a slow recirculating system which gradually lowers the water level. The gentle sound of moving water can be heard when walking through the cusp of the building section which remains open for passage year-round. The ponds are not intended to be drained. Instead, they are allowed to freeze in winter according to a detail first devised by Eliel Saarinen for the accommodation of the expansion of water during freezing. At night the west pond reflects the internal light radiating from the museum west pond which expresses a "spatiality of night." During the early evening hours of the winter months, glowing light escaping from the interior of the building along the west facade invite the public inside.

The Helsinki Museum of Contemporary Art, provides a variety of spatial experiences. We considered the range of contemporary artwork, and tried to anticipate the needs of a variety of artists including those whose works depend on a quiet atmosphere to bring out their full intensity. An exhibition space that works for an expressive and unpredictable artist such as Vito Acconci, must also work for artists such as Agnes Martin and Richard Tuttle. The general character of the rooms, which are almost rectangular with one wall curved, allows for a silent yet dramatic backdrop for the exhibition of contemporary art. These rooms are meant to be silent, but not static; they are differentiated through their irregularity.

Particular to Helsinki is the horizontal natural light of the northern latitudes. The slight variation in room shape and size due to the gently curving section of the building allows natural light to enter in several different ways. This asymmetrically drives movement through a series of spatial sequences. In this regard the overall design becomes a slightly warped "gallery of rooms," where the spatial flow emerges from the combination of the horizontal light-catching section and the continuity of the internal space. This curved unfolding sequence provides elements of both mystery and surprise—which do not exist in a typical single or double loaded orthogonal arrangement of

View toward main entrance

space. Instead, the visitor is confronted with a continuous unfolding of an infinite series of changing perspectives which connect the internal experience to the overall concept of intertwining or Kiasma.

This open-ended spatial system suggests an expanse that lies beyond, in contrast to rectilinear organization and "centered" composition that dictates the viewer's movement, or an expressionist dynamic that excludes the serenity necessary for viewing some types of work. The spaces of the intertwining curves in Kiasma avoid both the rigidity of a classical approach and the excessive complexity of expressionism. The dynamic internal circulation, with its curving ramps and stairs, allows for an open interactive viewing, inspiring the visitor to choose his or her own route through the galleries. Unlike a hierarchical sequenced or ordered movement, this open-ended casual circulation provokes moments of pause, reflection, and discovery.

Another concept behind the building's spaces is to create silence by eliminating the intermediate scale in the building's architecture. In this way, the art work can occupy the intermediate scale in contrast with the neutral mass of the walls. Rather than articulating columns, moldings, window openings, etc., the architecture expressed through details such as the twist of a door handle, the edge of a stair, the exposed thickness of a slab of glass.

A common problem in the design of an art museum with galleries on multiple levels is that the stacked section only permits natural light to enter the upper level galleries, leaving the lower levels exclusively dependent on artificial light. In the Museum of Contemporary Art, Helsinki, we address this problem in two ways. First, the curved roof allows secondary skylights while horizontal light is deflected down through the section along the center. Thus natural light is able to penetrate both upper and lower levels. Second, the curved roof section with its "refracting" skylight introduces another means for distributing light to galleries below the top level. Because of the building's curving and intertwining morphology, because of the interwoven torsion of space and light, we have allowed for the different levels to be naturally lit. There is a correspondence between the internal nearly rectangular spaces, and the exterior's continuous uninterrupted surface.

The Kiasma also serve as an "Art Forum," open and flexible for staged events, performances, dance, music, and seminars. The particular placement of the cafe at ground level—open to both the garden and the lobby—makes it adaptable to informal events, such as poetry readings or "round table" discussions. The auditorium, equipped with the latest video projection capabilities, has a continuous glass rear elevation, making it visible from the outside passage through the building. When there is a lecture taking place in the theater, this open view might draw in observers who are walking along the passage, to take part in the discussion.

With Kiasma, there is a hope to confirm that architecture, art, and culture are not separate disciplines but are all integral parts of the city and the landscape. Through care in development of details and the materials, the new museum provides a dynamic yet subtle spatial form, extending towards the city in the south and the landscape to the north. The geometry has an interior mystery and an exterior horizon which, like two hands clasping each other, form the architectonic equivalent of a public invitation. Referring to the landscape the interiors are reversible; and form the site which, in this special place and circumstance, is a synthesis of building and landscape...a Kiasma.

East elevation

Main entrance

Kiasmaヘルシンキ現代美術館

新しい現代美術館,「キアズマ」の敷地は,西に議事堂,東にエリエル・サーリネンのヘルシンキ駅,北にアルヴァ・アアルトのフィンランディア・ホールが近接するヘルシンキの中心部にある。設計意欲をかきたてられるこの敷地の性格は,さまざまな都市グリッドの合流点であること,記念碑的建築との近さ,遠くに見えるトューリョ湖に向かって開放できる可能性を持った三角形の形態から生まれている。

「キアズマ(交差)」というコンセプトによって,建物は都市と風景の持つジオメトリーと織り合わされ,それが建築形態に反映される。暗黙の内に文化性を含んだ曲線がこの建物をフィンランディア・ホールへと結び,一方で,背後の風景とトューリョ湖を結ぶ「自然のライン」ともかみ合っている。湖を建物まで引き延ばすという景観計画のなかで,この水の先細りになった広がりに沿って将来の都市開発エリアが提供されることになろう。それはまた,フィンランディア・ホールと水路の南端に位置する計画地のリフレクティング・プールとしての役割も果たす。北緯圏端の水平線近くの光が,都市の鏡となる水辺風景を強調し,新美術館をヘルシンキの,晴れた日には,アアルトの言葉を借りれば「ラップランドまで広がる」トューリョ湖の深奥部へつなぐ。水を引き入れることと共に提案された立面の変更とその浅い奥行きは,目下さまざまな計画が検討されている,パーキング・デッキやハイウェイとの連絡路を導入する余地を与えてくれるだろう。

トューリョ湖からのこの水の延長部は,新美術館と織り合わされ,通り抜けて行く。新しい建物の西面に沿って提案された長方形のプールは,水面の高さが徐々に低くなる緩やかな循環システムの水源となっている。一年中,通路として開放されている建物の先端部を歩いていると,流れる水のやさしい音色が聞こえる。これらの池は,排水することを意図していない。代わりに,エリエル・サーリネンが,凍っている期間の水の広がりの調整のために,最初に考案したディテールに従って,冬季には凍るままにされる。夜になると,西の池は,「夜の広がり」を表現するようにデザインされた美術館から放射する内部の光を反射する。冬の夕方のまだ早い時間には,西面に沿って建物の内部から漏れてくる内部の白熱光が,人々を内側へと招く。

ヘルシンキ現代美術館には多彩な空間体験が生みだされている。現代芸術の表現の幅の広さを考え,その緊

Atrium: view from entrance. Information on left

I-243

Concept sketch

張感を明示するためには静かな雰囲気に依存する作品を含め,多様な芸術家の必要とするものを予測するように努めた。ヴィト・アコンチのような表現的で予測不能な作品をつくるアーティストに対応する展示空間は,アグネス・マーティンやリチャード・タトルなどの作品にも対応しなければならない。一枚の壁だけが曲面のほぼ長方形の部屋は,現代美術の展示のための静かではあるがドラマティックな背景となる。これらの室内は静かであることを意図しているが,静止的ではない。その不規則性によって,個々に差異がつけられている。

ヘルシンキに特有なのは,北の緯度にある土地の水平線に近い太陽の光である。建物の緩やかにカーブする建物断面から生まれる部屋の形と大きさの微妙なバリエーションにより,自然光がいくつもの異なった経路を通って差し込んでくる。この不規則性が,空間のシークエンスを抜けて行く動きを進める。この点において,全体のデザインは,かすかにねじれを与えられた「部屋のギャラリー」となり,そこでは,空間の流れが,光を捕らえる水平の部分と内部空間の連続性の組み合わせから生まれている。このカーブしながら展開して行くシークエンスは,神秘性と驚きの両方の要素を与えてくれる——これは,よくある,単層や2層吹抜けの直交する空間構成にはあり得ないものである。その代わりに,訪問者は,内部体験を織り合わせ,つまりキアズマという全体のコンセプトに結びつく,変化するパースペクティブの無限の連なりが次々に展開して行くのを目にする。

オープン・エンドな空間システムは,その向こうに横たわる広がりを暗示する。それは,見る者の動きを支配する直線的な組立て,「中心性」を持った構成とも,ある種の作品の鑑賞に必要な静かさを排除してしまう表現主義者のダイナミズムとも対照的なものである。我々のキアズマのなかに織り合わされた曲面のつくる空間は,古典的なアプローチの硬直さも表現主義の過剰な複雑さ

Atrium: view toward entrance

Detail of handrail

Atrium: view from first floor

も避けている。湾曲する斜路と階段で構成されたダイナミックな内部の動線は相互に作用しあう開かれた眺めを提供し、来館者に、ギャラリー全体を抜けて行くルートを好きなように選択する気にさせる。階層的に構成されたシークエンスや秩序立った動きとは違って、このオープン・エンドで偶発性をもった動線は、休止、黙想、発見の瞬間を誘発する。

この建物の空間の背後にあるもうひとつのコンセプトは、この建物の建築的に中間的なスケールを消去することにより、静寂をつくりだすことである。これによって、美術作品は、壁のニュートラルなマッスに対比する中間的スケールを占めることができる。柱、モールディング、窓などの分節によるというより、むしろ、ドアの取手の捻れ、階段の端部、ガラス面の露出された厚みといった細部によってこの建築は表現されている。

ギャラリーが何層にも重なる美術館に共通する悩みは、積層する各レベルの上層にしか自然光が入らず、下階は人工照明に全面的に頼らなければならないことである。ヘルシンキ現代美術館では、二つの方法でこの問題に取り組んでいる。第一に、カーブする屋根は、水平に入る光が中央に沿って屈折して注ぐ一方で、補助的なスカイライトを設置することができる。この結果、自然光は上階と下階の双方に差し込む。第二に、「屈折」光を落とすスカイライトの付いた曲面屋根は、最上階より下の階のギャラリーに自然光を配分するもう一つの方法となる。建物の湾曲し、絡み合った形態構造によって、また、空間と光の織り合わされた捻れによって、各階はそれぞれ自然採光できる。ほぼ長方形の内部空間と外側の遮られるところのない連続する表皮の間には関係がある。

キアズマはまた、舞台を使うイベント、パフォーマンス、ダンス、音楽、セミナーといった催しに柔軟に対応できる「アート・フォーラム」としても機能する。1階にあり、庭とロビーの両方に開いたカフェは、その特別な配置により、詩の朗読や「ラウンド・テーブル」ディスカッションなどのインフォーマルな催しを開く場にもなる。最新のビデオ映写機器を備えたホールの背面は連続するガラス面とし、建物を貫く屋外通路からも中が見えるようにする。内部で講演が行われているときは、この開かれた眺めは、通路を歩いている人の興味を引き、ディスカッションへの仲間入りをさせることになるだろう。

キアズマには、建築、アート、文化は別々の原則を持つものではなく、都市と風景の切り離せない一部なのだということを確証したいという望みが込められている。細部と材料を注意深く展開することによって、この美術館は、南は街に向かって、北は風景に向かって広がる、ダイナミックでありながら、微妙な空間形態を提供するだろう。そのジオメトリーは、互いに握り締めた二つの手のように、内部の神秘性と外部の水平線を持ち、人々を招く建築的等価物をかたちづくる。風景に関係させて、インテリアはリバーシブルである。この特別な場所と環境のなかに、建物と風景の統合体を構成する。……それがキアズマである。

Auditorium lobby: staircase

Restaurant/cafeteria

View toward bookshop (door closed)

Bookshop (door opened)

Exhibition room on second floor

Door of exhibition room on first floor

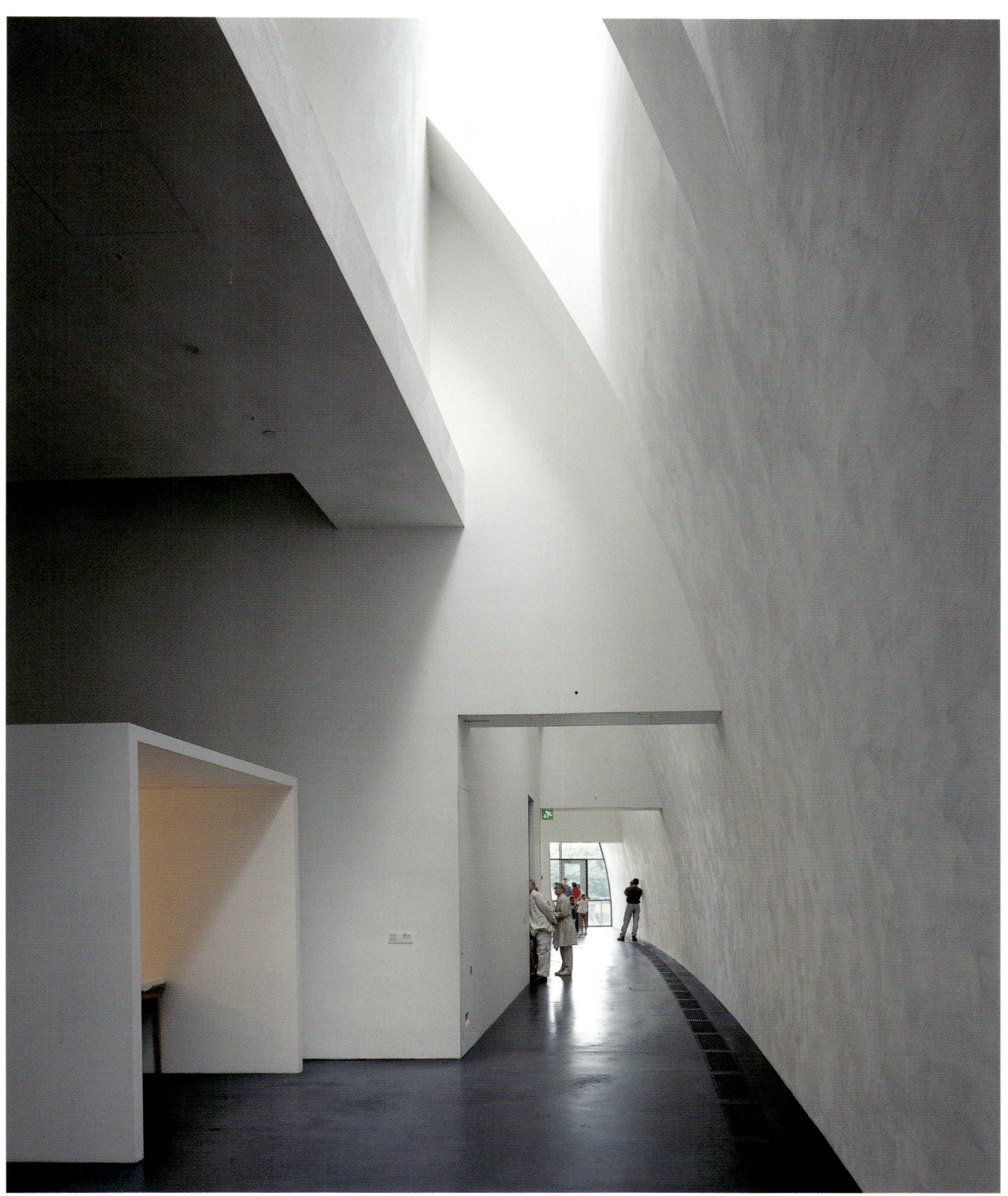

Exhibition room on second floor

1 INFORMATION
2 ATRIUM
3 CLOAK
4 AUDITORIUM LOBBY
5 AUDITORIUM
6 EXHIBITION ROOM
7 CORRIDOR
8 OFFICE
9 WORKSHOP FOR CHILDREN
10 STORAGE
11 PACKING/ASSEMBLING

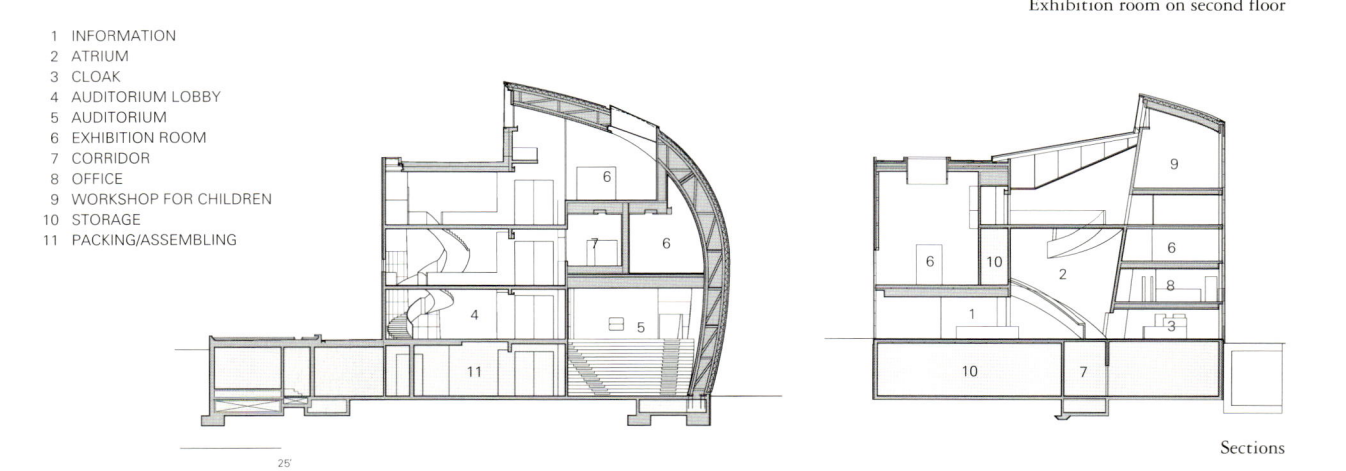

Sections

I-247

Exhibition room on fourth floor

Exhibition room on fourth floor

I-248

Exhibition room on fourth floor

1998-2005 Whitney Water Purification Facility and Park
Connecticut, U.S.A.

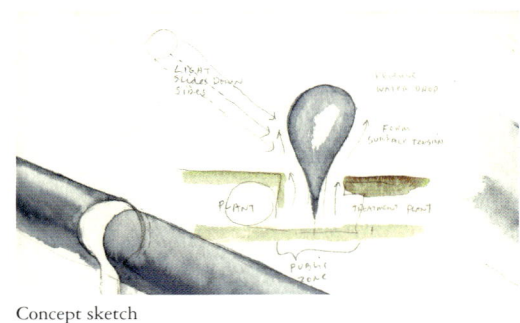

Concept sketch

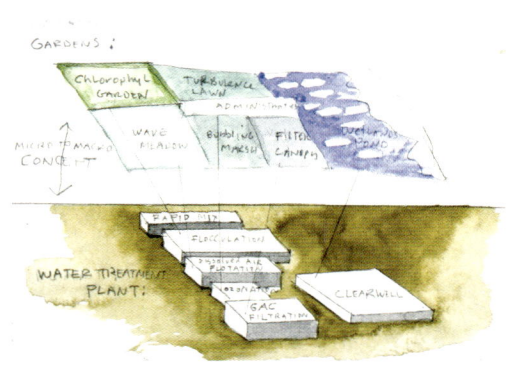

Concept sketch: analogy of water treatment plant and gardens

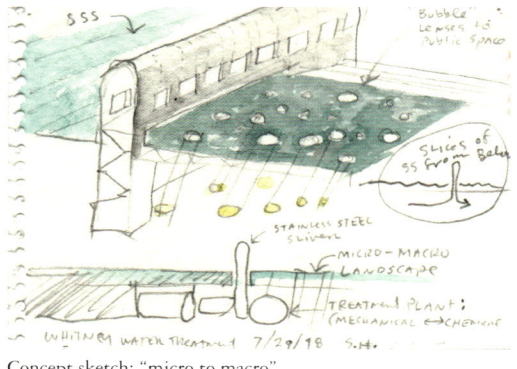

Concept sketch: "micro to macro"

Overall view

This water purification plant and park uses water and its purification process as the guiding metaphors for its design. Its program consists of water treatment facilities located beneath a public park and a 360-foot-long stainless steel sliver that encloses the client's public and operational programs. Like an inverted drop of water, the sliver expresses the workings of the plant below. Its shape creates a curvilinear interior space open to a large window view of the surrounding landscape while its exterior reflects the horizon in the landscape.

The public park is comprised of six sectors that are analogous to the six stages of the water treatment in the plant. The change in scale from molecular scale of the purification process below ground to the landscape above is celebrated in an interpretation of microscopic morphologies as landscape sectors. The park's "micro to macro" reinterpretation results in unexpected and challenging material-spatial aspects. For example, in a field formed by the green roof, which corresponds to ozonation bubbling, there are "bubble" skylight lenses that bring natural light to the treatment plant below. In the landscape area corresponding to filtration, vine wall elements on trellises define a public entrance court. Following the natural laws of gravity, water flows across the site and within the purification plant. As the water courses through its turns and transformations to-

View from east

ward its final clean state, it creates microprogram potentials within the vast space of the new park. Aligned along the base of the sliver are water pumps that distribute clean water to the region.

Given the urgent need to manage and conserve water resources, this project is an example of today's best sustainable design measures and water shed management practices. Indeed, it even includes the enlargement of an existing wetland into a vibrant microenvironment that increases biodiversity.

Low Environmental Impact Technology and Sustainable Design Measures

—Gravity Flow Operation
Setting the plant in the ground places the treatment process below lake level; this enables the purification plant to be driven by the lake's gravity pressure, eliminating the need for running energy-consuming pumps.

—Renewable Energy
A ground water heat pump system of 88 wells provides a renewable energy source for heating and cooling the building, and avoids the environmental impact associated with fossil fuel energy use, saving 850,000 kilowatt hours annually. The below grade plant's large thermal mass generates stable temperatures and minimizes the need for air-conditioning. A close collaborative effort with the local energy company to minimize energy usage resulted in the plant receiving significant monetary subsidies or Energy Credits. The building systems use no HCFCs, CFCs, or halons.

—Recycled Materials and Resources
All excavated earth and land clearing debris were salvaged and reused, and building materials were selected in keeping with sustainable design principals. A light-colored, recyclable, natural-finish stainless steel roof assists with heat absorption reduction. The terrazzo floor is comprised of recycled glass chip aggregate. The cork tile floor is of recycled wood content and tree bark. No VOC building products are used. Local concrete plants were selected to provide cast-in-place and pre-cast concrete which constitutes more than 40% of the overall building material, thus reducing the environmental impact of the building and transportation costs.

—Erosion and Sedimentation Control
The design team consulted the Connecticut Department of Environmental Protection, US Army Corp of Engineers and Inland Wetland Committee to develop an extensive erosion control/Plant dewatering strategy to prevent erosion.

—Reduced Site Disturbance/Landscape
The design minimizes site disturbance by preserving existing wetland conditions and natural vegetation. The landscape design supports biodiversity and preserves natural habitats. The existing site wetland has been documented as a recess point for certain species of migrating birds; this important feature has been preserved and enhanced. Trees and bushes provide shading throughout. The majority of the plant species are native grass and low shrubs, which greatly reduce maintenance and irrigation costs.

—Light Pollution Reduction
The design team demonstrated to the planning review board that due to the open nature of the landscape design, site lighting throughout the landscape was not required for security purposes. This reduces energy consumption and unnecessary off-site lighting.

—Storm Water Management
The storm water drainage system is managed though landscaping as opposed to piping. The surface pond to the east of the project is designed as a catchment area for detaining storm water. While paved walkways and a plaza are part of the design, they have been minimized in lieu of a net decrease in the rate and quantity of storm water run off from the existing developed site.

—Green Roof Design
The green roof increases the insulation R value by 3 points, prevents a heat island effect, and controls storm water runoff. The roof membrane is formed of a rubberized asphalt waterproofing system with an IRMA configuration. A root barrier fabric was installed on top of the insulation to optimize moisture management in the green cover and protect the insulation from water infiltration. The green roof is a low maintenance system and no "lawn cutting" or irrigation is required. Most of the plants will grow to about six-inches in height, and will spread to form full coverage within two growing seasons. The green roof design is expected to prolong the life of the roof membrane and protect it from normal wear and tear by buffering it from extreme freeze-thaw cycles and peak.

View from south

Entrance

Sketch: interior

ホイットニー浄水施設 ＋ 公園
この浄水施設公園の計画にあたっては、水質浄化プロセスがデザインを導くメタファーとして使用された。ここでは公園の地下に位置する水処理施設と、施設の運転プログラムを内包する360フィート(約108メートル)の薄い1片のステンレス仕上げの管理棟によって、プログラムが構成されている。水滴を逆さまにしたような形の管理棟は、地下の処理プラントの機能を象徴している。この形態がつくりだす曲線的な内部空間の大開口からは周辺のランドスケープを望むことができる。その一方、外壁には遠くまで広がるランドスケープが映り込んでいる。

公園を構成する6つの領域は、6段階に分けて行われるプラントの水処理に対するアナロジーになっている。地下の分子レベルの浄水プロセスから地上のランドスケープへのスケールの遷移の可否は、いかに微視的な形態構造をランドスケープ・セクターへと解釈しうるかにかかっていた。この公園の「マイクロからマクロへ」の再解釈は、思いもしない魅力的なマテリアルや空間の発見へとつながった。例えば、オゾン処理プロセスに対応する屋上緑化ゾーンでは、天窓の「バブル」レンズから自然光が地下処理施設へともたらされるようになっている。濾過プロセスに対応するランドスケープ・エリアでは、格子に蔓を這わせて緑化された壁面がパブリック・エントランス・コートの特徴になっている。敷地内の水は自然に流下し、浄水プラントに集められるようになっている。水が最終的に浄化されるまでいくつもの処理工程を経るように、水は新しい公園の広大な空間に対してマイクロ・プログラムによるさまざまな可能性を生み出している。細長い管理棟に沿って、地域一帯に上水を供給するため

Window detail

Exterior staircase

に送水ポンプが一列に設置されている。

　水資源の管理と保全が早急に求められている現在、このプロジェクトはサステイナブル・デザインを図る最高の流域管理事業モデルの一例である。実際にここでは、現存する湿地帯を種の多様性溢れる活発な微生物環境へと拡張することも意図されている。

[環境負荷低減技術およびサステイナブル・デザインへの評価]
〈自然流下方式〉
プラントを地下に計画したため、水処理プロセスは湖底よりも低いレベルに配置された。そのため、エネルギー消費量の大きいポンプを使用せずに、湖の水圧で浄化プラントを運転することが可能になった。
〈エネルギーの再利用〉
建築物の冷暖房のため、88本の地下水式ヒートポンプから再利用可能なエネルギーが供給される。その結果、年間850,000キロワット時のエネルギー消費を抑制し、化石燃料利用による環境負荷を回避している。地盤面下のプラントの巨大な熱質量は、室温を安定させ、機械空調の運転を最小限に抑えている。地域電力会社との緊密な協同作業によって電力利用を最小限に抑えることにより、財政面では助成金やエネルギー・クレジットの取得といった恩恵をもたらしている。また、建築設備には代替フロンやフロンガス、ハロンが使われてはいない。
〈再生材料と再生資源〉
地盤掘削や造成による排出岩土は回収のうえ再利用されるとともに、建築物の材料はサステイナブル・デザイン基準に従って選定が進められた。再生利用が可能なステンレス製の屋根には自然な肌合いで明度の高い塗装が施されているため、貫入熱量の低減に寄与している。テラゾ仕上げの床には再生ガラスのチップを骨材として使用し、コルク製のタイル・フローリングには木材や樹皮が再生利用されている。また、揮発性有機化合物は使われてはいない。建築物の総材料の40％以上を占める現場打ちコンクリート及びプレキャスト・コンクリートの調達には、現地のコンクリート・プラントが選定された。そのため、環境負荷を低減すると同時に輸送コストの抑制につながった。
〈浸食堆積管理〉
デザイン・チームはコネチカット州環境保護局、アメリカ陸軍工兵司令部、内陸部湿地委員会との協議に基づき、流水による土壌の浸食管理およびプラントの排水計画を詳細に検討した。
〈土壌保全／ランドスケープ〉
現存する湿地帯の状態や自然の植生を保全することで、土壌の変質を最小限に抑えるように計画されている。ランドスケープ・デザインは動植物の生息環境を保護し、種の多様性を確保する一助となっている。現存する敷地内の湿地帯は、渡り鳥といった特定の種の休息地として知られている。ここではそのような価値ある環境が積極的に保護されている。さまざまな高木や低木が、くまなく木陰を提供している。植物種の大部分は自生する芝草や灌木なので、保全や用水のコストを大幅に低減している。
〈光害低減対策〉
デザイン・チームは建築計画委員会に対して、ランドスケープ・デザインが開放的なのでセキュリティ上の観点からもランドスケープをくまなく照らすような外構照明は不要であるとの説明をおこなった。このことは不要な外構照明のエネルギー消費の抑制につながっている。
〈雨水排出管理〉
ここではランドスケープ化された雨水排水システムが排水管設備の代わりに使用されている。敷地東側に広がる池は、雨水を一時的に貯水することができるように調整池として計画された。周辺の開発区域から流れ込む雨水の表面流下はずいぶんと減少しているが、歩道やプラザの舗装範囲は最小限となるように計画された。
〈屋上緑化デザイン〉
屋上緑化は熱抵抗値を3ポイント向上させるとともに、ヒート・アイランド効果を防ぎ、雨水の表面流下を調節している。屋上スラブの防水被膜形成にはインバート塗膜防水工法によるゴム・アスファルト防水が使用されている。断熱材の上面には対根被膜が施されているため、緑化層への水分補給を最適化するとともに、断熱層への水分の浸透を防いでいる。「芝刈り」や用水が不要であるため、屋上緑化はメンテナンスを行う必要の少ないシステムである。植物の多くはほぼ6インチ（約15センチ）の高さにまで育ち、成長期を2回ほど迎えるうちに全てを覆うまでに一面に広がるようになるだろう。屋上緑化は屋根の耐用年数を延ばすことが期待されている。

1974-1998   Volume 1

List of Works

Term of design
Project title
Site
-
Program
-
Additional data:

1974–75
Residence
Manchester, Washington, U.S.A.
-
Program: private residence (two square ground plans with a pair of courtyards between them organize mass which is sheathed in cedar boards weathering to silver gray)
-
Clients: Helen and Myron Holl
General contractor: Myron Holl
Major materials: wood, plaster
Cost of construction: US$ 60,000

1975
Manila Housing
Daga Dagatan, Manila
-
Program: international competition for housing in Daga Dagatan
-
Client: International Architecture Foundation
Major materials: concrete
Site area: 147 ha

1975-77
Riverfront Flint Fountain
Flint, Michigan, U.S.A.
-
Program: three riverfront fountains
-
Associate architect: Lawrence Halprin (landscape)
Structural system: concrete

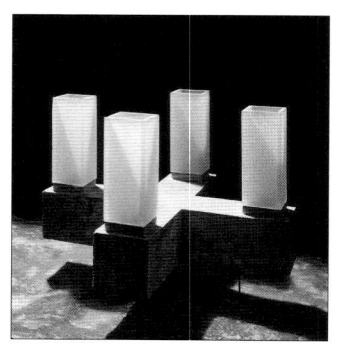

1976
Sokolov Retreat
St. Tropez, France
-
Program: an underwater retreat, anchored onto an existing house at the edge of the harbor in St. Tropez
-
Client: Michelle Sokolov
Major materials: concrete, glass
Total floor area: 780 sq.ft.

1976
St. Paul Capitol
St. Paul, Minnesota, U.S.A.

Program: competition for the State Capitol consolidating a museum for collecting and preserving the records of the past with governing functions in a subterranean structure

Client: State of Minnesota
Major materials: concrete, glass, granite, marble
Total floor area: 300,000 sq.ft.
Cost of construction: US$ 57 million

1977-78
Gymnasium Bridge
South Bronx, New York, U.S.A.

Program: hybrid building combining a gymnasium and bridge that condenses the activities of meeting, physical recreation and work into one structure while simultaneously forming a bridge from the community to the park on Randall's Island

Client: Wave Hill Center
Structural system: steel truss, concrete abutments
Major materials: steel, glass
Total floor area: 50,400 sq.ft.

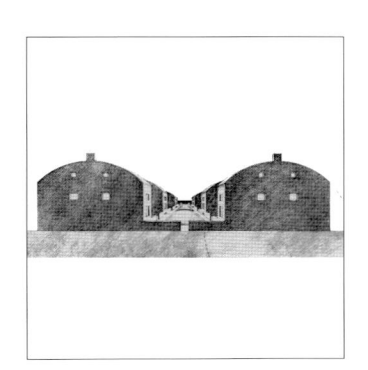

1977-78
Minimum Houses
Hastings-on-Hudson, New York, U.S.A.

Program: a proposed alternative to high-rise housing near Manhattan; each house has a small garden and a back porch

Major materials: single-span wood joists, concrete block walls, and rubber membrane roofing and wall covering
Total floor area: 1,300 sq.ft. each
Cost of construction: US$ 50,000 each

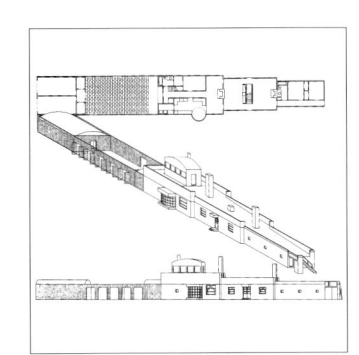

1978-79
Telescope House
Still Pond, Maryland, U.S.A.

Program: residence for a retired couple who wanted a versatile home that could be opened up or closed off according to the number of guests

Client: Gene Wyble
Major materials: concrete, wood
Site area: 160 ft. by 493 ft.
Total floor area: 4,300 sq.ft.
Cost of construction: US$ 280,000

1978-79
Millville Courtyard
Millville, New Jersey, U.S.A.

Program: the sunny side of an empty lot is organized into a courtyard

Client: an advertising agency
General contractor: Russel Sturgis
Major materials: concrete block, exterior cement plaster
Site area: 4,000 sq.ft.
Cost of construction: US$ 55,000

1979
Les Halles
Paris, France

Program: competition for housing, and an international meeting place on the former site of Les Halles pavilions of Baltard: trees are planted in the place of iron columns, walls are lined with arcades made of sandblasted glass

Client: City of Paris
Structural system: concrete frame
Major materials: concrete, steel, marble slabs, sandblasted glass

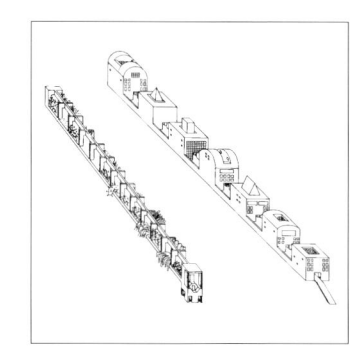

1979
Bridges of Melbourne
Melbourne, Australia

Program: Melbourne competition for a landmark to be built on a vast railroad yard dividing the central area of the city from the Yarra River, Bridge of Houses was part of an entry consisting of seven bridges proposed as "urban arms" extending the streets of Melbourne across the yards to the river; in this proposal the houses function as an ornate collection of urban villas with 4-6 apartments per block, facing green internal courts

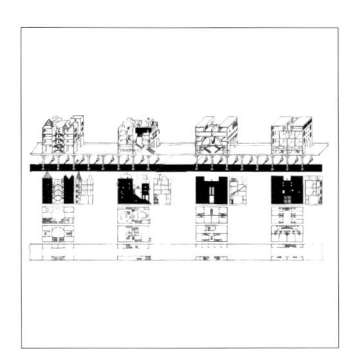

1979-82
Bridge of Houses
New York, New York, U.S.A.

Program: a variety of housing types and a public promenade on an abandoned elevated railroad

Consultant: Paul Gossen Structure
Major materials: lightweight metal frame, metal siding acid treated, wood doors with sandblasted glass
Total floor area: 147,500 sq.ft.

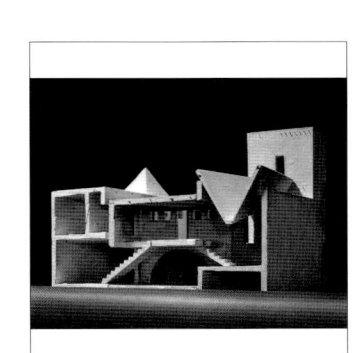

1980-81
Metz House
Staten Island, New York, U.S.A.

Program: a small house as a dwelling/working space for two artists and their daughter; conventional living/dining spaces are replaced by studios for sculpture and painting

Client: Mike Metz
Major materials: concrete block, pine, wood frame, slate, white marble
Total floor area: 2,350 sq.ft.

1980-81
Pool House and Sculpture Studio
Scarsdale, New York, U.S.A.

Program: a sculpture studio and bathhouse are sited next to an existing pool; the bathhouse provides an area for changing and refreshing; the sculpture studio that doubles as a guest room

Client: Rosen
Major materials: concrete block, stucco, marble
Total floor area: 682 sq.ft.
Cost of construction: US$ 80,000

1980-84
Autonomous Artisans' Housing
Staten Island, New York, U.S.A.
-
Program: an existing warehouse converted into housing and common workspace for artisans, including roof terraces and private gardens between each house
-
Major materials: concrete, wood
Total floor area: 9,828 sq.ft.
Cost of construction: US$ 1,500,000

1982-83
Guardian Safe Depository
Fair Lawn, New Jersey, U.S.A.
-
Program: renovation of an existing concrete building into a safe depository bank including a new facade, lobby, offices and security system
-
Client: Guardian Safe Inc.
Consultants: Paul Gossen
Major materials: concrete, steel, exterior cement plaster
Total floor area: 10,000 sq.ft.
Cost of construction: US$ 1 million

1982-83
Van Zandt House
East Hampton, New York, U.S.A.
-
Program: year-round weekend house with lap pool and guest bedroom
-
Client: Van Zandt
Major materials: stucco, wood frame, terne metal, double glazed windows
Total floor area: 1,600 sq.ft.
Cost of construction: US$ 260,000

1982-83
Cohen Apartment
New York, New York, U.S.A.
-
Program: apartment interior (all custom made fixtures, furniture, and carpets)
-
Client: Cohen
General contractor: Purdy Construction Company
Major materials: wood, plaster
Total floor area: 2,500 sq.ft.
Cost of construction: US$ 350,000

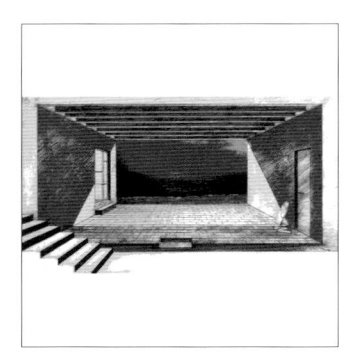

1984
Ocean Front House
Leucadia, California, U.S.A.
-
Program: the central portion of this private residence is open onto the oceanic horizon; the body of the house bridges this opening with a section of overlapping volumes topped by an arced roof
-
Structural system: wood frame
Major materials: wood and integral color stucco
Total floor area: 2,288 sq.ft.
Cost of construction: US$ 275,000

1984-88
Berkowitz-Odgis House
Martha's Vineyard, Massachusetts, U.S.A.
-
Program: private residence
-
Clients: Steven Berkowitz, Janet Odgis
General contractor: Doyle Construction Company
Major materials: wood
Total floor area: 2,600 sq.ft.
Cost of construction: US$ 275,000

1984-88
Hybrid Building
Seaside, Florida, U.S.A.
-
Program: building combining retail, office and residential uses
-
Client: Robert Davis
General contractor: New Creation Builders
Major materials: concrete, stucco, metal, wood
Total floor area: 17,665 sq.ft.
Cost of construction: US$ 2 million

1985-86
Pace Collection Showroom
New York, New York, U.S.A.
-
Program: commercial showroom
-
Client: Pace Collection
General contractor: C. Clark Construction Company
Major materials: steel windows, integral color plaster
Total floor area: 1,200 sq.ft.
Cost of construction: US$ 110,000

1986
Objects, Swid Powell
New York, New York, U.S.A.
-
Program: a series of objects designed for Swid Powell, which includes plates, candle sticks, and a picture frame, programs are imposed on the objects to explore new relationships between lines, planes, and volumes
-
Client: Swid Powell
Major materials: brass with green patina finish, glazed porcelain China

1986
Carpets, V'Soske
New York, New York, U.S.A.
-
Program: each of carpets are designed to uniquely express the concepts of the individual projects for which they are made
-
Client: V'Soske, New York

1986
Urban Proposal for Porta Vittoria District
Milan, Italy

Program: competition for mixed-use buildings for an open project that required forward-Looking, experimental urban plans

Client: XVII Triennale of Milan

1986-87
MoMA Tower Apartment
New York, New York, U.S.A.

Program: apartment interior

General contractor: C. Clark Construction Company
Major materials: integral color plaster
Total floor area: 1,800 sq.ft.
Cost of construction: US$ 180,000

1987
Giada Showroom
New York, New York, U.S.A.

Program: retail showroom

Client: Giada
General contractor: C. Clark Construction Company
Major materials: integral color plaster, brass, glass, terrazzo
Total floor area: 800 sq.ft.
Cost of construction: US$ 190,000

1987-88
45 Christopher Street Apartment
New York, New York, U.S.A.

Program: residential apartment

General contractor: Clark Construction Company
Major materials: plaster, steel, concrete
Total floor area: 2,000 sq.ft.

1987-88
Metropolitan Tower Apartment
New York, New York, U.S.A.

Program: apartment interior

General contractor: Woodworks Construction
Major materials: terrazzo, plaster
Total floor area: 1,200 sq.ft.

1988
Abrams Residence
Oxnard, California, U.S.A.

Program: private residence

Consultants: Robert Lawson, structure
Major materials: concrete, steel
Total floor area: 2,000 sq.ft.
Cost of construction: US$ 250,000

1988
Erie Canal Edge
Rochester, New York, U.S.A.

Program: new urban sector at canal edge providing housing, work space, cinemas

Major materials: steel frame, concrete frame

1988
Berlin AGB Library
Berlin, Germany

Program: competition for open-stack library; an addition to the Amerika Gedenk Bibliothek in Berlin

Client: Amerika Gedenk Bibliothek
Consultants: Guy Nordensen, structure
Structural system: concrete frame, steel truss
Major materials: concrete, sandblasted glass
Total floor area: 94,000 sq.ft.
Cost of construction: US$ 32 million

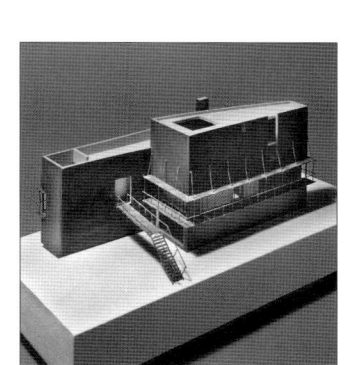

1988-90
Residence
Cleveland, Ohio, U.S.A.

Program: private residence for a lawyer and his wife, a painter

Major materials: steel, wood
Total floor area: 3,500 sq.ft.

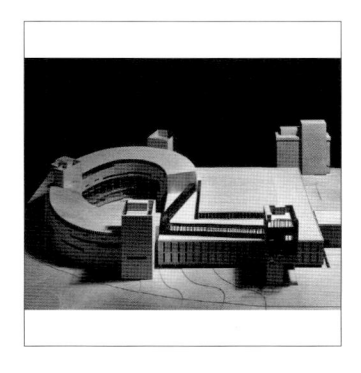

1988-91
College of Architecture and Landscape Architecture
University of Minnesota (early scheme)
Minneapolis, Minnesota, U.S.A.

Program: 90,000 sq.ft. addition to School of Architecture

Client: University of Minnesota
Consultants: Ellerbe Beckett, Inc., structure and HVAC
Major materials: concrete, steel, aluminum

1989
Spatial Retaining Bars
Phoenix, Arizona, U.S.A.

Program: new city edge (housing, work space, shops)

Structural system: concrete
Major materials: concrete

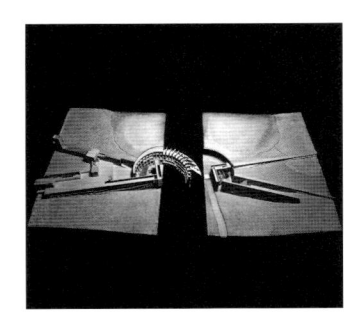

1989
Stitch Plan
Cleveland, Ohio, U.S.A.

Program: urban community (housing and commercial) at city edge

1989
Paris Tolbiac Project
Paris, France

Program: competition for urban ideas for the re-use of the Tolbiac rail yards in Paris explores new types of urban space; a section relational experiment; it was characterized by experiential phenomena with programmatic lines and correlation

1989
Exhibition at MoMA/Museum of Modern Art
New York, New York, U.S.A.

Program: exhibition 'two man show' showing drawings of MoMA's permanent collection

1989-91
Void Space/Hinged Space Housing
Fukuoka, Japan

Program: mixed-use complex with mostly residential apartments

General contractor: Shimizu Corp.
Structural system: concrete
Major materials: concrete, aluminum
Total floor area: 4,243 m^2
Cost of construction: US$ 7.8 million

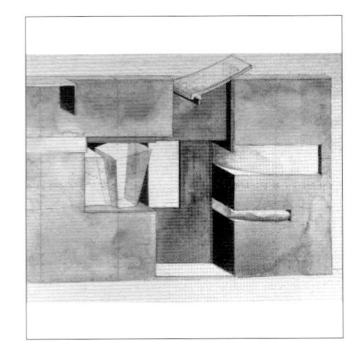

1989-91
Strand Theater Facade Renovation
New York Experimental Glass Workshop
Brooklyn, New York, U.S.A.

Program: facade renovation for a glass workshop studio

Client: E. D. C. New York
Major materials: cast glass, blown glass, bent glass, patinaed brass, aluminum

1989-92
Stretto House
Dallas, Texas, U.S.A.

Program: private residence

Local architect: Max Levy
Consultants: Datum Engineering
General contractor: Thomas S. Byrne Co.
Structural system: concrete block, steel pipe
Major materials: concrete, metal
Site area: 1 acre
Total floor area: 6,500 sq.ft.

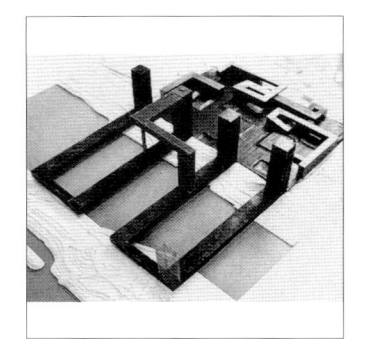

1990
1995 World Expo
Vienna, Austria

Program: competition for exhibits, public services, cafe, shops, hotels for a World Expo

Clients: City of Vienna
Structural system: steel frame

1990
Parallax Towers
New York, New York, U.S.A.

Program: an alternative proposal for Manhattan's 72nd Street Railyards including offices, apartments, hotel rooms, and the extension of Riverside Park

Structural system: steel tube truss
Major materials: steel, glass

1990
Spiroid Sectors
Dallas/Fort Worth, Texas, U.S.A.

Program: a proposal for a new hybrid building type sited in the partly settled area between Dallas and Fort Worth, these sectors would allow a densification of living quarters and workplaces, while enclosing and protecting large areas of Texas prairie

1990
Edge of a City Exhibition at Walker Art Center
Minneapolis, Minnesota, U.S.A.

Program: an exhibition exploring the limits of landscape and urban growth as developed in 6 projects with different locations; each project develops a different strategy

1991-92
Town Square, Four Houses and Chapel
Port Ludlow, Washington, U.S.A.

Program: a new town square in the shape of a parallelogram was proposed at the center of a new community on the site of a former saw mill; four houses are on one side of the square, while the chapel form expressed the duality of its function as a meeting house and a place of silence and reflection

Client: Port Ludlow Development
Structural system: wood frame

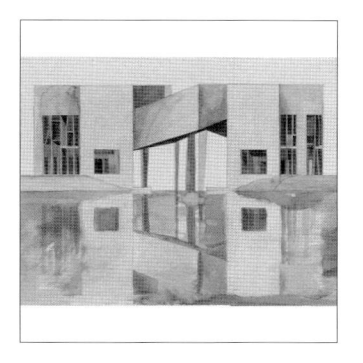

1990-91
Palazzo del Cinema
Venice, Italy

Program: competition for cinema complex

Client: City of Venice
Consultants: Guy Nordenson
Structural system: concrete
Major materials: concrete, metal alloy, sandblasted acrylic, cork, plaster, metal fabric
Total floor area: 25,200 m²
Cost of construction: US$ 28 million

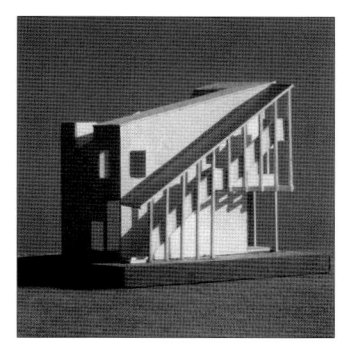

1991-92
Shop and Office
Langley, Washington, U.S.A.

Program: a two level experiment in corrugated metal accommodates a seed shop with shopkeeper's apartment upstairs; on the uppermost level an attic "dream space" is formed by the interior consequences of the "crumpled roof"

Major materials: wood, corrugated aluminum
Total floor area: 1,600 sq.ft.
Cost of construction: US$ 180,000

1990-91
Showroom for Anne Klein A-Line
New York, New York, U.S.A.

Program: retail showroom

Client: Anne Klein
General contractor: C. Clark Construction Company
Major materials: plaster, terrazzo, sandblasted glass
Total floor area: 10,000 sq.ft.
Cost of construction: US$ 1.1 million

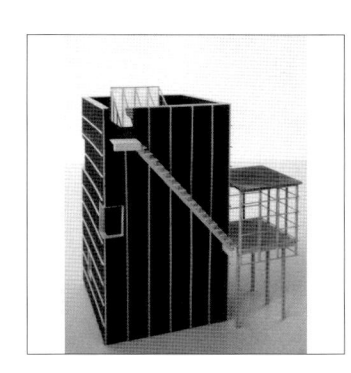

1991-92
Tower of Silence
Manchester, Washington, U.S.A.

Program: this building was planned as a silent retreat end architecture studio sited in a forested area overlooking the Puget Sound in Manchester

General contractor: Myron Holl
Total floor area: 256 sq.ft.
Cost of construction: US$ 20,000

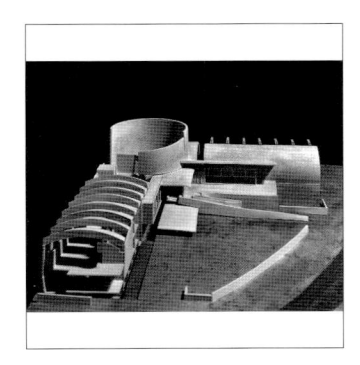

1991
Kemper Museum of Contemporary Art
Kansas City, Missouri, U.S.A.

Program: this proposal for a new art museum explores the problem of controlling and utilizing natural light by developing three alternate skylighting systems; diffused north light in a curved space and faceted south light in the two main gallery halls, and a "Laboratory of Light and Shadow" in the central atrium

Client: Kansas City Art Institute
Local architect: Divine Architects

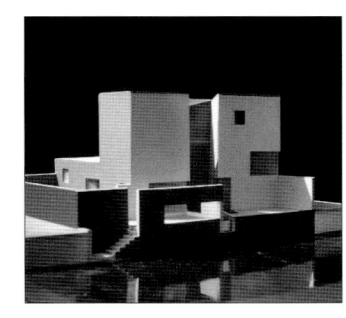

1992
Villa Den Haag
The Netherlands

Program: private residence

Client: Geerlings Vastgoed B.V.
Structural system: brick, concrete
Major materials: stained concrete bricks, wood windows, plaster
Site area: 248 m²
Total floor area: 270 m²

1991
D.E. Shaw & Co. Offices
New York, New York, U.S.A.

Program: offices for 65 employees on two floors of a 40-story midtown Manhattan tower

Client: D.E. Shaw & Co.
Consultants: Robert Director Associates, MEP; Scott Feuron, technologies
General contractor: Clark Construction Company
Major materials: drywall on metal studs, paint
Total floor area: 16,000 sq.ft.

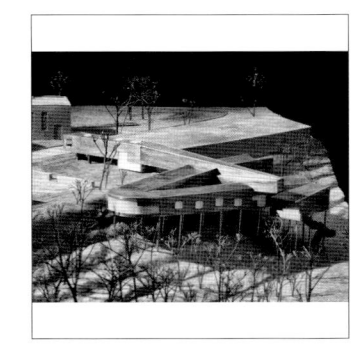

1992
Art and Architecture Buildings, Andrews University
Barrien Springs, Michigan, U.S.A.

Program: this project creates new art and architecture buildings on the campus of Andrews University

Client: Andrews University

1992-93
Storefront for Art and Architecture
New York, New York, U.S.A.

Program: facade renovation for art and architecture gallery

Clients: Storefront for Art and Architecture,
Shirin Neshat, Kyong Park (director)
Collaborator: Vito Acconci
Fabricator: Face Fabrications—Chris Otterbein
Structural system: steel studs

1992-96
Makuhari Bay New Town
Chiba, Japan

Program: 190 units of housing, retail and public facilities

Client: Mitsui Fudosan Group
Associate architects: Kajima Design,
K. Sone & Environmental Design Associates
General contractors: Kajima Design, Keisei, Mitsui Fudosan Group
Structural system: reinforced concrete (bearing wall system with flat-slab, partially steel)
Site area: 8,413 m^2

1992-98
Kiasma, Museum of Contemporary Art
Helsinki, Finland

Program: art museum including galleries, theater, cafe, shop, artist workshop

Client: Finnish Ministry of Public Building
Local architect: Juhani Pallasmaa Architects
Consultant: Insinööritoimisto Oy Matti Ollila & Co., Ove Arup, structure; Ove Arup, mechanical
General contractor: Seicon Oy
Building area: 12,077 m^2

1992-99
Cranbrook Institute of Science
Bloomfield Hills, Michigan, U.S.A.

Program: addition to and renovation of existing science museum and educational facility by Eliel Saarinen

Client: Cranbrook Educational Community
Consultant: Ove Arup & Partners, engineer;
Edmund Hollander Design, Cranbrook Architecture Office, landscape
Construction manager: O'Neal Construction (addition),
Barton Malow Construction Services (renovation)
Project area: 30,000 sq.ft. (addition), 64,000 sq.ft. (renovation)

1994
Manifold Hybrid
Amsterdam, The Netherlands

Program: 182-unit housing block

Building area: 23,630 m^2

1994
Hypo-Bank Offices and Art Hall
Munich, Germany

Program: competition for mixed-use building (retail, apartment, banking hall, offices, and art hall)

Clients: Hypo-Bank GmbH
Structural system: cast concrete
Site area: 16,000 m^2
Total floor area: 59,000 m^2

1994-97
Chapel of St. Ignatius, Seattle University
Seattle, Washington, U.S.A.

Program: Jesuit chapel for Seattle University

Client: Seattle University
Local architect: Olson Sundberg Architects
Consultant: Monte Clark Engineering, Datum Engineering, structure;
Linda Beaumont and Dora Nikolova Bittau, artists
General contractor: Baugh Construction
Footprint area: 567 m^2
Cost of construction: US$ 5,200,000

1994-2009
Knut Hamsun Center
Hamarøy, Norway

Program: historical museum for writer Knut Hamsun including exhibition areas, library, reading room, cafe and 230-seat auditorium

Client: Nordland Fylkeskommune (County)
Associate architect: LY Arkitekter AS
Consultant: Guy Nordenson and Associates,
Rambøll Norge, structure; Landskapsfabikken, landscape
Footprint area: 734 m^2
Total floor area: 2,908 m^2

1996
Museum of the City of Cassino
Cassino, Italy

Program: a historical museum (documenting the city through artifacts) and an art museum with permanent and changing exhibitions

Project area: approx. 12,000 m^2

1996-2000
Sarphatistraat Offices
Amsterdam, The Netherlands

Program: addition of new headquarters for housing developer

Client: Woningbouwvereniging Het Oosten
Local architect: Rappange & Partners
Consultant: Ingenieursgroep Van Rossum, structure
Major materials: perforated copper, perforated sheets of MDF and aluminium
General contractor: VOF Van Eesteren, Koninklijke Woudenberg
Total floor area: 4,645 m^2 (addition) and 325 m^2

I-260

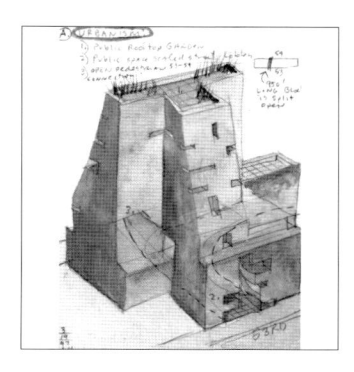

1997
MoMA/Museum of Modern Art Expansion
New York, New York, U.S.A.

Program: invited competition for the renovation and expansion of the Museum of Modern Art

Clients: MoMA, New York

1998-2005
Whitney Water Purification Facility and Park
Connecticut, U.S.A.

Program: water treatment facility and public park

Client: Regional Water Authority
Consultant: CH2MHill, Tighe & Bond Consulting Engineers, engineers; Michael Van Valkenburgh and Associates, landscape; Bioengineering Group, site sustainability
Structural system: induction bent steel tube hoop, cast-in-place and pre-cast concrete
Total floor area: 13,006 m^2

1997-99
"Y" House
Catskill Mountains, New York, U.S.A.

Program: private residence

Clients: Herbert W. Liaunig
Consultant: Edmond Hollander & Associates, landscape; L'Observatoire International, lighting

1997-2000
Bellevue Art Museum
Bellevue, Washington, U.S.A.

Program: galleries, classrooms, cafe, auditorium

Client: Bellevue Art Museum
Associate architect: Sclater Partners Architects, Seattle
Consultant: Skilling Ward Magnusson Barkshire, Guy Nordenson & Associates, structure; McKinstry, MEP
General contractor: Sellen Construction
Structural system: pneumatically placed concrete exterior walls, composite floor construction   Total floor area: 36,000 sq.ft.

1997-2002
College of Architecture and Landscape Architecture
University of Minnesota
Minneapolis, Minnesota, U.S.A.

Program: addition to and renovation of School of Architecture (library, auditorium, offices, classrooms)

Clients: University of Minnesota
Associate architects: Vincent James Associates (addition), Rozeboom Miller Architects (renovation)
Consultant: Ellerbe Becket Inc., engineer
Total floor area: 47,710 sq.ft. (addition), 107,220 sq.ft. (renovation)

1997-2005
Higgins Hall Center Section, Pratt Institute School of Architecture
Brooklyn, New York, U.S.A.

Program: center section of architecture school

Client: Pratt Institute
Consultant: Robert Silman Associates, P.C., structure
General contractor: F. J. Sciame Construction Co., Inc.
Structural system: pre-cast concrete columns and beams with pre-cast concrete plank floor slabs
Total floor area: 27,500 sq.ft. (22,500 sq.ft., actual building; 5,000 sq.ft., combined east and west courtyards)

STEVEN HOLL Architects

Awards, Exhibitions, and Published Writings

STEVEN HOLL ARCHITECTS

—

Steven Holl

–

Atsushi Aiba
Jacob Allerdice
Hideaki Ariizumi
Tim Bade
Gabriela Barman-Kraemer
Laurie Beckerman
Bryan Bell
Anault Biou
Molly Blieden
Sabina Cachero
Stephen Cassell
Pablo Castro-Estevez
Elsa Chryssochoides
Cory Clarke
Pier Copat
Martin Cox
Janet Cross
Lawrence Davis
Makram El-Kadi
Scott Enge
Erik Fenstad Langdalen
Joseph Fenton
Lisina Fingerhuth
Tod Fouser
Ben Frombgen
Thomas Gardner
Annette Goderbauer
Hal Goldstein
Mario Gooden
Friederike Grosspietsch
Yoh Hanaoka
Marie-Therese Harnoncourt
Kent Hikida
Michael Hoffmann
Vesa Honkonen
Paola Iacucci
Mark Janson
Thomas Jenkinson
Matthias Karlen
Bradford Kelley
David Kessler
Jun Kim
Jan Kinsbergen
Lucinda Knox
Justin Korhammer
Anderson Lee
Jennifer Lee
Linda Lee
Andy Lin
Rong-Hui Lin
Peter Lynch
Anne Malx
Julia Mandle
Chris McVoy
Anna Müller
Ralph Nelson
Stephen O'Dell
Lorcan O'Herlihy
Chris Otterbine
Suzanne Powadiuk
Melita Prieto
James Rosen
Justin Rüssli
Susi Sanchez
Florian Schmidt
Sebastian Schulze
Peter Shinoda
Gundo Sohn
Darius Sollohub
Teny Surjan
Tomoaki Tanaka
Sumito Takashina
Tapani Talo
Philip Teft
Audra Tuskes
Tom van den Bout
Heleen van Heel
Urs Vogt
Lynnette Widder
William Wilson
Adam Yarinsky

AWARDS

—

1982:
- Progressive Architecture Citation
for Metz House & Studio, Staten Island, NY
1984:
- Progressive Architecture Citation
for Van Zandt Weekend House, East Hampton, NY
1985:
- AIA New York Chapter Award
for Andrew Cohen Apartment, New York, NY
1986:
- AIA New York Chapter Award
for Pace Collection Showroom, New York, NY
- Progressive Architecture Citation
for Berkowitz-Odgis House, Martha's Vineyard, MA
1987:
- Progressive Architecture Citation
for Hybrid Building, Seaside, FL
1988:
- AIA New York Chapter Awards
for Urban Proposal for Porta Vittoria District, Milan,
for Giada Showroom, New York, NY
- NEA, Graham Foundation & NYSCA Grants
for MoMA Exhibit, New York, NY
1989:
- AIA National Honor Award
for Berkowitz-Odgis House, Martha's Vineyard, MA
1990:
- Progressive Architecture Awards
for College of Architecture and Landscape Architecture, University of Minnesota,
for American Memorial Library, Berlin, West Germany
- Arnold W. Brunner Prize in Architecture
for American Academy and Institute of Arts and Letters
1991:
- Progressive Architecture Award
for Void Space/Hinged Space Housing, Fukuoka, Japan
- AIA National Honor Award
for Hybrid Building, Seaside, FL
- NYC Art Commission Excellence in Design Award
for Renovation of the Strand Theater, Brooklyn, NY
1992:
- AIA New York Chapter Honor Award
for Void Space/Hinged Space Housing, Fukuoka, Japan
- AIA National Honor Award
for D.E. Shaw & Co. Offices, New York, NY
1993:
- AIA New York Chapter Architecture Project Award
for Makuhari Bay New Town, Chiba, Japan
- AIA National Honor Award
for Stretto House, Dallas, TX
1995:
- New York AIA Design Awards
for Cranbrook Institute of Science, Bloomfield Hills, MI,
for Chapel of St. Ignatius, Seattle University, Seattle, WA
1996:
- Progressive Architecture Awards
for Knut Hamsun Center, Hamarøy, Norway,
for Museum of the City of Cassino, Cassino, Italy
1997:
- New York AIA Medal of Honor Award
1998:
- National AIA Design Award
for Chapel of St. Ignatius, Seattle University, Seattle, WA
- Alvar Aalto Medal, Finland
- Chrysler Award for Innovation in Design, USA

EXHIBITIONS

—

1980:
- "Young Architects" at Yale School of Architecture Gallery, New Haven, CT
1981:
- "Window, Room, Furniture" (group show) at Cooper Union, New York, NY
- "Bridges" (one man show) at Architectura Arte Moderna, Rome, Italy
1982:
- "Bridge of Houses" at White Columns Gallery, New York, NY
1984:
- "Metamanhattan" at Whitney Museum Downtown, New York, NY
- "Cultural Connection and Modernity" (one man show) at Facade Gallery, New York, NY
- "Architecture in Transition", Berlin, Germany
1985:

Photographic Credits and Translator

- "Anchorage" (one man show) at Princeton School of Architecture, NJ
- "High Styles, American Design" at Whitney Museum, New York, NY

1987:
- XVII Triennale of Milan, "Urban Section", Milan, Italy
- "House/Housing" at John Nichols Gallery, New York, NY
- "The Emerging Generation in USA" at GA Gallery, Tokyo, Japan

1989:
- Museum of Modern Art, New York, NY
- Werkebund Gallerie, Frankfurt, Germany
- Fukuoka Jisho Gallery, Fukuoka, Japan
- Aedes Gallery, Berlin, Germany

1990:
- Harvard Graduate School of Design, Cambridge, MA

1991:
- Walker Art Center, Minneapolis, MN
- Venice Biennale, Venice, Italy

1992:
- Henry Art Gallery, Seattle, WA
- Canadian Center for Architecture, Montreal, Canada
- "Steven Holl" at GA Gallery, Tokyo, Japan
- "Contemporary Architectural Freehand Drawings" (group show) at GA Gallery, Tokyo, Japan

1993:
- Arc en Reve Centre d'Architecture, Bordeaux, France
- AR/GE Kunst—Galerie Museum, Bolzano, Italy
- Museum of Finnish Architecture, Helsinki

1994:
- Gallerie ROM, Oslo, Norway
- "Intertwining" at Galerie fur Architektur, Hamburg, Germany

1995:
- "Light Construction" at MoMA, New York, NY
- "Kiasma" at Architectural League, New York, NY

1996:
- Venice Biennale, "Sensing the future: Architect as Seismograph", Venice, Italy
- "Present and Futures: Architecture in Cities" at Centre de Cultura Contemporania de Barcelona, Barcelona, Spain

1997:
- GA Gallery, Tokyo, Japan
- "Dutch Architecture and the American Model" at Nederlands Architectuurinstituut, Amsterdam, The Netherlands
- "Shikiri: the Japanese and Their Homes" at Living Design Center OZONE, Tokyo, Japan

1998:
- "The Art of Building", at The Minories Art Gallery, Essex, UK
- "Present and Future: 100 Years of Architecture" at Museum of Contemporary Art, Los Angeles, CA

PUBLISHED WRITINGS

- "IAUS Report: A New Wave of European Architecture" *Architecture and Urbanism* (Aug. 1977)
- *Bridges*, Pamphlet Architecture Series #1, New York: Princeton Architectural Press (Dec. 1977)
- "Review of Blue Mountain Conferece", *Skyline* (Nov. 1978)
- "The Desert De Retz", *Student Quarterly* (Dec. 1978), Syracuse School of Architecture
- "USSR in the USA", *Skyline* (May 1979)
- *The Alphabetical City*, Pamphlet Architecture Series #5, New York: Princeton Architectural Press (March 1980)
- "Conversation with Alberto Sartoris", *Arcade* (Oct. 1981)
- *Bridge of Houses*, Pamphlet Architecture Series #7, New York: Princeton Architectural Press (July 1981)
- "Anatomy of a Skyscraper", *Cities* Cooper-Hewitt Museum, 1982 (pp. 68-69)
- *Urban and Rural House Types*, Pamphlet Architecture Series #9, New York: Princeton Architectural Press (Dec. 1982)
- "Foundations, American House Types", *Precis IV*, Columbia University, 1983 (pp.36-37)
- "Teeter Totter Principles", *Perspecta 21*, The Yale Architectural Journal, 1984 (pp.30-51)
- "Within the City: Phenomena of Relations", *Design Quarterly* (Spring 1988): Walker Art Center
- *Anchoring*, New York: Princeton Architectural Press, 1989
- *Edge of a City*, Pamphlet Architecture Series # 13 New York: Princeton Architectural Press, 1991
- *Intertwining*, New York: Princeton Architectural Press, 1996
- *Kiasma: Helsinki: Museum of Contemporary Art and the Finnish Building*, Helsinki, 1998

PHOTOGRAPHIC CREDITS

GA photographers:
except as noted

Provided by Steven Holl Architects:
pp.21-23, p.28, p.29 above, p.33 right, p.34, p.35 two photos (the second one from left/ right), p.37, pp.39-40, p.41 two photos (left/ right middle), pp.54-55, p.77 three photos (above middle/ above right/ below right), pp.82-83, p.111, pp.144-145, p.158, p.187, p.191, p.228, pp.236-237, p.254 except bottom, p.255 two photos (left bottom/ right top), p.256 left top and two photos on right (middle/ the second from bottom), p.257 two photos on left (middle/ the second from bottom), p.258 two photos on left (middle/ the second from bottom), and right middle, p.259 two photos on left (top/ middle) and four photos on right (except top), p.261 one photo on left (the second from bottom)

Paul Warchol:
p.29 below, pp.30-31, p.32 left, p.33 left, p.35 the third one from left, p.251

Mark C. Darley:
p.35 left, p.41 two photos (right top/ right bottom), p.257 one photo on left (the second from top)

Steven Turner:
p.250

Chris McVoy:
pp.252-253, p.261 right

TRANSLATOR

Hiroshi Watanabe:
pp.8-11

Kazumasa Tamai:
pp.12-17, p.19, p.23, p.31, p.35, p.37, pp.40-41, p.43, p.50, p.63, p.64, pp.66-67, p.69, p.73, p.79, p.83, p.89, p.103, p.107, p.109, p.111, p.119, p.123, p.129, p.147, p.151, p.157, p.161, p.217, p.222-223, p.225, p.227, p.229, p.231, p.233

Yasuko Kikuchi:
p.60, p.101, pp.170-171, p.179, p.199, p.207, p.213, pp.242-245, pp.252-253

Lisa Tani:
p.235

Masayuki Harada:
p.55, p.139, p.142, p.145, p.187, pp.194-195, p.237

Naoko Komeiji:
p.184

1999-2012   Volume 2   **STEVEN HOLL**

Copyright © 2012 A.D.A. EDITA Tokyo Co., Ltd.
3-12-14 Sendagaya, Shibuya-ku, Tokyo 151-0051, Japan
All rights reserved. No part of this publication may be reproduced,
stored in a retrieval system, or transmitted, in any form or by any means,
electronic, mechanical, photocopying, recording, or otherwise,
without permission in writing from the publisher.

Copyright of photographs except as noted
©2012 GA photographers
Copyright of drawings and renderings
©2012 Steven Holl Architects

Art direction (cover & logotype) : Gan Hosoya

Printed and bound in Japan

STEVEN HOLL
and CHRIS MCVOY

1999-2012   Volume 2

Edited by Yukio FUTAGAWA
Essay by Shlomi Almagor

企画・編集:二川幸夫　論文:シュロミ・アルマゴール

A.D.A. EDITA Tokyo

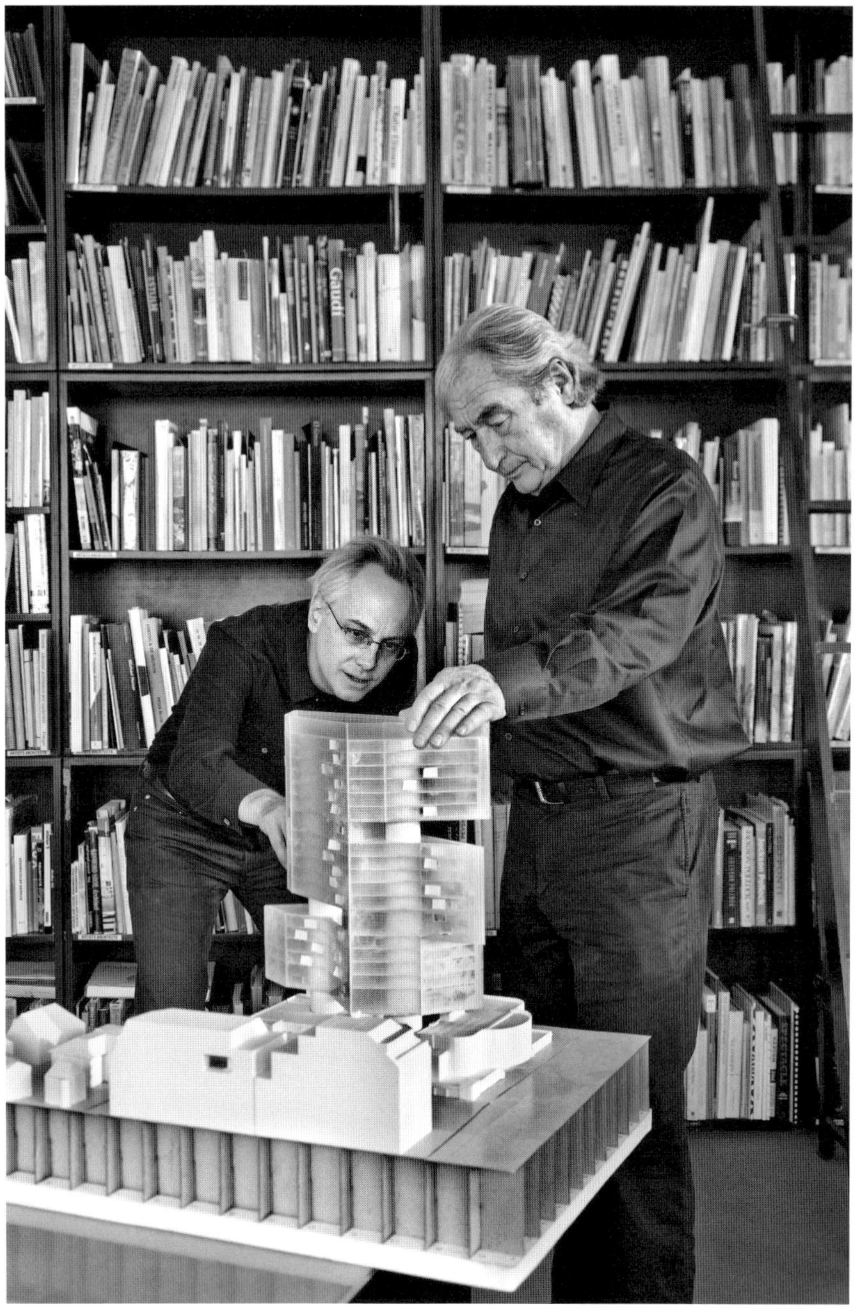
Gaudí

STEVEN HOLL

1947	Born in Bremerton, Washington
1970	Graduated from University of Washington; B. Arch
	Studied architecture in Rome
1976	Postgraduate studies at Architectural Association School, London
	Established Steven Holl Architects in New York
1981	Became Adjunct Professor at Columbia University
1985	AIA New York Chapter Award for Cohen Apartment, New York
1986	AIA New York Chapter Award for Pace Collection Showroom, New York
1988	AIA New York Chapter Awards for Urban Proposal for Porta Vittoria District, Milan and Giada Showroom, New York
1989	Became Tenured Professor at Columbia University
	Published *Anchoring*
	Participated in a Two-Man Show at Museum of Modern Art
	AIA National Honor Award for Berkowitz-Odgis House, Martha's Vineyard
1990	Arnold W. Brunner Prize for Achievement in Architecture for American Academy and Institute of Arts and Letters
1991	AIA National Honor Award for Hybrid Building, Seaside
	"Architecture Tomorrow" exhibit at Walker Art Center
1992	AIA New York Chapter Honor Award for "Void Space / Hinged Space" Housing, Fukuoka, Japan
	AIA National Honor Award for D.E. Shaw & Co., New York
1993	AIA National Honor Award for Stretto House, Dallas
1995	New York AIA Design Awards for Cranbrook Institute of Science, Bloomfield Hills
	Chapel of St. Ignatius, Seattle University, Seattle
1996	Published *Intertwining*
1997	New York AIA Medal of Honor Award
1998	National AIA Design Award for Chapel of St. Ignatius, Seattle University, Seattle
	Alvar Aalto Medal
	Chrysler Award for Innovation in Design
2000	Published *Parallax*
2001	France awarded Grande Médaille d'Or upon him, for Best Architect of Academy of Architecture
2002	Cooper Hewitt National Design Museum (Smithsonian Institute) awarded him their prestigious National Design Award in Architecture
	Published *Idea and Phenomena*
2003	Honorary Fellow of the Royal Institute of British Architects (RIBA)
2006	Received honorary degrees from Seattle University and Moholy-Nagy University in Budapest
2007	Published *House: Black Swan Theory*, and *Architecture Spoken*
2009	The First Ever Arts Award of the BBVA Foundation Frontiers of Knowledge Awards
	Published *Urbanisms: Working with Doubt*
2010	RIBA Jencks Award
	Published *Hamsun Holl Hamarøy*
2011	He was named the 2012 AIA Gold Medal winner
	Published *Horizontal Skyscraper*
2012	Published *Scale and Color Light Time*
	He is a tenured Professor at Columbia University's Graduate School of Architecture and Planning

CHRIS MCVOY

1964	Born Ankara, Turkey
1985	Graduated from University of Virginia; B.S. Arch
	Studied architecture in Venice; Solomon R. Guggenheim Fellowship
1992	Graduated from Columbia University; Master of Architecture
	Joined Tod Williams Billie Tsien Associates
1993	Studied architecture in Finland;
	William Kinne Research Grant;
	American Scandinavian Foundation Grant
	Joined Steven Holl Architects
1999	National AIA Design Award / Kiasma, The Museum of Contemporary Art, Helsinki
2000	Made first Partner Steven Holl Architects
2006	AIA Iowa Honor Award of Excellence / School of Art & Art History, Iowa City
2007	AIA/COTE Top Ten Green Project / Whitney Water Purification Facility and Park
	Published *Stone and Feather: Nelson-Atkins Museum Expansion*
2008	AIA National Honor Award / Nelson Atkins Museum of Art
2009	CTBUH Best Tall Building Overall / Linked Hybrid, Beijing, China
	Art + Architecture Symposium at the Pulitzer Foundation for the Arts
	Won Glasgow School of Art Competition
2010	Keynote speaker, Colombian Architecture Biennale
2011	Award for Excellence in Design / Queens Library, LIC, New York
	Awarded Virginia Commonwealth University, Institute of Contemporary Art Commission
2012	Won Museum of Fine Arts, Houston Competition

1999-2012 Contents
Volume 2

8	Steven Holl's Words, an Edited Selection
	Shlomi Almagor
30	**1. Light, Material and Detail**
32	Interior Renovation of New York University Department of Philosophy New York, New York, U.S.A., 2004-07
38	Experiments in Porosity "From Porosity to Fusion", Milan, Italy, 2005
42	Riddled Cabinet and Table for Horm, Italy, 2006, 2007
44	T Space, Dutchess County, New York, U.S.A., 2010
48	**2. Houses**
52	Little Tesseract, Rhinebeck, New York, U.S.A., 2001
56	Oceanic Retreat, Kaua'i, Hawaii, U.S.A., 2001-
60	Writing with Light House, Eastern Long Island, New York, U.S.A., 2001-04
66	Nail Collector's House, Essex, New York, U.S.A., 2001-04
72	Turbulence House, New Mexico, U.S.A., 2001-05
76	Swiss Residence, Washington D.C., U.S.A., 2001-06
84	Planar House, Phoenix, Arizona, U.S.A., 2002-05
90	Sun Slice House, Lake Garda, Italy, 2005-
94	Daeyang Gallery & House, Seoul, South Korea, 2008-12
102	**3. Housing and Hybrid Buildings**
104	Simmons Hall, Massachusetts Institute of Technology, Cambridge, Massachusetts, U.S.A., 1999-2003
116	World Trade Center Schemes 1 and 3, New York, New York, U.S.A., 2002
118	Loisium Visitors' Center, Loisium Hotel Spa Resort, Langenlois, Austria, 2001-03, -05
128	Zuidas, Amsterdam, The Netherlands, 2002
130	Linked Hybrid, Beijing, China, 2003-09
140	Sail Hybrid, Knokke-Heist, Belgium, 2005-
144	Meander, Helsinki, Finland, 2006-
146	Sliced Porosity Block, Chengdu, China, 2007-12
152	Benetton Tower, New York, New York, U.S.A., 2010
156	**4. Ontology of Institutions**
160	School of Art and Art History, University of Iowa, Iowa City, Iowa, U.S.A., 1999-2006
170	Nelson-Atkins Museum of Art, Kansas City, Missouri, U.S.A., 1999-2007
184	Museum of Human Evolution, Burgos, Spain, 2000
188	Musée des Confluences, Lyon, Lyon, France, 2001
192	Ile Seguin (Fondation Francois Pinault), Paris, France, 2001
194	College of Architecture, Cornell University, Ithaca, New York, U.S.A., 2001
198	Nanjing Museum of Art & Architecture, Nanjing, China, 2002-
202	Herning Center of the Arts, Herning, Denmark, 2005-09
214	Cité de l'Océan et du Surf, Biarritz, France, 2005-11
222	Center for Performing Arts, Princeton University, Princeton, New Jersey, U.S.A., 2008-
226	Campbell Sports Center, New York, New York, U.S.A., 2008-12
230	Glasgow School of Art, Glasgow, U.K., 2009-
236	V & A Dundee Museum and Design Nucleus, Dundee, U.K., 2010
240	Hangzhou Music Museum, Hangzhou, China, 2010-
244	New Art Building, University of Iowa, Iowa City, Iowa, U.S.A., 2010-
248	Cangqian Performing Arts Center, Art Museum and Arts Quadrangle, Hangzhou Normal University, Hangzhou, China, 2010-
252	Queens Library, New York, New York, U.S.A., 2010-
258	New Doctorate's Building, National University of Colombia, Bogotá, Colombia, 2010-
262	Institute for Contemporary Art, Virginia Commonwealth University, Richmond, Virginia, U.S.A., 2011-
266	**5. Edge of a City**
268	Centro JVD, Housing and Hotel, Guadalajara, Mexico, 1999
272	New Town: Green Urban Laboratory, Nanning, China, 2002
278	Toolenburg-Zuid, Amsterdam, The Netherlands, 2002
280	Beirut Marina & Town Quay, Beirut, Lebanon, 2002-
282	Akbuk Dense Pack, Akbuk, Turkey, 2006-
284	Vanke Center, Shenzhen, China, 2006-09
296	Ningbo Fine Grain, Ningbo, China, 2008
302	LM Harbor Gateway, Copenhagen, Denmark, 2008-
306	Shan-Shui Hangzhou, Hangzhou, China, 2009-
312	**6. Fusion: Landscape, Urbanism and Architecture**
314	World Design Park Complex, Seoul, South Korea, 2007
318	Triaxial Field, Hangzhou, China, 2008-
322	Visigoth Museum, Toledo, Spain, 2010
324	**List of Works 1999-2012**

8	スティーヴン・ホールの言葉——抜粋と考察——	194	コーネル大学建築学部棟　ニューヨーク州イサカ, 2001年
	シュロミ・アルマゴール	198	南京芸術・建築美術館　中国, 南京, 2002年〜
		202	ヘルニング芸術センター　デンマーク, ヘルニング, 2005〜09年
30	1章　光, 材料, ディテール	214	サーフ・オーシャン文化センター　フランス, ビアリッツ, 2005〜11年
32	ニューヨーク大学哲学学科インテリア改修　ニューヨーク州ニューヨーク, 2004〜07年	222	プリンストン大学パフォーミングアーツ・センター
38	ポロシティの実験「ポロシティから融合へ」　イタリア, ミラノ, 2005年		ニュージャージー州プリンストン, 2008年〜
42	ホルム社のためのキャビネット＆テーブル　イタリア, 2006年, 2007年	226	キャンベル・スポーツ・センター　ニューヨーク州ニューヨーク, 2008〜12年
44	Tスペース　ニューヨーク州ダッチェス郡, 2010年	230	グラスゴー・アート・スクール　イギリス, グラスゴー, 2009年〜
		236	V＆Aダンディー・ミュージアム　イギリス, ダンディー, 2010年
48	2章　住宅	240	杭州音楽博物館　中国, 杭州, 2010年〜
52	リトル・テッセラクト　ニューヨーク州ラインベック, 2001年	244	アイオワ大学新芸術学部棟　アイオワ州アイオワシティ, 2010年〜
56	オーシャン・リトリート　ハワイ州カウアイ, 2001年〜	248	杭州師範大学パフォーミングアーツ・センター, 美術館および広場
60	光に描かれた家　ニューヨーク州イースタン・ロング・アイランド, 2001〜04年		中国, 杭州, 2010年〜
66	釘収集家の家　ニューヨーク州エセックス, 2001〜04年	252	クイーンズ図書館　ニューヨーク州ニューヨーク, 2010年〜
72	タービュランス・ハウス　ニューメキシコ州, 2001〜05年	258	コロンビア国立大学博士課程棟　コロンビア, ボゴタ, 2010年〜
76	スイス・レジデンス　ワシントンDC, 2001〜06年	262	ヴァージニア州立大学現代美術研究所　ヴァージニア州リッチモンド, 2011年〜
84	プラナー・ハウス　アリゾナ州フェニックス, 2002〜05年		
90	サン・スライス・ハウス　イタリア, ガルダ湖, 2005年〜	266	5章　都市の周縁
94	デヤン・ギャラリー＆ハウス　韓国, ソウル, 2008〜12年	268	JVDセンター, 集合住宅およびホテル　メキシコ, グアダラハラ, 1999年
		272	ニュータウン：グリーン・アーバン・ラボラトリー　中国, 南寧, 2002年
102	3章　ハウジングとハイブリッド・ビルディング	278	トーレンブルグ・ツァイト　オランダ, アムステルダム, 2002年
104	マサチューセッツ工科大学シモンズ・ホール	280	ベイルート・マリーナ, 埠頭計画　レバノン, ベイルート, 2002年〜
	マサチューセッツ州ケンブリッジ, 1999〜2003年	282	アクビュク・デンス・パック　トルコ, アクビュク, 2006年〜
116	ワールド・トレード・センター跡地計画　ニューヨーク州ニューヨーク, 2002年	284	ヴァンケ・センター　中国, 深圳, 2006〜09年
118	ロイジウム・ビジター・センター／ロイジウム・ホテル・スパ・リゾート	296	寧波ファイン・グレイン（微粒子）計画　中国, 寧波, 2008年
	オーストリア, ランゲンロイス, 2001〜03年, 〜05年	302	LMハーバー・ゲートウェイ　デンマーク, コペンハーゲン, 2008年〜
128	ザイダス　オランダ, アムステルダム, 2002年	306	杭州「山水」計画　中国, 杭州, 2009年〜
130	リンクド・ハイブリッド　中国, 北京, 2003〜09年		
140	セイル・ハイブリッド　ベルギー, クノック＝ヘイスト, 2005年〜	312	6章　融合：ランドスケープ, 都市, 建築
144	メアンダー　フィンランド, ヘルシンキ, 2006年〜	314	ワールド・デザイン・パーク　韓国, ソウル, 2007年
146	スライスド・ポロシティ・ブロック　中国, 成都, 2007〜12年	318	三軸構造フィールド　中国, 杭州, 2008年〜
152	ベネトン・タワー　ニューヨーク州ニューヨーク, 2010年	322	西ゴート族博物館　スペイン, トレド, 2010年
156	4章　公共建築の存在論	324	作品リスト　1999〜2012年
160	アイオワ大学美術・美術史学部棟　アイオワ州アイオワシティ, 1999〜2006年		
170	ネルソン＝アトキンス美術館　ミズーリ州カンザスシティ, 1999〜2007年		
184	人類史博物館　スペイン, ブルゴス, 2000年		
188	コンフリューエンス（合流点）博物館　フランス, リヨン, 2001年		
192	セガン島計画　フランス, パリ, 2001年		

Steven Holl's Words, an Edited Selection
Shlomi Almagor

スティーヴン・ホールの言葉——抜粋と考察——

シュロミ・アルマゴール

* The following format of edition and comments on Steven Holl's texts is based on a PhD thesis in process in the UPC/Polytechnic University of Catalonia, Spain with the kind guidance of Professor Juhani Pallasmaa and under the direction of Professor José Antonio Ramos (ETSAM/Escuela Técnica Superior de Arquitectura de Madrid) and Professor Magda Saura (ETSAB/Escuela Técnica Superior de Arquitectura de Barcelona).

1 | ORIGINS AND FIRST INFLUENCES
2 | IDEAS AND THEORY
3 | THE POTENTIAL OF ARCHITECTURE
4 | BUILDING AND PLACE
5 | THE IDEA THAT DRIVES THE DESIGN
6 | PHENOMENON AND BODY
7 | MATERIALITY AND THE HAPTIC REALM
8 | LIGHT, SHADOW AND COLOR
9 | PROPORTIONS
10 | MOVEMENT IN SPACE
11 | TIME
12 | THE INTERTWINING OF IDEA AND PHENOMENA
13 | LANGUAGE
14 | HOLL'S METHOD OF WORK
15 | CONTEMPORARY CULTURE
16 | MODERN MEANS
17 | HOLL'S VISION - WHAT IS ARCHITECTURE? (OR WHAT IT SHOULD BE...)
18 | EDUCATION AND THE FUTURE

1 | ORIGINS AND FIRST INFLUENCES

Steven Holl grew up in a small town in the state of Washington, in the northwest of the United States. He studied at the University of Washington in Seattle, an institution that—during his years as a student—, as he claimed, lacked inspirational figures. He was lucky to have a stimulating teacher that, in addition to instilling in him and his fellow students ideas and passion, encouraged them to 'spread their wings' and see the world.

This professor was Herman Pundt, a fervent man of clear ideas about architecture.

According to Holl himself, it was there that his own belief in the need to 'live' the experience of architecture was cultivated.

He (Pundt) taught a theory and a history course in which students learned what he thought essential to equip a student in America for architecture. He traced the roots of modern architecture through the study of four figures in depth. Beginning with Brunelleschi and the Duomo in Florence, and he went to Schinkel, then to Louis Sullivan and the Chicago School and the last figure was Frank Lloyd Wright. This was the history of architecture and all we needed to know. We learned it by heart, every building, every problem and the various tragedies and so on.

The same professor Pundt helped Holl, in his final year of school, to receive a scholarship to study in Rome. There, he says, his attitude towards architecture changed completely.

I would even say that 1970 (the year in which Holl lived in Rome and travelled through Europe) was the first year I was inspired about architecture, before that I was so fed up with my professors that I almost dropped out of school in 1967 to become a painter.

Holl describes this move in a manner that leaves no doubt of the importance of this change for him:

... I won a position to study abroad and was suddenly air-lifted from the sleepy, shingled regionalism of Seattle to Rome....

Curiously, as had happened to Louis Kahn, a relatively long stay in Rome strongly influenced his way of thinking of architecture and about the phenomena related to the built environment.

I lived just behind the Pantheon, and I made a ritual of going inside the Pantheon every day for the months I was there to see the different ways light would come through the oculus—when it was raining, or when the light would change angle.
–
It took me two months to understand what I was looking at. At first I was just looking at it like a tourist. But after two months I was really analyzing and studying the historic layers that were built up underneath whatever building lay on the horizon. Rome was very important.

... And so important it was that, in relation to the Pantheon—one of the buildings most mentioned by Holl in his writings—, he presents us with the following sentence from which we can understand much of the work written and executed by this architect:

In the tremendous space of the Pantheon, I first felt the passion, the forceful capacity, of architecture to engage all the senses.

*以下のスティーヴン・ホールの文章に対する抜粋編集・コメントは，ユハニ・パッラスマー教授の助言，およびホセ・アントニオ・ラモス教授（マドリッド建築大学/ETSAM）ならびにマグダ・サウラ教授（バルセロナ建築大学/ETSAB）の指導の下，スペインのカタルーニャ工科大学（UPC）にて執筆中の博士論文に基づくものである。

1｜源流と初期の影響
2｜発想と理論
3｜建築のポテンシャル
4｜建物と場所
5｜設計を動かす発想
6｜現象と身体
7｜物質性と触知的領域
8｜光と影と色
9｜プロポーション
10｜空間内の運動
11｜時間
12｜発想と現象の絡まり
13｜言語
14｜ホールの仕事の進め方
15｜同時代的文化
16｜現代的手段
17｜ホールのヴィジョン―建築とは何か？
　　（あるいは何であるべきか……）
18｜教育と未来

1｜源流と初期の影響

スティーヴン・ホールはアメリカ北西部ワシントン州の小さな町に生まれ育った。彼が在学中の頃のシアトルのワシントン大学は，彼曰く，インスピレーションを与えられるような人物は少なかったようだが，それでも生徒達に知識と情熱を注ぎ込み「自分の力を試しに」世界へ羽ばたくことを大いに勧めてくれるような教師には出会うことができた。

　その教師とは，建築について明晰な思考を持った熱心な人物，ヘルマン・プントである。

　そこでホールは，建築とは「実体験」しなければならないものであるとの自身の信念を育んだ。

　彼（プント）は担当する理論と歴史の授業で生徒たちに，彼がアメリカの建築学生に必須であろうと考える事柄を教えました。4人の巨匠についての研究を通して近代建築のルーツをたどっていったのです。ブルネレスキとフィレンツェのドゥオーモにはじまり，シンケル，ルイス・サリヴァンとシカゴ派，そして最後にフランク・ロイド・ライト。それが建築の歴史であり，必要とされる知識のすべてでした。我々はそこに登場するすべての建物や問題やさまざまな事件などを暗記するまで学んだのです。

ホールが卒業年度にローマ留学のための奨学金を得られるよう奔走してくれたのもこのプント教授であった。彼の建築に対する姿勢はそこで大きく変化したという。

1970年（ホールがローマに住みヨーロッパを旅した年）になって初めて建築に触発されたと言ってもよいくらいです。それ以前の私は，あまりに学校の教授たちに嫌気がさしていて，1967年には絵描きになろうと大学を中退しかけていましたから。

この転機が彼に及ぼした変化の重要性はホールの語り口からも明らかである：

……海外留学の機会を得て，シアトルの眠たい片田舎からいきなりローマへと空輸され……

興味深いことに，ルイス・カーンの場合と同様，ローマでの比較的長期に渡る滞在は，彼の建築や建築環境に関する諸現象に対する考え方に強い影響を及ぼした。

パンテオンのすぐ後ろに住んでいたのですが，その数ヶ月間は毎日，それこそ儀式のようにパンテオンの中に入ってはその円形の天窓から差し込む光――雨が降る時や光の角度が変わったりするさま――を眺めていました。
―
その時見ていたものを理解するのに2ヶ月かかりました。はじめは観光客のようにただ眺めるだけ。2ヶ月後ようやく，この世に存在するどんな建物にもその下には積み重なる歴史の層があるのだと気付き，学ぶことになりました。ローマは自分にとって実に重要な場所でした。

……それがどれほど重要であったかは，ホールの著書の中で触れられることが多い建物の1つである「パンテオン」について記された以下の文章を見ても明らかである。この文章はまた，彼が手がけた作品や著作を理解する手がかりとなる：

パンテオンの途方もない空間の中でまず私は全感覚を引き込む建築の強い力，情熱を感じた。

ヨーロッパで過ごしたその年，ホールに深い印象を残したもう1つの建物が，ル・コルビュジエの「ロンシャンの教会」であった。初めてその地を訪れた際のことを回想する中で，ホールは素材や光について記述しており，ワシントン州からの一留学生がヨーロッパ滞在で経験した大きな変化を物語っている。

翌朝，木々に覆われカーブする長い道のりを歩き我々が辿り着くと，教会の大きな回転扉は開いていた。（中略）がらんとした空間に淡い太陽の光と共に足を踏み入れる。中は完全なる静寂，神秘的な光をゆらめかせるロウソクの燃える音がするのみ。対照的な質感（非常に粗い仕上げの漆喰対コンクリート）の上には天井の凹面が，光と空間と分厚い壁の上へと突き上げる力が織り成す曲線/逆曲線の対照によって形成されているようだった。（中略）3つの小礼拝堂のうちの1つの上に通る垂直な縦穴から降ってくる赤い光は生命を持っているかのように見え，液体のようでさえあった。3つの小礼拝堂はそれぞれ……異なるタイプの光を捕らえていた……。

2｜発想と理論

ヨーロッパからアメリカへ帰国しインターン期間を終えたホールは，思ったような職を見つけることができずヨーロッパに戻る。今度はイギリスに渡り，かのアルヴィン・ボヤスキーが校長を務めるロンドンのAAスクール/英国建築協会付属建築学校にて研究を続け，教鞭もとることになった。その頃のAAスクールはそれ自体が新しい発想を育てる豊かな土壌であり，ホールの教官や同僚達の中には当時そして後年，グローバルな建築的思考の中心人物と目されることになるジェームズ・スターリング，チャールズ・ジェンクス，レム・コールハース，エリア・ゼンゲリス，レオン・クリエ，ザハ・ハディッド，ベルナール・チュミといった面々がいた。

その年にもホールはヨーロッパ中を旅して回っている。1976年の終わりにニューヨークに帰国するも，やはり仕事は見つからず，教職に就く。舞い込んでくるわずかな仕事と教育活動の狭間で，ホールは研究者として実践・理論の両レベルでの思考を展開する。

自分の直感を形にしはじめたのはアンリ・ベルクソンの『物質と記憶』を読んでから。1979年のことでした。「プールハウス」のプロジェクトに着手しはじめようとしていたのですが，まだ生成的論点といったものはなく，ただ最先端の建築を古風な建築にリンクできたら，という思いしかありませんでした。当時読んでいたルドルフ・シュタイナーは，物理的な土地の歴史というものが実在し，それはちゃんとした意味も持っている，と書いていました。あなたがそれを認知しようが無視しようが関係なくそこに存在するものなのだと。それが私の作品における1つの極端な例を形づくったわけです……
―
1988年に『Anchoring（投錨）』を執筆しました。建築と土地と現象と発想と歴史のつながりについて語った私の初めてのマニフェストです。それはあくまで1つの運用哲学であり，何かうまいレシピがないか見つけてやろうというのではなく，予想不可能なものを受け入れる試みでした。1つとして同じ土地と情況はなく，いつも我々はその現場の条件に従い作業しないといけない，という意味で。

Another building, which left a great impression on Holl from that year in Europe was the church of Ronchamp by Le Corbusier. Holl recalls his first arrival to this site.

His descriptions of the materials and the light emphasize the profound change that Holl, the student from Washington, experienced in his stay in Europe.

Walking up the long, curving forested path the next morning, we arrived at the chapel to find its large pivoted door open. (......) We stepped into the empty space along a wash of sunlight. It was completely silent inside, except for the crackling of candles, all of which were mysteriously aglow. Above contrasting textures (extremely rough plaster against concrete) the concave ceiling appeared molded by light, space, and the upward thrust of the thick walls, in counterpoint of the curve-reverse curve. (......) The red light that filtered down from the vertical shaft above one of the three small chapels seemed alive, almost fluid. Each of the three chapels... had a different type of light captured....

2 | IDEAS AND THEORY

On his return to America from his stay in Europe, and after finishing his internship, Holl did not find the job he wanted and thusly returned to Europe. This time he went to England, joining the Architectural Association in London, with the famed Alvin Boyarsky as director. Holl studied and taught at the institute. At that time it was a fertile breeding ground for new ideas. Some of his teachers and colleagues in the AA were considered then and, even more so, in following years, as leading figures in architectural thinking globally including people like James Stirling, Charles Jencks, Rem Koolhaas, Elia Zenghelis, Leon Krier, Zaha Hadid and Bernard Tschumi.

—

In that year, too, Holl traveled through Europe. In late 1976, returning to New York, again, he did not find work and began teaching. Between academic activity and the little work that he had, Holl developed his thinking as a researcher on the practical level as well as the theoretical.

I began to formulate my intuitions when I read *Matter and Memory*, by Henry Bergson. It was 1979 and I was trying to begin the project for the Pool House without a generative argument except the hope that an ultra modern architecture could be linked to the archaic. I was reading Rudolf Steiner, who wrote that the history of the physical site has a presence and a meaning. You can choose to acknowledge it or you can choose to ignore it but it exists nevertheless. That became one extreme of my work...

—

In 1988 I wrote the text *Anchoring*, my first manifesto about the connection architecture, site, phenomena, idea, history. It was an operational philosophy; it did not try to find recipes, but to embrace the unpredictable, in the sense that we are always given a new site and situation, and we have to operate according to the conditions there.

For Holl all elements of the built environment—physical, psychological, and temporal—are all interconnected and interdependent. The experience of built space is a complex reality.

Maurice Merleau-Ponty described an 'In-Between' reality or 'ground on which it is universally possible to bring things together'. Beyond the physicality of architectural objects and practicalities of programmatic content, enmeshed experience is not merely a place of events, things and activities, but something more intangible, which emerges from the continuous unfolding of overlapping spaces, materials and detail. Merleau Ponty's 'in-between reality' is then perhaps analogous to the moment in which individual elements begin to lose their clarity, the moment in which objects merge with the field.

—

Architectural synthesis of changing background, middle ground and foreground with all subjective qualities of material and light forms the basis for an intertwining perception. When we sit at a desk in a room by a window, the distant view, light from the window, material on the floor, wood on the desk, and the near eraser in hand all begin to merge. This overlap is crucial to the creation of an intertwining space.

We must consider space, light, color, geometry, detail, and material in an intertwining continuum. Though we can disassemble these elements and study them individually during the design process, finally they merge.

—

The architectural synthesis of foreground, middle ground, and distant view, together with all the subjective qualities of material and light, form the basis of 'complete perception'. The expression of the originating idea is a fusion of the subjective and objective. That is, the conceptual logic which drives a design has an inter-subjective link to the questions of its ultimate perception.

Holl expresses his ideas about the components of the perception of built space. These consist of 'that which exists', 'what happens' and not 'that which is thought' or 'that which is devised'. Phenomenology (of perception) is a philosophy of lived experience.

Architecture intertwines the perception of time, space, light and materials, existing on a 'pre-theoretical ground'. The phenomena which occur within a space of a room, like the sunlight entering through a window, or the color and reflection of materials on a surface, all have integral relations in the realm of perception.

—

Experience of phenomena—sensations in space and time as distinguished from the perception of objects—provides a 'pre-theoretical' ground for architecture. Such perception is pre-logical i.e., it requires a suspension of a priori thought. Phenomenology, in dealing with questions of perception, encourages us to experience architecture by walking through it, touching it, listening to it.

—

Phenomenology as a way of thinking and seeing becomes an agent for architectural conception. While phenomenology restores us to the importance of lived experience in authentic philosophy, it relies on perception of pre-existing conditions. It has no way of forming a priori beginnings.

Holl explains that, in order to address these issues, one needs to first go through a certain mental process:

To open architecture to questions of perception, we must suspend disbelief, disengage the rational half of the mind, and simply play and explore. Reason and skepticism must yield to a horizon of discovery. Doctrines cannot be trusted in this laboratory. Intuition is our muse.

In many of his texts, Holl introduces explanatory examples from a wide variety of fields and it seems that his inspiring curiosity has no limits. His interests range from the physics of light and the chemistry of materials to music (from Bartok to John Cage), astronomy, philosophy and more.

In the following paragraph, for example, Holl explains how to increase the dynamics in a constructed space by the combination of weight and lightness, inspired by music.

A phenomenal architecture calls for both the stone and the feather. Sensed mass and perceived gravity

ホールにとって建物環境におけるすべての要素——物理的・心理的・経時的——はどれも相互に関連・依存し合うものであり，建物の空間を経験することは複合的な現実である。

モーリス・メルロー＝ポンティが記述した「狭間の」現実や「複数のものを1つにまとめることが普遍的に可能な領域」。建築的物体の身体性とプログラム内容の実用性を超えたところにある，網の中にとらわれるような体験とは，単なる事象や物事や活動の場ではなく，折り重なった空間や素材やディテールがどんどん広げられてゆく中で立ち現れる，何かもっと触れることのできないものです。とするとメルロー＝ポンティの「狭間の現実」とは，個々の要素が自身の明確性を失いはじめる瞬間，物体が領域と融合する瞬間と類似したものなのかもしれない。

変化する背景・中景・前景とそこにまつわるすべての素材と光の主観的性質の建築的総合が知覚認識の相関関係の基礎となる。部屋の窓の横にある机に座ると，遠くの眺め，窓からの光，床の素材，机の天板の木材，手に持った消しゴム等，すべてが融合し始める。こういった折り重なりは相関空間をつくるにあたり極めて重要である。

空間・光・色・形状・ディテール・素材を考えるとき，それらは連続する相関関係の中で捉えられなければならない。設計プロセスの中でばらばらに分解し要素を個別に分析することもできるのだが，最終的にはやはりそれらは融合してゆく。

——

前景・中景・遠景とそこにまつわるすべての素材と光の客観的性質の建築的総合が「完全な知覚」の基礎となる。そこに発生する「発想」の表現は主観と客観の融合である。つまり，設計を動かす概念的論理は，その究極的な知覚への諸問題への間主観的なリンクを有しているのだ。

ホールは建築空間の認識の構成要素について自身の考えをこう述べている。それは「そうだと思われているもの」や「考察されるもの」ではなく，「存在しているもの」と「起こるもの」から成っている。（知覚の）現象学は実体験の哲学なのだと。

建築は時間・空間・光・素材の知覚をからめとり，「前理論的基盤」に根ざしている。窓から差し込む太陽の光や平面に映り込む素材の反射や色彩といった部屋の空間内で起きる現象はすべて，知覚の領域内で一体となるような関連性を持っている。

——

現象の体験——物体の知覚とは区別される，空間と時間の感覚——は建築に「前理論的」基盤を提供する。かような知覚は前論理的，つまり先験的な考えの保留を要するものである。現象学において知覚の問題を扱うとき，我々は建築を体験するにあたり，その中を歩き，それに触れ，それに耳を傾けよと促されるのだ。

物の見方・考え方としての現象学は建築的構想の媒介となる。現象学が正規の哲学においては実体験の重要性を取り戻してくれる一方で，それは既存条件の知覚に依存するものであり，先験的なスタートを切りようがないのである。

こういった問題に取り組むには，まずある種の思考プロセスを経ることが必要だとホールは説明する：

建築における知覚の問題を扱う際，我々は疑念を保留し，頭の中の理性を解除し，単純に楽しみながら探検すべきである。発見の地平を前にして，理性や懐疑は一歩引くべきである。この実験室において原則などというものは当てにできない。直感こそが我々を導く女神なのだ。

ホールは自著のあちこちで幅広い分野における例を挙げて説明をしており，その示唆的な好奇心は尽きることがない。彼の関心は光の物理学から素材の化学，そして音楽（バルトークからジョン・ケージまで），天文学，哲学と多岐に渡る。

例えば次に引用する段落では，建物空間内のダイナミクスを高める方法を，音楽から着想を得たという重さと軽さの組み合わせを用いて説明している。

現象的建築とは，石と羽毛の両方を兼ね備えているもの。嵩を感じ重力を知覚することが，我々の建築に対する認識に直接影響を与える。

（中略）建築が重力・重さ・面圧・張力・ねじり力に応じた質量と素材を表現するとき，それらはオーケストラの楽器のような現れ方をする。素材をよりダイナミックに仕立てるには重さ（コントラバス，ドラム，チューバ）と軽さ（フルート，バイオリン，クラリネット）のコントラストを用いればよい。

3｜建築のポテンシャル

スティーヴン・ホールは熱心な建築の擁護者である。建築は人間に——今日，ともすれば欠如しがちな，生きている実感をフルに感じさせ体験させることのできる唯一の芸術であると言う。

良質な建築には生きる喜びと生活の質の向上への配慮がある。それは素材とディテールの中で囁かれ空間の中で繰り返し唱えられる。

ホール曰く，建築の素晴らしいところは，すべてのものにその可能性を提供するという点である……

建築は哲学や芸術や言語理論と違って誰にでもつながることができるポテンシャルを持っています。誰もがこのつながりの深さを理解できるかどうかはまた別の問題ではあります

が。それにしても真に強い建物に対して，人々はいろいろなレベルで応えてくる。インテリ層だけでなく，壁に手を触れただけの5歳の子供でさえも。自分にとっては，そこがとてもわくわくする点であり，真のチャレンジでもある……。プロジェクトの建築的意味合いを越え評価できる，あるいは教えられることは，建築を理解するやり方は他にもあるということなのです。一番よくあるのは空間や素材を直接体験して得られるもの。それは誰にでも感じることができます。

——

建築は実際に体験し感じる空間と時間の相関関係を形づくることができる，つまり我々の生活を変えることができる。現象学は本質の研究に関わるが，建築は本質に再び息を吹き込むポテンシャルを持っている。形と空間と光を織り成すことで，建築は，特定の土地・プログラム・建物から生まれる様々な現象を通じ日々の生活経験を高めることができる。発想の力が建築を駆り立てる，という面がある一方で，構造・素材・空間・色・光・影が絡み合い建築をつくり上げている，という面もある。

（中略）匂い・音・素材の幅——硬質な石とスティールから，たおやかな絹まで——が，毎日の生活に入り込みそれを形づくり，我々を始原的な体験へと立ち戻らせてくれるのだ。

ホールはこういった建築の他に類を見ない体験は，完全かつ直接的な複合的体験であると断言する。

2冊目の著書『Intertwining（絡まり）』の中では，古い石壁に射す真昼の太陽の動きの効果について，具体的な例を挙げて説明しながらこう述べている：

物体と領域の融合は網の目にとらわれるような体験を生む。それは建築独特の相互作用である。目をそらしてしまうことのできる絵画や彫刻とは異なり，またスイッチを切ってしまうことができる音楽や映画とは異なり，建築は我々を取り囲む。それは我々に，平面的そして深く立体的な視差的時空の絡まりの中で，位置を変えては融合する素材・質感・色・光との親密な触れ合いを約束するのだ。

ホール曰く，建築は我々を自然現象へと立ち戻らせ「人間的な体験」へと向かわせてくれる：

メディアからのイメージに満たされた今という時代は，ローカルな文化の特殊性が多国籍的なアイデンティティに取って代わられるというシュールな変化に立ち会っている。揺れ動く経済の混沌と不確実さが，絶え間なく供給される新技術が呼ぶ情報過多と相まって，自然現象からの乖離を引き起こしニヒリスティックな態度が生まれる原因となっている。

建築は，その物言わぬ空間性と実際に触れることのできる物質性をもって，人間的な体験になくてはならない本質的な意味と価値を取り戻してくれることができるのだ。

ホールは，彼が建築の基本因子と信じるものを提唱することに徹底的なこだわりを見せる。それが人々の

directly effect our perceptions of architecture.

(......) Architecture's expression of mass and materials according to gravity, weight, bearing, tension, and torsion reveal themselves like the orchestration of musical instruments. Material is made more dynamic through the contrast of heavy (bass, drums, tuba) and light (flute, violin, clarinet).

3 | THE POTENTIAL OF ARCHITECTURE

Steven Holl is a passionate proponent of Architecture. According to him, it is the only art that can, in an absolute manner, offer man the experience and sensation—sometimes absent at the present—of fully being alive.

The joy of living and the enhanced quality of everyday life is argued in a quality architecture. It is whispered in material and detail and chanted in space.

The exceptional thing about architecture, says Holl, is that it offers this possibility to all...

Architecture, unlike philosophy, art, or linguistic theory, has the potential to connect to everyone. Weather or not they understand the depth of this connection is another question. But if a building is really strong, people will respond on many levels; not only the intellectuals but also a five year old child who just touched the wall. To me this is very exciting; this is the real challenge... Beyond the architectural implications of the project, that I may appreciate, or that you can teach, there are other ways of understanding architecture. And maybe the most frequent one occurs through direct spatial or material experience, which can be felt by anyone.
—
Architecture can shape a lived and sensed intertwining of space and time; it can change the way we live. Phenomenology concerns the study of essences; architecture has the potential to put essences back into existence. By weaving form, space and light, architecture can elevate the experience of daily life through the various phenomena that merge from specific sites, programs, and architectures. On one level, an idea-force drives architecture; on another, structure, material, space, color, light, and shadow intertwine in the fabrication of architecture.

(......) A range of smell, sound, and material—from hard stone and steel to the free billowing of silk—returns us to primordial experiences framing and penetrating our everyday lives.

Holl assures us that this unique experience of architecture is a complex experience, total and direct.

In his second book, *Intertwining*, after describing—through a specific example—, the effects of the movement of the midday sun on an old stone wall, he says:

The merging of object and field yields an enmeshed experience, an interaction that is particular to architecture. Unlike painting or sculpture from which one can turn away, unlike music or film that one can turn off, architecture surrounds us. It promises intimate contact with shifting, merging materials, textures, colors, and light in an intertwining of flat and deep three-dimensional parallactical space and time.

Architecture, says Holl, can return us to natural phenomena and lead us back to the 'human experience';

The present moment, infused with media imagery, is witness to surreal changes of multinational identities replacing the specificities of local cultures. The chaos and uncertainty of fluctuating economies, combined with an information overload from the ever-increasing supply of new technologies, contribute to a detachment from natural phenomena, thus giving rise to nihilistic attitudes.

Architecture, with its silent spatiality and tactile materiality, can reintroduce essential, intrinsic meanings and values to human experience.

Holl seems to be persistent in his quest of advocating for what he understands as the basic factors of architecture, because he sees it as a crucial element in the lives of people...

I continue to enjoy doing lectures and writings about the philosophical potential of architecture; in the end it s an art form that has enormous consequences on our lives.

4 | BUILDING AND PLACE

One of the main principles of Holl's discourse is that a building is tied primarily to a specific site. The physical location of a project is one of the most important components in the design process.

One of the inspirations I drew from my early readings in phenomenology, particularly from Merleau-Ponty, was to grasp the profound uniqueness of each specific place, its light, its air, its smell, its ambient color, its history, or, I should say, many histories. I realized that each site on earth was a different beginning point, experientially, historically, intellectually, capable of joining us together in new ways as our bodies move through it and as it, the place, moved through our bodies. This simple but deeply moving fact opened my mind to the possibility of a radical eruption in architecture...
—
A building has one site. In this one situation, its intentions are collected. Building and site have been interdependent since the beginning of Architecture. In the past, this connection was manifest without conscious intention through the use of local materials and craft, and by an association of the landscape with events of history and myth. Today the link between site and architecture must be found in new ways, which are constructive transformation in modern life.
—
Architecture is bound to situation; it is intertwined with the experience of a place. The site of a building is more than a mere ingredient in its conception. It is its physical and metaphysical foundation.

In *Anchoring*, his first manifesto, Holl describes various buildings and places, dramatically inserted into their environment. These are two examples:

Standing in the courtyard of the Nunnery in Uxmal, time is transparent, function unknown. The path of the sun is perfectly ordered with the architecture. The framed views align with the distant hills. Descending through the ball court, ascending the 'House of Turtles', and looking again toward the great courtyard—the experience transcends architectural beauty. Architecture and site are phenomenologically linked.

At Louis Kahn's Salk Institute, there is a time of day when the sun, reflecting on the ocean, merges with light reflecting on the rivulet of water in the trough bisecting the central court. Ocean and courtyard are fused by the phenomenon of sunlight reflecting on water. Architecture and nature are joined in a metaphysics of place.

5 | THE IDEA THAT DRIVES THE DESIGN

One of the principal foundations of the theoretical work of Steven Holl is the 'guiding idea'. It is a concept (or various ones) that binds all the components of the work and places the design process on a track toward a clear direction.

生活において極めて重要な要素であると見ているからだ……

私は建築の哲学的ポテンシャルについて講演や執筆で述べることに今も喜びを感じています。つきつめれば，それは我々の生活に甚大な影響を及ぼす1つの芸術の形ですから。

4 | 建物と場所

ホールの論説の主要原理の1つに，建物は本来ある特定な土地に結び付けられている，というものがある。プロジェクトの物理的所在地は設計プロセスにおいて最も重要な構成要素の1つである。

現象学についての本を読みはじめた頃，特にメルロー＝ポンティから得たインスピレーションの1つが，個々の場所が持つ深遠なる特異性を把握することでした。その場所に特有の光・空気・匂い・基調色・歴史，そしていくつもの物語。私は，地上に存在するすべての土地はそれぞれの経験・歴史・知識により異なる起点となり，我々の身体がその中を通り抜け，またそういった場所がこの身体を通り抜けるに従い，今までにない形で我々を1つにつなぎ合わせていることを理解しました。この単純だが感慨深い事実が，私を建築の急進的爆発への可能性へと向かわせたのです……

―

建物には敷地がある。という状況下において，それが擁している意向はまとめられている。建物と土地は建築有史以来ずっと相互依存の関係にあり，過去にはこのつながりがローカルな素材や技術の使用，また風景と歴史上・伝説上の出来事との関連付けを通じ，意識的な意向なしに現れるものであった。今日，土地と建築は何か新たに別なつながり方をしているはずで，それは現代生活における建設的な変容なのである。

―

建築は状況につながっている。その場所の経験と絡み合っているのだ。建物の敷地は，その起源の単なる一成分にとどまらず，その形而下そして形而上的な根幹なのである。

彼の最初のマニフェストである『Anchoring(投錨)』でホールは，環境に対しドラマティックに挿入された様々な建物と場所について記述している。2つ例を挙げてみよう：

ウシュマルの尼僧院の中庭にたたずめば，時間は透明，機能は不明である。太陽の軌跡は建築と完璧に一致している。切り取られた景色は遠くの山々と並ぶ。球戯場を抜けて降り，「亀の館」を登り，再びその大きな中庭を振り返る体験は建築美を超越する。建築と土地は現象学的にリンクしている。

ルイス・カーンの「ソーク研究所」には，海に反射する太陽が，中央広場を両断する溝を流れる小川に反射する光と融合する，そんな時間帯がある。海と広場は水に映る太陽の光の現象によって融け合う。建築と自然が場所の形而上学により結ばれるのだ。

5 | 設計を動かす発想

スティーヴン・ホールの理論的著作の主要基盤の1つに"指針となる発想"がある。それは作品のすべての構成要素を束ね，設計プロセスに明確な方向性を与え軌道に乗せるようなコンセプト(複数ある場合もある)である。

コンセプトは設計プロセスを動かす「エンジン」。どんなプロジェクトにおいても初期段階では敷地とプログラムが分析され，時には出ばなをくじかれたりした後，漠然とした空間スケッチをともなった中心的コンセプト(複数ある場合もある)が決まる。土地はどれもそれ特有の状況を持っているため，我々はバランスを保ちつつも個別に独自な解を目指すことになる。ダイアグラムや言葉で表現されるコンセプトは，様々に異なる側面をまとめ上げるのに役立ち，プロジェクトの進行やクライアントとのコミュニケーションにも有用です。

……そして著書『Questions of Perception(知覚の諸問題)』ではこう記している：

(中略)「現象ゾーン」は多種のパーツのように機能し，他のどの構成要素よりも実質的な全体の問題を提示する。建築におけるチャレンジはどれも唯一無二なもの。どれも特有の敷地と状況，プログラムをかかえている。どれも土地・状況・多数の現象を融合させる系統だった発想……原動力となるコンセプト……を必要としている。全体の一貫性は多様なパーツを縫う糸のように浮かび上がるが，それは1つの分離した発想かもしれないし，いくつかのコンセプトの相関であるかもしれない。

―

(中略)発想は抽象ではない――が，建築プログラムと融合し，建物の任務原理として出現する。

そういった発想のほとんどをダイアグラムに集中させるホールは，自身の創作プロセスにとってそれが大切であると説明する：

私は全面的にコンセプト・ダイアグラムに頼っていて，自分の秘密兵器だと思っています。これのおかげで新規のプロジェクトへと，別の現場へと移行できるのです。

―

(中略)ダイアグラムは心構えを切り替える装置のようなもの。自分をリセットして，安定した発想から追い出してくれる。
(中略)私の描くダイアグラムは，単なる大まかな概要ではなく，それがないと想像し得なかったようなプロジェクトの方針の可能性を意識した，ある程度のレベルのディテールを伴っている。コンセプト・ダイアグラムが得られないことには，方向性が分からず途方に暮れてしまうのです。

6 | 現象と身体

もう1つ，ホールの理論において中心となる構成要素として，生命システム全般に作用するような現象を通じ建築が「ユーザー」に与えることのできる，総合的であり，かつ，活性化させるような体験がある。

―

設計時の思考プロセスについて問われたホールは，発想やコンセプトを練り上げるのに長い時間を掛けはするものの，鍵となるのはやはり身体的な体験であると語る。

私はこれまで敷地の一つひとつ，プログラム一つひとつに対し，その都度「限定的なコンセプト」を組み立てるというやり方をしてきました。20年以上の間，一般的な，包括的と呼んでよいような目標に努力を傾けてきました(中略)……が，建築の真の試金石は空間内を移動する身体の現象にあると思っています。それは建築のコンセプトや哲学の理解度とは関係なく知覚し感じることができる。つまり建築は素晴らしい普遍的な言語であると言えます。音楽と似て，哲学や理想をもって制作することができるもの。でもその本当の試金石は人々の体験にあるのです。

ホールは一連の発言を通じ，その場所で得られる肉体

Knut Hamsun Center (Hamarøy, Norway, 1994-2009): distant view

A concept is the 'engine' that drives the design process. Early in each project, after analyzing the site and program and sometimes after several false starts, a central concept (or concepts) is settled on, together with vague spatial sketches. As each site circumstance is unique, we aim for equally balanced and particular solutions. The concept, expressed in the diagram and words, helps focus a manifold of different aspects. It helps in the development of a project and communication with a client.

... and Holl writes in his book *Questions of Perception*:

... 'phenomenal zones', function like a manifold of parts, presenting the question of a whole more substantial than any of its components. Each challenge in architecture is unique; each has a particular site and circumstance or program; and for each, to fuse site, circumstance, and a multiplicity of phenomena, an organizing idea... a driving concept... is required. The unity of the whole emerges from the thread that runs through the variety of parts; whether it be one discrete idea or the interrelation of several concepts.
—
... ideas are not abstractions—but become fused with architectural programs and emerge as the working principles of a building.

Holl centers the majority of these ideas in diagrams and he explains the importance of those in his process of creation:

I depend entirely on concept diagrams; I consider them my secret weapon. They allow me to move afresh from one project to the next, from one site to the next.
—
... my diagrams are a device to put me in a different frame of mind, to recast me, to force me out of my stable mind set.... my diagrams cannot merely be a broad, sweeping gesture. They must have some quality of detail that sensitizes me to the possibilities of strategies for the project that I could not have otherwise imagined. Until I have the concept diagram, I do not know where to go, I'm lost.

6 | PHENOMENON AND THE BODY

Another central component of Holl's theory is the total and invigorating experience that architecture can offer the 'user' through phenomena that affect all vital systems.
—

Asked about the mental processes involved in his designs, Holl admits that despite spending a long time developing ideas and concepts, he still believes that the key remains the bodily experience.

I have been working with the strategy of a limited concept which is reformulated for each site and each unique program. Over twenty years, I have developed general, almost generic, aims (......)... yet I feel that the real test of architecture is in the phenomena of the body moving through spaces; which can be sensed and felt regardless of understanding the architect's concept and philosophy. In this sense architecture is a great universal language; like music it can be philosophically and idealistically produced but its true test is in public experience.

In a series of different quotes, Holl makes it clear that the real, direct and physical experience of a place cannot be substituted by any type of image:

I try to see recently championed work first hand and form my own opinions after walking through the spaces and experiencing the smell of the place. I have been incredibly disappointed by some recent feature buildings which do not hold up in a first hand experience. On the contrary, the work of Le Corbusier, Louis Kahn, Sigurd Lewerenz is always incredibly more in the physical reality than what can be communicated in photographs. Architecture is as much about an inner as outer world. Form and meaning become nominal when held up against the phenomena.

Of all the arts, Holl says, Architecture offers the most complete experience, a total experience...

Architecture, more fully than other art forms, engages the immediacy of our sensory perceptions. The passage of time; light, shadow and transparency; color phenomena, texture, material and detail all participate in the complete experience of architecture.... only architecture can simultaneously awaken all the senses—all the complexities of perception.

... and he describes the possibilities offered by this complete experience:

Architecture, by unifying foreground, middle ground, and distant views, ties perspective to detail and material to space. While a cinematic experience of a stone cathedral might draw the observer through and above it, even moving photographically back in time, only the actual building allows the eye to roam freely among inventive details; only the architecture itself offers the tactile sensations of textured stone surfaces and polished wooden pews, the experience of light changing with movement, the smell and resonant sounds of space, the bodily relations of scale and proportion. All these sensations combine within the complex experience, which becomes articulate and specific, though wordless. The building speaks through the silence of perceptual phenomena.
—
The smell of rain-wet dirt, the texture merged with the color and the fragrance of orange rinds, and the steel-iced fusion of cold and hard: these shape the haptic realm. These essences of material, smell, texture, temperature, and touch vitalize everyday existence.

The following quotes depict personal experiences of Holl in spaces and buildings that left an impression on him.

Holl speaks of the sensory experience and the differences between two separate visits, one in winter and another in summer, in the gardens of the Ryoanji Temple in Kyoto.

I noticed many sounds—the roaring cicada and ringing gongs—which had not revealed themselves during my winter visit, six years earlier. Like a projective lens, the hypnotically abstract spaces of Ryoanji magnified sensorial changes. The spatial-material seasonal connection seemed so intense and subtle as if it were revealing some hidden, vital force: a life-principle illuminated through the phenomenology of architecture. Merging and shifting perspectival views, details of joinery, the textures, smells and sounds all combined and expressed in this architecture of gravel, paper and wood.
—
The temple and gardens of Ryoanji stand as testament to the poetic intensity which—through subtle and inspired composition—can invoke mesmerizing and uplifting experience without excessive monetary or material means.

In the book *Questions of Perception*, after a series of detailed descriptions of his impressions during visits to places such as the Johnson Wax building by Wright, the city of Ferrara, the abandoned city of Uxmal (Yucatan) in Mexico and the City Hall of Säynätsalo by Aalto, Holl writes the following lines that reinforce his earlier mentioned comment about the importance of the experience 'in situ':

For me, these 'Archetypal Experiences' are not simply emotional encounters; nor are they strictly intellectual or academic... they are three and four dimen-

を伴う直接経験はどのような種類のイメージにも代えることが出来ないと明確に述べている：

最近注目を浴びている作品に実際に足を運び，その空間の中を歩き回り，その場所の匂いを体験して，自分なりの見解を持つようにしているのですが，近頃の「特徴のある建物」の中には直に体験してみると肩透かしを食うようなものがあり，ひどくがっかりさせられてしまう。それに引きかえ，ル・コルビュジエやルイス・カーンやシーグルド・レヴェレンツの作品はどれも写真が伝えられる以上のものを肉体的現実において与えてくれる。建築とは，外的な世界であると同じくらい，内的な世界なのです。形や意味は，現象に比べればちっぽけなものでしかない。

ホール曰く，全ての芸術の中で建築は最も完全な経験，トータルな体験を与えてくれる……

建築は他の芸術形態に比べ，我々の知覚認識により包括的かつ直接的に訴えかけるものである。時間の経過，光と影と透明度，色彩現象，質感，素材そしてディテールが総動員で建築の完全な体験を形づくる。(中略)建築のみが全知覚──感知するということの複雑さの隅々まで──を同時に呼び覚ますことができるのだ。

……そしてこの完全なる経験がもたらす可能性についてこう記している：

建築は，前景・中景・遠景を統合することで奥行きをディテールに，素材を空間に結びつける。石造りの大聖堂の映画を通した体験は，観る者をその内部や上空，果ては鮮明な過去へまでも引き込むのに対し，創意に富んだディテールの間を縫って自由に視線を散策させることを可能にするのは実際の建物のみである。ざらついた石の表面や磨かれた木のベンチの触感，動くに従い変化する光の体験，空間に響く音や匂い，スケールとプロポーションの身体的関係を与えられるのは実際の建物だけだ。こういった感覚がすべて組み合わさった複合的な体験は，言葉は持たずとも明瞭で具体的である。建物は知覚現象の沈黙を通し，話しかける。

──
雨に濡れた土の匂い，オレンジの皮の色と香りに溶け込む質感，氷のようなスティールの冷たさと硬さの融合。それらが形づくる触知的領域。その素材，匂い，質感，温度そして触感が日々の暮らしに生命を吹き込む。

以下の引用は，ホールの印象に残った空間や建物についての彼の個人体験を描いたものだ。
　京都の竜安寺の庭園を冬と夏の2回に分けて訪れた際にホールが感じた相違点とそれぞれの知覚的体験について語られている。

6年前の冬に訪れた際には無かった沢山の音に気付いた──うなるような蝉の声と鐘をつく音。催眠作用があるかのごとく抽象的な竜安寺の空間は射影レンズのように知覚的変化を拡大する。季節ごとの空間と素材の関係はあまりに強くそして繊細で，何か隠れた生命の力の存在を暗に示しているようだ。この砂利と紙と木でできた建築の中で，融合または移動する遠近感，建具のディテール，質感，匂い，音のすべてが組み合わさり表現されている。

──
竜安寺とその庭は詩的強度の証として存在する──その微かな，心に響くような構成を通し，過剰な金銭的・物的手段に訴えずとも，魅惑的で高揚感のある体験をもたらす。

著書『Questions of Perception(知覚の諸問題)』では，ライトの「ジョンソン・ワックス社ビル」，フェラーラの街並み，メキシコの打ち棄てられた都市ウシュマル(ユカタン)，アアルトの「セイナッツァロの町役場」といった場所を訪れた際の印象を詳細に記した後，「現場での」体験の大切さについて語った前掲のコメントに念押しするかのように以下の文章を続ける：

自分にとって，こういった「原型的体験」は単に感情を伴う出会いではなく，かといって厳密に知的あるいは学術的な出会いでもなく……それらは3次元・4次元の純粋な「知覚」なのだ。知覚を建築的思考の1モデルとすることで，(自分が目指し励むところの)建築を学ぶ者は「見る者」となるべく奮闘するのである。見るという術は，世界を明らかにする行為に取り組むことで何がしかの喜びをもたらしてくれるものだが，それは我々の洞察力を構成する自分自身の「ものの見方」の範疇を超えるものではない。

7｜物質性と触知的領域

ホール曰く，建築的空間をつくるディテールの物質性が明白になる時，触知的領域が開かれる。「触知的(haptic)」は触覚と関係した単語ではあるが，触知的領域はどうやら全感覚を巻き込むことができるらしい……

知覚者の感覚と連動する物質がもたらすディテールは我々を鋭い視覚を越え触覚へと向かわせる。線形性・凹面・透明性から硬さ・弾力性・湿気へと，触知的領域が開いてゆく。

──
建築における素材の体験は視覚のみならず触覚・聴覚・嗅覚によるもので，それらすべてが時間の中で我々の身体が描く軌跡と空間と絡み合っている。これほど多くの現象と感覚的経験に直接関わる領域は触知的領域をおいて他にはないかもしれない。

この「知覚領分」の中で重要な役割を負っているのが素材である。

Simmons Hall, Massachusetts Institute of Technology (Cambridge, Massachusetts, U.S.A., 1999-2003): natural light on 'tactile' surface

Herning Center of the Arts (Herning, Denmark, 2005-09): terrace in front of restaurant

Cranbrook Institute of Science (Bloomfield Hills, Michigan, U.S.A., 1992-99): water and glass effect

sional pure 'perceptions'. By taking perception as a model for architectural thought, a student of architecture (which I strive to be) struggles to become a seer. The art of seeing brings a certain joy in engaging the revealing of the world. Yet it remains in our 'perspective' from which we form our own visions.

7 | MATERIALITY AND THE HAPTIC REALM

According to Holl, the haptic realm opens up when the materiality of the details forming an architectural space becomes evident. The term 'haptic' has to do with the tactile, but the haptic realm, apparently, can involve all of the senses...

Matter interlocking with the perceiver's senses provides the detail that moves us beyond acute sight to tactility. From linearity, concavity and transparency to hardness, elasticity and dampness, the haptic realm opens.
—
The experience of material in architecture is not just visual but tactile, aural, olfactory; it is all of these intertwined with space and our bodily trajectory in time. Perhaps no other realm more directly engages multiple phenomena and sensory experience than the haptic realm.

Within this 'perceptive sphere', materials play a key role.

Reflection on perception in the design process considers all scales, including the micro scale of material properties. Even the most common seemingly inert material must be allowed to 'speak' its essence.
    Kandinsky addresses this approach:"... Everything has a secret soul, which is silent more than it speaks".
—
Materials produce a psychological effect such that mental processes, feelings and desires are provoked. They stimulate the senses beyond acute sight towards tactility. In the perception of details, colors and textures, psychological and physiological phenomena intertwine. Phenomena that can be sensed in the material and detail of an environment exist beyond that which can be intellectually transmitted...
—
The stuff of which something is made has emotive qualities. The transparency of a membrane, the chalky dullness of a wall, the glossy reflection of opaque glass and a beam of sunlight, intermesh in reciprocal relationships, forming the particular phenomena of a place. Given an architectural idea, the relationships of construction materials impose a dimension that penetrates perception through matter to tactility.

According to Holl, materials also constitute one of the means to express the guiding idea.

The materials of architecture communicate in resonance and dissonance, just as musical instruments in composition. Architectural transformations of natural materials, such as glass or wood, have dynamic thought and sense provoking qualities. Analogous to woodwinds, bras and percussion instruments, their orchestration in an architectural composition is as crucial to the perception and communication of ideas as the orchestration of musical instruments is for a symphonic work.

With a somewhat poetic description, Holl reminds us of the potential of materials...

The texture of a silk drape, the sharp corners of cut steel, the mottled shade and shadow of rough sprayed plaster or the sound of a spoon striking a concave wooden bowl, reveal an essence which stimulates the senses.

And, with these possibilities, he explains, 'phenomenal zones' are also those where materials 'work'.

... Cast glass seems to trap light within its material. Its translucency or transparency maintains a glow of reflected light, refracted light or the light dispersed on adjacent surfaces. This intermeshing of material properties and optic phenomena opens a field for exploration. Phenomenal zones likewise open to sound, smell, taste and temperature as well as to material transformation.

Apart from experimenting with glass and light, Holl also investigates the relation of the latter with liquid, mostly water. As in the image of a stick that appears crooked by water, the action of refraction, along with transparency, reflection and its materiality, can ignite the imagination.

An attention to phenomenal properties of the transformation of light through material can present poetic tools for making spaces of exhilarating perceptions. Refraction phenomena produce a particular magic in architecture that is adjacent to or incorporates water.
—
Liquid... in its lack of form... has phenomenal properties of rippling and reflection.

The refraction of sunlight in liquid in a glass... produces images that engages the psychological... The surface has texture, consistency, viscosity and color.
—
We might consider water a 'phenomenal lens' with the powers of reflection, spatial reversal, refraction and transformation of rays of light.
    ... reflection... in clear, still pond appear(s) more intense than (the) actual view.
    A flat plate of glass in a window... reflects the background with an amazingly sharp image. On the bottom of a pool, we can often see intense focal lines of sunlight projected by the crests of wavelets that act as lenses. The psychological power of reflection transcends the 'science' of refraction.

8 | LIGHT, SHADOW AND COLOR

Holl believes that natural light, along with the phenomena it conveys, grants architecture its soul and its value. Light, with its shadows and reflections, defines the elements and can grant them life or deprive them of it...

The perceptual spirit and metaphysical strength of architecture are driven by the quality of light and shadow shaped by solids and voids, by opacities, transparencies, and translucencies. Natural light, with its ethereal variety of change, fundamentally orchestrates the intensities of architecture...
—
Like a musician's breath to a wind instrument or touch to a percussion instrument, light and shadow bring out the rich qualities of materials which remain mute and silent in darkness.
—
Space remains in oblivion without light. Light's shadow and shade, its different sources, its opacity, transparency, translucency, and conditions of reflection and refraction intertwine to define or redefine space. Light subjects space to uncertainty, forming a kind of tentative bridge through fields of experience. What a pool of yellow light does to a simple bare volume or what a paraboloid of shadow does to a bone white wall presents us with a psychological and transcendent realm of the phenomena of architecture.
—
We hear the 'music' of architecture as we move through spaces while arcs of sunlight beam white light and shadow.

Holl's daily investigations of the Pantheon on his previously mentioned stay in Rome, taught

設計プロセスの中で知覚について熟考する際,材料特性のマイクロスケールを含むあらゆるスケールが対象となる。最もありふれた,一見不活性な素材でも,それ自体の本質を「語る」ことが許されていなければならない。

カンディンスキーの手にかかればこうなる：「(中略)あらゆるものには秘めたる魂があり,それは語るよりも無言である」。

—

素材は心理作用を生み,思考プロセスや気持ちや願望を喚起する。それらは感覚を刺激し,鋭い視覚を越え触覚へと向かわせる。ディテール・色・質感の知覚においては心理的現象と生理的現象が絡み合っている。環境の素材とディテールに「感じる」ことができる現象とは,知的側面において伝えることができるものを超えたところにある。

—

何か物を構成している素材というものは,感情に訴える属性を持っています。皮膜の透明度,白く粉をふいた壁の単調さ,すりガラスの光沢,一筋の陽光。それらが相関関係の中で噛み合い,その場所に特有な現象をつくり出す。建築的発想を加味された建材同士の相関関係が科してくる次元の中で知覚は物質を貫き触覚へと向かう。

ホールによれば,素材はまた,指針となる発想の表現手段の一つでもあるという。

建築のさまざまな素材は互いに共鳴したり不協を奏でたりしながら,さながら作品中の楽器のようにコミュニケートする。ガラスや木などといった自然素材の建築的変換は,思考や感覚を喚起するようなダイナミックな属性を持っている。木管や金管,打楽器と似て,それらを建築構造の中で編成指揮することは,交響曲におけるさまざまな楽器のオーケストレーションと同様に,アイディアのコミュニケーションと感知に不可欠である。

いくぶんと詩的な表現を用い,ホールは素材のポテンシャルについてこう指摘している……

絹のドレープの質感,切り出したスティールの鋭利な角,目の粗い吹付け漆喰のまだらな陰影,木のお椀に当たるスプーンの音,が明らかにする本質が感覚を刺激する。

そして,こういった可能性に加え,素材が「本領発揮」をするもう1つの土台として「現象ゾーン」があると説明する。

……鋳造ガラスは素材内部に光を閉じ込めるようだ。その半透明性あるいは透明性は反射した光や屈折した光や近接面に拡がる光などの輝きを維持する。素材の特性と光学的現象がこのように噛み合う時,新たな領域が開きさらなる探求がはじまる。現象ゾーンも同様に音・匂い・味・温度や素材の転換へと開かれる。

ガラスと光の実験の他にもホールは後者と液体,主に水との関係も研究している。水面で折れて見える棒のような屈折作用にはじまり,透明性,反射そして物質性は想像力に火をつけることができる。

素材を通した光の変容の現象的特性に着目すれば,心が浮き立つような感覚を与える空間を作るための詩的ツールが見つかるはずだ。特に屈折現象は,建築の近くに水を置いたり水を取り入れたりすることで魔法のような効果をあげる。

—

液体は……その形の無さゆえ……波紋と反射という現象的特性を持っている。

グラスに入った液体に屈折する太陽の光……は心理的側面に効果的なイメージを持っている。……その表面には質感・一貫性・粘性・色がある。

—

水は,反射・空間反転・屈折そして光線を変化させるといった力を持つ「現象的レンズ」だと言えよう。

風のない時の澄んだ池……に映る像……は実際の景色よりも強烈な印象を残す。

窓にはめられた平らなガラス板……に映りこむ背景は驚くほどシャープな像を結ぶ。たびたび目にする,さざ波の波頭がレンズの役割を果たしプールの底に落とす,くっきりとした日光の焦線。反射が持つ心理的影響力は,屈折の「科学」を凌駕する。

8│光と影と色

ホールは自然光とそれがもたらす現象が建築に魂と価値を与えると信じている。光は,その影と反射と共に,さまざまなエレメントを定義し,それらに生命を吹き込むことも,それらから生命を奪うこともできる……

建築の知覚的スピリットと形而上学的パワーは,立体とヴォイド,不透明性と透明性と半透明性によって形づくられる光と影の質が原動力となっている。自然光は,その多様で霊妙な変化と共に,建築の濃度の根本的な演出に一役買っている……

—

音楽家が管楽器に吹き込む息のごとく,あるいは打楽器に触れる手触りのごとく,光と影は,闇の中であれば静かに押し黙ったままなはずの素材の豊かな特質を引き出す。

—

光無くしては空間は忘却の淵に沈んだままだ。光の陰影,さまざまな光源,その不透明性・透明性・半透明性,そして反射・屈折の条件が絡み合い,空間を定義あるいは再定義する。光は空間を不確実性に晒し,いくつもの経験の領域の間に橋渡しをしようとする。黄色い光の泉がシンプルでがらんとしたヴォリュームにどう作用するのか,影の放物面が乳白色の

D.E. Shaw & Co. Office (New York, New York, U.S.A., 1991): reception with various colored lights

Chapel of St. Ignatius, Seattle University (Seattle, Washington, U.S.A., 1994-97): view toward altar in nave

him an important lesson on light...

(In the Pantheon) each day the light and shadow were very different. The Pantheon is a great teacher, a laboratory of light with dynamic umbra...

... And Holl puts his ideas and impressions into practice applying new technologies...

In the Light Laboratory at the Cranbrook Institute of Science, every day is different. Low winter sun refracts in luminous waves while a prismatic rainbow washes the blank wall... Diffraction in gentle waves suddenly merges with pulsing shadows that appear as inverted dancers near the ceiling.
—
... (it) is an experimental construction employing new glass lens techniques patterning light in motion for a living architecture.

Light, obeying the laws of science, crosses materials, breaks and bends and creates a broad range of shades and light tones. These effects of the rational obedience of the mathematical laws eventually have to do with the soul, says Holl.

In magnificent spaces, light changes and appears to describe form. An eclipse of white clarity suddenly gives way to a pulse with color; light is contingent, its shadows intermittent.
—
As light passes through small holes it spreads out, frays and bends...

The physics of light is evident in shadows. The boundary between light and shadow—usually the grey area of 'penumbra'—is filled with the mysteries of the mathematics of light.
—
Color is a property of light. Yet physics does not hold the key to unlocking the enigma of colors, as the experiences of chromatic space are bound up in mystical effects and philosophical potential.

... Astonishing advances in the physics of color may provoke us to rethink our everyday spatial experiences.

In his book *Parallax*, Holl talks about the chromatic project for the D.E.Shaw Offices in NY, where the backs of some walls separating the central area from the windows were painted in color. The natural light, hitting the tinted walls, left colorful reflections on the white surfaces that faced the room. In another book, talking about 'phenomenal zones', he explains this type of phenomenon:

Certain physical interactions offer zones of investigation: Color projection is experienced when light, reflected off a brightly colored surface, then bounced onto a neutral white surface, becomes a glowing phenomena that provokes a spatial sense. Reflected color is seen indirectly; it remains, with a ghostlike blush, the absent referent to an experience. In experiments with these phenomena we have discovered an emotional dimension that suggests a "psychological space".

The potential of color is, apparently, rich and complex...

Variation in reflectivity of glossy and matte surfaces, differences between opaque and transparent colors, and the unique properties of reflected and projected colors begin to suggest an enormous range in the phenomenology of color. Forces which impact on the experience of color function according to available light as well as traditional variable properties. Indeterminacy, in fact, might be the central condition of color.

Our perception of color cannot be fully explained through the mathematics of light waves and the physical action of vision.

9 | PROPORTIONS

According to Holl, human scale and proportion in relation to the human body have been disappearing from the architectural work towards the end of the twentieth century. These, he says, are part of the innate sensitivity of the human race and must be rescued.

Proportion can be felt more than directly perceived. It is, like cacophony and harmony in music, quite subjective and quite powerful.
—
One of the intuitive powers of humans is the perception of subtle mathematical proportions in the physical world.

... we have an analogous ability to appreciate visual and spatial proportional relations. In music, as in architecture and any of the visual arts, these sensibilities must be cultivated.
—
Historically a culture's particular building tradition often came with inherent balance. (... he gives the example of the *Tatami* in Japan)... Building was automatically scaled to the human in a proportional series.
—

Human scale, relative proportional scale and urban scale, all extremely important in architecture have been especially neglected in the last two decades.

A re-assertion of the human body as the locus of experience... as well as a firm aim to re-establish roots in the perceptual world with its inherent ambiguity presents us with new questions of proportion and scale in the development of future architectures.

10 | MOVEMENT IN SPACE

In his writings, Holl treats quite extensively the question of human movement within the built environment (both buildings and the city).

In many of his buildings, designed and constructed, one can detect what we might call 'processional spaces' or 'perceptible paths'. The viewer discovers the spaces while moving within them.

... The body incorporates and describes the world. Motility and the body-subject are the instruments for measuring architectural space.... only the criss-crossing of the body through space—like connecting electric currents—joins space, body, eye and mind.

In relation to movement in space, Holl defines the term 'Parallax':

The experience of Parallax (is) the change in the arrangement of surfaces defining space due to the change in position of a viewer...

... and 'Parallax' leads to the term 'Spatial field':

'... the spatial experience of parallax, or perspective warp, while moving through overlapping spaces defined by solids and cavities opens the phenomena of spatial fields. The experience of space from a point of view that is in perspective presents a coupling of the external space of the horizon and the optic point from the body. Eye sockets become a kind of architectural position grounded in a phenomena of spatial experience that must be reconciled with the concept and its absence of experiential spatiality.

An infinite number of perspectives projected from an infinite number of viewpoints could be said to make up the spatial field of the phenomena of a work of architecture.'

The analysis of movement shifts away from the historical term of the perspective towards a new dynamism. The change in position of the ob-

壁にどう作用するのかが，建築の現象の心理的そして超越的な領域を我々に見せつけてくれる。
—
太陽光線が孤を描き白い光と影を投げかける空間の中を歩けば，建築の「音楽」が聞こえる。

前述のローマ滞在中の日々のパンテオン研究が，ホールに光について大切なことを教えてくれた……

（パンテオンでは）光と影は毎日まったく異なる姿を見せた。パンテオンは偉大な師であり，ダイナミックな影と光の研究所でもあった……

……そしてホールはその発想と印象を実践に移し，そこに新しい技術を適用した……

「クランブルック科学研究所」の光の実験室には，1日として同じ日は訪れない。冬の低い太陽が明るい波となって屈折し，のっぺりとした壁にプリズムの虹が架かる……ゆるやかな波となり分散する光が突然，天井のあたりで反転したダンサーのように脈打っている影と融合する。
—
……（それは）生きた建築に動きのある光を導入する，新しいガラスレンズの技術を用いた実験的な構造である。

光は科学の法則に従い，素材を横断し折れたり曲がったりしながら多様な影と光のトーンをつくり出す。それは数学の法則を理性的に遵守した結果だが，ひいては魂に関わってくるものなのだとホールは言う。

すぐれた空間における光の変化は形を表現するかのようだ。白く鮮明な光が消えると突如として色彩の脈動が現れる。光は偶発的で，その影は断続的である。
—
光は小さな孔を通り抜けると拡散し，ほつれ，折れる……
　光の物理学は影にも明確に表れている。光と影の境界——だいたいは「半影」となる灰色の部分——は光の数学の不思議で満ちている。
—
色は光の属性の1つである。しかし色彩の謎を解く鍵を，物理学は持ち得ていない。彩色された空間の体験は神秘的効果と哲学的ポテンシャルに硬く結びついているからだ。
　……色の物理学における驚異的な進歩が我々に日常の空間体験の再考を促してくれるだろう。

著書『Parallax（視差）』の中でホールは，ニューヨークの「D・E・ショウ社オフィス」(1991)の彩色プロジェクトについて，中央エリアを窓から隔てる壁のいくつかは裏側に色がペイントされている件に言及している。着色された壁に自然光が当たると，部屋に面した方の白い壁の表面にカラフルな反射を投げかけた。別の著書では，「現象的ゾーン」について述べる際，このタイプの現象について説明している：

ある種の物理的相互作用には調査に値するものがあり，一例に色彩投影がある。鮮やかに着色された表面に光が反射し，それがニュートラルな白い表面に跳ね返ると，空間感覚を喚起するような発光現象が生じる。反射した色は直接見えるものではなく，指示対象が不在の，幻のようにほんのりとした色づきでしかない。こういった現象の実験を通して我々は"精神的空間"を示唆する感情的次元があることを発見した。

そしてどうやら色のポテンシャルは豊かで複雑であるらしい……

光沢ある表面とマットな表面の反射の差異，不透明な色と透明な色の違い，そして反射した色と投影された色に特有の属性は，色の現象学の途方もない領域の広さを暗示している。色の体験に影響を及ぼす様々な力は，そこで得られる光の種類と，従来の可変特性に左右される。つまり不確定性こそが色の主的条件なのかもしれない。
　我々の色に対する知覚を光波の数学と視覚という身体行動で完全に説明することはできないのだ。

9｜プロポーション

ホール曰く，20世紀終盤の建築作品から，人体に対応した人間的スケールとプロポーションが消えつつある。そして，それらは人類生来の感受性であり，救出されなければならないものであると語る。

プロポーションは知覚するよりもっと直接的に感じることができる，音楽における不協和音やハーモニーと同様にかなり主観的でかなり力強いもの。
—
人間の直感力の1つに，物理世界の中の微妙な数学的プロポーションを知覚できる能力がある。
　……我々には視覚的・空間的プロポーションの関係を認識する類似能力がある。音楽や建築など，どんな視覚芸術においても，そういった感受性の育成が必要だ。
—
歴史的に，ある文化に特有な建築伝統とは，それ固有のバランスを伴っていることが多い。（……ホールは日本の畳を例に挙げている）……昔，建造物は一連のプロポーションを通して人間のスケールに自動的に合致するようになっていた。
—
人間的なスケールと相対的比率のスケールと都市のスケールはすべて建築において非常に重要なものだがここ20年の間，特にないがしろにされてきている。
　体験の中心としての人間の身体の再考……そして知覚的世界とその特有の曖昧さの中に根を張りなおすという確固たる目的が，未来の建築の発達に向けてプロポーションとスケールにまつわる新たな課題を我々に投げかけてくる。

10｜空間内の運動

著作の中でホールは（建物と都市の両方の）建築環境の中での人間の動きの問題についてかなり詳しく触れている。
　彼が設計し建設された建物の多くには「行列的空間」や「知覚可能な経路」と呼べるようなものを見いだすことができる。見る者が空間内を動きまわるうちに空間を発見してゆく。

……身体は世界を取り込み，描く。運動性と，主題としての身体は，建築的空間を測定する道具である。……空間内を縦横に動く身体のみが，電流配線のように，空間と身体と眼と頭をつなぐのだ。

空間内の移動に関連して，ホールは「Parallax（視差）」という言葉をこう定義している：

「視差」体験（とは）見る者の位置の変化に起因する，空間を定義する表面配列の変化……

Kiasma, Museum of Contemporary Art (Helsinki Finland, 1992-98): slope

server, according to Holl, is no longer only in the horizontal plane...

Overlapping perspectives, due to movement of the position of the body trough space create multiple vanishing points, opening a condition of spatial Parallax. Perspectival space considered through the parallax of spatial movement differs radically from the static perspectival point of Renaissance space and the rational positivist space of modern axonometric projection. A dynamic succession of perspectives generates the fluid space experience from the point of view of a body moving along an axis of gliding change.
—
Parallax... is transformed when movement axes leave the horizontal dimension. Vertical or oblique movements through urban space multiply our experiences. Spatial definition is ordered by angles of perception. The historical idea of perspective as enclosed volumentrics based on horizontal space gives way to the vertical dimension. Architectural experience has been taken out of its historical closure. Vertical and oblique slippages are key to new spatial perceptions.

11 | TIME

Holl began experimenting with time in architecture in an early stage in his career. He notes that—inspired by the analysis of Bergson's Matter and Memory—, he designed in 1979 a Pool House in Scarsdale, NY. Holl sought to address the issue of time at various levels. One of the 'tools' he used was the location of two large openings in the longitudinal facades, indicating—daily and throughout the changing seasons—, the altering angle of the sun.

Space was perceived by the body moving through time. This experiment was, for us, crude space-time manifold.

Holl deals with the question of time in different ways. Architecture, he says, is a solid, eternal element, indicating the passage of time. The materials that compose it, the perceived natural phenomena and the movement within it, mark epochs and moments.

... architecture... serves as an index of time. Second, minute, hour, decade, epoch, millennium all are focused by the lens of architecture. Architecture is among the least ephemeral, most permanent expressions of culture.

—
... Materials that bear the marks of aging carry the messages of time.
—
Within its spatial frame a wealth of incidental and phenomenal experiences are time-contingent.

A wide range of experiments in time through his projects, along the years, has brought Holl to speak of seven different 'types' of time in architecture. From the chronological Creation time ('Duration of Conception' and Construction of the project) and the real Duration of the building; the ever-changing Diurnal Time and the Seasonal Time, the specificity of the Local Time of the site versus a global time; the Experiential Time unique to a work of architecture and the culture-dependent Linear Time.

Architecture (is) a vehicle for understanding and experiencing time... : a bridge, a metaphysical link allowing us a way to comprehend time. (......) The experiential, the relativistic, and the poetic may all be felt in architecture as an index of time.
—
With today's simultaneous, instant accessibility, our global time is pulverized: a time of bits. Local time, characterized by fixed place, is a stabilizing ground.
—
Global time and local time are like parallel universes that simultaneously make up the present. A challenge of today's architecture is to embrace both of these—anchoring in the particulars of the local while being forged in the innovations of the global.

12 | THE INTERTWINING OF IDEA AND PHENOMENA

Holl, in a phrase in the catalogue of an exhibition of his work in Switzerland, says that the union between idea and phenomenon is a creative act of architecture. According to Holl, that fusion is a procedure for setting the balance between the components during the design process.

Architecture is born when actual phenomena and the idea that drives it intersect... The concept acts as a hidden thread connecting disparate parts with exact intention. Meanings show through at this intersection of concept and experience. A structuring thought requires continuous adjustment in the design process... As dimensions of perception and experience unfold in the design process, constant adjustments aim at a balance of idea and phenomena.

In architecture, Holl says, all these different fields—these elements so diverse and sometimes even opposed—, are connected. Architecture is the art which, more than any other, connects different spheres.

Architecture is a transforming link. An art of duration, crossing the abyss between ideas and orders of perception, between flow and place, it is a binding force. It bridges the yawning gap between the intellect and senses of sight, sound, and touch, between the highest aspirations of thought and the body's visceral and emotional desires.

A multiplicity of times are fastened, a multitude of phenomena are fused, and a manifold intention is realized.

The balance in the creation of built space is achieved by training an intuitive thought, linking it with the logic of the processes of architectural planning.

The search for meaning (in architecture) demands a resistance to empty formalism, textual obfuscation and commercialism. Focusing on ideas early in the design process sets the substantial core ahead of the surface.... For what is an architectural concept if not the material and spatial expression of spiritual intentions?

Intertwining of intellect and feeling is inherent in thought intuitively developed... thought that searches and is open to the changing field of culture and nature that it expresses.

Although intuition cannot be explicitly expressed, we cannot condemn intuitive work to ambiguity.

Holl says his aim is "to realize space with strong phenomenal properties while elevating architecture to a level of thought". (......) This purpose is also explained in other words, as Holl sees it as a challenge of architecture in general, and while summing some of his own main principles.

Physical phenomena engage our 'outer perception', while mental phenomena involve our 'inner perception'. Mental phenomena have real, as well as intentional, existence. Empirically we might be satisfied with a structure as a purely physical-spatial entity but, intellectually and spiritually, we need to understand the motivations behind it. This duality of intention and phenomena is like the interplay between objective and subjective or, more simply, thought and

……そして「視差」は「空間領域」へとつながる：

「……固体と空洞に定義された空間の重なりの中を動き回る際の視差あるいは知覚的たわみの空間体験は，空間領域の現象を生む。遠近法に基づいた視点からの空間体験は，地平線上の外部空間と身体からくる視覚的位置とを結合させる。眼窩は空間体験の現象に根ざした建築的な位置のようなものとなり，経験的空間性の欠如とコンセプトとの和解を要する。
　無数の視点から発する無数のパースペクティブが，1つの建築作品の空間領域の現象を形成していると言ってもよいだろう。」

運動の分析はパースペクティブの歴史的表現から新たなダイナミズムへと移ってゆく。観察者の位置の変化は，ホールによると，もはや水平面のみにとどまらない……

重なり合うパースペクティブは空間内の身体の位置移動に伴いいくつもの消点をつくり，空間的視差の状態を生む。空間移動の視差を通して考える透視図法的空間は，ルネッサンス的空間の静的な透視点や現代の不等角投影法による合理的実証主義的空間とは根本的に異なるものである。パースペクティブのダイナミックな連続は，滑るような変化の軸に沿って動く身体の視点から得られる，流れるような空間体験を生む。

視差……は移動軸が水平方向の次元を逸脱するときに変化を見せる。都市空間内の垂直または斜めの移動は我々に多くの体験を与える。空間の定義は知覚の角度によって決まるのだ。水平空間に基づく屋内容積というパースペクティブの歴史的な捉え方は，垂直方向の次元へと取って代わられ，建築体験は自身の歴史的閉包から解放された。新たな空間知覚への鍵は，垂直や斜め方向の滑りにある。

11 | 時間

ホールはそのキャリアの初期から建築における時間について実験を重ねてきた。ベルクソンの『物質と記憶』の分析に触発され，1979年にニューヨーク州スカースデールに「プール・ハウス」を設計したと述べている。その中で様々なレベルから時間というテーマにアプローチしているホールだが，彼が用いた「ツール」の中の1つに，長手方向のファサードに設けた2つの大きな開口部の位置決め──つまり，1日そして季節を通じて変化する太陽の角度──がある。

時間の中を移動する身体に知覚される空間。我々にとってこの実験は，生々しい時空の多様体だった。

ホールはいろいろなやり方で時間の課題に取り組んでいる。彼曰く，建築とは，時間の経過を示す頑丈で不滅なエレメントである。それを形成する材料，知覚される自然現象とその中での移動が，様々な時代や瞬間に刻まれてゆく。

……建築は……時間の指標となる。秒・分・時・年代・時代・千年紀はすべて建築のレンズの焦点を通る。建築は刹那から最も遠く，最も永続的な文化の表現形態である。
──
……経年劣化の印を刻む素材は時間のメッセージを運ぶ。
──
空間という枠組みの中，豊富な偶発的・現象的体験は時間に依存する。

いくつものプロジェクトで試みてきた時間に関する幅広い実験を通し，ホールは建築における7つの異なる「タイプ」の時間について語るに至った。(中略)編年的な「創造時間」(プロジェクトの「構想と建設にかかる期間」)と実際の建物の「経過時間」，絶え間なく変化する「日周的時間」と「季節的時間」，グローバルな時間に対し土地特有の「ローカルな時間"，建築作品固有の「経験的時間」，そして文化に左右される「線形時間」。

建築(は)時間を理解し体験するための手段である……例えば橋は時間を理解するための一種の形而上学的なリンクである。(中略)経験的・相対論的・詩的なものはどれも建築において時間の指標として感じることができる。
──
同時／即時的アクセス性が我々のグローバルな時間を細かく粉砕してしまった現在，一定の場所に特徴づけられるローカルな時間は安定した基盤となる。
──
グローバルな時間とローカルな時間はパラレルワールドのように同時発生的に現在を形成している。今日の建築が取り組むべきは，その両方を受け入れること──ローカルの特有性に錨を下ろしつつグローバルなイノベーションの中で進化することだ。

12 | 発想と現象の絡まり

ホールは，スイスで開かれた自身の展覧会のカタログの中で，発想と現象の合体は建築における創造的行為であると述べている。ホール曰くその融合は，設計プロセスにおいて構成要素のバランスをとってゆくための手続きの1つである。

建築は実際の現象とそれを突き動かす発想が交差する時に生まれる……コンセプトは異質な物同士を明確な意向のもと繋いでゆく隠れた糸のような働きをする。このコンセプトと経

Knut Hamsun Center (Hamarøy, Norway, 1994-2009):
Orange glow of the horizon during winter weeks sheds a low reflection inside the museum. This building stands as a register of time's extremes in architecture, from its extended conception to its collapsed time of construction. ... the building is an instrument for the experience of unique seasonal and diurnal time. The register of light within the body of the building ... (provokes) ... a distinct and pronounced engagement with time.

冬の数週間に見られる水平線のオレンジ色の光は館内に低い反射を投げかける。この建物は，その長期間にわたる構想から畳み掛けるような建設期間まで，建築における時間の両極端の記録といえる。……また，固有の季節的・日周的時間を体験するための道具であり，建物本体の中の光の記録は……時間との明確かつ顕著な関係……(を促している)。

Nelson-Atkins Museum of Art (Missouri, U.S.A., 1999-2007):
An ever-changing daylight penetrates through the water of reflecting pools into the parking area

絶え間なく変化する陽光が，光が反射するプールの水を通り抜けて駐車場へと差し込む

feeling. The challenge for architecture is to stimulate both inner and outer perception; to heighten phenomenal experience while simultaneously expressing meaning; and to develop this duality in response to the particularities of site and circumstance.

The current tendency of segregation of specialties has facilitated, according to Holl, the distancing between logic and the feeling. The way to reunite these, he says, is the investigation—by architectural professionals, in every possible field...

(There is an) urgent need of a thought-to-feeling bridge today.... Three hundred years ago scientific ideas, perceptual phenomena, and their aesthetic and mystical effects could be discussed together. (......) Today, specialization segregates the fields (......) A scientist s world of statistics, cause and effect, and space-time—created with precise thought—is separate from the world of emotion and will. Thought and feeling should merge to provide a new catalyst for the imagination. (......) For architecture's inspirations every possible world at every scale must be explored.

13 | LANGUAGE

The architecture of which Steven Holl speaks, —these 'Phenomenal Zones'—are silent areas, areas without words.

According to Holl, words can guide, they can display things as a mirror, but they are not 'the things'.

And it seems that the use of the word 'language' can refer both to the descriptive language as to architectural style...

—

In a 1996 interview, having heard the comment that his architecture—since its beginning—not only avoided formal and linguistic manipulations, but has been exemplifying the physical qualities of architecture, Holl explains:

Intuition led me to this hybrid mode between a conceptual Framework and a phenomenological approach. I thought that light, texture, detail, and overlapping space, constituted a meaning that is silent and stronger than any textual manipulation.

In a different interview, years later, he would say:

As I aim for new ideas/concepts for each work, I have deliberately avoided developing a fashionable language.

... Postmodernism has come and gone. Deconstruction has likewise had its fashionable moment; now its light skins; I'm in favor of the original—if sometimes awkward—it always has a better chance to convey deeper meanings.

Another phrase of Holl's, regarding this matter...

Writing's relation to architecture affords only an uncertain mirror to be held up to evidence; it is rather in a wordless silence that we have the best chance to stumble into that zone comprised of space, light, and matter that is architecture. Although they fall short of architectural evidence, words present a premise. The work is forced to carry over when words themselves cannot. Words are arrows pointing in the right directions; taken together they form a map of architectural intentions.

But Holl does use a certain 'language'; an 'open vocabulary' of architecture.

Proto-Elements of architecture (an open language)
The open vocabulary of modern architecture may be extended by any compositional element, form, method or geometry. A situation immediately sets limits. A chosen ordering concept and chosen materials begin the effort to extract the nature of the work. Prior to site, even prior to culture, a tangible vocabulary of the elements of architecture remains open. Here is a beautiful potential: proto-elements of architecture.

Proto-elements: Possible combinations of lines, planes and volumes in space remain disconnected, trans-historical, and trans-cultural. They float about in a zero-ground of form without gravity but are precursors of a concrete architectonic form.

After a general overview, Holl mentions — under the definition of 'Lines', 'Plans' and 'Volumes'— specific elements that constitute his associative world.

Lines: stems of grass, twigs, cracks in mud, cracks in ice, veins in a leaf, woodgrain, nodal lines, spiderwebs, hair, ripples in sand... The astonishing Gothic stone tracery of King's College Chapel, of Westminster Abby, or of Gloucester Cathedral. The steel linearity of Paxton's Crystal Palace...

14 | HOLL'S METHOD OF WORK

One of the forms to understand Steven Holl's manner of seeing things is through the descriptions—by himself and by others—of his method of work.

—

Holl speaks of a systematic process in which the architectural design evolves progressively from the indeterminate to the precise and earthly...

The path of passage in architecture must lead from the abstract to the concrete, the unformed to the formed. While a painter or a composer might move from concrete to abstract, the architect must travel in the other direction, gradually incorporating human activities into what began as an abstract diagram.

Steven Holl's diagrams, in most projects, evolve through watercolor drawings and physical models.

His drawing—as part of his unique design process—, gives much weight to the user's movement and his perception of space, whether within a building or in urban context.

The traditional drawing of a plan is a blind notation, non-spatial and non-temporal. Perspectives of overlapping fields of space break this short circuit in the design process. Perspective precedes plan and section to give a priority to bodily experience and binds creator and perceiver. The spatial poetry of movement through overlapping fields is animated parallax.

In a conversation about his work, asked about the fact that—obviously—the process ends with complex computerized drawings, Holl explains about the force that the preliminary drawing has for him...

We use computerized techniques in almost every stage of the design process except the initial conception. For me the origin concept sketch must start with an analogue process intimately connecting mind-hand-eye. I feel this is the only way to be completely connected to the subtleties and qualities of the role intuition plays in conception. In the initial drawing, I feel a direct connection to spiritual meaning and the fusion of idea & space conception.

One of the basic means Holl uses in the process of creation and that serves as a 'bodily' connection of author—project-result are the models that aim to the materiality of the final spaces.

The models are not models for presentation; they are working tools to develop the concepts in materiality. The next step is going from the materiality of the model to the materiality of construction. The model is an in-between stage.

験の交差点に透けて見えてくるのが意味である。何かを構築しようという時，設計プロセスにおいては常に調整が必要となる……。設計プロセスにおいて知覚と経験の次元が展開するに従い，絶えず調整を加えることで発想と現象のバランスを目指す。

建築におけるこういった異なる領域——あまりに多様で時として相反するような要素——はすべて繋がっている，とホールは語る。建築は他のどの芸術よりも，異なる分野を繋げることができるものだと。

建築は物事を変化させるリンクである。それは発想と知覚の秩序，流れと場所の間に存在する溝を横断する，時間経過の芸術であり，結合力である。それは知性と視覚・音・触覚による認識の間や，思考の大志と身体に沸き上がる感情的な欲望の間に大きく開いた溝に，橋を渡す。
　様々な時間が結び合わされ，数々の現象が融合し，種々の意向が実現される。

建築空間の創造においてバランスをとるには，直感的な思考を鍛え，それを建築計画プロセスの論理にリンクすること。

（建築における）意味の探求は，空虚な形式主義や文章によるごまかし，営利主義といったものに抗えないとならない。設計プロセスの初期段階でアイディアに重点的に取り組むことで，実質的な核心を表面的なものから振り切ることができる。……建築コンセプトを持つことは，精神的な意向の実体的な空間表現以外の何者のためでもない。
　知性と感情の絡まりは，直感的に生成される思考につきものである……それが表現するところの変容する自然と文化の領域を探査すべくそれに向かって開かれた思考。
　直観を明示的に表現することはできないが，それを曖昧なものとして非難することはできない。

ホール曰く，自身の目標は「建築を思考のレベルまで持ち上げつつ，強い現象的特性を持つ空間を実現すること」であるとしている。（中略）この目標については別途，彼の主要原理をまとめるにあたり全般的な建築の課題としても説明されている。

物理的現象が我々の「外的知覚」の関与を促す一方で，心理的現象は我々の「内的知覚」を呼び起こす。心理的現象は現実的かつ意図的な存在である。経験上，我々は純粋に物理的・空間的実体としての構造物に満足できはするものの，そこに潜んでいる動機について，知的そして精神的に理解する必要がある。この意向と現象の二面性は客観／主観間，あるいはもっと単純に，思考／感情間の相互作用に似ている。建築にとっての課題は，内的そして外的知覚の双方を刺激すること，現象体験を高めると同時に意味を表現すること，そしてこの二面性を土地と状況の特性に応じ発展させることである。

ホール曰く，専門性の分離という現在の傾向が論理と感情との隔たりを増長しており，これらを再び結び合わせるには可能な限りの分野における研究調査（建築の専門家による）が必要であると語る……

今日，思考と感情をつなぐ橋が緊急に必要とされている。300年前であれば，科学的発見や知覚的現象，そしてそれらの美的・神秘的効果は一括して議論され得るものだった。（中略）今日では専門性が各分野を隔離してしまっている。（中略）科学者の統計・因果・時空の——明確な考えをもってつくられた——世界は，感情と意志の世界から分離している。思考と感情は想像力の新たな触媒となるべく融合すべきである。（中略）建築のインスピレーションのためには，可能な限りすべての世界とすべてのスケールを探索することが必要だ。

13 ｜ 言語

スティーヴン・ホールの語る建築——くだんの「現象的ゾーン」は，静寂のエリア，無言の場所である。
　ホール曰く，言葉は導くことができる。言葉は鏡のように物事を見せることができる。しかしそれ自体はその「物事」ではない。
　そして「言語」という言葉は，記述言語という意味でも，建築様式の意味でも使用されているようである……

1996年のインタヴューでは，彼の建築が——その初期の頃から，形式的・言語的操作を避けてきただけでなく建築の物理的特性を例示してきているとのコメントに対し，ホールはこう説明している：

直観が私をこのコンセプチュアルな枠組みと現象学的アプローチのハイブリッドへと向かわせたのです。光と質感とディテールと空間の重なりが形成する意味は，どんな言葉による操作よりも静かで力強いと思ったからです。

数年後，別のインタヴューではこう語った：

新しい発想・コンセプトを目指すたび，流行となるような言語を展開してしまうことを意図的に避けてきました。
　……ポストモダニズムはやって来たと思ううちに去って行きました。脱構築も同様に流行としての運命を辿った。今は軽量スキンがそうです。私はオリジナルなものの方がいい——時にぎこちなさがあったとしても，その方がより深い意味を伝える可能性を持っていますから。

この件に関して，ホールはこうも語っている……

建築にとって文章は，証拠と照らし合わす不確実な鏡としてしか機能しない。それはむしろ無言の沈黙の中にあり，我々に空間と光と物質でできたゾーン，つまり建築に足を踏み入れる絶好の機会を与えてくれる。建築の物証には及ばないものの，言葉は根拠を示すことができる。言葉自体には出来ないことでも作品はそれを引き継ぐことを強要される。言葉は正しい方向を指す矢印であり，それをもとに建築的意向の地図をつくることができる。

ただし，ホールは建築の「開かれた語彙」とも言うべきある種の「言語」を用いている。

建築の原始的要素（開かれた言語）
現代建築の開かれた語彙はいかなる構成要素・形態・方法あるいは幾何学に向けても拡張できる。状況が，直ちに制約を設け，選ばれた秩序化コンセプトと選ばれた材料が，作品の本質を抽出しようとし始める。土地よりも先に，それどころか文化よりも先に，建築要素の有形な語彙は開かれている。そこには建築の原始的要素という美しいポテンシャルがある。
　原始的要素：空間内で可能な線・平面・ヴォリュームはばらばらな状態のまま歴史をそして文化を超越している。それらはフォルムのゼロ地点を重力に関係なく浮遊しているが，建築学的フォルムの明確な前兆である。

総括に続きホールは——「線」「平面」「ヴォリューム」の定義の中で，彼の連想世界を形成する特定の要素につい

Whitney Water Purification Facility (Connecticut, U.S.A., 1998-2005): exterior stairs on stainless steel silver wall

It seems that Steven Holl's most potent tool in order to achieve the kind of diagram that serves his intentions are his watercolors. The architect, coming from a family of artists, was never strange to the art world and actually started painting in a very early age, himself.

According to Holl, the watercolors are:

... (a) playful activity... (of) 'chance operations'... transforming whatever one begins with—a diagram, a notion from a scientific journal or a word from Roget's thesaurus. Spontaneously, the painting takes on its own life and becomes an idea in the process. Non-intention is propelled forward by the will to form; it is driven by intuition.
—
As a method of catching intuition and first thoughts it is a technique which sets the imagination free.
—
Watercolor allows you to make bodies of light, to go from the bright to the dark. When I am making a series of perspectival views through a series of spaces and thinking about light, watercolor is a better media than line drawing.

According to Holl, these watercolors; these diagrams, apart from serving the evolution of the 'seed germ' (......) —the basic ideas of the building, they are also a channel; a medium through which Holl 'senses' the project as it advances.

... the play of light and shadow, ... the music of echoes and textures and smells, ... the aura and presence of real materials.... compellingly convey meaning in a building. I think of the diagram as an instrument that operates from the onset with the full spectrum of the architectural palette.

15 | CONTEMPORARY CULTURE

Steven Holl sees in some of the consequences of the major technological advances and their resulting cultural changes a danger to Architecture and the potential 'vigorous experiences' that the latter has to offer. But it is exactly in architecture, he says, where we can find an antidote for some of the contemporary ills.
—
'Phenomenal' architecture is which offers an authentic experience...

Phenomenology is a discipline that puts essences into experience. The complete perception of architecture depends on the material and detail of the haptic realm, as the taste of a meal depends on the flavor of its ingredients. As one can imagine being condemned to eating only artificially flavored foods, so one can imagine the specter of artificially constituted surroundings imposing themselves in architecture today.
—
As a catalyst for change, architecture s ability to shape our daily experiences in material and detail is subtle yet powerful. When sensory experience is intensified, psychological dimensions are engaged.

Among the consequences caused by some of the current architecture, technology and culture— is the growing separation of man from natural phenomena and, therefore, the erosion of man's natural being.

Holl says that according to the author Henry Bergson, the term 'Duration' should be used these days, instead of the term 'time'.

The idea of lived time (durée réelle) is particular to each culture and has no universal definition. However, (today...)...ongoing historical time s ever shorter spans have become, in our media-conscious, sensationalist culture, especially tedious, and misleading.

These definitions of time, he says, influence in what space means for us...

It is important to think and to act on our thinking in the present. We are not merely of our time, we are our time. In our time the nature of speed itself transformed the definition of space.

... Architecture, when brought about well, can serve as a remedy for some modern ills

Our modern concept of time is based on a linear, and perhaps disjunctive, model. The problem of temporal fragmentation of modern life; the destructive effects of increasing levels of media saturation resulting in stress and anxiety, might be countered in part by the distension of time in the perception of architectural space. The physical and perceptual experience of architecture is not a scattering or dispersion—but a concentration of energy. This physically experienced 'lived time' is measured in the memory and the soul in contrast to the dismemberment of fragmented messages of media.

Holl gives an example of these moments of optimism...

Today's harshest experiences of scattered and negative dispersal of energy exist side by side with transcendent impressions. For a moment as one looks up at the vault over Grand Central Terminal in New York, as the beams of dusted light pour in through the huge arched windows, one's perception modifies consciousness, attention is broadened, time is distended...

16 | MODERN MEANS

Between high-technologies and new material handling systems, Holl calls to seek and get the best out of these with the purpose of keeping the 'phenomenal potential' of architecture.

I think architecture offers the hope of returning to us all those experiential qualities; light, material, smell, texture, that we have been deprived of by the increasingly synthetic environment of images on video screens. Architecture is an antidote to an existence which is synthesized in the space of TV and lived out in sheet rock apartment buildings with low ceilings and synthetic carpets.... The challenge is to raise architecture back up to its role of framing our daily lives.
—
I believe that the potential for phenomenology as a departure point for an architectural practice becomes more poignant in the face of the prevalence of the synthetic in our lives. How is phenomenological experience compatible with these new technologies? Those technologies can potentially create new forms of experience.

Holl himself uses new systems applied to different materials such as metals and glass and even water...

Materials may be altered trough a variety of new means, which may even enhance their natural properties. For example, new developments in translucent insulation have given a new life to structural glass plank systems developed over forty years ago. The translucent insulation white glass planks that constitute the west wall of the Helsinki Museum of Contemporary Art allows for new hybrid techniques.
—
Raindrops range in size according to their surface tension... there is a natural range of size, a natural limit.

The Cranbrook Institute of Science's House of Vapour atomizes water drops...Each drop is pressurized into 4,000 droplets with a special nozzle... Technology stretches the capabilities of natural materials, transforming them. Materials are coerced into new natures..

Inspired by nature and natural phenomena that he seeks to apply by modern technology, Holl

て言及している。

線：草の茎，小枝，泥に入ったひび，氷に入ったひび，葉脈，木目，節線，蜘蛛の糸，髪の毛，砂漣……。「キングスカレッジの礼拝堂」や「ウェストミンスター修道院」や「グロスター大聖堂」の石造りの窓の驚異的な透かし細工。「パクストンの水晶宮」のスティールでできた直線性……

14｜ホールの仕事の進め方

スティーヴン・ホールの物事の捉え方を理解するにあたり，彼の仕事の進め方についての描写——彼自身によるものと他者によるもの——を通して見てみるのも1つの手だ。

ホールは，建築設計が不確定なものから緻密で現世的なものへと徐々に発展するような系統的プロセスについて語っている……

建築の歩む道筋は抽象的から現実的へ，未定形から定形へと向かわねばならない。画家や作曲家が現実から抽象へと向かうこともある一方で，建築家はその逆へと向かい，抽象的なダイアグラムとして生まれたものに人間の様々な活動を徐々に組み込んでゆく。

スティーヴン・ホールのダイアグラムは，ほとんどのプロジェクトにおいて水彩画から物理的モデルへと進化する。
　彼のドローイングは——彼独自の設計プロセスの一環として，それが建物であろうと都市的文脈であろうと，彼の空間に対する認識やユーザーの動きに随分と重きを置いている。

昔ながらの設計図は目隠し状態の表記法であり，非空間的かつ非時間的だ。設計プロセスにおけるこの短絡を，重なり合った空間領域のパースペクティブが打破してくれる。パースペクティブは平面図と断面図に先立ち身体的経験を優先し作者と受け手を結びつける。重なり合う領域内での運動の空間的ポエトリーは，動く視差である。

自身の作品についての対話の中で，そのプロセスが——当然のこととして，最終的には複雑なコンピュータ化されたドローイングとなる事実について問われた際，ホールは準備段階でのドローイングが持つ力についてこう説明している……

コンピュータ技術は，構想の初期段階を除く設計プロセスのほぼ全局面において使用しています。私にとって，最初のコンセプト・スケッチはいつも必ず頭と手と眼を密接につなぐアナログなプロセスから始まる。構想の中で直観が担っている役目の繊細さと質に完全につながっておくためには，これが唯一の方法なのだと思っています。最初のドローイングを通じ，精神的な意味や発想＆空間構想の融合に直につながっているという実感を持つのです。

ホールが創作過程に用いる，そして作者／プロジェクト／成果間の「身体的な」つながりとしての機能を果たす基本的な手段の1つに，最終的な空間の物質性を目指したモデルがある。

ここでのモデルとはプレゼンテーションのためのモデルではなく，コンセプトに具体性を持たせるための作業ツールとしてのモデルを指しており，その次の段階ではモデルの物質性から建設の具体性へと移行する。モデルはある種の中間的段階なのだ。

スティーヴン・ホールにとって，己の意向に役立つようなダイアグラムを作成するために最も有効なツールは彼の水彩画であろう。芸術家の血筋をひくこの建築家にとって芸術の世界は馴染みが深く，実際に幼少時から絵を描いてきている。
　ホール曰く水彩画とは：

……「偶然性」に彩られ（た）……遊び心に満ちた活動……で，ダイアグラムや科学誌に載っていた記事やロジェ類語辞典から引いてきた単語など，始まりが何であれそれを変化させてしまうもの。絵画は自ら命を絶ち，その過程でアイディアとなる。非意図的であることが，形づくることへの意志によって前へと推し進められる。直観に突き動かされているのだ。
—
直観や最初の考えを捉える方法として，それは想像力を自由に解放するテクニックである。
—
水彩を用いれば，明るさから暗さまでの光の集まりをつくることができます。いくつもの空間を通じて透視画法的な考え方を案じたり光について考えたりするとき，水彩は線描よりも優れたメディアとなるのです。

ホール曰く，こういった水彩画やダイアグラムは，「種の胚芽」——建物の基本となるアイディア——の進化に役立つ以外に，水路ともいえる媒介であり，それを通じホールはプロジェクト自体を，それが進行するに連れ，「感じる」ことができるのである。

……光と影のたわむれ，……反響音と質感と匂いが奏でる音楽，……リアルな素材が持つオーラと存在感……が建物に意味を惹きつける。ダイアグラムは，建築要素が持つ幅の全域においてのっけから機能する道具なのだと思っています。

Sketch by architect

15｜同時代的文化

スティーヴン・ホールは，主要な技術的進歩とその結果としての文化の変容がもたらした影響の一部は，建築を，またそれが提供する「生き生きとした経験」への可能性を，危険にさらしていると目している。しかし建築の中にこそ，そういった現代の病に対する解毒剤を見いだすことができる，とも語っている。

—
「現象的な」建築とは本物の体験を与えてくれるもの……

現象学は本質を経験に変える学問である。建築の完全な知覚は，料理の味がその材料の風味に左右されるように，触知的領域のディテールや素材に依存している。人工的な味付けの食べ物だけを食べさせられることを想像してみれば，今日の建築において押しつけられる人工的につくられた環境が及ぼす悪影響のほどがわかるはずだ。

建築が素材とディテールをもって我々の日々の経験を形づくる能力は，変化を促進させる触媒としては控え目でありながらも強力である。感覚的経験が濃くなるにつれ心理的な次元も関わってくる。

現在の建築や技術，文化による影響の1つに，自然現象からますます分離する人間，つまり人間の自然な生命の浸食，がある。
　アンリ・ベルクソン曰く，昨今では「時間」よりも「経過」という言葉が使われるべきだ，とホールは述べる……

実際に経た時間という概念（durée réelle）は文化に特有なもので，普遍的な定義は持ち得ない。ただし，（今日では）……これまでになく短くなってきている歴史的時間のスパンは，メディア意識が高く扇情的な現在の文化においては，非常に退屈で人を惑わせやすいものになっている。

seems to never cease investigating...

... Similarly, new composite construction methods can create superstrong, lightweight shells... New fusing methods and new engineering technologies will reshape the haptic realm.

Holl puts no limit to his imagination, seeking innovation. He is inspired by physical phenomena, chemical reactions and even by the dark matter that holds galaxies together...

Through his research, Holl reaches the following conclusion (quoting Dr. Lawrence Krauss, director of the Physics Department at Case Western Reserve):

Nature comes up with possibilities that no science fiction writer would dare suggest.

But, still, despite the new possibilities, Holl is aware that the vast majority of new media and the culture involving it are an obstacle to the perception of built space.

... our ordinary lives are laden with devices which divide our attentions, and cajole our desires, rerouting them to specious commercial ends. Modern commercial existence muddles the question of what is essential. As our technological means multiply, are we growing—or becoming stunted—perceptually? We live our lives in constructed spaces, surrounded by physical objects. But, born into this world of things, are we able to experience fully the phenomena of their interrelation, to derive joy from our perceptions?

... and he suggests a way to overcome the obstacles:

To advance toward these hidden experiences, we must penetrate the omnipresent veil of mass media. We must fortify our defenses to resist the calculated distractions, which can deplete both psych and spirit. Everything which is tangibly present must receive attention. If the media make us passive receivers of vacuous messages, we must firmly position ourselves as activists of consciousness.

17 | HOLL'S VISION — WHAT IS ARCHITECTURE? (OR WHAT IT SHOULD BE...)

Within the context of the situation—mentioned above—, of expansive marketing and excess of image, Holl points out a phenomenon parallel to the globalization of architecture and he proposes the merger of the two phenomena in a new architecture...

While a global movement electronically connects all places and cultures in a continuous time-place fusion, the opposite tendency coexists in the uprising of local cultures and expression of place. In these two forces —one a kind of expansion, the other a kind of contraction—time-space is being formed. A new architecture must be formed that is simultaneously aligned with transcultural continuity and with a poetic expression of individual situation and community.

Such an architecture, given the circumstances of the times, tends towards abstraction...

It is precisely the realm of ideas—not forms or styles—that presents the most promising legacy of twentieth-century architecture. The twenty-first century propels architecture into a world where meanings cannot be completely supplied by historical languages.... The increased size and programmatic complexity of buildings amplify the innate tendency of architecture toward abstraction.

This abstraction makes part of an architectural language. In an interview he gave in 1995, Holl relates to the definition of such a language by the end of the century.

What is a language of architecture? This is a dilemma at the end of the twentieth century. In the 1920s there was a syntax and a language of modern architecture, now we have what some people would call chaos. I would say it's a wide-open, exciting freedom. It's possible that architecture could be more interesting than it ever has been in history because we have such latitude. In any given project I want to be open to whatever the potentials. I think our lives today could be enhanced by the kind of emotional variety spaces could give—the different kinds of tectonic, the different kinds of material, the different kinds of light.

Holl adds...

Architecture... differs with every circumstance and site. It is at once difficult to make and also infinitely open and free. An attitude reaching toward the full extension of those earliest freedoms of modern architectural thought could take architecture beyond neo-modernities and post-modernities into a realm where ideas have no boundaries—and the final measure of architecture lies in its perceptual essences, changing the experience of our lives.

18 | EDUCATION AND THE FUTURE

In an assertion about the education of architects, Holl defends—perhaps because of his own experience—a method similar to that which was instilled in him as a student—the profound investigation of a specific work as opposed to a wide range of—almost unattainable—, information.

Today the overload of information brings with it an atmosphere of exhaustion and superficiality. A great breadth of digital information is instantly available. What is lacking is not information but a solid knowledge that can cultivate†and encourage an intuitive wisdom.
—
This overload of information often leads to a recurring and deeper confusion in the student. Rather than breadth I would propose depth; a depth of knowledge achieved through the exhaustive study of a specific work of architecture and its development could lead the student to a better personal evolution.
—
... from the sense of education, we are 'keepers of the flame'. Great past examples, when deeply understood, provide an inspired educational platform. The fresh and original depends on keeping experimentation alive —which is fundamentally unpredictable. If it is fully predictable, it is not experimental. With the growing commercialization of architecture, 'safe' work can be culturally worthless. I would fight for the feeling that architecture is a vital activity related to ideas and to life.
—
Certainly as architects we have to keep moving; we have to improve our curiosity, but we must bring architecture back to what we really feel when we apprehend it. The fluid time of phenomena and movement—rather than the fixed time of form—gives impetus to the content.

In addition to encouraging intuitive knowledge and the importance of research for students, Holl emphasizes the need for the development of individual consciousness about 'the things', certain sensitivity to the world, in order to participate actively—as architects and as users—, in the experience of perception.

To open ourselves to perception, we must transcend the mundane urgency of 'things to do'. We must try to access that inner life which reveals the luminous intensity of the world.

An awareness of one's unique existence in space is essential in developing a consciousness of

こういった時間の定義が，我々にとって空間が何を意味するかという点に影響を与えると彼は語る……

今現在の判断を元に考えたり行動したりすることが大事である。我々は時間に帰属するだけの存在ではなく，我々自身が時間を体現してもいる。今の時代，速度自体の特性は空間の定義を変化させた。

……建築は，きちんとつくられたものであれば，現代の病の特効薬として役立つことも可能である。

我々の時間に対する現代的な概念は線形な，ともすれば分離的な，モデルに基づいている。現代生活の時間的断片化の問題や，深まるメディア浸透がもたらす破壊的影響とその結果としてのストレスと不安には，建築空間の知覚における時間の膨張をもって，ある程度は抗うことができよう。建築の物理的・知覚的体験はエネルギーの集中であり，拡散や分散ではない。この物理的に経験される「実際に経た時間」は，メディアの断片的なメッセージとは対照的に，記憶や魂の中で測定される。

ホールはそういった楽観的な瞬間の例を挙げる……

今日のエネルギーの拡散・マイナス分散というもっとも過酷な経験は，先験的な印象と隣り合わせにある。ニューヨークのグランドセントラル駅の円天井をふと見上げる時，巨大なアーチ形窓から埃っぽい光の筋がこぼれる中で，人の知覚は意識を修正し，注意を拡張し，時間を膨張させる……

16 | 現代的手段

建築の「現象的ポテンシャル」を保つためには，先端技術と新しいマテリアル・ハンドリング・システムの狭間でそれらを最大限に活用する術を探すべきであるとホールは呼びかける。

建築は，ビデオスクリーンが映し出す，ますます人工的な環境により奪われてしまった光・素材・匂い・質感といった経験に基づく特質を我々の手に取り戻してくれる，そんな希望を与えてくれると思っています。建築は，テレビの中で合成され，低い天井と化繊のカーペットと薄っぺらい壁のアパートの中で生き延びている存在への解毒剤。……建築を，我々の日常生活の枠組みという本来の役割に押し上げることが課題となるのです。
―
建築の実践の出発点としての現象学のポテンシャルは，我々の生活の中にある人工的な物事の蔓延を前にして，ますます痛切な状況になっていると思います。現象学的経験がそんな新技術と両立できるのか？　こういった技術は，新しい形の経験を創造する潜在能力を持っています。

ホール自身，新しいシステムを，金属やガラス，はたまた水といった素材へと適用している。

素材は様々な新手段を通じた変更が可能で，それにより元の特性を改良することも可能である。例えば半透明な断熱材の開発は，40年以上も昔のガラス板構造に新たな息吹を与えている。「ヘルシンキ現代美術館」の西壁を構成する白いガラス板と半透明な断熱材は，新しいハイブリッド技術を可能にした。
―
雨粒のサイズは表面張力に左右され……自然なサイズの振り幅，天然の限界がある。

「クランブルック科学研究所」の「蒸気の家」は水滴を原子化する……水滴一つひとつに特殊ノズルが圧をかけ4,000滴に分解する……。技術は自然素材を変化させ，その可能性を伸ばす。素材は新たな特性を持つことを強要される。

彼が現代技術に適用しようとしている自然と自然現象に触発され，ホールの探求はつきない……

……同様に，新しい複合構造法は非常に強く軽量なシェルを可能にする……新しい溶融法や工学技術が触知的領域を再形成することだろう。

ホールは想像力に限界を設けず革新を追求する。物理的現象や化学反応，星雲を1つにまとめている暗黒物質にまでインスピレーションを受けるのだ……。

研究を通じ，ホールは次の結論へと到達した（ケース・ウェスタン・リザーブ大学物理学部長ローレンス・クラウス博士の言葉を引用して）：

自然はどんなSF作家も思いつきもしないような可能性を用意してくる。

しかし，新しい可能性の影で，新しいメディアやそれに関わる文化のほとんどが，建物空間の知覚にとっては障害となることにホールは気付いていた。

……我々の普段の生活は，我々の注意を分断し，欲望を掻き込み，それらを見かけ倒しの商業目的へとルート変更させようとする装置で満載である。現代の商業的存在は何が本質なのかという質問を混乱させる。技術的な手段が増えるに従い，我々は知覚という側面で成長してゆくのか，はたまた成長不良をおこすのか。我々は建造された空間の中に生き，物理的な物体に囲まれて暮らしている。しかし，この"物の世界"に生まれた我々は，それらの相関関係の現象を存分に経験し，己の知覚から喜びを得ることができるのだろうか？

……そして障害を克服する方法を提案する：

Interior Renovation of New York University, Department of Philosophy (New York, New York, U.S.A. 2004-2007): stair hall

こういった隠れた経験へと進むには，我々はマスメディアの偏在するベールの中に忍び込まないとならない。気力と精神の両方を消耗させかねない計算ずくの撹乱に抗う力を強化しなければならない。触れることのできる状態で存在するものすべてに注意を注がなくてはならない。メディアが我々を空虚なメッセージの従順な受容者に飼い慣らそうというのなら，我々は毅然として自覚を持った活動家として自分を位置づけなければならない。

17 | ホールのヴィジョン——建築とは何か？
（あるいは何であるべきか……）

上述の状況にあるような拡張するマーケティングやイメージの過剰という文脈の中で，ホールは建築のグローバリゼーションに並行するある現象を指摘し，この2つの現象を新しい建築の中に融合することを提案する……

あらゆる場所と文化を，時間と場所の連続した融合の中で電子的につなげるグローバルな動向がある一方で，ローカル文化や場所の表現の蜂起という逆の傾向も共存している。この2つの力——ある種の拡散と，ある種の縮小——の中に時空

perception.

Holl, who speaks of the need to become 'activists of conscience' (Paragraph of 'modern means') against the distractions of the media, advocates an awareness of that consciousness in order to be able to live such authentic experiences...

Architecture holds the power to inspire and transform our day-to-day existence. The everyday act of pressing a door handle and opening into a light-washed room can become profound when experienced through sensitized consciousness. To see, to feel these physicalities is to become the subject of the senses.

Within the current times of advanced technology and strong influences of media—among others—, Holl adapts himself without renouncing his principles and writes these optimistic, unsurrendered affirmations...

Today, working with doubt is unavoidable; the absolute is suspended by the relative and the interactive. Instead of stable systems we must work with dynamic systems. Instead of simple and clear programs we engage contingent and diverse programs. Instead of precision and perfection we work with intermittent, crossbred systems, and combined methods. Suspending disbelief and adopting a global understanding is today an a priori condition, a new fundamental for creative work in science, urbanism, and architecture. Working with doubt becomes an open position for concentrated intellectual work.
—
The epistemology of our time, the potential of knowledge, presents us with a new optimism.† New channels of acquiring knowledge and recombining ideas and facts into new knowledge open up with modern technology s connective speed. Enormous issues of our epoch, for example the case of shrinking biodiversity, should not be framed fatalistically, ... a fresh look acquiring new knowledge, expanding our horizon of thought suggests there are no inherent limitations to thought.

To raise architecture to the potential of thought, carries with it curious and optimistic questions of new knowledge.

REFERENCES:

Anchoring, Steven Holl
(Princeton Architectural Press, New York, 1989)
p.9, p.11

Steven Holl—Catalogue
(Artemis, cop, Zürich, 1994)
p.21, p.22, p.23, p.25, p.26, p.28, p.29, p.31

Intertwining, Steven Holl
(Princeton Architectural Press, New York, 1996)
p.9, p.11, p.12, p.13, p.16

GA Document Extra #6—Steven Holl
(A.D.A. Edita Tokyo, Tokyo, 1996)
p.11, p.33, p.25

Questions of Perception
Steven Holl, Juhani Pallasmaa, Perez-Gómez
(a+u, Tokyo, 1998)
p.40, p.41, p.42, p.45, p.58, p.63, p.74, p.80, p.116, p.119, p.122, p.123, p.127, p.134

Parallax, Steven Holl
(Birkhäuser, Basel, 2000)
p.26, p.38, p.68, p.71, p.75, p.86, p.90, p.98, p.108, p.112, p.132, p.140, p.144, p.184, p.252, p.345

Written in Water, Steven Holl
(Lars Müller Publishers, Baden, 2001)
p.2, p.3, p.4

El Croquis 78+93+108—Steven Holl 1986-2003
(El Croquis Editorial, Madrid, 2003)
p.14, p.15, p.21, p.23, p.32, p.33, p.36, p.37, p.42, p.51, p.54, p.58, p.63, p.66, p.67, p.69, p.81, p.86, p.87

Steven Holl, Urbanisms: Working With Doubt
(Princeton Architectural Press, New York, 2010)
p.13

Color Light Time, Steven Holl
(Lars Müller Publishers, Baden, 2012)
p.103, p.104, p.105, p.110, p.116, p.118

Steven Holl, Architecture/Knowledge, Essay
(to be published in 2012)
courtesy of Steven Holl Architects

が形成される。文化を超えた連続性と個別な状況とコミュニティーの詩的表現と同時に足並みを揃えることのできる新しい建築が形成されなければならない。

かような建築は，時代の状況を前提とすれば，抽象へと傾く……

最も有望な20世紀建築の遺産が提示するのは，フォルムでもスタイルでもなく，発想の領域に他ならない。21世紀が建築を駆り立てる先の世界では，歴史的言語が意味を完全にカバーしきれなくなっている……。建物の肥大化したサイズとプログラムの複雑さが，建築が生来持っている抽象への傾向を増幅する。

この抽象化が建築言語の一部を構成している。1995年に行われたインタヴューでホールは世紀末におけるそのような言語の定義について言及している。

建築の言語とは何か？　それは20世紀末のジレンマです。1920年代には現代建築の構文や言語がありましたが，今我々にあるのは，それをカオスと呼ぶ人もいるような代物です。私に言わせれば，それは大きく開かれた，心躍る自由。これだけの自由度があれば，建築が有史以来もっとも面白くなるという可能性だってある。どんなプロジェクトにおいても，あらゆるポテンシャルを受け入れたいと思っています。今日の我々の生活を，いろいろな種類の地層構造，いろいろな種類の素材，いろいろな種類の光といった，空間が与え得る感情の多様性のようなものを通じて向上させることができると思っています。

ホールはこう付け加える……

建築……は，様々な事情や土地によってその都度異なるもの。それはつくるのが難しいと同時に無限にオープンで自由なものでもある。現代建築の思考が最初の頃に持っていた自由の完全な延長線上に向かうような姿勢が，建築を，ネオモダンやポストモダンを越え，限界のない発想の領域へと導く──建築にとっての最後の方策はその知覚的本質にあり，我々の生活体験を変化させる。

18 | 教育と未来

建築家の教育についての言明の中でホールは？　自身の体験からか？　学生時代に受けた教えと似通ったメソッドを擁護している。つまり，手が届かないほどの幅広い情報ではなく，特定の作品について深く掘り下げる研究である。

今日の情報過多は消耗と見かけ倒しの気配をまとっている。

幅広いデジタル情報を即座に得ることはできるが，足りないのは情報ではなく，直感的英知を育み後押しできる確かな知識なのです。
—
この情報過多はしばしば学生に再発性の深い混乱を招きます。幅よりもむしろ深さが大切なのだと，私は言いたい。特定の建築作品についての徹底的な研究を通じて得られる深い知識とその開発は，学生をより良い個人的進化へと導くのです。
—
教育の本来の意味で言えば我々は「炎の守り手」です。過去の偉大なお手本は，深い理解を得られれば，インスピレーションに満ちた教育基盤となり得る。新鮮さやオリジナリティは実験を絶やさずにいることにかかってくる──それは予測不可能なもの。もしも完全に予測可能であるならば，それは実験ではなくなる。ますます商業化の進む建築にとって，「安全な」作品など文化的に価値がない。私は建築が思考と生命に関わる不可欠な活動であるという想いのために戦うことも辞さないと思っています。
—
もちろん建築家として動き続けること，自分の好奇心を磨くことは大事ですが，建築を，我々が理解したと思った当初に本当に感じたことへと呼び戻さなければならない。フォルムの固定された時間よりも，現象と運動の流動的な時間が内容に弾みをつけるのです。

直感的知識と研究の重要性を学生に薦めるのに加え，ホールは知覚の体験に──建築家として，ユーザーとして，積極的に参加するための世界に対するある種の感受性，「物事」に対する個々の意識を育てる必要性を強調する。

知覚に向かって己を開くには，「しなければならないこと」の俗世の緊急性を超越しなければならない。世界の輝きを明かしてくれる内面的な生活に到達する努力が必要だ。
　空間における自己の存在は唯一無二のものであるという自覚が，知覚の意識を育てるにあたり不可欠なのだ。

メディアの妨害に抗う「良心の活動家」である必要性について語る（「16. 現代的手段」参照）ホールは，そのような本物の体験を生きるには，自覚的にその意識を持つべきであると提唱する……

建築には我々の日々の存在を変え，そこにインスピレーションを吹き込む力がある。ドアの取っ手を押して光に満ちた部屋へと踏み入る日々の行為は，感作された意識を通じて体験することで深遠なものになり得る。こういった身体性を見て感じることは，感覚の対象となることである。

昨今の先進技術，とりわけメディアの強い影響力の時代において，自身の信条を放棄することなく自らをそこに適応させるホールは，以下のような楽観的かつ不屈の主張を記している……

今日，疑いを抱えながら仕事に向かうことは不可避である。絶対的なものは相対的で相互作用的なものに留保される。選ぶべきは安定したシステムよりもダイナミックなシステム。単純で明快なプログラムよりも偶発的で多様なプログラムに取り組み，精度や完成度よりも断続的な異種交配のシステムや複合的な方法を採用すること。今日，不信感を保留しグローバルな理解を持つこと自体，先験的な状況であり，科学・アーバニズム・建築における創造的な営為にとっての新たな基本となる。疑いを抱えながら仕事に向かう限り，知的作業が集結する場に居場所は無い。
—
この時代の認識論，知識のポテンシャルは，新たな楽観を我々に提示する。現代技術の接続速度と相まって，知識獲得の新たな経路や，発想や実態を再結合し新たな知識を形成する道が開かれる。この時代の膨大な課題，例えば生物学的多様性の縮小などは，運命論の枠組みに押し込めてはならず，……新たな知識を獲得し思考の地平を拡張するような新鮮な眼差しは，思考には先天的な限界などないことを教えてくれる。
　建築を思考のポテンシャルまで引き上げれば，それと一緒に新たな知識の興味深く楽観的な問題がついてくるのだ。

1 Light, Material and Detail
光, 材料, ディテール

Architecture, by unifying foreground, middle ground, and distant views, ties perspective to detail and material to space. While a cinematic experience of a stone cathedral might draw the observer through and above it, even moving photographically back in time, only the actual building allows the eye to roam freely among inventive details; only the architecture itself offers the tactile sensations of textured stone surfaces and polished wooden pews, the experience of light changing with movement, the smell and resonant sounds of space, the bodily relations of scale and proportion. All these sensations combine within one complex experience, which becomes articulate and specific, though wordless. The building speaks through the silence of perceptual phenomena.

It is not surprising that some architects have written that the entire intention of their work revolves around light, just as some painters have focused completely on the properties of color. The perceptual spirit and metaphysical strength of architecture are driven by the quality of light and shadow shaped by solids and voids, by opacities, transparencies, and translucencies. Natural light, with its ethereal variety of change, fundamentally orchestrates the intensities of architecture and cities. What the eyes see and the senses feel in questions of architecture are formed according to conditions of light and shadow.

The haptic realm of architecture is defined by the sense of touch. When the materiality of the details forming an architectural space become evident, the haptic realm is opened up. Sensory experience is intensified; psychological dimensions are engaged.

Steven Holl

建築は前景，中景，そして遠くの眺望をひとつに総合することで，視線をディテールに，素材を空間へと結びつける。石造りの聖堂に対する映画的経験は，鑑賞者をその表層へと惹きつけ，内部へと誘い，あるいは過去へと写真的回帰を促す。その一方で，独創的なディテールのあいだで視線が浮遊するのは，現実の建築においてである。すなわち，石の表面の質感や磨き上げられた木製の座席の触感，移ろいゆく光を経験すること，空間に響き渡るざわめきや匂い，スケールやプロポーションと身体との関係性。これらを私たちに与えてくれるのが建築というものである。全ての感覚は，明瞭で固有のひとつの複合的経験へと，沈黙のうちに結実する。建築が私たちに語りかけてくるのは，そのような知覚の現象の沈黙を通してである。

　ある画家が色を表現することに全てを注いできたように，ある建築家にとっては光のあり方が建築の目的の全てであったとしても，それはごく自然のことである。精神的知覚と建築の形而上学的な強靭さは，ソリッドやヴォイド，不透明性や透明性，透過性といった概念が生み出す光と影の本質によって決定される。優美に移ろいゆく自然の光は，その本質において，建築と都市の強靭さをひとつに融合させる。目に映り，感覚で感じる建築の諸問題とは，光と影の状態によって構成されるものである。

　建築の触覚的領域は，手に触れた質感が決める。建築空間を構成するディテールの物質性が明らかになると，触覚の領域が現れる。知覚的経験は強められ，そこでは心理的側面が関与する。

（スティーヴン・ホール）

Riddled Cabinet

Evening view from street

Interior Renovation of New York University Department of Philosophy

2004-07　　New York, New York, U.S.A.

Lounge on sixth floor: stair hall is behind white wall

Lounge on sixth floor

The Dean of the Faculty of Arts & Sciences and a committee of Philosophy Professors collaborated in the selection of Steven Holl Architects to design the complete interior renovation of a 1890 corner building at 5 Washington Place for the consolidation of the NYU Department of Philosophy within a concept which organizes the new spaces around light and phenomenal properties of materials. A new stair shaft below a new skylight joins the 6-level building vertically with a shifting porosity of light and shadow that change seasonally. The Ground level, utilized by the entire University, contains a new curvilinear auditorium on a cork floor. The upper level floors contain Faculty Offices and Seminar Rooms which are done in different shades and textures of black & white, according to the texts in Ludwig Wittgenstein's book "Remarks on Colour".

The building exits within the NoHo Historic District and is within the jurisdiction of the New York City Landmarks Preservation Commission. The building is part of the main NYU campus within New York City's Greenwich Village and is sited on-access to Washington Square Park.

Entry lobby

Downward view of stair hall

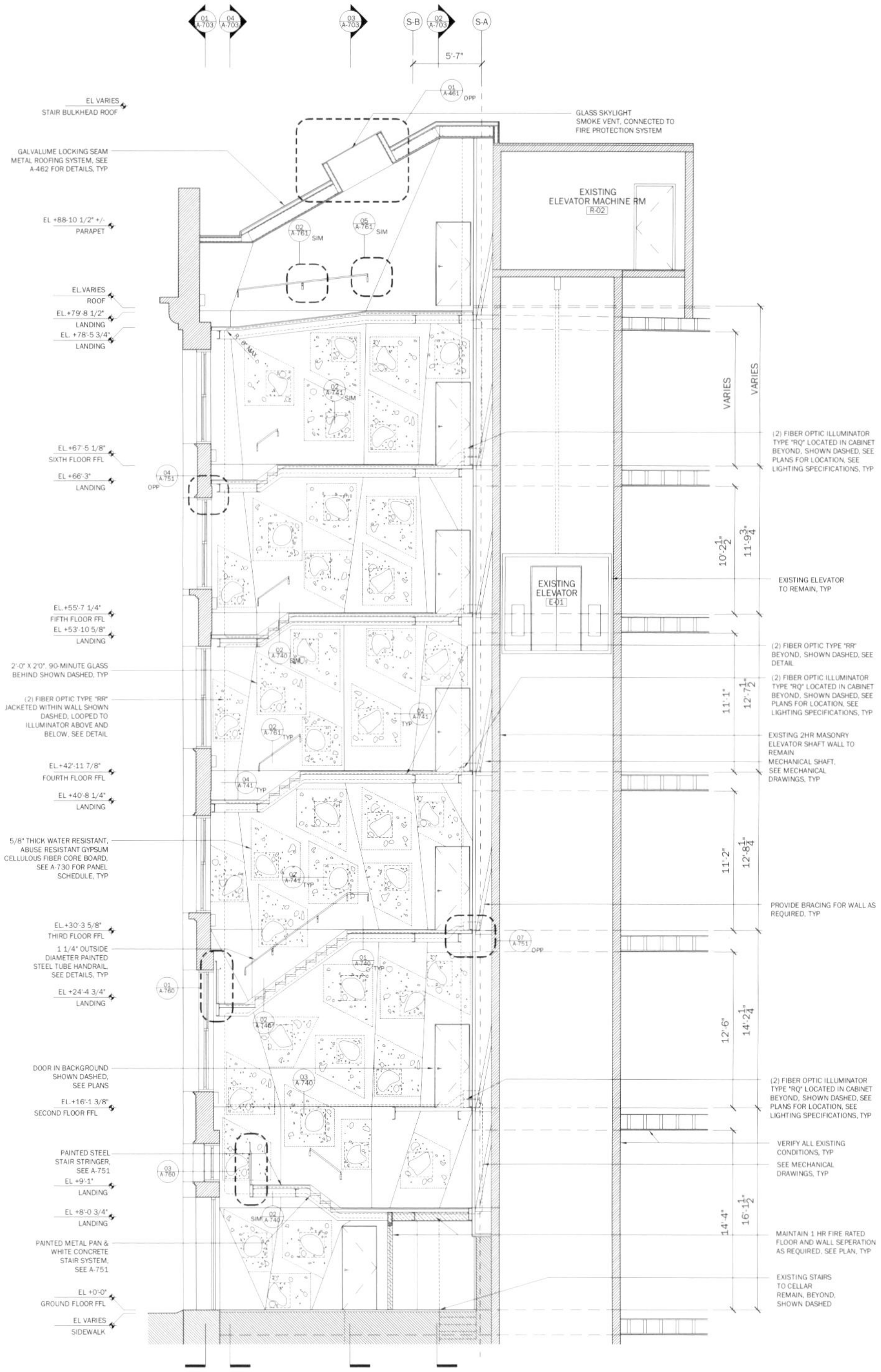

Stair hall: interior wall

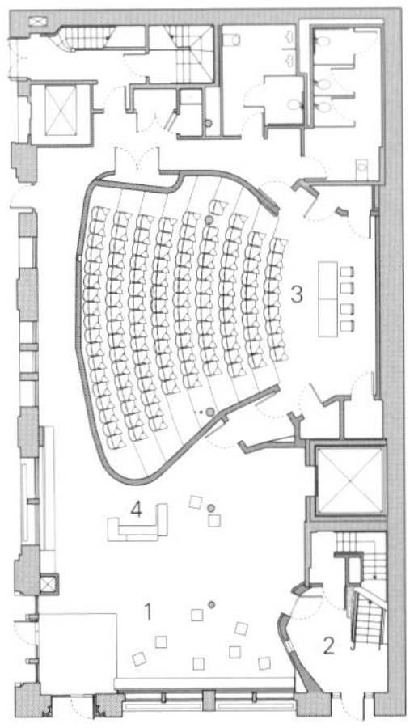

First floor 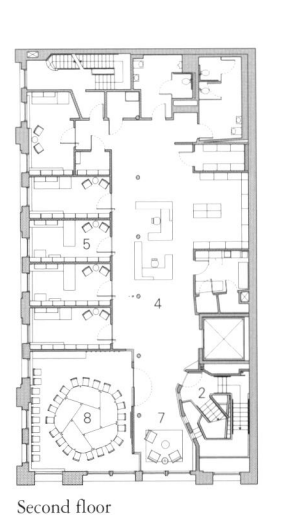 Second floor 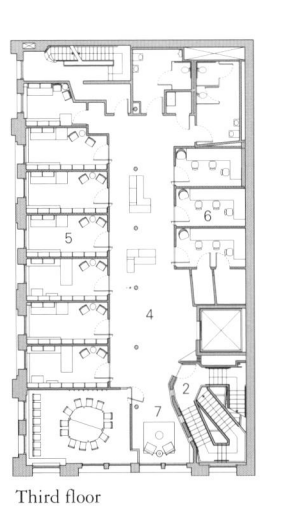 Third floor 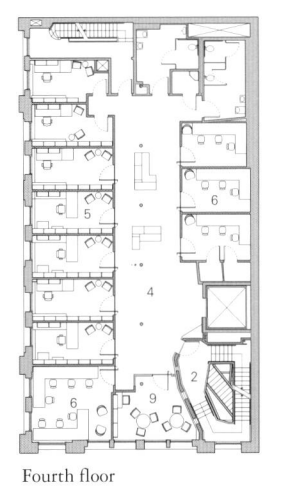 Fourth floor 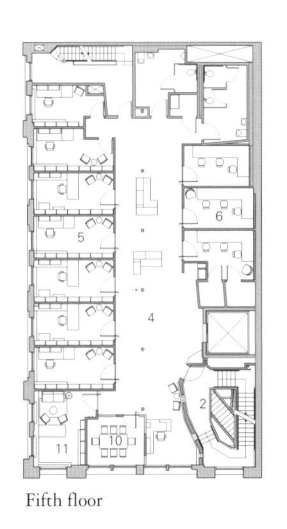 Fifth floor 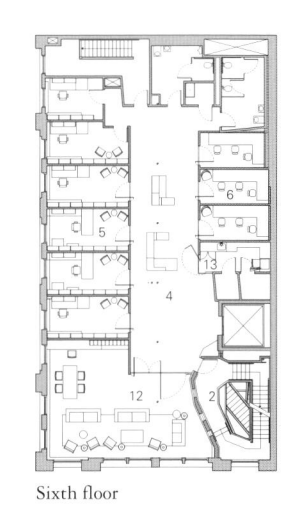 Sixth floor

1 ENTRY LOBBY
2 NEW STAIR HALL
3 AUDITORIUM
4 RECEPTION
5 FACULTY OFFICE
6 GRADUATE OFFICE
7 READING AREA
8 SEMINAR ROOM
9 LIBRARY
10 MEETING ROOM
11 CHAIR'S OFFICE
12 LOUNGE
13 KITCHEN

II-34

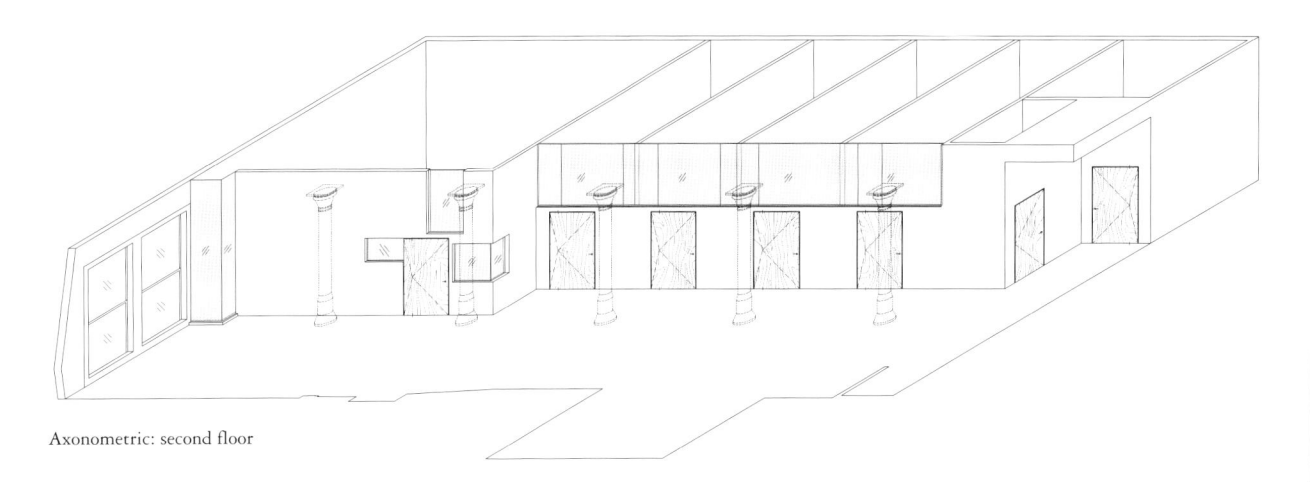

Axonometric: second floor

Second floor: textures of black and white

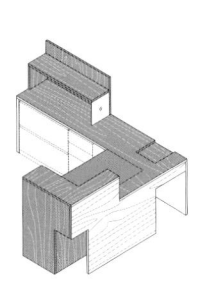

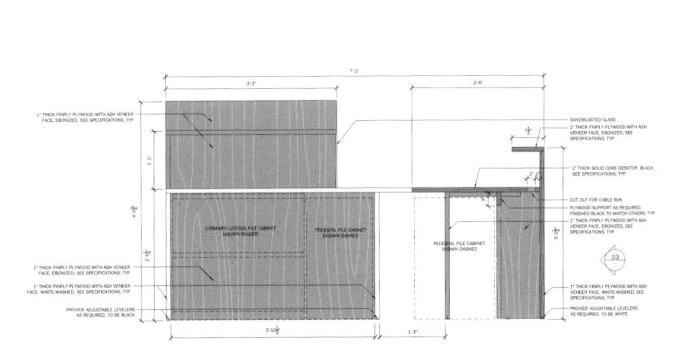

Millwork details

Reception on fifth floor: furniture designed by architect

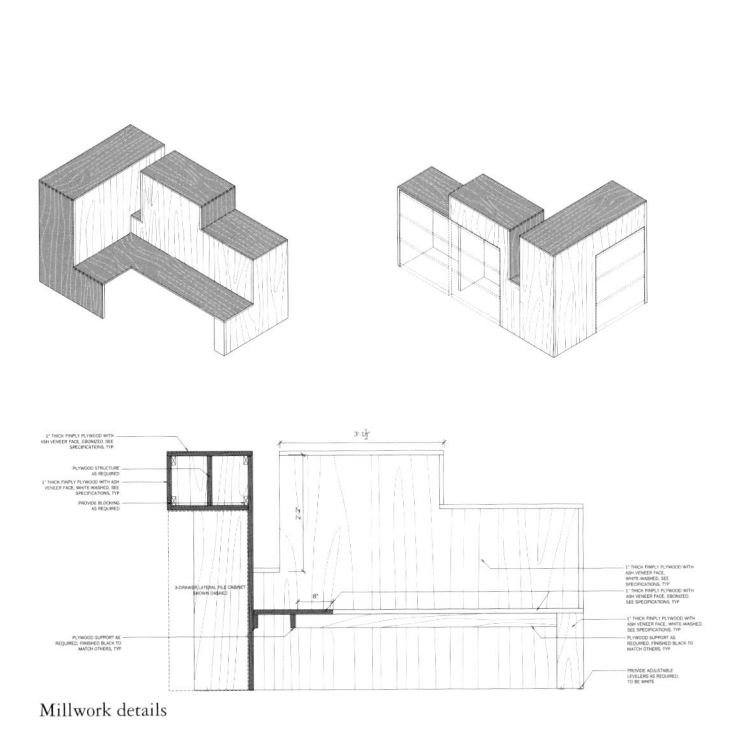

Millwork details

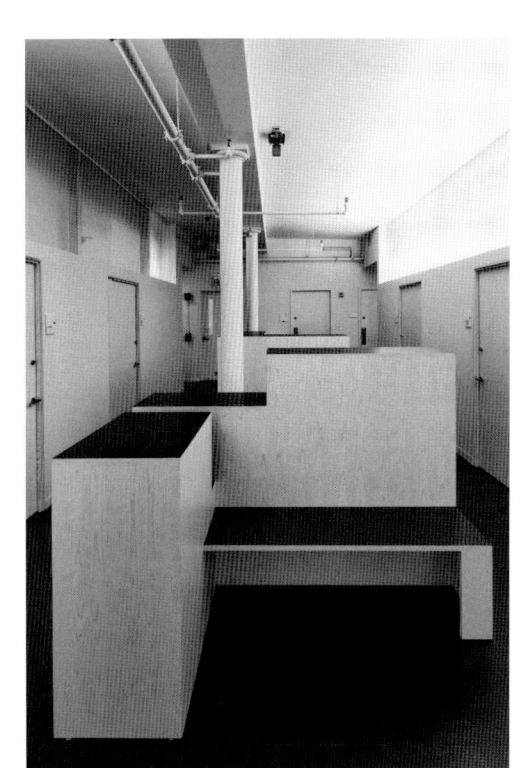

Millwork designed by architect

II-35

Rainbow projected on wall of stair hall

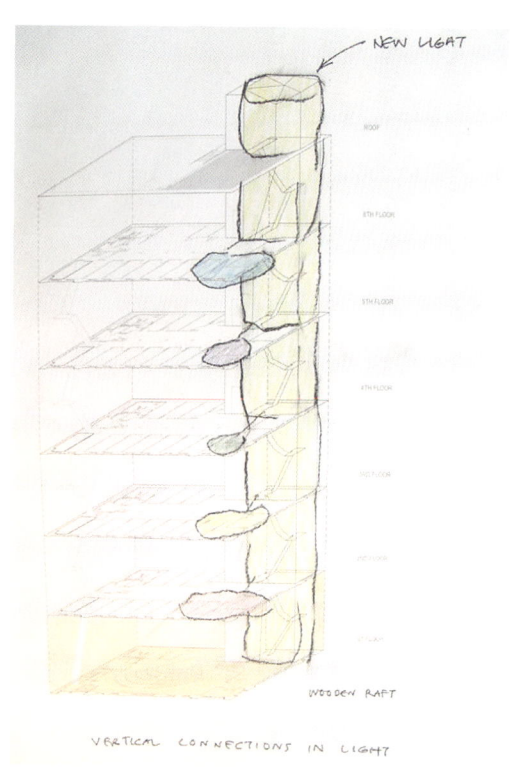

Concept sketch: diagram of stair hall

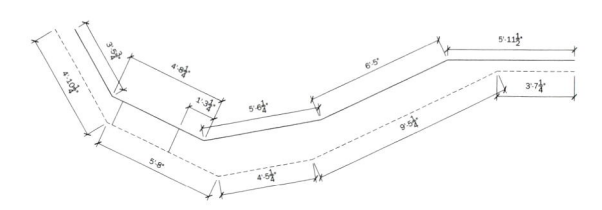

Plan geometry: plywood stair wall at second floor

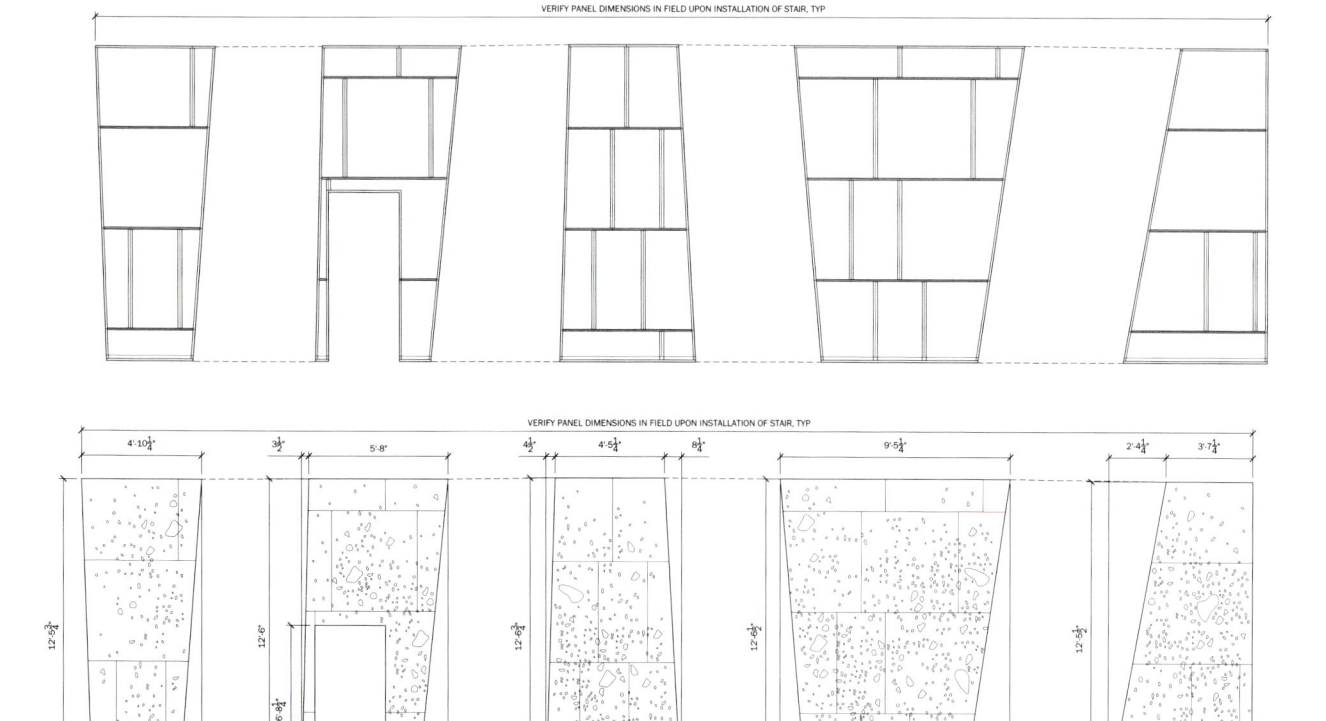

Details: unfolded elevations of plywood stair wall at second floor and perforation pattern

ニューヨーク大学哲学学科インテリア改修
人文理学部長と哲学科教授会は，ニューヨーク大学哲学科の強化を図り，光と物質の現象的性質の周囲に新しい空間を配置するというコンセプトに従って，ワシントン・プレイス5番地角の1890年代の建築の内装リノベーションをデザインするために，スティーヴン・ホール・アーキテクツを共同で選定した。新しいスカイライトの下の新しいシャフト状階段室では，季節とともに変化する光と影の無数の孔が見せる移ろいが，6階建ての建築を垂直方向につないでいる。全学が使用する1階には，コルク床の曲線形をした新しいオーディトリアムが含まれている。上層階には，ルートヴィヒ・ウィトゲンシュタインの著書『Remarks on Colour（色彩について）』の文章に従って，多様なニュアンスとテクスチャーの白黒で仕上げられた学部事務室とセミナールームがある。

この建築はノーホー歴史地区の内部に出口があり，ニューヨーク市歴史的建物保存委員会の管轄下にある。この建築は，ニューヨーク市グリニッジ・ビレッジのニューヨーク大学メインキャンパスの一部であり，ワシントン・スクエア・パークに直結した場所に位置している。

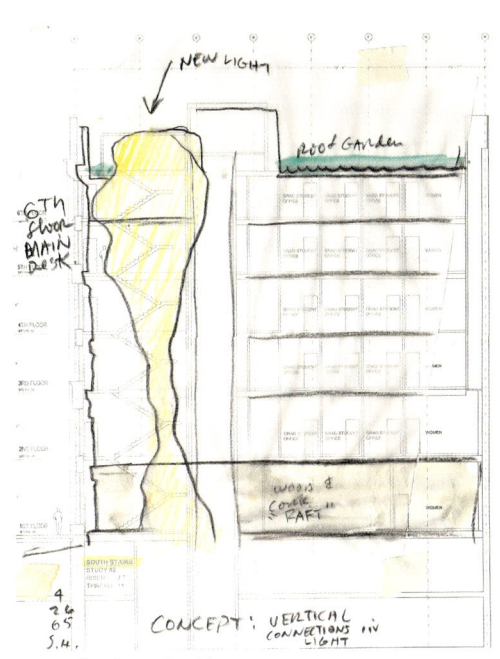

Concept sketch: sectional images

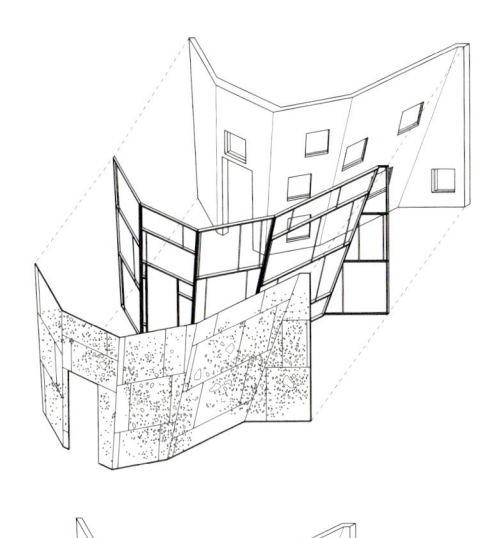

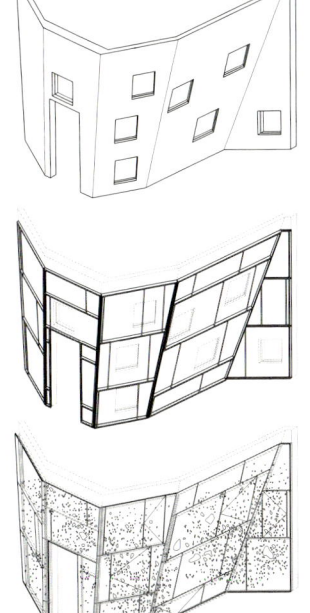

Diagram: paneling system of stair wall

Stair hall with rainbow

II-37

2005

Experiments in Porosity
"From Porosity to Fusion"
Milan, Italy

Part 1: Porosity: Alvar Aalto's Villa Mairea

In 1938 when Alvar Aalto was experimenting with the designs for the Villa Mairea, Le Corbusier's Villa Savoye had been completed for seven years. While both of these villas became iconic examples of modern architecture, their approach is almost opposing, regarding the connection between the architecture and the site. Poised in the center of a great field the Villa Savoye is the extreme autonomous object sitting on pilotis in a geometric and pure contrast to the landscape.

Merged with the birch forest, the Villa Mairea, with its lashed poles and partially sod roofs, fuses with the landscape. These two villas, though nearly the same size and program are antithetical as a white cube and a sponge; as distinct as the typological is from the topological.

Decades before, the "organic architecture" of Frank Lloyd Wright's Usonian houses, aspired to deep integration of house and landscape but somehow Aalto had made this aspiration into a new icon with the Villa Mairea. Was it the witty and irreverent collage technique which seemed so free compared to Wright's geometric consistency? Was it the purposely primitive detailing in lashed-together pole clusters lattice work and leather-wrapped door handles? Was it the quote of new "white architecture" blurred with partially plastered and lumpy brick finish? Somehow Villa Mairea came to symbolize fusion with the landscape in a new way expressing Frank Lloyd Wright's earlier principle.

The elevated cube of Savoye had radicality—with the free façade, free plan, roof gardens, pilotis and horizontal strip windows. In fact, Le Corbusier's 1926 manifesto, The Five Points of the New Architecture were virtually and literally characterized in the Villa Savoye. But the Villa Savoye had vanishing points; normal perspectives. Aalto had built a villa without vanishing points. Aalto's Villa Mairea keeps dilating space, merging and interlocking with the landscape outside.

You cannot turn around in Aalto's Villa Mairea without sensing these multiple vanishing points. Western perspective is time-fixed while eastern perspective exists outside of time. This "time porosity", this episodic and partial perspective, seems to be everywhere in Aalto's merging of birch forest and villa. While a walk through the Villa Savoye's strict geometry evokes the fixed certainty of a manifesto on Purism, a walk through the Villa Mairea is to experience phenomenological acceptance of uncertainty—as if Aalto was working with uncertainty itself. And here is where the doubts begin, when trying to elevate the work to a Model.

Part 2: Porosity to Fusion

As a Thought Experiment, we organize a few of

Piece 1: exploded elevations

Piece 2: exploded elevations

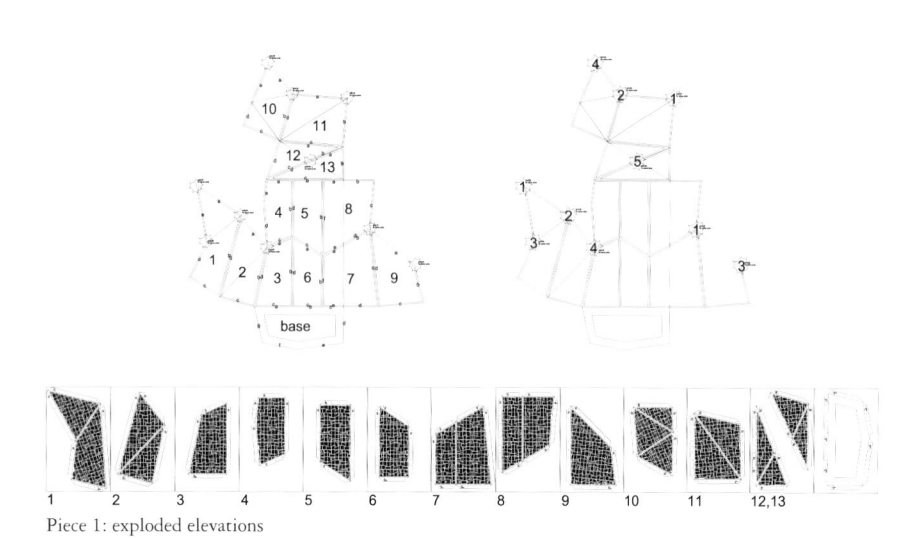

Detail of parts (no.10)

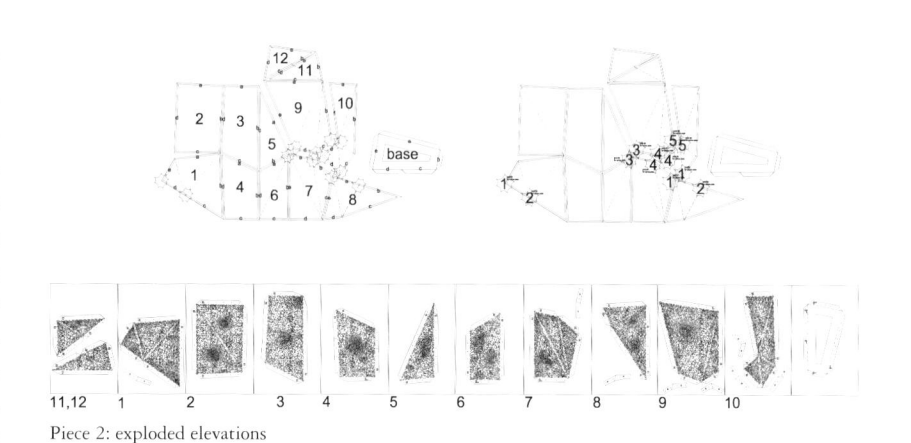

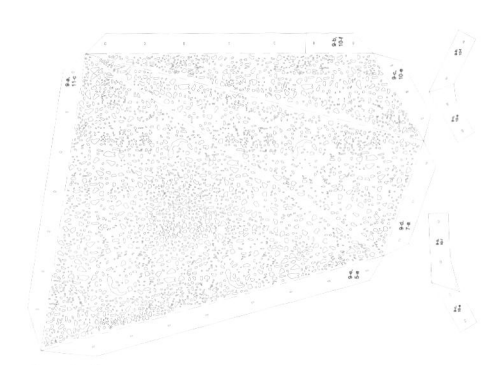

Detail of parts (no.9)

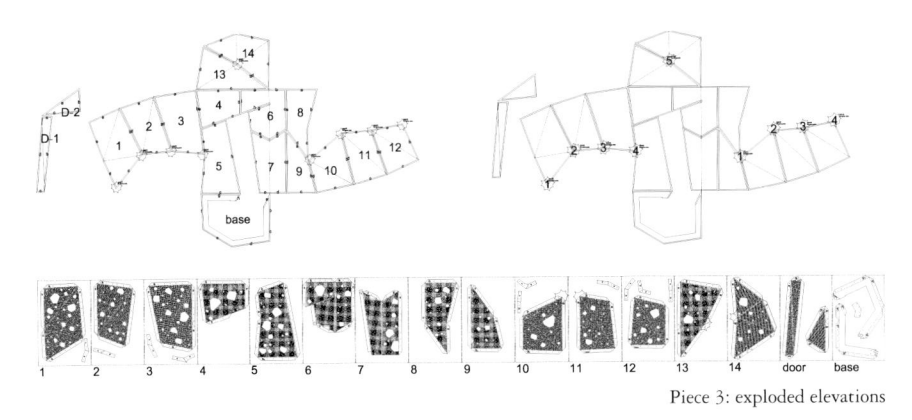

Piece 3: exploded elevations

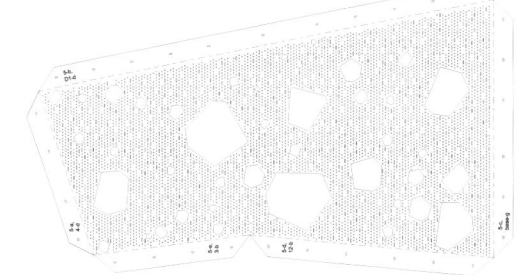

Detail of parts (no.5)

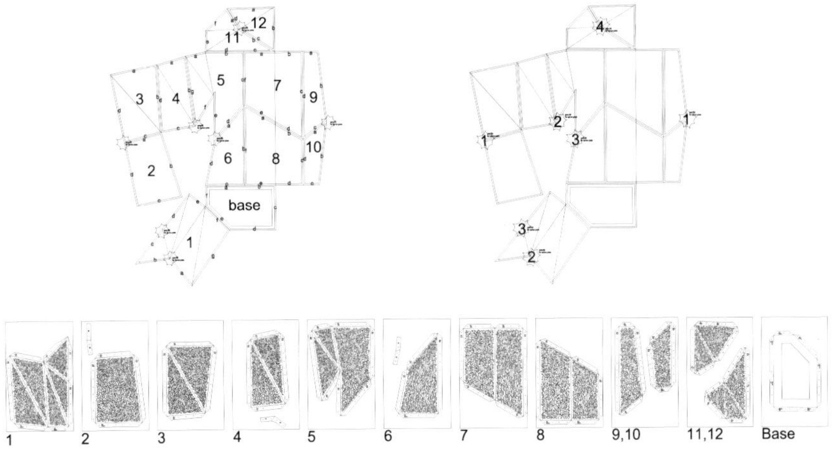

Piece 4: exploded elevations

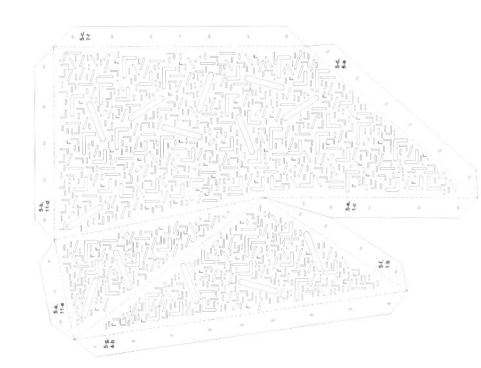

Detail of parts (no.5)

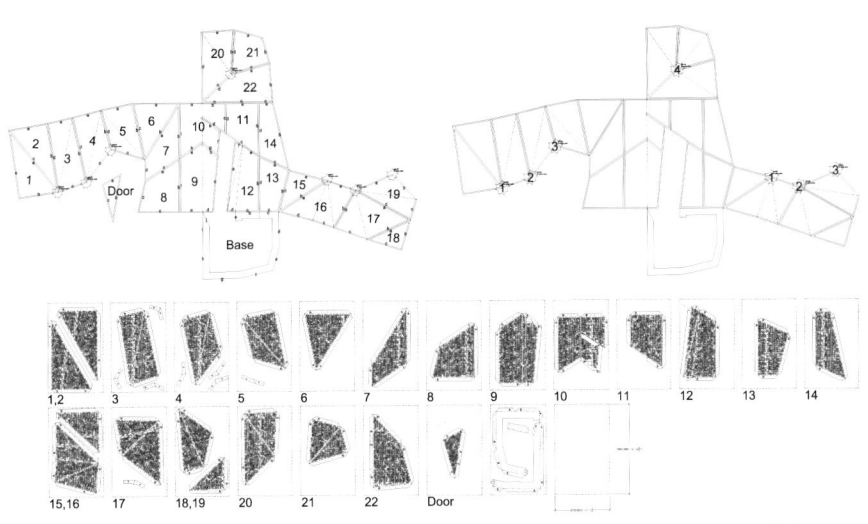

Piece 5: exploded elevations

Detail of parts (no.9)

our projects in relation to this "Fusion" model.

The former arguments for fusion of architecture, urbanism and landscape can be reinforced with a testament for the fusion of spirit and matter as well as fusion of light with form, shade and shadow. Rather than a pre-occupation with independent object-like forms, it is experiential phenomena of spatial sequences within, around and between which triggers emotions and joy in the experience of architecture. The phenomenal properties of light reflected or refracted over a delicately faceting form transcends the formal aspects of the making of the faceted forms when it picks up the glowing yellow-orange light of the setting sun which changes every day in its faceted surfaces.

Likewise, a digitally perforated porous skin penetrated by low horizontal sun multiplies its presence in pins of light with a corresponding web of shadows. When sunlight is projected through trees in a dapple of white light and black shadow on a wall, this dancing variegation exhilarates. Natural light and shadow have the psychological power to inspire and encourage. When the seasonal change of the sun angle is multiplied by variations from sunrise to sunset, porosity when fused with light attains choreographic phenomena.

New, digitally driven techniques have provided a previously unattainable degree of porosity in membranes, surfaces and solids, opening up possibilities for a 21st Century architecture of new phenomenal properties.

However, power of technique no matter how omnipotent requires a human motive; requires a connection of spirit and matter. Otherwise all our works are relegated to empty show or the dilettante facile act of manipulating fashion. If the digitally activating hardware and software are of the objective side and the mind originating thoughts are on the subjective side, it is a fusion of objective-subjective which connects matter and spirit.

How can this simple principle be given teeth? Especially problematic is the fact that language misrepresents the phenomenal effects of our conceptual acts. Some sort of intuition or "subjective ideal" is necessary as a force to drive the objective. Power of technique in the final physical forms is devoid of character in itself—sensory experience of the mind completes its existence.

In writing about the "Transvaluation of Architectural Principles" (Steven Holl and Nihilism, *Domus*, February, 2004), Pierluigi Nicolin wrote "The challenge involves crossing, albeit symbolically, a strong and ancient boundary—that between nature and artifice, between what is there because it comes from within and what is there because it has been constructed." Aalto's Villa Mairea opens a porous lens on the "ancient boundary".

Downward view: one work is consisted of 5 pieces

Detail: inside of piece

Exhibition at Milano Salone 2005: eight modern-day architects reinterpret the eight residential houses by modernist architects.
Steven Holl designed for "Villa Mairea" by Alvar Aalto

ポロシティの実験「ポロシティから融合へ」
[第一部：ポロシティ：アルヴァ・アアルト マイレア邸]
ル・コルビュジエのサヴォア邸が完成して7年後の1938年，アルヴァ・アアルトは実験的なマイレア邸の設計に取り組んでいた。これらの住宅は共に近代建築を象徴する作品として見なされているが，建築と敷地との関係性という点においてはそれぞれの方法論は正反対といってよいものである。広大な敷地の中央に落ち着き払うサヴォア邸はジオメトリや純粋性という点で，自然とは対照的なピロティによって支えられた極度に自律的な存在である。

　樺の木の林の中に溶け込むマイレア邸は一束の柱と植栽の茂る屋根によって，住宅が自然と融合している。タイポロジーとトポロジーが概念として互いに峻別されるように，これらのふたつの住宅はほぼ同規模のプログラムであるにもかかわらず，ホワイトキューブとスポンジという点で対照的である。

　数十年前まではフランク・ロイド・ライトのユーソニアン住宅の「有機的建築」が，住宅と自然の完全な統合の願望を表現したものであった。そのような願望を新しい象徴性へと導いたのはアアルトのマイレア邸である。ライトの均整のとれたジオメトリと比べるとマイレア邸は自由である。知的で無作為なコラージュ技法と言うべきだろうか？　あるいは幾束もの柱を格子状に細工してドアハンドルを革で包むといった，素朴なディテールを意図したものなのだろうか？　部分的には漆喰を使い，粗のある煉瓦仕上げで輪郭を馴染ませた，新しい「白の建築」の引用だろうか？　マイレア邸は

Detail of surface

Inbetween space

ある意味,フランク・ロイド・ライトの初期の理論を表現しうる新しい方法論で自然との融合を象徴した存在である。

ル・コルビュジエが1926年に表明した通り,サヴォア邸の中空に浮くキューブには自由な立面,自由な平面,屋上庭園,ピロティ,及び水平連続窓の実験的性格がある。近代建築の五原則は視覚的にも字義的にもサヴォア邸に描写されている。しかしサヴォア邸には通常の遠近技法の消失点が存在している。アアルトが建築したのはそのような消失点のない住宅である。アアルトのマイレア邸では空間は拡張され,外部の自然と一体となって相互の関係性が生み出されている。

複数の消失点の存在を知覚することなく,アアルトのマイレア邸を巡ることはできないだろう。西欧文化では遠近技法とは時間に対して固定的である。東洋の技法は時間概念の外部に存在している。この「時間のポロシティ」,挿話的,個別的な遠近技法は,樺の林とひとつになったアアルトの住宅のあらゆる側面に表れている。サヴォア邸の厳格なジオメトリはピューリズム宣言の不変の確実性を想起させる。その一方でマイレア邸を歩くと,不確定性に対する現象学的是認を経験することができる。それはあたかも,アアルトが不確実性それ自体と取り組んでいたかのようにも見える。作品をモデルへと昇華させるにあたり疑念が生じるのは,その一点においてである。

[第二部:ポロシティから融合へ]
「融合」モデルに関わる幾つかのプロジェクトが思考実験として計画された。

建築の融合に関する以前の議論では,精神と事象,光と形態,光の陰翳がそれぞれ融合することで,その誓約の定めるところ,アーバニズムとランドスケープは相互に強め合うものと理解された。独立したオブジェ的形態という先入観から離れて,これは建築を経験することの感性と喜びをその内部や周辺,中間領域で誘起する空間シークエンスの経験的現象である。繊細にファセットされた形態の表面で反射し,屈折する光の持つ現象学的属性は,ファセットされた表面で毎日変化する黄橙色の落日の光の輝きを捉える度に,形態を単に操作するというフォルムとしての側面を超越するのだ。

同様に,デジタル的に穿孔されたポーラス構造の表皮を水平線からの光が貫くと,光の点とそれと呼応する陰翳の綾の存在が何重にも現れる。木漏れ日が木々の間から斑紋様に白い光と黒い影を壁面に落とし,踊るような光と影が一層豊かな彩りを与えてくれる。自然の光と影は人々の心を鼓舞し,勇気づけてくれるものである。季節を通して日が昇り,落ちる度に,太陽光は一層豊かに変化する。ポロシティと光の融合は,そこでは踊るような現象へと結実する。

新しいデジタル制御技術によって以前は不可能だった密度でポロシティを膜構造,表皮,ソリッドに与えることができるようになった。これは21世紀の建築に新しい現象学的属性の可能性を切り開くものである。

その一方で,技術力の如何にかかわらず,そこで必要とされるのは人の心を惹起するもの,精神と事象との結びつきである。さもなければ上辺を取り繕うか,あるいは安易にファッションを操作するディレッタントな振る舞いに終始することになるだろう。デジタル技術がもたらすハードウェアとソフトウェアという客観的側面,知的思考の主観的側面を両輪としたこの方法論は,事象と精神を結びつける客観性と主観性の融合である。

このように単純な原則論に,如何にして効力を付与すべきだろうか? 特に問題となるのは,言語が私たちの概念的行為に対する現象学的影響を誤読するという点である。ある種の直観的理解,あるいは「主観的発想」は客観性にとって欠くべからざるものである。最終的な物理的形態の持つ技術力は自己にその本質を内在させるものではない。知性の感覚的経験こそが,存在を全きものとするのである。

「建築の諸原則の再評価」(『スティーヴン・ホールとニヒリズム』,Domus,2004年2月)において,ピエルルイジ・ニコリンが記述したように,「挑戦は象徴的ではあるが,強くて古い境界線に対する越境行為が内包されている。それは自然と技巧とを分け隔てるもの,内部性に由来するが故に存在するものと所与に建設されたが故にそこに存在するとの境界線である」。

アアルトのマイレア邸は「過去の境界線」に穿孔されたポーラス構造のレンズである。

2006, 2007 Riddled Cabinet and Table for Horm
Italy

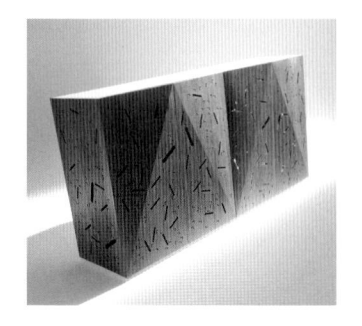

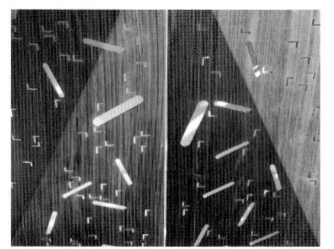

Hingeless Front Cabinet (2007)

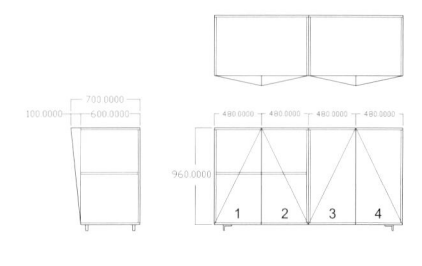

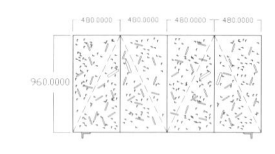

Drawings of Hingeless Front Cabinet: plan/ elevations with porosity pattern

Riddled Table (2006, 2007)

Recently our work has focused on a series of experiments in porosity. We have spent a number of years conducting research into the multiple identities and forms of this concept. Arguments for the porosity of architecture, urbanism and landscape can be reinforced with a testament for the porosity of spirit and matter as well as light's effect through form, shade and shadow. Rather than a pre-occupation with solid, independent object-like forms, it is experiential phenomena of spatial sequences within, around and between which triggers emotions and joy in the experience of space. The phenomenal properties of light reflected or refracted over a delicately faceting form transcend the formal aspects of the making of faceted forms. The forms pick up the glowing yellow-orange light of the setting sun which changes every day in their faceted surfaces. Likewise, a digitally perforated porous skin penetrated by low horizontal sun multiplies its presence in pins of light with a corresponding web of shadows. When sunlight is projected through trees in a dapple of white light and black shadow on a wall, this dancing variegation exhilarates. Natural light and shadow have the psychological power to inspire and encourage. When the seasonal change of the sun angle is multiplied by variations from sunrise to sunset, porosity, when fused with light, attains choreographic virtuosity.

Our latest experiment in porosity is at the specific scale of furniture. Made of a laminated 4-ply composite material developed by Albeflex, the furniture's shapes are based on the best performance qualities of the material. The riddled furniture celebrates the materiality and phenomenal properties of this new unique composite, while exhibiting and demonstrating its unique capabilities for flat fabrication and volumetric assembly.

Storage Unit
The 'Riddled Cabinet' is based on the installation 'Experiments in Porosity' consisting of five delicately faceted forms which exist not as independent objects, but rather as phenomenal experiences of spatial sequences within and around as parts of a whole. In the "Riddled Cabinet" the five porous boxes snap together influencing the geometries of each adjacent box. The cabinets are inscribed in an orthogonal frame defining the limits of the piece as furniture and densely perforated with five unique porous patterns. Each of these patterns reveals the contents of that specific box in a differentiation of light and shadow.

Table
The 'Riddled Table' takes advantage of closely folded double membranes to produce the legs and table top. The layering of the faceted porous surfaces produces a gradated phenomenal effect of light and shadow as the distance between folded over planes tightens and widens. The table-top seems to hover above the ground as the heavily perforated legs dissolve into an organic pattern of glowing light and transparency.

About Horm
From here comes the strongly evocative name "Horm". "Sacred enclosure with right of asylum" is the meaning of this ancient Arabian word. Continuous exploration, deepening of aesthetics and technological contents, synergies: this is the dynamic reality lying behind Horm which has taken the firm, established in '89, to so far havens.

In Horm, design is expressed through clean shapes, from which any superfluous ornament has been wiped away thus reaching a smoothness not pursuing sensationalism but rather shrinking away from it. Along an onward path that relies on unswerving and on the harmony of the numerical elements, lines and thickness keep on relating to each other. Although in the diversity of spaces and of planning solutions, minimalism proves itself to be the leitmotiv of the aesthetics where the inner and external order have a precise correspondence.

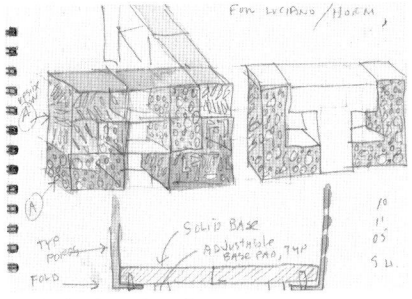

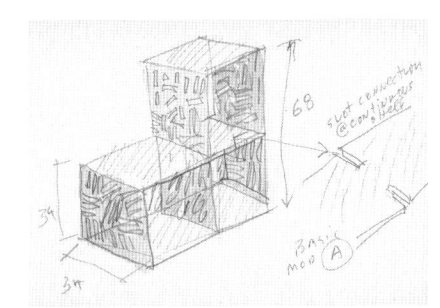

Riddled Cabinet (2006)

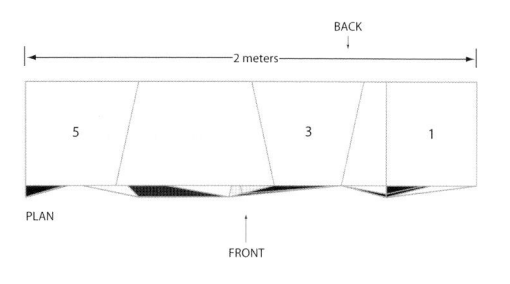

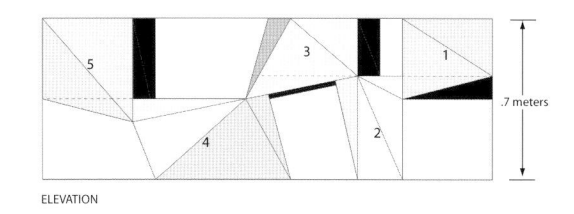

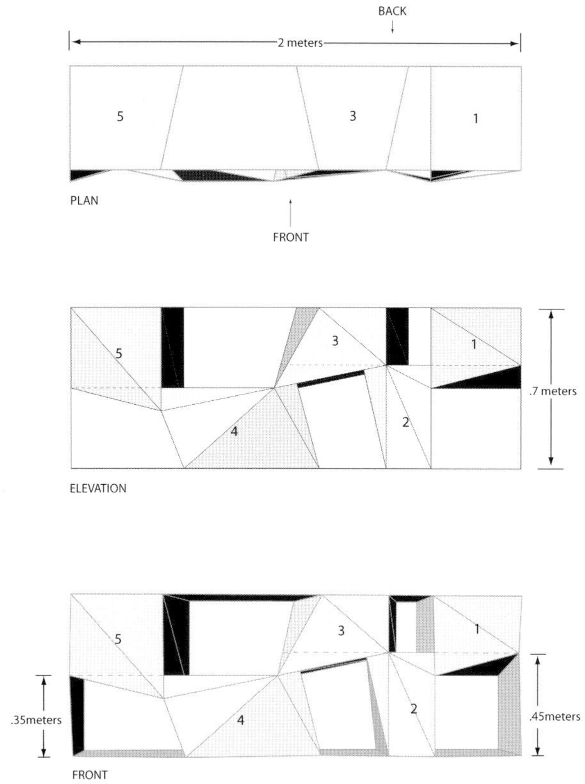

Drawings of Riddled Cabinet

ホルム社のためのキャビネット＆テーブル
近年関心を払い続けてきたポロシティに関わる実験。何年もの時間を費やし、この概念の持つ複合的アイデンティティや形態について、研究が進められてきた。建築、都市、ランドスケープのポロシティに関わる議論を一層強めるのは、形態を通過する光や陰影、精神や物質に宿るポロシティの確固たる存在の証によるところである。重厚で完結したオブジェのようなフォルムといった先入観よりはむしろ、空間シークエンスの内部や外部、あるいはその中間領域の現象学的経験こそが、空間を経験するなかで感情や喜びを引き起こすのだ。繊細なファセット状の形態に反射屈折する光の現象学的特性は、単にファセット面を構成するという物質的側面を越えた意味を持つものである。黄橙色の夕日に輝く形態は、毎日、ファセットの表面に異なった表情見せる。同様に、水平方向から入る太陽の光がデジタル加工で穿孔されたポーラス状の表皮を貫くと、光の点や周囲の網目のような影に、表皮の存在感がより一層際立って見える。太陽光が木々を通して壁面に白い光と黒々とした影の模様を描くと、踊るような斑の模様はより一層の彩りを見せる。自然の光と影には人々にインスピレーションを与え、気持ちを鼓舞する心理的な力が備わっている。太陽の角度が季節毎に変化し、朝日や夕日が一層豊かな彩りを与えるようになると、ポロシティは光と融合し、精緻に躍動するのだ。

ポロシティに対する最新の実験的試みは家具のスケールによるものである。素材はアルベフレックス社が開発した4層のラミネート積層材によるもので、素材の特徴を最も生かすように家具の形が決められている。リドルド・ファーニチャーとは、この新しく独創的な複合材の素材の性格と現象学的特性への称揚であるとともに、平面ファブリックを立体に組み立てる独創的な可能性を示し、表現したものである。

［収納ユニット］
「リドルド・キャビネット」とは、「Experiments in Porosity（ポロシティの実験）」のインスタレーションのためにつくられたもので、繊細なファセット面を持つ5つのフォルムは独立したオブジェとしてではなく、空間シークエンスの内外で全体を部分的に構成する現象学的経験として存在している。「リドルド・キャビネット」では5つのポーラス状のボックスが一体となり、隣接したボックスのジオメトリに干渉している。キャビネットは家具として、それぞれのピースの境界を決定する直交フレームに内接し、それぞれのボックスは5つの独自のポーラス状のパターンで緻密に穿孔されている。これらのパターンは光と影の微分的差異によって、それぞれのボックス独自の特徴を表している。

［テーブル］
「リドルド・テーブル」では複層皮膜を折り曲げ、閉じることによって、足と天板が構成された。重なり合うように折り曲げられた平面同士の距離は狭く、また、広く変化する。ファセットのポーラス状の表面が複層的に生み出すのは、次第に表情を変える現象学的な光と影の効果である。密実に穿孔された足は透明に光輝く有機的パターンへと溶けるように消失し、天板は床から浮遊して見える。

［ホルム社について］
「Horm/ホルム」の名は、強烈なイメージを惹起する。この古代アラビア語は「アサイラムの権利と聖なる場所」を意味する。たゆみない挑戦、美的感性と技術への探究、相乗効果が生み出すもの。これこそが89年の設立以来、ホルム社を支え、遥か遠くの安息の地へと導いてきた。

ホルム社は明快なフォルムに特徴がある。余分な装飾もなく、センセーショナリズムを拒否し、滑らかなフォルムを追求する。たゆまぬ前進と、相互に作用する数的要素、ライン、厚みの調和。空間の多様性とプランニング・ソリューションの一方で、ミニマリズムは自らを美学におけるライトモチーフであることを示し、内部と外部のオーダーが明瞭に調和するのだ。

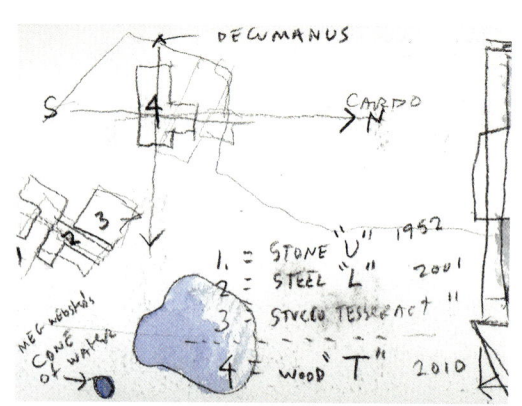

Sketch: disposition on site

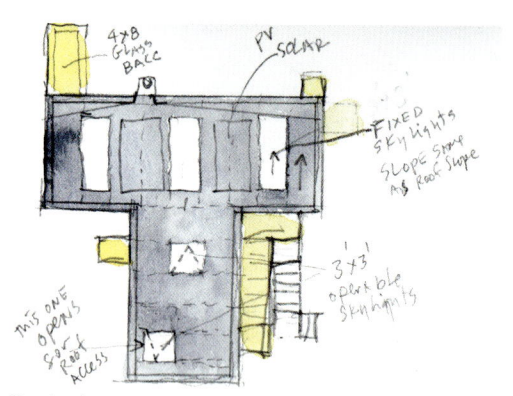

Sketch: plan

On a four acre site in Dutchess County, New York, a new wooden "T" space sits near a stone "U" house from 1952, which has a steel "L" addition from 2001.

The new gallery floats over the natural landscape. It has nine steel columns and nine elevations, all integrated via proportions of 1:1.618.

A rain skin of natural 2 x 2 cedar is suspended on stainless steel screws. There is no plumbing, or sheetrock. The interiors are painted plywood and the floor is sanded marine plywood with all the stains of the 4-month construction process exposed.

Wooden windows, doors and skylights were specifically built for this space. The gallery is reached from the east by a gently sloping wooden ramp, and exited on a wooden ramp through the south elevation which is a large pivoting wall.

Light comes from skylights, cut to achieve 25 foot candles of natural light on the walls, eliminate the need for electricity.

Entrance on southwest

T Space
2010
Dutchess County, New York, U.S.A.

Model: T Space (front) and Steel L (behind)

Site plan S=1:8000

1 ENTRANCE
2 BRIDGE

First floor S=1:500

Northwest elevation

Bridge on southeast

Detail of bay window on northwest

II-45

View from southwest: corner detail

View toward entrance

Interior: looking various corners with natural light

Detail of entrance

Tスペース
ニューヨーク州ダッチェス郡の4エーカーの敷地に、新しく木造の「T」スペースが建つ。すぐ傍の1952年に建てられた石造の「U」ハウスには、2001年にスティールの「L」が増築された。

新しいギャラリーは自然のランドスケープに浮遊する。9本のスティール柱と9つの立面を持ち、全ては1：1.618のプロポーションにまとめられた。

2インチ角の天然杉による雨曝しの表皮は、ステンレス・スティールの釘で留められている。水道も、石膏ボードもない。内装には塗装合板が、床には、4ヶ月の建設過程でできた傷は全てそのままに、磨き仕上げの船舶用合板が使用されている。

木窓や扉、天窓が、この空間のために特別に製作された。ギャラリーには東側から傾斜の緩い木製スロープを通って入り、南壁面の回転式の大開口から木製スロープを通って出てくることができる。

天窓から光が入るため、電気を必要とせず、蝋燭のように自然光が25フィート（約7.6メートル）の壁面を照らす。

2 Houses
住宅

One of the exciting things about designing houses is that every house presents the possibility of a fresh and new idea and expression. The beginning point of making of a house often comes directly out of the land in the relation of the building to the site— of the building to the particular place.

For example, at the site of Oceanic Retreat (2001-) in Hawaii, the fact that tectonic plates on the floor of the ocean are moving about five centimeters per year became the jumping off point for the design of the house. The house is in two parts, which slide apart from each other almost like tectonic plates that have slipped past one another. They are sitting on a kind of precipice overlooking the horizon of the vast Pacific Ocean. Kaua'i being the foremost island on the tectonic plate is the promontory. The stairs in the main building are rising at that same five centimeters that the tectonic plates move per year. The house is in moss green stained concrete and is completely powered by solar energy. It becomes a precipice on which you look out across this vast oceanic horizon. The notion of the immensity and the silence of that place is embedded in how the house is developed.

You can find the opposite site condition on Mecox Bay in Long Island near Watermill. This is a house for a brain surgeon, a house that's really more introspective. It is not very far from the Jackson Pollock studio in Springs. When I was beginning the project I thought about those strips of light that came through the barn where Jackson Pollock painted some of his greatest action paintings. The idea began of making a house which was about the phenomena of light coming through strips of wood. This house is called 'Writing with Light' House (2001-04). Light writes patterns on the floors and walls. We conceived the whole house as a box of wooden strips that get carved away in terms of the movement of the sun during the day. The swimming pool is on the roof over the garage. At that point in the house the walls fall away and light comes through strips directly onto the swimming pool. You can see right through the top of the house. The idea being linear, being lightweight—the entire house is constructed of wood; very different from the concrete slipping plates of the Oceanic Retreat House in Kaua'i.

A very particular place in Essex, New York was the site of the Nail Collector's House (2001-04). The client is a writer who asked for a "poetic utterance". He said 'I really want a place as a retreat, a place where I can keep all of my library books. I would

あらゆる住宅には新しい思考と表現の可能性がある。これこそが住宅の設計で素晴らしい点である。住宅をつくるということは, 建物と敷地との関係において, また, 建物と特定の場所との関係において, その土地と直接向き合うことがその出発点である。

例えばハワイのオーシャン・リトリート(2001-)の敷地では, 海底のテクトニクス・プレートが毎年約5cm移動しているという事実がこの住宅を設計するきっかけとなっている。この住宅はふたつに分かれて計画された。あたかも相互に隣接したテクトニクス・プレート同士のように, お互いにスライドして配置されている。この住宅は広大な太平洋を望み, 水平線を見下ろす断崖に立地する。カウアイ島はテクトニクス・プレートの先端に位置する断崖の島である。主要棟では, テクトニクス・プレートが一年間に動くのと同じ5cmで階段が構成されている。この住宅は苔の色に染色されたコンクリートに包まれ, 電力は全て太陽光発電から供給される。この住宅は広大な海の向こうの水平線へと視線を誘う, 断崖の一部となっている。この住宅に内包されているものは, 広大で静寂に包まれた, この土地に対する理解である。

ウォーターミル近くのロングアイランド州メコックス湾の敷地条件は正反対である。この住宅は脳神経科医のためのものである。この住宅は, 一層内向的に計画されている。程遠くない場所にはジャクソン・ポロックのスプリングスのスタジオがあった。細く延びる幾筋もの光が納屋に差し込んでくる。ジャクソン・ポロックはアクション・ペインティングの名作の幾つかを, このスタジオで制作していた。この住宅の契機はそのような光についてである。木板のあいだから差す光の現象性が, この住宅計画の発想の原点である。「光に描かれた」家(2001-04)。これが住宅の名である。光が床面や壁面に, 紋様を描く。住宅全体は縞状の木の箱として計画されている。そこには日中の太陽の動きにあわせて, 幾筋もの光が刻み込まれるのだ。ガレージを覆う屋根の上にはスイミング・プールが設けられている。住宅のその場所には壁がない。スイミング・プールに縞状の木板を通して直接, 光が差すのはそのためである。住宅の上からは全てを見渡すことができる。直線的であるということ, 軽いということ——カウアイ島のオーシャン・リトリートの滑らかなコンクリートのプレートとは対照的に, 住宅はすべて木造で計画された。

釘収集家の家(2001-04)の敷地は, ニューヨーク州エセックスのなかでも非常に特殊な場所に位置している。作家であるクライアントは, 「詩的言語」を求めていた。「休息のための場所, 自分の蔵書を全て保管することのできる場所, 『詩的言語』のような建築が欲しい」。これがクライアントの言葉

Turbulence House

like the architecture to be a "poetic utterance"'. I went to the site which is in a nineteenth century town where it feels as if nothing has been built in a hundred years. On a promontory where the ferry goes across Lake Champlain, the site is on ruins of an old nail factory that produced square headed nails. The client had lived there and collected these nails that still remained on the site, which is why we call it 'Nail Collector's House'. The house comes out of this notion of expressing nails. The house is sheathed in cartridge brass secured by exposed nails which give a dented texture to the thin brass. The house is organized by the number twenty-four, the number of chapters in both the *Iliad* and the *Odyssey*. The client, Alan Wardle, was excited about connecting the design to myth and the sea. Homer's twenty-four chapters became the twenty-four square windows that float over the walls in drifting pattern, giving light to the interior and giving the body of the building definition. The house is organized by a sequence of movement up in three levels where you walk right through the library and pass up into the sleeping loft.

Turbulence House (2001-05), the guest house for Richard Tuttle and Mei-mei Berssenbrugge, has a very unique site on top of a mesa in Abique, New Mexico. The design was based on the idea that the wind could blow right through the center of this house. If you look at the section of the building, it becomes a kind of tip of the iceberg sitting on the mesa. I imagine a much larger form below. The house, which is pre-fabricated in stress-skin panels, was built in twenty-one pieces in Kansas City and shipped to the site. There it was bolted together so that local craftsmen could plaster and finish the inside. Through the combination of a prefabricated house and the local craftsman's hand in fitting out the interiors on a special site on the mesa, the very unique condition for this particular house was expressed.

At the Planar House (2002-05) in Arizona, where the site faces Camelback Mountain, the program was for a gallery that the owners could also inhabit. The house takes on the expression of the construction in planes of tilt-up concrete. These planes define an orthogonal, gallery-like, condition. The way these structural planes come together shapes the fenestration. One sees a tilt-up section next to another and there's a slot that turns into a small window. It is a very hot climate so we envisioned 'cool pools' that extend to form stacks on the roof that bring light down, exhausting the warm air vertically. The light brought down to the single

であった。敷地は19世紀につくられた町で、この百年間のあいだ、何も新しく建てられていないかのようであった。この住宅の敷地は、フェリーがシャンプレイン湖を横切る岬の上の、角釘の製造工場の跡地にある。クライアントは以前からここに住み、敷地にそのまま残されていた釘の収集を行っていた。そこでこの住宅は「釘収集家の家」と名付けられたのだ。釘をどう表現するかが、この住宅の始まりである。この住宅は薬莢に使われる真鍮で被覆され、露出した釘によって留められている。そのことが、薄い真鍮に窪みのある質感を付与している。この住宅はイリアスとオデュッセイアの両方の章の数、24という数字で構成されている。クライアントのアラン・ワーデル氏は、住宅を神話と海に結びつけるという発想を大変気に入っていたようだ。ホメロスの詩編は24の正方形の窓となり、壁面を漂うように浮遊する。光はそこから内部空間に取り込まれ、この建築を定義する身体となる。住宅は書庫を抜け、スリーピング・ロフトに至るまで、三層にわたって延びる動線シークエンスで構成される。

リチャード・タトルとメイメイ・ベルセンブルグのゲストハウス、タービュランス・ハウス(2001-05)が建つのは、ニューメキシコのメサの台地の、非常に特殊な敷地である。計画において発想の契機となったのは、この住宅の中央を吹き抜ける風である。建築の断面を見てみると、ある意味、メサに建つ氷山の一角のように見える。その下には一層巨大な形態が広がっている。この住宅はモノコックパネルのプレファブリケーションによるもので、カンザスシティで21の部材が製造され、敷地へと搬入された。現地ではボルトで組み立てられ、内部空間は土地の職人のプラスターで仕上げられている。メサという特殊な敷地でプレファブリケーションで住宅をつくり、その土地の職人の手仕事で内部空間が仕上げられる。非常に特異な状況を表現した結果が、この特別な住宅である。

キャメルバック山に面したアリゾナ州のプラナー・ハウス(2002-05)は、ギャラリーのためのプログラムである。また、オーナーが居住することも可能である。ティルトアップ工法のコンクリートの平面がこの住宅の表現となった。これらの平面が直交することで、ギャラリーとしての性格が与えられた。これらの面構造をひとつに構成することで、開口部が形成される。隣り合うティルトアップ工法の断面の細長い隙間が、小さな窓となる。ここは非常に暑いところなので、屋根の煙突に対応した「冷却プール」が計画された。煙突は光をその下に導き入れるとともに、暖気を垂直に抜くことができるようになっている。この住宅のメインギャラリーの床一面に落ちる光は、非常に独創的なものである。斜路はプールのある中庭を通り過ぎ、キャメルバック山を遠くに望む屋上の彫刻庭園へと至る。

floor of the main gallery section of the house is special. A ramp leads past the enclosed pool court to a roof top sculpture garden with a view of Camelback Mountain.

A completely different condition characterizes the site on the edge of Lake Garda, Italy where we designed a house for a lighting executive. It is a house organized around natural light; we call it Sun Slice House (2005-). The condition of natural light slices the body of this building, giving it different characters at different times of the day and different seasons. The relation to Lake Garda is very sensitive, shaping how the house could be fit on the site. It could only be fit in a very particular way, so there was a plastic-like stretching of the cor-ten body of the building to form courtyards and spaces that look out on Lake Garda.

In the case of the house for Daeyang Shipping Company (Daeyang Gallery & House, 2008-12) in Seoul, South Korea the idea driving the design comes from a musical score. The program called for a house that is also a gallery and a performance space for musical events. There is the gallery below and from the gallery rises three pavilions through a sheet of water. It is in that condition of the relationship of below and above that the pavilions themselves were transformed. The shapes of the pavilions are derived from the musical score, "Symphony of Modules", written in 1967 by a composer Istvan Anhalt. It was a piece of music that was never played because the orchestra was so large, it never could be assembled. In transforming the graphic score we made it into strips of light. There are three pavilions which have fifty-five skylight strips that mark the space in changing ways. It is musical how the light comes into the space sometimes dancing on reflections of the large sheet of water from which the pavilions rise. There are concerts, poetry readings, there is the Daeyang Shipping Company art collection—this house really is a semi-public space. Its character arises from the uniting of the below grade gallery system, the sheet of water and the three pavilions, organized via a musical score.

Each house has a particular beginning which can be unique. Expression of materials and structure and the condition of light and movement through the space is driven by an idea. Each house is a unique statement about a particular site or the conditions of a program or a place on this earth. This strategy was clarified in *Anchoring*, written in 1988, "there is a universal in the specific and specific in the universal."

Steven Holl

イタリアのガルダ湖の畔の敷地の状況は，これらとはまた完全に異なっている。ここでは照明会社の幹部のための住宅が計画された。自然光のなかに構成される住宅で，この住宅はサン・スライス・ハウス(2005-)と名付けられている。自然の光がこの建築の身体を切断し，一日を通して，また，季節を通して，建築に異なった表情を与えてくれる。ガルダ湖との関係は，住宅をいかにこの敷地に馴染ませるかという点で，非常に繊細なものである。そのためには特別の方法が必要とされた。彫塑的に延びるコールテン鋼の建築の身体が中庭と空間を構成し，そこからはガルダ湖が一面に広がっている。

韓国ソウルのデヤン商船の住宅（デヤン・ギャラリー＆ハウス，2008-12）では，ある楽譜が計画を発想するきっかけとなった。求められたプログラムは，音楽のためのギャラリー兼パフォーマンス・スペースとしても使うことのできる住宅であった。ギャラリーは地下にあり，そこから3棟の建築が水盤を貫くように立ち上がる。それぞれの棟の形態が変化するのは，上下の階層の関係性によるところである。建築の形は作曲家イシュトヴァン・アンハルトが1967年に作曲した"Symphony of Modules"という楽曲の譜面がモチーフとされた。この楽曲は非常に大きなオーケストラの編成を必要としたために，これまでに一度も演奏されることがなかった。ここでは絵のような楽譜を変形させて，光の筋がつくり出されている。3棟の建築には55本のストライプの天窓がある。時間とともに移ろう空間がその特徴である。光は時折，巨大な水盤に反射して踊るように空間に彩りを与える。これこそがひとつの音楽である。そして建築は，その水盤の上に聳えるのだ。デヤン商船の美術品のコレクションがあり，コンサートや詩の朗読が催される。ここは実際にはセミパブリックの住宅である。地階のギャラリーのシステム，水盤，そして3棟の建築が，楽譜の譜面を通してひとつに統合される。それこそがこの住宅の特徴である。

各々の住宅には，その住宅にしかない出発点が存在している。素材と構造に対する表現，光の入り方，そして空間の動き。これらを生み出すのはただひとつのアイディアである。各々の住宅はその敷地の固有性，プログラム，あるいは地球上の特定の敷地条件に対する，固有の意志の表明である。この方法論は1988年に執筆した『Anchoring』のなかで理論化された。すなわち「固有性のうちに普遍性は宿り，普遍性のなかに固有性が宿る」のだ。

（スティーヴン・ホール）

2001 Little Tesseract
Rhinebeck, New York, U.S.A.

Wall detail

North elevation

A hollow charcoal cube is warped by distorting forces opening a triangle of light from above. This cubic wooden structure is linked by an exoskeletal steel "L" to an existing stone "U". The link, like a porch, is a temperate zone with operable glass. From the central room of the stone "U" one moves down a slight ramp in the steel "L"; space then overlaps diagonally connecting upward toward the triangle of light. This central spatial connection fuses outward contrasting materials.

A solar stack wall in structural glass planks heats the cube in winter and cools via stack effect in summer. PV cell assist the electrical. Steel windows slice through the dark stucco on steel plate blades forming special viewing frames from the interior with unified white plaster head/jamb/sill.

Two projects in New York: Little Tesseract (Rhinebeck) and College of Architecture, Cornell University (Ithaca)

リトル・テッセラクト

捻れるように作用する力が濃灰色のキューブを歪め，頂部の開口から三組の光を落とす。木構造のキューブはスティールの「L」と呼ばれる外骨格によって，「U」と呼ばれる既存部へと連続する。ポーチのような連結部には，可動式ガラスの落ち着いた空間がある。「U」と呼ばれる石造部の中央の居室からは，緩やかな斜路を下ってスティール構造の「L」へと至る。そこでは対角線上に重なり合う空間が，三組の光に向かって連続する。中央にあるこの空間の連続性は，外部の素材のコントラストへと融合する。

厚板の構造ガラスは太陽熱を集め，冬の間はキューブを暖めるとともに，夏の間は煙突効果で冷気をもたらしてくれる。補助電力には太陽電池が利用される。スティール窓はその細枠で黒スタッコの空間を切断し，白プラスターの框／抱枠／下枠と一体となって，内部空間からの眺望をその枠に収めている。

View from northeast

Living room

Model: existing wing (left) and new wing (right)

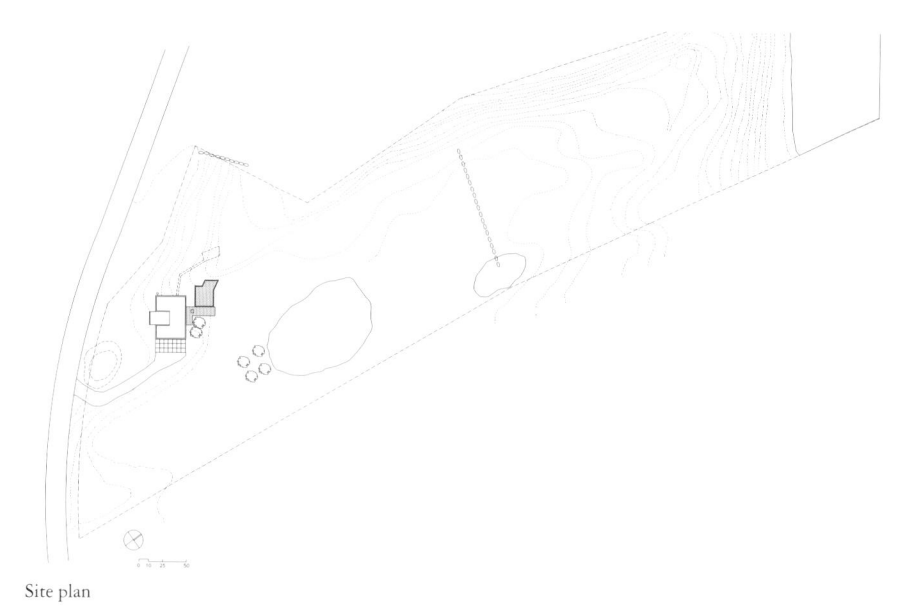

Site plan

View from north: steel structure with glazed wall connecting new wing (right) and existing wing (left)

Reflecting pool on south

CONCEPT: stone "U" + steel "L" + TESSERACT

Concept sketch: new cubic wooden structure is linked by steel "L" to an existing stone "U"

1 LIVING ROOM
2 BEDROOM
3 REFLECTING POOL

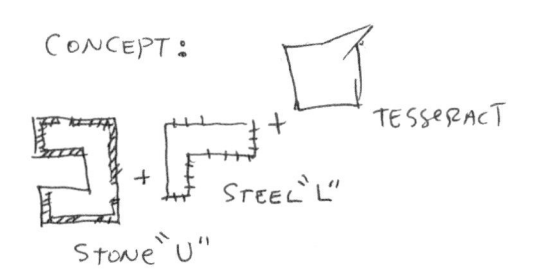

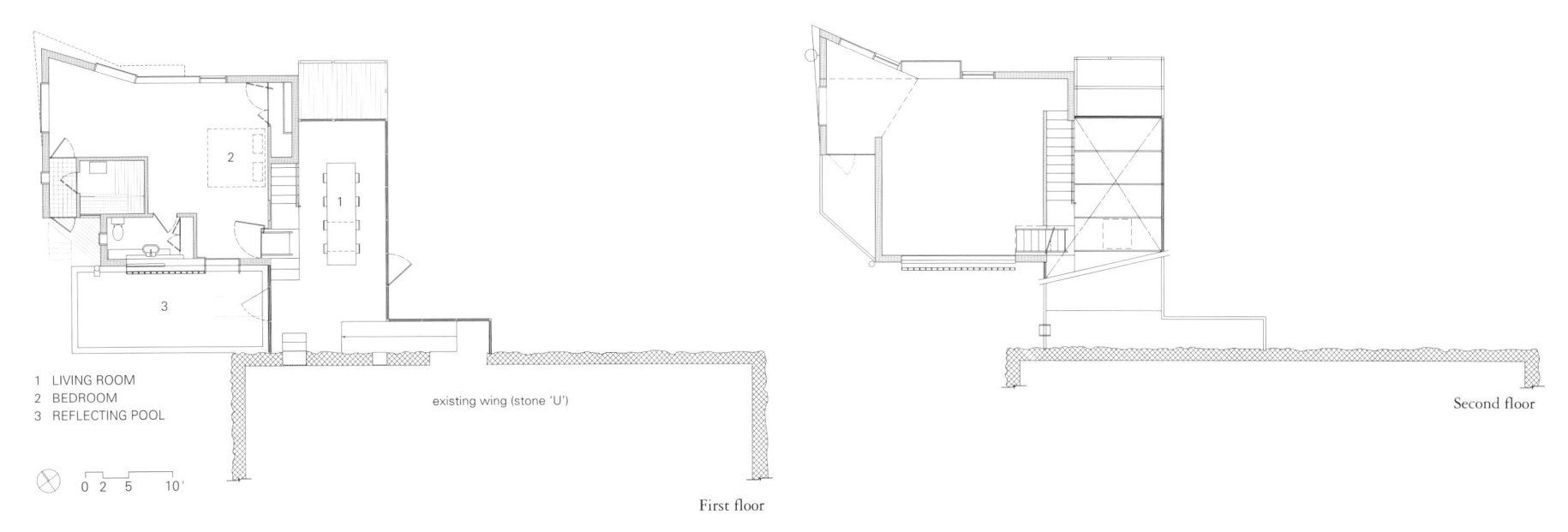

existing wing (stone 'U')

First floor

Second floor

Living room: staircase to second floor

East elevation

West elevation

South elevation

North elevation

2001- **Oceanic Retreat**
Kaua'i, Hawaii, U.S.A.

Distant view from northeast

Sketch: overall image

View from south

Overall view from south

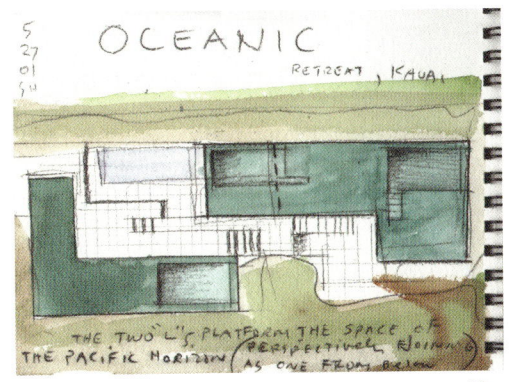

Plan

View from east: edges of two wings

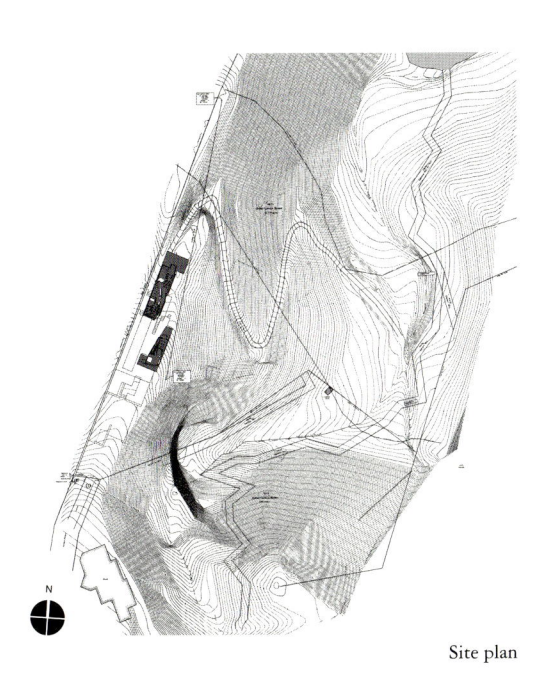

Site plan

II-57

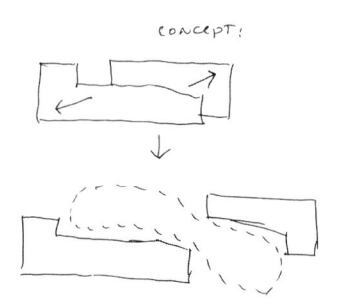

Concept sketch

Model: view from northeast

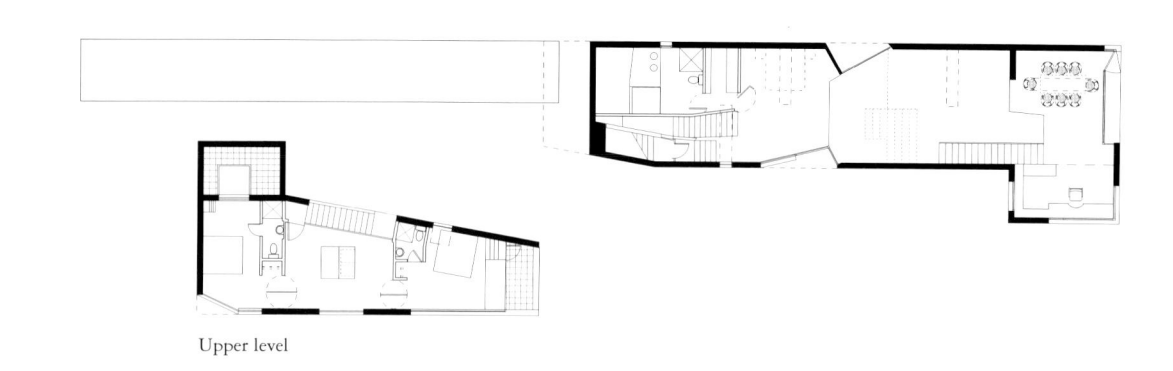

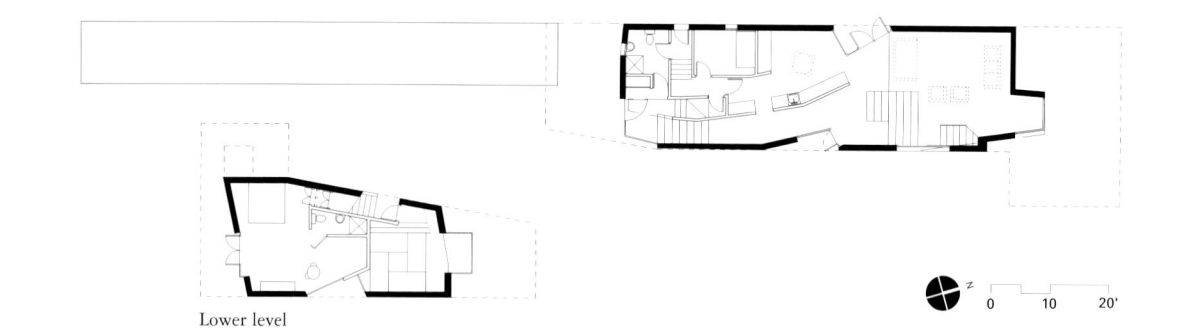

Upper level

Lower level

Site
The Hawaiian Islands, the earth's most isolated islands were one of the last places on earth to be occupied by humans. Kaua'i, the oldest of the eight major Hawaiian Islands occupies the leading edge of the Pacific tectonic plate which has moved across the volcanic hotspot at a constant rate of 3.5 inches per year. The site for this retreat is on the northwest "prow" of Kaua'i with Japan 3,600 miles over the distant Pacific horizon. The 18 acre site is 90% natural preservation area. The house, retreat is limited even further to a bracketed zone of two "L"s around an inner court. The present habitant of the Lycyan Albatross on the tip of the site will remain natural and undisturbed. (These mysterious birds nest on the site 6 months, spending the other 6 soaring across the open ocean—apparently sleeping on air currents, dropping occasionally for a bite of fish .)

Program
This is a special place of retreat and reflection to be occupied in special visits by the owner and his son and daughter. Included are special observation deck with a telescope for stargazing, a room for yoga and calligraphy, and 3 bedrooms in a studio pavilion. The inner court has a 3 m x 25 m lap pool.

Concept
The absolute and severe qualities of the site are continued in two "L"s forming a platform like the space of the horizon. The house, occupying the space below this datum is carved out for the best views and flow. While the extreme promontory of the site is left for the birds, the geometric line is continued in a way that the house builds back the eroded part of the site.

While the plan's master axis is perpendicular to the horizon due to the natural topography, views of the ocean connect all interior spaces like a dotted line horizon.

Arrival is in an auto court framed in local lava stone walls. The floors of this court is a local gravel which naturally compacts. Passing through interlocking red and green endemic flower gardens, one arrives in a sheltered court with natural overhangs of the house geometry marking the route.

If space is like water, the plan and section contains, drops, embanks and then releases the space down the curvilinear path through the natural gardens finally to the ocean horizon (like the ancient concept of Zen garden organization with a pool at the end—but here it is the pounding ocean).

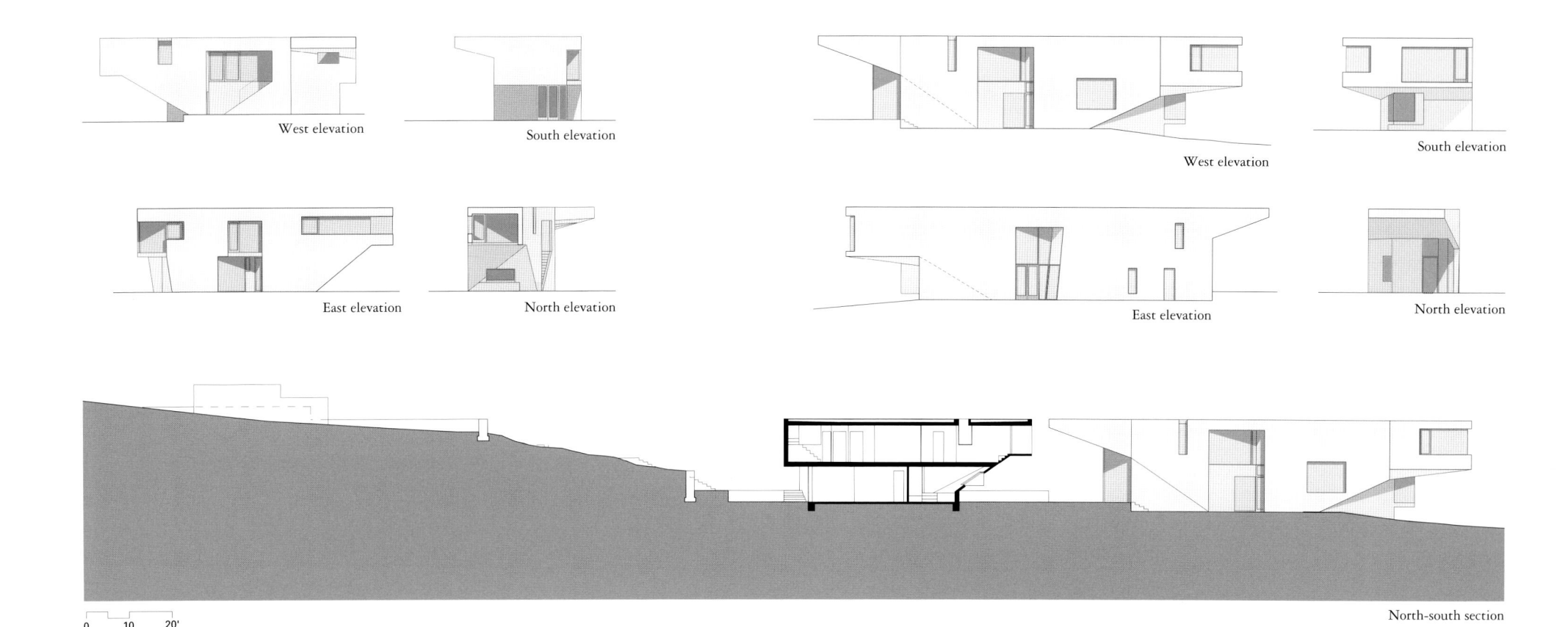

West elevation　　South elevation　　　West elevation　　South elevation

East elevation　　North elevation　　　East elevation　　North elevation

North-south section

オーシャン・リトリート

[敷地]
地球上で最も孤立した島々であるハワイ諸島は，人が住み着いた最後の場所であった。ハワイ諸島の主要な8つの島のなかで最も古いカウアイ島は，毎年3.5インチずつ火山のホットスポットを横断して動いている太平洋プレートの最先端を占めている。隠遁の場所であるこのプロジェクトの敷地は，カウアイ島の北西の"舳先"に位置し，水平線の彼方3,500マイル先に日本がある。18エーカーある敷地の90%は自然保護地区である。この家，つまり隠れ家の場所は，内側にあるコートを囲む2つのL型によって挟まれた領域にさらに限定されている。敷地の先端に宿る，現在の住民，アルバトロス（アホウドリ科の海鳥）は自然のまま，邪魔されずに生息できるだろう。（このミステリアスな鳥たちは，6ヶ月をこの敷地で休み，残りの6ヶ月は広い海原を空高く舞い飛びながら過ごす—どうやら気流に乗りながら眠り，ときどき急降下して魚に食いついているらしい。）

[プログラム]
隠棲のための特別な場所であり，オーナーと彼の息子と娘が一定の時期に訪れることを考えた住まいである。天体観測用の望遠鏡が置かれた特別な観察デッキ，ヨガと書道のための部屋，3つの寝室があるスタジオ・パビリオンなどが含まれる。内側のコートには3m×25mのラップ・プールがある。

[コンセプト]
純粋で，厳しい敷地の性格は，水平線がつくった空間のようなプラットフォームを形成する2つの"L"の中へ続いて行く。この基準線の下の空間を占める住宅は，一番良い眺めと空間の流れを得るように土地を刻み出す。敷地最先端の崖は鳥たちのために手をつけずに残される一方，建物の幾何学的な輪郭線は，この家が，敷地の浸食部を取り戻すかのように続く。

平面上の主軸線は地形のために，水平線に垂直に通る一方で，大洋の眺めは，すべての部屋を，点々と連なる水平線のように連結する。

家への到着地点は，この土地の溶岩壁に囲まれたオート・コートである。コートの表面は自然に密集した地元の小石である。赤と緑のこの地に固有の花々が互いに重なり合う庭を過ぎると，この道筋の目印となっている，形態として自然にせり出したヴォリュームに覆われたコートに出る。

もし空間が水のようであるとすれば，平面と断面は，その空間を内包し，滴らせ，囲み，次に，自然の庭を抜けて，最後に水平線に向かって解き放つ。（最後に枯れ山水がくる禅の庭を組み立てる古来の構成概念のように——但し，ここではそれは，打ち寄せる大洋ではあるが。）

2001-04 Writing with Light House
Eastern Long Island, New York, U.S.A.

Sketch

The concept of this linear wooden beach house evolved from the inspiration of the site's close proximity to the studio of the painter Jackson Pollock. Several free-form designs were made based on the 1949 painting "Seven in Eight". Opening up the interior to the free expanse of the bay and the north view of the Atlantic Ocean required closing the south side for privacy from the street.

The final scheme brackets the internal energy into an open frame, which the sun shines through in projecting lines. The strips of white light inscribe and seasonally bend internal spaces dynamically with the cycle of the day.

The wooden balloon frame construction is comparable to the strip wood sand dune fencing along the ocean. Several guest rooms swirl around the double level living room from which one ascends to a pool suspended over the garage. From this upper pool court, the Atlantic Ocean is visible.

View from southeast: deck (right) and garage (left)

Entrance on south

View from east: north elevation facing Atlantic Ocean

View from northeast: outside staircase to roof terrace

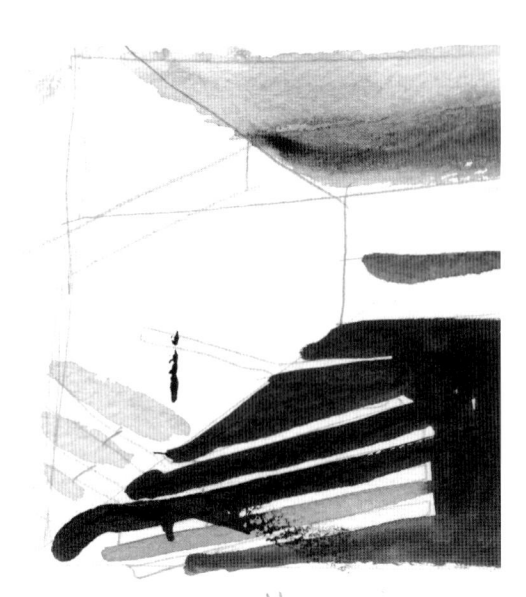

Concept sketch

Concept = "Writing with Light"
Linear strips of sunlight inscribe and bend internal spaces dynamically in time

North elevation

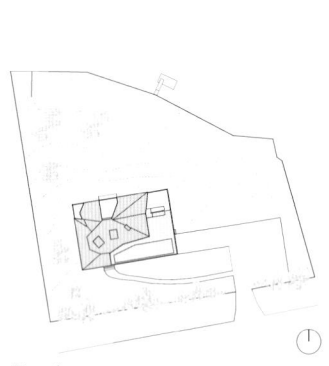

Site plan

1 ENTRANCE
2 LIVING ROOM
3 DINING ROOM
4 KITCHEN
5 GUEST ROOM
6 LIBRARY
7 GARAGE
8 DECK
9 BATHROOM
10 MASTER BEDROOM
11 DRESSING ROOM
12 POOL
13 ROOF TERRACE

First floor

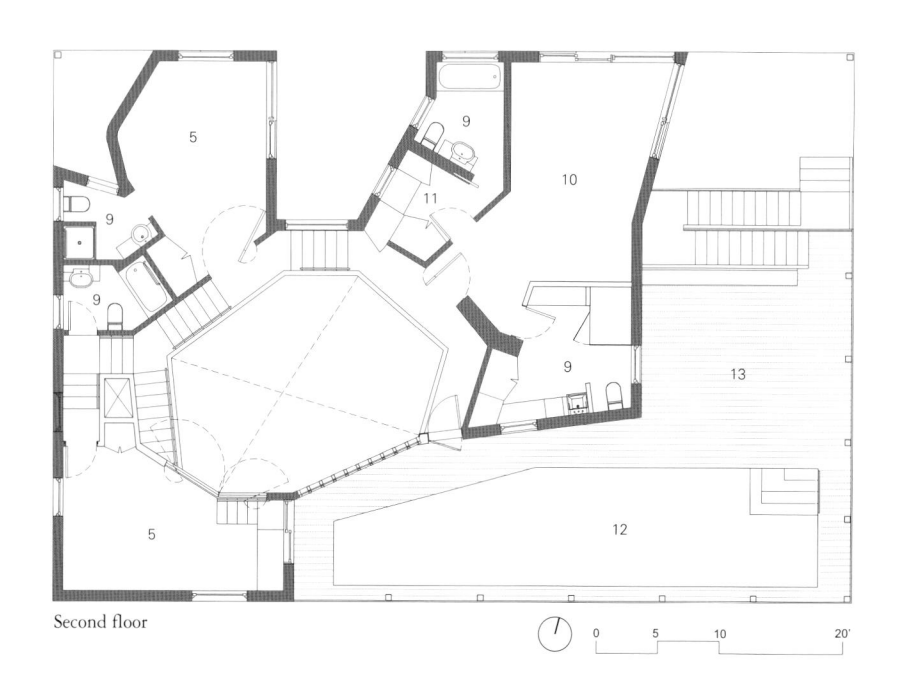

Second floor

II-62

View from deck on northeast

光に描かれた家
この線形をした木造のビーチ・ハウスのコンセプトは，敷地が画家ジャクソン・ポロックのアトリエに近いことから得た発想をもとに展開されている。幾つかの自由な形は，1949年の"セブン・イン・エイト"と題するポロックの絵に基づいてデザインした。屋内を湾と北側の大西洋の眺めに開放するためには，道路からのプライバシーを守るために，南側を閉ざすことが必要だった。

オープン・フレームのなかに内部のエネルギーを挟みこみ，射し込む陽光はストライプを描いて輝く。その白い光の縞模様は季節の推移と共に屈曲し，一日の循環に従ってダイナミックに内部空間を刻む。

木造のバルーン・フレーム構造は，海辺に沿って続く細い木片でつくられた砂丘のフェンスに似ている。ゲストルームが幾つか，2層吹抜けたリビングルームをぐるりと巡って配置され，そこからガレージの上のプールに出られる。この上階にあるプール・コートからは大西洋が見える。

Northeast corner: view toward dining room

Sketch: interior

Living room: looking from entrance toward east

View from dining room: deck on east

Roof terrace: looking north

Dining room: stairs to kitchen

Dining room: looking living room

Living room: looking west

II-65

2001-04 Nail Collector's House
Essex, New York, U.S.A.

Overlooking the expanse of Lake Champlain in the 19th Century town of Essex, this 1,200 sq. ft. house for a writer is sited on a former nail factory foundation. The owner has a collection of square head 19th Century nails gathered over the years on this site.

Windows correspond to the 24 chapters of Homer's *Odyssey* and are organized to project "Fingers of Light" into the interior volume. The main northeast wall has 14 windows; the southeast and southwest walls contain 5 windows, while the northwest wall is blank.

The largely open interior ascends counter-clockwise through a series of spaces pierced by the light of the windows. A "prow" thrust toward Lake Champlain completes this upward spiral of space.

White plaster walls, hickory floors and "cartridge brass" siding nailed in pattern over a wood frame create a tactile weathering for this structure, a poetic reinterpretation of the industrial history of the site and the pre-Civil War architecture of Essex.

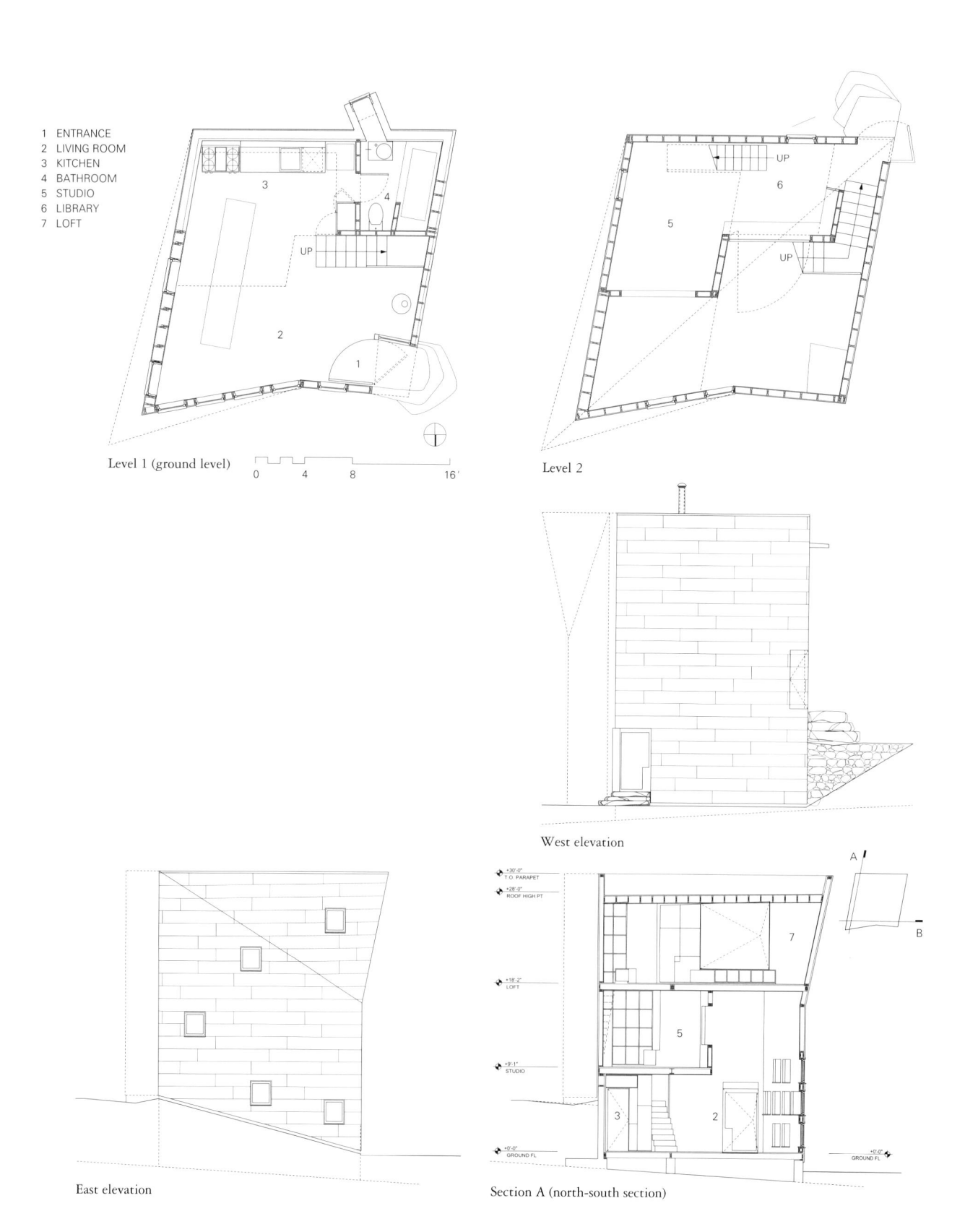

1 ENTRANCE
2 LIVING ROOM
3 KITCHEN
4 BATHROOM
5 STUDIO
6 LIBRARY
7 LOFT

Level 1 (ground level)

Level 2

West elevation

East elevation

Section A (north-south section)

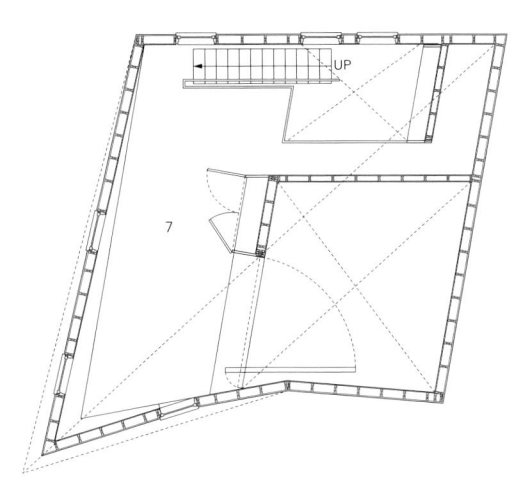

Level 3 (loft level)

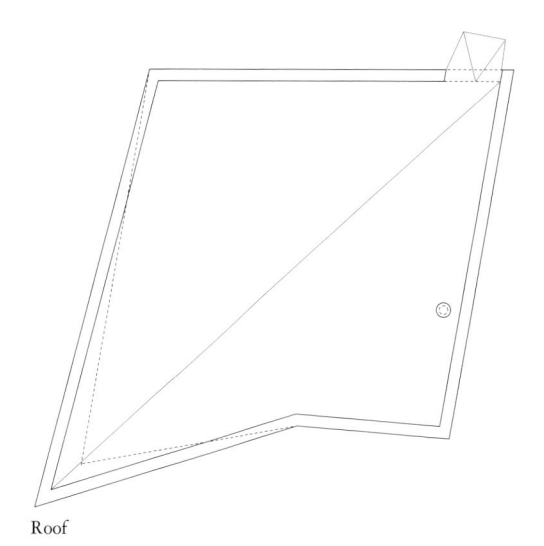

Roof

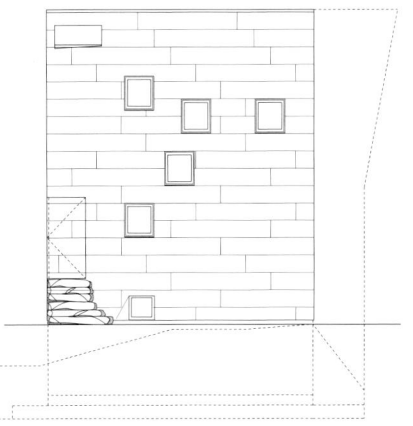

South elevation

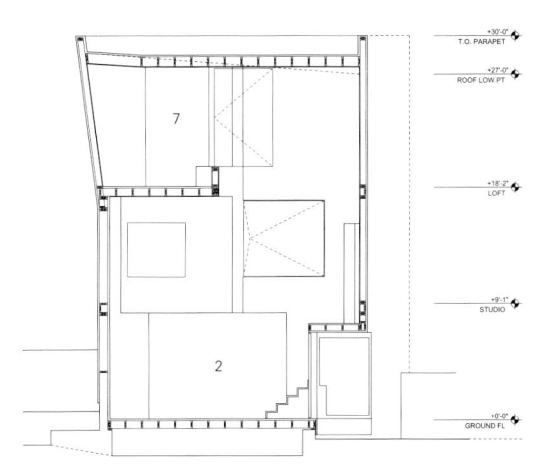

Section B (east-west section)

North elevation

釘収集家の家

ニューヨーク州北部地方にある,19世紀の町エセックス。シャンプレイン湖を見晴らす1,200平方フィートの住宅で,かつて釘をつくっていた工場跡の基礎の上に建てられている。著述家であるオーナーは,何年にも渡ってこの敷地で集めてきた,頭が四角い19世紀の釘のコレクションを持っている。

家の窓はホメロスの『オデュッセイア』の24の章に対応し,内部空間に"光の指"が差し込むように構成されている。正面にあたる北東の壁には14,南東と南西の壁には5つの窓があり,北西の壁に窓は無い。

大きく開放された内部は,窓から射し込む光にうがたれた空間を辿りながら時計と逆回りに上っていく。シャンプレイン湖に突き出た"舳先"が,この上昇する螺旋空間をしめくくる。

プラスターの白い壁,ヒッコリー材の床,そして木枠の上に模様を描いて釘打たれた"カートリッジ・ブラス"(薬莢に使われる真鍮)の下見板がつくる触感的な水切り勾配。ここでは,敷地にかつてあった工場と,独立戦争前のエセックスの建築の歴史が,詩的に翻訳し直されている。

Sketch: north elevation and plan

Northeast corner and plan

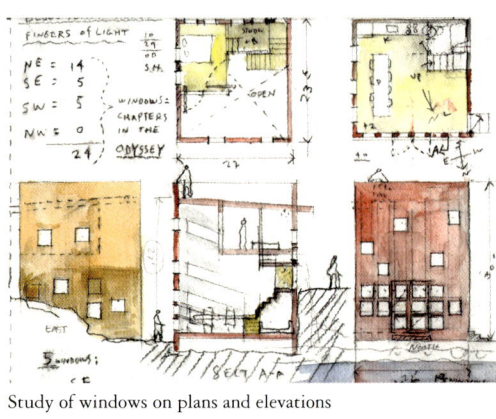

Study of windows on plans and elevations

View from east: Champlain Lake on right

II-68

Site plan

Entrance on northwest corner

II-69

Entrance on north

Level 1: kitchen (below) and studio and library (above)

Loft on level 3

View toward northeast corner of loft

Library on level 2: looking void over living room

Windows on north

Level 3: railing of stairs

II-71

2001-05 Turbulence House
New Mexico, U.S.A.

Sketch

Adjacent to adobe courtyard houses built by the artist Richard Tuttle, this small construction is sited atop a windy desert mesa. It's form, imagined like the tip of an iceberg indicating a much larger form below, allows turbulent wind to blow through the center. The artist's friend Kiki Smith calls it a "brooch pinned to the mesa".

The stressed skin and aluminum rib construction will be digitally prefabricated in Kansas City—then bolted together on site. P.V. cells covering the roof allow overflow power for the existing adobe constructions.

Snow view

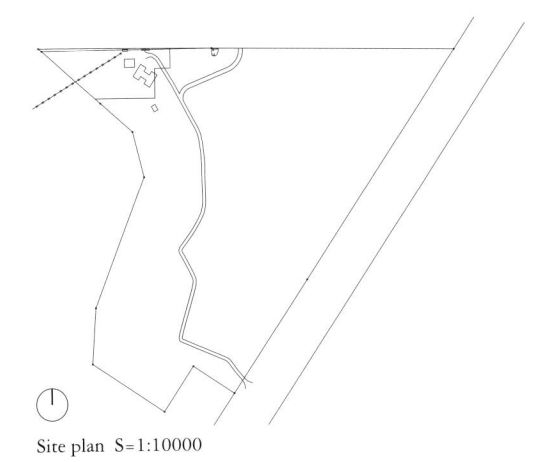

Site plan S=1:10000

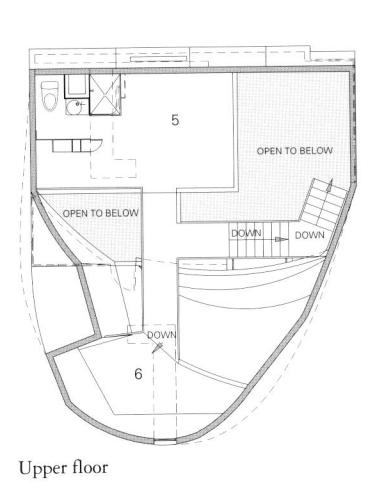

Upper floor

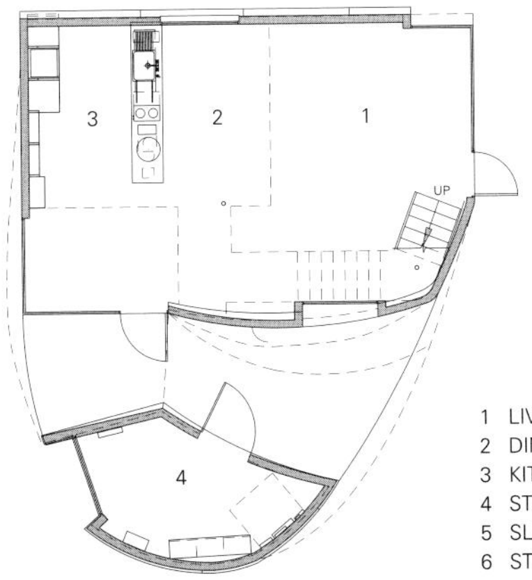

Lower floor S=1:200

1 LIVING ROOM
2 DINING ROOM
3 KITCHEN
4 STORAGE
5 SLEEPING LOFT/BATH
6 STUDY

View from south: structure is placed in desert

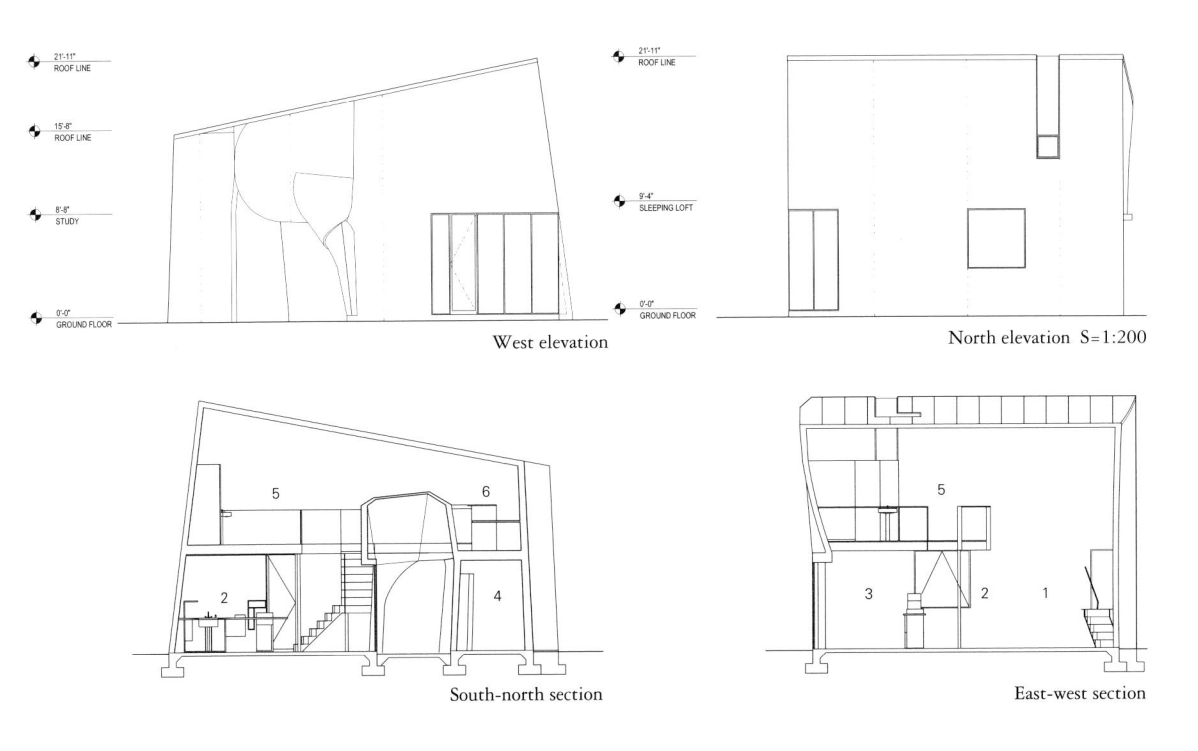

West elevation

North elevation S=1:200

South-north section

East-west section

Evening view: hollow of volume

Upper floor: looking sleeping loft with bath

Lower floor: view from living room toward kitchen/dining area

Living room: staircase to upper floor

タービュランス・ハウス
アーティストのリチャード・タトルが建てた日乾し煉瓦のコートヤード・ハウスに隣り合って建てられるこの小さな建物は、風が強い、砂漠のメサ（頂上が平らで周囲が崖になった台地）の頂上に置かれる。その下にもっと大きな形があることを暗示する氷山の先端を想わせるその形状は、荒れ狂う風にその真ん中を吹き抜けさせる。アーティストの友人であるキキ・スミスは、それを"メサに留めたブローチ"と呼んでいる。

モノコック構造とアルミのリブで構成された建物は、カンサス・シティでデジタル方式で造られたプレハブ部材を現場で組み立てる。屋根の光電池は、余剰電力を既存の日乾し煉瓦の建物に供与する。

2001-06 Swiss Residence
Washington D.C., U.S.A.

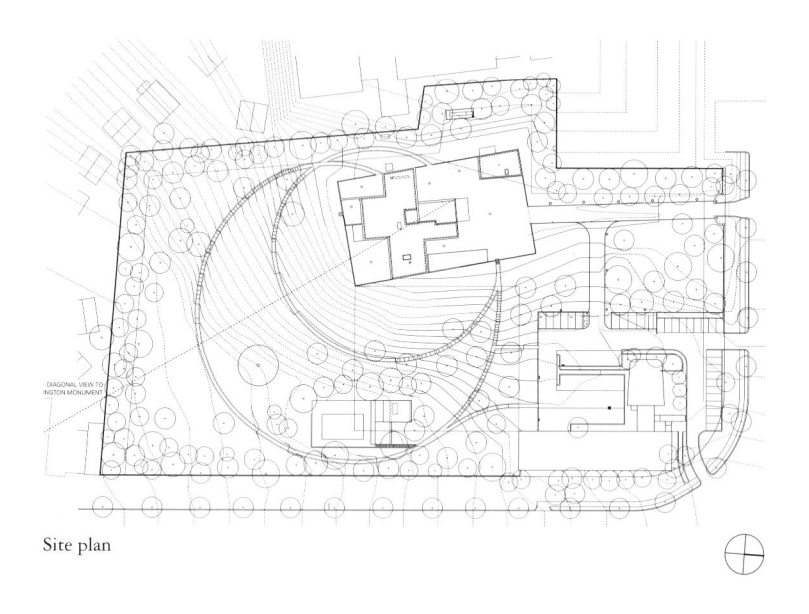

Site plan

The scheme placed first in the competition of ten Swiss-American team's designs for the replacement of the Washington D.C. residence of the Swiss Ambassador.

It is not only to be a private house but also a cultural gathering place on which standards and self-image of a country are measured.

Sited on a hill with a direct view through the trees to the Washington monument in the distance, a diagonal line of overlapping spaces drawn through a cruciform courtyard plan was the conceptual starting point. Official arrival spaces and ceremony spaces are connected along this diagonal line on the first level, while private living quarter functions are on the level above.

Materials are charcoal integral color concrete trimmed in local slate and sand-blasted structural glass planks.

Constructed according to Swiss "Minergie Standard", the south facades use passive solar energy. The roof is a "sedum" green roof with PVC panels.

The existing natural landscape will be clarified with new walkways and trees, while the plateau of the residence defines an arrival square: a reception courtyard and an herb garden with sub-floor wiring flexibilities.

スイス・レジデンス

ワシントンD.C.のスイス大使公邸を建て替えるために，スイス，アメリカ両国から選ばれた建築家10人によるコンペの1等入選案。

私邸であると同時に，スイスの国家水準とセルフイメージが試される文化的な集いの場所となる。

木立を抜けて真っ直ぐ前方にワシントン・モニュメントを望む丘に位置し，十字形の中庭型プランから引き出された折り重なる空間がつくる対角線が基本構想の出発点となった。公的な訪問客が到着する場と儀式用のスペースはこの対角線に沿って1階に並び，私的な生活空間は2階にある。

材料には，地元産のスレートで縁取りしたチャコール色のカラー・コンクリート，サンドブラストした構造用ガラス厚板を用いる。

スイスの省エネルギー基準に従って，南面にはパッシブソーラーを使用。塩化ビニル・パネルと，"シーダム(ベンケイソウ)"の緑色の屋根。

もとの自然景観は，新しい歩行路と木立で整え，建物の建つ台地は，訪問客が到着する広場である，レセプション・コートヤード，フレキシブルな第二の大地を持つハーブ園を明快に分けるだろう。

1 MAIN ENTRANCE HALL
2 DINING ROOM / RECEPTION AREA
3 SERVICE
4 HERB GARDEN
5 RECEPTION TERRACE
6 REFLECTING POOL
7 CARETAKER HOUSE
8 AMBASSADOR PRIVATE QUARTERS
9 GUEST ROOM
10 STAFF ROOM

First floor

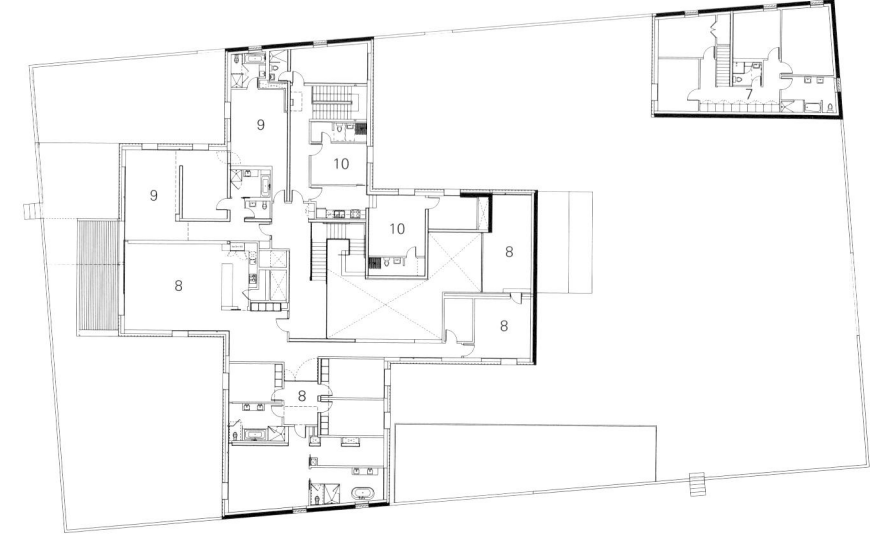

Second floor

View from southeast: house situated on a hill

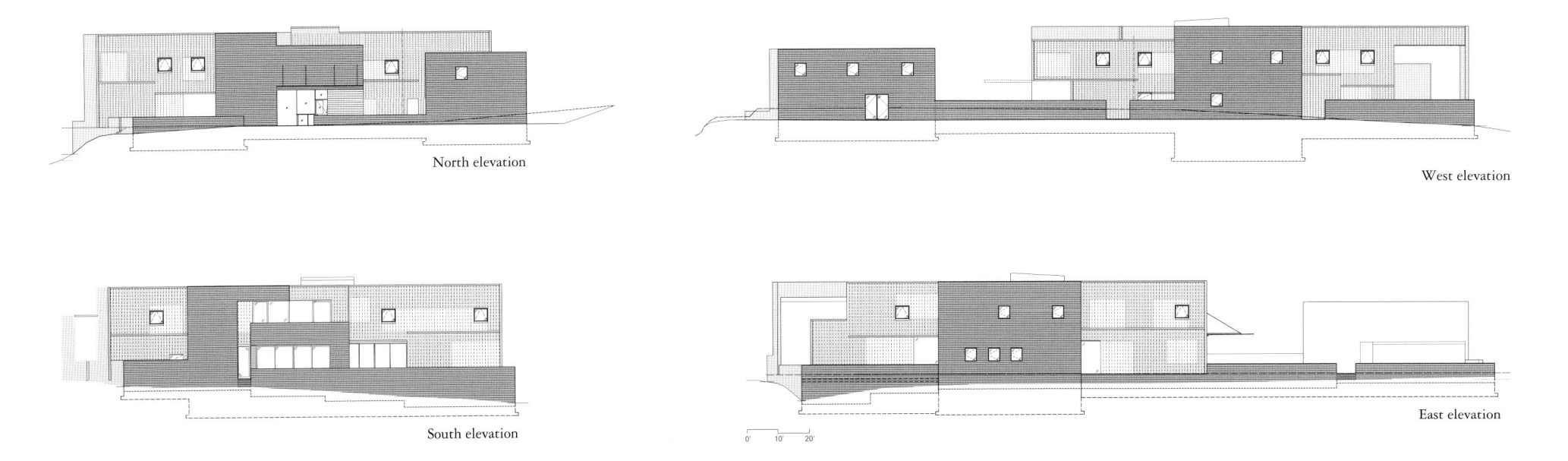

North elevation

West elevation

South elevation

East elevation

Southwest corner: view toward terrace enclosed by walls

East elevation facing reflecting pool

Entrance

Evening view from north:
entrance (right) and reflecting pool (left)

Main entrance hall: looking entrance

Main entrance hall: looking north

Reception area

Main entrance hall: view toward dining/reception area

Reception area

Reception area: reception terrace on right

II-81

Sketches: interior

Main entrance hall: staircase to second floor

Downward view of main entrance hall

Dining room

Staircase with skylight

Entry of private quarters on second floor

2002-05 Planar House
Phoenix, Arizona, U.S.A.

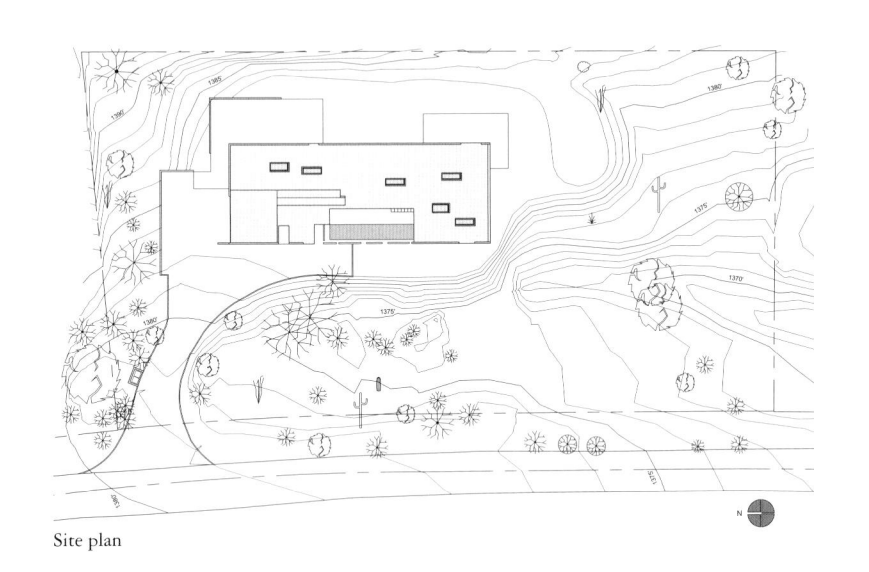

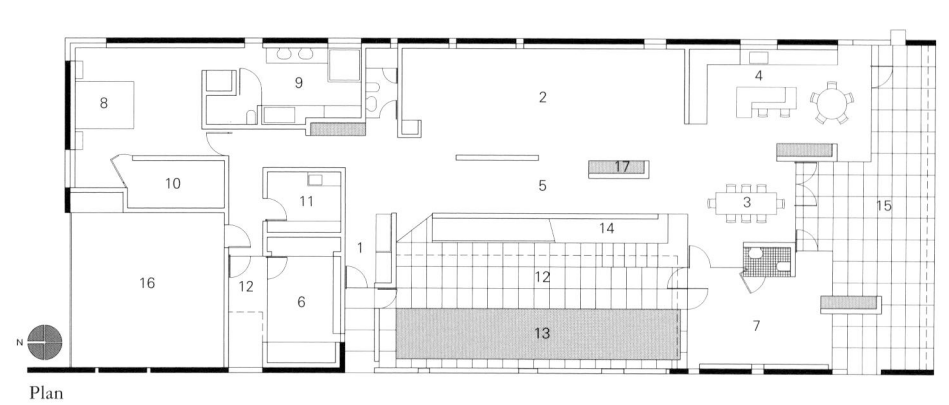

Site plan

Plan

1. ENTRANCE
2. LIVING ROOM
3. DINING AREA
4. KITCHEN
5. GALLERY
6. LIBRARY
7. STUDY
8. MASTER BEDROOM
9. BATHROOM
10. CLOSET
11. LAUNDRY
12. COURT
13. LAP POOL
14. RAMP
15. PORCH
16. GARAGE
17. COOLING POOL

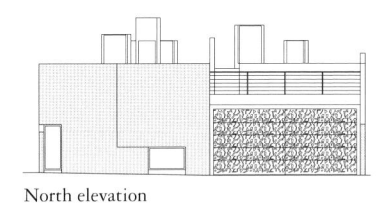

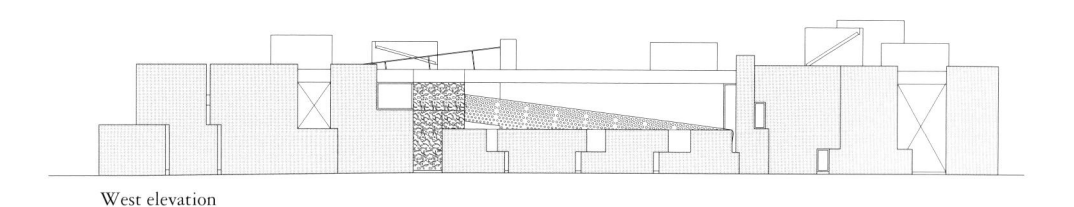

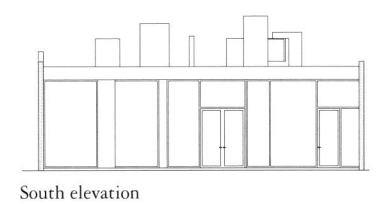

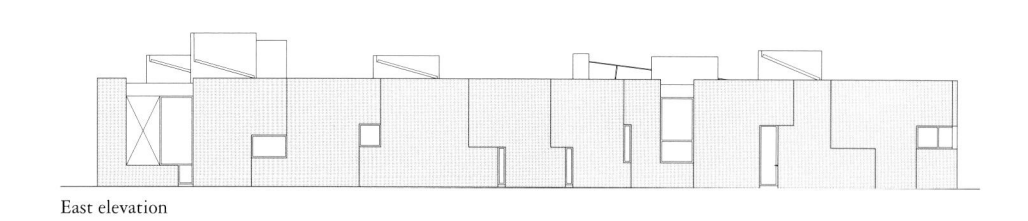

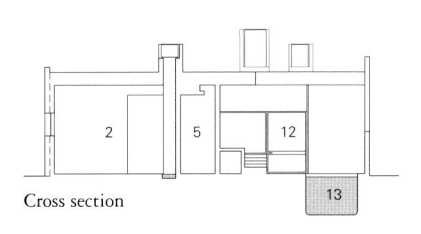

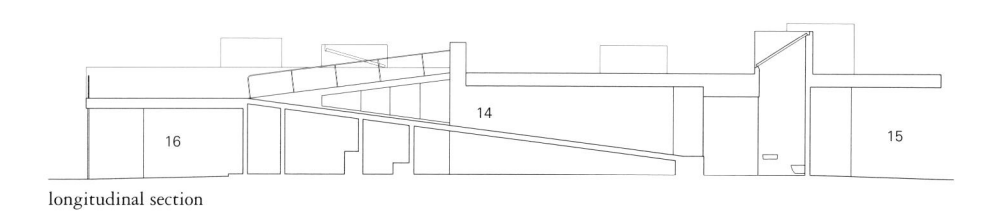

North elevation

West elevation

South elevation

East elevation

Cross section

longitudinal section

Sketch: court with pool

View from southwest: porch on south

Entrance

Court: ramp to rooftop (right) and pool (left)

II-85

Sited in Paradise Valley with a direct vista to Camelback Mountain, this house is to be a part of, and vessel for, a large contemporary art collection. Great 20th century works by Bruce Nauman, Robert Ryman and Jannis Kounellis are part of the collection which includes important video artworks.

Constructed of tilt-up concrete walls, the nature of the walls merges with the simple orthogonal requirements of the interiors for art.

Shape extensions and light and air chimneys connected to cooling pools articulate the planar geometry. From a courtyard experienced at the entry of sequence, a ramp leads to a rooftop sculpture garden—a place of silence and reflection.

West elevation: court is behind low walls

East elevation: tilt-up concrete walls

Southeast corner: detail of concrete and glazed walls

Entrance

View from entrance hall toward south: living room (left) and gallery (center)

Skylight along wall: cooling pool at the bottom

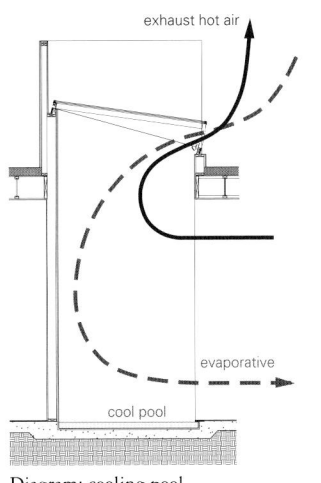

Diagram: cooling pool

プラナー・ハウス
パラダイス・ヴァレーにある敷地からはキャメルバック山が真っ直ぐ前方に望める。膨大なコンテンポラリーアート・コレクションの一部であると共にその器となる住宅である。ブルース・ノーマン,ロバート・ライマン,ジャニス・コルネリスの素晴らしい20世紀美術が,重要なビデオアート作品を含めたコレクションの一部を占めている。

ティルトアップ工法で建てられた壁は,美術作品の展示に必要な,四角形の簡素な内部空間に同化する。

形の広がりと,クーリング・プールに続く光と外気を通す筒状の空間が,平面的な形態に明快なリズムをつける。内部空間が展開してゆく起点となる中庭から,静かに思いに浸る場所である屋上の彫刻庭園までスロープが続いている。

Sketch: skylights and walls

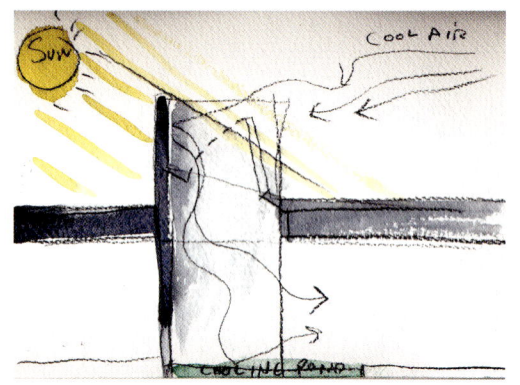

Concept sketch: cooling pool

View from study toward dining area and kitchen

Living room: looking south

II-88

View from kitchen toward study: court (right) and porch (left)

Library

Master bedroom

Master bedroom

Bathroom

II-89

2005- Sun Slice House
Lake Garda, Italy

View from approach

Model: view from northwest

This weekend house on Lake Garda for an Italian lighting company owner and his family is organized to frame slices of sunlight. While the owner's profession revolves around artificial light, slices of natural light and their change in space throughout the day and year is the focus of the house. While most elevations are simple rectangles strategically sliced and cut for the play of light within, the north facade is made of glass with views of Lake Garda. In order to emphasize the bends and changes in the strips of sunlight, simple cubic volumes form the basic building geometry. These are loosely joined in topological sheet rubber-like geometry, which also inscribes wind-protected courts on both sides of the house. Changes of season and weather allow different courtyard opportunities.

The steel frame and concrete structure is skinned with an alloy of copper, steel, chromium, and nickel, which weathers to a leathery red color. Interiors are white plaster with terrazzo floors on the ground level while bamboo floors cover the second. Natural ventilation and geothermal heating and cooling are part of the energy plan.

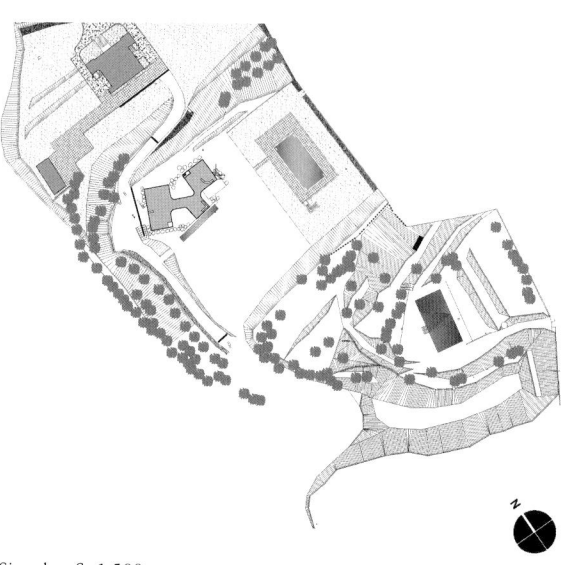

Site plan S=1:500

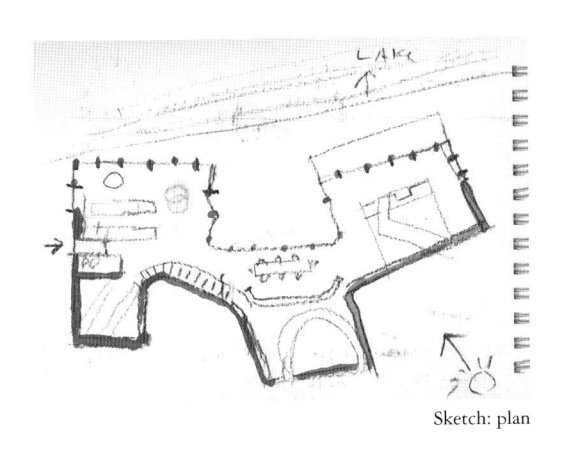

Sketch: plan

First floor

Ground floor

Lower floor S=1:150

1 ENTRANCE
2 KITCHEN
3 DNING ROOM
4 STUDIO
5 LIVING ROOM
6 GARAGE
7 MASTER BEDROOM
8 MASTER BATHROOM
9 BEDROOM

Sections S=1:150

サン・スライス・ハウス

イタリアの照明会社のオーナーとその家族のためのガルダ湖に面するこの週末住宅は、陽光を細長く切り取って内部に採り込むように構成されている。人工照明を中心に展開しているオーナーの仕事から、自然光の切片と、一日や一年を通してのその変化をデザインの焦点とした。

立面の大半は、光の戯れをその内部に薄くあるいは広く、戦略的に切り取るために単純な長方形をしているが、北面はガラスで構成され、ガルダ湖が見晴らせる。

細長く切り取られた陽光の曲折と変化を強調するために、単純な立方体が建物の基本形をかたちづくる。この基本形は、ゴム製のシートを思わせるトポロジカルな幾何学形態と緩やかに合体し、家の両側に風から守られた中庭を刻み出す。季節や天候の変化は、さまざまな雰囲気の中庭を楽しませてくれる。

鉄骨フレームとコンクリートの躯体は、銅、鋼、クロム、ニッケルの合金で覆われ、革のような赤褐色に風化する。内部は白いプラスター塗りの壁と天井に、1階はテラゾー、2階は竹を敷き詰めた床である。自然換気と地熱利用の暖冷房がエネルギー計画の主要素となる。

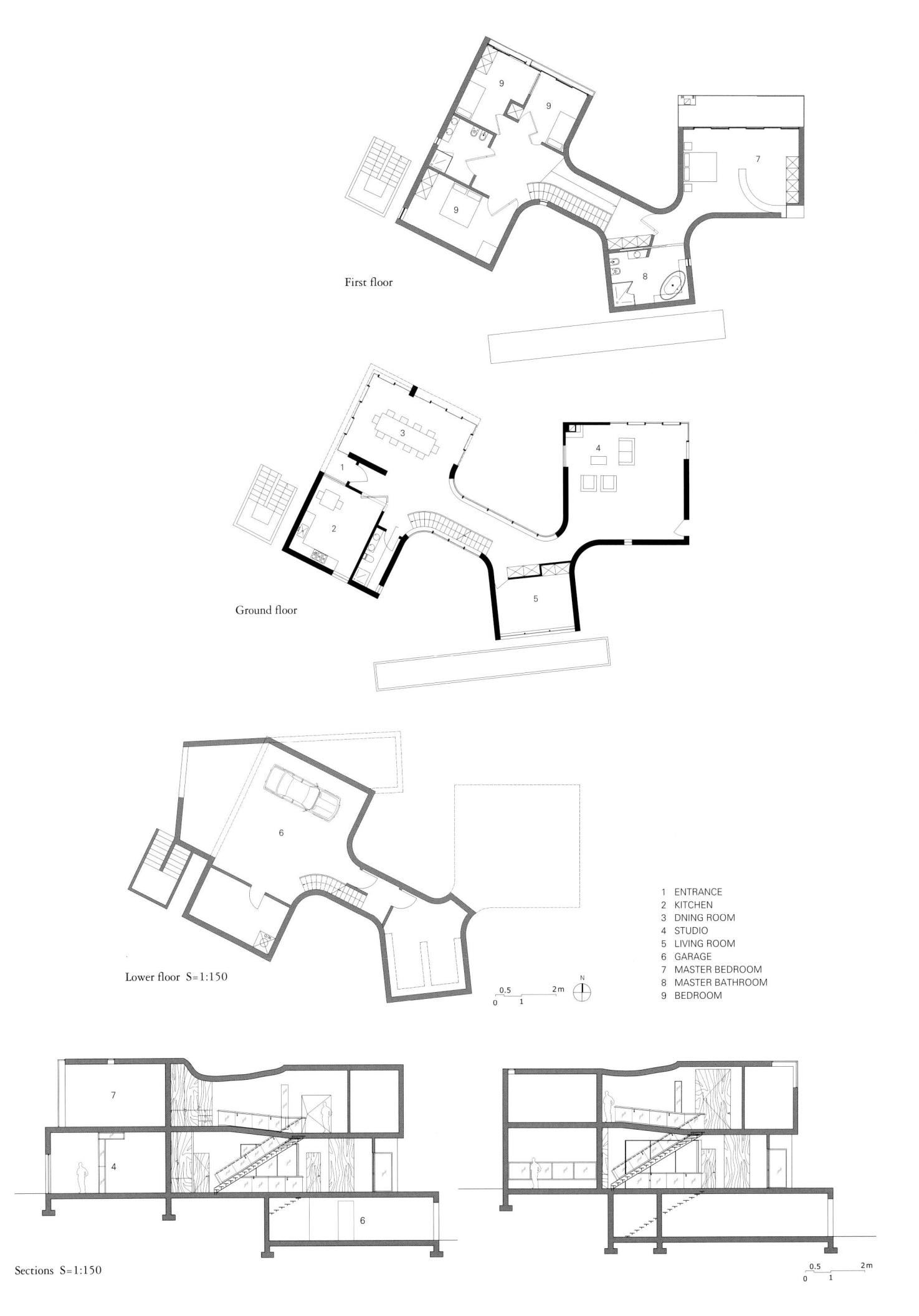

Overall view from south

Concept sketch

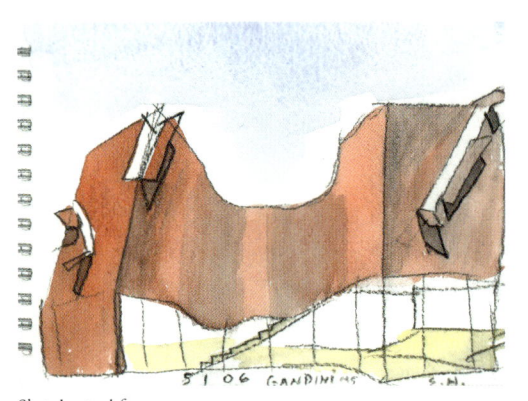

Sketch: steel frame

East elevation

North elevation

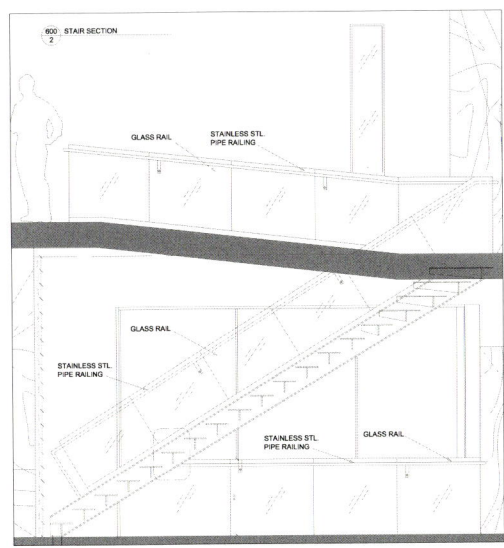

Sectional detail of staircase

Staircase

10 am

10 am

12 am

12 am

Inteiror model: sunlight through slit

II-93

2008-12 Daeyang Gallery & House
Seoul, South Korea

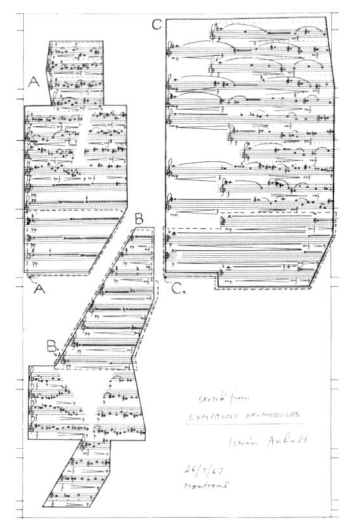

"Symphony of Modules"

1 LIVING ROOM
2 DINING ROOM
3 KITCHEN
4 MEETING ROOM
5 MASTER BEDROOM
6 LIBRARY/BEDROOM
7 EVENT SPACE
8 FOYER/ENTRANCE
9 GALLERY
10 GARAGE
11 STORAGE
12 MECHANICAL
13 HOUSE KEEPER ROOM
14 REFLECTING POOL

Symphony of Modules

The private house and gallery is sited in the hills of the Kangbuk section of Seoul, Korea. The project was designed as an experiment parallel to a research studio on "the architectonics of music". The basic geometry of the building is inspired by a 1967 sketch for a music score by the composer Istvan Anhalt, "Symphony of Modules," discovered in a book by John Cage titled "Notations".

Three pavilions; one for entry, one residence, and one guest house, appear to push upward from a continuous gallery level below. A sheet of water establishes the plane of reference from above and below.

The idea of space as silent until activated by light is realized in the cutting of 55 skylight strips in the roofs of the three pavilions. In each of the pavilions, 5 strips of clear glass allow sunlight to turn and bend around the inner spaces, animating them according to the time of day and season. Proportions are organized around the series 3, 5, 8, 13, 21, 34, 55.

Views from within the pavilions are framed by a connecting reflecting pool which is bracketed by gardens that run perpendicular to the skylight strips. In the base of the reflecting pool, strips of glass lenses bring dappled light to the white plaster walls and white granite floor of the gallery below.

A visitor arrives through a bamboo formed garden wall at the entry court, after opening the front door and ascending a low stair. He or she can turn to see the central pond at eye level and take in the whole of the three pavilions floating on their own reflections.

The interiors of the pavilions are red and charcoal stained bamboo with the skylights cutting through a red bamboo ceiling. Exteriors are a rain skin of specially treated brass, which ages naturally within the landscape.

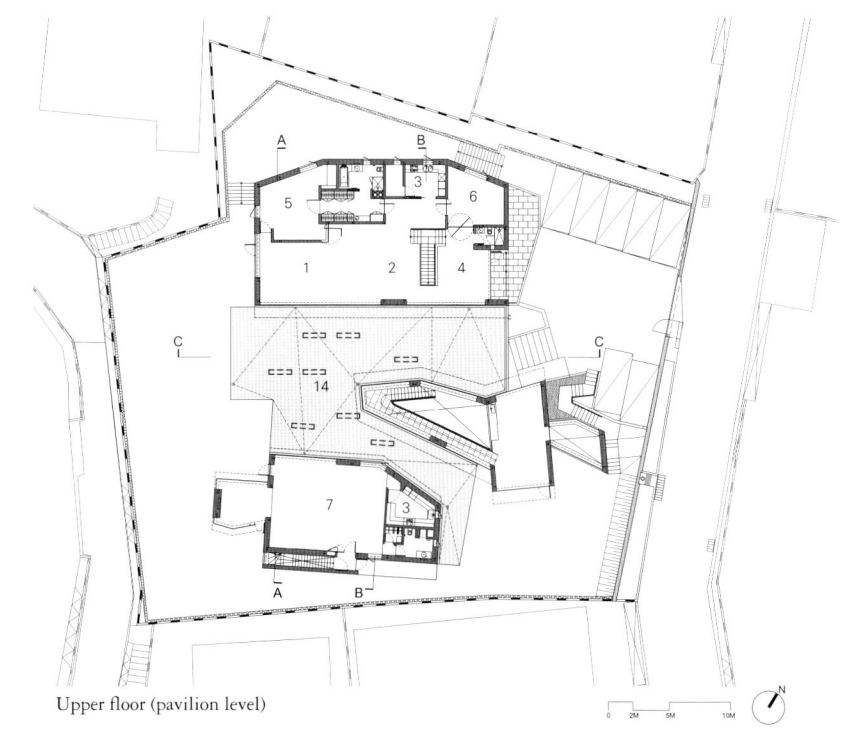

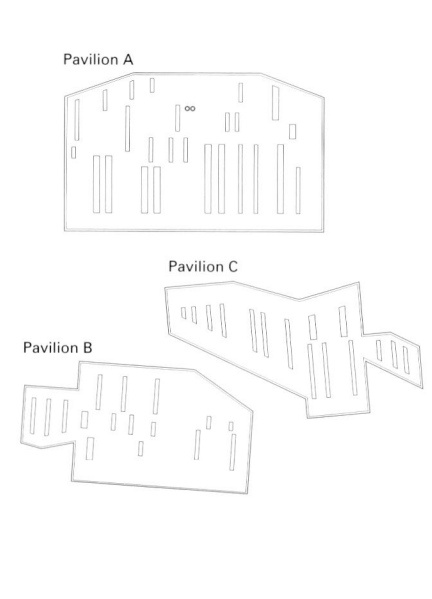

Lower floor (gallery level) S=1:600

Upper floor (pavilion level)

Roof

デヤン・ギャラリー＆ハウス
[Symphony of Modules]
このプライベートハウスとギャラリーは韓国ソウルの江北区の丘に位置している。プロジェクトは「音楽の建築学」と題された研究スタジオと併行して行われた実験のために計画された。建築の基本ジオメトリーは，作曲家イシュトヴァン・アンハルトが1967年に残した譜面のスケッチ"Symphony of Modules"からインスピレーションを受けている。このスケッチはジョン・ケージの『Notations』と題された一冊の本に収録されていた。

エントランス，住宅，ゲストハウスからなる三つの棟は，連続するギャラリーのある下階レベルから上に向かって押し上げられるかのように見える。それぞれの水盤は上下階のレファレンスとしての役割を果たす。

静寂な空間が光によって躍動を始める。この考え方は3棟の屋根に設けられた55本のスカイライトの切れ込みによって実現される。いずれの棟も5本の細長い透明ガラスを通して，太陽光が内部空間に沿って回転し，あるいは曲がりながら差し込み，一日の時間や季節を通して空間に生気を与えている。空間のプロポーションは3，5，8，13，21，34，55と続く級数によって構成されている。

細長いスカイライトに対して直交する庭に囲まれた，棟と連続するリフレクティング・プールが，棟の中から見える眺望を構成する。リフレクティング・プールの底にある細長いガラスレンズは，まだら模様の光を下階ギャラリーの白いプラスター壁と白い御影石の床に落とす。

来訪者はエントランス・コートで竹で型取られた庭の壁をくぐり，フロント・ドアを開いて，低い階段を上がる。振り返ると視線の先には中央の池が広がり，3棟の建築が水面に自ら反射させながら漂うのに気がつくだろう。

各々の棟のインテリアには赤もしくは濃灰に染められた竹が使用され，赤い竹製の天井の切れ込みにはスカイライトが覗く。真鍮の外壁には雨に濡れたような特殊加工が施され，時間とともに周囲の景観に馴染む。

East elevation

South elevation

West elevation

North elevation S=1:300

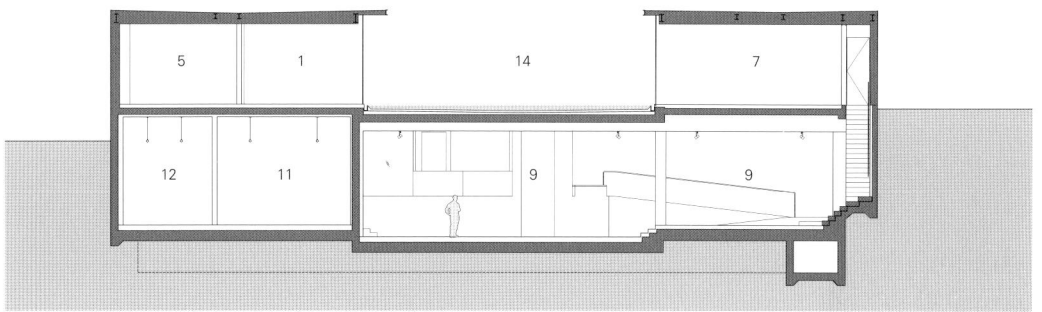

Section A-A

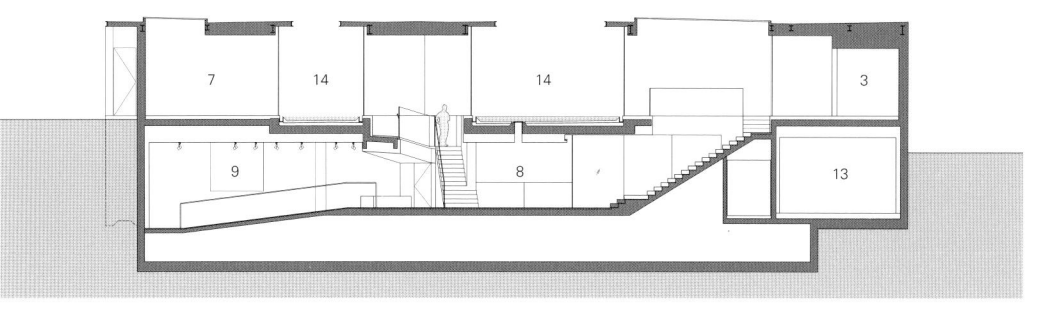

Section B-B

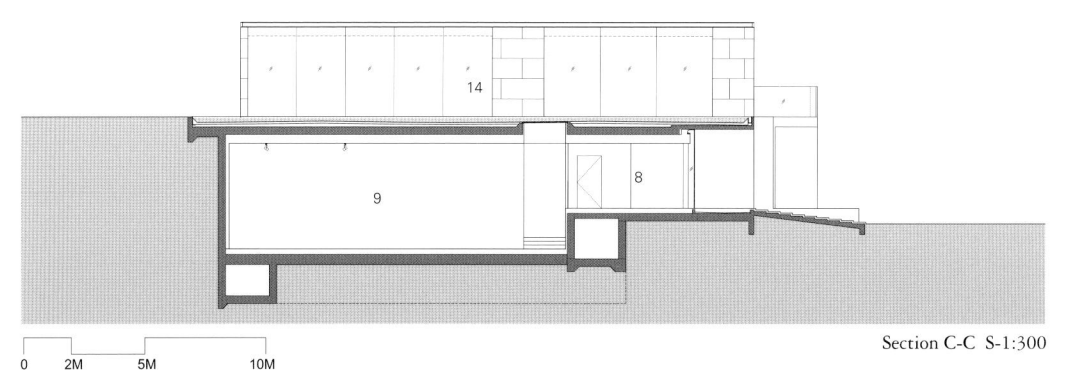

Section C-C S=1:300

Entrance: Pavilion C (left) and Pavilion A (right)

Entrance gate

Fountain at entrance

Door handle: shape of reflecting pool

II-96

Reflecting pool: view from southwest

View from Pavilion A: Pavilion C (left) and Pavilion B (right)

View from east: Pavilion B (left) and Pavilion C (right)

Lower floor, gallery on south: view toward ramp and entrance

Gallery on south: staircase to Pavilion B on upper floor

Pavilion C: view toward northeast. Entrance/foyer on lower floor

Pavilion C: view toward west

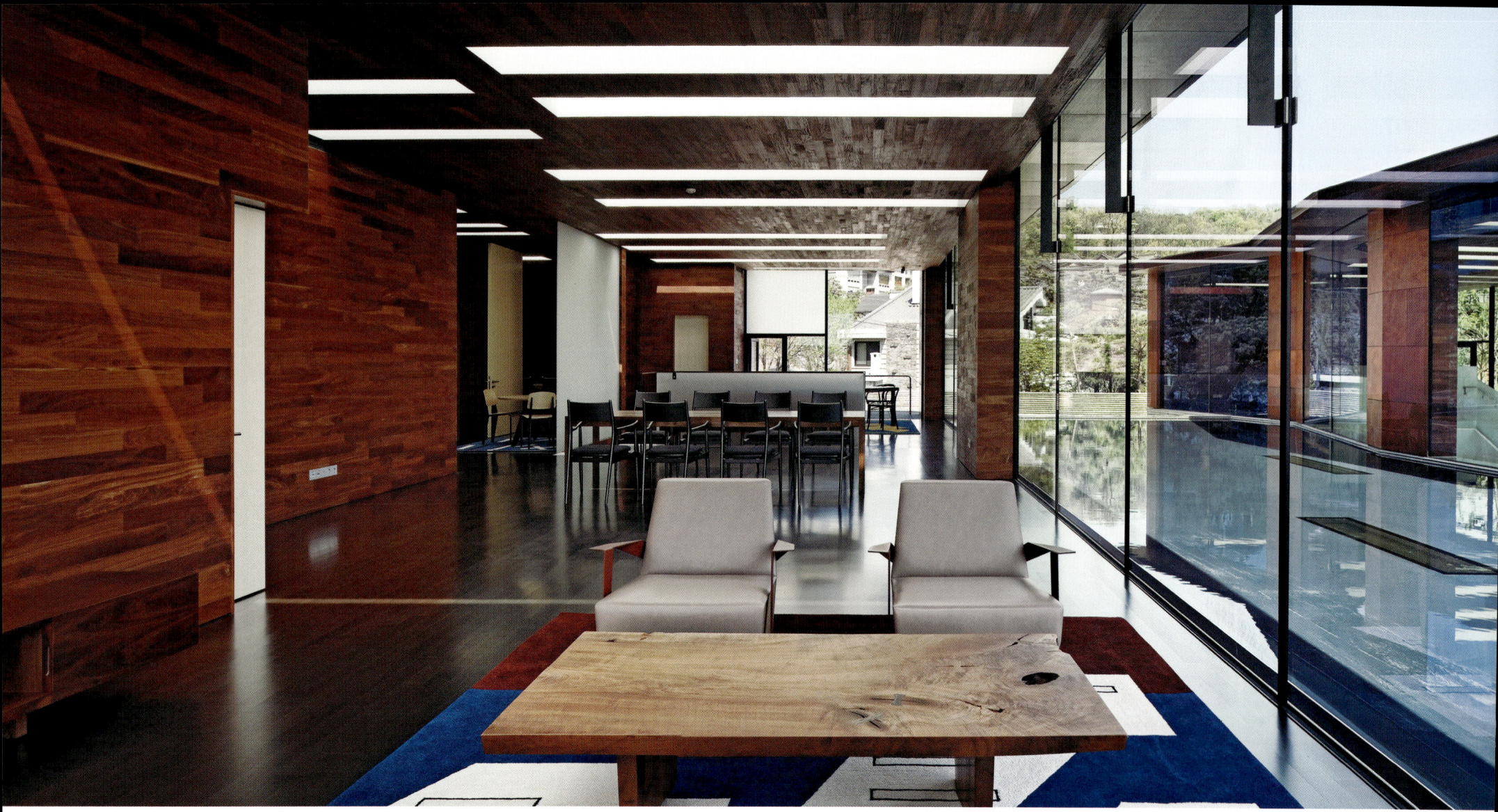

Pavilion A: view from living room toward dining room

Pavilion A: view toward Pavilion C (left) and Pavilion B (right)

Pavilion A: cabinet at meeting room. Staircase to gallery on lower floor is behind

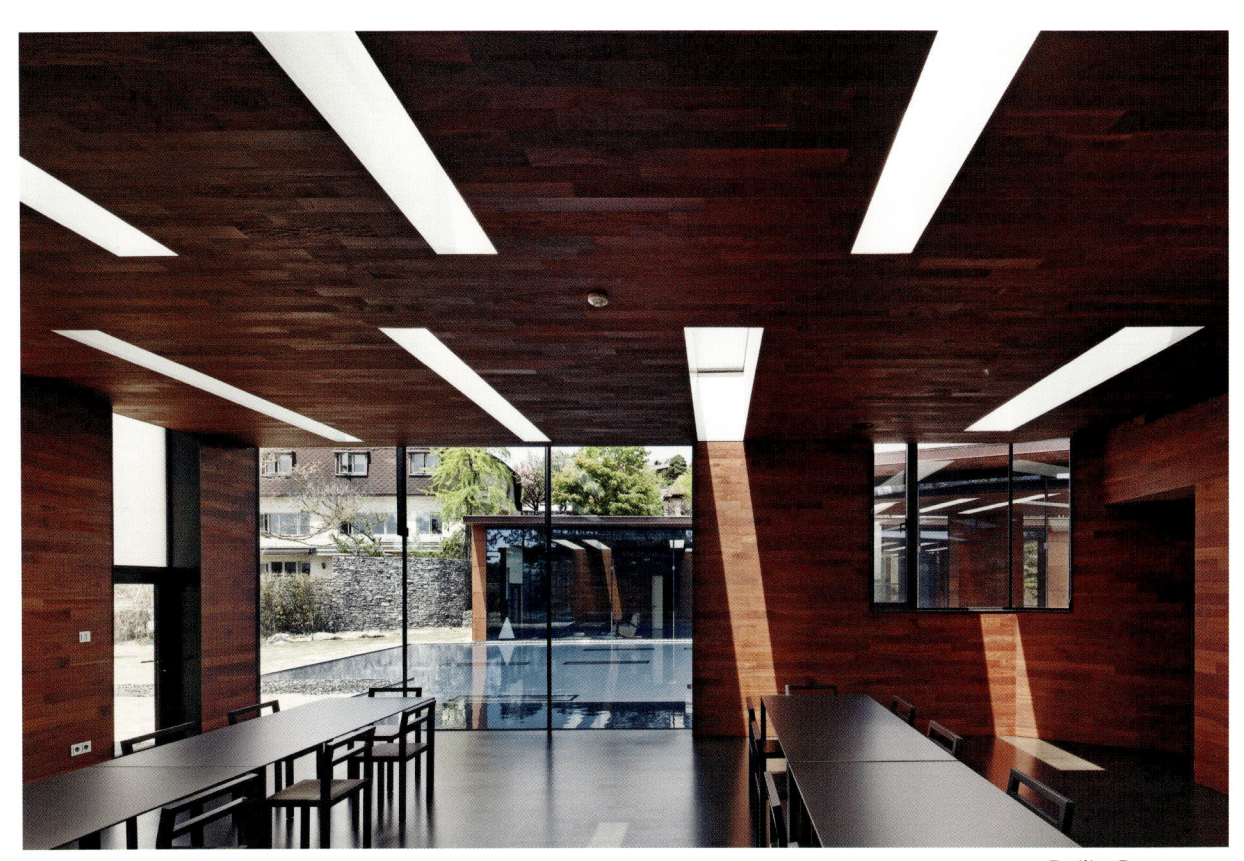

Pavilion B: event space

Pavilion B: glazed floor at west end

Pavilion B: event space. Looking west

II-101

"What pressures specific to the twentieth century does the combination of programs impose on architectural form? Concentration of many social activities within an architectural form distend and warp a pure building type. Certain previously neglected forms of associations have been wrenched together in the modern city so as to generate buildings which might stand as an anti-typology, if examined under current theoretical preoccupations. Building functions are mixed, disparate uses combined; these structures are "Hybrid Buildings" with respect to use. Although there are examples of combined function buildings throughout history, Hybrid Buildings developed most rapidly in the twentieth century. The modern city has acted as fertilizer for the growth of architectures from the homogeneous to the heterogeneous in regard to use. Urban densities and evolving building techniques have affected the mixing of functions, piling one atop another, defying critics who contend that a building should "look like what it is.""

—Steven Holl and Joseph Fenton
Hybrid Buildings, Pamphlet Architecture 11, 1984.

In the 21st century, what is the potential of Hybrid Buildings? Certainly the hyper-urbanization of cities in China, such as Shenzhen, Beijing and Chengdu, can act as catalyst incubators for new and experimental architectural types. These urban circumstances provoke unorthodox combinations and particular ideas related to specific places. In the first decades of the 21st century, China is experiencing the most radical migration from rural to urban sites in human history. Six hundred million people are in the process of moving into urban places. Instead of developers building huge, bland apartment buildings without service programs or public space, new building types are needed.

These new hybrid types can shape public space. Urban porosity is a key intention for large hybrid buildings with the aim of pedestrian oriented urban places. Each new public space formed by hybrid buildings contains living, working, recreation and cultural facilities. These new pedestrian sectors eliminate the need for automobile transfer across the city. They become localized "social condensers" for new communities.

Sections of Hybrid buildings take precedent over the planimetric. As urbanists and architects of metropolitan densities we must think first of building sections for the qualities of sunlight

「20世紀という特別な時代に，建築の形態は複合的プログラムによって，どのような強制を受けるようになったのか？　建築形態内部では様々な社会活動が集中し，純粋なビルディング・タイプを拡張し，包含する。現在の理論的命題という観点によると，かつては注意の払われることがなかった特定の組織形態が近代都市では捻れるように一体化し，ともすればタイポロジーを無視して存在する建築を生み出してきたことが分かる。建築の機能は複合的なものとなり，本質的に異なる利用形態がひとつに結びつけられる。「ハイブリッド・ビルディング」とは，利用形態に即したこれらの構造体のことである。歴史上，確かに複合的機能を組み合わせた建築は存在してきた。一方で，20世紀を中心に急速に発達してきた建築がハイブリッド・ビルディングである。現代の都市は均質的空間から異質的空間へと指向する。利用形態に即した建築の発展にとって，この時代は発展の良き土壌であった。都市の過密と建設技術の発展は，機能の融合に作用し続けてきた。これらの機能がひとつずつ積み重ねられることで，『建築とはそれ自身の表明である』と論ずる批評家を拒絶してきたのだ。」

—スティーヴン・ホール及びジョセフ・フェントン
『ハイブリッド・ビルディング』，Pamphlet Architecture 11, 1984年

21世紀のハイブリッド・ビルディングの可能性とは何か？　確かに深圳，北京，成都といった中国都市群の超近代化は，新しい実験的な建築のプロトタイプを促す孵化器の触媒としての役割がある。これらの都市環境が異端を組み合わせ，その場所に関する固有の発想を喚起してきたのだ。21世紀の初めの10年間，中国は農村部から都市部へと，歴史上最も急激な人口の流入を経験してきた。現在では6億人という人口が，都市部へと流入し続けている。サービス・プログラムやパブリック・スペースのない，巨大で退屈な開発会社の集合住宅の代わりに，新しいビルディング・タイプが求められている。

新しいハイブリッド・タイプがパブリック・スペースをつくり出す。アーバン・ポロシティとは，歩行者を中心とした都市空間，巨大なハイブリッド・ビルディングの中核となる概念である。ハイブリッド・ビルディングが構成する各々の新しいパブリック・スペースには，居住空間，オフィス，レクリエーション，及び文化施設が内包される。これらの新しい歩行者のセクターは，自動車で都市を移動する必要性を排除する。これらは新しいコミュニティのための，土地に根差した「社会的凝縮器」である。

ハイブリッド・ビルディングでは，断面が平面に対して優先する。過密した大都市の都市計画家や建築家として，十分な太陽光と対角線方向の動線力学のために，まず建築の断面を検討する必要がある。近代の都市の生

3 Housing and Hybrid Buildings
ハウジングとハイブリッド・ビルディング

Sliced Porosity Block (under construction)

and the dynamics of diagonal sectional movement. The old conditions of linear perspective (from planimetric projections) disappear behind us as modern urban life presents multiple horizons and multiple vanishing points. The further affirmation of the diagonal and the vertical in new spatial experience is the challenge of 21st century metropolitan density. Hybrid Buildings may be super green architecture utilizing geothermal and solar energy, water recycling and micro climate vegetation.

Freedom of invention is a particular potential of hybrid buildings. Unprecedented ideas may drive the design of new building types. In certain ways, these new buildings might illuminate the unique character of the site and city they arise in.

In summary, Hybrid Buildings today have the following potentials:

- 21st century cities as incubators
- Public space formation
- Programmatic juxtapositions
- Living/Working/Recreating and Cultural social condensers
- Dynamics of section
- Super green architecture
- Freedom of new concepts

All these aspects characterize the positive path of Hybrid types in the creation of inspiring and active new urban spaces.

Steven Holl

活が複合的な水平面と，複合的な消失点を提供すると共に，(平面への投影による)直線的パースペクティブといった旧来の方法は我々の背後へと消失する。対角線と垂直線といった，新しい空間経験へのさらなる是認は，過密した21世紀の大都市が取り組まなければならない挑戦である。ハイブリッド・ビルディングは地熱，太陽光，再利用水，微気候の植栽を利用した，スーパーグリーンな建築ともなりうるだろう。

自由な発想は，ハイブリッド・ビルディングの潜在的可能性である。かつてない発想が新しい建築の類型を生み出すきっかけとなる。確かにこれらの新しい建築は，建築の敷地と都市の持つ独特の性格に，豊かな彩りを与えるだろう。

要約すると今日のハイブリッド・ビルディングには，次のような潜在性がある。

——21世紀の都市の孵化器
——パブリック・スペースの形成
——プログラムの併置的関係性
——居住／オフィス／レクリエーション／社会的文化的凝縮器
——断面の力学
——スーパーグリーンな建築
——新しいコンセプトへの自由

これらの側面は全て，新しい都市空間の創造性を積極的に触発するという点で，ハイブリッド・タイプへの道を切り開くものである。

(スティーヴン・ホール)

1999-2003 **Simmons Hall**
Massachusetts Institute of Technology
Cambridge, Massachusetts, U.S.A.

Overall view from southwest

South elevation (right)

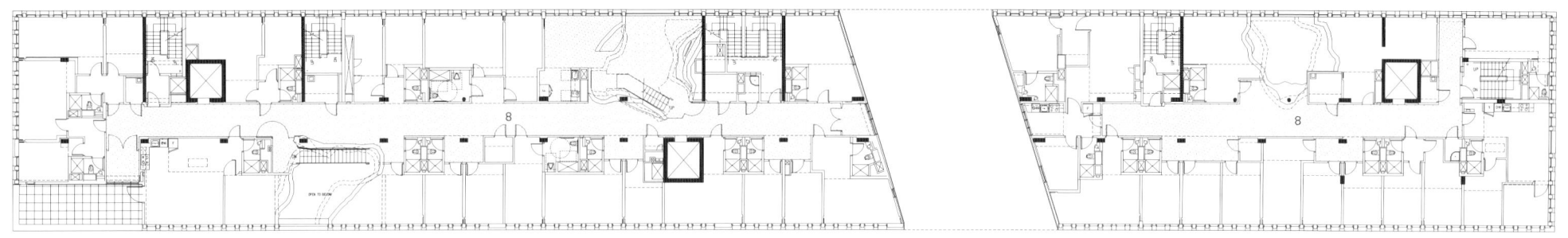

Fourth floor

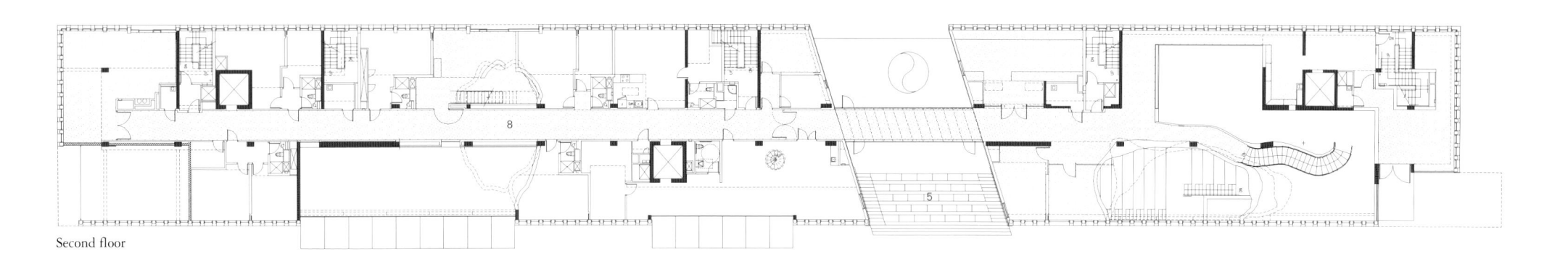

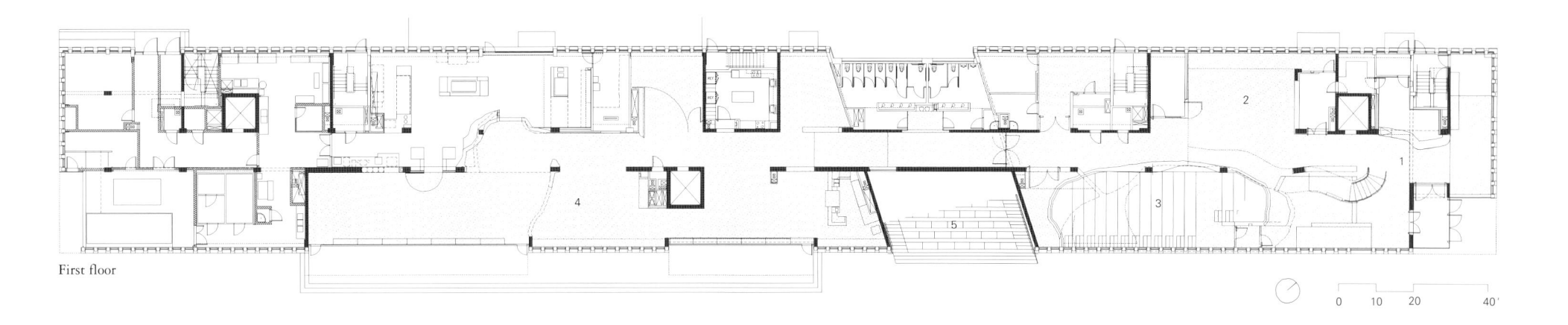

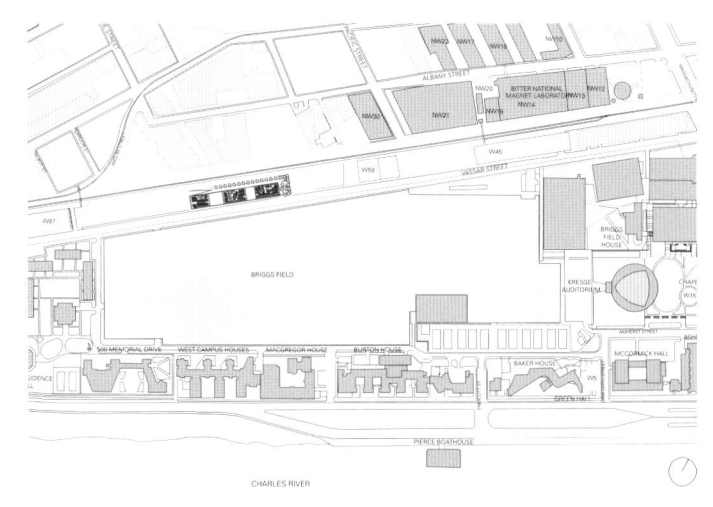

Second floor

First floor

Site plan

Concept

The 350-bed residence is envisioned as part of the city form and campus form with a concept of "Porosity" along Vassar Street. It is a vertical slice of a city ten stories tall and 330 feet long. The Urban Concept provides amenities to students within the dormitory such as a 125-seat theater, as well as a night cafe. House dining is on street level, like a street front restaurant with a special awning and outdoor tables. The corridors connecting the rooms are like streets (11 feet wide) which happen upon urban experiences. As in Aalto's Baker House, the hallway can be more like a public place, a lounge.

The Sponge concept for the new Undergraduate Residence Hall transforms a porous building morphology via a series of programmatic and bio-technical functions.

The overall building mass has five large scale openings. These roughly correspond to main entrances, view corridors, and the main outdoor activity terraces of the dormitory connected to programs such as the gymnasium.

The next scale of opening creates vertical porosity in the block with a ruled surface system freely connected to sponge prints, plan to section. These large, dynamic openings (roughly corresponding to the "houses" in the dorm) are the lungs of the building bringing natural light down and moving air up through the section.

The "PerfCon" structure is a unique de-

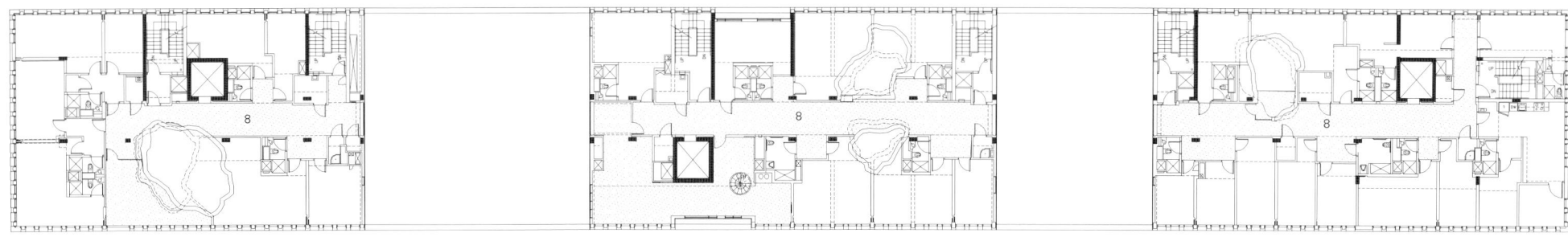

Ninth floor

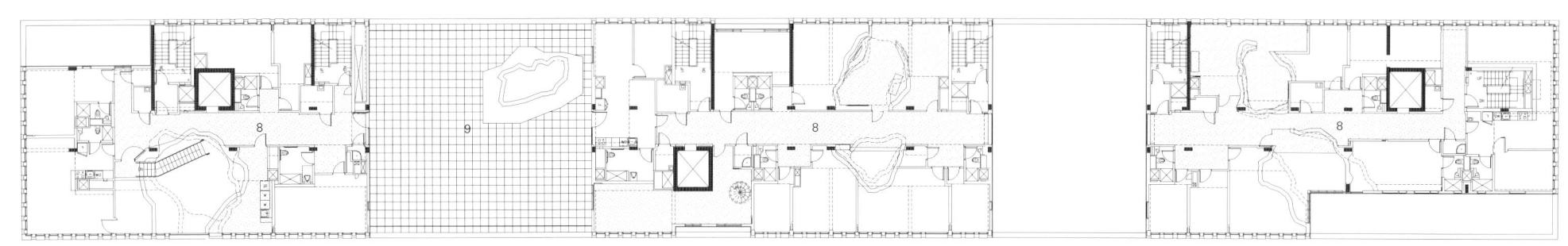

Eighth floor

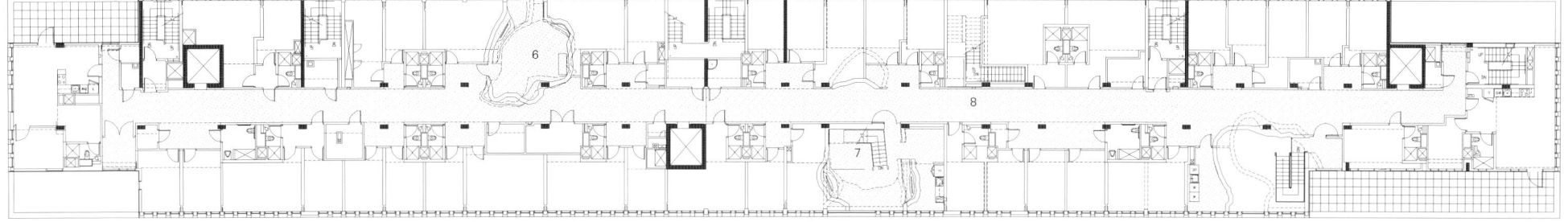

Sixth floor

sign, allowing for maximum flexibility and interaction. Each of the dormitory's single rooms has nine operable windows over 2 feet x 2 feet in size. The 18 feet depth of the wall naturally shades out the summer sun, while allowing the low angled winter sun in to help heat the building. In the deep setting of the numerous windows color is applied to the head and jamb creating identity for each of the ten "houses" within the overall building. The night light from the 9-window rooms will be magical and exciting.

Foundation
With bedrock too deep to reach and soil too unstable to support friction piles, the building was designed to "float" like a boat in water. A volume of soil, equal to the weight of the building above, was excavated. Once complete, the pressure exerted by the building equals the pressure from the soil that had been removed. A 4 feet thick solid concrete matt foundation evenly distributes the building load to the soil below.

Infill Windows
Computer generated structural models of the PerfCon structure showed areas that were critically overstressed due to long spans and bent spans over open corners. Select windows in these areas were filled in to resolve the overstressed conditions.

Colored Window Jambs
Based upon a structural diagram used to coordinate the size of reinforcing steel in the PerfCon panels, the colored jambs express the anticipated maximum stresses in the structure. The colors reveal the size of the reinforcing steel cast within the PerfCon panels. Blue=#5, Green=#6, Yellow=#7, Orange=#8, Red=#9 and #10. Uncolored areas are #5 or smaller.

Natural Ventilation
9 operable windows per single room allow students options for ventilation, views and privacy. Opening high and low windows takes advantage of the natural rise of warm air within the high-ceiling rooms.

1 LOBBY
2 LOUNGE
3 MULTI-PURPOSE ROOM
4 HOUSE DINING
5 "BLEACHER SEATING"
6 GROUP STUDY
7 GROUP LOUNGE
8 CORRIDOR
9 TERRACE

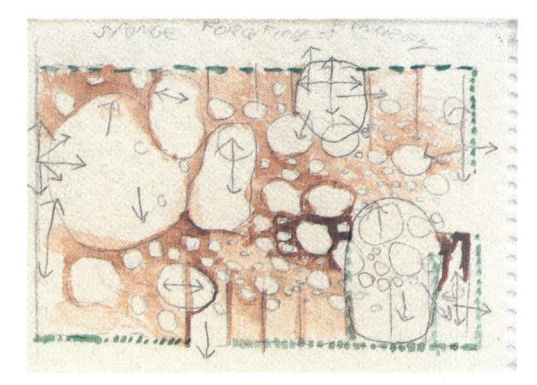

Concept sketches

Main entrance on southeast corner

Glazed wall of house dining

II-108

View from south: "Bleacher Seating"

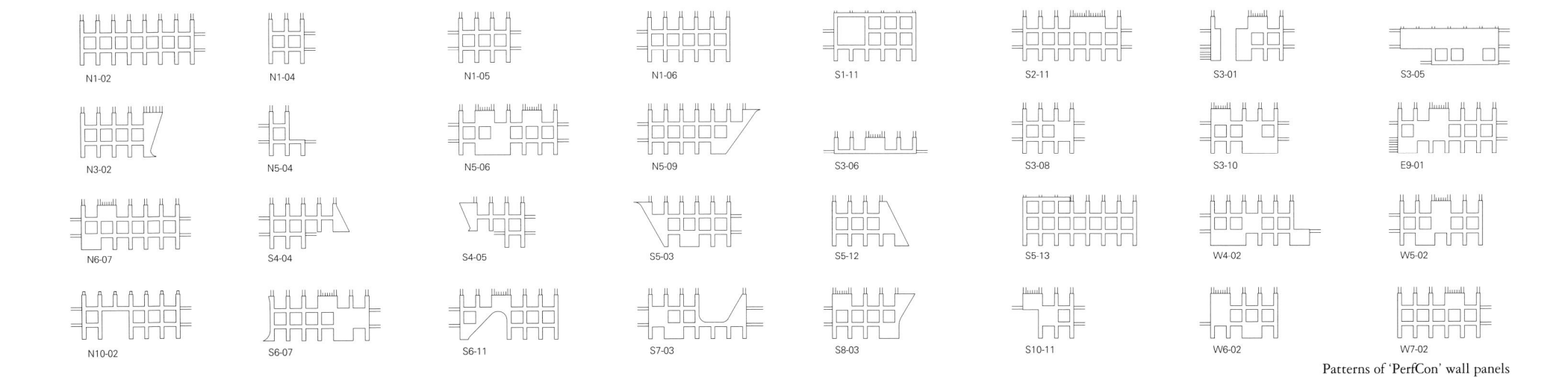

Patterns of 'PerfCon' wall panels

II-109

Lobby

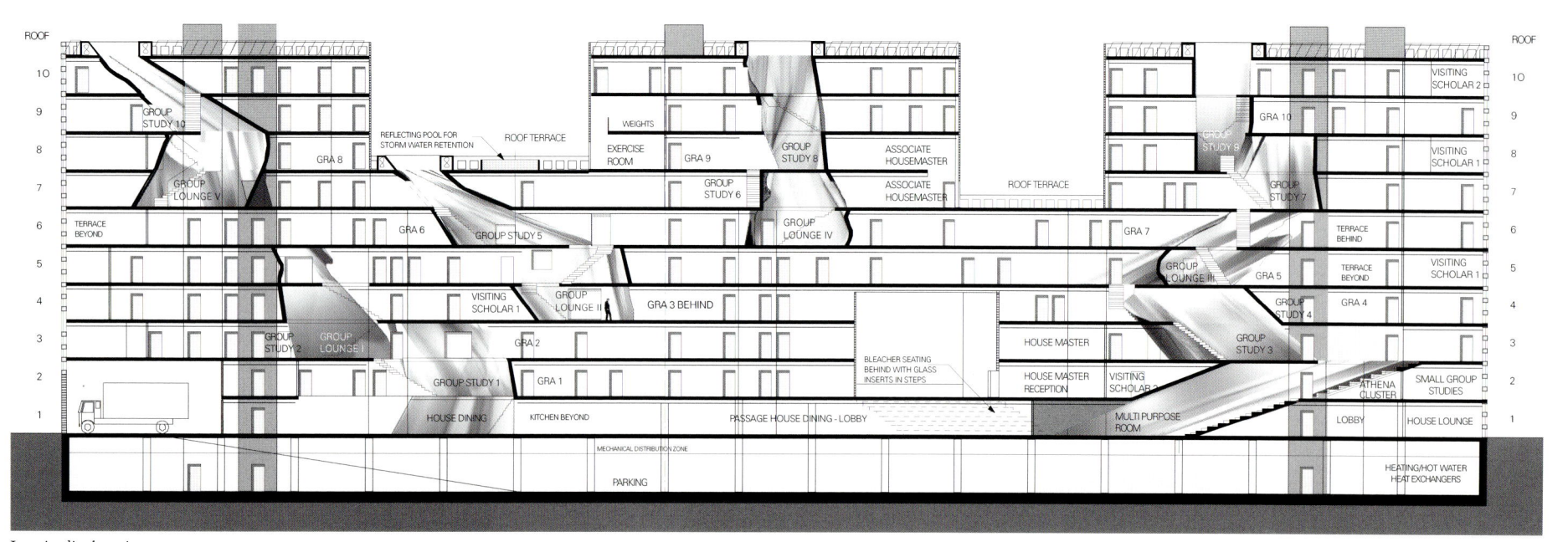

Longitudinal section

Cross sections

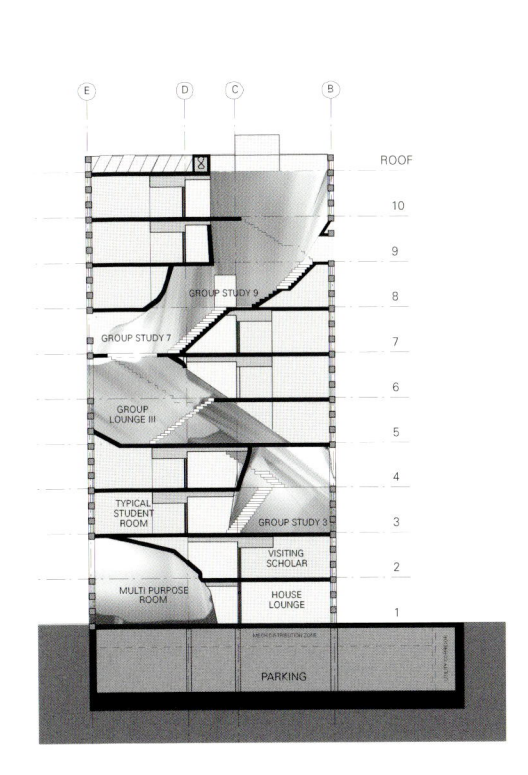

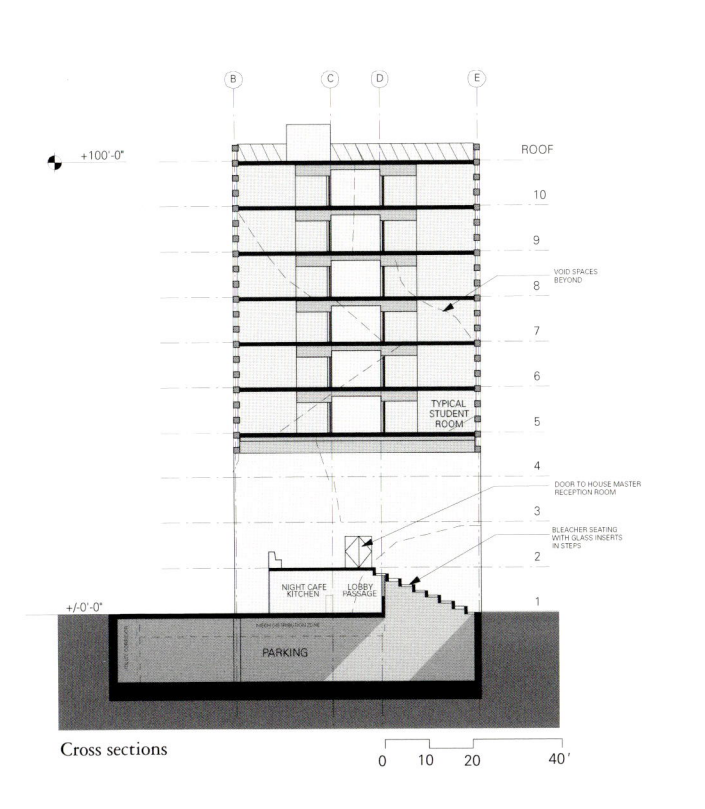

Lounge on first floor

House dining on first floor

マサチューセッツ工科大学シモンズ・ホール
［コンセプト］
このベッド数350の寄宿舎は,街の一部でもありキャンパスの一部でもあるかたちを,"多孔性"コンセプトにより,ヴァッサー・ストリートに沿って構想したものである。建物は10階建て,全長330フィートの垂直に切り取られた都市の一片である。街の一部という考えから,寄宿舎内に125席のシアターとナイト・カフェを設置することで,学生にアメニティを提供する。学生食堂は街路レベルにあり,街路に面したレストランのように,特製の日除けの下,戸外にもテーブルが置かれている。各部屋を結ぶ廊下(幅11フィート)は,都市的な体験に遭遇する街路に似ている。アアルトのベーカー・ハウスのように,廊下は,むしろパブリック・スペースであり,ラウンジのようなものになるだろう。

この新しい学部学生寄宿舎に適用されたスポンジ・コンセプトは,多孔性の建築類型を,一連のプログラムに基づいたバイオテクニカルな機能を介して変貌させる。

建物全体のマッスには,大きな開口が5つある。これらは,メイン・エントランス,ビュー・コリドー,体育館などのプログラムと連結した戸外活動のためのメイン・テラスに,ほぼ対応している。

それより小さなスケールの開口は,平面から断面へと,スポンジ型の場所に自在につながる表面システムによって,ブロック内に垂直に通る孔をつくりだす。これらの大きく,ダイナミックな開口(ほぼ寄宿舎内の"ハウス"に対応している)は,建物の肺であり,断面に沿って,自然光を落とし,空気を上昇させる。

"PerfCon"構造は,最大限の柔軟性と相互作用を与えてくれる独創的なデザインである。寄宿舎の個室には,それぞれ2×2フィートを超える大きさの開閉できる窓が9つ付いている。18フィートの奥行きを持つ壁は,夏の日射しを自然に遮り,冬の低い日射しを入れて,建物を暖めてくれる。壁のなかに深く後退して設置されている夥しい数の窓には,上枠と竪枠に色が塗られ,建物全体で10ある"ハウス"のそれぞれを個別化する。9つ窓のある部屋から流れ出る夜の灯りは,魅力的で,心浮き立つものになるだろう。

［基礎］
岩盤まで達するにはあまりに深く,土壌は摩擦杭を支えるにはあまりに軟弱なため,建物は水のなかのボートのように"浮かんでいる"。上に載る建物の重量に等しい量の土壌が掘削された。それが終わると,建物に

Multi-purpose room: upward view

Multi-purpose room: downward view

Ceiling of multi-purpose room

よって加わる圧力は，取り去られた土壌からの圧力と等しくなる。4フィート厚のコンクリートのべた基礎が，建物の荷重を下の土壌に均等に分散する。

［充填された窓］
コンピュータで作成されたPerfConの構造モデルは，ロングスパンとコーナーの開口部を覆うベントスパンのために，危険なほど過度の荷重がかかる部分があることを示していた。これらの部分にある窓を選んで，過度な荷重を解決するために充填材で補強した。

［着色された窓の枠］
PerfConパネルの鉄筋のサイズを調整するために使われた，構造ダイアグラムに基づいて着色された枠は，構造内にかかる最大限の予測荷重を表現している。色彩は，PerfConパネルに打ち込まれた鉄筋のサイズを表す。青＝＃5，緑＝＃6，黄＝＃7，オレンジ＝＃8，赤＝＃9及び10。無着色のエリアは＃5あるいはそれ以下である。

［自然通気］
それぞれの個室にある9つの開閉できる窓は，通気，眺め，プライバシーを学生に与える。高い位置や低い位置にとられた窓は，天井の高い部屋のなかで，暖められた空気が自然に上昇する助けとなる。

Group lounge

Group study room

Downward view of group study room

Corridor

II-114

Group lounge with skylight

SCHEME 1

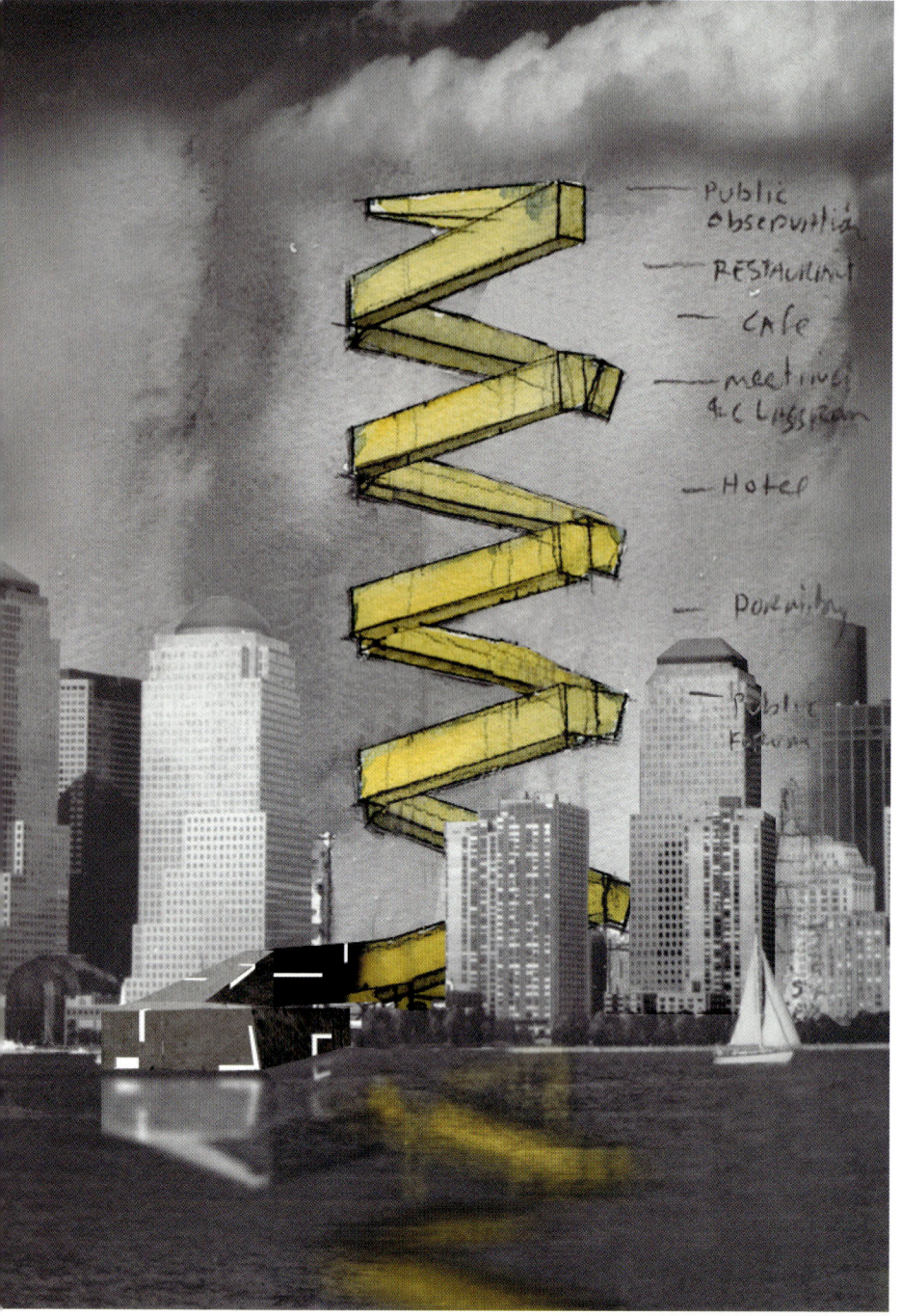

Concept sketch

Site

Upper part of tower: truss structure of translucent glass

Sketch: light through slit

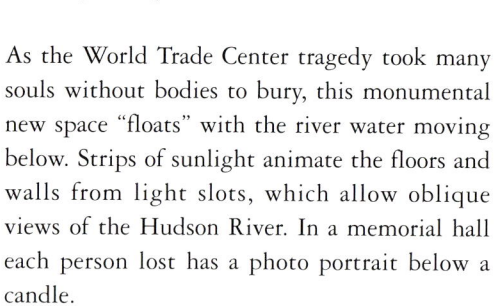

Observation decks

As the World Trade Center tragedy took many souls without bodies to bury, this monumental new space "floats" with the river water moving below. Strips of sunlight animate the floors and walls from light slots, which allow oblique views of the Hudson River. In a memorial hall each person lost has a photo portrait below a candle.

Scheme 1
The memorial ramps up to a new bridge over West Street, connected to a "folded street" which ascends over the site. Along the ascending "street" are a number of functions: galleries, cinema spaces, cafes, restaurants, a hotel, classrooms for a branch of New York University.

Sheathed in translucent glass the truss construction allows for grand public observation decks.

A new street level plan allows north-south and east-west streets to go through the site while accommodating auditorium halls for concerts and events.

The footprints of the original towers are formed into 212 feet x 212 feet reflective ponds, with thousands of glass lenses allowing light to spaces below.

Scheme 3
Our third proposal for the design of the World Trade Center site was developed with Richard Meier and Partners, Eisenman Architects, and Gwathmey Siegel. As a reminder that the mag-

World Trade Center Schemes 1 and 3
2002   New York, New York, U.S.A.

II-116

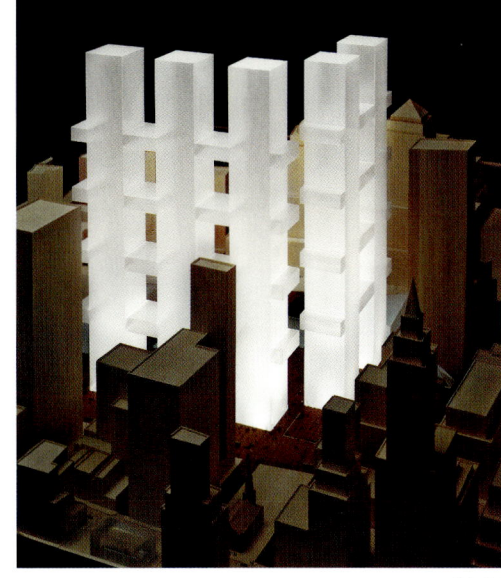

SCHEME 3

Sketch: night view over Hudson River

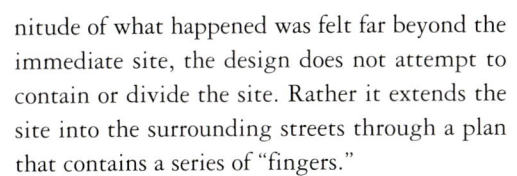

Model

Sketch: lower levels

nitude of what happened was felt far beyond the immediate site, the design does not attempt to contain or divide the site. Rather it extends the site into the surrounding streets through a plan that contains a series of "fingers."

Instead of individual iconic buildings, the creation of urban space in the spirit of Rockefeller Center was our aim as a team. The most visible signs of renewal are the proposed hybrid buildings, rising 1,111 feet to restore the Manhattan skyline with geometric clarity in glowing white glass. The horizontal and vertical field of buildings sustain activities from a hotel and conference center to offices, cultural spaces, and residences.

Comprised of five vertical sections and interconnecting horizontal layers, the two buildings represent a new typology in skyscraper design. At ground level, these forms become ceremonial gateways into the site. In their quiet abstraction as solids and voids, the buildings appear as screens, suggesting both presence and absence, and encouraging reflection and imagination. Their cantilevered ends extend outward, like the fingers of the ground plan, reaching toward the city and each other.

ワールド・トレード・センター跡地計画

埋葬するべき幾つもの肉体なき精神を奪ったワールド・トレード・センターの悲劇。そのためこの新しい記念碑的空間はたゆみなく流れる川の水面に「浮遊」している。細長い隙間から入る太陽光が帯のように床や壁へと彩りを与え、斜めに視線を向けるとハドソン川への眺望が広がっている。メモリアル・ホールでは犠牲者の肖像写真が蝋燭の下に飾られている。

［第1案］

ウエスト・ストリートに新しく架けられる橋へと続くメモリアル・ランプは「折り畳まれるように」敷地の上空を走る通路へと連結する。ギャラリー、映画スペース、カフェ、レストラン、ホテル、ニューヨーク大学支部の教室など、上へと延びる「通路」に沿って数多くの機能が配置されている。透過性のあるガラスで被覆されたトラス構造には誰もが眺望を得られるようにデッキが備えられた。

道路レベルの平面計画では南北と東西の通りが敷地を通り抜けるように走り、コンサートやその他の催しのためにオーディトリアムが配置されている。元々のタワーの跡地には212×212フィート（約64m×64m）のリフレクティング・ポンドが計画された。何千ものガラスレンズを通し、光はその下部へと引き込まれる。

［第3案］

我々が行ったワールド・トレード・センターの敷地に対する3番目の提案はリチャード・マイヤー、ピーター・アイゼンマン、及びグワスミー・シーゲルと共に進められた。実際に起きたことに対する衝撃は、その場所を越えて遠く離れた土地に居ても感じることができた。その記録としてこの計画は、敷地をひとつに囲い、あるいは分割することがない。敷地に対して何本もの「指」が周囲のストリートへと延びてゆくように、提案が行われた。

象徴的建築を個別に計画するよりも、ロックフェラー・センターの精神に基づき都市に空間を創造することがひとつの共通した目標であった。これは再建にあたって高さ1,111フィート（約340m）のハイブリッド・ビルディングを、白く輝くガラスのジオメトリの明晰性でマンハッタンのスカイラインに再生することが最大の視覚的特徴である。水平垂直の建築のアクティビティは、ホテルやコンファレンス・センター、オフィス空間や文化的空間、及び住宅に至る様々な活動に充てられている。

5つの垂直断面で構成され水平のレイヤーを相互に連結することで、2棟の建築はスカイスクレーパーの形態に新しいタイポロジーを付与している。地上レベルではこれらのフォルムがメモリアルのために、敷地へのエントランスを構成する。ソリッドとヴォイドへの静謐な抽象化のなかに、建築は沈思黙考し創造を促しつつ、存在と非存在を暗示するスクリーンとして現出する。キャンティレバーの終端部は外部に向かって広がり、地上階の平面計画のように、お互い都市に向かってその「指」を伸ばす。

2001-03 Loisium Visitors' Center
-05 Loisium Hotel Spa Resort
Langenlois, Austria

VISITORS' CENTER

View of entrance on northwest corner. Elevation is segmentalized by panels and tiled with rectangular aluminum panels

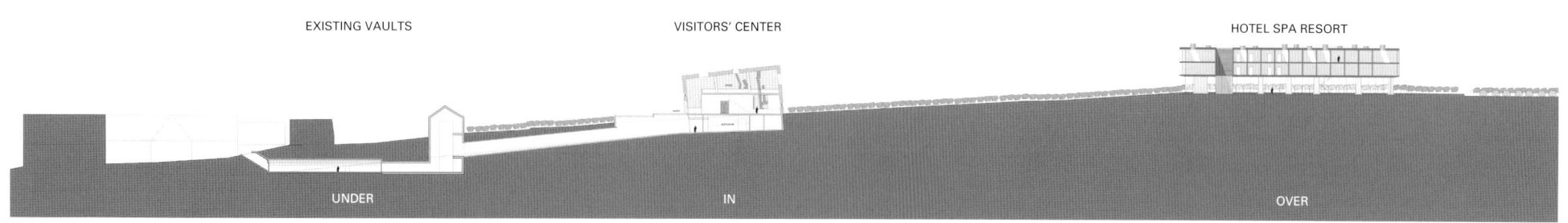

EXISTING VAULTS — VISITORS' CENTER — HOTEL SPA RESORT

UNDER — IN — OVER

Site section/elevation

Site plan

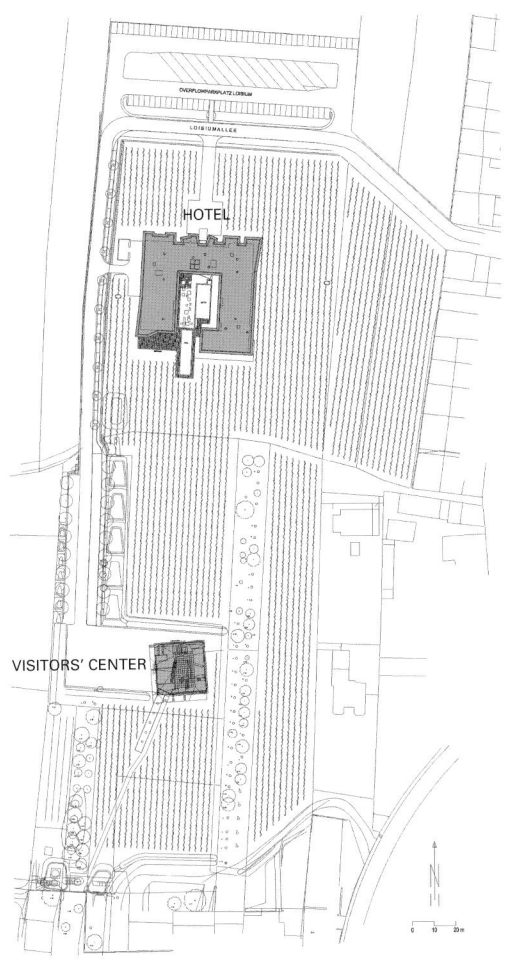

View from southwest: building is surrounded by vineyard

On the edge of the picturesque town of Langenlois, one hour west of Vienna, a new wine center and visitors' facility was built on a gently south-sloping vineyard to celebrate the rich local heritage of a magnificent wine vault system. This historic subterranean network, which includes 900 year old stone passages, underlies the urban plan of the town. The north-south axis of the network echoes that of the Baroque houses above and suggests the existence of a second town below that which is visible.

The project is composed of three parts: the existing vaults, which were made accessible to visitors, the Visitors' Center, and the Hotel Spa Resort. The vault system's geometry is transformed into an abstract three dimensional spatial language. This language forms the basis of the architecture of the Visitors' Center and Hotel, wherein each project element is derived from and related to the unique spaces of the vaults, while simultaneously having individual qualities of space, materials, light and experience.

The three elements of the project stand in relation to a geometric field of vineyards, the landscape of wine production:

1. Under the ground——Existing Vaults
2. In the ground——Visitors' Center and Ramp Connection
3. Over the ground——Wine and Spa Resort Hotel

Visitors' Center

The Visitors' Center's design concept is derived from the geometry of the wine vaults. The simple 24 m x 24 m x 17 m volume is cut and sliced to create a rich geometry. Some of the deep cuts are glazed in recycled bottle glass with rich green hues that cast their lustrous light on the interior.

Partially set into the earth of the vineyard, the slight forward tilt of the structure indicates its subterranean connection by ramp to the antique vault system. Upon entering, the visitor perceives a wonderful volume of space and steps out to the vineyard and past a cafe. A foot path leads down to the entrance of the vault system. The return journey is made through a ramped passage dappled with light refracted through a reflecting pool. The visitor then arrives on the lowest level of the building which houses a wine bar, a multi-purpose area and a shop with local products and books. Stairs and ramps connect to ground level with a generous wine shop and an upper floor with seminar rooms and offices. The roof terrace with spectacular views over the surrounding landscape and town can be made accessible on special occasions.

The Hotel Spa Resort

Like the grid of the city, the geometric spacing of the vineyard rows is continuous through the landscape connecting the three elements. The 53 m x 53 m square plan is aligned with the strict geometry of the surrounding vineyard rows. Offering a variety of activities and room types, the Loisium Spa Resort Hotel offers guests and visitors a variety of experiences. Earthlike materials and palette combined with the views of the surrounding landscape create a strong connection and relationship of the hotel to its context.

Public functions including the lobby, a wine themed restaurant, bar, cigar lounge, conference and meeting facilities, and wellness and spa area are located on the ground floor with views open to the surrounding vineyard. An inviting courtyard and terrace provides outdoor seating. 82 guest rooms are located in two upper floors. While the ground floor is transparent and open, the upper floors are more private.

Atrium: inner wall surface is exposed concrete and cork finish

Detail: colored glazed wall of recycled bottle glass

II-120

View toward west from wine shop

View from event area on basement

First floor

Ground floor

Basement

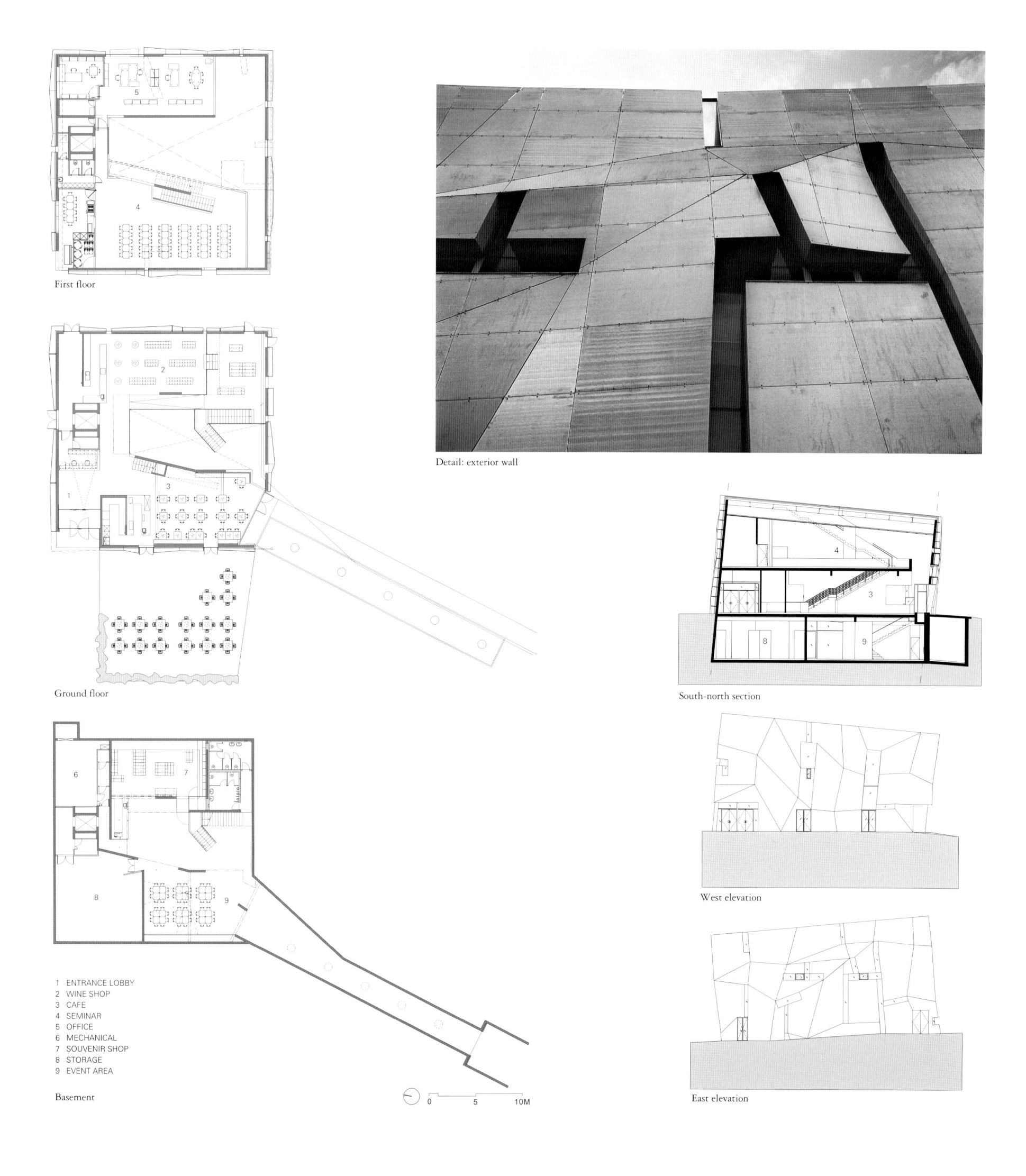

1 ENTRANCE LOBBY
2 WINE SHOP
3 CAFE
4 SEMINAR
5 OFFICE
6 MECHANICAL
7 SOUVENIR SHOP
8 STORAGE
9 EVENT AREA

Detail: exterior wall

South-north section

West elevation

East elevation

Entrance

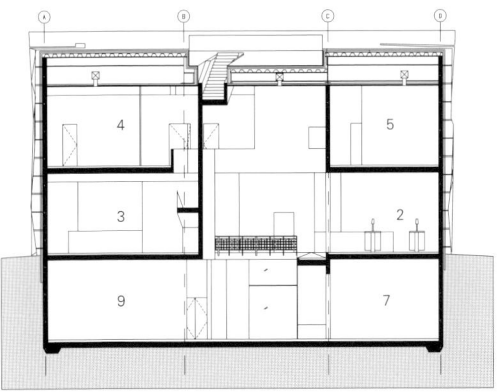

East-west section

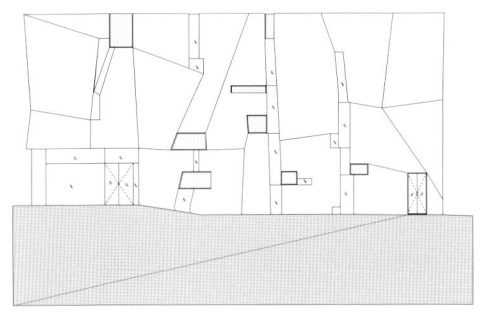

South elevation

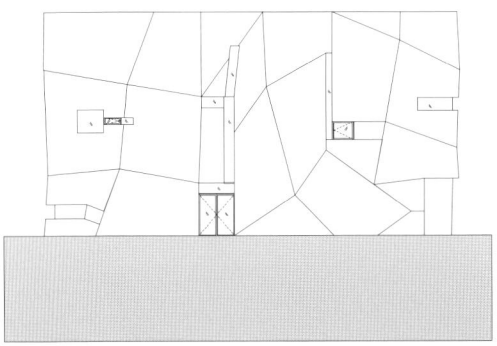

North elevation

0 5 10M

Natural light is inserted through openings of varied sizes and forms

II-123

Overall view from south vineyard: swimming pool on center

HOTEL SPA RESORT

Overall view from southeast (above) and northwest (below)

Upper floor: guest rooms

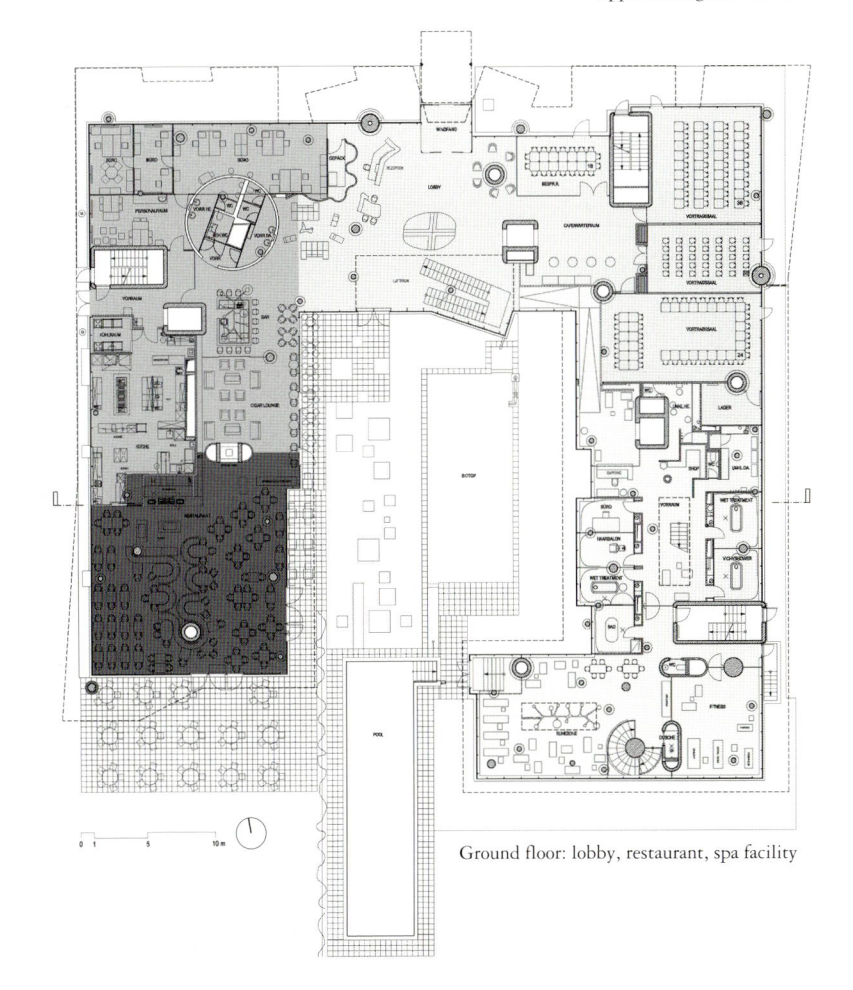

Ground floor: lobby, restaurant, spa facility

Swimming pool between two wings of guest rooms

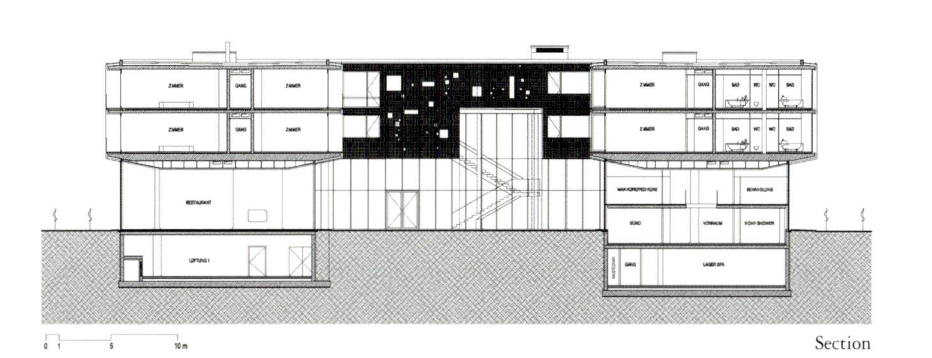

Section

II-125

Entrance lobby: view toward visitor's center through window

Entrance lobby

ロイジウム・ビジター・センター／
ロイジウム・ホテル・スパ・リゾート

ウィーンから西に1時間行った所にある,絵のように美しいランゲンロイスの町外れに,この地方の豊かな遺産である地下の素晴らしいワイン貯蔵システムを公開するために,緩やかな南斜面の葡萄畑に,ビジター・センターと観光客のための施設が建てられた。900年は経た石敷の通路を含む,古い歴史を持つ地下のネットワークは町の都市計画の基底となっている。ネットワークの南北軸は,地上のバロック風の家々を追って延び,目に見える町の下にある第2の町の存在を暗示する。

全体は3つの部分で構成されている。観光客も入ることができるようにつくられた既存の地下貯蔵庫,ビジター・センター,ホテル・スパ・リゾートである。地下貯蔵庫システムを構成する幾何学は三次元の抽象的な空間言語へと変換される。この言語はビジター・センターとホテルの建築の基本をかたちづくり,そこでは各エレメントは地下貯蔵庫の独得な空間に由来するか,関係づけられる。同時に,空間,材料,光,そこで得られる体験にはそれぞれに固有の質が付与される。

3つの棟は,葡萄畑の幾何学的な構成,ワインづくりの風景との関係のなかに立っている。

1) 地下——既存の地下貯蔵庫
2) 地中——ビジター・センターとスロープの接続部
3) 地上——ワイン＆スパ・リゾート・ホテル

［ビジター・センター］

ビジター・センターのデザイン・コンセプトはワイン貯蔵庫の幾何学に由来している。24×24×17メートルの単純なヴォリュームは豊かな幾何学形態をつくりだすために切り取られ,薄く切り分けられる。深い切り口には濃い緑色の瓶を再生利用したガラスが嵌め込まれ,内部に魅力的な光を投げかける。

葡萄畑の地中に一部が埋め込まれ,わずかに前方に傾斜する建物は,スロープで古代の地下貯蔵庫システムと結ばれていることを暗示する。エントランスで,客は空間の素晴らしいヴォリュームを感知し,葡萄畑にちょっと出て行き,カフェを過ぎる。歩行路が地下貯蔵庫のエントランスへ降りて行く。帰路はリフレクティング・プールを通って屈折する光が斑模様を描くスロープを辿る。そして客は建物の一番下の階に出る。そこにはワイン・バー,多目的エリア,地元の物産や本を集めた

View from courtyard toward Visitors' Center over vineyard

店がある。階段やスロープが、広いワイン・ショップのある1階、そして、セミナー室やオフィスのある上階に通じている。周囲の風景や町の素晴らしい眺めを見晴らせるルーフ・テラスは、特別な機会には公開される。

［ホテル・スパ・リゾート］
都市グリッドのように、葡萄畑の列の幾何学的な間隔は風景全体を貫き3つのエレメントを連結する。53×53メートルの方形平面は、周囲の葡萄の木の列がつくる厳格な幾何学形態と整列する。多彩な活動エリアと部屋のタイプを設定することで、ロイジウム・スパ・リゾート・ホテルは宿泊客や観光客に多彩な体験を提供する。大地に似た材料と色調は周囲の風景と組み合わされて、ホテルのコンテクストとの強いつながりをつくりだす。

　ロビー、ワインをメインとしたレストラン、バー、喫煙ラウンジ、会議や集会施設、ウェルネスやスパなどのパブリックな機能は、周囲の葡萄畑を広々と望める1階にある。感じの良い中庭やテラスが戸外での座席を提供する。82の客室は、上の2層に収まる。1階は透明で開放的である一方、上階はよりプライベートなスペースになっている。

Guest room

Guest room: looking bathroom

Corridor between guest rooms

2002 Zuidas
Amsterdam, The Netherlands

Over the next decade the Zuidas masterplan will create a new 21st century center for Amsterdam. International high-speed rail links will terminate at a new station, around which extensive urban functions including residential, commercial and cultural space will be developed. On a key site in this new urban center a triangular "Glass Flatiron in Two Scales" is projected.

Containing 89 apartments, hybrid living/office lofts and retail space, the building offers unique possibilities for global living. With a short walk to the new station, and six minutes from Schiphol airport, one can effectively live a few hours away from London, Paris, Frankfurt or New York. Similarly the building will offer a home to peripatetic global citizens seeking a European base.

The 17,800 square meters, eighteen-story high building is a Glass Flatiron characterized by two opposing scales of openings. Three openings in a "giant" urban scale offer shared terraces and elevated gardens for the residents, and locate the main entry to the building. The smaller "human" scale of openings create terraces for individual units. The syncopated disposition of these on each floor allows for maximum variation in the six basic apartment types while creating a unique rhythm on the building facades. The building mass is sheathed in a monolithic structurally-glazed curtain wall of greenish glass, while the openings find their expression in yellow membrane, vibrant against the cool overcast Dutch sky. The rhythmic counterpoint of flush glass and the yellow creates a unique urban experience.

View from street

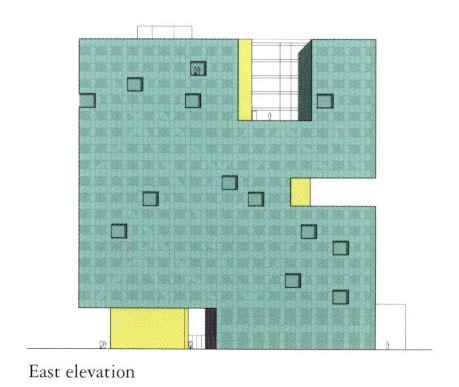

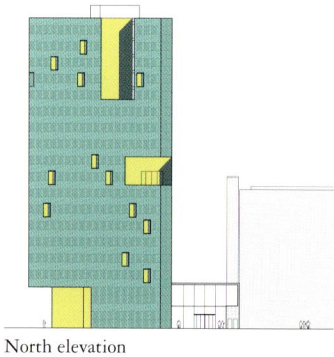

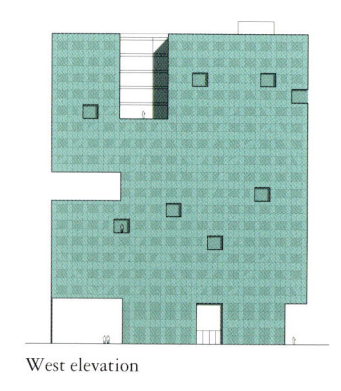

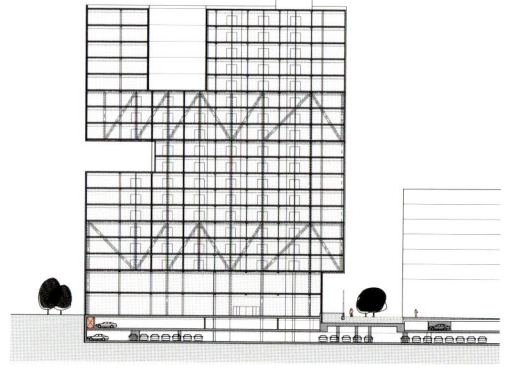

East elevation

North elevation

West elevation

Longitudinal section

Concept sketch

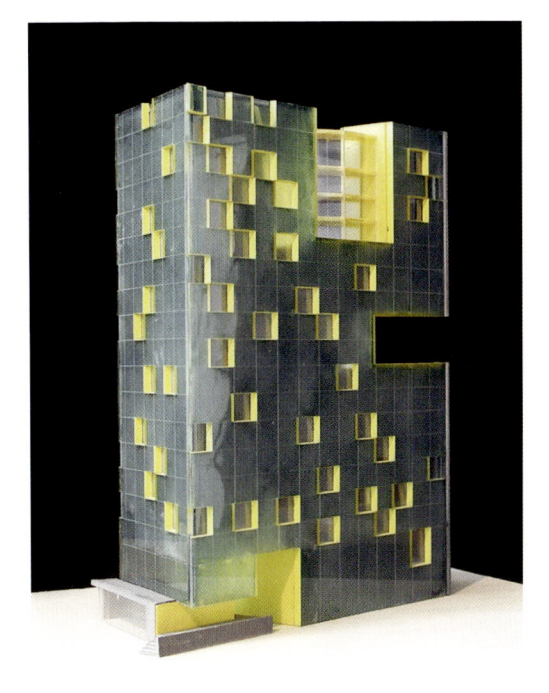

Model: glazed curtain wall of greenish glass

Model: entrance lobby

Entrance lobby

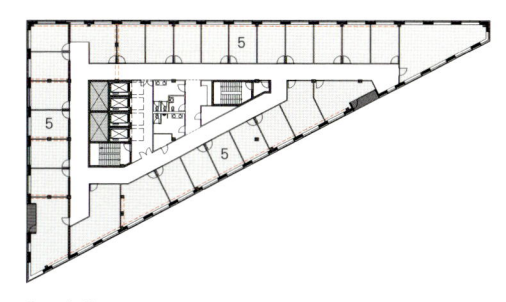

Fourth floor

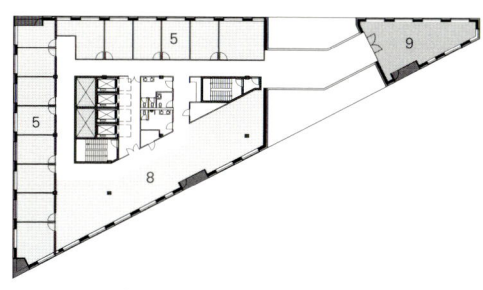

15th to 18th floors (typical floor)

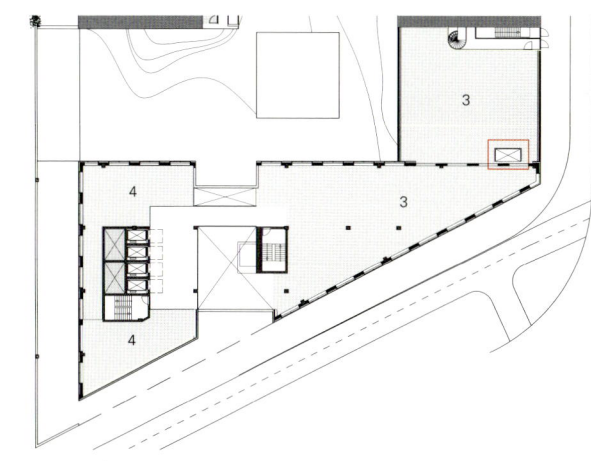

Second floor

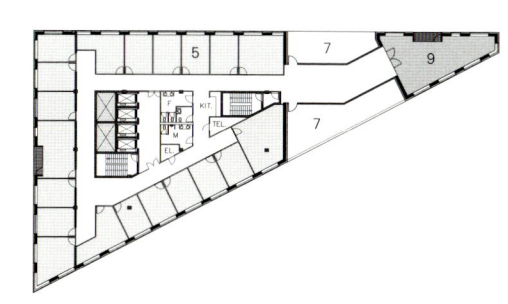

14th floor

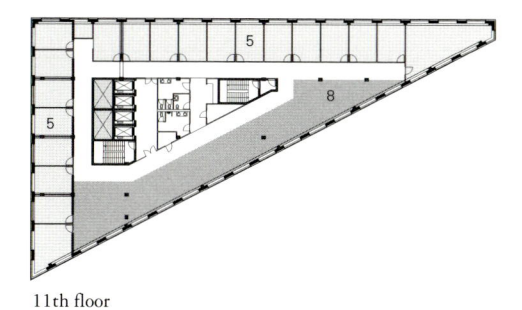

11th floor

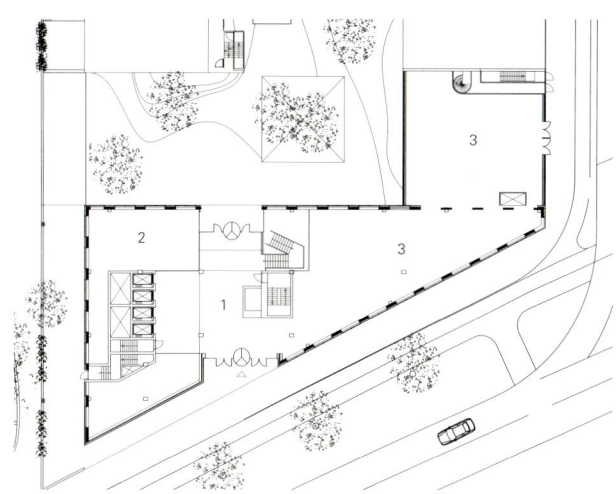

Site plan/ground floor

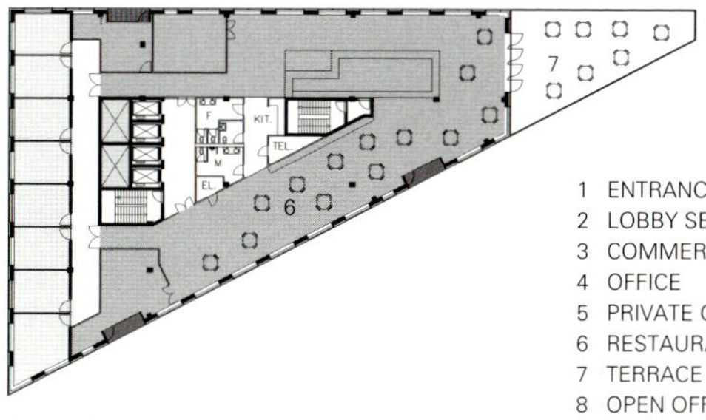

Ninth floor

1 ENTRANCE LOBBY
2 LOBBY SERVICE
3 COMMERCIAL SPACE
4 OFFICE
5 PRIVATE OFFICES
6 RESTAURANT
7 TERRACE
8 OPEN OFFICE SPACE
9 CONFERENCE ROOM

ザイダス

10年間のうちに，ザイダスのマスタープランは21世紀のアムステルダムの新しい中心拠点となるだろう。新しい駅舎は国際高速鉄道網のターミナルとなり，周囲には住宅，商業施設，文化スペースといった都市機能が集中的に開発される予定である。中心にはこの都市の新しい拠点となる三角形の「ガラス・フラットアイアン」が，2つのスケールに沿って計画されている。

89住戸，住宅・オフィス一体型のロフト，及び商業空間のあるこの建築は，国際生活に相応しい独自の可能性を追求するものである。新しい駅舎まで歩いて程近く，スキポール空港からは6分で着く。ここにはロンドンやパリ，フランクフルト，ニューヨークからわずか数時間の生活がある。また同様に，この建築はヨーロッパに拠点を求める，世界中を旅する市民のための住宅でもある。

床面積17,800平米，高さ18階に及ぶガラス・フラットアイアンは，2種類の開口部の持つ正反対のスケール感がその特徴である。「巨大な」都市のスケールの3つの開口部には，居住者用の高層庭園，共用テラス，及び建築へのメインエントランスが配置計画されている。ずっと小さく「ヒューマン」なスケールの開口部は，個々の居住ユニットのテラスとなる。各々のフロアのシンコペーションのリズムは，6種類の基準となる住居タイプから配置計画に最大限の多様性を引き出すと共に，建築のファサードに独自のリズムを生み出している。冷たく雲のたれ込めるオランダの空と色鮮やかな対照をなすように，建築のマッスは緑がかったモノリシックな構造ガラスのカーテンウォールで覆われ，開口部は黄色の皮膜として表現されている。輝くようなガラスと黄色の面のリズミカルな対位法が生み出すのは，独自の都市経験である。

2003-09　Linked Hybrid
Beijing, China

View from roof of Cinematheque (public garden) surrounded by towers

Sketch: pond and Cinematheque volumes

The 220,000 square-meter Linked Hybrid complex in Beijing, aims to counter the current privatized urban developments in China by creating a twenty-first century porous urban space, inviting and open to the public from every side. A filmic urban experience of space; around, over and through multifaceted spatial layers, as well as the many passages through the project, make the Linked Hybrid an "open city within a city". The project promotes interactive relations and encourages encounters in the public spaces that vary from commercial, residential, and educational to recreational; a three-dimensional public urban space.

The ground level offers a number of open passages for all people (residents and visitors) to walk through. These passages include "micro-ur-

Bridge between towers

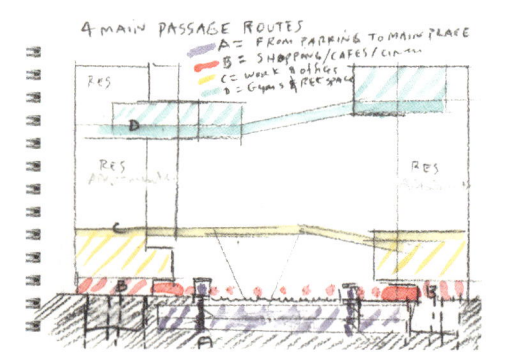

Evening view: looking from northwest. Tower 1 (left) and Tower 2 (right)

4 main passage routes connecting towers

II-132

A CINEMATHEQUE
B HOTEL
C POND/PARKING BELOW

Site plan

Typical floor

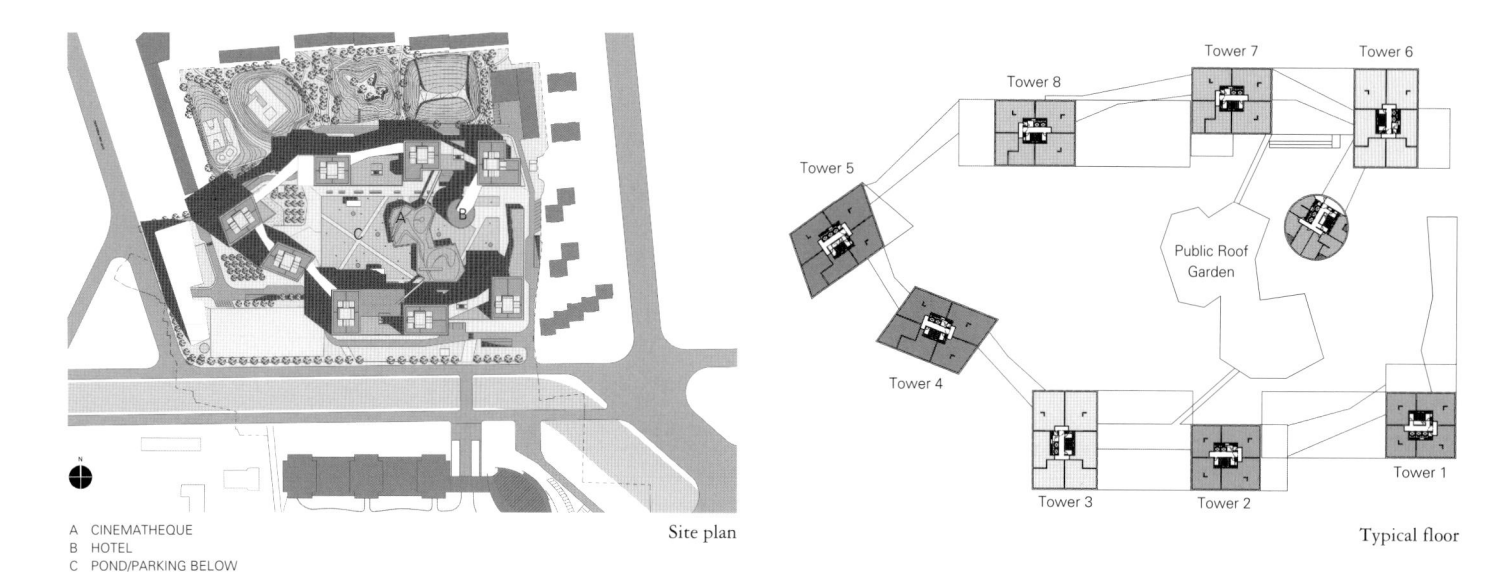

banisms" of small scale shops which also activate the urban space surrounding the large central reflecting pond. On the intermediate level of the lower buildings, public roof gardens offer tranquil green spaces, and at the top of the eight residential towers private roof gardens are connected to the penthouses. All public functions on the ground level,—including a restaurant, hotel, Montessori school, kindergarten, and cinema— have connections with the green spaces surrounding and penetrating the project. Elevators displace like a "jump cut" to another series of passages on higher levels. From the 12th to the 18th floor a multi-functional series of skybridges with a swimming pool, a fitness room, a cafe, a gallery, etcetera connects the eight residential towers and the hotel tower, and offers views over the unfolding city. Programmatically this loop aspires to be semi-lattice-like rather than simplistically linear. We hope the public sky-loop and the base-loop will constantly generate random relationships; functioning as social condensers in a special experience of city life to both residents and visitors.

Focused on the experience of passage of the body through space, the towers are organized to take movement, timing and sequence into consideration. The point of view changes with a slight ramp up, a slow right turn. The encircled towers express a collective aspiration; rather than towers as isolated objects or private islands in an increasingly privatized city, our hope is for new "Z" dimension urban sectors that aspire to individuation in urban living while shaping public space.

Geo-thermal wells (655 at 100 meters deep) provide Linked Hybrid with cooling in summer and heating in winter, and make Linked Hybrid one of the largest green residential projects. The large urban space in the center of the project is activated by a greywater recycling pond with water lilies and grasses in which the cinematheque and the hotel appear to float. In the winter the pool freezes to become an ice-skating rink. The cinematheque is not only a gathering venue but also a visual focus to the area. The cinematheque architecture floats on its reflection in the shallow pond, and projections on its facades indicate films playing within. The first floor of the building, with views over the landscape, is left open to the community. The polychrome of Chinese Buddhist architecture inspires a chromatic dimension. The undersides of the bridges and cantilevered portions are colored membranes that glow with projected nightlight and the window jambs have been colored by chance operations based on the 'Book of Changes' with colors found in ancient temples.

The water in the whole project is recycled. This greywater is piped into tanks with ultraviolet filters, and then put back into the large reflecting pond and used to water the landscapes. Re-using the earth excavated from the new construction, five landscaped mounds to the north contain recreational functions. The 'Mound of Childhood', integrated with the kindergarten, has an entrance portal through it. The 'Mound of Adolescence' holds a basketball court, a roller blade and skate board area. In the 'Mound of Middle Age' we find a coffee and tea house (open to all), a Tai Chi platform, and two tennis courts. The 'Mound of Old Age' is occupied with a wine tasting bar and the 'Mound of Infinity' is carved into a meditation space with circular openings referring to infinite galaxies.

Sustainable Design Intent

Linked Hybrid's intended experience of spatiality and passage has a tremendous impact on its sustainability. Envisioned as an "open city within a city", it is a pedestrian-oriented combination of public and private space that encourages the use of shared resources and reduces the need for wasteful modes of transit. It is an urban oasis, proving that peaceful, green spaces can exist in an exploding metropolis such as Beijing.

Water Efficiency

An estimated 220,000 liters of gray water from all apartment units will be recycled each day and reused for landscape and green roof irrigation, toilet flushing, and rebalancing pond water—resulting in a 41% decrease in potable water usage.

Energy Flows

Linked Hybrid's ground source heat pump system, one of the largest in residential construction, is its most groundbreaking innovation. Shouldering 70% of the complex's yearly heating and cooling load, the system is comprised of 655 geothermal wells, 100 meters below the basement foundation. Additionally, the underground wells have taken the place of above-ground space normally needed for cooling towers, increasing available green areas, minimizing noise pollution and significantly reducing the CO_2 emissions created by traditional heating/cooling methods.

High Performance Building Systems

The project boasts exterior window louvers and low-e coated glass for solar gain and heat control, as well as a high-performance building envelope and integrated slab heating and cooling system.

Indoor Environmental Quality

Linked Hybrid makes use of a technique called displacement ventilation, in which air that is slightly below desired temperature in a room is released from the floor. The cooler air displaces the warmer air, causing it to be released from the room and resulting in a cooler overall space and a fresh breathing environment.

View from south: from right to left, Tower 1, Tower 2, Tower 3, and Tower 4

Towers connected by bridges

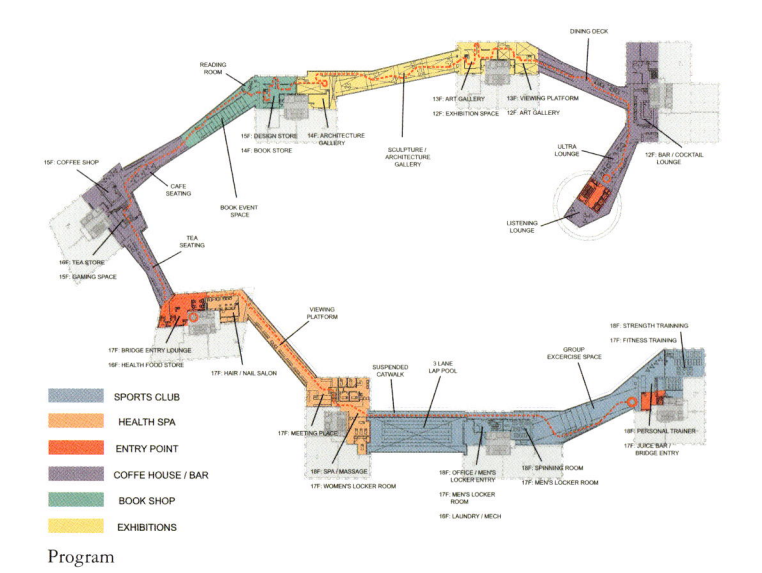

Program

Diagram: pedestrian circulation on public space level

II-134

Evening view from Cinematheque toward west

Pond: Cinematheque on right

リンクド・ハイブリッド

北京における、220,000平米規模のリンクド・ハイブリッド・コンプレックスは、全方位的に人々を迎え入れ、人々に開かれた、21世紀の新しい多孔性の都市空間をつくることによって、中国で現在進んでいる都市開発へ対抗することを目標においている。多面的な空間のレイヤーの廻りや、上方やその中を貫通する映像的な都市空間の体験は、プロジェクト全体を通り抜ける数多くの通路と共にリンクド・ハイブリッドを「都市の中の開かれた都市」につくりあげる。プロジェクトは、双方向の関係を押し進め、商業、住宅、教育からレクリエーションまで多彩な公共空間内での出会いを促す。それは三次元の都市空間となる。

地上レベルには、すべての人(住民も訪問者も)が隅から隅まで歩き廻れる、沢山の開放された通路が巡らされる。これらの通路は、小規模な店舗によるミクロ=アーバニズムを含み、それらは敷地中央部の大きなリフレクティング・ポンド廻りの都市空間を活気づける。低層棟の中間レベルでは、パブリックな屋上庭園が静かな緑地を提供し、8棟の住居タワーの頂上ではプライベートな屋上庭園がペントハウスとつながる。レストラン、ホテル、モンテッソーリ法で教える学校、幼稚園、映画館などを含め、地上レベルに置かれたすべての公共施設は、プロジェクトを囲み、浸透する緑地につながる。エレベータはより高いレベルにある一連の別の通路へと映画の「ジャンプカット(急激な場面転換)」のように転置する。12階から18階へ、スイミング・プール、フィットネス・ルーム、カフェ、ギャラリーなどがある多機能な一連のスカイ・ブリッジが8棟の住居タワー、ホテル・タワーを連結し、市街を見晴らせる眺めを提供する。プログラム上は、このループはあまりにも単純な線形よりも半格子状とすることが望ましい。私たちは、公共的な上方のスカイループと基部のベースループが常に無作為な関係を生み出してほしいと願っている。ループは住民にも、訪れる人にも都市生活の特別な体験をもたらす社会的なコンデンサーとして機能する。

タワーは、空間を通り抜けて行く身体の通路体験に照準を合わせ、動き、タイミング、シークエンスを考慮に入れて構成されている。視点はわずかにスロープを上がり、ゆるやかに右へ曲がるにつれて変化する。丸く囲まれたタワーは集合体への願望を表現している。我々が理想とするのは、個別化を強める都市における孤立したオブジェクトや私的な島のようなタワーというよりも、都市空間を形成しながら同時に都市住居としての特徴を生みだす未知の次元の都市セクターなのである。

地熱利用の井戸(100mの深さで655基)が、夏と冬の冷暖房設備を提供し、リンクド・ハイブリッドをクリーン・エネルギーを使用する、大規模な住宅プロジェクトにする。敷地中央にある大きな都市空間に、シネマテークとホテルが浮かぶように姿を現し、睡蓮や水草が生え、排水を再利用した池によって活気づく。冬にはプールの水面が凍り、アイススケートのリンクとなる。シネマテークは集いの場所であるばかりでなく、このエリアの視覚的な焦点である。シネマテークは浅い池にその姿を反射させながら池の上に浮かび、建物ファサードへの映写は、内部で上映されているフィルムを暗示させる。風景を見晴らせる建物の1階はコミュニティに開放されたまま残される。中国の寺院建築に見られる多色彩飾にインスピレーションを得て、色が決められた。片持

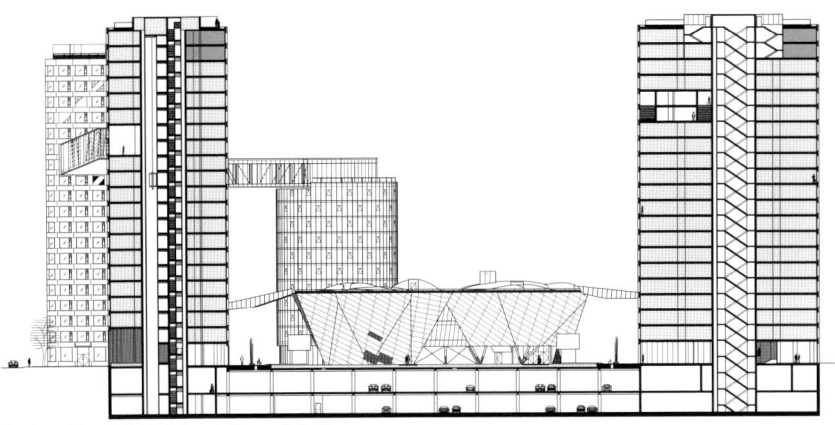

Section: Tower 3 (right) and Tower 8 (left)

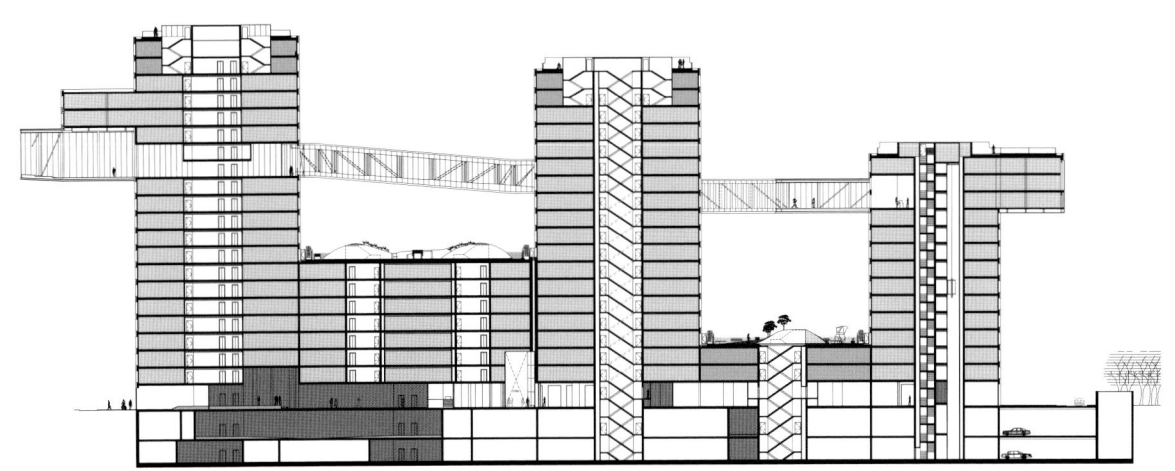

Section: Tower 6 (right), Tower 7 (center), Tower 8 (left)

Towers (left) and Cinematheque on pond (right)

ち部分とブリッジの下側は着色された薄膜で,夜間照明の中で光り輝き,窓の竪枠は,古代寺院で見つけた色彩を『易経』に基づいて無作為にあてはめている。

　敷地全体で使われる水は再利用される。この雑排水は紫外線フィルターのついたタンクへと管で流され,大きなリフレクティング・ポンドへ戻され,後にランドスケープへの散水として使われる。新しい工事で掘り起こされた土を再利用した,敷地の北側に景観構成された五つのマウンドにはレクリエーション機能が配される。幼稚園に一体化された「幼児のマウンド」には,入口となる通り抜けの門があり,子供の安全のためにフェンスで囲まれている。「青年期のマウンド」にはバスケットボール・コート,ローラー・ブレードやスケートボード用の場所,もちろん音楽とTVのラウンジもある。「中年期のマウンド」には,カフェと茶店(すべての人に開かれている),太極拳用の壇,2面のテニスコートがある。"老年期のマウンド"はワインのテイスティング・バーと,無限の小宇宙からイメージした円形の開口部付きの,瞑想空間がある"無限のマウンド"で占められる。

[サステイナブル・デザインの取り組み]

リンクド・ハイブリッドの綿密に計画された空間的広がりや通路空間は,サステイナビリティの向上に重要な役割を果たしている。「都市の中の都市」の構想のもと,歩行空間を中心とした複合的なパブリック・スペースとプライベート・スペースが資源の共有を促し,環境負荷の高い交通方式の需要を抑制している。ここは都市のオアシスとして,爆発的な成長を続ける北京のような大都市においても,落ち着いた緑あふれる空間が存在しうることを示している。

[節水対策]

すべての住戸から1日に排出される220,000リットルの生活排水は,植栽や屋上緑化の散水,トイレの洗浄水,池の水位調整用として再生・再利用される予定である。その結果,上水使用量が41%低減される見込みである。

[エネルギー利用]

住宅建設としては最大規模の地熱利用式ヒートポンプ・システムは,リンクド・ハイブリッドに採用された最新の先端技術である。複合施設の年間熱負荷の70%を負担するこのシステムは,基礎の地下100mに達する655本の地熱井によって構成される。また,この地中井のおかげで,通常であればクーリング・タワーの設置に必要とされる地上空間を緑化し,騒音公害を抑え,従来型の冷暖房方式によって排出されるCO_2を大幅に削減している。

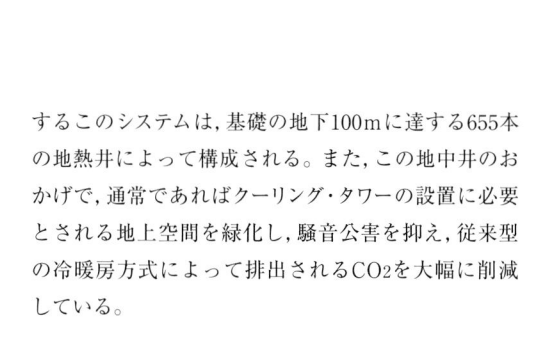

[ビル・システムの熱効率]

太陽熱取得や熱制御のため,断熱性能の高い建築外皮やスラブ一体型の冷暖房システムとともに外部ルーバーやLow-Eガラスが計画されている。

[屋内環境品質]

リンクド・ハイブリッドでは置換換気という技術が使用されている。そのため,床面からは目標室温よりもやや低く設定された空気が吹き出される。冷気と暖気が置換されることで,排気が促され,空間全般の室温を低く保ち,新鮮で快適な環境がもたらされる。

Downward view of pond: Looking toward Tower 7 to Tower 9 on north. Cinematheque with public roof garden, and cylindrical volume of Hotel (right)

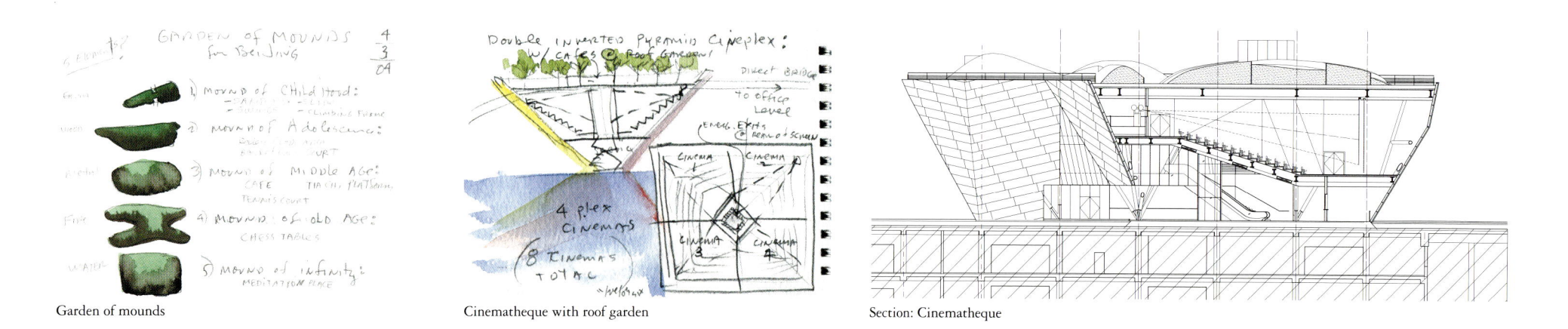

Garden of mounds

Cinematheque with roof garden

Section: Cinematheque

Sketch: swimming pool

Bridge between Tower 3 and Tower 4: viewing platform

Cinematheque: auditorium

Bridge between Tower 2 and Tower 3: swimming pool below (right)

II-139

2005–   Sail Hybrid
Knokke-Heist, Belgium

Site plan

Night view

Located on the North Sea coast, the Belgian seaside resort town of Knokke-Heist required a renovation and transformation of their existing casino. Following a request for proposals, five firms were shortlisted for an international design competition, including Herzog & de Meuron and Zaha Hadid Architects; with the jury unanimously selecting Steven Holl Architects' Sail Hybrid design. With an enhanced program intended to provide an iconic landmark and bolster the town's stature and urban spaces, the project will transform the seaside resort into a premiere travel and architectonic destination. The new three-part hybrid transformation rebuilds one of Belgium's great architect's fine works, becoming a glowing new beacon on the Atlantic wall and interconnecting the ensemble of city buildings in Knokke-Heist with new urban porosity.

The Sail Hybrid design was inspired by the Rene Magritte mural, *The Ship Which Tells the Story to the Mermaid*, one of eight original Surrealist masterpieces in the series called Le Domaine Enchanté, which was commissioned for the Casino in 1953. The murals are housed in the Magritte Room, a protected monument located in the original Albert Place Casino built in 1930 by Leon Stynen. The Sail Hybrid concept expressly preserves the Magritte Room and restores the Stynen Casino facades. The mural inspired a hybrid transformation of the casino into three architectures: Early Modern Restored Volumetric Architecture (white restored, reprogrammed casino), a Porous Bridge Hybrid Architecture (perforated congress hall), and a Sail-like Planar Architecture (glass planes—hotel and apartment Tower) to create a synergy of new functions.

The new design occupies the single point in Knokke-Heist coastline with an opening in the Atlantic Wall. The seaward orientation and resulting thin profile ensures unobstructed sea views for all tower residents and does not impinge on the views of the adjacent residential context. Porosity is achieved through the design of the congress hall curtain wall as well as the ground level of the casino which opens to the sea on the north side, and continues through con-

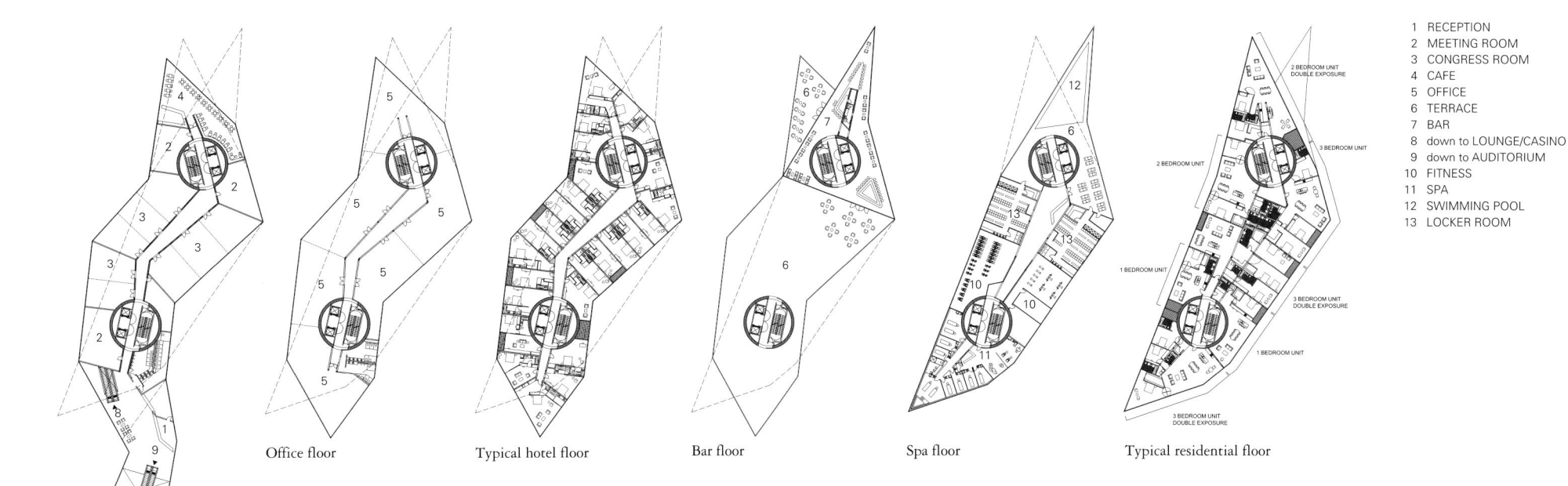

	Office floor	Typical hotel floor	Bar floor	Spa floor	Typical residential floor	1 RECEPTION 2 MEETING ROOM 3 CONGRESS ROOM 4 CAFE 5 OFFICE 6 TERRACE 7 BAR 8 down to LOUNGE/CASINO 9 down to AUDITORIUM 10 FITNESS 11 SPA 12 SWIMMING POOL 13 LOCKER ROOM

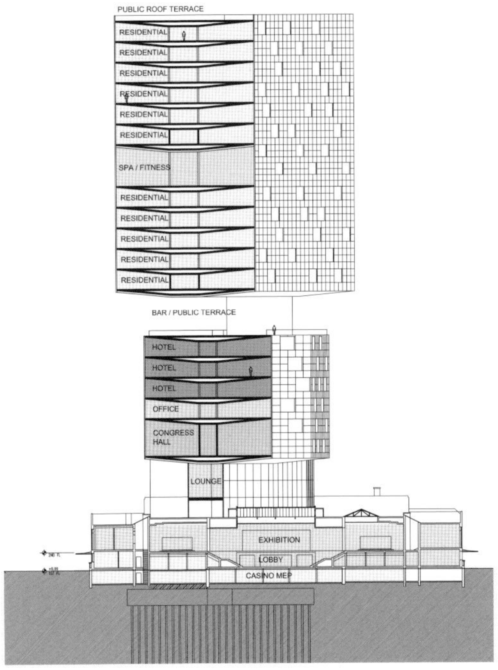

Congress Hall floor

Cross section: Sail Building

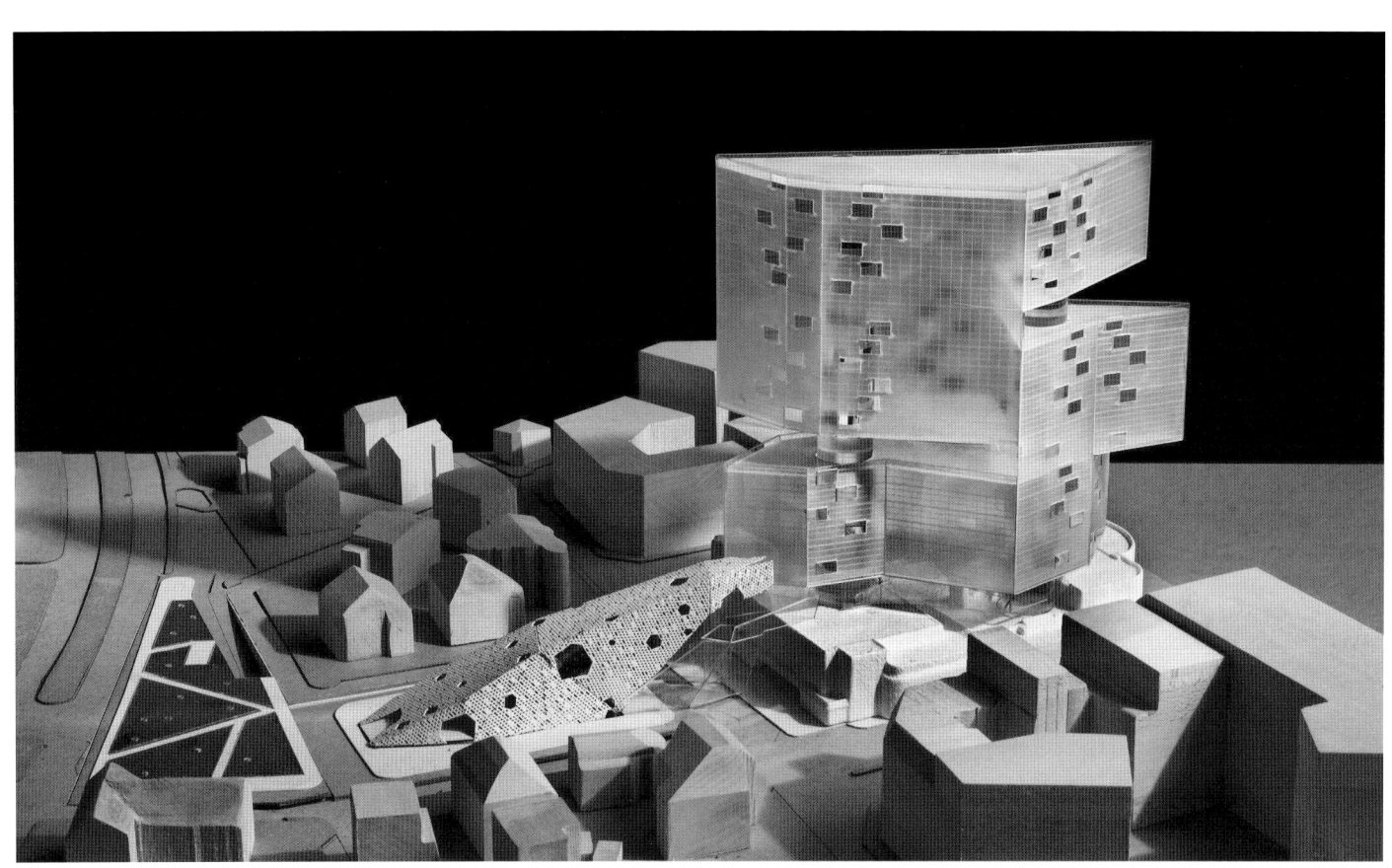

Model: view from east

gress hall to the south avenue facing entrance.

Priority was given to public areas including a spa, rooftop terrace, pool and restaurant which were located on the highest tower floors. Congress hall includes another roof terrace, pool and cafe, accessible from both the exhibition and casino areas. A predominantly pedestrian public space, casino square, paved in Belgian bluestone and enhanced with landscaping and public art, fronts the boardwalk and creates a sense of place in the city's urban fabric.

The synergistic integration of various functions including dining, meeting, leisure and congress are combined in the program: casino, flagship hotel, congress facilities, events hall, exhibition facilities, restaurant, cafe, Magritte room, nightclub, apartments, galleries, spa facility, retail and below ground automated parking are included in more than 71,000 square meters of area on 19 floors with two rooftop terraces and two pools. Building materials include glass, steel and recycled terrazzo, glass aggregate and locally produced concrete. A geothermal energy plant under the parking garage, automated parking that eliminates theft, damage and emissions while maximizing capacity, and the use of a high performance curtain wall to provide insulation and control solar gain are implemented to achieve optimum sustainability. The restoration and re-use of the original Stynen Casino eliminates waste, minimizes demolition, manufacture and energy consumption.

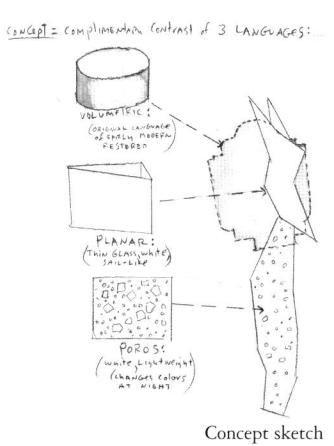

Concept sketch

II-141

Distant view over sea

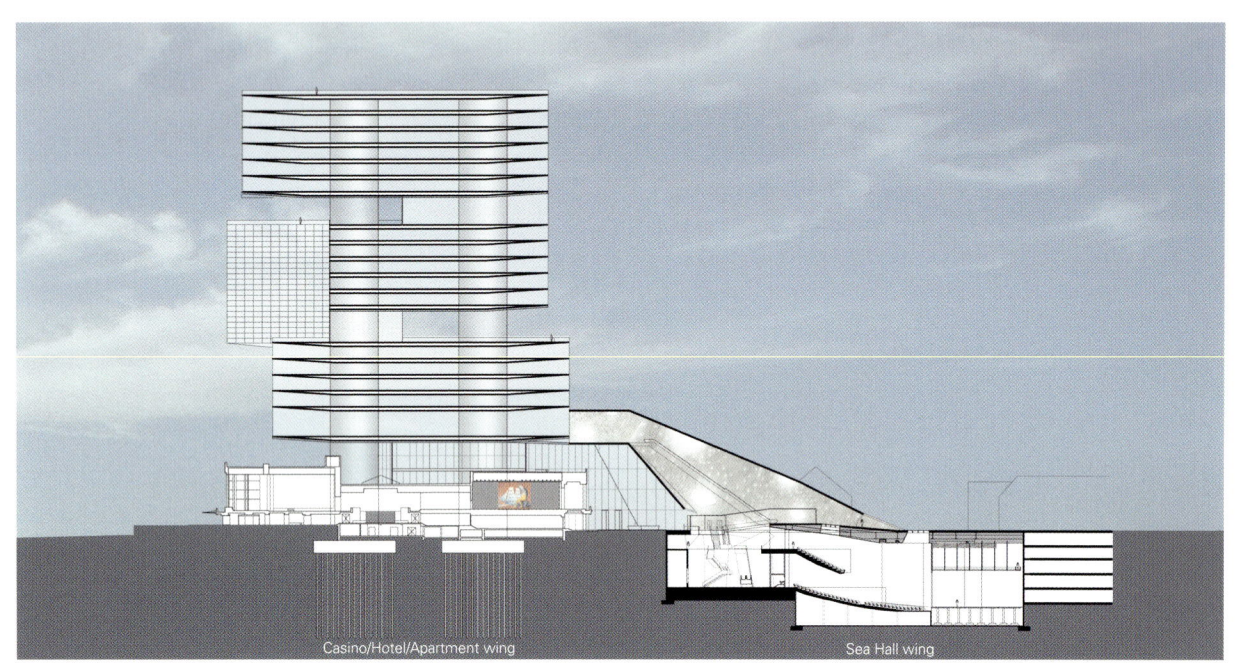

Longitudinal section

Site model and cross section: auditorium of Sea Hall

セイル・ハイブリッド
北海沿岸に位置するベルギーの臨海リゾート都市であるクノック＝ヘイストに現存するカジノは，改修とプログラムの変更を必要としていた。計画案の募集に引き続いて，ヘルツォーク＆ド・ムーロンやザハ・ハディドを含む5つの事務所の作品が国際コンペの最終選抜候補に挙げられ，その結果として，我々のデザイン「セイル・ハイブリッド」が満場一致で選ばれることとなった。アイコニックな特色をもつ建物を提供し，街の成長や都市的空間を補強するよう意図された拡張プログラムにより，プロジェクトがこの臨海リゾートを旅先として，また建築的に魅力ある目的地へと変容させることを目論んでいる。三つの部分の混合からなる建築によって既存状況を変容させるこのプロジェクトは，ベルギーの偉大な建築家の作品の中の一つを改築するものであり，クノック＝ヘイストの街の様々な混成建物群を，この都市性を持った新しい多孔性建築で結びつけ，「大西洋の壁」の間にあって光り輝く新たな灯台となることを目指している。

「セイル・ハイブリッド」のデザインはルネ・マグリットのあるだまし絵にヒントを得ている。1953年にこのカジノより依頼され製作された「魅惑の領域」と名付けられた8つの傑作，シュールレアリスト絵画連作の中の一つ「物語を人魚に語る帆船」である。これらの絵は，レオン・スタイネンによって1930年に建てられた，オリジナルのアルバート・プレイス・カジノにある保護記念文化財である「マグリット・ルーム」に収められている。「セイル・ハイブリッド」のコンセプトでは明白な形でマグリット・ルームを保存し，スタイネンによるカジノのファサードを復元している。このだまし絵は，混合することでカジノの変容を目指すこのプロジェクトにおいて，全体を三つの建築で構成するようヒントを与えてくれた──初期モダン建築の復元ヴォリューム（復元された，新規プログラムによる白いカジノ），多孔性の陸橋型ハイブリッド建築（多数の穴の開けられた会議場），そして帆のようなフラットな建築（ガラス面──ホテルと共同住宅タワー）といった，新しい機能の相助作用を生み出すための建築群である。

新しいデザインは「大西洋の壁」の切れ目があるクノ

Swimming pool

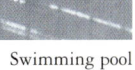

Sea Hall: entrance

1 ENTRANCE TO SEA HALL
2 PLAZA
3 FOYER
4 BALCONY
5 MAIN HALL
6 STAGE
7 BAR
8 SERVICE

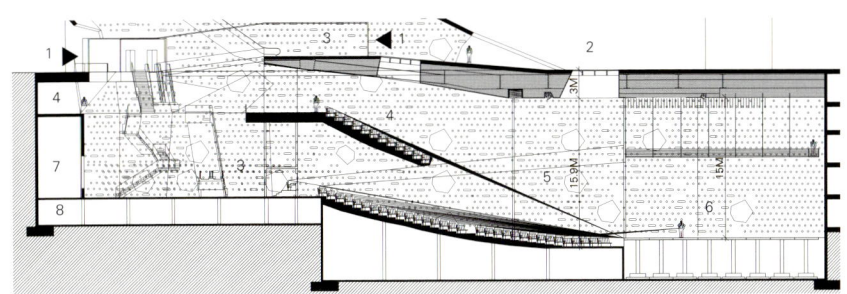

Longitudinal section: Sea Hall

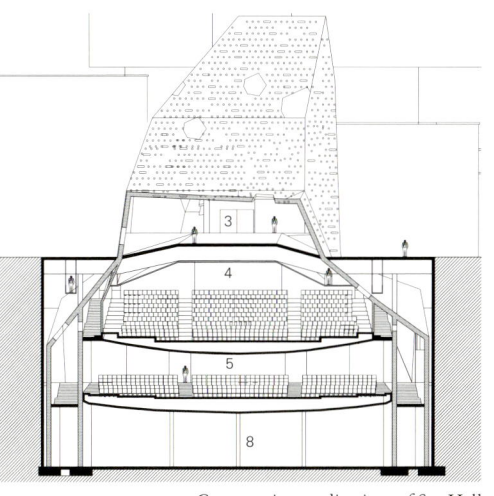

Cross section: auditorium of Sea Hall

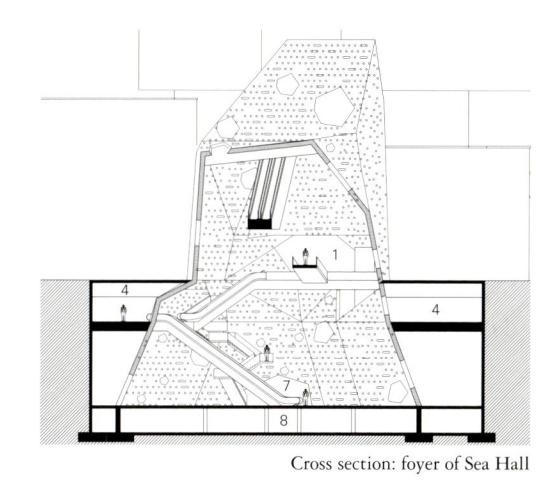

Cross section: foyer of Sea Hall

ック＝ヘイストの海岸線の中の一点を占めている。海に面した建物の向きと結果としての薄い外形は、タワーの全居住者の海への視界を妨げずに確保し、また隣接する居住環境の視界に影響を与えないものとなっている。多孔性質は会議場のカーテンウォール、及び北側において海へと開いているカジノの地上レベルで用いられており、会議場からエントランスに面した南側大通りへと続いている。

スパや屋上テラス、プールやレストランといったタワーの最上層階に位置する公共空間に重点が置かれている。会議場には別の屋上テラスとプール、カフェなどが与えられ、展示場、カジノエリアの両方からアクセス可能である。大部分が歩行者用の公共スペースである「カジノ広場」はベルギーの青石で舗装され、造園や公共アート作品などで拡張されているが、板張りの遊歩道に面し、街の都市的構成の中に織り込まれた場としての存在意義をつくり出している。

ダイニングの場や会合、レジャー、議会といった様々な機能が相助作用をもって統合され、プログラムの中で組み合わされている。カジノ、主力の高級ホテル、会議施設、イベントホール、展示場設備、レストラン、カフェ、マグリット・ルーム、ナイトクラブ、集合住宅、ギャラリー、スパ施設、店舗、それに地下全自動型駐車場などが71,000平方メートル、19階建ての建物の中に、二つの屋上テラスと二つのプールと共に提供されている。建物の素材はガラス、鉄鋼や再利用のテラゾ、ガラス破片や地元産出のコンクリートなどが含まれる。地熱発電の施設が駐車ガレージの下に設けられ、自動化された駐車場は盗難や損害、ガス放出などを排除しつつ収容能力を最大化している。また高能率のカーテンウォールは太陽光による温度上昇をコントロール、断熱するよう建物に組み込まれ、環境維持性能を最適化している。スタイネンによるカジノのオリジナルを復元、再利用することで廃棄を避け、取り壊しや新規部材製作、エネルギー使用量を最小限に留めていく。

2006- Meander
Helsinki, Finland

Distant view from Taivallahti Bay

Located in Helsinki's cultural and historical (Sibelius lived nearby) district Taka-Töölö along the Taivallahti Bay, the site is enclosed by the Taivallahti Barracks, two apartment buildings and an office block. Out of the bounded inner block Steven Holl Architects' 8,886 m² Meander rises in section towards the sea horizon, providing breathing space to the historic barracks and maximizing views and sunlight to the 49 apartments in the new building. The 180-meter long glass building with a height varying from two to seven floors, meanders across the rectangular courtyard like a musical score, shaping garden void spaces within the block. Meander is carried by load bearing perpendicular concrete walls, and glazed with horizontally hinged panels of intelligent glass to maximize control of light and solar gain. This glass skin of the building slightly varies in shade from transparent to opaque with thermal elements and functions like a chameleon skin. During the evenings, the building glows like an ice sculpture. The apartments, ranging from 62 m² to 222 m², all have private saunas, balconies, and views of the sea or of Hesperia Park. Pivoting walls maximize user control on spatial variations. Among the public spaces for residents is a rooftop sauna with sea views, which opens onto a jogging track spanning the full building length.

For the design and construction of Meander, Steven Holl Architects is collaborating with Vesa Honkonen Architects (Helsinki, Finland). Meander is the second project for Steven Holl Architects in Helsinki; in 1998 the Kiasma Museum of Contemporary Art opened its doors to the public. This museum, considered as one of Steven Holl Architect's major works, received the National AIA Design Award in 1999.

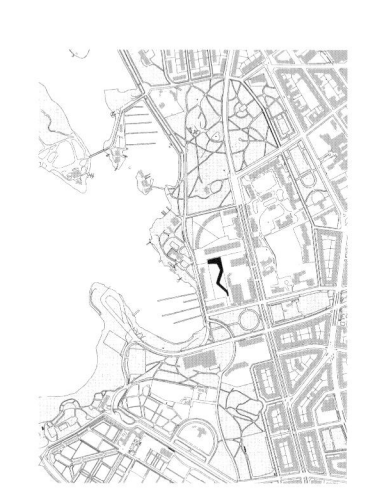

Location

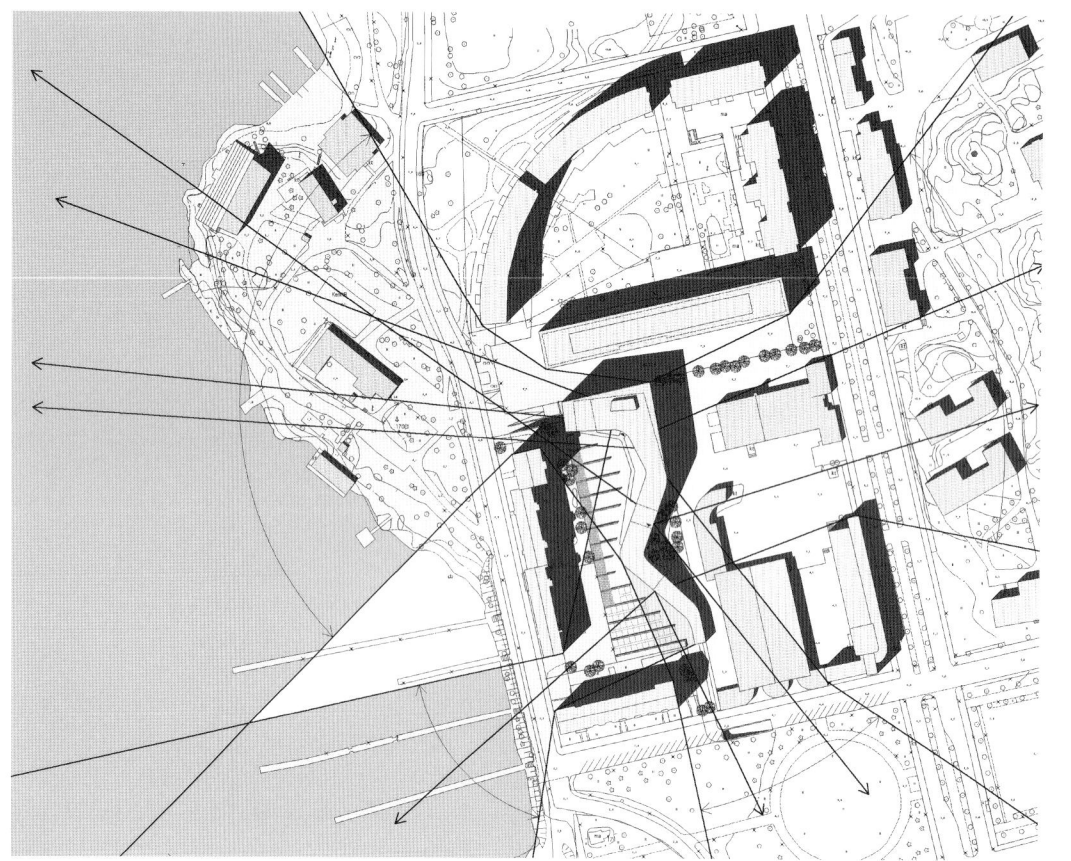

Site plan: all apartments have views of the sea or the bay or the park

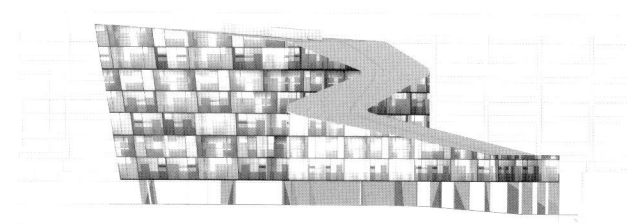

South elevation

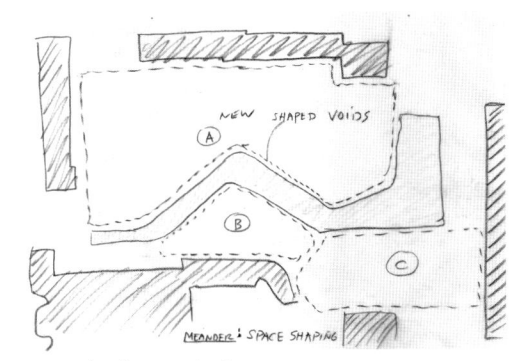

Concept sketch: space shaping

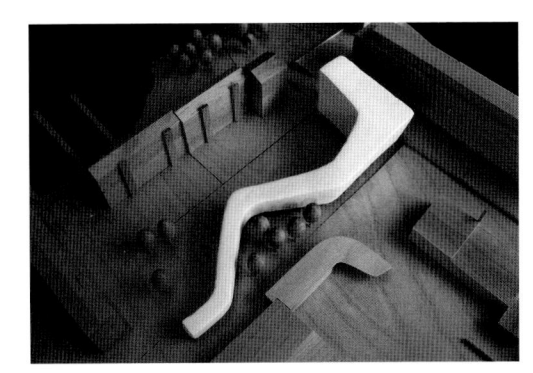

Model

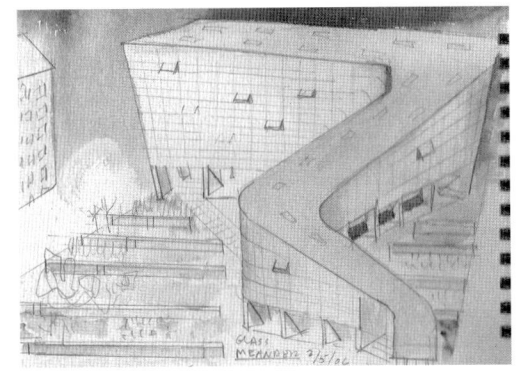

Sketch: south view

Sketch: pool garden

メアンダー

(シベリウスがその傍に住んでいた)ヘルシンキの文化歴史地区タカトゥーロ。この敷地はタイバラハティ湾に面し、周囲をタイバラハティ兵舎の2棟の集合住宅と、1棟のオフィス・ブロックによって囲まれている。スティーヴン・ホールの8,886平米のメアンダーは、兵舎によって阻まれたブロックから水平線に向かって立ち上がり、古い兵舎には息吹を、新しい建築の49の住戸には眺望と太陽を最大限に確保する。2層から7層へと高さの変化する全長180メートルに及ぶこのガラス建築は、長方形の中庭を楽譜のように蛇行し、ブロックに庭園となるヴォイド空間を構成する。メアンダーは垂直の耐震コンクリート壁で支えられ、光と熱負荷を最大限に調節するため、水平に回転するスマートガラスで覆われている。建築のガラスの表皮は熱によって陰影が透明から不透明へとゆっくりと変化し、カメレオンの皮膚のように機能する。夜になると、建築は氷の彫刻のような輝きを放つ。集合住宅の住戸は62平米から222平米に及ぶ。全ての住戸にはプライベート・サウナとバルコニーがあり、海か、あるいはヘスペリア・パークへの眺望を臨む。間仕切り壁を回転させることで、居住者は自由に空間を使うことができる。住民用のパブリック・スペースのなかでも、屋上のサウナからは海を眺め、建築の全長にわたって延びるジョギングコースを見渡すことができる。

メアンダーでは(フィンランド・ヘルシンキの)ヴェサ・ホンコネンとの共同作業を通して、設計と建設が進められる。メアンダーは1998年にキアズマ現代美術館が公開されて以来の、スティーヴン・ホールにとってヘルシンキで取り組む第二の計画である。この美術館はスティーヴン・ホールの代表作のひとつとして見なされ、1999年にはアメリカ建築家協会建築賞を受賞するに至っている。

1 LOBBY
2 POOL AREA
3 CLUB ROOM
4 GAME & RELAXING AREA
5 RENTAL SPACE
6 BICYCLE STORAGE
7 STORAGE
8 PARKING
9 MECHANICAL
10 SPARE ROOM
11 JOGGING TRACK
12 SAUNA
13 ROOF TERRACE

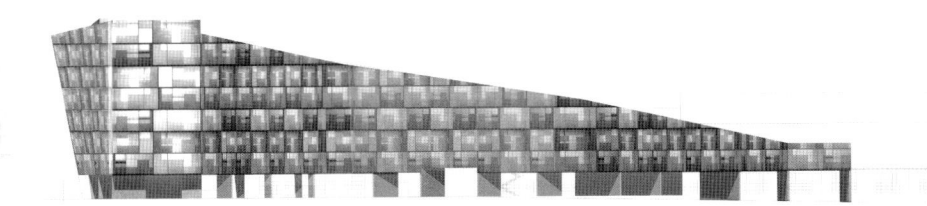

East elevation

Level 8
Level 6
Level 4
Level 3
Level 2
Level 1
Level 0

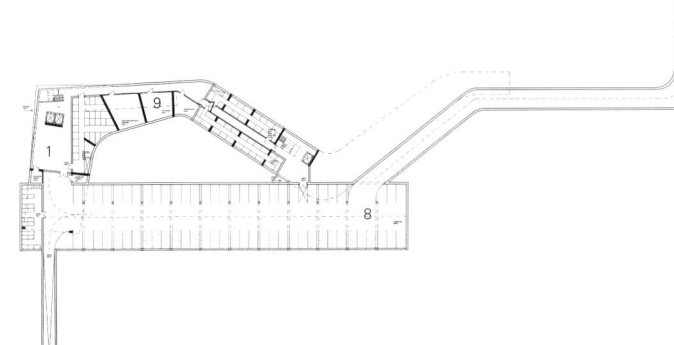

Model: view from southwest

Sliced Porosity Block
2007-12 Chengdu, China

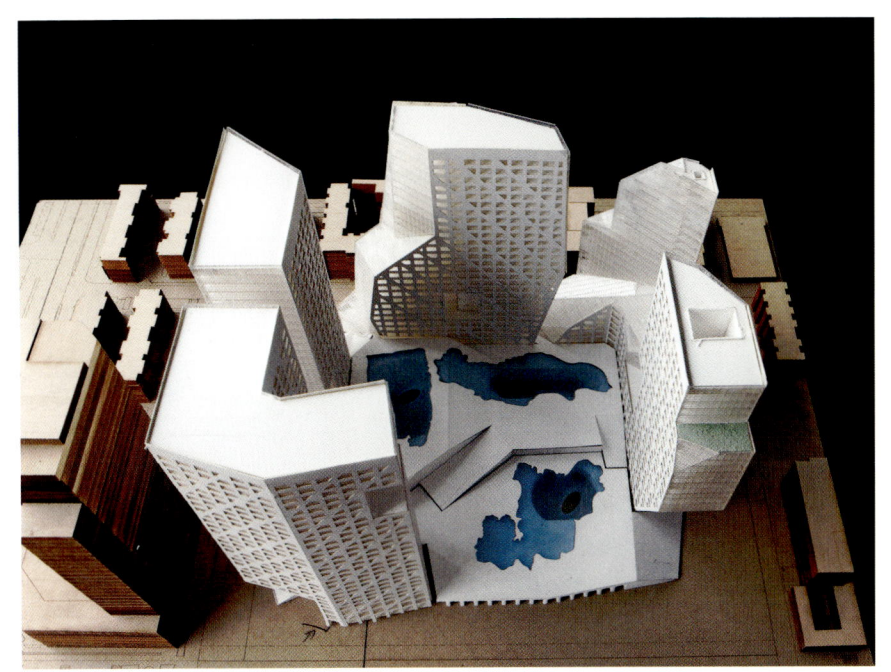

Model: downward view

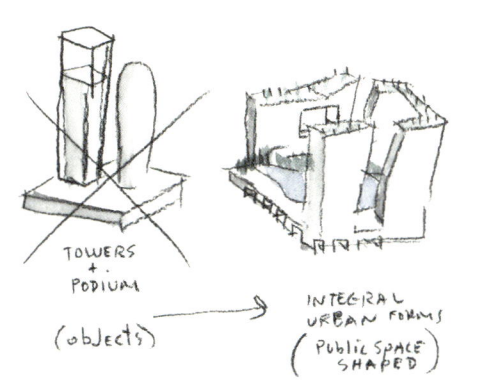

Concept sketch: integral urban functions shape public space

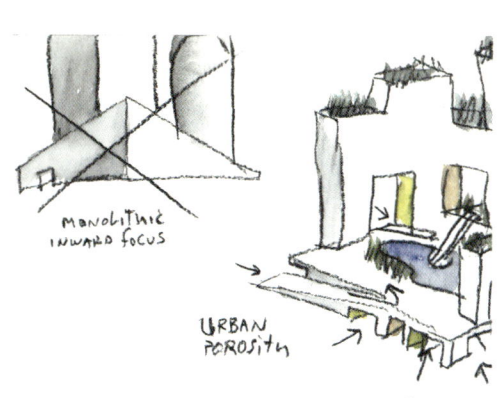

Urban porosity

Microurbanism

Super-green architecture

The Sliced Porosity Block, CapitaLand China's new Raffles City in Chengdu, is a hybrid of different functions like a giant chunk of a metropolis. It will be located just south of the intersection of the First Ring Road and Ren Min Nan Road. Its sun sliced geometry results from required minimum daylight exposures to the surrounding urban fabric prescribed by code and calculated by the precise geometry of sun angles.

The large public space framed by the block is formed into three valleys inspired by a poem of Du Fu (713-770). In some of the porous openings chunks of different buildings are inserted. Our micro urban strategy will create a new terrain of public space; an urban terrace on the metropolitan scale of Rockefeller Center. This new terrain is sculpted by stone steps and ramps with large pools that spill into stepped fountains. Trees, plantings and benches are flanked with cafes. Roof gardens are cultivated through their individual connections to hotel cafes.

At the shop fronts there will be luminous color, neon, backlit color transparency. Like the wash of color that suddenly appears in the great black and white films by Andrei Tarkovsky. The aim for the Sliced Porosity Block is to form new public space and to realize new levels of green construction in Chengdu. The complex is heated and cooled geothermally by 400 wells. The large podium ponds harvest recycled rainwater with natural grasses and lily pads creating a cooling effect.

Concept sketch: 'Three Valleys' inner garden

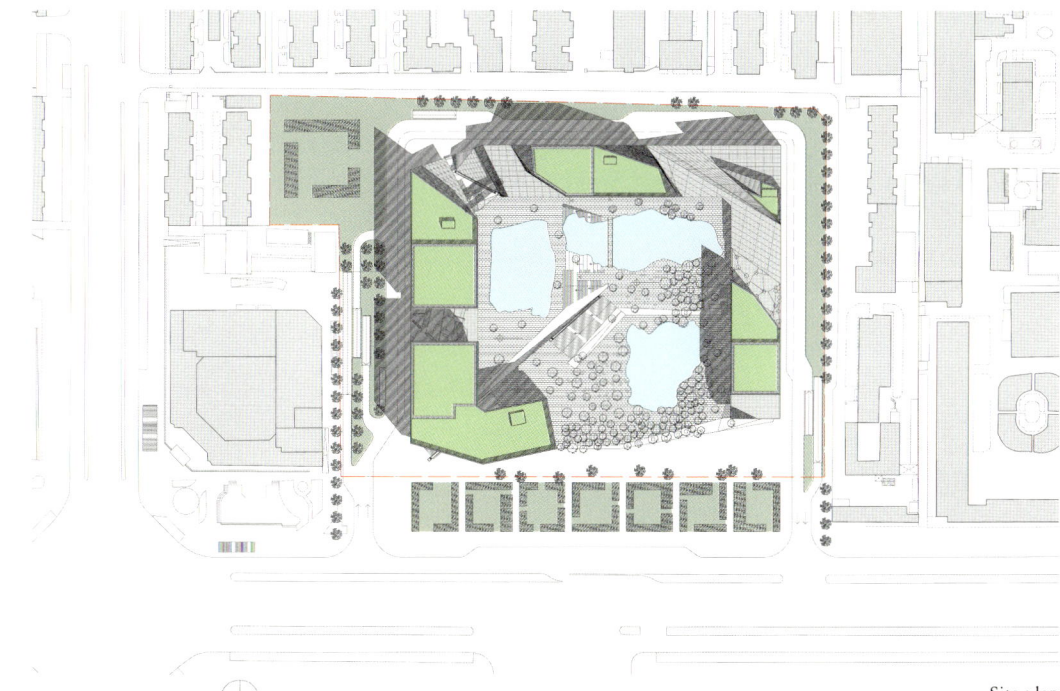

Site plan

II-147

View from southwest (under construction)

View toward tower on northwest corner (under construction)

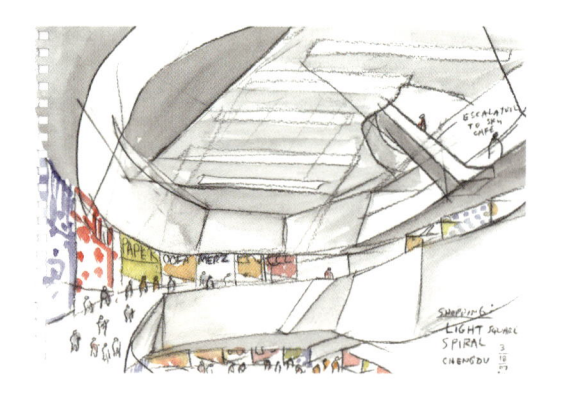

Sketch: retail area

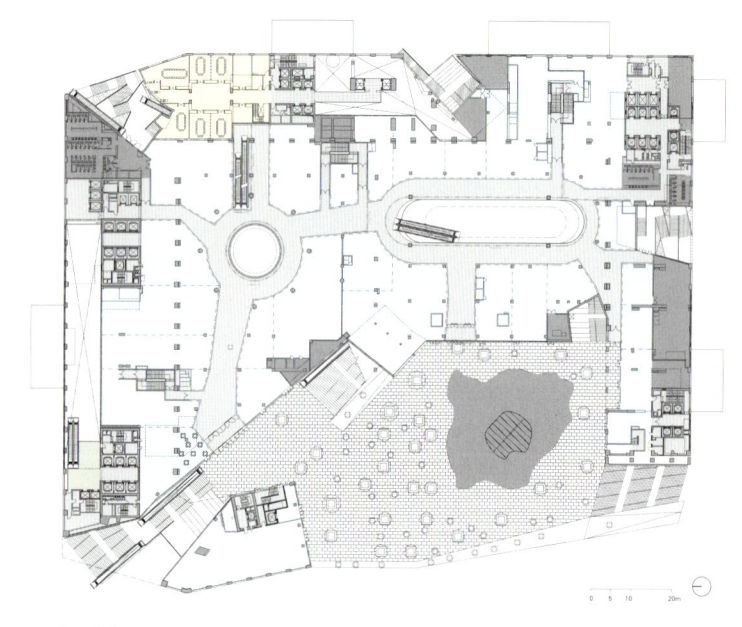

Level 2

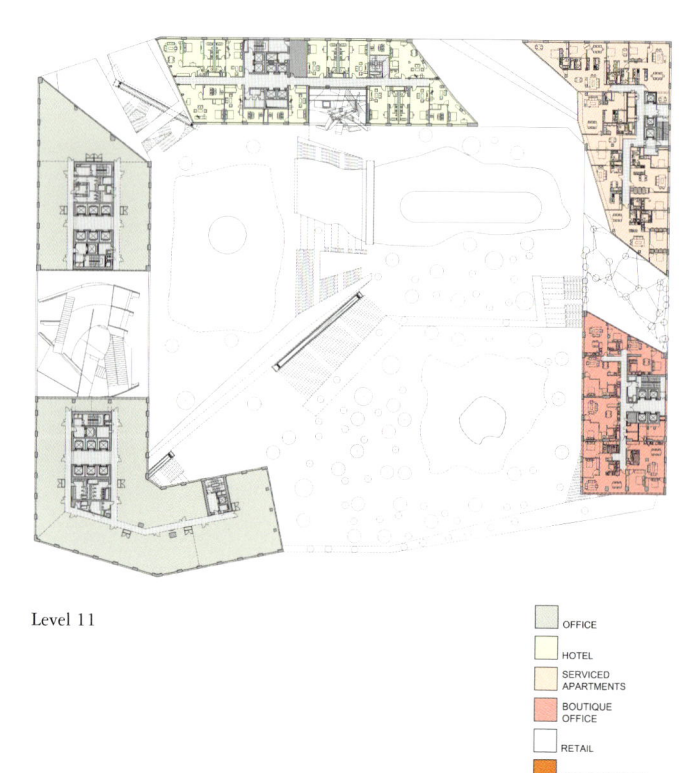

Level 11

OFFICE
HOTEL
SERVICED APARTMENTS
BOUTIQUE OFFICE
RETAIL
PUBLIC PROGRAM
SEMI PUBLIC PROGRAM
CIRCULATION
SERVICE AREA

スライスド・ポロシティ・ブロック
Sliced Porosity Block—キャピタランド・チャイナ(シンガポールを拠点とするアジア最大規模の不動産開発業者)が手掛ける,中国,成都市における新しい「ラッフルズ・シティ」は,大都会に塊を成して存在している異なった機能を一カ所に混合させたものである。この建物は第一環状道路と人民南道路交差点のすぐ南に位置することになる。

太陽に「削ぎ取られた」形になる建物の幾何形態は,条例によって規定された周辺都市環境への最低日照要求に対応するもので,太陽高度や角度の正確な幾何計測に基づいたものである。

大きな量塊の建物群に囲まれた広い公共スペースは,杜甫(713〜770年)のある詩に触発されて,三つの谷を形づくるというヒントを得た。建物ヴォリュームにうがたれたいくつもの穴には,別の建物の量塊が挿入されている。我々の考える極小都市という方法論は,公共スペースという考え方に新たな地平空間を創造する。それは,庭園空間を,ロックフェラー・センターのような都市建築レベルのスケールに落とし込むことである。この新しい地平空間は,石段の階段や傾斜路,壇上になった噴水池に流れ込む大きな水盤などによって彫り込まれ削り取られている。幾つかのカフェが樹々や植栽,ベンチなどの側に並ぶ。点在する屋根付きの庭園は,ホテルの各カフェにそれぞれ独自につながるように切り開かれている。

店舗の店先は華やいだ色,ネオンや背面から照らされ透過された透明な光などで彩られている。それはまるでアンドレイ・タルコフスキーの素晴らしい白黒映画の中に,突然色が溢れ出したかのようだ。この量塊を削ぎ落とすことで生まれた多孔性ブロックの狙いは,新しい公共の空間を形成し,環境に配慮した建築を新たな水準で成都市に実現することである。この複合建築においては,400もの井戸による地熱効果を用いた冷暖房が行われる。基壇にある大きな池の並びにより集められた雨水は,自然の芝生に覆われた地表を潤すことによって再利用され,池に浮かぶ睡蓮の葉は,周辺の空気の冷却効果をもたらしている。

Tower on northeast corner (under construction)

© Lebbeus Woods

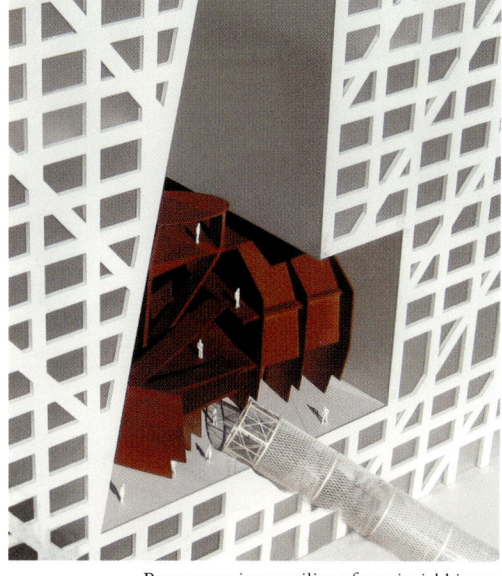

Porous opening: light pavilion

Porous opening: pavilion of provincial history

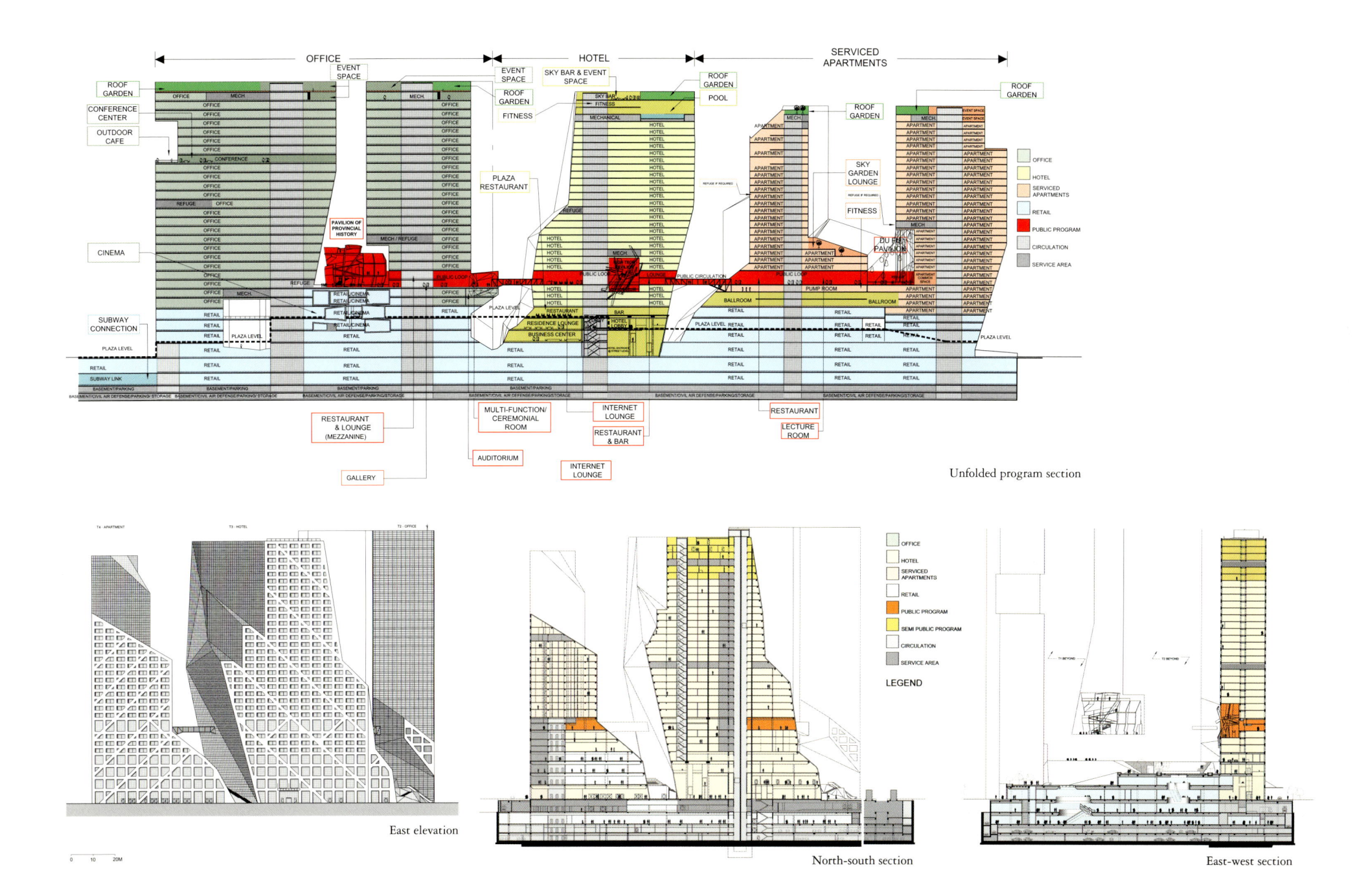

Unfolded program section

East elevation

North-south section

East-west section

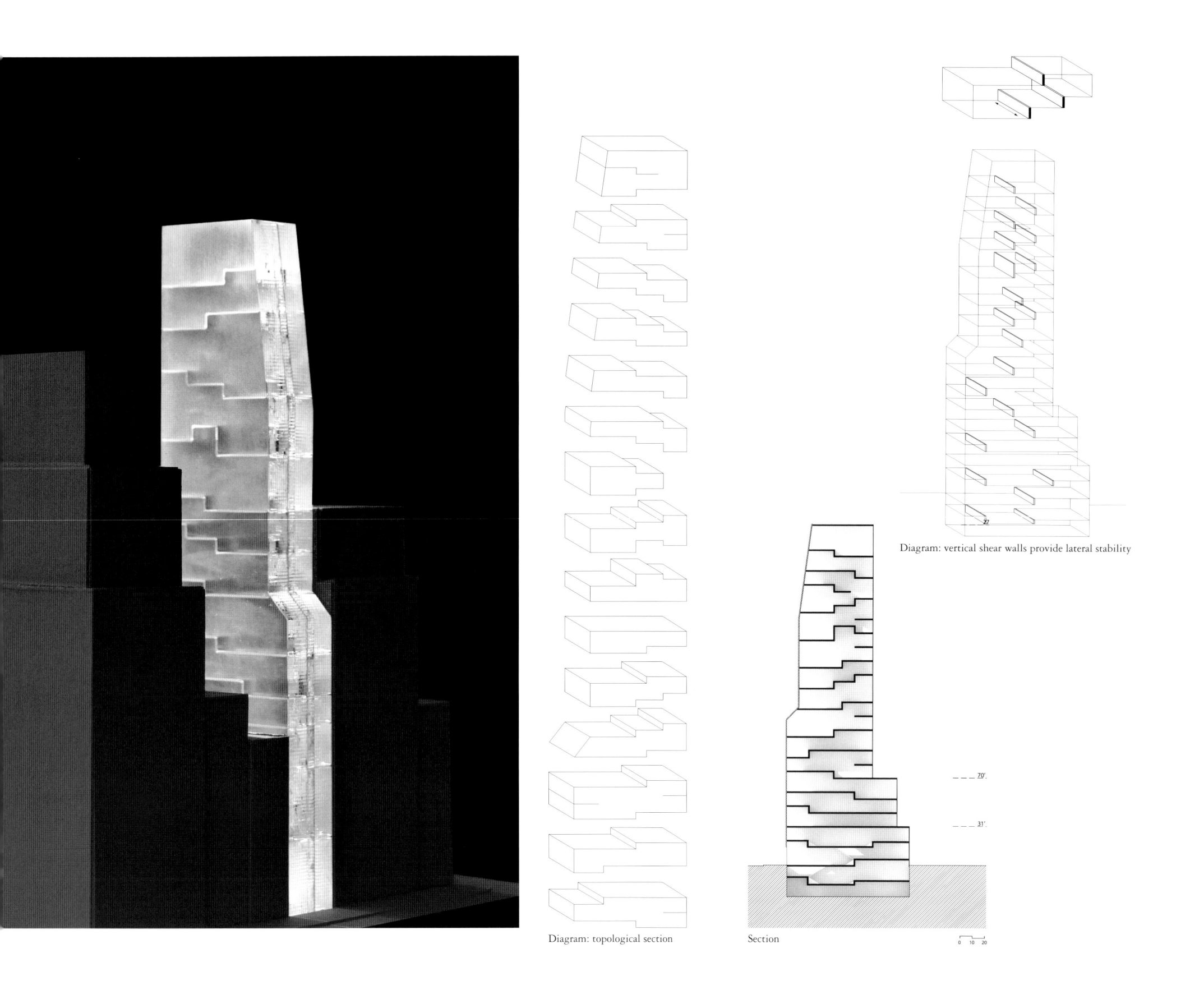

Diagram: topological section

Diagram: vertical shear walls provide lateral stability

Section

Benetton Tower
2010 New York, New York, U.S.A.

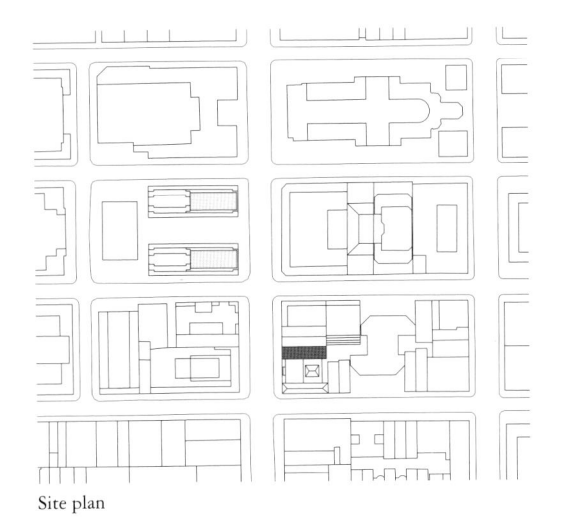

Site plan

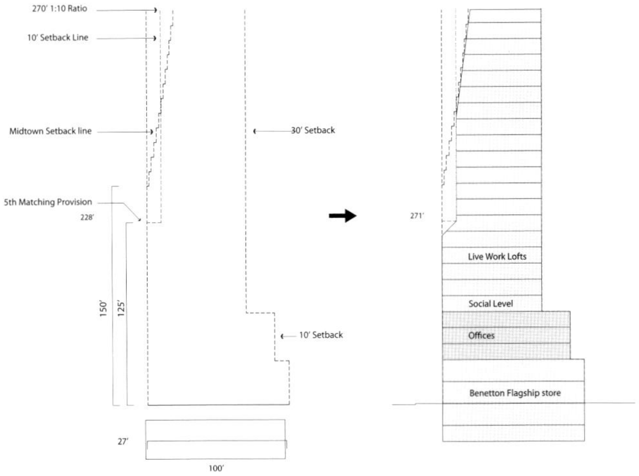

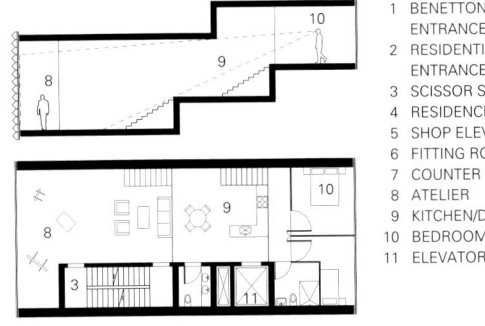

1 BENETTON STORE ENTRANCE
2 RESIDENTIAL ENTRANCE LOBBY
3 SCISSOR STAIRS
4 RESIDENCE ELEVATOR
5 SHOP ELEVATOR
6 FITTING ROOMS
7 COUNTER
8 ATELIER
9 KITCHEN/DINING ROOM
10 BEDROOM
11 ELEVATOR

Topological artist loft:
plan (below) and section (above) S=1:400

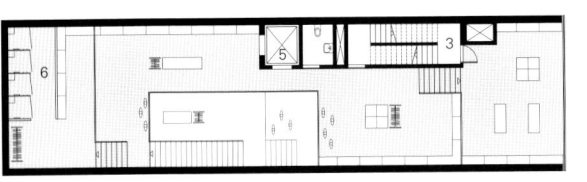

Second floor

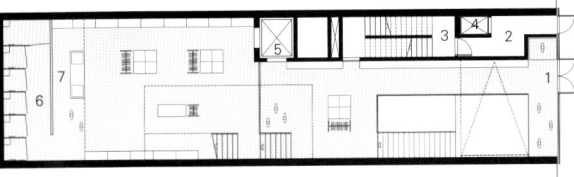

First floor

Basement S=1:400

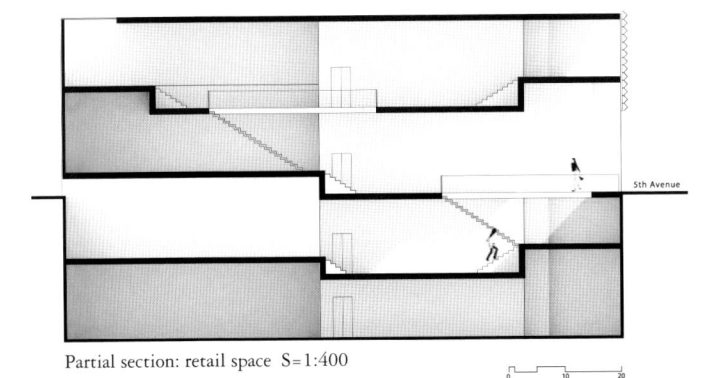

Partial section: retail space S=1:400

Section diagram: zoning code (left) and proposed area (right)

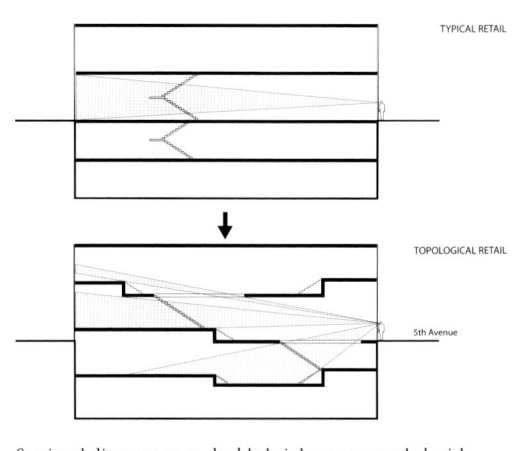

Sectional diagram: open double height space coupled with level changes allow shoppers to see all floors simultaneously from the street, bringing them in contact with all products

"Topological Section/Topological Retail"
The Tower/Topological Section

Located at 601 5th Avenue, diagonally across from Rockefeller Center, Benetton's flagship store and residential tower has the rare opportunity to make an exemplary tower for New York.

The shape of the building is informed by the strict zoning laws and building codes of midtown Manhattan, but avoids the typical stepped facade produced by setbacks. Instead a continuous glass surface folds between the setback lines.

The folded facade is made out of a special prismatic glass in structural planks; a new material that refracts white sunlight into a spectrum of colors, and at the same time harvests solar energy for the building. This new material will resonate with Benetton's image of diversity, innovation, and color.

The interior walls and floors are fused together to produce a topological section. Instead of the typical extruded floor plans, where every level is the same, the topological section allows for every level to be different and unique, creating double-height spaces and level changes.

The FAR on the site is 15. With the given site of 27 feet x 100 feet and added setbacks, this typically would allow for a 228 feet tall building with 20 floors. The topological section, with double height spaces and level changes, allows the building with the same FAR of 15 to be 270 feet tall, exploiting a loophole in the zoning law.

The topological section on the interior is expressed on the exterior side elevations; floors are pulled through to connect with white translucent glass. These side elevations, typically rendered blank as a result of New York City building codes, here will expresses the spatial logic of the building.

The Flagship Store/Topological Retail

Prismatic glass cascades down to the street level, merging the tower's expression with Benetton's retail identity. The tower and store will be recognized as one and the same.

The retail space is again configured with a topological section. Open double height spaces coupled with level changes allow shoppers to see all floors simultaneously, and encourage them to use the stairs, bringing them in contact with all of the products.

The specialness of the topological retail space with its unique architectural spatial concept merges with the image of Benetton.

At the front of the store, a vertical open space connecting the various levels gives a moment of inspiration to shoppers and allows them to take in the breadth of clothing that is available to them. In addition, it presents the opportunity for large scale projections that define the identity of Benetton.

International Live/Work Lofts

Benetton's rich connection to the visual arts and extensive patronage through existing grants, suggests a new international artist grant based in New York, sponsored by Benetton. Live/Work lofts would provide space for young artists from around the world to spend six months in one of the most inspiring cities in the world.

Apartments

Every loft is unique and different. The topological loft offers an open and free-feeling space, as well as providing a distinct separation of functions through its variation in section—a distinct and unprecedented type of apartment building for New York.

Structure

The fused planar floors and walls, which define the topological space, also perform structurally. With a 1:10 floor to elevation ratio, the very slender tower gains lateral stability through the folding concrete floors and walls.

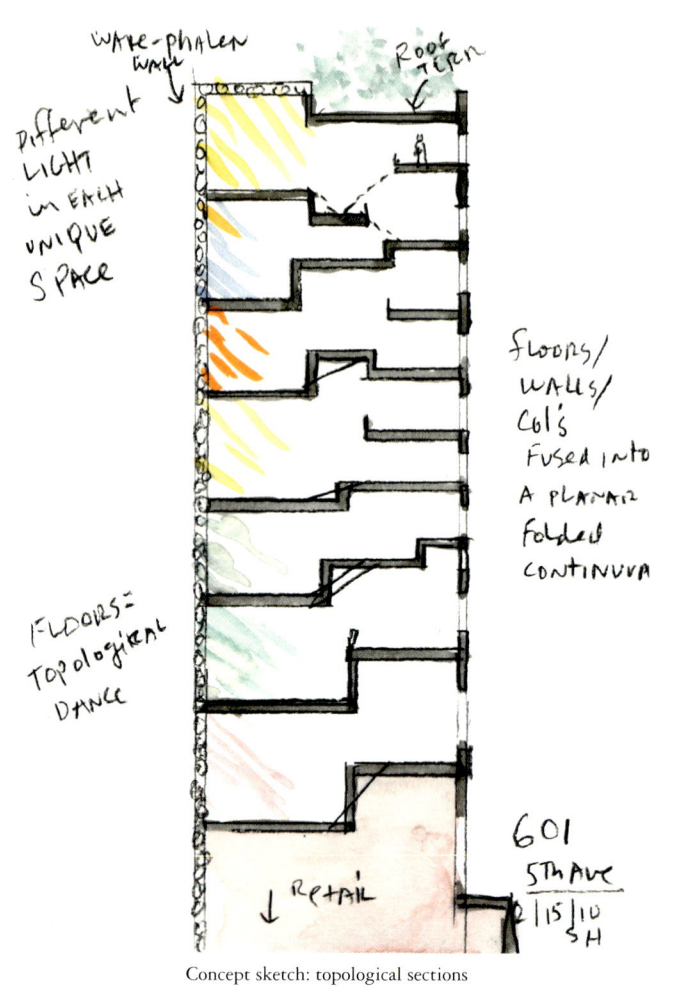

Concept sketch: topological sections

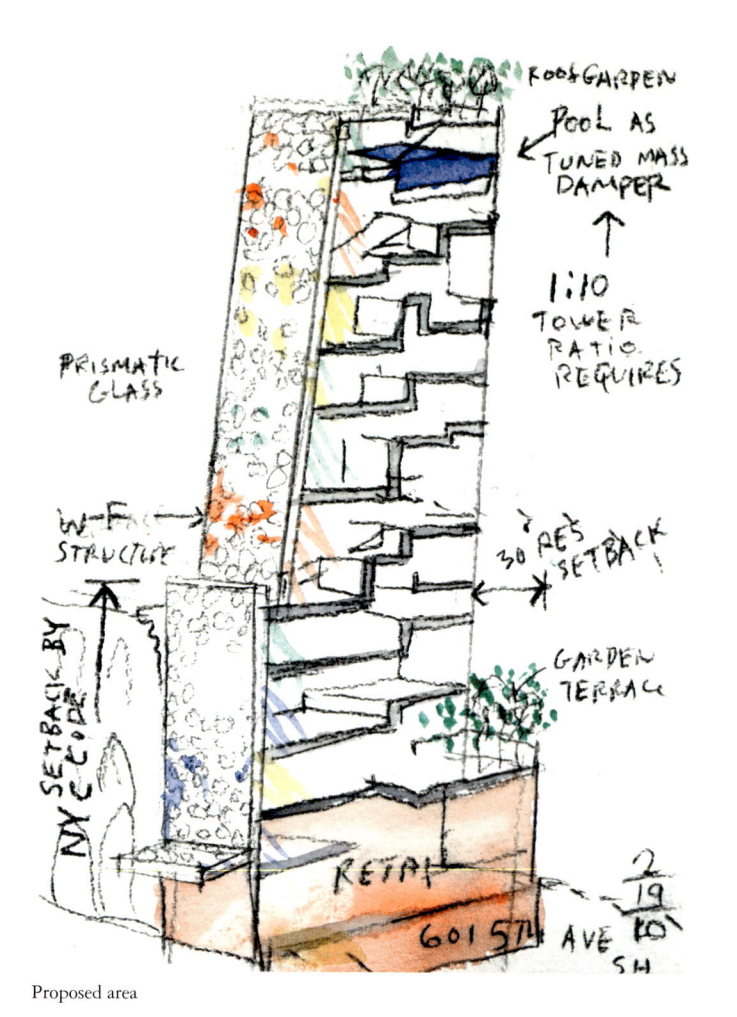

Proposed area

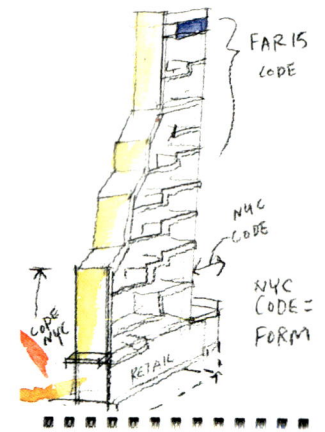

New York City building codes

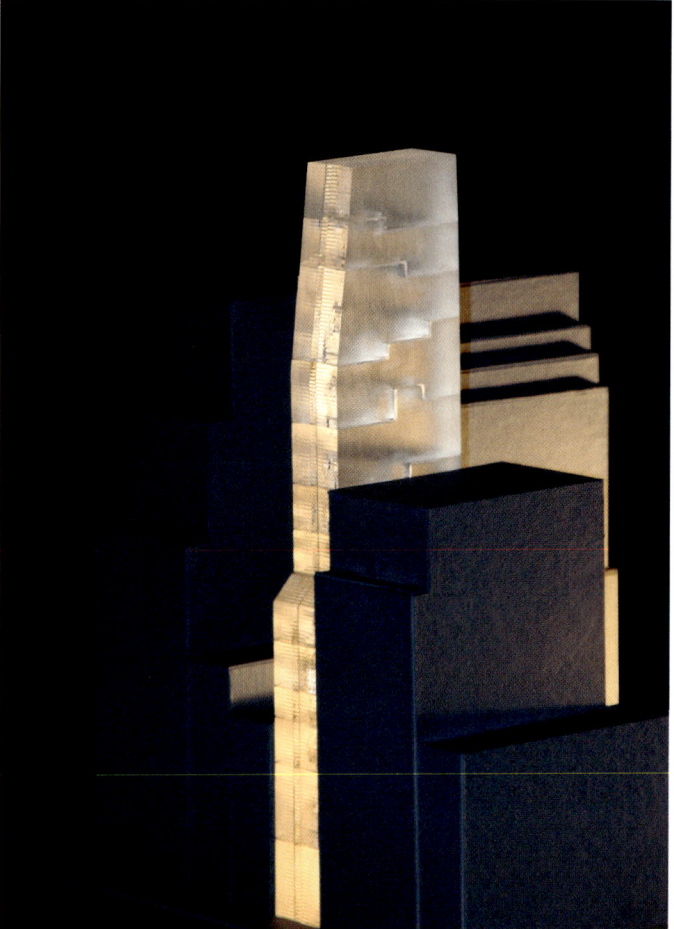

Model: prismatic glass facade

Topological section

ベネトン・タワー
「トポロジカル・セクション／トポロジカル・リテール」
［ザ・タワー／トポロジカル・セクション］

5番街601番地はロックフェラー・センターの筋向いである。ベネトン旗艦店とレジデンシャル・タワーは，ニューヨークを代表する希有の高層建築となるだろう。

マンハッタン・ミッドタウンの厳格なゾーニング法と建築基準で決定される建築形態。斜線制限による典型的なステップ型ファサードを回避する方法が模索された。ガラスは連続することなく，その表面は斜線制限のなかで屈折する。

太陽の白色光はスペクトルに分解される。太陽光発電を行う新しい素材，構造面に取り付けられた特殊なプリズム・ガラスが屈折したファサードを構成する。この新しい素材はベネトンの持つイメージの多様性，革新性，そして鮮やかな色彩と共鳴するようになるだろう。

内部空間は壁と床がひとつに融合し，トポロジカル・セクションを構成する。典型的な平面計画では全てが同じ基準階で構成され，垂直方向へと引き延ばされる。それとは逆に，トポロジカル・セクションの階層は全てが異なり，それぞれ独自の吹き抜け空間とスキップフロアを生み出している。

敷地の容積率は1500％。27×100フィート（約8.2m×30.5m）の敷地と斜線制限を考慮すると，一般的には高さ228フィート（約69.5m），20階の建築が可能になる。トポロジカル・セクションでは吹き抜け空間のレベルが

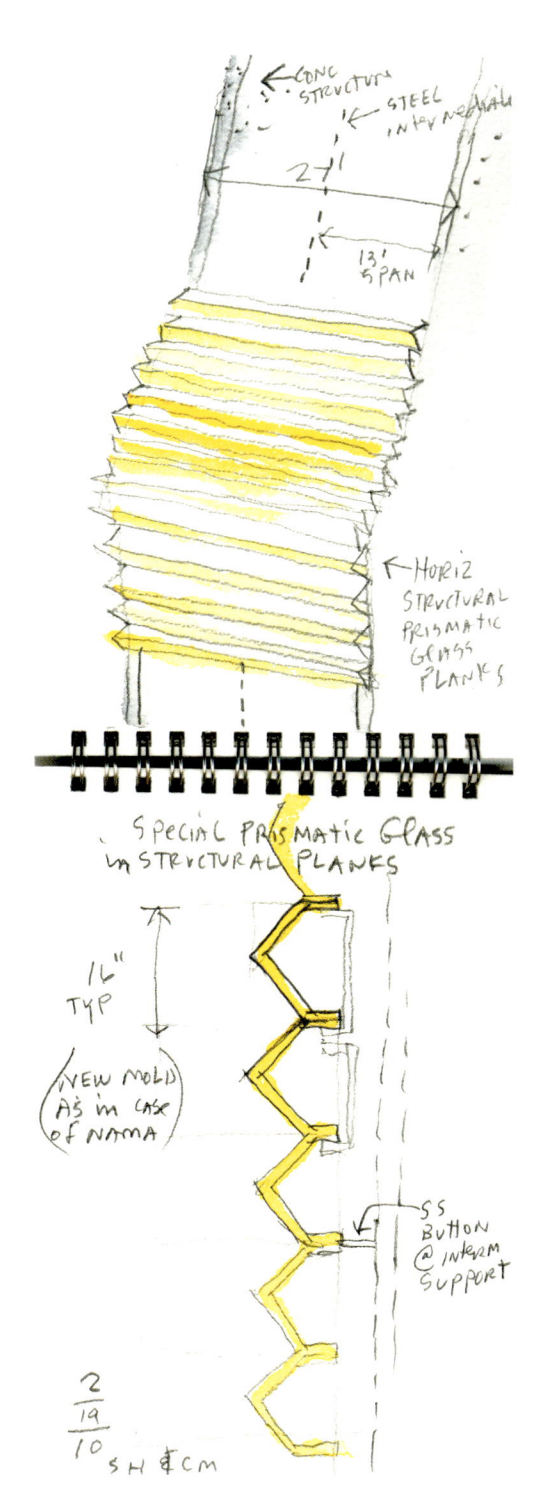

Sketches: detail of prismatic glass

Concept sketch: prismatic glass harvests solar energy for building

Mock-up model: prismatic glass

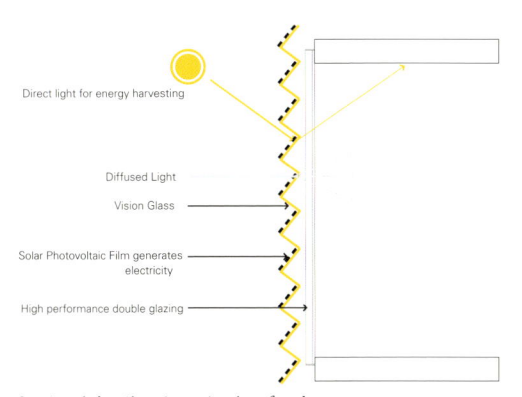

Sectional detail: prismatic glass facade

変化する。ゾーニング法の優遇措置を利用することで，同じ容積率で15階層，高さ270フィート(約82.3m)の建築が可能となった。

　外部の立面は，内部のトポロジカル・セクションを表現したものである。床スラブは外部へと引き出され，そこで白く透過するガラスへと接合される。ニューヨーク市の建築基準では一般的に，これらの側面は無彩色とすることが定められている。そのためここでは，建築の空間の論理構造が表現されている。

[旗艦店／トポロジカル・リテール]
プリズム・ガラスによる光の滝はストリートレベルに達し，建築表現とベネトンの企業理念はひとつに融合する。そこでは建築とベネトンは，完全に同一のものとしてみなされるだろう。

　店舗空間もまた，トポロジカル・セクションを構成する。開放的な吹き抜け空間のスキップ・フロアからは，消費者は全てのフロアを同時に見渡すことができる。階段の利用を促すことで，全てのプロダクトを手に取って確かめることができる。

　トポロジカル・リテールの空間的特殊性と建築空間の独自の理念が，ベネトンというひとつのイメージに融合する。

　垂直に延びる開放的な店舗のフロントは，様々なレベルをひとつに結びつけることで，服を買おうとする消費者を刺激し，あるいは息をつくことのできる空間を提供する。さらにこの空間は，ベネトンのアイデンティティとして，巨大なイメージを空間に映し込むことができる。

[国際的な居住／制作ロフト]
ベネトンとビジュアル・アートとの豊かな関係性や，助成を通した現在の幅広い支援活動は，ニューヨークを本拠地としたベネトンによる国際的な新しい芸術家支援活動を連想させる。居住／制作ロフトでは，世界中で最も刺激的な都市に6ヶ月間滞在するための空間が，世界中の若手芸術家に提供される。

[集合住宅]
全てのロフトはひとつずつ異なっている。トポロジカル・ロフトは開放され，自由に寛ぐことができる。その一方で，多様な断面に従って機能は完全に分離されている。ニューヨークの集合住宅で，これは他に類のないタイプの住宅である。

[構造]
床と壁は一体的に融合してトポロジカル・スペースを定義するとともに，構造としても機能する。フロアと立面の比率は1：10。折れ曲がるコンクリートの床と壁によって，非常に細長い高層建築は水平方向の安定性を確保している。

4 Ontology of Institutions
組織の存在論

To give expression to an institution which is in a dynamic condition of change is a great challenge for architecture today.

For example, what is the role of the branch library with what is currently happening to the book? We are in a volatile and changing time, where books are disappearing and electronic media are replacing them. This is one of the conditions that we are faced with in the design of a library in Queens (2010-), which is a very small building. What is the expression of the building? What can it be as an experience to solidify the notion of this as the institution of a small community library? Certainly the most important aspects are social; the building is a place for meeting, a place for generating ideas, a place for the community to come, interact and connect. There is a relation to the book that we tried to achieve where the section of the building is really a section through a series of book stacks. The work spaces are horizontal computer tables. As you walk into the building you will see stacks of books, but in fact actual conditions will find most people on computers. There is a balance between the book and the digital which is very flexible and that was something we came to early on in the section. The fact that the library is surrounded by towers, some twenty times taller, requires this small public building to have a large public presence. The client asked for an iconic presence for this thirty-five thousand square foot facility in the middle of residential skyscrapers. Luckily the site is on the edge of the waterfront of the East River. We carved the facade, which aligns with the movement through the section of the building. It inscribes the Manhattan view in the distance but is also inscribes the nature of the balance of books and the digital on the interior along the stepped section. It creates a figure cut into the foamed aluminum prism of a building that's only forty feet wide by eighty feet tall. The building glows at night, giving a special reflection over the river. As an institution it becomes a new kind of expression of all these different forces that are at play; from the internal forces, the flexible ground floor, the public meeting room, to the fact that it's very small for its size but needs to be large in terms of its presence in the community, to the relation of the digital and the book. When thinking about an ontology of institutions or the expression of institutions, in many cases, one has to imagine a new way to concretize a meaningful expression that can be understood as a public building.

ダイナミックに変化する状況の渦中で公共建築にかたちを付与することは，今日の建築にとって偉大な挑戦である。

例えば，本の世界で今起きている変化を前にして，小さな図書館の果たすべき役割とは何だろうか？　めまぐるしい変化の時代に，本というものは消えてゆき，電子メディアがその代わりの役割を果たす。クイーンズの図書館(2010-)を計画する際に私たちが直面したのはこのような問題である。この図書館は非常に小さい。建築表現とは何か？　コミュニティのための小規模図書館。理念を強化し，建築をあるひとつの経験とするためにはどうすればよいか？　最も重要な側面は，社会的なものである。建築とは，人と人とが出会い，アイディアを生み出し，コミュニティへと人々を誘い，交流し，結びつきを確かめる場所である。本との関係性。ここで追求されたのは，幾重にも積層された本棚が建築の断面となることであった。ワークスペースにあるのは，コンピュータのための水平なテーブルである。この建築のなかを歩いてゆくと，山のような本が目の前に飛び込んでくる。その一方で，実際にはほとんどの人はコンピュータと向き合っている。本とデジタル・メディアのあいだには非常にフレキシブルなバランスがある。これは当初から，建築の断面で検討を行ってきたものである。この図書館は，時には20倍もの高さの高層建築によって囲まれている。それゆえに，この小規模の公共建築は，社会にとって大きな存在である必要があった。周囲には高層集合住宅が立ち並ぶ。その中心に，クライアントは象徴的存在感を秘めた35,000平方フィート(約3,250平米)の建築を求めていた。この敷地がイーストリバーのウォーターフロントの際に面していたのは幸いである。建築の断面方向の動線に併せて，ファサードには切り込みが入れられている。その結果，遠くマンハッタン島への眺望が躯体に刻まれ，同時に段状の断面を持つ内部空間に，本とデジタル・メディアとの本質的調和が刻印されている。切り込みを入れることで，幅40フィート(約12m)，高さ80フィート(約24m)しかない発泡アルミニウムの建築が，結晶のように生み出された。夜になり輝きを増すと，この建築は川面に美しく反射する。内部空間の力学，フレキシブルな地上階，開放的なミーティング・ルーム。小規模であるにもかかわらず，コミュニティでは大きな存在感を示すという事実。デジタル・メディアと本との関係性。公共建築として，この場所に作用する全ての力学に対する新しい表現が追求された。公共建築の存在論や，それらの建築の表現について考える際には多くの場合，その建築が公共建築として意義あるものとして確実に理解されるために，新しい方法論を想像する必要がある。

小さな美術館。傑出した芸術家としてよく知られたピエロ・マンゾーニ

Herning Center of the Arts

A Small Art Museum: when a museum is related to one collection of a body of work—like in the case of the Herning Center of the Arts (2005-09) where a collection of some fifty works of the great artist Piero Manzoni resides, a special expression is required. Connecting this institution, (a small museum in Denmark's Jutland peninsula), to its site and to the artist who was one of the most important figures of the Arte Povera movement, became a central aim. The idea driving our design is a way of giving expression to this institution but also giving it meaning vis-à-vis the site, a particular place in the Jutland peninsula in Denmark. The building is white concrete which had fabric imbedded in the formwork to give it texture. We folded truck tarps so that when they were inserted into the concrete formwork you get this feeling of the building being made out of fabric. The form of the building itself is related to the original factory construction across the street which was built in the shape of a shirt collar. We imagined shirt sleeves thrown over the "treasure boxes" that hold the galleries to form a light-catching section. Light comes in under the curves of these sleeve shapes and creates a perfect twenty-five foot-candles of natural light at 5'-6" on the walls of the galleries. Transforming a flat field, the building is fused with the surrounding landscape with mounds and pools integrated into the overall geometry of the site. The expression of this museum as an institution comes out of the history of this place in the Jutland peninsula and the relation of Piero Manzoni's work, creating a flow of galleries in the glow of natural light.

A Literature Center in Norway: With the Knut Hamsun Center (1994-2009) in Hamarøy, there is a unique expression which is related to building as a "body of invisible forces". This vertical black form takes on a torsion, takes on this notion from a section of the novel *Hunger* where Hamsun describes the "building as a body of invisible forces." A literary passage became a conceptual figure around which the form of the architecture takes its shape. Incorporating local aspects, such as tarred wood skin and sod roofs, the building builds its site.

What is interesting about the question of the expression of institutions today is the potential of meaningful uniqueness. This is very different from even fifty years ago when one might begin a design with a relationship to architectural history as a way of symbolically connecting to the nature of the institution. Today architecture can begin from anything. It can begin from the spirit of a figure like Knut Hamsun. It can begin from the notion of fabric in the work of Piero Manzoni, it could begin from an idea of the relation of the book and the digital together with the notion of carving a view through a section. We inherit a much more open field. Architecture is in a more open way able to make original expressions for institutions and give them a meaningful relationship to their sites and their contents.

の作品が50点ほど展示してあるヘルニング美術館(2005-09)の場合のように，あるまとまった作品のコレクションのための美術館では，それに相応しい表現が要求される。ここでは小さな美術館を，(デンマークのユトランド半島にある)土地と，アルテ・ポーヴェラの芸術運動において最も重要なひとりの芸術家へと結びつけることが，主な目的だった。敷地はデンマークのユトランド半島にある。計画の発想の中心はこの公共建築に表現を付与する方法と，敷地に意味性を付与することであった。これは型枠に布生地を敷き詰め，打設して質感を表現したホワイトコンクリートの建築である。トラック用防水布を折り曲げコンクリートの型枠に取り付けることで，ここではファブリックの質感が表現されている。建築の形態自体は，通りの向かいのシャツの襟の形をした当時の製造工場に由来している。私たちはギャラリーを内包し，断面から光を捉えるために，「宝箱」の上に投げるようにして置かれたシャツの袖のような形を想像した。光はこれらの袖の曲面の下から入射し，ギャラリーの壁面5フィート6インチ(約1.7m)のところから見ると，25フィート(約7.6m)の自然光の燭台となって見える。平面を変形することで，建築は小高い土手や水盤といった周囲のランドスケープに溶け込み，敷地全体のジオメトリへと統合される。この建築はユトランド半島の場所の歴史と，ピエロ・マンゾーニの作品との関係性によってもたらされたものである。そこでは，ギャラリーは流れるように自然光のなかで輝くのだ。

ノルウェーの文学センター。ハマロイのクヌート・ハムスン・センター(1994-2009)の独創的表現は，建築を「不可視の身体」として見なすものである。ハムスンは建築を「不可視の力の作用する身体」として語る。垂直の黒の形態が捻れているのは，『飢え』と題した小説のなかから発想を得たものである。文学の小径という抽象的なかたちを取り巻くように，建築形態がその姿を現す。タール塗りの木素材の表皮や，草屋根といった土地の固有性がひとつになって，建築はこの土地に建つ。

固有の意味の可能性こそが，今日の公共建築の表現の面白さである。50年前の状況とすら，現代は非常に異なっている。当時は建築史との関係が，計画の端緒となった。それこそが，表現を公共建築の本質と象徴的に結びつけるための方法論であった。今日の建築は，その契機をあらゆる場所に求めることができる。クヌート・ハムスンという人物の精神性や，ピエロ・マンゾーニの作品に見られるファブリックの概念がその起点となる。本とデジタル・メディアとの関係性といった発想や，断面を切断して得られる眺望といった概念が，発想の原点となる。眼前には，より広大な視野が広がっているのだ。現代では社会に対して，より開かれた方法で，公共建築に独創的な表現を行っている。そのことが，結果として建築に敷地やその土地の文脈に深い意味性を付与しているのだ。

サーフ・ミュージアムについてはどうか？　ビアリッツのサーフ・オーシャン・文化センター(2005-11)に先行して，このような公共建築の前例はない。これは元々，市長が提案したプログラムで，サーフィンに関するミュージアムをつくり，海洋環境について学ぶというものであった。初めのプログラムはサーフィンの人気や楽しさと海洋文化をひとつに結びつけることで，人々を

A Surf Museum? In the case of the Cité de l'Océan et du Surf (2005-11) in Biarritz there is no institution that you could say is a precedent. This was an original program by the mayor to create a museum that would be about surfing, but it would also be about the health of the ocean. The original program was to combine the joy and the popularity of surfing and surf culture to attract people to this institution and teach them about the ecology of the ocean. The notion of science becomes as important as surfing. Our concept drawing "Under the Sky and Under the Sea" was about the forming of a space which could at once shape the public experience and point the view to the ocean horizon. The whole building is built around a convex/concave shape that tilts the main public space towards the ocean horizon. It gives you a condition of the oceanic horizon as the main feeling of occupying the space. The building takes on this shape and takes on a very specific character and a specific experience, creating a new expression for a new institution; one that fuses with the landscape beyond. It fuses with the immediate foreground, with the ocean horizon and with the two giant stones that are on the beach, bringing those two stones back as glass pavilions for a café and surfers kiosk. The white concrete has been cast with flake board texture as if worn by the sea. The exposed Okalux insulation between the glass is like the foam of the sea. "L'ecum de la mer!"

A Large Museum Expansion: In the case of the Nelson Atkins Museum (1999-2007) in Kansas City, the relation of the original building to the new expansion is primary. From an original 1937 Greco-Roman neoclassical building in stone, a new addition is doubling the size of the institution. The meaning and the relation between the two is based on the idea of "the stone and the feather", the idea of the heavy and the light, the idea of uniting opposites. When I first went to the site for that project I read in the old neoclassical façade 'the soul has greater need for the ideal than for the real' and that gave me the courage to break the rules of the competition and propose lenses of glass that bring light down through the landscape into a continuous system of galleries that are fused into the site. This relationship between the new and the old is of contrast, one light and one heavy, one open and one closed circulation, one hermetic and one opening out to the landscape in all directions. The new expression of the Nelson Atkins does not ignore the original neoclassical building but makes a complimentary contrast between the new and the old. The expression of the institution becomes the complimentary contrast between these points in time and the space they create.

To shape the architecture of an institution toward meaningful expression is a challenge which presents the potential of engaging expression unique to the site, circumstance and program.

Steven Holl

この施設に引きつけ，海洋の生態環境について学習するというものであった。ここで科学という概念は，サーフィンと同じく重要なものである。「空と海の下に」は，海の向こうの水平線を眺めながら社会的経験を行うことのできる空間を構成するというコンセプト・ドローイングである。主要パブリック・スペースが海に向かって傾くように，建築全体は凹凸形状につくられている。中に入って海の向こうの水平線を見ると，空間を独占していると感じられるだろう。建築の持つこのような形態，非常に特殊な性格，そして特別な経験が，新しい公共建築に対する新しい表現を生み出している。建築は，遠くのランドスケープへと融合するのだ。また建築は，眼前の前景や，海の彼方の水平線や，海岸に浮かぶ二つの巨大な岩礁と融合し，これらの二つの岩礁を手元へと引き寄せ，カフェとサーファー施設の二つのガラス棟に帰結させる。ホワイトコンクリートは木毛板で打設され，海で洗われたかのような質感を見せる。ガラスのあいだで露出するオカルクス社の断熱材は，"L'ecum de la mer！（海の泡）"である。

大規模美術館の拡張。カンザスシティのネルソン＝アトキンス美術館(1999-2007)では，既存建築と新しい建築との関係性が主題である。石造による1937年当時のギリシャ・ローマ新古典主義建築に始まり，この増築計画は施設の規模を2倍へと増強するためのものである。これら二つの空間の意味性と関係性は，「石と羽」という着想に基づいている。重いものと，軽いもの。これら正反対のものが，ひとつに結びつけられている。この計画のために初めて敷地を訪れた時のことである。旧館の新古典主義のファサードは「精神は現実(real)よりも理念(ideal)を求む」の言葉そのものであった。そこでこの計画では，コンペの規則を破り，敷地へと融合する連続したギャラリー構成のなかに，自然を通して光を落とすガラスレンズの提案を行った。新しいものと古いものとの関係性は対照的である。一方は軽快に，他方は重厚に。一方は開放的な，他方は閉鎖的な動線で構成される。一方は密封され，他方は自然に向けて，あらゆる方向に空間が開放されている。ネルソン＝アトキンス美術館の新しい表現は，本来の新古典主義建築を無視せずに，新しいものと古いものとのあいだの修辞的対称性を指し示すものである。この施設は時間と空間の両面において，これらの点が生み出す修辞的対称性を表現している。

ある公共建築をその意味の本質において建築化するということは，敷地や環境，プログラムにとって，固有の表現に関わる潜在的可能性を指し示すひとつの挑戦である。

（スティーヴン・ホール）

East view from Riverside Drive

School of Art and Art History, University of Iowa
1999-2006 Iowa City, Iowa, U.S.A.

Concept: A Hybrid Instrument of Open Edges and Open Center

The site presented special conditions: an existing 1937 brick building with a central body and flanking wings located along the Iowa River in addition to two existing morphologies: a lagoon and a connection to the organic geometry of nearby limestone bluffs which form the edge of the Iowa City grid. The new building straddles these two morphologies.

The new University of Iowa Art and Art History Building is a hybrid instrument of open edges and open center; instead of an object, the building is a "formless" instrument. Implied rather than actual volumes are outlined in the disposition of spaces. Flat or curved planes are slotted together or assembled with hinged sections. Flexible spaces open out from studios in warm weather. The main horizontal passages are meeting places with interior glass walls that reveal work-in-progress. The interplay of light is controlled through shading created by the overlapping planar exterior. Exposed tension rods of the partial bridge section contribute to the linear and planar architecture. Interior floors are framed in exposed steel and concrete planks, with integrated air and services distribution in the core voids. The resulting architecture is a hybrid vision of the future, combining bridge and loft spaces, theory with practice and human requirements with scientific principles.

Architecture for an Art School

In Formless: A User's Guide, (Zone Books 1997) Rosalind Krauss and Yves Alain Bois explore the ideas of "Informe" first undertaken by Georges Bataille. Bypassing the battle between 'form and content', "Formless" constitutes a third term outside of the binary thinking which is itself formal. Analyses of the work of Jackson Pollock, Cy Twombly, Lucio Fontana, Robert Smithson, and Gordon Matta-Clark, among others, set the framework for understanding avant-garde and modernist art practices. (One of Jackson Pollock's most important works belongs to the University of Iowa.)

The Architecture of the Art School explores "formless" geometries in its disposition of spaces and combinations of routes. A working and flexible teaching instrument, the building connects interior functions in spatial overlap at its center which acts as "social condenser" where ongoing work can be observed. Around the perimeter, spaces overlook, overlap, and engage the surrounding natural landscape. The dispersion and "fuzziness" of the edges is seen as way to embrace natural phenomena such as sunlight reflected off the lagoon water or off newly fallen snow in winter.

Prefabricated steel building principles, the most economical building type in America, are employed throughout the structure and materials. Steel in suspension is highly efficient. Due to its low relative height, interiors gain their character through the composition of exposed steel structure and HVAC. Metal sheets are folded, creating strength while minimizing the amount of material used.

A rich architectural language is achieved through the inventive use and combination of basic elements, such as fluorescent lighting tubes hidden by the bottom flange of steel beams, or the merging of painted ductwork with the steel structure.

The red coloring of the new building relates it to the original red brick structure, as does its relatively low landscape-embracing profile. We envisioned a new facility of inspiring interior spaces and natural light working like a formless instrument toward cultural production of past, present and future art. This first-rate art facility firmly positions the University of Iowa at the pinnacle of art education in America.

West elevation of library

View from south: lagoon under library

Overall view from north

View from northeast: entrance on Riverside Drive

Entrance on south: staircase

Entrance hall: looking east

アイオワ大学美術・美術史学部棟

[コンセプト：オープン・エッジとオープン・センターから成るハイブリッドな道具]

敷地条件は特徴的である。中心部を2つの翼棟が挟む，1937年に完成した煉瓦造建築がアイオワ川に沿って建ち，加えて2つの地形的な形態が存在する。小さな沼と，アイオワの都市グリッドの端部を形成する，近くの石灰岩の崖が持つ有機的な幾何学形態との結びつきである。新しい建物はこれら2つの地形にまたがっている。アイオワ大学美術・美術史学部棟はオープン・エッジとオープン・センターから成るハイブリッドな道具である。物体ではなく，この建物は"不定形な"道具である。具体的なヴォリュームの代わりに，暗示されたヴォリュームが空間の配置のなかにその輪郭を浮かび上がらせる。平坦な面や湾曲する面が，合わさって細長い空隙をつくり，あるいは蝶番のような接合部で組み合わされる。フレキシブルなスペースは暖かい日にはスタジオから外に開放される。水平に延びる主要通路は，制作中の作品が見えるガラス張りの内壁に面した人々が集まる場所である。交錯する陽射しは，重なり合う平坦な外面がつくりだす日よけで調節される。沼の途中まで延びるブリッジを支持する露出したテンション・ロッドは，リニアで平坦な建築構成を特徴づける。内部の床は露わしスティールとコンクリート板で枠取られ，コア・ヴォイドのなかに通気管とサービス関係の配管がまとめられる。結果として生まれた建築は，ブリッジとロフト・スペース，実践と理論，人間の要求と科学的原則を合体させた，ハイブリッドな未来像となった。

[美術学校のための建築]

『フォームレス：ユーザーズ・ガイド』（ゾーン・ブックス，1997年）のなかで，ロザリンド・クラウスとイヴ・アラン・ボワは，ジョルジュ・バタイユが最初に試みた"アンフォルム（形をなさない）"という概念を探求している。"形態と意味"の間の戦いを迂回しながら，"不定形"は，それ自身"形態的"である二元思考の外に第3の用語を形成する。ジャクソン・ポロック，サイ・トゥオンブリー，ルチオ・コスタ，フォンタナ，ロバート・スミッソン，ゴードン・マッタ＝クラークなどの作品の分析は，前衛やモダニストの芸術的実践を理解するための枠組みを設定した（ジャクソン・ポロックの最も重要な作品の一つはアイオワ大学が所蔵している）。

美術学校の建築では，空間の配置と動線の組み合わせのなかに"不定形な"幾何学を探求している。制作するため，フレキシブルな教育を行うための道具である建物は，進行中の作品を観察できる"ソーシャル・コンデンサー"として働く，中央部の空間の重なりのなかに内部の諸機能を連結する。周縁では，空間は周りの自然風景を見晴らし，重なり合い，そこに加わる。周縁部の分散と"曖昧性"は沼の水に反射する陽射しや，冬に新しく降った雪のような，自然現象をとらえる方法と見なされる。

アメリカでは最も経済的な建物であるプレファブの鉄骨造の原則を，構造と材料全体を通して採用する。サスペンション構造の鉄骨は非常に効率的である。比較的低い天井の高さによって，内部空間は露出された鉄骨構造と暖房・通気・空調の構成を通してその特性を獲得する。メタル・シートは折り曲げられて，使用材料の量を最小限にしながら，強度を持たせる。鉄骨梁の底部フランジによって隠された蛍光灯の照明管や，鉄骨造にペイントした配管を混ぜるといった，基本要素の創意工夫のある使い方や組み合わせを通して，豊かな建築言語が生まれる。

新しい建物の赤い色調は，風景に取り囲まれた比較的低い外形と同様，出発点にあるオリジナルの赤煉瓦の建物と結びつく。私たちは，精神を鼓舞する内部空間と，過去・現在・未来にわたる芸術の文化的な創出に向けて不定形な道具のように作用する，自然光で構成された新しい施設を構想していた。この第一級の芸術施設は，アイオワ大学をアメリカの芸術教育の頂点に立たせるだろう。

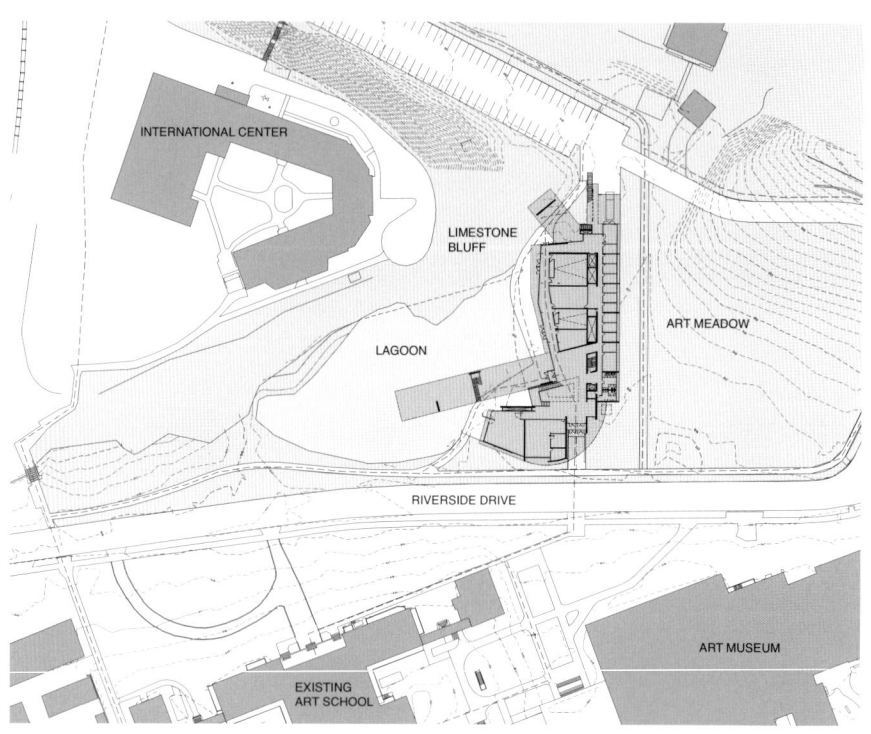

Site plan

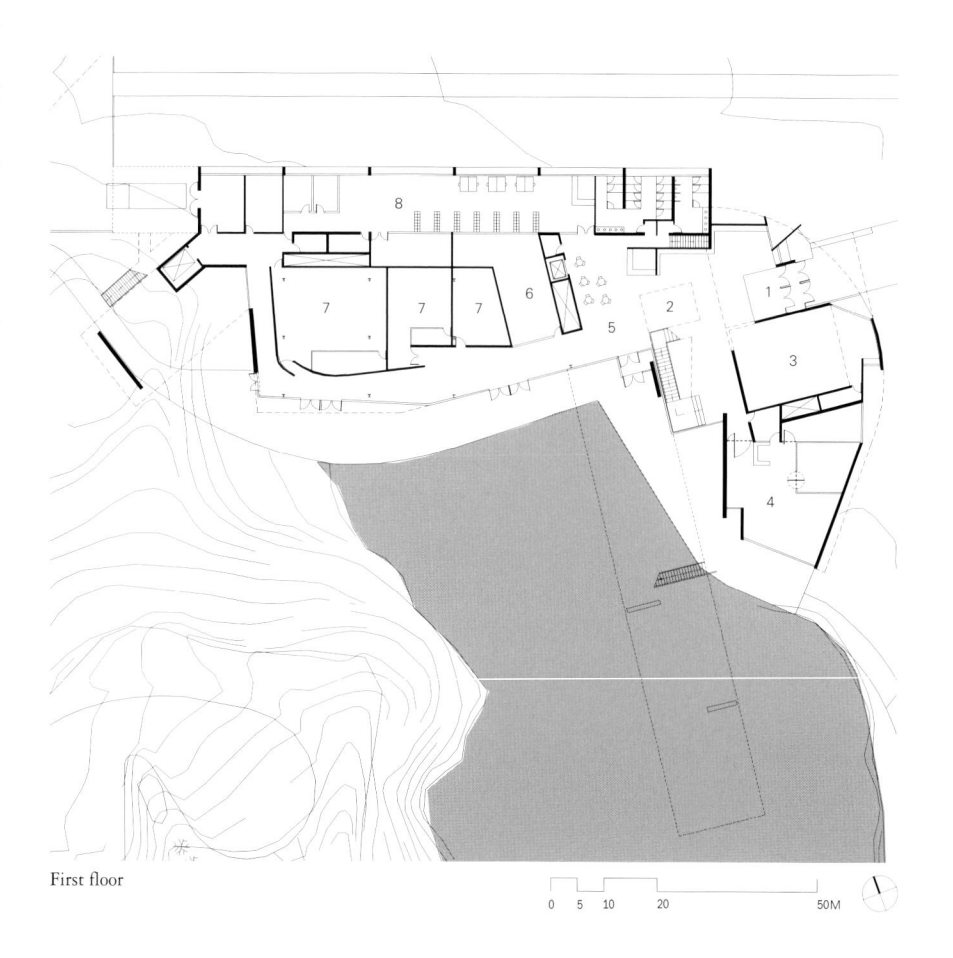

First floor

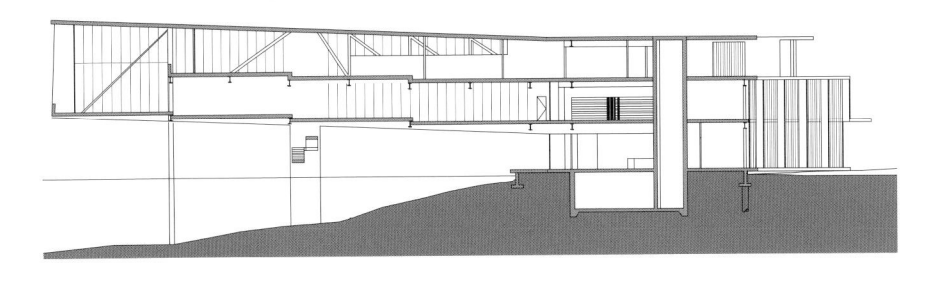

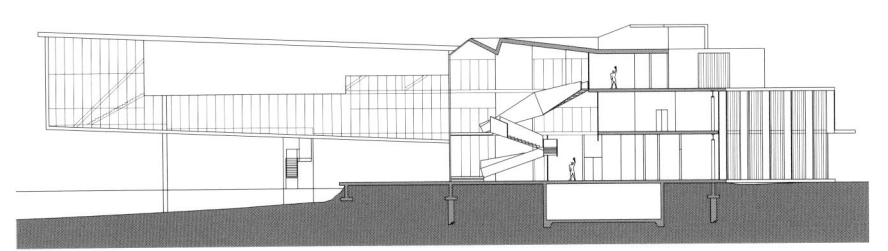

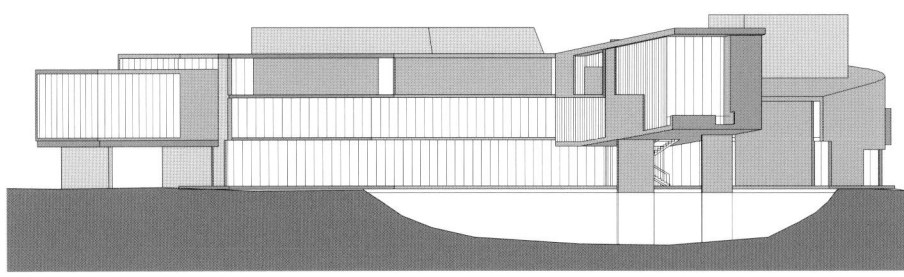

Longitudinal sections

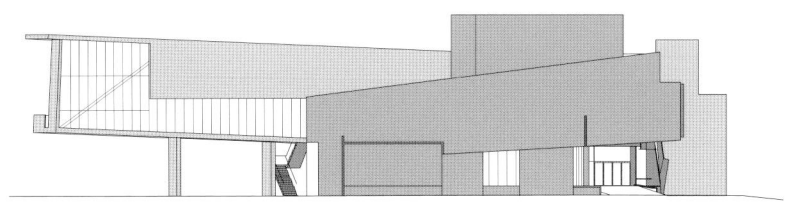

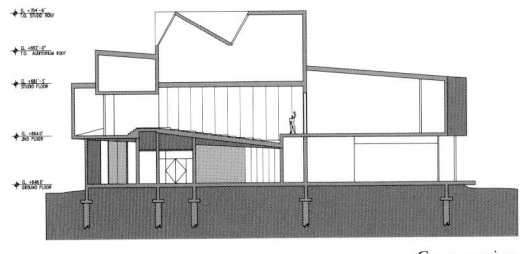

Cross section

South elevation

East elevation

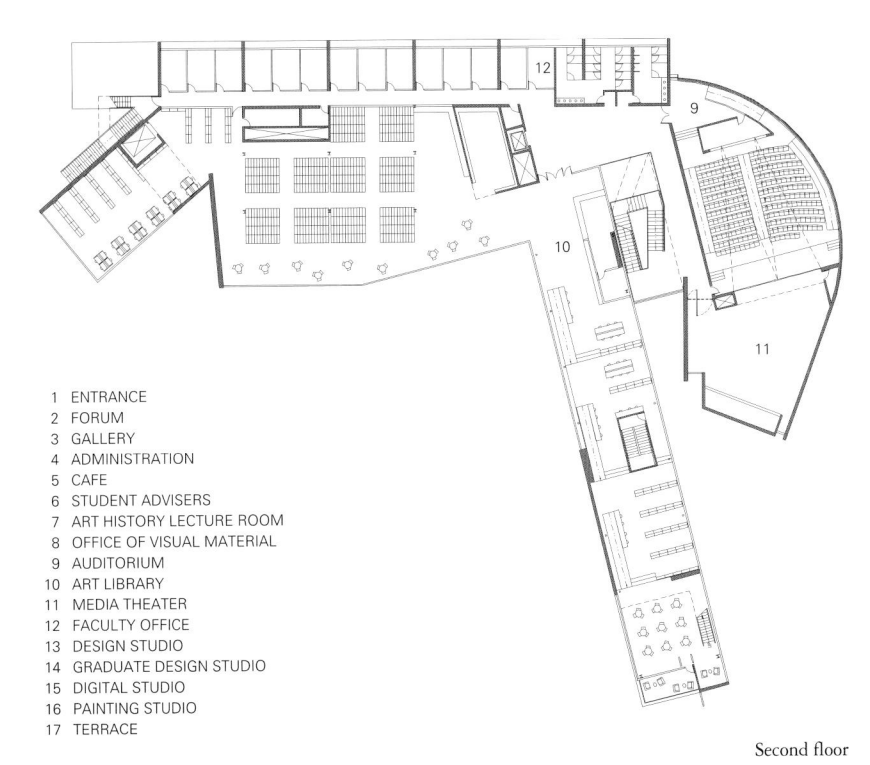

1 ENTRANCE
2 FORUM
3 GALLERY
4 ADMINISTRATION
5 CAFE
6 STUDENT ADVISERS
7 ART HISTORY LECTURE ROOM
8 OFFICE OF VISUAL MATERIAL
9 AUDITORIUM
10 ART LIBRARY
11 MEDIA THEATER
12 FACULTY OFFICE
13 DESIGN STUDIO
14 GRADUATE DESIGN STUDIO
15 DIGITAL STUDIO
16 PAINTING STUDIO
17 TERRACE

Second floor

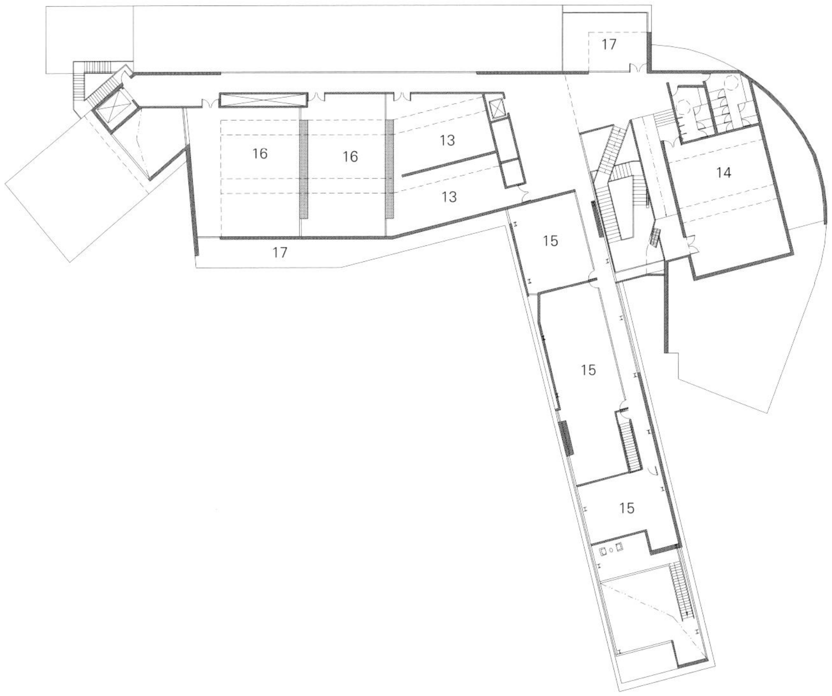

Third floor

II-165

Forum: looking south

Concept sketch

Forum: west corner facing lagoon

II-166

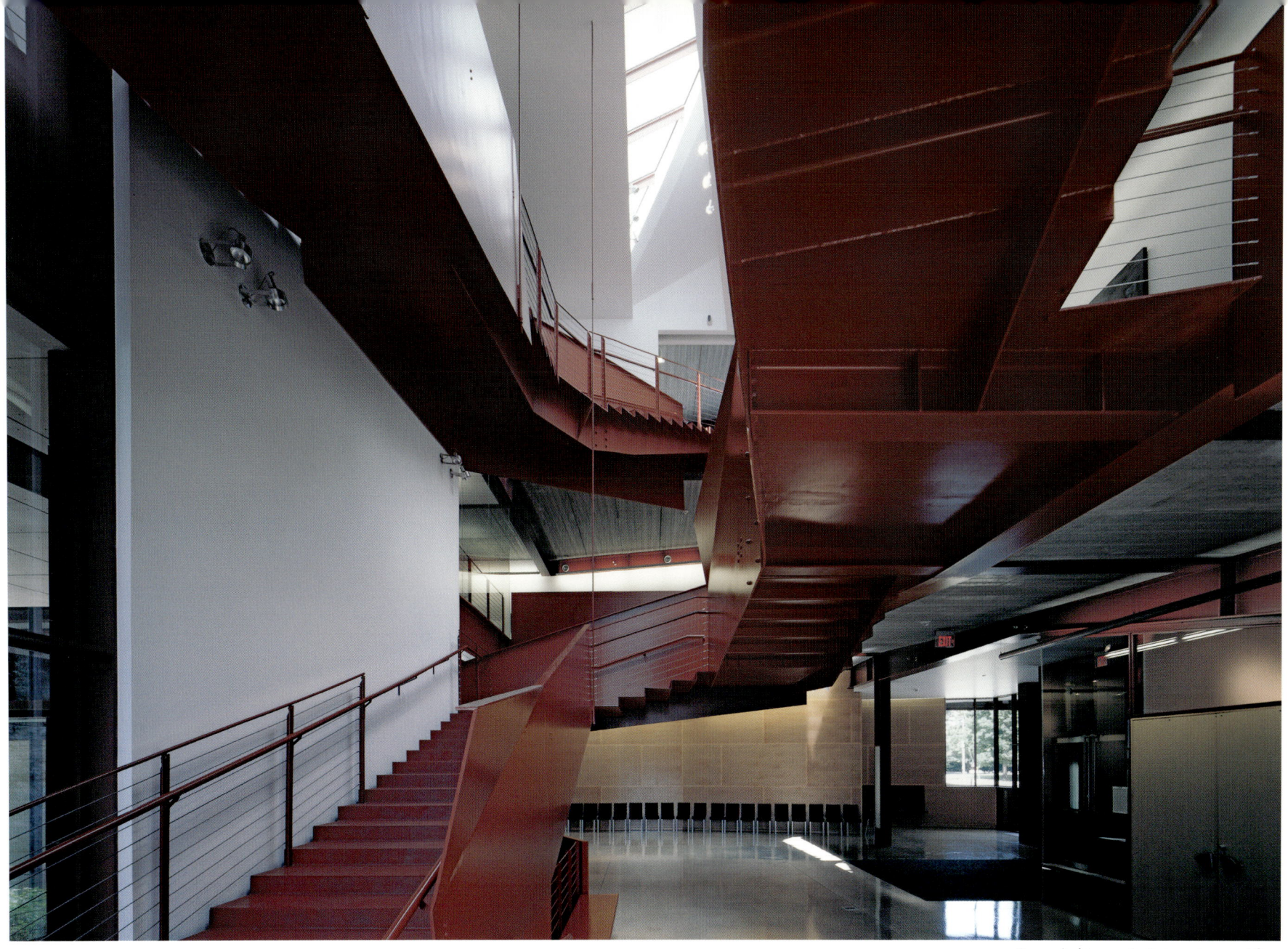

Forum: looking north. Staircase to second floor

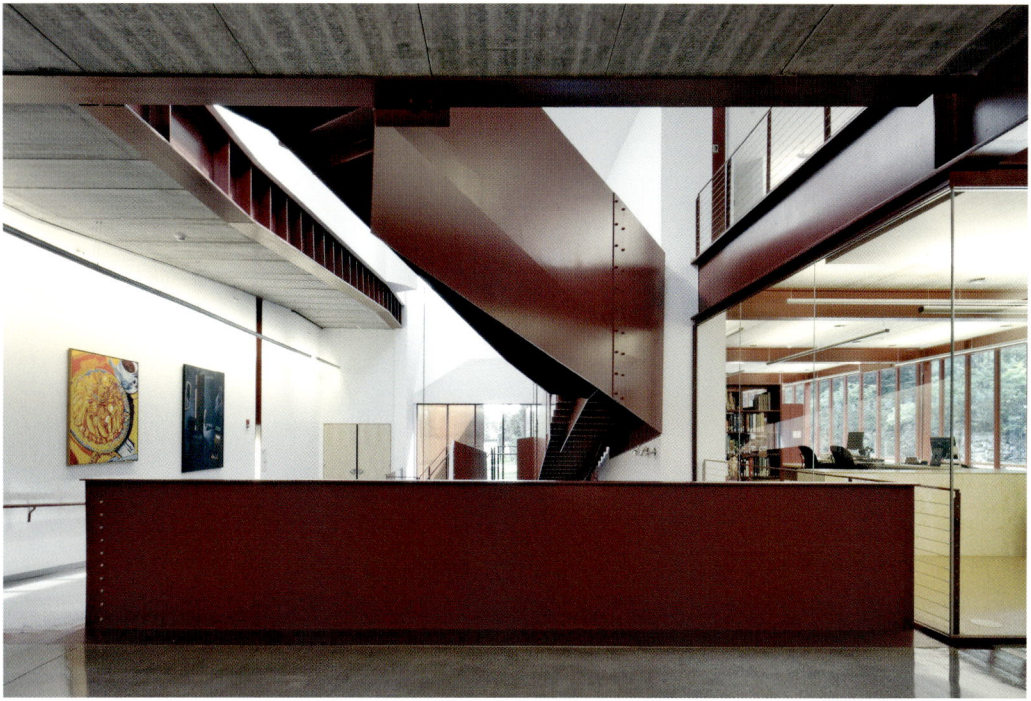

Second floor: library on right

Library on second floor: glazed wall facing lagoon below

South side of library

South end of library

Wall detail

Office of visual material on first floor

Graduate design studio on third floor

Auditorium on second floor

Reflecting pool of entry plaza: new addition, "Bloch Building" (left) and original museum (right)

Nelson–Atkins Museum of Art
1999-2007   Kansas City, Missouri, U.S.A.

View toward Lens 1 over reflecting pool: main entrance on second floor

Evening view of Lens 2

II-171

Site plan

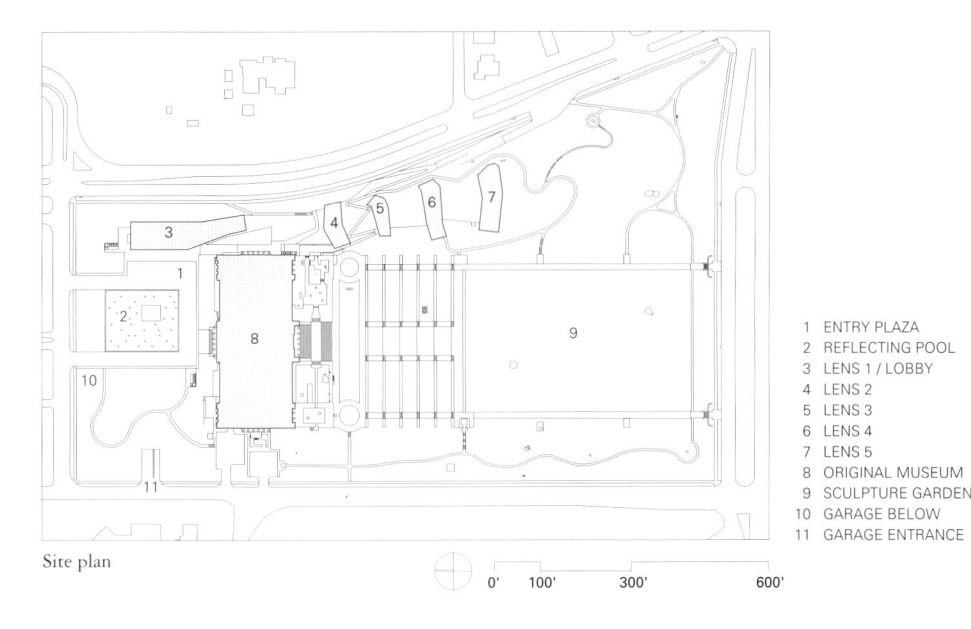

1 ENTRY PLAZA
2 REFLECTING POOL
3 LENS 1 / LOBBY
4 LENS 2
5 LENS 3
6 LENS 4
7 LENS 5
8 ORIGINAL MUSEUM
9 SCULPTURE GARDEN
10 GARAGE BELOW
11 GARAGE ENTRANCE

The expansion of The Nelson Atkins Museum of Art fuses architecture with landscape to create an experiential architecture that unfolds for visitors as it is perceived through each individual's movement through space and time. The new addition, named the Bloch Building, engages the existing sculpture garden, transforming the entire Museum site into the precinct of the visitor's experience. The new addition extends along the eastern edge of the campus, and is distinguished by five glass lenses, traversing from the existing building through the Sculpture Park to form new spaces and angles of vision. The innovative merging of landscape, architecture and art was executed through close collaboration with museum curators and artists, to achieve a dynamic and supportive relationship between art and architecture.

As visitors move through the new addition, they will experience a flow between light, art, architecture and landscape, with views from one level to another, from inside to outside. The threaded movement between the light-gathering lenses of the new addition weaves the new building with the landscape in a fluid dynamism based on a sensitive relationship to its context. Rather than an addition of a mass, the new elements exist in complementary contrast with the original 1933 classical "Temple to Art":

Original Building	New (complementary contrast)
Opaque	Transparent
Heavy	Light
Hermetic	Meshing
Inward views	Views to landscape
Bounded	Unbounded
Directed Circulation	Open Circulation
Single Mass	Transparent lenses

The first of the five "lenses" forms a bright and transparent lobby, with cafe, art library and bookstore, inviting the public into the Museum and encouraging movement via ramps toward the galleries as they progress downward into the garden. From the lobby a new cross-axis connects through to the original building's grand spaces. At night the glowing glass volume of the lobby provides an inviting transparency, drawing visitors to events and activities.

The lenses' multiple layers of translucent glass gather, diffuse and refract light, at times materializing light like blocks of ice. During the day the lenses inject varying qualities of light into the galleries, while at night the sculpture garden glows with their internal light. The "meandering path" threaded between the lenses in the Sculpture Park has its sinuous complement in the open flow through the continuous level of galleries below. The galleries, organized in sequence to support the progression of the collections, gradually step down into the Park, and are punctuated by views into the landscape.

The design for the new addition utilizes sustainable building concepts; the sculpture garden continues up and over the gallery roofs, creating sculpture courts between the lenses, while also providing green roofs to achieve high insulation and control storm water. At the heart of the addition's lenses is a structural concept merged with a light and air distributor concept: "Breathing Ts" transport light down into the galleries along their curved undersides while carrying the glass in suspension and providing a location for HVAC ducts. The double-glass cavities of the lenses gather sun-heated air in winter or exhaust it in summer. Optimum light levels for all types of art or media installations and seasonal flexibility requirements are ensured through the use of computer-controlled screens and of special translucent insulating material embedded in the glass cavities. A continuous service level basement below the galleries offers art delivery, storage and handling spaces, as well as flexible access to the "Breathing-Ts".

The ingenious integration of art and architecture included a collaborative effort with artist Walter De Maria, one of the great minimalist artists of our time. De Maria's sculpture, *One Sun /34 Moons,* is the centerpiece of the expansive granite-paved entrance plaza with a reflecting pool that forms a new entry space shaped by the existing building and the new Lobby "Lens". The "moons" of the art work are circular skylight discs in the bottom of the pool that project water-refracted light into the garage below. Conceived as a vehicular Arrival Hall, the garage is generously proportioned, directly connected to the new museum lobby on both levels, and spanned with continuous undulating vaults by an innovative pre-cast concrete 'wave-T'.

A strong relationship between the architectural concept and the Museum's important oriental art holdings is illustrated by works in the permanent collection such as *Verdant Mountains* (12th century) by Chiang Shen or *The North Sea* (16th century) by Chou Ch'en, which demonstrate the timeless merging of art, architecture and landscape. The new addition celebrates this fusion with the new Isamu Noguchi Sculpture Court, setting a binding connection to the existing Sculpture Gardens.

Third floor

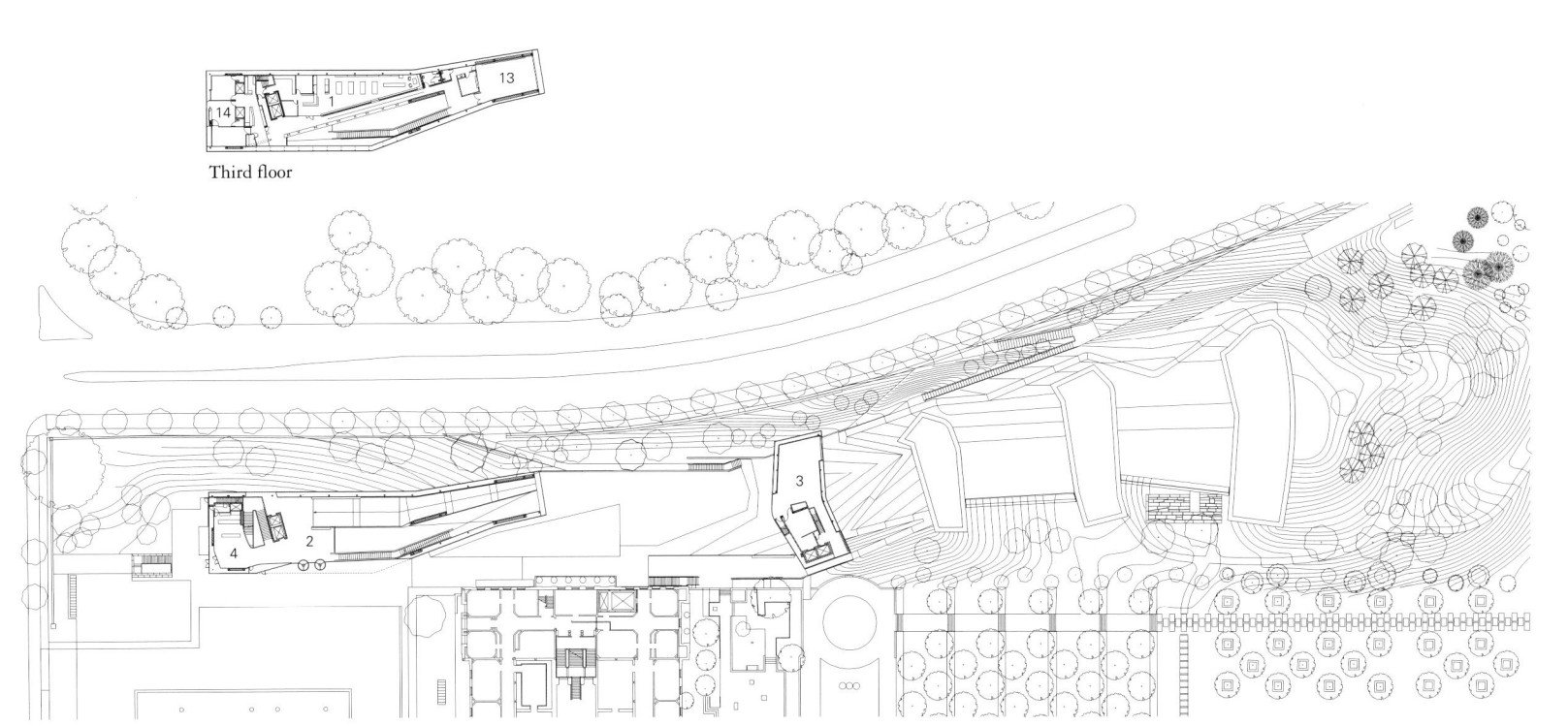

Second floor

1 LIBRARY
2 MAIN ENTRANCE/UPPER LOBBY
3 GARDEN DINING ROOM
4 CAFE
5 LOWER LOBBY
6 MODERN & CONTEMPORARY ART GALLERY
7 PHOTOGRAPHY GALLERY
8 AFRICAN ART GALLERY
9 SPECIAL EXHIBITIONS
10 NOGUCHI COURT
11 AUDITORIUM
12 PARKING
13 ASSEMBLY SPACE
14 EXECUTIVE OFFICES

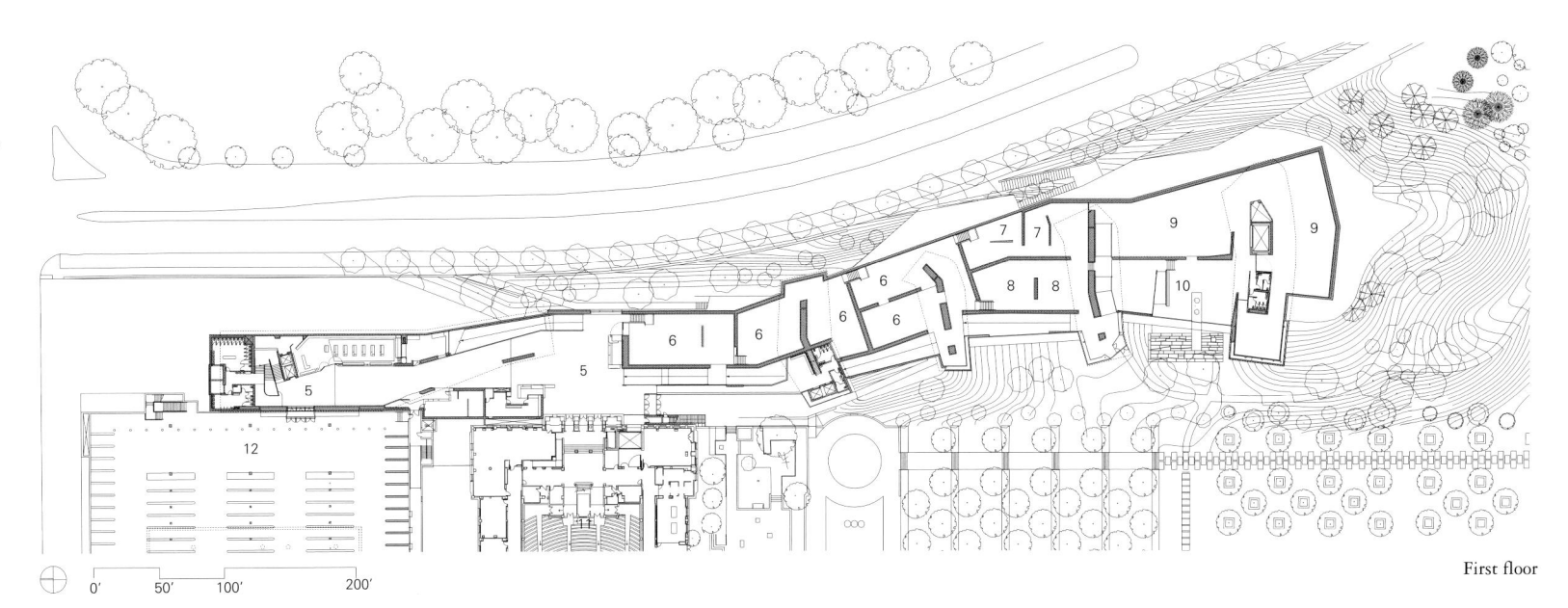

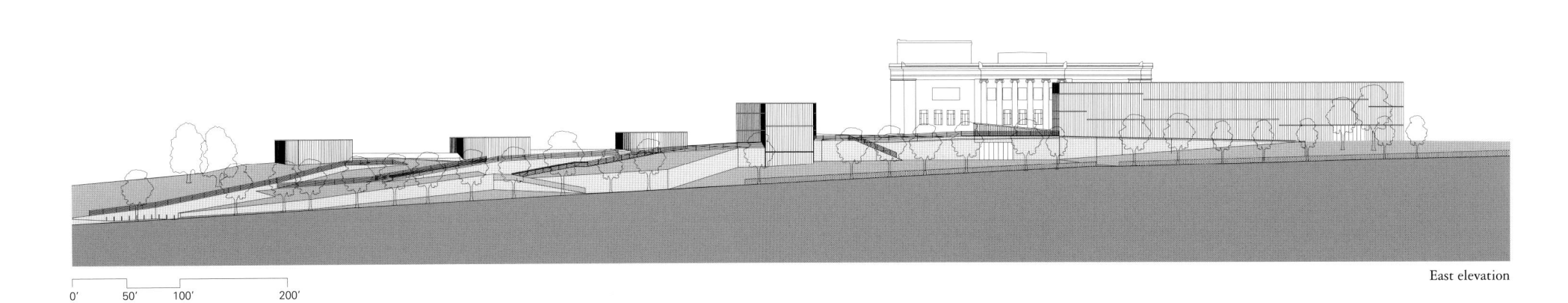

First floor

East elevation

II-173

Sculpture garden: view from southwest. Original museum (left) and new addition "Bloch Building"

View of Lens 1 from north

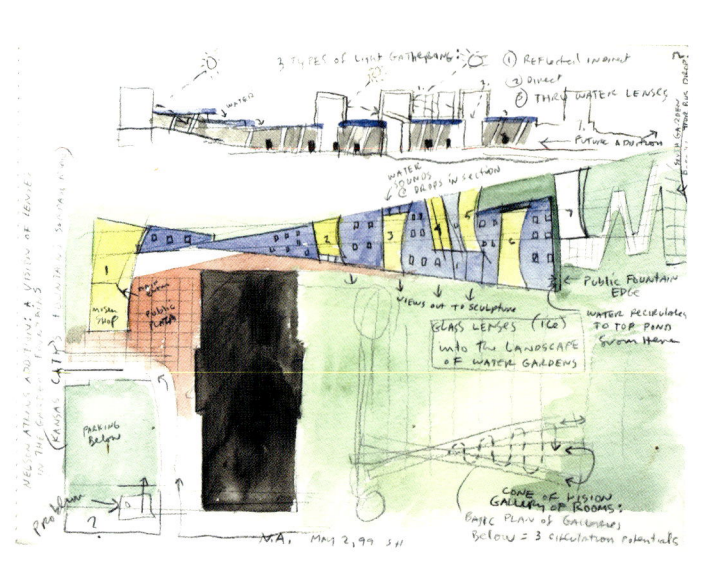

Concept sketch: new addition 'glass lenses'

II-174

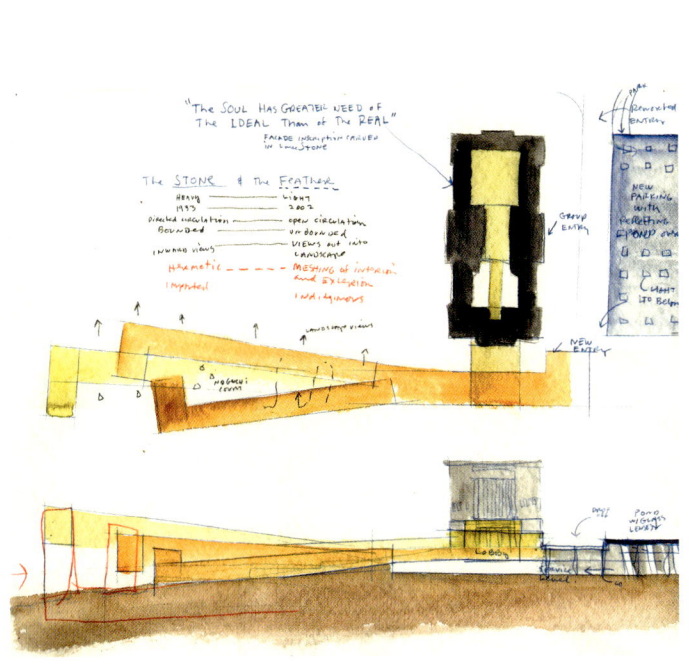

New addition and original museum

View from southeast: Lens 1 (right) and Lens 2 (left). Original museum between them

Parking under reflecting pool with skylight discs in the bottom of pool

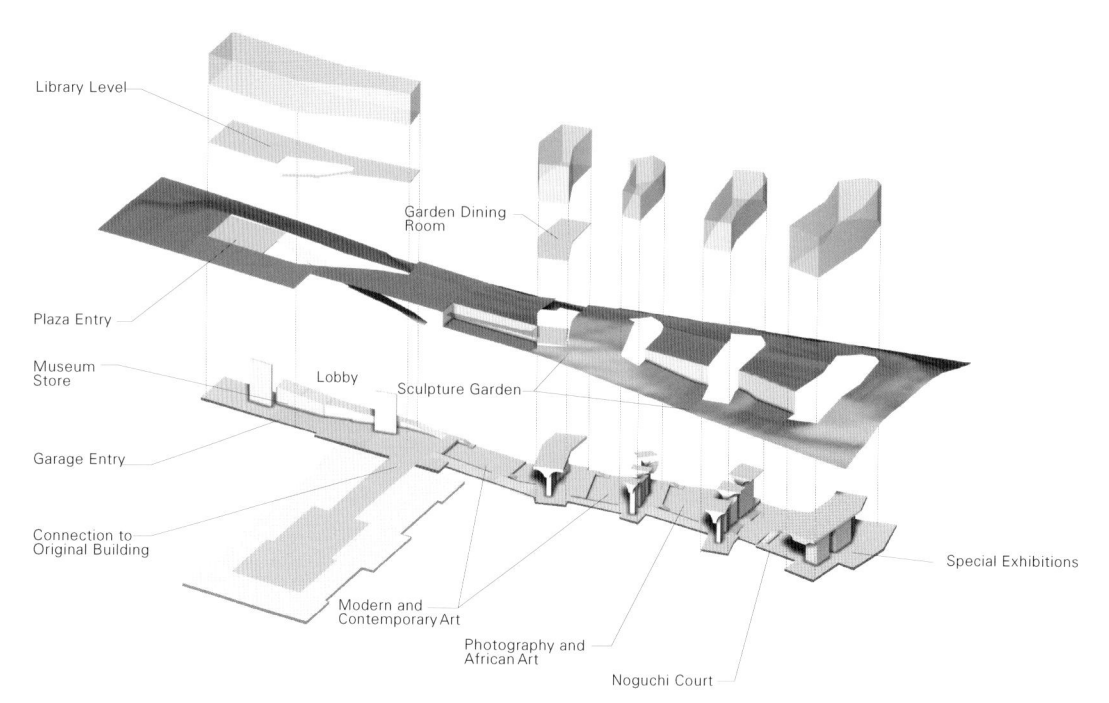

Diagram: program of new addition

ネルソン=アトキンス美術館

ネルソン=アトキンス美術館の拡張計画では、来館者が空間と時間のなかを進んで行くにつれて次々に展開し、一人ひとりの体験のなかで捉えられる建築をつくるために、建築と景観の融合を試みている。ブロック・ビルディングと名付けられた新棟は、既存の彫刻庭園と組み合わされて、美術館サイト全体を、来館者が身体で様々に感じる領域へと変える。新棟を際立たせているのは、敷地の東端に沿って、旧棟から彫刻庭園を横切って延び、新しい空間と視点を形成する5つのガラス"レンズ"である。芸術と建築のダイナミックで補完的な関係をつくりあげるために、景観、建築、芸術作品の創造的な融合が、美術館のキュレーターとアーティストの密接な協力を得て実現した。

建物のなかを進むにつれて、光、芸術作品、建築、景観の間の流れを、一つのレベルから別のレベルへ、内部から戸外への眺めと共に経験するだろう。光を集める"レンズ"の間を縫いながら進む動きは、そのコンテクストとの微妙な関係に基づいた流れるようなダイナミズムの中に、建物を景観と一つに編み上げる。新棟は重々しい量塊として加わるのではなく、1933年に建てられた、古典的な"芸術の殿堂"である旧棟の補完的な対比として現れる。

〈旧棟〉　　〈新棟（補完的対比）〉
不透明　　　透明
重厚　　　　軽快
密閉　　　　メッシュ
内向する眺め　景観へ向かう眺め
限定　　　　無限
統制された動線　開かれた動線
単体　　　　透明なレンズ

5つの"レンズ"の最初の1つは、明るく透明なロビーをかたちづくる。ここにはカフェ、アート・ライブラリー、書店があり、人々を美術館へ招き入れ、庭へ向かってスロープを降りながらギャラリーへ進むように誘う。ロビーから新しい軸線が横方向に延び、旧棟の大空間をつなぐ。夜には、照明に輝くガラス張りのロビーが魅力的な透明性を帯びて、人々をイベントや様々な活動に引き寄せる。

"レンズ"の半透明ガラスの層は光を集め、拡散し、屈折させ、時に、氷塊のようなかたちを与える。日中、"レンズ"は様々な質を持つ光をギャラリーに注ぎ込み、夜はその内部の照明によって彫刻の庭を照らす。彫刻庭園の中、"レンズ"の間を縫いながら進む"曲がりくねる道"を補完するように、ギャラリーの連続する流れも同じように曲折して続く。コレクションの展開に合わせて連なるギャラリーは、緩やかに彫刻庭園に向かって降りて行くが、その連続性を中断して戸外の眺めが挟み込まれる。

新棟のデザインには、持続可能な考え方が組み込まれている。彫刻庭園は、ギャラリーの屋根へと続き、屋根を覆って"レンズ"の間に彫刻の中庭をつくりだす。緑化された屋根は断熱効果も高く、豪雨の際の雨水も調節する。新棟を特徴づけている"レンズ"の中心にあるのは、光と空気を運ぶという発想と融合させた構造コンセプトである。この"呼吸するT"型ストラクチュアは、下側の湾曲に沿ってギャラリーに光を運び、同時にガラス面を支持し、HVACダクトの設置スペースを提供する。"レンズ"を構成するペアガラスの空隙は、冬には陽射しに暖められた空気を集め、夏には熱気を排出する。あらゆる種類の芸術作品やメディア・インスタレーション、季節の変化に対応した最適な強さの光を、コンピュータ制御のスクリーン、ガラスの空隙に埋め込んだ半透明の特別な断熱材を使用することで確保する。ギャラリーの下、連続するサービス・レベルを構成する地階は、作品の搬送、収蔵、取り扱いスペースであり、また"呼吸するT"へもアクセスできる。

芸術と建築の独創的な統合には、現代の偉大なミニマリスト・アーティストの一人、ウォルター・デ・マリアとの共同制作が含まれる。デ・マリアの彫刻、「一つの太陽／34の月」は、旧棟と、新棟のロビーを構成する"レンズ"によって囲まれ、水盤のある、花崗岩敷きの広いエントランス・プラザの中心を飾る。アート・ワークの"月"は水盤の底に設置された円形のスカイライト・ディスクで、下のガレージに水中で屈折する光を注ぐ。車の到着ホールとしてゆったりと構成されたガレージは、新しい美術館ロビーの2つのレベルに直接つながり、架け渡されたプレキャスト・コンクリートの革新的なストラクチュア、"ウェーブT"の波打つヴォールト群で支えられている。

建築コンセプトと美術館の重要な東洋美術の収蔵品との強い結びつきは、芸術・建築・風景の永遠の融合を感じさせる、チャン・シェンの「Verdant Mountains（緑の山）」(12世紀)やチョウ・チェンの「The North Sea」(16世紀)などのパーマネント・コレクションに明らかにうかがえる。新棟は、この融合を、彫刻庭園との緊密な結びつきをかたちづくる新しいイサム・ノグチ・スカルプチュア・コートと共に謳い上げる。

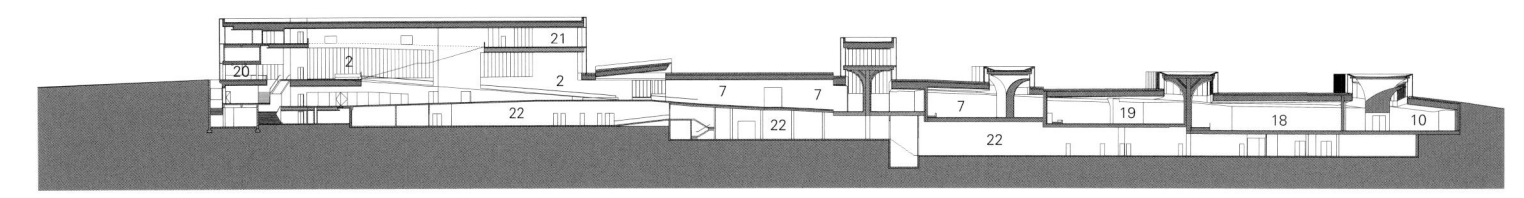

Longitudinal section

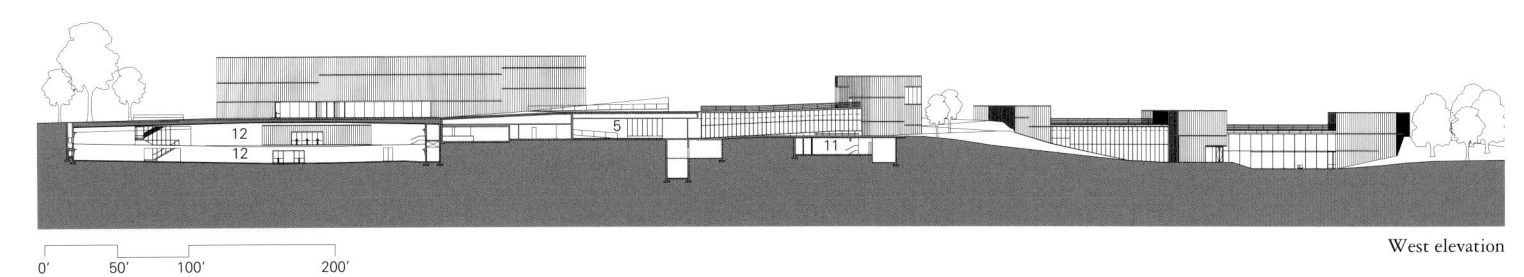

West elevation

1 PARKING GARAGE
2 LOBBY
3 MUSEUM SHOP
4 LIBRARY
5 STACKS
6 MECHANICAL
7 MODERN & CONTEMPORARY ART GALLERY
8 COLLECTION STORAGE
9 NOGUCHI COURT
10 SPECIAL EXHIBITIONS
11 ART RECEIVING
12 ORIGINAL BUILDING
13 NEW OPENING & STAIR
14 EUROPEAN ART GALLERY
15 ASIAN ART GALLERY
16 AMERICAN ART GALLERY
17 AUDITORIUM
18 AFRICAN ART GALLERY
19 PHOTOGRAPHY GALLERY
20 CAFE
21 ASSEMBLY SPACE
22 ART SERVICE LEVEL

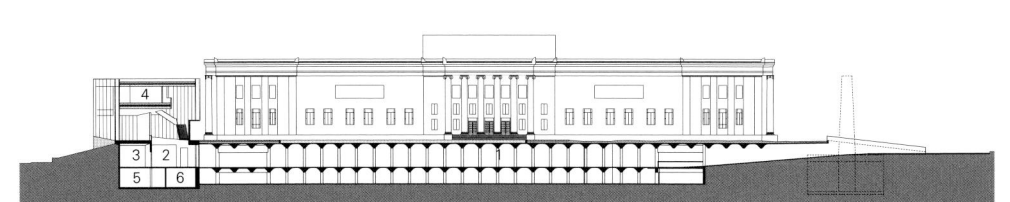

Cross section: main lobby and garage

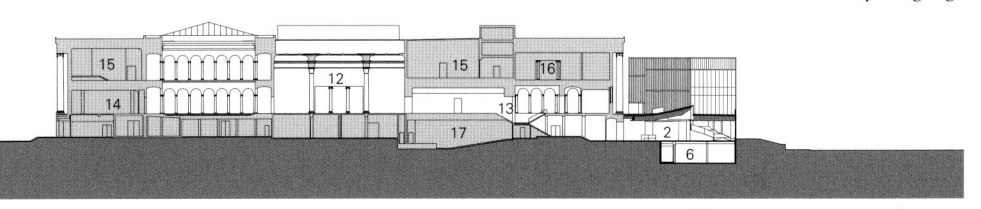

Cross section: lower lobby (Lens 1) and original building

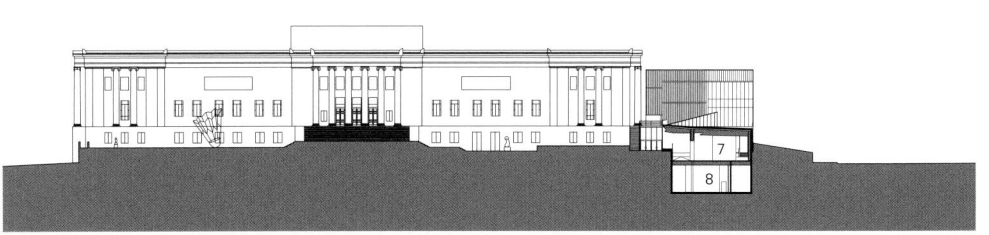

Cross section: modern and contemporary gallery

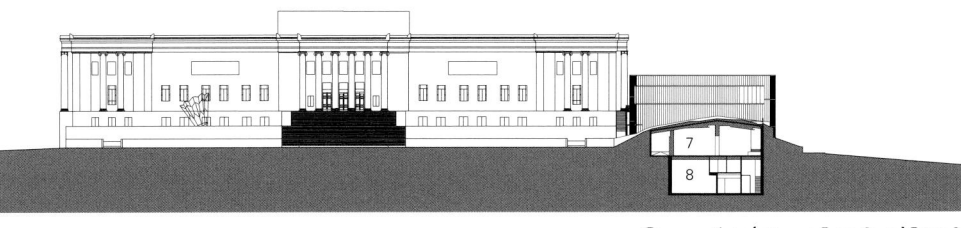

Cross section: between Lens 2 and Lens 3

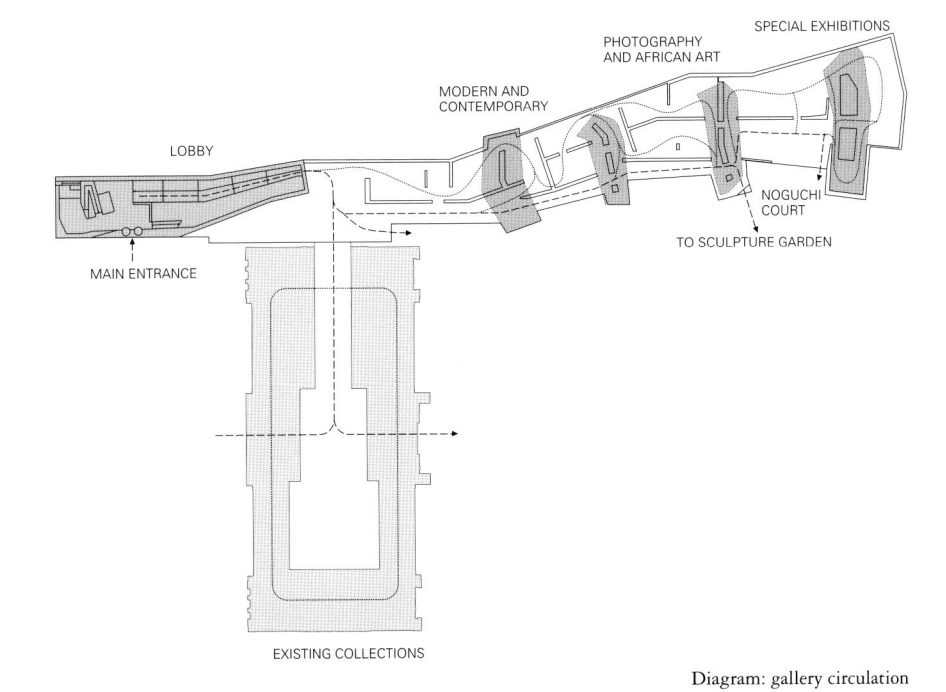

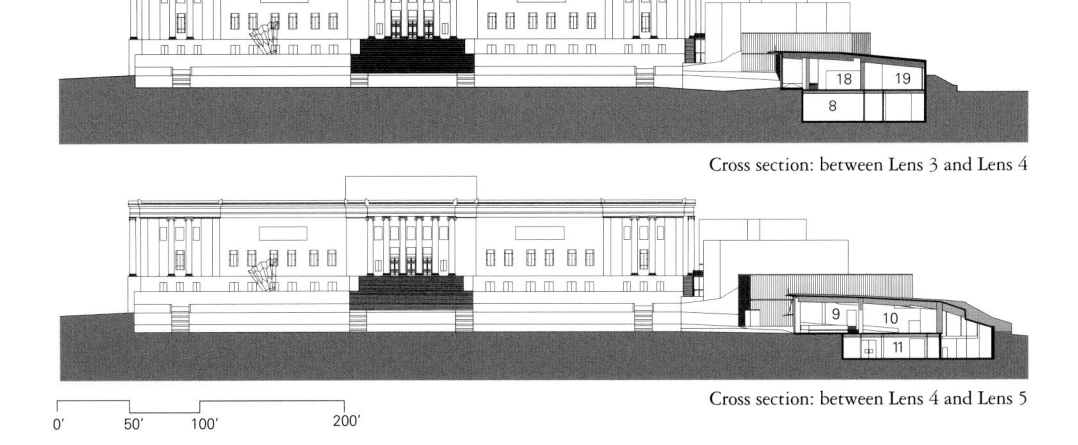

Cross section: between Lens 3 and Lens 4

Cross section: between Lens 4 and Lens 5

Diagram: gallery circulation

II-177

Lens 1: lobby on second floor. Main entrance on right

Entry of contemporary gallery from lobby

Lens 1: lobby on first floor. Looking north

Sloped corridor along galleries

Lobby: looking north

"Breathing Ts" under Lens 4

Special exhibition under Lens 5

Contemporary gallery between Lens 2 and Lens 3

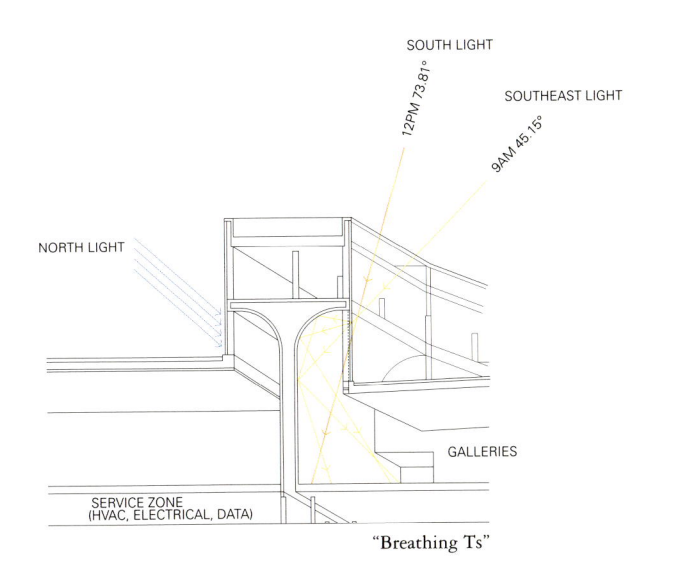

"Breathing Ts"

Sketch: "Breathing Ts"

II-181

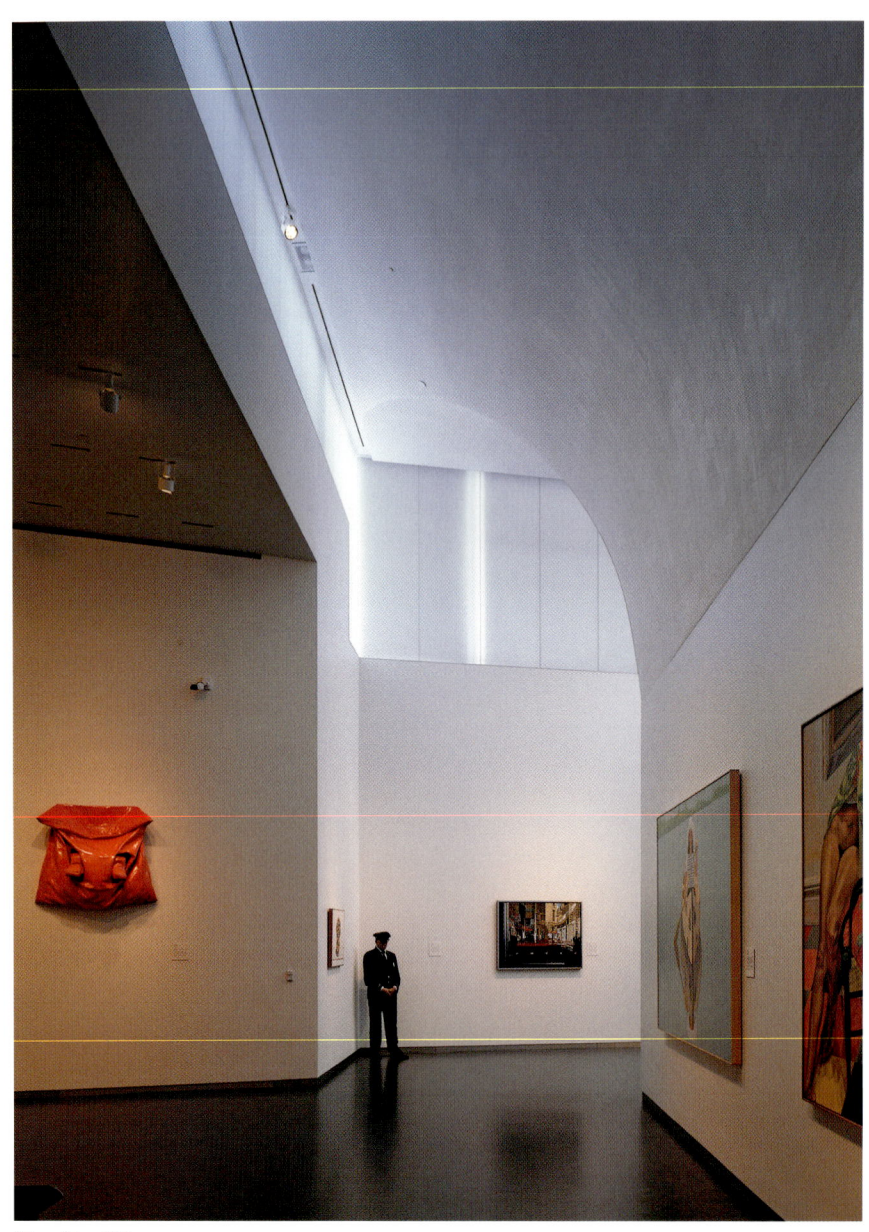

"Breathing Ts" structure

"Breathing Ts" under Lens 3

II-182

Noguchi Court: looking north

Sketch: Noguchi Court

Noguchi Court: view toward sculpture garden on west

II-183

2000 # Museum of Human Evolution
Burgos, Spain

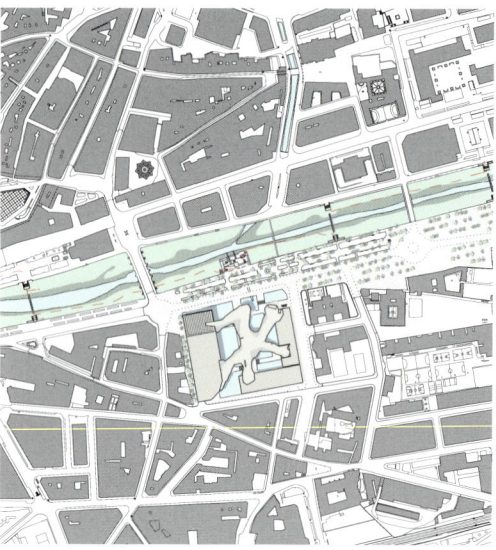

Site plan

1 MAIN ENTRY	13 AUDITORIUM
2 LOBBY	14 LOUNGE
3 PARKING ENTRY	15 GREEN ROOM
4 CONFERENCE HALL ENTRY	16 LIBRARY
5 REHEARSAL ROOM	17 PROJECTION/MEETING ROOM
6 WORKSHOP	18 LAB MODULE A
7 SERVICE ZONE	19 EXHIBITION HALL
8 ATAPUERCA ROOM	20 EVOLUTION ROOM
9 ATAPUERCA MAIN CAVE REPLICA	21 TEMPORARY EXHIBITION
10 LAB MODULE B	22 PRESS CONFERENCE
11 LAB MODULE C	23 RESTAURANT
12 CONFERENCE HALL	24 OFFICE

—Concept A
The body of the Museum of Human Evolution hovers above an "Urban Mirror"—a platform of water recycled from the Arlazon River. The river branches to the north, bringing water from the Atapuerca caves, thereby connecting the site to the caves, just as origin myths from the world's cultures are connected to water.

—Concept B
A "Chromatic Space" is created between the urban mirror and the undersides of the museum and auditoriums. This dramatic urban space, with open walkways over water, serves as an enormous entry space from which one can see the entrances to all the lobbies. The Chromatic Space corresponds to the long span of time before humans first became conscious of their own evolution—this "layer of unconsciousness" is a place for reflection.

—Concept C
For a visitor experiencing the museum, the content of exhibits is gradually revealed using different formulations of space, first, by recreating the actual environment of the Atapuerca caves and second, a "Score of Darkness" is created alongside the cave reconstruction by light piercing the dark background spaces. Finally, advanced digital exhibition techniques explore new information and future projections.

—Concept D
5 points of fusion occur where the organic form, inspired by the Atapuerca caves, merges and overlaps with the orthogonal forms derived from urban Burgos. These merging points allow 5 places of programmatic flexibility and overlap. Circulation and exhibits can be rerouted according to the needs of specific events.

—Concept E
The unity of man and nature is expressed in the void-solid reversal of the central museum geometry which extends out from the cave reconstruction. This argument against a non-dualistic consciousness is also expressed in the Arlazon River water connection at the urban mirror platform.

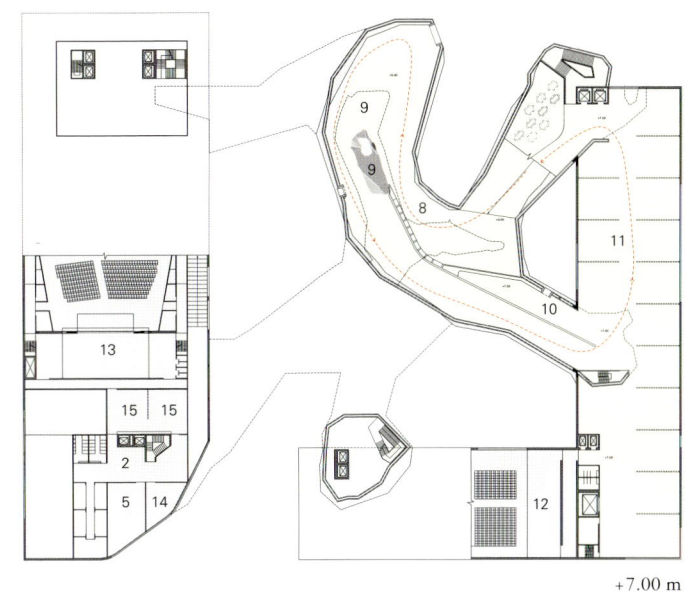

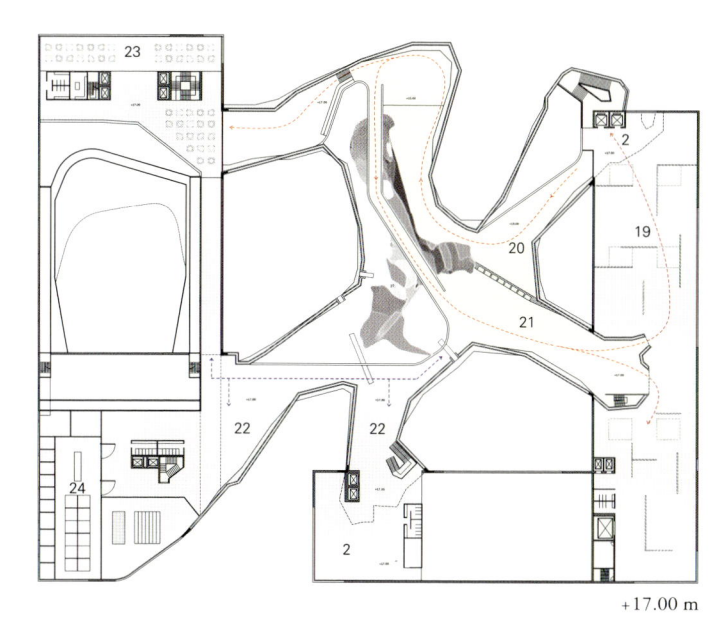

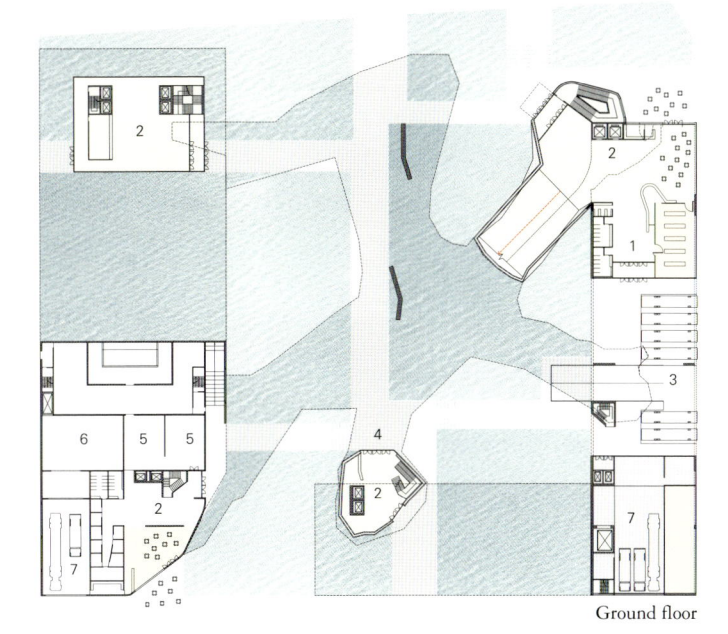

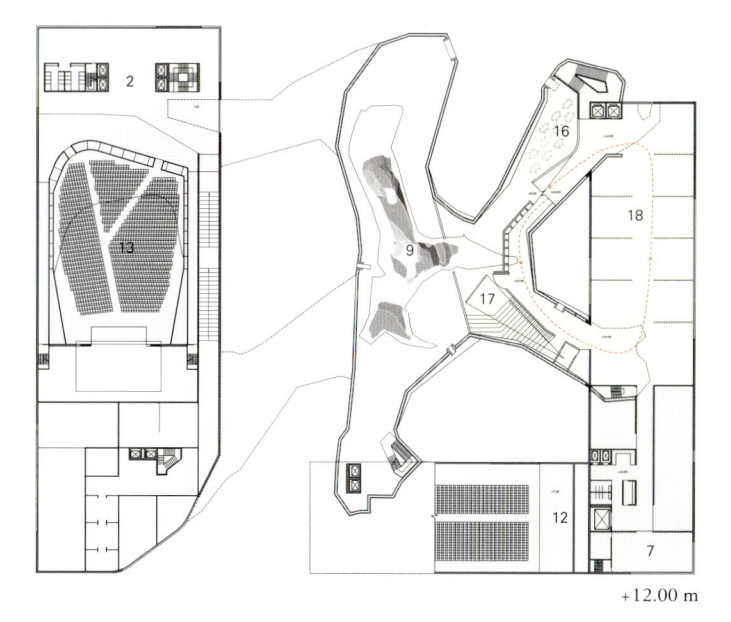

+7.00 m

+17.00 m

Ground floor

+12.00 m

Elevation

Concept sketches

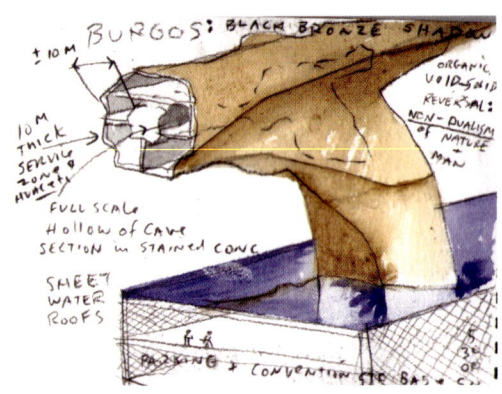

Atapuerca Room section

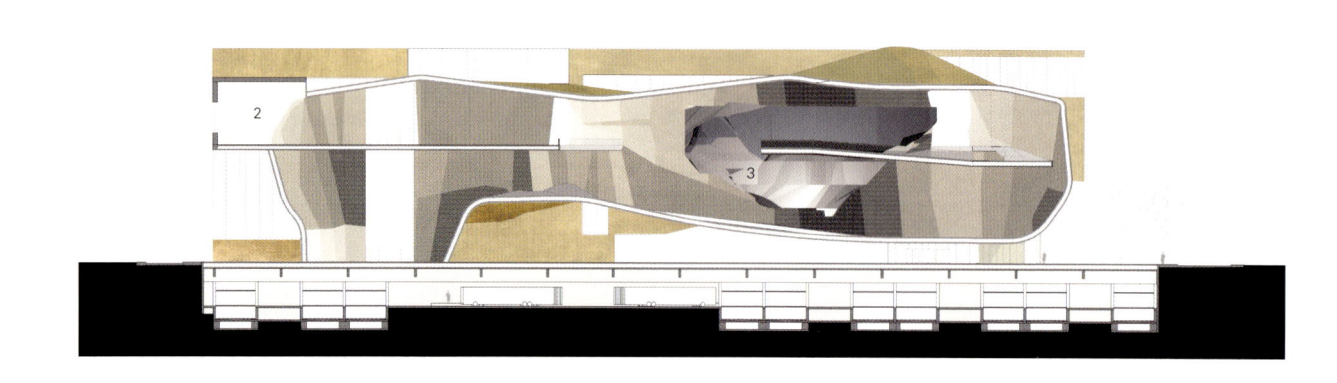

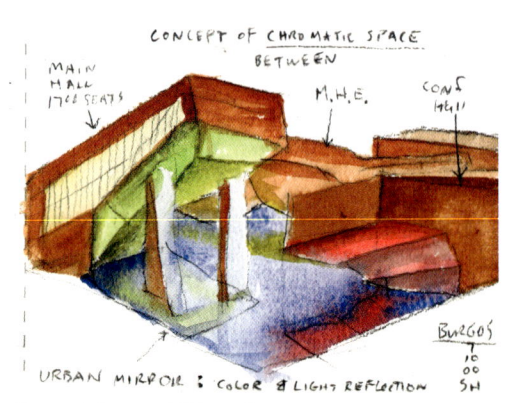

Chromatic Space and Urban Mirror

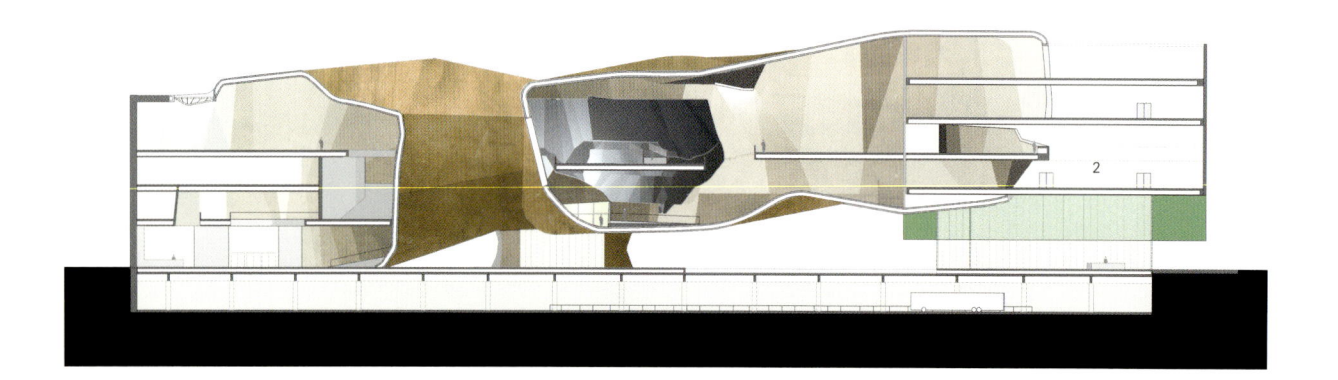

1 AUDITORIUM
2 LOBBY
3 ATAPUERCA ROOM
4 EXHIBITION HALL

Sections

II-186

Atapuerca Room

人類史博物館
〈コンセプトA〉
「アーバン・ミラー」はアルランソン川の水を再利用した水盤である。人類史博物館の躯体はその上に浮遊する。川は北へと分岐し，アタプエルカの洞窟から水を運ぶ。世界中の文化の創造神話が水と結びついているように，この川は敷地と洞窟とを結びつける役割を果たしている。
〈コンセプトB〉
「クロマティック・スペース」はアーバン・ミラーと，ミュージアム及びオーディトリウムの底面とのあいだに生み出される。躍動的な都市空間と水上の開放的な歩道は，巨大なエントランス空間の役割を果たす。そこからはロビーへのエントランスを全て見渡すことができる。クロマティック・スペースは人類が初めて自己の進化を意識するようになる以前の長い時間の流れに応答するものである。この「潜在的レイヤー」は沈思黙想の場である。
〈コンセプトC〉
それぞれ異なった方法によって定式化された空間が，ミュージアムを体験する来館者に展示内容を徐々に明らかにする。まず初めにアタプエルカの洞窟の実際の環境が再現される。次に背後の暗闇の空間を差し貫く光によって，再現された洞窟に沿って「暗闇のスコア」が生み出される。最後に最先端のデジタルの展示技術によって，新しい情報と未来へのヴィジョンが探究される。
〈コンセプトD〉
5つの融合点で，アタプエルカの洞窟に着想を得た有機的形態がブルゴスの町から導かれた直角形の形態とひとつに同化して重なり合う。これら5つの融合点ではプログラムがフレキシブルに重なり合っている。順路と展示方法はそれぞれのイベントの要求に従い，変更することができる。
〈コンセプトE〉
中央ミュージアムのジオメトリは再現された洞窟から外に向かって広がり，ヴォイドとソリッドの反転した空間に人間と自然の調和が表現される。非二元論的な知覚に対するこれらの議論は，アーバン・ミラーの水盤にアルランソン川の水を利用するという点においても，同時に表現されている。

Urban Mirror

Temporary exhibition room

Atapuerca Room

Musée des Confluences, Lyon
Lyon, France

2001

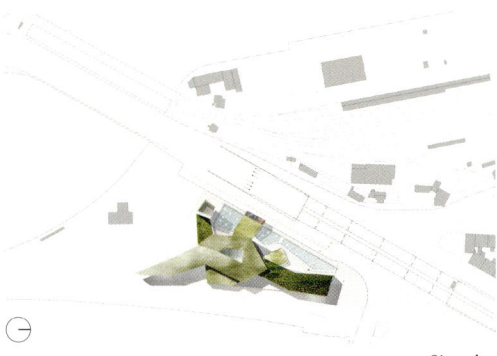

Site plan

The building form is a response to the unique aspects of the site. Its thinness and tapering off, the wide space of flow of the converging Rhone and Saone Rivers, the horizontality and organic turbulence are all aspects responded to in the building section of the new museum. The building's geometry moves toward horizontal vectors like that of the rivers.

The concept aims for a convergence of four geophysical aspects:
1. Matter—the in and out of physical exhibition materials
2. Energy—the main entry hall of public flow
3. Configuration—the auditorium and main orientation
4. Correlation—the education tower-classrooms for study and deeper evaluation

These four vectors join in a central horizontal turbulence from which a suspended taper emerges horizontally cantilevered above with the flowing rivers reflected on its underside. It is an open concept of flowing within the architecture with spaces in liquid discourse. Interior passages should intervene and cross-cut. Exhibitions are held within parentheses walls bounded by intersecting potential. The building sections aim at relationships working at the root level, where things and formulations merge.

The steel framed structure utilizes standard sections due to new computer programs producing each joint effortlessly in complex geometries. The building skin is a special golden patina copper alloy with a natural patina's positive response to typical urban air pollution. Glass walls are double with an energy recycling of the inner air space.

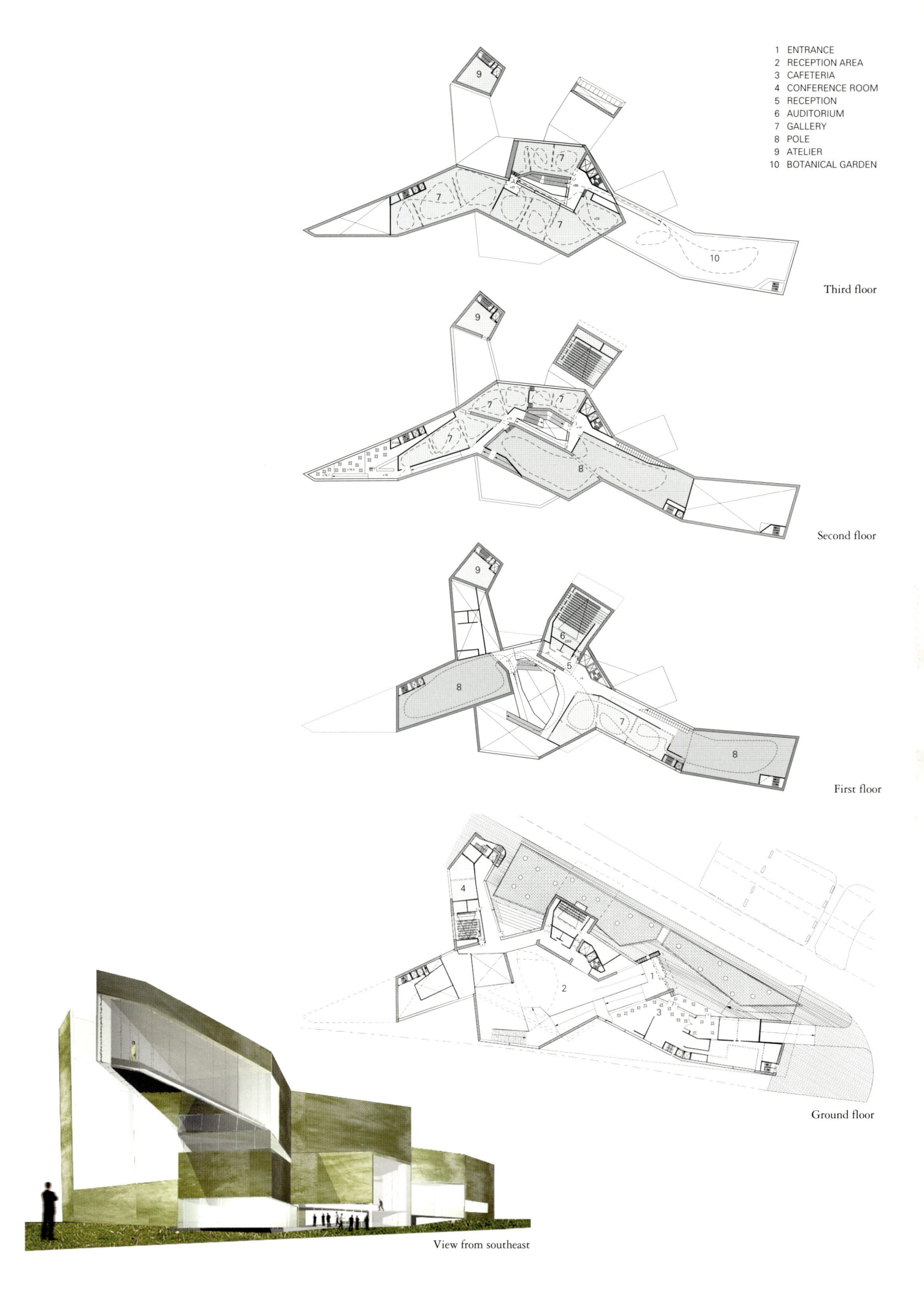

1 ENTRANCE
2 RECEPTION AREA
3 CAFETERIA
4 CONFERENCE ROOM
5 RECEPTION
6 AUDITORIUM
7 GALLERY
8 POLE
9 ATELIER
10 BOTANICAL GARDEN

Third floor

Second floor

First floor

Ground floor

View from southeast

West view

Sketch: night view from Saone River

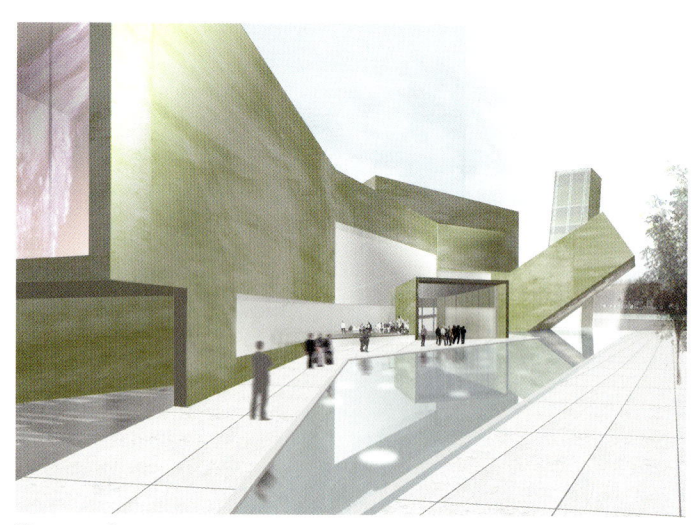

View toward entrance on west

II-190

Sketch: reception area

First floor

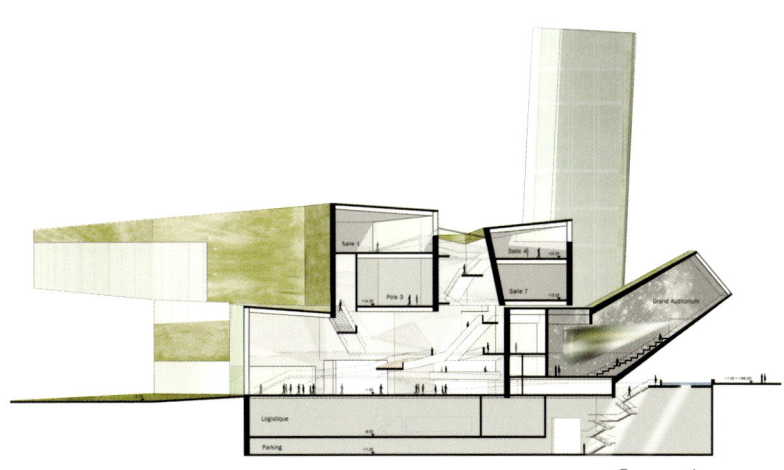

Cross section

Sketch: gallery

West elevation

First floor

コンフリューエンス(合流点)博物館

建物の形態はこの敷地ならではの特性に基づいて決められている。幅が狭い上に先に行くほど細くなる土地で,ローヌ川とソーヌ川が合流することで大きな流れが生まれる地点でもある。建物のジオメトリーは,これらの川のように水平方向に展開する。新たな美術館の空間構成を導くにあたり,水平性と有機的な乱流というテーマが,ここでの特性全てに対応できるようにした。

コンセプトは,以下4つの地球物理学的な性質を併せ持ったものを目指している。

1) 事象——物理的な展示品の全て
2) エネルギー——一般の人も訪れるメイン・エントランスホール
3) 各要素の配置——オーディトリアムと主要な動線
4) 相互関係——教育施設のタワー=学習,および熟考の為の教室

これら4つのベクトルが,建物中央に起こる水平方向の乱流と合体する。ここから,宙吊りになった先細の形状が,その姿を映し込む2つの川の上に水平に伸びて片持ち状に突き出る。これこそが2つの流体の対話の間に置かれた建築空間の流動性という開放的なコンセプトである。この空間を内部通路が介入し横断する。展示は交差する可能性に満ちた挿入壁の内側で行われる。建物断面は,状況と方法が融合する下の階において,その関係性に照準を合わせる。

各ジョイントの複雑な幾何学形態を簡単に製作する,新しいコンピュータ・プログラムのために,鉄骨枠組構造には標準接合部材を利用する。建物の被膜は,独特の,緑青を帯びた金色の銅合金で,都市に典型的な大気汚染への積極的対応として自然の錆をつける。二重のガラス壁は内側の空気層によりエネルギーを再利用するためである。

2001 Ile Seguin (Fondation Francois Pinault)
Paris, France

Sketches

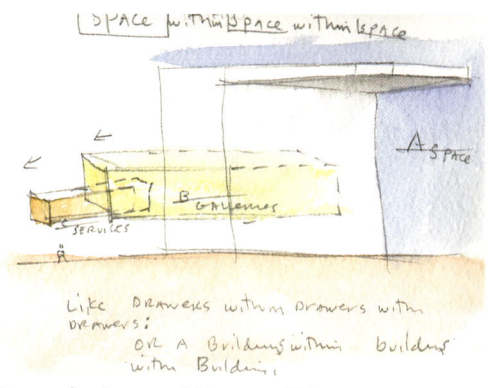

Concept sketch: space within space within space

The concept for the Pinault Foundation on Ile Sequin, Paris is a salute to Stephane Mallarme's epic poem Un Coup De Des (A Throw of the Dice). Simple rectangular galleries in a range of sizes in fine proportions and light are joined around five "thrown" armature spaces. These shaped voids form a vast internal spatial sequence.

Here we imagine collaborating on new permanent artworks with artists such as Walter de Maria, James Turrell, Richard Serra, etc. Around the Foundation at the edge of Ile Seguin are located cafes and terraces connected by a continuous electric tram. The activities of the sitting and moving crowds loop the site and are near the water's edge, while the heart of the Foundation is a 'spiritual refuge'.... a place of personal reflection.... a place free of the noise and smell of automobiles. Free in a zen-like emptiness of poetic reverie.

While the overall reads as one building, the internal concept is of three types of major spaces each inserted into the other (thing within a thing within a thing). The transformation of the Renault Factory site which built out Île Seguin will have a social/public ideal equal to the Art Foundation's ideals.

Access from water bus

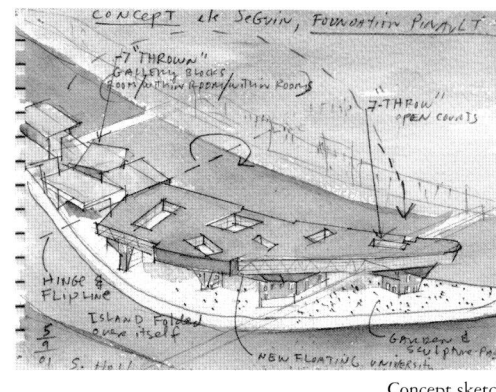

Concept sketch

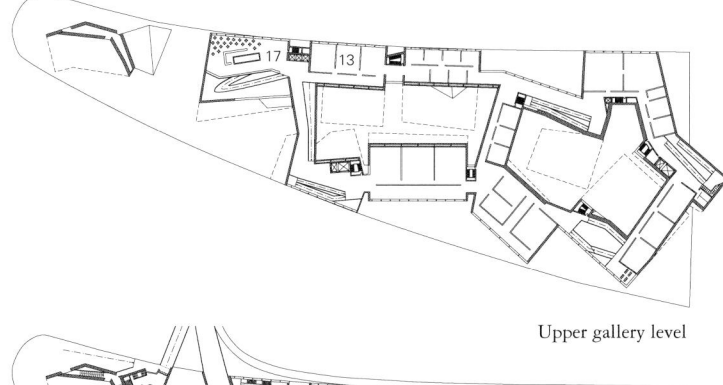

Upper gallery level

Lower gallery level

1	RECEPTION	7	COMMUNICATION OFFICE	13	GALLERY AND BREATHING SPACE
2	TRAIN STATION	8	EDUCATIONAL WORKSHOPS	14	CHILDREN'S SALON
3	BOOKSHOP	9	VIDEO CAFE	15	LIBRARY
4	CONVENIENCE	10	MANAGEMENT	16	BOOKSHOP+ORIENTATION
5	LIBRARY	11	ADMINISTRATION OFFICE	17	CAFE
6	TV STATION	12	DIRECTION OFFICE		

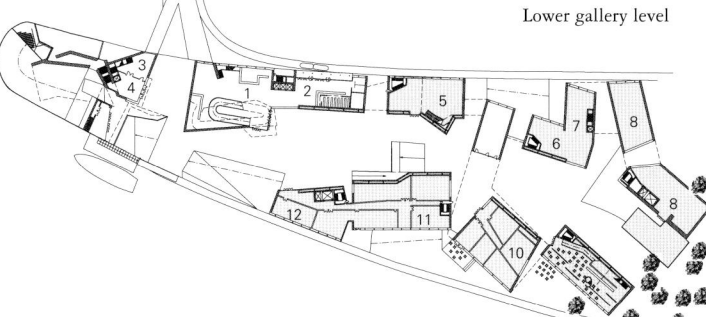

Ground floor S=1:4000

セガン島計画

ピノー財団のパリ・セガン島のコンセプトは, ステファヌ・マラルメの叙事詩 Un Coup De Des(骰子一擲)に対する敬意の表明である。単純な長方形のギャラリーに光が入る。5つの空間が建築の骨格となる。「骰子を振るように」計画されたその空間の周囲に, 様々な規模, 端整なプロポーションをしたギャラリーが結びつく。これらのヴォイド形態は, 内部空間に深いシークエンスを構成する。

ウォルター・デ・マリア, ジェームズ・タレル, リチャード・セラといった芸術家との共同作業を通して, ここに恒久的な新しい美術作品をつくることを想像したい。財団施設を取り巻くように, セガン島の川縁ではカフェやテラスが電気式トラムによって, 連続して結ばれている。腰を下ろし, 歩き回る人々は敷地を活発に巡り, 水辺に親しむ。その一方で財団の中心部にあるのは, 「精神の休息の場」……, 沈思する空間……騒音や車の排ガスの匂いから自由な場所である。禅のように空虚な, 詩的幻想の空間に佇む。

全体計画はひとつの建築である。(空間の中の空間の中の空間という)互いに入れ子になった3種類の主要空間が, 内部空間のコンセプトである。セガン島に増築されたルノー社の工場の敷地に手を加えることは, 美術財団の理想と等しく, 社会的/公共的理念の追求である。

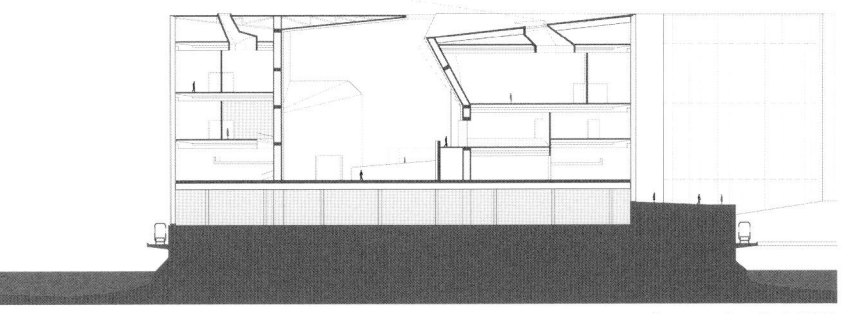

Cross section S=1:1200

East view

College of Architecture, Cornell University
2001　　Ithaca, New York, U.S.A.

Studio and shop

Campus passage

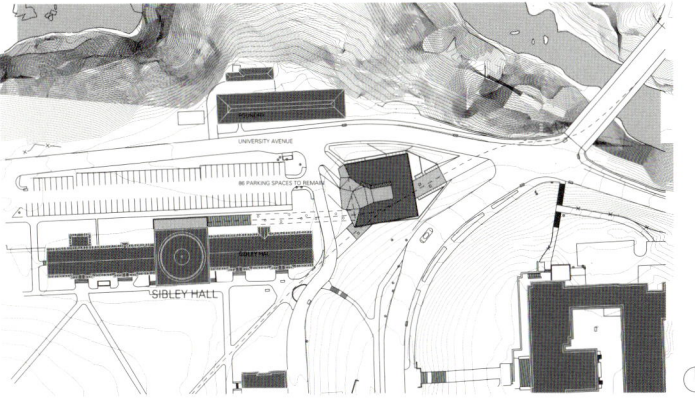

Staircase

Site plan S=1:3000

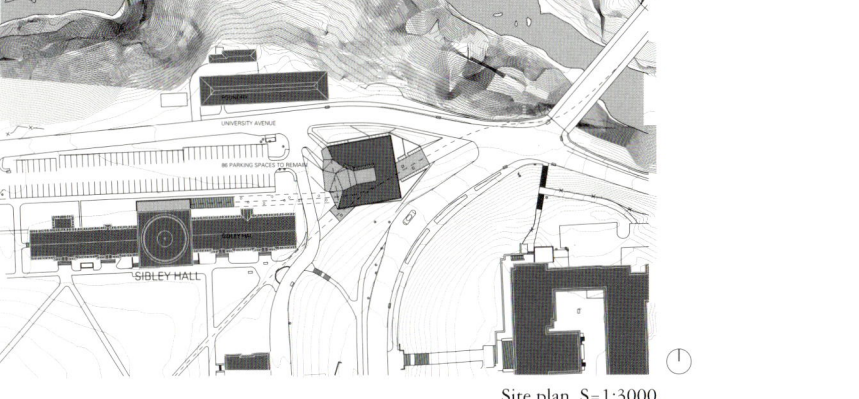

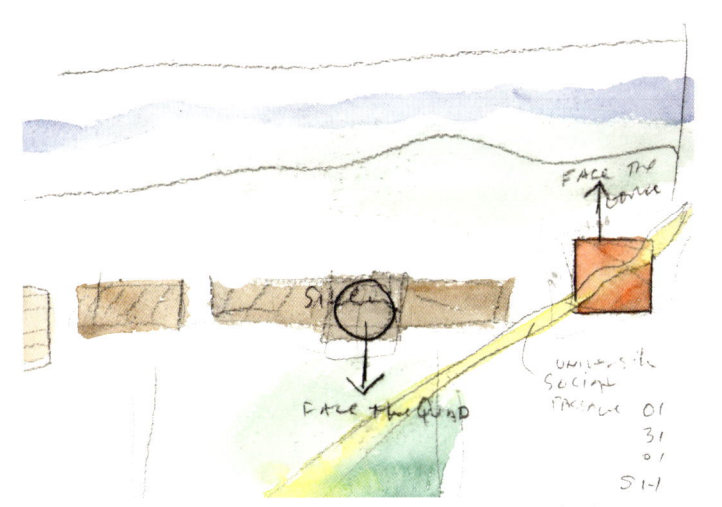

Concept sketch: thoroughfare for pedestrian

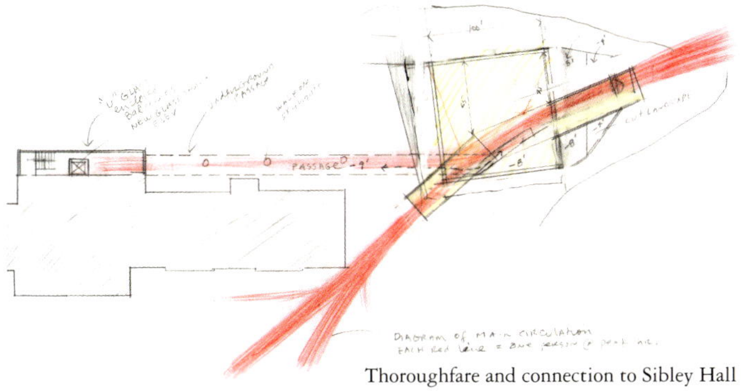

Thoroughfare and connection to Sibley Hall

Diagram

The site for the new Department of Architecture building, Milstein Hall, is located at the northeast corner of the Arts Quad, north of the Fall Creek Gorge Bridge, a main thoroughfare for pedestrian traffic onto campus. The new Milstein Hall offers a campus passage at its ground plane which is open to all and makes a new connection to the existing architecture school building, Sibley Hall. Students traveling through the Arts Quad can encounter exhibits of ongoing work in the school, see student projects in the shop, or attend an architecture lecture which is announced along the passage. The shop and lecture hall open directly to the new campus passage, facilitating the "social condenser" aspect of this passage.

The upper levels of the new Architecture School provide a special view connection to the gorge, the campus, and the distant views of Lake Cayuga. This view connects to the Finger Lakes Region's amazing topography.

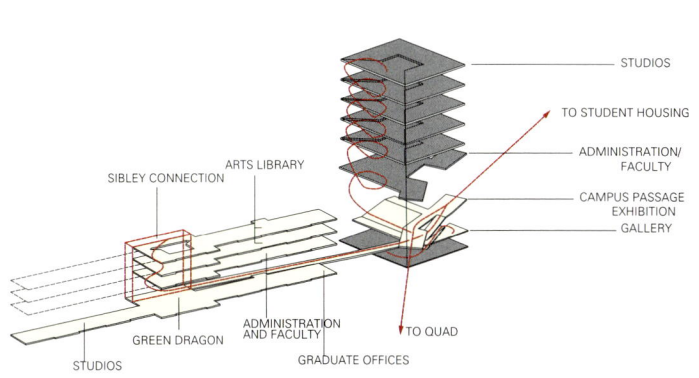

Concept: Tesseract or Hypercube (An Open Bracket)

Scientifically a Tesseract is the four dimensional analogue to a cube (a square is to a cube as a cube is to a Tesseract). Internally this cube3 develops non-Euclidean properties which are experientially evident in the overlapping interior perspectives. The Review Rooms, the heart of an architecture studio education, are in the central overlapping cubes.

The loft-like studio spaces form an Open Bracket made operative by the infrastructural Tesseract Zone which is pulled inside out forming the west facade. The Tesseract Zone is embedded in the Open Bracket as a shifting intermittent section with alignments to the landscape of the site: The bottom of Fall Creek Gorge, the distant view of Lake Cayuga, the angle of the sun (47.5° at Equinox).

Construction in precast concrete planks and beams is complimented by the simplicity of structural channel glass planks on three facades (with translucent insulation) and juxtaposed with aluminum in different states for the Tesseract wall (foamed aluminum, bead-blasted, and direct digital-cut sheets). The translucent insulation in the glass planks brings softly molded light into the studios, while the rooms of Tesseract wall can be fully darkened to accommodate digital media.

The design incorporates many sustainable building elements, such as a ventilated cavity between the channel glass along the east and south facades. During the summer, a natural chimney effect exhausts the facades at the parapet. Closed in winter, these walls bring in solar heat. Natural cross ventilation is via 3' x 3' operable windows in shadow boxes which let in the winter sun and shade out summer sun. Photovoltaic cells on the roof are directly connected to ceiling fans in the studios for summer cooling.

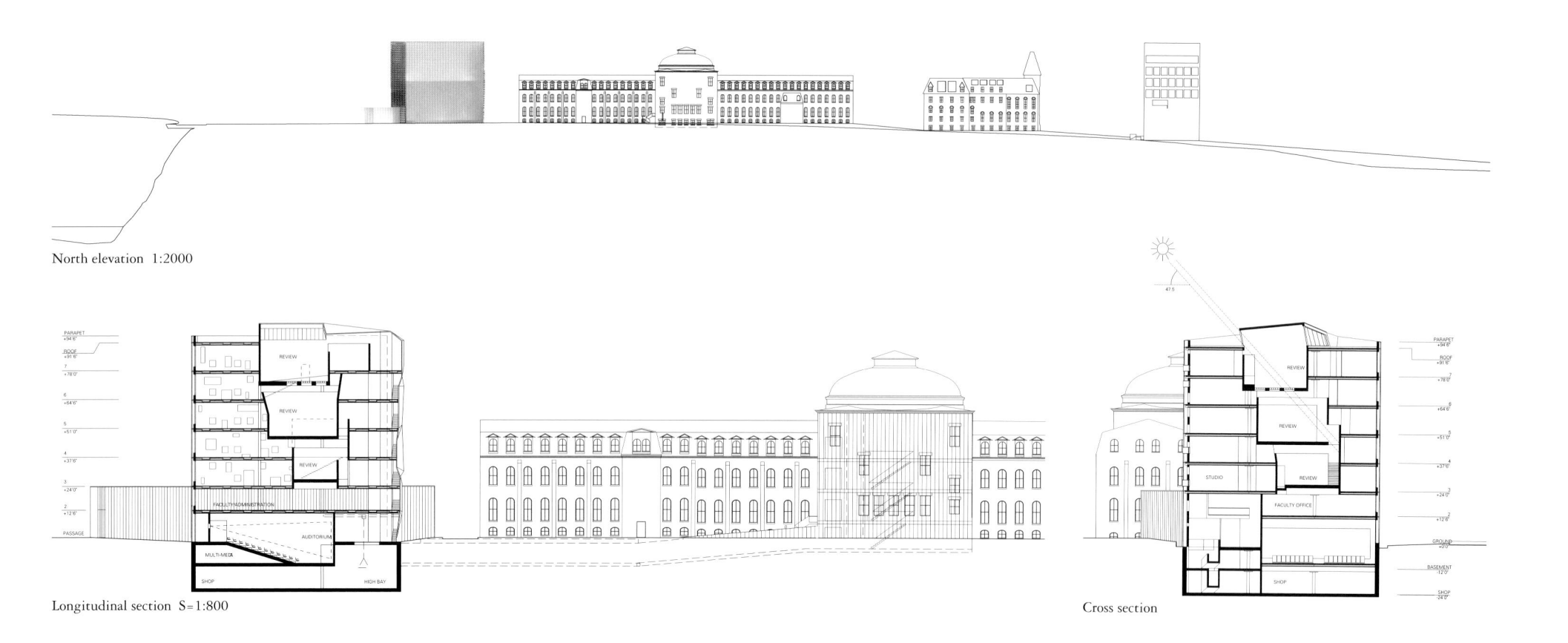

North elevation 1:2000

Longitudinal section S=1:800

Cross section

Model: south view

West view

コーネル大学建築学部棟

新しい建築学部棟ミルスタイン・ホールの敷地はアーツ・クワッドの北東の角，キャンパスに向かう歩行者が使うフォール・クリーク・ジョージ・ブリッジの大通りの北に位置している。新しいミルスタイン・ホールは地上レベルに街路を通し，全てをキャンパスに対して開放することで，既存の建築学部棟シブリー・ホールとの新しい連続性を生み出している。アーツ・クワッドを通る学生は，大学でその時々に行われている展示と偶然に出会い，ショップでは学生の作品を見たり，あるいはこの通路で告知される建築のレクチャーに参加する。ショップとレクチャー・ホールはこのキャンパスの新しい街路に直接開放されることで，街路に「社会凝縮器」としての側面を付与している。

新しい建築学部の上層階からは，キャンパスの峡谷への優れた眺望の連なりや，遠くカユーガ湖への眺めを得ることができる。さらにこの眺望は，フィンガー・レイク地方の素晴らしい地形へと向かう。

[コンセプト：テッセラクト，超立方体（オープン・ブラケット）]
正方形が立方体に，立方体がテッセラクト（正八胞体）になるように，数学的にはテッセラクトとは，四次元における立方体を指す概念である。この三次元立方体は非ユークリッド幾何学の発展によるもので，内部空間のパースペクティブの重なりという点で経験的によく知られている。建築スタジオの教育の中核となるレビュー・ルームは，オーバーラップする立方体の中心に位置している。

ロフト状のスタジオ空間はオープン・ブラケットと呼ばれている。インフラを収容するテッセラクトによって，内部は外部へと突出し，西側ファサードを構成する。フォール・クリーク渓谷の谷底，カユーガ湖，（春分や秋分では47.5°に相当する）太陽角。テッセラクト・ゾーンは敷地の自然に合わせて断続的に変化する断面を構成し，オープン・ブラケットに内包される。

建設工法はパネルと梁のプレキャスト・コンクリートによる。ファサード3面は（透過性断熱材と一体の）単純な構造用溝型ガラスによって補完され，テッセラクトの壁面は（発泡アルミニウム，ビーズブラスト加工，デジタル加工といった）様々な表情のアルミニウムが併設される。ガラス面の透過性断熱材は柔らかい光を成形面に合わせてスタジオに取り入れる一方で，テッセラクト壁の諸室はデジタルメディアを収容するため，完全に遮光されている。

計画では東と南のファサードに沿って設けられた溝型ガラスの通気層のように，サステイナブルな建築要素が数多く採用されている。夏期は自然の煙突効果によって，パラペットからファサードの空気を排気する。冬期，密閉すると太陽熱が蓄熱される。自然通気はシャドーボックスに取り付けられた3×3フィート（0.9×0.9m）の可動式窓から行われ，冬は太陽光を取り入れ，夏は太陽光を遮る役割を果たす。屋根の太陽光発電は直接，スタジオのシーリング・ファンへと接続され，夏は涼気をもたらしてくれる。

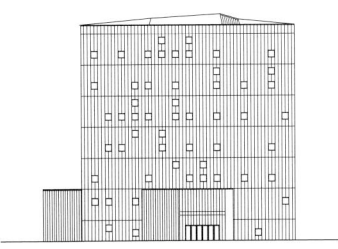

East elevation S=1:1000

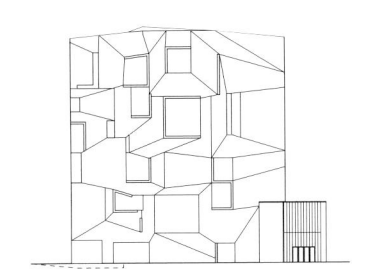

West elevation

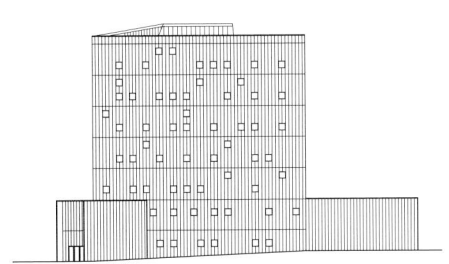

South elevation

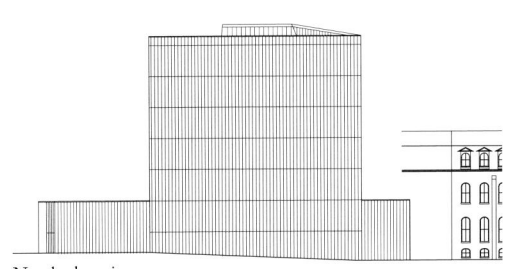

North elevation

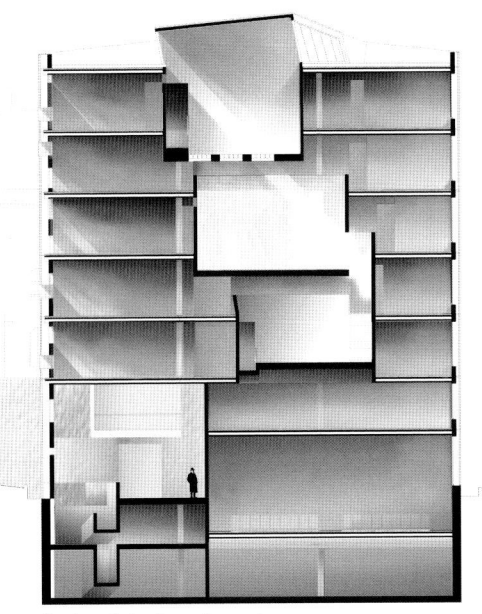

Section: light through openings

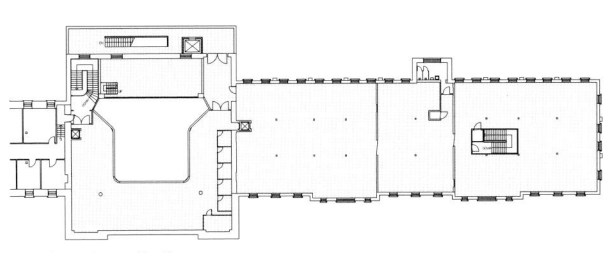

Third level (+24'-0")

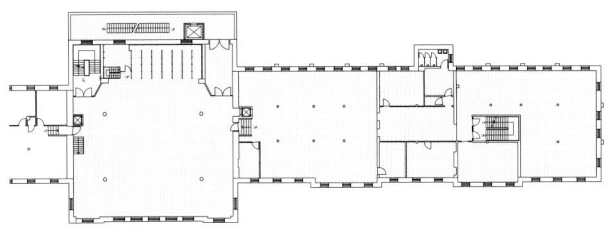

Second level (+12'-6")

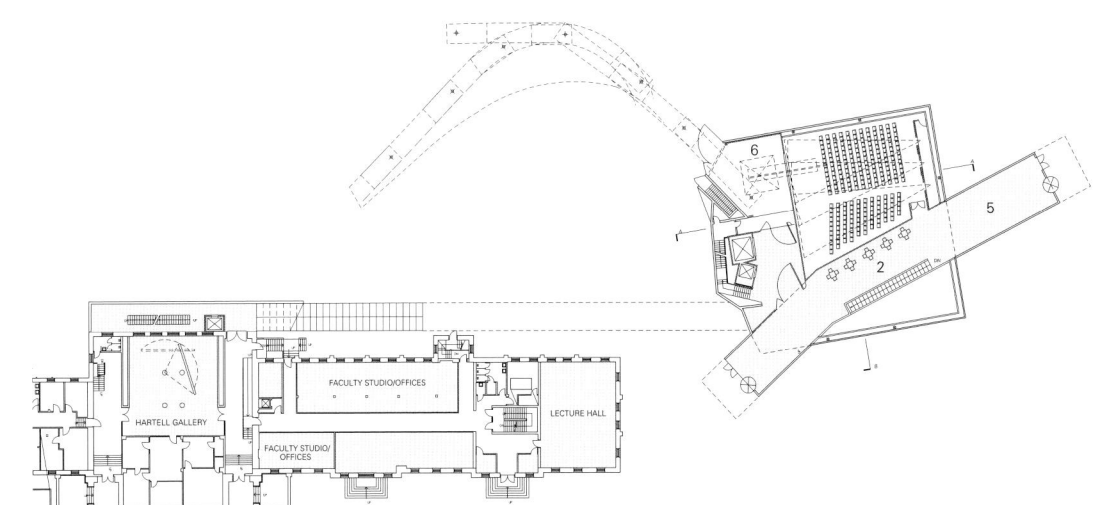

First level (+0'-0")

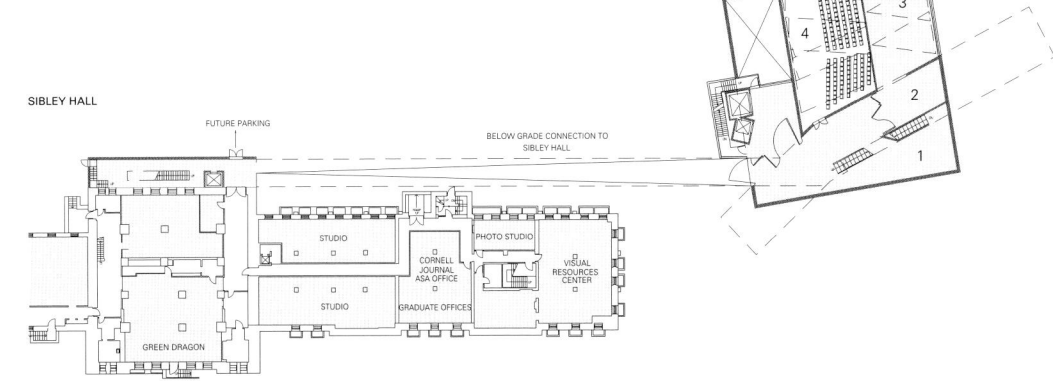

Gallery level (-12'-0") S=1:1000

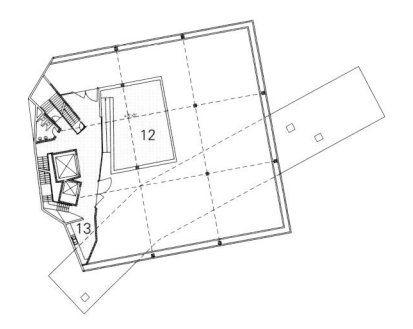

Seventh level (+78'-0")

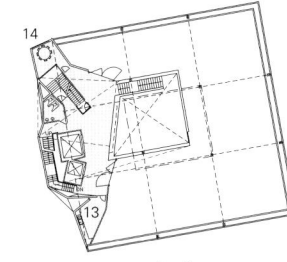

Sixth level (+64'-6")

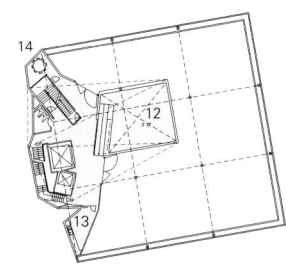

Fifth level (+51'-0")

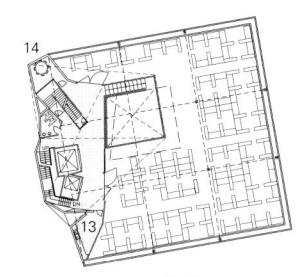

Fourth level (+37'-6")

1 GALLERY
2 EXHIBITION
3 MULTI-MEDIA ROOM
4 AUDITORIUM
5 CAMPUS PASSAGE
6 COVERED WORK AREA
7 FACULTY OFFICE
8 RECEPTION
9 OFFICE
10 COMMITTEE ROOM
11 DEAN'S OFFICE
12 REVIEW
13 SHOP
14 SEMINAR
15 DISPLAY

II-197

2002- Nanjing Museum of Art & Architecture
Nanjing, China

Perspective is the fundamental historic difference between Western and Chinese painting. After the 13th Century, Western painting developed vanishing points in fixed perspective. Chinese painters, although aware of perspective, rejected the single-vanishing point method, instead producing landscapes with "parallel perspectives" in which the viewer travels within the painting.

The new museum is sited at the gateway to the Contemporary International Practical Exhibition of Architecture in the lush green landscape of the Pearl Spring near Nanjing, China. The museum explores the shifting viewpoints, layers of space, and expanses of mist and water, which characterize the deep alternating spatial mysteries of early Chinese painting. The museum is formed by a "field" of parallel perspective spaces and garden walls in black bamboo-formed concrete over which a light "figure" hovers. The straight passages on the ground level gradually turn into the winding passage of the figure above. The upper gallery, suspended high in the air, unwraps in a clockwise turning sequence and culminates at "in-position" viewing of the city of Nanjing in the distance. The meaning of this rural site becomes urban through this visual axis to the the great Ming Dynasty capital city, Nanjing.

The courtyard is paved in recycled Old Hutong bricks from the destroyed courtyards in the center of Nanjing. Limiting the colors of the museum to black and white connects it to the ancient paintings, but also gives a background to feature the colors and textures of the artwork and architecture to be exhibited within. Bamboo, previously growing on the site, has been used in bamboo-formed concrete, with a black penetrating stain. The Museum has geothermal cooling and heating, and recycled storm water.

Site plan

View from southwest

View from south (under construction)

Sketches

West elevation

II-199

Roof

Upper floor (flooting gallery)

East elevation

West elevation

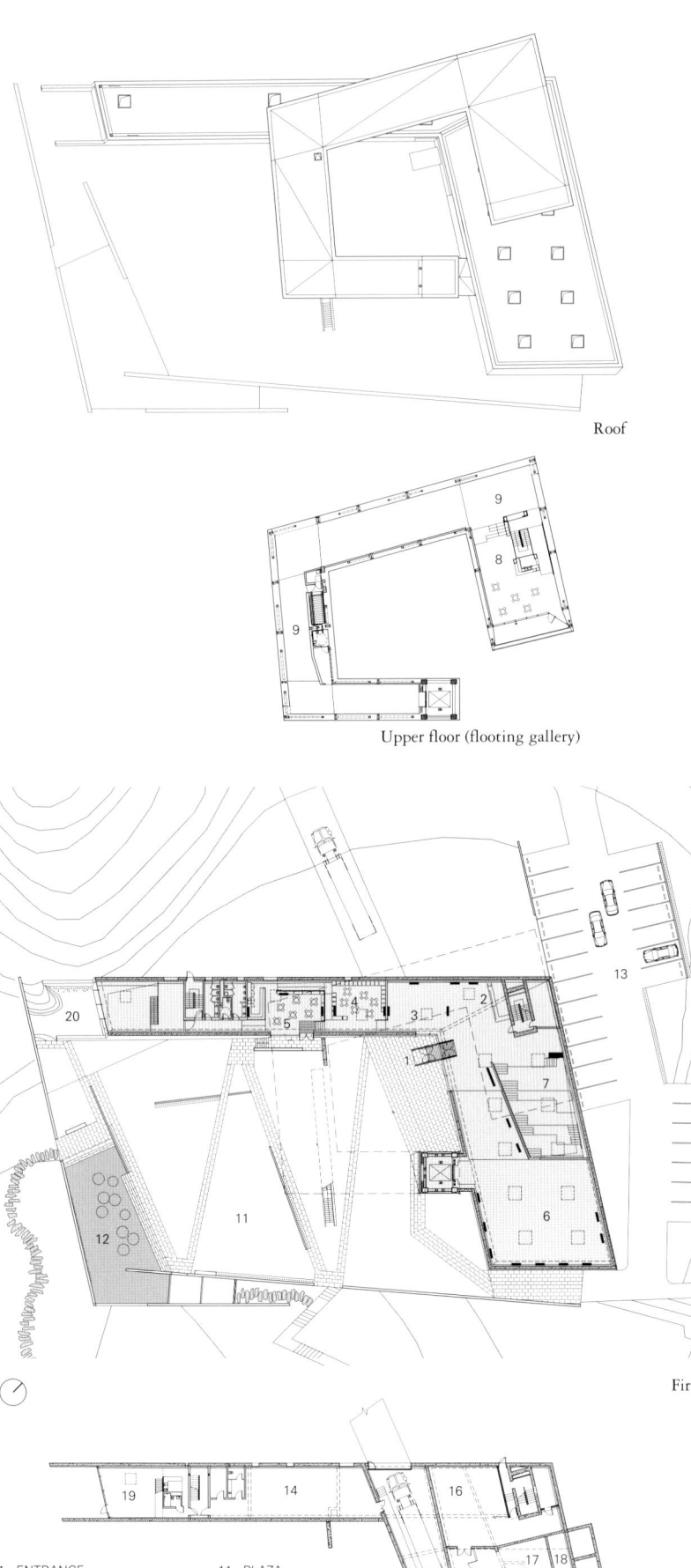

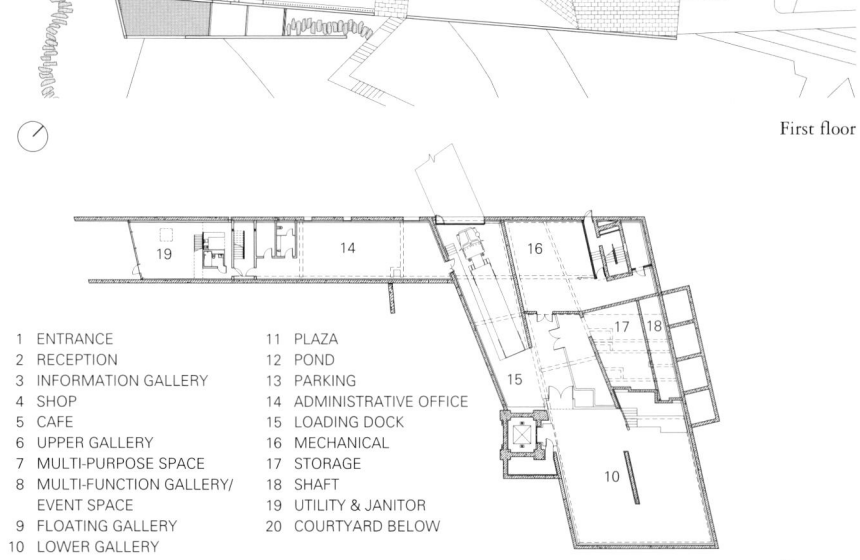

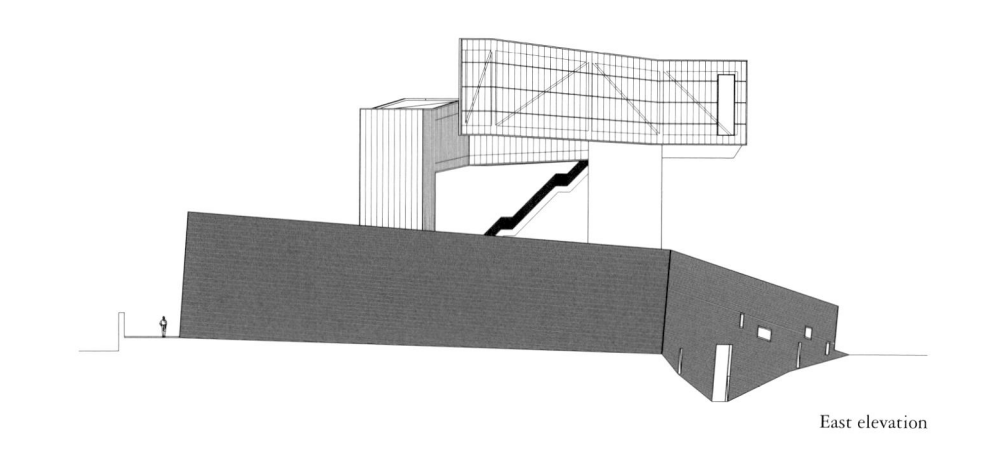

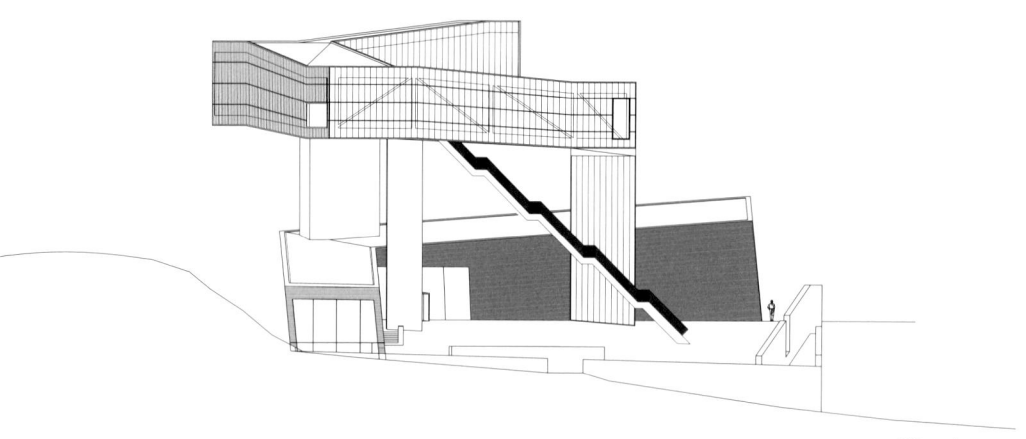

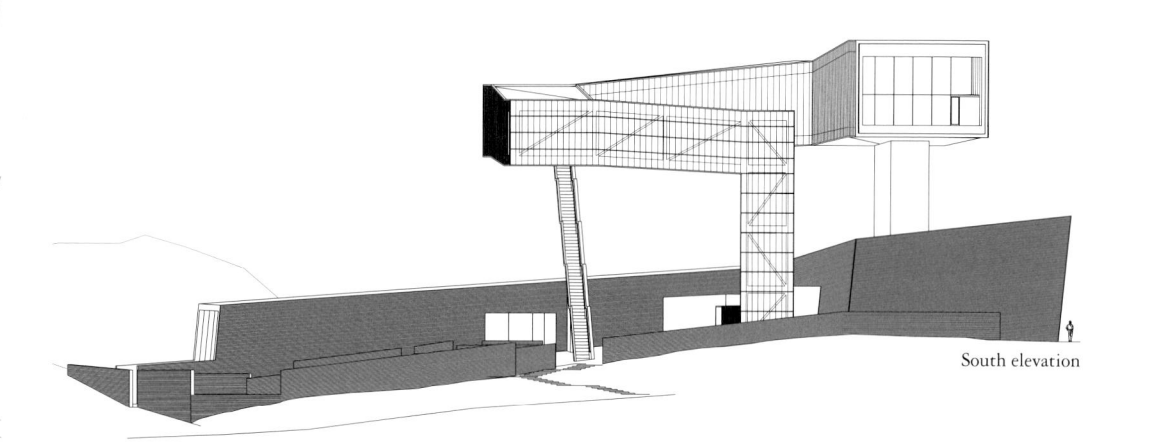

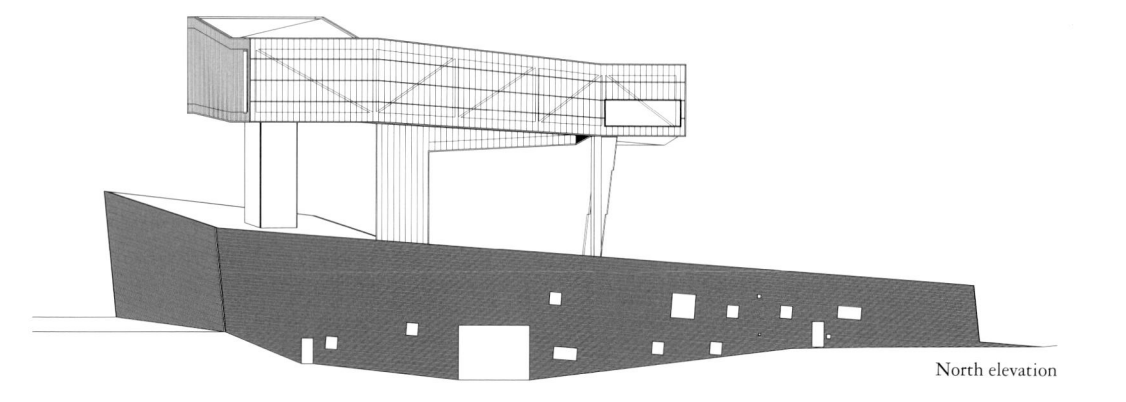

First floor

South elevation

1 ENTRANCE	11 PLAZA
2 RECEPTION	12 POND
3 INFORMATION GALLERY	13 PARKING
4 SHOP	14 ADMINISTRATIVE OFFICE
5 CAFE	15 LOADING DOCK
6 UPPER GALLERY	16 MECHANICAL
7 MULTI-PURPOSE SPACE	17 STORAGE
8 MULTI-FUNCTION GALLERY/ EVENT SPACE	18 SHAFT
9 FLOATING GALLERY	19 UTILITY & JANITOR
10 LOWER GALLERY	20 COURTYARD BELOW

Basement

North elevation

First floor: upper gallery

Interior model: basement and first floor

Gallery on upper floor: floating gallery

南京芸術・建築美術館

透視図法は, 西洋と中国の絵画の間で歴史上根本的な相違を示すものである。13世紀以降, 西洋絵画では固定された遠近関係の中で消滅点の概念を発展させた。これに対し, 中国の画家達は遠近の相関関係には気付きながらも一点透視図法の描画方法を拒否し, 代わりに「平行透視図法」で表現することで見る者が, 絵画の中に入り込んで辿ることのできる風景を創出した。

この新しい美術館は, 中国は南京にほど近い珍珠泉の青々とした緑の景観内に位置する, 現代国際実践建築展示場への入り口に建つ。建物は視点の移動や空間の重なり, 霞や水の拡がりといった中国絵画の構成の妙を探求し, 平行透視図法的な空間の「視界」や, 庭にある, 竹で型取りされた黒いコンクリート壁の上に浮かぶ軽やかな「図形」によって形づくられる。地上レベルの直線の通路は徐々に変化し, 曲がりくねって, 上部の「図形」の通路となる。空中に高く浮かぶ上部ギャラリーは時計廻りのシークエンスを辿って開放されていき, 南京を遠景として見晴らす「内部視点」となる場所で完結する。偉大な明王朝の首都へとつながるこの視覚的な軸を介して, 都会から離れた敷地が都市的なものとなる。

敷地内の中庭は, 南京中心部にあった庭を取り壊した際の, 古い胡同 (フートン) のレンガを再利用したもので舗装される。美術館の配色を黒と白に限定することによって過去の水墨画を連想させているが, 同時に展示される美術品の色や素材感などの背景としても機能する。敷地に植わっていた竹をコンクリートの型枠にして, 壁の表面に竹の模様を残し, 黒の透明な染料で仕上げる。建物は地熱利用の冷暖房と雨水を再利用するシステムも備えている。

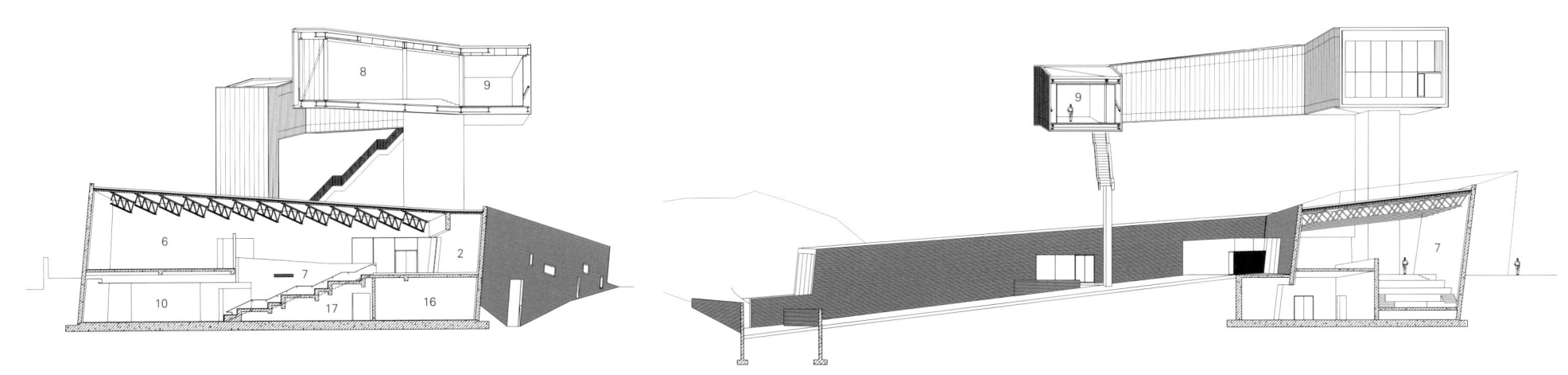

North-south section

East-west section

2005-09 Herning Center of the Arts
Herning, Denmark

Overall view from southeast

Monochrome, Achrome, Malevich & Manzoni

Thinking of the more than 46 original works by Piero Manzoni in the Herning Museum, we could look back; from the monochrome obsessions and writings of Malevich there is a spirit bridge to the achrome works of Piero Manzoni.

Holger Reenberg has written about the links between Malevich and Manzoni, who wanted, "to reach the zero point from where anything is possible…". While I had been familiar with Piero Manzoni, I first discovered that he had created many of his most important works in Herning, Denmark while I read the extended booklet produced for the competition for the Herning Center of the Arts.

This site in the center of Denmark's Jutland Peninsula seemed charged with the mysterious energy of 1960s Arte Povera, Gruppo Zero and the monochromatic desert ground of Malevich.

We were among six other architects invited to compete for the new Herning Center of the Arts to be sited near the museum-occupied original shirt factory. The plan of this 1950s building was made in the shape of a shirt collar…. Herning was an interesting, idiosyncratic place. In late August, I reread the competition brief and enthusiastically accepted proposed building constraints which included a height limit of eight meters and the color white.

I studied Piero Manzoni's work at length as a way into the competition. The "Socle du Monde" had inspired me years before, during my studies of the work of Robert Smithson, Michael Heizer, and other conceptually focused artists working with land. Piero Manzoni had preceded them all with "Socle du Monde", which had been made at Herning. The famous canned series: "The Artist's Shit" had been produced at the Herning factory, as had many fabric explorations in the "Achrome" series. As a connection to these, we imaged the building in white tilt-up concrete with the forms lined to capture a fabric wrinkle texture.

It was a coincidence to find my favorite Danish architect Jørn Utzon had built one of his prototypical buildings of 1972 next to the museum site. Occupied now as a residence and beautifully maintained, its relation to the new building was important in our initial thinking.

Treasure Boxes/Shirt Sleeves

I decided to accept the galleries as two "treasure boxes"—rectangles at the center of the plan which would then have curvilinear light gathering roof elements loosely displaced. The flat featureless landscape was partially shaped in the reverse-curved of the geometry of the roof—fusing the architecture and the landscape. From the air the forms resembled shirt sleeves thrown onto boxes. The loose edges of the plan could be adjusted for the cafe, auditorium and lobby. On a single level, the building would have excellent circulation and be geothermally heated and cooled.

Clearly anchored to its site, this seemed an inspired concept. The interior spaces would come

View from northeast: entrance on center

Evening view from south: restaurant on left

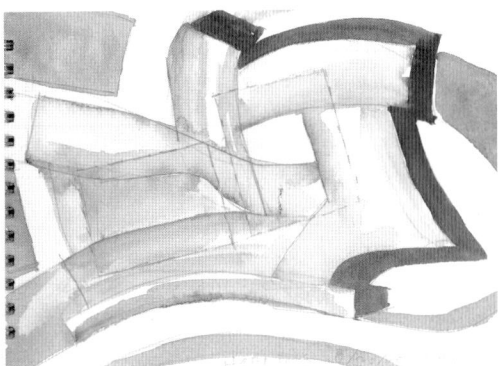

Sketch: "shirt sleeves" over boxes

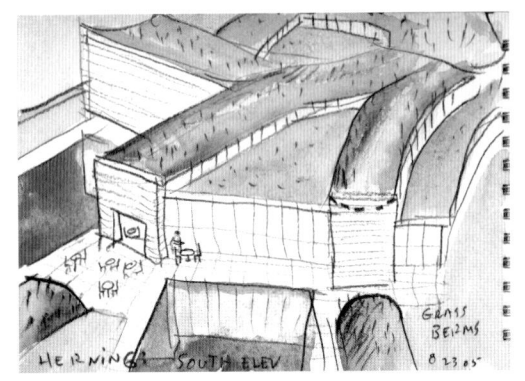

South side with restaurant

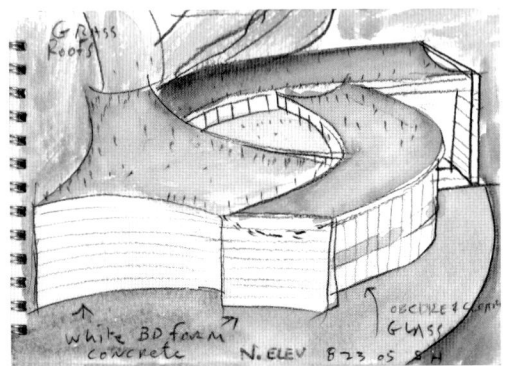

North elevation

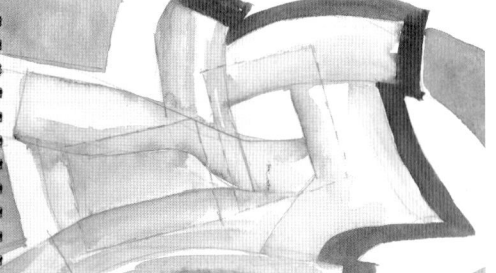

1 ENTRANCE FOYER
2 PERMANENT EXHIBITION
3 TEMPORARY EXHIBITION
4 AUDITORIUM
5 MUSIC REHEARSAL
6 LIBRARY
7 DISCOVERY CENTER
8 RESTAURANT
9 ADMINISTRATION
10 TOWN SQUARE AT BIRK
11 SCULPTURE STORAGE
12 PAINTING STORAGE
13 PRINT STORAGE
14 WORKSHOP ROOM
15 GENERAL STORAGE
16 MECHANICAL

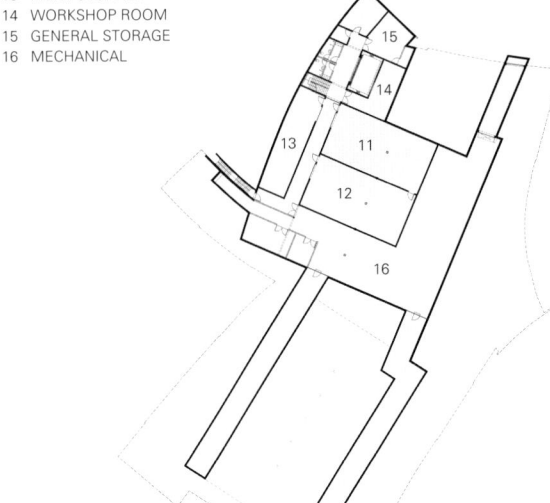

Basement

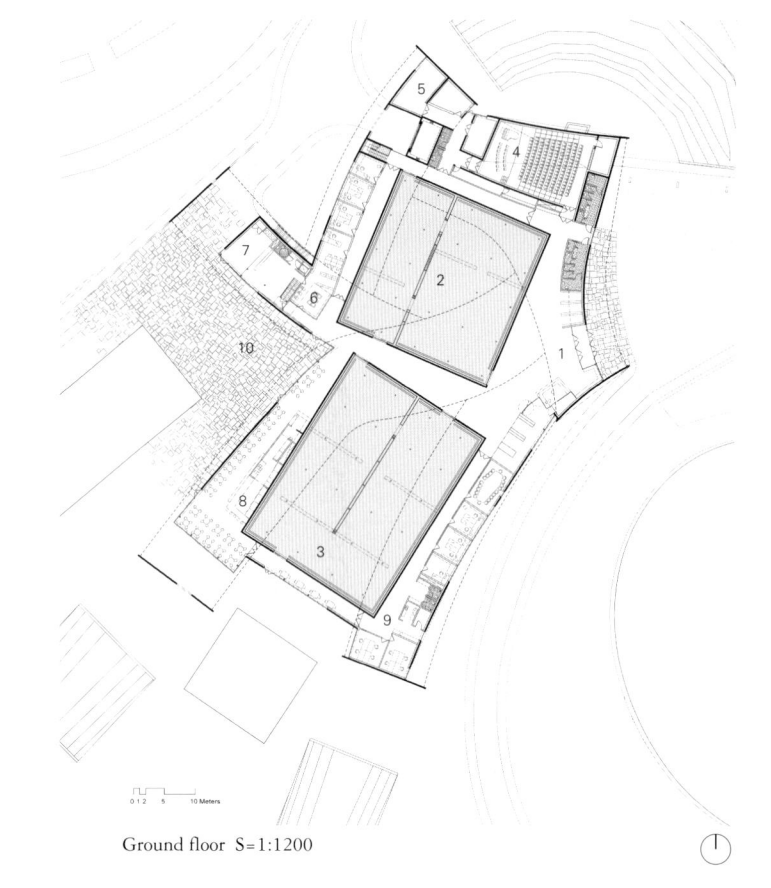

Ground floor S=1:1200

alive with a gradual curved light. The presentation boards with black and white photos of the little model looked stunning. I imagine an amazing quality of light within the orthogonal walled galleries. The cliché arguments today revolve around new art museums being either too expressive for good gallery space, or the other extreme; a collection of white boxes which suck the life out of art, we had a third way. The entire presentation—all seven boards—was limited to black and white.

Scandinavian Blood/Northern Light

My grandfather was born in Tønsberg, Norway. My father, a full-blooded Norwegian, raised us on the edge of Puget Sound, near Seattle. The low angle of northern sunlight in the winter has a special inspiring power similar to the light in Scandinavia. In 1993, we were invited to compete for the contemporary art museum in Helsinki. The concept of intertwining northern light, the city fabric and landscape in our scheme —"Kiasma", prevailed as our project was selected over 516 entries. Attention to the low angle of Helsinki sunlight was developed in a "light catching" section.

These building experiences and my Scandinavian blood gave me a head start to conceive the Herning building with a special quality of light connecting to its site. The curved planar "shirt sleeve" roofs turn up with strips of skylight to catch the low angle of the sun and allow it to slightly grace across the down curving ceiling. The geometry in light reflecting curves distributes the light so wonderfully in the gallery spaces that they can be used without artificial light. The space is animated and alive when a cloud moves in front of, or away from, the sun—as often happens in this region.

Planar Architecture/Fabric Forms

The planar nature of the curved roof elements draped over the treasure boxes of the galleries was followed by the planar development of other spaces in white concrete. Truck tarps were inserted into the concrete formwork to yield a fabric texture that swallows the imperfections of rapid construction. Floors of integral color charcoal concrete unify the ground plane into a continuous patina with a wax finish. Diffused light in areas like the cafe was achieved in sandblasted channel glass. Earth mounds, which carry the building geometry into the landscape, form spaces around the building. At the entry the curved mound forms a space protecting from the adjacent highway. On the south side large reflecting pools gather and reflect the sunlight onto soffits. The landscape architect Torben Schønherr has developed our competition concept with his own delicate porous paving and plantings.

Realization: Luminist Space of Surprise

The Herning building is rather than a building experienced first as an object, it has a series of exterior experiences fused with the landscape. As

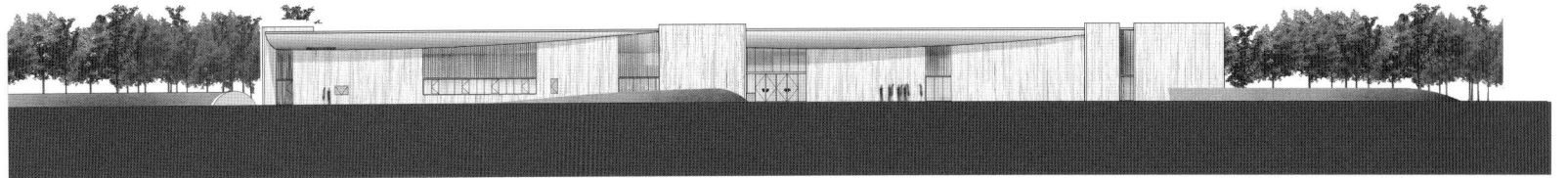

East elevation

South elevation

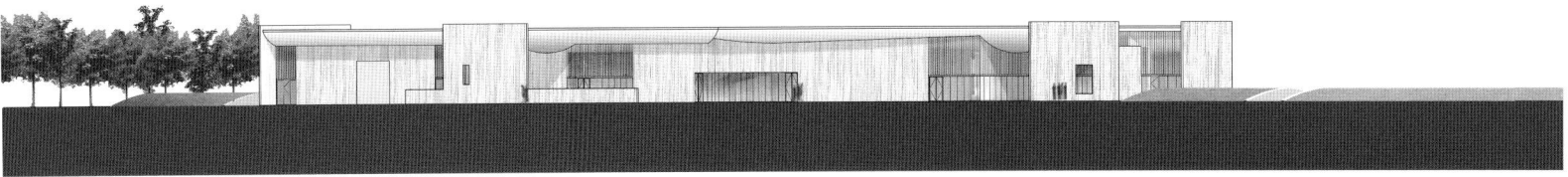

West elevation

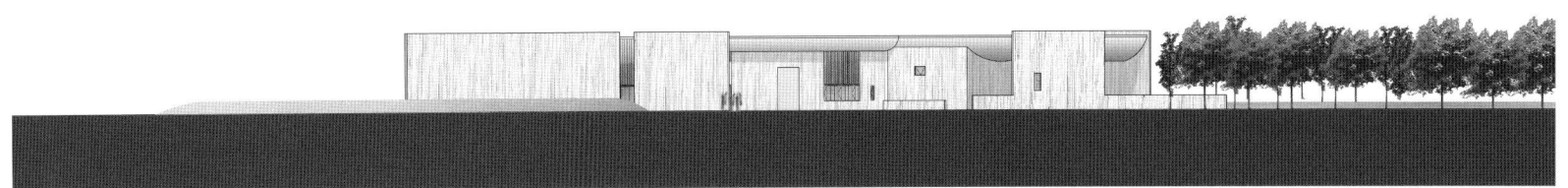

North elevation

you move around the exterior of the building, you experience very different spaces none of which add up into an object or a singularity. Going into the building is quite a different experience. There is a sense of surprise on entering, especially if you enter at the end of the day around 5:30 pm when the low angle of the western sun seems to blow through the two low slung curves capturing the light at the ceiling.

Moving forward through the splayed rectilinear walls containing the galleries, the space glides into one or the other where the glowing curve of the ceiling follows a direction of flow through a sequence of spaces. The gallery spaces where walls always meet floors at right angles are shaped for focus on the art, while at the perimeter of the building edges become more fuzzy, interacting with the landscape. The cafe spaces spill out onto terraces. The Concert Hall for the Midwest Ensemble opens to its own practice rooms and service space while connecting to the main lobby. The galleries at the center of the building can be easily closed while all peripheral spaces remain open for after-hours use. The monochrome frame foregrounds the color of the art which charges the space differently according to each artist and each exhibition. The rectilinear spaces of the galleries have been fine-tuned according to the ratio of 1 : 1.618—as in all our projects. In his seminal book, *The Geometry of Art and Life*, Matila Ghyka puts forth an argument for proportion based on mathematical principles found in nature; the Golden Section ratio 1 : 1.618 is the key ratio in organic growth.

As one walks around the spaces threading through the administrative offices; the presence of the curved planar roofs above again energizes the space—but in an upswinging curve toward the landscape outside. In the everyday tasks of all who work in this museum, the planar and light-catching geometry of the architecture will enliven activities within, embracing the landscape. The monochromatic frame of the museum architecture is animated by the change of light angles everyday and throughout the seasons. With its Concert Space, which can act as an events auditorium, its Children's Center, restaurant, and outdoor gathering areas, the hope is for the museum to act as a social condenser for the community. The core of the museum—the galleries—aim at a "luminist" space for changing art.

On first encounter the artist Iannis Kounellis said the spaces remind him of sheds with hanging fisherman's nets. Perhaps here one can read a bit of the ocean in the continuous flatland site of the Jutland Peninsula. A swelling of landscape turning into waves of light marking a "zero point" as Piero Manzoni said… "where anything is possible".

Steven Holl, June 2009

East elevation: administration office on left

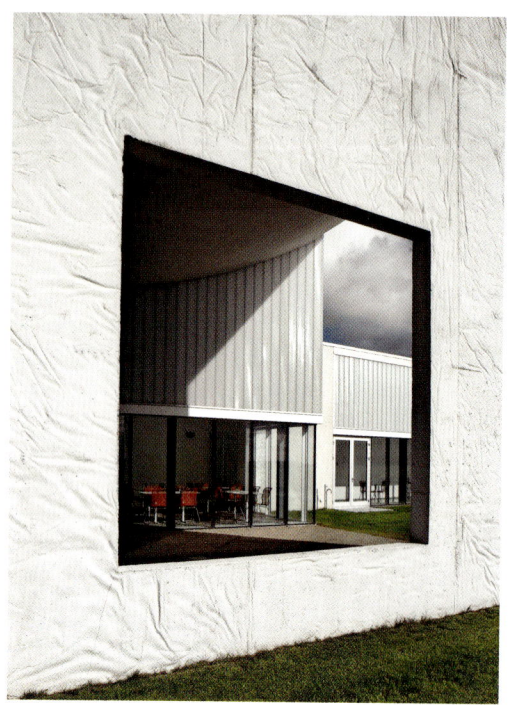

View toward restaurant

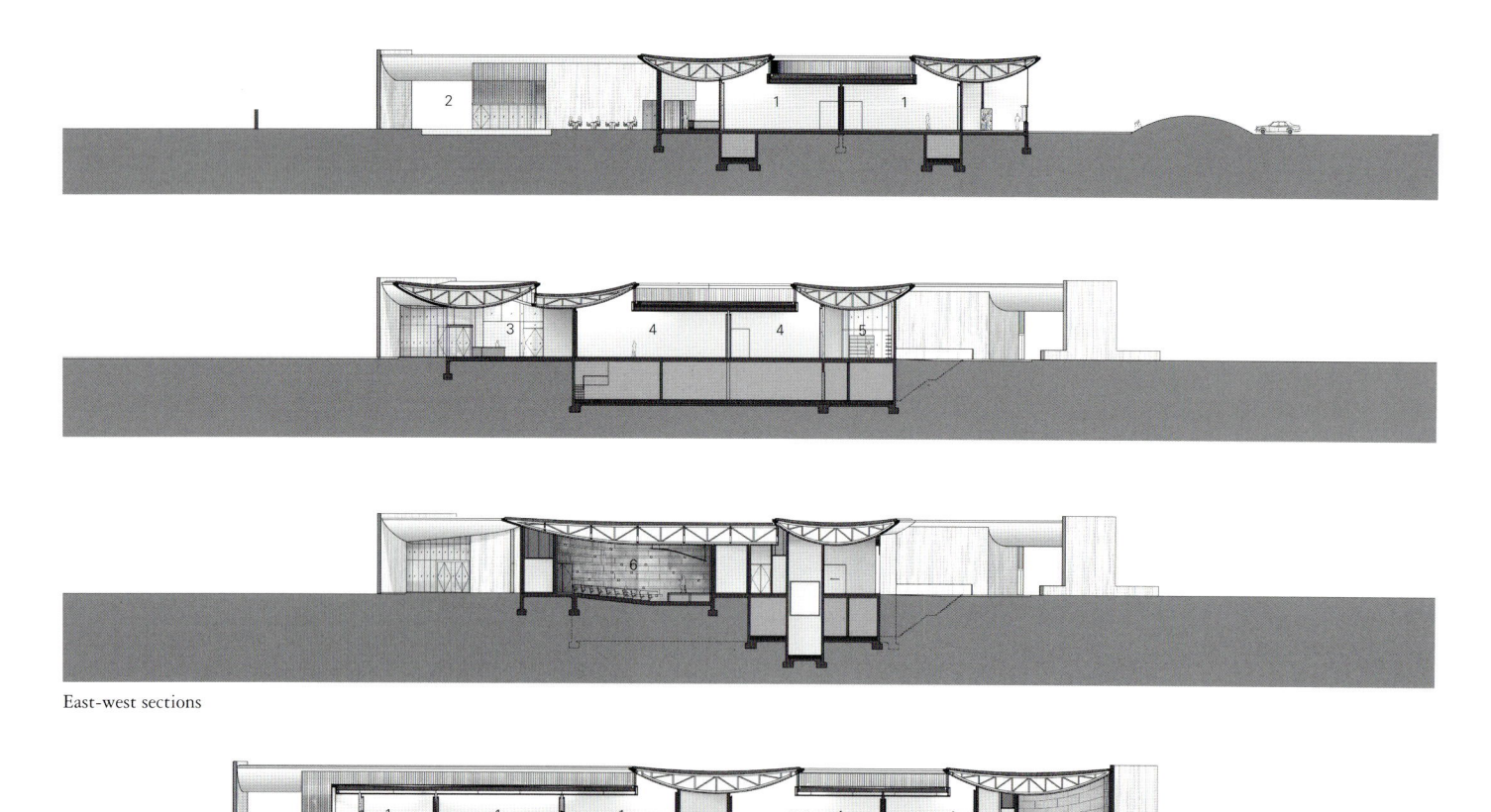

East-west sections

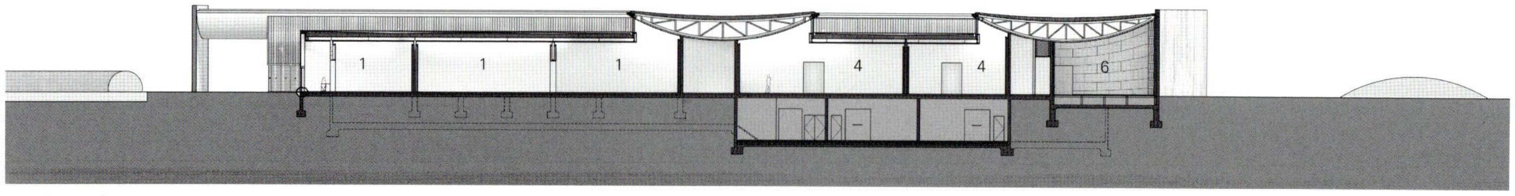

North-south section

1 TEMPORARY EXHIBITION
2 TOWN SQUARE AT BIRK
3 ENTRANCE FOYER
4 PERMANENT EXHIBITION
5 LIBRARY
6 AUDITORIUM

Entrance foyer: looking main entrance on northeast, permanent exhibition on left

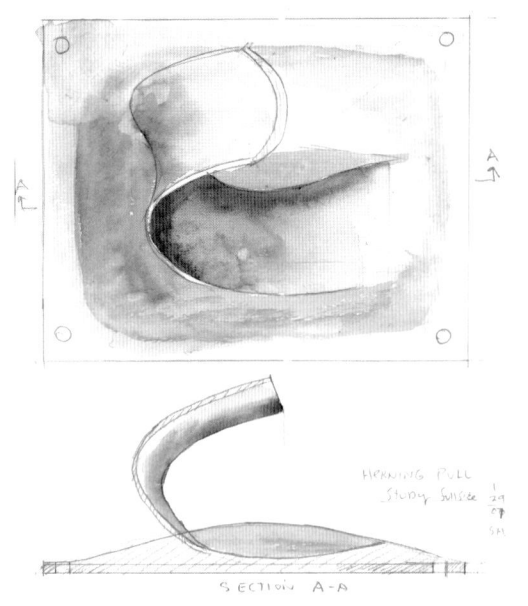

Detail of door handle at main entrance

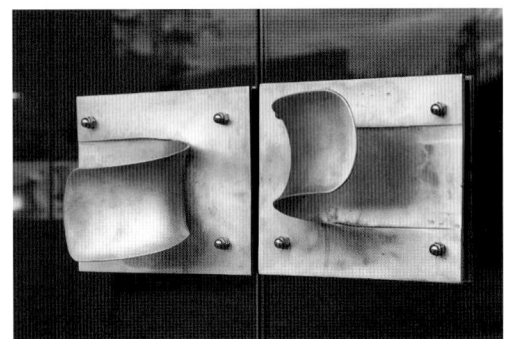

Door handle at main entrance

Entrance foyer: temporary exhibition (left) and permanent exhibition (right)

ヘルニング芸術センター
[モノクローム, アクローム, マレーヴィチとマンゾーニについて]

ヘルニング美術館に収蔵されている46点以上にも及ぶピエロ・マンゾーニの作品からは, マレーヴィチのモノクロームへの執着や言説からピエロ・マンゾーニのアクロームへと続く精神の架け橋を見てとることができる。

ホルガー・レーエンベアはマレーヴィチとマンゾーニとの共通点についてこう書き記している。彼らは「そこからすべてが始まるゼロに到達する」ことを望んでいたのだ, と。ピエロ・マンゾーニについては以前からよく知ってはいたが, 最も重要と見なされている作品の多くがデンマークのヘルニングで制作されたと知ったのは, ヘルニング美術センターのコンペティションに関連してつくられた一冊のパンフレットを読んでからだった。

デンマークのユトランド半島中央に位置するこの土地は, 1960年代のアルテ・ポーヴェラ, グループ・ゼロ, あるいはマレーヴィチの寂寞としたモノクローム地の持つ神秘的な熱気に満ち溢れているかのようであった。

私たちは他の6名の建築家とともに, 今では美術館となっている当時の衣料品工場の近くに建てられる予定の, 新しい「ヘルニング美術センター」のコンペティションに招待されていた。1950年代に建てられたこの建物の平面はシャツの襟の形をしていた。ヘルニングとは, かくも興味深く独特の気風を持った土地柄である。高さを8mに抑える, 色を白とするなどといった建築制限は, 私にとって非常に魅力的だった。

コンペティションにあたって, 私はピエロ・マンゾーニの作品を詳細に見直すところから始めることにした。ロバート・スミッソンやマイケル・ハイザー, あるいは抽象表現でアースワークに取り組む他の芸術家の研究を通して, Socle du Monde（地球の台座）は何年も前から私の興味をかき立てる存在だった。ピエロ・マンゾーニは彼らよりもずっと早くから, ヘルニングでSocle du Mondeを制作している。有名な「芸術家の糞」の缶詰は, 一連の「アクローム」における布生地への試みと同じく, ヘルニングの工場で制作されていた。これらの作品から, 皺のある布生地のような質感のコンクリートに白く包まれた建築を私たちは想像した。

隣の敷地には, 私の好きなデンマークの建築家ヨーン・ウッツォンが1972年に建てた, 彼の原点となる建築を見つけることができた。このことは私にとって全くの偶然であった。当初の考えでは, 美しく手入れが行き届き, 現在では住宅として使用されているこの建築との関係性が重要なものになりそうだった。

[宝の箱／シャツの袖]

私はギャラリーを二つの「宝箱」のようにすることに決めた。平面計画の中央にはこれら二つの長方形があり, むくりのついた屋根は光を捉えることができるようにずらして配置されている。建築とランドスケープが一体化するように, 平坦でのっぺりとしたランドスケープの一部は屋根の曲面を逆さまにしたような形になっている。空から見ると, まるで二つの箱の上に覆いかけられたシャツの袖のように見える。平面計画のゆるやかな輪郭に沿って, カフェやオーディトリアム, ロビーが収められるようになるだろう。一層なので, この建築物は空気循環に優れ, 地表熱による冷暖房環境を有するようになるはずだ。

土地にしっかりと根差していること。まさにこのことが, コンセプトを決めるインスピレーションになった。曲面に沿う柔らかな光が, 内部空間に躍動感を与えるだろう。小さな模型のモノクローム写真のプレゼンテーション・ボードは素晴らしい出来ばえだった。垂直の壁で囲まれたギャラリーには魅惑的な光がはいってくるはずだ。今日, 新しく美術館が建てられるたびに, 展示空間としての表現が行き過ぎているといったありきたりの主張から, ホワイト・キューブは芸術からその生を奪い取るものだといった極端な主張まで, 様々な議

論が繰り返されてきた。私たちが選んだのは，第三の道だった。私たちはプレゼンテーション・ボードを7枚ともすべて，モノクロームで仕上げたのだった。

[スカンジナビアの血／極北の光]
私の祖父はノルウェーのトンスベルグに生まれている。父は生粋のノルウェー人だったが，シアトルにほど近いピュージェット湾の畔の町で私たちを育ててくれた。冬の間，低く差し込むシアトルの太陽の光は，スカンジナビアの光とよく似て，私に多くのインスピレーションを与えてくれた。1993年に招待されたヘルシンキの現代美術館のコンペティションでは，極北の光，都市構造，ランドスケープとが絡み合う「キアズマ」というコンセプトが認められ，516もの応募作品の中から私たちのプロジェクトが選出された。低く差し込むヘルシンキの太陽の光への関心が，今回の計画では「光を捉える」断面構成に結実している。

ここにしかない素晴らしい光で「ヘルニング・センター」を構想することができたのは，このような建築体験と私の体に流れるスカンジナビアの血のおかげである。滑らかな曲面の「シャツの袖」の細長い隙間からは，スカイライトを通して太陽光が低く差し込み，むくりのついた天井面に沿ってわずかな彩りを与えている。天井のジオメトリーからは，光が反射して素晴らしい光が室内にもたらされる。そのため，ギャラリー・スペースでは人工照明を使う必要がない。この土地の移り気な気候では雲が太陽を遮り，通り過ぎるたびに，空間に生が与えられ，躍動するのである。

[平坦な建築／布生地の形]
宝箱のようなギャラリーに覆い掛けられている滑らかな屋根の曲面に続いて，別の場所ではホワイト・コンクリートの平面性に対する操作が行われている。布生地の質感を表面に出すために，トラック用防水布がコンクリートの型枠に挿入された。おかげで突貫工事の粗い仕上がりも目立たなくなった。隅々まで着色された墨色コンクリートの床面はワックスで仕上げられ，フロアに風格ある統一感を与えている。サンドブラスト加工の溝型ガラスを通して，カフェなどのエリアには柔らかい光が入ってくる。小高い土手は建築のジオメトリーをランドスケープへと引き延ばし，建築の周りに空間をつくりだしている。エントランスはむくりのつ

Entrance foyer: view from auditorium

Permanent exhibition

Permanent exhibition with clerestory windows

Temporary exhibition

いた土手により,隣接する高速道路から守られている。軒裏は,南側にある大きなリフレクティング・プールに反射する太陽の光を受けて輝いている。ランドスケープ・アーキテクトのトーベン・ショーンヘルが私たちのコンペティションのコンセプトを,彼自身の繊細なポーラス状の舗装と植栽とでさらに発展させてくれた。

[実現に向けて:意外な空間の光と影]
この建築はオブジェクトとして瞬時に経験されうる建築物というよりは,ランドスケープと一体化した外部空間の経験の連続体である。ここでは建物の周辺を歩いても,様々な空間経験は決してひとまとまりの形象として結実することはない。建築物の内部には全く異なった空間経験がある。内部空間は感動的である。特に日の落ちる午後五時半頃になると,光をうまく捉えられるように低くむくりのつけられた二つの曲面に沿って,西に低く傾いた太陽の光が一斉に流れ込んでくる。

斜めに配置されたギャラリーの直線的な壁に沿って歩いてゆくと,空間同士が滑らかに連続している。そこでは建築のシークエンスに従い,むくりのついた天井が空間の流れに沿って輝くように連続している。ギャラリー空間の壁面は常に床から垂直に直立している

ので作品に視線が集中するようになっている。その一方,建築物の周辺の輪郭はより緩やかな形をしているためランドスケープと相互作用を及ぼし合っている。カフェ・スペースはテラスへと溢れ出し,メインロビーからはミッドウェスト・アンサンブルのためのコンサート・ホールを通って練習室やサービス空間に抜けることができる。建物中央に配置されたふたつのギャラリーが閉まった後も,周りの施設はすべて利用することができるようになっている。モノクロームのフレームは展示作品の色合いを引き立たせ,空間は各々の芸術家や展覧会ごとに様々な色で満たされてゆく。ギャラリーの直線的な空間は,私たちの他のプロジェクトと同じく,その比率が1:1.618となるようにきめ細かく計画されている。マティラ・ギカは名著『The Geometry of Art and Life』で,自然界に存在するプロポーションに潜む数学的法則についての議論を行なっている。すなわち,黄金分割比の1:1.618とは有機的成長にとって重要な比率である。

歩きながら管理事務室を通り抜けると,ここでも頭上でむくりのついた滑らかな屋根の存在が,空間に躍動感を与えている。違いはここが外部のランドスケープに向かって開放されているということだろうか。毎日この美術館で働く人々のために,ランドスケープを

包容し,滑らかに光を捉える建築のジオメトリーが内部空間の活動に生気を与えるようになるだろう。季節を通して毎日変化する光の角度が,この美術館建築のモノクロームのフレームに彩りを与えている。イベント・オーディトリアムとしても使用できるコンサート・スペース,チルドレン・センター,レストラン,屋外活動スペースなどと一緒に,コミュニティの社会的凝縮器としてここが機能することを私は望んでいる。美術館の中核となるギャラリーは,様々な作品のための「ルミニスト」となるのだ。

初めて出会ったときにヤニス・クーネリスは私にこう語った。ここにくると漁網を吊った漁師小屋を思い出す,と。おそらくはどこまでも続くユトランド半島の平原に,大洋の名残を見いだすことができるのかもしれない。大地がふくれあがり「ゼロ」を指し示す光の大波となる。ピエロ・マンゾーニが語ったように「そこからすべてが始まるのだ」。

(スティーヴン・ホール,2009年6月)

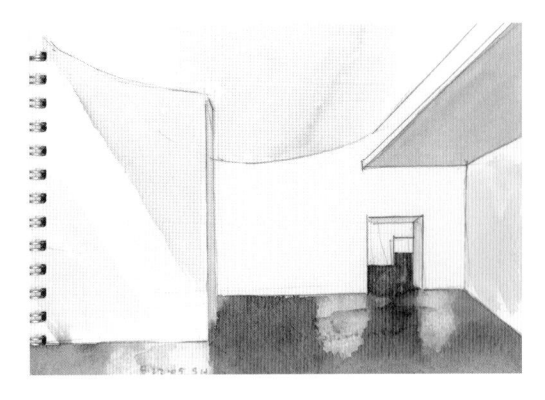

Sketches: interior with clerestory windows

Permanent exhibition

II-212

Kt. 64.000

Channel glass facade system 60 W with translucent insulation split in two.

Steelmesh in grid 80 x 80 mm og 80 x 120 mm RHS hanger for flatroof area above galleries integrated between shins of channelglass

Black out screen

Kt. 61.100
UK. ceiling

Steelframe with mesh 80 x 80 mm and 80 x 120 mm RHS hanger to be integrated between channel glass

Sectional detail: clerestory window

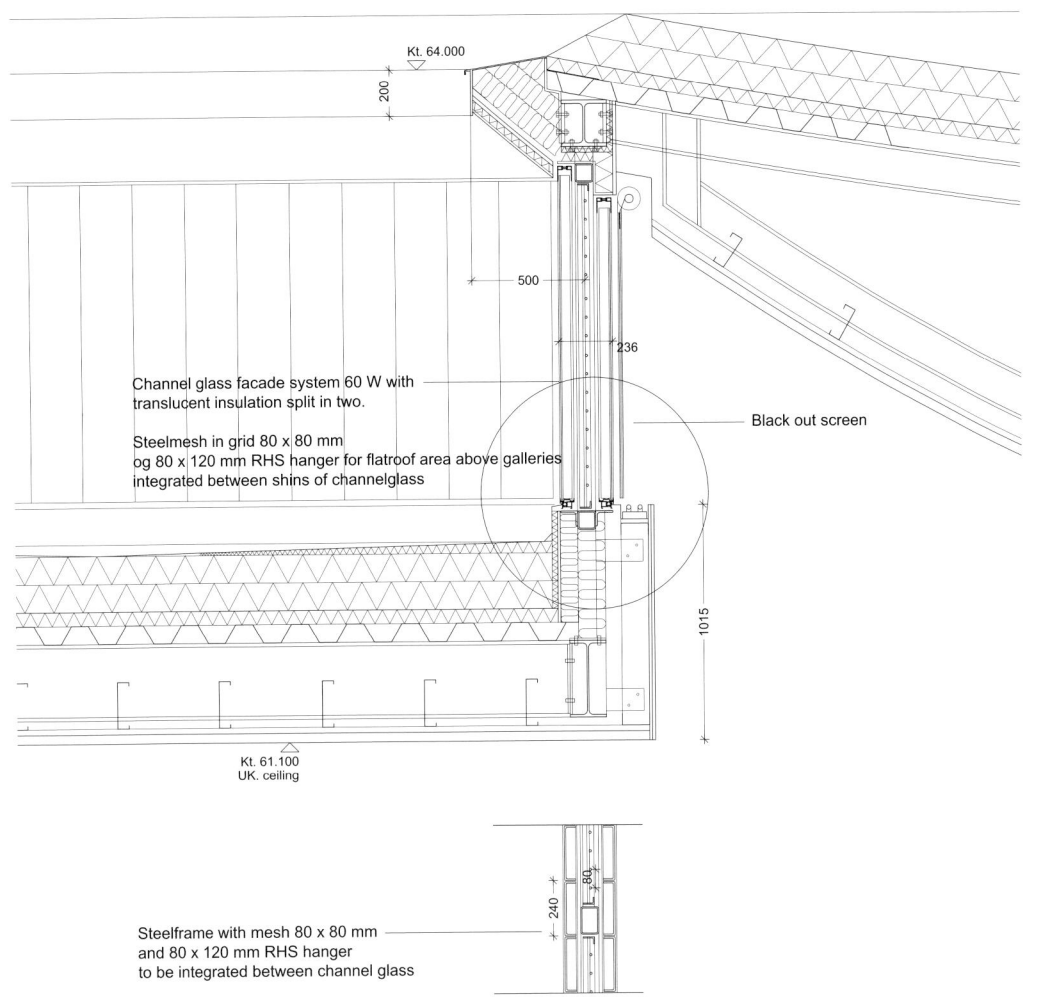

Restaurant

Skate pool at roof plaza. View toward Atlantic Ocean

Cité de l'Océan et du Surf
2005-11   Biarritz, France

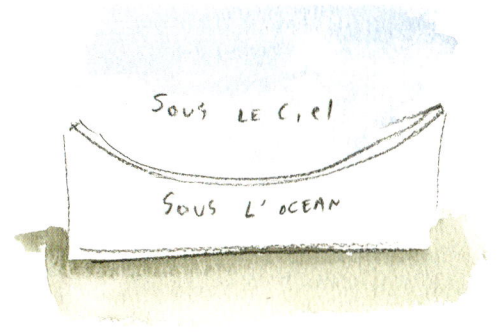

Overall view from east

Sous le ciel
Sous l'océan

Place de l'océan, Biarritz

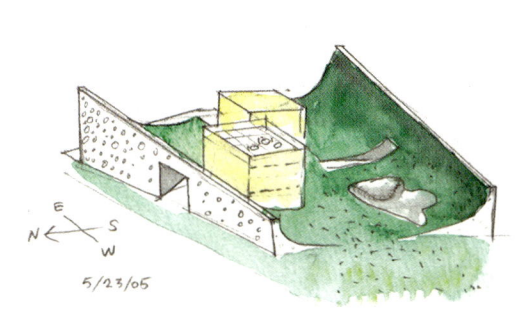

5/23/05

Sketches

II-215

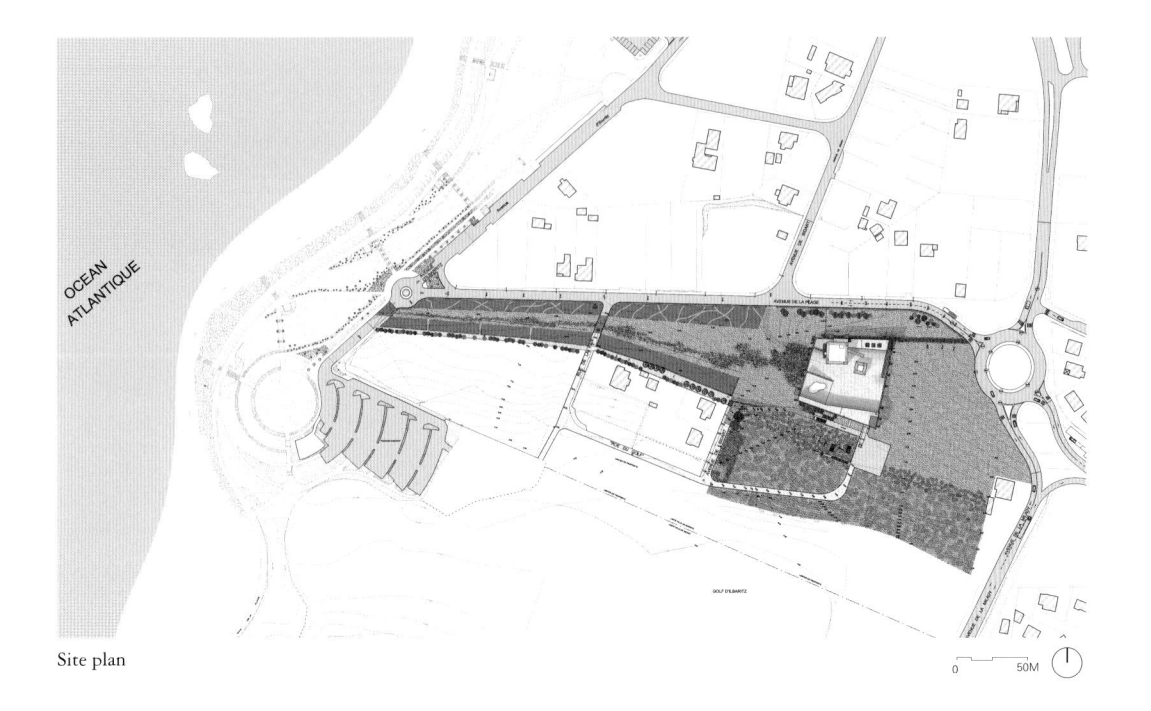

Site plan

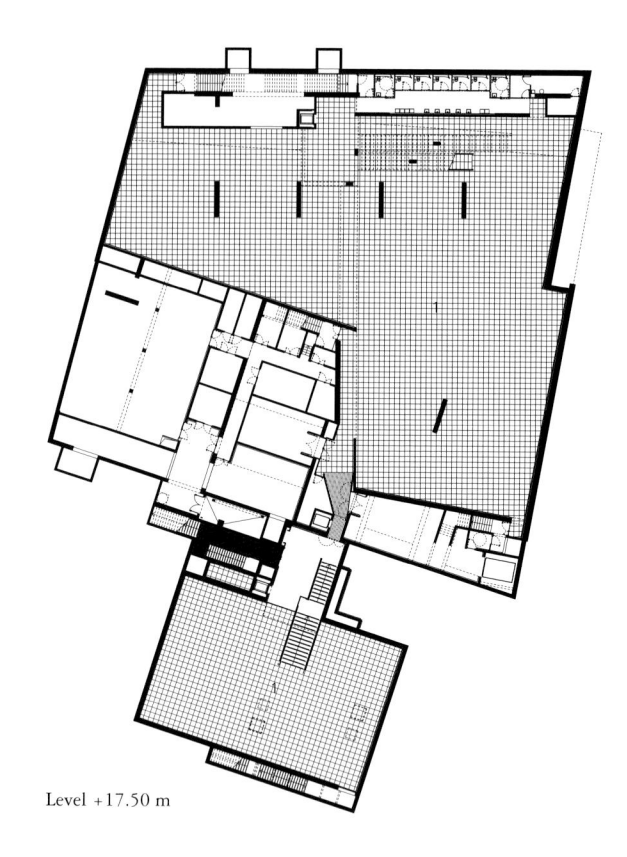

Level +17.50 m

The Cité de l'Océan et du Surf is a museum that explores both surf and sea and their role upon our leisure, science and ecology. The design by Steven Holl Architects in collaboration with Solange Fabiao is the winning scheme from an international competition.

The building form derives from the spatial concept "under the sky"/"under the sea". A concave "under the sky" shape forms the character of the main exterior space, the "Place de l'Océan."

The convex structural ceiling forms the "under the sea" exhibition spaces. The building's spatial qualities are experienced already at the entrance where the lobby and ramps give a broad aerial view of the exhibition areas, as they pass along the dynamic curved surface that is animated by moving image and light.

The precise integration of concept and topography gives the building a unique profile. Towards the ocean, the concave form of the building plaza is extended through the landscape. With slightly cupped edges, the landscape, a mix of field and local vegetation, is a continuation of the building and will host festivals and daily events that are integrated with the museum facilities.

Two "glass boulders", which contain the restaurant and the surfer's kiosk, activate the central outdoor plaza and connect analogically to the two great boulders on the beach in the distance.

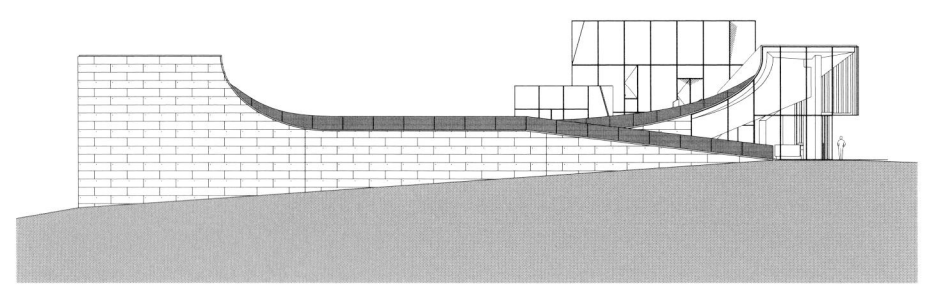

East elevation

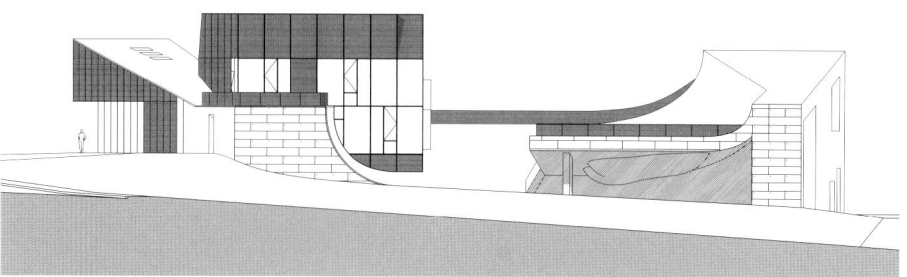

West elevation

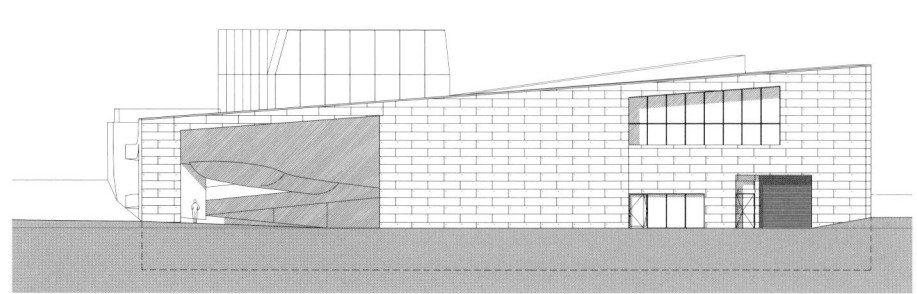

South elevation

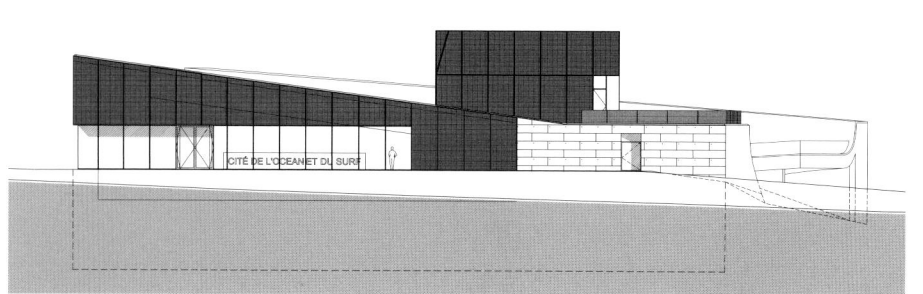

North elevation

Level +20.70 m

Level +25.10 m

Level +28.70 m

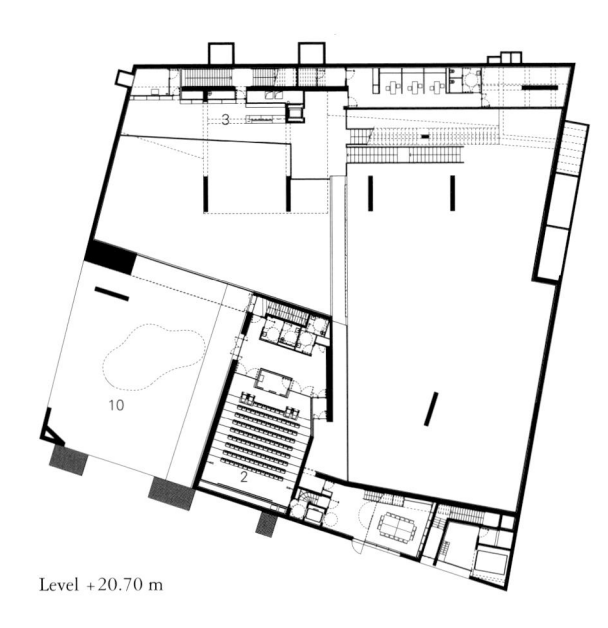

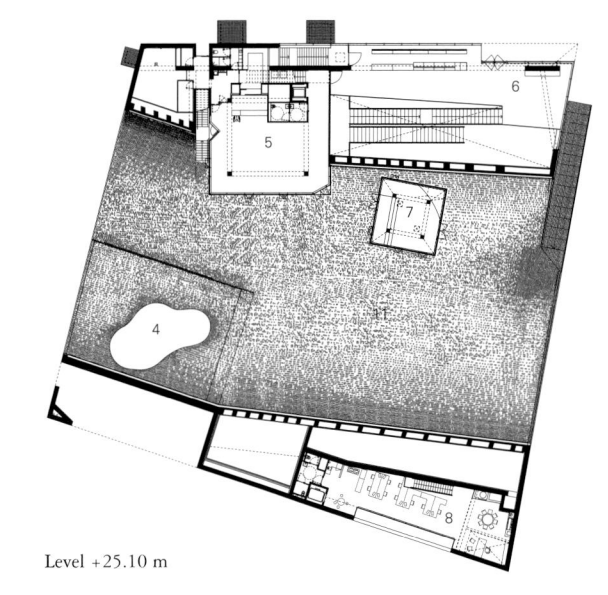

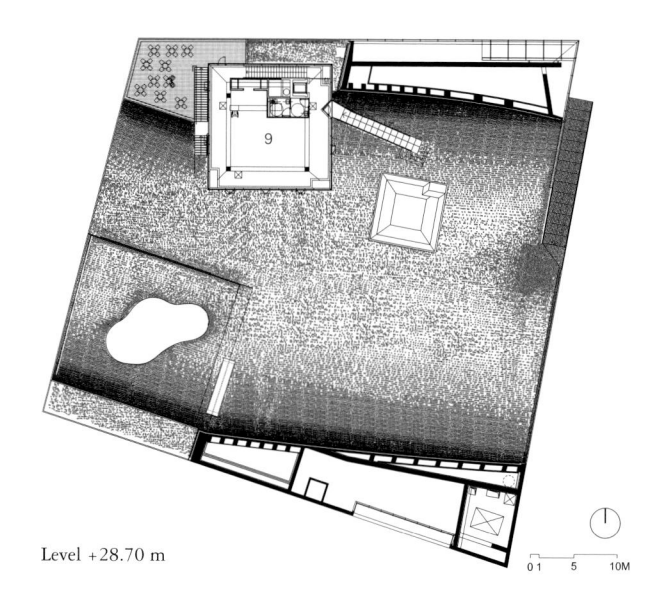

The glass boulders can be reached through the main entry lobby, which connects the street level to the cafeteria and surfer's kiosk, and but are also accessible independently through the plaza, which serves as a main gathering space open to the public.

The museum store is located at the intermediate level of the exhibition spaces, with direct access to the entry lobby and the auditorium. The more intimate restaurant and the elevated outdoor terrace are at the top level of the museum, providing open ocean views.

At the building's southwest corner, there is a skate pool dedicated to the surfers' hangout on the plaza level and an open porch underneath, which connects to the auditorium and exhibition spaces inside the museum. This covered area provides a sheltered space for outdoor interaction, meetings and events.

The exterior of the building is a textured white concrete made of aggregates from the south of France. Materials of the plaza are a progressive variation of Portuguese cobblestones paving with grass and natural vegetation. A combination of insulated glass units with clear and acid-etched layers animates the visual dynamics enhancing interior comfort. The interior of the main space is white plaster and a wooden floor provides under-floor wiring flexibilities.

1 EXHIBITION ROOM
2 AUDITORIUM
3 MUSEUM SHOP
4 SKATE POOL
5 CAFE
6 ENTRANCE LOBBY
7 SURFER'S KIOSK
8 OFFICE
9 RESTAURANT
10 PORCH
11 ROOF PLAZA

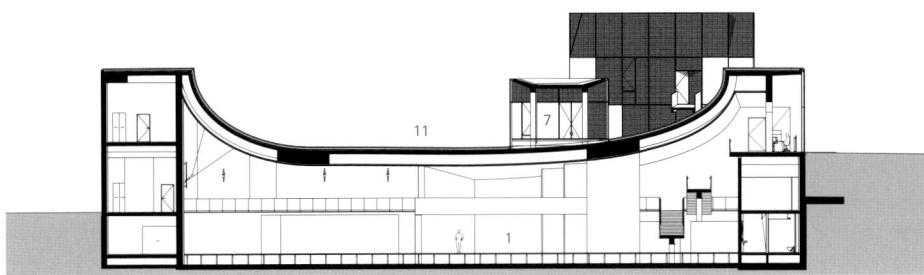

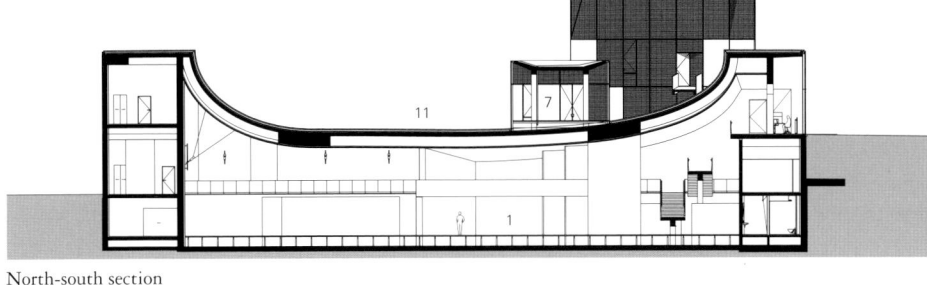

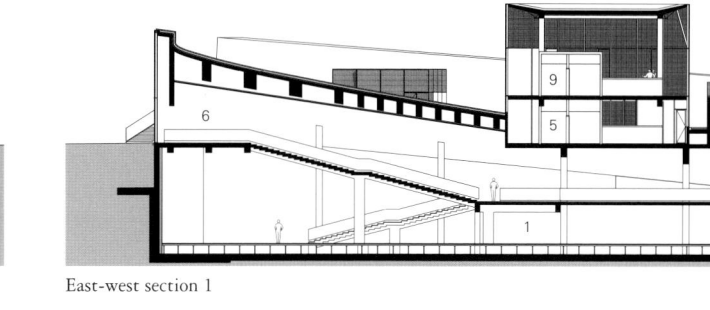

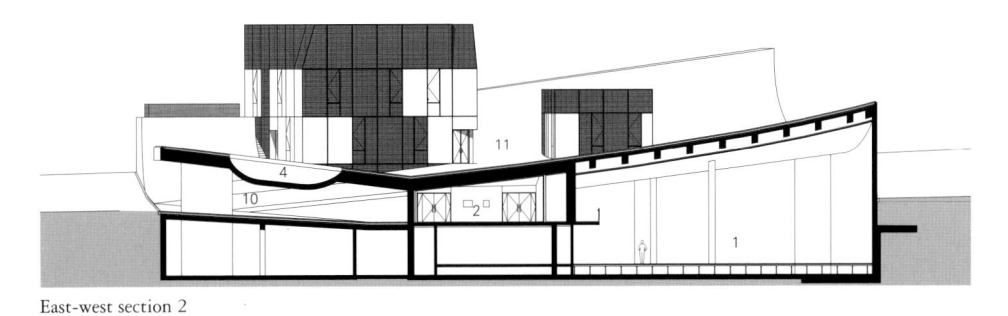

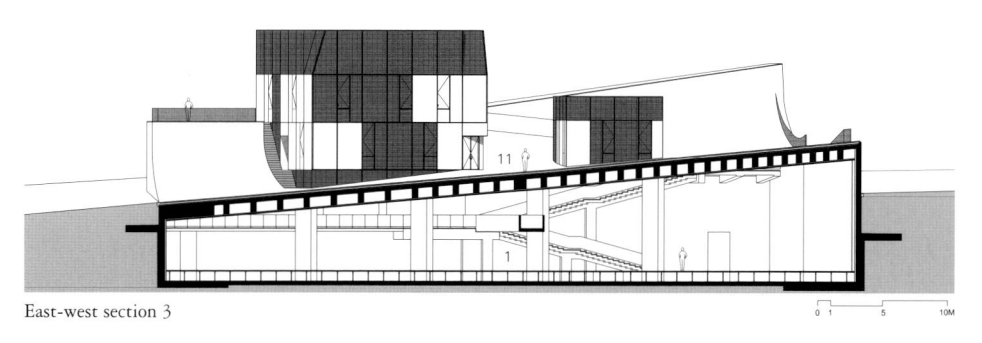

North-south section

East-west section 1

East-west section 2

East-west section 3

Skate pool at roof plaza

Porch under skate pool at southwest corner. Entrance to auditorium (right)

サーフ・オーシャン文化センター

サーフ・オーシャン文化センターは,打ち寄せる波や海と,これらがレジャーや科学,環境に果たす役割への理解を深めるためのミュージアムである。ソランジ・ファビアオと共に手掛けたスティーヴン・ホールの計画は,国際コンペの最優秀案である。

建築形態は「空のしたに」/「海のなかへ」という空間コンセプトに由来する。「空のした」の凹型の形状が,「海の広場」と呼ぶ主要外部空間を規定する。「海のなか」の凸型の構造の天井面は展示空間を構成する。空間の質はエントランスを通して経験される。移ろうイメージや光の映える躍動的な曲面に沿って歩くと,ロビーと斜路からは展示空間が一面に広がっている。

この建築の独創的な形状はコンセプトとトポグラフィーの精緻な統合によるものである。海に向かって,建築の凹形状の広場がランドスケープへと延びる。碗状にわずかに窪んだエッジのついた建築へと連続する,原生の植物と大地を組み合わせたランドスケープは,フェスティバルやミュージアムと一体になって日々のイベントに利用することができる。

二つの「ガラスの標石」にはレストランとサーファー・ショップが収容され,中央の屋外プラザに活気を与えている。これは遠く離れた海岸のふたつの巨大な岩へと結びつけられたアナロジーである。このガラスの標

North elevation: night view toward entrance

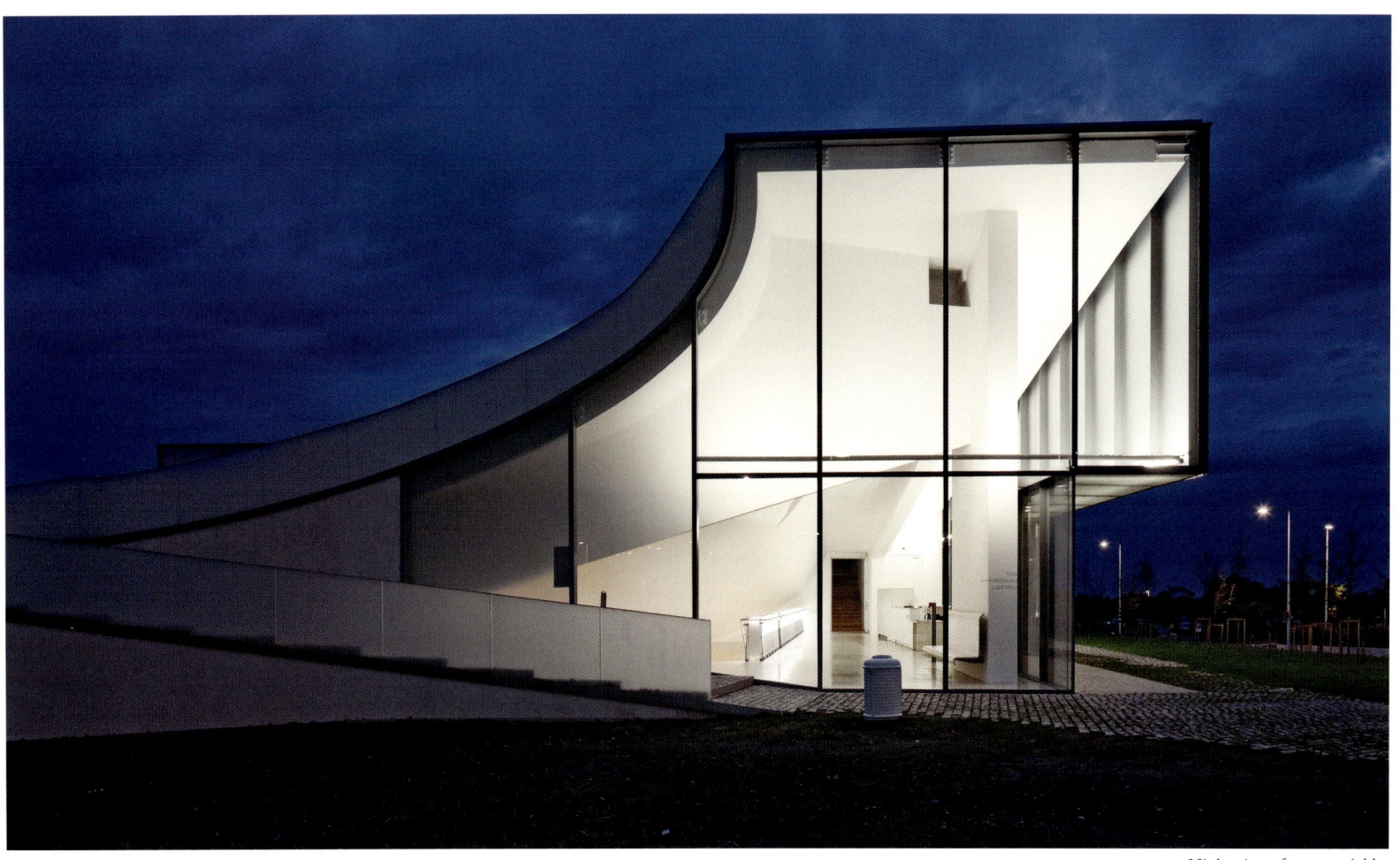

Night view of entrance lobby

Entrance lobby: exhibition room below

View toward entrance

石へは，ストリート・レベルとカフェテリア，サーファー・ショップをつなぐ主要エントランス・ロビーから迪ることができる。その一方で，一般に開放され人々が集まるプラザからも個別にアクセスすることが可能である。
　ミュージアム・ショップは展示空間の中間階に位置し，エントランス・ロビーやオーディトリアムに直接アクセスすることができる。ミュージアム最上階の，いっそう落ち着きのあるレストランと空中の屋外テラスからは海に向かって眺望が広がっている。
　建築の南西の角のプラザレベルには，サーファーの集まるスケート・プールがある。また，その下部は開放的なポーチとして，ミュージアム内部のオーディトリアムと展示空間へと連続している。この覆いのある空間は屋外の交流活動やミーティング，イベントのためのシェルターの役割を果たす。
　建築の外観は南フランス産の骨材の質感豊かな白色のコンクリートで仕上げられている。広場の素材にはポルトガル産の敷石が，芝と植栽の間に様々な表情を見せる。透明ガラスとエッチングガラスによる断熱ユニットの組み合わせが視覚的ダイナミズムを引き立て，内部空間をより一層快適なものにしている。主要空間の内部仕上げは白プラスターである。また，木フローリングなので床下配線を可能にしている。

Exhibition room

Auditorium

Level +20.70 m: exhibition room below

2008- Center for Performing Arts, Princeton University
Princeton, New Jersey, U.S.A.

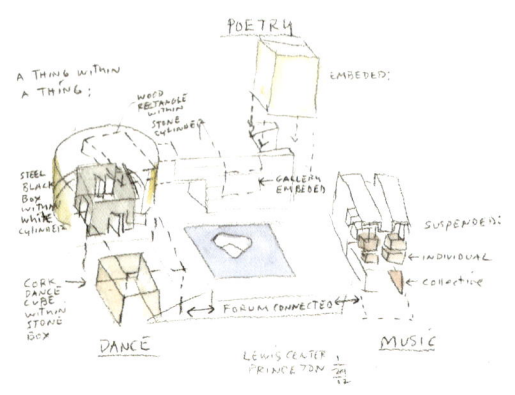

Concept sketch: a thing within a thing

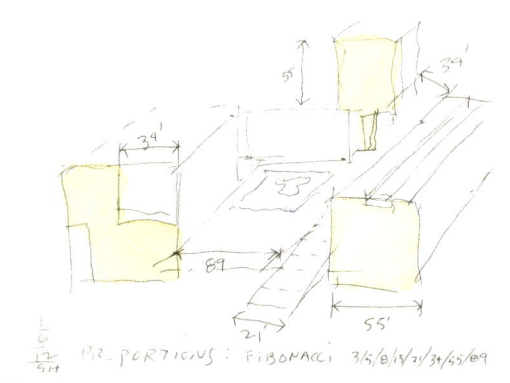

Propotion

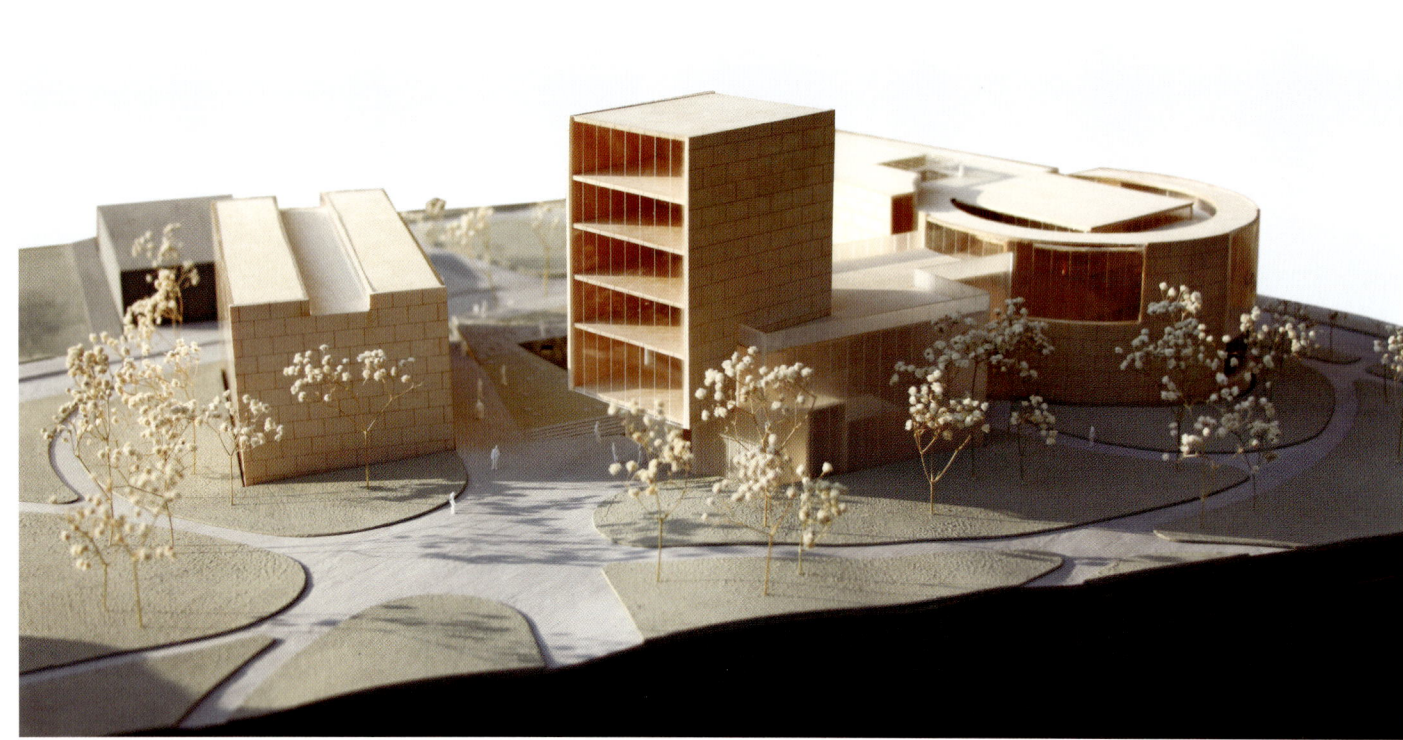

Model: Music Building (left), Arts Center (center), Theater + Dance Building (right)

Plaza paving

Night view of Music Building

II-222

Aerial view

Forum: moss garden on right

Forum

View toward plaza

Theater and dance building: stair hall

II-223

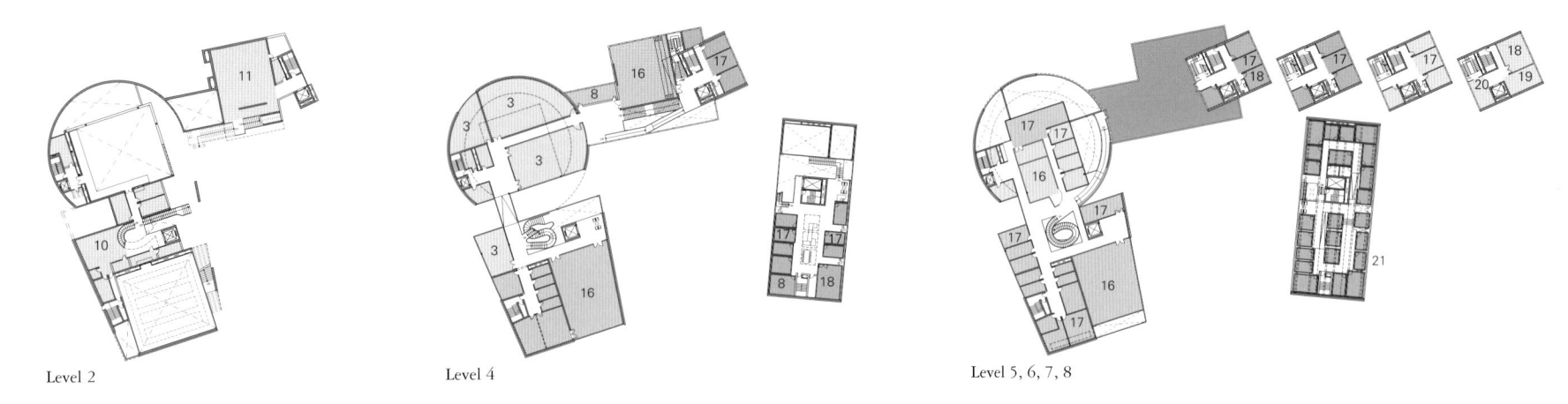

1	DANCE THEATER
2	BLACK BOX THEATER
3	ACTING STUDIO
4	FORUM
5	MOSS GARDEN
6	PROP SHOP
7	CO-LAB
8	STUDIO
9	INSTRUMENTAL REHEARSAL ROOM
10	COSTUME SHOP
11	LEWIS CENTER GALLERY
12	LOBBY
13	JAZZ STUDIES STUDIO
14	PERCUSSION STUDIO
15	SEMINAR ROOM
16	DANCE STUDIO
17	OFFICE
18	CONFERENCE ROOM
19	LIBRARY
20	LOUNGE
21	PRACTICE ROOM

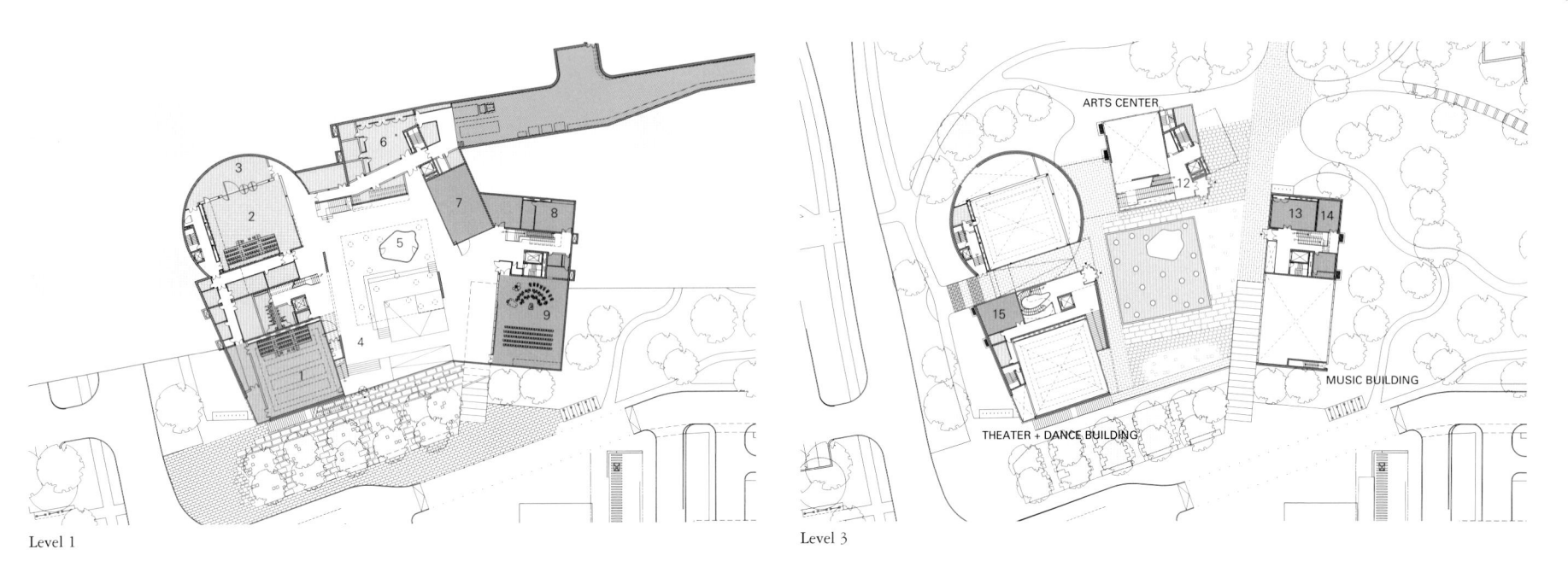

Level 2

Level 4

Level 5, 6, 7, 8

Level 1

Level 3

The program for this building complex includes, a theatre and dance building, an arts building, and a music building with orchestral rehearsal and practice rooms. All three buildings are integrated in a forum below ground. The project aims to create a new campus gateway; shaping campus space while maximizing porosity and movement from all sides.

Overlook views into the dance and theatre practice spaces and the orchestral rehearsal space are aimed at provoking curiosity and interaction. As an open public invitation, this gateway space aims to connect the local community to the University.

The structures are formed in concrete frame and stone from Lecce, Italy, with several types of translucent glass.

Each of the three buildings' interiors is developed uniquely.

The Theatre and Dance Building is developed according to the idea of a "thing within a thing". Within the overall concrete frame, the black-box theatre is comprised of steel, while the dance theatres are felt, bamboo, and cork. A "dancing stair" connects all levels.

The Arts Building is developed with an embedded concept by its concrete and stone tower connecting to Princeton's historic Blair Arch.

The Music Building is developed according to an idea of "suspension". Above the large orchestral rehearsal room individual practice rooms are suspended on steel rods. Acoustically separate, these individual wooden chambers have a resonant quality.

Ceramic fritted glass walls allow views out to the campus. At night, a warm and lively glow from these wooden practice chambers gives a joyful musical presence.

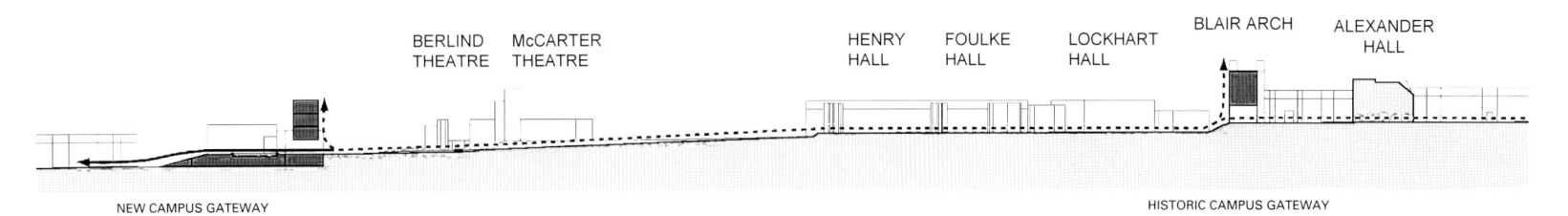

Diagram: vertical gateway of the new center for performing arts

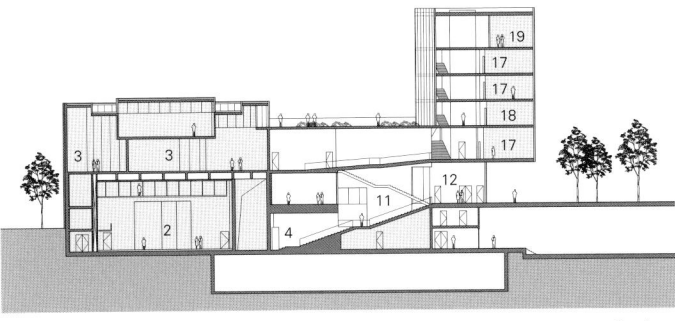

Sections

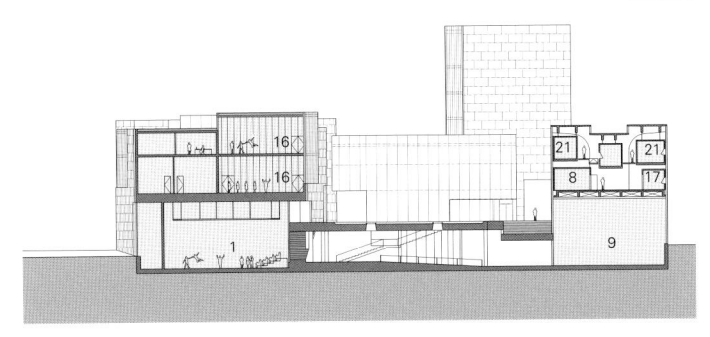

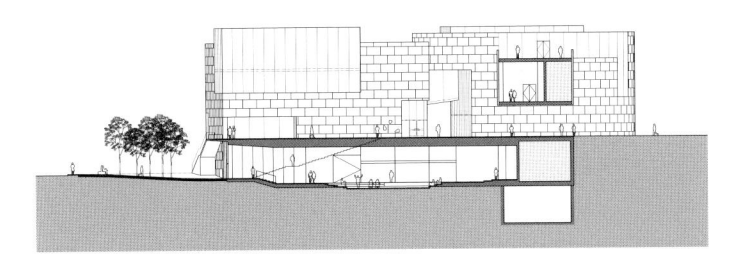

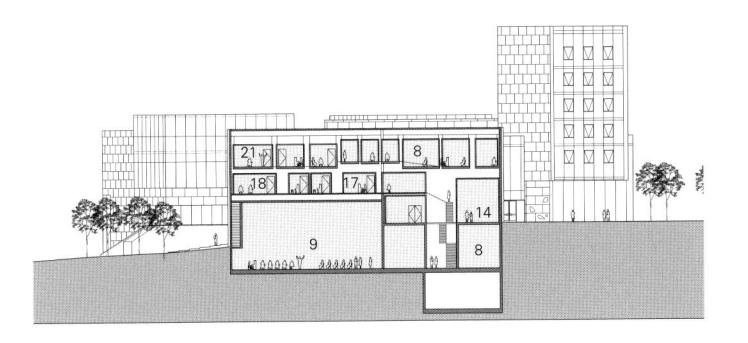

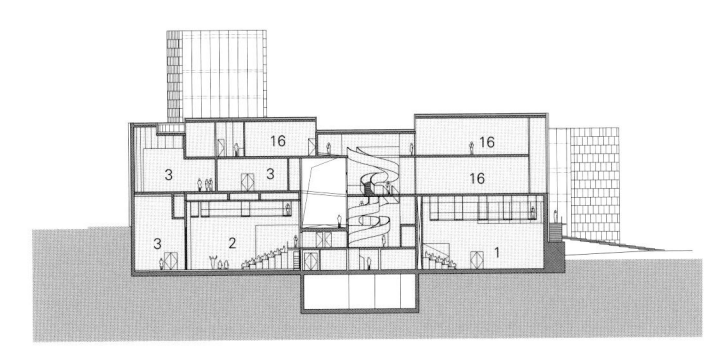

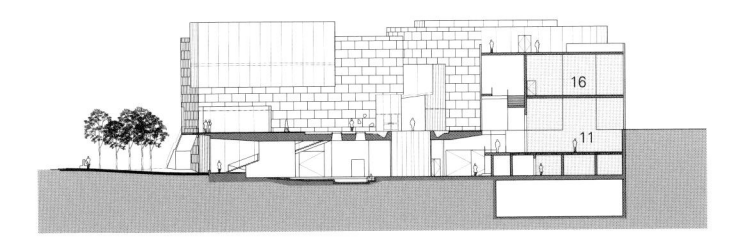

Model: Theater + Dance Building (left), Arts Center (center), Music Building (right)

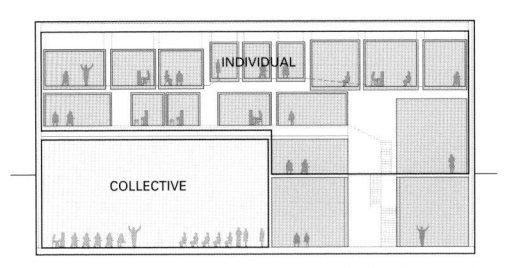

Music Building: section

Concept sketch: Music Building

プリンストン大学パフォーミングアーツ・センター
この複合建築のプログラムにはシアター・ダンス棟，芸術棟，及びオーケストラのリハーサル室と練習室を備えた音楽棟が内包されている。3棟の建築は全て，地階のフォーラムへと統合されている。この計画の目的はキャンパス空間をつくり，ポロシティを最大化して全ての方向からのアクセスを可能にする新しいキャンパスへの入り口を生み出すことにある。

ダンス・シアターの練習室とオーケストラのリハーサル室の風景を見下ろすことができるのは，好奇心や相互交流を惹起するためのものである。一般に広く開放されたこの空間は，地域社会と大学とを結びつけることを目的としている。

構造にはコンクリート・フレームとイタリア・レッチェ産の石材，さらに幾つかの種類の透過ガラスが使用されている。

3棟の建築の内部空間は，各々独特の特徴を持つ。
シアター・ダンス棟の計画は「入れ子状の空間」として構想された。全体のコンクリート・フレームの内部はスティールのブラックボックス・シアターで構成され，さらにダンス・シアターはフェルト，竹，及びコルクで仕上げられている。「舞踏階段」が，ここでは全ての階層を結びつ

けている。

芸術棟はプリンストン大学の由緒あるブレア・アーチへと続くコンクリートと石の塔状建築として構想された。

音楽棟の発想は「サスペンション」にある。巨大なオーケストラのリハーサル室の上部では個別の練習室がスティールのロッドで支持されている。音響的に分離したこれら個別の木の小空間には高い音響性能が与えられている。

陶磁の釉薬が施されたガラスの壁面からはキャンパスを眺めることができる。夜になるとこれらの木の練習室から溢れる暖かく活気に満ちた輝きが，美しい音楽の存在を引き立ててくれる。

II-225

2008-12 Campbell Sports Center
New York, New York, U.S.A.

The new 48,000 square foot Campbell Sports Center at the corner of 218th Street and Broadway aims to:
- Create new visibility for Columbia Athletics
- Form an inviting new gate for Baker Athletics Complex
- Shape state of the art athletic spaces with interconnecting flow
- Extend Field Play onto and into the building with stepped ramps
- Sustainability and ecological innovation

The Campbell Sports Center serves as a new "gateway" to Baker Athletics Complex at the prominent urban corner where Broadway meets 10th Avenue and the 1 Subway line—the northernmost crossing of Broadway with avenues that run the length of Manhattan.

The design concept "points on the ground, lines in space"—like field play diagrams used for football, soccer, baseball—develops from point foundations on the sloping site. Just as points and lines in diagrams yield the physical push and pull on the field, the building's elevations push and pull in space. External stairs, "lines in space," and terraces extend the field play up and into the building and give views from the upper levels over the Baker Athletics Complex and Manhattan with the Empire State and Chrysler buildings in the distance.

Evening view from subway line

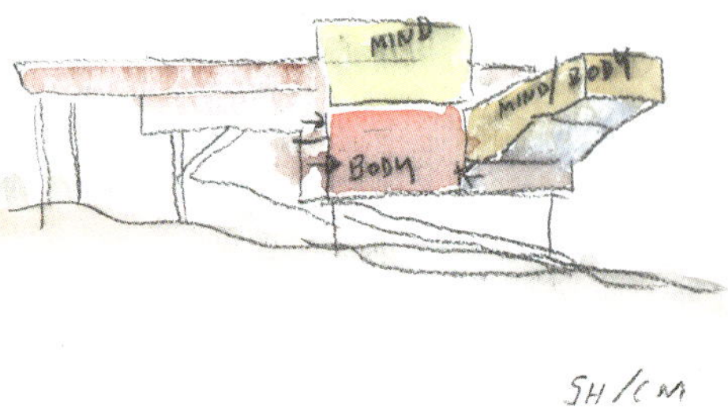

Diagram

Model: building is placed at the corner

Concept sketch: structure with stepped ramps

キャンベル・スポーツ・センター
218丁目とブロードウェイの交差点に建つ48,000平方フィート（約4,500平米）の新しいキャンベル・スポーツ・センターの目標は下記の通り：

——コロンビア・アスレチックスの新しい視覚的象徴となること
——ベーカー・アスレチックス・コンプレックスの新しいエントランス・ゲートとなること
——相互に動線の連続した，最先端のアスレチック・スペースとなること
——フィールド競技を屋上や室内でできるように，建築にはステップ状の斜路を設けること
——サステイナビリティと環境に対する革新的試み

キャンベル・スポーツ・センターは，ベーカー・アスレチック・コンプレックスの新しい「エントランス・ゲート」の役割を果たす。ブロードウェイ，10thアベニュー，及び地下鉄1号線が出会う名の通った場所として知られ，ブロードウェイがマンハッタン島の全長を走るアベニューと交差する最も北側の交差点である。

　フットボールやサッカー，ベースボールではプレイ・ダイアグラムが使われる。設計コンセプト「地表の点と空間の線」もまた，傾斜した敷地の一つひとつの基礎の点から連続的に発展させたものである。ダイアグラムの点や線がフィールドの動きを示すように，建築の立面も空間に対して前後に動く。外部階段，「空間の線」，そしてテラスは，フィールド競技を建築の屋上や室内へと拡張したものである。上階からはベーカー・アスレチックス・コンプレックスとマンハッタン島を越えて，エンパイア・ステート・ビルディングとクライスラー・ビルディングを遠くに眺めることができる。

Site

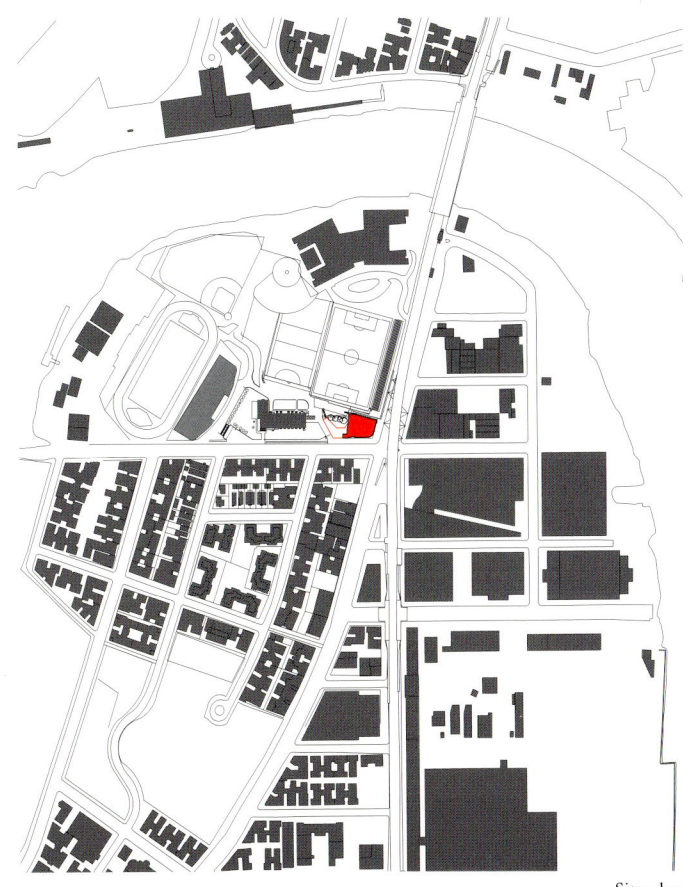

Site plan

Cantilevered volume

Site (under construction)

Steel structure (under construction)

Third floor

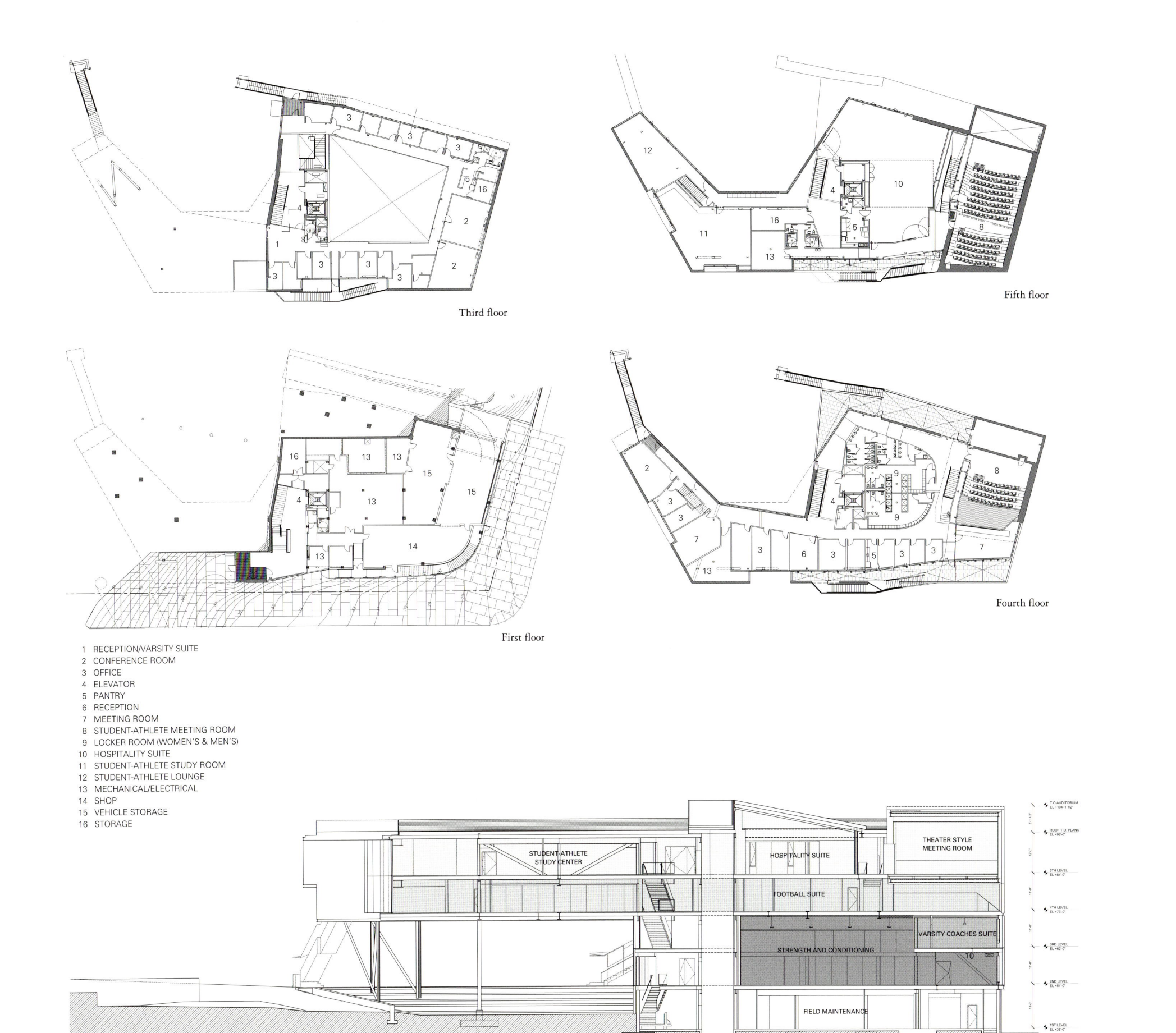

Fifth floor

First floor

Fourth floor

1 RECEPTION/VARSITY SUITE
2 CONFERENCE ROOM
3 OFFICE
4 ELEVATOR
5 PANTRY
6 RECEPTION
7 MEETING ROOM
8 STUDENT-ATHLETE MEETING ROOM
9 LOCKER ROOM (WOMEN'S & MEN'S)
10 HOSPITALITY SUITE
11 STUDENT-ATHLETE STUDY ROOM
12 STUDENT-ATHLETE LOUNGE
13 MECHANICAL/ELECTRICAL
14 SHOP
15 VEHICLE STORAGE
16 STORAGE

Section

2009- Glasgow School of Art
Glasgow, U.K.

We aim for a building in complementary contrast to Charles Rennie Mackintosh's 1909 Glasgow School of Art—forging a symbiotic relation in which each structure heightens the integral qualities of the other. We envision a thin translucent materiality in considered contrast to the masonry of the Mackintosh building—volumes of light which express the school's activity in the urban fabric embodying a forward-looking life for the arts.

This project's unique interior and exterior forces on the design are the catalysts for creating a new 21st century model for the art school. Working simultaneously from the inside out—engaging the functional needs and psychological desires of the program—and the outside in—making connections to the city campus and relating to the Mackintosh building opposite—the design will embody the school's aspirations in the city's fabric.

The new Glasgow School of Art building's special site, on top of one of Glasgow's Drumlins and opposite one of the United Kingdom's greatest works of art and architecture, offers unique potential to transform the GSA's presence in the city to a 21st century vibrant, cutting-edge art school that simultaneously values continuity with history.

Mackintosh's amazing manipulation of the building section for light in inventive ways has inspired our approach towards a plan of volumes in different light. We see the studio/workshop as the basic building block of the building. Spaces have been located not only to reflect their interdependent relationships but also their varying needs for natural light. Stu-

East elevation

Site model

dios are positioned on the north facade with large inclined north facing glazing to maximize access to the desirable high quality diffuse north light. Spaces that do not have a requirement for the same quality of natural light, such as the refectory and offices, are located on the South facade where access to sunlight can be balanced with the occupants needs and the thermal performance of the space through application of shading.

"Driven voids of light" allow for the integration of structure, spatial modulation and light. The "Driven Void" light shafts deliver natural light through the depth of the building providing direct connectivity with the outside world through the changing intensity and color of the sky. In addition, they provide vertical circulation through the building, eliminating the need for air conditioning.

Along the South elevation, at the same height as the Mackintosh main studios, a landscape loggia in the form of a Machair gives the school an exterior social core open to the city. The natural vegetation with some stone work routes the water into a small recycling water pond which will reflect dappled sunlight onto the ceiling inside.

A 'Circuit of Connection' throughout the new GSA encourages the 'creative abrasion' across and between departments that is central to the workings of the school. The open circuit of stepped ramps links all major spaces—lobby, exhibition space, project spaces, lecture theater, seminar rooms, studios, workshops and green terraces for informal gatherings and exhibitions.

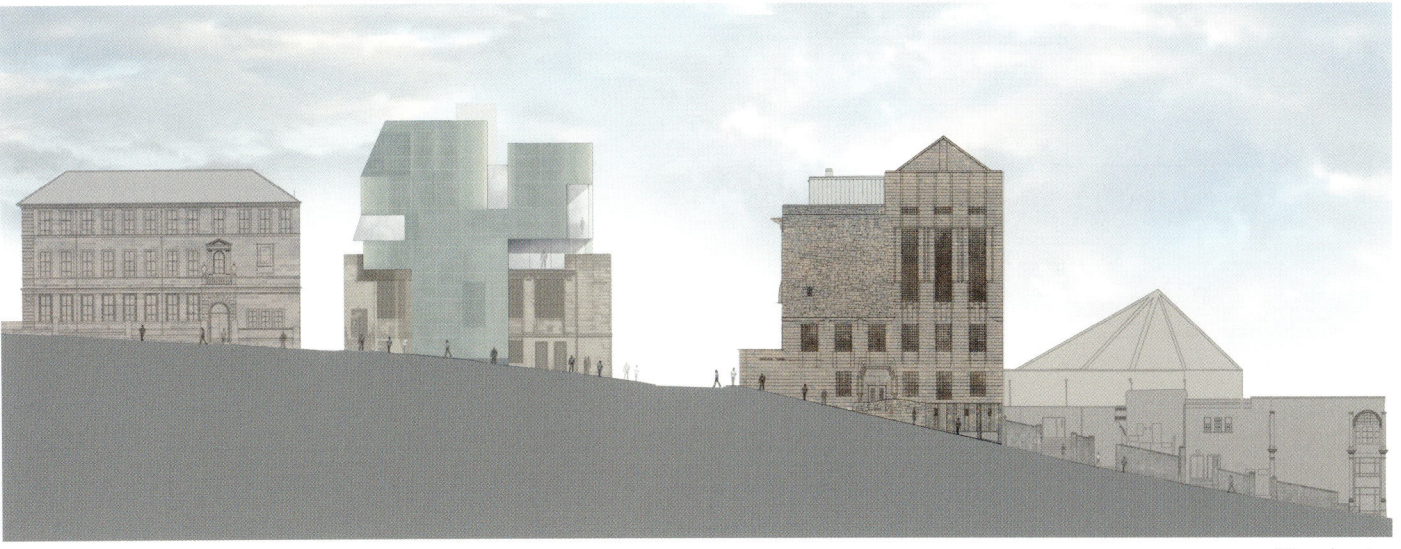

West elevation

Evening view

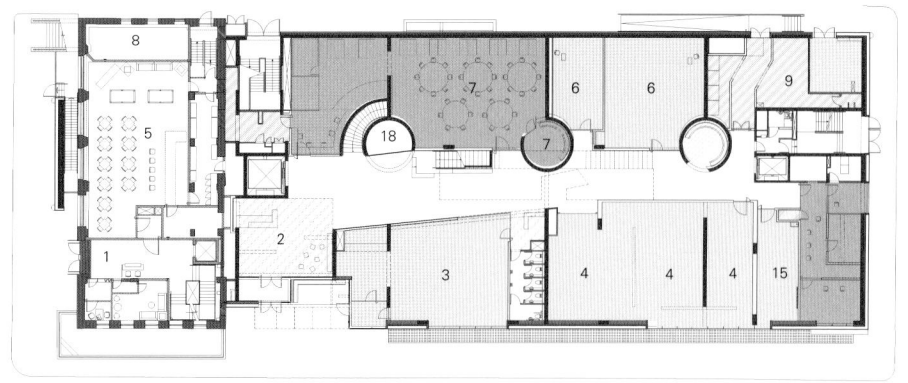

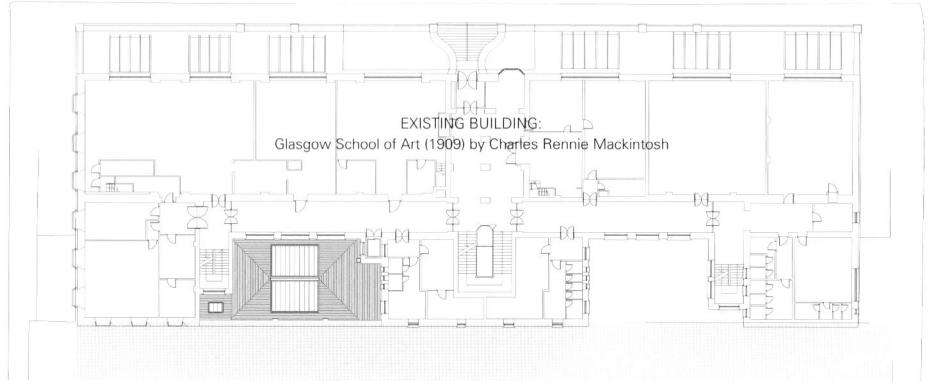

Ground floor S=1:700

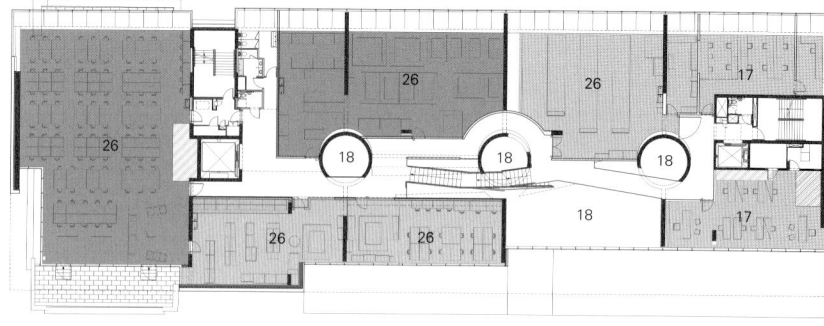

1 ENTRY HALL
2 MAIN LOBBY
3 'WINDOW ON MACKINTOSH'
4 EXHIBITION/GALLERY
5 VENUE
6 PRINCIPAL SEMINAR ROOM
7 DIGITAL WORKSHOP
8 MECHANICAL PLANT
9 STORAGE
10 MAIN LECTURE THEATER
11 PHOTO STUDIO AND DARK ROOM
12 LECTURE THEATER LOBBY
13 WORKSHOP SPACE
14 ASSEMBLY SPACE
15 PROJECT SPACE
16 DIRECTORATE ROOMS
17 STAFF ROOM/ADMINISTRATION OFFICE
18 OPEN TO BELOW/LIGHT VOID
19 STAGE
20 GENERAL SEMINAR ROOM
21 VISUAL COMMUNICATIONS ROOMS
22 CAFE
23 STAFF DINING
24 REFECTORY SPACE
25 KITCHEN/SERVERY
26 FASHION TEXTILE STUDIO
27 PRODUCT DESIGN STUDIO

Third floor

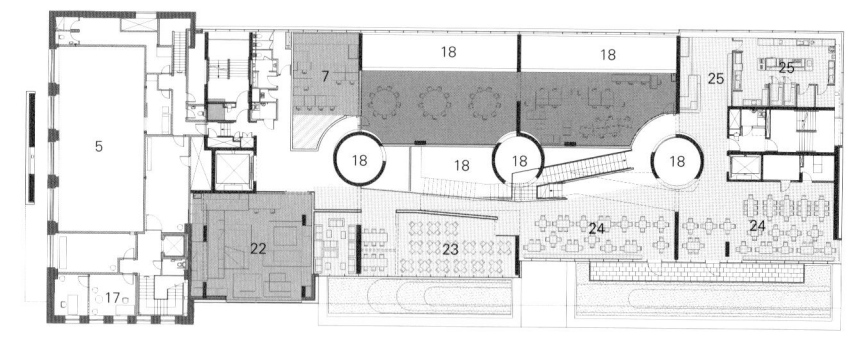

Second floor

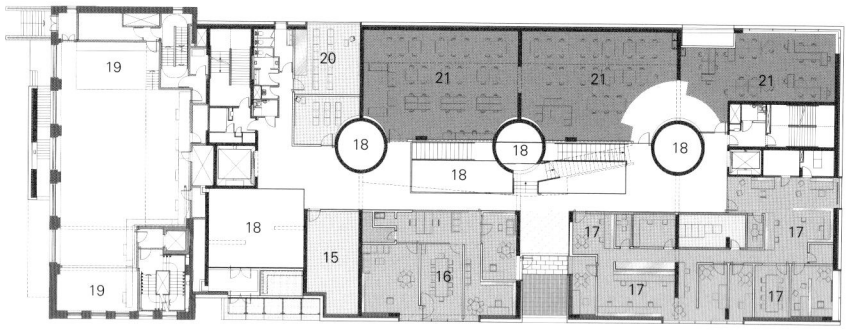

First floor

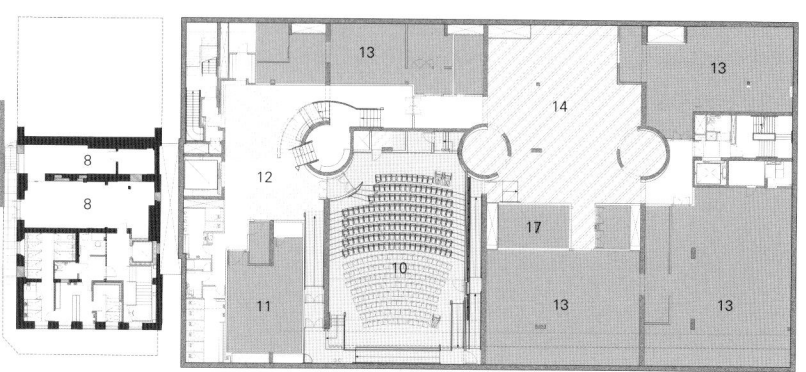

Basement

Refectory space on second floor

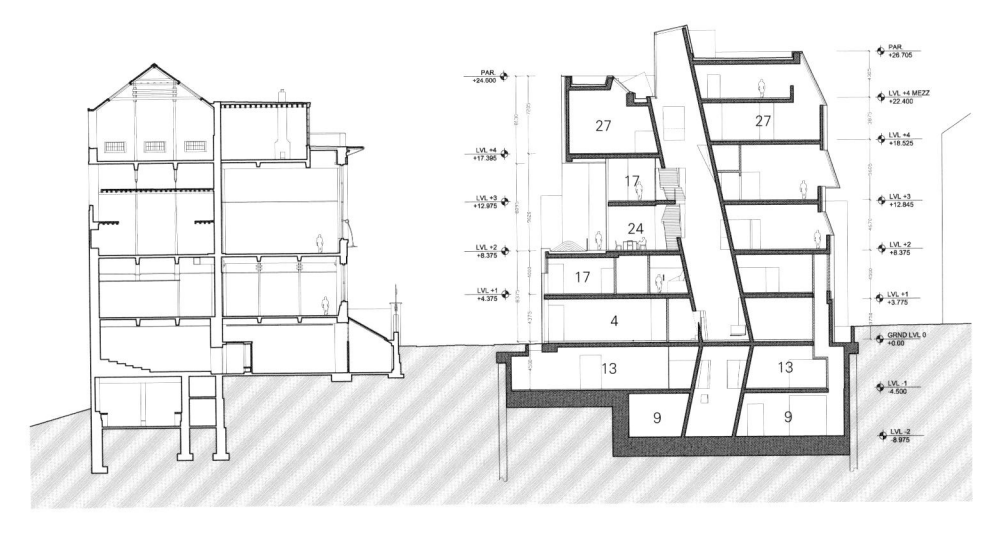

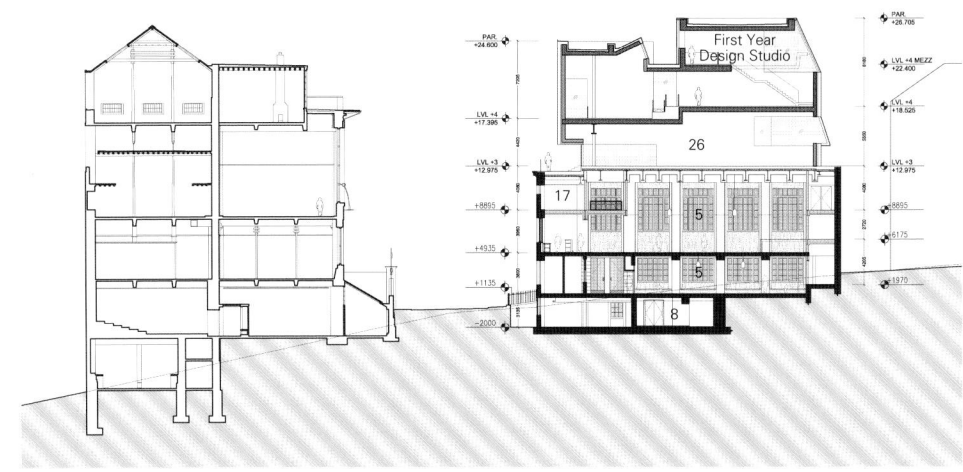

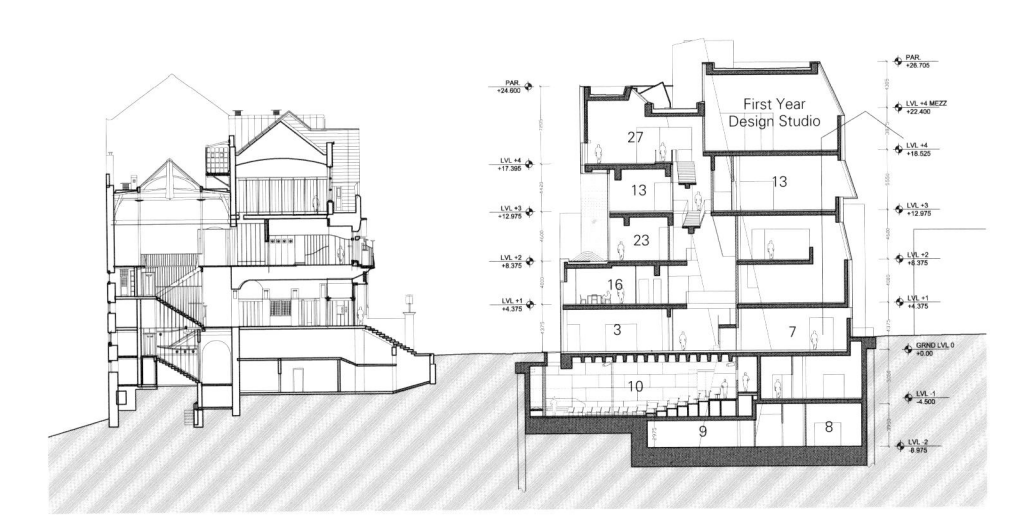

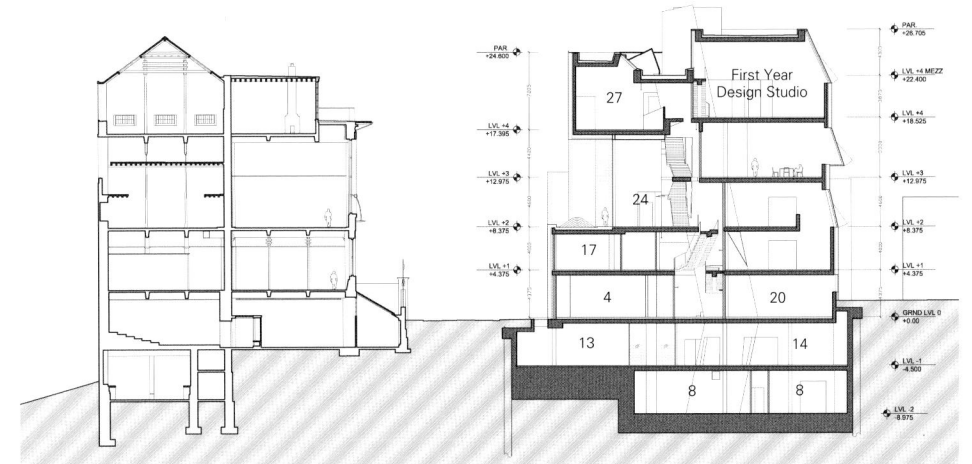

Sections S=1:700

グラスゴー・アート・スクール

チャールズ・レニー・マッキントッシュの1909年のグラスゴー芸術大学とは対照的な現代の建築を計画することで，全体を構成する相互の本質を互いに引き立てる象徴的関係性を構築することが計画の目的である。マッキントッシュの石造建築との対比を考慮して，薄く透過的な素材による建築が構想された。光のヴォリュームは都市の大学活動を表現し，芸術の新しい日常を実現させるためのものである。

この計画の内外部の独創的な空間力学は，21世紀の新しい芸術大学の規範を創造する触媒としての作用を持つ。一方ではプログラムに内包される機能的要求と心理的欲望を組み合わせ，他方ではシティ・キャンパスとこの建築を結びつけながら，その背後ではマッキントッシュの建築との関係性が構築される。内部から外部へ，外部から内部へと同時に計画を進めるなかで，この計画はこの都市における大学の情熱を具象化するだろう。

グラスゴーのドラムリンの頂部に位置し，その反対側ではイギリスで最も偉大な芸術と建築の造作物を構える，新しいグラスゴー芸術大学の敷地の特殊な性格は，躍動感に溢れた21世紀の最先端の芸術学校としてGSAを再生し，かつ，歴史との連続性に価値を置く独創的な潜在的可能性を付与するものである。

光を取り入れるためにマッキントッシュが行なった空間断面の優れた新発見は，様々な光を取り入れるヴォリュームを計画するためのアプローチとして十分に刺激的なものである。ここではスタジオ／ワークショップは建築の基礎となるブロックとして見なされた。相互依存の関係にある空間や，自然光に対する異なった要求を反映するように配置計画が行われた。スタジオは北面に配置され，北から入る安定した望ましい拡散光を，北側に傾斜した巨大なガラスから最大限取り入れることができる。スタジオと同じ品質の自然光を必要としない食堂やオフィスといった空間は南側に配置され，利用者の要求やその空間の熱的効率性に見合うように日除けを応用して太陽光の入射が調節されている。

「光を打込むヴォイド」は構造，モジュール空間，及び光を統合する役割を担う。「打込みヴォイド」の光のシャフトは建築深くに自然光を引き込み，光や空の色の変化を通して外部の世界との繋がりを内部空間に提供する。さらに建築を通した垂直動線によって，機械空調は不要なものとなっている。

マッキントッシュのメインスタジオと同じ高さの南立面の周囲ではマハルの形をした自然のロッジアが，都市に開かれた屋外の社会活動の拠点としての役割を大学に付与している。幾つかの石積みの水路と自然の植物によって，水は再生水を利用した小さな池へと導かれ，斑模様の太陽光を内部の天井へと映す。

新しいGSAを貫通する「循環動線」は，大学の中枢機能とも言うべき学科同士の「創造的摩擦」を促す役割を果たす。ロビー，展示空間，プロジェクト・スタジオ，講義室，セミナー・ルーム，スタジオ，ワークショップ，及び寛いだ会合や展示のための緑のテラスといった主要な全ての空間は，段状の傾斜路で構成される開放動線によって連結されている。

Circuit of connection

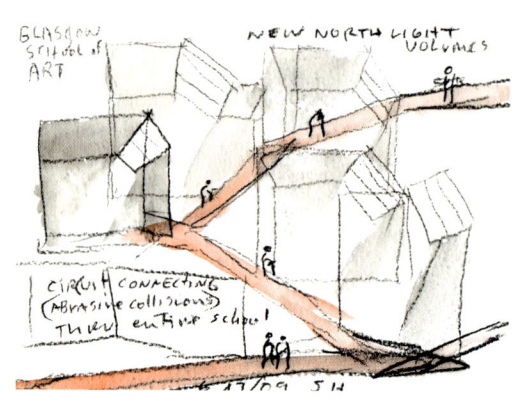

Sketch: circuit

Lobby

Study interior-model: corridor is pierced by three cylindrical structures for light void

Upward view of light void

Upward view of existing Mackintosh building (west facade)

Studio on upper floors with skylight

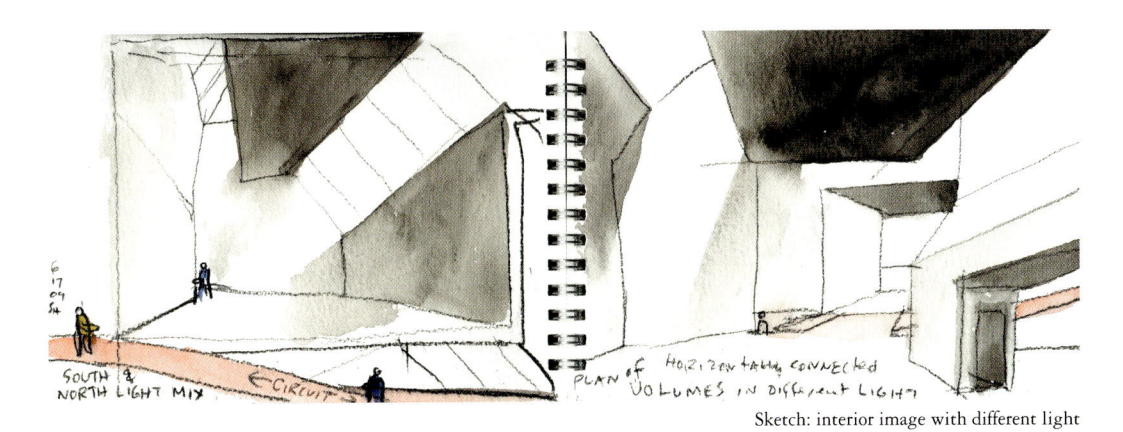

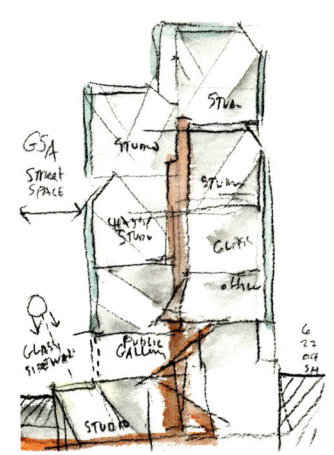

Sketch: interior image with different light

Flexible studio

Concept sketch: section

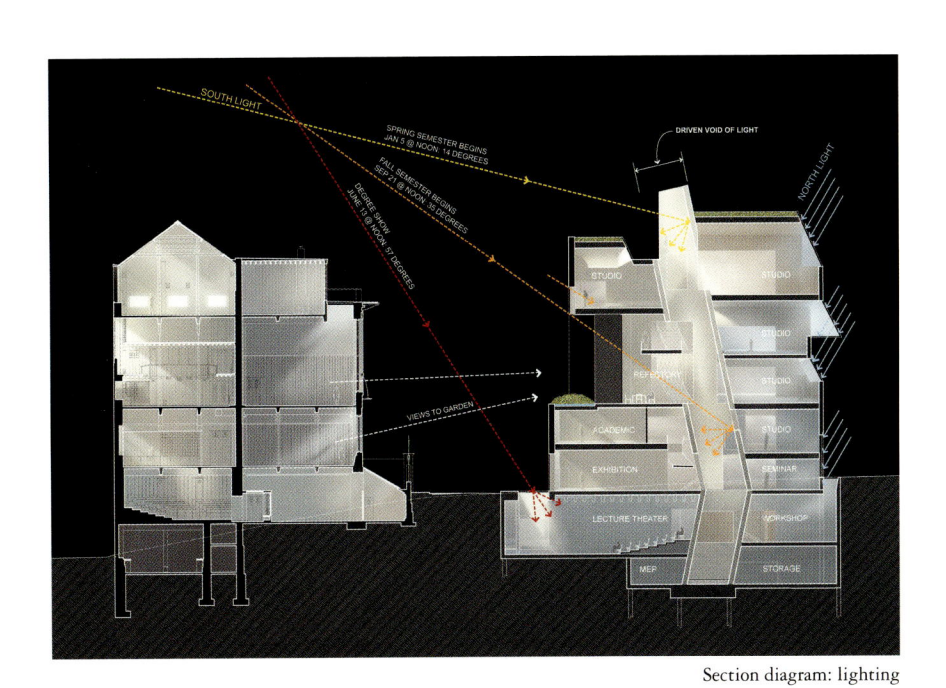

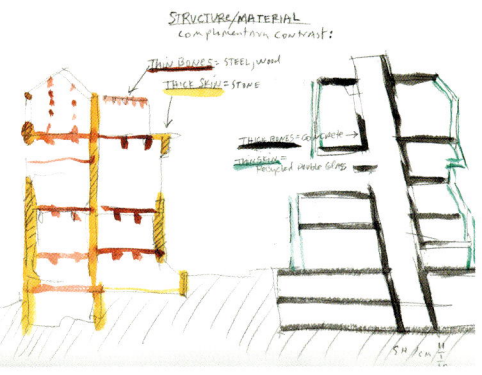

Light

Section diagram: lighting

Existing building and new building: contrast of structure and material

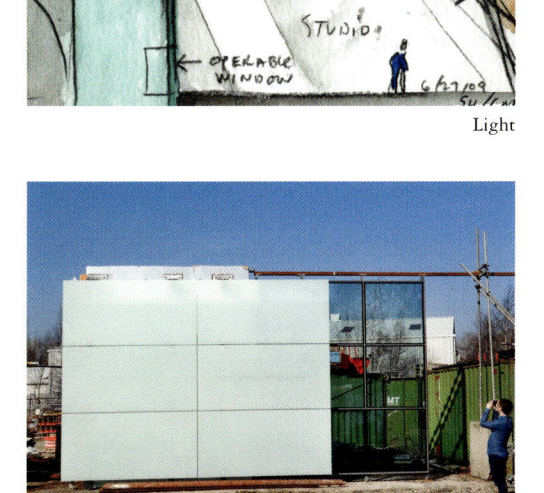

Glass mock-up

II-235

2010 V & A Dundee Museum and Design Nucleus
Dundee, U.K.

Site
Around 1900, Dundee had a wonderful riverfront with many rectangular water harbors. We propose to restore the Earl Grey Harbour as a foreground to the new V&A Museum and Design Nucleus. The original large stone harbor edges can be utilized after removal of the existing 1960s construction. Together with the harbor next to the ship, "Discovery," a new landscape and water public space can link the new Museum to the city.

In 1853, the Royal Arch was built in Dundee as a monumental gate to commemorate the visit of Queen Victoria and Prince Albert. Our new architecture, floating on its own reflection in the River Tay, is an apparition that will be vertically equal to the original gate. Our aim is for a new architecture of changing light fused with the river.

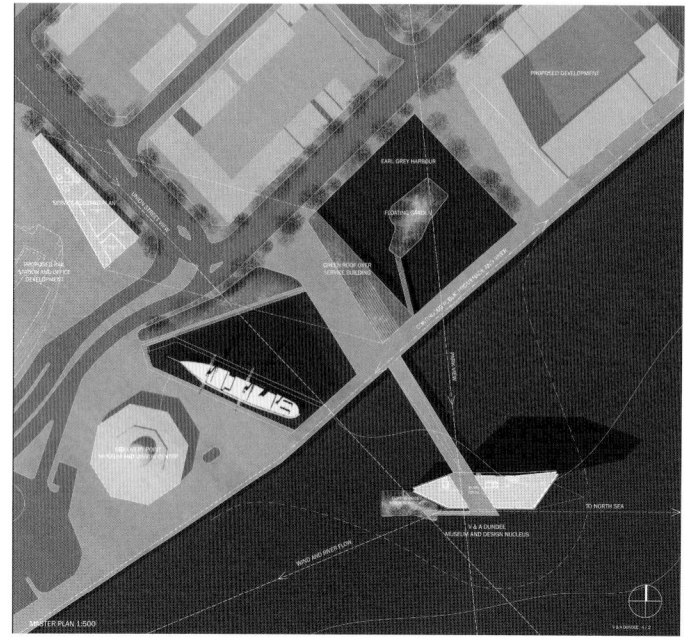

Site plan

Gossamer Architecture
At night the building casts a white shadow on the Tay. A floating image it measures time by how the building shimmers with the passing river's rushing water. Transformed by the river and the weather, it is a gossamer architecture in rivery air. Suspended in ripples of sparkling light. During winter, the building's form glistens and merges with ice and snow.

The inner spaces are formed around a cascade of light and are promising like a blank canvas on which the future can be creatively fabricated. The open, flexible loft-like galleries are accessed via an open stair and ramp circuit and central elevators for maximum connectivity between the various exhibition and design activities.

Material and Construction
The new building's sail-shaped geometry has a floating translucent skin of fine, stainless steel mesh. This screen provides a windshield and a semi-transparent membrane over light openings to the galleries. At night this screen will glow with reflected light. The steel structure of the technology used in oil platforms from local builders will be the most economical, as it terminates on pile caps of collected driven concrete piles. Interiors will include floors of local wood, plaster walls on plywood backing, and an excellent flexible lighting system.

Landscapes
There are three "floating landscapes." The first is at the river level, where a landscape platform with a cafe will rise and descend with the tide, allowing visitors an intimate connection with the river. The second is along the entry, where a landscape of local vegetation floats above a utility space for museum receiving and storage. The third is in the restored Earl Grey harbor where a floating park brings the public to water level.

Sustainable Design Strategies
We envision an exemplary demonstration of renewable energy technologies with geothermal heating and cooling, solar photovoltaic cells on the roof, skylights for daylighting purposes, and river-propelled turbines for electricity generation.

Circulation and Organization
From the shore promenade a wide bridge leads to the museum's open Portal overlooking the River Tay. The inviting Main Hall extends vertically to begin the visitor circuit linking all public activities through the building. The open loft-like galleries and 'Design In Action' studios with high ceilings and controlled natural light offer flexibility for exhibitions and design workshops. The central glass-walled elevators and open stair circuit provide clear orientation and connectivity between the various exhibition and design activities, while allowing for gallery re-installation closings without interruption of public flow. Along the circuit the restaurant opens out to a sunset view terrace, the Design in Scotland galleries open to a North Sea facing terrace, and at the top a Cafe/Wine Bar opens to a roof terrace overlooking Dundee and the River Tay. The public's free flow up through the building offers the visitor choice and unexpected discoveries of both the applied arts and design, and the river cityscape's changing atmospheric light of this special site.

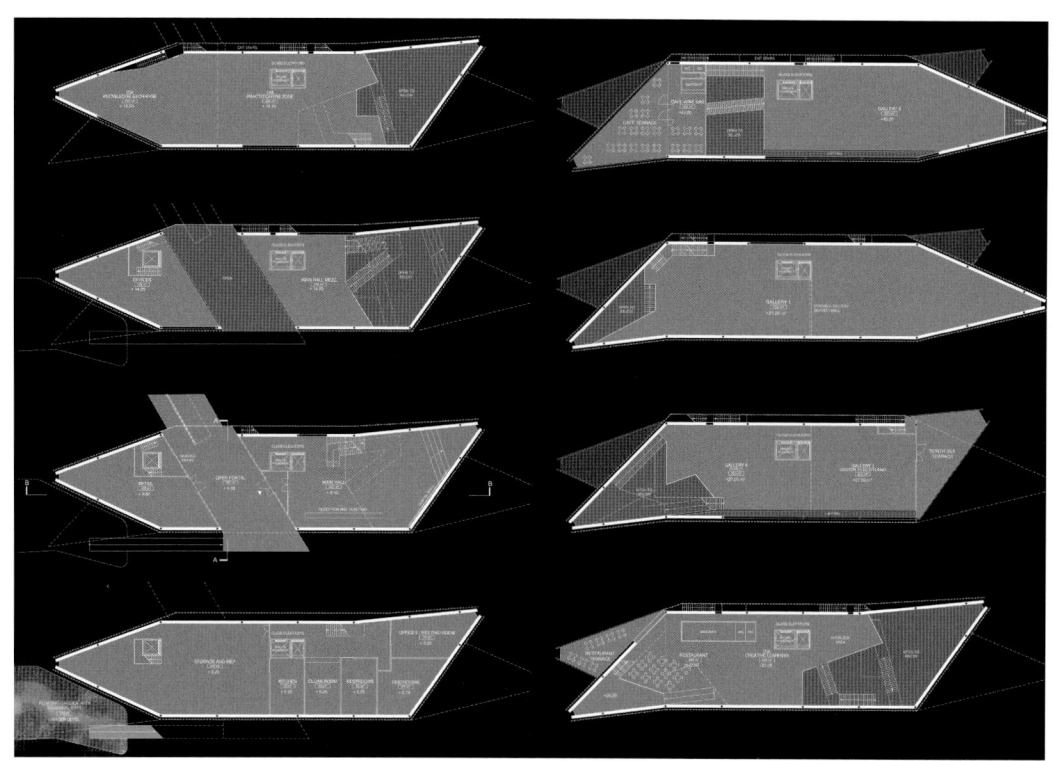

Plans

Ｖ＆Ａダンディー・ミュージアム

［敷地］

1900年頃のダンディーは長方形の港の多い，素晴らしいウォーターフロントであった。新ヴィクトリア＆アルバート博物館とデザイン・ニュークリウスを前に，ここではアール・グレイ・ハーバーの改修提案が行われた。本来の巨大な石造の港の埠頭は，1960年代の既存建造物を撤去した後に，再利用される予定である。「ディスカバリー号」という名の船の係留する港と共に，新しいランドスケープと水際のパブリック・スペースが，新しい博物館をこの町へと結びつける。

1853年にはヴィクトリア女王とアルバート王子の訪問を記念し，ダンディーを象徴するゲートとしてロイヤル・アーチが建設された。新しい建築はテイ川の水面に自らを写して浮遊する。建築は本来のゲートの幻影として垂直に立ち上がるのだ。川とひとつに融合する，移ろいゆく新しい光の建築が，計画の目的である。

［薄布のような建築］

夜になると建築は，テイ川の水面に白い陰影を放つ。素早く流れゆく川面に揺らめき，時の流れを見定めるかのように浮遊するイメージ。川と天候によって建築は姿を変える。川の空気に佇む薄布のような建築。水面の細波に浮かぶ建築。冬になるとこの建築の形は氷や雪とひとつになって輝きを放つ。

内部空間を構成する，滝のように流れ落ちる光。この建築はひとつの希望。創造力をかき立てる白いカンヴァスに未来を描く。自由で開放的なロフト・ギャラリーは，外からの階段と斜路動線によってアクセスする。中央のエレベータは可能な限り，様々な展示とデザイン活動をひとつに結びつけている。

［素材と建設工法］

帆のようなジオメトリを覆うのは，透過性のある，きめの細かいステンレス・メッシュの表皮の浮遊感である。このメッシュは風をよけるのと共に，半透明の皮膜でギャラリー開口部に光を取り入れる役割を果たす。夜になるとこのメッシュは反射光で輝きを放つ。鉄骨構造には地元の建設会社の石油採掘用プラットフォームの技術が最も経済的であるように思われた。コンクリート杭は集中して打設され，フーチング基礎で固定されている。内部には地産材のフローリング，合板下地のプラスター壁，及びフレキシブルで優れた照明システムがある。

［ランドスケープ］

ここには3つの「浮遊するランドスケープ」がある。第一の川の水面のレベルでは，カフェのあるランドスケープ・プラットフォームは潮の満ち引きによって上下し，来館者は川との距離を楽しむことができる。第二はエントランス部分で，搬入口や収蔵庫など，美術館の管理施設の上に現地の植栽がそよぐ。第三はアール・グレイ・ハーバーを改修した公園で，波のあいだに浮遊するように，人々を水面まで誘う。

［サステイナブル・デザインの方法論］

地熱冷暖房，屋上の太陽光発電，採光のための天窓，水力タービン発電といった，再生可能エネルギー技術を代表する実例となることが構想された。

［動線と組織構成］

海岸のプロムナードから幅のあるブリッジを通ると，博物館の開放的なエントランスにテイ川への眺望が広がっている。広大なメイン・ホールが垂直に人々を誘う。来館者はここから動線を辿り，建築のなかのあらゆる活動はこの動線に全て結びつけられる。背の高い天井と調光された自然光に恵まれた開放的なロフト型のギャラリーと「デザイン・イン・アクション」スタジオは，展示やデザイン・ワークショップにフレキシビリティを与えている。中央のガラス・エレベータと開放的な階段動線によって，様々な展示やデザイン活動が一目で分かる。一方で展示を入れ替える際にギャラリーを閉鎖しても，パブリック動線が遮られることのないように計画された。動線の先には夕日の見えるテラスに向けてレストランが開放されている。スコットランド・デザイン・ギャラリーはテラスに面して北海に開かれ，最上階のカフェ・ワインバーは，ダンディーとテイ川を見渡す屋上テラスに向かって開放されている。パブリック・スペースの流れるような空間は，建築を通して来館者に選択の自由を与え，応用芸術やデザインに思いもよらない発見をもたらしてくれる。川面に映えるシティ・スケープには，この特別な場所ならではの空気が漂っている。

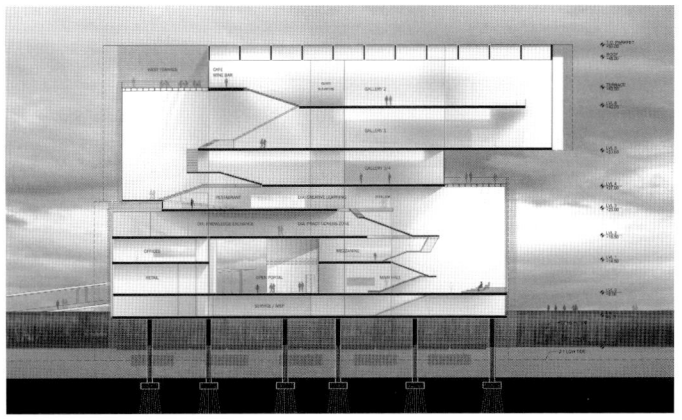

Longitudinal section

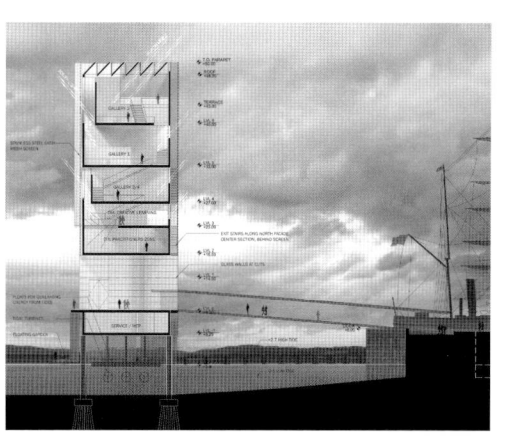

Cross section

View from northeast. Building on River Tay

View from harbor on northwest

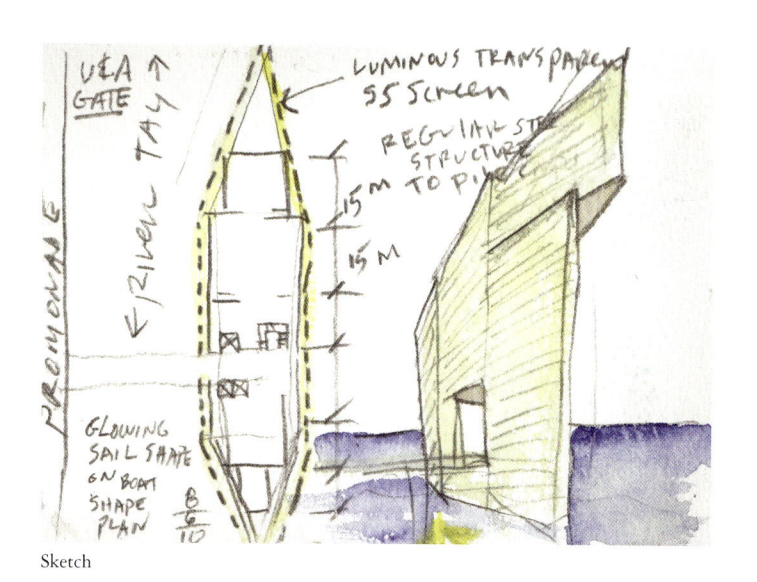

Sketch

Gallery: view of main hall and River Tay through slit

Main hall

Entrance

Gallery

2010- Hangzhou Music Museum
Hangzhou, China

In order to unify the scattered cluster of buildings on the existing campus, the scheme identifies five voids to form the overall morphology—like a caesura in music. The first void is the great ancient garden with beautiful existing trees. The second void is the new Music Plaza with reflective pond and arrival space. The third, fourth, and fifth voids utilize the spaces between buildings with different programs, providing open areas for music performance, discussions, cafes, restaurants, and recreation.

These voids are formed by simple wooden pergolas, which hark back to Song Dynasty architecture when the first wood construction standards were published. The pergolas have a cast glass shingled roof embedded with translucent solar PV cells and LED lights. During the day, the sun shines on the pergolas and PV cells collect the energy. At night, the lighting of the pergolas comes from the LEDs, bringing life to the whole campus.

The new Music Plaza is flooded in a thin layer of water and framed by a glass orientation pavilion and the new music library. Skylights at the bottom of the pond bring light down to a large gallery space below. This space is flexible and the reflecting pond can also be drained to accommodate a larger audience.

The existing library and the north piano building, which currently occupy the most prominent edge of the site, will be demolished and be the site for a new Music Museum Pavilion as the anchor point of the new campus. The Pavilion is based on the idea of the "Eight Sounds" in traditional Chinese music: silk, bamboo, wood, stone, metal, clay, gourd, and hide. Inside each of the eight different pieces, there is a watching/listening chamber, showing not just a great sounding music but the production of it. Each of the pavilions is made of one of these materials, while the exterior of the building is clad in the same wood as the pergolas.

To improve and unify the existing buildings on the campus—many of them built between the 1950s and 70s without proper insulation—a layer of high performance insulation and typical grey Chinese bricks with tight mortar joints will be added. New energy efficient windows will help to bring the existing buildings to the current highest environmental standards. These renovation strategies will transform the whole campus into a unified energyefficient entity.

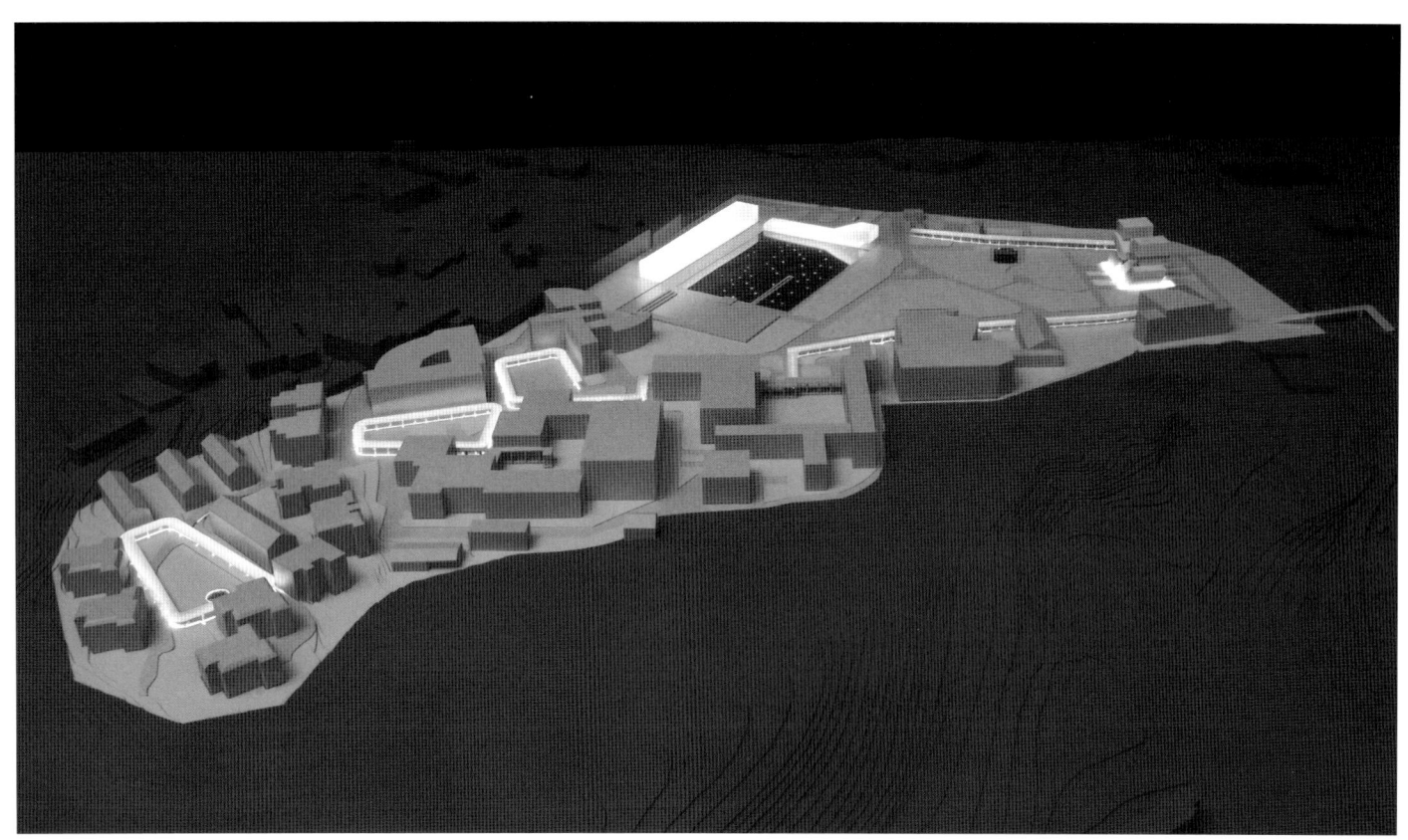

Site model: new buildings (Museum and Library) and pergolas

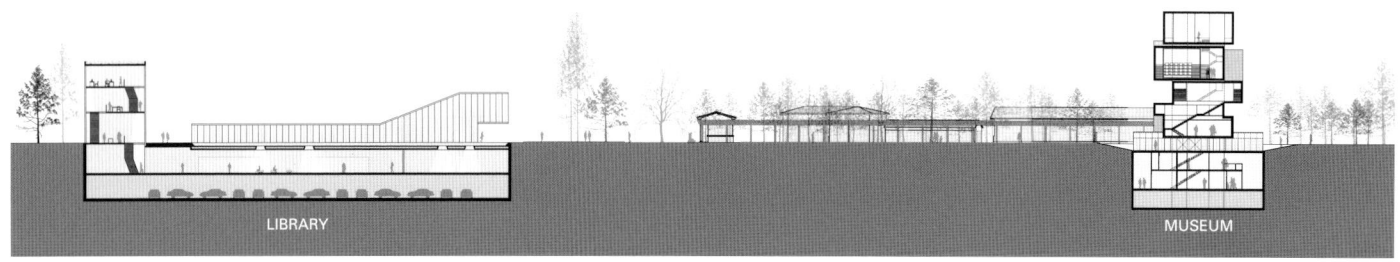

Section S=1:1200

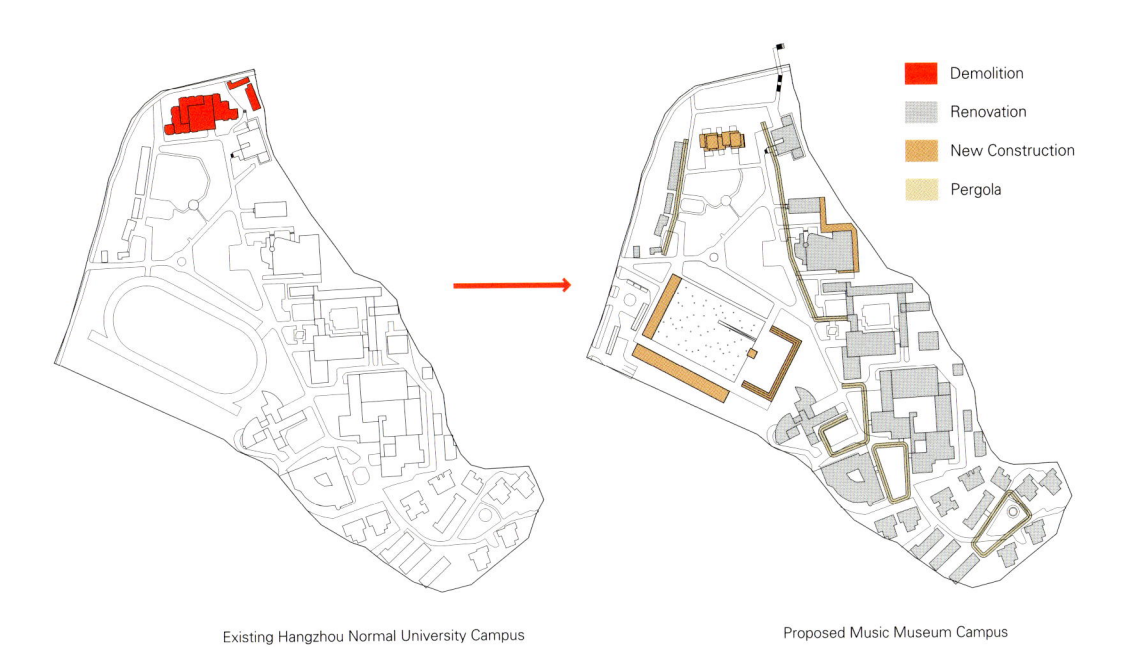

Diagram: proposed campus

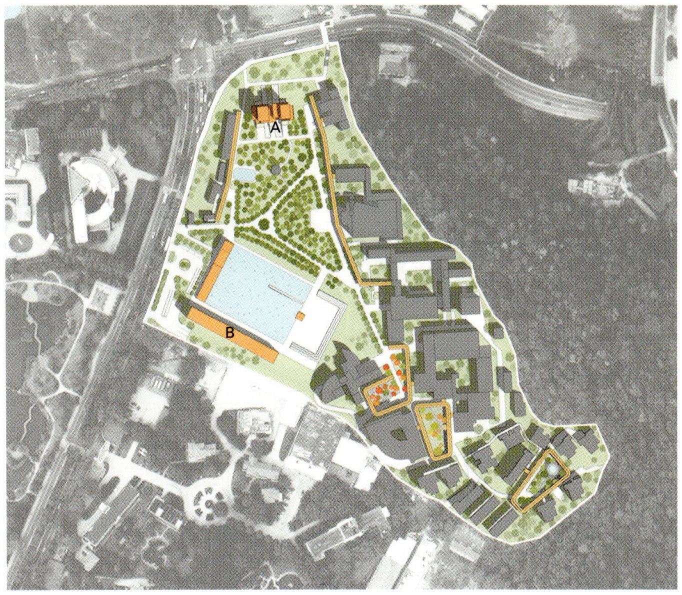

Existing Hangzhou Normal University Campus

Proposed Music Museum Campus

- Demolition
- Renovation
- New Construction
- Pergola

A MUSEUM
B LIBRARY

Site plan　S=1:6000

MUSEUM

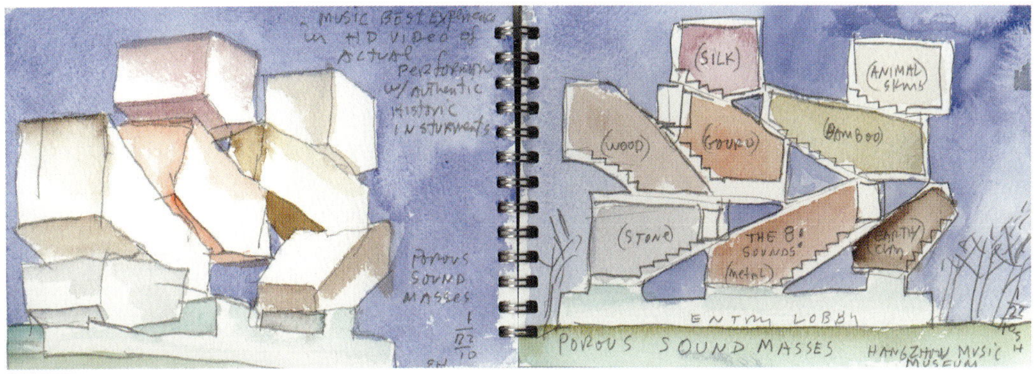

Sketch: museum

A　EIGHT SOUNDS PAVILION
B　MUSIC BAR
C　PERMANENT EXHIBITION
D　MAKE-UP BUILDING

Site plan　S=1:2000

杭州音楽博物館

現存するキャンパスに分散している一連の建築を統合する。この計画の特徴は全体の形態を構成する五つのヴォイド，いわば楽曲におけるカエスーラ(休止)である。第一のヴォイドは美しい木々の現存する古代の大庭園である。第二のヴォイドはリフレクティング・ポンドとエントランス・スペースのある新しいミュージック・プラザである。第三，第四，第五のヴォイドは異なるプログラムの建築のあいだの空間を利用した，演奏会やディスカッション，カフェ，レストラン，レクリエーションのための屋外空間である。

これらのヴォイドを構成する質素な木製のパーゴラは，木造建築様式が初めて確立した宋の時代の建築を想起させるものである。これらのパーゴラの鋳造ガラス葺きの屋根には半透明の太陽光発電セルとLED照明が埋め込まれている。日中は太陽がパーゴラの上で輝き，太陽光発電セルにエネルギーが蓄えられる。夜間はLEDがパーゴラを照らし，キャンパス全体に活気

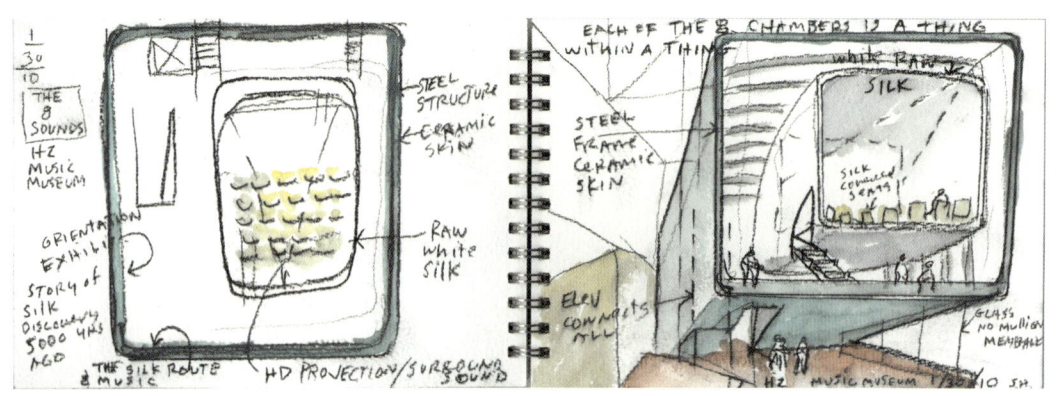

Museum: auditorium

Basement (mezzanine)

Second floor

Fourth floor

Basement S=1:600

First floor

Third floor

Museum: auditorium

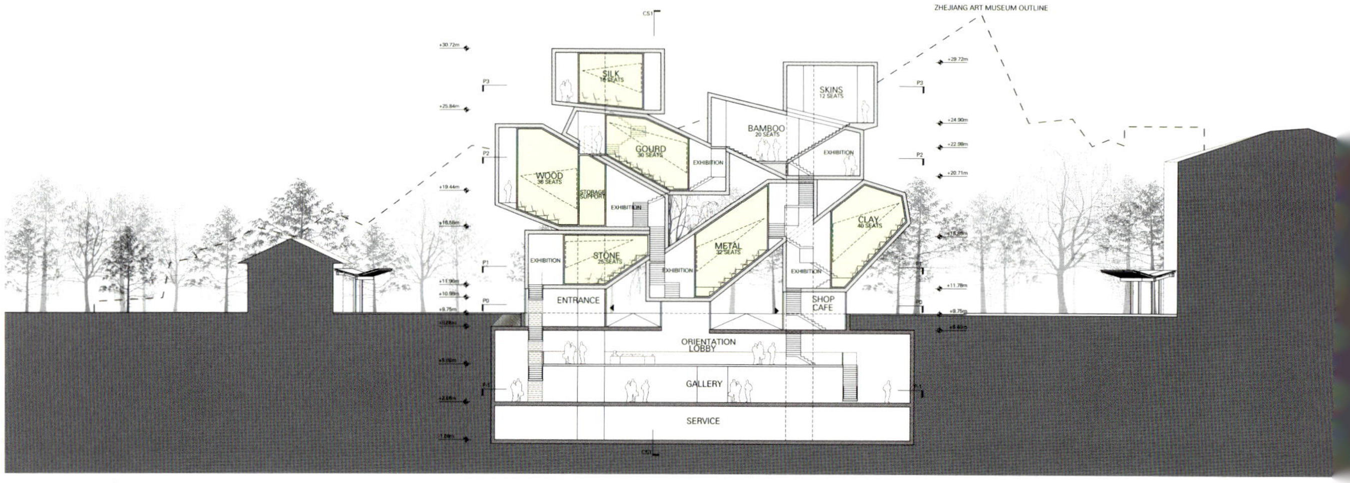

Section S=1:600

II-242

LIBRARY

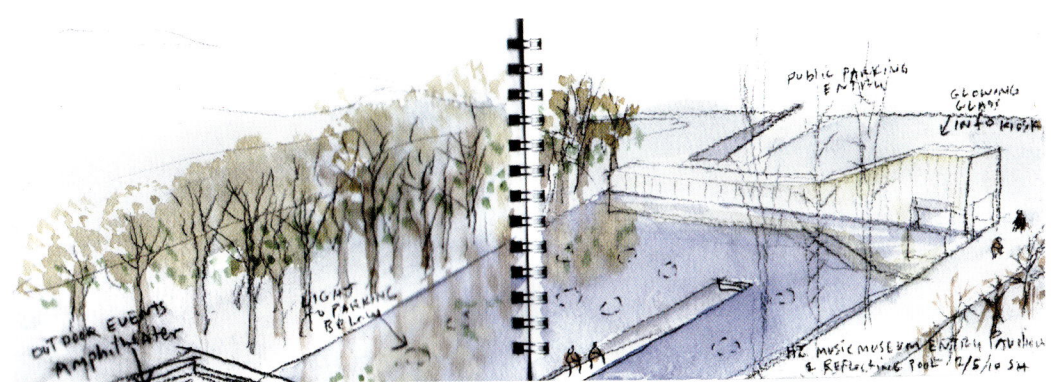

Sketch: library

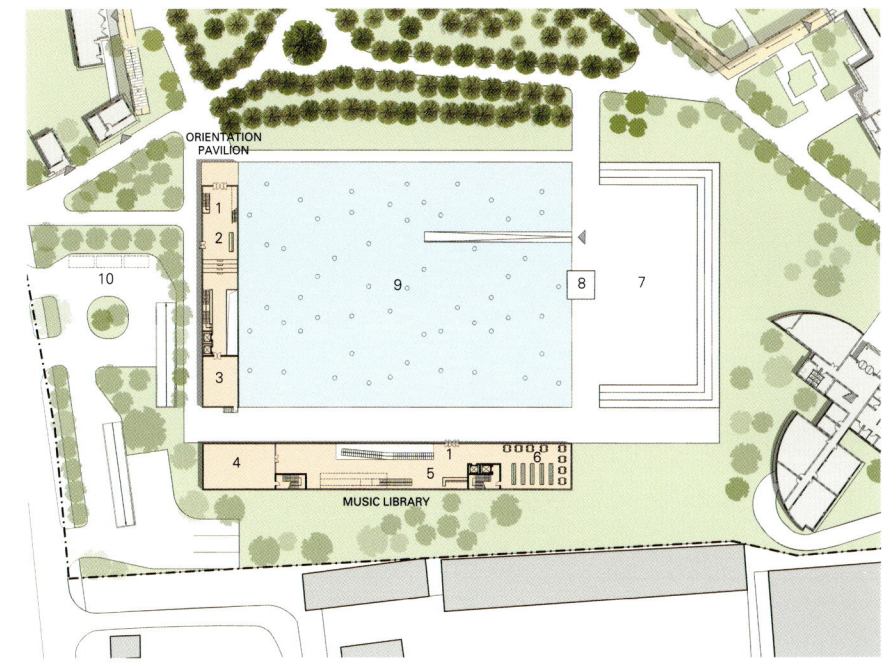

First floor S=1:1600

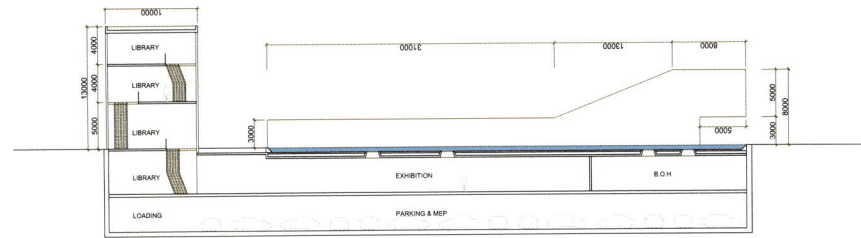

Section S=1:800

Upper floor 2

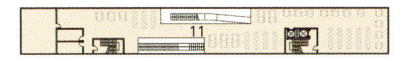

Upper floor 1

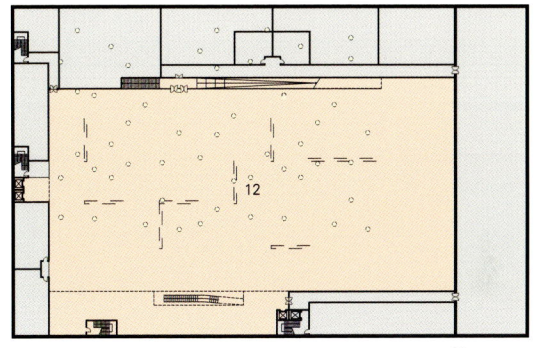

Basement

Movable stage on reflecting pond

1 LOBBY
2 INFORMATION
3 PUBLIC SEMINAR
4 CAFE
5 CHECK-OUT
6 REFERENCE
7 AMPHITHEATER
8 MOVABLE STAGE
9 REFLECTING POND
10 DROP-OFF
11 LIBRARY
12 EXHIBITION

をもたらしてくれる。

　新しいミュージック・プラザは薄い水盤に水を湛えて，ガラスのオリエンテーション棟と新しい音楽図書館に囲まれている。リフレクティング・ポンドの底の天窓からは光が地下の大ギャラリー・スペースへもたらされる。この空間は自由に使うことができる。また，リフレクティング・ポンドの水を抜くことでより多くの聴衆を収容することもできる。

　現在，敷地の主要な境界線のほとんどを占めているのは既存の図書館と北のピアノ棟である。これらの建築は完全に解体され，新しいキャンパスの基準点として，新しい音楽博物館のための敷地となる予定である。この棟は中国の伝統楽器の「八音」という考え方に基づいている。すなわち，糸，竹，木，石，金，土，匏，革である。八つの異なる建築要素の内部は卓抜した音楽を紹介し，上演することのできる鑑賞室である。各々の棟はこれらの素材のうちのいずれかでつくられている。その一方，建築の外壁はパーゴラと同じく木で覆われている。

　キャンパスの既存棟を改修・統合するにあたっては（多くは1950年代から70年代にかけて建てられたもので，適切な断熱が施されていない）性能のよい断熱層と中国特有の薄墨色のレンガがモルタル目地でしっかりと貼られ，エネルギー効率の高い新しいウィンドウが最新の環境基準を既存棟にもたらす予定である。こうした改修方法により，キャンパス全体はエネルギー効率の面で有利な，一つにまとめ上げられた環境になっていくであろう。

2010-   **New Art Building, University of Iowa**
Iowa City, Iowa, U.S.A.

Concept sketch: campus space definition, porosity

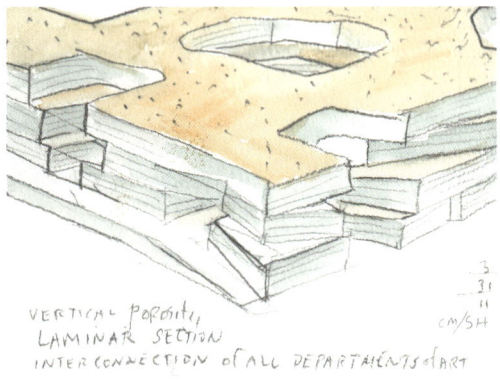

Vertical porosity

Multiple centers of light

Northwest elevation

Site model: New Art Building (right) and School of Art and Art History Building (by Steven Holl, 2006, left)

Concept sketch: stairs as "Social Condensers"

Atrium as one of seven cutouts for 'Multiple Centers of Light'

Interior image with various openings

Atrium with skylight

Corridor between cutouts

First floor

Second floor

Third floor

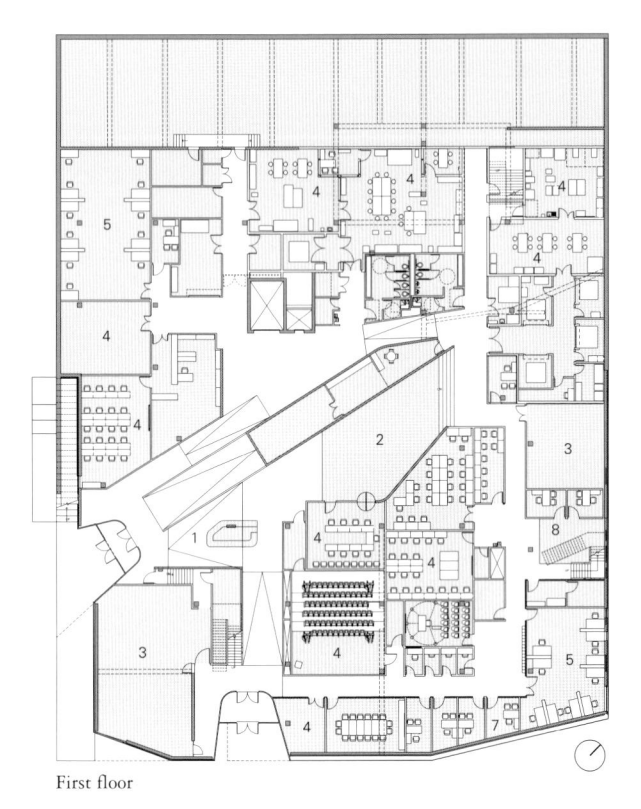

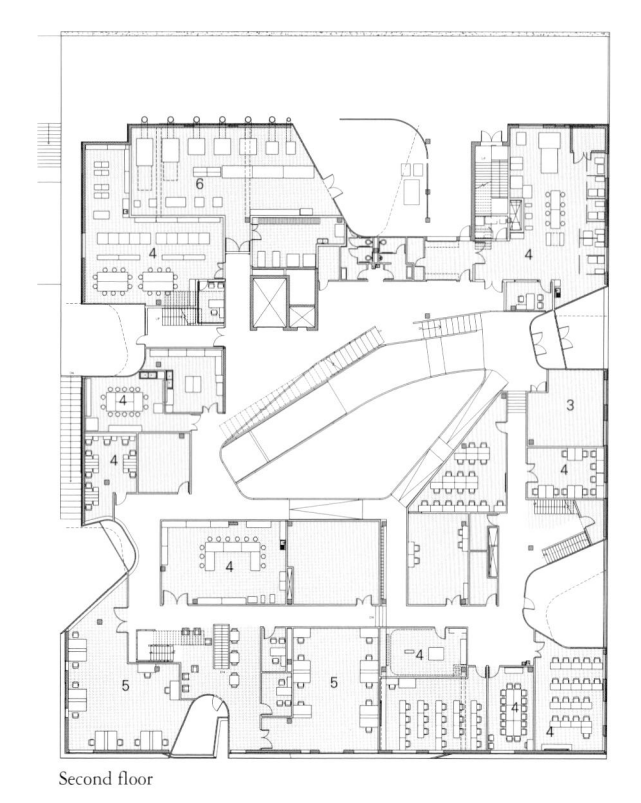

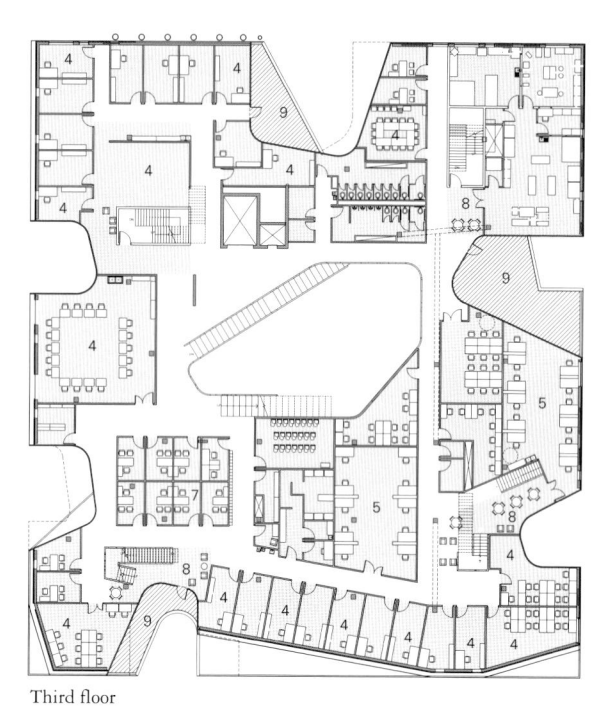

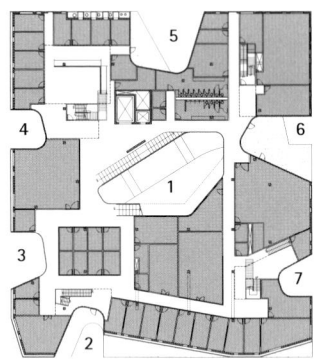

Multiple centers of light: seven vertical cutouts

1. RECEPTION
2. FORUM
3. GALLERY
4. CLASSROOM/ STUDIO/ SEMINAR ROOM
5. GRADUATE STUDIO
6. KILN ROOM
7. OFFICE
8. COMMON AREA/ STAGING
9. TERRACE

The new facility for the University of Iowa's School of Art and Art History will contain 126,000 sq.ft. of loft-like space for the departments of printmaking, painting, photography, intermedia, and three-dimensional art. A four story structure is aimed at the interconnection between the arts. While the 2006 Arts West building is horizontally porous and of planar composition, the new building will be vertically porous and volumetrically composed.

"Concept"
1. Interconnection: Horizontal Programs, Vertical Porosity
In a school for the arts today, interconnection and crossover are of fundamental importance. Today digital techniques open up increased interconnection between all the arts. The essential tools of working now have a boundarycrossing, interconnected impact. Interconnection between all of the departments is facilitated in the vertical carving out of the large open floor plates. Students can see activities ongoing across these openings and be encouraged to interact and meet.

Further interconnection is facilitated by glass partitions along the studio walls adjacent to internal circulation.

2. Multiple Centers of Light
Natural light and natural ventilation are inserted into the deep floor plates via the "multiple centers of light." Seven vertical cutouts encourage interaction between all four levels. These spaces of glass are characterized by a language of shifted layers where one floor plate slides past another. This geometry creates multiple balconies, providing outdoor meeting spaces and informal exterior working space.

3. Stairs as Vertical "Social Condensers"; Corridors as Horizontal Meeting Spaces
Stairs are shaped as "social condensers," encouraging meeting, interaction and discussion. Some stairs stop at generous landings with tables and chairs, others open onto lounge spaces with sofas. The aim of interaction between all departments of the school takes shape in these social circulation spaces.

4. Campus Space Definition/Porosity
The original grid of the campus breaks up at the river, becoming organic as it hits the limestone bluff. The Arts West building reflects this irregular geometry in fuzzy edges. The new building picks up the campus grid again in its simple plan, defining the new campus space of the "arts meadow."

5. Material Resonance, Ecological Innovation
A geothermal well system serves the new building via radiant cooling and radiant heating in the concrete slab and natural ventilation is achieved via operable windows. A punched concrete frame structure provides thermal mass at the exterior while "bubble" slabs provide radiant cooling and heating. A Rheinzink skin in weathering blue-green is perforated for sun shade on the southwest and southeast.

Fourth floor

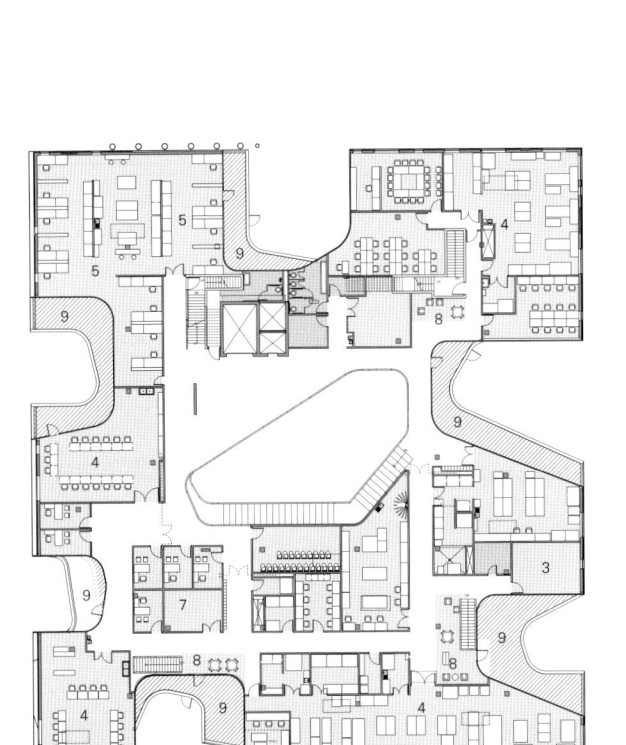

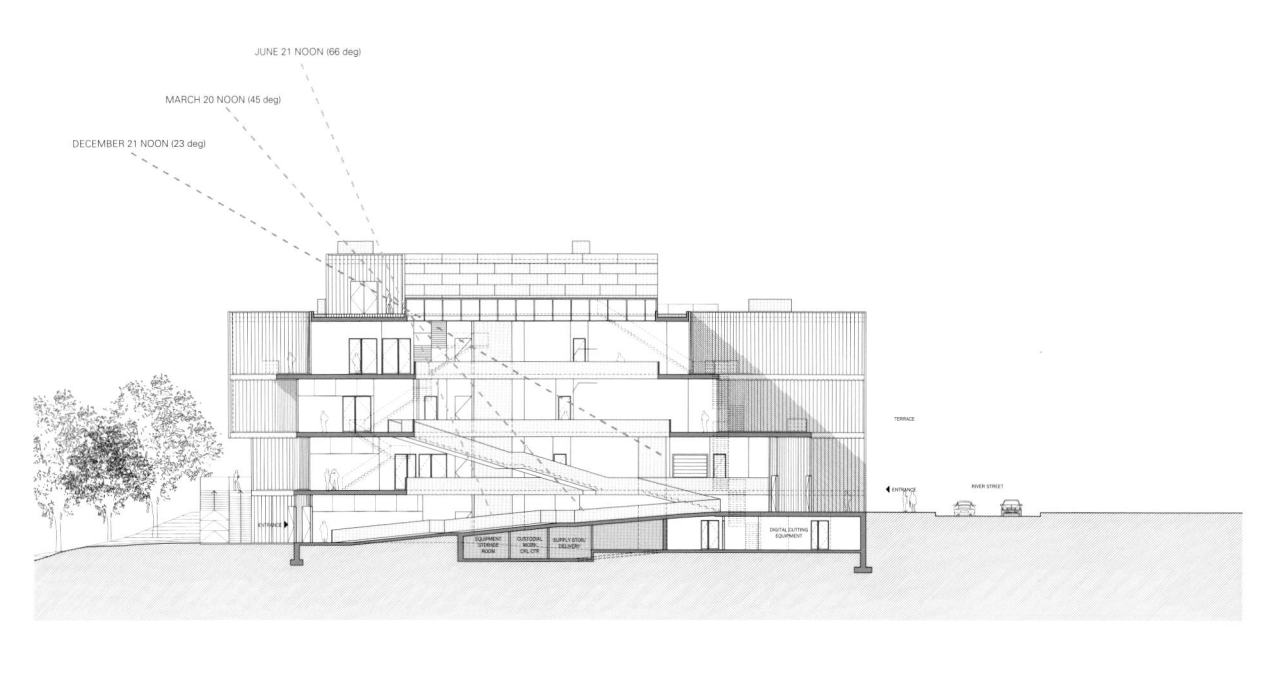

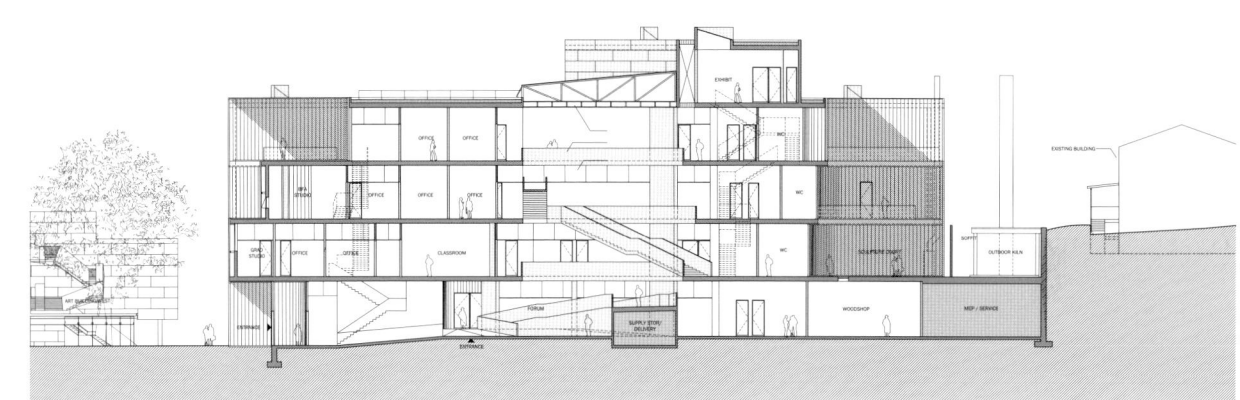

Sections

アイオワ大学新芸術学部棟

アイオワ大学芸術・芸術史学部の新しい施設には版画, 絵画, 写真, インターメディア, 及び立体芸術の各学科のために126,000平方フィート（約11,700平米）のロフト状の空間が収容される予定である。4層の構造体は各芸術の相互交流を促すことを目的として計画された。2006年のアーツ・ウェスト棟が水平のポーラス構造による平面のコンポジションをなす一方で, この新しい建築は垂直のポーラス構造として, 立体的に構成されている。

構想

[1. 相互交流：水平のプログラム, 垂直のポロシティ]
今日の芸術大学では相互交流やクロスオーバーが本質的重要性を担う。今日ではデジタル技術によって芸術のあらゆる分野で相互交流が進んでいる。制作の基本的技法は, 現在では領域横断的に相互に影響を与えている。巨大で開放的なフロアスラブを垂直に切り開くことで, 全ての学科で相互交流が生み出される。学生にとってこれらの開口部を通し, 他のフロアの制作活動を見ることは相互交流のきっかけとなるだろう。さらに内部動線に隣接したスタジオ壁面のガラスのパーティションが, より一層相互交流を促している。

[2. 多様な光の中心点]
自然光と自然換気は幾つもの「多様な光の中心点」を通してフロア深くまで導かれる。7つの垂直の切開部は4層の全ての階層の相互作用を促している。プレートが他のプレートとスライドしながらシフトする。これこそがこのガラス空間の言語的特徴である。このジオメトリは屋外ミーティング・スペースや屋外の私的な制作空間といった, 多様性のあるバルコニーを生み出している。

[3. 垂直の「社会凝縮器」としての階段, 水平のミーティング・スペースとしてのコリドール]
階段はミーティングや相互交流, 議論を促すための「社会凝縮器」として構成されている。いくつかの階段は幅広くテーブルや椅子を誂えた踊り場へと続き, その他の階段はソファのあるラウンジに向かって開放されている。大学の全ての学科に相互交流を促すという目的は, この社会的動線空間に結実している。

[4. キャンパス空間の定義／ポロシティ]
キャンパスの元々のグリッドは川に沿って断たれ, ライムストーンの断崖との際で自然へと溶け込んでいる。アーツ・ウェスト棟はこの不規則的なジオメトリを柔らかなエッジで反映したものである。新しい建築はグリッドを再び単純な平面計画へと取り込み, 新しいキャンパス空間を「芸術の草原」として定義している。

[5. 共鳴する素材, 環境のイノベーション]
新しい建築は地熱井システムによるコンクリートスラブの輻射冷暖房を備え, 可動式窓による自然換気を取り入れている。穿孔されたコンクリートの軸組構造は外周部に熱容量を与え, 「泡状の」スラブは輻射冷暖房として機能する。南西部と南東部にはラインツィンク社の風化した緑青のような表皮がサンシェードとして穿孔されている。

2010-

Cangqian Performing Arts Center, Art Museum and Arts Quadrangle, Hangzhou Normal University
Hangzhou, China

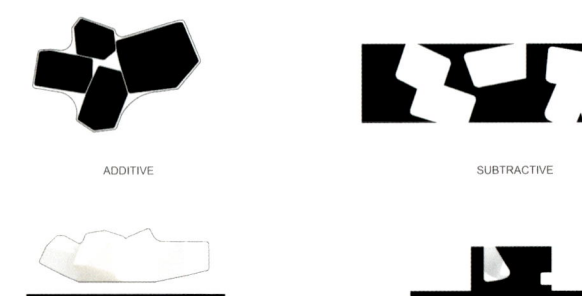

ADDITIVE

SUBTRACTIVE

OF THE SKY

OF THE EARTH

Concept diagram

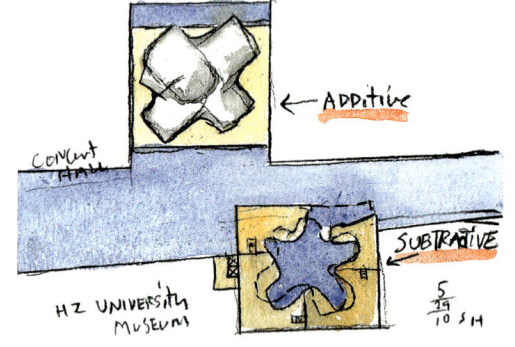

Concept sketch: additive/subtractive

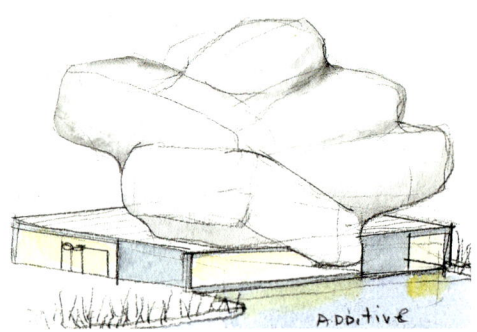

Performing Arts Center: additive

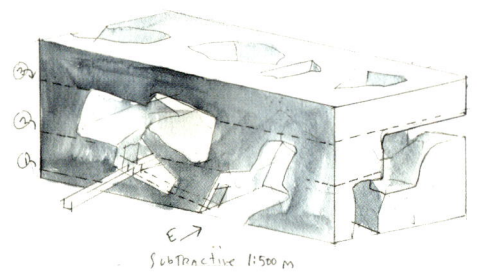

Art Museum: subtractive

Art Museum (left) and Performing Arts Center (right)

On the new campus for Hangzhou Normal University a pair of buildings central to the new campus identity have a unique concept.

Sited on either side of an existing canal, one functions as the new university art museum with instructional spaces, while the other functions as the performing arts center with a 1,200-seat opera house, a 750-seat concert hall, a 600-seat television studio, a 200-seat auditorium and a 120-seat auditorium.

An "additive form" concept generates the unique geometry of the Performing Arts Center, with the different halls stacked up freely and pulled away from each other to form a special public access hall at the center. The slightly rounded edges of the different halls are pierced by escalators in this dramatic arrival space. The spatial energy itself here adds drama even when silent.

Sitting on a glowing glass "socle" base, the auditorium bodies are "shrink-wrapped" with a translucent membrane skin which allows a soft light to all public and circulation spaces. Inside the auditoriums are of curved and laminated bamboo, with perforations in some panels to achieve perfect acoustics. In the opera house

PERFORMING ARTS CENTER

Sketch: lobby

some panels are adjustable for different acoustic requirements. Seats have bamboo backs with blue-green mohair upholstery.

On the other side of the canal, the University Art Museum has a "subtractive" geometry with the voids carved in special glass bars, bringing diffused light to the galleries within. The concrete structural walls at the exterior minimize columns on the interior for exhibition flexibility. The charcoal-stained bamboo-formed concrete exterior gives a special texture to the walls, which are broken at the voids, lined in glowing planks of glass. These voids are also outdoor teaching spaces in their amphitheatre stepping, providing real variety and spatial energy in a museum of orthogonal walls designed to feature the art within.

United by a pedestrian bridge, the unique relationship of these buildings—one "additive", the other "subtractive"; one of the sky, the other of the earth—alludes to many ancient Chinese concepts while being the most ultra-modern and high-tech instruments for teaching at the new Hangzhou Normal University.

Lobby

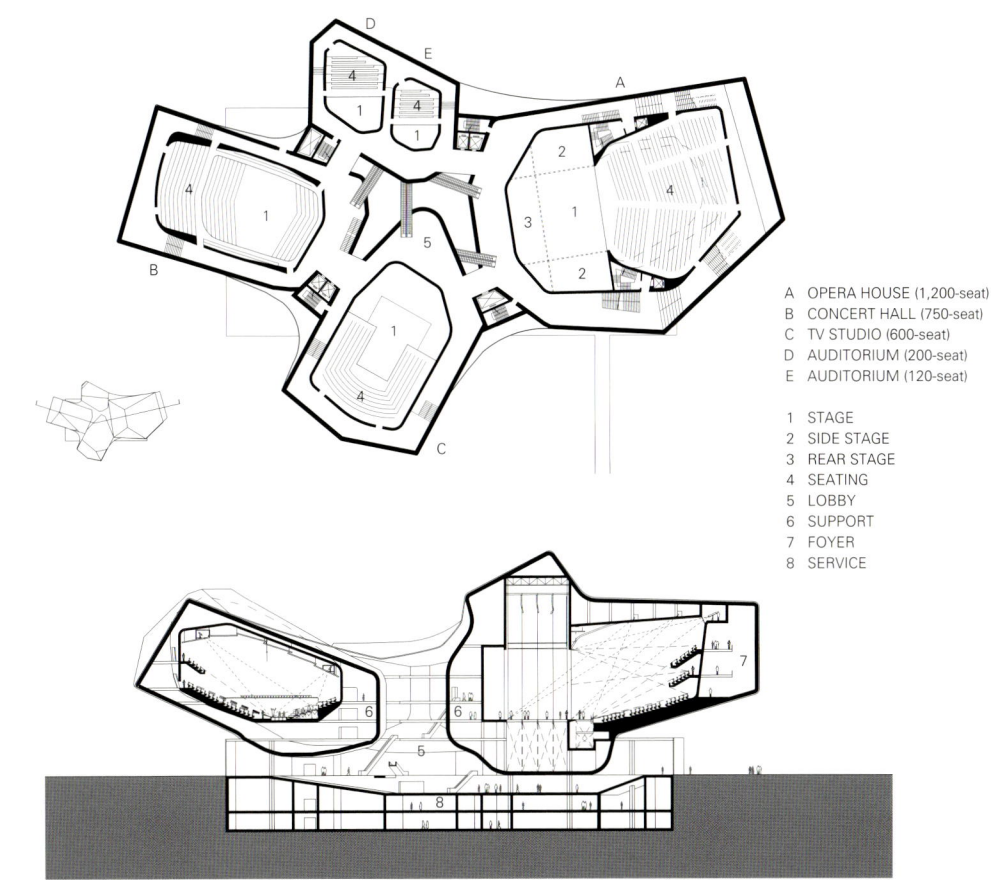

A OPERA HOUSE (1,200-seat)
B CONCERT HALL (750-seat)
C TV STUDIO (600-seat)
D AUDITORIUM (200-seat)
E AUDITORIUM (120-seat)

1 STAGE
2 SIDE STAGE
3 REAR STAGE
4 SEATING
5 LOBBY
6 SUPPORT
7 FOYER
8 SERVICE

Plan/section

Opera House

ART MUSEUM

A ENTRY COURTYARD
B LANDSCAPE GARDEN
C WATER GARDEN
D OUTDOOR TEACHING SPACE

1. CHILDREN'S EDUCATION CENTER
2. CAFE
3. MUSEUM SHOP
4. CONTEMPORARY ARTS
5. LOBBY
6. DIGITAL MEDIA
7. GENERAL MATERIALS
8. CHINESE PAINTINGS & CALLIGRAPHY
9. CHINESE & OVERSEAS OIL PAINTINGS
10. DONATED ART EXHIBITION HALL
11. METAL/WOOD WORKSHOP
12. CERAMIC WORKSHOP
13. TRADITIONAL ARTS & CRAFTS WORKSHOP
14. ART HISTORY MULTI-MEDIA DISPLAY
15. CALLIGRAPHY & SEAL-CUTTING MULTI-MEDIA DISPLAY
16. HANGZHOU CONTEMPORARY OIL PAINTINGS
17. ZHEJIANG ARTISTS WORKS
18. HANGZHOU CALLIGRAPHY & SEAL-CUTTING
19. ARTS FROM HAN DYNASTY
20. TEACHER'S ART (100-year old normal university)
21. OFFICE
22. WORLD CONTEMPORARY
23. TRADITIONAL ARTS & CRAFTS

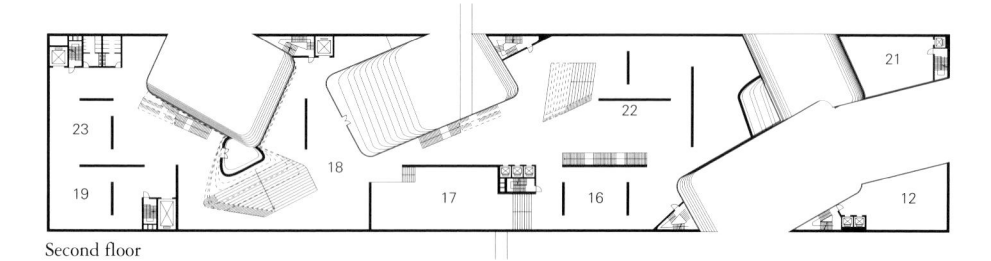

Second floor

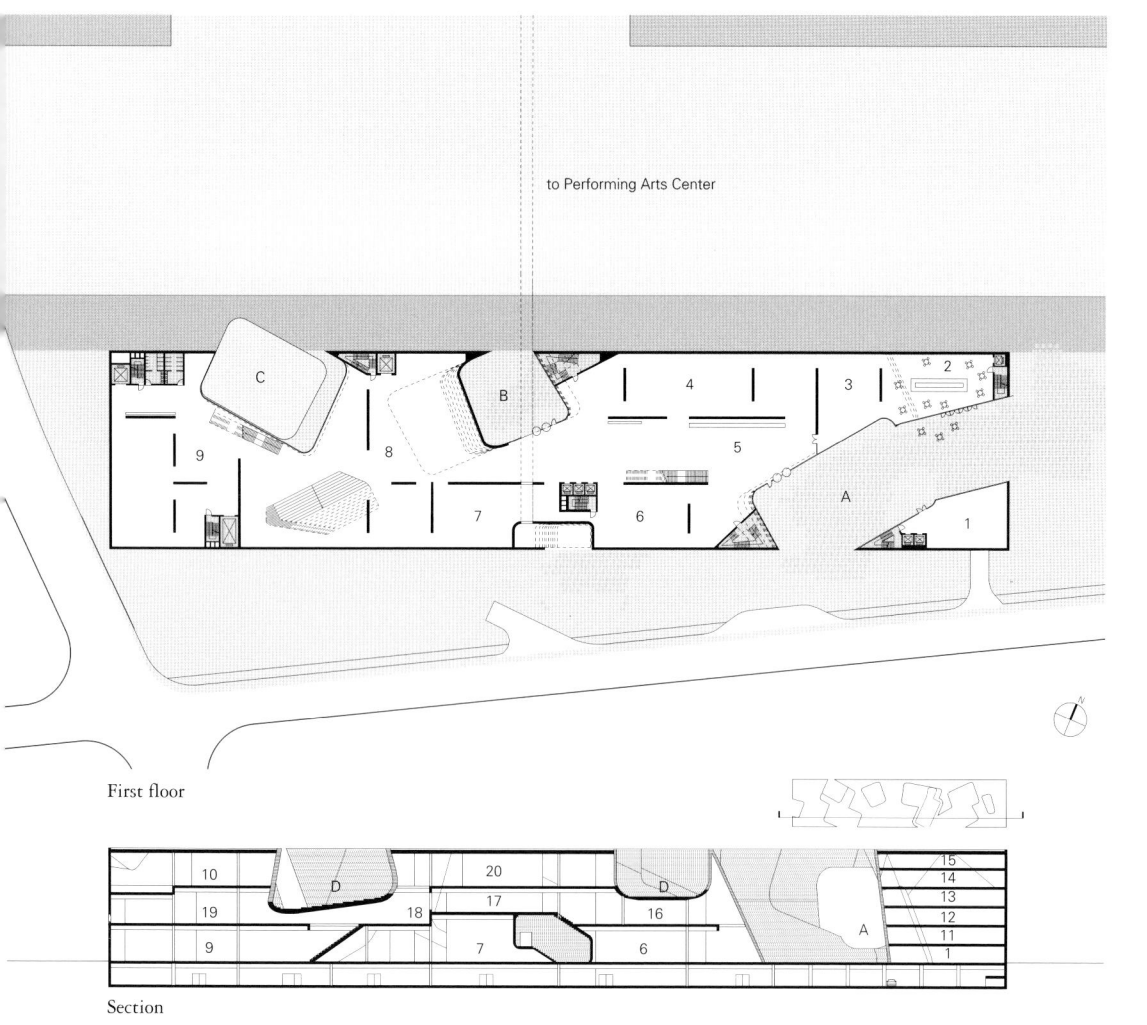

First floor

Section

Entry courtyard

Gallery

Gallery

杭州師範大学
パフォーミングアーツ・センター, 美術館および広場
杭州師範大学の新キャンパスに建てられる一対の建築。新キャンパスの中心として, 独創的なコンセプトが込められている。

古くからある運河の両側に計画された建築は, 一方は教育施設を備えた大学の新美術館として機能し, 他方は1,200席のオペラハウス, 750席のコンサートホール, 600席の映像スタジオ, 200席のオーディトリアム, 120席のオーディトリアムのあるパフォーミング・アーツ・センターとして機能する。

「形態を加算する」という発想から, パフォーミング・アーツ・センターに独自のジオメトリーが付与された。異なるホールが次々と積層し, お互いから引き離されることで, 中央に特別なエントランホールが生み出される。この躍動的なエントランホールでは各々のホールのわずかに丸みを帯びたエッジに対し, エスカレータが貫通する。静寂のなかに強靭な空間が躍動感を与えている。

光を放つガラスの「基壇」の上に建つオーディトリアムは, 透光性のメンブレイン膜で「ラッピング」されている。オーディトリアムは動線上のパブリック空間のあらゆる場所に柔らかい光を落とす。竹を積層した曲面のオーディトリアム内部では, そのいくつかのパネルに孔が開けられ, 音響効果を完全なものとしている。オペラハウスではそれぞれの劇に必要な音響効果に合わせて, 可動式パネルが採用された。竹の背板の座席には, 青緑の生地が張られている。

運河の反対側では, 大学の美術館棟の「減算による」ジオメトリーが, 幾筋もの特殊ガラスでつくられたヴォイドを通して拡散光を内部のギャラリーに導いている。コンクリート構造の外壁には内部空間の展示の自由度を高めるため, 柱の数を最小化する役割がある。竹の型枠の, 墨色に染められた外部コンクリートは壁面に独特の風合いを与え, ヴォイドの際では光を放つガラスの積層材が一本の列をなす。これらのヴォイドは同時に屋外教育の場でもある。この段状の円形広場は, 内部の美術作品を引き立てるように設計された直角の壁の美術館に, 真実の多様性と空間の力強さを付与している。

歩道橋で連結されたこれらの建築の独特の関係性, すなわち「加算」と「減算」, あるいは空と大地の建築という関係性は, 非常に現代的かつ先端的な杭州師範大学の新しい教育施設であるのと同時に, 古代中国に見出される多くの思想に対する暗喩でもある。

Performing Arts Center (left) and Art Museum (right)

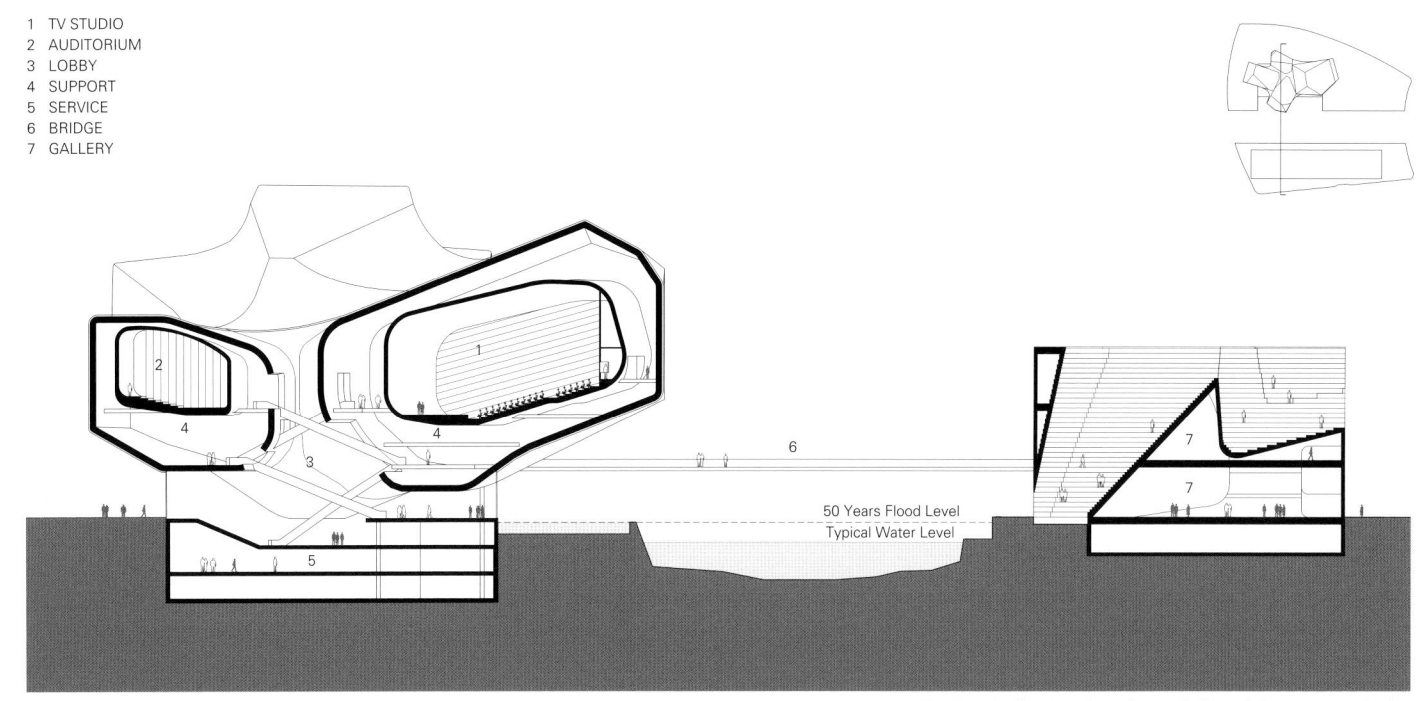

1 TV STUDIO
2 AUDITORIUM
3 LOBBY
4 SUPPORT
5 SERVICE
6 BRIDGE
7 GALLERY

50 Years Flood Level
Typical Water Level

Section: Performing Arts Center (left) and Art Museum (right)

Night view: site facing the East River

Location

Site plan

2010-

Queens Library
New York, New York, U.S.A.

Sketches: open movement along facade (left) and interior (right)

Model: overall view from river

Evening view over river

II-253

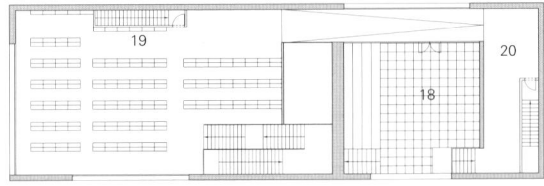

Level 4

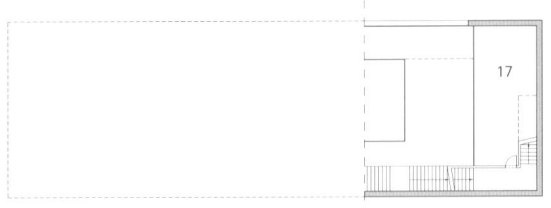

Mezzanine on level 3

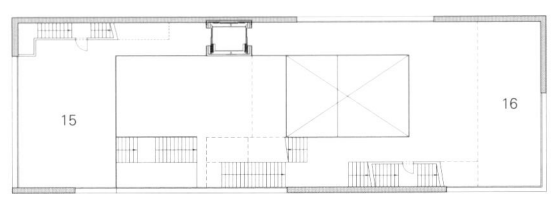

Level 3

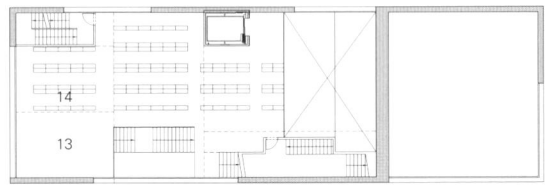

Mezzanine on level 2

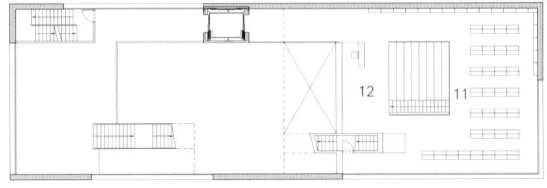

Level 2

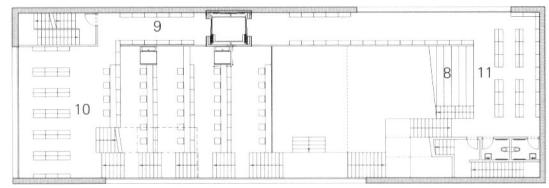

Level 1

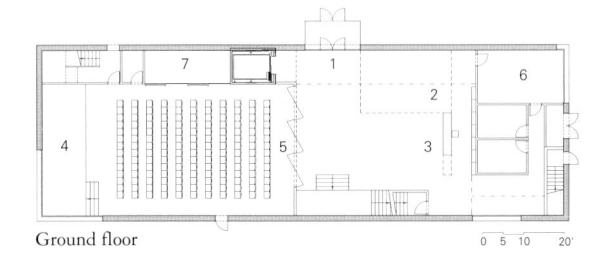

Ground floor

1 ENTRANCE
2 CIRCULATION & INFORMATION
3 CURRENT PERIODICALS
4 STAGE
5 MEETING ROOM
6 WORKROOM
7 STORAGE
8 CHILDREN'S ACTIVITY AREA
9 INFORMATION LIBRARIAN
10 ADULT READING COLLECTION
11 CHILDREN'S AREA
12 CHILDREN'S LIBRARIAN
13 QUIET ROOM
14 ADULT COLLECTION
15 LOUNGE OFFICES
16 CYBER CENTER
17 MECHANICAL
18 TERRACE
19 TEEN AREA
20 CAFE

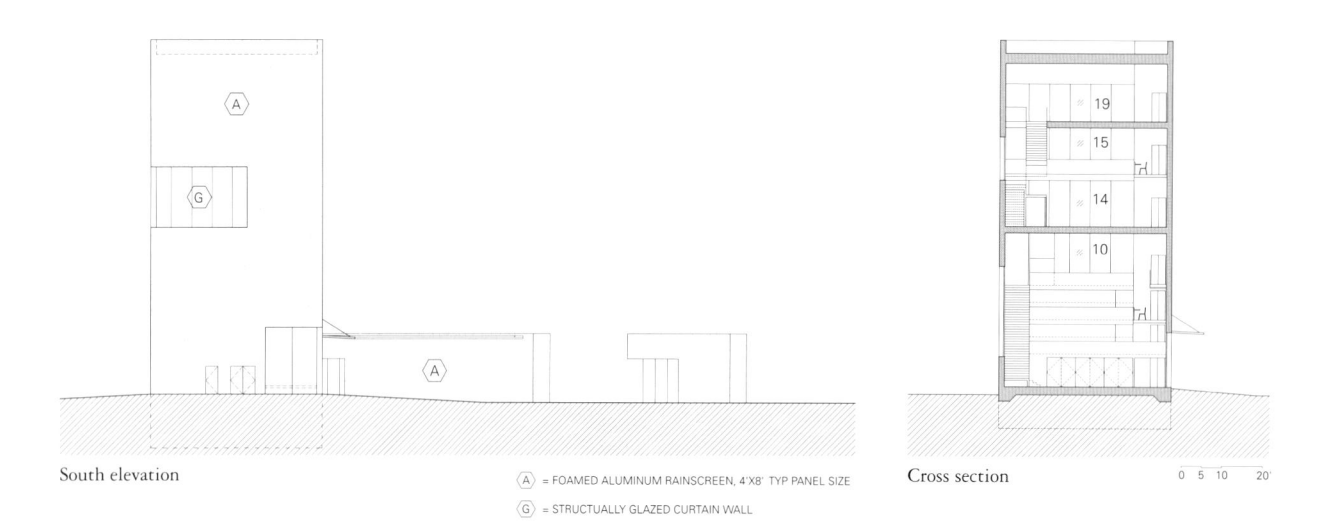

North elevation

South elevation

Ⓐ = FOAMED ALUMINUM RAINSCREEN, 4'X8' TYP PANEL SIZE
Ⓖ = STRUCTURALLY GLAZED CURTAIN WALL

Cross section

The prominent site on the East River, facing a magnificent view of Manhattan, inspired the design, which cuts the lines of the main interior circulation route into the west façade. A "Manhattan view" stair rises up from the open arrival space, allowing the users a great view toward the city, flanked perpendicularly by reading tables in ascending sections backed with bookcases. While users may be on computers, the view from the entry is of books, and the view on the way up is of the East River and Manhattan.

The program's separation into children's area, teen area and adult area, can be read in the carved cuts of the east face of the building, one façade opening for each area. Yet the programmatic divisions are fluid: not "this is that," as childhood can return. The building section of the new library is open and flowing, while the plan is compact, allowing for the most energy-efficient design and the greatest amount of public space on the site.

Along the west is an elongated reflecting pond of recycled water, which is edged in the natural grasses that once grew at the bank of the East River. Frogs, turtles, and fish inhabit this year-round natural water strip. On the east entrance side, the library together with a low park office pavilion forms a public reading garden with a bosque of ginko trees. Ascending the stair inside one can reach the rooftop reading garden with amazing panoramic views. At night the glowing presence of the new library along the waterfront joins the Pepsi sign and the "Long Island" sign at the old Gantry to become a beacon and inviting icon for this new community place.

The fabric-formed concrete structure is exposed and painted white inside, while exterior insulation and a foamed aluminum rainskin give the exterior a subtle sparkle and glow, without being overly shiny. As the material is 100 percent recycled aluminum, this outer layer relates to all the green aspects in the new facility.

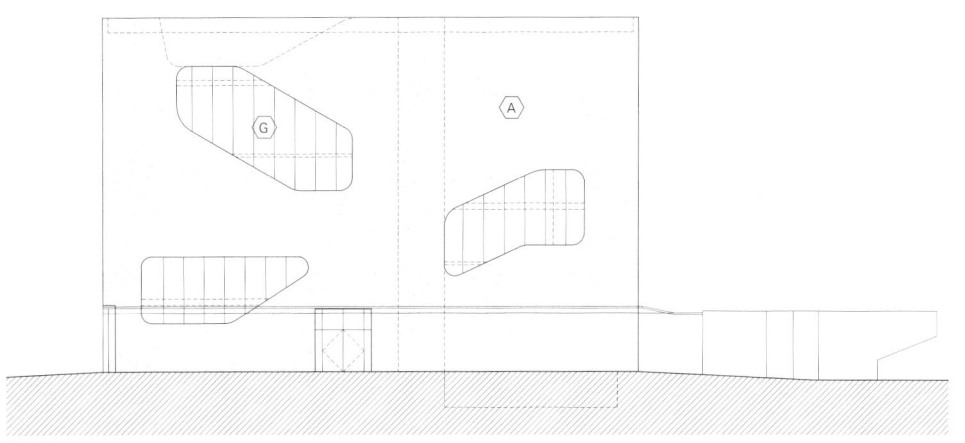

East elevation

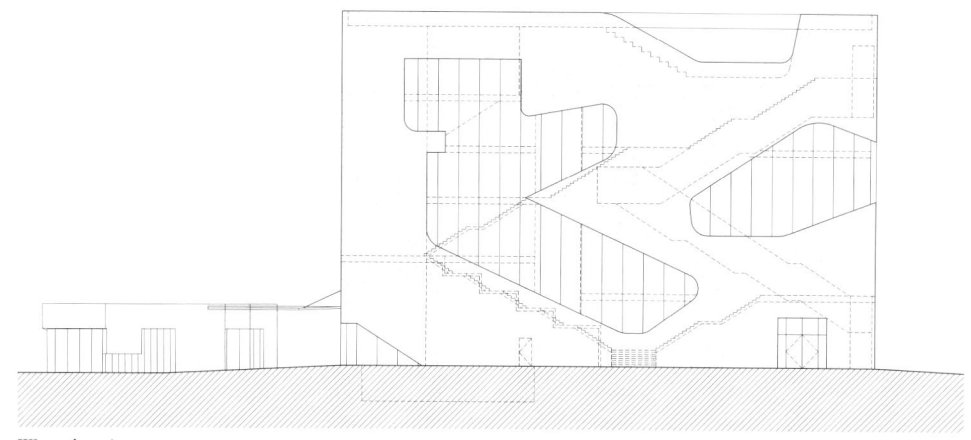

West elevation

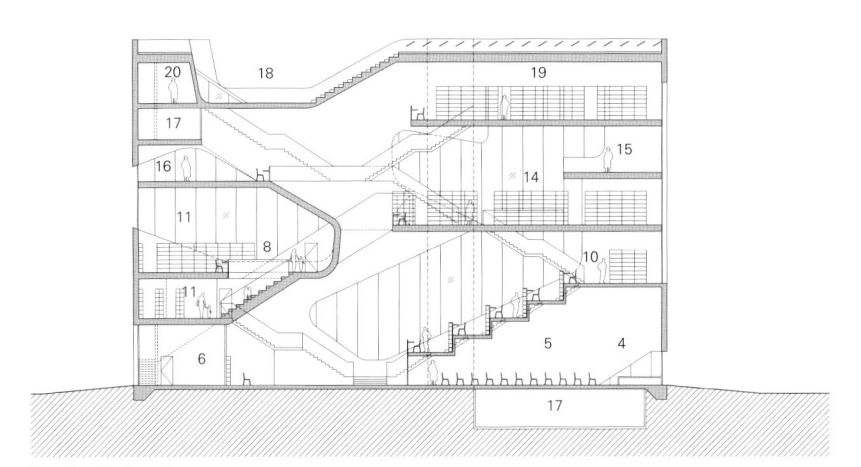

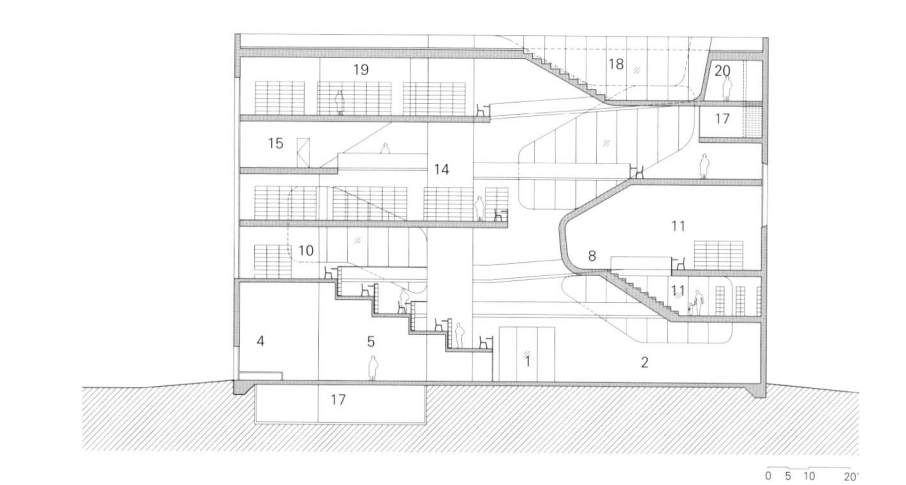

Longitudinal sections

クイーンズ図書館

イースト・リバーに面した絶好の敷地はマンハッタンの壮大な眺望と向かい合い,インスピレーションをかき立てる。内部の主要動線は,西側のファサードへと切り開かれている。開放的なエントランス空間からは「マンハッタン・ビュー」と名付けられた階段が続く。上がるにつれて,書架を背にした閲覧用机とは直角に,利用者の眼前にマンハッタンの眺望が広がる。利用者はPCを使うものの,エントランスから入ると一面には書架が,階段を上がるとイースト・リバーとマンハッタンへの眺望が,広がっている。

プログラムは子供用,ティーン用,一般用に分かれ,それぞれのエリアごとに開口部のある東ファサードに,内包するプログラムを読み取ることができる。その一方で,初めから「これはここ」とは決めず,プログラムは流動的に配置された。新しい図書館の断面は流れるように開放した計画とする一方で,平面計画はコンパクトなものとしたため,エネルギー効率がよく,敷地のパブリック・スペースを大きく確保することが可能になった。

西側に沿っては,再生水を利用したリフレクティング・プールが細長く延び,イースト・リバーの河岸に育った自然の緑で縁取られている。蛙,亀,あるいは魚が,年間を通してこの細長い水盤に生息する。エントランスの東側では図書館が,低層の公園管理棟とともに,イチョウ木立の中に読書のためのパブリック・ガーデンを構成している。内部階段を上がると,屋上のリーディング・ガーデンからは素晴らしい眺望を眺めることができる。夜になるとこの新しい図書館は水際で鮮やかに輝く。旧来のガントリー・プラザにあるペプシや「ロング・アイランド」のサインと共に,この新しいコミュニティ空間へと人々を誘う灯台のような象徴的存在である。

布地のように成形されたコンクリート構造は,内部では打放しに白く塗装されている。一方,外断熱と発泡アルミニウムによる雨曝しの外皮は,艶を抑えて,繊細に煌めく輝きをその表面に残す。100%の再生アルミニウムが使用された外皮の層は,この新しい施設の環境評価と全面的に結びついている。

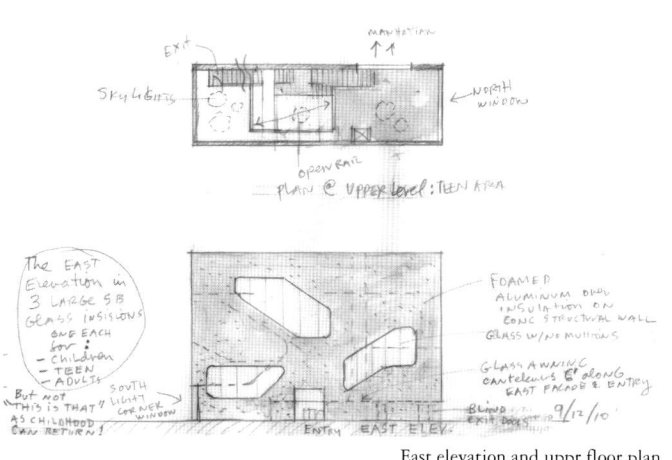

East elevation and uppr floor plan

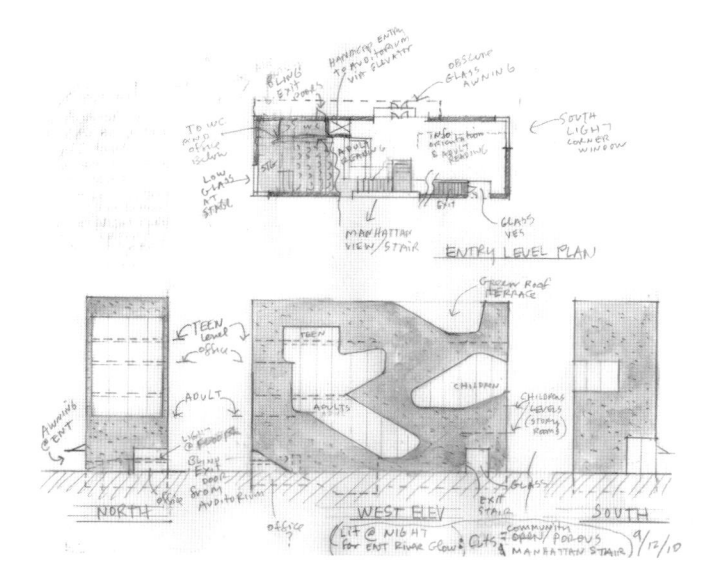

North, west, south elevations and ground floor plan (entry level)

Children's activity area

Children's area on level 2

Interior model of upper floor: Manhattan view on west

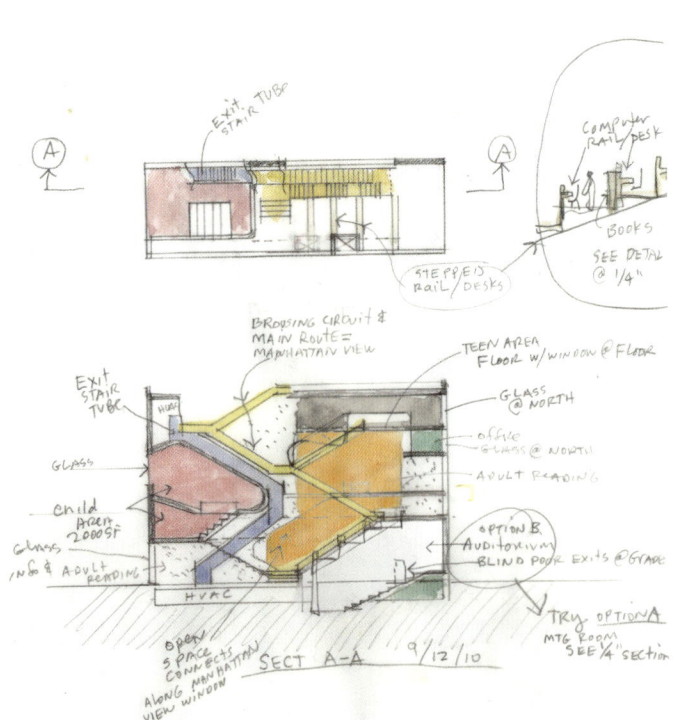

Section

Cyber center on level 3: Manhattan view over East River

II-256

Model: window of adult reading collection area

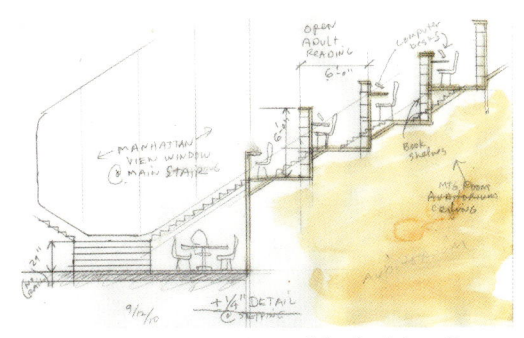

Sectional detail: adult reading area

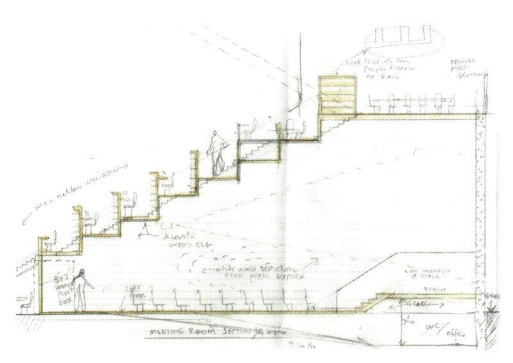

Sectional detail: meeting room (below) and adult reading area (above)

Adult reading collection area on level 1

Interior model: looking corner on upper levels

II-257

2010-

New Doctorate's Building, National University of Colombia
Bogotá, Colombia

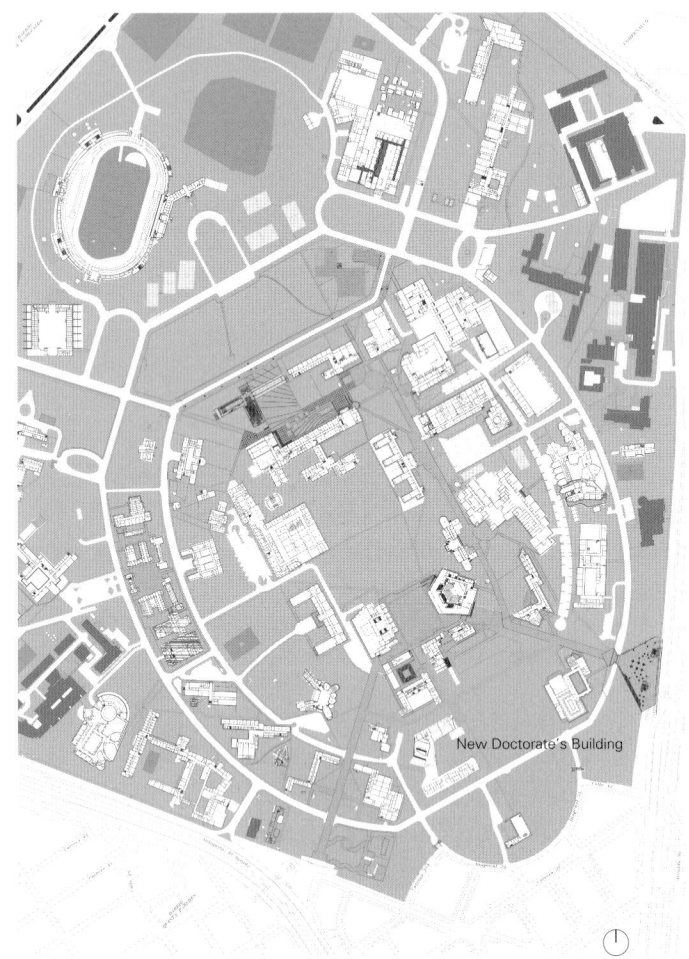

Site plan S=1:10000

Site model: view from southeast

The importance of the National University of Colombia campus began with its enlightened master plan by the architect Leopold Rother in the 1930s. With its green center, classical axiality, and layered concentricity, the campus contains some wonderful examples of architecture.

We envision the new Doctorate's Building re-energizing the original master plan, shaping campus green space. While buildings of the 1970s clogged the inner green of the original master plan, our new building aims to turn that closure inside out, re-establishing green space definitions.

The moderate climate of Bogotá (cool summers and temperate winters) allows for space turned "inside out" to be at the heart of the new building section. The life of the school, with students moving back and forth on exterior walks, is evident in this central open social space.

The 6,400 m² two-story building rises in section at the main gathering space. From the building's 600-seat auditorium, a roof begins to warp upwards, shaping a campus gate-like pergola. Here sun-protected social space is aligned to one of the original diagonals of the Rother plan. The campus entry approaches and the central axis are linked in the new building and its green space, opening up new porous routes of movement.

The south arm of the building rises up in a cantilevered restaurant with roof terraces and mountain views. The north arm turns down into the landscape opening to an "upside-down" portion, shaping a grotto water garden. A continuous flow of rain water and grey water are linked in this lower basin; a reflecting pool at the auditorium emits the sound of slowly pouring water.

The water recycle system is driven by solar photovoltaic cells on the roof, which also provide 15% of the electrical power for the new structure. High-performance reinforced concrete joins local woods and Bogotá stone in a palette of material resonance and ecological innovation.

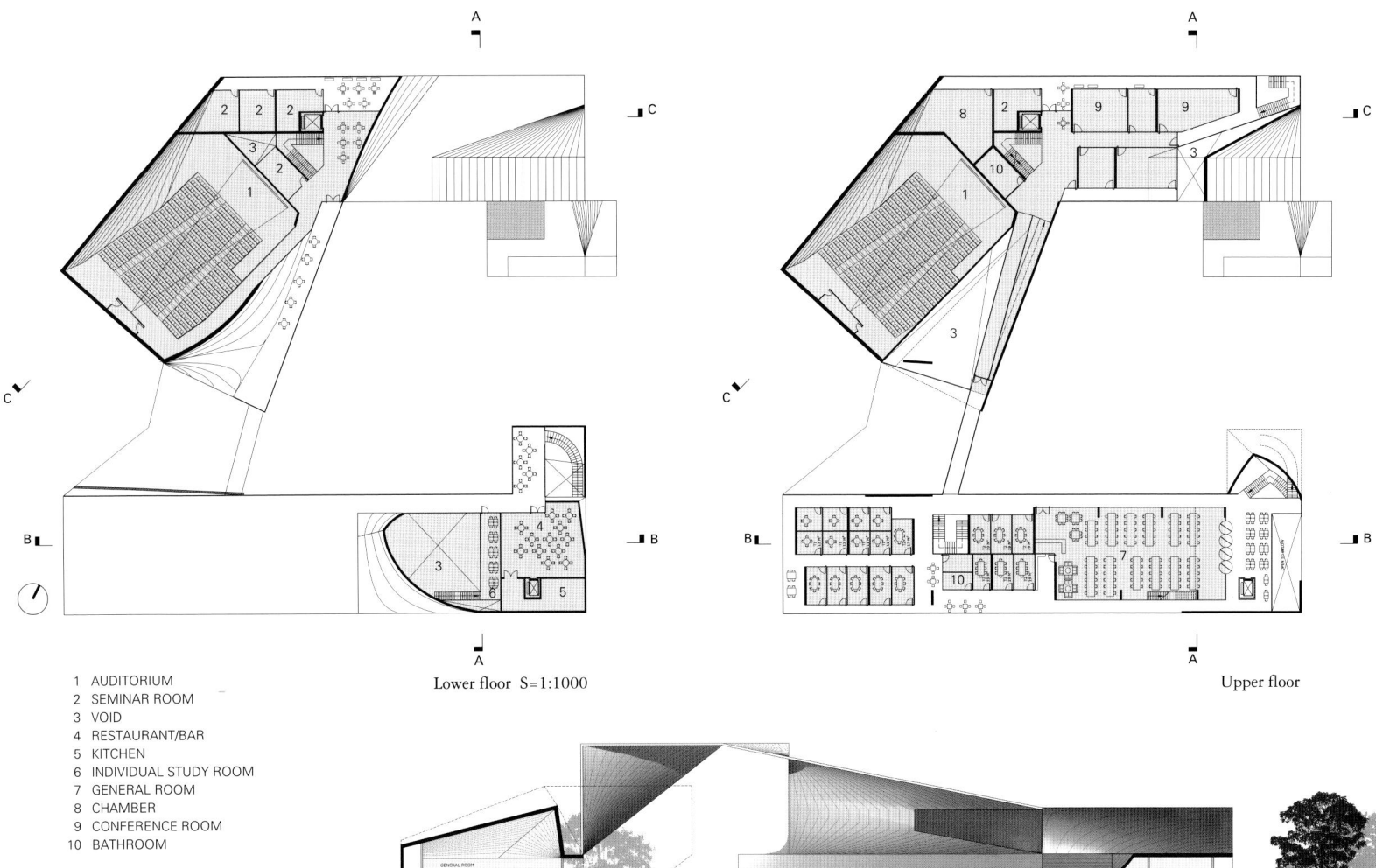

1 AUDITORIUM
2 SEMINAR ROOM
3 VOID
4 RESTAURANT/BAR
5 KITCHEN
6 INDIVIDUAL STUDY ROOM
7 GENERAL ROOM
8 CHAMBER
9 CONFERENCE ROOM
10 BATHROOM

Lower floor S=1:1000

Upper floor

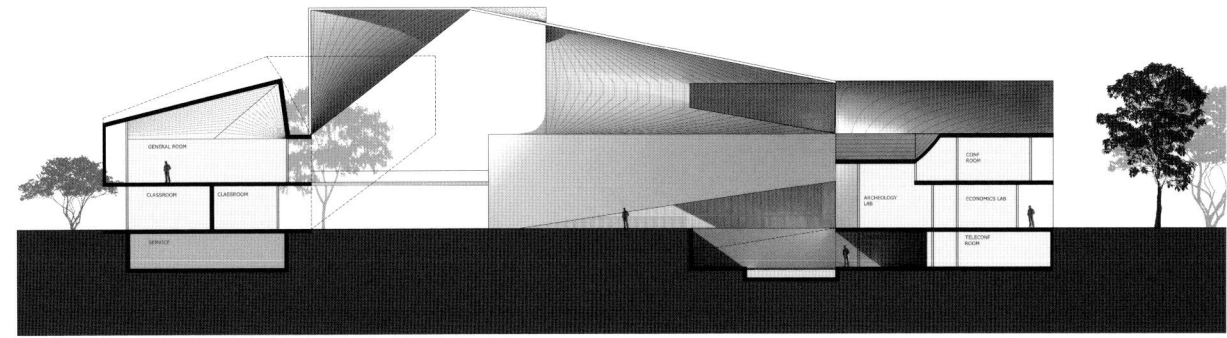

Section A-A

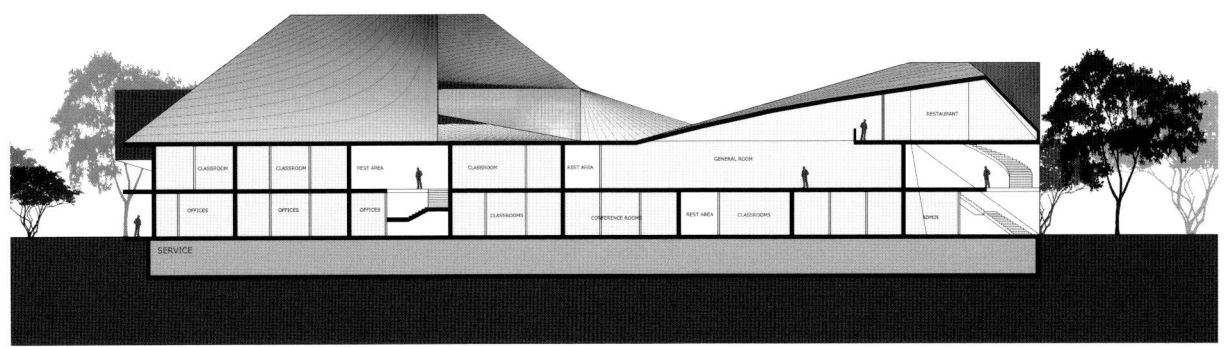

Section B-B

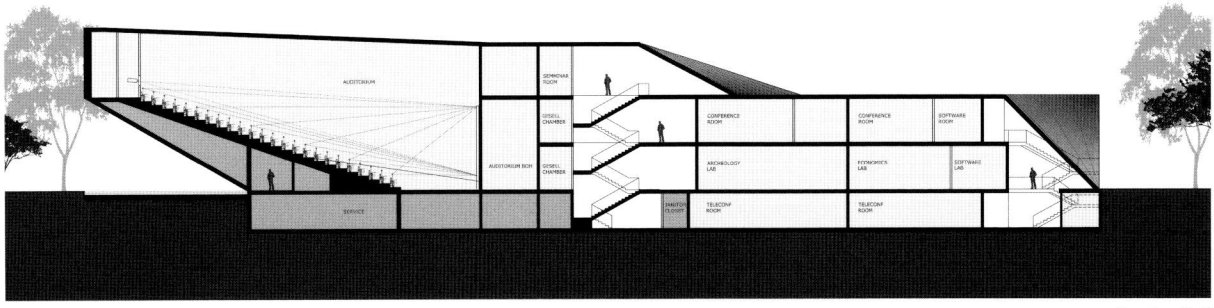

Section C-C

II-259

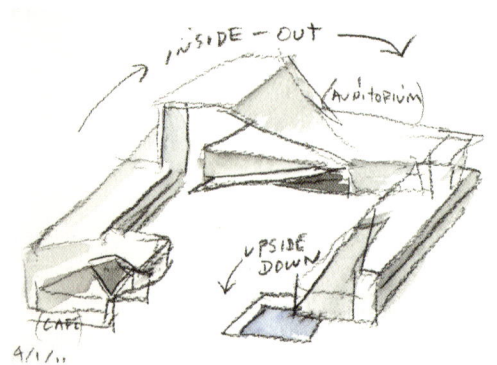

Concept sketch: "inside-out" space

View toward restaurant

View from west: "inside-out"

View from south

Inner court

Concept model

コロンビア国立大学博士課程棟

コロンビア国立大学キャンパスの価値は，建築家レオポルト・ローターによる啓蒙主義的な1930年代のマスタープランにその端を発する。中心部の緑，古典的な都市軸，及び複層的な同心円構造とともに，キャンパスには優れた建築が散在している。

新しい研究棟の構想は，キャンパスを緑の空間として構成し，当初のマスタープランの再生を行うものである。当初のマスタープランの緑は，1970年代に建てられた建築によって中庭として塞がれてしまっていた。この新しい建築はそのような囲いの表裏を逆転し，緑の空間を再定義することを目指している。

（夏は涼しく，冬は温暖な）ボゴタの穏やかな気候は，「表裏を裏返した」空間が新しい建築断面の中心となることを可能にしている。外部通路を行き交う学生が，この開かれた中央の社会的空間で大学生活を過ごすのは明らかだろう。

6,400平米の2層の建築は，人の集まる主要空間で断面方向に立ち上がる。屋根は建築の600席のオーディトリアムから上に向かって折れ曲がり，キャンパス・ゲートのようなパーゴラを形成する。この太陽から守られた社会的空間は，ローターの当初のマスタープランの対角線上の軸線に沿ったものである。キャンパスのエントランスからのアプローチと中央の軸線は，この新しい建築と緑の空間へと連続し，新しいポーラスの動線へと開放される。

南の翼棟はキャンチレバーのレストランとして立ち上がり，ルーフ・テラスと共に山並みを望む。北の翼棟は大地へと埋め込まれ，「逆さまに」開放された洞窟のような水中庭園を形成する。雨水と中水は連続した流れとなって，この下層階の水盤に集められる。オーディトリアムのリフレクティング・プールからは緩やかに流れる水音が響く。

水の再処理システムは新しい建築の消費電力の15%を供給する屋根面の太陽光発電によって運転される。高強度鉄筋コンクリート，この土地の木材，及びボゴタ・ストーンといった素材の取り合わせは，環境面での新たなる技術革新である。

2011– Institute for Contemporary Art, Virginia Commonwealth University
Richmond, Virginia, U.S.A.

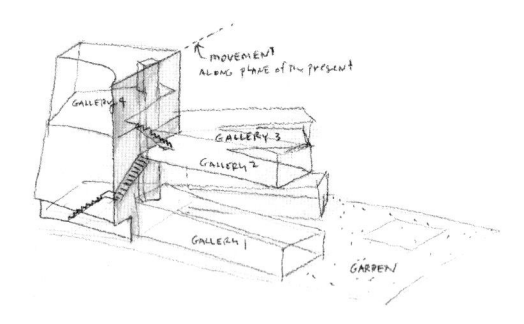

Program

Model: section and elevation view

Sited at the edge of the Virginia Commonwealth University campus in Richmond, Virginia, the new Institute for Contemporary Art will link the University with the surrounding community. On the busiest intersection of Richmond at Broad and Belvidere Streets, the building will form a gateway to the University with an inviting sense of openness. The main entrance is formed by an intersection of the performance space and forum, adding a vertical "Z" component to the "X-Y" movement of the intersection. The torsion of these intersecting bodies is joined by a "plane of the present" to the galleries in "forking time."

The idea of "forking time" suggests that in the world of contemporary art there are many parallel times. The notion of one ongoing time and its "grand narrative" of history is questioned.

The new Institute for Contemporary Art is organized in four galleries, each with a different character. Flexibility allows for four separate exhibitions, one continuous exhibition, or combinations. Galleries can be closed for installations without affecting the circulation to the others. One can begin the sequence through the four galleries by taking the oversized elevator to the top and circling down, or by beginning at the lower gallery of the forum and moving up. Exposed concrete beams and planks in the galleries complement the concrete floors. As flexible spaces, the galleries can accept suspended art or projects anchored to the floor slab.

Vertical movement along the "plane of the present" links the galleries, the performance space, sculpture garden, and forum. Along this architectural promenade, the integration of all the building elements can be experienced in changing views.

The 38,000 sq.ft. building has a double front: one side opens from the city, the other from the sculpture garden to the forum, linking city and campus. On the ground level, the cafe opens directly onto the sculpture garden, as does the ground level gallery. Pivot doors allow opening events to spill out into the garden. Paved in bluestone gravel, the garden is planted with gingko trees. A large reflecting pond of recycled water shapes the sense of this garden as a "thinking field."

The building is an experience of movement in time around the exterior as well as the interior. Approaching on foot from the west (from

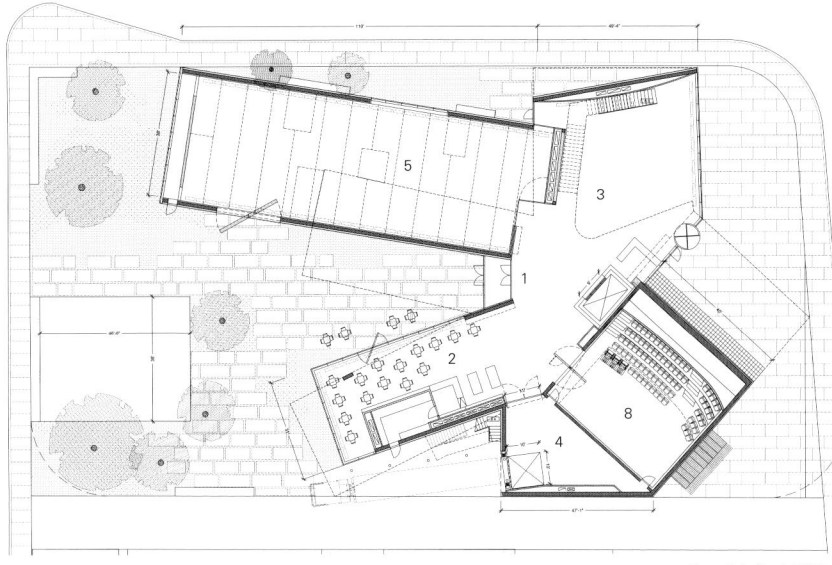

1 ENTRY
2 CAFE
3 FORUM
4 LOADING DOCK
5 GALLERY 1
6 GALLERY 2
7 GALLERY 3
8 PERFORMANCE SPACE
9 STORAGE
10 ART STORAGE

Level 1 S=1:700

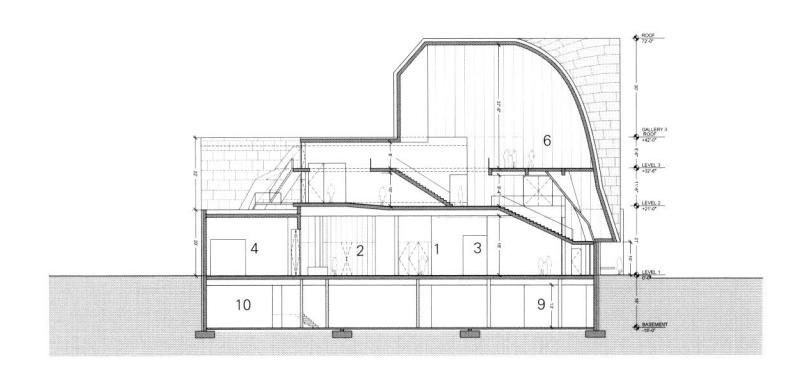

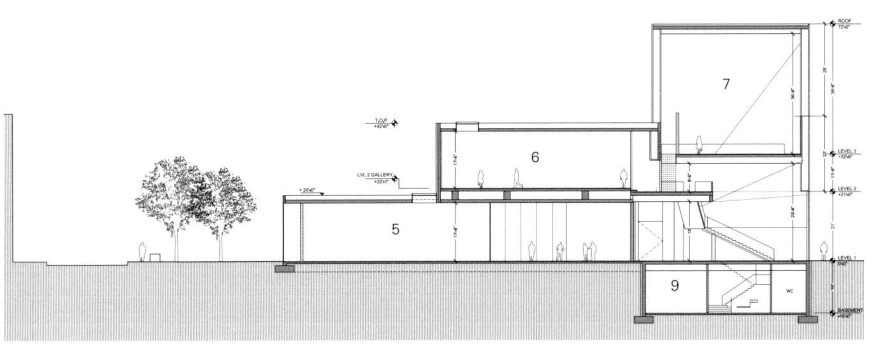

Sections S=1:700

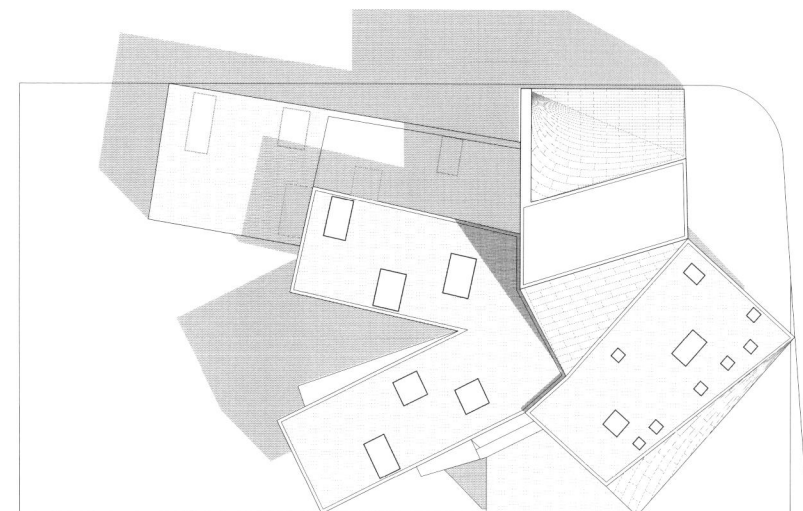

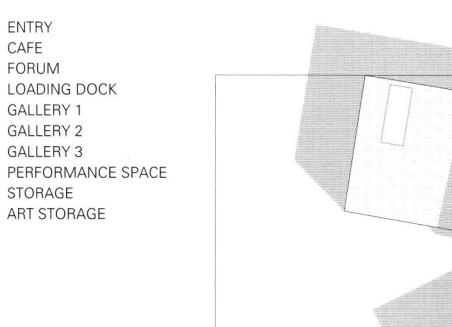

Roof

Level 3

Level 2

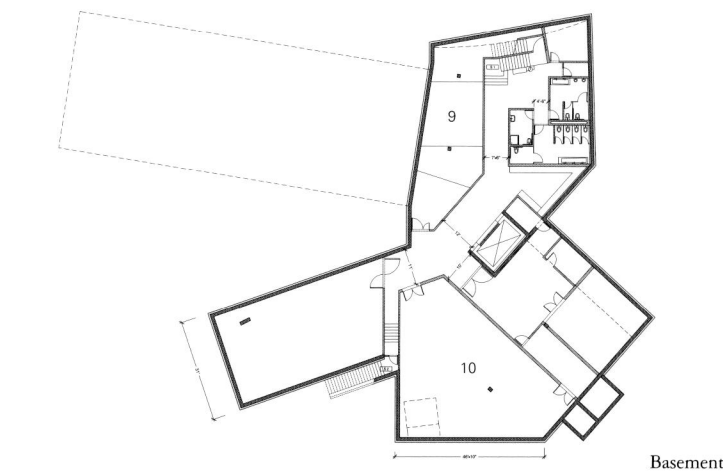

Basement

the University), the building unfolds in the parallax of changing perspectives. As you walk, the crunch of gravel under your feet is complemented by a view that gradually opens to reveal the lobby. If you arrive by car from the north, east, or south, the double vertical geometry in torsion marks a gateway presence, which changes shape as the car passes by. At night glowing planes of obscure glass activate the exterior. Video projections may appear on these obscure glass walls, animating the garden with art.

The flexible performance space has 247 seats and a sprung floor for dance performances. The rear stage wall opens to allow the loading dock to double function as a deeper back stage.

The concrete floors and exposed concrete beams of the building are complemented by the greenish-grey skin (Rheinzink).

The garden roofs include a sculpture terrace on the second level. The building is heated and cooled with geothermal wells. In developing the garden, we envision collaboration with artists for semi-permanent works.

The Institute for Contemporary Art will be a new gateway and catalyst, linking the University and the city of Richmond. With its inviting double-fronted forum opening to a serene sculpture garden, it will provide spatial energy for the most important cutting-edge contemporary art exhibits. Propelled by VCU's top-ranked School of the Arts, the ICA's architecture is an instrument for exhibitions, film screenings, public lectures, performances, symposia, and community events, engaging the University, the city, and beyond.

Concept sketch

Evening view: entrance on center

Evening view: forum facing the busiest intersection of Richmond at Broad and Belvidere Streets

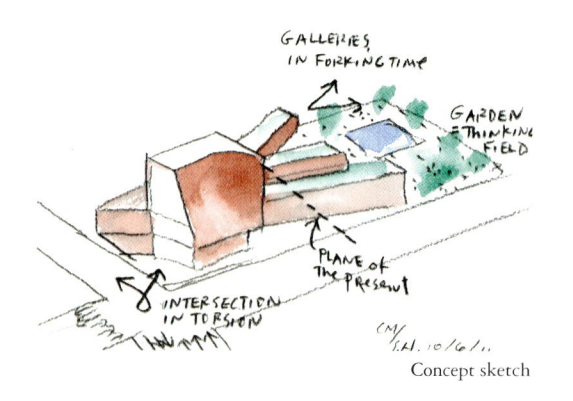

ヴァージニア州立大学現代美術研究所
ヴァージニア州リッチモンドのヴァージニア州立大学キャンパスに位置する新しい現代美術研究所は、大学を地域社会へと結びつけるものである。ブロード・ストリートとベルヴィディア・ストリートの角にあるリッチモンドで最も交通量の多い交差点に面して、この建築は開放性で親しみのある大学への入り口を構成する。主要エントランスはパフォーマンス空間とフォーラムの交差する地点に設けられ、ここではX－Y軸の交差動線に垂直のZ軸が付加されている。これらの空間の交差に対し、「現在平面」によって「分岐時間」のギャラリーに捻れが加えられている。

「分岐時間」の構想は、現代美術の世界に数多く平行する時間軸の存在を暗示するものである。唯一の時間が流れ、そこに「大きな物語」の時代があるという感覚は、正しいものではない。新しい現代美術研究所はお互いに異なる性格の四つのギャラリーで組織されている。ここでは四つの個別展示や、一つの連続した展示、あるいはそれらを組み合わせた展示を柔軟に行うことができる。ギャラリーは他の動線に影響を与えることなく作品の設置のために閉鎖することが可能である。来館者は特大のエレベータで最上階に上がり、そこから四つのギャラリーを見ながら下階へと下り、あるいはフォーラムの低層部のギャラリーから上へと昇るシークエンスを通ることができる。打ち放しコンクリートの梁やギャラリーの厚板が、コンクリートの床を補完している。フレキシブルな空間として、これらのギャラリーでは作品を宙に吊し、床スラブに留めることができる。

「現在平面」に沿って移動する垂直動線は、ギャラリー、パフォーマンス空間、彫刻庭園及びフォーラムを結びつける役割を果たす。このような建築的プロムナードでは構成要素がひとつに統合されて、異なる視線の中に全てを経験することができる。

38,000平方フィート（約3,500平米）の建築は二つのファサードを持つ。一つは都市に開放されたもの、他方は彫刻庭園からフォーラムへと続き、都市とキャンパスとを繋ぐものである。地上レベルではギャラリーと共に、カフェが直接彫刻庭園に開放されている。回転扉によってオープニングイベントの際は、人々は庭園へと溢れ

出ることができる。青石を敷き詰めた庭園にはイチョウの木々が植えられている。再生水による巨大なリフレクティング・ポンドはこの庭園に「思考の場」の雰囲気を与えている。

　この建築は内外部にわたり，時間のなかで身体の動きを経験するためのものである。(大学のある)西側から歩いてゆくと，建築は視線の変化とともに広がり様々なパースペクティブを見せる。歩くにつれて足の下の砂利石が音を立てるのと相まって，視線が緩やかに開かれロビーがその姿を現す。車で北や東，あるいは南側から到着すると2層にわたって垂直に捻れるジオメトリがエントランスとしての存在を示し，車が通り過ぎるのに従いその姿を変える。夜になると不透明なガラス面が輝き，外部に活気をもたらしてくれる。これらの不透明なガラスの壁には映像を投影し，庭園を芸術で彩ることも可能である。

　フレキシブルな247席のパフォーマンス空間にはダンスパフォーマンスのため，防振床が用意されている。また，舞台の背後の壁面を開放すると荷捌き用デッキをバックステージとして利用することもできる。

　この建築のコンクリートの床面と打ち放しのコンクリートの梁は(ラインツィンク社の)緑灰色の表皮と対をなしている。

　庭園の屋根には，2階部分に彫刻テラスが設けられている。この建築は地熱井によって冷暖房を行うことができる。庭園の計画では，半永久的に作品を展示するため芸術家と共同作業を行うことが構想された。

　現代芸術研究所は大学の新しい入り口として，大学をリッチモンドの町へと繋ぐ触媒としての役割を果たすようになるだろう。人々を誘う二つの正面を持つフォーラムは落ち着きのある彫刻庭園へと開放され，最も価値ある最先端の現代芸術の展示を行うために，空間に強度を与えている。

　芸術学部はヴァージニア州立大学を率いる頂点の学部である。現代芸術研究所の建築は，展示，フィルム上映，講義活動，パフォーマンス，シンポジウム，及びコミュニティ活動を，大学と都市とを越えてひとつに結びつけているための道具となる。

Gallery 2 on level 2

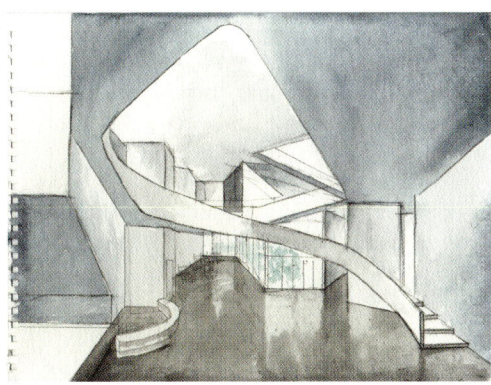

Sketch: forum

Forum with light through opening

Forum: staircase to upper floors. Cafe and entrance on left

In thinking about urbanism and about the growth of cities, and the fact that now more than half the population of the 7 billion people on this earth will be living in cities, one of the most exciting new zones of development is the edge of the city.

Our "Edge of a City" projects are different cases with different forms and typologies, but they all have the strategies of maximum preservation of the landscape, condensing hybrid functions, making green buildings and shaping public space. The first projects, made between 1986 and 1990, were experiments in strategies to counter sprawl at the periphery of contemporary cities. Each of these projects proposed living, working, recreation, and cultural facilities through the utilization of hybrid buildings in new pedestrian sectors that act as social condensers for new communities. Each site was different, requiring a unique architectural response.

The projects in this volume (1999-2012) collect work in China, Turkey and Europe. While China continues to undergo one of the largest population migrations in human history (with 600 million moving from rural to urban living), we focused on proposing new urban typologies which might shape public space and set environmental examples.

In large scale urban works like our Linked Hybrid project in Beijing, we shaped public space with eight skyscrapers linked by bridges; we aimed to make a place of living, working, recreation and culture where we added programs like the cinemateque, the Montessori school, the hotel, and the restaurants. While this project was subject to many regulations, at the edge of cities, typologies might be more open.

At the edge of the city of Ningbo, China we had the opportunity to propose a new city fragment (Ningbo Fine Grain, 2008). We proposed the grain of this new giant project would be very fine. Rather than big box buildings, rather than programs that become unwieldy and create a lack of public space we envisioned the entire project as a fine grain. A random process, computer-driven, gave form to public space and hybrid buildings. Ningbo is a water city where canals and living by water can become one of the great qualities. The condition of being by the canal, the condition being by water is really primary to the fine grain urban plan.

In Hangzhou we won a large competition based on the idea of "Shan-Shui," which is "mountain-water" (Shan-Shui Hangzhou, 2009-). The aim is to reuse these old factory buildings at the edge of Hangzhou that were once used for oxygen manufacturing and boiler manufacturing. The idea is to unite them in a condition of merging landscape and architecture and creating a balance between landscape and architecture. Hangzhou is a water town with many canals; there was just one main canal on our site, so we introduced the concept of "canal spreaders" to multiply the canals into five and create a new

アーバニズムや都市の成長に関する考察において、また、70億人という地球上の人口の過半数がやがて都市居住を始めるようになるという事実において、都市開発の分野において最も新しく、刺激的な場所は都市の周縁部である。

「都市の周縁」とは、形態やタイポロジーが様々に異なる条件における複数の計画である。これらには全て、自然をできる限り保護し、ハイブリッドな機能を凝縮し、グリーン・ビルディングとパブリック・スペースをつくりだすという共通の方法論を備えている。初めてのプロジェクトは1986年から1990年にかけて計画されたもので、現代の都市の外縁のスプロール化に対抗する方法論に関する実験である。これらの計画ではいずれも、新しいコミュニティの社会的凝縮器として機能する歩行空間を通して、ハイブリッド・ビルディングを利用した居住、オフィス、レクリエーション、及び文化施設が提案された。それぞれの敷地条件ごとに、その場所に固有の建築的応答が引き出された。

この作品集第2巻(1999-2012)には、中国、トルコ、及びヨーロッパの計画が集められている。(農村部から都市部への居住者が6億人に及ぶ)中国が最も激しい人口移動を歴史上初めて経験する一方で、私たちはパブリック・スペースを構成し、環境保護の例証となるような、新しい都市のタイポロジーを提案することに集中してきた。

アーバン・スケールの計画では、北京のリンクド・ハイブリッド(2003-09)で、パブリック・スペースとブリッジで繋げられた8棟のスカイスクレーパーを設計した。居住、オフィス、レクリエーション、及び文化施設といった目的の他に、ここではシネマテーク、モンテッソーリ教育の学校施設、ホテル、及びレストランといったプログラムも加えられている。都市の周縁のこの計画には多くの規制がかけられていたものの、開放的なタイポロジーが模索された。

中国の寧波の都市周縁部では、新しい都市的断片を提案する機会に恵まれた(寧波ファイン・グレイン(微粒子)計画、2008)。ここでは、新しい大規模計画に一粒の種を播くことができれば非常に素晴らしいものになると考えられた。巨大な箱型の建築や、不便でパブリック・スペースの欠如したものになりがちなプログラムではなく、全体計画は微粒子的に構想された。コンピュータによって生成されるランダムなプロセスが、パブリック・スペースとハイブリッド・ビルディングに形態を付与する。寧波は水の都である。ここでは運河や水のある生活が、価値あるもののひとつとなるように思われた。運河がすぐ近くにあるということ、水辺がすぐ近くにあるということ。これらが一粒の種となり、都市計画の骨格となった。

杭州では「山水」思想で、大規模コンペに勝利することができた(杭州「山水」計画、2009-)。これはかつて酸素やボイラーの製造を行っていた杭州の周縁の古い工場建築を再利用するためのものである。これらの工場群を結びつけることで、自然と建築が融合し、自然と建築のあいだに関係性が生み出される。杭州は運河の多い水の都である。ここではちょうど、1本の大運河が敷

5 Edge of a City
都市の周縁

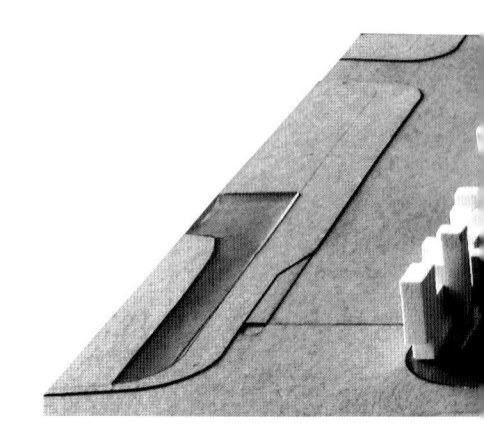

morphology. The linearity of canal spreaders then rise up to form what we call "lantern towers", which refer back to the great stone lanterns at Westlake in Hangzhou. Shan-Shui will be a new sector of living by the water, connecting to the restored and reprogrammed factory buildings, the group on the south will be by David Chipperfield and the group on the north is by Herzog and deMeuron. The transformation of this old industrial city edge site into a vibrant quarter of living, working, recreation, and culture has an inspiring balance of old and new; a balance of architecture and landscape.

Our Dense Pack project for Akbuk (2006-), Turkey is sited on a blank landscape on the Aegean Sea. The program is for an independent community with living, working and cultural facilities. In order to preserve the maximum natural landscape, the project is arranged in three "dense pack" elements of typological variety. These islands of architecture float in a restored natural landscape and utilize solar power, recycled water and solar desalination. As an exemplary construction, recycled materials are used. The adjacency of diverse programs and the preservation of a fragile natural landscape set this project as an example of a balance of architecture and landscape.

At the edge of the city of Nanning, China, we proposed a Green Urban Laboratory (2002) reconfiguring a ruined peninsula into a linear town in a figure-eight form, which would preserve the existing mountain topography. A pedestrian community of low buildings with living space above and working space and shops below characterize the main typology. Rising above along this linear strip there are seven "mountains" which include a variety of cultural programs. This Edge city is connected to the center of Nanning via high-speed light rail.

Our most ambitious realization the Horizontal Skyscraper (Vanke Center, 2006-09) in Shenzhen is a hybrid building containing offices, a hotel, condominiums, a conference center, a 500-seat auditorium, restaurants and cafes. The strategy to raise the building to the height limit of 35-meters creates a large public space at grade. As Shenzhen has a tropical climate, the shade and shadow of the hovering building are positive attributes. Due to its height of 20 meters, tropical vegetation has room to thrive everywhere in this public space.

Countering sprawl and preserving and creating natural landscapes were primary aims of the American Edge of a City projects, In Shenzhen, China, the city has grown up around the horizontal skyscraper so rapidly that it is no longer an edge, but a center with large tropical gardens of much needed public space.

Steven Holl

地の中を流れていた。そこでこの運河を5本に分岐して新しい形態構造を生み出すために,「キャナル・スプレッダー」という概念が導入された。直進的なキャナル・スプレッダーは垂直に延びて,「ランタン・タワー」を形成する。これは杭州西湖の巨大な石灯籠からの引用である。「山水」は水際の新しい居住セクターになる予定である。修復され,新しくプログラムされた工場建築は居住区と結びつけられ,デヴィッド・チッパーフィールドは南街区を,ヘルツォーク&ド・ムーロンは北街区を担当する予定である。この古い工業都市の周縁の敷地は,住み,働き,休息し,文化に触れることのできる活気ある地域へと変化する。これは新旧の関係性,建築と自然の関係性を刺激する計画である。

トルコのアクビュクにあるデンス・パック(2006-)は,エーゲ海の何もない自然のなかに位置している。プログラムは居住,オフィス,文化施設のある独立したコミュニティのためのものである。自然のランドスケープを最大限保護するために,この計画は多様なタイポロジーを持つ3つの「デンス・パック」に従って配置されている。これらの建築は太陽光発電,再利用水,太陽熱脱塩を利用し,再生された自然のランドスケープに浮遊する。この地域を代表する建築として,再生材が使用された。多様なプログラムは近接し,繊細な自然のランドスケープが保全される。この計画は建築と自然との関係性の例証として位置づけられている。

中国の南寧の都市周縁部では,グリーン・アーバン・ラボラトリー(2002)として,荒廃した半島を8の字型の直線的な市街地として再整備するように計画を提案した。ここでは現存する丘陵の地形の保全が試みられている。上層階の居住空間と,下層階のオフィス空間と商業店舗で構成される低層建築による歩行者のコミュニティが,このタイポロジーの特徴的である。直線的な帯状の空間に沿って7つの「山脈」が立ち上がり,多様な文化的プログラムが内包される。この周縁都市は,南寧市中心部と高速LRTによって結ばれている。

深圳のホリゾンタル・スカイスクレーパー(ヴァンケ・センター,2006-09)は,実現した最も大胆なハイブリッド・ビルディングである。ここにはオフィス,ホテル,コンドミニアム,コンファレンス・センター,500席のオーディトリアム,レストラン,及びカフェが収容されている。建築を35mの高さ制限まで持ち上げるという方法論は,巨大な一つのパブリック・スペースを生み出している。深圳は熱帯気候である。そのため,浮遊する建築が落とす陰影は,積極的なものとして捉えられている。パブリック・スペースの高さは20mに及ぶため,熱帯植物はあらゆる場所に繁茂することができる。

都市のスプロール化に対抗し,自然のランドスケープをつくり保存することが,アメリカの「都市の周縁」の計画の主な目的である。中国の深圳では都市がホリゾンタル・スカイスクレーパーを取り巻くように急速に成長し,もはや周縁を形成することはないが,その中心にあるのは巨大な熱帯の庭園と,より一層重要なパブリック・スペースの存在である。

(スティーヴン・ホール)

1999 Centro JVD, Housing and Hotel
Guadalajara, Mexico

Aerial Range (behind) and Terrene Range (front)

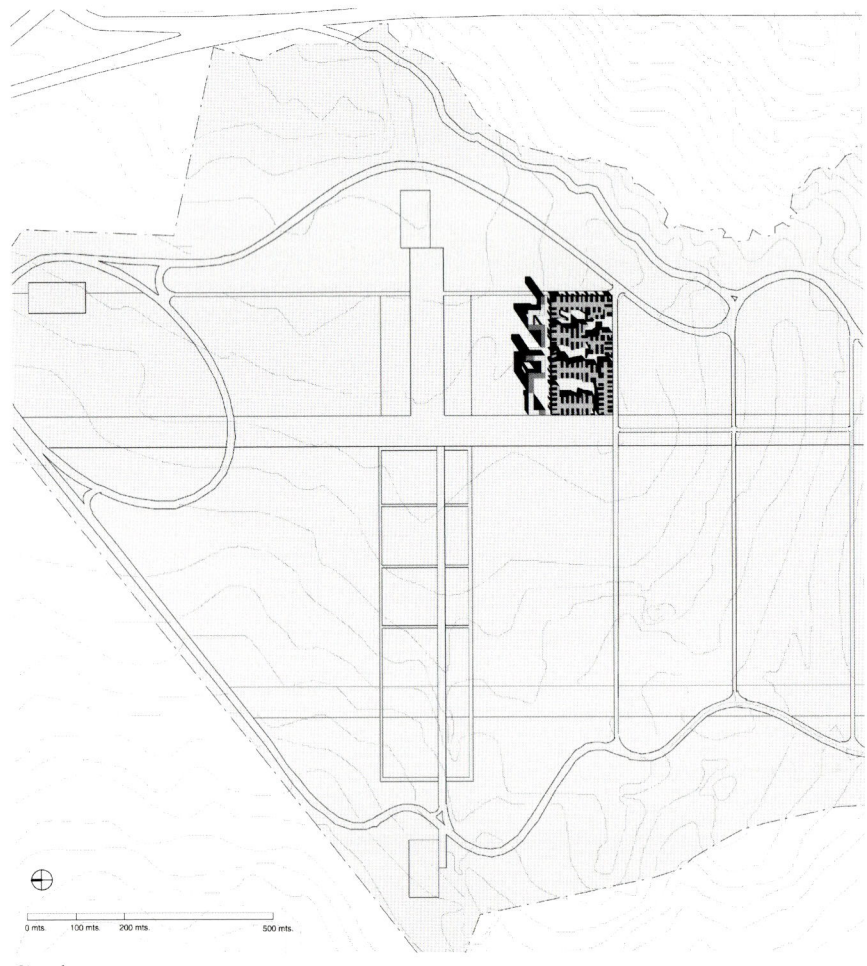

Site plan

Living on Two Horizons. As part of the initial phase of the new Cultural Center project, this sector of 200 housing units and 150 hotel rooms is divided into an Aerial (upper) Range and a Terrene (lower) Range. As one approaches the town from above, the distinct character of the two horizons charges a sense of arrival. One stands as a field, the other as frame; solids throwing shadows and voids catching light.

The Aerial Range hovers 20 meters above the ground of the former cornfield. Close views of the new museum and its sculpture garden as well as distant views of the green hills are framed. The interlocking sections offer each apartment and hotel room north and south views. The Aerial Range is extroverted toward distant views and the Terrene Range is introspective focusing towards garden courts. The Ranges contain a hybrid of hotel and housing with garden hotel rooms along the north of the Terrene Range and permanent apartments in the Aerial Range. This allows for adjustment and flexibility.

Silent Interval Spaces are cut through the mat of the Terrene Range using the geometry of the shadows from the Aerial Range. In each of the Interval Spaces, back-reflected color gaps mark the entry to the garden houses and project light and a wash of color to the parking level below, facilitating orientation.

Two spatial horizons suggest two time horizons. The ancient Mexican Calendar has 18 months of 20 days each. There are 18 arms in the Aerial Range. The five "interval spaces" carved from the Terrene Range correspond to the ancient Mexican Epochs. Each of these spaces give entry to 20 houses.

The in-between space of the Aerial Range frames an east-west perspective. This magnified spatial center has no ends.

Construction is in white tilt-up concrete, cable trusses and bead-blasted aluminum.

Sketch: house perspective

House perspective

Aerial Range

Sketch: upper stratum/lower stratum and shadow

JVDセンター、集合住宅およびホテル

住むための2本の水平線。新しい文化センターの第一期計画の一部として、200の住居ユニットと150のホテルの客室からなるこのセクターは、(上部の)空中レンジと(下部の)地上レンジに分かれている。飛行機でこの町に到着すると、くっきりとした2本の水平線が人々を暖かく迎えてくれる。一方はフィールドとして、他方はフレームとして、ソリッドは影を落とし、ヴォイドは光を受け止めている。

空中レンジはかつてのトウモロコシ畑の地表面から20m上空に浮遊している。間近には新しいミュージアムと彫刻庭園を、遠景には緑の丘への眺望を眼中に収めることができる。各々のブロックを組み合わせることで、集合住宅とホテルの客室からは南北に眺望が広がっている。空中レンジは遠くの眺望に対して開かれ、地上レンジは中庭に向けて閉じられている。地上レンジの北側には庭付きのホテルの客室が、空中レンジには定住型住宅がある。それぞれのレンジはホテルと住宅の複合体である。この空間は適応性とフレキシビリティを備えている。

空中レンジの落とす影の持つジオメトリーによって、地上レンジを中間領域が静かに貫通している。各々の中間領域では、色の異なるバックライトがガーデン・ハウスへの入り口を示す。光と溢れるような色彩が階下の駐車場を照らし、方向表示の役割を果たしている。

空間の2枚の水平線はタイム・ホライゾンを暗示する。古代メキシコ暦はひと月20日、1年は18ヶ月ある。空中レンジには18の部門がある。地上レンジに刻まれた5本の「中間領域」は、古代メキシコ時代に対応するものである。これらの空間には各々20ずつ、住居エントランスが割り当てられている。

空中レンジのあいだの空間は、東西への視線を生み出している。この誇張された空間の中心には終わりというものがない。

建設には白色のティルトアップ・コンクリート、ケーブルトラス、及びビーズブラスト加工のアルミニウムが用いられる。

Eighth floor

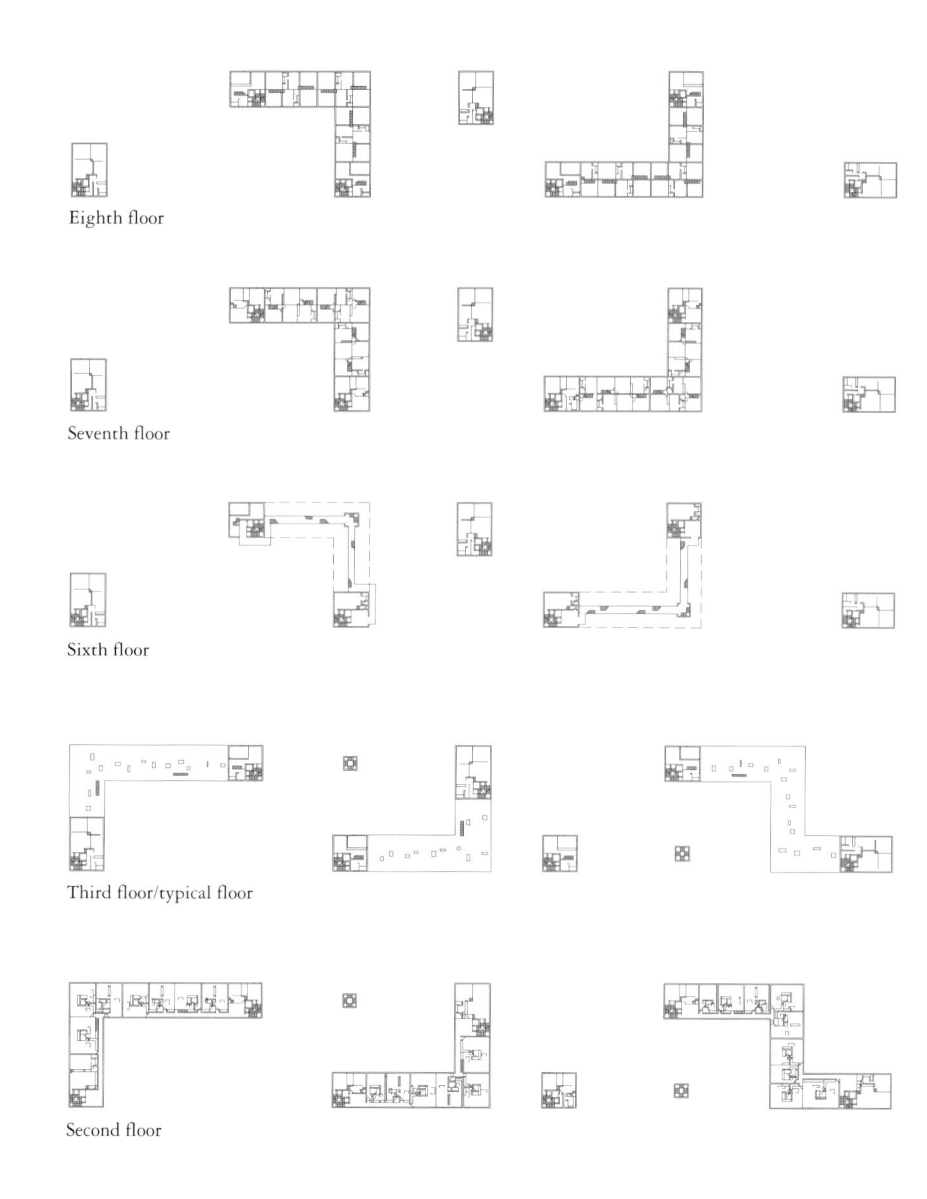

Seventh floor

Sixth floor

Third floor/typical floor

Second floor

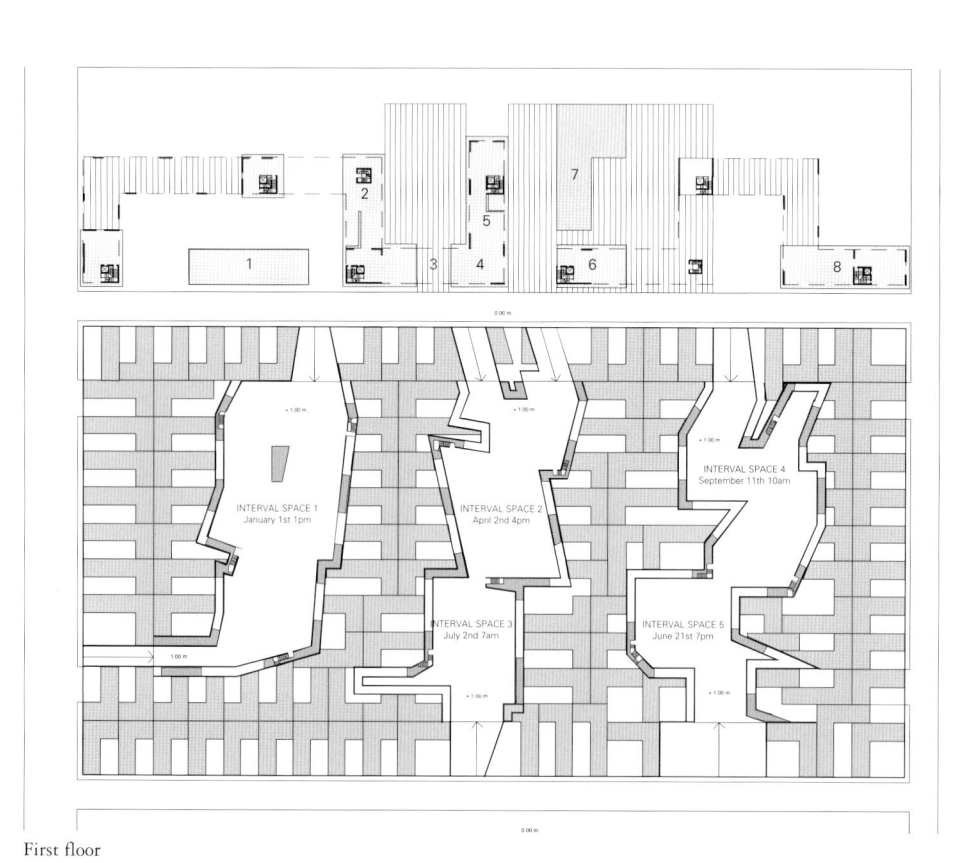

First floor

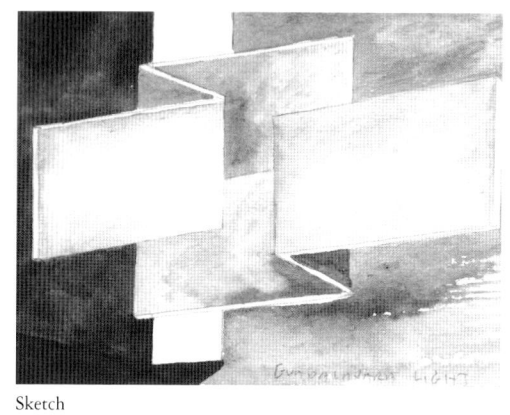

Sketch

INTERVAL SPACE 1
January 1st 1pm

INTERVAL SPACE 2
April 2nd 4pm

INTERVAL SPACE 3
July 2nd 7am

INTERVAL SPACE 4
September 11th 10am

INTERVAL SPACE 5
June 21st 7pm

1 CHILDREN DAY CARE CENTER
2 CHECK IN
3 ENTRY
4 WAITING
5 BAR/CAFE
6 POOL EQUIPMENT
7 POOL
8 COMMUNITY ROOM
9 LAUNDRY
10 WORKSHOP
11 STORAGE
12 KITCHEN

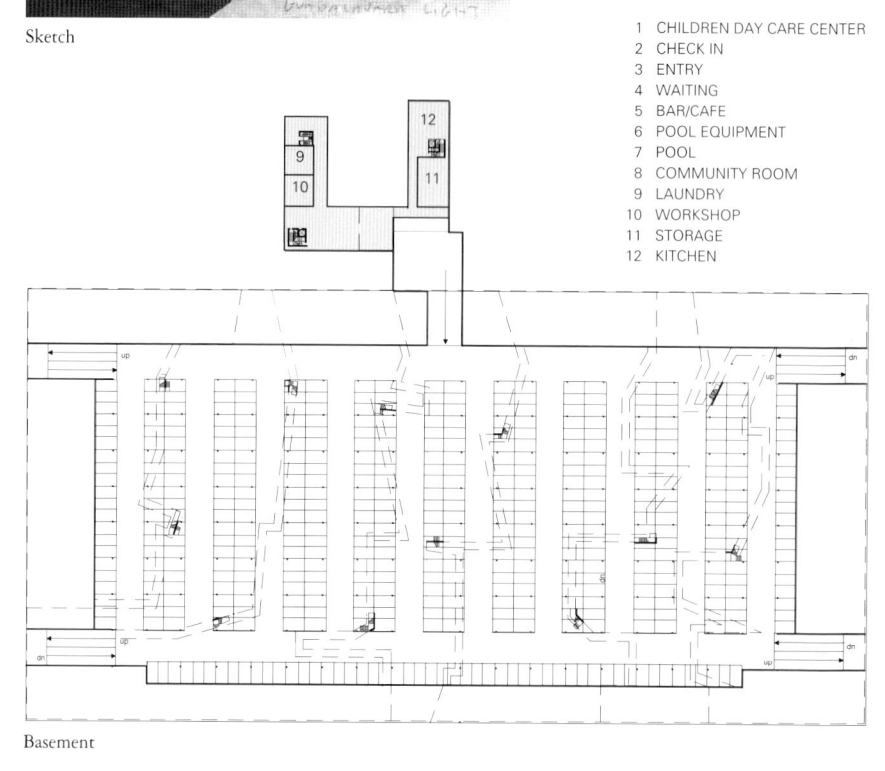

Basement

II-270

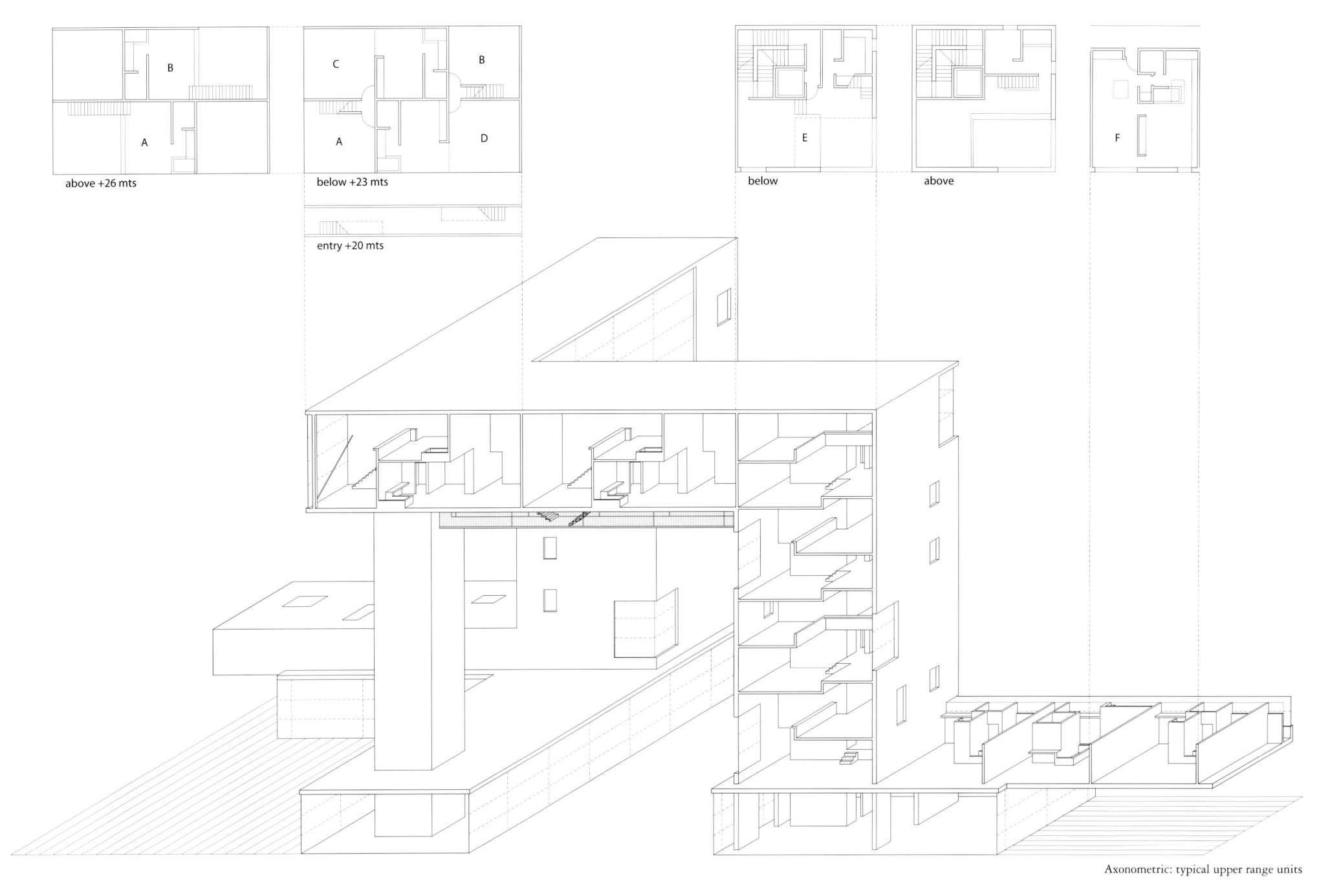

above +26 mts

below +23 mts

entry +20 mts

below   above

Axonometric: typical upper range units

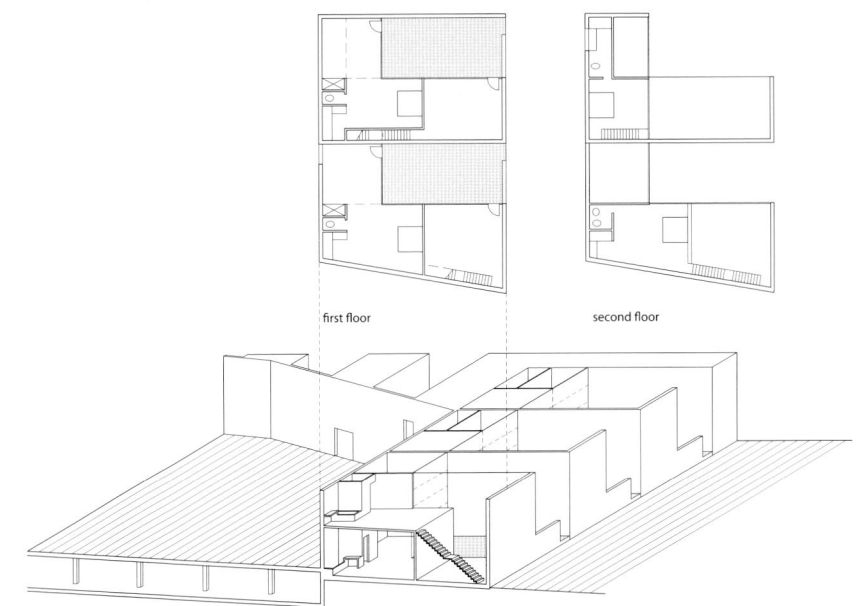

first floor   second floor

second floor

3-bedroom apartment   2-bedroom apartment
first floor

Axonometric: typical hotel rooms

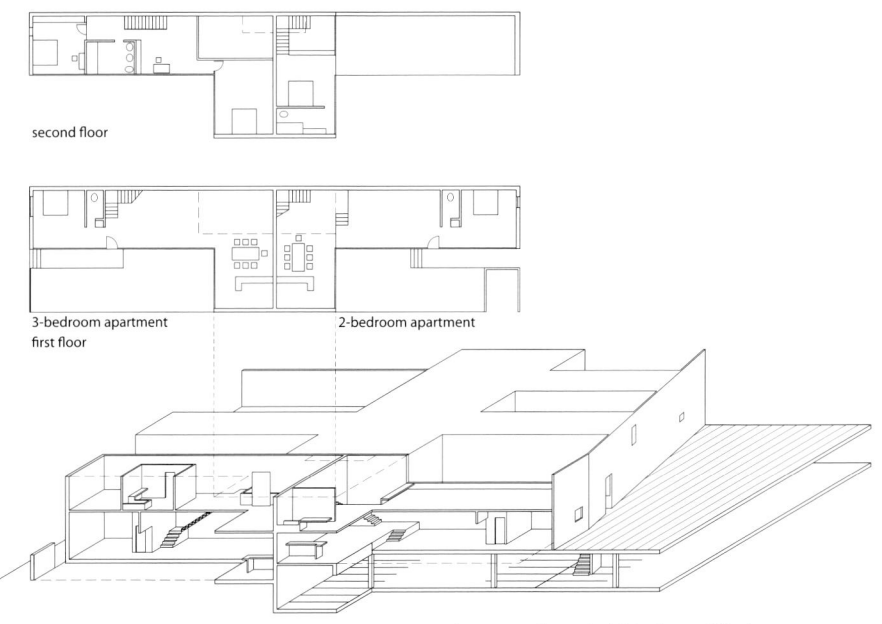

Axonometric: typical 3 bedroom/2 bedroom apartment

II-271

New Town: Green Urban Laboratory
2002 Nanning, China

Athletic Park

SEVEN MOUNTAINS

DENSE PACK TOWN

URBAN STREET

FOUR LANDSCAPES

Sketches: dense pack town

1 FOLDED STREET MOUNTAIN	8 LIGHT RAIL TRAIN
2 CULTURAL MOUNTAIN	9 NEW CHINESE GARDEN
3 ROCK MOUNTAIN	10 CAFE PAVILION
4 KNOWLEDGE MOUNTAIN	11 SCHOOL PLAYGROUND
5 IMPLOSION MOUNTAIN	12 ATHLETIC PARK
6 SUBTRACTION MOUNTAIN	13 ORGANIC GOLF COURSE
7 GATE MOUNTAIN	

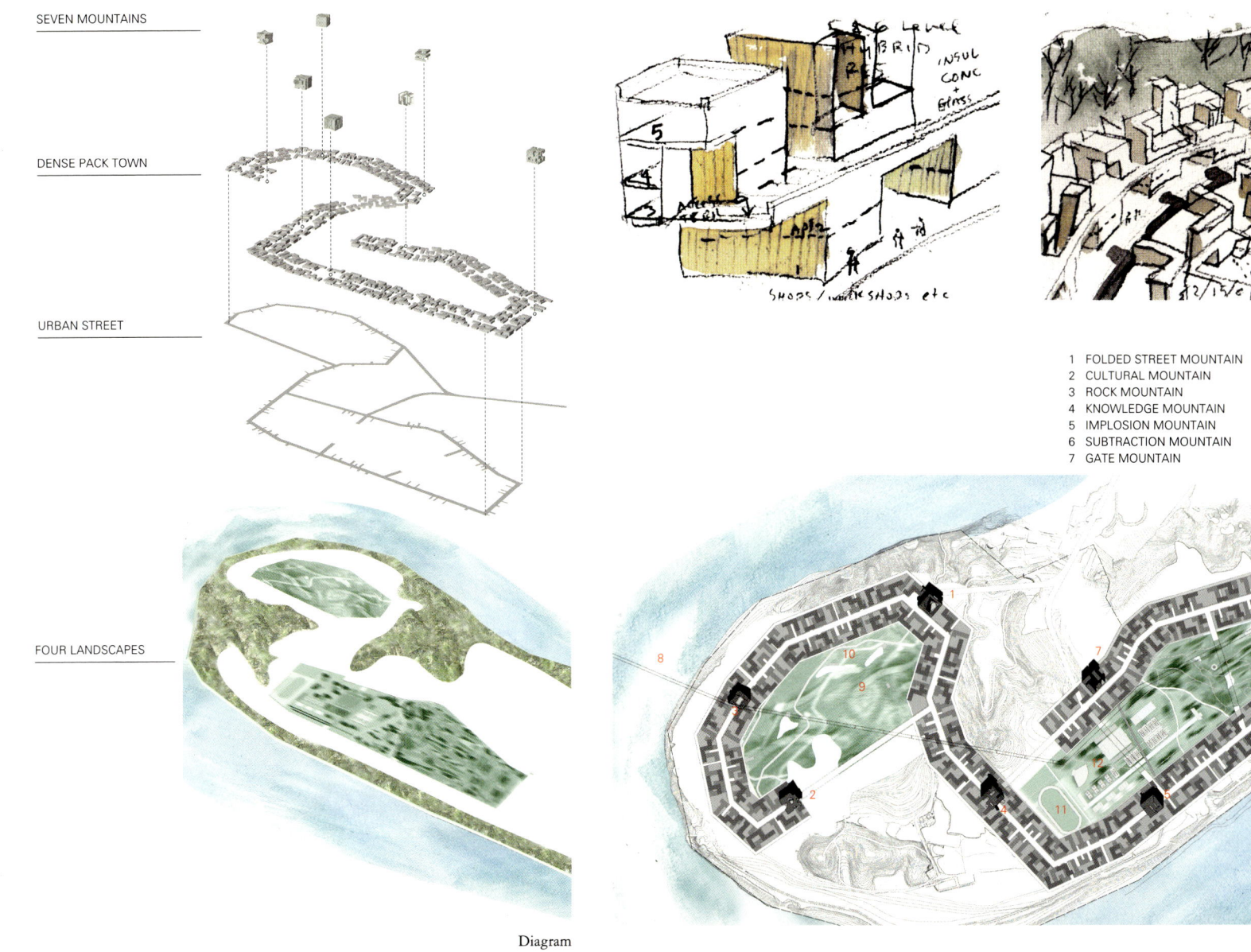

Diagram

Site plan

II-273

Folded Street Mountain

Site
Liusha Peninsula in Nanning was once a beautiful rolling ridge of green which was likened to the tail of a dragon whose head lay in Qingxiu Mountain Park. The green dragon was sliced by an aborted development in the early 1990s leaving a muddy flat plateau in its midst.

Program
For this new town of approximately 27,000 residence, 9,000 units of housing (of 120 square meters per unit on average) are planned. The town will also include schools, shops, hotel and recreational facilities, as well as a Beiqiu anthropology museum and the rebuilt Tianning Buddhist Temple.

Concept
The overall shape of the town results from an organic link between idea and form. A figure-8 plan takes its form from the shape of the peninsula together with the preservation of two large existing green hills. The linear city loops back over itself like nature's cycles.

Two new central parks are contained by the linear looped form. One offers recreational and athletic activities; the other has cultural elements such as modern Chinese gardens, meditation pavilions, cafes, and school playgrounds.

A new light rail line is proposed to connect to the heart of Nanning with three stops within the new town and continuing to Qingxiu Mountain Park, the great feature of the peninsula. Together the old and new form an expanded tourist destination.

Low Scale (grass roofs)
The main housing aims for a maximum porosity with natural ventilation and shading.

Precast concrete sections with 50% wall and 50% window are basic structural elements forming porous architecture. Deep set operable windows allow for natural sun shading. Green roofs are hydroponic vegetable gardens accessible to the residents.

Within a strictly defined building envelope, the aim of individuation in housing is achieved through overlapping spatial configurations.

High Scale (mountains)
Hybrid buildings of multiple stories (with a defined cubic envelope of 60 m x 60 m x 60 m) yield rich urban experiences with multiple functions and views over the garden city. The master plan allows for the eventual construction of 7 mountain buildings, which could be constructed in phases.

Following the proposed mountains are described in order of construction:

1. Folded street mountain
   - Shops connected by a stepped ramp
   - 100 room hotel
   - Public observation roof with café (Tourist destination: Green Town scientific exhibition ongoing)
2. Cultural mountain
   - Schools
   - Bieqiu anthropology museum
   - Monastic cells & Tianning Temple at top
3. Rock mountain
   - Clad in local rough cut stone
   - Train station
   - Bike and auto garage
   - Offices
   - Community meeting room
   - Rooftop observation deck
4. Knowledge mountain
   - Schools / classrooms
   - Auditoriums
   - Faculty offices
   - Offices / workspaces
   - Rooftop library and reading rooms
5. Implosion mountain
   - Media Center
   - Cinemas
   - Digital health club
   - Parking
6. Subtraction mountain
   - Train station
   - Schools at ground level adjoining playground
   - Offices, work and studio space
7. Gate mountain
   - Schools at ground level
   - Workshop / shops
   - Luxury apartments
   - Hotel

Green Laboratory
The new city is to be a model of the underlying principles that govern natural cycles on earth; and in the universe. The most advanced ecological/architectural systems and techniques will be explored, creating an added attraction to eco-tourists (with economic consequences).

Some aspects include:

a. Solar power by arrays of Gallium arsenide cells; 30% more efficient than current silicon cells.
b. Natural ventilation through natural passive solar shading walls boosted by solar powered fans.
c. Geothermal cooling from river
d. Recycled water system using the latest treatment technologies
e. Ecosystem standards of non-polluting transportation; light rail connection, electrical hybrid cars, bike and pedestrian paths

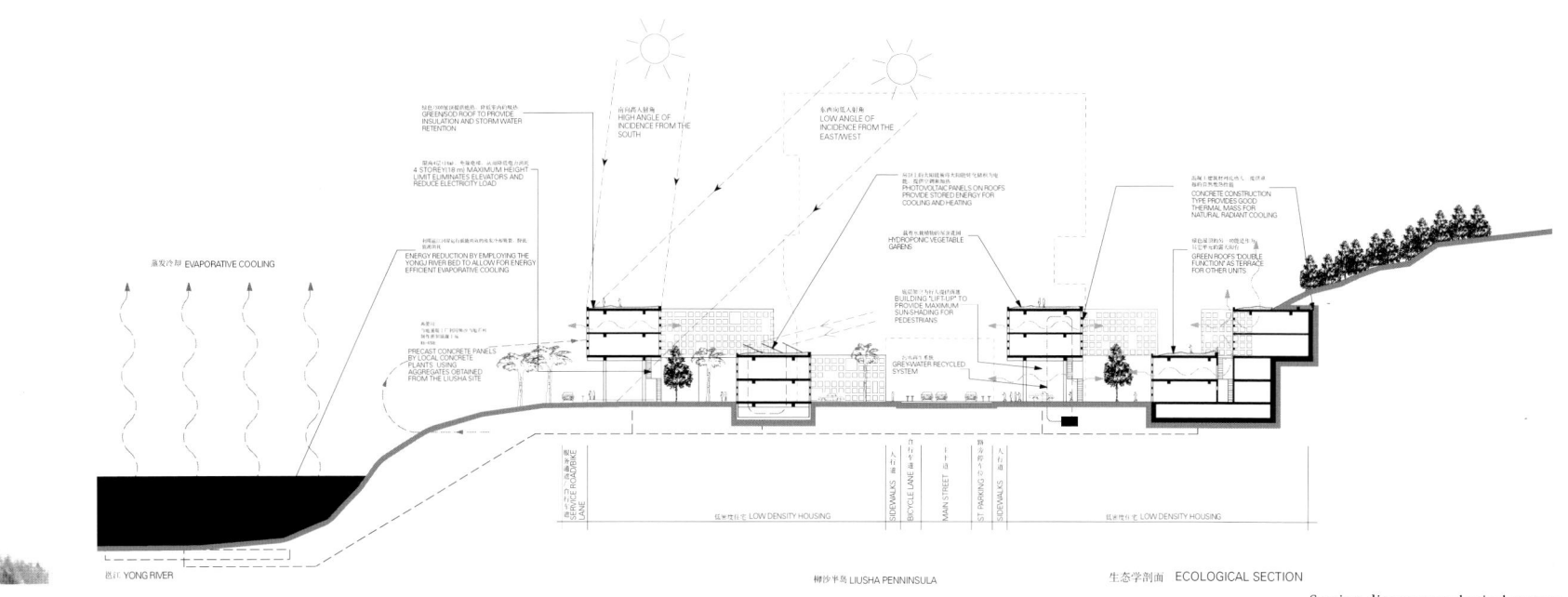

ニュータウン：グリーン・アーバン・ラボラトリー
[敷地]
南寧市の, 川に突き出た柳沙半島は, かつては緑に包まれた起伏する美しい尾根を構成し, さながら, 頭を青秀山公園に横たえる竜の尾のように見えた。緑の竜は, 1990年代初頭の, 中断されてしまった開発で切り刻まれ, その真ん中に泥土の平らな台地を残したままになっている。

[プログラム]
このニュータウンには, 約27,000戸の低層住宅, 9,000戸から成るハウジング (平均面積は120m²) が計画されている。この町には, 学校, 店舗, ホテル, レクリエーション施設, 貝丘人類学博物館, 再建された天寧寺も含まれることになるだろう。

[コンセプト]
町全体の形は, アイディアと形態の有機的な連携から生まれている。8の字型のプランは, 半島の形と, 緑に包まれた大きな2つの丘を保存することから考えられた。線形の都市は, 自然の循環のように輪を描いて自らの上に戻ってくる。

　輪を描くリニアな形態によって, 新しい中央公園が2つ, そのなかに納められる。一方はレクリエーションや運動の場を提供し, 他方は, 現代的な中国庭園, 瞑想のパビリオン, カフェ, 学校の運動場などの文化的な場を備える。

　南寧の中心を結び, ニュータウン内で3つの駅に停まり, 半島の大きな特徴である青秀山公園へ続く新しい軽鉄道が提案されている。新しいものと古いものが一つになって, 大きな広がりを持つ, ツーリストの目的地を形成する。

[低いスケール (草屋根)]
メインのハウジングは, 自然通気が可能で日除けのついた, 最大限多孔性の建物を目指す。

50％が壁, 50％が窓となったプレキャスト・コンクリートの部材が, 多孔性建築を構成する基本的な構造要素である。深く後退させて設置した開け閉めできる窓が, 自然の日差しを遮る。緑の屋根は, 住民が入れる水耕法による菜園である。

厳格に既定された建物外壁のなかで, ハウジング内の独立性は, 重なり合う空間配置によって達成される。

[高いスケール (山)]
高層で構成されたハイブリッド・ビル (60m×60m×60mの明瞭な輪郭を持つキュービックな外壁に包まれている) は多様な機能とガーデン・シティを見晴らす眺めによって, 豊かな都市体験をもたらす。マスター・プランは, 最終的には段階的に7棟のマウンテン・ビルの建設を予定する。

　以下に提案しているマウンテン・ビルを建設の順に説明する。

1. 折り畳まれたストリート・マウンテン
—階段を刻んだランプによってつながれた店舗
—100室のホテル
—カフェのあるパブリックな屋上展望台 (ツーリストの目的地：グリーン・タウンの科学展覧会が進行中)

2. 文化の山
—学校
—貝丘人類学博物館
—頂上に, 僧坊と天寧寺

3. 岩の山
—地元産の切石で被覆
—鉄道駅
—バイクと車のガレージ
—オフィス
—コミュニティの集会室
—屋上の展望デッキ

4. 知識の山
—学校／教室

—オーディトリアム
—教職員室
—オフィス／ワークスペース
—屋上図書室と閲覧室

5. 内部破裂する山
—メディア・センター
—シネマ
—デジタル・ヘルスクラブ
—パーキング

6. 減法の山
—鉄道駅
—運動場に隣接して1階に学校
—オフィス, ワーク／スタジオ・スペース

7. 門の山
—1階に学校
—ワークショップ／店舗
—高級アパート
—ホテル

[グリーン・ラボラトリー]
新しい街は, 地球と宇宙の自然の循環を支配する法則を強調するモデルとなるだろう。最新のエコロジカルな建築システムと技術を探求し, エコ＝ツーリスト (経済的帰結と共に) に対するさらなる魅力をつくりだす。

含まれるいくつかの局面：

a. ガリウムと素電池の配列による太陽光発電。現在のシリコン電池より30％効率がよい。

b. 自然のパッシブソーラーの日除け壁を通した自然換気。太陽光発電によるファンによって効果を高める。

c. 川からの地熱冷房。

d. 最新の処理技術を使用した水の再利用システム。

e. 汚染のない交通によるエコシステム規格：軽鉄道による接続, ハイブリッドな電気自動車, 自転車と歩行者道路。

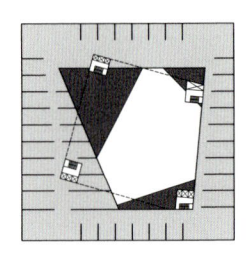

Implosion Mountain (left) and Knowledge Mountain (right)

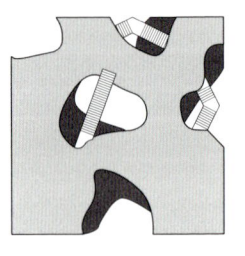

1. 交叠街道之山
各种商店沿续步台阶螺旋面上，最后到达具有100个房间的宾馆，以及设有咖啡茶室的观景平台。持续的绿色城市科技展览成为旅游景点。

FOLDED STREET MOUNTAIN
- THE STEPPED RAMP SECTION SPIRALS UP WITH SHOPS OF ALL KINDS ARRIVING AT A 100 ROOM HOTEL AND OBSERVATION ROOF WITH CAFÉ.
(TOURIST DESTINATION: GREEN TOWN SCIENTIFIC EXHIBITION ONGOING)

2. 文化之山
- 学校
- 贝丘人类学博物馆
- 顶部为禅房和天宁寺

CULTURAL MOUNTAIN
- SCHOOLS
- BEIQIU ANTHROPOLOGY MUSEUM
- MONASTIC CELLS & TIANNING TEMPLE AT TOP

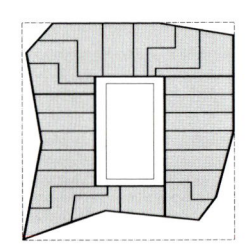

3. 岩石之山
(用当地毛坯岩石作墙面)
- 轻轨电车站、自行车停放处和停车房
- 办公室
- 社区会议室
- 楼顶观景台

ROCK MOUNTAIN
(LOCAL ROUGH CUT STONE FACED)
- RAIL STATION AND BIKE AND AUTO GARAGE
- OFFICES (TOWN OFFICIALS' OFFICE)
- COMMUNITY MEETING ROOM
- ROOFTOP OBSERVATION DECK

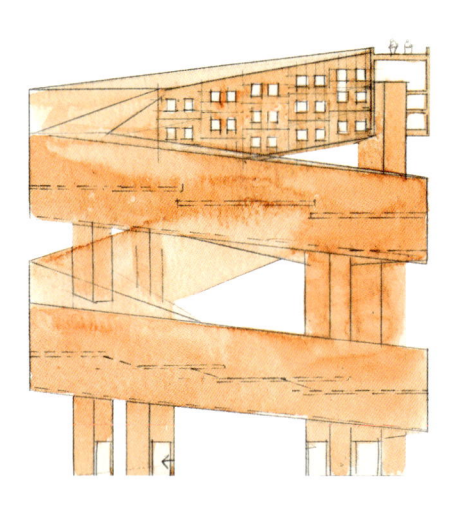

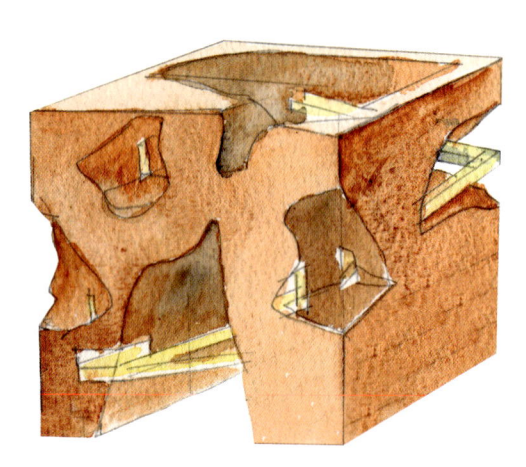

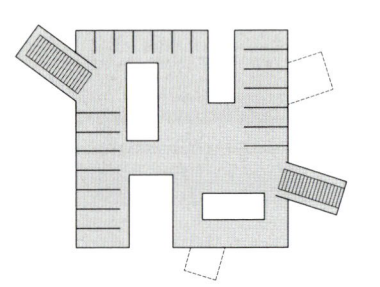

4. 知识之山
- 学校 / 教室
- 大礼堂
- 教师办公室
- 其它办公和工作空间

KNOWLEDGE MOUNTAIN
- SCHOOLS / CLASSROOMS
- AUDITORIUMS
- FACULTY OFFICES
- OTHER OFFICES / WORKSPACES

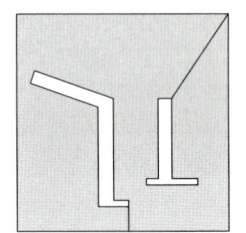

5. 内聚之山
- 媒体中心
- 影剧院
- 数码化健身房
- 地下停车房

IMPLOSION MOUNTAN
- MEDIA CENTER
- CINEMAS
- DIGITAL HEALTH CLUB
- PARKING BELOW

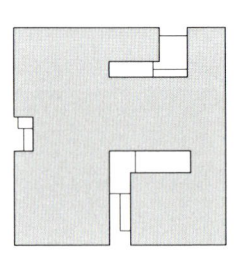

6. 减法之山
- 轻轨电车站
- 办公室、工作室和艺术创作室
- 低层为与室外活动场所邻接的学校

SUBTRACTION MOUNTAIN
- TRAIN STATION
- OFFICES, WORK AND STUDIO SPACE
- SCHOOLS AT BASE NEXT TO PLAYGROUND

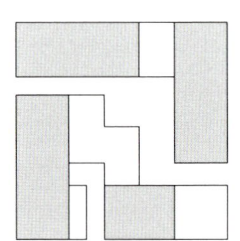

7. 城门之山
- 豪华公寓
- 宾馆
- 作坊 / 商店
- 低层为学校

GATE MOUNTAIN
- LUXURY APARTMENTS
- HOTEL
- WORKSHOP / SHOPS
- SCHOOLS AT BASE

Seven Mountains

Dense pack town

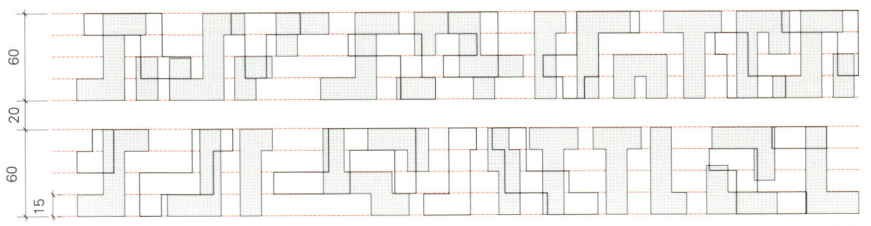

Standard urban module

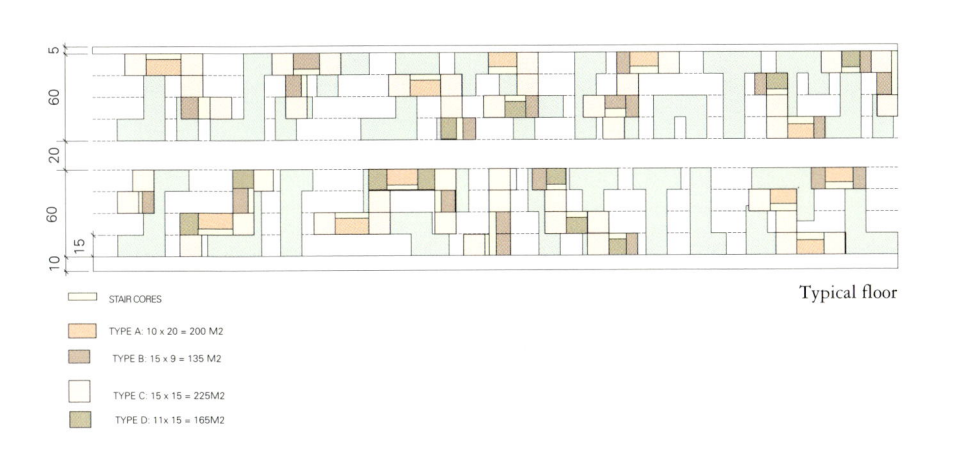

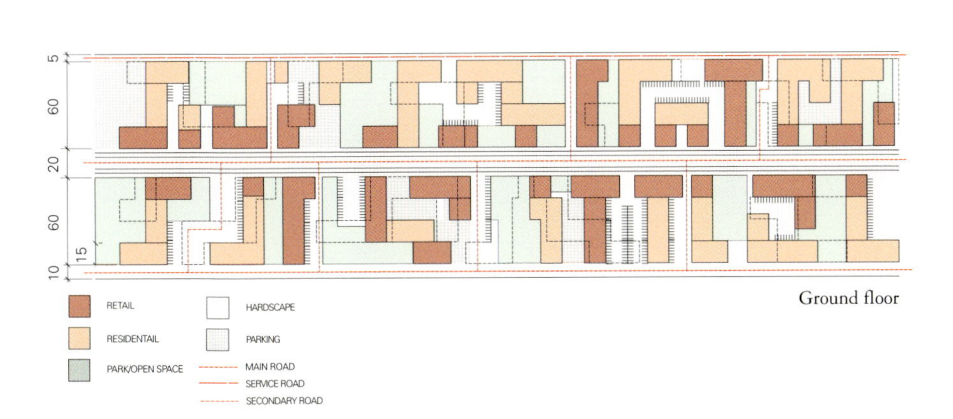

Typical floor

STAIR CORES
TYPE A: 10 x 20 = 200 M2
TYPE B: 15 x 9 = 135 M2
TYPE C: 15 x 15 = 225M2
TYPE D: 11x 15 = 165M2

Ground floor

RETAIL
RESIDENTIAL
PARK/OPEN SPACE
HARDSCAPE
PARKING
MAIN ROAD
SERVICE ROAD
SECONDARY ROAD

Urban Street: view toward Folded Street Mountain

Interior

II-277

2002 Toolenburg-Zuid
Amsterdam, The Netherlands

The competition-winning scheme for Toolenburg-Zuid was based on three principle planning concepts.

-20 Percent Water
The polder is returned to 20 percent water in the form of a large calligraphic cut. The earth displaced for the water calligraphy is used to create a topological earth calligraphy.

-Ascending Section
Like the distant ascending jets, an ascending section moves across the site at a 5 degree angle, reaching a total height of 80 meters in the Cactus Towers, which overlook the adjacent site's lake recreation area. This sectional ascent, with the bearing angle from north to south, maximizes sunlight in all sections.

-Six Housing Types for 21st Century Living
This series of six different building types present a diversity of programs on a large scale. The range of variables in each basic type is digitally stretched to the point of transforming (almost morphing) into other types: Cactus Towers, Polder Voids, Co-Housing Arms, Floating Villas, Checkerboard Villas, and House-Factories.

Five Ideals for the Twenty-First Century

1. Space-Time-Information
Toolenburg-Zuid is envisioned as a hybrid zone oriented toward world citizens. As a global site, home owners will be able to remain virtually connected to their homes across space and time.

2. Combinatory & Crossbred Living
Toolenburg-Zuid is designed as a site for programmatic hybridization, allowing for varied lifestyles and living arrangements. The project provides tower-lofts for the global commuter, courtyard houses for the family commuter with two children and a dog, and the house factory for the young sculptor in need of workspace. The variety of specialized housing types, such as co-housing for groups of single-parent families, celebrate the vital and dynamic residential community that results from the contemporary diversity of family arrangements.

3. Live-Work-Leisure
The integration of working, living, and recreation is an ideal.

4. Global Living without Automobile Dependency
Minutes by train from Amsterdam Airport Schiphol, the new housing is connected by an inner tram loop, allowing for life free of the automobile.

5. Ecology & Metonymy
Ecological goals of each part of the project relate to the environment of the whole, with each part designed to optimize its particular design. Throughout the project, maximum use is made of passive solar, natural ventilation, and other renewable forms of energy. Recycling and composting facilities provide nutrients to the landscape.

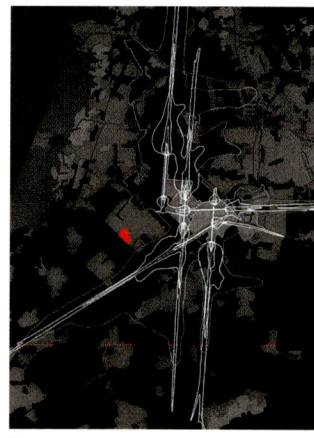

Site

トーレンブルグ・ツァイト

コンペに優勝したトーレンブルグ・ツァイトの計画は，3つの設計コンセプトの原則に基づいている。

——20パーセントの水面

敷地ではポルダーの20％が，大きな筆記体のような形の水面に戻される。水面をつくるために掘削された土を使い，今度はトポロジカルな筆記体がポルダーへと描かれる。

——上昇する断面

遠くで上昇を続けるジェット機のように，敷地を通して傾斜は5度ずつ上がり，カクタス・タワーで80mの高さに至る。そこから隣接する敷地の親水公園を見渡せる。北から南に向かう傾斜は，全ての断面で最も多く太陽光を取り入れることを可能にしている。

——21世紀の生活のための
　　6種類のハウジング・タイプ

6種類の異なるビルディング・タイプは，巨視的なスケールで

Cactus Tower (right) and Polder Void (center)

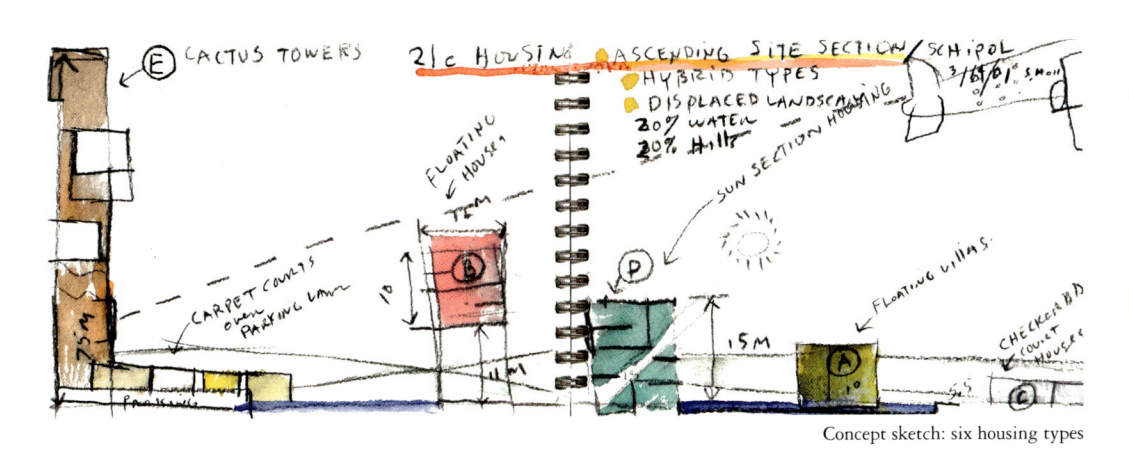

Concept sketch: six housing types

View from garden

プログラムに多様性を与えている。デジタル処理で各々の基準タイプの変数幅を引き延ばし，(ほぼ別の形になるまで)変形される。カクタス・タワー，ボルダー・ヴォイド，コー・ハウジング・アームズ，フローティング・ヴィラ，チェックボード・ヴィラ，そしてハウス・ファクトリーである。

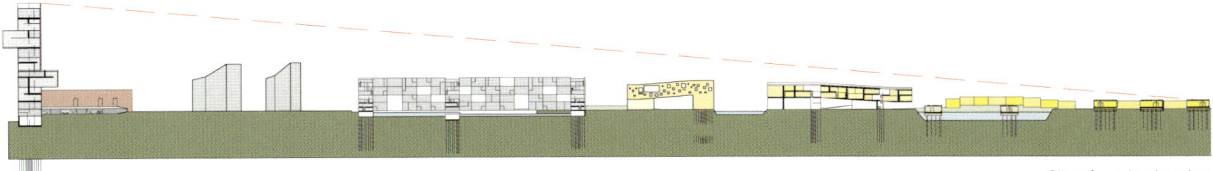

[21世紀のための5原則]
1．空間─時間─情報
トーレンブルグ・ツァイトは世界中の市民に向けたハイブリッド・ゾーンとして構想される。住宅の所有者は空間と時間を越えて，グローバルな場所という仮想的な意味において，これらの住宅に住むことができる。

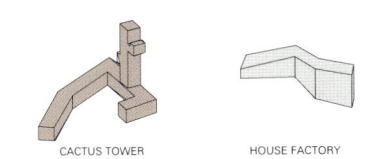

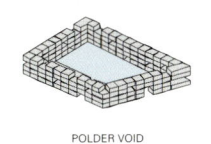

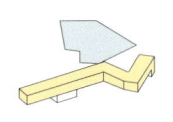

2．結合と雑交配
トーレンブルグ・ツァイトはハイブリッドにプログラムされた敷地として計画され，様々な生活様式が居住空間に配置されている。提供されるのはグローバルなコミューターのためのタワー・ロフト，2人の子供と犬のいる家族のコートヤード・ハウス，そして若手彫刻家の作業場として使うことのできるハウス・ファクトリー。単親家族同士のコー・ハウジングなど，様々に特化したハウジング・タイプの存在は，現代の家族構成の多様性がもたらす，活気と躍動感に溢れる住民コミュニティへの祝辞である。

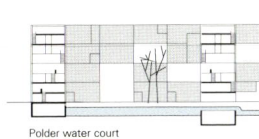

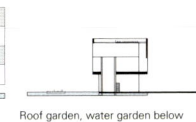

3．居住─オフィス─レジャー
オフィス，居住，レクリエーションの統合がひとつの目標である。

4．車に依存しないグローバルな居住
アムステルダムのスキポール空港から鉄道で数分の場所に立地し，構内は環状トラムで結ばれているため，ここでは自動車が必要とされることはない。

5．エコロジーと換喩
各々の計画におけるエコロジーへの取り組みは，環境全体としてのあり方と結びついている。計画では個々の特殊性を最適化するように設計が行われている。最大限利用されるのはパッシブ・ソーラー，自然換気，及びその他の再生可能エネルギー資源である。再資源化，堆肥化を行う施設からは土壌に養分が供給される。

Site elevation/section

CACTUS TOWER HOUSE FACTORY POLDER VOID CO-HOUSING FLOATING VILLA CHECKERBOARD GARDEN HOUSE

Six housing types

Terrace garden Braqueted garden space Polder water court Roof garden, water garden below Floating garden nearby Private courtyard and roof garden

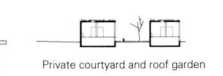

Relationship to green spaces

1 CACTUS TOWER
2 HOUSE FACTORY
3 POLDER VOID
4 CO-HOUSING UNIT
5 FLOATING VILLA
6 CHECKERBOARD GARDEN HOUSE

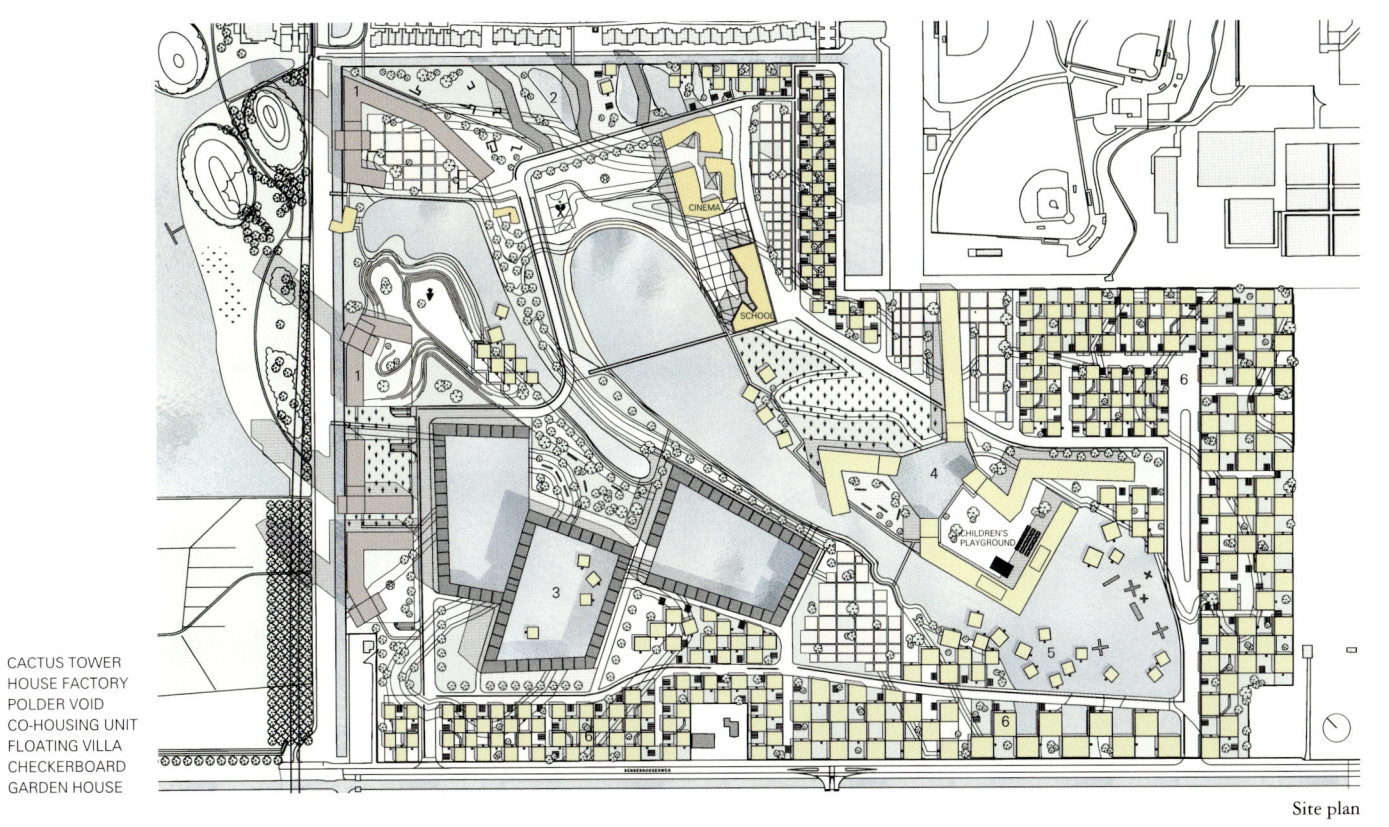

Site plan

2002- Beirut Marina & Town Quay
Beirut, Lebanon

Location

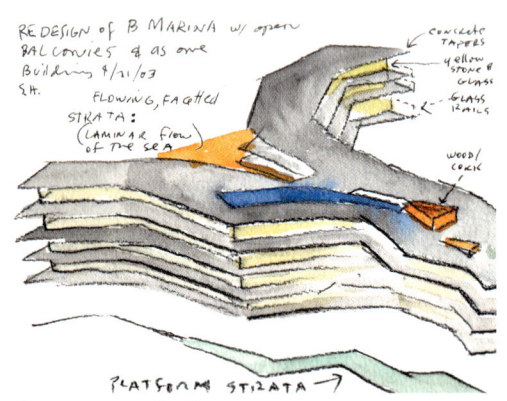

Sketch: apartment building

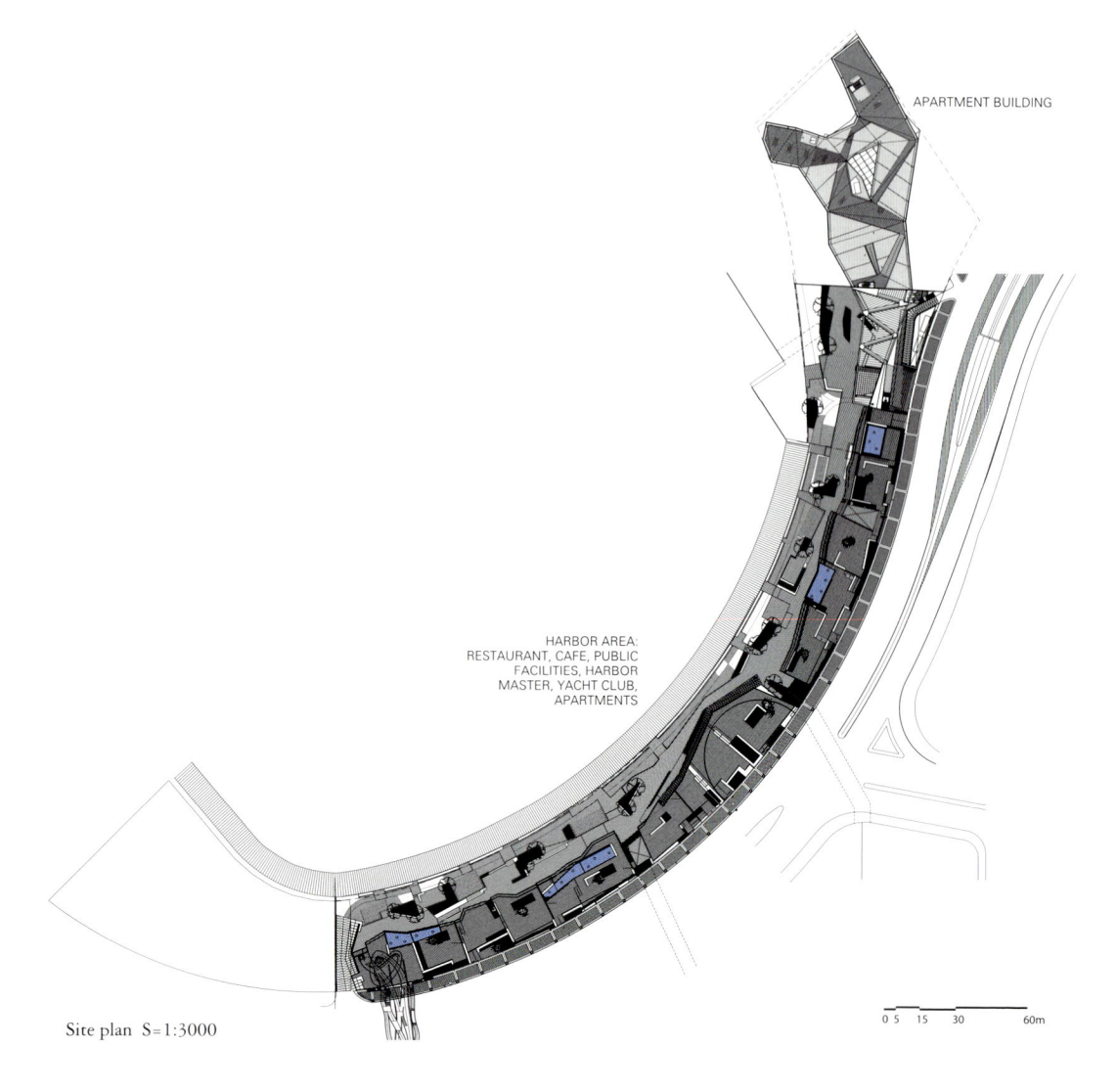

Site plan S=1:3000

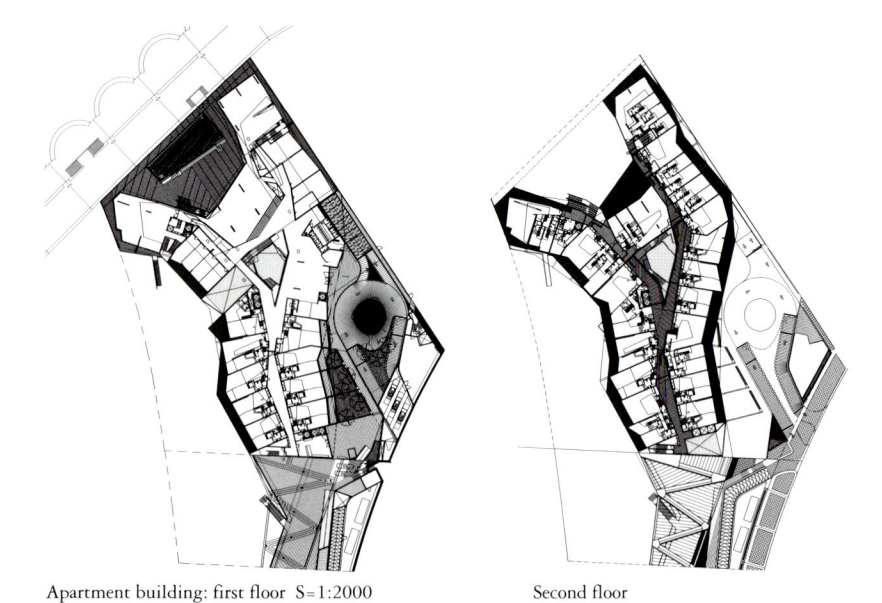

APARTMENT BUILDING

HARBOR AREA: RESTAURANT, CAFE, PUBLIC FACILITIES, HARBOR MASTER, YACHT CLUB, APARTMENTS

Apartment building: first floor S=1:2000

Second floor

The Beirut Marina building takes its shape from strata and layers in forking vectors. Like the ancient beach that was once the site, the planar lapping waves of the sea inspire striated spaces in horizontal layers, as distinct from vertical objects. The horizontal and the planar become a geometric force shaping the new Harbor spaces. The form allows a striated organization of public and private spaces which include; restaurants and shops, public facilities, harbormaster, yacht club, and apartments above. The apartment building hinges to create a "y". The form produces a high ratio of exterior surface area offering a maximum amount of views, rising to form a public observation roof to the sea.

The building is situated along a new fabricated terrain, that is extended from Beirut's Corniche, the seaside promenade, to create an 'urban beach' of public spaces overlooking the Marina. Stairs and ramps are integrated to provide access to the waterfront level. The syncopated rhythm of platforms is achieved by constructing the overall curve of the Corniche in 5 angles related to the 5 reflection pools. Due to the variations in height along the Corniche, the platform levels and pools vary slightly in height allowing quiet, gravity-fed fountains to connect each pool level.

Celebrating the sea horizon, the terraces are sculpted in local stone. The simple geometry of the upper platforms is in contrast to the colorful activity of restaurants below. The colored walls and fabrics below have their monochromatic and organic complement in awnings over the tables by the reflecting pools on the upper level. The building roof forms a public observation platform for the sea horizon.

Sketch: view from terrace

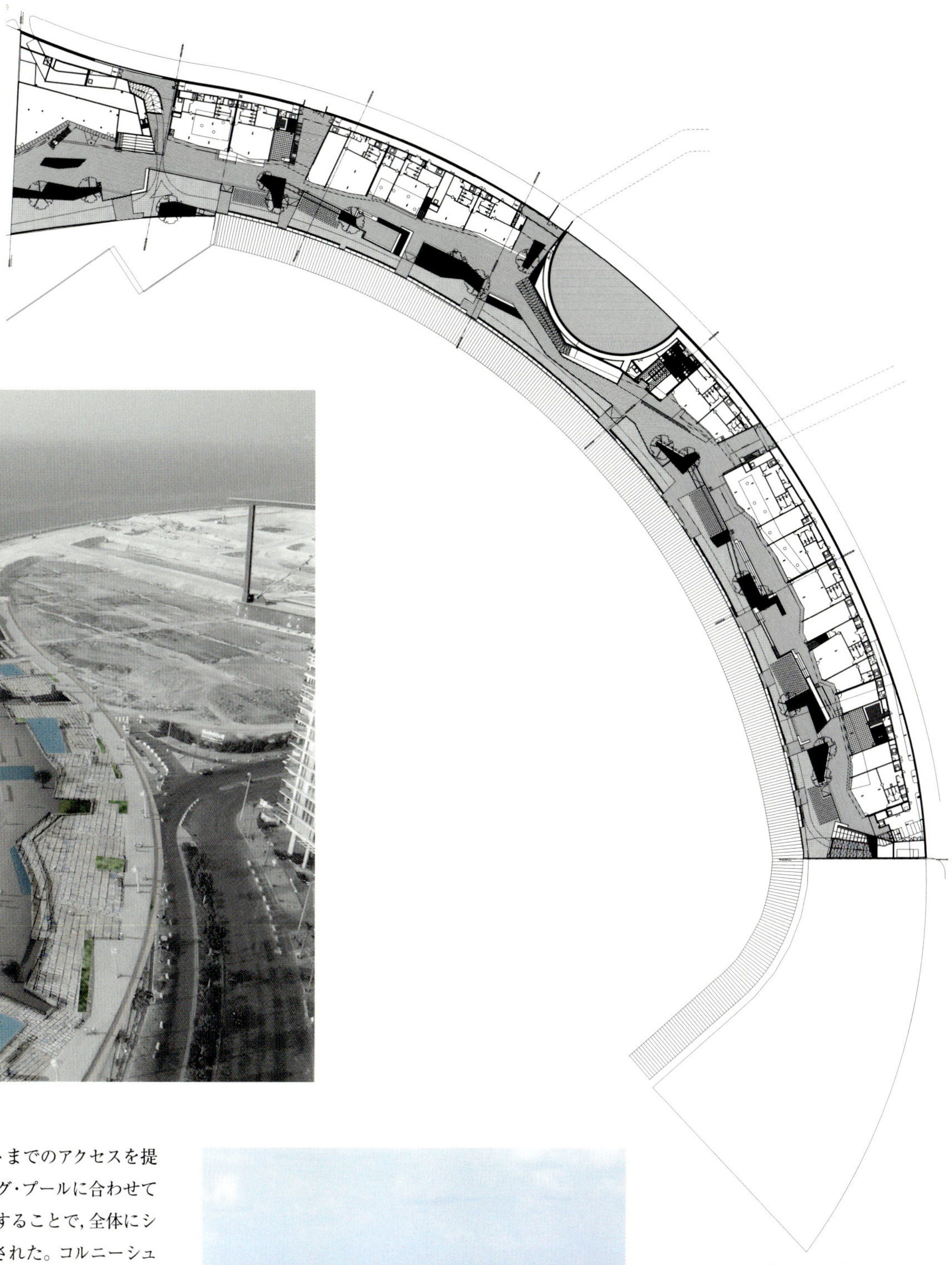

Harbor area: plan S=1:2000

Balcony of aparment building

ベイルート・マリーナ, 埠頭計画

ベイルート・マリーナは, 様々に分岐し, 積層する地層がそのモチーフである。かつて砂浜だった頃のように, この敷地には滑らかな波が常に打ち寄せる。そのことが, 垂直のオブジェとは対照的に, 水平に積層する縞状の空間を惹起するのだ。水平性と平面性がジオメトリを規定し, 港湾空間には新しい形態が付与される。レストラン, ショップ, 公共施設, 港湾管理棟, ヨットクラブ, 及びその上階の集合住宅。これらのパブリックな, あるいはプライベートな空間が, 水平に堆積される。集合住宅棟は「Y」字型に屈折する。そのため外壁は, 面積が大きく, 眺望を最大限にもたらしてくれる。建築の屋根は展望台として開かれ, 海への眺望を臨む。

建築は新しい人工の地形として計画される。これはベイルートのコルニーシュ, 海岸の大通りから延伸したもので, マリーナを見下ろすパブリック・スペースとしての「アーバン・ビーチ」を構成している。階段と斜路は一体となって, ウォーターフロントまでのアクセスを提供している。5つのリフレクティング・プールに合わせてコルニーシュを5つの角度で建設することで, 全体にシンコペーションのリズムが生み出された。コルニーシュはそれぞれ高さが異なっている。各々のプラットフォームや水盤の, 僅かなレベルの違いが, 水盤から水盤へと静かに流下する水の流れを生み出している。

原産石で彫塑された屋外テラスは, 水平線に広がる海を祝福している。落ち着きのある上階プラットフォームのジオメトリとは対照的に, 下階フロアは色彩豊かなレストランが映える。下階の色鮮やかな壁面とファブリックは, 上階のリフレクティング・プールの傍にあるテーブルの上に延びる単色で有機的なオーニングと, 補完的関係にある。建築の屋上は水平線を眺める展望台として開放されている。

II-281

Site plan S=1:7500

Site plan and site section:
three dense-pack "islands" are located in relation to the site's topography

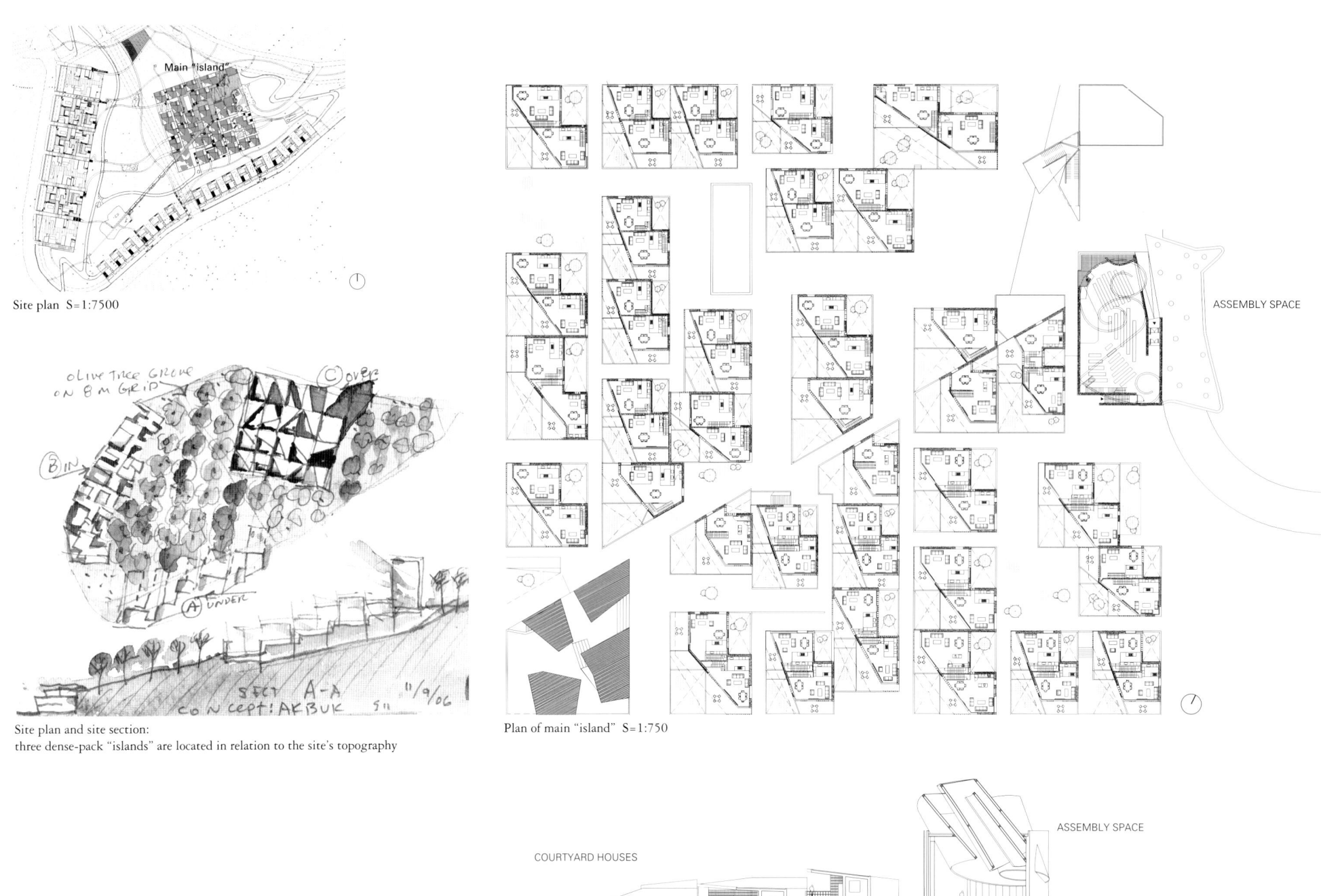

Plan of main "island" S=1:750

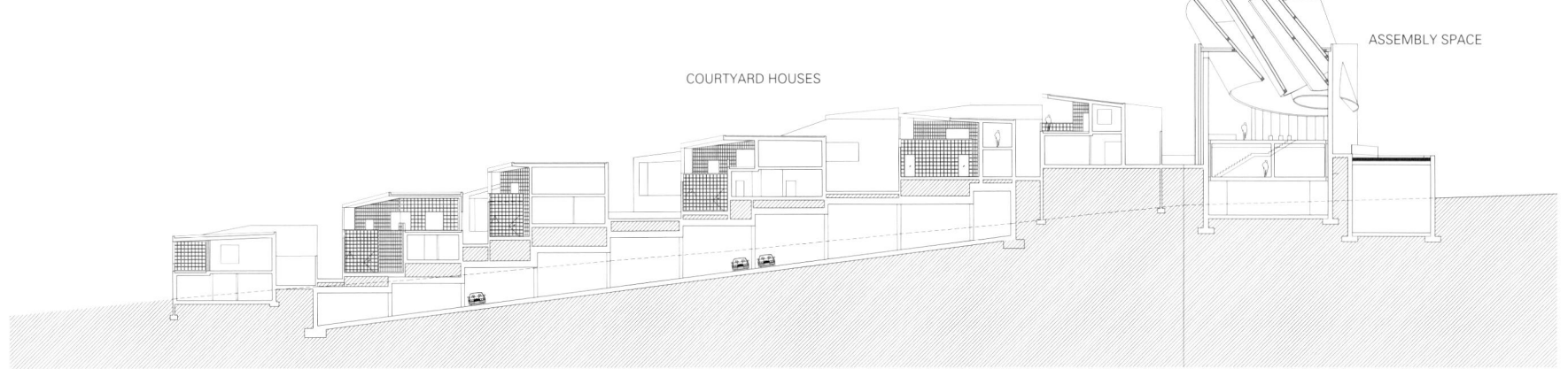

Section of main "island" S=1:750

Akbuk Dense Pack

2006-   Akbuk, Turkey

Concept sketch

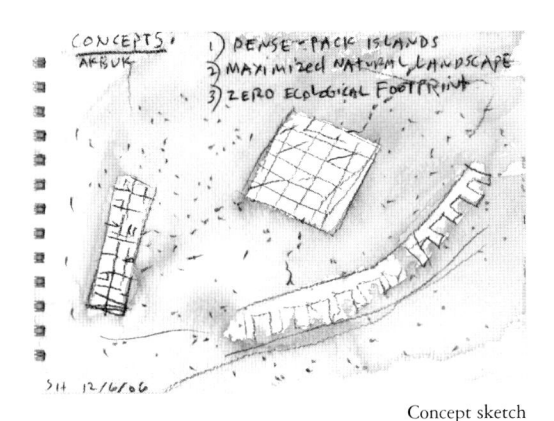

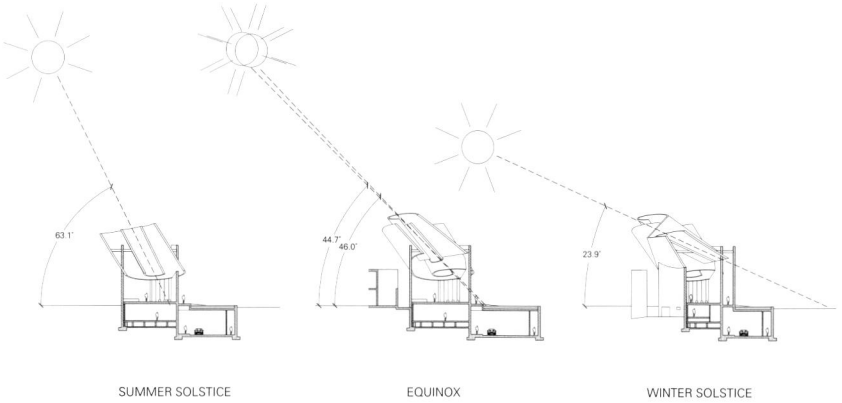

Model: assembly space

SUMMER SOLSTICE   EQUINOX   WINTER SOLSTICE

Diagram: assembly space with sun lighting

Overlooking the Aegean Sea, a new eco-reserve of small town fragments, like islands in a preserved landscape of cultivated natural vegetation, will be characterized by advanced technologies in sustainability, while also anchored in the poetic reverie of this ancient site.

The nearby ancient Greek town of Miletus inspires a compact gridded plan.

Three dense-pack "islands" are strategically located in relation to the site's topography, maximizing the natural landscape and minimizing roads, surface parking, and infrastructure: under the ground, a spa and townhouses cut into the earth; in the ground; courtyard villas with pools; and over the ground, a dense pack precinct with apartments around courtyards on a platform over a parking and cistern level below.

This main urban "island" has a special assembly space shaped by three solstice spiral skylights. Courtyard houses in two-story-high dense-pack construction in white concrete (mixed with local stone) have solar shades of Turkish chestnut, prefabricated in North Turkey by local craftsmen continuing ancient woodworking traditions.

With optimized solar shading, natural ventilation, thermal rock storage, and thermal mass construction, a seawater radiant-slab system supplies all heating and cooling. Solar water heating and gray- and storm-water recycling via ponds and cisterns further minimize the ecological footprint.

Site model: view from southwest. Main "island" is right behind

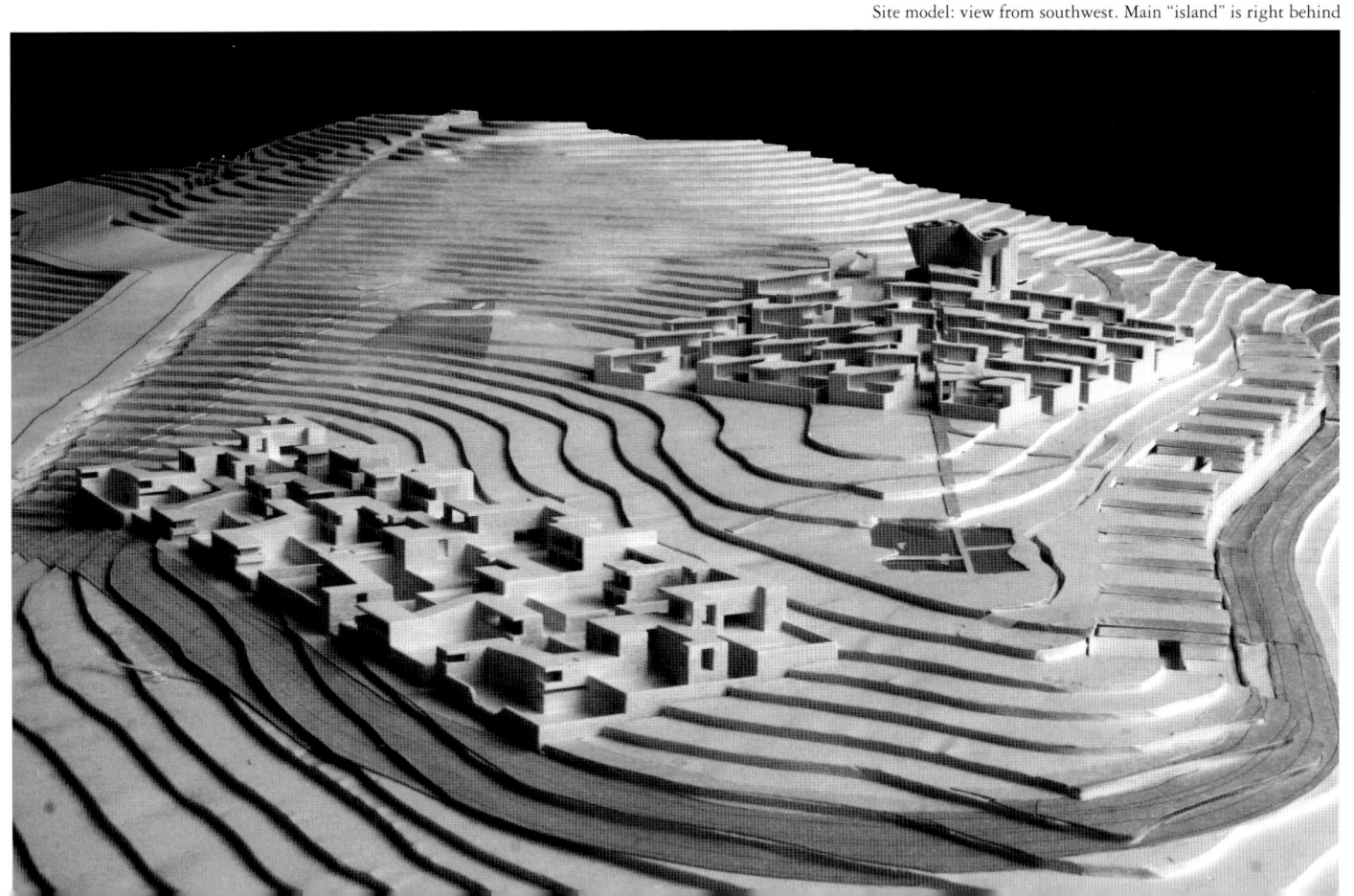

アクビュク・デンス・パック

小さな町の断片のような新しい環境保護地区は、エーゲ海を見下ろす、植物の自然な生態が残っている景観の中で島のように見える。この地区は、進歩的な環境共生技術を特質としつつ、同時に、この詩趣に富む幻想的な歴史ある敷地に、しっかりと根付くこととなろう。

近隣の古代ギリシャ都市ミレトスは、グリッド状の都市計画で有名なヒッポダモスの故郷であり、密度の高いグリッド状プランを着想する源となった。

三つの「島」から成る高密度集積体は、敷地形状との関係により、綿密な計画に従って配置されている。自然の景観を最大限に生かしつつ、道路、地上の駐車場、インフラを最小限に抑えるよう、地下には、スパ施設と低層集合住宅が地面に切り込んで配され、地中には、プールと中庭のあるヴィラがあり、地上には、階下の駐車場と貯水槽とを覆うプラットフォームに載った、中庭を囲む賃貸集合住宅の高密度区域がある。

このうち、メインとなる都市的な「島」には、3つの至点スパイラル状のスカイライトによって特徴づけられている集会スペースがある。中庭を囲む2階建ての高密度住宅は、地元産の石を取り混ぜた白いコンクリート造で、トルコ名産の栗材の日除けがついている。この日除けは、昔ながらの木工の伝統を守っている地元の職人たちの手によって、トルコ北部で取り付け部品として製造されたものである。

日除け、自然換気、石を利用した蓄熱システム、保温性能のある躯体構造を最大限に利用して、海水を用いた放射スラブ・システムが、全体の冷暖房をコントロールしている。さらに、貯水池や貯水槽を介して、太陽熱温水器の水と、雑排水、雨水をリサイクルすることによって、エコロジカル・フットプリント(生態学的足跡指数)は、最小限に抑えられるのである。

2006-09 Vanke Center
Shenzhen, China

Overall view from south

Sketch

Diagram: maximize landscape

Reflecting pond

View from Vanke Center lobby

Site plan

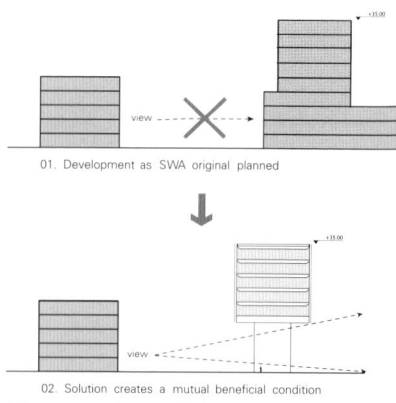

Diagram

Diagram: unobstructed views

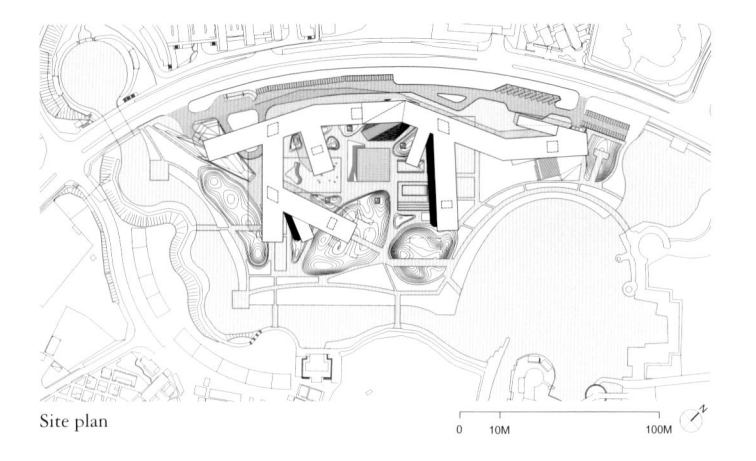

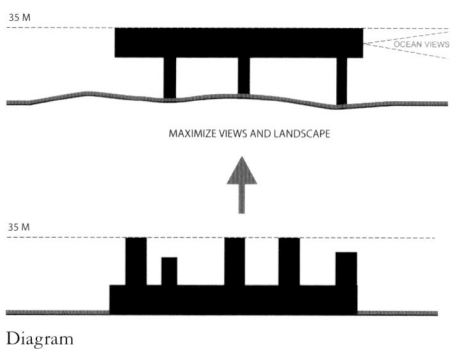

Hovering over a tropical garden, this 'horizontal skyscraper'—as long as the Empire State Building is tall—is a hybrid building including apartments, a hotel, and offices for the headquarters for Vanke Co. ltd. A conference center, spa and parking are located under the large green, tropical landscape which is characterized by mounds containing restaurants and a 500-seat auditorium.

The building appears as if it were once floating on a higher sea that has now subsided; leaving the structure propped up high on eight legs. The decision to float one large structure right under the 35-meter height limit, instead of several smaller structures each catering to a specific program, generates the largest possible green space open to the public on the ground level.

The underside of the floating structure becomes its main elevation—the sixth elevation—from which 'Shenzhen Windows', offer 360-degree views over the lush tropical landscape below. A public path beginning at the "dragon's head" will connect through the hotel and the apartment zones up to the office wings.

As a tropical strategy, the building and the landscape integrate several new sustainable aspects. A micro-climate is created by cooling ponds fed by a greywater system. The building has a green roof with solar panels and uses local materials such as bamboo. The glass facade of the building will be protected against the sun and wind by porous louvers. The building is a Tsunami-proof hovering architecture that creates a porous micro-climate of public open landscape.

The Vanke Center will be the first, highest rated USGBC, LEED Platinum Certified Project in China.

Renewable materials Vanke HQ wing

- Bamboo:

This highly renewable material, which is easily available in China, is used for doors, floors, and furniture throughout the Vanke Headquarters instead of using raw materials or exotic woods.

- Green Carpet:

InterfaceFLOR Carpet tiles are used throughout the open office area. This carpet is a cradle-tocradle product, meaning that it is not only produced from recycled materials, but that the manufacturer agrees to collect any damaged carpet and to recycle it into other carpet or products. This carpet contains a GlasBac® RE backing that has an average of 55% total recycled content with a minimum of 18% post-consumer recycled content. It uses recycled vinyl backing from reclaimed carpet tiles and manufacturing waste.

- Non toxic Paint:

All paint finishes, as well as the millwork and adhesives are to be low or free of V.O.C. (Volatile Organic Compounds)—like phenols and formaldehyde—which can cause various health and environmental problems.

- Greenscreen Shading:

The Vanke Headquarters uses Greenscreen solar shading fabrics from Nysan —a PVC free product that contains no V.O.C. (Volatile Organic Compounds). Not only does the product not "off-gas" during its life time, but it is also easier and quicker to recycle and divert to landfills.

Sustainable site

The building is sited on reclaimed/stabilized land that forms part of the municipal storm water management system. The lagoon functions as bio-swale/retention pond connected to several adjacent creeks. Part of the landscape architecture water edge proposal designed by Steven Holl Architects is the redesign the municipal hardscape bulkhead into a soft-edge planted estuary. As a restorative ecology, the Vanke center landscape works to maintain native ecosystems minimize run-off, erosion and environmental damage associated with conventional modes of development.

The project is both a building and a landscape, a delicate intertwining of sophisticated engineering and the natural environment. By raising the building off of the ground plane, an open, publicly accessible park creates new social space in an otherwise closed and privatized community.

The site area is approximately 60,000 square meter: of which 45,000 square meter is planted. With the addition of the planted roof area of the main building (approximately 15000 square meter) —the total planted area of the project is roughly equal to the site before development.

Stormwater management/Heat island effect

A large portion of the ground plane forms the roof on top of the program spaces above and below grade. In order for these landscaped roof areas to absorb large quantities of rainfall in the same way that natural soil would; sunken gardens, courtyards, ponds and planted mounds create a circulatory system to regulate and redistribute storm water throughout the site.

In addition to the planted areas, several types of permeable pavement; local river stones, crushed gravels, open joint stone pavers, grasscrete and compressed sand pavers are being used. These will retain a lot of rainfall before secondary gutters redirect overflow into a series of ponds and wetlands that are planted with marsh grasses and lotus. These systems function collectively as a bio-swale that filters, aerates and irrigates the landscape. No potable or municipal water will be used for maintenance or irrigation.

Regional connectivity

Two public transportation stops (bus) are located within 500 meter of the site. Separate areas for bicycle storage, and electric vehicle parking/charging stations have been provided. Throughout the project, all waste is collected and sorted into recyclables. Currently we are considering to compost organic compounds to be used as fertilizer for the landscape.

Water efficiency

To conserve potable water use; low-flow, high efficiency plumbing fixtures have been specified throughout the project. Greywater is recycled through dual-flush toilets. Waterless urinals have also been specified.

Ground floor

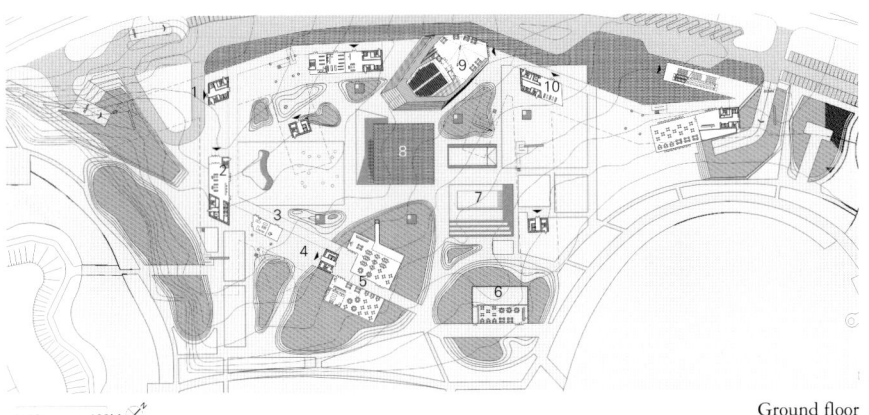

1 SOHO DROP OFF
2 VANKE CENTER LOBBY
3 SHOP
4 VANKE CENTER ENTRY
5 CHINESE CAFE
6 BAR/KITCHEN
7 HOTEL POOL
8 MARBLE PAVERS
9 AUDITORIUM
10 SPA LOBBY

Energy efficieny
Each face of the 26 faces of the building has been calculated based on solar heat gain throughout the year and its louvers are fine-tuned to the orientation of the sun. Some louvers are fixed horizontally, some have apertures of differing size, and some are dynamically controlled by sensors, opening and closing according to the sun. The full height glass curtain wall brings daylight deep into all interiors spaces, and the latest high-performance glass coatings (double silver Low-E) are used throughout the project. These coatings have several advantages over conventional coatings because they have higher visible light transmittance which ensures better natural lighting and extremely low solar heat transmittance. This saves energy by reducing cooling loads. 90% of interior spaces have direct views to the exterior.

In addition to the high-performance coatings, a secondary layer of perforated aluminum louvers is hung from the glass to create a double skinned facade. The interstitial cavity created by these two layers creates a convective stack-effect, drawing cool air in through the underside of the building and hot air out at the top of the structure near the roof. The perforated louvers provide extensive primary sun protection in closed condition. They reduce up to 70% of solar heat gain at its peak load, yet still provide 15% of light transmittance through the perforations. Given the intensity of the tropical sunlight, field measurements have calculated that this 15% light transmittance in closed mode is sufficient natural lighting to perform routine office functions without the need for secondary artificial lighting in most (75%) of spaces.

In the office portion of the project the operation of the exterior louvers, interior shades, air conditioning and lighting systems are coordinated by a series of interior and exterior sensors which balance ambient light levels, solar heat gain and ambient temperatures for maximum energy efficiency. There are individual controls for lighting and shade operation in most offices. Individual task/spot lights are provided for off hour, additional use.

Indoor environmental quality
The shallow floor plate of the upper building is organized in a branching pattern lifted high off the ground to allow for unimpeded views to the ocean, mountains and surrounding landscape. Prevailing ocean (day) and mountain (evening) breezes circulate underneath and through the building. Exceptionally large operable windows of two meters wide provide natural ventilation and generous cross breezes for the interiors during the cooler months of the year.

From November to March the outdoor conditions in Shenzhen are calm and window ventilation can take over the role of the mechanical ventilation in most of the building (and in the condominium part completely). It is estimated that during this season mechanical ventilation systems can be switched off for at least 60% of the time. This will reduce electric energy consumption annually by 5 kWh per square meter.

Sky gardens, sunken courtyards, balconies at the ends of each floor, and terraces throughout the building create micro-climates that bring the landscape further indoors and create passively cooled tertiary zones.

In addition to natural ventilation, filtered outside air (MERV-13) is added to all the mechanical systems prior to conditioning and interior-CO_2 levels are constantly monitored to control the fresh air exchange rate. A heatrecovery unit exchanges the conditioned exhausted air temperature with the incoming fresh air, and prevents any cooling energy from being lost.

Renewable energy/Green power
1,400 square meter of photovoltaic panels installed on the roof of the building provide 12.5% of the total electric energy demand for Vanke Headquarters.

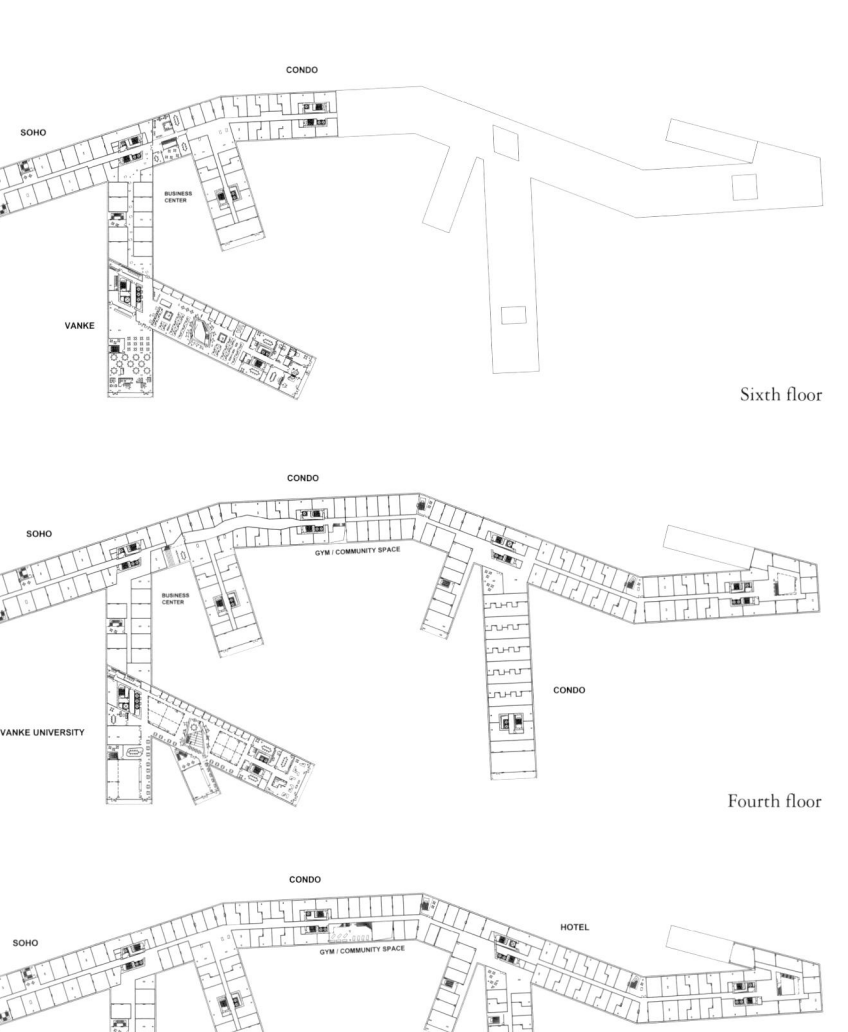

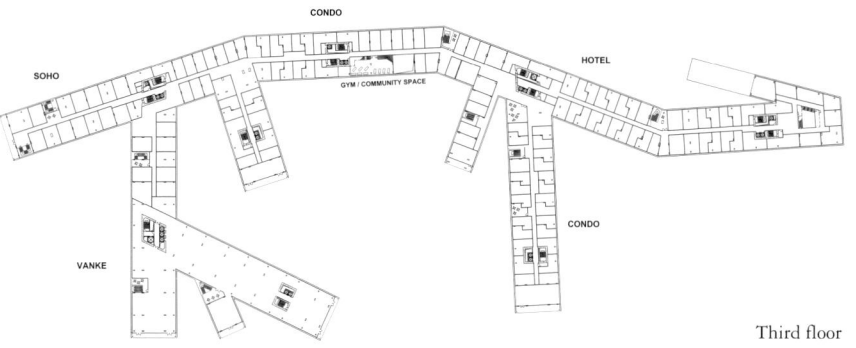

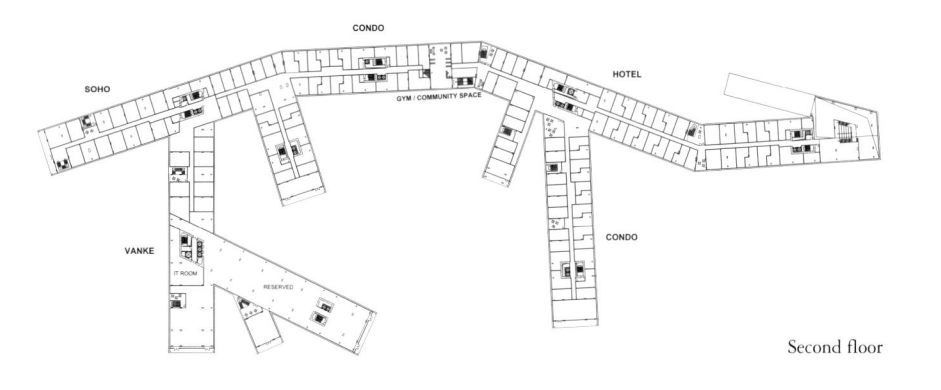

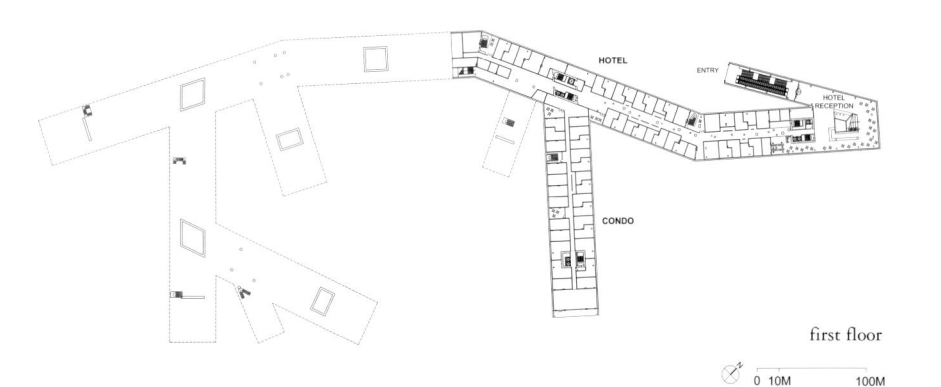

Sixth floor

Fourth floor

Third floor

Second floor

first floor

Office wing (left), condominium wing (center), hotel wing (right)

Office wing

Steel structure under office

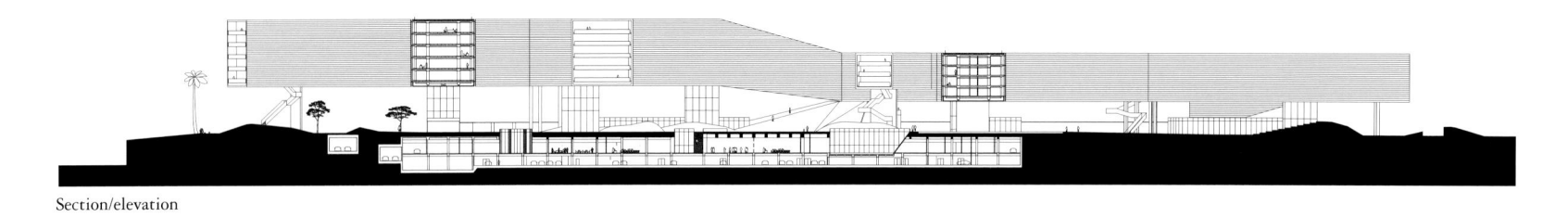

Section/elevation

| VANKE CAFE CENTER | PASSAGE W/ LIGHT FROM ABOVE | BUSINESS CENTER | PASSAGE W/ MORPHING TYPOLOGY | GYM / COMMUNITY SPACE | PASSAGE W/ VIEWS | PASSAGE W/ LIGHT FROM BELOW | HOTEL LOBBY |

Path section

ヴァンケ・センター

高くそびえるエンパイア・ステート・ビルとは対照的に,「ホリゾンタル・スカイスクレーパー」はトロピカル・ガーデンの上空に浮かぶ集合住宅,ホテル,およびヴァンケ・コーポレーション本社によって構成される複合施設である。コンファレンス・センター,スパおよび駐車場は広大で緑あふれるトロピカル・ランドスケープの地下に計画され,地上部分はレストランと500席のオーディトリアムを内包する小丘が特徴的である。

この建築物は,あたかも現在より高いところに海面があった頃の名残であるかのように,8本の構造体によって丈高く支えられている。ここでは小規模の構造物を各々のプログラムに合わせて提供する代わりに,ひとつの巨大な構造体を制限高さ35メートルのレベルに浮遊させている。そのため,地上レベルでは可能な限り最大限の大きさの緑地が社会に対して開放されている。

浮遊する構造体の下面もまた,重要な立面要素である。この6番目の立面にある「深圳ウィンドウ」からは,360度にわたってその下に青々と茂るトロピカル・ランドスケープを見渡すことができる。「ドラゴンズ・ヘッド」と呼ばれる一画から始まる歩道はホテルと集合住宅ゾーンを抜けて,オフィス・ウィングへとつながっている。

熱帯に建てられることを考慮して,建築物とランドスケープにはいくつかの持続性に関わる新しい試みが統合されている。中水を利用したクーリング・ポンドによって,局所的気候が生み出されている。建築物にはソーラーパネルとともに屋上緑化が施され,竹のような地域素材も使用されている。この建築のガラス・ファサードは,多孔ルーバーによって太陽や風から守られるようになるだろう。津波にも耐えられるように浮遊するこの建築は,社会に対して開放されたランドスケープに局所的気候を提供している。

ヴァンケ・センターは中国では初めてとなるUSGBC(グリーン・ビルディング評価制度)最高水準の,またLEED(環境評価基準)プラチナ認証のプロジェクトになるだろう。

[ヴァンケ・コーポレーション本社におけるリサイクルの試み]

——竹
再生材として,中国では入手が容易な素材である。ヴァンケ・コーポレーション本社では建具や床材から家具に至るまで,他の木材や外国産材に代わって随所で使用される。

——グリーンカーペット
オフィスのオープンエリアにはインターフェースフロア社のカーペットタイルが使用される。このカーペットの思想は「ゆりかごからゆりかごへ」である。この製品はリサイクル材から製造されるばかりではなく,製造会社は傷んだカーペットを全て回収し,他のカーペットや製品に再利用することを約束している。カーペットに使用されるGlasBac® REの裏打ち材は,全成分の平均55%がリサイクル材で構成されている。また,使用済みリサイクル材が最低18%は含まれている。この裏打ち材には,再生カーペットタイルや製造廃棄物から回収された再生ビニル樹脂を使用している。

——無公害塗料
木製品や接着剤と同様,塗装仕上げには,健康被害や環境汚染を引き起こすフェノール樹脂やホルムアルデヒドなどVOC(揮発性有機化合物)の含有量が低濃度か,あるは全く含まれないものを使用することが求められた。

——グリーンスクリーンによる日射遮蔽
ヴァンケ・コーポレーション本社では,Nysan社のグリーンスクリーンが日光を遮蔽するために使用される。これはVOCを含まない非塩化ビニル製品である。この製品はライフサイクルにおいて「非揮発性」であるばかりではなく,リサイクルや埋め立てが容易な素材である。

[持続可能な敷地環境]

この建築物の敷地は,地方行政の雨水管理事業の一部を構成する土壌の安定した埋め立て地にある。ラグーンは,隣接する用水路へとつながるバイオ・スウェイル(生物湿地)やバイオ・レテンション(生物滞留池)として機能する。ランドスケープ・デザインの一部として私たちが提案する水辺環境は,地方行政のコンクリート護岸を植生豊かな入り江へと再計画するものである。生態環境の回復という点では,ヴァンケ・センターのランドスケープには,従来の生態系を維持しながら表面流下や流域の浸食,従来型の開発手法によってもたらされる環境破壊を抑制する機能がある。

建築とランドスケープの両面において,このプロジェクトでは洗練された環境工学と自然環境が繊細に絡み合っている。地表面から建築物を離して計画し緑地を社会に開放することで,閉鎖的でプライベートになりがちなコミュニティに新しい社会的空間を生み出している。

敷地エリアは約60,000平方メートルに及ぶ。そのうちの45,000平方メートルには植栽が施される。約15,000平方メートルに及ぶ主要建築物の屋上緑化部分を含めると,このプロジェクトの植栽される部分の総面積は開発が行われる前の敷地面積とほぼ等しくなる予定である。

[雨水管理計画／ヒートアイランド現象]

緑化面の大部分は,地盤面の上下にわたって配置されたプログラム・スペースの屋根面で構成されている。自然界の土壌のように,ランドスケープ化された屋根面は降水の大部分を吸収することができる。サンクンガーデンや中庭,池,植栽された小丘は雨水を調節して敷地全体に再分配する循環システムを形成している。

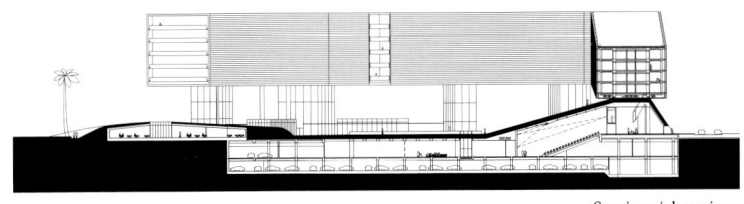

Sections/elevations

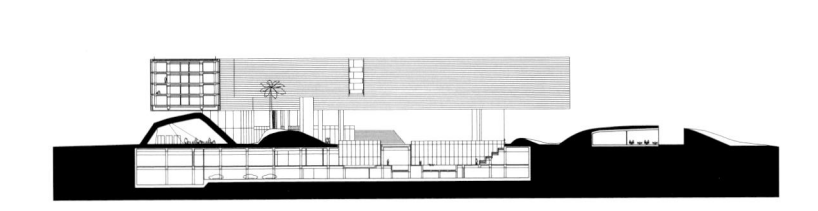

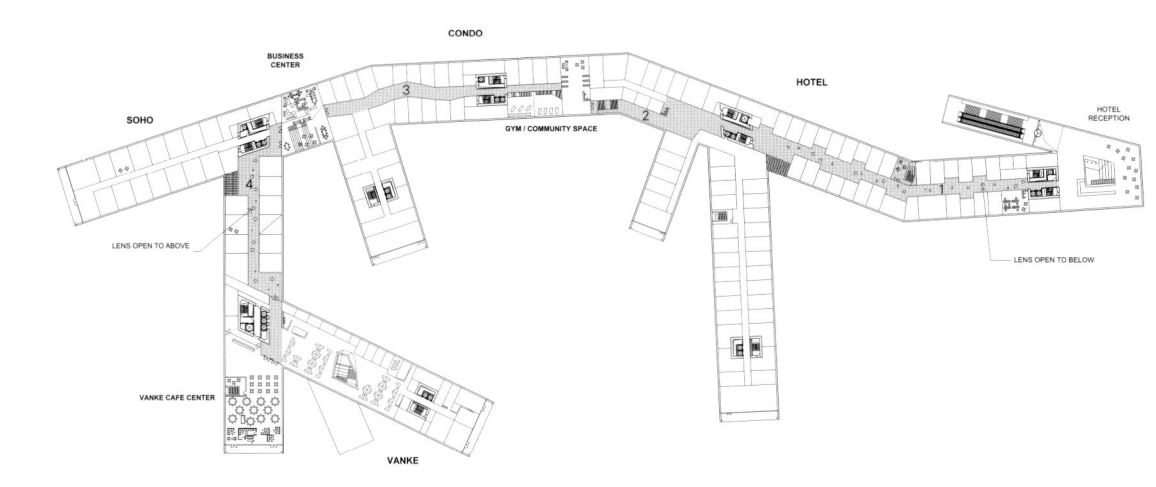

Path plan

　ここでは植栽の施された区画に加え，現地の河川で採取された石，砕石，目透かし貼りの敷石，植生ブロック，締め固められた敷砂などの浸透性舗装が使用されている。これらには，補助排水溝に流れ込む雨水が，葦や水蓮の生い茂るいくつもの池や湿地を氾濫させることがないように大量の雨を一旦保持する役割がある。これらのシステムは雨水を濾過，活性化し，ランドスケープを潤すためのバイオ・スウェイルとして一体的に機能する。飲用水や公共水道水を使わずに，ランドスケープの維持や用水がなされる予定である。

[地域社会との関係]
敷地内には公共交通機関(バス)の停留所が2ヶ所，500メートル離れて設けられる。別の敷地には，駐輪場と電気自動車のための駐車場とチャージ・ステーションが用意されている。すべての廃棄物は分別収集のうえ，リサイクルされる。現在，ランドスケープで肥料として使用するために，有機廃棄物のコンポスト化を検討中である。

[節水対策]
飲用水を節約するため，プロジェクトを通して使用水量が少なく高効率の衛生器具が採用された。中水はデュアル・フラッシュ型トイレに再利用されている。また，無水小便器も採用された。

[エネルギー効率]
建築物の外壁面は26面とも年間を通して太陽熱取得量の測定が行われている。また，壁面のルーバーは太陽の向きに合わせて調整される。いくつかのルーバーは水平に固定され，別のルーバーは異なる間隔で取り付けられる。また，太陽に合わせてセンサーで開閉調節されるよう，可動式になっているものもある。全面ガラスのカーテンウォールからは内部空間にくまなく日光が入るようになっている。また，最新の高効率ガラス・コーティング(Low-E複層ガラス)が全面的に採用されている。より自然な光を取り入れることを可能にする高い光透過性や，非常に低い熱貫流率など，このコーティングは通常のものと比較して様々な点で優れている。このことは冷房負荷を低減し，エネルギー消費の抑制につながっている。内部空間の90%からは直接外部を見渡すことができる。

　高効率のコーティングに加え，ダブルスキン・ファサードを形成するため副次的にアルミニウムの多孔ルーバー層がガラス面に取り付けられる。これら二つの層の間の空隙は対流による煙突効果を生み出し，建築物の下面から冷気を吸い込み屋根面に近い構造体の上部からは暖気を排出する。多孔ルーバーは閉じることによって，太陽からの入射熱を遮るため重要な役割を果たしている。最大負荷時には70%に上る太陽熱取得を低減しながら，ルーバーの穴からは太陽光の15%が透過するようになっている。熱帯地方の強い太陽光の下では，ルーバー閉鎖時に透過する15%の自然光でも，執務空間のほぼ75%で補助的な人工照明を使用せずに日常業務を十分に行えることが実地計測で確認された。

　このプロジェクトのオフィス部門では，外部ルーバー，内部シェード，空調設備，照明システムが内外部に設置されたいくつものセンサーによって連携し，エネルギー効率が最大化されるようにアンビエント照明の照度，太陽熱取得および室温を調節する。オフィスルームの多くでは，照明やシェードを個別に調節することが可能になっている。休日や特別な作業のためにタスク・ライティングやスポット照明が用意されている。

[屋内環境品質]
奥行きの浅い建築上層部のフロアプレートは，海や山あるいは周囲のランドスケープへの視線を遮ることがないように地上から高く，いくつにも分岐した形状をしている。日中は海からの，夜間は山からのそよ風が建築物の中やその下を吹き抜けてゆく。涼しい時期になると，非常に大きな幅2mに及ぶ可動式ウィンドウから，自然換気と心地良い風通しが内部空間にもたらされる。

　11月から3月までの間，深圳では穏やかな気候が続くので，全てのコンドミニアムを含めて建築物の大部分では機械換気の代わりに窓からの自然換気が利用される。この季節になると，一日のうちの少なくとも60%の時間帯で機械換気システムの使用を停止することができるものと予測されている。そのため，電気消費量を1平方メートルあたり通年で5キロワット時抑制できる見込みである。

　スカイ・ガーデンやサンクン・コートヤード，各階の端部にあるバルコニー，建築物の至る所にあるテラスがつくり出す局所的気候は，屋内活動をランドスケープへと開放し，自然を利用した第三の空間をつくりだしている。

　自然換気に加え，機械換気の外気取り入れ口にはMERV(フィルター最小効率値)13レベルのフィルターが設置されている。また，外気の換気効率を調節するために室内の二酸化炭素濃度が常時監視されている。熱回収ユニットは，排気と外気とを熱交換することで熱損失を防いでいる。

[再利用可能なエネルギー／グリーン・パワー]
建築物の屋上に設置された1,400平方メートルに及ぶ太陽光発電パネルは，ヴァンケ・コーポレーション本社の電力総需要量の12.5%を供給している。

Vanke Center lobby on right

Vanke Center lobby

View from Vanke Center lobby toward condominium and hotel wing

Elevator hall on first floor

Sixth floor

II-293

Staircase on sixth floor

Staircase on fifth floor

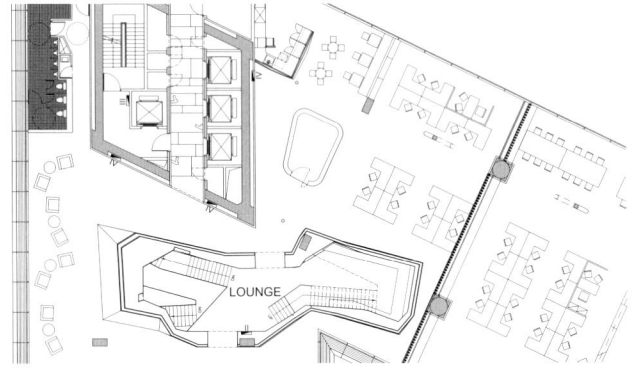

Fourth floor

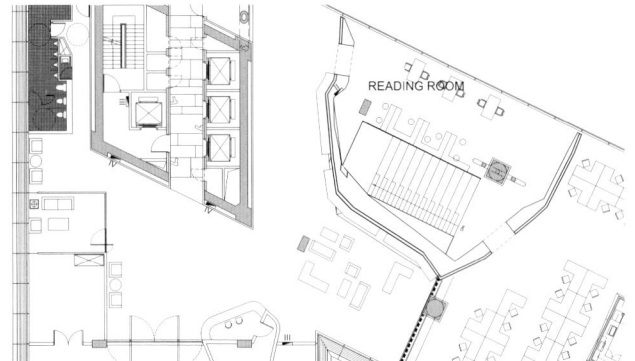

Sixth floor

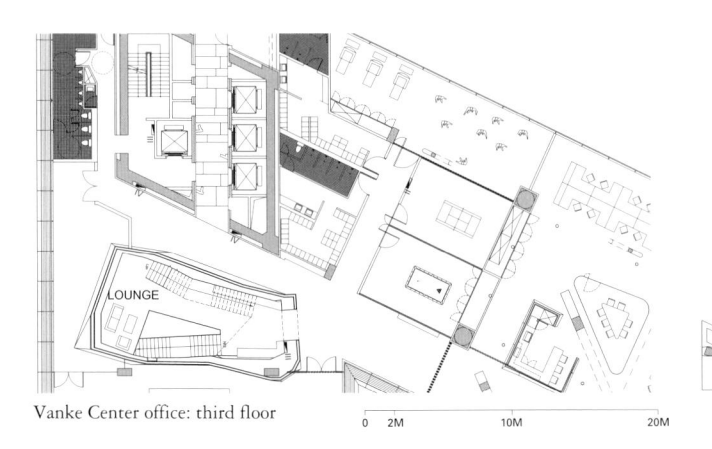

Vanke Center office: third floor

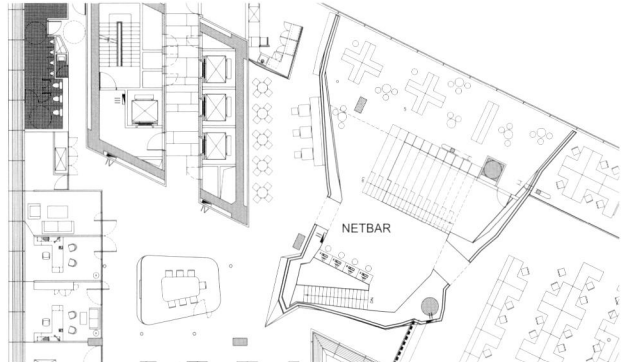

0 2M 10M 20M

Fifth floor

Staircase on third floor

Wall detail

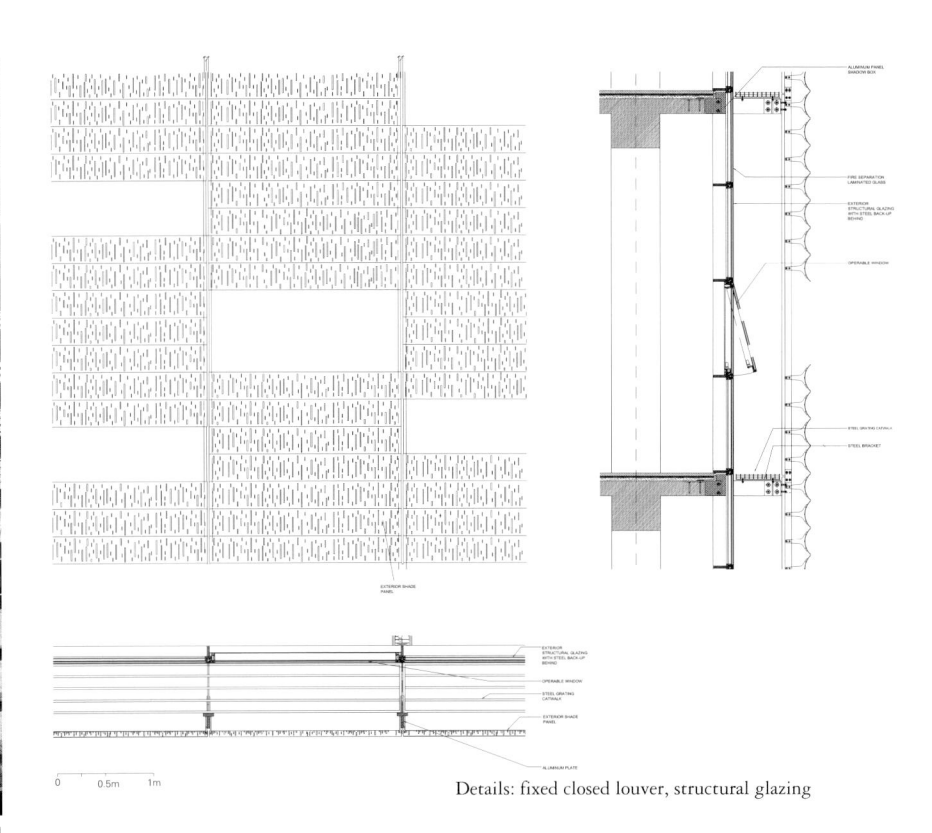

Details: fixed closed louver, structural glazing

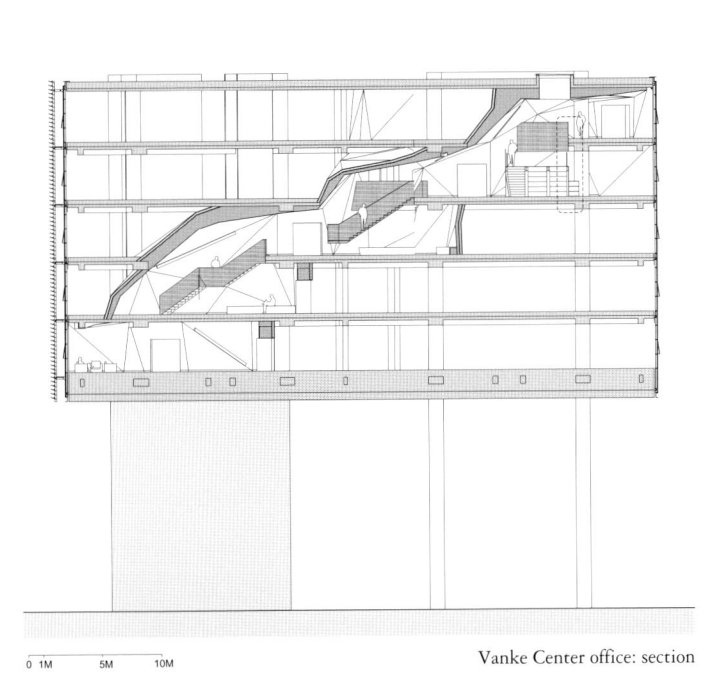

Vanke Center office: section

Sixth floor

II-295

Ningbo Fine Grain
Ningbo, China

2008

Plan: 0. grid

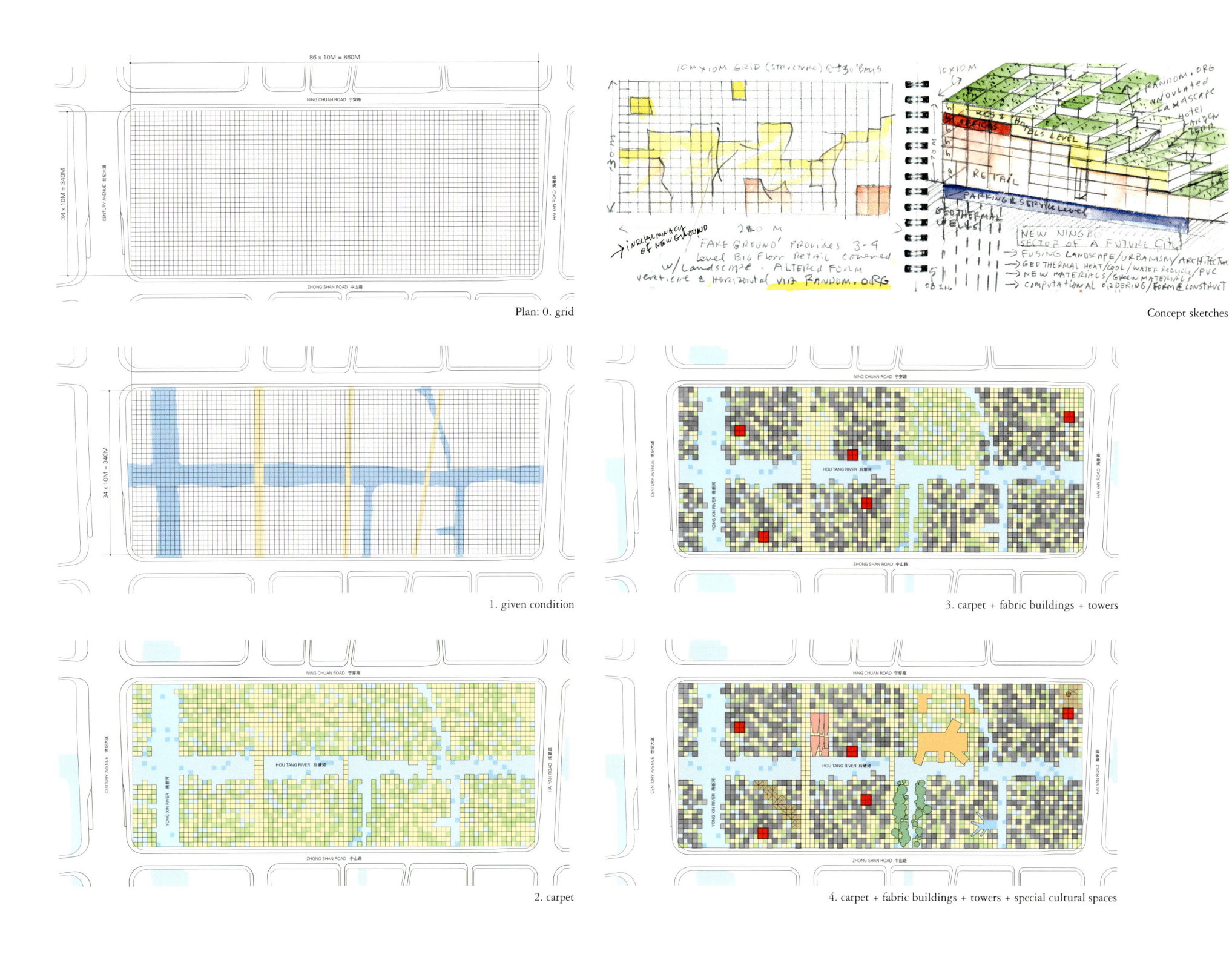

Concept sketches

1. given condition

3. carpet + fabric buildings + towers

2. carpet

4. carpet + fabric buildings + towers + special cultural spaces

Concept sketch: super green urbanism

Axonometric

The proposal for Ningbo consists of a twenty-first century "water town" based on five strategies:

1. Ecological Urbanism
Transportation by solar-powered water taxis minimizes dependence on automobile transportation. Parking is located at perimeter areas with a typical walking distance of 200 meters. There is geothermal cooling and heating, supplemented by solar panels at roof garden terraces, and complemented by green Sedum roofs and a storm-water and gray-water recycling system.

2. Integration of Functions for 24-hour life
Live /work /shop /entertaining functions are integrated across the site in a gentle mix.

3. Fine Grain Morphology/ Water Edge Architecture
Aimed at close integration to the unique water edge character of this new Ningbo sector, a special fine grain urban morphology is invented. Based on the typical spacing in construction of 10 meter by 10 meter bays, the entire site is gridded. A chance-based process aimed at achieving the build out area of 500,000 square meters is introduced via a computer program (www.random.org). This allows for maximum variety of spatial experience and variety of new water-edge architecture. The chance-based process allows for maximum functional flexibility and program adjustment within a fine grain.

4. Reflection Phenomena
The architecture has been envisioned with the reflection in the canal water from its inception. Color and light in reflection are a unique urban experience here.

5. Unique Parks and Cultural Architecture
Marking the main north-south axis connecting this new sector to the larger master plan, a unique grouping of architecture, housing, cinemas, and concert halls have been envisioned. Unique parks such as the park of solar pergolas (powering fountains) shape spaces inside the overall fine grain.

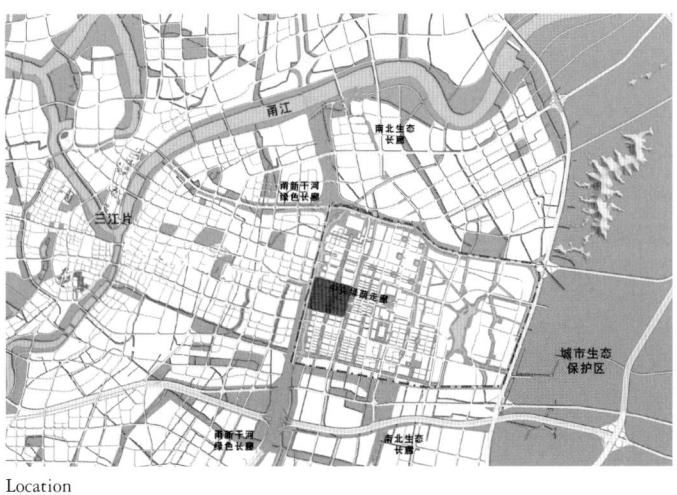

Location

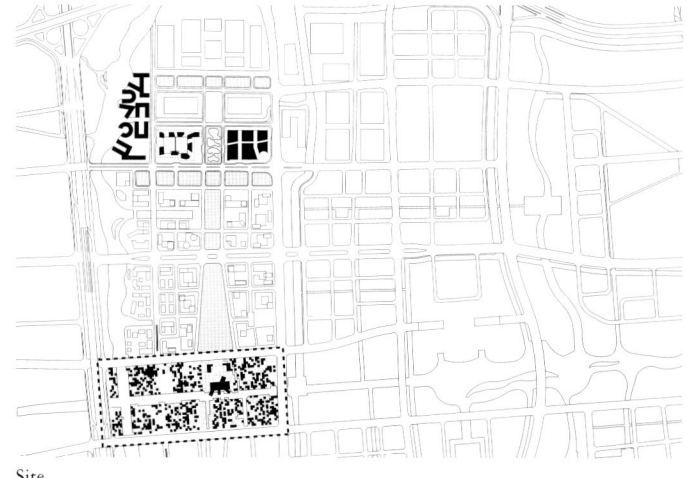

Site

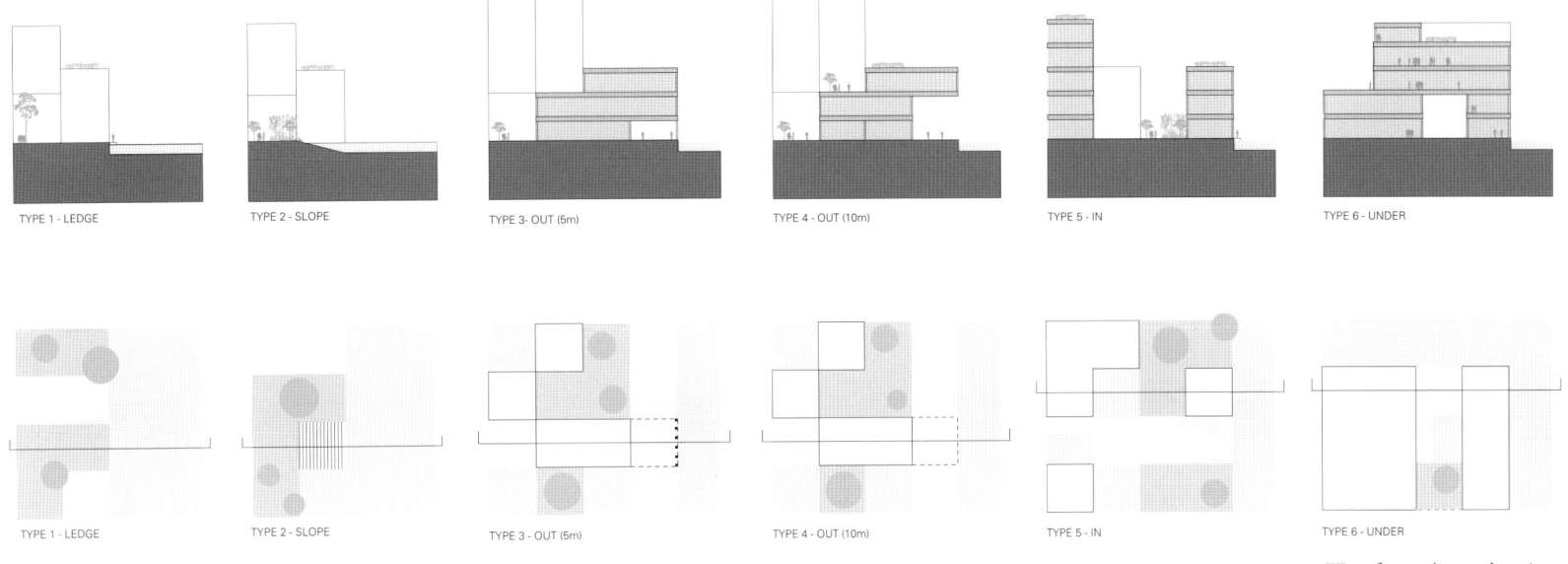

| TYPE 1 - LEDGE | TYPE 2 - SLOPE | TYPE 3 - OUT (5m) | TYPE 4 - OUT (10m) | TYPE 5 - IN | TYPE 6 - UNDER |

Waterfront: plans and sections

寧波ファイン・グレイン（微粒子）計画

この寧波市での提案は, 以下五つの方法をもとに考え出された, 21世紀における「水郷都市」というアイディアから構成される。

［1．環境に配慮した都市生活］
太陽光発電を動力とした水上タクシーでの移動により, 車への依存を少なくする。水上タクシーの駐車場は, 一般に考えられている歩行近距離である, 徒歩200メートル圏内の敷地周縁部にある。地熱を利用した冷暖房のシステムがあるが, 屋上庭園のテラスに設置された太陽光発電パネルにより補充され, 雨水及び生活排水の再利用システムを備えベンケイソウに覆われた屋根がさらにこのシステムを補完している。

［2．24時間ライフスタイルのための機能統合］
生活, 仕事, 買い物, 娯楽などの機能が敷地内で穏やかに混じり合い, 統合される。

［3．微粒子形成学／水際の建築物］
寧波市地区の, 水際に面した地域の特徴と調和することを目指し, 特別な「微粒子都市形成学」と呼べるコンセプトを考案した。建設では一般的な10メートル×10メートルのスパンを基準に, 敷地全体が基準メッシュによりグリッド化された。500,000平米に及ぶ建設エリアを無作為なプロセスで実現するため, コンピュータ・プログラム (www.random.org) が導入された。これにより出来得る限りの, 様々な空間体験と多様な水辺の建築が生まれる。この言わば偶然とも言えるプロセスは, 微粒子状に広がる敷地において, 機能的フレキシビリティとプログラムの適応を最大限可能にする。

［4．反射現象］
このプロジェクトでは, 当初より運河水面の映り込みを思い描いてきた。反射の中に見いだす色や光が, この場所特有の都会的経験となるだろう。

［5．特徴のある公園と文化的建築物］
この新しい地区と, さらに大きなマスタープランとをつなぐ南北に走る主軸を印象づけるため, 住宅, 映画館, コンサートホールなどの建築物を特殊な方法でまとめることを思い描いた。ソーラー・パーゴラ (噴水を稼働させる電力を供給可能) を持つような特徴ある公園が, このプロジェクトにおける微粒子の総体の中で, 様々な空間を生み出していくことだろう。

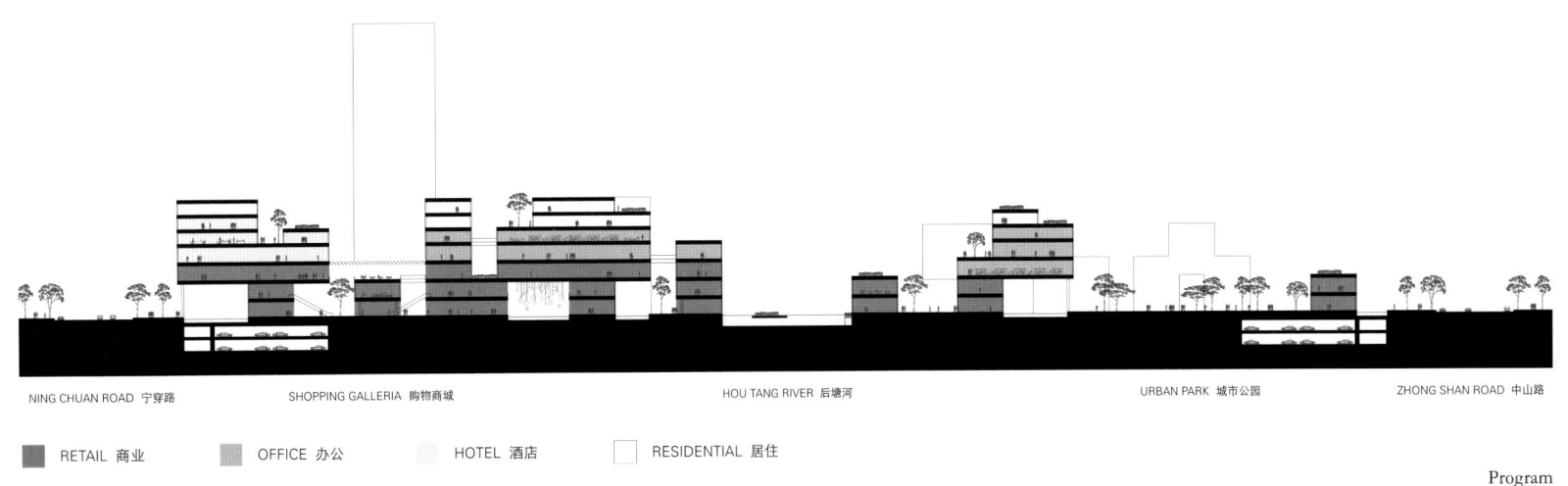

NING CHUAN ROAD 宁穿路　　SHOPPING GALLERIA 购物商城　　HOU TANG RIVER 后塘河　　URBAN PARK 城市公园　　ZHONG SHAN ROAD 中山路

■ RETAIL 商业　　▨ OFFICE 办公　　▨ HOTEL 酒店　　□ RESIDENTIAL 居住

Program

Green roof

Sketch: fountain murals at water edge

Canal

Reflection in canal water

Plaza with solar pergolas

Sketches: study for plaza with solar pergolas

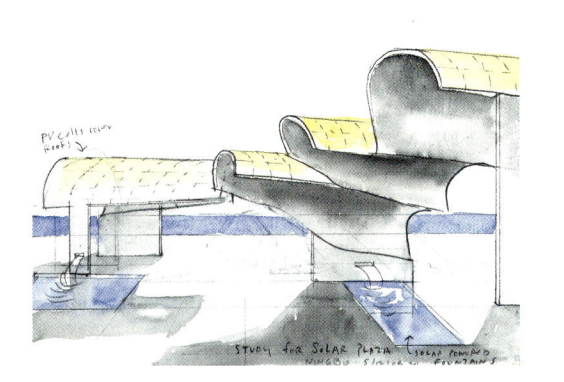

II-301

2008- LM Harbor Gateway
Copenhagen, Denmark

Overall view: Langenlinie-Tower (left) and Marmormolen-Tower (right)

Diagram: urban concept

The LM Project design for the dramatic new harbor entrance to the great city of Copenhagen is based on a concept of two towers carrying two bridges at two orientations all connecting back to the unique aspects of the site's history.

The Langenlinie site, a berth for ocean ships for decades, is expressed in the Langenlinie Tower with geometry taken from the site's shape. A prow-like public deck thrusts out to the sea horizon. This deck is the level of public entry to the bridge elevators and has public amenities such as cafes and galleries. It can be reached by a wide public stair as well as escalators.

The Marmormolen Tower connects back to the City with a main terrace that thrusts out towards the city horizon shaped by a public auditorium below. It can also be reached by escalators and is adjacent to the public bridge elevator lobby.

Each tower carries its own cable-stay bridge that is a public passageway between the two piers. Due to the site geometry, these bridges meet at an angle, joining like a handshake over the harbor. The soffits below the bridges and under the cantilevers pick up the bright colors of the harbor; container orange on the undersides of the Langenlinie, bright yellow on the undersides of the Marmormolen. At night the uplights washing the colored aluminum reflect like paintings in the water.

The project utilizes a variety of progressive sustainable solutions to ensure this important international landmark is rooted in Denmark's identity as one of the world leaders in alternative energy. Both towers have high performance glass curtainwalls with a veil of solar screen made of photovoltaics; collecting the sun's energy while shading. They are connected to a seawater heating/cooling system with radiant heating in the floor slabs and radiant cooling in the ceiling. Natural ventilation is provided on every floor with windows opening at the floor level and ceiling level for maximum air circulation. Optimum natural light is provided to all offices due to the reflective light performance of the screens. Wind turbines line the top of the pedestrian bridge roof; providing all electricity for lighting the public spaces. Due to wind power, this inviting harbor front gateway is always glowing.

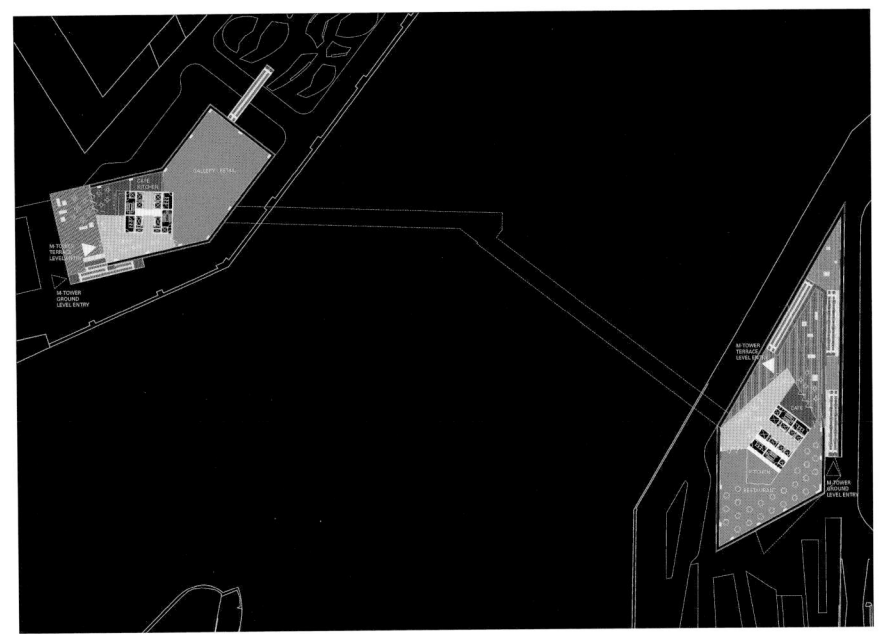

Terrace level: Marmormolen-Tower (left) and Langenlinie-Tower (right)

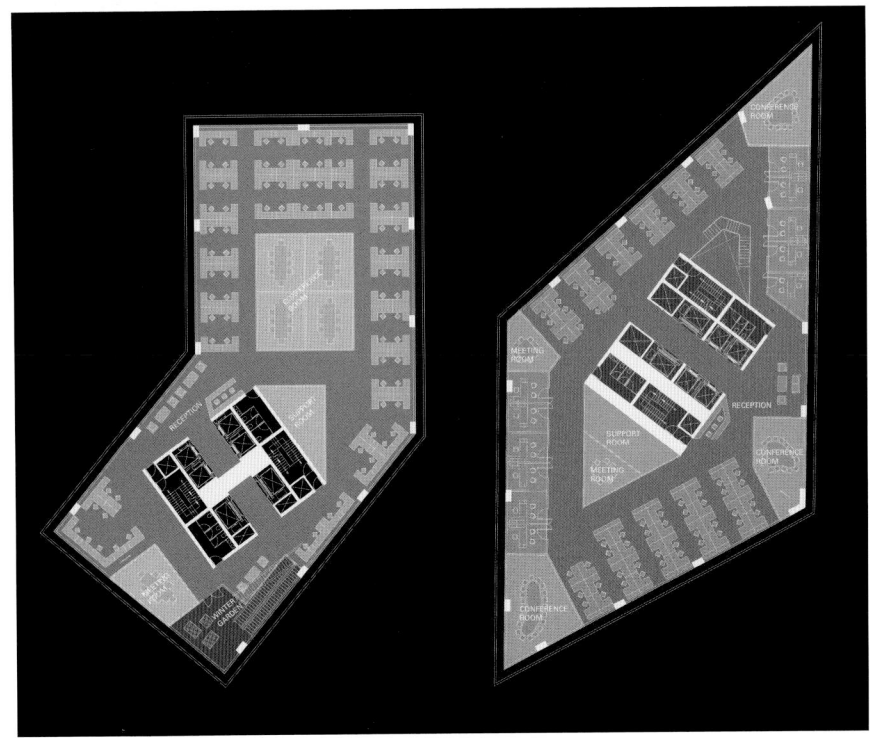

Site plan

Office level: Marmormolen-Tower (left) and Langenlinie-Tower (right)

LMハーバー・ゲートウェイ

新しくドラマティックな，偉大なる都市コペンハーゲンへの港湾玄関となるこのプロジェクトは，二つのタワーが支える二つのブリッジが，敷地特有の歴史的要素に結びつくようなそれぞれの方角を向いて接続する，というコンセプトに基づいている。

ランゲリニーの敷地は，数十年に渡って大洋航海船の停泊地となってきたが，その特徴は「ランゲリニー・タワー」として，敷地の形状から読み取られた幾何学形態によって表現されている。船首のような公共の甲板デッキが海に向かって水平に伸びており，これがパブリック・エントランス・レベルとなっている。この階にはブリッジ・レベルへと昇るエレベータがあり，カフェやギャラリーといった公共の娯楽施設も設けられている。この場所は，幅の広い一般階段とエスカレータでアクセスできる。

「マルモルモーレン・タワー」は，下層部にある公会堂の形態が反映され，都市の地平線へ向けて突き出されたメイン・テラスによりコペンハーゲンの街と接続している。このテラスもブリッジへと昇る公共のエレベータ・ロビーに隣接しており，エスカレータでアクセスできる。

各タワーは，それぞれが二つの桟橋の間を結ぶ公共通路となる斜張橋を擁している。敷地の幾何形態の制限により，これらの橋はある角度をもって接続しており，港湾の上方で握手するかのように合流する。橋梁の底面と建物の片持ち梁下部は，港湾に用いられた明るい色が反映され彩色されている――「ランゲリニー」の片持ち梁の下部は貨物コンテナのオレンジ，「マルモルモーレン」では明るい黄色が用いられている。夜間には，アップライト照明が色付きアルミニウムを照らし出し，水中の絵画のように反射する。

この重要な国際的ランドマークが，世界でも代替エネルギー利用における先駆者であるデンマークの独自性に根ざしたものということを証明するように，ここでは環境維持のための進歩的な解決策を数多く取り入れている。どちらのタワーも，太陽光エネルギーを収集しつつ日除けが可能な，光電変換・起電工学による太陽光遮蔽のスクリーンに覆われた高性能なガラス・カーテンウォールを採用している。これらタワーは海水冷暖房システムに接続されており，放射暖房を床面に，放射冷房を天井に組み込んでいる。各階には，床レベルと天井レベルに設置された窓による自然換気が備わり，最大限の空気循環を可能にする。スクリーン・システムの反射光により，全てのオフィス空間において最適化された自然光が取り入れられている。歩行者橋の屋根面には風力タービン・システムが並べられており，公共空間を照明するための全電力はこのシステムでまかなっている。風力発電エネルギーにより，この魅力的な港湾関門は常に発光し輝くことだろう。

Langenlinie-Tower (left) and Marmormolen-Tower (right)

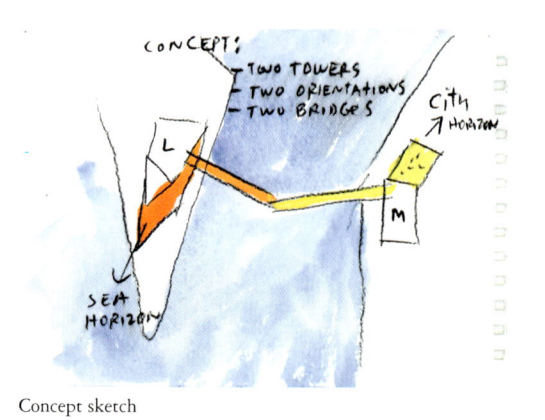

Concept sketch

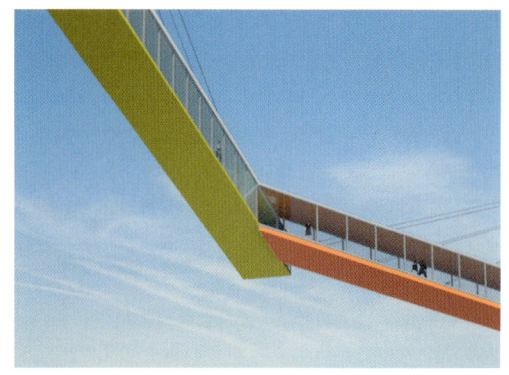

Bridge 'handshake'

Interior: bridge 'handshake'

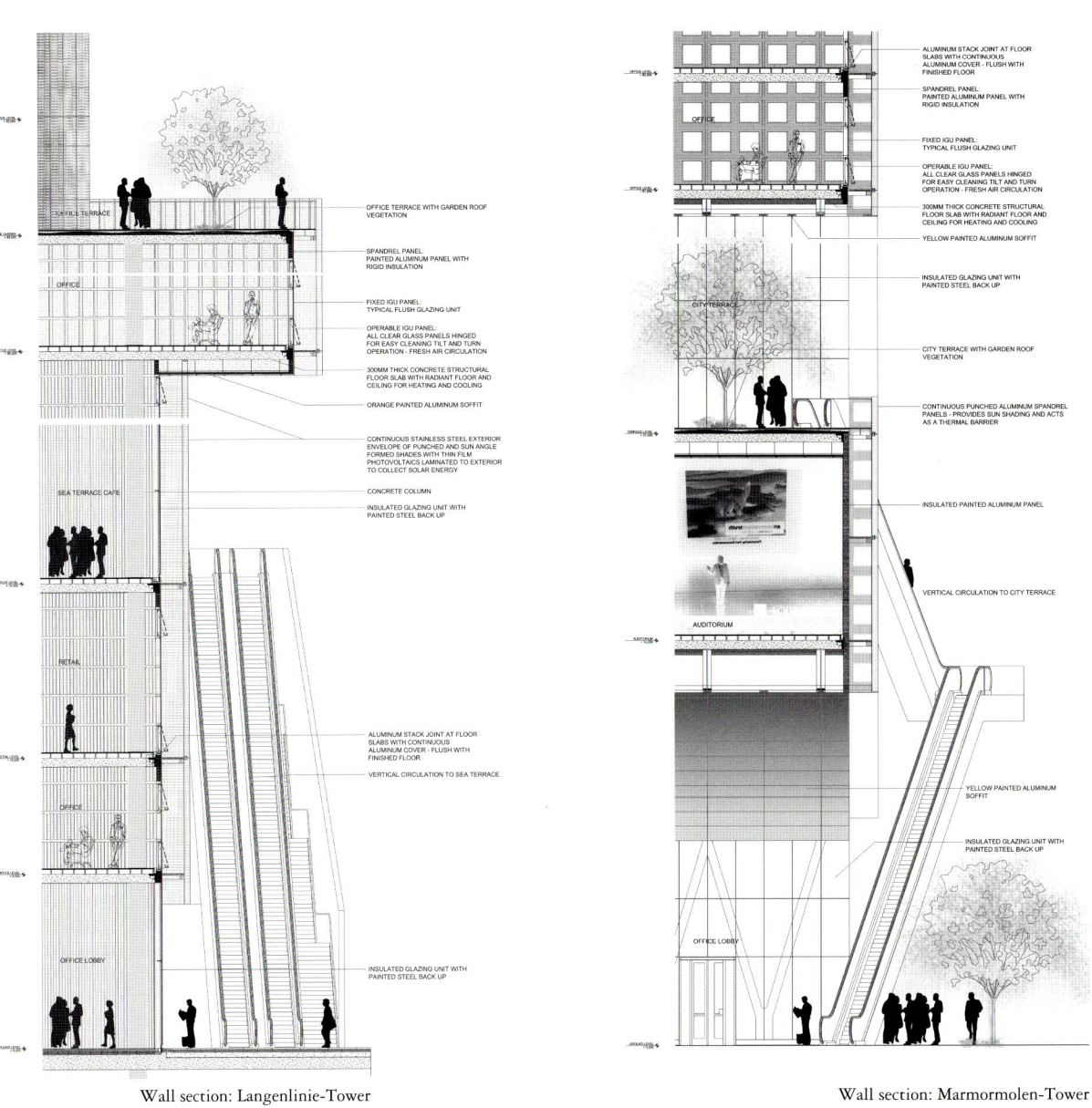

Sketch: public circulation

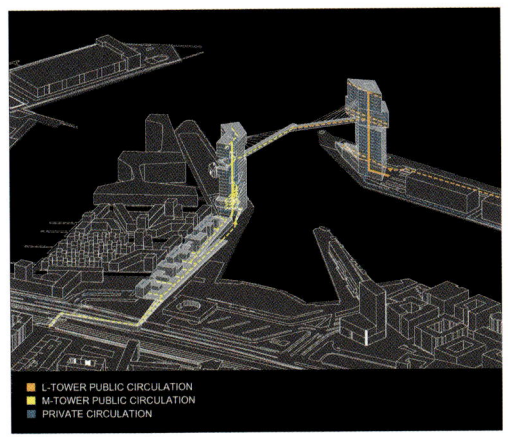

Diagram: public circulation

Program

Wall section: Langenlinie-Tower

Wall section: Marmormolen-Tower

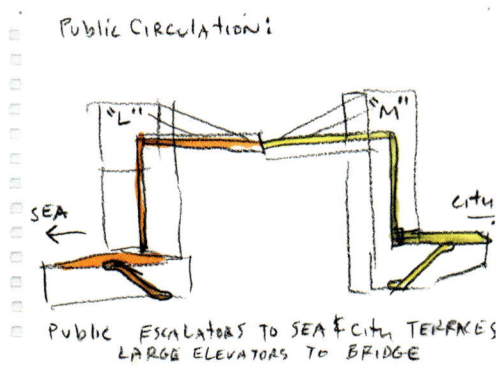

Section: Langenlinie-Tower (left) and Marmormolen-Tower (right)

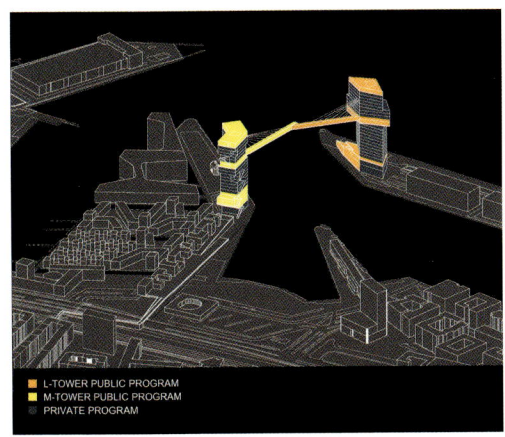

II-305

2009– **Shan-Shui Hangzhou**
Hangzhou, China

Evening view: one of Lantern Towers (left), Canal Spreaders (center), Water Tower and Mountain Tower (right behind)

Model: Mountain Tower and Water Tower, Canal Spreaders, and Lantern Towers (from left to right)

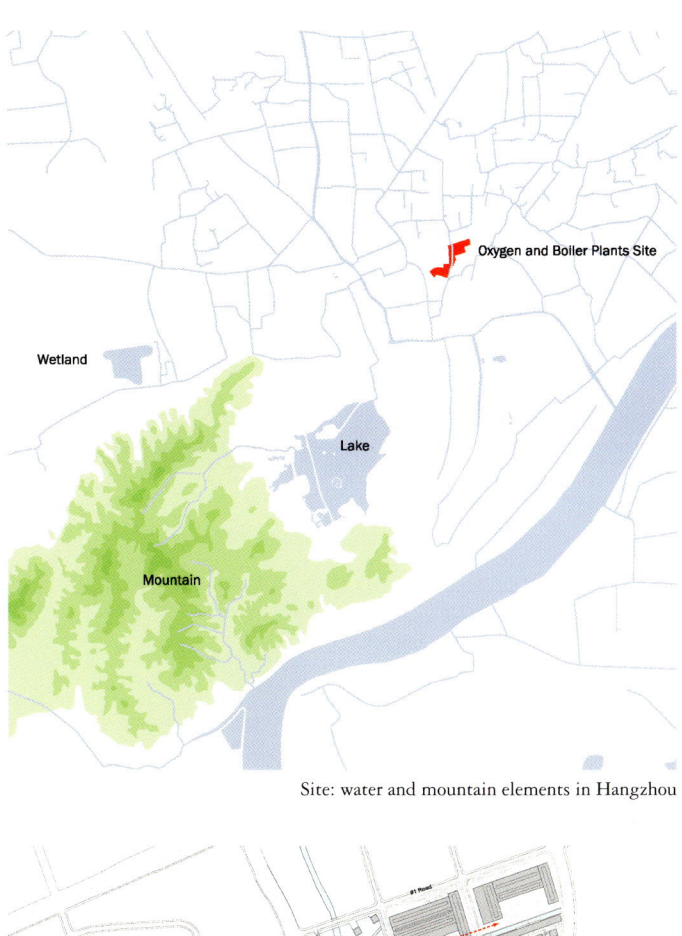

Site: water and mountain elements in Hangzhou

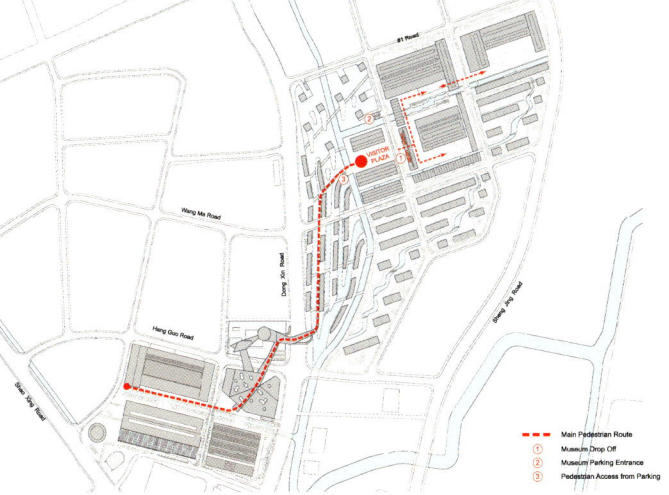

Pedestrian circulation

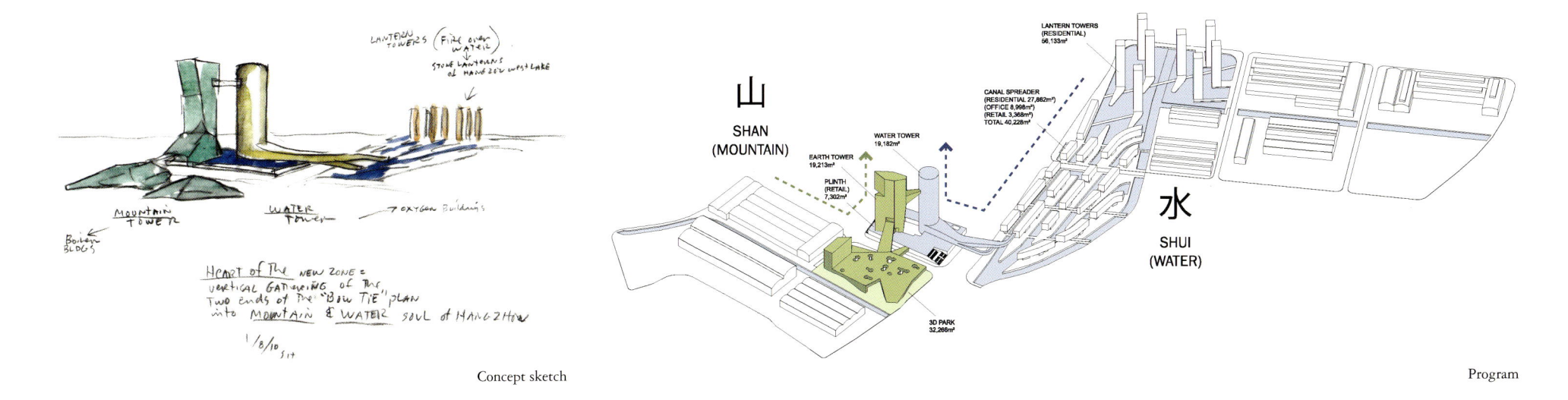

Concept sketch

Program

II-307

LANTERN TOWERS CANAL SPREADERS

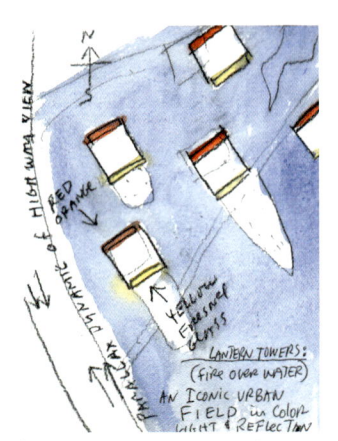

Sketch: Lantern Towers on canal

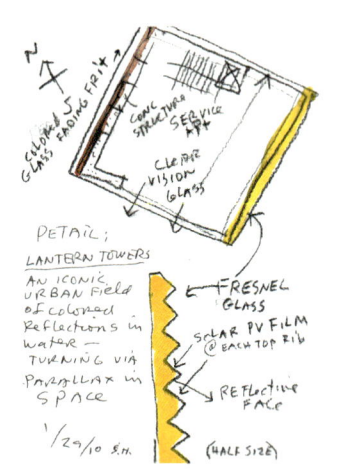

Facade of Lantern Towers: glass curtain wall

View toward Lantern Towers over Canal Spreaders

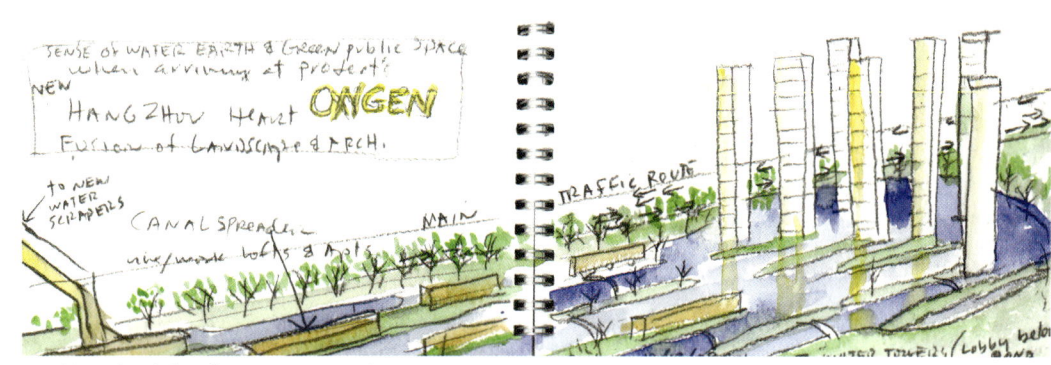

Canal Spreaders (left) and Lantern towers (right)

Lantern Towers

Steven Holl Architects (SHA) won the master plan for this international competition in 2009. In the current development, the SHA site brings together an urban constellation with David Chipperfield Architects's design for the reuse of the boiler factory buildings on the southern portion of the site, and Herzog & de Meuron's reuse of the former oxygen factory buildings to the north.

The heart of the "bowtie" plan is a "Water Tower" and a "Mountain Tower," alluding to the spirit of Hangzhou. The Water Tower branches into tributary forms connecting to the north, while the Mountain Tower connects via landscape forms to the south.

There are five large scale elements in the SHA design, which hover between landform and architecture, connecting to the factory buildings at each end of the site.

1) Water Tower
The round water tower rises from a sheet of water, connecting with a curved bridge crossing Dong Xing Road to the north. This diffused glass tower houses serviced apartments and offices with retail space at the base, and a restaurant and event space at the top.

2) Canal Spreaders
An existing canal feeds five new canals, lined with new hybrid buildings. These "Canal Spreaders" characterize a new zone of living by the water. They offer a variety of housing types as well as offices, cafes, restaurants and shops along the public paths at the water's edge.

3) Lantern Towers
The lantern towers take inspiration from the old stone lanterns in West Lake, setting "fire over

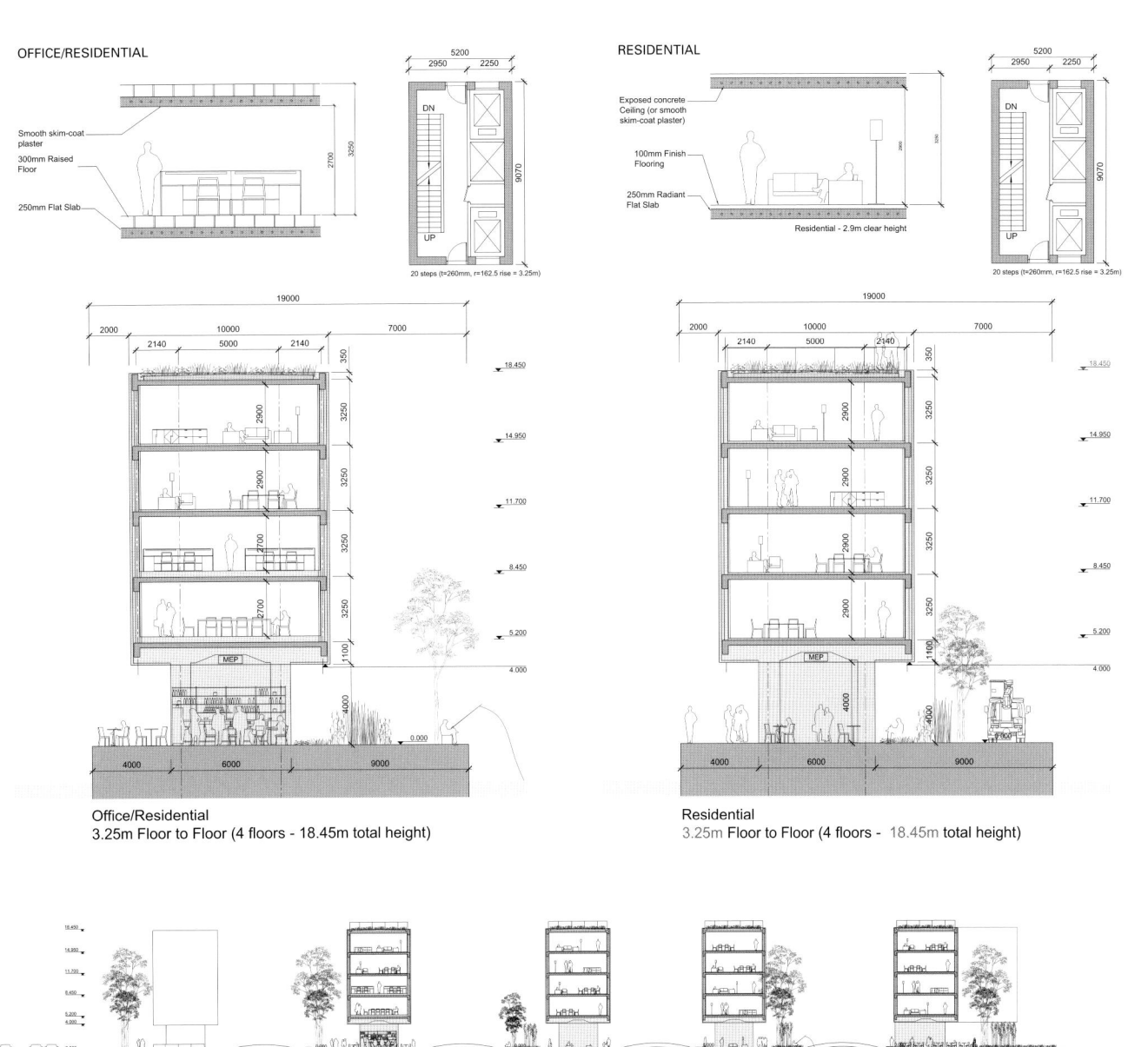

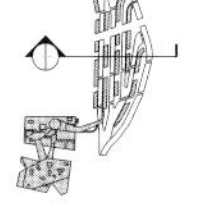

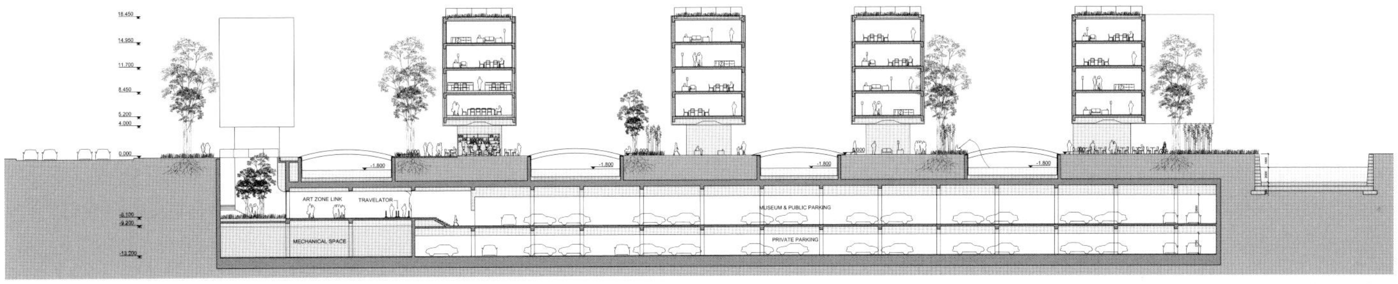

water." Photovoltaic glass curtain walls gather the sun's energy during the day. At night, one elevation of each tower glows via special Fresnel glass, reflecting the day's energy in the water. One loft apartment per floor is connected by an elevator to collective lobbies below the pond. Health club, spa, retail shopping and parking levels connect the lower levels.

4) Mountatin Tower
At the center of the site, the Mountain Tower is joined via an escalator bridge to an event space at the top to the Water Tower. This tower of translucent ceramic skin and green roofs branches to the landscape of the 3D Park.

5) 3D Park
A fusion of landscape and architecture in the 3D Park yields public green-space roofs with openings; as "gardens within gardens," bringing nature and light to the lower levels. It is flanked by a 200-room hotel, served by a spa and restaurants opening to roof gardens, and bisected by a pedestrian link, lined with shops.

Hybrid buildings, the mix of functions, the merging of architecture and landscape, and the invigorating programs inserted into the re-used factory buildings, characterize this unique urban constellation.

Aspiring to a twenty-first century urban vitality in balance with landscape, Shan-Shui will be a magnificent and inspiring new section of the great city of Hangzhou.

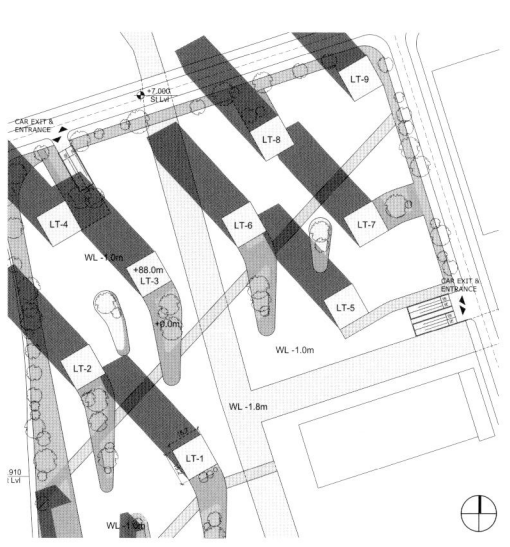

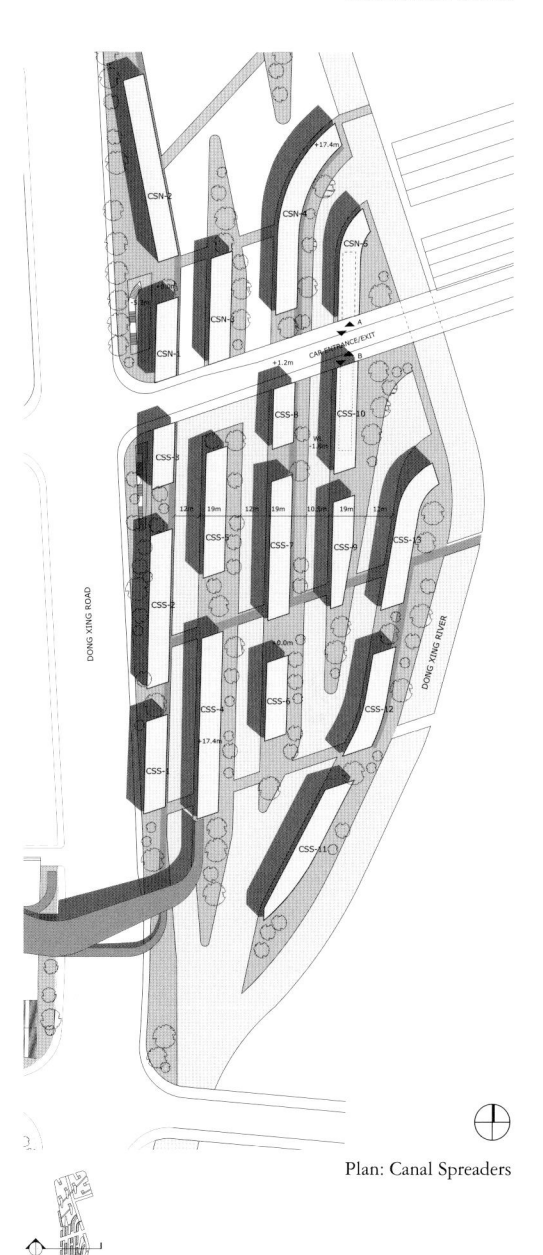

WATER TOWER
MOUNTAIN TOWER
3D PARK

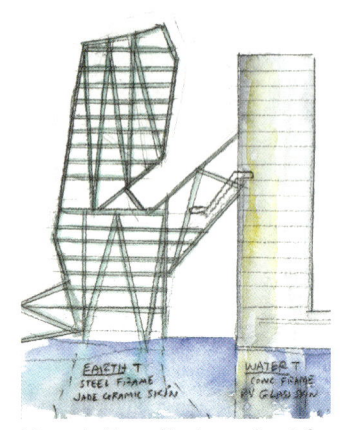

Mountain Tower (Earth tower) on left and Water Tower on right

Night view: Moutain Tower and Water Tower on left. Water Spreaders on right

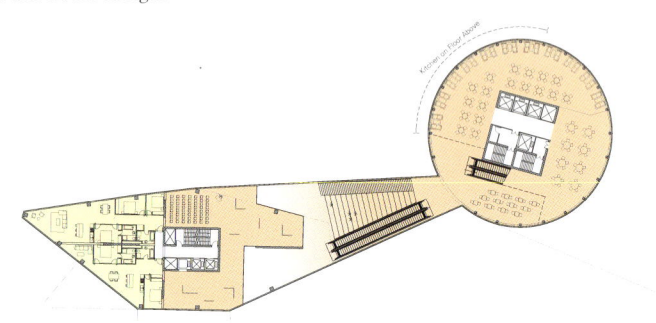

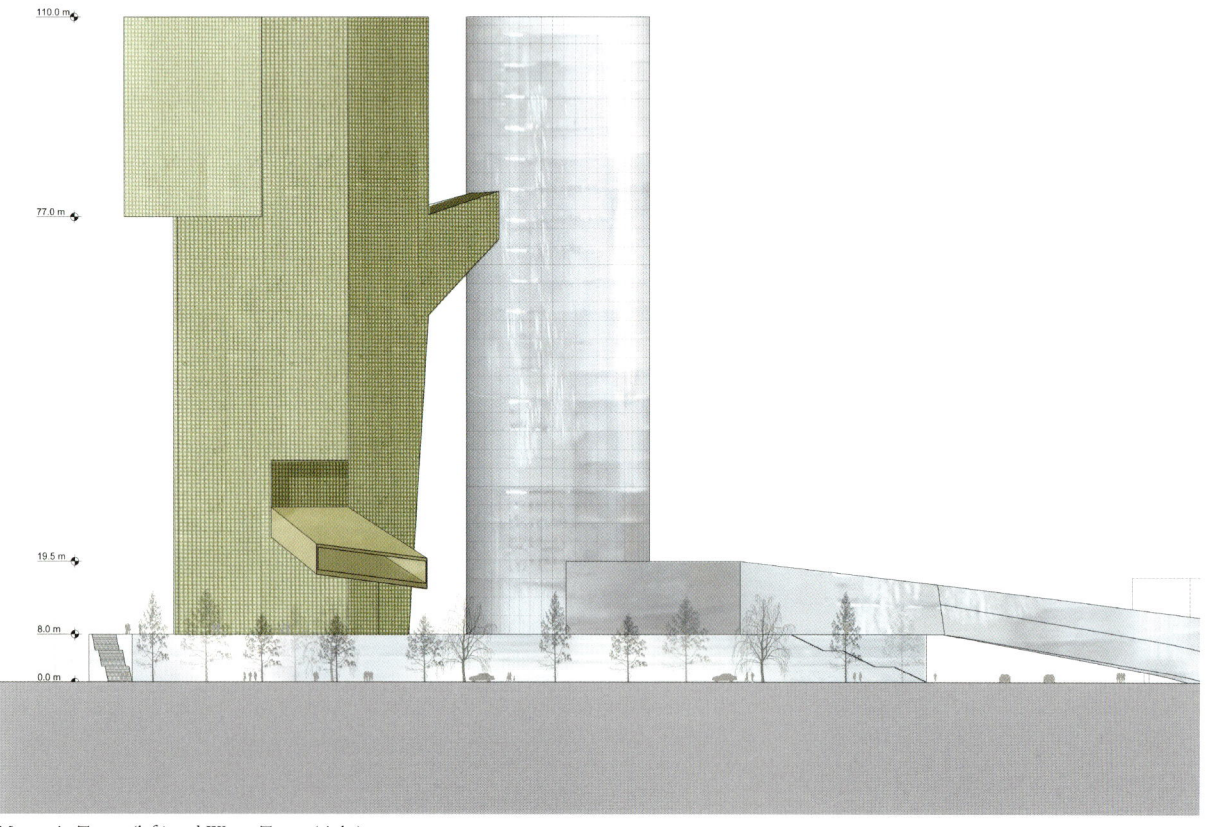

Mountain Tower (left) and Water Tower (right):
typical floor plan (above) and elevation (below). Mountain Tower is joined to Water Tower via an escalator bridge on upper level

杭州「山水」計画

2009年の国際コンペで優勝したマスタープランである。南側の敷地ではデヴィッド・チッパーフィールドがボイラー工場の再利用計画を、北側ではかつて酸素製造工場として使われてきた工場の再利用計画をヘルツォーク&ド・ムーロンが手掛けている。この開発は、これらの計画を都市へとひとつに布置させるためのものである。

「蝶ネクタイ」のような平面計画の中心にある「ウォーター・タワー」と「マウンテン・タワー」は、杭州の精神文化への暗喩である。ウォーター・タワーは川の支脈のように分岐し、北側の敷地へと連続する。マウンテン・タワーはランドスケープを通して、南の敷地へと繋がる。

スティーヴン・ホールの設計では、大地と建築のあいだで浮遊し、敷地の両端の工場建築へと連続する空間要素が5つ、巨大なスケールで計画されている。

1. ウォーター・タワー
丸い形のウォーター・タワーは水盤の上に立ち上がり、北側は東新路と交差する曲線状のブリッジへと接続している。拡散ガラスを使用したこのタワーには、滞在型ホテル、オフィス、足廻りには商業空間、最上階にはレストランとイベントスペースが収容される。

2. キャナル・スプレッダー
既存の運河は新しいハイブリッド・ビルディングの5本の運河に分岐する。これらの「キャナル・スプレッダー」は、水辺の新しい居住空間の特徴である。ここでは水辺の通路に沿って様々な種類のハウジング・タイプ、オフィス、カフェ、レストラン、及びショップが立ち並んでいる。

3. ランタン・タワー
水盤に炎を灯す。ランタン・タワーは西湖の古い石灯からインスピレーションを受けたものである。PVガラス・カーテンウォールは昼間、太陽光の集光が行われる。夜になると、それぞれのタワーのファサードが1面ずつ、特殊なフレネルガラスを通して輝きを放ち、昼間蓄えた光を水中に放つ。階ごとに一住戸ずつ設けられたロフトと水盤の下にある共用ロビーは、エレベータによって結ばれている。ヘルスクラブ、スパ、ショッピング、駐車場は、低層部で繋がっている。

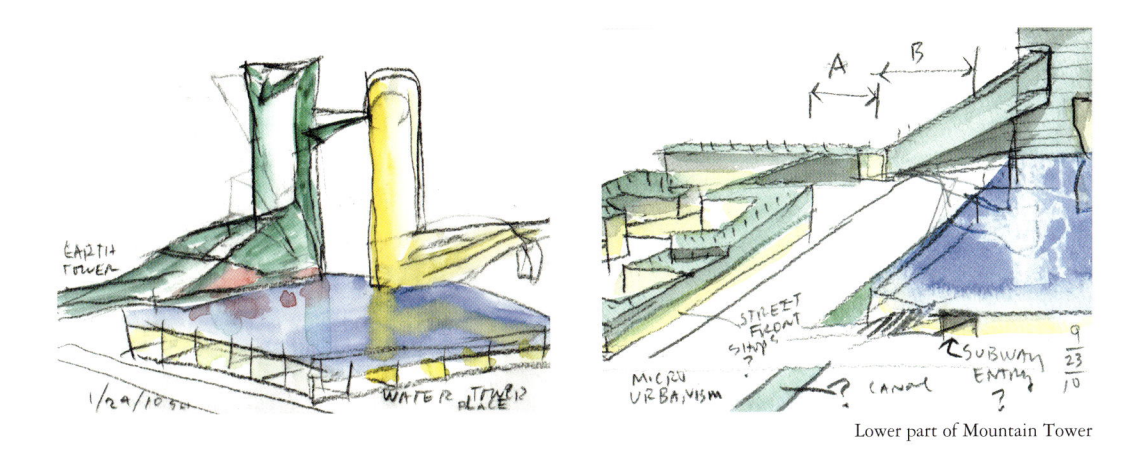

Lower part of Mountain Tower

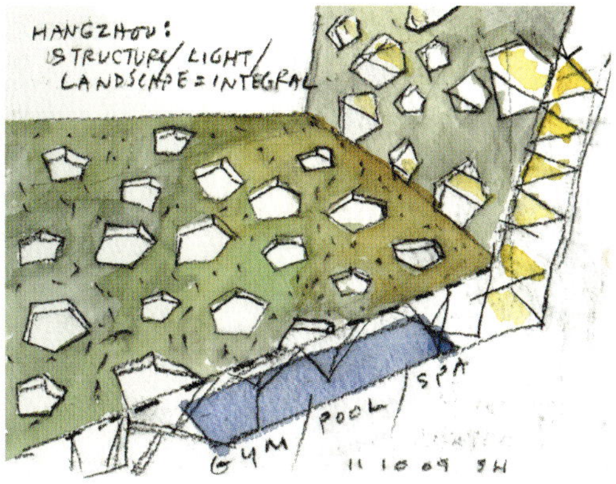

3D Park: green-space roofs with openings

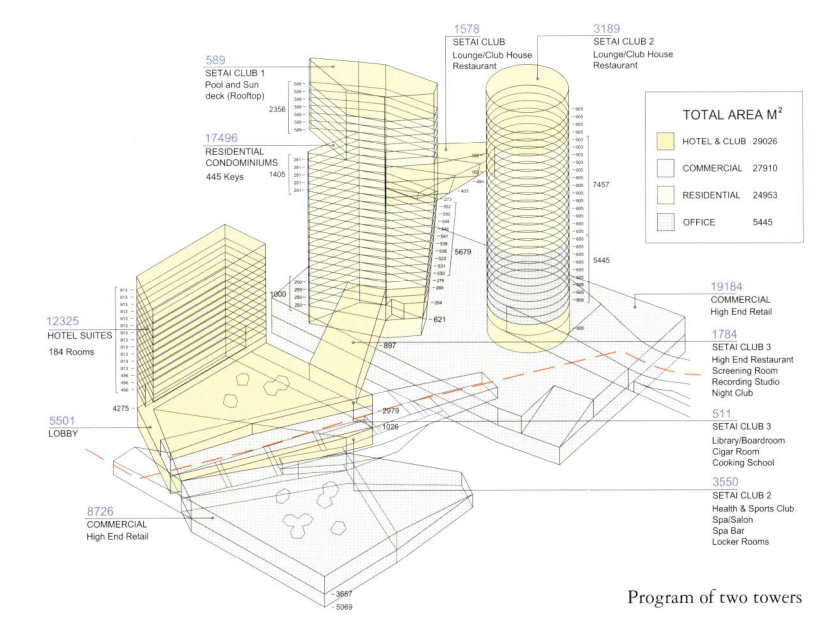

Program of two towers

Pool under 3D Park

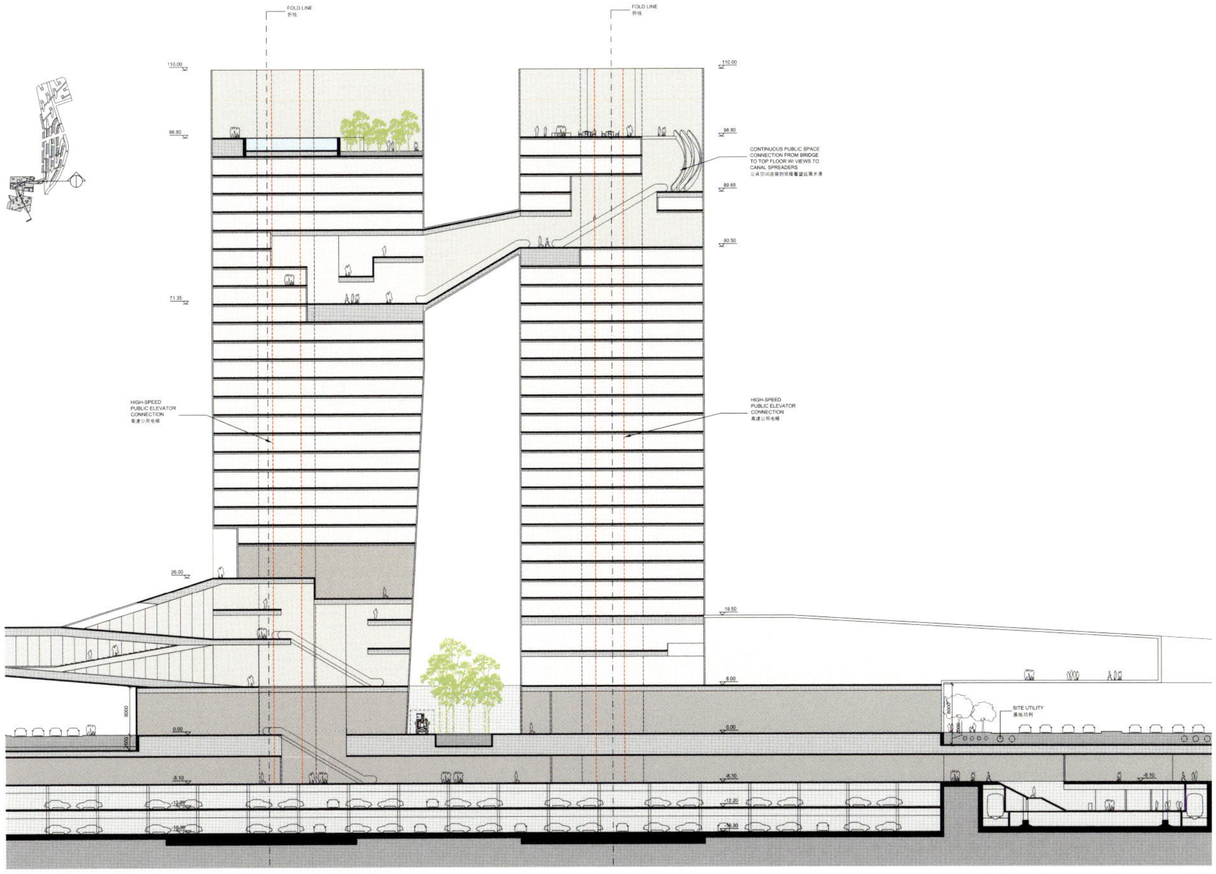

4. マウンテン・タワー
敷地の中央のマウンテン・タワーからは，エスカレーターブリッジを経由して，ウォーター・タワーの最上階のイベントスペースにゆくことができる。透過性セラミックの表皮と屋上緑化されたタワーからは，3Dパークのランドスケープへと動線が延びる。

5. 3Dパーク
3Dパークのランドスケープと建築の融合は，開口部を持ち緑化されたパブリックな屋根面に結実する。「庭園の中の庭園」として自然や太陽光が，下層階にまで届く。3Dパークは200室のホテルに隣接し，ルーフガーデンへと開放されたスパとレストランを利用できる。ショップに沿って走る歩道が空間を二分する。

ハイブリッド・ビルディングの複合的機能，建築とランドスケープとの融合，そして再生された工場建築に挿入される刺激的なプログラム。これらが都市的な布置に独自の特徴を与えている。

ランドスケープも調和のとれた21世紀の都市の生命力をかき立てる山水のプロジェクトは，壮大に人々を鼓舞する杭州という大都市の新しい側面となるだろう。

Section: Mountain Tower (left) and Water Tower (right)

6 Fusion: Landscape/Urbanism/Architecture
融合：景観／都市／建築

Parallel to the aim of enhancing and invigorating the experience of the body moving through urban space, is an aspiration for new composite configurations of landscape, urbanism & architecture. Different routes of movement in shifting ground planes through light, water, and vegetation characterize architecture melting into landscape. This interlacing of landscape and urban infrastructure provokes new building types where sections take precedent over plans.

The porous and green skin of the earth, combined with the spatial energy of architecture might yield a new synthesis of fused disciplines. The hope is for new experiential, environmental and social potential.

This conflation of landscape, urban form and architectonic space is aligned with the hybrid combination of metropolitan programs. Just as a hybrid building might contain apartments, offices, retail and cultural facilities, defying any reference to being singularly "this or that"—so the combination of landscape, urbanism and architecture yields a new amalgam; a hybrid type.

In Seoul, Korea, in the middle of the city we were invited to the competition for the World Design Park Complex (2007). From our very first sketches we felt that all the programmatic aspects inserted into this central area should be fused with the landscape. The concept of a tri-axial structure supporting a condition of landscape in several layers becomes a 3D landscape. The programmatic aspects, structure and light were united with planting and with different pools of recycled water. The tri-axial system creates a series of hexagons that drop light down in several layers into different programs or into the different 3-dimensional landscapes. We wanted to erase the notion of 'where does architecture begin and landscape end'. It becomes a fusion of landscape and architecture.

In the Lake Whitney Water Purification Plant (1998-2005) in Connecticut, the project was dedicated to purifying and supplying water to New Haven. 90% of the building is tucked in under the landscape. Only the administration wing emerges as a sliver in the landscape. We collaborated with Michael Van Valkenburgh Landscape Architects to create the largest green roof in the state of Connecticut. While accommodating all of the pragmatic functions of a large water treatment plant, we created a new kind of landscape experience.

In the case of the Visigoth Museum (2010) in Toledo, Spain, we were working with this notion of extreme heat in Spain and the mystery of the history of the Visigoth culture. It is a culture that comes out of the shadows of the past; still today there are many mysterious connections. The idea is a "pergola of shadows." The whole building would rise up and become another layer of the landscape with perforations, but also something that folds back into the land and becomes a kind of grotto below with shadows and water. On a hot afternoon, the experience of arriving at the Visigoth Center would be cool and refreshing with reflections of vegetation and circles of light rippling on water. Space, color, texture and light are integrated as in El Greco's great painting "Visions of Toledo", where sunlight pierces holes in the clouds.

The fusion of landscape, urbanism and architecture is an integral approach which might set the frame for a comprehensive way to think about particular projects. New hybrid building types might be realized with the aim of building a meaning into a site; forging an inspiring relation of a particular program and a unique place.

Steven Holl

Visigoth Museum

都市空間を歩くことを通して身体的経験を拡張し、活性化させる。そのような企図と平行するのは、ランドスケープ、アーバニズム、および建築の、新しい配置構成に対する願望である。光、水、植物によって地表面は遷移する。そのような様々な運動の方法の存在こそが、ランドスケープのなかへと融合してゆく建築の特徴である。そのようなランドスケープと都市構造の交錯は、断面が平面に先行する新しいビルディング・タイプを誘発する。

建築の空間的強度と共にポーラス状に大地を覆う緑が生み出すのは、融合した諸原則による新しい総合のかたちである。これは新しい実験的、環境的、社会的潜在性に秘められた希望である。

ランドスケープ、都市形態、そして建築空間の融合は、都市的なプログラムの複合的結合と並列的な関係にある。ハイブリッド・ビルディングは集合住宅、オフィス、商業店舗、文化施設を内包し、「これか、さもなければ、あれか」といった単純な言及を拒絶する。その結果、ランドスケープ、アーバニズム、そして建築は、新しい空間の融合体、すなわちハイブリッドという類型を生み出すのだ。

韓国ソウルでは、市街中心部のワールド・デザイン・パーク(2007)のコンペに招待された。最初のスケッチの段階から、この町の中心部に挿入されるプログラムは、あらゆる側面においてランドスケープと融合するべきであるように思われた。複数の階層でランドスケープのあらゆる状態を支持する3軸構造が、3次元のランドスケープへと結実する。プログラム、構造、光といった建築要素は、再生水を使った様々な種類の水盤や植栽とひとつに結びつけられる。3軸構造が生み出す六角形のレンズの組み合わせは、様々な種類のプログラムや3次元ランドスケープに、複数の階層にわたって光を落とす。「建築はどこから始まり、ランドスケープはどこで終わるのか」。そのような概念を消失させることで、ランドスケープと建築はひとつに融合される。

コネチカット州のホイットニー湖の浄水施設(1998-2005)では、水資源を浄化し、ニューヘイヴンに上水を供給することが計画された。建築のうちの90%はランドスケープのなかに埋め込まれている。ここでは管理棟のみが、ランドスケープのなかで細長い切片のように存在している。コネチカット州で最大規模の屋上緑化は、ランドスケープ・アーキテクトのマイケル・ヴァン・ヴォルケンバーグとの共同作業によるものである。大規模水処理施設に要求される実務的なあらゆる機能を収容する一方で、ランドスケープに対する新しい経験が生み出された。

スペイン、トレドの西ゴート族博物館(2010)は、スペインの灼熱の気候と、西ゴート族文化の歴史の神秘への取り組みである。西ゴートとは、歴史の影から生まれてきた文化である。その神秘性は、今日にも数多く引き継がれている。コンセプトは「パーゴラの落とす影」。建築全体は宙に浮き、多孔質のランドスケープに新しい階層が生まれる。その一方で、一部は下部に向かって折れ曲がり、影と水の洞窟をつくる。暑日の午後、西ゴート族研究センターに着くと、涼しく、気持ちをリフレッシュさせてくれる。植栽は水盤に映り、光の輪が水面にさざ波をたてる。雲の隙間から太陽光が差し込むエル・グレコの名作「トレド眺望」の風景のように、空間、色彩、質感、そして光は、ひとつに統合される。

ランドスケープ、都市、そして建築を融合するということは、個別の計画の検討に対する包括的方法論に方向性を示す上で必要なアプローチである。ある敷地に意味性を付与すること。個別のプログラムと場所の固有性のあいだに、挑発的な関係性をつくりだすこと。これらが契機となり、ハイブリッド・ビルディングという新しい類型が現実のものとなるのだ。

(スティーヴン・ホール)

2007

World Design Park Complex
Seoul, South Korea

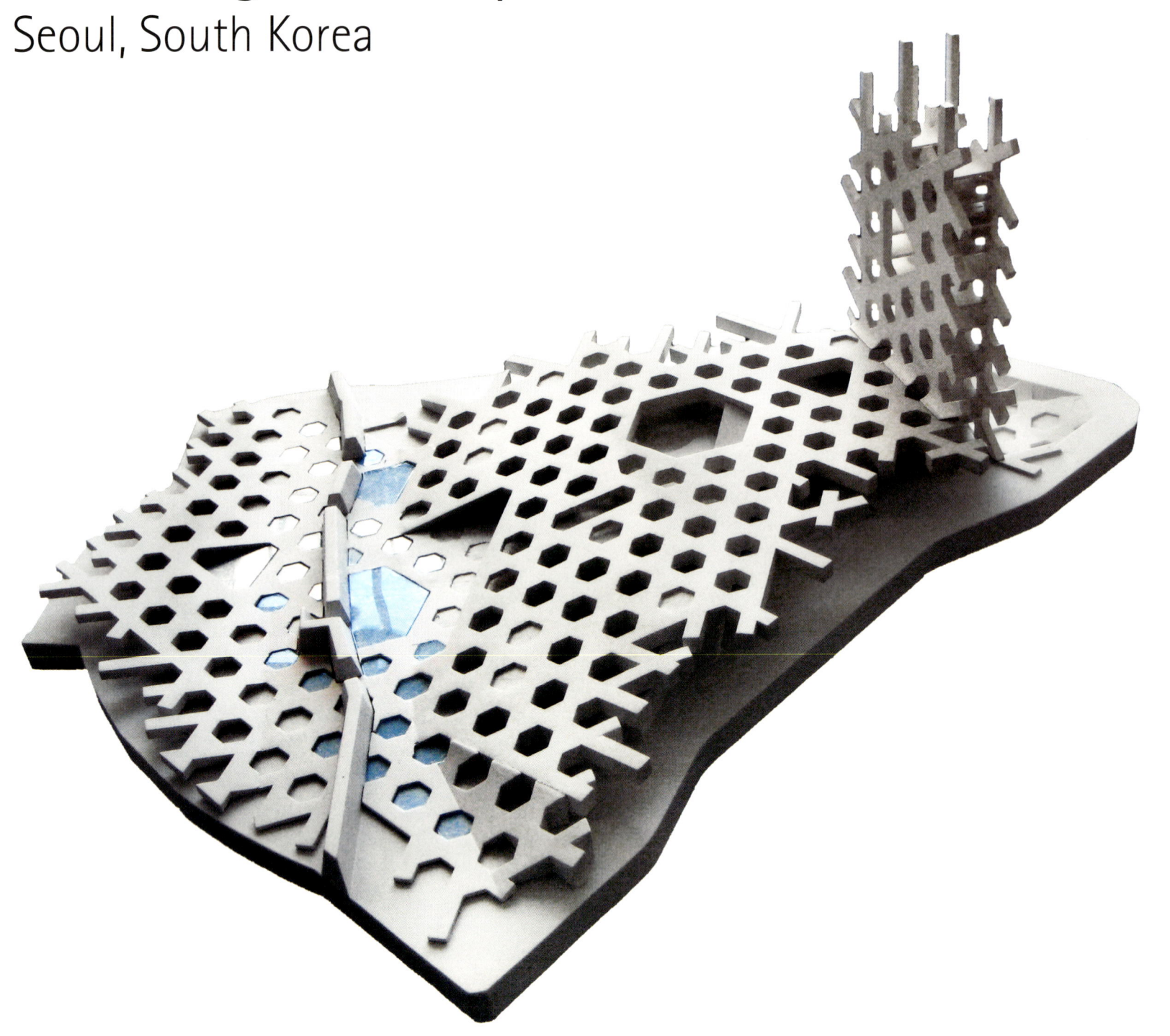

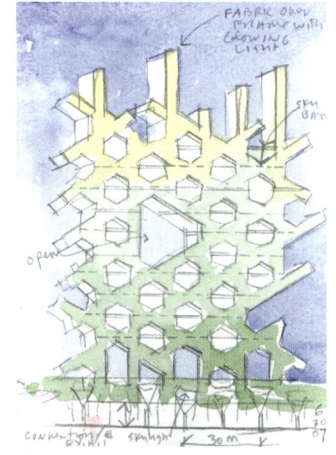

Sketch: vertical park

Double layered park

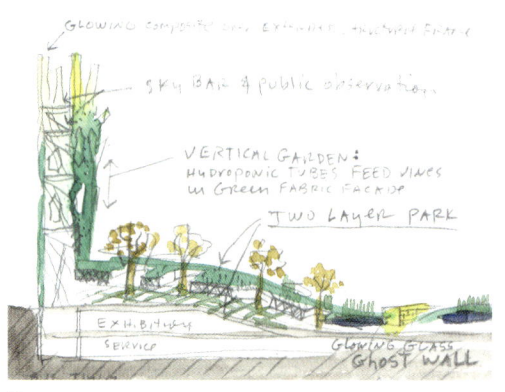

Program

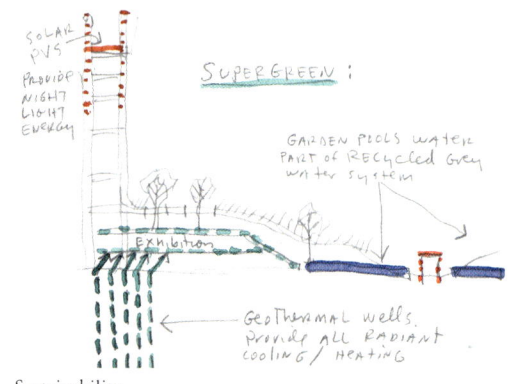

Sustainability

Distant view

Section

Double layered park

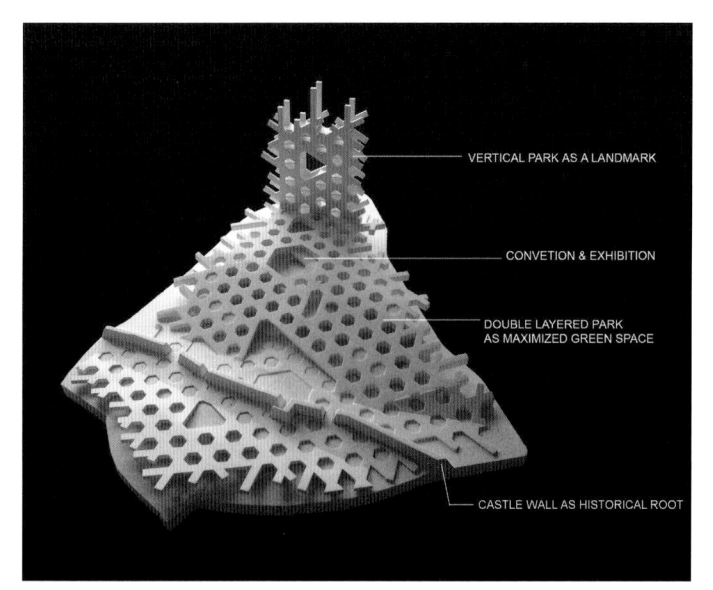

Diagram

Ground level

1 SHOP ENTRY
2 SHOPPING CENTER
3 COLLECTION STORAGE
4 PARKING
5 CONVENTION HALL
6 SPECIAL EXHIBITION
7 EXHIBITION
8 LOBBY
9 DESIGN INFORMATION CENTER

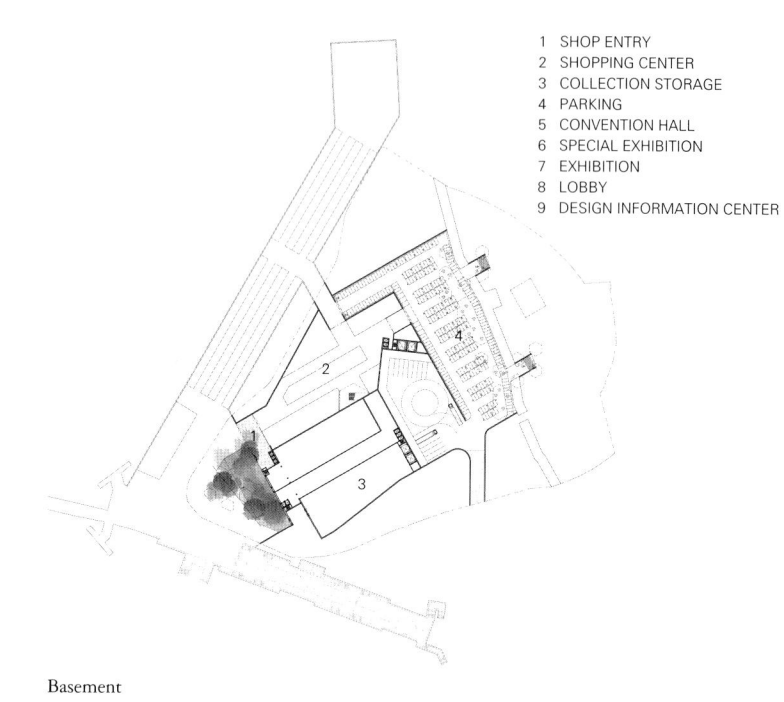

Basement

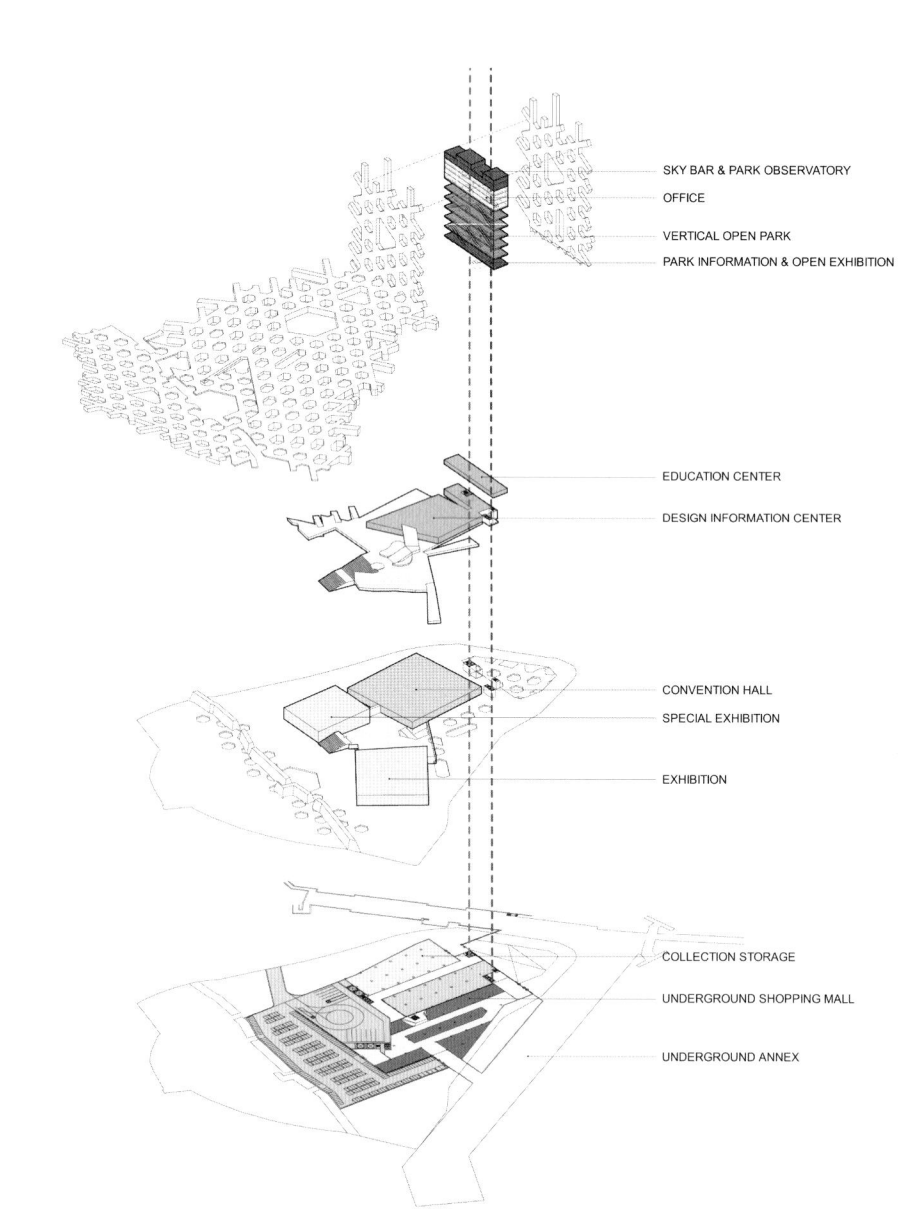

Program

The "weave" concept for this project refers to four different meanings: a double level and Vertical Park in the form of a weave; the old historic morphology of Seoul's Kangbuk district with its intricate weave of streets, historic structures and gardens; the new role of the surrounding fashion district and textiles; and a 21st century aspiration to fuse landscape, urbanism and architecture.

The site's historic trace of the ancient castle wall is envisioned to be reconstructed in cast glass blocks which are the same size and dimensions of the original stones. At night, these glass blocks will glow and add a special quality to the new landscape.

The basic morphology of the macro scale "weave" is based on a tri-axial fabric which yields six-sided voids. These spaces take on various configurations—skylights, gardens, water ponds, fountains—as the phase change of the "weave" responds to variations over the landscape.

At the site's southwest corner, the "weave" suddenly turns vertical, forming an open porous framework for the relocation of a vertical section of the Park. The tri-axial structure is open with an open air carbon fiber weave curtain. On the upper level, elevators serve a sky bar and cafe, public observation deck and visitors information centre, while a large below grade public lobby joins all public circulation to the subway stations and underground shopping malls.

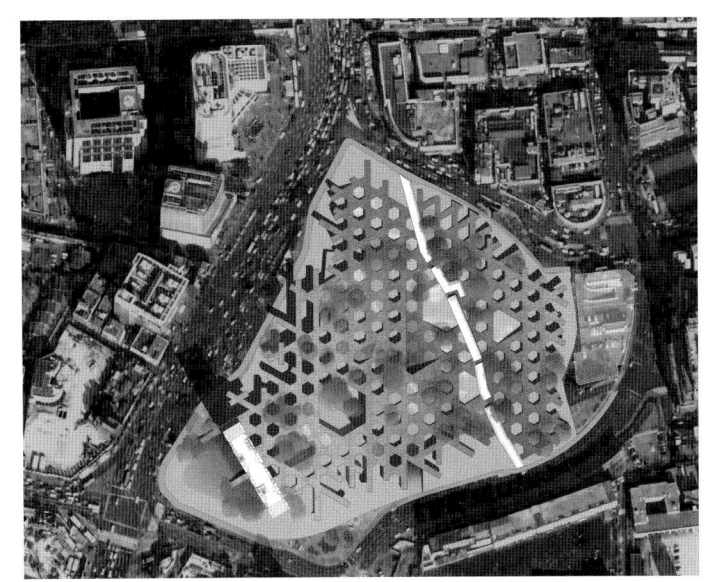

Site plan/roof

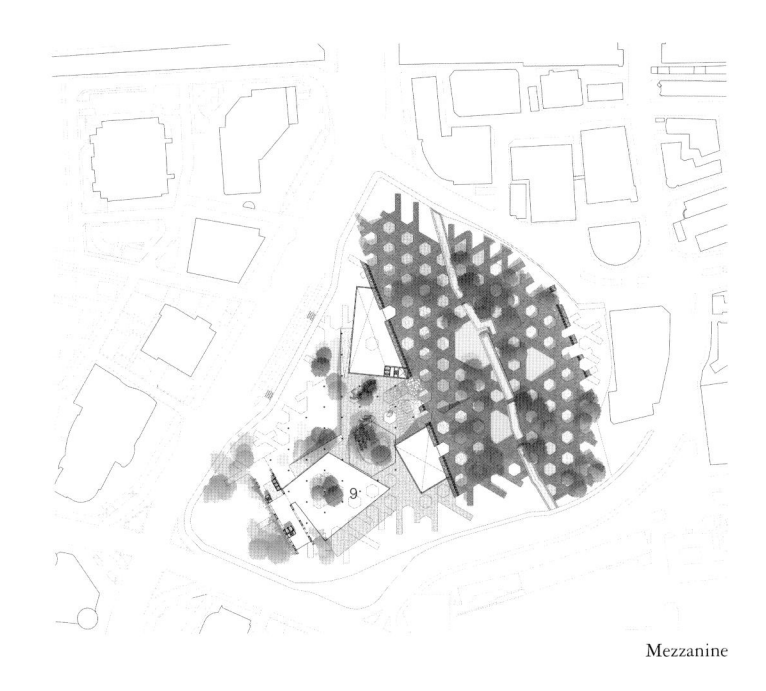

Mezzanine

Double layered park: view toward staircase to lobby

Double layered park

ワールド・デザイン・パーク
このプロジェクトにおける，「織物」というコンセプトには，次の四つの意味がある。水平方向の二つの階層と，バーティカル・パークが，織物のような形状をしていること。この歴史あるソウル市カンブック(江北)地区では，街路，歴史的建造物，庭が，入り組んだ形態を織りなしていること。周辺の服飾問屋街と繊維産業が，新しい役割を担うということ。景観，都市計画，建築を融合させようという，21世紀的な，熱烈な願望があるということ。

敷地に残る歴史的な城壁の跡は，縦・横・高さともオリジナルの石材と同じサイズの，鋳造ガラスブロックで再構築されることによって描き出される。夜になると，ガラスブロックの壁が光り輝き，この新しい景観に格別な素晴らしさを加えることとなる。

マクロなスケールにおける「織物」の基本的な形態は，六角柱状のヴォイドをもたらす，3軸構造体を基にしている。地形の変化に対応し，「織物」の姿が変化していくにつれて，これらのヴォイドは，スカイライト，庭園，池，噴水など，様々な構成要素となっていく。

敷地の南西の角部で，「織物」は突如として垂直に立ち上がり，屋根の無い，たくさんの穴が開いた構造を形づくり，パークの垂直部分がここから展開していく。この3軸構造体は，メッシュ状のカーボン・ファイバー製の織物で覆われているが，オープンなものである。上層階にはカフェ・バー，公開の展望デッキ，観光案内所があり，複数のエレベータが通じている。地下には公共のロビーがあり，地下鉄の駅と，地下のショッピング・モールへの，一般の動線をつないでいる。

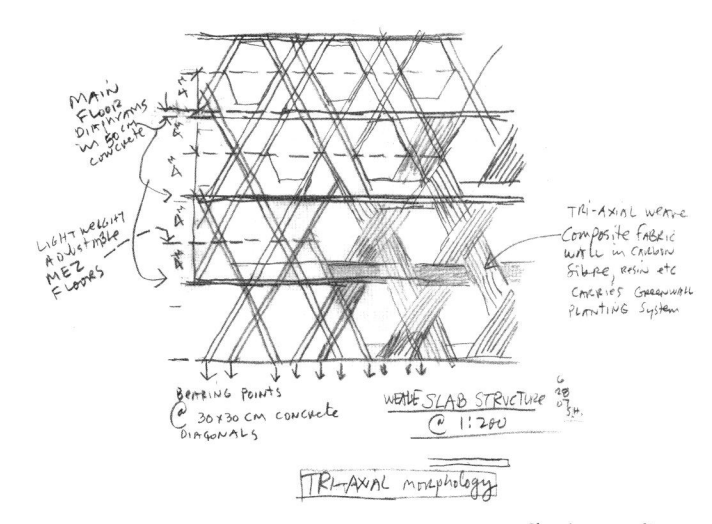

Skecth: tower diagram

2008– Triaxial Field
Hangzhou, China

Entrance

Site
The site at a wetland edge of the water city of Hangzhou, is part of a larger development of hotels and villas. The view to natural wetlands to the west will be inspiring.

Program
The program is for a unique event space which can have a chapel-like atmosphere for weddings, musical and dramatic events. The space can also service large banquets or conferences and presentations.

Concept/Strategy
Rather than make an "object" building we propose to make a field; to merge the landscape and architecture. Light from above for the main event space is formed by voids cut through a triaxial structure. Structure is integral to the light as it was in many historical examples of sacred architecture throughout history.

This new field-like form is integrated with water ponds that are higher on the east edge, gently dropping in elevation to the west which are analogous to ponds in the adjacent wetland preserve. A stair to this roof/field leads to selected areas with wire guard rails. The laminated glass skylights with integral solar PVC film can also be walked on.

Geothermal wells provide heating and cooling for the space via radiant floor slabs. A few skylights open automatically at the uppermost area of the space inducing natural ventilation and supplementing cooling.

The structural concept a triaxially reinforced post-tension concrete plane, is gently folded to shape space and sliced for the main entrance and openings to landscape.

Due to the post-tensioning of the white concrete structure the roof slab is naturally water-tight. Among the many green aspects of the building is the new generation of white concrete with its ability to scrub CO_2 from the atmosphere.

Along the west elevation doors can be opened out for activities which spill out into the landscape.

Concept

Program

Circulation

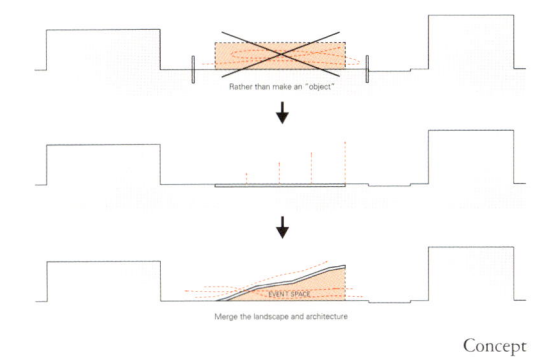

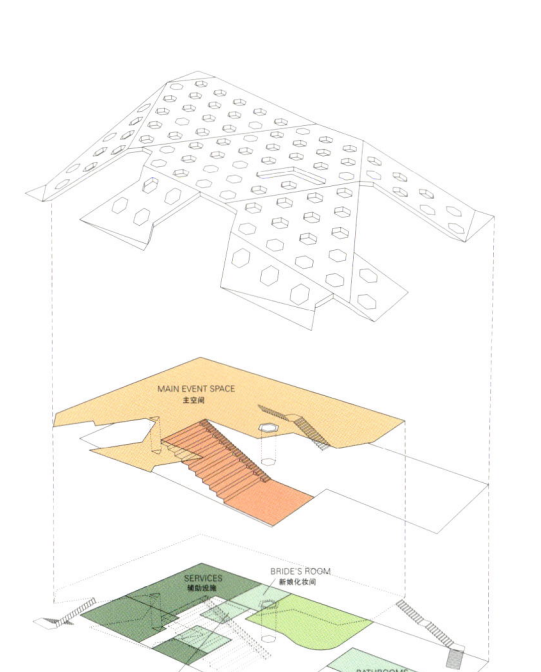

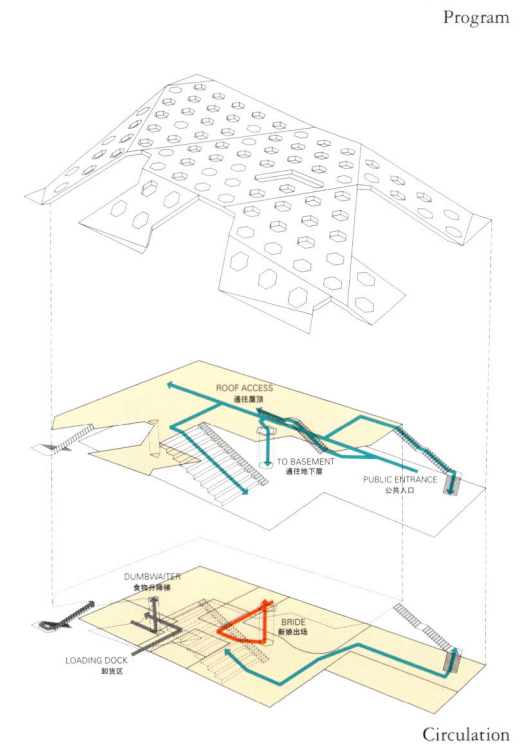

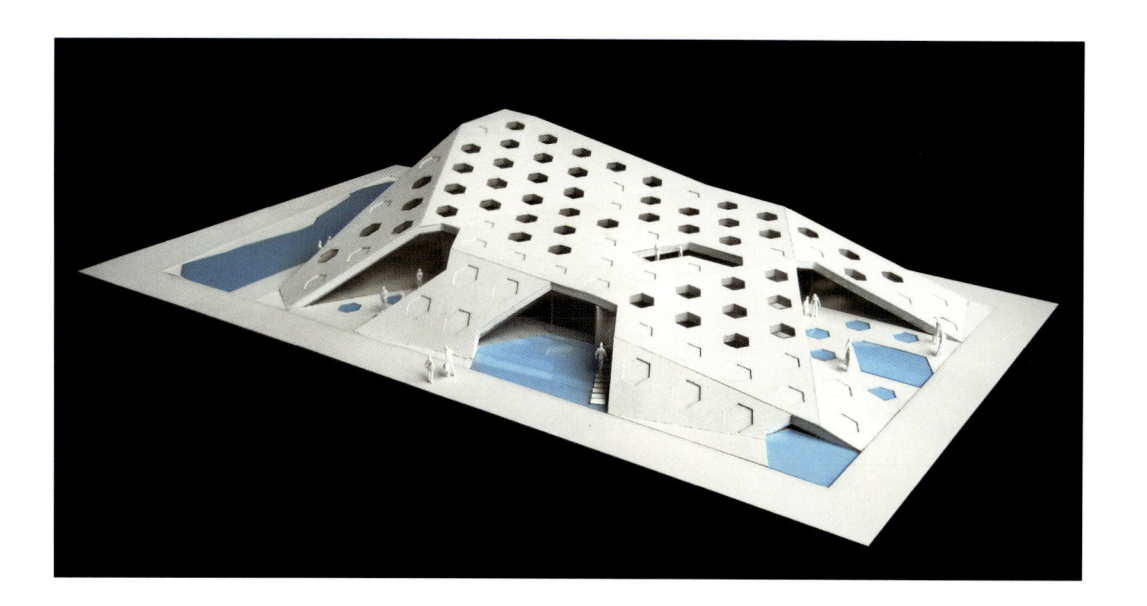

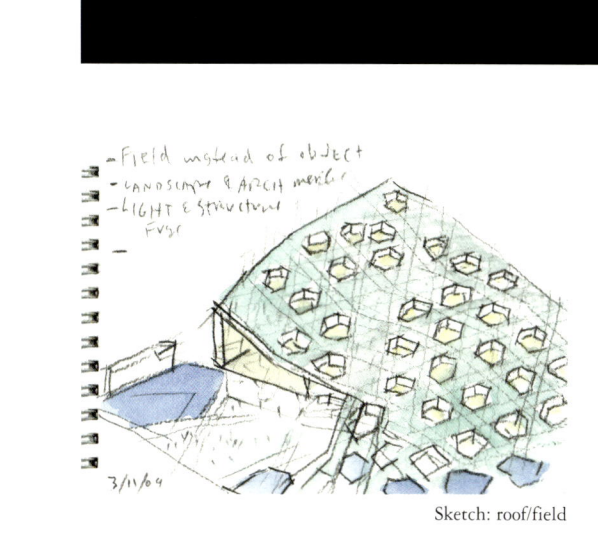

Sketch: roof/field

Multi-function space

Main event space

II-319

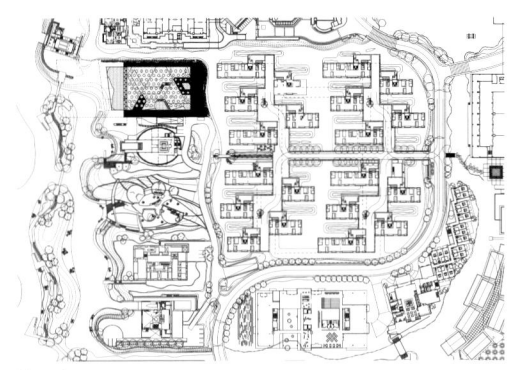

Site plan

3軸構造フィールド
［敷地］
敷地は水の都，杭州にある湿地帯の端に位置し，ホテルや別荘地のための大規模な開発地の一部である．西に向かって広がる湿地帯の自然の景色が，想像力をかきたてる．

［プログラム］
計画されているのは，ユニークなイベントスペースである．そのスペースは教会のような雰囲気を持ち，結婚式や音楽・演劇のイベントを催すことができる．また，大きなパーティや会議，あるいは説明会の場としても利用可能である．

［コンセプト／計画］
「物体」としての建物ではなく，ランドスケープと建築が一体になった場を提案する．メインイベントスペースに差し込む上方からの光は，三つ軸を持つ構造体をくり抜いた吹抜けによって形作られている．歴史上の多くの神聖な建築物がそうであるように，構造は，建築において光を決定する要素として不可欠なものである．

地面のような形状をしたこの建物は，東端部の方が高くなっており，隣接する湿地帯にある池と一体化するように，西側に向かってそのレベルを徐々に下げている．フィールド／屋根に通じる階段は金網の手摺で囲われる限定されたエリアに通じている．太陽光を調節する塩化ビニール製フィルムでラミネートされたガラスの天窓の上も，歩くことができる．

冷暖房は，地熱井による床スラブの放射熱で行われる．また最上部の天窓の数カ所は自動で開き，自然換気させて冷却を補う．

構造のコンセプトである三つの軸で補強されたポストテンション・コンクリートの面は，全体を形づくるために緩やかに折り曲げられ，またメインエントランスとランドスケープへとつながる開口部では，切り込まれる．

ポストテンションのホワイト・コンクリート構造の屋根スラブは，そのままでも防水性がある．環境に配慮した数々の材料の中でも，大気から二酸化炭素を削減する効果を持つ，ホワイト・コンクリートの新しい世代が始まる．

西面の扉は外に向かって開放することができ，ランドスケープへと溢れ出す屋外の活動を可能にしている．

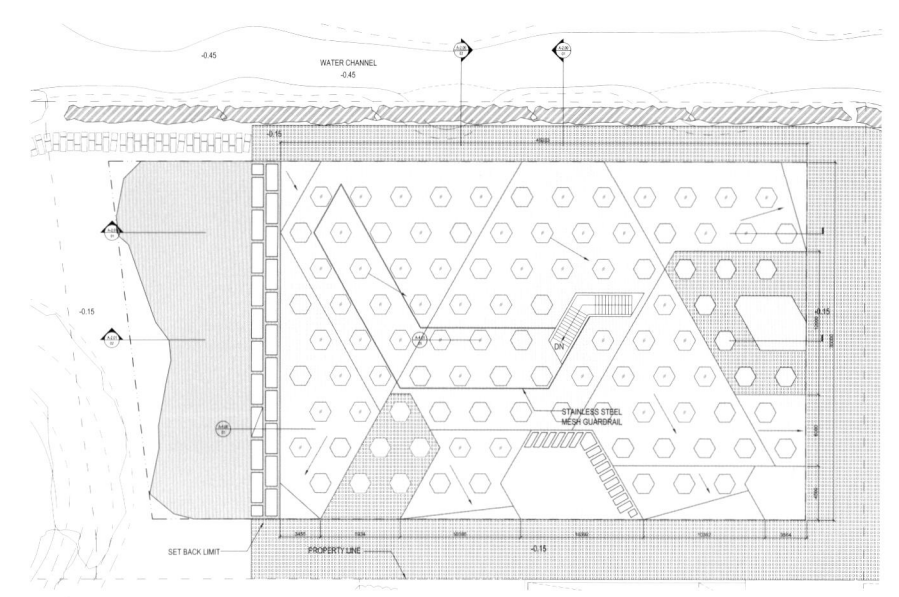

Roof

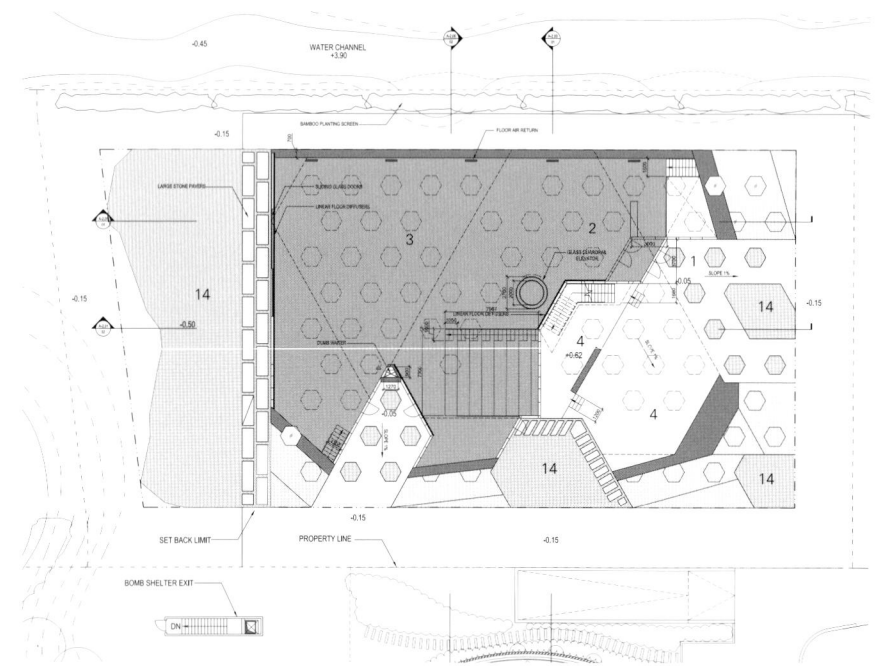

Ground floor

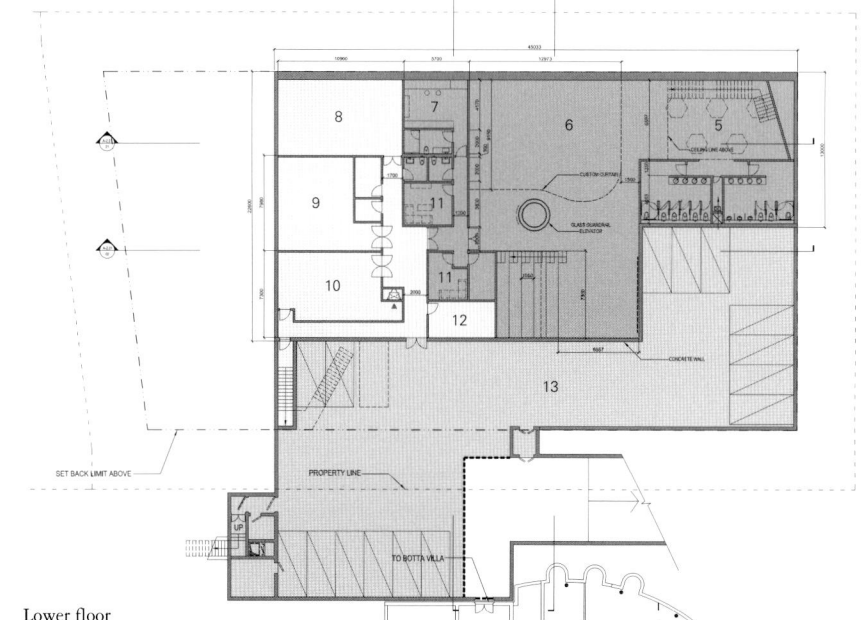

Lower floor

1 ENTRANCE
2 LOBBY
3 MAIN EVENT SPACE (OPEN AREA)
4 PORCH
5 FOYER
6 MULTI-FUNCTION SPACE
7 BRIDE'S ROOM
8 MECHANICAL
9 STORAGE
10 FOOD PREPARATION
11 GUEST ROOM
12 STAFF ROOM
13 CIVIL DEFENSE SPACE
14 POOL

Porch

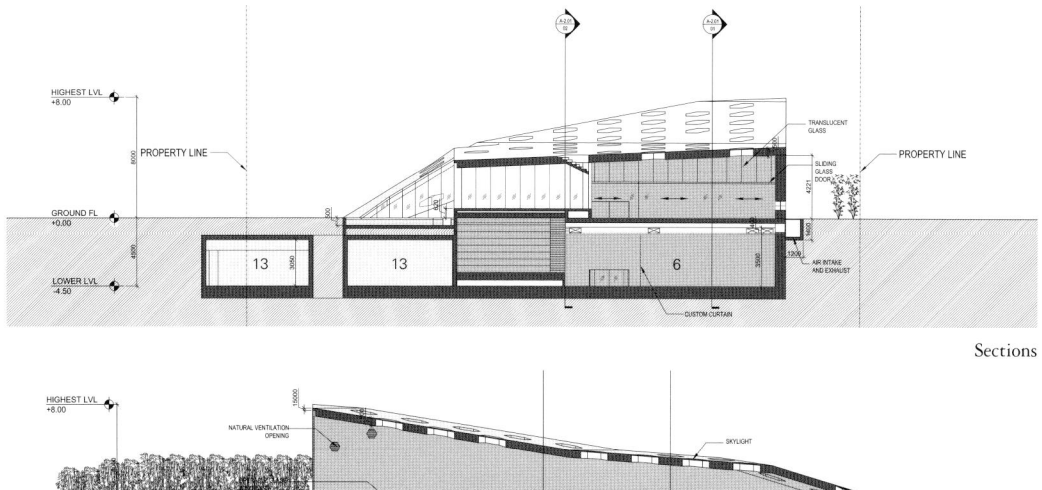

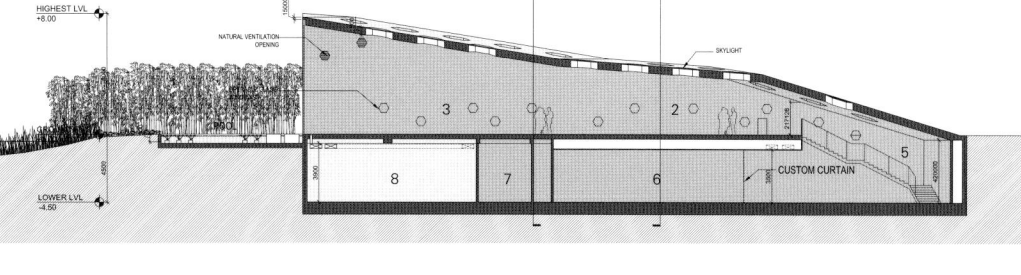

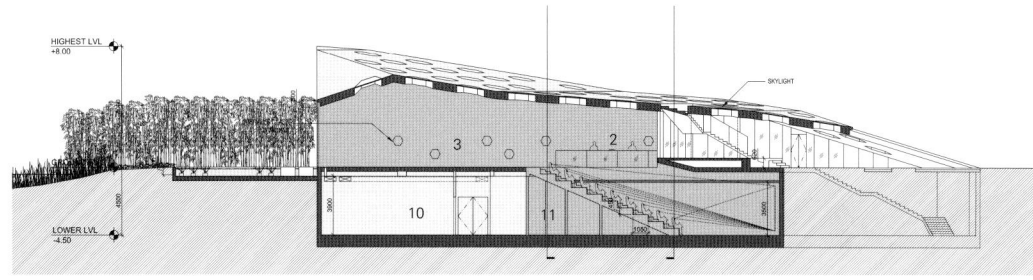

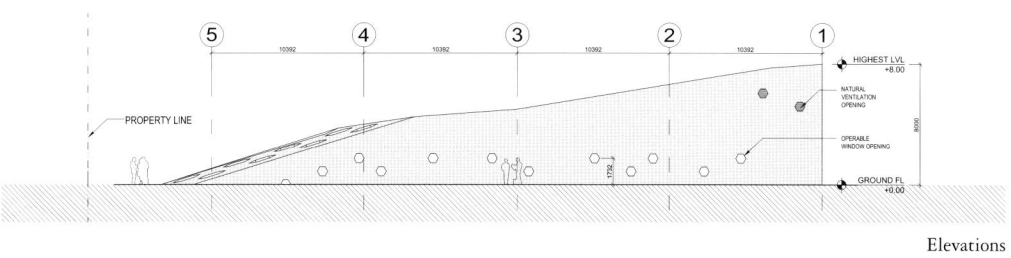

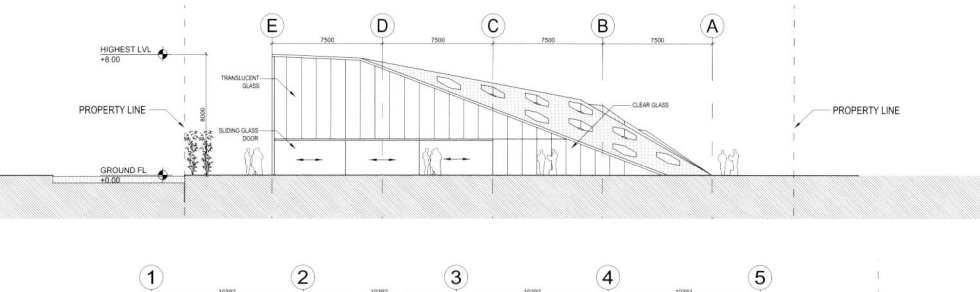

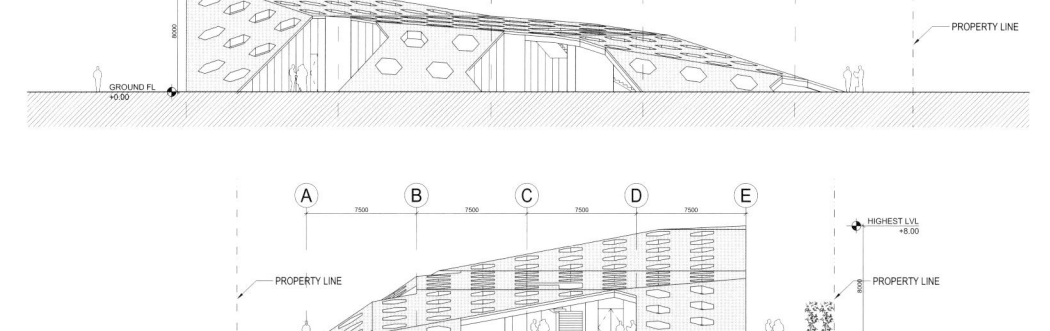

View from pool toward porch

Sections

Elevations

2010 Visigoth Museum
Toledo, Spain

Model: concrete columns and floating volume

Site model

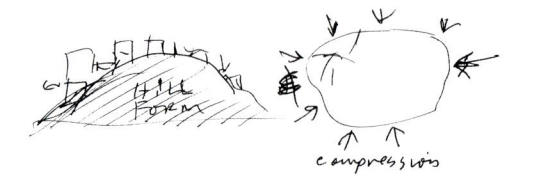

Concept sketches

While the Tajo River embraces Toledo, causing a geometric condensation of the town, the site for Visigoth Museum, located adjacent to Toledo, is excavated and elevated. The building is a fold in the earth that rises up with a sedum roof to form a "Pergola of Shadows."

The building takes its inspiration from El Greco's painting, View of Toledo. As holes in the clouds pierce the sky, the surface of the new ground is punctured, bringing natural light to the Pergola of Shadows below. This new outdoor space provides a shaded public plaza and forms the entry to the new museum and Interpretation Center.

Concrete columns catch the south sun and bring it down to the plaza, where it reflects in a channel of Tajo River water, the "Channel of Three Cultures."

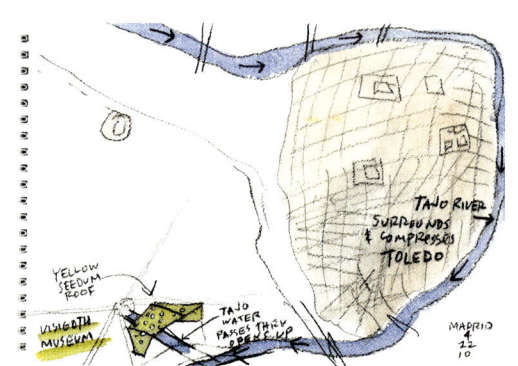

Plaza: concrete columns catch south sun and bring it down on water

西ゴート族博物館

タホ川はトレドの町を取り囲むように流れ、密集した町並みを形成している。トレドに程近い西ゴート族博物館の敷地では、土地は掘削されて立ち上がる。建築は地中に折れ曲がり、ベンケイソウの生える屋上は宙に浮き「陰影のパーゴラ」となる。

建築はエル・グレコの絵画「トレド眺望」からヒントを得たものである。雲の隙間から空を見るように、新しい大地の表面は穿孔され、自然光がその下の「陰影のパーゴラ」へともたらされる。新しい屋外空間はパブリック・プラザに日陰をつくり、新しい博物館と解析センターへのエントランスとなる。

コンクリートの柱は南の太陽の光を受け止め、プラザへと引き入れる。太陽光は、タホ川の水を引き込んだ「三文化の水路」に煌めきを落とす。

Channel of Tajo River water flows to plaza

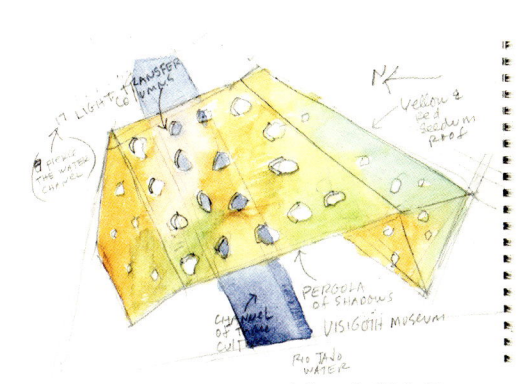

Museum and channel of Tajo River water

Exhibition space

1999-2012 Volume 2   List of Works

Term of design
Project title
Site
-
Program
-
Additional data

1999
Centro JVD, Housing and Hotel
Guadalajara, Mexico
-
Program: 200 housing units and 150 hotel rooms
(as part of the initial phase of new Cultural Center project)

Consultant: Guy Nordenson Associates, structural;
Ove Arup & Partners, mechanical
Structural system: white tilt-up concrete, cable trusses and bead-blasted aluminum

1999
Center for Contemporary Art
Rome, Italy
-
Program:
international competition for contemporary art museum

1999
XKY Xcraper
Vuossari, Finland
-
Program:
competition for residential, retail facilities, public observation deck

1999-2003
Simmons Hall, Massachusetts Institute of Technology
Cambridge, Massachusetts, U.S.A.
-
Program: dormitory for university students with theater and cafe
-
Clients: MIT/Massachusetts Institute of Technology
Associate architects: Perry Dean Rogers Partners (Boston)
Consultant: Guy Nordenson and Associates, Simpson Gumpertz & Heger Inc., structural; Ove Arup & Partners, mechanical
General contractor: Daniel O'Connell's Sons
Structural system: precast concrete
Total floor area: 195,000 sq.ft.

1999-2006
School of Art and Art History, University of Iowa
Iowa City, Iowa, U.S.A.

Program: art and art history building, including facilities for sculpture, painting, printmaking, graduate studios, administrative offices, gallery, and library

Clients: University of Iowa
Consultant: Guy Nordenson and Associates, structural
General contractor: Larson Construction
Structural system: steel
Total floor area: 70,000 sq.ft.

1999-2007
Nelson-Atkins Museum of Art
Kansas City, Missouri, U.S.A.

Program: museum addition and renovation

Clients: Nelson-Atkins Museum of Art
Local architect: Berkebile Nelson Immenschuh McDowell Architects
Consultant: Guy Nordenson and Associates, structural; Ove Arup & Partners with W.L. Cassell, mechanical; Walter De Maria, artist; Gould Evans and Olin Partnership, landscape
Total floor area: 165,000 sq.ft., new addition; 234,000 sq.ft., renovation; 22 acres, sculpture park

2000
Museum of Human Evolution
Burgos, Spain

Program: competition for museum including galleries, conference hall, auditorium

Clients: City of Burgos
Consultant: Guy Nordenson and Associates, structural; Ove Arup & Partners, mechanical
Total floor area: 28,500 m^2

2001
Little Tesseract
Rhinebeck, New York, U.S.A.

Program: solarstack prototype

Consultant: The Orchard Group, fabricator

2001
Musée des Confluences, Lyon
Lyon, France

Program: competition for museum with auditorium, education tower-classrooms

Associate architect: Pierre Vurpas Associates
Consultant: Jacobs Serete (Paris), Phillipe Averty, structural; Guy Nordenson and Associates, associate structural engineer
Structural system: steel frame

2001
Ile Seguin—Foundation Francois Pinault
Paris, France

Program: invited competition for the Foundation Francois Pinault including galleries, university, cafes and public amenities

Clients: Pinault Foundation
Consultant: Guy Nordenson & Associates, structural; Ove Arup & Partners, mechanical

2001
College of Architecture, Cornell University
Ithaca, New York, U.S.A.

Program: building for College of Architecture, Art & Planning

Client: Cornell University
Consultant: Guy Nordenson and Associates, structural; Ove Arup & Partners, mechanical; The Orchard Group, model fabrication
Building area: 70,000 sq.ft. (6,503 m^2)

2001
Los Angeles County Museum of Art
Los Angeles, California, U.S.A.

Program: competition for art museum

2001-04
Writing with Light House
Eastern Long Island, New York, U.S.A.

Program: private residence

Consultant: Robert Sillman & Assoc., structural
General contractor: Koral Bros., Southampton
Structural system: wood frame
Major materials: weathered cedar slats over cedar boards and vertical cedar batten, exterior; stained concrete floors, pine wood floors, plaster walls, interior
Total floor area: 5,500 sq.ft. including basement

2001-04
Nail Collector's House
Essex, New York, U.S.A.

Program: private residence

Clients: G. Alan Wardle
Total floor area: 1,200 sq.ft.

2001-03
Loisium Visitors' Center
Langenlois, Austria

Program: cafe, wine shop, souvenir shop, seminar rooms, event spaces, offices

Clients: Kellerwelt Betriebs GmbH & Co. KG
Local architects: ARGE Architekten
Consultant: Retter & Partner GmbH, structural; Altherm Engineering, mechanical
Total floor area: 1,200 m²
Cost of construction: 2.2 million euro

2001-05
Loisium Hotel Spa Resort
Langenlois, Austria

Program: vineyard hotel with lobby, bar, cigar lounge, restaurant, conference rooms, Aveda spa, 82 hotel rooms

Clients: Loisium Hotelbetriebs GmbH & Co. KG
Local architect: ARGE Architekten
Consultant: Retter & Partner GmbH, A-Krems, structural
Structural system: concrete
Total floor area: 7,000 m²
Size: 12.50 meters (building height), 4-floor

2001-05
Turbulence House
New Mexico, U.S.A.

Program: guest house (including study, sleeping loft)

Clients: Richard Tuttle, Mei Mei Berssenbrugge
Local architect: Kramer Woodard Architects
Consultant: Delapp Engineering, structural; A. Zahner Company, metal panel fabricator
Structural system: stressed skin and aluminum rib
Major materials: pre-constructed aluminum panels
Building area: 900 sq.ft. (84 m²)

2001-06
Swiss Residence
Washington D.C., U.S.A.

Program: residence including living spaces of the ambassador, representational spaces, staff quarters

Associate architect: Ruessli Architekten AG
Consultant: A. F. Steffen Engineers, Robert Silman Associates, P.C., structural; ZedNetwork Hannes Wettstein, interior
General contractor: James G. Davis Construction, Niersberger Gebäudetecnik
Structural system: reinforced concrete
Site area: 25,000 sq.ft.   Total floor area: 28,000 sq.ft.

2001-
Oceanic Retreat
Kaua'i, Hawaii, U.S.A.

Program: private residence

Local architect: Peter Vincent & Associates LLC
Consultant: Guy Nordenson and Associates, engineer
General contractor: Krekow-Jennings Inc.—Steve Farrell, PM
Building area: 5,400 sq.ft. (502 m²)

2002
World Trade Center Schemes 1 and 3
New York, New York, U.S.A.

Program: monumental new space for World Trade Center tragedy (memorial hall, and galleries, cinema spaces, cafes, restaurants, a hotel, classrooms for a branch of New York University)

Associate architect (scheme 3): developing with Richard Meier and Partners, Eisenman Architects, and Gwathmey Siegel

2002
Zuidas
Amsterdam, The Netherlands

Program: new headquarters for prominent European law firm; offices, conference room, terrace, lobby, restaurant

Associate architect: BSC Architecture, Tim Bade, Martin Cox
Local architect: Claus en Kaan Architecten
Consultant: Infocus, project manager; Goudstikker-DeVries, structural; Huygen Installatie Adviseurs BV, mechanical
Building area: 191,598 sq.ft. (17,800 m²)

2002
New Town: Green Urban Laboratory
Nanning, China

Program: competition for new town of approx. 27,000 residence, 9,000 housing units (including schools, shops, hotel and recreational facilities, museum; rebuilding Tianning Buddhist Temple)

Clients: Guangxi Runhe estate Development Co., Ltd.
Structural system: concrete
Major materials: pre-cast concrete
Site area: 1,865,000 m²
Footprint area: 480,000 m²   Total floor area: 1,350,000 m²

2002
Toolenburg-Zuid
Amsterdam, The Netherlands

Program: competition (1st place) for six housing types for 21st century living

2002-05
Planar House
Phoenix, Arizona, U.S.A.

Program: private residence

Consultant: Rudow & Berry, structural; Roy Otterbein, mechanical
General contractor: The Construction Zone
Structural system: tilt-up precast concrete panels, wood framing
Major materials: concrete, wood, glass
Site area: 50,000 sq.ft.
Footprint area: 5,200 sq.ft.
Total floor area: 3,400 sq.ft.

2002-
Nanjing Museum of Art & Architecture
Nanjing, China

-

Program: museum complex with galleries, tea room, bookstore, and a curator's residence

-

Associate architect: Architectural Design Institute, Nanjing University
Consultants: Guy Nordenson and Associates, structural;
L'Observatoire International, lighting
Site area: 9,408 m²
Footprint area: 1,529 m²
Total floor area: 3,124 m²

2002-
Beirut Marina & Town Quay
Beirute, Lebanon

-

Program: apartments, restaurants, outdoor public spaces with site specific art installations, specialty stores, harbormaster, yacht club, and public facilities

-

Clients: Solidere
Associate architect: Nabil Gholam Architecture
Building area: 220,000 sq.ft. (20,439 m²)

2003
Musée des Civilisations de l'Europe et de la Méditerranée
Marseille, France

-

Program:
galleries, auditorium, cafe and restaurants, offices, support facilities

2003-09
Linked Hybrid
Beijing, China

-

Program: 644 apartments, public green space, commercial zones, hotel, cinemateque, kindergarten, Montessori school, underground parking

-

Clients: Modern Green Development Co., Ltd. Beijing
Associate architect: Beijing Capital Engineering Architecture Design Co. LTD.
Consultant: Guy Nordenson and Associates, China Academy of Building Research, structural
General contractor: Beijing Construction Engineering Group
Site area: 61,800 m²   Footprint area: 16,826 m²   Footprint area: 221,426 m²

2004
Lombardia Regional Government Center
Milan, Italy

-

Program:
competition for offices, public plaza, press conference and exhibition and debate facilities, cafes, public observation deck

2004
The High Line
New York, New York, U.S.A.

-

Program:
competition for renovation and transformation of the High Line into public space

2004-07
Interior Renovation of New York University, Department of Philosophy
New York, New York, U.S.A.

-

Program: faculty offices and graduate student offices, seminar rooms, periodicals library and lounge with a 120-seat auditorium

-

Clients: New York University
Consultant: Robert Silman Associates, structural; Ambrosino, DePinto & Schmieder (ADS Consulting Engineers), MEP;
F.J. Sciame Construction Co., Inc., construction manager;
Renfro Design Group, lighting
Building area: 30,000 sq.ft.

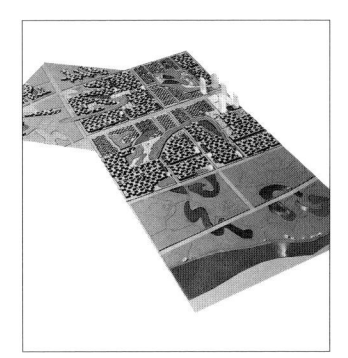

2005
Xi'an New Town
Xi'an, China

-

Program: competition for urban planning project including housing, cultural spaces, offices, public services, school and commercial spaces

2005
Experiments in Porosity
Milan, Italy

-

Program: exhibition at Milano Salone 2005 (eight modern-day architects reinterpret the eight residential houses by modernist architects)

-

Contributors: Garrick Ambrose, Makram El-Kadi,
Consultant: Alberto Martinuzzo, material consultant and fabricator

2005
Denver Justice Center
Denver, Colorado, U.S.A.

-

Program:
competition (1st Place) for 35 court rooms, offices and public spaces

2005-09
Herning Center of the Arts
Herning, Denmark

—

Program: temporary exhibition galleries, 150-seat auditorium, music rehearsal rooms, restaurant, media library and administrative offices

—

Clients: Herning Center of the Arts
Local architect: Kjaer and Richter A/S
Consultant: Niras, structural; Niras, Transsolar, mechanical; Schønherr Landskab, landscape
Site area: 12,000 m²
Building area: 5,600 m²

2005-11
Cité de l'Océan et du Surf
Biarritz, France

—

Program: museum, plaza, exhibition areas

—

Clients: City of Biarritz/Adim Sud Ouest
Associate architects: Rüssli Architekten,
Agence d'Architecture X. Leibar JM Seigneurin
Consultant: Betec & Vinci Construction Marseille, structural
Site area: 20,000 m²
Footprint area: 2,830 m²
Total floor area: 4,081 m²

2005-13
Sail Hybrid
Knokke-Heist, Belgium

—

Program: three architectures—'Sail-Like Planar' (hotel and apartment tower); 'Volumetric' (restored, reprogrammed casino); 'Porous' (congress hall)

—

Clients: Knokke-Heist
Local architect: Buro II
Consultant: Robert Silman Associates, structural
Site area: 14,000 m²   Footprint area: 7,200 m²
Total floor area: 44,000 m²
(including tower, casino, sea hall; excluding parking)

2005-
Sun Slice House
Lake Garda, Italy

—

Program: private residence

—

Local architect: Luca Pellegrinelli
Consultant: Gianni Pellegrinelli, structural
Site area: 12,900 m² (total site including guest house)
Footprint area: 160 m²
Total floor area: 399 m²

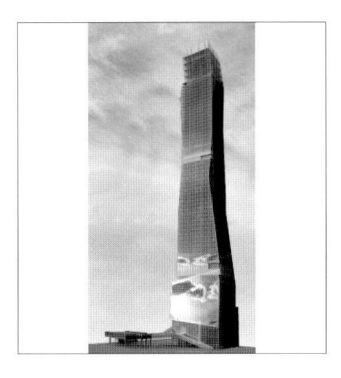

2005-
Highline Hybrid Tower
New York, New York, U.S.A.

—

Program: mixed use; offices, hotel, and condominiums

2006
T-Husene
Copenhagen, Denmark

—

Program:
Five towers of mixed-use (residential and commercial), and landscape

2006, 2007
Riddled Cabinet and Table for Horm
Italy

—

Riddled Cabinet:
Materials: lasercut Canaletto walnut and aluminum with vegetal oil finish
Dimensions: 200 x 50 x 70 cm
Specifics: limited edition (pieces numbered and signed)

Riddled Table:
Materials: lasercut Canaletto walnut with a vegetal oil finish
Dimensions: 180 x 85 x 73 (H) cm

2006-09
Vanke Center
Shenzhen, China

—

Program: mixed-use building including hotel, offices, condominiums, and public park

—

Clients: Shenzhen Vanke Real Estate Co.
Associate architect: CCDI
Consultant: CABR, CCDI, structural; CCDI, mechanical
Site area: 61,729.7 m² Landscape area: 52,000 m² Public green space: 47,288 m²
Building area: 120,445 m² (8,292 m², conference center; 25,704 m², condominiums; 11,113 m², hotel; 13,591 m², Soho offices; 13,874 m², Vanke headquarters)

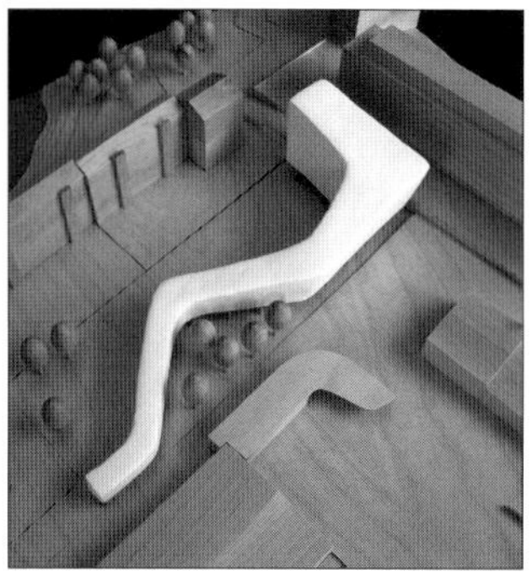

2006-
Meander
Helsinki, Finland

—

Program: competition (1st prize) for 49 apartments, 500 m² rental space, garage, rooftop sauna and running track

—

Clients: City of Helsinki & Senate Properties
Local architect: Vesa Honkonen Architects
Consultant: Tero Aaltonen, Matti Ollila & Co.
Consulting Engineers Ltd., structural
Site area: 29,146 sq.ft. (8,886 m²)

2006-
Akbuk Dense Pack
Akbuk, Turkey

—

Program: mixed-use master plan including apartments, townhouses, villas, hammam, and assembly space

—

Clients: TK
Project area: 355,209 sq.ft.

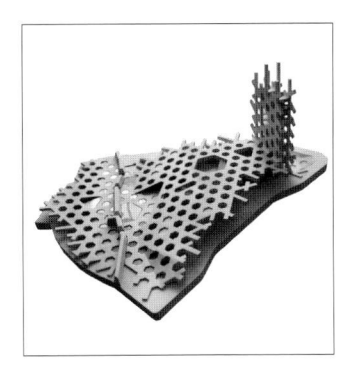

2007
World Design Park Complex
Seoul, South Korea
-
Program: competition for mixed-use complex with offices, retail, cafe, sky bar, exhibition space, and double level vertical park
-
Clients: Seoul Metropolitan Government
Local architect: Samoo Architects & Engineers
Site area: 61,585 m²

2007
Campidoglio Due
Rome, Italy
-
Program: City Hall and Offices

2007
Hudson Yards
New York, New York, U.S.A.
-
Program: competition for master plan mixed-use project

2007-08
Franz Kafka Society Center
Prague, Czech Republic
-
Program:
cultural center with exhibition, lecture and concert space, as well as offices and a library

2007-12
Sliced Porosity Block
Chengdu, China
-
Program: five towers with offices, serviced apartments, retail, hotel, cafes, and restaurants
-
Clients: CapitaLand Development
Associate architect: China Academy of Building Research
Consultant: China Academy of Building Research, structural; Ove Arup & Partners, MEP
Site area: 17,500 m²   Footprint area: 310,000 m²
Total floor area: 195,000 m², above; 115,000 m², below

2008
Ningbo Fine Grain
Ningbo, China
-
Program: competition for mixed-use development with retail, entertainment, cultural, offices, hotels, and residential
-
Clients: Ningbo Yaxin Investment Consultants Co., Ltd.
Site area: 31 hectares
Total floor area (above ground): 400,000 m²

2008-12
Daeyang Gallery & House
Seoul, South Korea
-
Program: residence and art gallery
-
Clients: Daeyang Shipping corp.
Local architect: E.Rae Architects
Consultant: SQ Engineering, structural
General contractor: Jehyo
Structural system: RC structural wall and steel
Major materials: exposed concrete and copper panel
Site area: 1,760 m²   Footprint area: 382 m²   Total floor area: 994 m²

2008-12
Stadgenoot Campus
Amsterdam, The Netherlands
-
Program: offices, reception area, lobby space

2008-12
Triaxial Field
Hangzhou, China
-
Program: multi-purpose event space
-
Clients: Hangzhou Westbrook Investment Co., Ltd.
Consultant: Guy Nordenson and Associates, structural
Structural system: post-tensioned concrete, triaxial reinforcements
Major materials: concrete
Site area: 2,721 m²
Footprint area: 847 m²
Total floor area: 1,483 m²

2008-12
Campbell Sports Center
New York, New York, U.S.A.
-
Program: sport center
-
Clients: Columbia University
Consultant: Robert Silman Associates, structural; ICOR Associates, MEP; W.J. Higgins, curtain wall consultant
Major materials: exposed steel structure, exposed precast concrete plank, marine aluminum rainscreen wall, flush glazed curtain wall
Building area: 48,000 sq.ft. (4,459 m²)

2008-14
Center for Performing Arts, Princeton University
Princeton, New Jersey, U.S.A.

Program: campus complex (three buildings—Theatre and Dance building, Arts building, and Music building with orchestral rehearsal and practice rooms)

Clients: Princeton University
Structural system: concrete frame and stone with several types of translucent glass

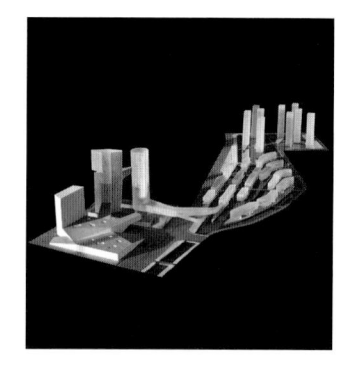

2009-
Shan-Shui Hangzhou
Hangzhou, China

Program: master plan (apartments and offices, retail space, restaurant and event space, hotel, and others)

Clients: Hangzhou Urban Planning Documentation Center
Consultant: CABR, structural; Lisa Maione, graphic consultants; Michael Bell, Peter Lynch, MOS, Francois Roche

2008-16
LM Harbor Gateway
Copenhagen, Denmark

Program: office towers and civic spaces with a public walkway 65 meters above harbor

Clients: ATP Ejendomme, CPH City and Port Development
Consultant: HNTB Corporation, structural; Niras, mechanical
Site area: 7,500 m^2
Footprint area: 3,488 m^2 (both towers)
Total floor area: 58,018 m^2

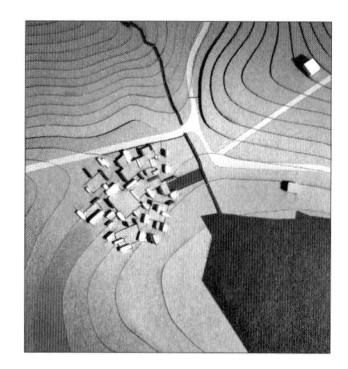

2010
Klanghaus, Swiss Musical Center
St. Gallen, Switzerland

Program: music rehearsal, recording, experimentation and research spaces

2009
Youth Wellness Center
Bremerton, Washington, U.S.A.

Program: community wellness center with nutrition wing, health wing and fitness wing

2010
SF MoMA
San Francisco, California, U.S.A.

Program: competition for museum addition

Clients: San Francisco Museum of Modern Art

2009
Columbia Business School
New York, New York, U.S.A.

Program: competition for academic building

2010
T Space
Dutchess County, New York, U.S.A.

Program: gallery space

Consultant: Silman Associates, PC., structural;
JLP Home Improvement, fabricator
Major materials: cedar, plywood, steel

2009-
Glasgow School of Art
Glasgow, U.K.

Program: art, design, and architecture school (studios, project spaces, lecture theater, seminar rooms, cafe, exhibition, and academic administrative spaces)

Clients: Glasgow School of Art
Associate architect: JM Architects
Consultant: Arup, engineer;
Michael Van Valkenburgh and Associates, landscape;
Building area: 121,094 sq.ft. (11,250 m^2)

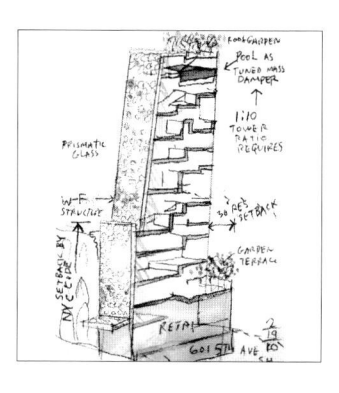

2010
Benetton Tower
New York, New York, U.S.A.

Program: competition for Benetton's flagship store and residential tower with work loft for young artists from around the world

2010
V&A Dundee Museum and Design Nucleus
Dundee, U.K.

-

Program: museum

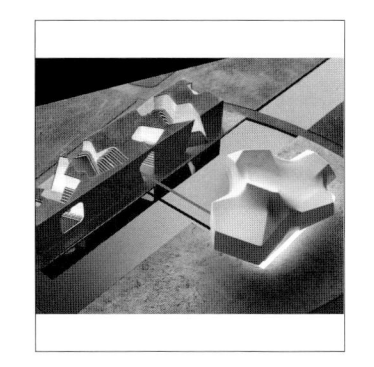

2010-
Cangqian Performing Arts Center, Art Museum and Arts Quadrangle, Hangzhou Normal University
Hangzhou, China

-

Program: Performing Arts Center (pac), Art Museum (am), and Arts Quadrangle (aq)

-

Consultant: China Academy of Building Research/CABR, structural
Site area: 27,700 m^2 (pac), 12,700 m^2 (am), 82,161 m^2 (aq)
Footprint area: 12,900 m^2 (pac), 20,000 m^2 (am), 113,189 m^2 (aq)
Total floor area: 28,100 m^2 (pac), 28,200 m^2 (am), 113,189 m^2 (aq)

2010
Visigoth Museum
Toledo, Spain

-

Program:
competition for museum, research center and interpretation center

-

Clients: Toletum Visigodo
Project area: 166,840 sq.ft. (15,500 m^2)

2010-
New Doctorate's Building, National University of Colombia
Bogotá, Colombia

-

Program: classrooms, offices, lab space, study rooms, cafe, restaurant, auditorium

-

Clients: National University of Colombia, Bogotá
Major materials: high performance fiber-reinforced concrete
Building area: 70,000 sq.ft. (6,503 m^2)

2010-13
Queens Library
New York, New York, U.S.A.

-

Program: Library with adult reading collection, children's area, teen area, cybercenter, conference room and outdoor amphitheater

-

Clients: Queens Library, New York City Department of Design and Construction
Consultant: Robert Silman Associates, ICOR Associates, engineers
Building area: 21,000 sq.ft.

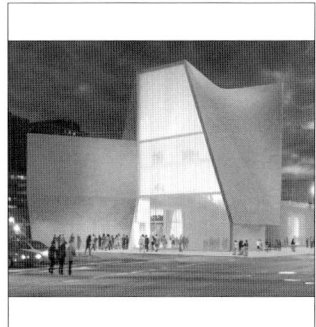

2011-15
Institute for Contemporary Art, Virginia Commonwealth University
Richmond, Virginia, U.S.A.

-

Program: gallery spaces, 247-seat performance space, cafe, administrative offices, classroom, sculpture terrace, art storage

-

Clients: Virginia Commonwealth University
Associate architect: BCWH Architects
Consultant: Robert Silman Associates, structural
Strucutral system: cast-in-place, precast, reinforced concrete
Building area: 70,000 sq.ft. (6,503 m^2)

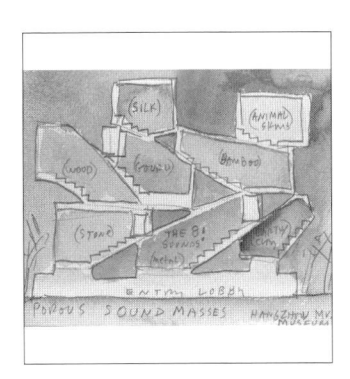

2010-
Hangzhou Music Museum
Hangzhou, China

-

Program: museum and library

-

Clients: Hangzhou City Planning Bureau
Consultant: Ethan Spigland and Raphael Mostel, musical consultants; Yehuda Safran, project consultant
Site area: 68,000 m^2
Footprint area: 14,532 m^2
Total floor area: 48,220 m^2 (3,000 m^2, museum)

2010-
New Art Building, University of Iowa
Iowa City, Iowa, U.S.A.

-

Program: new facility for the University of Iowa's School of Art and Art History (space for the departments of printmaking, painting, photography, intermedia, and three-dimensional art)

-

Clients: Iowa University
Building area: 126,000 sq.ft. (four story)

STEVEN HOLL
Architects

STEVEN HOLL ARCHITECTS

1999-2012
—
Steven Holl
–

Peter Adams
Masao Akiyoshi
Justin Allen
Garrick Ambrose
Jason Anderson
Tim Bade
Sarah Bai
Roberto Bannura
Lei Bao
Francesco Bartolozzi
Gabriella Barmen
Gisela Baurmann
Robert Benson
Arnault Biou
Janine Biunno
Matthias Blass
Molly Blieden
Nikole Bouchard
Johanna Cressica Brazier
Chris Brokaw
Sabina Cachero
Kefei Cai
Tei Carpenter
Marcus Carter
Pablo Castro
Aaron Cattani
Lesley Chang
Yimei Chan
Yen-ling Chen
Xi Chen
Regina Chow
Tynnan Chow
Sofie Christensen
Haiko Cornelissen
Frank Cottier
Martin Cox
Guido Cuscianna

J. Paul Dallas
Elsie Dedecker
Christiane Deptolla
Rodolfo Dias
Margot Dirks
Gong Dong
Jennifer Drumgoole
Rob Edmonds
Clemence Eliard
Makram ElKadi
Peter Englaender
Esin Erez
Rychiee Espinosa
Ayat Fadaifard
Iben Falconer
Nicole Fox
Nathalie Frankowski
Jason Frantzen
Priscilla Frasier
Scott Fredericks
Forrest Fulton
Mingcheng Fu
Mike Fung
Nick Gelpi
Annette Goderbauer
Inge Goudsmit
Cao Guanlan
Runar Halldorsson
Yoh Hanaoka
Gary He
Hideki Hirahara
Eleanore Ho
Mimi Hoang
Yunsung Hong
Vesa Honkonen
Emran Hossain
Wenny Hsu
Li Hu
Erica Jackson
Ziad Jamalledine
Young Jang
Kelvin Jia
Liang Jing
Matt Johnson

Seung Hyun Kang
Joseph Kan
Gabriella Karl
Hollyamber Kennedy
Justin Korhammer
Alex Knezo
Maren Koehler
Max Kolbowski-Frampton
Sofia Krimizi
Katarina Kristic
Martin Kropac
Gyong Kwon
Edward Lalonde
Erik Langdalen
Anderson Lee
Jennifer Lee
Jongseo Lee
Bin Li
Christine Li
Eric Li
John Lim
Andy Lin
Tz-Li Lin
Ted Lin
Wan-Jen Lin
Jessica Liu
Richard Liu
Vivien Liu
Yan Liu
Ruth Lo
Yichen Lu
Jackie Luk
James Macgillivray
Clark Manning
Emily Marchesiello
Maki Masubayashi
Fiorenza Matteoni
Chris McVoy
Brian Meltzer
Woosik Min
Giorgos Mitroulias
Anna Muller
Johanna Muszbek
Daijiro Nakayama

Ernest Ng
Rafael Ng
Sarah Nichols
Alisa Ochoa
Stephen O'Dell
Alessandro Orsini
Linda Pellegrini
Lautaro Pereyra
Pietro Peyron
Gabriela Pinto
Jose Carlos Quelhas
Ryan Quinlan
Julia Radcliffe
Roberto Requejo
Garrett Ricciardi
Nathan Rich
Elena Rojas-Danielsen
Michael Rusch
Kyra Safranoff
Susie Sanchez
El-Rashid Satti
Olaf Schmidt
Honora Shea
Lee Pei Shyun
Jay Siebenmorgen
Dominik Sigg
Clare Smith
Brett Snyder
Elissa Swanger
Ida Sze
Filipe Taboada
Asami Takahashi
Zhiying Tan
Shen Jiang Tao
Sanjay Thakur
Richard Tobias
Benadict Tranel
Quang Truong
Dimitra Tsacherielia
Judith Tse
Matt Uselman
Julia Van Den Hout
David Van Der Leer
Johan Van Lierop

Irene Vogt
Urs Vogt
Kitty Wang
Christian Wassmann
Aislinn Weidele
Manta Weihermann
Jeanne Wellinger
Ariane Weigner
Nelson Wilmotte
Ebbie Wisecarver
Human Wu
Lan Wu
Su Xia
Noah Yaffe
Christina Yessios
Martin Zimmerli

II-332

Awards, Exhibitions, and Published Writings

AWARDS

1999:
- National AIA Design Award
  for Kiasma—The Museum of Contemporary Art, Helsinki
- New York AIA Project Award
  for Nelson-Atkins Museum of Art, Kansas City, MO
- New York AIA Design Award
  for Cranbrook Institute of Science, Bloomfield Hills, MI

2000:
- Progressive Architecture Awards
  for Nelson Atkins Museum of Art;
  for MIT Undergraduate Residence

2001:
- Seattle AIA Design Award
  for Bellevue Art Museum, Bellevue, WA
- L'Academie D'Architecture's Grande Medaille d'Or (Paris)

2002:
- New York AIA Design Award
  for Simmons Hall, MIT Undergraduate Residence;
  for College of Architecture and Landscape Architecture, University of Minnesota
- Cooper Hewitt National Design Award for Architecture

2003:
- AIA National Honor Award
  for Simmons Hall, MIT Undergraduate Residence
- Honorary Fellow of the Royal Institute of British Architects
- NY AIA Project Award
  for Loisium Visitors' Center, Langenlois, Austria

2004:
- International Parking Institute, Award of Excellence
  for best design of a parking facility
  for Nelson Atkins Museum of Art, Kansas City, MO

2005:
- Benjamin Moore Hue Award
- New York Chapter American Institute of Architects Honor Award
  for Lake Whitney Water Purification Plant

2006:
- New York Chapter American Institute of Architects Citation
  for Sail Hybrid, Knokke Heist, Belgium
- New York Chapter American Institute of Architects Merit Award
  for Planar House
- Roger H. Corbetta Merit Award, Concrete Industry Board
  for Central Section Higgins Hall
- AIA Iowa Honor Award of Excellence
  for School of Art & Art History, Iowa City, IA
- Maholy-Nagy University of Art and Design, Budapest, Hungary
- Honorary Doctorate, Seattle University, Seattle

2007:
- AIA Institute Honor Award
  for School of Art & Art History, University of Iowa, Iowa City, IA
- AIA NY Architecture Merit Award
  for School of Art & Art History, University of Iowa, Iowa City, IA
- AIA NY Architecture Honor Award
  for New Residence at the Swiss Embassy, Washington, D.C.
- AIA NY Architecture Honor Award
  for Higgins Hall Center Section at the Pratt Institute, Brooklyn
- AIA/COTE Top Ten Green Project
  for Whitney Water Purification Facility and Park
- AIA Central States Architecture Award, USA
  for Nelson Atkins Museum of Art, Kansas City, MO

2008:
- AIA National Honor Award
  for Nelson Atkins Museum of Art, Kansas City, MO
- AIA New York Chapter Architecture Honor Award
  for Nelson Atkins Museum of Art, Kansas City, MO
- AIA NY Educational Design Award
  for NYU Department of Philosophy, New York
- AIA NY Sustainable Design Award
  for Linked Hybrid, Beijing, China

2009:
- BBVA Foundation Frontiers of Knowledge Award
  in the Arts Category
- AIA New York Chapter Citation
  for D.E. Shaw Supercomputer 32nd floor lobby, New York, NY
- CTBUH Best Tall Building in Asia and Australia
  for Linked Hybrid, Beijing, China
- CTBUH Best Tall Building Overall
  for Linked Hybrid, Beijing, China

2010:
- Good Design is Good Business, Best Green Project Award
  for Horizontal Skyscraper, Shenzhen, China
- Good Design is Good Business, Best Residential Project Award
  for Linked Hybrid, Beijing, China
- Progressive Architecture Award
  for LM Harbor Gateway, Copenhagen, Denmark
- AIA NY Honor Award
  for Horizontal Skyscraper-Vanke Center, Shenzhen, China;
  for Knut Hamsun Center, Hamarøy, Norway
- RIBA International Award
  for Herning Center of the Arts, Herning, Denmark
- North Norwegian Architecture Award
  for Knut Hamsun Center, Hamarøy, Norway
- International Architecture Award
  for Herning Center of the Arts, Herning, Denmark
  for Knut Hamsun Center, Hamarøy, Norway
- RIBA Jencks Award
- Green Good Design Award
  for Horizontal Skyscraper-Vanke Center, Shenzhen, China

2011:
- AIA Institute Honor Award
  for Horizontal Skyscraper-Vanke Center, Shenzhen, China
- Byggeskikk Prize
  for Knut Hamsun Center, Hamarøy, Norway
- Award for Excellence in Design
  for Queens Library, LIC, New York
- American Architecture Award
  for Horizontal Skyscraper-Vanke Center, Shenzhen, China
- Emirates Glass LEAF Award
  for Océan et du Surf, Biarritz, France
- Annual Design Review Award
  for Océan et du Surf, Biarritz, France

2012:
- AIA Gold Medal

EXHIBITIONS

1999:
- San Francisco Museum of Modern Art, San Francisco, CA
- "The Un-Private House"
  at Museum of Modern Art, New York, NY

2000:
- "1st Design Triennial"
  at Cooper-Hewitt Museum, New York, NY
- "Open Ends: Architecture Hot and Cold"
  at Museum of Modern Art, New York, NY
- "Parallax" at Max Protetch Gallery, New York, NY

2001:
- "Architecture + Water" at Van Alen Institute, New York, NY
- "Parallax" at American Academy in Rome, Italy

2002:
- "A New World Trade Center"
  at Max Protetch Gallery, New York, NY
- "A New World Trade Center"
  at National Building Museum, Washington, D.C.
- "Idea and Phenomena"
  at Architekturzentrum Wien, Austria
- "A New World Trade Center"
  at Venice Biennale (American Pavilion), Venice, Italy
- "Next" at Venice Biennale (Arsenale building), Venice, Italy
- "City to Desert: Density in the Landscape"
  at Basilica Palladiana di Vicenza, Vicenza, Italy

2003:
- "Idea and Phenomena"
  at Arkitekturmuseet Stockholm, Sweden
- "Idea and Phenomena" at Garanti Gallery Istanbul, Turkey
- "Works in Progress" at University of Minnesota, MN

2004:
- "'Cities, Corners' within Universal Forum of the Cultures"
  at Forum Universal De Las Culturas Barcelona, Spain
- "Annual Exhibition of Contemporary American Art"
  at The National Academy of Design, New York, NY
- "Tall Buildings: MoMA"
  at Museum of Modern Art, New York, NY
- "The China Art Museum"
  at International Architectural Art Biennal Exhibition

2006:
- "Esto Now: Photographers Eye New York"
  at Center for Architecture, New York, NY
- "Luminosity/Porosity" at Gallery MA, Tokyo, Japan
- "L'eau, Source d'Architecture"
  at Electra Gallery, Paris, France
- "Inside the Sponge" at CCA, Montreal, Canada
- "The Green House"
  at National Building Museum, Washington, D.C.

2007:
- "Steven Holl / Antonella Mari"
  Lecce Otranto, Italy

2008:
- "Rapid Urbanization—New Public Spaces"
  at Hong Kong-Shenzhen Biennale,
  Architecture & Urbanism, China
- "Casa Per Tutti"
  at Triennale Architettura Milano, Milan, Italy
- "Dreamland: Architectural Experiments Since the 1970s"
  at Museum of Modern Art, New York, NY
- "Pre"
  at Museum of Modern Art, New York, NY

2009:
- "Design USA"
  at Cooper Hewitt National Design Museum, New York, NY
- "Urbanisms: Steven Holl + Li Hu 4 Projects in China"
  at Horizontal Skyscraper-Vanke Center, Shenzhen, China

2010:
- "Urbanisms: Steven Holl + Li Hu 4 Projects in China"
  at Linked Hybrid, Beijing, China;
  at Urban Planning Exhibition Hall, Hangzhou, China
- "Su Pietra" at Castello di Acaya, Lecce, Italy

2011:
- "194X-9/11: American Architects and the City"
  at Museum of Modern Art, New York, NY
- "Highrise—Idea and Reality"
  at Museum of Gestaltung Zurich, Zurich, Switzerland
- "Imperfect Health"
  at Canadian Centre for Architecture, Montreal, Canada
- "8 Urban Projects"
  at Hong Kong & Shenzhen Bi City Architecture and
  Urbanism Biennale, Shenzhen, China

2012:
- "Steven Holl Architects: Forking Time"
  at Meulensteen Gallery, New York, NY

PUBLISHED WRITINGS

- *El Croquis 93—Steven Holl 1996-1999*
  Madrid: El Croquis Editorial, Eds. Fernando Marquez Cecilia
  and Richard Levene, 1999
- *The Chapel of St. Ignatius* Intro. Gerald T. Cobb, S.J.
  New York: Princeton Architectural Press, 1999
- *Parallax*
  New York: Princeton Architectural Press, 2000
- *Density in the Landscape*
  "City Fragments: Seven Strategies for Making an Urban
  Fragment in the Hudson Valley"
  New York: Columbia University Press (Columbia Books of
  Architecture), 2001
- *El Croquis 108—Steven Holl 1998-2002*
  "Thought, Matter and Experience"
  Madrid: El Croquis Editorial, 2001
- *Written in Water*
  Baden: Lars Müller Publishers, 2002
- *Idea and Phenomena*
  Baden: Lars Müller Publishers, Ed. Architekturzentrum
  Wien, 2002
- *Steven Holl Architect* Intro. Kenneth Frampton
  Milan: Electa Architecture, 2002
- *El Croquis 78+93+108—Steven Holl 1986-2003*
  Madrid: El Croquis Editorial, 2003
- *Steven Holl*
  New York: Universe-Rizzoli, Ed. Francesco Garofolo, 2003
- *GA Document 82—special issue: Steven Holl Competitions*
  Tokyo: A.D.A. Edita Tokyo, 2004
- *Simmons Hall: Source Books in Architecture 5*
  New York: Princeton Architectural Press, Ed. Todd Gannon,
  2004
- *Experiments in Porosity*
  Buffalo: University at Buffalo, School of Architecture and
  Planning, Eds. Brian Carter and Annette W. LeCuyer, 2005
- *Steven Holl—special issue of Contemporary Architecture 62*
  Korea: CA Press, Ed. Ji-seong Jeong, 2005
- *Alvar Aalto: Villa Mairea, Noormarkku/Porosity to Fusion*
  (Entrez Lentement)
  Milan: Lotus Eventi, Ed. Lorenzo Gaetani, 2005
- *Luminosity/Porosity*
  Tokyo: TOTO Shuppan, 2006
- *Hybrid Instrument*

Photographic Credits and Translator

Iowa City: University of Iowa School of Art and
Art History, 2006
- *World Architecture*
"Trips to China—Selected Journals of Steven Holl"
(Jan. 2007)
- *area 91* "Steven Holl: Sail Hybrid, Knokke-Heist" (Apr. 2007)
- *Steven Holl—Architecture Spoken*
New York: Rizzoli International Publications, 2007
- *House—Black Swan Theory*
New York: Princeton Architectural Press, 2007
- *World of Wine: Loisium*
Ostfildern: Hatje Cantz Verlag, 2007
- *Imagining MIT: Designing a Campus for the 21st Century*
Cambridge: MIT Press, 2007
- *Bold Expansion: The Nelson-Atkins Museum of Art Bloch Building*
London: Scala Publishers, 2007
- *Questions of Perception: Phenomenology of Architecture*
San Francisco: William Stout Books, 2007 (reprint)
- *Stone and Feather: Steven Holl Architects/Nelson Atkins Museum Expansion*
New York: Prestel, 2007
- *El Croquis 141—Steven Holl 2004-2008*
Madrid: El Croquis Editorial, 2008
- *Urbanisms: Working with Doubt, Steven Holl*
New York: Princeton Architectural Press, 2009
- *Pamphlet Architecture 3: Ner Haiti Villages*
New York: Princeton Architectural Press, 2010
- *Hamsun Holl Hamarøy,*
Baden: Lars Müller Publisher, 2010
- *GA Document 110—special issue: Steven Holl*
Tokyo: A.D.A. Edita Tokyo, 2010
- *This is Hybrid*
Aurora Fernandez Per, Javier Mozas, Javier Arpa
a+t architecture publishers, 2011
- *Three Days in Biarritz*
Fernando Guerra, 2011
- *Horizontal Skyscraper, Steven Holl*
William Stout Books, 2011
- *Scale, Steven Holl*
Baden: Lars Müller Publisher, 2012
- *Color Light Time, Steven Holl*
Baden: Lars Müller Publisher, 2012

PHOTOGRAPHIC CREDITS

GA photographers:
except as noted

Provided by Steven Holl Architects:
p.15 (top and bottom), p.21, p.40 (above two images), p.41, p.45 one image (above), p.54, p.58, p.90, pp.92-93, p.117, p.129, p.142, p.145, p.152, pp.154-155, p.186, p.190, p.196, p.198 (below), p.201, p.222, p.225, p.226, p.228 above, p.230, pp.234-235, pp.244-245, p.239, p.240, p.248, pp.250-251, p.253, pp.256-257, p.258, p.260, p.262, pp.268-270, p.283, p.307, p.314, pp.318-319, p.322, p.324 one photo (top), p.325 two photos on left (middle and the second from bottom), and two photos on right (middle and the second from bottom), p.326 one photo on left (the second from bottom), p.327 two photos on left (middle and bottom), and one photo on right (middle), p.328 two photos on right (bottom and the second from bottom), p.329 two photos on left (top and the second from bottom), and two photos on right (middle and the second from bottom), p.330 two photos on left (top and middle), and two photos on right (top and middle), p.331 three photos on left (the second from top, middle, and bottom), and one photo on right (top)

Courtesy of Horm and Steven Holl Architects:
p.30, pp.42-43, p.328 one photo on right (the second from top)
Steen Gyldendal:
p.15 middle
Sholomi Almagor:
p.19
Susan Wides:
pp.44-47 (except one image of p.45 above), p.52 right, p.330 one photo on right (the second from bottom)
Bilyana Dimitrova:
p.52 left, p.53 left, p.55
Hisao Suzuki:
p.53 right
Andy Ryan:
p.27, p.73, p.74, p.75 (left above), p.228 (two images on right)
Paul Warchol:
p.72, p.75 (left below and right)

Iwan Baan:
p.13, p.146
Chris McVoy:
p.23, p.228 left below

TRANSLATOR

Yasuko Kikuchi:
p.59, p.63, p.67, p.75, p.76, p.87, p.91, pp.112-113, pp.126-127, pp.136-137 (except paragraphs after 'Sustainable Design Intent'), 164, p.176, p.189, p.191, p.275
Lisa Tani:
pp.8-29, p.31, pp.49-51, pp.102-103, p.157-159, pp.266-267, p.313
Masayuki Harada:
pp.40-41, p.43, p.47, p.53, p.95, p.117, p.129, p.137 (paragraphs after 'Sustainable Design Intent'), p.145, pp.154-155, p.187, p.193, p.196, pp.208-211, p.225, p.227, p.233, pp.241-243, p.247, p.251, p.255, p.261, pp.264-265, p.269, pp.278-279, p.281, pp.290-291, p.299, pp.310-311, p.323
Kei Sato:
pp.142-143, p.150, p.201, p.303
Kanae Yoshiimura:
p.36, p.283, p.317
Naoko Komeiji:
pp.218-220
Makoto Kanchiku:
p.320

スティーヴン・ホール作品集 1975-2012
2012年10月26日発行

企画・編集	二川幸夫
撮影	GA photographers
序文	伊東豊雄／シュロミ・アルマゴール
アート・ディレクション	細谷巖（表紙,ロゴ・デザイン）
発行者	二川幸夫
印刷・製本	大日本印刷株式会社
発行	エーディーエー・エディタ・トーキョー
	東京都渋谷区千駄ヶ谷3-12-14
	TEL.(03) 3403-1581(代)

禁無断転載

ISBN978-4-87140-432-7 C1352